Mark H. McCormack's The World of Professional Golf 1996

An IMG PUBLISHING Book

An IMG PUBLISHING Book

All rights reserved
First published 1996
© IMG Operations, Inc. 1996

Designed and produced by Davis Design
Appendixes prepared by Bronwyn Harris

ISBN 1-878843-15-X

Printed and bound in the United States of America.

Contents

1. The Sony Ranking

Greg Norman has been the best player in professional golf over the past 10 years, a fact which has been well-documented by the Sony Ranking. There were 507 weeks from the start of the Sony Ranking in April, 1986 though 1995. Norman was ranked No. 1 in the world for 238 of those 507 weeks, and no other golfer was No. 1 for as many as 100 weeks.

Seven golfers have held the No. 1 position in the history of the Sony Ranking: Norman, Bernhard Langer, Seve Ballesteros, Nick Faldo, Ian Woosnam, Fred Couples and Nick Price. Faldo, second to Norman with 97 weeks as No. 1, holds the record of 81 consecutive weeks in the top position, from July, 1992, to January, 1994.

Norman is the only golfer never ranked outside the top 10 (his lowest: seventh in 1992) and Langer is the only other never ranked outside the top 20 (his lowest: 20th in 1989). Woosnam, Ballesteros and Tom Watson are the only others never ranked outside the top 50.

Price, the most recent challenger to Norman, took over No. 1 in August, 1994, after victories in the British Open and PGA Championship. He held that position for 43 weeks until Norman reclaimed it in June, 1995, with a stretch in which he tied for third place in the Masters Tournament, won the Memorial Tournament, tied for fourth in the Kemper Open and placed second in the U.S. Open. The week after that, Norman won the Canon Greater Hartford Open, the second of his five worldwide victories for the year.

Meanwhile Price, who had 17 victories over the previous three years, did not win until taking two late-year titles in Africa. He finished 1995 as No. 2 in the world.

Norman, of course, is from Australia and Price, from Zimbabwe. The next three players on the final Sony Ranking for 1995 were Langer of Germany, Ernie Els of South Africa and Colin Montgomerie of Scotland. It marked the second consecutive year in which no golfer from the United States was ranked in the top five.

U.S. Open champion Corey Pavin was ranked No. 6, the leading American, and Couples was No. 8. Between them was Faldo of England, who fell four positions from No. 3 during the year. Completing the top 10 were Masashi (Jumbo) Ozaki of Japan and Steve Elkington of Australia, winner of the PGA Championship.

As most people know by now, the Sony Ranking is a specially developed computerized method of evaluating the relative performances of the world's leading players. The Sony Ranking is sanctioned by the Championship Committee of the Royal and Ancient Golf Club of St. Andrews, and is endorsed by the major professional tours.

Some of the most respected people in golf worldwide bring their opinions to bear on the workings of the system. The Sony Ranking Advisory Committee meets at St. Andrews each October, and its recommendations are passed on to the R&A for approval. In addition to myself, the Sony Ranking Advisory Committee consists of:

Brenda Blumberg (advisor to South African PGA), Tim Finchem (U.S. PGA Tour), Peter Dobereiner (Association of Golf Writers), Taizo Kawata

(Japan Golf Association), Kosaku Shimada (PGA of Japan), Colin Phillips (Australian Golf Union), Richard Rahusen (European Golf Association), Pat Rielly (PGA of America), Ken Schofield (PGA European Tour), Frank Tatum (past president, United States Golf Association), Colin Maclaine (past captain and chairman of the Championship Committee of the R&A), and Peter Townsend (PGA European Tour Policy Board).

All tournaments from the world's golf tours are taken into account and points are awarded according to the quality of the players participating in each event. The number of points distributed to each golfer is dependent upon his finishing position.

The four major championships (Masters Tournament, U.S. Open, British Open and PGA Championship) and the flagship events of the major tours (The Players Championship (U.S.), Volvo PGA Championship (Europe), Japan Open and Australian Open) are weighted separately to reflect the greater prestige of the events and strong fields participating.

Through 1995 the Sony Ranking was based on a *three-year* "rolling" average weighted in favor of more recent results, but starting in 1996 the system has been changed to a *two-year* "rolling" average with the points accumulated in the most recent 52-week period doubled.

Each player is ranked according to his average points per tournament, which is determined by dividing his total number of points by the number of tournaments he has played over that two-year period. There is a minimum requirement of 20 tournaments for each 52-week period. For example, if a player were in 32 tournaments in the most recent 52 weeks and 15 tournaments in the previous 52 weeks, his divisor would be 52 (32 plus 20). A player who was in 32 tournaments in each year would have a divisor of 64 (32 plus 32).

The winners of the major championships are awarded 50 points (doubled to 100 points in the current year) and the winner of The Players Championship is awarded 40 points (80 points in the current year), which is also the most points possible to be earned from winning any other tournament in the world. The winner of a tournament with a relatively strong field would probably receive approximately 25 to 30 points (50 to 60 points in the current year).

Minimum points for the winners of official tour events have been set at six points for Asia and South Africa, eight points for Australasia and Japan, and 10 points for Europe and the United States. In addition, the Volvo PGA Championship in Europe has a minimum of 32 points for the winner, and the Open Championships of Australia and Japan have a minimum of 16 points for the winner (minimum points doubled in the current year). Points are reduced proportionately for tournaments reduced to 36 or 54 holes because of inclement weather or other reasons.

Points to be awarded above the minimum levels for these events are determined by the strength of field. This is determined by the number and ranking of players in the tournaments who are among the top 100 golfers on the Sony Ranking. Each player ranked in the top 100 of the Sony Ranking is assigned "ratings points" ranging from 50 points for the No. 1 player, then down to two points each for those ranked 81st to 100th.

The total of the ratings points is then applied to the table on pages 8 and 9 to adjust the Sony Ranking points to reflect the quality of the field.

As a by-product, the Sony Ranking system is able to identify the strongest tournaments in the world. Many tournament organizers use the Sony Ranking to determine qualifiers or as a basis for issuing invitations. For example, the top 50 players on the Sony Ranking are exempt from having to qualify for the British Open. The PGA of America has also made effective use of the Sony Ranking in issuing invitations to the PGA Championship.

Following were the highest-rated tournaments in the world for 1995:

	Event	No. of Sony Ranked Players Participating					Sony Rating Points
		Top 5	Top 15	Top 30	Top 50	Top 100	
1	PGA Championship	4	14	28	48	79	734
2	British Open	5	13	27	46	74	708
3	The Players Championship	5	15	30	44	71	702
4	U.S. Open Championship	5	15	30	42	67	688
5	Masters Tournament	5	15	30	45	61	677
6	The Nestle Invitational	5	15	27	39	65	648
7	Memorial Tournament	4	9	22	37	62	559
8	MCI Classic	4	9	21	29	49	475
9	Colonial National Invitational	2	5	19	31	53	447
10	NEC World Series of Golf	4	11	18	24	35	420
11	Doral-Ryder Open	3	7	18	26	46	412
12	Tour Championship	4	9	17	23	30	381
13	Motorola Western Open	2	7	17	24	46	378
14	Kemper Open	2	7	12	23	38	370
15	Sprint International	2	4	10	19	43	334
16	AT&T Pebble Beach Nat'l	1	6	16	23	39	325
17	GTE Byron Nelson Classic	2	5	11	22	38	316
17	Phoenix Open	1	3	13	24	43	316
19	Honda Classic	2	7	13	18	30	306
20	Andersen Consulting World Ch.	1	7	13	23	26	275
21	Scottish Open	1	5	9	15	40	265
22	Johnnie Walker Classic	3	8	8	11	21	262
23	Buick Open	3	5	9	15	28	257
24	Volvo PGA Championship	2	7	7	13	35	253
25	Dubai Desert Classic	3	6	6	10	22	247
26	Nissan Open	-	2	10	16	33	243
27	Northern Telecom Open	1	2	7	16	40	242
28	Buick Invitational of California	1	2	9	17	34	240
29	Johnnie Walker World Champ.	3	8	10	15	19	236
30	Nedbank Million Dollar Chal.	4	9	12	12	12	230

Age Groups of Top 100 Sony Ranked Players

Under 25	25-27	23-30	31-33	34-36	37-39	40-42	43-45	Over 45
				Pavin				
				Couples		Norman		
				Lehman	Price	Roberts		
			Montgomerie	Frost	Langer	Torrance		
			Elkington	Gallagher	Faldo	Jacobsen		
		Olazabal	Singh	Calcavecchia	Rocca	Hoch		
		Mayfair	Janzen	Faxon	Ballesteros	Haas		
		Parnevik	Love	Nobilo	Stewart	McNulty		
		Parry	Maggert	Glasson	Woosnam	Simpson		
		Daly	Jimenez	Senior	O'Meara	Stadler		
	Els	Estes	Triplett	Perry	Mize	James		
	Mickelson	Gilford	Austin	Lane	Funk	Weibring		
	Campbell	Watts	Waldorf	Tway	Sluman	Strange		
	Furyk	Johansson	Ogle	Azinger	Edwards	Clark		M. Ozaki
Duval	Maruyama	Jobe	Riley	Forsbrand	Sutton	Bryant	Crenshaw	Watson
Leonard	Clarke	Stricker	Turner	Huston	N. Ozaki	Nakajima	McCumber	Kite
Allenby	Haeggman	O'Malley	Fehr	Lowery	Clements	Romero	Zoeller	Irwin
Cejka	Gamez	Hamilton	Tomori	Higashi	Cook	Rivero	Lietzke	Morgan

As the graph above illustrates, the players who have dominated professional golf for the past decade have finally entered the downside of their careers. The columns for age groups 37-39 and 40-42 — including such players as Norman, Price, Langer, Faldo, Ballesteros and Woosnam — have been overtaken for the first time by a younger (age 34-36) group led by Pavin and Couples. They are closely followed by a wave of even younger (age 31-33) players including Montgomerie, Elkington and Vijay Singh.

The top 200 players on the Sony Ranking as of December 31, 1995 (the final list based on the three-year "rolling" average) are to be found on pages 6 and 7, and in greater detail in the Appendixes. The opposite page makes note of the trends which occurred during the year.

Three of the 1995 major champions — Elkington, Pavin and Ben Crenshaw — made significant gains within the top 50, as did Sam Torrance and Lee Janzen, who each had three victories on the PGA European Tour and U.S. PGA Tour, respectively. The injured Jose Maria Olazabal had the largest fall within the top 50.

Peter Jacobsen and Billy Mayfair, with two victories each on the U.S. PGA Tour, were the leaders among those advancing into the top 50, while Tom Kite was foremost among those exiting the top 50.

David Duval made the most impressive debut in the history of the Sony Ranking. His final No. 39 position was the best ever by a rookie. The previous best first-year performances were by Els (No. 40 in 1992), Olazabal (No. 43 in 1986), Phil Mickelson (No. 47 in 1993) and Robert Gamez (No. 53 in 1990).

Two other rookies on the U.S. PGA Tour, Woody Austin and Justin Leonard, are listed among those advancing into the top 100 of the Sony Ranking. Chip Beck and Rodger Davis were probably the most prominent of those losing top-100 positions.

1995 Sony Ranking Review

Major Movements Within Top 50

Upward Name	Net Points Gained	Position 1994	1995	Downward Name	Net Points Lost	Position 1994	1995
Steve Elkington	366	43	10	Jose Maria Olazabal	532	5	12
Sam Torrance	307	38	15	Nick Price	513	1	2
Lee Janzen	214	32	16	David Frost	335	11	24
Corey Pavin	182	10	6	Nick Faldo	315	3	7
Scott Hoch	177	30	20	Ian Woosnam	262	16	41
Ben Crenshaw	127	34	19	Fuzzy Zoeller	233	12	32
Jay Haas	116	47	25	Seve Ballesteros	223	14	27
Mark Calcavecchia	109	49	30	Fred Couples	158	7	8
Colin Montgomerie	107	8	5	Mark McNulty	156	18	36
Greg Norman	95	2	1	Mark McCumber	86	19	23

Major Movements Into Top 50   Major Movements Out of Top 50

Name	Net Points Gained	Position 1994	1995	Name	Net Points Lost	Position 1994	1995
Peter Jacobsen	375	123	18	Tom Kite	347	13	54
Billy Mayfair	373	166	35	John Cook	279	24	98
Michael Campbell	369	209	28	Paul Azinger	234	21	61
David Duval	353	427	39	Rick Fehr	161	50	97
Costantino Rocca	262	63	21	John Huston	153	40	72
Jim Gallagher, Jr.	182	65	26	Larry Mize	148	28	55
Kenny Perry	177	101	48	David Edwards	128	45	77
Mark O'Meara	175	83	44	Tommy Nakajima	117	46	78
Payne Stewart	123	54	29	Barry Lane	116	35	52
John Daly	114	72	45	Hale Irwin	114	29	56
Scott Simpson	103	57	38	David Gilford	95	33	53
Peter Senior	25	53	47	Robert Allenby	77	48	64
Craig Stadler	12	59	46	Bruce Lietzke	68	41	63

Other Major Movements

Upward Name	Net Points Gained	Position 1994	1995	Downward Name	Net Points Lost	Position 1994	1995
Woody Austin	292	–	66	Mark Roe	185	51	105
Bob Tway	285	308	57	Gordon Brand, Jr.	171	60	117
Justin Leonard	264	351	59	Chip Beck	169	62	125
Satoshi Higashi	235	258	80	Tony Johnstone	165	64	118
Jim Furyk	228	261	81	Rodger Davis	158	81	181
Alexander Cejka	204	367	85	Mike Springer	149	77	160
Brandt Jobe	170	226	74	Keith Clearwater	145	117	275
Shigeki Maruyama	157	184	84	David Feherty	127	89	178
Hidemichi Tanaka	152	–	112	Steve Pate	123	114	231
Wayne Riley	146	190	88				
Jarmo Sandelin	128	–	154				
John Morse	121	260	111				
Kirk Triplett	120	99	60				
Steve Stricker	119	133	75				
Fred Funk	117	110	70				

The Sony Ranking

(As of December 31, 1995)

POS.	NAME, CIRCUIT	POINTS AVERAGE	POS.	NAME, CIRCUIT	POINTS AVERAGE
1	Greg Norman, ANZ 1	21.97	51	Mark James, Eur 11	4.63
2	Nick Price, Afr 1	16.26	52	Barry Lane, Eur 12	4.51
3	Bernhard Langer, Eur 1	15.68	53	David Gilford, Eur 13	4.50
4	Ernie Els, Afr 2	13.98	54	Tom Kite, USA 29	4.46
5	Colin Montgomerie, Eur 2	13.86	55	Larry Mize, USA 30	4.45
6	Corey Pavin, USA 1	13.58	56	Hale Irwin, USA 31	4.38
7	Nick Faldo, Eur 3	13.16	57	Bob Tway, USA 32	4.31
8	Fred Couples, USA 2	12.02	58	Brian Watts, USA 33	4.24
9	Masashi Ozaki, Jpn 1	10.82	59	Justin Leonard, USA 34	4.22
10	Steve Elkington, ANZ 2	10.48	60	Kirk Triplett, USA 35	4.19
11	Tom Lehman, USA 3	9.62	61	Paul Azinger, USA 36	4.17
12	Jose Maria Olazabal, Eur 4	9.26	62	Anders Forsbrand, Eur 14	4.11
13	Loren Roberts, USA 4	8.55	63	Bruce Lietzke, USA 37	4.08
14	Vijay Singh, Asa 1	8.41	64	Robert Allenby, ANZ 7	4.02
15	Sam Torrance, Eur 5	8.28	65	D.A. Weibring, USA 38	3.90
16	Lee Janzen, USA 5	8.25	66	Woody Austin, USA 39	3.89
17	Davis Love III, USA 6	7.67	67	Curtis Strange, USA 40	3.79
18	Peter Jacobsen, USA 7	7.53	68	Per-Ulrik Johansson, Eur 15	3.78
19	Ben Crenshaw, USA 8	7.23	69	Duffy Waldorf, USA 41	3.76
20	Scott Hoch, USA 9	7.18	70	Fred Funk, USA 42	3.74
21	Costantino Rocca, Eur 6	7.02	71	Howard Clark, Eur 16	3.72
22	Phil Mickelson, USA 10	6.89	72	John Huston, USA 43	3.70
23	Mark McCumber, USA 11	6.79	73	Jeff Sluman, USA 44	3.70
24	David Frost, Afr 3	6.66	74	Brandt Jobe, USA 45	3.70
25	Jay Haas, USA 12	6.47	75	Steve Stricker, USA 46	3.67
26	Jim Gallagher, Jr., USA 13	6.36	76	Brad Bryant, USA 47	3.65
27	Seve Ballesteros, Eur 7	6.36	77	David Edwards, USA 48	3.65
28	Michael Campbell, ANZ 3	6.28	78	Tsuneyuki Nakajima, Jpn 2	3.64
29	Payne Stewart, USA 14	6.09	79	Steve Lowery, USA 49	3.63
30	Mark Calcavecchia, USA 15	6.08	80	Satoshi Higashi, Jpn 3	3.59
31	Brad Faxon, USA 16	6.00	81	Jim Furyk, USA 50	3.53
32	Fuzzy Zoeller, USA 17	5.97	82	Hal Sutton, USA 51	3.52
33	Tom Watson, USA 18	5.95	83	Brett Ogle, ANZ 8	3.51
34	Jeff Maggert, USA 19	5.82	84	Shigeki Maruyama, Jpn 4	3.47
35	Billy Mayfair, USA 20	5.80	85	Alexander Cejka, Eur 17	3.42
36	Mark McNulty, Afr 4	5.79	86	Darren Clarke, Eur 18	3.40
37	Frank Nobilo, ANZ 4	5.61	87	Gil Morgan, USA 52	3.31
38	Scott Simpson, USA 21	5.54	88	Wayne Riley, ANZ 9	3.25
39	David Duval, USA 22	5.49	89	Peter O'Malley, ANZ 10	3.21
40	Jesper Parnevik, Eur 8	5.46	90	Eduardo Romero, SAm 1	3.16
41	Ian Woosnam, Eur 9	5.31	91	Naomichi Ozaki, Jpn 5	3.05
42	Bill Glasson, USA 23	5.30	92	Greg Turner, ANZ 11	3.01
43	Craig Parry, ANZ 5	5.25	93	Joakim Haeggman, Eur 19	3.01
44	Mark O'Meara, USA 24	5.15	94	Todd Hamilton, USA 53	2.96
45	John Daly, USA 25	5.00	95	Lennie Clements, USA 54	2.95
46	Craig Stadler, USA 26	4.83	96	Jose Rivero, Eur 20	2.89
47	Peter Senior, ANZ 6	4.81	97	Rick Fehr, USA 55	2.77
48	Kenny Perry, USA 27	4.79	98	John Cook, USA 56	2.76
49	Bob Estes, USA 28	4.77	99	Katsuyoshi Tomori, Jpn 6	2.76
50	Miguel Angel Jimenez, Eur 10	4.70	100	Robert Gamez, USA 57	2.72

POS.	NAME, CIRCUIT	POINTS AVERAGE	POS.	NAME, CIRCUIT	POINTS AVERAGE
101	Peter Baker, Eur 21	2.72	151	Sven Struver, Eur 33	1.91
102	Frankie Minoza, Asa 2	2.71	152	David Ishii, USA 74	1.85
103	Jim McGovern, USA 58	2.70	153	Lucas Parsons, ANZ 15	1.83
104	Jay Don Blake, USA 59	2.67	154	Jarmo Sandelin, Eur 34	1.83
105	Mark Roe, Eur 22	2.67	155	Paul McGinley, Eur 35	1.81
106	Mark Brooks, USA 60	2.64	156	Eduardo Herrera, SAm 4	1.80
107	Mike Heinen, USA 61	2.62	157	Pierre Fulke, Eur 36	1.79
108	Wayne Westner, Afr 5	2.60	158	Guy Boros, USA 75	1.79
109	Nolan Henke, USA 62	2.60	159	Grant Waite, ANZ 16	1.78
110	Masahiro Kuramoto, Jpn 7	2.57	160	Mike Springer, USA 76	1.78
111	John Morse, USA 63	2.54	161	Yoshinori Mizumaki, Jpn 18	1.78
112	Hidemichi Tanaka, Jpn 8	2.53	162	Paul Eales, Eur 37	1.78
113	Andrew Magee, USA 64	2.51	163	Don Pooley, USA 77	1.74
114	Philip Walton, Eur 23	2.49	164	Ignacio Garrido, Eur 38	1.74
115	Hisayuki Sasaki, Jpn 9	2.46	165	Kazuhiro Hosokawa, Jpn 19	1.73
116	Carlos Franco, SAm 2	2.41	166	Mike Hulbert, USA 78	1.72
117	Gordon Brand, Jr., Eur 24	2.40	167	Rocco Mediate, USA 79	1.71
118	Tony Johnstone, Afr 6	2.35	168	Ted Tryba, USA 80	1.69
119	Scott Verplank, USA 65	2.28	169	Hajime Meshiai, Jpn 20	1.67
120	Mike Clayton, ANZ 12	2.27	170	Wayne Grady, ANZ 17	1.66
121	Andrew Oldcorn, Eur 25	2.27	171	Donnie Hammond, USA 81	1.65
122	Billy Andrade, USA 66	2.26	172	Russell Claydon, Eur 39	1.62
123	Retief Goosen, Afr 7	2.24	173	Kiyoshi Maita, Jpn 21	1.62
124	Nobuo Serizawa, Jpn 10	2.22	174	Katsunari Takahashi, Jpn 22	1.60
125	Chip Beck, USA 67	2.22	175	Russ Cochran, USA 82	1.60
126	Paul Broadhurst, Eur 26	2.18	176	Mathias Gronberg, Eur 40	1.57
127	Blaine McCallister, USA 68	2.18	177	Fulton Allem, Afr 9	1.57
128	Sandy Lyle, Eur 27	2.17	178	David Feherty, Eur 41	1.55
129	Bob Lohr, USA 69	2.15	179	Santiago Luna, Eur 42	1.54
130	Hideki Kase, Jpn 11	2.14	180	Jean Louis Guepy, Eur 43	1.54
131	Andrew Coltart, Eur 28	2.13	181	Rodger Davis, ANZ 18	1.54
132	Tomohiro Maruyama, Jpn 12	2.10	182	Glen Day, USA 83	1.54
133	Roger Wessels, Afr 8	2.08	183	Robin Freeman, USA 84	1.54
134	Masayuki Kawamura, Jpn 13	2.05	184	Peter Hedblom, Eur 44	1.52
135	Robert Karlsson, Eur 29	2.04	185	Jay Delsing, USA 85	1.49
136	Jose Coceres, SAm 3	2.03	186	Michael Jonzon, Eur 45	1.48
137	Carl Mason, Eur 30	2.02	187	Steve Jones, USA 86	1.48
138	Roger Mackay, ANZ 13	2.02	188	Ryoken Kawagishi, Jpn 23	1.47
139	Joey Sindelar, USA 70	2.01	189	Mark Wiebe, USA 87	1.46
140	Dan Forsman, USA 71	2.01	190	Dillard Pruitt, USA 88	1.46
141	Gene Sauers, USA 72	2.01	191	Marco Dawson, USA 89	1.46
142	Ronan Rafferty, Eur 31	2.00	192	Stephen Ames, SAm 5	1.46
143	Toru Suzuki, Jpn 14	1.99	193	Raymond Floyd, USA 90	1.45
144	Patrick Burke, USA 73	1.98	194	Mike Standly, USA 91	1.44
145	Kazuhiro Takami, Jpn 15	1.97	195	Nobumitsu Yuhara, Jpn 24	1.43
146	Rick Gibson, Can 1	1.97	196	Paul Moloney, ANZ 19	1.42
147	Toshimitsu Izawa, Jpn 16	1.97	197	Steven Richardson, Eur 46	1.42
148	Peter Mitchell, Eur 32	1.96	198	Gary Orr, Eur 47	1.41
149	Terry Price, ANZ 14	1.94	199	John Adams, USA 92	1.40
150	Tsukasa Watanabe, Jpn 17	1.92	200	Mike Sullivan, USA 93	1.40

Detailed Structure For Allocation of Sony Ranking Points

Special event minimums noted in the headings:
- 451–475 — Europe PGA Champ. Minimum
- 96–105 — Austr & Japan Opens Minimum
- 36–45 — Eur & USA Minimum
- 16–25 — Austr/NZ & Japan Minimum
- 5 — Asia & SAf Minimum

Pos.	MAJOR CHAMPIONSHIPS	Players Championship	776-825	726-775	676-725	626-675	576-625	526-575	501-525	476-500	451-475	426-450	401-425	376-400	351-375	326-350	301-325	276-300	251-275	226-250	201-225	176-200	151-175	126-150	116-125	106-115	96-105	86-95	76-85	66-75	56-65	46-55	36-45	26-35	16-25	6-15	5	4	3	2	0
1st	50	40	40	39	38	37	36	35	34	33	32	31	30	29	28	27	26	25	24	23	22	21	20	19	18	17	16	15	14	13	12	11	10	9	8	7	6	5	4	3	2
2nd	40	24	24	23	23	22	22	21	20	20	19	19	18	17	17	16	16	15	14	14	13	13	12	11	11	10	10	9	8	8	7	7	6	5	5	4	4	3	3	2	1
3rd	30	24	23	22	22	21	20	20	19	18	18	17	17	16	16	15	15	14	14	13	13	12	12	11	11	10	10	9	8	8	7	7	6	5	5	4	4	3	2	2	1
4th	24	19	19	18	17	17	15	15	14	14	13	12	12	11	12	11	10	10	10	9	9	8	7	7	7	6	6	5	4	4	4	4	3	3	3	3	3	2	2	2	1
5th	22	17	17	16	15	15	14	14	13	13	12	12	11	11	11	10	10	9	8	8	7	7	6	6	5	5	4	4	3	3	3	3	2	2	2	2	1	1	1	1	1
6th	20	16	16	15	14	14	13	13	12	12	11	10	10	10	9	8	8	8	7	7	6	5	5	4	4	4	3	3	3	3	3	3	2	2	2	2	1	1	1	1	
7th	19	15	15	14	14	13	13	12	11	11	10	10	9	9	8	8	7	7	6	6	5	4	4	4	3	3	3	3	2	2	2	2	2	2	1	1	1				
8th	18	14	14	14	13	12	12	11	10	10	9	9	8	8	7	7	7	6	5	5	4	4	4	3	3	3	3	2	2	2	2	2	2	1	1	1					
9th	17	13	13	14	11	11	11	10	9	9	8	8	7	7	6	6	6	5	4	4	4	3	3	3	3	2	2	2	2	2	2	2	2	1	1	1					
10th	16	12	12	10	10	10	10	9	8	8	7	7	6	6	5	5	5	4	4	3	3	3	3	3	2	2	2	2	2	2	2	2	1	1	1	1					
11th	15	11	11	11	11	10	9	9	8	8	7	7	6	6	5	5	4	4	3	3	3	3	2	2	2	2	2	2	2	2	2	1	1	1							
12th	14	11	11	11	11	9	9	8	8	8	7	6	6	6	5	5	4	4	3	3	3	2	2	2	2	2	2	2	2	2	1	1	1	1							
13th	13	10	10	11	11	9	8	8	8	7	6	6	6	5	5	4	4	3	3	3	2	2	2	2	2	2	2	1	1	1	1	1									
14th	12	9	9	11	11	8	8	7	7	7	6	6	5	5	4	4	3	3	3	2	2	2	2	2	2	1	1	1	1	1											
15th	11	9	9	9	9	8	7	7	6	6	5	5	5	4	4	3	3	3	2	2	2	2	2	2	2	1	1	1	1	1											
16th	11	8	8	9	7	7	7	6	6	6	5	5	4	4	4	3	3	2	2	2	2	2	2	2	2	1	1	1	1	1											
17th	10	8	8	9	7	7	6	6	6	5	5	4	4	4	3	3	3	2	2	2	2	2	2	2	2	1	1	1	1												
18th	10	7	7	9	7	6	6	6	5	5	4	4	4	3	3	3	2	2	2	2	2	2	2	2	1	1	1	1													
19th	9	7	7	9	7	6	6	6	5	5	4	4	3	3	3	2	2	2	2	2	2	2	2	1	1	1	1														

TOTAL RATING POINTS

RATING POINTS

Current Rank of Players	Rating Points
1st	50
2nd	34
3rd	30
4th	27
5th	24
6th	21
7th	20
8th	19
9th	18
10th	17
11th	16
12th	15
13th	14
14th	13
15th	12
16th to 30th	11
31st to 34th	10
35th to 38th	9
39th to 43rd	8
44th to 50th	7
51st to 55th	6
56th to 60th	5
61st to 70th	4
71st to 80th	3
81st to 100th	2
Total Available	825

51st plus all making 36-hole cut in major championships

World Golf Rankings 1968-1995

Year	No. 1	No. 2	No. 3	No. 4	No. 5	No. 6	No. 7	No. 8	No. 9	No. 10
1968	Nicklaus	Palmer	Casper	Player	Charles	Boros	Coles	Thomson	Beard	Nagle
1969	Nicklaus	Player	Casper	Palmer	Charles	Beard	Archer	Trevino	Barber	Sikes
1970	Nicklaus	Player	Casper	Trevino	Charles	Devlin	Coles	Jacklin	Beard	Huggett
1971	Nicklaus	Trevino	Player	Palmer	Casper	Barber	Crampton	Charles	Devlin	Weiskopf
1972	Nicklaus	Player	Trevino	Crampton	Palmer	Jacklin	Weiskopf	Oosterhuis	Heard	Devlin
1973	Nicklaus	Weiskopf	Trevino	Player	Crampton	Miller	Oosterhuis	Wadkins	Heard	Brewer
1974	Nicklaus	Miller	Player	Weiskopf	Trevino	M. Ozaki	Crampton	Irwin	Green	Heard
1975	Nicklaus	Miller	Weiskopf	Irwin	Player	Green	Trevino	Casper	Crampton	Watson
1976	Nicklaus	Irwin	Miller	Player	Green	Watson	Weiskopf	Marsh	Crenshaw	Geiberger
1977	Nicklaus	Watson	Green	Irwin	Crenshaw	Marsh	Player	Weiskopf	Floyd	Ballesteros
1978	Watson	Nicklaus	Irwin	Green	Player	Crenshaw	Marsh	Ballesteros	Trevino	Aoki
1979	Watson	Nicklaus	Irwin	Trevino	Player	Aoki	Green	Crenshaw	Ballesteros	Wadkins
1980	Watson	Trevino	Aoki	Crenshaw	Nicklaus	Pate	Ballesteros	Bean	Irwin	Player
1981	Watson	Rogers	Aoki	Pate	Trevino	Ballesteros	Graham	Crenshaw	Floyd	Lietzke
1982	Watson	Floyd	Ballesteros	Kite	Stadler	Pate	Nicklaus	Rogers	Aoki	Strange
1983	Ballesteros	Watson	Floyd	Norman	Kite	Nicklaus	Nakajima	Stadler	Aoki	Wadkins
1984	Ballesteros	Watson	Norman	Wadkins	Langer	Faldo	Nakajima	Stadler	Kite	Peete
1985	Ballesteros	Langer	Norman	Watson	Nakajima	Wadkins	O'Meara	Strange	Pavin	Sutton
1986	Norman	Langer	Ballesteros	Nakajima	Bean	Tway	Sutton	Strange	Stewart	O'Meara
1987	Norman	Ballesteros	Langer	Lyle	Strange	Woosnam	Stewart	Wadkins	McNulty	Crenshaw
1988	Ballesteros	Norman	Lyle	Faldo	Strange	Crenshaw	Woosnam	Frost	Azinger	Calcavecchia
1989	Norman	Faldo	Ballesteros	Strange	Stewart	Kite	Olazabal	Calcavecchia	Woosnam	Azinger
1990	Norman	Faldo	Olazabal	Woosnam	Stewart	Azinger	Ballesteros	Kite	McNulty	Calcavecchia
1991	Woosnam	Faldo	Olazabal	Ballesteros	Norman	Couples	Langer	Stewart	Azinger	Calcavecchia
1992	Faldo	Couples	Woosnam	Olazabal	Norman	Langer	Cook	Price	Azinger	Davis
1993	Faldo	Norman	Langer	Price	Couples	Azinger	Woosnam	Kite	Love	Love
1994	Price	Norman	Faldo	Langer	Olazabal	Els	Couples	Montgomerie	M. Ozaki	Pavin
1995	Norman	Price	Langer	Els	Montgomerie	Pavin	Faldo	Couples	M. Ozaki	Elkington

(*The World of Professional Golf* 1968-1985; Sony Ranking 1986-1995)

Sony Ranking of Leading Players 1986-1995

Player	1st Ranking	1986 Aug 31	1986 Dec 28	1987 Apr 26	1987 Aug 30	1987 Dec 27	1988 May 1	1988 Aug 28	1988 Dec 25	1989 Apr 30	1989 Aug 27	1989 Dec 31	1990 Apr 29	1990 Aug 26	1990 Dec 30	1991 Apr 28	1991 Aug 25	1991 Dec 29	1992 Apr 27	1992 Aug 30	1992 Dec 27	1993 Apr 25	1993 Aug 29	1993 Dec 26	1994 May 1	1994 Aug 28	1994 Dec 25	1995 Apr 30	1995 Aug 27	End of 3-Year System
Norman	6	2	1	1	1	1	1	1	2	2	1	1	1	1	1	4	4	5	7	7	5	4	2	2	1	2	2	3	1	1
Price	52	40	54	57	46	47	50	33	41	27	43	38	45	47	38	43	41	24	20	10	8	5	4	4	3	1	1	1	2	2
Langer	1	3	2	3	3	3	4	9	15	18	20	16	14	17	14	9	8	7	6	4	6	2	3	3	4	4	4	4	4	3
Els																			95	80	40	53	27	20	14	7	6	5	5	4
Montgomerie												162	158	107	81	83	36	36	32	24	20	16	16	14	12	9	8	7	6	5
Pavin	9	15	19	11	17	24	45	56	46	63	59	85	91	65	54	30	15	18	18	16	16	19	14	10	10	10	10	10	7	6
Faldo	24	28	48	62	22	14	12	5	4	3	3	2	2	2	2	3	3	2	2	1	1	1	1	1	2	3	3	2	3	7
Couples	42	62	73	80	53	46	31	27	19	14	16	15	12	11	11	18	9	6	1	2	2	3	6	5	5	5	7	6	8	8
M. Ozaki	96	35	23	22	19	18	15	18	11	13	13	12	11	12	17	16	22	30	24	20	15	13	13	12	13	12	9	9	9	9
Elkington								175	163	138	143	142	86	80	62	47	46	44	41	27	18	18	18	19	34	40	43	29	10	10
Lehman																			140	115	74	57	47	48	21	14	17	19	11	11
Olazabal		166	43	46	38	49	49	36	20	8	9	7	9	3	3	2	2	3	3	3	4	7	8	15	7	6	5	8	12	12
Roberts										151	128	105	110	69	59	65	74	88	99	128	104	105	96	107	29	20	20	17	9	13
Singh										175	130	87	76	64	76	62	56	77	50	37	38	26	20	16	16	19	15	18	19	14
Torrance	23	29	46	48	50	44	55	70	99	82	64	60	66	75	50	46	40	55	59	90	108	73	44	37	39	41	38	49	13	15
Janzen																		183	125	85	70	45	21	22	27	29	32	26	23	16
Love	30	44	56	78	60	60	69	82	91	74	62	65	79	59	44	23	25	23	8	12	10	11	11	9	15	18	25	21	18	17
Jacobsen	46	51	38	64	123	116	120	60	62	52	58	46	27	28	29	38	67	50	73	93	123	124	138	136	134	111	123	25	17	18
Crenshaw	37	36	33	18	11	10	7	6	7	9	15	17	26	23	28	25	58	52	81	44	51	30	56	64	53	44	34	22	21	19
Hoch				32	24	27	21	26	41	26	24	24	29	39	39	52	42	41	54	101	116	110	87	88	61	36	30	32	24	20

2. The Year In Retrospect

Professional golf in 1995 probably will not be remembered because of any single person, as was 1994 for Nick Price and his seven victories including two major championships. This year, Price had only two late-year victories in Africa and dropped to No. 2 on the Sony Ranking.

Greg Norman, who advanced to No. 1, set an earnings record on the PGA Tour in the United States but did not win any of the four major championships. Corey Pavin won the U.S. Open and Steve Elkington won the PGA Championship, and both had other victories as well, but neither was measurably better than the other. Masashi (Jumbo) Ozaki added to his formidable record, but only in Japan.

Perhaps the person who came closest to putting their mark upon 1995 was a young woman from Sweden, not 25 years old until October, Annika Sorenstam, who became the first to win money titles in the United States, Europe and Australasia in the same year, and who won six tournaments.

Among the men, my assessment of the year would be Elkington first, followed by Pavin and Norman, then a second tier of comparable achievers consisting of Ernie Els, Colin Montgomerie and Bernhard Langer. Two major champions were not included on this list, Ben Crenshaw and John Daly, because they did little else.

Crenshaw had an emotional victory for his second Masters title one week after his mentor, Harvey Penick, died at age 90. Crenshaw had only three other top-five finishes on the U.S. PGA Tour, although he won the late-year MasterCard PGA Grand Slam of Golf. Whether it was because Daly was at St. Andrews, or some other reason, the week of the British Open was the exception to his year. He did not have a single top-10 finish and missed the 36-hole cut eight times on the U.S. PGA Tour.

Nevertheless, it was a year to be savored by Daly on at least three counts. He won the British Open, went for a second entire year without an alcoholic drink, and did nothing to merit a reprimand from the game's authorities. Considering his troubles in the past, it was his best year as a professional golfer. "I'm just trying to regain some friends out here," Daly said. "There's no way I would be here today if I was still drinking."

The Ryder Cup was the most memorable event of the year, as the Europeans came from a 7-9 deficit entering the final-day singles to post a 14½-13½ victory. Everyone knew the European (and earlier, British and Irish) teams had won the singles only once in 30 previous competitions, to which European captain Bernard Gallacher had a snappy response, "History is for amateurs, professionals only think of the future."

The Europeans then went out and won seven matches, halved one and lost only four. It came down to two matches, Nick Faldo (Europe) versus Curtis Strange and Philip Walton (Europe) versus Jay Haas. Faldo hit a wedge shot to within about three feet of the 18th hole for "the best scrambling par of my life" and won as Strange bogeyed the last three holes. The last American hope, Haas fought off elimination for two holes then lost when he and Walton halved the 18th with bogeys.

While the emotion-charged European team regained the Ryder Cup with only their second victory ever in America, critics in the United States were quick to blame captain Lanny Wadkins and Strange, who was a captain's choice, rather than acknowledging that the two teams were more even than the American media and spectators wanted to believe.

Rare sparks also flew when Norman refused to sign Mark McCumber's scorecard after the first round of the NEC World Series of Golf. Norman believed McCumber had tapped down a spike mark on his line before putting. McCumber said he was only removing a bug. A tournament official signed McCumber's scorecard, since there was no evidence other than the word of the two players. Norman considered withdrawing from the tournament on principle, but was convinced to stay — and went on to win.

That aside, it was virtually a crisis-free year on the administrative side of the U.S. PGA Tour. The World Tour, proposed in late 1994 with Norman at the fore, faded away with little further mention. Meanwhile Commissioner Tim Finchem and the heads of the world's other tours held meetings from time to time, and among their considerations was the possibility of world events, probably after 1998, when the current U.S. television contracts have expired.

Not only did Finchem not have any problems with Daly, but also Finchem was relieved of an investigation by the Federal Trade Commission into the U.S. PGA Tour's rules regarding conflicting events and releases for televised golf appearances. In August, 1994, the Tour had refused a proposal from the FTC to voluntarily eliminate these rules. In a statement released in September, FTC secretary Donald S. Clark wrote, "... the investigation has been closed."

The controversy of the year occurred on the U.S. LPGA Tour. Television commentator Ben Wright was quoted in May by a newspaper reporter in Wilmington, Delaware, as saying "lesbians in the sport hurt women's golf" and making other comments along those lines. That touched off a wave of protest, including from Wright himself, who denied the remarks. The reporter had only written notes, not a taped recording, and Wright escaped criticism from the LPGA and retained his CBS employment.

Later in the year, however, *Sports Illustrated* quoted a witness to the interview and also reported that at a party in June Wright had confirmed making the remarks. Wright also was reported to have made derogatory comments about the Wilmington reporter, which the magazine said were untrue. This created more protest, and the sources of the article made retractions.

It took until the first week of January for CBS to respond with a statement that there were "no plans for Wright's return" to the network's golf telecasts. Wright began his own statement by saying, "Despite the fact that I have been widely misquoted, there is no doubt I have been guilty of making insensitive remarks."

Commissioner Charles Mechem, as he had planned from the start, retired at the conclusion of his five-year LPGA contract at the end of 1995. His replacement, announced in June, was communications executive Jim Ritts.

The World Money List for 1995 was led by Pavin with $2,746,340, followed by Ozaki, Montgomerie and Norman — all with more than $2 million — then by Langer, Elkington and Els just short of that figure. Pavin's total, including $1,000,000 from the Nedbank Million Dollar Challenge, was the fourth highest ever. Els won $2,862,854 in 1994, Price won $2,825,280 in 1993 and Nick Faldo won $2,748,248 in 1992.

Pavin was the first American to lead the World Money List since 1982, after U.S. players dominated the first 17 years of the compilations. There were 32 players who earned more than $1 million this year, eight more than the previous high in 1994.

The Senior World Money List was led by Raymond Floyd — the last previous American to lead the World Money List — and he broke his own senior record with $1,811,049. Eight other seniors earned more than $1 million. Sorenstam led the Women's World Money List with $1,043,121, breaking the record of $1,006,143 set by Laura Davies in 1994.

The complete lists are in the Appendixes.

The figures do not include skins games, pro-ams or shootouts, which would add, for example, $240,000 to Pavin's total from the Skins Game and $750,000 to Floyd's, since Floyd won the Senior Skins Game as well as two new pro-am events, the Office Depot Father/Son Challenge and Lexus Challenge.

Now, our review of 1995 in professional golf, starting with the leading players of the year.

STEVE ELKINGTON

Event	Position
Mercedes Championship	1
Phoenix Open	T-26
AT&T Pebble Beach National Pro-Am	T-19
Buick Invitational of California	MC
Nissan Open	T-14
Doral-Ryder Open	T-4
The Players Championship	WD
Masters Tournament	T-5
Kmart Greater Greensboro Open	MC
Shell Houston Open	MC
GTE Byron Nelson Classic	T-32
Buick Classic	T-18
Colonial National Invitational	T-15
Memorial Tournament	T-2
U.S. Open Championship	T-36
Motorola Western Open	T-29
British Open Championship	T-6
PGA Championship	1
Ernst Championship	T-8
Fred Meyer Challenge	5
NEC World Series of Golf	DQ
Buick Challenge	MC
Toyota World Match Play Championship	2

Event	Position
Alfred Dunhill Cup	T-5
Tour Championship	T-2
MasterCard PGA Grand Slam of Golf	T-2
Franklin Templeton Shark Shootout	1
Heineken Australian Open	T-29
Andersen Consulting World Championship	T-9

The year started well for Steve Elkington — with a 25-foot birdie putt in a playoff to win the Mercedes Championship — and would only get better. Elkington defeated Bruce Lietzke on the second extra hole of the U.S. PGA Tour's season-opening event, formerly known as the Tournament of Champions. He claimed his first major title in the PGA Championship with a final-round 64 and another 25-foot birdie putt in a playoff, this time on the first hole against Colin Montgomerie. The PGA victory came three weeks after Elkington could have won the British Open but for his putting. He tied for sixth place. He also tied for fifth place in the Masters and for 36th in the U.S. Open.

In addition, Elkington was runner-up in two well-regarded American events, the Memorial Tournament and Tour Championship, and lost in the final of the Toyota World Match Play Championship to defending champion Ernie Els. He lost by one stroke in the late-year MasterCard PGA Grand Slam of Golf, but won a team event the next week, the Franklin Templeton Shark Shootout, with partner Mark Calcavecchia.

Long regarded as having the best swing in golf, Elkington won the Vardon Trophy for having the lowest scoring average, was fifth on the U.S. money list with $1,254,352 and sixth on the World Money List with $1,914,135. During the year he advanced from No. 43 to No. 10 on the Sony Ranking.

Although Elkington had won four tournaments, including The Players Championship in 1991, plus the Australian Open in 1992, this was the first year he could demonstrate his ability while healthy. He was hospitalized early in 1994 with a virus and, while there, had a malignant growth removed from his shoulder. In May, Elkington underwent sinus surgery, which helped alleviate a longtime breathing problem.

Elkington, who reached his 33rd birthday in December, is from Australia but has become well-acclimated in Texas since going there to attend the University of Houston. He met his wife, Lisa, while attending Houston and they now have a home there, near Champions Golf Club.

COREY PAVIN

Event	Position
Mercedes Championship	T-12
United Airlines Hawaiian Open	T-36
AT&T Pebble Beach National Pro-Am	MC
Bob Hope Chrysler Classic	T-70
Nissan Open	1
The Nestle Invitational	T-37
The Players Championship	T-3
Masters Tournament	T-17

Event	Position
MCI Classic	T-53
BellSouth Classic	MC
GTE Byron Nelson Classic	T-16
Colonial National Invitational	MC
Memorial Tournament	MC
Kemper Open	2
U.S. Open Championship	1
Canon Greater Hartford Open	T-11
Motorola Western Open	T-60
British Open Championship	T-8
PGA Championship	MC
NEC World Series of Golf	T-20
Canon European Masters	T-31
Suntory Open	T-5
Walt Disney World/Oldsmobile Classic	T-49
Volvo Asian Masters	1
Tour Championship	T-2
MasterCard PGA Grand Slam of Golf	T-2
Nedbank Million Dollar Challenge	1
Andersen Consulting World Championship	T-9

Corey Pavin had a year that was arguably the equal of Elkington's — and better than Elkington's if only the money or the number of tournaments won are counted. Pavin led the World Money List with $2,746,340 and had four individual victories to Elkington's two. He was just ahead of Elkington with $1,340,079 on the U.S. PGA Tour.

Pavin, who advanced from No. 10 to No. 6 on the Sony Ranking, earned more Sony points for the year than Elkington (688 to 624) but Elkington played in three fewer events and had the higher Sony points average for the year (27.13 to 26.46). Each could say he was the best golfer of 1995.

Like Elkington, Pavin had an impressive victory early in the year and his first major championship. He won the Nissan Open for the second year in a row and secured the U.S. Open title with the Shot of the Year. He scored late-year victories in the Volvo Asian Masters by nine strokes and in the Nedbank Million Dollar Challenge by five strokes. The week before the U.S. Open, Pavin lost a playoff in the Kemper Open, and he tied for second with Elkington later in the Tour Championship and MasterCard PGA Grand Slam of Golf.

In the other major championships, Pavin tied for 17th place in the Masters, tied for eighth (one stroke behind Elkington) in the British Open and missed the 36-hole cut in the PGA Championship.

Pavin's four-wood shot into the 18th green at Shinnecock Hills will stand as one of the greatest ever hit on the final hole of the U.S. Open. From 228 yards out, and with the wind gusting up to 20 miles an hour, Pavin's shot settled only five or six feet from the cup. Although Pavin missed the putt, it did not matter, because Greg Norman bogeyed the 17th hole behind him and would have to hole his second shot to the 18th to tie him, which of course he did not.

It was an appropriate finish for Pavin, whose nickname is "Bulldog" because of his tenacity, despite being one of the shortest drivers on the U.S. PGA Tour (ranked 159th in 1995). Pavin, age 36 in November, entered the year with 14 career victories, including two when he was the leading U.S. money winner with $979,430 in 1991.

GREG NORMAN

Event	Position
Mercedes Championship	18
Dubai Desert Classic	6
Johnnie Walker Classic	T-4
Doral-Ryder Open	T-2
The Nestle Invitational	T-11
The Players Championship	T-37
Masters Tournament	T-3
MCI Classic	WD
Memorial Tournament	1
Kemper Open	T-4
U.S. Open Championship	2
Canon Greater Hartford Open	1
Murphy's Irish Open	11
British Open Championship	T-15
PGA Championship	T-20
Sprint International	T-8
Fred Meyer Challenge	1
NEC World Series of Golf	1
Canon European Masters	MC
Buick Challenge	T-20
Tour Championship	T-9
Alfred Dunhill Cup	T-5
Sumitomo Visa Taiheiyo Masters	T-15
Franklin Templeton Shark Shootout	5
Heineken Australian Open	1
Greg Norman's Holden Classic	T-13

If Greg Norman had won a major championship, he would have had the best year of all. He won three times and led the U.S. PGA Tour with record earnings of $1,654,959. He became the circuit's career money leader with $9,592,829. He was fourth on the World Money List with $2,001,285 and padded his record career worldwide total at age 40 to $16,413,101.

In addition to his three U.S. PGA Tour victories, Norman won his fourth Heineken Australian Open, his first home-country win in five years, and had a team victory with Brad Faxon in the Fred Meyer Challenge. He now has 71 career victories.

Most remarkable was how close Norman came to greater accomplishments. He was the only player to finish in the top 20 of all four major championships and could have won the Masters and U.S. Open. He pulled a sand wedge approach shot on the 17th hole of the Masters and three-putted for a bogey to tie for third place. He shot 68-67 to lead the U.S. Open, then 74-73 to finish second. He pulled six-iron shots into the water at the 18th hole of the Doral-Ryder Open to tie for second place and at the 17th of the Kemper Open to tie for fourth.

His biggest regret in 1995 was at the MCI Classic. He had a painful back, but tried to start the second round and withdrew after one swing. The incomplete round made him ineligible for the Vardon Trophy, although he finished with the lowest scoring average, 69.06 to Elkington's 69.59.

The injury kept Norman out for six weeks but he returned with a vengeance, in successive weeks winning the Memorial Tournament, tieing for fourth in the Kemper Open, placing second in the U.S. Open and winning at the Canon Greater Hartford Open. That surge enabled Norman to regain No. 1 on the Sony Ranking from Nick Price, and Norman held the top position for the rest of the year.

His Memorial victory was by four strokes, but he needed a 40-foot eagle chip shot on the 15th hole to win at Hartford, and he holed another chip shot for a birdie from 66 feet for his third U.S. victory at the NEC World Series of Golf in a playoff against Price and Billy Mayfair.

ERNIE ELS

Event	Position
Bell's Cup	1
Dubai Desert Classic	7
Johnnie Walker Classic	T-43
Philips South African Open	2
Lexington PGA Championship	1
Doral-Ryder Open	T-17
The Nestle Invitational	T-42
The Players Championship	T-68
Masters Tournament	MC
MCI Classic	T-7
GTE Byron Nelson Classic	1
Buick Classic	T-4
Colonial National Invitational	MC
Memorial Tournament	T-13
U.S. Open Championship	MC
Westinghouse-Family House Invitational	1
FedEx St. Jude Classic	T-26
Motorola Western Open	MC
British Open Championship	T-11
Buick Open	T-3
PGA Championship	T-3
Ernst Championship	T-8
Sprint International	2
Fred Meyer Challenge	T-9
NEC World Series of Golf	T-28
ANA Open	2
Toyota World Match Play Championship	1
Alfred Dunhill Cup	T-5
Tour Championship	T-16
Gene Sarazen World Open	T-10

Event	Position
Dunlop Phoenix Tournament	T-20
Nedbank Million Dollar Challenge	T-7
Johnnie Walker World Championship	T-9

A year after winning the U.S. Open, now age 26, Ernie Els continued to distance himself from other golfers of his age by defending his title in the Toyota World Match Play Championship and contending for both the British Open and PGA Championship titles.

In addition to the World Match Play, where he beat Elkington 3 and 1 in the final, Els won two early-year events in South Africa, the Bell's Cup and Lexington PGA Championship (sanctioned by the PGA European Tour), and won the GTE Byron Nelson Classic while playing an extensive schedule in the United States for the first time. He also won the two-day Westinghouse-Family House Invitational, for a total of five victories and 17 in his four-year career.

At the British Open, Els was tied with John Daly entering the final round but shot 75 to Daly's 71 and took a share of 11th place. He was three strokes ahead entering the final round of the PGA Championship, then shot 72 and fell to a third-place tie, two strokes behind. He also was second in three tournaments.

Although climbing from No. 6 to No. 4 on the Sony Ranking, Els also had periods in which he played miserably. He missed the 36-hole cuts in both the Masters and U.S. Open. After a fine start in South Africa, Els struggled in his first four U.S. starts then had three top-10 finishes, including the Byron Nelson victory. He followed that with a stretch in which he missed cuts in three out of five tournaments before regaining his form at the British Open. He worst showing after that was a 28th-place tie.

COLIN MONTGOMERIE

Event	Position
Dubai Desert Classic	2
Johnnie Walker Classic	7
Doral-Ryder Open	T-17
Honda Classic	T-53
The Nestle Invitational	T-42
The Players Championship	T-14
Masters Tournament	T-17
Air France Cannes Open	T-13
Tournoi Perrier de Paris	3
Benson & Hedges International Open	T-4
Peugeot Open de Espana	T-15
Volvo PGA Championship	T-9
Murphy's English Open	2
Deutsche Bank Open	T-20
U.S. Open Championship	T-28
Murphy's Irish Open	T-4
Scottish Open	3
British Open Championship	MC

Event	Position
Heineken Dutch Open	T-7
Volvo Scandinavian Masters	2
PGA Championship	2
Volvo German Open	1
Canon European Masters	T-11
Trophee Lancome	1
Collingtree British Masters	T-7
Smurfit European Open	T-3
Mercedes German Masters	WD
Toyota World Match Play Championship	T-5
Alfred Dunhill Cup	1
Volvo Masters	2
Sumitomo Visa Taiheiyo Masters	4
Nedbank Million Dollar Challenge	11
Johnnie Walker World Championship	T-16

Colin Montgomerie birdied the last three holes in the PGA Championship, including a 20-foot putt to finish with 65, but Elkington birdied to win the playoff. Montgomerie congratulated the winner, then noted, "All I can say is that I did nothing wrong. Having to birdie the last three holes of a major championship and succeeding is a positive note. I'm taking that away positively, as I did from the other playoffs that I've managed to lose in."

Otherwise, Montgomerie had another tremendous year as he won two tournaments, was third on the World Money List with $2,153,211 and led the PGA European Tour money list for the third consecutive year. He won £835,051 to runner-up Sam Torrance's £755,706 total, and his victories in the Volvo German Open and Trophee Lancome were taken at the expense of his rival for the money title. He was on Scotland's winning team in the Alfred Dunhill Cup, along with Torrance and Andrew Coltart, and won one of the crucial singles matches as Europe regained the Ryder Cup from the United States.

At age 32, Montgomerie climbed from No. 8 to No. 5 on the Sony Ranking, in ideal position to remain as one of the world's top golfers for another decade. There is hardly any question that Montgomerie will win several major titles along the way.

While Montgomerie has nine career victories, all in Europe, he has placed second 20 times and lost all five playoffs he has entered, including the 1994 U.S. Open. This year he was second five times and lost a playoff to Philip Walton in the Murphy's English Open. He was runner-up by three strokes in the Dubai Desert Classic, by five in the Volvo Scandinavian Masters and by two in the Volvo Masters.

BERNHARD LANGER

Event	Position
Dubai Desert Classic	T-16
Johnnie Walker Classic	T-23
Doral-Ryder Open	T-40
Honda Classic	T-13

Event	Position
The Nestle Invitational	T-31
The Players Championship	2
Masters Tournament	T-31
Benson & Hedges International Open	T-19
Peugeot Open de Espana	T-8
Volvo PGA Championship	1
Deutsche Bank Open	1
U.S. Open Championship	T-36
BMW International Open	T-2
Murphy's Irish Open	T-20
British Open Championship	T-24
Heineken Dutch Open	T-35
Volvo German Open	T-37
Trophee Lancome	5
Smurfit European Open	1
Mercedes German Masters	2
Toyota World Match Play Championship	4
Volvo Masters	T-5
Sumitomo Visa Taiheiyo Masters	T-9
Nedbank Million Dollar Challenge	3
Johnnie Walker World Championship	T-4
Andersen Consulting World Championship	T-9

No one has been more consistent than Bernhard Langer over the past two decades, and 1995 was another year of sustained excellence for the 38-year-old German. He equalled Seve Ballesteros' European record by winning for the 17th consecutive year and put himself in position to set a world record in 1996. Arnold Palmer and Jack Nicklaus also had 17-year winning streaks on the U.S. PGA Tour.

Langer also broke Neil Coles' European record of 56 consecutive tournaments without missing the 36-hole cut and extended his string to 66 in a row at the year's end. The world record is 113 consecutive tournaments by Byron Nelson in the 1940s.

With three victories, raising his career total to 46, Langer was third on the European money list with £655,854 and fifth on the World Money List with $1,923,554. He remained second behind Greg Norman on the Career World Money List with $14,467,643.

Langer's wins were in the Volvo PGA Championship (for the third time), Deutsche Bank Open and Smurfit European Open, where he holed a 70-foot eagle putt on the 18th hole to tie Barry Lane, then won with an 18-foot birdie on the second playoff hole. He was second three times, including a one-stroke loss to Lee Janzen in The Players Championship. In the major events, however, his best was a tie for 24th place in the British Open.

He improved his Sony Ranking by one position to No. 3. He was at his best in the autumn, was a top-10 finisher in his last eight tournaments and contributed two points in the foursomes towards Europe's victory in the Ryder Cup.

Among the other stars of the 1995 U.S. PGA Tour, Billy Mayfair, who earlier won the Motorola Western Open, took the season-ending Tour Championship and was second to Norman on the American money list with $1,543,192 (and 12th on the World Money List with $1,635,599). He also was second three times. Mayfair, age 29, had only one previous career victory and made a large advance on the Sony Ranking from No. 166 to No. 35.

The only one besides Norman to win three U.S. tournaments was Lee Janzen, who was third on the money list with $1,378,966 (and ninth worldwide with $1,705,392). The 1993 U.S. Open champion, Janzen won The Players Championship under difficult conditions, and later won the Kemper Open and Sprint International, going from No. 32 to No. 16 on the Sony Ranking.

Other than a ninth-place tie in the Mercedes Championship, Janzen did not have another top-10 finish and did not earn enough points to qualify for the U.S. Ryder Cup team. He won his third title the week after being passed over as a captain's choice for the Ryder Cup, and there was much second-guessing then and after the American team lost. But the 31-year-old Janzen got his chance on the U.S. team for the Alfred Dunhill Cup and lost all three of his matches.

There were nine players who won over $1 million on the U.S. PGA Tour alone, and 21 of the 32 million-dollar winners on the World Money List played most of their tournaments in America. Eight players each won two official events.

Peter Jacobsen struck early with back-to-back victories in the AT&T Pebble Beach National Pro-Am and Buick Invitational of California. He just missed a chance for his third victory with a 60-foot birdie try to gain a playoff at the Doral-Ryder Open. He also was third in The Nestle Invitational and second by one stroke in the Kmart Greater Greensboro Open, but did not have another top-10 finish for the year.

Nevertheless, Jacobsen proved he was not just a mimic of great players, a hugely popular under-achiever, but also quite a golfer in his own right. It was unexpected since Jacobsen, at age 41, entered the year with only four career victories, the last in 1990. He zoomed from No. 123 to No. 18 on the Sony Ranking and had $1,186,337 in worldwide earnings.

Other two-time U.S. winners were Mayfair, Elkington, Pavin, Vijay Singh, Mark O'Meara, Jim Gallagher, Jr. and Fred Funk. Most prominent among those not previously mentioned in this chapter, Singh, No. 15 on the Sony Ranking, won the Phoenix Open and Buick Classic while placing ninth on the money list with $1,018,713.

Singh's 21 American starts would have been close to a full schedule for most players, but not the 32-year-old Fijian. He played 17 more events around the world, with stops in 11 countries, even in Korea on the new Omega Tour, where he won the Passport Open. His worldwide earnings were $1,674,913, including a playoff loss in the Johnnie Walker World Championship in Jamaica.

An oversight led to O'Meara's first victory since 1992. He failed to enter the Nissan Open and added the Honda Classic to his schedule, where he won. He went to a playoff later in the year to win the Bell Canadian Open and cracked the $1 million barrier for the first time with $1,018,957 worldwide while taking No. 44 on the Sony Ranking.

For the second time in three years, Gallagher won two American tournaments, the Kmart Greater Greensboro Open and FedEx St. Jude Classic, and also was second twice, placing No. 26 on the Sony Ranking and earning $1,098,442 worldwide. Funk won two of the weaker-field tournaments, the Ideon Classic at Pleasant Valley and Buick Challenge.

Third on the Sony Ranking when the year began, Nick Faldo committed to a full American schedule to improve his chances in the major championships. He won the Doral-Ryder Open in a promising start, but a 24th-place tie in the Masters was his best in the majors as he placed 19th on the U.S. money list with $790,961 (and $1,105,218 worldwide) and his Sony Ranking fell to No. 7. Faldo and his wife, who remained in England, announced their separation late in the year. He would remain in America in 1996.

Davis Love III won the Freeport-McMoRan Classic, which was his last opportunity to qualify for the Masters, where he placed second. It was his 28th major championship as a professional, and the first in which he had even a top-10 finish. He then tied for fourth in the U.S. Open, but was not a factor in the other two major events. Love was the individual winner in the World Cup of Golf, and he and Fred Couples won the team title for the United States for a record fourth consecutive year. He finished No. 17 on the Sony Ranking and had $1,646,995 in worldwide earnings.

Couples finished No. 8 on the Sony Ranking and won $1,462,009 worldwide despite having recurring back problems and not winning on the U.S. PGA Tour. He went three-for-three on the PGA European Tour. He won back-to-back in the season-opening Dubai Desert Classic and Johnnie Walker Classic in the Philippines, then won the last event of the year, the Johnnie Walker World Championship, with an eagle-birdie finish then another birdie on the second playoff hole.

Also more successful off the U.S. PGA Tour, Scott Hoch won the Heineken Dutch Open and West Coast Classic in Canada before wrapping up a six-week surge with a victory in the Greater Milwaukee Open. Hoch, No. 20 on the Sony Ranking, earned $1,192,071 worldwide.

Tom Lehman and Loren Roberts, who won their first tournaments in 1994 after a combined 31 years of trying, continued their winning ways with Lehman (No. 11 on the Sony Ranking) taking the Colonial National Invitational title and Roberts (No. 13) repeating as champion in The Nestle Invitational. Both also won over $1 million worldwide.

Several players who had not won for several years achieved victories: Hal Sutton (1986) at the B.C. Open, Bob Tway (1990) at the MCI Classic, Payne Stewart (1991) at the Shell Houston Open and Mark Calcavecchia (1992) at the BellSouth Classic. Calcavecchia also won the Argentina Open and the Franklin Templeton Shark Shootout with Elkington. Brad Bryant, who had not won in 17 years as a professional, took his first victory in the Walt Disney World/Oldsmobile Classic.

Three first-year players — David Duval, Justin Leonard and Woody Austin — were among the U.S. PGA Tour's top-25 money winners. Duval also was among the worldwide million-dollar winners, and Austin had a victory in the Buick Open.

In addition to Montgomerie and Langer, the headliners of the PGA European Tour were Sam Torrance, Alexander Cejka, Costantino Rocca, Michael Campbell and Philip Walton.

Long-time stars Seve Ballesteros, Ian Woosnam, Sandy Lyle and Jose Maria Olazabal were less successful. None of those former major champions were among even the top 30 European money winners although Ballesteros won the Peugeot Open de Espana, for his 71st career victory, and the Tournoi Perrier de Paris with Olazabal, who had foot problems requiring surgery.

Surprising for different reasons, Torrance and Cejka each won three European tournaments, the same number as Langer and one more than Montgomerie, the leading money winner.

At age 42, Torrance probably was considered to be past his best years as a golfer. He won the Conte de Florence Italian Open, Murphy's Irish Open and Collingtree British Masters, battling Montgomerie to the end for the money title before placing second. He improved from No. 38 to No. 15 on the Sony Ranking and won $1,788,798 worldwide.

Cejka, age 34, had not placed better than ninth since becoming a professional in 1989, but the Czech-born German won the Turespana Open de Andalucia, Hohe Bruche Austrian Open and Volvo Masters to place sixth in Europe, 68th worldwide with $603,485, and he reached No. 85 on the Sony Ranking.

Rocca, No. 21 on the Sony Ranking, was one of the worldwide million-dollar winners despite not having a victory. The 38-year-old Italian, whose only two European victories were in 1993, finished second five times and placed in the top five a total of 11 times. He will always be remembered for the improbable putt he holed on the 18th at St. Andrews in the British Open to tie Daly. He lost the playoff but won legions of fans with his delightful spirit.

Also gaining recognition at the British Open, Campbell led after three rounds before finishing in a third-place tie. The 26-year-old New Zealander, who won the Alfred Dunhill Masters on the Australasian Tour, had six finishes in second or third place and came from outside the top 200 to finish the year at No. 28 on the Sony Ranking.

Walton won two tournaments, the Turespana Open de Catalonia and Murphy's English Open, and the Irishman had the honor of playing the decisive match in Europe's Ryder Cup victory. Also of particular note, no Swedish player won more than one tournament, but together they posted five victories. The Swedish winners were Jarmo Sandelin, Robert Karlsson, Jesper Parnevik, Mathias Gronberg and Anders Forsbrand.

Although not winning in Europe, Barry Lane took home a $1,000,000 prize on New Year's Eve when he defeated David Frost in the final match of the Andersen Consulting World Championship. Lane's worldwide total was $1,585,140 for 13th place.

The rich late-season tournaments on the Japan Tour were established in hope of attracting the world's best golfers who then went away with many of the victories. For the first time within memory, those stars left without a single trophy.

Japan's best golfer, Masashi (Jumbo) Ozaki, maintained his No. 9 position on the Sony Ranking while earning $2,169,824, the second highest total in the world, and there were four other Japanese golfers who earned more than $1 million in 1995, despite having only meager results outside their homeland.

The 48-year-old Ozaki, who now has 74 career victories in Japan, won the Chunichi Crowns, Yonex Open Hiroshima, ANA Open, Dunlop Phoenix Tournament and Japan Series of Golf. He also was second in the U.S. Open after a 69-68 start, but finished 80-71 to share 28th place. It was his best placing in six tournaments outside Japan.

Ozaki had a surprising challenger in Japan, 34-year-old Satoshi Higashi, who had three victories in the previous 12 years but won four times and earned $1,500,401. Masahiro Kuramoto won $1,269,739 (including $300,000 for fourth place in the Andersen Consulting World Championship), Shigeki Maruyama won $1,131,532 and Katsuyoshi Tomori won $1,057,642.

Despite those riches, the only multiple winners in Japan, besides Ozaki and Higashi, were young American Brian Watts and Frankie Minoza of the Philippines, who each won twice and had earnings of over $800,000. Both Watts and Minoza were former No. 1 money winners on the Asia Tour. Four other former Asia Tour leaders also played — and won — in Japan: Rick Gibson of Canada, Carlos Franco of Paraguay and Americans Todd Hamilton and Brandt Jobe. The 1995 Asia Tour leader, Jobe arrived in Japan with three victories by April.

There were two tours in Asia this year, the long-time circuit of the Asia-Pacific Golf Confederation, which concluded early, and the new Asia PGA Tour, which began in June and went through the rest of the year, acquiring a sponsor in October and becoming the Omega Tour. Lin Keng-Chi of Taiwan, with three victories, was the only multiple winner on the Omega Tour. American Clay Devers had victories on the Asia and Omega circuits, and Hamilton won in Asia and Japan.

Unlike the Asian and Japanese golfers, those from Australasia and Southern Africa, with limited schedules on their home circuits, were forced to seek competition elsewhere and were prominent on every other tour in the world. The accomplishments of Norman, Elkington, Els, Price and Campbell have already been noted.

David Frost of South Africa and Peter Senior of Australia also won more than $1 million each. Frost, No. 24 on the Sony Ranking, played mostly on the U.S. PGA Tour, where his best was a second-place tie in the MCI Classic, and also won $500,000 as runner-up in the Andersen Consulting World Championship. Senior, ranked No. 47, won the Australian Masters and Dunlop Open in Japan, and was runner-up in Japan's rich Dunlop Phoenix Tournament.

The leading money winner on the 14-event Australasian Tour was Craig Parry, No. 43 on the Sony Ranking, with A$334,803 and victories in the Canon Challenge and Norman's Holden Classic. He also earned $293,413 in the United States and had a worldwide total of $717,189.

Frank Nobilo of New Zealand, No. 37 on the Sony Ranking, had an even more profitable year with $800,967 worldwide including his European victory in the BMW International Open. Other Australasian winners in Europe were Greg Turner in the Turespana Open de Baleares and Wayne Riley in the Scottish Open. Stewart Ginn won the Golf Digest Open in Japan.

There were seven tournaments in South Africa plus the Nedbank Million Dollar Challenge and the new Alfred Dunhill Challenge, in which the Southern Africa team defeated Australasia in Johannesburg. There also was the Hassan II Trophy in Morocco and the Zimbabwe Open.

The leading money winner of the South African circuit with $57,447 was Roger Wessels, who earned $168,136 worldwide and gained the top 200 in the Sony Ranking at the No. 133 position. Zimbabwe's Mark McNulty had a poor year by his standards, winning $433,686 worldwide and slipping from No. 18 to No. 36 on the Sony Ranking.

Just as in their younger days, American golfers have dominated senior play, even though some of the names have been different. This could begin to change in about 10 years provided, of course, that the leading international players want to continue extensive tournament schedules, which may not be the case, just as in 1995 when American stars Jack Nicklaus, Raymond Floyd and Tom Weiskopf were only willing to be part-time performers.

Their absences opened the way for such former steady, but not stellar golfers as Jim Colbert, Dave Stockton and Bob Murphy to lead the U.S. Senior PGA Tour. Colbert led the U.S. money list with $1,444,386, about $25,000 more than Floyd won while playing in only 21 official events to Colbert's 34. Also playing 34 tournaments, Stockton was third on the list, and Murphy was fourth after 29 starts. Colbert and Murphy each had four victories.

Floyd won three official tournaments, including the PGA Seniors' Championship, and also won the Senior Grand Slam to lead the Senior World Money List with $1,811,049 to Colbert's $1,645,011. Nicklaus played only seven official tournaments and won a senior major championship at The Tradition. Other senior major titles were won by Weiskopf in the U.S. Senior Open and by J.C. Snead in the Ford Senior Players Championship, with Nicklaus placing second both times.

Another Hall of Fame golfer, Lee Trevino, the 1994 Player of the Year, had two victories — raising his total to 26, a Senior PGA Tour record — plus the unofficial Legends of Golf with partner Mike Hill. Trevino finished seventh on the money list, his worst placing ever, as he recovered from neck surgery in late 1994 and also had an ailing shoulder.

There were nine players who earned more than $1 million on the Senior World Money List, including Isao Aoki of Japan and Graham Marsh of Australia, who were also very prominent international golfers while in their primes. Aoki won once in America and twice in Japan. He and John Bland of South Africa, who won in America and Europe, were the only seniors to win on more than one tour.

Hale Irwin became eligible for senior golf in June, played in 12 tournaments and won twice. He was one of five first-time winners in 1995 on the Senior PGA Tour. The others were Marsh, Bland, Walter Morgan and Bruce Devlin.

Weiskopf, who played in just 19 events, achieved a lifetime goal when he won the U.S. Senior Open. Four other veterans — Gary Player, Bob Charles, George Archer and Don Bies — ended dry spells extending back at least to 1993. Archer was one of six multiple winners during the year.

Chi Chi Rodriguez, now age 60, went winless for the second year in a row.

Another 60-year-old had a big week. At the First of America Classic, Jimmy Powell became the first player ever to win both the Super Senior sidelight competition and the main event in the same week.

With perhaps the round of the year, Arnold Palmer shot his age — 66 — for the first time, on his birthday, September 10, at the GTE Northwest Classic.

Brian Barnes won the Seniors British Open, the premier tournament of the 11-event European Seniors Tour, and Brian Huggett had two victories there. In Japan, Aoki began and ended the 10-event circuit with victories in the two most important tournaments, the American Express Grand Slam and Japan Senior Open.

It took longer than in men's golf, but the women's game has also become international. First, Japanese stars Ayako Okamoto and Hiromi Kobayashi were successful in America. By the end of 1995, European players had won more events on the U.S. LPGA Tour than on the men's PGA Tour — 33 to 30 over the histories of the respective organizations.

The world's No. 1 woman golfer, Laura Davies of England, was challenged at the top this year, as was noted in the opening of this chapter, by Annika Sorenstam, a 24-year-old from Sweden. Davies won seven tournaments to Sorenstam's six, but Sorenstam became the first ever to be the leading money winner in the United States, Europe and Australasia in the same year.

Sorenstam got her first victory in America at the U.S. Women's Open (coming from five strokes behind in the final round), then won the GHP Heartland Classic (by 10 strokes) before dueling with Davies in the Samsung World Championship of Women's Golf. Sorenstam won in a playoff with a 45-foot birdie chip-in. She also won twice in Europe and once in Australia and led the Women's World Money List with a record $1,043,121.

Second on the Women's World Money List with $932,246, the 32-year-old Davies won twice in the United States, four times in Europe and once in Japan. Other Europeans to win in America were Alison Nicholas of England, who had two victories plus one in Europe, and Kathryn Marshall of Scotland. It was the second consecutive year in which the Europeans won eight events in America.

Ikuyo Shiotani, with five Japanese victories, was third on the Women's World Money List with $822,334, and was followed by Japanese players Mayumi Hirase with $808,176 and Akiko Fukushima with $743,131. Beth Daniel was the leading American, holding seventh place on the Women's World Money List with $681,219.

Other major championship winners were Nanci Bowen in the Nabisco Dinah Shore, Kelly Robbins in the McDonald's LPGA Championship and Jenny Lidback in the du Maurier Ltd. Classic. Another promising international newcomer, 20-year-old Australian Karrie Webb, won the Weetabix Women's British Open.

Betsy King qualified for the LPGA Hall of Fame with her 30th career victory, which came 19 months after her 29th title, in the ShopRite Classic. Michelle McGann, like Nicholas, had three victories over two tours, winning twice in America and once in Japan. Dottie Mochrie and Patty Sheehan each won twice in America.

3. Masters Tournament

It was a story that warmed the hearts of golf fans the world over — Gentle Ben, one of the most popular golfers in history, coming from behind, holding on against surging emotions, and winning the 1995 Masters Tournament. It was a charming story to the millions, but a strange one to Ben Crenshaw himself.

Crenshaw hadn't been playing well before the Masters. At the Freeport-McMoRan Classic, where he was the defending champion, he missed the 36-hole cut. He left New Orleans and headed for Augusta National Golf Club early. Fate had thus set the stage. Sunday night, Crenshaw was having dinner in the clubhouse when the grim message arrived. Tom Kite called him to tell him that Harvey Penick had died.

Penick was the patriarchal golf pro, kindly teacher and their coach from the University of Texas who had become famous in his later years with the best-selling *Little Red Book*. He meant the world to a couple of kids from Austin, from their youth to this day. He died at age 90. They flew to Austin Wednesday morning to be his pallbearers, and then flew back to Augusta that night. In some special way that no one will ever understand, it would be Crenshaw's week. From the moment he received the call to the instant a week later, on the final 18th green, when he doubled over and sobbed into his hands, he had a silent, invisible force with him. "I believe in fate," Crenshaw said later. "Fate has dictated another championship here."

Crenshaw, the 1984 Masters champion, wasn't among the favorites. He had been struggling, and he was anxious about his game. But a strange peace had come over him after the funeral. "There was this calmness to him that I have never seen before," said his wife, Julie.

"It was like someone put their hand on my shoulder and guided me through," Crenshaw said.

In a way, it was true. Penick was bedridden and very ill when Crenshaw visited him two weeks before the Masters. And it was then that Crenshaw, who got his first lesson from Penick at the age of about 6½, received his last at age 43.

Crenshaw would work his way through the pack and win with a 70-67-69-68–274 total, 14 under par, but it wasn't until he began coming to the press interviews in the second round that his story would begin to emerge. Until then, no one had heard much about him this year. He last won almost a year to the day earlier. So far in 1995, his best finish was third in the Phoenix Open in January. Things went downhill from there. He missed two cuts just before the Masters, and that made three misses in four outings. So except for his place in the Harvey Penick story, Crenshaw did not register on the media scale, and this was a "media Masters" if there ever was one.

There was, for example, the enduring question of whether an American could break the European grip on the Masters. Fred Couples, in 1992, was the last American to win. Europeans had won six of the last seven, seven of the last 10, nine of the last 15. Seve Ballesteros, Nick Faldo and Bernhard Langer had won two Masters each, and Ian Woosnam, Sandy Lyle and Jose

Maria Olazabal one each. Also on the agenda: Could Olazabal, the 1994 champion, retain his crown? He was still limping from toe surgery. Could Nick Price, the No. 1 golfer in the world, win his third major in a row? (He had won the last two in 1994, the British Open and PGA Championship.) And would Davis Love III have enough energy left to do anything? He had needed a victory to qualify, and he played an awesome schedule trying to get it — nine of the last 11 tournaments. He made it on the last gasp, with a playoff victory in New Orleans. Smart money said he had to be flat. Smart money was wrong. Love chased Crenshaw all the way with a final-round 66, finishing second by one stroke, his best Masters ever and his first top-10 finish in a major championship. Then there was the Chip Beck's compass flap, another Masters' first. Then there were two eagles by Jack Nicklaus, both at the fifth hole, to say nothing of his opening 67 that stirred things up, and two birdies and a plaque by Arnold Palmer at the 16th hole.

A media Masters it was, and it opened like a stampede. Of the 86 starters, 42 shot par or better in the first round, 33 broke par, and 15 were in the 60s. Crenshaw was deep in the pack with his 70, along with Faldo, the pre-tournament favorite, who never was a factor on his way to a tie for 24th place. Other favorites didn't get that close. Reigning U.S. Open champion Ernie Els missed the cut by two strokes. Price missed the cut by four.

For all of this, the Masters belonged at the outset to 19-year-old amateur Eldrick (Tiger) Woods, making his first appearance in a major championship. The world was waiting. He was the finest amateur in the United States at the time, probably in the world, and he was a freshman on the Stanford University golf team. He had won three straight U.S. Junior championships (1991-93) and the 1994 U.S. Amateur, the youngest ever to win that title — which got him into this Masters — and practically everything else worth winning. He was considered a cinch to become the next great golfer.

"I had no idea how long he was," Nicklaus said. In practice rounds, he was outhitting Couples and Greg Norman by as much as 30 yards. At the par-five 15th, he was hitting eight irons and nine irons — for his second shots. In the end, the iron play did him in. It wasn't quite under control. Still, with a 72-72-77-72–293 total, he was the only one of five amateurs to make the cut.

With the storybook surge of Nicklaus and his 67, and the debut of Woods, hardly anyone noticed that David Frost, Phil Mickelson and Olazabal had tied for the first-round lead at the imposing score of six-under-par 66. It was a Masters-low for all three. Frost and Olazabal went bogey-free, and Mickelson's score — six birdies, an eagle and two bogeys — was a record for a left-hander, three better than the 69 he had shared with Russ Cochran. He also was the first left-hander to lead the Masters.

Woods was on the leaderboard from the start, as the U.S. Amateur champion. He didn't stay there long. As one American writer put it: "About 1:30 p.m. in the first round, the future came down off the Masters leaderboard, and the past went up." Woods was hovering at or over par, and was never under par. Soon his name had to come down to make room for Nicklaus.

Was this going to be 1986 all over again? Nicklaus was 46 then, the oldest ever to win the Masters. He was 55 now, but fresh from winning on the Senior PGA Tour the week before. He was on his game.

Nicklaus launched his 67 with an eagle at the par-four No. 5, flying a 180-

yard five iron right into the hole. Nicklaus and his son, Jackie, his caddie, didn't know what happened to the ball. "Where did it go?" Nicklaus asked. The stunned crowd soon told them. "It took about a second, and then the gallery erupted," Nicklaus said. It was his 20th Masters eagle, and the sixth different Augusta hole he had eagled. Nicklaus bogeyed the par-five eighth, and birdied four holes on the back nine, including the par-three 12th. Maybe the best sign came at No. 2. He parred it. The sweeping, downhill par-five is a birdie hole for most, but it has tormented Nicklaus for years. This time he pulled his drive into the little creek on the left, chopped an eight iron across the fairway, put a seven iron to 16 feet, and two-putted for par.

This wasn't 1986 revisited, Nicklaus said. Credit the rain that softened the wicked greens, he said. "It probably helped me as much as anybody," Nicklaus said, noting that his talent wasn't what it used to be. "Rain makes a golf course easier. The course doesn't separate people out as much."

Woods shot an even-par 72 despite a bogey at No. 1, where he putted off the green from 30 feet. He had other difficult moments. "I lost my focus," he explained. "I went more or less brain-dead." He was two over par after five holes, but steadied himself. "I kept on saying to myself, the game hasn't changed — you play one shot at a time, and the low score wins," he said. For Tiger-watchers of the future, here's how the rest of the round went: He birdied No. 2 from four feet, bogeyed No. 3 from three, and No. 5 after a poor drive. He birdied the par-five No. 8 from seven feet to make the turn in one-over 37.

Fans got another show of his power at the tough par-four, 485-yard 10th, which he reached with a three wood and nine iron to 12 feet. He made the birdie putt. He bogeyed the 485-yard, par-five 13th, hitting a three wood off the tee, a 185-yard six iron into the bank, then chipping on and three-putting. At the 500-yard, par-five 15th — which he had played with driver and nine iron from 155 yards twice in practice — he went over the green with an eight iron from 170 yards. He chipped to four feet and holed his fourth and final birdie of the day. Woods left his first round in the Masters a contented young man. "I hit my driver really well, played a few loose iron shots, and I made some really good saving putts," he said. "I'm pretty happy with it."

Woods played with Olazabal, who was astounded by his power. "I had to wear binoculars to see how far the ball was going," Olazabal said. Woods, on the other hand, was astounded by Olazabal's touch. "His short game was unbelievable," he said. Olazabal birdied No. 5 going out, then shot 31 coming back. He birdied the entire Amen Corner — an 18-foot putt at the 11th, a chip-in from 25 feet at the 12th, a six-foot putt at the 13th. Then he eagled the 15th with another 25-foot chip-in.

"I was surprised," Olazabal said. "I haven't been playing well in the last few tournaments." He didn't blame the surgery he had on his right big toe in January. "It can hurt when I'm walking, but not when I'm hitting shots," he said.

Beck was happy. The compass flap had come to a harmless end. When Beck was going over his 68 with the media, he mentioned what a great help it was that his caddie used a compass to determine wind direction. Just how it helps to know the direction of the wind remained a puzzle, but now a crucial question was before the house. It's against the rules to use such a device during play. Had Beck signed a scorecard that didn't include a penalty? If so, he would be disqualified. The issue was finally resolved when Beck explained that he used the compass only during practice. The crisis over, the episode goes into the record book as the first known use of a compass in the Masters.

So order was maintained on the congested leaderboard, which found Beck tied with Mark O'Meara at 68, a stroke behind a threesome at 67 — Nicklaus, Corey Pavin and England's David Gilford, in his first Masters, who eventually tied for 24th, assuring himself of an automatic invitation for the 1996 Masters. Pavin was a darkhorse favorite who finished third in 1992 and eighth in 1994. He birdied three of the first four holes, each from at least 15 feet. But he was doomed not to win this time, either. A final-round 75 dropped him to 17th place.

Some other observations from the leaders:

Woosnam (69), the 1991 champion, was pleased that he was drawing the ball again, noting that Augusta suits his right-to-left shots — except for the eighth, which doglegs right. "I ought to get a big saw and cut down some of those trees," Woosnam said. Scott Hoch (69) three-putted the 10th, which raised the ghost again. That's where he blew an 18-incher, which cost him the 1989 Masters in a playoff against Faldo. Can he ever get away from it? "I can," he said, "but you (media) can't."

If the first round was any indication, this was going to be an awesome Masters. Crenshaw was safely in that crowd of 33 who broke par, but he had given no hint of what was coming. He started with a bogey at No. 1, birdied Nos. 4, 5 and 9, then parred his way home for an uneventful 70.

For all of the fireworks, attention was on just two: Could Woods make the cut? Could Nicklaus do it one more time?

The first-round leaderboard:

David Frost	66	Ian Woosnam	69
Phil Mickelson	66	Wayne Grady	69
Jose Maria Olazabal	66	Scott Hoch	69
Corey Pavin	67	Hale Irwin	69
Jack Nicklaus	67	David Edwards	69
David Gilford	67	Lee Janzen	69
Chip Beck	68	Davis Love III	69
Mark O'Meara	68		

There are plaques to Palmer all over, even one to a 12 he once took in the Los Angeles Open. Now there's a new one, a heavy bronze slab bolted to the side of a new, big stone fountain behind Augusta National's 16th tee. It was dedicated on "Arnold Palmer Day," Tuesday, commemorating his four Masters victories and his career. "From the day he first set foot on the grounds, this tournament has never been the same," Masters chairman Jackson T. Stephens said at the ceremonies. "His style captured the American fancy."

Palmer was 65 now. This was his 41st straight Masters. He won in 1958, 1960, 1962 and 1964, and this would be his 12th straight missed cut. He shot 79-73–152, but he left them laughing.

"Is the water in that fountain any good?" he asked the gallery at the 16th tee. Cracked a matron, "You made it holy, didn't you?" Arnie chuckled. He fired a six iron to 10 feet, and birdied the hole for the second straight day. He had hit a five iron to five feet in the first round. "They put a plaque up to me here," he told his caddie. "I had to do something." Later, another thought struck him. "If we could put a plaque on every hole," he said, "maybe I could play here."

The end also came early for Els, the 1994 U.S. Open champion, and for the slumping Price. Both missed the cut, Price for the second time in three years. Augusta baffles him. "I don't know what goes on here," Price said. "I wish someone would tell me." He shot the course record, 63, in 1986. "That seems like 400 years ago," he said. Other surprise departures: Kite, Larry Mize, Vijay Singh and Fuzzy Zoeller.

The pleasant Friday started out with a 45-minute fog delay, and also with an odd surprise for Jay Haas. He found a dead beaver on the roof of his car at the home he was renting. It probably came from a nearby pond. "Someone hit it with a car, and put it on my car as a kind of joke," he said. Then Haas, pleasant 41-year-old from Greenville, South Carolina, played a little joke of his own on everyone else. He birdied the last four holes, and shot 64, the tournament's best score in five years. He held a one-stroke lead over John Huston (66) and Hoch (67). No one was paying attention to him much of the day. The galleries were swarming Nicklaus and Olazabal. But this wasn't their day.

Olazabal's driver acted up and he shot 74–140. Nicklaus zoomed to 78 that just got him under the cut at 145. "There's nothing wrong with my golf game that my head won't fix," Nicklaus said. Things were iffy from the start. At No. 1, Olazabal drove behind a tree on the left, and made a wonderful save. Nicklaus also saved par, after a wide approach and a weak first putt. Olazabal saved par again at the par-five No. 2. His tee shot was wide to the left and hit a tree. It was a 130-yard drive. The second hole got Nicklaus again. He put his second wide to the right, beyond the big greenside bunker, chunked his wedge only a few yards, to the middle of the bunker, came out only so-so, and two-putted for a bogey. That stung. It was the easiest hole of the day. Out of 85 players, 37 birdied it, and only six bogeyed it. Then things got worse. At the par-three 12th, Nicklaus shanked his tee shot. "The last time I did that was in 1964," he said. "I almost killed Bobby Jones and Clifford Roberts." The two Augusta National founders were sitting in a cart. Nicklaus whistled an eight iron over their heads. He tied for second that year. But this time, with 78, he barely made the cut. It came at one-over-par 145. With Doug Ford having withdrawn, that left 47 players in the field.

Woods, with 72–144, was the only amateur to make it, and the first since 1992. "Am I low amateur?" he said. "Wow! Being low amateur was one of my goals. I should be a couple under par right now, but I'm still happy just to make the cut." It was, he noted, the first time he had made the cut in nine pro events. His short irons were still bothering him, but his length was paying off. He made four birdies, all on the par-fives. In the first round he birdied three and bogeyed one.

With the weather pleasant and the greens still receptive, the day was ideal for scoring. There were 20 rounds in the 60s, which was bad news for Frost and Mickelson, co-leaders with Olazabal in the first round. Both shot solid 71s and slipped two strokes off the lead. Mickelson was up-and-down with four birdies and three bogeys. Frost carded two birdies and one bogey playing a cautious game he termed "positive-defensive."

Haas took the opposite approach. Call it positive-aggressive. "I got in position and I felt like I could fire at the flags," he said. Haas used to play Augusta with his uncle, Bob Goalby, the 1968 Masters champion, both for real and in their minds. Haas had a solid if unspectacular career, with nine victories in his 19 years on the PGA Tour. But he was laboring this year. He had missed the cut five times in eight outings. He felt at home at Augusta, though. In 15 Masters, he had a fifth, a sixth and two sevenths, and he missed the cut only twice. "Most of the holes appeal to my eye," he explained. "I can see the shots."

Haas started the day five strokes off the lead. He made three birdies on the front nine, at Nos. 1, 6 and 8, on putts of seven, three and one feet. He even birdied the dangerous 10th, from eight feet. Then came four pars, then a closing streak of four birdies. It started with a gamble at the 15th, a 243-yard four-wood shot off an uphill-sidehill lie atop a mound. It was a layup situation, but Haas cleared the fronting pond easily, chipped back to four feet, and holed the putt for a birdie. The rest was easy — at the 16th, a six iron to four feet; at the 17th, a wedge to 12 feet, and at the 18th, a seven iron to 15 feet for the 64. Funny thing, though, is that Haas didn't fully realize what he was doing until he was swamped by a huge ovation as he marched up the 18th fairway. Then later, in the scoring tent. "I was signing my card," he said, "when it hit me that this was the first time I made four birdies in a row."

A most unlikely twosome moved up right behind him. Tied for second, one stroke back, were Huston, who had missed the cut in the last three PGA Tour events and who was about empty of confidence, and Hoch, who missed the cut twice and withdrew once in his last three events.

"I don't think I've ever come into this tournament with less confidence," Huston said, after matching his all-time Masters low with 66. The problem had been putting, and nothing solves that problem like a handful of 20- and 30-footers for birdies, including a run of three starting at No. 9, from three, 30 and two feet. Huston was chatting with the press and paused for a sip of water. He began sputtering. "I'm going to choke," he said. The press corps broke up at the double meaning. So did Huston. "I know how you guys love that word," he said.

Hoch highlighted his 67, his Masters low, with an eagle three at the 13th, holing an 80-yard sand wedge shot from across the creek — thanks to a mistake. "I set my eagle up with a bad drive," he said. He had to lay up after driving into the trees. "I needed to leave a full shot," he said. "I laid it up 80 yards — perfect." He followed the eagle with birdies at the 16th and 17th.

A new name appeared on the leaderboard. This was Brian Henninger. A burst of four straight birdies from No. 7 carried him to 68 and a tie for seventh at 138 with, among others, Love, who had a bogey-free 69. After that grinding sprint to get to Augusta, Love should have been on the ropes with exhaustion. The pressure may have added something to his game. "I'm a little sharper on my concentration now," he said. And he discovered a flaw in his game, which could account for two missed cuts and nothing better than 25th in five Masters. The flaw? "I was thinking more about results," he said, "than just playing the shot at hand."

Elsewhere on the course, Ballesteros rebounded from 75 to 68, but not without one of his adventures at the 13th. He hooked his drive into the creek, took a penalty drop, smacked his third across the fairway to the right and hit a spectator in the head, and finally got on the green and two-putted for a double-bogey seven. Faldo hadn't faded completely, but he was drifting. A second 70 for 140 put him one stroke further off the lead, and five behind. "I'm waiting for a spark," he said.

Crenshaw was hit by his spark two weeks earlier, only he was just starting to realize it. It hit when he visited Penick for the last time. Crenshaw, one of the greatest putters ever in the game, needed a putting lesson. This would be the last lesson he would ever get from Penick. "Can you please get a putter and show me how you're stroking that ball?" Penick said from his sickbed. "Now," Penick said, "I want you to take two good practice strokes, and then trust yourself and don't let that clubhead get past your hands in the stroke." That was the essence of Penick: Simplicity, confidence. Was it that simple? Maybe so. Crenshaw bogeyed twice but still matched his all-time Masters low with 67. The 137 total was his low for the first two rounds, and it was just one stroke off his low for any two rounds. He was now tied for fourth place, two strokes off the lead.

It was more than just putting, though. True, there was the 25-footer at the 11th and the 12-footer at the 16th. Crenshaw authored some terrific iron play as well. Five of his birdie putts came from six feet or closer, including a pair of two-footers at the seventh and eighth holes. "As Harvey always said," Crenshaw offered, "there's nothing that can boost your confidence like holing a couple of putts."

The second-round leaderboard:

Jay Haas	64 - 135	Phil Mickelson	71 - 137
John Huston	66 - 136	Brian Henninger	68 - 138
Scott Hoch	67 - 136	Davis Love III	69 - 138
Ben Crenshaw	67 - 137	Lee Janzen	69 - 138
David Frost	71 - 137	Corey Pavin	71 - 138

The third round of the Masters was pure rush hour.

"You just can't think about all the players — it's too draining," Mickelson said. He finished the day a healthy nine under par and was no better than just one of the guys.

It's said the Masters really begins on the back nine of the final round, but Steve Elkington took one look at the jammed leaderboard and noted, "I don't think there will be a clear-cut leader going into the back nine."

"We haven't had this much crowding in as long as I can remember," said Crenshaw, who kept on holing those confidence-builders. He shot 67 and tied for the lead at 10-under-par 206 with the bright, bubbly Henninger, who posted 68. Five players were just one stroke behind them, three more another stroke back, and so it went. Overall, Augusta National had taken another thumping. Of the 47 players who made the cut, only six were over par for the tournament, three were at even par (216), and 38 were under par. More to the point: 23 (nearly half the field) were within six strokes of the lead. There were 16 within five strokes, 14 within four and 12 within three. No matter how you sliced the numbers, the final round would be a shootout.

The cast did change a little. Haas, the halfway leader, got off to a rocky start. First came an unfortunate double bogey at No. 3. Just as he was addressing his par putt, the ball moved about a quarter-inch. He called the one-stroke penalty on himself, replaced the ball, then two-putted for a six. That knocked him out of the lead. "I wasn't listening if I was talking to myself," he said. Maybe the incident rattled him. He started playing his worst golf of the tournament, adding bogeys at the fourth and sixth holes. He was four over par after just six holes. But he pulled himself together, made a fistful of birdies, and finished with 72, one stroke off the lead. Haas had followed the advice his good friend Curtis Strange had left in a note of encouragement in his locker. "Patience!" the note said.

Huston, who joked about choking the day before — he meant that sip of water — seemed bent on fulfilling his unintended prophecy. He triple-bogeyed No. 1 and was out in 40. He, too, pulled himself together, played the last 18 holes in five under par for a gutsy 72, and finished two strokes back. Norman shot 68, and moved to within three of the lead, and had no doubt who would be on top on Sunday. "Me," he said.

Nicklaus, after going 67-78, rebounded with 70 that included another eagle — at No. 5 again, a record 21st in the Masters. In the first round, he flew a five iron 180 yards into the cup. This was a seven iron from 163 yards and landed short and rolled in. No green jacket, but another crystal goblet to find room for at home. "I give the crystal to Barbara and let her do what she wants," he said.

Couples moved to within one stroke of the lead with 67 that included a fitful back nine. After a birdie at No. 12, he bogeyed the 13th, and it was the reverse of the miracle at No. 12 that won for him in 1992, his ball clinging to the bank just above the water. This time, his seven-iron approach to the 13th hit in front of the green and rolled back into the water. "I guess they can't all hang up on the bank," Couples said. He birdied the next three holes. Elkington also was one stroke off the lead with 67 — one of four bogey-free rounds of the day — but his mind remained elsewhere. His first child, a girl, arrived a month early. He withdrew from The Players Championship two weeks ago and went home to Houston to be with his wife, Lisa, for the arrival. "I call home every chance I get," Elkington said. "If this was any other tournament, I would have stayed home."

Haas, with Strange's reminder to be patient guiding him in defense of his slender lead, teed off at 2:16 p.m. He noticed something interesting on the leaderboard. Strange was four under par after six holes. "Well," Haas said, "he's not being very patient out there."

"This caught me off guard," Strange said. "I was rooting for Jay, then all of a sudden I got going myself." He finished with a day's-best 65, a nine-birdie, two-bogey performance that left him two strokes off the lead. He bagged birdies in bunches, at the first three holes, his longest putt a five-footer at No. 1, and then four in a row from the 13th, from 30, 30 and three feet, and four inches at the 16th. At the par-fives, where gambles cost him the 1985 Masters, he gambled again, and made birdies. He reached the 13th green in two, and he missed the green at the 15th but pitched close.

Elsewhere, Ballesteros, after 75 in the second round, fell even harder in the third. He was one under par through No. 3, then played the next nine holes in seven over par, including two double bogeys. He shot 78 and was last going into the final round. Woods, after a 72-72 start, shot 77. "I just couldn't get the right distance with my short irons and middle irons," he said. He was tied with Ballesteros at 221. Olazabal's flickering hopes of a repeat championship all but died when he limped to 72 and finished six strokes off the lead. Frost continued to be Mr. Consistency. He took only his second bogey in three rounds, shot another 71 for a 208 total, two off the lead, and said he wouldn't be taking any chances. "Plod along, don't do anything stupid," he said. Love kept plugging away, shot 71 for 209, and noted, "If I had numbers in my head at the beginning of the week, I would have thought seven under would be leading." Instead, seven under was three strokes off the lead.

Henninger climbed to the top now in his first Masters with 68 and a three-round total of 206. He got into the Masters through a back door. His victory came in the Deposit Guaranty Classic, which used to be played opposite the Masters. In 1994, it was opposite the British Open. After three victories on the developmental Nike Tour, it was his first victory on the PGA Tour. In this 1995 season, he missed four cuts in 10 events, had a best finish of 12th, and was 94th on the money list with a modest $56,250. Would he now add the 1995 Masters?

His putting said yes — in the third round, anyway. "I made a couple today that were just phenomenal," he said. It was almost accidental, he conceded. "You're only trying to hit it six feet, and it ends up doing something else — you know, six feet here, three feet there." A three-putt and a missed green cost him two bogeys. Going out, he holed birdie putts of 20, 25 and 25 feet. He had two birdies coming home, including a monster at the 16th, a 55-footer with about 12 feet of break that gave him a share of the lead with Crenshaw. Nicklaus made one like it when he won the 1975 Masters. "I always feel the presence of Jack Nicklaus at that hole," Henninger said. The question had to be asked. What size would you take in a green jacket? "I don't care what size," Henninger said. "I could swim in it."

Crenshaw had none of Henninger's thrills, nothing but a clean three-birdie 69 — a 15-footer at No. 4, an eight-footer at the 11th and two putts from the fringe at the 13th. The only thing resembling trouble came at No. 5, where his bunker shot left him eight feet from home. True to form, he holed the putt and saved par. The question for Crenshaw now was patience. "I'm trying to play one shot at a time and not get ahead of myself," Crenshaw said. There was no getting away from the Harvey Penick story. Crenshaw said he would like to talk to his old friend again. "I would probably call him," Crenshaw said. "He would tell me, 'Trust your swing, trust your judgment and play hard and hope for the best.'"

And are you trying to win one for Harvey?

"I'm trying — I'm trying awfully hard," Crenshaw said. "You want to do things like that for someone who has helped you so much, and I'm trying like the dickens."

The third-round leaderboard:

Ben Crenshaw	67 - 206		Curtis Strange	71 - 208
Brian Henninger	68 - 206		David Frost	71 - 208
Jay Haas	64 - 207		John Huston	66 - 208
Steve Elkington	67 - 207		Greg Norman	68 - 209
Fred Couples	69 - 207		Davis Love III	69 - 209
Phil Mickelson	71 - 207		Duffy Waldorf	69 - 210
Scott Hoch	67 - 207		Corey Pavin	71 - 210

Crenshaw seemed calm and composed as he made his way through the fourth round, but one has to believe that inside, he felt the way Ken Venturi looked in the last round of the 1964 U.S. Open, staggering and reeling in the dense heat and humidity. The proof came on the final green, when he dropped the winning putt, then broke down. In the final round, more than ever before, Crenshaw would feel Penick's hand on his shoulder.

"We dreaded this day for a long time," Crenshaw had said. "He was in pain for the last 10 years, really. I don't know how he made it as long as he did, but it has been emotional. You're losing somebody who you owe your life to."

The last act still had to be played out.

The debut of Woods came to an interesting close. Shaking off that third-round 77, he birdied three of the last four holes — chipping close at the 15th, and 15-foot putts at the 16th and 18th holes — for 72, a five-over-par 293 total, and a tie for 41st out of the 47 finishers. "Just give me a few years and a lot of hard work," Woods said. "I have to get back here as an amateur."

The anticipated shootout never materialized. It fell apart, man by man. Henninger, the boyish rookie, was the first to go. He was paired with Crenshaw in the final grouping, the two of them at 10 under par. He bogeyed No. 2 to Crenshaw's birdie, and soon he was gone. But at least he guaranteed himself a return trip with a top-24 finish. A 76–282 total tied him for 10th with Couples, who had a strange day. Couples pulled within one stroke of Crenshaw with an eagle at the par-five eighth. He trailed by two through the 10th, then bogeyed the entire Amen Corner. He was on his way to 75. Cross off another challenger. Elkington (72), Hoch (73), Frost (71) and Strange (73) got left behind. They couldn't get anything going.

Next, scratch Mickelson. He got to 10 under par with a birdie at No. 4, but at the par-three sixth, his tee shot went over the green and his return putt went down over the front. He double-bogeyed, and not even an eagle at the 13th could revive him. He shot 73–280 and tied for seventh place. Now it was a four-man battle.

Make it three. Haas picked up two strokes and was 11 under and still a threat until he bogeyed the 16th.

It came down to Crenshaw, Love and Norman.

Norman and Love, the last two challengers, were on the same stage. They were paired together, three strokes behind Crenshaw, but five groups and nearly 50 minutes ahead of him.

Norman birdied the second and sixth holes, then chipped in at the 10th to start a three-birdie back nine. "Anybody who writes that the 10th is my nemesis," he said, with particular gusto, "I'll wring their neck." The 10th had hurt him in the past. Now he got even. He also birdied both par-fives, two-putting the 13th from 18 feet and the 15th from seven, and tied Crenshaw for the lead briefly at 12 under par. Then he tripped at the 17th. He pulled his sand wedge approach shot into a swale back-left on the green, about 60 feet from the pin, and three-putted for his only bogey of the day. He shot 68–277 and tied Haas for third. Another Masters had slipped by. But he didn't lose this one. It was kept from him. "You have to do something special to win here," he said.

For Love, it was close, and the good-natured guy put a wry twist on his gallant try. "Maybe you still have to throw me in with Corey Pavin and the guys who've never won a major," he said, "but I won't get any more questions about not finishing in the top 10 in the majors." He shot 66, the low round of the day, for a 13-under-par 275 total. He was second to Crenshaw by one stroke, but it really wasn't that close. Crenshaw had a two-stroke cushion coming to the last hole, and only his emotion-packed bogey there made the race look tighter. Things would have been different for Love, though, except for two crucial points. The first came at the par-five 13th hole. Five of the top eight finishers, including Crenshaw, birdied it, and one, Phil Mickelson, eagled it. Love missed the green with his seven-iron approach and parred it. That's lost ground. Add the three-putt bogey at the tough par-three 16th, and that was the story for Love.

Given the big gap between him and Crenshaw, Love had the comforting but empty satisfaction of tying Crenshaw on the first nine with birdies at the second, fifth and eight holes. He didn't let up. He birdied the 10th from 10 feet, and the 14th from two after nearly holing his wedge for an eagle two. He birdied the 15th, too, from 12 feet, and fell to 13 under par. But the 16th cost him dearly. His seven-iron tee shot ended up on the slope behind the flag. "Sometimes you wonder if things are meant to be," Love said. "That shot went four or five yards farther than I should have been able to hit, and it stayed on top of that hill. No way it should stay up there." But it did, and the only way to stop the ball from up there was to hole it. He didn't. He three-putted for his only bogey of the day.

He bounced right back at the 17th. For the second time in four holes, he nearly holed a wedge shot for an eagle two. This one stopped just a foot away. Then came a great scrambling par at the 18th. Not wanting to risk the fairway bunkers at the dogleg with a one iron, he used his driver. He hit it more than 300 yards, but wide to the left. "I've been over there a few times," Love said, grinning. "It's the place to be, really. I had 116 yards to the front, and you just can't beat that. I just didn't hit it far enough." He missed the green to the left, and used his putter brilliantly from there to get up and over the mound, and had a two-footer left for his par. Now he had to wait out Crenshaw.

Prospects were hardly promising.

"You're watching Ben looking at 10-footers," Love said, "and you know he's going to make some."

As things turned out, Crenshaw missed only two makeable putts, and they cost him two bogeys as against six birdies in his 68. He took the lead at No. 2 with a birdie from four feet while co-leader Henninger started his slide with a bogey. Crenshaw suffered his first bogey at No. 5, two-putting from eight feet after a weak chip. Up ahead, Couples started to apply some pressure with a birdie at No. 6 and an eagle at No. 8. Couples wouldn't last long, but Love jumped in to take up the chase. Crenshaw birdied two more going out, on a five-footer at No. 6 and a one-footer at the ninth. Down the back nine, the issue still hung very much in doubt. These duels often take on the look of match play, and this one did, too, except that the competitors were so far apart. The impression was that only some gross error could cost Crenshaw this Masters. The truth was, merely standing still could have done him in. But he didn't stand still.

At the 13th, Crenshaw just missed the green with a five-iron approach, but chipped to 15 feet and holed the birdie. And at the 15th, almost an automatic birdie, he parred.

"I'll never forget 16 and 17 as long as I live," Crenshaw was to say. Few would forget them. They settled this Masters.

At No. 16, where Love's tee shot stayed up on the slope and cost him a bogey, Crenshaw's tee shot came rolling lazily down to within five feet of the hole. He made the birdie. Next: "I played 17 like a dream," Crenshaw said. "I hit a little nine iron pin-high left, and hit the prettiest putt I've ever hit. The second it came off my putter, I could tell it was heading home." Home it was, and Crenshaw had a two-stroke lead. But there was one little twitch in his triumphal march up the 18th. "Fortunately, I had two shots to play with," he said. Indeed. He missed the green at the 18th, chipped poorly to about 10 feet, and missed the par putt.

Crenshaw had just 18 inches left. He rolled it in for a bogey and his second Masters. And then everything that was holding him together let go. He pulled off his golf cap and threw it down, and bent over, his elbows on his knees and his face in his hands, and he sobbed.

"I let it all go," Crenshaw said. "I couldn't wait any longer."

4. U.S. Open Championship

The United States Golf Association celebrated its centennial year in 1995. Considering that the country itself had been around not quite 220 years by then, a centennial seemed worth celebrating. Observances began in December of 1994 with a black tie dinner that brought together some of the celebrated elite of the game to New York, where the association was founded in December of 1894. Other celebrations continued throughout the year.

In a move to draw attention to its roots, the USGA took its three original championships to its founding clubs. The Amateur went to Newport for the first time since 1895, the Women's Amateur went to The Country Club in Brookline, Massachusetts, and the Open went to Shinnecock Hills, near the village of Southampton, New York, on the eastern extremes of Long Island.

Taking the Open to Shinnecock turned out the most fortunate choice of all. Jim Foulis, an immigrant Scot based in Chicago, had won the 1896 Open, the first ever played at Shinnecock Hills. It didn't return for 90 years, but when it came back, in 1986, it ended in an atmosphere of mystical wonder.

In the Lerner and Loewe fairy tale, the enchanted Scottish village Brigadoon awakens for one day every hundred years, then disappears into the mist. On the morning after the 1986 Open, Shinnecock Hills lay under a blanketing fog as if it, like Brigadoon, had gone back to sleep for another century.

The USGA uncovered the trail leading back to Shinnecock Hills after only nine years. The organization has made some important and justified decisions in its first century; the decision to bring the Open to Shinnecock Hills stands among its most sound. Sitting among the sandy hills of eastern Long Island, Shinnecock is about as close as we come in this country to the conditions common to the Scottish linksland where golf developed into the game as we know it today. It is furthermore such a supreme and enjoyable test of the game that every one of the golfers looked forward to every round.

While the Open has been played over this wonderful golfing ground three times now, this was only the second at the modern course, which dates back only to 1931. Each of the last two have been revelations. Everyone knew this was a fine course — it had been tested in the 1967 Senior Amateur Championship and again at the 1977 Walker Cup Match — but it took the Open to show just how good it is.

Its serpentine fairways wind for 6,944 yards through rolling sand hills, exposed to winds from the Atlantic Ocean to the south and Long Island Sound to the north. It offers every type of hole — long par-fours, short par-fours, two par-fives, both reachable with the second shot under the proper wind conditions, and four par-threes ranging from the 226-yard second to the 158-yard 11th. Both the seventh and the 17th follow the classic principles of a redan hole.

The holes run helter-skelter through every point of the compass, following no steady direction, so wind from any direction assures a variety of effects. Some holes will play downwind, others into headwinds, some will play through winds crossing from left to right, others from right to left. The next day everything might be reversed, or perhaps the downwind holes will play through crosswinds. Winds are probably the key to playing Shinnecock, for they blow even under normal conditions.

While the golf course it is played over is often the making of an Open, the championship means more than great courses; it means great shotmaking as well.

In its 100 years, the Open's final few holes have seen profound heroics. In the more significant moments, there was Francis Ouimet laying his jigger shot within 15 feet of the cup and birdieing The Country Club's 17th hole, which sealed his playoff victory over Harry Vardon and Ted Ray back in 1913. Ten years later Bobby Jones played a glorious 195-yard mid iron to six feet on the last green at Inwood as he won his first Open, and seven years later holed a 40-foot putt on the last green at Interlachen as he won his fourth.

Twenty years later Ben Hogan ripped a one iron into the last green at Merion in 1950, climaxing his return to national competition 16 months after the terrible automobile accident that could have ended his career and his life. Five years after that, as Hogan seemed to have a fifth Open in hand, Jack Fleck played a nerveless seven iron within eight feet of the cup on the 18th at the Olympic Club in San Francisco, setting up the birdie that caused a tie, then he beat Hogan in the playoff.

As a celebration of the Open's 100th year, the four wood Corey Pavin played into the 18th at Shinnecock on the last day of the 1995 Open should stand among the most decisive shots ever struck on the Open's final hole. On a hole that measured 450 yards, and in winds gusting up to 20 miles an hour, with a flick of his hands Pavin maneuvered his ball within five or six feet of the cup, tucked in the far left corner of the green. The shot set up what everyone assumed would a final birdie and a fitting climax to a gritty round of golf played under difficult conditions.

It was a stunning shot played under tension Pavin had never felt before, the kind of shot that showed him that after years of threatening to win an important tournament, he indeed had the stuff of champions, and that he could play the shots he needed when he needed them most.

When the ball settled so close to the hole and the gallery began chanting, "Corey, Corey, Corey," Norman, the only man left with a thin chance of catching up, knew that if Pavin holed the putt he would have to birdie both the 17th and 18th to tie.

When Pavin missed and finished his round in 68 and the 72 holes in 280, it was hardly a reprieve, for by then Norman had plopped his seven-iron tee shot into a bunker and bogeyed the 17th. Now Greg found himself in the same position as Macdonald Smith back in 1930; both men had to hole their second shots on the last green to tie. Neither succeeded. Norman went for it, but his seven iron bounced over the green and he had to chip and putt to save his par four and second place.

Norman finished with 282, two strokes behind Pavin after a round of 73, and one ahead of Tom Lehman, who stumbled over the last nine holes and shot 74 and 283. He and Norman had gone into the last round tied for first place.

Six others shot 284, among them Neal Lancaster, a 32-year-old North Carolinian who set an Open record by playing Shinnecock's second nine in 29 strokes and closing with 65, the best round of the week.

While Pavin's 280 was one stroke higher than the 279 that Ernie Els, Loren Roberts and Colin Montgomerie had shot at Oakmont in 1994, and eight strokes above Lee Janzen's winning 272 at Baltusrol in 1993, it was five below Tom Kite's winning 285 at Pebble Beach in 1992. Skeptics will moan that Pavin did no better than even par, and that while Kite did indeed win with 285, his score bettered par at Pebble Beach by three strokes. They will say further that Pavin became the first player to win with an even-par score since Hale Irwin shot 284 at Inverness, a par-71 course, in 1979.

They shouldn't, because under the conditions of the last two rounds, with strong winds blustering in from the Atlantic and with greens becoming more firm and unfriendly each day, par had become an irrelevant figure. By then Shinnecock Hills had transformed the game into what it had been in the beginning by challenging golfers not so much to target a specific figure but to play each hole in as few strokes as possible — as it should be played.

After he had settled down following a frustrating and draining day, Norman proposed that instead of the posted par of 70, a figure of 72 or 73 might have been more realistic. I don't think Norman meant some holes had been undervalued but that the course must be judged as a whole. Shinnecock Hills was simply that difficult a course.

At the same time it was that good. The players themselves offered the most striking confirmation — no one complained, as the modern professional golfer is accustomed to doing when his scores soar as they did at Shinnecock.

At the end of the first round, for example, we had nearly as many scores in the 80s as we had in the 60s. Eight men shot 80 or higher and 10 broke 70. The high scores can be blamed partly on the modern player's methods of preparation. They believe they can come to an Open site two days before the opening round, play a couple of practice rounds and then know everything they have to know. The formula didn't work at Shinnecock because of the weather.

Caught in a pocket of low pressure for about a week, the course had absorbed quite a bit of moisture before the weekend leading up to the Open. Then four inches of rain fell from Sunday through Wednesday afternoon. As a result, Shinnecock's greens, suitably firm and fast with a week to go, had turned to pudding. Shots that would have been rejected by the hard greens pulled up quickly and occasionally spun back off some of those with moderate slopes. Those golfers who arrived on Tuesday and played their practice rounds through the rain and muck had only a vague notion of what Shinnecock was really like when the cloud cover broke, the sun shone through the overcast, and the sandy soil dried out. Six of Shinnecock's 12 par-four holes measure more than 440 yards. Playing Wednesday, Nick Price said that he and Norman played wooden clubs for their second shots on three of them — the third, which measured 453 yards; the sixth, at 471 yards, and the 14th, at 444 yards. Playing into the wind as well, the second, a 229-yard par-three, demanded three woods of most players and drivers from others.

"Under these conditions," Price said, "this is one of the longest Open courses I've ever seen. I can't see its getting firm and fast soon, either. To win — and this is my favorite oxymoron — you need cautious aggression."

Consequently, when the day of the first round dawned under clear skies and a drying breeze, Shinnecock's character had changed. The greens grew progressively firmer each day and the afternoon winds common to the region began flinging balls off line and into what seemed like virgin grasslands.

For the most part, the USGA had set up Shinnecock about the way it does most courses. The fairways may have seemed a little wider but they really weren't. Like most Open setups they ranged from 30 to 32 yards, bordered by a six-foot width of intermediate rough cut to an inch and a half, and then by the primary rough, cut to five inches, that reached anywhere from 10 to 30 yards.

Beyond that, though, rather than giving the appearance of the typical U.S. Open setup, Shinnecock looked like Muirfield, the great Scottish course, where every blade of grass that ever grew on that ancient ground is still there, sometimes hip high and always impossible not only to play from but to walk through. If a ball strayed into that stuff, the player could do no more than draw his wedge and hack it back into play. This somewhat shaggy grass not only gave Shinnecock an unkempt and natural look, it is what helped set it apart.

At first the course looked as if it might be too much for Pavin, which wasn't surprising since he had such a grim Open record to begin with. Since 1981, when he played in his first, he had failed to qualify for four, missed the 36-hole cut in six others, and in the five he actually played all the way through, he had placed among the 10 low scorers in two — sixth at Hazeltine in 1991 and ninth at Oakland Hills in 1985. The following year at Shinnecock he shot 80 in the first round, 79 in the second, and ran for cover.

It looked like more of the same as the 1995 Open began. Among the early starters, leaving the first tee at 8:15 Thursday morning, grouped with Davis Love III and Vijay Singh, Corey began with a bogey on the first, scraped out a par three on the second, and then bogeyed the third. This was not starting out well, but Pavin is a resilient player who had learned from his earlier rocky starts. He is also deadly within 100 yards of the green. Reaching the fifth hole, a 535-yard par-five heading dead into the stiffening wind, Pavin played two good wood shots within 100 yards of the green, then holed his wedge. With the eagle three he had snapped back to even par and perhaps signaled the start of a significant round.

It didn't, though. Missing fairways and missing greens, Pavin played mediocre golf from then on, bogeying four more holes, birdieing two, and shooting 72, two over par. He hit only seven greens, perhaps because he hit only seven fairways; one cannot play Shinnecock from the rough.

This was nowhere close to being good enough on this day, for others seemed to have Shinnecock's measure. Price, playing the golf that had made him one of the game's three best players over the last three years, shot 66, Scott Simpson shot 67, and Norman and Phil Mickelson shot 68s. Six others shot 69, and 18 more matched the par of 70. Pavin's 72 left him in a tie for 46th place.

While Norman could never be dismissed, Price looked the more dangerous. He had played exceptional golf over the previous three-year period when he had won 17 tournaments, among them the PGA Championships of 1992 and 1994, along with the 1994 British Open, but his touch seemed to have left him as the 1995 season opened. Where he had been expected to at least challenge in both The Players Championship and the Masters, he had struggled through The Players, eventually placing 37th, and in his next tournament shot 76 and 73 and missed the cut at Augusta. The past year had put too much of a strain on him.

Looking back on it, Price admitted the interviews, the autographs, the constant demands on his time ground on his nerves.

Reminded that Palmer and Nicklaus had gone through more than he had ever thought of, Nick said, "I can't speak for Jack or Arnold, but I know there weren't as many TV crews in the '60s. I just did seven TV interviews.

"I had it for 18 months. Signing 3,000 autographs a day ... I was starting to resent people wanting things from me rather than feeling honored by it. After a period of success, not many people ask if they can do something for you. It can really be taxing if you can keep playing well and stay in the limelight. I'm an easy-going person, but I was fed up with it."

His golf had become so loose that in the middle of a round of 75 at Houston, Jeff (Squeeky) Medlen, his caddie, told him, "Nick, you really should take some time off." The next day he missed the cut and went home for three weeks.

"Sometimes," he said, "someone has to tell you that. I needed to let the urge to play build up again."

He returned a new man, placed 12th at the Colonial, 10th at the Memorial, where he closed with 65, and then tied for ninth place at the Kemper Open the week before the Open. Even more encouraging, he played half his rounds in the 60s, shooting one 65, one 66, two 68s and two 69s, and shot over 71 only once.

On the other hand Price had never done well in the Open. He had missed the cut at Oakmont in 1994, and he indeed looked shaky on the early holes at Shinnecock. As the current British Open champion he was grouped by tradition with Els, the defending U.S. Open champion, and Eldrick (Tiger) Woods, the Amateur champion. Off at 9:15, hours before the wind rose to full force, he saved a wonderful par on the second. After rifling a two iron into the right greenside bunker, he recovered within five feet of the cup and holed the putt.

He hit every other green through the first four holes and two-putted each of them then had his first break on the fifth, where he looked for a time as if he might bogey. After a long and straight drive, he reached the right greenside bunker with an arrow-like three wood. His recovery, though, caught a downslope and glided off the green, settling at least 30 feet from the cup. Taking a deep breath to steady himself, Price chipped in. One under par.

Three more routine pars and then a three wood and a sand wedge to 12 feet on the eighth and another putt fell. Two under now, he had gone out in 33, and he was playing the steadiest kind of golf. Through the first 11 holes he had hit nine greens, but he had holed only those two putts on the second and eighth. Now for the 12th, a devilishly hard par-four, Shinnecock's longest at 472 yards and playing even longer, since it headed directly into the wind, which by now was gathering strength. He had needed a three wood to reach it the previous day, and now he needed another. He pulled it; the ball settled in an ugly lie, deep in the heavy rough left of the green. Wondering if he could dig it out at all, Nick pitched to 10 feet, which may have been his best shot of the day, and then missed the putt. A bogey; his first mis-played hole.

Safely past the 13th, a short par-four, where he hit still another green, Nick played the last five holes in three under par. A driver and a five iron to six feet on the 14th set up one birdie, a driver and another three wood to the edge of the green on the downwind 16th and a chip to five feet set up another, and then a four iron into the 17th that settled 25 to 30 feet away and Price holed his only sizable putt of the day.

Four under now, on his way to 66, but another birdie would match the Shinnecock record of 65, shared by Lanny Wadkins, Mark Calcavecchia and Chip Beck from the 1986 Open. A driver and a glorious four iron to the 18th pulled up within six feet of the hole. If the putt fell he would not only match the record, he would give himself a little breathing room for the following day. Nick steadied himself over the ball, gave it a firm rap, but the putt slipped past the hole. He settled for the 66.

Price had played a wonderful round of golf. Over a long and difficult course, he had hit 12 of the 14 fairways on driving holes and 15 greens. No one could ask more on this course.

One round, though, is only the beginning. He would need more first-rate golf to win the Open, because a field of experienced and determined pursuers lurked close behind him. Besides Simpson, Mickelson and Norman, Fuzzy Zoeller, who had been so close in the 1994 British Open, was among those at 69, along with Bob Tway, who had led after the first round in 1986. Janzen, the 1993 champion who had shot only one of his previous eight rounds in the 70s and had won the Kemper Open, was among the large crowd at 70, along with Watson, 45 years old and still playing wonderful golf. He had threatened throughout both the 1994 U.S. and British Opens, and here he was again.

Watson had wrung the most he could from what had truly been a mediocre round. He hit just seven fairways, but he reached 13 greens, and even though he holed nothing to speak of, he fought his way to a 70. He had his finest moment on the 18th after starting out with a pulled drive that settled in a fairway bunker about 175 yards short of the green. From that sandy lie he played an exquisite six iron that hit a slope rising inside the right rear of the green, jumped on, and rolled 12 feet from the cup. He holed it for the birdie.

Meantime, Nicklaus had shot 71, along with Montgomerie, who had come so close to winning both at Pebble Beach in 1992 and at Oakmont the previous year. Ben Crenshaw, who had won at Augusta in April, Faldo, Ian Woosnam and Love were groped with Pavin at 72; and Roberts, who lost the 1994 Open to Els on the 20th hole of a playoff, shot 73, along with Billy Ray Brown, who had nearly tied Hale Irwin and Mike Donald at Medinah in 1990.

While Price and some of the others had played first-class golf, others had struggled through the long day. Fred Couples, frustrated by problems with his back, stumbled around in 77. Payne Stewart, Bernhard Langer, Raymond Floyd and, most disappointing of all, Els, all shot 74s and found themselves in danger of missing the 36-hole cut.

The first-round leaderboard:

Nick Price	66	Fuzzy Zoeller	69
Scott Simpson	67	Bill Glasson	69
Phil Mickelson	68	Steve Lowery	69
Greg Norman	68	Bob Tway	69
Jeff Maggert	69	Jumbo Ozaki	69

All the promise Price had shown in the opening round turned out to be an illusion; he was never the same again. Where he had played early in the first round, he played late in the second, teeing off just before two o'clock under conditions he hadn't seen since he arrived at Shinnecock. The wind had shifted overnight, sweeping in now from the southwest off the Atlantic, almost the opposite direction from what he had known. Now the holes that had played into the wind on Thursday played downwind on Friday, confusing club selection and giving the players a different look at the golf course. The scores, however, were puzzling. Where only 10 men had broken par under the easier conditions of the first round, 14 shot in the 60s in the second, and where 18 had shot even-par 70 in the first, just 10 matched it in the second. On the other hand, where only eight men shot in the 80s on Thursday, 12 couldn't break 80 in the second.

Price began steadily enough, running off four consecutive pars, and he looked as if he might begin padding his lead when he birdied the fifth once again, which was reachable now in the following wind. Then his game fell apart. Mis-clubbing in the unfamiliar wind, Nick bogeyed five of the next 10 holes, shot 73, and dropped out of first place with 139 for the 36 holes.

Before Price had even teed off, Norman had seized the day with a stirring 67, the best round of the day, matched only by Langer, who needed it, and by Bob Estes, for whom it did no good; the weight of his first-round 80 dragged him under and he missed the cut.

When the day ended, Norman held the 36-hole lead at 135, which fell one stroke short of the Open's 36-hole record of 134. His near-record score notwithstanding, Norman couldn't feel particularly relaxed because so many of the game's leading players stood close behind him and so many of them seemed to have found their games. Besides Price, just four strokes behind him, and Langer, whose 67 had jumped him within six, Faldo and Love had sprung to life with 68s, leaving them at 140, Tway had shot a second consecutive 69 and tied Mickelson at 138, and 48-year-old Masashi (Jumbo) Ozaki, the long-driving Japanese golfer, hung closest to the leader with 137 following a round of 68.

Seeing Norman at the top seemed normal, since he had been so close on so many of the big occasions over the last 10 years. He had, however, been bothered by injuries that affected him in the Open. He withdrew in the second round at The Country Club in 1988 with an injured wrist after hitting a tree root, and with a hip injury at Hazeltine in 1991.

Earlier in 1995 he had complained his back was sore at the MCI Heritage Classic in mid-April, went home to Florida and took five weeks off. The rest had an even better effect on Norman than a similar rest had had on Price. Back again two weeks before the Open, Greg shot 66-70-67-66–269 and won the Memorial, and he nearly won the Kemper Open again, though his gambling nature cost him strokes he couldn't afford. Two strokes behind Janzen with two holes to play, and with no interest in second place, Norman tried to reach a difficult pin position on the 17th and missed his target by about 10 feet. His ball splashed into a water hazard and he double-bogeyed.

Nevertheless, he played the round in 68, his 11th consecutive round of par or better since his opening 73 in the Masters. Over that stretch he had shot 42 under par.

He seemed to be continuing the streak in the Open. He had made no bogeys at all through the first 18 holes, and he began the second round as if he never would. After a routine par on the first he drilled a three iron to 20 feet on the second and holed the putt, then played a stunning seven iron inside eight feet on the third for another birdie. Two under for the round now and five under for 21 holes. Norman was hot.

He missed a birdie opening on the fifth when his four iron ran off the back of the green and his pitch ran off the front, but he chipped back to no more than a foot and saved his five. Two more routine pars on the sixth and seventh, and then he ran into the first trouble he couldn't solve. He missed the eighth green and took his first bogey of the Open. Back to one over for the day and four under for 26 holes. Another routine par four on the ninth and he had gone out in 34.

Quickly, though, he dropped another stroke at the 10th, an unusual par-four that runs up and down hills like a rollercoaster for 409 yards. His second missed the green, and he missed the par-saving putt from five feet.

With the lost stroke, Norman stood at even par for the day, but now he struck back on the 11th with a stinging nine iron inside two feet. The putt fell; one under once again. Routine pars on the 12th and 13th, then a three wood and eight iron to 25 feet on the 14th and another putt fell. Two under once more and Norman was set for a spectacular finish. Still two under through the 17th, Norman drove to the right side of the 18th fairway and followed with a strong three iron. Helped along by a quartering wind, the ball hit the green and rolled onto the rear collar and settled about 18 feet from the cup but up against a cut of taller grass.

Since the grass might snag a putter, Norman played a shot he had often practiced on the putting green of his home. He opened the blade of his wedge, and using a putting stroke, he tapped the ball with the flange. The ball rolled into the hole.

This was his fifth birdie of the round, his third on the second nine. Back in 33, he had his 67, and once again he stood at the top of the standings, the fifth time he had led at the halfway stage of one of the four major championships.

Others weren't so lucky. Second after the first round, Simpson shot 75 and fell to 21st place, Zoeller shot 74 and dropped from fifth to 30th, Jeff Maggert went from fifth to 11th with 72, and Watson skidded from 11th to 30th with 73. Crenshaw, though, gained a little ground, climbing from 46th place into a tie for 30th with Watson and Zoeller.

The 36-hole cut fell at 146, six strokes over par, and it caught some of the finest players in the game. Making a hash of his defense, Els shot 73 and missed by one stroke; with 147 as well, Seve Ballesteros failed for the third time in five years; and the cut caught Irwin, Beck, Calcavecchia, Paul Azinger, still recovering from his cancer scare, and, sadly, Nicklaus.

After a sound opening round, Nicklaus had fallen apart in the second. One over par through the fifth, he played the remaining 13 holes in 10 over par, went out in 39, came back in 42, shot 81, and matched the highest score he had ever made in a U.S. Open.

This was his 39th consecutive Open. He had played in every one from 1957 on, more than anyone had ever played. As he left Shinnecock that evening, most of us wondered if we would ever see him in another. He had been given a special exemption from qualifying for this and for 1994 in recognition of his incomparable record. Would he be given another for 1996, which would be his 40th? He said he would never again try to qualify, and no one could see any fault in this. Hogan hadn't, either. It would be a shame if he weren't invited again, but then the Open is played to decide the national champion, and while we would miss him, finally, after so many years, we had to accept that this remarkable man could no longer compete.

The second-round leaderboard:

Greg Norman	67 - 135	Nick Price	73 - 139
Jumbo Ozaki	68 - 137	Davis Love III	68 - 140
Phil Mickelson	70 - 138	Nick Faldo	68 - 140
Bob Tway	69 - 138	Curt Byrum	70 - 140
Bill Glasson	70 - 139	Mark Roe	69 - 140

The prevailing southwesterly wind seemed mild early in the morning of the third round, but it picked up strength as noon approached, and before anyone was quite ready, it began blustering in from 20 to 25 miles an hour, transforming Shinnecock from a hard and trying course into a brutal test of patience and control, both of shots and of emotions.

The wind had two effects. First, it flung flying balls into the deep, untended rough outside the normal lines, where its wispy tendrils reach knee-height but where down below it is the devil to play from; there is only one recovery — dig it out as best you can and aim for the shortest route back to safer ground.

Second, it helped dry the greens, which had already begun firming up. Now they would become progressively more difficult to hold.

The scores showed it, humbling some of the leading players of the time. Kite, who had won the 1992 Open on a windy afternoon at Pebble Beach, shot 82 and matched his worst score in the 24 Opens he had played. His scorecard showed three sevens, one of them on the 18th, where he was penalized two strokes, one for causing his ball to move on the putting green and another for not replacing it.

With a triple-bogey seven on the 10th hole, where two of his pitches didn't carry quite far enough and rolled back down a steep hill to his feet, Crenshaw played the second nine in 43 and shot 79. Faldo started with a six on the first hole, went out in 40, and shot 79 as well. Watson shot 77, and Ozaki, who had gone into the round in second place, played the last four holes in five over par, had 44 on the second nine, and shot 80, which dropped him to 32nd place with two others. Even though he shot 72, quite a respectable score this day, Mickelson had troubles as well, and he indeed might — perhaps should — have scored better. He did birdie five holes, more than anyone else, but he threw those strokes away with seven bogeys.

Where 24 men had shot in the 60s in the first two rounds, only three managed in the third. Both Gary Hallberg and Ian Woosnam shot 69s, Hallberg because he holed his five-iron tee shot to the seventh and Woosnam because he eagled the fifth. Lehman, on the other hand, shot 67 with nothing better than a birdie.

Lehman played truly remarkable golf. Off a few minutes before one o'clock, an hour and a half before Norman and Ozaki, the last pairing, Lehman made standard pars on the first two holes, and then began his march by birdieing three of the next four. Playing through a left-to-right crossing wind, Lehman lofted a nine iron within 10 feet on the third and holed it, reached the fifth green with his second and got down in two from 40 feet, then played his best hole of the day on the sixth, Shinnecock's strongest hole. On what is at best a difficult driving hole, Lehman let his tee shot slide right into the deep rough, which under ordinary circumstances meant he would probably lose one stroke. When he arrived at his ball, though, he saw it sitting up in wispy grass, and with 185 yards left to cover, he took a gamble and ripped into the ball, going for the green. It shot off like a rocket, rolled about 30 feet from the cup, and he holed the putt — a birdie where a bogey seemed likely.

Speaking about it later, Lehman said, "I felt like I stole two shots on that hole."

Three under now, Tom finished the first nine in 32, overshot the 11th green but chipped back to a foot and saved his par, then played the 12th as well as it had ever been played. With the wind coming from behind him, the hole played much shorter than its 472 yards, and so after a solid drive he had only a nine iron left. His pitch hit the hard green and rolled less than three feet from the cup. When the putt dropped, Lehman stood four under par for the day and two under for the distance. He might even take the lead if Norman slipped further, for Greg was already struggling.

That was as far as Lehman could go, though, and now he began struggling as well. A 10-foot putt dropped on the 14th to save a par, but then he bogeyed the 15th. His approach was off target, and with the greens hard and fast now, his first chip ran across and off the other side. Another chip to a foot saved a bogey. Standard pars on the last four dangerous holes salvaged his 67.

This was the best round of the Open, played under such difficult circumstances that when Norman heard of it he said it was like 59. It jumped Lehman from a tie for 21st place into a share of the lead with Norman, who struggled throughout the day.

Usually a first-class putter, Norman couldn't hole anything, and he needed good putting on a day when he hit only five greens in the regulation strokes. Playing wonderful recovery shots, though, he one-putted the first eight greens and made his way through the first nine with the loss of only one stroke. After missing the green of the seventh, a par-three, Norman pitched all the way over and then chipped back within a foot of the hole and saved the bogey.

Ozaki had played the first nine in 36 as well, but then they both threw away two strokes on the 10th, the hole that had bedeviled Crenshaw earlier. Norman's was the more spectacular crash. He pulled his drive into the deep stuff and had no option but to chop his way back to the fairway. His ball rolled to the base of the hill below the steep grade climbing upward to the green.

Even under normal conditions Norman puts extreme spin on his pitches, but although the hole had been cut so dangerously close to the front edge of the green that a ball short of the pin might roll back down the hill, Norman felt he could not waste a stroke with a safe shot. He went for the flag. Another foot or two and the shot would have been perfect. Instead the ball dug into the green, took the backspin, and tumbled back down the hill.

A stroke gone. Now Greg played the safer shot, pitched on and took two putts. A double-bogey six, three over for the day but still two under for 46 holes.

Still he struggled on, saving pars with striking work around the greens. He saved his three from a bunker at the 11th, missed each of the next three greens and yet didn't lose a stroke, and finally played a standard par on the 15th, only the second green he had hit.

It was here that Ozaki reached the height of his frustrations. Playing from the rough through most of the day, Jumbo pushed his drive into the deepest grass, but already five over par for the day, he felt he couldn't afford to play safe. Instead of playing a safe shot, he tried to reach the green. It was a bad decision. The grass grabbed his club and the ball shot across the fairway into the rough on the other side. Another bogey.

The heart seemed to go out of him then. He double-bogeyed the 16th and dropped strokes on both the 17th and 18th. He was finished.

Norman struggled on, finished with 74, and fell into a tie with Lehman, at 209, still a stroke under par for 54 holes. He might have held onto the lead, but after he nearly rattled the flagstick with his seven-iron approach to the 18th, he missed from four feet.

His had been an uncommon round. Never in command of his shots, he had nevertheless saved what could have been a dreadful round by one-putting 13 greens. He had two-putted only four and three-putted the 16th, which cost him his final bogey, and he had escaped from bunkers on both par-three holes on the second nine. Now, though, where he had begun the day with some breathing room, he could see he might be in trouble, for Lehman would not give in easily, and seven others had climbed within three strokes of him.

The third-round leaderboard:

Greg Norman	74 - 209		Ian Woosnam	69 - 212
Tom Lehman	67 - 209		Scott Verplank	71 - 212
Bob Tway	72 - 210		Steve Stricker	71 - 212
Phil Mickelson	72 - 210		Vijay Singh	72 - 213
Corey Pavin	71 - 212		Davis Love III	73 - 213
Nick Price	71 - 212			

As the last round began under a clear and cloudless sky, nine men were bunched within three strokes of one another, with Love and Singh a further stroke behind. The last round held the promise of a tight and tense day, for these nine men made up an interesting cast.

Recovering from a long and debilitating slump, Tway had shown flashes of his former first-class game along with the hope he might return to the form that won him the 1986 PGA Championship. Price was still dangerous, even after two rounds of 73. Woosnam still had to be watched along with Steve Stricker, who had shown unexpected staying power with two 71s and 70, and Scott Verplank, who had shown so much promise as an amateur, winning a PGA Tour tournament, and yet fizzled as a pro, still hung on.

Then there was Pavin. After his opening 72, Pavin had followed with 69 in the second round and then 71 in the third, one of the fine rounds of the day. He had played the last two rounds in even par, then, which left him two over par and in a tie for fifth place, just three strokes behind Norman and Lehman. Before long, though, he fell even further behind, for Lehman birdied the third after Pavin had bogeyed. Now Corey stood five strokes out of first place; his cause seemed hopeless, but he had 15 holes to play, and anything could happen.

Nevertheless, Norman remained the man to beat. A tough competitor, superb driver and a superior putter, Norman is a force wherever he plays, either in the four major championships or the weekly Tour events. He has taken lots of abuse for not having won more, but at the same time he is always there; anyone who would win on the big occasions must deal with him.

Norman had had opportunities to win the U.S. Open twice by 1995. He had holed a long, breaking putt on the final green at Winged Foot and tied Zoeller in 1984 but had lost the playoff, and two years later led after 54 holes at Shinnecock, then closed with 75 and dropped to 12th place, six strokes behind Floyd. Now, with the force of the wind only slightly eased from Saturday, still coming in from the southwest at about 15 to 20 miles an hour, Norman once again lost his lead quickly.

Bad luck dogged him on the early holes. His approach to the first green smacked against the top of the flagstick and bounced 20 feet away, which might have cost him one stroke, and a short putt for a par on the second caught the rim of the hole and spun back toward him. By then Tway, playing one hole ahead of him, had birdied the second, and Greg fell to second place, behind both Tway and Lehman, who had made his three on the second. Then Lehman birdied the third to dip two under par for 57 holes, one ahead of Tway and two ahead of Norman.

By the time Lehman birdied the third, Pavin had played through the fifth. He still lay five strokes behind, but he made no more mistakes after the third, and had indeed been playing solid golf. A driver and four iron set up a par from four feet on the sixth; his four iron missed the seventh green, but a sand wedge to eight feet and a good putt saved a par; a driver and eight iron to 20 feet on the eighth and another par, and then he hit a good drive and a stunning six iron within six feet of the cup on the difficult ninth with its blind green sitting atop Shinnecock's highest hill, close by the old wooden clubhouse. The putt fell; back to two over par but still not quite in the hunt.

As Pavin headed toward the 10th tee, Norman, Lehman and Tway were all tied at even par, Tway through the eighth, where he had birdied, and Norman and Lehman one hole behind. From then on it became difficult to follow.

Now, as Norman and Lehman turned for home, they shared the lead, for Tway had bogeyed the 10th.

The 12th played a pivotal role. A straightaway par-four of 472 yards, beginning from a high tee to falling ground and then uphill once more to a fairly open green sitting on a gentle rise, it played downwind in the southwesterly breeze. Not among the game's long drivers (he ranks about 150th in the PGA Tour's statistics), Pavin reached the green with a smart eight iron to about 12 feet from the hole. Also among the Tour's deadliest putters, he ran the putt home.

At about that time, as Norman and Lehman stepped onto the 11th tee, the scoreboard beside the green showed a score of one over par for a player at the bottom. Someone else had climbed within a stroke of Norman. The

Norman-Lehman gallery obscured the name at first, but when the spectators shuffled for position, the letters "IN" showed though. It was Pavin.

Now the gallery began to murmur; Corey had birdied the 12th, and now he stood one under par for the day; he was closing in.

Just then both Norman and Lehman began stumbling. Both men missed the 11th green with their tee shots, but Norman saved par with a magical pitch from the base of the upslope that caught the high grass bordering the green in just the right spot, then ghosted down the slight incline within two or three feet of the cup. It was a wonderful shot to watch, and of course he holed the putt. Lehman, though, bogeyed from the right greenside bunker. Still even par, Norman led by one stroke over Pavin and Tway and by two over Lehman and Love.

Quickly, just as he gave one stroke away, Lehman picked up two on Norman, whose driving began to waver. He drove into the rough on the 12th and bogeyed just as Lehman birdied. Now Pavin, Norman, Lehman and Tway all stood one over par.

The deadlock didn't last. Minutes later and all at about the same time, Tway bogeyed the 14th, Norman bogeyed the 13th, and Pavin lofted a soft wedge inside 12 feet and birdied the 15th.

Two under par for the day now, Corey had dropped to even par for 69 holes and held the lead to himself. Tway was finished. He gave away strokes on the last three holes, finished with 75, and fell back into a tie for 10th place. Meanwhile, Lehman, Norman and Love were hanging on by their fingernails, Lehman one stroke behind, and Norman and Love two. Love, though, had played through the 16th by then; the holes had just about run out.

The gallery knew it and began their rush to catch Pavin, moving on now to the 16th, the par-five that weaves for 544 yards to a green guarded by five bunkers. They had no trouble finding him for Pavin was easy to identify. To begin with, he looked out of place in an Open field. Standing, he claimed, five-foot-nine, which he may have exaggerated by a couple of inches, and weighing no more than 150 pounds, he appeared to hide behind a bushy black mustache and a baseball-type cap whose bill tilted so far downward it hid his eyes. He walked with a splay-footed stride and went through an awkward-looking routine as he set up to play his shots. After a series of flatish practice swings more common to a 20-handicapper, he rocked back and forth from one foot to the other before he settled into his stance and swung. When he moved into the shot, though, his hands, so low in the practice motion, rose to the proper position, and he whipped them through with terrific speed. It was not a pretty sight, but it worked for him.

His physical appearance and his mannerisms, though, masked a sound and at times exceptional golf game. With the remarkable coordination and hand action that gave him the ability to create more shots than most players only dreamt of, he was one of those golfers who loved to move the ball around. He hit it left-to-right, right-to-left, some shots high, others low, whatever the situation called for. He was altogether a joy to watch, for he played the game with such intelligence, he was the only first-class player of his time who revived memories of Lee Trevino. He demonstrated that shotmaking skill there on the 16th.

Two good woods had left him within a pitch of the green, but with the wind in his face, Pavin played one of those shots that proved intelligence pays off. Rather than risk a high-flying wedge or nine iron that might end up anywhere, Pavin played a low eight iron. It was a wonderful shot to watch. The ball bored through the wind, hit a little short of the flagstick and curled left, then settled 10 or 12 feet from the cup. He could have settled the championship there if the putt had fallen, but it didn't, and now both Norman and Lehman still clung to life. They needed birdies, though. Norman had picked up a stroke on the 15th, but that had been his first birdie since the 18th hole on Friday; you don't win the Open playing like this. Within the next two holes, though, Norman, Lehman and Love were finished.

Love double-bogeyed the 18th, the 16th destroyed Lehman, and it almost killed Norman as well. Struggling all the way from the tee to the green, Lehman made seven and Norman played the same shot Pavin decided against, a high pitch played with tremendous backspin that climbed into the brisk wind, hit close to the flagstick, then drew back off the green. Instead of the birdie he needed, Greg had to work for his par.

Still, he stood just one stroke behind Pavin, and if he birdied both the 17th and 18th he could force another playoff.

Corey had made a hard-working par on the 17th, holing a tense five-footer, then played a solid drive down the right side of the 18th fairway. His drive had run only about 225 yards, which left him a little less than 210 yards to the front of the green and perhaps 230 to the flagstick. It was then he played that magnificent four wood, watched it bounce three times before reaching the green, then ease within holing distance. When the ball stopped rolling, Pavin dropped to his knees and said a prayer of thanks. The Open was his.

Pavin had taken the first prize the way it should be taken; he had gone out and won it. On a day when the principal challengers couldn't play the shots they needed, and where all around him men of greater reputation could not, Pavin had found the will and the control to play his best golf. He had played 72 holes over a trying and demanding course and had beaten the best players in the game without ever dipping below par for the number of holes he had played. He had, in fact, begun the long journey with a bogey on the first hole and had not recovered from it until he birdied the 15th hole of the last round.

As Pavin stood among a select group gathered in the old clubhouse for a ceremonial toast, Judy Bell, the chairman of the USGA's championship committee, read a passage that tried to explain the meaning of the Open. It read:

"Clearly it isn't the money.

"It is fame, certainly, for the names of Open champions are never forgotten, and the designation of Open champion stays with a man throughout his lifetime.

"To the golfer who strives for it, winning the Open offers the ultimate satisfaction and the pride of knowing that for one week when it mattered most, he was the best player of them all."

As Pavin clutched the gleaming silver trophy, a tear ran down his cheek. He had indeed been the best of them all.

5. British Open Championship

St. Andrews — the town as well as its golf courses — holds a special attraction for Americans. While in Oakmont Country Club Americans can claim the second oldest course where either the British or United States Open is still played, Oakmont was founded only in 1903, perhaps 60 or 70 years after Allan Robertson gave the Old Course its final shape. The game had been played in the United States no more than a decade or so when Oakmont opened, but the Scots had been playing golf for centuries by then.

Perhaps Americans flock to shrines such as St. Andrews because, compared to Scotland, the game has such shallow roots in the United States, but I believe it amounts to more than that. It is simply the fascination most of us feel for this special town. Whatever it is, the town and the Old Course draw Americans to St. Andrews like the voice of the river maiden echoing off the Lorelei.

As the sailors of myth were drawn to the Lorelei, golfers are drawn to St. Andrews and show their compulsion to go in the strangest circumstances. A stroke behind Mike Donald playing the ninth at Medinah during the 1990 U.S. Open, Billy Ray Brown, a big, rawboned Texan, walked beside Grant Spaeth, the president of the USGA, and told him he had entered the Scottish Open because he had heard a certain number of high finishers would be invited into the British Open, again over the Old Course, and "I sure want to play at St. Andrews."

He was not alone, for the American entry to the British Open is never so high when it is played anywhere else. When it returned to St. Andrews in 1995, Americans made up nearly one-third of the field. Of the 159 who were to start, 55 were Americans, three more actually than the total number of British golfers. It could have been more, but five others who were exempt from qualifying withdrew for various reasons — Fred Couples and Fuzzy Zoeller because of painful backs, and Tom Lehman because his wife had delivered a baby.

Some of those Americans were old and treasured Open hands, principally among them Arnold Palmer, who breathed new life into this oldest championship in 1960, and Jack Nicklaus, the winner of two Opens at St. Andrews. Although no one expected either man to take a significant part in the outcome, they always add something to any golf event simply by playing.

Sixty-five years old in July of 1995, Palmer had come to play a ceremonial farewell to the Open, which he had revived from a moribund state in 1960. Palmer lost to Kel Nagle by one stroke after having won both the Masters Tournament and the U.S. Open earlier in the season. This was the first effort to win what has become known as the modern Grand Slam, modeled after the 1930 Grand Slam of Bobby Jones, an amateur. Palmer did win the next two Opens, at Royal Birkdale in 1961 and at Royal Troon 1962.

Nicklaus played his first Open in 1962, shortly after beating Palmer at Oakmont in the U.S. Open, but it took him 10 strokes to play the 11th, the Railway Hole, and he missed the halfway cut. Later, of course, he won three British Opens, his first at Muirfield in 1966, and then his two at St. Andrews in 1970 and in 1978.

Perhaps Americans are attracted to St. Andrews because the Old Course is one of the few venues the public can play, since, for example, with only one exception the U.S. Open is played at highly private clubs. The Masters is always at the Augusta National Golf Club, where few have ever trod except during Masters week, and I can't imagine a stranger's wandering to Muirfield unannounced and being put into the ballot.

Americans love to browse in the Quarto Book Shop where they might find Spenser's *Fairie Queen* sandwiched between Bernard Darwin's *Golf Between Two Wars* and Ben Hogan's *The Modern Fundamentals of Golf*. They love to wander into the shop where Tom Morris made his gutta percha balls, and where young Charles Blair Macdonald became so stricken with the game that he came home to the United States bursting with the enthusiasm. They stand outside the shop where in happier times Laurie Auchterlonie turned out such wonderful clubs and yearn for a set of their own. They climb to the top of the cathedral ruins and look over the old town, then roam about the cemetery, stand beside Allan Robertson's grave and gaze at the bas-relief of Young Tom Morris. Then, back at the golf course again, they stare through the big windows of the Royal and Ancient's clubhouse and find members staring back at them.

An Open at St. Andrews is also a time to reflect that this game is perhaps the richest of all for memories that tie those of us today with the great figures of the past. We look back at how Jones so loved this course and indeed this town, and how that affection was returned when he was made a freeman of St. Andrews. How guests at St. Salvador sang *Gaudeamus Igatur* as a begowned Nicklaus strode from the hall bearing an honorary degree from the University of St. Andrews not because of academic achievement, but because this town, so ingrained in golf, believes that what he and his fellows accomplish in their pursuits warrants recognition as well.

We look back as well on the great moments: Jones led from the course by a phalanx of policemen after his victory over Cyril Tolley in the 1930 British Amateur, the first step toward the Grand Slam, Palmer so close to winning and yet losing by one stroke to Nagle, Nicklaus taking off his sweater on the 18th tee and then driving the green in 1970, Seve Ballesteros birdieing the 18th after Tom Watson mis-played his approach to the devilish 17th into the road, Sam Snead stepping off a train and winning the first post-war Open in 1946, Dick Burton, who held the title through the war years, driving out of bounds from the first tee when he finally had the chance to defend, and the lamented Tony Lema giving the championship his own sense of grace four years later, and Bobby Locke and Peter Thomson adding to the legend.

From the end of the First World War through 1990, seven of the 13 Opens played at St. Andrews had been won by American golfers. Besides Nicklaus' two, and Snead's and Lema's, Bob Jones won there, along with Jock Hutchison, a St. Andrean by birth but an American citizen, and Denny Shute won there as well. Then in four remarkable days in July of 1995, John Daly raised the count to eight American victories in 14 championships.

Each of those others had its moments, but for those who were there, nothing could match the closing moments of the 1995 championship as first Daly thought he had the championship won, then had his heart ripped from him when Costantino Rocca holed the most improbable putt within living memory. Later Daly defeated Rocca in the four-hole playoff.

Rocca's putt followed what must have been his most embarrassing moment. He had just saved his par on the 17th with an astonishing shot from the road, then played a fine drive that settled to the left of the green and left him a simple pitch to the pin set, as usual, close to the edge of the Valley of Sin, a diabolical depression in the left front of the home green. With the huge gallery hushed, Rocca played a risky shot. Trying to nip the ball cleanly with enough backspin to brake quickly, he stubbed it; with perhaps 40 yards to the hole the ball carried perhaps 15 and rolled to the bottom of the Valley. Rocca was crushed, believing he had thrown away the Open.

He took a minute or two to compose himself, and then stroked his putt. The ball rolled at least 40 feet through the Valley, climbed a gentle slope, and suddenly found the hole directly in its line. It dived in; if it hadn't, it would have run yards past. Rocca had tied Daly at 282, six strokes under a difficult par.

This was an astonishing Open in another respect. St. Andrews has always brought the best players to the top. In 1984, for example, Ballesteros and Watson, two of the best players of their age, battled to the end. In 1990, Nick Faldo, the game's foremost player then, had to beat off Greg Norman in the third round and won by five strokes over Payne Stewart and Mark McNulty.

By contrast, those with the biggest reputations weren't within sight of the lead. Rocca's high finish caught everyone by surprise, but not so much as Steve Bottomley's taking third place. Not one of the bright lights of European golf, Bottomley had missed the cut in seven of his eight previous tournaments on the PGA European Tour. He had never placed higher than 10th since he joined the Tour in 1988, had gone through the qualifying tournament seven times, and made it into the Open field by holing a nine-foot putt on the final hole of qualifying. Then he shot 69, one of the day's two rounds under 70, and tied Mark Brooks, an American, and Michael Campbell, a New Zealand Maori, for third place, at 283.

Vijay Singh and Steve Elkington tied at 284, and Corey Pavin, the U.S. Open champion, shot 285 and tied Mark James and Bob Estes for eighth place. Then Stewart shot 286, along with Sam Torrance and Ernie Els, Norman and Ben Crenshaw shot 287, Bernhard Langer 289, Jose Maria Olazabal and Watson 290, and Ballesteros and Faldo 291.

If this was not a week for the big names, it had other compensations; it forced us to realize that with all his flaws Daly is indeed a three-dimensional player who is good enough to win anything at all. He became only the second American winner of the championship in the past 12 years, joining Mark Calcavecchia, who won in 1989.

The whole world knew Daly could hammer the ball beyond reason, but at St. Andrews he astonished us with his all-around ability, especially his delicate touch around and on the greens. He has a surprising flair for playing the running shots so necessary for success in links golf.

For at least a week he overcame an unfortunate behavioral pattern as well. He had been known to sulk and play as if he didn't care when the ball didn't run his way, but when he played a hole or two poorly here, he gathered himself and struck back. His reaction when Rocca holed his shocking putt on the 18th showed he had the will to win. As soon as it fell, Daly grabbed his own putter and began readying himself for the playoff.

When he arrived at St. Andrews, no one knew quite what to expect. An alcoholic who hadn't had a drink since December 21, 1992, he claimed, he had been divorced twice, suspended from the PGA Tour twice, and he nearly killed his brother once. Driving at 80 miles an hour, he lost control of his car on a bend in a road. His brother was thrown clear and came out of it without a serious injury. Another time he was stopped by police who suggested he might have been drinking a little.

Indignant, Daly said, "Certainly not. I've been drinking a lot."

Daly has had the shakes, the sweats, and he was still suffering withdrawal headaches as the Open began, hardly the proper condition for a potential champion, but in some measure his winning seemed pre-ordained. Certainly it didn't surprise Michael Bonallack, the Secretary of the Royal and Ancient Golf Club of St. Andrews. Remembering that Daly had played five rounds over the Old Course in one under par in the 1993 Alfred Dunhill Cup, Bonallack began looking on him as a potential champion. He had seen how quickly John had adapted to links conditions and noted how adroitly he played the short game.

A few years earlier Lee Trevino had told Daly that if he were ever to win a British Open he would probably win it over the Old Course, because, Trevino said, "It's the only course with enough room," for Daly did not always hit where he aimed. David Feherty, the Irish wit, needled him at the Alfred Dunhill Cup by saying, "Don't worry, John. There are five courses out there; you're bound to hit one of them."

Then Daly added another weapon to his arsenal, a new driver with loft of about eight degrees, two degrees less than the allowable loft for a putter. With this new artillery piece, Daly hit the ball lower and straighter. He also did just about everything else right in the first round. Driving extraordinary distances, playing the running shots as if he had been to the manner born, and putting like a dream, he shot 67 and finished the day tied with Watson, Crenshaw and McNulty. The gallery couldn't have been more pleased.

Surprisingly, considering his history, Daly had drawn an enthusiastic following in Britain, principally because of his Brobdingnagian driving, but just as well, perhaps, because of his touch. No golfer, though, is more appreciated by the Scots than Watson, the winner of five British Opens, four of them in Scotland, and no one is appreciated by more golf fans anywhere than Crenshaw, who had yet to win one. Both Watson and Crenshaw were playing in their fourth St. Andrews Opens, and even though they were both in their 40s, they had shown they could still compete. Watson had played very well at Turnberry in 1994 and could have won with a better closing round, and Crenshaw had won the Masters in April.

Opening rounds of any big occasion usually have their moments of surprise. Besides the low scores of the leaders, we saw disappointing moments as well, one of them wrenching. Nicklaus had taken 10 strokes to play Troon's 11th hole in his first Open in 1962; now he took another on the 14th of the Old Course. Caught in Hell Bunker, a deep sand pit 80 yards short of the green, he took four strokes to get out and shot 78, which beat only four other golfers.

Palmer was one of them. With a frustrating 83, he placed last.

Those high scores were the exceptions, because the Old Course had seldom been battered so badly as it was on this day. When it ended, 59 men had broken par 72, another 25 had matched it, and only 75 had shot 73 or higher. Considering what lay ahead, these were strange figures indeed.

Moistened by early morning fogs, the fairways looked lush and green but this was an illusion that masked hard, fast-running ground that had taken only scattered rain for the previous two months. Although the greens were not fast, they were firm and hard to hold, as they should be for a championship. Still, the 1990 Open had confirmed that the Old Course needs weather to stiffen its defenses. Under mild and warm conditions, the 1990 field had driven scoring to alarming levels. At the height of his powers then, Faldo had opened with 67 and 65, and Norman had kept up with two 66s. Both men had matched the record 67-65 of Henry Cotton in the unforgettable 1934 championship at Sandwich. Of the 72 men who survived the cut, 62 shot par or better, and Faldo shot 270, fully 18 strokes under par.

As scores began coming in from the early starters, it looked as if we might see 1990 all over again. Russell Claydon, a former English Amateur champion, birdied three of the first seven holes, Jim Gallagher shot 32 going out, and Pavin stood three under par after 12 holes. Both Gallagher and Pavin held on to shoot 69s, and Claydon finished with 70.

A 10- to 15-mile-an-hour breeze had begun rising in early morning, but only a stronger wind could have checked the scoring trend. Even though Watson had said he preferred a windy day because it created another hazard, he shot an uneasy par 36 through the first nine, then, with the slight wind crossing from his right to his left and from slightly behind, he raced home in 31 with sensational golf. Some of his shots were wonderful to watch, especially his seconds to the 13th and 14th.

By then he had birdied both the 10th and 12th with stunning pitches to eight and six feet. A three wood short of the hill rising beyond the drive zone left him a seven-iron approach to the 13th. Aiming to a point perhaps 30 yards right of the flagstick, Tom played the shot just right. It curled back as it rode the wind, came at the green almost sideways, and settled perhaps four feet from the cup. Always pleased to applaud genius, the gallery roared. Watson looked toward them with his usual tight-lipped smile and holed the putt.

Totally confident in his swing now, Watson drove straight ahead to the Elysian Fields on the 14th rather than taking the safe route to the left, played a three wood outside the stone wall defining out of bounds on the right, and once again turned his ball back to the green about 15 feet from the flag. His putt for an eagle three dropped, and when he birdied the 18th as well, he turned in the day's first 67.

McNulty's was the second, which was perhaps the major surprise of the day, even though he had finished second to Faldo in 1990. This had been a difficult year, though. He had been playing terrible stuff after changing his swing. His game had worsened so he had missed more cuts than he had made — seven in succession on the PGA Tour — and had grown so disheartened he had consulted David Leadbetter, his lifelong friend and teacher. The results were startling.

Even par approaching the swing of holes at the far end of the course, McNulty suddenly began playing exceptional irons, ran off four consecutive birdies from the seventh through the 10th, then added another on the 14th, where he reached the green with a three-wood second and got down in two from 20 feet.

A remarkable shot saved him from a bogey on the 17th. From a rough lie on the road after a mis-played five iron, McNulty ran the ball up the bank of the green, then holed from 15 feet.

Daly was next. Although he has a tendency toward impatience, he seemed completely under control, perhaps because he rattled off three quick birdies, the first two from the reasonable distance of eight feet on the third and fourth, then another on the fifth that took his breath away. Covering the 567 yards from tee to green with a drive and a three iron, Daly paced off his putt at 120 feet. In danger of three-putting, he coaxed his first putt within five feet, then holed it.

With another birdie on the ninth, partially offset by two bogeys, Daly went out in 34, but he came back with three more birdies, his last on the home hole under unusual circumstances. As everyone else, Daly aimed his drive left to avoid out of bounds along the right, but when he pulled the shot it ran on and on and into the gallery beyond the metal fencing blocking the spectators from the fairway. After taking a free drop, Daly played a neat little running shot within seven feet of the cup and holed the putt.

Taking stock, Daly claimed this round was, "The most patient golf I've ever played. Certainly it's the best I've hit the ball since I don't know when, and I had more birdies today than I've had all season."

Crenshaw, too, played better than he had in some time, racing out in 33 with three birdies, and home in 34. One of the great putters of his generation, Ben holed only one putt of any length, running in a 20-footer on the fifth and another from 12 feet on the 15th, but he also three-putted the fourth. Ben hit what may have been the best shot of the day on the 17th, playing a sweeping hook with a two iron that ran into the heart of the green.

Several others played exceptional rounds as well. Feherty, who had finished high at Turnberry, shot 68, along with Vijay Singh, Bill Glasson and Mats Hallberg. A young American, David Duval, was looking to join them until he took seven on the 17th and finished with 71. It was the first of eight scores of seven or worse on the Road Hole during the championship.

With 69, Pavin left himself in good position, and defending champion Nick Price, who seemed edgy after his great year in 1994, shot an erratic 70. Norman kept himself in range with 71 after wondering if his tender back would keep him from playing at all, but Faldo shot 74 on a day when he could neither drive nor putt and summed up his day neatly by saying. "I just didn't make anything out of anything."

The first-round leaderboard:

John Daly	67	David Feherty	68
Mark McNulty	67	Vijay Singh	68
Tom Watson	67	Bill Glasson	68
Ben Crenshaw	67	Mats Hallberg	68

Faldo managed to make something of something the next day and thrust himself back into the championship with a stirring 67. At the same time Price confirmed that he would give up his championship by shooting 74. It was a day when Daly held himself together, shot 71, and kept his share of the lead at 138, when Brad Faxon, with 67, and Katsuyoshi Tomori, with 68, rose to the top with Daly, when Watson and McNulty began their fall, when Crenshaw hung on by his fingertips, when Els might have moved ahead and yet blundered on the late holes, and when Palmer played his last strokes in the championship.

It was furthermore a day that ended with the field so closely bunched that 103 golfers completed 36 holes within 10 strokes of one another. They would all play the last two rounds. Furthermore, Faxon, Daly and Tomori were being pressed by six others just one stroke behind, at 139, and three more just two behind, at 140. Some of them were the most dangerous men in the game — Crenshaw, who had dreamed of winning the Open, slipped from 67 to 72, but he stood five under par along with Pavin, one of the game's better wind players, Els, the 1994 U.S. Open champion, Brooks and Rocca, a likable 38-year-old Italian who had placed second in two tournaments earlier in the season.

The wind had strengthened overnight, whipping in from the southwest once again at velocities approaching 30 miles an hour, which made the more imaginative hole locations difficult to reach. The freshening wind had other effects, not only flinging high-flying balls about but blowing putts off line and drying out the greens as well. By day's end they had become firm and difficult to hold. It was a day for the low, running approach shots, the genius of links golf.

Strangely enough, Watson, who everyone knows as one of the game's best wind players, slumped to 76, ruined by three double bogeys on par-four holes. McNulty shot 76 as well, and together they dropped from first to 31st, along with Langer, Feherty, Calcavecchia and Ken Green. Green, incidentally, had been involved in a bizarre incident. Among them Green, Hisayuki Sasaki and Jose Rivero completed the 12th, a 316-yard par-four, in only eight strokes. Both Green and Sasaki drove the green and eagled while Rivero could do no better than a par four. Sasaki shot 71, Green and Rivero 72s.

Meanwhile, Daly's round, and indeed his whole week, hinged on his reaction to the fifth hole, which he had reached with a three-iron second shot in the first round. He had learned in his practice rounds that he could use his driver on every one of the 16 driving holes except the 12th, where a one iron would put him on the green. He had kept control of his driver throughout the first round and through the opening holes of the second, but his drive on the fifth got away from him and plunged into a nest of bunkers spotted along the right side of the fairway. From where his ball lay he had no option but to pitch out safely. Then he took two more shots to reach the green and made seven, dropping two strokes. His gallery held its breath, perhaps remembering Turnberry the previous year where a wild drive on the 10th hole cost him another double bogey, and he followed by four-putting the little 11th for another. He was never the same, shot a petulant 80 in the fourth round and finished dead last.

This, evidently, was a new Daly, though. He brushed off his seven and went back to work, played the next four holes in pars, then birdied four of the next five and came back in 33. Once again he had to struggle with a monstrous putt. His one iron into the 12th actually rolled closer to the hole of the sixth on one of the Old Course's huge double greens, but he lagged his first putt close enough to save the birdie. He had played the last 13 holes in four under level fours, exceptional golf under any circumstances.

By the time Daly began, Faxon had been on the course for an hour playing the steadiest kind of golf. Faxon had been threatening to win something of merit for some time. A year earlier he had played 41 consecutive holes at Turnberry without a bogey and shot 67-65 in the second and third rounds and went into the final round tied for first with Zoeller. Neither man had anything more to give, though, and gave way to Price. Now Faxon was at it again. Out in 34, he turned for home by holing from seven feet on the 10th, lost a stroke on the 11th by three-putting from 70 feet following a loose six-iron tee shot, then holed from seven feet once more on the 12th.

Three under for the day now, he reached the 14th green with two big woods, and from 100 feet coaxed his first putt within two feet and holed it. Another birdie; four under. Four more pars brought him to the 18th needing another birdie to match his 36-hole score of a year earlier. A pitch to 10 feet and another solid putt for his sixth birdie of the day, his ninth in two rounds. He had birdied one of every three holes he had played and once again threatened to win an important championship.

Tomori had played 36 holes with only three bogeys, quite good scoring for a man who believed the Old Course too difficult for his game. He had gone out in 34 with birdies on the fifth, where he reached the green with his second, and the seventh, where he lofted a sand wedge to four feet. He came back with three more birdies and had only one blemish, a bogey on the 13th, where he three-putted from what he guessed was 100 feet.

A mis-played shot or two wrecked Els and Glasson. Four holes from the finish, Els needed only pars to shoot 66 and lead the field, but he tried to play too fine a shot into the 15th and three-putted, then nearly saved his par after missing the 17th green but missed from four feet and bogeyed once again. Instead of 66 he shot 68 and slipped to a tie for fourth.

Even with his loose finish, Els was luckier than Glasson. Playing on gimpy knees so fragile he often wears braces, Glasson stood two under par for the round and six under for 34 holes. Two more pars and he would join the leaders, but then he made eight on the 17th without going into either the road or the Road Bunker, finished with 74, and dropped to 142 and a tie for 20th.

Daly had run his second shot within six feet on the 18th but missed the putt. Had he made it he would have saved the R&A a considerable amount of money, because then the field for the last two rounds would have been reduced by nine players. Since those within 10 strokes of the leader qualify for the last two rounds, scores of 148 and better made the cut, rather than 147. The missed putt reprieved Nicklaus, who rebounded from his opening 78 with 70 in the second.

One other mighty veteran qualified without help from the 10-stroke rule. With 144, Gary Player made the cut for the 26th time in a career dating back to 1956. At 59, he became the oldest man to play the last two rounds since the Second World War. Nicklaus, by the way, survived for the 30th time.

Others weren't so lucky. Ian Baker-Finch, the 1991 champion, missed with 153; Paul Azinger, recovering from cancer, shot 149; Colin Montgomerie shot two rounds of 75 and missed by two strokes, and Palmer missed as well.

Nevertheless, the day belonged to Palmer. As he strode along those final few fairways the gallery applauded his every step, and when he marched up the 18th, the crowd lining the fairway pressed so tightly together straining for a glimpse of the man, those caught in the crush couldn't move. Then, as he putted out, Faldo walked to him and shook his hand. He had finished 25 minutes ahead of Arnold, but he and a few others had waited to see him close his Open career.

"He's done everything for the Open here," Faldo said. "But for Palmer in 1960, who knows where we'd be; probably down in a shed on the beach."

Palmer reflected on that final walk as well, saying, "When I came up the 18th I kept thinking about 1960 and what that led to — a lot of great years and a lot of happy times for me, both in golf and socially ... It was a warming and happy time."

The second-round leaderboard:

John Daly	71 - 138	Ben Crenshaw	72 - 139
Brad Faxon	67 - 138	John Cook	70 - 139
Katsuyoshi Tomori	68 - 138	Ernie Els	68 - 139
Costantino Rocca	70 - 139	Corey Pavin	70 - 139
Mark Brooks	69 - 139		

At dusk on Saturday evening it had become clear none of the old heroes would claim the championship. Price had fallen to 16th place even though he had shot 70, Faldo sank to 29th with a frustrating 75, and Norman dropped to 40th with 72. They had too many strokes to make up and too few holes to do it in.

The leading contender at the moment was Campbell, a 25-year-old Maori descended from a Scotsman who had emigrated to New Zealand in the middle of the 19th century. Campbell startled the field by shooting 65 on a windy, gusty day when the ground dried out and some greens turned to stone. Somehow Campbell managed them and climaxed his round with a stunning and lucky shot from the Road Bunker that barely cleared the high face and rolled within 18 inches of the hole.

With his 65 he posted a 54-hole score of 209, nine strokes under par, two head of Rocca, who persisted in holding on, and three ahead of Elkington, and four ahead of Pavin, Els, Tomori and Daly, who showed signs of cracking toward the end of the round. Campbell's 65 beat the next best score by three strokes. James, Barry Lane and Per-Ulrik Johansson shot 68s, but at 213 Lane lagged six strokes behind Campbell, and James and Johansson trailed by eight. Faxon, meantime, dropped six behind with 75 and slid out of the race; Frank Nobilo, another New Zealander, fell apart in the rising wind and shot 80, and John Cook, just one stroke behind when the round began, shot 75 and dropped to 16th place with Price.

At the same time Brooks slipped back with 73, but he would be heard from later.

Once again the wind had to be dealt with, rising from the southwest once more but now at velocities up to 30 miles an hour, the strongest yet. It tore dead into the faces of those playing the first, and it shortened the 18th considerably.

Campbell had gone into the third round tied for 20th place and had teed off just before one o'clock, two hours before Faxon and Tomori, the last men off. By the time they had played the first, Campbell had already birdied four holes and had turned for home in 32. Six under par for 45 holes, he had caught the leaders.

He had played marvelous golf on the outward nine, fighting the wind crossing from left to right, yet still birdieing four holes, and now, beginning the homeward nine with the wind at his back, Campbell missed from 10 feet on the 11th, the difficult par-three Eden Hole, where the pin was set more than 15 feet behind the Strath Bunker, but then he ran off three more birdies. He drove the 12th green and got down in two from 40 feet, lofted a sand wedge to 10 feet on the 13th, overshot the 14th with a four-iron second but chipped back and holed from 10 feet once again. He had birdied seven of his last 12 holes.

When his score went up on the leaderboard, others couldn't believe it. Playing three holes behind him, Torrance said, "I couldn't keep my eyes off the scoreboard. Every time I looked, his score kept getting better."

Now he stood seven under for the day, nine under for 50 holes. Finally leading the field, he saw no one making a run at him. Faxon had double-bogeyed the sixth and gone out in 39, Tomori was on his way to 37, Daly and Crenshaw were both stumbling, and although Rocca continued to play steady golf, he lagged four strokes back and needed something better.

Then Campbell almost gave it to him on the 17th, where his nine-iron approach missed the narrow green and splashed into an impossible position in the Road Bunker. The ball sat in such a confining space he couldn't play to the left, he couldn't play to the right, and he didn't have room to play backwards away from the green. It seemed unlikely he could play any kind of shot at all because the bunker's high front face apparently blocked any shot toward the hole.

Back in the clubhouse, Player was watching on television. One of the game's finest bunker players, Player checked with R&A members to be sure Campbell could invoke the unplayable ball rule and drop away from the steep front bank. Assured that he could, Player said, "Then that's what he should do."

Campbell indeed considered it, but with the confidence of youth he felt sure he could chop his ball out. He dug in his feet, aimed left of the flagstick, set just 15 feet from the bunker, then swung into the shot. The ball popped up quickly, but as it climbed it grazed against the layered sod forming the front face. Campbell sucked in his breath, afraid the ball would drop back into the sand, perhaps even hit him, and cost two penalty strokes. Instead the ball cleared the bunker, took the slope of the ground, and glided toward the cup. The huge gallery thundered approving cheers, Campbell took a deep breath, and Player rose from his chair, clapped a few times, then bowed toward the television set.

With a par four on the 18th, Campbell came back in 33 and shot the lowest score of the championship. While his position at the top of the standings may have surprised most of the gallery, others more familiar with European golf knew that Campbell was making a success of his career. He had placed second to Langer in the Volvo PGA Championship eight weeks earlier and had finished among the leading 10 scorers in four other tournaments. Still, they weren't the Open; he would face severe pressure the next day.

The third-round leaderboard:

Michael Campbell	65 - 207	Ernie Els	72 - 211
Costantino Rocca	70 - 209	Katsuyoshi Tomori	73 - 211
Steve Elkington	69 - 210	Mark Brooks	73 - 212
John Daly	73 - 211	Sam Torrance	71 - 212
Corey Pavin	72 - 211		

This was the 124th playing of the Open, which began in 1860, a century before Palmer arrived. In all the preceding 123, few had finished with so much crammed into the last day. First, although he didn't say it outright, Nicklaus hinted that this, too, may have been his last appearance in the championship he had graced every year since 1962. Then there was the sudden blossoming of Bottomley, the stumbling start of Campbell, which cost him the championship, the gritty play of Rocca throughout the day, culminating with his two outlandish finishing holes, and transcending them all the determination, fighting spirit and strength of will of Daly.

Of the nine men bunched within five strokes of one another, Pavin and Els probably drew the most support. When the wind came up early in the day, Faldo had said, "It's the worst wind I can remember in a British Open. Balls on the green were likely to move, and trying to judge the wind when you're putting is so difficult." Nicklaus felt conditions like these would hurt Daly because he hits his shots so high.

"Look for Watson," Jack cautioned. "He's the best bad weather player out there." Jack turned out to be a poor prophet; Watson shot 77 and tied for 31st place, and Daly obviously had learned to cope.

Playing together, Daly and Els ran off three pars, and then Daly made a move on the fourth, at 463 yards the longest par-four on the Old Course. A nicely gauged nine iron aimed left of the flag drifted with the wind and pulled up 15 feet right of the cup. Daly holed it. He was six under par now, just three behind Campbell, who was struggling.

Campbell had given nothing away yet, but he had holed a couple of five-footers to save pars on the first two holes and had missed the flag so badly on the third he played his third shot with a pitching wedge even though his ball lay on the green.

Meanwhile play had become so agonizingly slow players had trouble keeping their rhythm. Usually a deadly putter, Pavin could hole nothing and gradually gave ground; Els played loose golf; Tomori was on his way to 78, and Torrance, five strokes behind when the day began, birdied the third, but then gave away strokes on the eighth and ninth when he needed more birdies.

The wind was causing nagging problems, whipping trouser legs and bending flagsticks, it blew putted balls off line and indeed became such a threat to move balls at rest on the green, some players cautiously avoided grounding their putters so they couldn't be penalized if the ball moved. Then a lashing rain fell from time to time. What part the conditions played in Campbell's first mistake can't be judged, but the wind howled across the fifth fairway from left to right as Michael played his second shot.

From a good position in the fairway, about 220 yards out, Campbell ripped into his one iron. The shot was a disaster. Caught up in the wind, it soared off line, carried over the prickly gorse bushes bordering the right, passed behind the grandstand beside the green, and settled in a clean lie on the fourth fairway of the New Course, which runs parallel, more than 100 yards from the green. A nine iron into the wind pulled up 30 feet short, and he three-putted. He had made his first bogey since the 17th hole of the second round, but he still stood eight under par.

At about the same time, Daly played a beautifully judged low running shot within six feet on the seventh and holed it. He was seven under, one behind Campbell.

Now the tempo changed as Campbell and Rocca fell back and Daly surged ahead. An eight iron to 12 feet on the eighth, then another good putt and Daly went to nine under just as Campbell drove into one of the Coffin bunkers on the sixth. With no hope of reaching the green, he slipped to seven under par and dropped behind Daly, who was running ahead of the field.

Bottomley, meanwhile, was having a day players of his caliber only dream of. One under par after the eighth, he had one of those breaks that make all the difference between a good round and a bad one. Playing a running shot to the ninth green, he hit the shot fat and left his ball 75 feet short of the hole. Then he holed the putt. Out in 34, he had surged to four under par for 63 holes, not contending yet, but moving closer.

Six holes later he rolled in another giant putt from 65 feet. He was five under now, but he would go no lower. A shot into the Road Bunker cost him one stroke, but he made it up with a birdie from about six feet on the home hole, shot 69, and became the only player within 20 strokes of the lead to break 70. With 283, he had the best 72-hole score of those who had finished; let the others try to match it.

Brooks was the first. Beginning the day at 212, he was still four under par through the 13th. Now, playing downwind, he reached the 14th green with his second and saved the birdie from 10 feet, then punched a low seven iron into the 15th and holed from 25 feet. Now he stood at six under, just two behind Daly, who was playing two holes behind.

Gambling now as he fought to make up strokes, Brooks threw himself into his drive on the 16th, which has two primary hazards on the left — the Principal's Nose, three small bunkers clustered around a knob, and Deacon Sime, another bunker just beyond it — and an out-of-bounds fence ranges along the right. The conservative route is to the left of the Principal's Nose, but this was no time for caution. Brooks took the direct route, between the bunkers and the fence. The ball streaked toward the green, missed the Principal's Nose, but somehow it kicked into Deacon Sime. With no escape except a pitch back to the fairway, Brooks made six.

A closing birdie on the 18th helped, but who knows what might have happened if he had missed the bunker on the 16th. Still, he matched Bottomley at 283 and had some hope left, because Daly suddenly began losing strokes.

John had nearly wrecked his round with a wild drive into the gorse left of the ninth fairway, but with luck found his ball lying on a shell road clear of the bunkers and saved par. He was still two strokes clear of the field at eight under for 63 holes. He made pars on No. 10 and 11, then pulled his drive up short of the 12th green, but he putted up the slope of the severely tiered green within six feet of the cup. Another birdie and he could run away with the championship. The ball caught a piece of the hole and spun away. Three holes later he had another chance, but once again his 30-footer hit the hole and jumped out.

Rocca, meanwhile, had steadied himself after nearly ruining his day with bogeys on the seventh, eighth and 10th holes. Seven under par at the start, he had fallen back to four under, but a birdie on the 14th and he stood at five under par, three behind Daly, who was playing the 16th, and tied with Brooks, Bottomley, who had finished, and Elkington, who still had holes to play.

Now Daly nearly threw it all away once more. His approach to the 16th just missed reaching the green's upper level and he three-putted from 70 feet. Then his approach to the 17th bounced into a terrible lie close to the steep face of the Road Bunker.

But Daly wouldn't be denied. Laying the blade of his wedge nearly flat, he swung into the ball with all he had. It jumped clear of the steep face and bounded onto the green about 30 feet from the cup. Two putts and he had bogeyed once again. Six under now, only one stroke ahead of Rocca and Elkington, who had somehow become the only men who might catch him. When Daly missed from 25 feet on the 18th and Elkington bogeyed the 17th, Rocca alone had an opening.

He missed one chance on the 16th, and then he looked finished when his approach to the 17th skirted the front of the green, raced across the road, slammed into the stone wall beyond, and rebounded back onto the road. Only a miracle shot could save him now.

Somehow, though, Rocca played that miracle shot. With his ball sitting in a little depression on the tarmac, which eliminated a pitch, he had to play the shot with his putter. When he struck the ball, it popped up as if he had indeed played a wedge, carried over the road, hit a piece of turf that shot it forward, climbed the bank, jumped onto the green, and rolled within four feet of the cup. He saved his par and remained five under with only the 18th left.

Then he played that bizarre series of shots. By then Daly had signed his scorecard and come back to watch Rocca finish. When he stubbed his pitch, Daly's wife threw her arms around John, certain he had won. With more restraint, Daly warned her, "It's not over yet."

Indeed it wasn't, for then Rocca holed his improbable putt, which set off an incredible scene. When it fell, the roar of the gallery echoed through the town and Rocca fell to the ground, buried his face in the sacred turf, and pounded the ground with his fists. Eventually he stopped pounding and covered his head with his arms and lay there while the cheering went on. When finally he stood, tears glistened on his cheeks.

Daly, meanwhile, picked up his putter and walked to the practice green.

Brooks had been watching the finish on television in the R&A clubhouse. When Rocca's putt fell, he rushed out and found Daly. John had lost his yardage book. Brooks gave him his, and both Pavin and Faxon said, "Go get him."

The four-hole playoff, scheduled for the first, second, 17th and 18th holes, ended almost as it began. Rocca three-putted the first, and Daly holed from about 35 feet on the second. Then Rocca's approach to the 17th tumbled into the Road Bunker, and he took three strokes to get out against Daly's immaculate four. Now Daly led by five strokes; the 18th had turned into nothing more than the quickest route back to the clubhouse.

6. PGA Championship

With five holes to play in the British Open, Steve Elkington stood three strokes behind eventual winner John Daly, closer than he had ever been to winning one of the game's four major championships. Within the next four holes he threw away his chance of winning.

Facing a blind shot to the 13th green at St. Andrews, Elkington pitched to five feet but missed the putt. Following another first-class pitch to the 14th, one of the two par-fives on the Old Course, Elkington missed again from 15 feet. His putt from 10 feet or so on the 15th ran true to the hole but pulled up two or three inches short of the cup. Then from about 18 feet, his putt on the 16th grazed the cup but wouldn't fall. Where he might have won, Elkington slipped into a tie with Vijay Singh for sixth place at 282, just two strokes behind Daly and Costantino Rocca, who tied for first place.

Elkington was disappointed of course, but aside from his showing in the British Open, he had won the Mercedes Championship to open the year, tied for fifth in the Masters Tournament, and while he had fallen to 36th place in the U.S. Open, he had tied for second in the Memorial Tournament.

He felt he was having a good year, and so after he returned home to Houston, Elkington strolled out to the Champions Golf Club expecting encouragement and congratulations from Jack Burke, who owns not only the club but an impressive playing record of his own. Burke had won both the Masters and the PGA Championship in 1956, and so his opinions carried weight. He had watched the British Open on television and had noted Elkington's finish. He skipped praise and told him instead, "Your putting is pitiful."

That comment didn't help Elkington's ego at all, but then Burke laid out what Steve had to do and the thoughts he had to take with him to the PGA Championship at Riviera Country Club in Pacific Palisades, California, in three weeks. Going into the fourth round at Riviera, Steve stood six strokes behind Ernie Els, the young South African who had won the 1994 U.S. Open. Now his putting could hardly have been better. He played the first nine in 31, came back in 33, tied Colin Montgomerie at 267, then rolled in a 20-foot putt on the first playoff hole and won the championship.

The 267s were monumental scores. They not only bettered the PGA Championship record by two strokes, they matched the lowest 72-hole score in any of the four major championships as well. Greg Norman had set the British Open record with 267 at Sandwich in 1993.

It was quite a week. While Elkington's 31 on the first nine and his closing 64 might have won raves at most tournaments, they were nearly lost among a consistent stream of exceptional rounds here. His was just one of four 64s in the four rounds, and all four were beaten by the 63s of Michael Bradley in the first round and Brad Faxon in the fourth.

Statistics can be pretty dry stuff, but what happened at Riviera, one of the country's finest and most testing golf courses, not only amazed us, it illustrated that a professional golfer using modern equipment is capable of shooting any score at all. Mark O'Meara, Jay Haas and Jim Gallagher also shot 64s, while Els, Montgomerie, Michael Campbell, Jeff Maggert, John Adams and Naomichi (Joe) Ozaki shot 65s. Altogether, 12 men shot 65 or better and another 14 shot 66. Furthermore, Elkington's 31 simply didn't rank. Faxon shot 28, Adams shot 29, and Bradley, Ozaki, Justin Leonard, Jose Maria Olazabal and Fred Couples shot 30s.

The scoring level was startling, especially over a course so revered as Riviera, the most popular tournament course in Southern California. The field shot 143 rounds in the 60s over the four rounds, a little over 32 percent, which is kind of scary. Then there were an additional 25 rounds at 70, one under par.

Just off Sunset Boulevard in the western suburbs of Los Angeles, Riviera was built in the 1920s by George Thomas, one of the pioneers of American golf course architecture. For years his book *Golf Architecture in America* was the only serious study of the craft. Born into a wealthy Philadelphia family, Thomas seemed headed for a career in banking and finance, but was drawn to golf through his interest in landscape gardening. Like Donald Ross, he became an expert on roses and wrote several small books on their care and breeding.

Thomas moved to California following World War I and did most of his best known work there. Although he didn't lay out a great many courses, he did some of the game's lasting jewels. Three of his works have remained pillars of the game in Los Angeles. Aside from Riviera, he also designed Bel-Air and the North Course of the Los Angeles Country Club.

The North Course is considered the best in the Los Angeles basin, even though the club has a reputation of nearly paranoiac privacy. For a time, though, it wasn't quite so reclusive. The inaugural Los Angeles Open was played there in 1927, and it returned in 1934, 1935, 1936 and then again in 1940. Quickly, though, the club decided to abandon tournament golf and in recent years has stoutly resisted persistent requests to hold the U.S. Open.

While LACC may have been Thomas' best design, Riviera has been his best known. In a game that prizes its past, Riviera had more tradition than any club in California south of Pebble Beach. The only course in California where both the Open (1948) and the PGA (1983) had been played, Riviera had been the site of many Los Angeles Opens as well. From the 1920s through the 1990s, some of the more memorable moments in golf had taken place there, and some of the game's greatest figures had won there — Macdonald Smith, Denny Shute, Lawson Little, Tommy Bolt, Lloyd Mangrum, Ben Hogan, Sam Snead, Byron Nelson, and in later years Tom Watson and Johnny Miller.

Above all, perhaps, Riviera has been closely linked with Hogan.

Golf was just returning to normal following World War II when the Los Angeles Open kicked off the 1947 season. Hogan shot 280 at Riviera and beat Toney Penna by three strokes. A year later he shot 275 and beat Lloyd Mangrum by four strokes. Six months after that, the U.S. Open came to Riviera and Hogan shot 67-72-68-69–276, bettered the scoring record of 281 by five strokes and beat Jimmy Demaret by two strokes. The record had stood since Ralph Guldahl set it in 1937, when he had, incidentally, beaten Snead in the first Open Sam had entered. Hogan's record lasted 19 years, until Jack Nicklaus shot 275 at Baltusrol in 1967. Because of his command of the course, Riviera had been nicknamed Hogan's Alley.

Hogan's Riviera legend didn't end there, though. While he tied for 11th place the following January, beaten eight strokes by Mangrum, Ben was nearly killed in an automobile accident three weeks later and didn't play again in 1949. After struggling for months to build his strength and return to the game, Hogan entered the 1950 Los Angeles Open, in January, opened with 73, followed with three 69s, and seemed to have the tournament won. Snead, though, birdied the last two holes, closed with 66 and tied Hogan, then beat him in a playoff.

As the 1995 PGA Championship approached, some parallels were drawn between Ben Hogan in 1948 and Corey Pavin in 1995. Pavin had won the PGA Tour events at Riviera in 1994 and 1995. Had he followed the pattern drawn for him he would have won the 1995 PGA Championship as well, since it was played at Riviera. Instead he followed by winning the 1995 U.S. Open, the same three Hogan had won. The Open, however, had been played at Shinnecock Hills, and Pavin played no significant part in the PGA. Nor, for that matter, did many of the game's best.

Greg Norman for example, who must be dealt with in any tournament, started nicely but had no finishing kick. Ben Crenshaw, who had won the Masters, Nick Faldo, Couples and Nick Price, the 1994 PGA champion, couldn't keep up with the exceptional pace of scoring. Both Pavin and Daly played badly enough to miss the 36-hole cut.

On the other hand, others played exceptionally well. Elkington made up for his disappointment in the British Open, and Montgomerie continued to demonstrate he is indeed a player of the first quality, even though his record in playoffs is grim. He has now lost playoffs for the U.S. Open of 1994, the PGA Championship of 1995, and Europe's Volvo PGA of 1991. Els had the championship in his hands until the last nine of the last round, and Brad Faxon kept alive the prospects that one day he will win a major title. He could have won the 1994 British Open at Turnberry, and he made a remarkable climb with his closing 63 at Riviera, although he had no chance of winning the way Elkington, Montgomerie, Els and Maggert played.

Looking back on the week, it seems strange indeed that so many scored so well under such difficult putting conditions. No one could remember such poor greens for an important championship since the 1963 U.S. Open, when sheets of ice that lay for months on the greens at The Country Club in Brookline, Massachusetts, killed the grass, and then vandals carved up the fifth green twice.

Riviera didn't have those problems, but the greens became so spike-marked, every putt looked like it had to run an obstacle course. The problem developed from the best intentions. The original greens had shrunk and contours changed over the years as Riviera's notorious kikuyu grass, a coarse-bladed strain, moved in on them and sand piled up from bunker shots. After the PGA awarded Riviera the 1995 championship, the club's management decided to rebuild the greens and bunkers to their original configuration. Crenshaw and his organization were brought in and set up a two-year program. Crenshaw took measurements and studied old photographs before the work began, then reshaped the greens' surfaces and reconfigured the bunkers. Then the trouble began.

Crenshaw wanted to seed the greens and allow the grass time to establish a deep root system. Management though, as management sometimes will, decided against the advice they had paid for and ordered sod instead. Sod, though, doesn't root as easily as seed, and the new grass didn't take hold.

The greens were in marginal condition for the Nissan Open, the PGA Tour event in January, and they hadn't improved much by August, the dates of the PGA Championship. They were soft and easily damaged, and, as it turned out, difficult to putt.

They did, though, hold everything that hit them, a condition that had more effect on scoring than the minefields the players had to putt through. Then, when the championship began, 57 men broke par 71 in the first round, matching the PGA record set two years earlier at the Inverness Club in Toledo, Ohio. Ten men shot 66 or better, 15 more shot 67 or 68, and another 18 shot 69. Some of the nine-hole scores were frightening.

Gil Morgan, who had played wonderful golf through the first 43 holes of the 1992 U.S. Open before an equally sensational collapse, left the first tee a little before seven o'clock, birdied the first two holes and shot 66. Two hours later Norman birdied the first three holes, went out in 31 and shot another 66, and O'Meara, playing in the next group, went out in 31 as well, and shot 64. O'Meara had barely signed his scorecard when Gallagher followed him in with another 64. It was only 1:45, and already Riviera was being ripped apart.

The 64s looked safe, though, until late in the day when Bradley, an obscure, 29-year-old player from Florida, went out in 30 and just behind him Adams, who was equally obscure, turned for home in 29. Bradley held on and came back in 33, but Adams slipped to 36 on the home nine and shot 65. It had been quite a day.

Part of the reason behind the low scoring lay in the weather and in the layout of the course itself. It was glorious. If a perfect day can be described as clear blue skies without a hint of clouds, a bright warm sun, and a slight cooling breeze, then that is what we had at Riviera throughout the week.

Furthermore, instead of 71, par was more realistically 70. The first hole was no more than a medium-tough par-four. It may measure 501 yards, but the tee is set high on a hill, which adds perhaps 20 to 25 yards to the drive and brings the green within range of a medium iron for players of this caliber, often a shorter club than they played into the second hole, a par-four. Haas, for example, had a little over 200 yards into the first green but 225 yards to the second, which measured 40 yards less. The contrast went even further. In the first round, 72 men birdied the first and another six eagled. Haas scored a three; those who made fives could be sure they lost at least one stroke to the field. Over the four rounds the first hole gave up 347 birdies and 19 eagles, more than twice as many sub-par scores as any other hole.

Even with his 64, O'Meara had an uneasy feeling. Off the 18th green before Bradley had begun his round, O'Meara said, "I'm thrilled to shoot 64, but it's still early. You could see a lot of low scores this week. The way the greens are holding, there's a good chance someone will break a record."

Of his eight birdies, O'Meara holed only one sizable putt. A one iron and sand wedge left him 20 feet from the cup on the 10th, at just 315 yards Riviera's shortest par-four, and he holed the putt. Earlier he had holed from six feet on the first, from 15 feet on both the fifth and sixth, a par-three with a bunker in the middle of the green, and from six feet on the eighth, a simple little par-four of 370 yards.

Four under par then, he birdied the 10th, dropped a sand wedge within eight feet on the 11th, a reachable par-five of 564 yards, and after losing a stroke at the difficult 12th, where he bunkered his nine-iron approach, picked up two more birdies with first-class irons to eight feet on the 16th, a nice par-three of 165 yards, and to four feet on the 17th, a par-five of 576 yards that would be critical in the late stages of the championship.

No one scores anywhere without well-struck irons. Of Gallagher's seven birdies, six were from 15 feet or less, and two of those were from three feet. He made his most spectacular on the seventh, where he drove into a difficult lie in the rough, played his approach short, then chipped in from perhaps 45 feet.

For a time no one really threatened to catch Gallagher and O'Meara. Lee Janzen had gone out in 32, but he bogeyed the 12th, failed to birdie either of the par-fives on the home nine, and shot 66. Crenshaw birdied only one hole on the first nine and shot 68; Larry Nelson went out in 33 but slipped to 37 coming back; Faldo shot 69; Rocca, the surprise of the British Open, shot 70, Price 71, and Olazabal 72. Daly went out in 35, level par, even with a double-bogey five on the sixth; but he made seven on the 12th after playing one shot left-handed and then taking a penalty stroke for an unplayable ball, came back in 41, and shot 76. Pavin double-bogeyed the sixth as well and shot 71.

Then along came Bradley, in the fifth group from the end. No one knew what to expect of him since he had never played in the PGA and had missed the cut in all three of his U.S. Open starts. On the other hand he had shown some improvement earlier in the year by tying for eighth place in two tournaments, although he had never threatened to win anything.

Grouped with Guy Boros, a son of Julius Boros, a former U.S. Open and PGA champion, and Jay Don Blake, Bradley was just beginning his round when Gallagher climbed the steep slope from the 18th green to the clubhouse. Driving with his three wood, Bradley played a long and straight drive and then rifled a six iron within 20 feet of the flag, holed the putt, and began the day with an eagle three. A nine iron to 12 feet on the third, a seven iron to four feet on the fifth, and then a nine iron to eight feet on the ninth set up three birdies, and Bradley had gone out in 30.

Three more birdies on the second nine — from 20 feet on the 12th after a long and well-placed drive left him only a pitching wedge, another long putt from 25 feet on the 16th after a seven-iron tee shot, and then an 18-footer on the 17th — brought him to the home hole eight under par, one stroke from establishing a record for the lowest score in either the PGA, Masters, U.S. or British Opens.

His approach left him within 20 feet, but his putt seemed to skip across the bumpy green and missed by at least a foot.

Bradley admitted later that he had heard a spectator say something about his having a chance to set the record, "and I got to thinking that Johnny Miller had shot 63 at Oakmont (in 1973). So, yeah, when I got to the 18th tee I was thinking, 'Boy, if I can make birdie and shoot 62 ...,' so if I give myself a chance that's all I can ask."

The first-round leaderboard:

Michael Bradley	63	Chip Beck	66
Mark O'Meara	64	Jeff Maggert	66
Jim Gallagher, Jr.	64	Gil Morgan	66
John Adams	65	Lee Janzen	66
Greg Norman	66	Ernie Els	66

As a parting comment as he left Riviera that night, Bradley looked ahead and said, "I'm more comfortable at even par or one, two or three under than I am at seven, eight or nine under, but that's not a good attitude because you're not going to win golf tournaments shooting one, two or three under. You've got to throw in that 64, 65, and then that 66 and 67. You need that to win tournaments. I don't know what to expect tomorrow. I'll give it 100 percent, and whatever happens happens."

What happened wasn't good. Bradley slipped back into his comfort zone, went from 63 to 73 and suddenly found himself five strokes behind Els and O'Meara, who continued to batter Riviera.

On another flawless day, one record fell and another was tied. Fifty-eight men broke par, one more than in the opening round, and although no one shot in the 20s, both Leonard and Olazabal shot 30. At the end of the day we had seen eight eagles, a double eagle by Per-Ulrik Johansson on the 11th, and a hole-in-one by Janzen, who holed a six iron on the sixth.

The 131s of Els and O'Meara tied the previous 36-hole PGA record set by Hal Sutton in 1983, once again at Riviera, and the 142 needed to survive the 36-hole cut broke new ground, the lowest since the PGA switched to stroke play for the 1958 championship. It had been another spectacular day.

The standings were reshuffled, of course. Bradley fell from first into a tie for ninth, O'Meara climbed from second into a tie for first with Els, who jumped from a tie for fifth into a share of first place. With 66, the 23-year-old Leonard, two years removed from winning both the U.S. Amateur and the NCAA Championship, moved into third place, with 134, three strokes behind the leaders.

Meanwhile, Gallagher went from 64 to 72, Adams from 65 to 76, Morgan from 66 to 73, and Beck from 66 to 74. At the same time, Janzen, Norman and Maggert managed to hold form, although all three shot higher scores than they had in the opening rounds. Janzen followed his 66 with 70, while both Maggert and Norman shot 69s and moved into a tie for fourth place, at 135, with Montgomerie, who climbed 15 places, Elkington and Brian Claar. All three had opened with 68s and followed with 67s.

Bradley struggled through a disappointing day, especially after he opened by birdieing the first and dropping to nine under par. His round was wrecked by the fourth hole, the very difficult par-three. His tee shot flew left of the green, hit a cart path, then leaped into the rough and lay closer to the 17th fairway than to the fourth green. Standing in deep kikuyu grass, Bradley warned the gallery, "Look out, guys, this could go anywhere," then played one wedge short, another to the green, and made his first double bogey. Then he stepped onto the fifth tee, pushed his drive out of bounds, and made another. By then he had scored seven strokes worse than he had through the first five holes of the first round.

On the other hand, Bradley showed he knows how to fight back. Taking a deep breath, he pulled himself together, played the remaining 13 holes in one under par, and shot 73. He never contended again.

While Els' 65 wasn't the best score of the day — Steve Stricker shot 64 — it was the most significant. It jumped him to the front, where he would hold on until the late stages of the championship. One of the early starters, teeing off just before 8:30, Ernie knew scores would be low once again because Leonard had birdied the first three holes by then, on his way to going out in 30. Els began with an eagle three on the first after a big drive and a four iron to eight feet, but he gave one of those strokes away on the fifth. Prone to hooking when he plays a bad shot in tight situations, Els drove into the left rough, caught a tree branch with his second shot, missed the green with his third, pitched to five feet and nursed the putt home, barely saving a bogey.

Out in 34, one under par, Els birdied four of the next five holes. He ran in a putt from eight feet on the 10th, where his wedge second hit the flagstick, left his three-wood second short of the 11th green but chipped to two feet, holed from 25 feet on the 13th, then hit a stunning six iron to seven feet on the 14th. Five under for the day then, Ernie tried to reach the green of the 17th, a 576-yard par-five, by forcing a three-wood second. He pushed it into the right rough, but saved his birdie with a pitch over the right greenside bunker within two feet of the cup. A routine par four on the difficult 18th and he had come back in 31. No one played a better second nine throughout the week, and only three others played it as well.

O'Meara was just beginning as Els finished, and like everyone who hopes for a good round, he birdied the first, playing a four iron to 18 feet and holing the putt. He lost the stroke on the seventh where he hooked his drive into the rough, then holed another 18-footer on the eighth and went out in 34.

A six-footer fell on the 11th, and then O'Meara ran off four consecutive pars before closing with birdies on the 16th and 18th and shooting 67.

With better luck Leonard might have shared the lead with Els and O'Meara instead of ending the day in fourth place at 134, three strokes behind them. While he played the first nine in 30, he played his shots just as well on the home nine, made nothing at all, and came back in 36. His 66 was a superb score, of course, but as it is with all low scores, it might have been better. A bad drive on the 18th, his only truly unfortunate shot of the day, cost him a bogey. Still, he hadn't shot a lower round since joining the PGA Tour in 1994.

Montgomerie's 67 could have been one stroke or two better as well had he coaxed in a few more putts. Out in 32, he birdied the 11th to slip to four under par for the day, but he could go no lower. A 12-foot putt from the back of the 12th green ran dead on line but stalled an inch or so short of the cup, and he parred in.

As it turned out, Johansson needed that double-eagle two on the 11th, where his three-wood second dropped short of the green, rolled on, took a slight break to the right, and tumbled into the cup. With it he shot 69 and finished at 141, one stroke below what he needed. As it was, the cut caught many better-known players, including Pavin. Corey's 76 was his worst round at Riviera since he shot 77 in the second round of the 1987 Los Angeles Open. Starting out at 12:30, Corey played the first nine in 35 and stood at even par after 27 holes, knowing he had to match par coming in to survive the cut. Then he bogeyed the 10th, failed to birdie the 11th, bogeyed the 14th, and double-bogeyed the 15th. Instead of shooting 36, he shot 41 and missed by five strokes.

He wasn't alone, of course. Daly missed as well, which eliminated both the U.S. and British Open champions. David Duval, the PGA Tour's hottest rookie, shot 143, along with Davis Love III. Larry Mize made a game try by going out in 31, but he needed 35 coming back, shot 37 instead, and missed the cut by two; Sutton, who won the only other PGA at Riviera, shot 144; Tom Lehman missed the cut with 147; and Phil Mickelson shot 148.

Among the foreign threats, Ian Woosnam shot 143, Vijay Singh, who nearly won at Inverness two years earlier, went out with 148, and Seve Ballesteros shot 151.

The second-round leaderboard:

Ernie Els	65 - 131		Brian Claar	67 - 135
Mark O'Meara	67 - 131		Steve Elkington	67 - 135
Justin Leonard	66 - 134		Jeff Maggert	69 - 135
Colin Montgomerie	67 - 135		Greg Norman	69 - 135

Golf fans are drawn to big hitters, which is understandable, but they are so hypnotized by their rocketing drives they often miss other, more important, parts of their games. Think of Sam Snead, for example, and his soaring drives spring to mind. Jack Nicklaus, like Snead the longest straight driver of his time, attracted his early fans with his length, just as Norman and Daly drew later galleries. With the exception of Nicklaus, whose wedge play wasn't as effective as the rest of his game, all these men worked wonders around the greens.

Els was the equal of any of them in length, but his real strength lay in his short game. Long as he was, it wasn't his driving that accounted for his 66 in the third round; his sand wedge deserved most of the credit. Using it from a greenside bunker on the first hole, for example, he pitched to five feet and birdied; from another greenside bunker on the third, he pitched into the hole for another birdie; from deep kikuyu grass left of the fourth green he pitched to three feet and saved his par three; from the wrong side of the bunker in the middle of the sixth green, he pitched across and saved another par; after overshooting the 11th green he chipped into the cup for an eagle three, then pitched to five feet from the light rough alongside the 17th green and birdied once more.

More records fell. Els' 66 not only earned him a three-stroke lead over O'Meara, who shot 69, and Maggert, with 65, it set the PGA record at 197 for 54 holes as well, the lowest three-round score of any of the four major championships. Until then, Faldo had been the only man to shoot under 200 in any of them. Nick shot 199 at St. Andrews in 1990 and matched it at Muirfield two years later. (At Riviera, though, he stood at 212, tied for 49th place, 15 strokes behind Els.) Raymond Floyd had set the previous PGA record with 200 at Southern Hills in Tulsa in 1982. Even though Riviera's greens had dried out under the warm California sun and no longer held every shot that hit them, the players continued their assault. Thirty-eight men broke par — 28 shot scores in the 60s — another 13 shot 71, and only 21 of the 72-man field finished over par.

Haas shot 64, the best round of the day; Ozaki, who went out in 30, and Maggert shot 65s; Els and Craig Stadler shot 66, and five others shot 67.

Maggert's 65 moved him into a tie for second place with O'Meara at 200; Montgomerie, one of the 67 shooters, took over fourth place at 202, and Stadler climbed from 16th after 36 holes into fifth at 203, tied with Elkington, who shot 68.

While some players moved up, others fell back. Leonard shot 70 and dropped from third place into a tie for seventh, along with Haas and Sluman, the 1988 PGA champion. Norman shot 70 as well and fell to 10th, and Brian Claar shot 73 and skidded from fourth to 21st. Players had to shoot in the middle 60s just to hold position.

No one will ever know how Haas managed his 64. While he hit 13 of the 14 fairways on driving holes, he missed eight greens. His chipping and putting, though, were of another world. He needed only 21 putts on the 18 holes. Nicklaus, who was paired with him, claimed he holed everything he looked at, and Haas agreed he basically didn't miss a putt under 20 feet.

At one stage, watching Haas save a series of pars after misplayed approaches, Nicklaus asked, "Why don't you try hitting a couple of greens?" When Jay finally hit a few and made a couple of birdies, Nicklaus smiled and said, "That's the way you're supposed to do it."

Who knows what Nicklaus might have said had he been paired with Els. Those who did follow Els saw not only some of the best recovery shots they had ever seen, they also witnessed a tense duel most of the way between him and O'Meara, who remained even through the first 10 holes. They both birdied the first, O'Meara getting down in two from 55 feet, and then Els moved ahead with his birdie on the third, where he holed from the bunker. He had hooked his drive and then threaded his second through the trees into a deep bunker alongside the green. As he took his stance, Ernie could see only the top part of the flagstick, and when he hit his sand iron, he turned away, thinking he had done nothing more than play a decent shot. Suddenly, though, when the crowd began to roar and his caddie jumped up and down, Els knew he had holed it and moved a stroke ahead of O'Meara.

Mark caught up by rifling a six iron to four feet on the fifth, and they both made their par threes on the sixth, where Els pitched across the mid-green bunker to four feet and holed as O'Meara made an orthodox par.

Els moved one stroke ahead once more at the seventh, where from a sidehill lie O'Meara pulled his approach, played a weak chip, ran his first putt past, then missed coming back.

Both men were having problems playing those delicate little chips from the kikuyu, because Els played a weak shot after overshooting the eighth green and fell back into a tie. After 44 holes, both men stood at 12 under par, and although they were leading, they were being threatened by Maggert. Seven under par when the day began, Jeff had gone out in 32 and stood 10 under, then reached the fringe of the 11th with his second and birdied again. Now he stood at 11 under par, just one stroke behind. Meantime, Norman had birdied the 11th and gone to eight under, Montgomerie stood eight under through 10, and Elkington nine under through the ninth after going out in 33.

Then O'Meara played a lovely pitch to three feet on the ninth and holed while Els pulled his approach and struggled to save his par. As Mark's putt fell, the gallery cheered wildly, for O'Meara grew up in California and attended Long Beach State College, not far from Los Angeles. Now O'Meara dropped to 13 under par and led Els by one stroke.

Ernie caught Mark once again with a birdie on the little 315-yard 10th, then headed for the 11th, a vulnerable par-five which had already given up one double eagle and 135 birdies. Everything changed there.

Much the longer hitter, Els rolled his second shot over the green while O'Meara's second stopped a few yards short and he pitched to 12 feet, putting himself in position for another birdie. While O'Meara marked his ball, Els stood behind the green taking a series of practice strokes. As he tested his stroke, the grass consistently grabbed his sand wedge; it looked as if he might have the same trouble he had on the eighth, where he had barely nudged his ball onto the green.

Not here, though. Els made clean contact. The ball popped up from the grass, jumped onto the green, ran toward the hole, and tumbled into the cup. He had eagled. Now O'Meara would have to hole his birdie putt to stay within a stroke of Els. Instead he three-putted. As his second putt glided past the cup, O'Meara stood with his left hand on top of his putter grip and his head bowed while he tugged at his visor with his right hand. From battling Els stroke for stroke, he had fallen three strokes behind.

He couldn't catch up, even though Ernie bogeyed the 12th with another mis-played drive. Els closed with birdies on both the 17th and 18th, shot his 66, and stood at 16 under par for 54 holes. O'Meara matched Ernie's birdie on the 17th, shot 69, and fell into a tie with Maggert.

Montgomerie could have caught them, but he left birdie putts short on both the 17th and 18th and fell five strokes behind the leader.

The third-round leaderboard:

Ernie Els	66 - 197	Craig Stadler	66 - 203
Jeff Maggert	65 - 200	Jay Haas	64 - 204
Mark O'Meara	69 - 200	Justin Leonard	70 - 204
Colin Montgomerie	67 - 202	Jeff Sluman	68 - 204
Steve Elkington	68 - 203		

Late in the afternoon of the third round, someone in the press tent asked Els if he thought his three-stroke lead put him beyond the reach of the rest of the field. Surprised by the apparent naivete of the question, Els stared for a moment and then asked, "Where have you been?," implying that, no, he didn't feel unbeatable. Everybody laughed.

On the other hand, a little study showed the question might not have been so silly as it seemed at the time. Els had already shot two 66s and 65. If he shot no better than 70 the next day, four strokes over his worst score so far, then O'Meara and Maggert would have to shoot 66 to catch him; Montgomerie would need 64, and Elkington and Stadler 63. Beyond them there was little hope at all, although few players had given up.

At 204, Leonard, Haas and Sluman stood seven strokes behind, but they believed miracles could happen. Leonard summed it up by saying, "Tomorrow is Sunday of a major championship; anything can happen." Sluman said he didn't consider himself finished because the way Riviera was playing, low scores were definitely possible.

"I'm nine under par," Sluman said, "and Jay Haas shot seven under today, so you never know. Obviously," he went on, "Ernie is going to finish well."

Els, however, didn't finish well. On a day of torrid scoring, Els played tentative, defensive golf while others attacked, and let the championship slip away.

It was clear early that this would be a day of low scores. Teeing off just after 7:30 following a five-minute delay while a blanket of fog cleared, Couples birdied seven of the first 11 holes, went out in 30, and shot 66 before Els and Maggert, the last two men to start, had begun warming up. A few minutes earlier Crenshaw had played the second nine in 32 even with a double-bogey six on the 18th and shot 67. Their rounds did neither Couples nor Crenshaw much good. Couples finished in a tie for 31st place at 279 and Crenshaw capped a frustrating week in a tie for 44th place at 281.

On the other hand, Faxon startled everyone by shooting the lowest nine-hole score in any of the major championships, and even threatening for a time to steal the championship. Off at 10:20, two hours before Els and Maggert, and trailing Els by 11 strokes, Faxon began with an eagle three on the first, holing a 10-foot putt after a stunning five iron.

A 20-footer almost fell on the second and he settled for a par four, and then he played another lovely iron to five feet on the third and birdied. A solid par three on the fourth, and then a seven iron to 25 feet on the fifth. The putt fell; he was four under par for the round.

He hit a six iron to 12 feet on the sixth, and then a nine iron to three feet on the seventh; both putts fell. He hit another pitch to eight feet on the eighth, but the putt slipped past, and then Faxon dropped a nine iron about 20 feet from the cup on the ninth. He read the putt to break about four feet and played it perfectly. He was seven under par with a score of 28 for the first nine. Now Faxon stood 13 under par, within three strokes of Els, who was just beginning.

As Faxon began running in his birdie putts, word spread through the gallery and the crowd began racing to him, cheering him on, chanting "59, 59," urging him to become the first player to break 60 in a major championship. Others called "Ryder Cup," encouraging him to win a place on the U.S. team that was to play the Europeans the following month in Rochester, New York. The even more fanciful called, "Win, Win," as if he actually stood a chance.

If he could keep up his momentum on the home nine he just might, though, but those at the top must waver and give him an opening.

After a routine par four at the 10th, Faxon rifled a three wood from 280 yards onto the green and got down in two from about 20 feet. He was eight under for 11 holes, and 14 under for the tournament.

This was as far as Faxon could go. Suddenly the putts that had been seeking out the holes began turning away. He missed from 20 feet on the 13th, from 15 feet on the 14th, and then he three-putted the 15th from 15 feet. A stroke was lost when he could afford to give nothing away; he was seven under once again. He struck back with a birdie from 20 feet on the 16th, a par-three of 165 yards, but then he struggled to save his par four on the 18th, where he holed from 15 feet after missing the green.

Faxon came back in 35 and shot 63, the second 63 Riviera had given up that week, and also the lowest fourth-round score ever in the PGA Championship. While Faxon jumped from 21st place to within a few strokes of the leaders, and, incidentally, earned himself a place on the U.S. Ryder Cup team, he needed a much better score to challenge the leaders, because by then Elkington, Els and Montgomerie had the championship to themselves.

Three strokes ahead when the day began, Els increased his lead to four strokes when both Maggert and O'Meara bogeyed the second and O'Meara failed to birdie the first. Neither Maggert nor O'Meara could gain any more ground, and they gradually gave way.

Meantime, Elkington was making his move. A 32-year-old Australian who went to the University of Houston, which is known for strong golf teams, he knew what had to be done to win. He had begun with the mandatory birdie four on the first, birdied the third from 15 feet after a fine eight-iron approach, then holed from eight feet on the sixth. Not one of the game's top putters, Elkington had found a way to get the ball into the hole. He ran in another putt from 18 feet on the eighth and made a steady par four on the ninth. Out in 31, Elkington stood at 14 under par for 63 holes.

Six strokes behind Els when the round began, Elkington had cut deeply into Ernie's lead, for Els was not having one of his better days. His tournament began unraveling on the fourth. Going for the green with a two iron, Els barely cleared the big frontal bunker, then three-putted from 45 feet. He was back to even par for the day and 16 under for 58 holes. Safely past the fifth, Ernie hooked his six-iron tee shot left of a cart path on the sixth, and with no way to pitch close to the hole, he bogeyed once again. He was one over for the day, 15 under for 60 holes.

Now Els looked uncertain. His confidence shaken, he missed birdie putts on both the seventh, from five feet, and the eighth, from six feet. At the same time, Elkington was growing stronger as the holes passed. Then his caddie spotted a scoring standard showing Els at 15 under par.

"That's a nice number," the caddie said. Elkington agreed. Once four strokes ahead, Els led Elkington by only one now. Then Elkington pitched to two feet on the 10th, chipped to two feet on the 11th, and holed from eight feet on the 12th, making three consecutive birdies that Els couldn't answer. Elkington had played the first 12 holes in seven under par and suddenly sprinted ahead, moving to 17 under par for 65 holes. Els stood 15 under after failing to birdie the 11th for the first time, and Montgomerie had caught him by going out in 32 and birdieing the 11th.

Still, there were holes to be played, and Elkington couldn't feel safe, for now the birdies wouldn't come. He hit a six iron to 10 feet on the 13th and the putt glided past, a six iron to 20 feet on the par-three 14th and made another par, another six iron to 10 feet on the 15th and still another putt was missed. He was having no luck, and finished his round with three consecutive pars. Out in 31, he had come back in 33, shot 64, scored 267 for the 72 holes, and let the others try to match it. They could after all, for Els wasn't finished yet.

After missing his birdie opening on the 11th, Ernie birdied the 12th to reach 16 under par, then lofted his tee shot within 12 feet of the cup on the 16th. A birdie here and he would catch Elkington. He studied the line, then set himself over the ball. He thought he stroked the putt perfectly. The ball broke toward the hole, caught the left lip, ducked into the cup, then quickly spun all the way around the rim and slid out. Els was shaken. "I couldn't believe it," he said later. He was still 16 under, one stroke behind.

Els' tournament ended on the 17th, another par-five he had birdied in every round. Els had missed on the 16th because he had tapped his putt a little too hard. Now, facing a six-footer to save a par five, he stroked it too softly. The ball ran toward the hole, but just before it reached the cup it took a sharp break to the left and rolled past. He bogeyed, his only six in four rounds, and dropped back to 15 under par, two strokes behind with only the 18th to play. He was finished.

Montgomerie wasn't, though. He had been playing the best tee-to-green golf of anyone in the championship through the first three rounds, hitting 37 of the 42 fairways on driving holes and had placed his ball on the putting surface on 45 of 54 greens and had putted from the collars of five others. Then, through the first 15 holes, he had missed only one fairway and two greens, one of them seriously damaging. His pitch to the 13th settled in the deep rough and he chipped poorly, costing him a bogey five.

Montgomerie had gone out in 32 and stood 14 under par. A birdie at the 11th dropped him to 15 under, but when he missed that par putt on the 13th he slipped back to 14 under, and he still stood 14 under after the 15th and needed three more birdies to catch Elkington. Some players crack under this kind of pressure while others live for it. Here Montgomerie showed he has the courage to play his best under trying conditions. He hit his tee shot to four feet on the 16th, pitched to four feet on the 17th, and with one more birdie to go, played an eight iron to 20 feet on the 18th and ran the ball toward the hole. It bounced over the spike marks but never left its line, then dived into the cup. Back in 33, he shot 65 and caught Elkington at 267, forcing a playoff. They would play the 18th hole to settle matters.

Elkington ended it quickly. A perfectly placed drive and then another eight iron from about 175 yards left him 25 feet from the cup. He holed it, Montgomerie missed from 20 feet, and Elkington had won the championship.

Elkington had been a bit of an enigma through his professional career, principally because of his health. He is allergic to grass, of all things. He entered the hospital in January of 1994 and spent the first part of the year recuperating from a virus infection. While he was in the hospital for the infection he had a malignant growth removed from his shoulder, and went back in again in May for surgery on his sinuses, which had hampered his breathing most of his life.

Otherwise, he is a joy to watch. He dresses impeccably and he has one of those uncomplicated swings Dave Marr describes as having no moving parts. He simply turns away from the ball, then turns into it. At 6-foot-2 and about 200 pounds, he has the strength to hit the ball long enough to bring most par-fives into range, and this week he putted like a dream.

He drove well, too, hitting 43 of the 56 fairways on driving holes. In his last two rounds, Elkington hit 29 of 36 greens, and was on the putting surface of 50 in the four rounds, which isn't bad.

Montgomerie, on the other hand, played exceptionally well from tee to green. He hit 61 greens, 17 of them in the second round. He also hit 50 of the 56 fairways. In the end, though, one putt made the difference — and Elkington holed it.

7. The Players Championship

Talk about ironic.

The man who sent his putter flying into the lake between the sixth green and seventh tee in 1992, then had to beg the grounds crew to retrieve it, used that same putter to make a dramatic 25-foot putt to save par at the 14th hole. Then, the same man — the one who leads the PGA Tour in hitting the island, but not the green at the famous 17th hole at the TPC at Sawgrass — saved par from the bunker there.

Call it justice or Lee Janzen's day. But whatever term you choose, the result was the same — Janzen stepped up and out of the crowd to win the second biggest tournament of his career when he beat Bernhard Langer by one stroke in The Players Championship in Ponte Vedra Beach, Florida.

The 1993 U.S. Open champion did it with that old Ping Zing 2 putter and an unflappable set of nerves that did their jobs so well that, on a day when everyone on the star-studded leaderboard struggled Open-style, Janzen could afford to let his mind wander to the Orlando Magic basketball team as he walked down the 18th fairway.

That Janzen had won his Open under survival-of-the-fittest conditions at Baltusrol three years earlier didn't hurt. While most players beat themselves, Janzen concentrated on beating the course — the same course, it must be noted, that yielded Greg Norman's 24-under-par romp in the park a year earlier. Any resemblance between the two courses — 1994 and 1995 — was on schematic drawings only.

Where Norman charged, Janzen maneuvered. Where Norman crowed about his winning total of 264, Janzen was happy to walk away with a meager five-under-par 283.

Is there any wonder talk of The Players Championship as a major was back in vogue? With a mine field of a course, this "major wannabe" became more of a major compilation. This was a Masters with rough; an Open where the stimpmeter ran in the we-don't-talk-about-it numbers. Those greens that once had dinosaurs buried underneath were now just sadistic. The wind was whipping like it was coming off the Firth of Forth. Just look at the scores. For the week there were more rounds over 80 (38) than under 70 (23). And, as is a major custom, there were more trainwrecks on the final day than you would care to count.

Tops on the list was Davis Love III, whose quest to win a tournament and qualify for the Masters ran amok at the 17th hole. After two-putting the 16th for a birdie to tie Janzen, Love floated a tee shot to the island green and it one-hopped over and into the water. "I double-crossed it," Love said. "I hooked it when I tried to cut it. It summed up my whole week. I thought I should have won. I threw away enough shots."

Love was hardly alone. The perfect weather, hard fairways and concrete greens turned what could have been a runaway by Langer or Pavin into a constant blur of great shots and great flops. It all started in the opening round when Nick Price put a pair of sevens on his card, including a quadruple bogey at the 17th. Ben Crenshaw, the best putter in the land, four-putted the 18th. Then there was Nick Faldo, who took a seven on the 17th on his way to 80.

Norman ended his chances Saturday with a double-bogey finish; Tom Kite in the opening round with a bogey, double bogey ending. The water at the 17th swallowed 41 golf balls in the first round under 49 mile-per-hour wind gusts and 58 balls in all, while the 18th didn't give up one birdie in the third round. How tough was it? Consider that Langer ran off a string of nine pars Saturday to take the lead.

The week started with talk once again of a World Tour. But this time it wasn't of Norman's ill-fated attempt to start up a global tour, but rather a meeting of the heads of the five major tours (United States, European, Australasian, South African and Japanese). Norman was rather quiet on the matter, saying of his tour idea "... the can of worms fell over ... and everyone started scrambling to pick up the worms." The group met, then decided to table further discussions until they looked further into the matter. That done, the tournament began.

The wind was howling when the players took to the course and the players were howling when the day was over. That Pavin led with 66 was an amazing afterthought. The news of the day? Try 23 rounds in the 80s and an aggregate worst ball of 122. The average score was 75.32 and there were those 41 balls in the water at the 17th hole.

The field knew then there would be no flying the ball to the hole; no quick pluck of a club from the bag. Downwind from the tee was, more often than not, into the wind at the green. The flagsticks weren't just flapping, some were bending halfway to the ground. Others looked as though they were about to snap or flip out of the cup. As for putts, reading the break was only half of it. Try calculating that plus the angle and speed of the wind gusts.

Hit it solid like Pavin or Gene Sauers or even Payne Stewart — all of whom played in the less breezy morning — and you lapped the field. Pavin, who led by one stroke at the end of the day over Sauers and by three strokes over Janzen, Langer, Stewart, Larry Mize and Steve Stricker, birdied the 132-yard monster 17th with an eight-iron shot that settled 20 feet from the pin. He made the putt, one of the four birdies he slipped in from 20-plus feet in his opening round. But even he left shaking his head.

"I can't remember the last time we played under these kind of conditions here," Pavin said. "I has been this windy, but we haven't played with the greens this firm and this fast." The last time Pavin shot 66 here was in 1983 when he closed with that score to finish seventh at the qualifying tournament. "I haven't played all that well when I've come back here," he said. "The first times I came back, I felt like the ghosts from the tour school were out there." If it wasn't them or the wind, it was something, because things got crazier on the second day.

As Ian Woosnam was three-putting from 10 feet at the sixth hole and watching his ball hit four feet from the flagstick at the seventh then skid off the green, Phil Mickelson was taking advantage of lucky bounces. He started the day 12 strokes off the lead, considered withdrawing, then banked in a seven-iron shot for an ace at the par-three 13th hole en route to 66.

But by the end of the day Pavin and Sauers shared the lead going into the weekend at five-under-par 139. They also shared a little trivia. For the first time this season on the U.S. PGA Tour, the leading score after the second round was higher (relative to par) than it was after the first round.

Sauers could have changed that had he parred the final hole, but he didn't. Standing on the 18th tee with a two-shot lead, he hooked his tee shot into the water for a double bogey. Love, Langer and Stricker were tied for third place, one shot back at 140.

"The course is playing really hard," Pavin said after the second round. "If it keeps playing like this, the winning score won't be much lower." How right he was. With the average score hovering at 74.319 on the second day, 74 players made the cut at 149 — the highest cut of the year by four strokes. Contrast that with Norman's score in 1994. He was 14 under par at the halfway point in 1994.

The question of the week wasn't how many birdies you could make, but rather how many double bogeys and trips to the drop circle you could avoid, which explained why Pavin and Langer, two of the more meticulous and precise players in the field, shared the lead at five-under 211 going into the final round. "Sometimes you have to be aggressive, but with certain pins, it is still pretty much impossible to get the ball somewhere nearby the hole," Langer said after his charge to the top began with nine consecutive pars. "Patience is the key every day."

By the end of Saturday's round, there were 19 semi-patient players within five shots of the lead and 23 within six. From the sound of things, they would need all the patience they could muster for the final round. The tough conditions, players said, were only going to get tougher since the already hard greens were dried out by the windy conditions. "Can you hear them calling?" Stewart said to a member of the grounds crew. "They're starving for water out there." Added Janzen, "The greens are very close to being extinct."

All of which caused balls to skip over hill, dale and 40 more yards before coming to rest in a back bunker or the rough or even the water. No one was safe. Least of all Sauers. The third-round co-leader made the turn one over par for the day after eight pars and one bogey, then things fell apart. He four-putted the 10th hole, then hit into the water at both the 17th and 18th to finish with a pair of double bogeys and a nasty 78. He left without saying a word.

Pavin's day started strong with a chip to eight feet for birdie — and the lead — at the second hole, but then it stagnated. A two-putt here, a 15-foot birdie there and back-to-back bogeys at the 14th and 15th, where he failed to get up and down, left him trailing Langer. Then, quicker than you could say final round, Pavin slipped in a 10-foot birdie at the 17th and Langer two-putted the 18th for a bogey and they left the course tied for the lead.

"I played all right," said Pavin. "I hung in there. It was just like yesterday — tough conditions."

Langer spent the front nine saving par four times from ugly places, then, after bogeying the 10th, he birdied the 11th with a sand wedge to three feet, then dropped a 22-footer at the 12th. The highlight to his day, however, was a 78-foot birdie at the 15th. "It was one of the longest of my career," he said. "It was tough. It broke three different directions and I played it two feet to the left of the pin."

The surprises of the day? Faldo got to one under for the tournament, then dumped two balls in the water at the 17th, and Mike Heinen bogeyed the final hole, but still shot himself into contention with 67.

Still, given the conditions, the one to watch going into the final round was Janzen. A third-round 69 left him just one stroke behind the leaders and confident. "The greens are so hard it's easy to misjudge the wind. You can hit a very good shot and be in big trouble," Janzen said. "The harder, the better. You have to pick out a spot and try to land the ball. Usually, we're just firing at the pin no matter what we have in our hands. You have to be a thinker out there and Bernhard Langer's one of the best. So is Corey Pavin. That's probably a good reason they're at the top of the leaderboard."

The same goes for Janzen, who was just about to start earning his reputation as one of the best closers in the game. Consider that Pavin went into the round as one of the best players never to win a major (he finally did three months later at the U.S. Open) and Langer went in as the most meticulous player to have won two. Janzen, meanwhile, went in with that one major and an Open mindset.

Langer unraveled early because his driver couldn't seem to find the fairway. His wild closing 73 included five bogeys, a double bogey and still left him tied with Janzen after 12 holes. "Every hole can grab you and catch you," Langer said.

Pavin's ride was equally crazy as he closed with 74 that left him tied for third with Stewart (72) and Sauers (68) at 285. "Bernhard and I had a big adventure out there today," Pavin said. "We still had a chance to win the golf tournament. We never were out of touch with the leaders ... but it just wasn't happening today."

What was happening? Janzen. And for a while at least, Love. That bid for the Masters was looking good after Love caught Janzen with a birdie at the 16th hole. Then he one-hopped his tee shot at the 17th into the lake. "Even if I don't miss putts, I'm two or three swings away a day from blowing it open," said Love, whose closing 72 left him tied with Brad Bryant at 286.

While others succumbed to the wild rides, Janzen was focused. After a bogey at the 13th hole, he holed a 25-foot par putt at the 14th. "I had just bogeyed 13, so (bogeying) 14 would have sent me the wrong direction," Janzen said. "It was tremendous to be able to make that putt." After a birdie at the 16th gave him a two-stroke lead, he saved par from the bunker on the 17th. Then, he rolled in a five-foot par putt at the 18th.

Justice? Perhaps. In his previous four trips to this event, Janzen's record was just on the other side of so-so. He had ties for 34th and 36th (1993 and 1994, respectively) and two missed cuts. It was during that second missed cut (1992) that he tossed away his putter.

Playing with Price and Peter Persons, Janzen missed another makeable putt, got mad and tossed his putter in the lake. Later that day, Janzen realized his mistake and teamed up with TPC grounds crew member Don Branske to save the putter. A few months later, Janzen won the U.S. Open with it. Now The Players Championship.

"Golf is full of tradition and it is hard to break the barrier of four majors," Janzen said after collecting the $540,000 winner's check. "But I consider this a major. This is a hard golf course. It is hard and fast like a major, the best field in the world you could possibly assemble. Everybody here, at the end of their career would love to say they won The Players Championship as much as they would want to say they won the Masters, U.S. Open, British Open, PGA. I think it is a great thing to put on my resume."

8. Ryder Cup

It was a foregone conclusion. Before anyone teed it up, before a crowd of 25,000 descended on Rochester, New York, and even before the grounds crew started turning Oak Hill Country Club into a training ground for U.S. Open course preparation, the Ryder Cup Matches were being handed to the Americans. There was no way they could lose. Then they did.

While everyone was pointing fingers at Curtis Strange, who couldn't save par on any of the last three holes Sunday, and United States captain Lanny Wadkins for selecting him in the first place, the Europeans were pointing champagne bottles at anyone within shake-and-spray range. They didn't care that Seve Ballesteros found only three fairways all week or that Nick Faldo made only two birdies in three days. All that mattered was that they rallied on the final afternoon and blindsided the cocksure Americans on their own soil.

The gold cup that — win or lose — inspires grown men to cry was on its way back to Europe. "I can't tell you what this means to me," said European captain Bernard Gallacher, both fists clutching glasses of champagne. "It's just ... I can't." Gallacher was 0-10 in Ryder Cups coming into this one. He had been questioned and criticized. After all, playing in eight losing matches and captaining two others wasn't the way to come into what was being profiled as an American runaway. It was generally believed that he needed a miracle.

If so, he got it. The Europeans staged the most stunning comeback in nearly four decades as they turned a foregone conclusion into an outrageously brilliant afternoon. The United States went into the final day needing five victories and got just four and one half. "We needed good performances from the whole team and we got them," Gallacher said. "All the team played majestically. It's getting almost too much to bear, this Ryder Cup."

Once every two years the Americans and Europeans get together to wave flags, have cozy dinners and posture, then play for bragging rights as the best players in the world. That the Europeans had lost the last two Cups by centimeters — it was 14½-13½ in 1991 and 15-13 in 1993 — didn't seem much of a factor going into the fnal day. The U.S., after all, held a 9-7 lead and a Ryder Cup deathgrip on the singles matches. The Americans just don't get beat in singles. Especially not on their home turf.

Yet, that's exactly what happened. While many were nodding in agreement that Ballesteros should captain — not play on — the next European team, his teammates did what most observers thought they could not do. Philip Walton beat Jay Haas. Mark James beat Jeff Maggert. Howard Clark beat Peter Jacobsen. David Gilford beat Brad Faxon. Strange couldn't save par.

Too much? Too much hype and myth, perhaps. The Americans were supposed to be young but experienced. The Europeans were thought to be too experienced and fading fast. The home crowd bought into it. Its team simply bit the dust. "We're still going to win," Gallacher was saying late Saturday night, down 7-9. But no one was listening. Except his team.

The European crew wasn't as glitzy as the Americans. Outside of Europe's top four — Faldo, Ballesteros, Ian Woosnam and Bernhard Langer — the American spectators in Rochester needed programs to pick out the players.

To the Americans, Colin Montgomerie was a man who had come up short. Costantino Rocca followed a miracle with a playoff loss at St. Andrews. Walton and Gilford were just names; Clark, James and Sam Torrance were graying players whose time was past.

So how do you explain what happened at what cynics immediately labeled as Choke Hill? The immediate reaction was to point to Wadkins, who chose Strange and Fred Couples as his captain's choices and left two of America's hottest players, Lee Janzen and Jim Gallagher, Jr., on the sidelines. Strange hadn't won on the U.S. PGA Tour since 1989 and Couples was thought to still be nursing a sore back. Gallagher and Janzen had each won twice in 1995, but had not collected enough points to make the team outright.

Strange went 0-for-3 during the week, the most critical loss coming to Faldo on Sunday. Strange, who won the 1989 U.S. Open at Oak Hill, led most of the day and all he needed was one par in the last three holes to win the match. He couldn't do it. Three bogeys, one huge loss. The Gallagher-or-Janzen-wouldn't-have-done-thats were loud and long. So was the conjecture over how much Ben Crenshaw played, considering the state of his game, which was just about on sub-par with Ballesteros'. At least Ballesteros was 1-2. Crenshaw was 0-3.

The real problem? The two teams were more even than the American media and spectators wanted to believe. The Europeans were more experienced than the fresh-faced Americans who earned their spots with clusters of top-10 finishes during the 20-month selection process. Not victories. Add it up. James had 17 European wins; Maggert, one victory. Clark had won a dozen times, Jacobsen only half as many. Torrance had 21 victories, Loren Roberts had two. And the list went on.

Wadkins didn't have a player who had won a tournament since June. Four of his players hadn't won since at least 1993.

Everyone wanted to talk about the U.S. without Janzen and Gallagher. No one seemed to mention the Europeans were missing Jose Maria Olazabal, who was sidelined with foot problems. Would Janzen have won it for the U.S.? Better yet, would Olazabal have made it a runaway for the Europeans?

As it was, the enduring memory of this Ryder Cup won't be the tears streaming down Ballesteros' face as he and Faldo embraced. It won't be Gallacher jumping for joy. It will be the picture of Strange at the closing ceremonies, his left hand cradling his bowed head. "I probably deserve what I'm going to get now (from the press)," Strange said. "No matter how bad you beat me up, it's not going to hurt as much as what I'm going to do to myself."

The irony is that these two teams were well matched. They played three days of golf and the Europeans won by one point. The Super Bowl should be so lucky.

The hints were there, but few saw them. Oh, the Americans did neatly dispose of Montgomerie and Faldo twice on the first day, but Rocca led a spirited Saturday morning comeback. In the afternoon, Faldo gave one away, then Corey Pavin took one with a chip-in at the 18th hole. A 9-7 lead with a day to go? The Americans were banking on it.

The U.S. won two of the first three matches Sunday, then the bottom fell out. "I know these guys are disappointed," Wadkins said. "I've sat in their seats before and it's not fun. They haven't even gotten to the toughest part yet — the dinner. But they're champions. The Europeans played inspiring golf. We didn't play as well as we could play. The Europeans just played awfully well. Sometimes you just have to hand it to the guys who win."

Had the Ryder Cup been a one- or two-day affair, the Americans would have kept it once again. They led 5-3 after the first day and 9-7 after the second.

A cold front blew through the area and the Ryder Cup Matches opened with a day of rain — both drizzle and downpours — and chilly winds. The biggest dilemma Wadkins faced, however, was how to manage his rookies. He wanted all five of them — Tom Lehman, Phil Mickelson, Roberts, Faxon and Maggert — to play that first day and gain confidence. The veterans, he didn't worry about. Maybe he should have.

The American rookies finished the day 5-1 with Maggert helping with two wins and the U.S. dominated the fourballs for the first time since 1979 when the opponents expanded to include all of Europe, not just Great Britain and Ireland.

While Lehman, who teamed with Pavin, was hitting a pressure shot on the final hole to beat Faldo and Montgomerie in foursomes, Couples and Haas were losing to Rocca and Torrance, and Crenshaw and Strange were beaten by Langer and Per-Ulrik Johansson. But the players causing the most concern were Jacobsen and Faxon.

The criticism of Jacobsen had been his supposed tendency to lose concentration. He fought back at the press before the event saying the reports were wrong. Then he up and lost his concentration. In Friday afternoon's fourball competition, he made a blunder at the par-four seventh hole. Paired with Faxon, Jacobsen chipped his third shot five feet past the pin, then scooped up his ball and high-fived Faxon. "Great four," he said.

Faxon gulped. "That was a five."

Jacobsen said he never knew Faxon had to take a drop after his tee shot went in the water. He didn't see it. Faxon didn't tell him. He didn't ask. The incident shook Jacobsen's confidence. He blocked his tee shot on the next hole, bladed a chip and picked up. The duo lost 4 and 3 to Gilford and his cheerleader/partner Ballesteros. "I feel like an idiot," Jacobsen said. "I want to cry."

Lehman, meanwhile, showed he was tough as nails. Not only did he pull off some awesome shots — his first tee shot was a 280-yard three wood and he had a 200-yard five-iron approach off soggy ground to the eighth green — but he also narrowly avoided being distracted by a misunderstanding. When Faldo said something to the effect that Lehman's putt at the second hole was good, Lehman asked him to repeat it. Faldo said something else, then made a gesture toward him to pick up the ball. "Well, if you would speak clearly," Lehman shot back.

Pavin, who emerged as the team's leader, took Lehman aside and calmed him down. Three holes later, the U.S. was 4 up. Lehman said after he and Pavin held off a Faldo-Montgomerie comeback, "Nick's gesture was like he was saying, 'You stupid little idiot.' I was hot."

So were the Americans. Behind a strong performance by Mickelson and Pavin, the U.S. won the afternoon matches 3-1 to take a 5-3 lead. That turned out to be Europe's wake-up call. At dinner Friday night, Gallacher chewed on his team as well as his dinner, giving them a good old-fashioned "tongue lashing." Whatever he said worked.

Europe started out hot and got better. Putts started falling and Rocca added a hole-in-one at the par-three sixth hole. "It was a very great moment for me and for my partner because with the hole-in-one, it's very difficult to lose the hole," Rocca said with a grin. Or the match. He and Torrance blitzed Maggert and Davis Love III 6 and 5.

Jacobsen and Roberts were the lone American winners in the morning as the Europeans took three of the four matches. If that wasn't enough, the winless duo of Montgomerie and Faldo found their games and beat Strange and Haas 4 and 2.

That done, Gallacher shook things up in the afternoon. He broke up Montgomerie and Faldo, pairing Montgomerie with Torrance in a futile match against Couples and Faxon who won 4 and 2. Faldo teamed with Langer and lost to Pavin and Roberts 1 up.

The tough match for the Europeans was the pairing of Gilford and Ballesteros against Haas and Mickelson. Ballesteros couldn't find Rochester, let alone a fairway, and was basically there to keep Gilford's spirits up. "I think you could put Seve with the paper boy," Jacobsen said, "and Seve would probably bring him through." Still, Haas and Mickelson took the match 3 and 2. Then came the drama.

With the final match tied going into the 18th hole, Faldo put his approach shot 17 feet from the pin. Then Pavin pulled off a great four-iron approach shot from the right rough — "Unbelievable," Maggert said. "I got a chill after that shot." — and topped that when he chipped in from off the green.

"Corey's our go-to guy," Faxon said of the only player to win four matches (4-1). "You know how Michael Jordan wants the ball? Corey has that. He wants it, and when he makes a birdie it jacks everyone up." Added Wadkins, "My first thought when he grabbed the iron was he was laying up. Then I saw the loft and I said, 'Wow, you know he's going to really try and pull something off here.'"

The shot landed within 10 feet of the cup, but rolled 18 feet from the pin and into the fringe. It was not going to be easy to stop the chip, but when the ball caught the cup, it circled the hole and fell in. That gave the U.S. a 9-7 lead and the American victory seemed nothing short of a formality. The U.S. had lost the singles just twice since 1940 — the last time in 1985 — and this didn't seem to be shaping up as the third.

"Nobody was down," Faldo said. "In a way, it's a good position to come from. Nobody can muck about it."

Gallacher had nothing to lose so he gambled when he made the final pairings. The man who is wound tighter than a 100 compression golf ball chose inspiration over fairways; emotion over birdie putts. He put a struggling Ballesteros in the lead-off spot in singles where he would meet Lehman Sunday morning.

Talk about risks. Ballesteros in his prime was daunting. He and Olazabal were *the* team to beat. For the longest time, Olazabal was lost without Ballesteros. Now Ballesteros was lost. He couldn't find a fairway and the only thing that kept his ball somewhat in play were the trees that often stopped it from rolling into an adjacent fairway. But could he still scramble.

The man who won the 1979 British Open from the car park was getting up and down from everywhere Sunday. A chip shot over a bunker for birdie at the second hole. A brilliant up-and-down from what seemed like the banks of Lake Ontario. A halved hole. The man with no game wasn't going to win, but he refused to let go.

Ballesteros made the turn 1 down and eventually lost 4 and 3, but it didn't matter. That his scrambling front nine inspired the biggest comeback in Ryder Cup history did. Instead of looking at the leaderboard and seeing Ballesteros gone after nine holes, Clark and James — Europe's second and third players — saw their spiritual leader hanging tough. It couldn't help but inspire their victories over Maggert and Jacobsen or Torrance's upset of Roberts. Torrance, after all, had a miserable 6-15-6 Cup record coming into the match.

Ballesteros didn't hit a fairway until the 10th when his gallery erupted in applause. But while he struggled, his teammates wiped up. Given the match-ups, the U.S. likely should have been no worse than 4-1 after the first five matches. Instead, it was 2-2-1 with Couples coming back to halve the match with Woosnam.

Ballesteros, who was finished after 15 holes, turned cheerleader. "The only contribution I made was the one before we played," Ballesteros said with a grin. "We were supposed to wear green today, but I said we had to wear blue if we wanted to win." Why? "It's my lucky color."

Three hours later, no one could argue.

Five matches came down to the final hole and the Americans went 0-4-1. Strange bogeyed the final three holes to watch a 1-up lead turn into a 1-down loss to Faldo. Faxon missed putts at the 16th and 17th holes while Gilford saved tremendous pars twice. At the 18th, Gilford made his 10-footer for bogey, then Faxon missed a six-footer for par. "They had to play better than we did," Faxon said, "and they just drummed us. No question about it."

Couples managed to halve his match with Woosnam at the 18th with a scrambling par. He cut a nine-iron approach that landed in the bunker, then got up and down for par while Woosnam's 20-foot birdie putt stopped at the edge of the cup. Couples was the last American to par the hole. The Europeans didn't even need birdies to win the hole. Par did just fine. The U.S. kept a two-point lead. Just not for long.

Montgomerie defeated Crenshaw 3 and 1, and Faxon failed to save par from the same bunker that Couples did. Gilford bogeyed the 18th, too, but won the match when Faxon's six-foot downhill putt didn't come close. "I was nervous as a cat," Faxon said. "I didn't read (the putt) well enough. If I had one thing to do over, I would have taken longer to read the putt." The matches were tied at 11½ points each.

Strange capped his rocky finish (he was 1 up through 15 holes) with a poor approach shot that came up short of the green. After chipping short, he missed a six-foot putt. Faldo hit a wedge shot to within three feet of the hole and made the putt. "It was as good as Muirfield in 1987 (his first British Open win)," Faldo said. "Actually, it was tougher because if I miss, it goes four feet past and I have to start negotiating with Curtis." With that, Europe took the lead 13½-12½.

"I don't have to beat him," said Strange, who stared down Faldo in a playoff to win the 1988 U.S. Open, the first of his back-to-back titles. "I just have to make four on the last hole and that probably wins the match. I'm disgusted with myself. It's a frightening thought how I'm going to wake up tomorrow knowing 11 guys fought their hearts out and I didn't play very well."

Not long after, Haas found the left woods off the 18th tee and was forced to punch out. His wedge to the green spun back off then he ran his par chip six feet past the pin. Walton lagged his putt to within six inches of the hole and Haas, who had battled back from 3 down with three holes to play, conceded. The Ryder Cup belonged to Europe.

Haas called the approach shot "just a bad swing. I needed to hit a hard sand wedge and fanned it. It's nothing I haven't done a hundred times before." Just not something he had done with the Ryder Cup riding on it. "In golf," Wadkins said, "things don't always happen like they're supposed to."

The final match of the day was anti-climactic, but still spoke volumes as former Arizona State teammates Mickelson and Johansson went at it. Johansson led 3 up after six holes. Mickelson charged back, however, with birdies at the 10th, 11th and 12th holes to take a 1-up lead he never relinquished. He closed Johansson out 2 and 1.

"This has been a terrific achievement," Gallacher said. "There's nothing (no difference) between these teams. I've been saying that for three Ryder Cups. It's the team that's on the day of the match."

When Haas conceded the putt, Ballesteros broke into tears. So did Faldo. Strange hung his head.

"I just didn't finish very well," Strange said. "I was escaping with Band-Aids on my swing. And that's what happens under a lot of pressure — the swing doesn't hold up. You keep plugging away and hope it doesn't fall apart. I have no excuses. My swing didn't hold up."

Neither did a lot of others, but Strange was still the controversial focal point. Had been since Wadkins announced his selection back in August. "I knew what would happen if I didn't perform," Strange said. "I probably deserve what I get in the press the next couple of days, but no matter how hard they beat me up, it won't come close to how hard I'm beating myself up."

He wasn't alone. At the closing ceremonies, Wadkins broke down. The words got caught in his throat; the tears rolled down his cheeks. Gallacher stood and put his arm around Wadkins. He had been there and done that. The gesture broke the tension and drew a round of laughs. It provided composure for Wadkins, who hopes to be playing with the 1997 U.S. team in Spain. "Enjoy your time with that pretty little thing," Wadkins said, pausing to peer over his glasses. "Because two years from now, we're coming to get it."

9. Toyota World Match Play

What to think of Ernie Els? Is he really the next Nick Faldo or Greg Norman, or is he just another first-class player? Will he go along from year to year, winning tournaments but never realizing the potential the rest of us see in him, or will he develop into a genuine star?

While at times in 1995 Els showed he has the game to compete at any level, at others he needed to play much better. By winning his second Toyota World Match Play Championship in October, Els temporarily climbed to second place in the Sony Ranking behind Norman, which isn't bad for someone barely 26 years old, but at the same time the World Match Play must be considered the highlight of a year that left behind some sour memories.

Els won the GTE Byron Nelson Classic in the spring, but he played listless golf both at Augusta and at Shinnecock Hills and missed the cut in the Masters and U.S. Open. Three weeks later, though, he nearly won the British Open, and in August he could have won the PGA Championship. Had he played only slightly better in the last rounds, he would have won both.

He went into the fourth round at St. Andrews tied with John Daly in the British Open, but where Daly shot 71 and won, Els slipped to 75 and tied for 11th place. He looked unbeatable in the PGA Championship, taking a three-stroke lead into the fourth round, but once again he slipped and shot 72 while all around him others were ripping Riviera apart. Needing a birdie four on the 17th, which was eminently doable, he bogeyed and dropped to third place, two strokes behind Steve Elkington and Colin Montgomerie. Elkington won the one-hole playoff.

Even when Els beat Elkington in the final of the World Match Play he played so poorly on some holes that the gallery left feeling Elkington could have won had he played anywhere near as well as he had in the PGA Championship. At the same time there is another, more positive way to look at Els. While it is true that he had missed opportunities to win in 1995, hadn't all the great players failed sometimes?

Els was only the fourth player to have won two World Match Play titles in succession and only the second to have won the first two he played. Hale Irwin won in 1974, the year he won the first of his three U.S. Opens, won again the following year, then went to the final in 1976, losing to David Graham on the 38th hole.

In his six matches over two years Els had beaten Elkington, Montgomerie, Seve Ballesteros, Jose Maria Olazabal, Lee Janzen and Bernhard Langer, all but Montgomerie a winner of at least one of the four majors. He won in style as well, beating Ballesteros, 2 and 1, when both stood 11 under par for 35 holes, and then shooting seven-under-par golf against both Olazabal, whom he beat by 2 and 1, and Montgomerie, who fell by 4 and 3.

He was even sharper against Janzen in his first match of 1995, playing 32 holes in 12 under par and winning by 4 and 3, and again scoring 68 and 69, seven under, in his one-hole victory over Langer. Ernie lost some of his edge against Elkington, although he played the first round of the final in five under par for the 17 holes he actually played out (he conceded the 16th when he lay three in a ditch). He was two under after his birdie on the 35th, the last hole of the match.

For the 208 holes he had played out over six matches, Ernie stood 51 under par, a birdie every fourth hole, strong golf for the Burma Road course of the Wentworth Golf Club, which winds 6,957 yards through wooded heathland in Virginia Water, England.

With Els being given a first-round bye as the defending champion, along with Nick Price, who had played such wonderful golf in 1994, Elkington, the PGA champion, and Ben Crenshaw, the Masters winner, most of the first-round interest settled around the match between Sam Torrance and Langer, who had won the Volvo PGA Championship at Wentworth in May. Janzen, winner of The Players Championship, was to meet Katsuyoshi Tomori, who had gone into the last round of the British Open tied with Daly, Montgomerie was to meet David Duval, the best new player on the American Tour, while Costantino Rocca, who won everyone's heart at the British Open, played Vijay Singh, who had nearly won the 1993 PGA Championship.

As the day played out, Janzen, Langer and Rocca advanced easily, but Montgomerie threw away a big lead and struggled to beat Duval on the last hole.

The first round was to begin at 8:15, but Wentworth lay under an early morning fog that delayed play more than two hours. The mist gradually dissipated in the warming sun, and the matches finally began a little after 10:15, still too soon for Tomori.

He figured to be no pushover since he had played so well at St. Andrews, but he had been weakened by a slight fever and called a doctor. Instead of medication, the doctor told him to take a shower, "Not too hot, not too cold." Tomori arrived on the first tee feeling all right, but he said his putting had been affected. He indeed missed a number of putts from inside 15 feet in the morning round — one from less than two feet on the 16th — but he won two of the first four holes before the missed putts began costing him. He didn't win another until the afternoon. By then Janzen led by three holes, and even though Tomori birdied three of the first 11 holes, he couldn't catch up. Janzen ended the match, 7 and 6, by holing a 25-foot eagle putt on the 12th. His reward was a second-round match with Els.

Meantime, Langer was having an easy time with Torrance. Sam had played in two previous World Match Plays, although not since 1985, and so far hadn't beaten anyone. His prospects looked grim even before play began for a number of reasons. First, he was age 42 and he had played for 10 consecutive weeks, the Ryder Cup a month earlier had taken something out of him, and he wasn't hitting the ball especially well. Then, Langer is an especially difficult man to beat; he fights for every stroke, and he doesn't know when he's beaten.

Running off four birdies on the first eight holes, Langer let Torrance know who was boss from the start. He led by four holes after the first nine and opened his lead to six after 16. There Sam dug in, birdied both the 17th and 18th, and went to lunch still four holes down. Langer struck back in the afternoon when Sam played some sloppy stuff, stood seven holes up after the fifth, and eventually won by 5 and 4.

Meantime, Rocca was playing with striking confidence. With his engaging smile he had become a folk hero to the spectators, and he responded to their cheers with some of the best golf of the day. As his wife called, "Forza, Italia" (Go, Italy), from behind the gallery ropes, he went out in 31, came back in 34 and took a three-hole lead to lunch, then fought off Singh in the afternoon and won by 4 and 3.

Among the winners only Montgomerie struggled, and he shouldn't have. He opened with 66 in the morning, which put him five holes ahead at lunch. Duval, though, battled to the end. Only 24, he had already shown he could play at this level — in his first full year on the PGA Tour, he had placed second in three tournaments, including the Memorial, third in another, sixth in a fourth and eighth in a fifth — and now he struck back, and suddenly the match changed direction.

Duval birdied the 10th with a five iron to eight feet, Montgomerie conceded the 11th after he drove into the woods, and Duval eagled the 12th by holing from 15 feet following a solid three iron into the heart of the green. From five holes ahead, Montgomerie now had only two in hand, and very quickly they had almost gone as well.

He won the 13th when Duval missed the green with a seven iron, but then he let two more holes slip away with shoddy work around the greens. He three-putted the 15th from just 12 feet, and took three from the collar of the 16th green and lost to Duval's par four. He was just one hole ahead now.

Both birdied the 17th after missing little pitches that might have fallen, and Montgomerie saved the day by birdieing the 18th.

The flaws in Montgomerie's game carried over into the second round, when the four seeded men played their first matches. Montgomerie met Elkington, who had beaten him in a playoff for the PGA, and beat him again, 3 and 1. He and Els were the only winners among the four seeds. Langer defeated Price by one hole, and Rocca continued his steady and reliable golf and beat Crenshaw, 3 and 2.

Rocca certainly could have won by a larger margin, since he led by eight holes with 16 to play, but Crenshaw fought back to 3 down before Rocca put the match out of reach.

Crenshaw came to Wentworth late because of a kidney infection. Scheduled to fly to London on Monday, he canceled the flight when he noticed blood in his urine. His family doctor prescribed an antibiotic, and Ben made reservations for Tuesday. Two canceled flights caused more delays, and he didn't arrive until Thursday, the day before his first match

When he finally played, he didn't look sharp. He shot 74 against Rocca's 67 in the morning, untypically missing a series of holeable putts, and went to lunch down by seven holes. His putting picked up in the afternoon after he opened his stance a little and gave himself a better look at the hole, and he picked up five holes from the third through the 10th. Now he stood just 3 down with eight holes to play, but Rocca hit a five iron within six feet on the 12th and eagled. Back to 4 up; even though Crenshaw won the 14th with a par three, he was finished. Rocca won, 3 and 2. One seeded player was gone.

Price was the other. He had held control of the match through the first 16 holes of the morning, indeed leading by two holes, but then Langer came to life while Price let opportunities slip away. You must birdie one of Wentworth's last two holes, both par-fives. Price birdied neither, Langer birdied both, and they went to lunch all-square. Langer began the afternoon with a salvo of birdies, went out in 32, and moved two holes ahead. That was all a player with his strength of will needed. Even though Price fought back and played the second nine two strokes under par, it wasn't good enough. Langer won by one hole.

Just as Langer birdied the 17th and 18th to turn his match around, so did Elkington. All-square with Montgomerie after the 16th, Elkington pulled two holes ahead when Montgomerie made two fives, and was never caught. Once again Montgomerie's short game cost him holes. For example, both he and Elkington bunkered their approaches to the 15th in the afternoon. Montgomerie came out decently but, as he had against Duval, he missed his putt, but Elkington saved his par. Had Montgomerie holed, the match might have turned out differently because he won the 16th by holing a 30-footer. Instead of 1 down, though, he was 2 down, and when he couldn't beat Elkington's birdie on the 17th, the match ended, 3 and 1.

There was no question about Els' match with Janzen. His golf was of another world and left Janzen trying to do nothing more than play good shots and hope he could win a hole here and there. Janzen actually did beat Els by one hole in the afternoon, but he had gone to lunch down by five holes and lost the match, 4 and 3.

Ernie set the early tone with some superb iron play — a six iron to seven feet on the first, a seven iron to nine feet on the second, and another seven iron to four feet on the third. He missed the seven-footer on the first, but he holed the other two to stand 2 up after three holes, went out in 32 and back in 32, and shot 64. Janzen, meantime, had played a solid round of 70 but had won only the 16th, with a nine iron to two feet.

Five down after the first 18, Janzen played 14 holes of the afternoon round in four under par and won five holes, but he lost four others and went out. The tournament was down to four men.

Langer had complained he was tired after two matches. He said that at 38 he had reached the age where he wasn't up to the physical and mental grind of 36-hole matches. He is nevertheless one of the game's most dangerous players. There was no doubt, though, that Els was the fresher man. He had played only one tournament in five weeks while Langer had just played five matches in the Ryder Cup, won in Ireland, and the next week placed second in Germany. Yet Els had to go the full 36 holes to win a tough match by one hole.

Elkington labored to win his match as well, taken to the 35th hole by Rocca, who finally lost by 3 and 1 when Elkington birdied the 17th.

The morning rounds, delayed an hour by fog, were remarkably similar in that both ended with the eventual winners one hole ahead. Both Els and Elkington had gone around in 68s while Langer and Rocca had shot 69s. Els and Elkington still led by one hole at the end of 27 holes, but Elkington and Rocca were playing the better golf. They had cut two strokes from par and shot 33 on the first nine while Els and Langer had gone out in 36s, one over par.

Now Els and Langer played a series of remarkable holes that left the gallery gasping. With Els safely on the 10th green with his six-iron tee shot, Langer missed, chipped 10 feet past, then holed for a half. From the left rough on the 11th, Els hit his nine-iron approach to a foot while Langer's ball lay 20 feet away. Once again Langer holed for the half.

Now Els' bunkered his second shot to the 12th, pitched to 10 feet and holed for another half. Next Langer played a marvelous shot into the 13th, a six iron that drew around the corner of a hill and settled within five feet of the cup. He holed the putt and drew level with Els. When he birdied the 15th, running in a putt from about 20 feet, he had birdied four of his last five holes, played the last six with five threes and a four, and gone ahead for the first time since the 14th hole of the morning round.

Realizing he was in danger of losing, Els responded with a birdie of his own on the 16th and followed with a birdie at the 17th that Langer couldn't match. After Bernhard left a short pitch nine feet short and missed the putt, Els holed from five feet and moved ahead by one hole.

Langer could have sent the match to extra holes when Els couldn't reach the green from a fairway bunker. Langer did reach it, though, but he left himself a putt of nearly 60 feet, ran his first putt fully 10 feet past, then missed coming back. They halved in par fives.

Els had played marvelously consistent golf. In 36 holes he had bogeyed only the eighth in the afternoon and birdied seven holes. Langer, on the other hand, had bogeyed four holes, birdied seven and eagled the fourth in the morning. He shot two rounds of 69 while Els shot 68 and 69. It had been a very close match.

Meantime, Elkington and Rocca were marking up better scores and playing just as tense a match until the holes began running out. Neither man won a hole until Rocca birdied the eighth from six feet, but he lost his edge when Elkington birdied the 10th. Rocca reached his peak on the 12th hole, where he rifled a four-iron second within two feet and eagled, pulling one hole ahead once more, but just as quickly he bogeyed the 13th and never led again.

Elkington pulled ahead at the 17th, and still led by one hole after the 11th in the afternoon. Then, just as Rocca had eagled the 12th in the morning, Elkington rifled a three iron onto the green and holed from 30 feet for an eagle of his own.

Two up now, it went back and forth until Elkington holed an 18-footer on the 16th to go ahead by two holes, then birdied the 17th, where, with a chance to match him, Rocca played a sloppy pitch and missed the putt. Instead of playing for the championship, Rocca would beat Langer by 2 and 1 in an 18-hole match for third place the next day. The tournament would be decided by Els and Elkington.

Both are tall men — Els stands 6-foot-3 and Elkington 6-foot-2 — and they both have exquisite swings. Els moves smoothly into the shot while Elkington has perhaps the most economical swing of all the leading players; he simply turns away from the ball, then turns back. Unfortunately neither of those swings worked very well in the final. Both sprayed shots all over the place, missed greens they had no business missing, and in general played uninspiring golf.

For example, ahead by one hole, Elkington played an indifferent seven iron into the seventh that settled on the lower level of the two-tiered green more than 50 feet short of the hole. He three-putted, missing the second from three feet or less. He was never ahead again. On the next hole he missed the green completely, pulling an eight iron dangerously close to a pond and losing to a par four. Then he missed the ninth green from a short distance but saved a half with a deft little pitch inside two feet.

Later Els began playing even worse. Three up after birdies on the 11th and 12th that Elkington couldn't match, he missed the green on the 14th, an uphill par-three of 179 yards and bogeyed, won the 15th when Elkington drove into the trees lining the right side of the fairway (Steve was lucky his ball didn't fly out of bounds), and then played two wild hooks that cost him both the 16th and 17th. His drive on the 16th sailed so deep into the trees he would have declared the ball unplayable in a stroke-play tournament and gone back to the tee. Instead, he tried to hack it out but conceded after Elkington played an eight iron to 20 feet.

Then Els stepped onto the 17th tee and hit another wild hook that was going nowhere but out of bounds and lost the hole to a par five. From 3 up he had gone to 1 up with the 18th to play.

This could be considered the key hole of the match, for if Elkington had halved, he would have gone to lunch just one hole down. Instead he played a timid pitch about 12 feet short of the cup, missed the putt, and Els holed from eight feet for the win. Back to 2 up.

As the afternoon round began, Els picked up two more holes. He won the second with a birdie and the third when Elkington threw it away. From a clean lie in the fairway, Elkington played a shot that squirted off to the right and settled behind a knob short of the green. Els scrambled for a par and Elkington bogeyed; now Els led by four holes.

Back and forth they went, first one playing a bad shot, and then the other. Els three-putted the fourth, bunkered his tee shot to the fifth, then lost the seventh to Elkington's birdie three. Now Elkington was just one hole down, but he missed the eighth green once again, playing a worse eight-iron shot than he had in the morning. Els went 2 up.

Ernie's driving had improved substantially in the afternoon after he had changed to a driver with eight degrees of loft and teed the ball lower. Then, instead of veering out of control to the left, his drives flew with just a hint of a drift to the right. He made no more mistakes after the fifth, and Elkington couldn't gain ground, even when he seemed in position. With the holes running out and needing birdies, Elkington played a perfectly placed three-wood shot from the tee that flew over a bunker on the left, setting up an open shot to the pin, but he played a mediocre pitch to 20 feet, and his last chance had gone.

By then Els hadn't used his driver since the 13th hole and had driven with irons. On the 17th, though, he ripped into a three wood and followed with a screaming two iron that hit short of the green, jumped forward, ran directly at the hole, for one heart-stopping moment looking as if it might fall for a double eagle, then died 15 feet past the cup. He made his birdie and defeated Elkington, 3 and 1. He had learned a valuable lesson: How to win without playing at his best. It was a fitting end.

10. Alfred Dunhill Cup

Late on Sunday afternoon, while Scotland and Zimbabwe played in the final match for the Alfred Dunhill Cup, spectators clustered around the 18th green at St. Andrews heard the unmistakable melody of *Flower of Scotland* rising from behind the British Golf Museum, across the road from the Royal and Ancient Golf Club. A band rehearsing for the presentation ceremonies evidently had its collective eyes on the scoreboard, for with the holes running out, Scotland had strokes in hand.

Nevertheless, some of the more superstitious cringed when the first wavering notes floated across the old links; they feared the band tempted the demons that for so many years had plotted against the land where the game had begun. Scotland hadn't won in 10 previous Dunhill Cups, and indeed in the two instances when it had reached the final match it had been beaten by England, the old enemy.

This, though, would be a moment of glory, for as the end drew close, Andrew Coltart and Sam Torrance stood strokes ahead of Tony Johnstone and Mark McNulty, and only Colin Montgomerie had no hope, too far behind Nick Price with too few holes to play. That is how it ended, two matches won by Scotland and one by Zimbabwe.

It had been quite a week for the Scots, especially for Coltart, who had come into the Dunhill Cup with far less impressive credentials than his teammates. Yet it was Coltart who played the best, shooting rounds of 66, 68, two 75s and a final 67 when it mattered most. Furthermore, twice Scotland won all three daily matches and never lost more than one individual game.

To refresh your memory, the Alfred Dunhill Cup is an international match among three-man teams from 16 countries broken down into four groups, each group comprising two seeded and two unseeded teams. Seedings are based on individual players' standing in the Sony Ranking. All the matches are by three individual games over 18 holes, one match on each of the first three days. This is not strictly a match-play format, though. All games go 18 holes, and the player with the lower medal score is declared the winner. The team winning the most individual games, either two or three, wins one point.

Each country plays every other country in its group. The four teams with the most victories in its group — or who have won the most individual games if there is a tie — advance to the Sunday morning semi-finals, and those winners meet in the final match the same afternoon.

Strong winds gusted to more than 30 miles an hour and the temperature dropped as the tournament began, which could only be expected since this was late October. The favorites had a decent first day. Of the eight seeded teams, five won, and only the United States, Canada and England lost. The Canadians and Americans were beaten in all three of their games, and the English lost, 2-1, to Spain, which was playing without either Seve Ballesteros or Jose Maria Olazabal.

Even though Montgomerie and Torrance were battling for first place in the PGA European Tour's money list, Scotland was seeded fourth, dragged down because Coltart stood 121st on the Sony Ranking. The United States, runner-up to Canada in 1994, was seeded first, Australia was second, and Zimbabwe third. In the end, though, neither the United States, Canada nor Australia reached the semi-finals, and only Australia won two matches.

By luck, Scotland was drawn into Group 2, one of the weaker divisions. Only South Africa, led by Ernie Els and David Frost, could be considered on the same level, since neither Germany, without Bernhard Langer, nor China, whom the Scots drew as their first opponent, had sent players with international reputations. The Chinese certainly weren't up to challenging Scotland. Two of their team shot 80 or higher, and the Scots won easily.

By the time the Scots had their match under control, the Americans and the Irish were locked in a close battle. With a team made up of Ben Crenshaw, Lee Janzen and Peter Jacobsen, the United States had gone into the first round not only seeded first but feeling confident as well. All that optimism disappeared quickly; the Irish won every game and shut out the favorites, 3-0. Ronan Rafferty birdied the 17th from 40 feet and shot 70 against Crenshaw's 71. Jacobsen hit his approach onto the road alongside the 17th green, shot 73, and lost to Philip Walton's 72; and with a chance to beat Darren Clarke if he could birdie the 18th, Janzen sliced his drive out of bounds and lost by two strokes. Not only had the Americans lost to the Irish for the third time in four meetings, the margin of their beating by itself assured they had only slim prospects of reaching the semi-finals.

Similarly, the Sony Ranking aside, nearly everyone felt Australia had fielded the strongest team, headed by Greg Norman and Steve Elkington and backed up by Craig Parry, but while the second-seeded Australians beat Argentina, they could just as easily have lost. Off first, Norman shot 75 and lost by three strokes to Jose Coceres, who was not widely known outside Buenos Aires, but Eduardo Romero pushed his drive out of bounds on the 14th, losing two strokes, and fell to Elkington's 72, and Parry birdied the last two holes, shot 70, and beat Vicente Fernandez by one stroke.

With the temperature rising under glorious sunshine on the following day, Coltart continued to play first-class golf, shot 68, and Scotland won all three games once again, although not as easily as they had against China. Germany fought to the end. Alexander Cejka double-bogeyed the 17th and lost to Coltart by two strokes; Torrance shot 71 and won by three over Heinz Peter Thul, and Montgomerie, playing last, shot 72 and beat Sven Struver by one.

Meantime, South Africa inherited China and won all three games, although not so easily as Scotland had the previous day. Zimbabwe, behind McNulty's 66 and Price's 68, won two matches from Japan; and Ireland, with 69 by Clarke and 71 by Walton, beat Canada, 2-1, and eliminated the defending champion.

At the same time, the United States learned how to lose while winning, Australia kept itself alive as Norman found his form, and England lost to Argentina, leaving a bitter Mark James declaring the Old Course an unfit place to play golf. He summed it up by saying, "It's a bleak course, the crowd's nowhere near you, and it's freezing cold."

After its loss to Ireland, the United States had only one chance to advance beyond the round-robin stage — win all three games against Sweden. For a good part of the day the Americans looked as if they might pull it off.

Crenshaw and Jacobsen shot a pair of 67s against Jarmo Sandelin and Jesper Parnevik, but once again Janzen let his match slip away. Three strokes behind Per-Ulrik Johansson with only two holes to play, Janzen picked up two strokes when Johansson double-bogeyed the 17th hole, then caught him by birdieing the 18th. They would play extra holes. After fine drives, Johansson floated a wedge within six feet of the cup on the first, but Janzen, 90 yards from the flagstick, a distance he claimed the absolute limit of his sand wedge, overshot the pin by 30 feet, and missed his putt. Johansson holed, and the Americans were finished. They had won only two of their six games, a dismal record for the top seed.

Australia still had a chance, though, especially since Norman had revived his game and shot 67, one stroke better than Miguel Jimenez, Olazabal's replacement, who shot 68. Out in 31, Parry shot 67 as well and left Ignacio Rivera three strokes behind, but Elkington shot another 72 and fell to Jose Rivero's 70.

Still, the Scots had captured the galleries. The spectators warmed especially to Coltart, who in two games had been outscored by his opponents on only five holes. He had 11 birdies in 36 holes and had gone 34 holes without a bogey. Even three-putting the 17th cost him nothing, because Cejka drove into the grounds of the Old Course Hotel and made six.

According to the common belief, only four matches mattered when the third round began, because the winners would then advance to the semifinals and the other eight teams would head for home. Ireland, the surprise team so far, would play Sweden with Group 1 at stake; Scotland would play South Africa for Group 2; Zimbabwe would play New Zealand for Group 3, and Australia would play England for Group 4. The common wisdom was wrong — the match between Spain and Argentina mattered as well, although no one realized it until later in the day.

Playing first, the Argentines looked as if they would run away from Spain when Fernandez raced out in 31, four strokes better than Jimenez, and shot 68, but the Spaniards struck back. Rivero shot 70 and beat Romero's 72, and Coceres could not make up for his rocky 38 on the first nine and fell to Garrido's 71. Spain won, 2-1, then walked into the R&A clubhouse and hoped for England to beat Australia in all three games.

Surprising everyone, the English accommodated the Spaniards, although they struggled to the end. Elkington had played rather erratic golf in the first two rounds, birdieing eight holes, bogeying six, and double-bogeying the fourth in the second round. He was drawn against Barry Lane in the first game, ran off 16 consecutive pars, and stood level after both he and Lane bogeyed the 17th. When Lane birdied the 18th, England had won its third game of the week.

Minutes later Norman came to the 18th one stroke behind James and played a wonderful pitch inside four feet. A birdie here would send the match to extra holes. While James stood at the edge of the green looking downhearted, Norman missed the putt. His 69 fell one stroke short of James' 68.

Just about then, Parry missed an even shorter putt on the 17th that would have moved him one stroke ahead of Howard Clark, then fell to his knees when a 20-footer glided past on the 18th. Next, Clark's putt from about 10 feet was clearly headed past the cup, but his ball suddenly turned sharply left, hung on the lip for an instant, then tumbled in. A 69 against Parry's 70. England had shut out the Aussies.

Watching from inside the clubhouse, the Spaniards smiled. They were in the semi-finals because they had won five individual games and Australia only four, even though two of those four had been against Spain.

While Australia took its lumps, Ireland barely squeezed past Sweden and Scotland battled to beat South Africa. Wielding his 54-inch driver, Sandelin shot 67 and beat Clarke by three strokes, but Rafferty shot 68 and won by three over Johansson. Once again Walton held the key. One stroke behind with four to play, he pulled ahead when Parnevik bogeyed the 15th and 16th, and saved a half in bogeys with a deft chip from off the road on the 17th. Still one stroke ahead, but Sweden wasn't finished yet, for Parnevik sent the game to extra holes by birdieing the 18th from more than 20 feet. Once again Walton showed his resolve by holing from six feet on the first after Parnevik missed from not much farther way.

Avoiding the usual platitudes, Walton slumped in a chair and admitted, "To be honest, I didn't enjoy it one bit. I'm not sure anyone enjoys that kind of pressure. Obviously, though, you enjoy it more when you get through."

Leading off for Scotland, Coltart played his first loose round, stumbled home in 40 with an unfortunate run of four consecutive bogeys, shot 75, and was no match for Els, who shot his third consecutive 70. Torrance was running away from Retief Goosen, five strokes ahead after the 12th, but suddenly the Scots were in trouble. Montgomerie had fallen two strokes behind David Frost after the first nine; while up ahead Goosen gained two strokes on Torrance when he birdied the 13th and Sam bogeyed, another when he birdied the 16th, and still another when Torrance bogeyed the 17th.

By then Montgomerie had rallied. He pulled even with birdies from eight feet on the 10th and 35 feet on the 11th, then moved ahead when Frost three-putted the 12th. When Frost drove into a pot bunker on the 15th, which cost him a six, Montgomerie had won his game, but Torrance still had the 18th to play with one stroke in hand. Curiously, Goosen drove with an iron and left his ball lying on Granny Clark's Wynd, the public road that knifes across the first and 18th fairways. He wasn't through just yet. Facing a very difficult shot from the blacktop, he pitched to 25 feet, then almost made Torrance's heart stop when his putt caught the lip of the hole. It stayed out, though, and Sam holed his birdie, shot 68 against Goosen's 70, and all of Scotland cheered. The Scots would play the Irish the following morning.

Spain, meanwhile, could look forward to playing Zimbabwe, which had moved quietly along behind Price and McNulty, neither of whom had scored as high as 70 in the first two rounds. After shooting 69 and 66, McNulty slipped to 70 in the third round, but that was still good enough to beat New Zealand's Michael Campbell by two strokes, and Price shot his second consecutive 68 and beat Frank Nobilo by three. Tony Johnstone's 73 was good enough to beat Greg Turner by one stroke.

While the United States lost 2-1 to Canada, I should mention Crenshaw. He had played the best golf of anyone over the last two rounds, shooting 67 on Friday trying to keep his team alive, and 68 on Saturday, with honor his only reward. Both scores might have been better except for two lapses. He was penalized two strokes on Friday for not declaring a second drive on the 17th a provisional (his first drive was in bounds but he had to play the second) and another one-stroke penalty on Saturday when he moved his marker a putter-head's length but didn't replace it.

As the semi-finals shaped up, with one seeded and one unseeded team in each match, Scotland, the fourth seed, figured to have more trouble with Ireland than Zimbabwe, seeded third, would have with Spain. While Scotland had struggled to beat South Africa, the one strong team it had faced, Ireland, by contrast, had beaten three tough opponents — the United States, Canada and Sweden. At the same time, Spain had survived a group that included Australia, the second seed, England and Argentina; while Zimbabwe, with Price playing exceptional golf, had lost only one game in beating Wales, New Zealand and Japan.

Then Spain gave Zimbabwe more of a battle than anyone expected, and Scotland barely got by Ireland.

The weather had worsened overnight, and rain fell through the morning. The golfers walked under umbrellas as the matches began, but the dull gray clouds gradually drifted away and the temperature climbed as the sun broke through.

While he hadn't shot sensational scores, Walton had played steady, reliable golf, never wavered, and won each of his three games. Then he gave away his game with Coltart, who was playing some dull stuff. Two over par after the 14th, Walton stood two strokes ahead of Coltart, who was having a dreadful day, but Walton played the next three holes in two over par, lost each of them, shot 76, and Coltart won by one stroke.

A missed birdie putt at the 15th held the key. Ten feet from the cup, Walton assumed he would have to birdie since Coltart would surely hole his putt from half that distance. Walton missed, Coltart holed, and then Walton played three miserable holes. He three-putted the 16th, drove into the rough on the 17th and smothered his second shot, and with a chance to even the match by birdieing the 18th, he hit his approach fat and left his ball in the Valley of Sin, the deep depression on the front left of the home green.

While Coltart and Walton were stumbling around, Montgomerie and Clarke were playing remarkably steady golf; Montgomerie just out-birdied him, shot 70, and won by two strokes. Playing his best golf of the week, Montgomerie set himself up with birdie opportunities on every hole, and indeed lipped out a 20-footer on the second and three-putted the fifth from 70 feet for a par five. Once again the final holes were decisive. Clarke had caught up by birdieing the 14th, but Montgomerie pulled ahead once more by holing from 30 feet on the 16th, and added another stroke when Clarke three-putted the 17th from off the green.

Only Rafferty won for Ireland, beating Torrance, 73-74, but his victory came too late; Ireland had lost.

So had Spain, although its match with Zimbabwe had been a close-run thing. Shooting 70, Jimenez eased past Johnstone, who led with two holes to play. Johnstone dropped back to level by three-putting the 17th from 12 feet, and Jimenez birdied the 18th with a lovely pitch to two feet.

That left it up to Price, because McNulty was running away from Garrido. Five strokes ahead after the first nine, and still ahead with two to play, McNulty shot 73, evidently winning by four strokes, but Garrido was disqualified later for signing a scorecard showing a par five on the 14th where he had actually scored a six.

In the critical match, Price had been playing another sub-par round and stood three strokes ahead of Rivero with four holes to play. Suddenly, though, he lost two of those strokes when Rivero holed from 12 feet on the 15th and Price missed from eight, and Rivero ran in another birdie on the 16th as Price scrambled to save his par four. Rivero almost tore the heart from Price when his putt from off the 17th green rolled dead two inches from the cup. Rivero shot 70, Price 69, and Zimbabwe was in the final.

Scotland had advanced even though Montgomerie's left wrist had been sore for weeks and Torrance had been taking medication for a chest infection. It is part of golf legend that sick men are often dangerous; these two certainly were. Even though every wristy swing had pained him, Montgomerie had never flinched, and Torrance, coughing and wheezing his way around, had never given in. If Scotland were to win, it seemed logical those two would have to carry most of the weight.

They had the tougher assignments as well. Torrance was drawn against McNulty in the second game and Montgomerie against Price in the third. Coltart would lead off against Johnstone.

Andrew made it easier on his teammates. One stroke ahead after birdieing the fifth, he shocked Johnstone by holing in one at the eighth. When his six iron dived into the cup and the largely Scottish gallery roared, Johnstone was stunned; three behind now, he never challenged again. Coltart shot 67 while Johnstone shot a credible 71 and lost by four strokes.

Now, if either Torrance or Montgomerie would win his game, Scotland would have the cup. Playing just one hole behind, both Torrance and McNulty went out in 33s, but Sam birdied the 12th from five feet after McNulty had missed from eight, and McNulty bunkered his drive on the 13th and bogeyed. When Torrance birdied the 14th, he had moved three strokes ahead and was left with nothing to do but make his figures. He shot 68, beat McNulty by two strokes, and Scotland had won; Montgomerie's loose 74 against Price's 68 didn't matter.

His eyes flooded with tears, Torrance climbed the old stone steps behind the home green, threw his arms around Coltart, and muttered, "Well done, mate."

It had been a tough 11 years for the Scots, losing final matches to England in 1987 and 1992, also losing a further three semi-finals. But no one could deny they deserved to win. Each man had won four of his five matches, and Coltart had been a revelation. In his two years on the Scottish team he had won eight of his nine games, and even with those two shaky 75s, he had played the Old Course in nine under par. Torrance, meanwhile, had shot five under and Montgomerie four under.

Price, though, had played the best of anyone, shooting rounds of 67, 68, 68, 69, 68, and beating par by 19 strokes — wonderful golf.

Basking in the afterglow, Torrance said, "This was my proudest moment. To win at St. Andrews after 11 years is unbelievable. We knew this was our best chance of winning. We came here very confident, we got a good draw, and we did it."

Speaking for Zimbabwe, Johnstone said, "To lose to Scotland at the home of golf is no disgrace."

Price agreed. "Hats off to the Scottish guys," he said. "They're something else."

11. Johnnie Walker World Championship

There was something quite familiar about the 1995 Johnnie Walker World Championship. Fred Couples ended the five-year Johnnie Walker sponsorship of the event the way he started it — with a victory — and with his performances in between, the accounting became impressive. He won the $550,000 first prize from the $2.3 million purse, boosting his winnings to $1,517,500 in five tournaments. Between the two victories, Couples finished seventh, second and 17th. "The first million I made here is gone," Couples said. "Maybe I can hang on to this $550,000."

In 1995 alone, Couples was making a pretty fair living off Johnnie Walker — and wearing out his welcome on the PGA European Tour. Couples started in January, winning the season-opening Dubai Desert Classic, then the Johnnie Walker Classic in the Philippines. Then he ended the year with his victory at the Tryall Golf Club near Montego Bay, Jamaica. In between, Couples was on the American PGA Tour, and because of his back problems he had an indifferent year. In 15 tournaments, his best finish was a tie for fifth in the Mercedes Championship in January. Late in the year, he teamed with Davis Love III to win the World Cup in China for the fourth successive year.

Couples' back was still bothering him in Jamaica, to one degree or another. Sometimes it was sore, sometimes tight, sometimes not, but always a concern. But on he played, and never was the real Fred Couples more visible than when he found himself three strokes down with two holes to play in the final round.

"I told my caddie that if I finish 3-3, we've got a chance to get into a playoff," Couples said. A 3-3 finish at Tryall? Right, Fred. Just an eagle and a birdie, that's all. But Couples did it, tied Vijay Singh and Loren Roberts, and then beat them with a birdie on the second extra hole.

The Tryall golf course can have a pretty good bite. In the calm, at a short 6,760 yards, it is no match for the modern professional. But with the wind up, buffeting the flat shoreline and zipping through the abrupt coastal hills, it could be maddening. Couples shot rounds of 70-67-71-71, Singh 69-68-72-70 and Roberts 70-70-70-69, as they tied with five-under-par 279 totals. They were the only players in the 20-man field to finish under par. The next best, six strokes behind with one-over-par 285 totals, were Bernhard Langer (68) and Mark Calcavecchia (73).

The field for this finale was the smallest of all. The format called for a maximum of 28 players who won certain designated events plus qualifiers based on their standing on the Sony Ranking. There were 20 players this time, and when Anders Forsbrand had to be hospitalized in the early stages of pneumonia after the second round, the field was down to only 19 players.

It might have been an 18-player field if John Daly, the British Open champion, had had his druthers. There may not be a worse performance of any consequence on record. Day after day, Daly continued to flail away, but he was sinking deeper into the morass with each swing. He shot a staggering 80-80-84-80–324, fully 40 over par, and 23 strokes more than the next highest, Toshimitsu Izawa (301), the Japan Open champion.

A player had to play the entire tournament to receive prize money. The rule was added after Daly's performance in the inaugural event in 1991. He opened with 77, then was disqualified for signing an incorrect scorecard in the second round. He shot 87 but signed for 86. He still received $50,000, the last-place money.

"This course is not made for me, and I know it," Daly said. "It takes the driver out of my hands. But it's a hell of a challenge."

Daly put himself into dubious historical company. Records showed that the last former British Open champion to post a score as high as 324 was Arnaud Massy, the 1907 champion, who had a 324 total in the 1920 Open. Coincidentally, while Massy was winning in 1907, amateur John Ball, the 1890 champion, was posting a 327 total, which was the most recent score higher than 324 by a former champion. The 1907 Open was the last in which gutta-percha was the golf ball of preference.

The competitive fire may have gone out of Daly in the first 10 minutes of the tournament. He never recovered from his quadruple-bogey eight on the first hole in the first round. All told, he had two quintuple bogeys, one quadruple bogey, two triple bogeys, 10 double bogeys and 13 bogeys. He had a total of 14 penalty strokes. After his third-round 84, someone asked whether he would apologize. "I can't apologize for trying," Daly said. "In 1991, I didn't try, but this time I tried."

Wayne Riley, the Scottish Open champion, also struggled on the first hole, but with happier results. He chipped in from 35 feet for a birdie, and was on his way to a five-under-par 66 and the first-round lead. "You hole a few putts and play the par-fives as you should," the good-humored Australian said. He birdied two of the three par-five holes, with another chip-in at No. 4 and two putts at No. 17, the easiest hole on the course. He bogeyed just once, at the 10th, where he missed the green after an errant drive forced him to lay up short of the ditch. "I'm surprised to be well ahead — surely someone would be within a couple of shots," said Riley, who was in the first pairing.

Singh, finishing more than an hour later, came the closest. He was second with 69, three strokes behind Riley. He bogeyed twice, and both were inexcusable, he said. "I've got 70 yards to the flag and make bogey at No. 6," he said, "and I literally missed it from less than three feet at the 13th." He got somewhat even with Tryall with birdies at two of the par-fives and then a birdie at the brutal par-four No. 8. It was the only birdie there in the first round (and one of only five all week). He drove cleanly across the gully, and then facing the wind off the Caribbean not far in the distance, he fired a six iron to six feet.

Only two others broke par the first day, both at one-under 70. Roberts, the former U.S. Open runner-up, offset an opening bogey with two exciting birdies. He chipped to one foot at the par-five No. 4, and he drained a 40-foot putt for a three at No. 9. Couples, in contrast, turned in an adventure. He had two birdies and a bogey going out. Coming in, he double-bogeyed the par-four 12th, bogeyed the par-three 13th, and eagled the par-five 14th. He finished his round with a birdie at the 18th. Perhaps that was an omen. He would birdie the 18th three of the four rounds. He birdied it in the last round to get into the playoff, then birdied it again to win.

Other expected challenges fell short. Langer, for one, a three-time winner on the 1995 PGA European Tour, ran afoul of the 11th in the seaside gaunt-let — the 10th, 11th, 12th, 14th and 15th holes, all in a line running parallel to the Caribbean and so almost constantly affected by the wind off the sea to the left. "I paid a heavy penalty for my drives into the rough at 11 and 18," Langer said. At the par-four 11th, his drive was almost unplayable, and it cost him a double bogey, the first of only two the entire tournament. He birdied the 16th and 17th, then bogeyed the 18th from the rough.

Nick Faldo had two birdies and five bogeys for 74, and refused to blame the elements. "The wind wasn't that bad," he said. "But two fliers didn't help." Faldo, the 1992 champion, was still searching for the perfect swing. This time it was a "bad hip action" that was bothering him. Playing the U.S. PGA Tour full-time, he won the Doral-Ryder Open and had five other top-10 finishes in his first 12 starts. Now his goal was to correct that hip action. Maybe that explained his second-round 75 on the day the wind had eased.

There are two ways to measure the wind at Tryall. One is to consult a wind gauge. The other is to check the scores. The average score in the first round was 74.25 — 3.25 strokes over par. The average in the second was 72.85, almost a stroke and a half better. Three players had the same scores, five were worse, and 12 improved. The improvement averaged a whopping 3.5 strokes, led by the huge swings of Izawa (80 to 71), Colin Montgomerie (77 to 70) and defending champion Ernie Els (79 to 73). Even so, the 1995 Johnnie Walker World Championship looked like a five-man chase, and maybe that was being liberal.

Couples was trying to make it a one-man chase. He exploded for four birdies over the last five holes, the last three in a row — the hottest stretch by anyone all week — for 67 and a share of the 36-hole lead. He was not recommending it, but his back problem did wonders for his game. "Early on, it felt great," Couples said, "and when I started making all those birdies, it stiffened up." He played the first nine in even par, with two birdies and two bogeys. Except for a bogey at the treacherous par-three 13th, with its over-water carry into the wind, he dominated the second nine. He started with a 25-foot chip-in at the 10th, birdied the par-five 14th from five feet, parred the mean 15th (which is about the same as a birdie), then birdied the last three — a sand wedge to three feet at the 16th, two putts from 10 feet at the 17th, and a sand wedge to two feet at the 18th. "As I tightened up, I started hitting the ball better," Couples said. "I don't know why."

Riley, the first-round leader, hung on by his fingernails and took the rosy outlook. "I can't complain," he said. "After that start, I still shot 71 — and that's a lot better than some guys shot." It was better than 13 others, actually, but it dropped him out of the solo lead and into a tie with Couples and Singh at five-under-par 137. Riley started with two bogeys out of the rough on the front, then got three birdies coming in, including a chip to six inches at the 17th that left Riley applauding himself. "Someone's got to clap," he said. "It might as well be me."

Singh was miffed at his driving in the first round, but he stuck with it, strong wind or weak. "If you can manage the wind, you should be able to make a good round," he said. Tryall took the driver out of Daly's hands, but not out of Singh's. "I hit my driver where I planned to hit it," he said. He hit it nine times in the 14 driving holes in a three-under-par 68. That paid rich dividends at the par-fives. He birdied the fourth and 14th holes on three-wood approaches, and eagled the 17th with a seven-iron shot to 20 feet. After bogeys at the 10th and 18th, it was a net gain of three strokes.

Roberts logged four birdies, but like Singh and Riley, he fell victim to the 18th for his third bogey and settled for another 70. At two-under 140, he was the fourth and only other man under par. Mark Calcavecchia started the round with two bogeys, but birdied the 16th and 17th to move to fifth place at 70-142. It was time for the other big names to get moving, but the silence was deafening. Colin Montgomerie bogeyed the 18th for 72 and 147 total, 10 strokes off the lead. Faldo was even par for the round, then double-bogeyed No. 7 and No. 10 for 75 and a 149 total, 12 strokes behind.

"Basically, it's down to four or five guys," Couples said after the second round. "Anybody down to (Alexander) Cejka and Riley, anybody at even par can win it." That was a span of five strokes, hardly a safe spread.

There were two big surprises in the third round. One was Riley, solo leader in the first round and co-leader in the second. He knocked himself out of the lead with 76, for an even-par 213 total, just at the five-stroke limit Couples spoke of. The other surprise, now tied with him, was Cejka, the fast-rising young German, a three-time winner on this year's PGA European Tour. He posted a six-under-par 65 that would stand as the best round of the week.

Riley had an awful time. He was out in 39 that included six bogeys. The damage rolled on. After bogeys at the eighth and ninth holes, he double-bogeyed the 10th. He was out of contention.

Cejka, meanwhile, was working on his 65, the only bogey-free round of the tournament. "The weather was quieter and I played much better," Cejka said. It was the kind of golf that brought Cejka victories in the Turespana Open Andalucia, Hohe Brucke Austrian Open and Volvo Masters on the PGA European Tour this year. Cejka launched his attack at the par-three No. 5, with a tee shot from under a tree limb to a green sloping from left to right. Cejka struck his five iron to 10 feet and holed it. He birdied the eighth from six feet, one of only three to do it all day. Then he birdied the 10th, 11th, 14th and 16th for an inward 32, bettered only by Els' tourna-ment-best 31. He was five strokes off the lead.

"It's going to be tough, but five or six shots is not impossible, even in one round," Cejka said. He got no arguments.

Singh was up and down to 72 with three bogeys and two birdies. He got one birdie on two-putts from 20 feet at No. 4, the other on a 15-footer at the 16th. "I struck the ball better today, but I had a bad feel on the greens," he said. "Thank goodness it was today and not tomorrow."

Roberts, the steadiest man in the field, turned in his third straight 70. He took advantage of the less demanding holes. He birdied No. 4, and was the only one among the leaders to birdie both the 11th and 12th.

For Couples, this was beginning to look like the Ghost of Christmas Past — his victory in 1991. It also looked like the Ghost of Masters Past. He got another of those hanging breaks, as when the ball clung to the bank above the water at Augusta's 12th hole long enough for him to win the 1992 Masters. This time he got the break at Tryall's wicked par-three 15th hole. He was ahead by three strokes coming to the tee. He came off a five-iron shot, his ball just cleared the Flint River and ended up to the right of the green, in a mess. He got a free drop from the cart path, which left him with a baseball swing at the ball, to the green just some 30 feet away.

"It bounced around, down there to the corner, and should have gone into the hazard," Couples said. "I don't know how it stayed there." But it did, and he was happy to escape with a double-bogey five. "I could have made anything," he said. He got the stroke back with a two-putt birdie at the 17th, and saved par from off the green at the 18th for his 71 and a one-stroke lead on Singh.

It turned out that Couples was right, but not for long. Maybe anyone within five strokes could have won. That meant only five players, but the possibilities shrank to three in a hurry. Cejka double-bogeyed the second and eighth holes. Riley made two bogeys and a double bogey in four holes from No. 5. Calcavecchia flirted with being a contender for a while, but two first-nine bogeys and a double bogey at No. 11 put him out of the race. So it became a three-man chase, but even that didn't seem certain.

Singh appeared to be doomed early, with bogeys at the first two holes, but he got the strokes back with birdies on the next two. Couples jumped to a three-stroke lead on both with a birdie at No. 1 to Roberts' par and Singh's bogey. Then Couples started a self-destructive binge that looked like the end of him. After the birdie at No. 1, he bogeyed four of the next six holes — No. 2 from a bunker, No. 4 from a creek, No. 5 after missing the green and No. 7 on three putts from 20 feet. Roberts, with a birdie at the ninth, led Singh by one stroke and Couples by two.

Roberts bogeyed the 10th and slipped back into a tie with Singh, the two of them one stroke ahead of Couples. Roberts was in the driver's seat. He birdied the 11th and 14th, staying one ahead of Singh, who also birdied there, and three ahead of Couples.

Leaving the 16th green, Couples trailed Singh, his playing companion, by two strokes, and Roberts in the group ahead by three. Remember what Couples said to his caddie as they approached the 17th tee? "… if I finish 3-3, we've got a chance to get into a playoff." Couples' caddie didn't even grin. He knew his man.

What led Couples to such a wild conclusion was what he saw on the 17th green ahead. "Loren didn't make too many mistakes, and walking down the 17th, I watched him make that little putt. I thought for birdie," Couples said. "But there was no reaction from the gallery." Roberts had made a par. His lead wasn't four strokes, it was still three. That meant Couples still had a chance, even if trailing by three strokes with two holes to play.

Roberts almost saw it coming. "I said after three 70s that another 70 wouldn't be enough," he said. "It looked as if 69 would make it, but the 17th turned it all around for Freddie and Vijay."

Singh didn't see Couples coming, though. "When I birdied 17 to tie for the lead, I was ready for a playoff — at least with Loren," Singh said. "But Freddie's putt on 18 just dropped, and it was three-way."

The par-five 17th, the easiest hole on the course for the week, was the first critical hole down the stretch. In the final found, it yielded three eagles and 13 birdies. Par was the worst score, and there were only three, one by Roberts after he drove into the rough.

Couples, playing with Singh just behind, took heart. The indifferent gallery up ahead told him that Roberts' short putt was only for a par. That's when he told his caddie that a 3-3 finish had a chance. Singh had a chance to eagle the 17th, but birdied and tied Roberts at five under par. Couples hit his eight-iron approach just over the back of the green, about 25 feet from the flag. It was a downhill putt with a slight bend. Couples, who had missed a number of short putts on the front nine, rolled this one in for the eagle. He was one behind Singh and Roberts. At the 18th, Roberts parred for 69 and was in with 279.

At the 18th, Singh put his approach shot to 25 feet. He missed the winning birdie putt. He would settle for a par and 70, and a tie with Roberts. Couples had put his wedge shot to 20 feet. He coolly rolled the putt in for the birdie and 71 to join the playoff.

The playoff would be at the scenic 18th with its water wheel and aqueduct off the tee. All three made pars the first time. Roberts was the only one to hit the fairway. He two-putted from 27 feet. Singh came out of a fairway bunker and two-putted from 24 feet. Couples escaped the left rough, and he two-putted from 22 feet.

The second time around, all three hit the fairway. Roberts hit first to the green and put his approach shot 18 feet above the hole. Singh hit next and seemed to lock up the victory. His shot stopped about five feet above the hole. Then Couples flipped a sand wedge to 15 feet below the hole.

Roberts missed his birdie try. He tapped in for his par.

Couples was next. With never a change of expression or pace, he lined up the 15-foot putt, tapped, and down the ball went for the birdie.

Now Singh had to match him with that five-footer. His birdie try never touched the hole.

"I felt when I made mine," Couples said, "Vijay might give his a little extra boost and it wouldn't take the break."

"It's been a long day," Singh said.

"It's been a great day," Couples said.

12. American Tours

Let's start with what Greg Norman did not do in 1995. He did not win a major championship and he did not win the Vardon Trophy for the lowest scoring average on the PGA Tour in the United States. He could have, possibly should have done both. He tied for third place in the Masters and was second in the U.S. Open. He indeed had the lowest scoring average — 69.06 to winner Steve Elkington's 69.59 — but was ineligible for the title because he withdrew after hitting his first tee shot in the second round of the MCI Classic.

What Norman did was to lead the PGA Tour with record earnings of $1,654,959 and become the Tour's all-time money leader with $9,592,829. He won three American tournaments — Memorial Tournament, Canon Greater Hartford Open and NEC World Series of Golf — raising his total to 15 victories since joining the circuit in 1983. It was by far his best year ever in the United States, and one of his best worldwide with five victories as he regained the No. 1 position on the Sony Ranking.

He also was in his customary spot as the center of attention, starting the year at the fore of a doomed World Tour concept, conceding long putts with Nick Price in the Alfred Dunhill Challenge, viewing a billboard of himself in New York's Times Square from his limo seat en route to the U.S. Open, engaging Mark McCumber in a rules dispute at the World Series, debating appearance money and course conditions overseas, and at year's end, riding in a jet fighter and landing on an aircraft carrier in the Pacific Ocean off San Diego.

Just another year in the life of golf's Great White Shark.

Other enduring images of 1995 would include Ben Crenshaw sobbing as he bent over and buried his face in his hands after winning the Masters a week after the death at age 90 of his mentor, Harvey Penick, a golf professional and best-selling author in his last several years. There was the triumph of Corey Pavin with his marvellous four-wood shot on the 72nd hole of the U.S. Open, and of Elkington in a playoff with Colin Montgomerie to conclude a grueling PGA Championship. The year's other major title, the British Open, went to John Daly, who did not otherwise distinguish himself.

The Ryder Cup, played in alternate years, has become as important as the major championships, and the European team produced one of the strongest memories with its final-day comeback to stun the Americans in Rochester, New York. It was only the second time the United States had ever lost the Ryder Cup at home.

Nick Price, the PGA Tour's leading money winner of the past two years, did not have a victory in the United States and was 30th on the money list. Back problems again affected Fred Couples, who was also winless and placed 63rd on the money list. However, both were successful overseas.

Nine players won over $1 million on the PGA Tour, with Billy Mayfair taking second place to Norman with $1,543,192, having two victories including the season-ending Tour Championship. Lee Janzen won The Players Championship and two other events, one just after he was omitted from the Ryder Cup team, and placed third with $1,378,966. Others over $1 million for their American play were Pavin, Elkington, Davis Love III, Peter Jacobsen, Jim Gallagher, Jr. and Vijay Singh.

Jacobsen, who had four career victories and none since 1990, took back-to-back titles at the AT&T Pebble Beach Pro-Am and Bob Hope Chrysler Classic. Other drought-breakers included Hal Sutton (1986) at the B.C. Open, Bob Tway (1990) at the MCI Classic, Payne Stewart (1991) at the Shell Houston Open, and Mark Calcavecchia (1992) at the BellSouth Classic. Never a winner in 17 years, Brad Bryant won the Walt Disney World/Oldsmobile Classic.

In addition to Norman and Janzen with three victories each, there were eight two-time winners: Jacobsen, Singh, Pavin, Gallagher, Elkington, Mayfair, Mark O'Meara and Fred Funk. Among other notables, England's Nick Faldo played full-time in the United States and won the Doral-Ryder Open, Paul Azinger placed 100th on the money list in his first full season following treatment for lymphoma in his right shoulder, and Curtis Strange remained without an American victory since 1989, although he was 49th on the money list.

David Duval led the rookie class with $881,436 to place 11th on the PGA Tour money list, Justin Leonard was 22nd and Woody Austin was 24th with the only first-year victory in the Buick Open.

Tom Kite, whom Norman replaced as the No. 1 career money winner, fell to 104th on the 1995 money list but ended the year by being chosen captain of the United States team for the next Ryder Cup in 1997.

U.S. PGA Tour

Mercedes Championship—$1,000,000
Winner: Steve Elkington

Steve Elkington proved to be rustproof in the rain. While other last-round leaders showed the effects of year-end layoffs, Elkington held on for a playoff victory over Bruce Lietzke in the weather-disrupted, season-opening Mercedes Championship, an elite gathering of winners only, previously known as the Tournament of Champions at the La Costa Resort in Carlsbad, California.

Elkington, the 1992 playoff winner of this event, took the 1995 version with a 25-foot birdie putt on the second extra hole. He reached the playoff when Lietzke blew sole control of the lead with a bogey on the 17th hole after a drive into soppy, soggy rough. Elkington and Lietzke each finished regulation play with 278 totals. Each had a five-under-par 67 over the last round.

"I realized this was my best chance to win a tournament," said the veteran Lietzke, who has built a highly successful career on little more than a part-time basis and absolutely no practice whatsoever. "Everybody was just as rusty as I am. I've made a career out of that. That's the way I play all the time."

After two days and three rounds (Thursday's play was rained out and 36 holes were played Friday), John Huston held a four-stroke lead. But after a one-hour rain delay on Sunday, he blew himself out of the lead and out of contention with a double bogey from the water on the fifth, a three-putt bogey on the next and double bogey on the next after he putted into a pond. Fred Couples and Lee Janzen each had a share of the last-round lead at one point or another, Janzen dropping back with a bogey on the 10th and Couples with a three-putt. Craig Stadler missed the playoff by two shots, the number he was penalized for missing his Saturday starting time by 90 seconds. Stadler was on the tee, talking with friends, while his starting time came and went.

John Daly returned to action after sitting out the last four months of the 1994 season in a "voluntary" suspension. He tied for 20th in a field of 31.

United Airlines Hawaiian Open—$1,200,000
Winner: John Morse

A certain air of mystery surrounded John Morse, both before and after his upset victory in the Hawaiian Open. When he seized control with a pair of 65s in the middle rounds, everyone was wondering either "Who is he?" or "Where has he been?"

Tom Lehman was among the latter group. "I thought maybe he had quit golf after college," Lehman said. They played against each other when Morse won the Big Ten title for the University of Michigan. Since then, the graying 36-year-old played the Florida mini-tours, on the Canadian circuit, in Australasia and on the 1993 Nike Tour, from which he graduated to the PGA Tour.

An even greater mystery, however, involved the manner in which he achieved his first victory on the American circuit: an overwhelming domination of the par-five holes. Even Morse couldn't explain it. The man who shifts back and forth between conventional and cross-handed putting, is among the shorter hitters on the PGA Tour, ranking 161st in driving distance in 1994. He scored only two eagles in the entire season. But in four rounds he played the four par-fives with 12 birdies, a par and three eagles: 18 under par on those 16 holes and an average of 3.87 on each and every long hole. "I can't explain it," Morse shrugged. "Par-fives usually aren't my forte."

But he was only one under par on all the other holes, finishing with a 68 and a 19-under-par 269 total. Lehman and Duffy Waldorf shared second at 272. Morse wasn't headed over the last 18 holes and finished with a flourish, hitting a five-wood second shot to six feet and dropping the putt for a last-hole eagle, his second of the day. The victory was worth $216,000, which compares with the $146,137 he collected for the entire 1994 season.

Northern Telecom Open—$1,250,000
Winner: Phil Mickelson

Despite some erratic action off the tee and uncharacteristically indifferent putting, Phil Mickelson set a golfing "first" with his scrambling, one-stroke decision over Jim Gallagher and Scott Simpson in the Northern Telecom Open in Tucson, Arizona. The triumph went with his 1991 victory to make

Mickelson the first man to win the same tournament as a professional and as an amateur. And the 24-year-old lefthander also became the youngest since Jack Nicklaus in 1963 to acquire his fifth PGA Tour title.

For the second time in as many years, an early victory provided Mickelson with the opportunity for an outstanding season. And, recognizing what he may have squandered when a skiing accident cost him three months and a Masters appearance in 1994, Mickelson appeared more determined to capitalize on this fast start.

"It had been a year since I won. I was really looking forward to winning again," Mickelson said after the unnecessary confirmation that he was fully recovered from his injuries. Any questions about his physical state had been answered earlier in his late-season heroics in the 1994 Presidents Cup and a final-round 63 at Las Vegas.

That Mickelson led or shared the lead at the end of each round may be deceptive. This one did not come easily. As an illustration, take that stretch beginning on the seventh hole of the third round. Mickelson went bogey, eagle, birdie, double bogey, eagle. He shot 70, one under par, for the day and dropped back into a three-way tie for the lead. "I was awfully upset," Mickelson said. "I made too many stupid mistakes. I had a chance to build a cushion and instead I made it a shootout." The last-round shootout failed to materialize, however. Mickelson, aided by a save of par from the water on the 11th, remained in a tie for the lead with Gallagher going to the 18th. Gallagher three-putted from 60 feet and Mickelson became a winner with a two-putt par.

Phoenix Open—$1,300,000
Winner: Vijay Singh

Vijay Singh, who turned his game around with a little help from swing guru Mac O'Grady, two-putted from long range for a winning par on the first extra hole for a playoff victory over Billy Mayfair in the Phoenix Open. Singh secured his second American title with a two-and-a-half-foot second putt. "To lose a playoff with a bogey is very disappointing," Mayfair said.

The seeds of Singh's victory were sown two weeks earlier in Hawaii where the tall man from got a refresher course from O'Grady, who helped Singh with some swing changes in 1994. The changes worked for a while, but Singh lost control at the end of the year, couldn't find a fairway, played very poorly. A little brush-up work with O'Grady in Hawaii sorted things out almost immediately, however.

As a result, Singh missed only four fairways in as many rounds at Phoenix and missed only one green over the final 18 holes of regulation, which he played in five-under-par 66. Both he and Mayfair started the last 18 one shot back of leader Ben Crenshaw, with Hale Irwin and Tom Watson among the contenders.

Singh and Mayfair, who also had a closing 66, quickly separated themselves from the rest of the pack and Mayfair took the upper hand when Singh bogeyed the 12th after hitting a three iron in the water. "I never looked at the boards," Mayfair said. "I knew Vijay was playing good and I was playing good. I was just trying to get as many birdies as possible."

But he came up one short. Singh caught Mayfair on the par-four 17th, where he very nearly drove the green and got up and down for birdie. Both made scrambling pars on the 18th to finish regulation play in a tie at 269. Crenshaw was third alone, missing the playoff by two shots.

AT&T Pebble Beach National Pro-Am—$1,400,000
Winner: Peter Jacobsen

There's never been any doubt that Jack Lemmon is a better actor — probably even a better cheerleader — than golfer. A 21 handicap gives a clue. And then there's his woeful record in the AT&T Pebble Beach National Pro-Am, the storied old tournament once known as the Crosby Clambake on California's Monterey Peninsula. On more than one occasion Lemmon has said he would rather make the 54-hole cut than win an Oscar. In approximately 28 tries — the records are incomplete and Lemmon says he doesn't know the exact figure — he hasn't made it yet.

This time, however, he stuck around on Sunday to serve as a cheerleader for his long-time partner, Peter Jacobsen, in title contention for the individual title. Lemmon watched Jacobsen play the first three holes at Pebble Beach before he had to leave for a meeting. And Jacobsen birdied them all, using the fast start as the springboard to a two-shot victory over David Duval. Jacobsen's first victory in five years came on a mastery of Pebble Beach. He played the last two rounds there in 66 and 65 and did not make a bogey in those 36 holes. "Hall of Fame stuff for me," Jacobsen said.

Jacobsen's 271 total also broke Tom Watson's tournament scoring record by two shots. Jacobsen, however, had an edge. After rain on 26 of the 30 days preceding the tournament, players were allowed to lift, clean and place balls in the fairway. The pre-tournament weather was so bad, in fact, that Spyglass Hill, Poppy Hills and Pebble Beach all were closed to practice entirely; no player set foot on them until the start of play. There was some concern that the tournament would be cancelled. But when tournament dates came around, so did the weather — four days of near ideal conditions, another aid in the shattering of Watson's scoring mark.

"I'd say Watson's record is still in place," Jacobsen said. "I'd place an asterisk on my score. I'm not delirious enough to think I'm in Tom Watson's league."

Watson and Jack Nicklaus, who earlier said "this is the year I start playing golf or I quit playing golf," at one time or another got in sight of the lead and were paired together in the final round. After climbing to within one stroke of the top through 36 holes, Watson failed to break par over the last 36, however. Nicklaus tied for sixth after a last-round 70. Duval was second at 67–273, while Davis Love III and Kenny Perry tied for third at 275.

Buick Invitational of California—$1,200,000
Winner: Peter Jacobsen

It's understandable that Peter Jacobsen may have had a personal identity crisis. After all, at one time or another the 40-year-old has been a television commentator, a musician, an author, a comic-mimic, a tournament promoter and a member of the PGA Tour policy board. But none of those, he discovered, was his real role. "What I've learned is that I want to be remembered as a golfer," Jacobsen said. "To do that, I've got to go out and win tournaments. That's the whole deal."

Jacobsen took a big step in that direction when he followed up his triumph at Pebble Beach with a runaway, four-shot, 19-under-par victory in the Buick Invitational of California in La Jolla. His 269 total, on four rounds in the 60s at Torrey Pines, made him the first since David Frost in 1993 to win consecutive tournaments on the American Tour.

It also set up the next target for Jacobsen. "A lot of guys have come out early and won a couple of times, then gone on to have monster years," Jacobsen said. "That's what I'm hoping to do; win at least once more, maybe a major championship. I would love to make the Ryder Cup team again." He's well on his way. Two victories in as many weeks put him in the top 10 on the Ryder Cup selection list. With $470,961 in earnings only six tournaments into the schedule, he led the Tour and had surpassed his yearly earnings in all but two of his 18 previous seasons.

Playing steady, solid golf, Jacobsen moved out to a three-shot lead after three rounds. In the final round, however, Mike Hulbert caught him. Briefly. Using his one-handed putting style, Hulbert birdied the first three holes. Jacobsen, playing behind him, regained sole control with a 20-foot birdie putt on the third and wasn't in real danger again. Hulbert tied for second at 273 with Mark Calcavecchia, Hal Sutton and Kirk Triplett.

Bob Hope Chrysler Classic—$1,200,000
Winner: Kenny Perry

Rarely — if ever — has the winner of a PGA Tour tournament been so completely overshadowed. But consider Kenny Perry's competition in the five-day, 90-hole, four-course Bob Hope Chrysler Classic in Palm Desert, California. The low-key, soft-spoken Perry was struggling for recognition against a line-up that included the current and two former Presidents of the United States, the world's most famous comedian and the last man to win consecutive U.S. Opens.

While Perry won with a solid, creditable, 25-under-par 335 total, the tournament probably will be best remembered as the event in which President Bill Clinton teed it up in the first round with the host comedian, along with former Presidents Gerald Ford and George Bush. And in the last round, attention centered on a faltering finish that killed Curtis Strange's chances for his first American victory since the 1989 U.S. Open.

Hope, the three Presidents and defending champion Scott Hoch drew a gallery of 15,000 to 20,000 for their first-round fivesome at Bermuda Dunes, an exercise that proved to be more interesting than artistic. After almost six hours of play, "official" scores for the three chief executives were reported, quite generously, as Bush 92, Clinton 93 and Ford 108. A witness who walked all 18 holes with them observed, however, "You could erase the national deficit overnight with addition like that." A golf writer for a nationally circulated magazine called the exhibition of shanks and hooks, balls into the gallery, out of bounds and off golf carts as "the funniest thing I ever saw."

Perry, 34, winner of two earlier titles in an eight-season career, wrested the lead from long-shot Harry Taylor with 67 at Indian Wells in Saturday's fourth round. Strange moved into a tie for second, one back, with the best round of the tournament, 63 at Bermuda Dunes that included birdies on seven of his last eight holes.

In the final round at Bermuda Dunes, Perry birdied three of the first five holes and led Strange by three with 11 holes to go. Strange birdied Nos. 8 and 12 to close to within one, then tied for the lead when his approach hit the flagstick for a tap-in birdie on the 13th. His second shot ran through the green on the 16th, however, and Strange bogeyed, restoring Perry to sole control. And Strange's last hope drowned when his fairway wood second shot from 228 yards out drifted into the water on the right of the par-five finishing hole. The steady Perry won with a finishing 70 and Strange's last-hole bogey dropped him back into a tie for third behind David Duval.

Nissan Open—$1,200,000
Winner: Corey Pavin

The gesture is more than a half-century old, made famous during the dark days of the Battle of Britain by Winston Churchill. Cigar jutting from his bulldog face, Churchill stubbornly held aloft two fingers in the V-for-victory sign as he toured the bomb-blasted rubble of London. Another bulldog, smaller but equally indomitable, flashed the same sign after winning the Nissan Open at famed old Riviera Country Club in Pacific Palisades, California. But Corey Pavin intended a different meaning. His raised fingers signified "2" or even "II," after a successful defense of his title.

"Corey played terrific. He's a gutty little performer. He just flat won the golf tournament," Kenny Perry said after a near-miss in his own quest for a "2" or even a "II." Perry, the winner a week earlier in the Bob Hope event, led through the second and third rounds in this one in a bid for a second consecutive victory but could not hold off Pavin's last-round run. "I was very close to making it happen again," Perry said following his tie for second, "but it just didn't happen."

It didn't happen because Pavin, a graduate of nearby UCLA and playing one of his favorite courses in the world, had "one of my best tournaments ever on the tour" and elevated himself into some Hall of Fame company, Ben Hogan and Arnold Palmer. Hogan won two Los Angeles Opens and the U.S. Open at Riviera in a 17-month period in 1947-48, and Palmer, in 1967-68, was the last previous successful defending titleholder in this tournament. "It's just amazing to hear my name mentioned in the same sentence with theirs," said Pavin, who also stamped himself as the early favorite for the PGA Championship scheduled at Riviera in August.

Pavin, who won this one with a closing 67 and a 16-under-par 268 total, started the final round one behind Perry. But Perry's putting deserted him — he missed makeable birdie putts on four of the first eight holes — and Pavin was three under par on the first seven holes. He went ahead to stay with a birdie on the sixth. When Pavin bogeyed the 15th, Jay Don Blake was within two, but he missed a six-footer for birdie on the 17th and, effectively, it was over. Blake and Perry tied for second at 271, while Craig Stadler, who had an ace in his last-round 70, and Scott Simpson followed at 272.

Doral-Ryder Open—$1,500,000
Winner: Nick Faldo

Originally, the "Blue Monster" label referred only to the 18th hole at Doral Country Club in Miami, that water-guarded finishing horror of a par-four that ranks as one of the most dangerous, difficult and intimidating holes on the PGA Tour. Later, the term was expanded to include the entire Blue course, but the truth of the original definition was confirmed — again — when Nick Faldo hit into the lake in the final round and won the Doral-Ryder Open. The English star won when he executed a magnificent third shot and saved bogey, and Greg Norman, needing only a final par to force a playoff, followed Faldo into the water.

Faldo, who transferred his playing base from Europe to the United States this year, appeared to have the tournament in his hands when he went to the 18th tee on Sunday. But he dunked his tee shot into the edge of the water on the 13th. Disappointed but undaunted, he promptly played a 230-yard three-wood third into the wind, over the lake to an angled green for a five, a final round of three-under-par 69 and a 273 total. Then came Norman, in his search for a third Doral title. He drove into the deep rough, missing the fairway by about two yards. He came up with a nasty lie. He overswung on his approach and pull-hooked into the water, some 30 yards out in the lake.

"I tried to kill a six iron," Norman said. "I thought I could carry the water. There was a clump of grass right behind the ball. It was just sitting in the wrong place. I thought if I hit it solid, I'd have enough to carry the water, but I just yanked it and the club turned over on me. It wasn't a good shot by any means." The bogey completed a last-round 73 and left Norman tied for second with Peter Jacobsen at 274. The victory was Faldo's first in the United States since his 1990 Masters triumph and, he said, confirmed his decision to move his base to America was the right one. "I'm very pleased and surprised," he said after the turn-around triumph. "It's exactly what I've worked for and wanted to do over here. Now I've done it. Hopefully, it's going to take a lot of pressure off me and I can get on with it, see what I can do."

While the tournament turned on the 18th hole drama, Faldo's putting made it all possible. He dropped five putts from 25 feet or longer in the third round and made every clutch putt he faced Sunday, including a 20-footer for the go-ahead birdie on the 14th. Jacobsen, who have himself a 41st birthday present with 64 in the third round, went to the final hole with a long-shot chance. He had a 60-foot putt for birdie and a playoff. It just missed. "It was one of those putts you dream about," said Jacobsen, who was seeking a third victory of the year. "You don't expect to make it, but if you do, it's a storybook ending."

Honda Classic—$1,200,000
Winner: Mark O'Meara

Mark O'Meara's selection of the Honda Classic event provided an end to his frustrating slump and three-year non-winning string. Three weeks earlier, O'Meara showed up in Pacific Palisades, California, for the Nissan Open, only to discover he had forgotten to commit for the tournament and thus was not eligible to play. Only then did O'Meara hastily add the Honda to his schedule as a substitute for the Nissan. "Fate," he said after holding off last-gasp challenges by Nick Faldo and Ian Woosnam for his first victory since winning the AT&T Pebble Beach National Pro-Am for the fourth time in 1992.

His mastery of Pebble Beach proved O'Meara's ability as a wind player, a fact that stood him in good stead in the extremely difficult conditions at Weston Hills. Hurricane-force winds on Wednesday destroyed the tournament's skyboxes and forced cancellation of half the pro-am. The winds diminished — at least slightly — for the tournament proper but remained a major, troubling, disturbing factor. "I've never seen a British Open with wind like this. Not consistently like this for three days," Faldo said after the third round. "This is Irish Open stuff. When you're over putts, you're thinking, 'wait for the wind to go calm and then hit it.' You can feel yourself moving."

For the first three rounds O'Meara did most of the moving. He led by three at the end of the second and third rounds, by as many as seven during Saturday's play and by six after five holes of the final round. But he bogeyed the 10th and 11th and watched from the 12th fairway as Woosnam dropped a 30-foot putt for eagle and a tie for the lead. The little Welshman, coming off a two-month break, couldn't keep it together, however. A poor chip cost him a bogey on the 13th, he missed a short birdie putt on the 16th and bogeyed the last, going from bunker to bunker.

Faldo, meanwhile, was making a windblown bid for a second consecutive victory. After missing an 18-inch putt on the 13th — "I tweaked it; it bobbled or I wobbled, I'm not sure which," he said — he birdied the 15th and 16th to pull to within one. He hit a great two iron to eight feet but missed the putt to tie O'Meara, who was grinding out par after par. On the par-five 18th, needing a birdie to tie, Faldo bunkered his third. O'Meara was on in three and lagged his 15-footer to 12 inches. After gaining permission from Faldo, he finished it off, completing a final round of 71 and a 275 total. "After three years, I didn't want to wait around for a one-footer," he said. Faldo's closing 69 gave him second alone at 276 and Woosnam slipped back to third at 69–277.

The Nestle Invitational—$1,200,000
Winner: Loren Roberts

His mind was bordering on blank. The putts were somewhat out of focus. He was facing the strongest field in golf to date this year. The weather was positively disruptive; the golf course long and very difficult. Everything was just the way Loren Roberts wanted in The Nestle Invitational. "For some reason I get here and my attitude changes," Roberts said after a two-stroke triumph made him the first man to successfully defend his title at Arnold Palmer's Bay Hill Club in Orlando, Florida. "I can visualize the shots off the tee. It's framed out for you."

That, of course, is off the tee and from the fairway. Putting is an entirely different matter and a critical factor in his rise to golfing respectability. Roberts led the PGA Tour in putting last season when he broke through to his first career victory in this event, lost a playoff for the U.S. Open and had a $1 million-plus season. Roberts, 39, who honed his putting skills as a former club pro — "the putting green was right outside the pro shop and I could putt for hours," he said — described his unorthodox approach to that part of the game. "My eyes go out of focus, and my brain kind of goes out of focus a little, too," he said. "So I don't get hung up on trying to hit anything on a perfect line. It's a hard thing to explain. I kind of let my eyes go into a blank stare."

Whatever the method, it was effective in the storm-disrupted tournament. Roberts took 27, 25, 27 and 29 putts in the four rounds against a field that included the top 24 players in the Sony Ranking. In the 10-year history of the rankings, it was only the second time outside the major championships that so strong a field had been assembled. And that was just fine for Roberts, too. "When you come up with the lowest score against the best players in the world, that makes me proud," he said. And the victory, he said, confirmed his place in golf. "I feel I finally got where I want to be. I finally feel good enough to have a chance. That's where I want to be."

Both the second and third rounds were interrupted by afternoon storms and both had overnight delays with 69 players stranded on the course Friday, 40 on Saturday. The steady Roberts led after each. He was among those who had to come back Sunday to complete third-round play and helped his cause with a chip-in eagle three on the 16th hole. He took a two-shot lead into the final round. Brad Faxon's early charge brought him even, but Roberts regained control just before the turn. He holed a 15-foot par-saving putt on the eighth while Faxon was lucky to escape from a variety of problems with a bogey. Roberts birdied the ninth from 10 feet while Faxon three-putted. That put Roberts' lead at three and he really wasn't threatened again, finishing with a round of 71 and a 16-under-par 272 total. Faxon finished 71–274 and Peter Jacobsen, a two-time winner already this season, was third at 69–275.

The Players Championship—$3,000,000
Winner: Lee Janzen

See Chapter 7.

Freeport-McMoRan Classic—$1,200,000
Winner: Davis Love III

Seven hours before he died, Harvey Penick learned that Davis Love III was leading the Freeport-McMoRan Classic in New Orleans. Penick was pulling for Love to win and thus earn a berth in the Masters Tournament the following week, so when Tom Kite told him of Love's bid, Penick raised his feeble hands and clapped. Twice. The legendary teacher never saw Love win. He died just minutes after Love beat Mike Heinen on the second play-off hole, but you knew the 90-year-old was smiling when Love said later he never once doubted he would win.

It was a bittersweet win for Love, whose father Davis, Jr., idolized Penick. On one hand, he was ecstatic about his first win in 17 months and the spot in the Masters. On the other, he was saddened by Penick's death. "I just kind of grew up with everything in *The Little Red Book*," said Love, whose father died in a plane crash in 1988. "He was just a part of my dad. I kind of feel like the last bit of my dad is gone now."

Love didn't make the win easy on himself. A third-round 66, which included a pair of eagles, put him up by two strokes over Mike Standly and Steve Jones going into the final round and, thanks to a double-bogey finish by Heinen, he even retained that margin with three holes to play. But he couldn't hold on. Heinen, who closed with 66, eagled the 11th hole, then birdied the 13th from four feet to tie for the lead. But he pushed his drive at No. 18 into a bunker, his approach found the water and he two-putted from 12 feet for double bogey. The best thing that happened to Love was the eagle. "It spurred me on, got me grinding," he said. The worst? Heinen's double bogey. "I started protecting (his lead)" he said.

Love, playing an hour behind Heinen, scrambled for par at the 16th, then pulled a five-foot par putt at the 17th. Then, at No. 18 — the toughest finishing hole on the PGA Tour in 1994 — his eight-iron approach found the bunker. His third shot flew 15 feet past the pin and he two-putted to tie. Both players parred the first playoff hole, then Love won with a six-iron approach to three feet for the win. "I just never let it cross my mind that I wasn't going to win and get to Augusta," said Love, who shot 14-under-par 274. "Today, I kept telling myself, 'You're doing to go to the Masters.' I just don't like to be left out."

Masters Tournament—$2,000,000
Winner: Ben Crenshaw

See Chapter 3.

MCI Classic—$1,300,000
Winner: Bob Tway

There were tears in his eyes as Bob Tway tried to explain that, yes, this win in the MCI Classic was bigger and tougher and more important even than holing that bunker shot to beat Greg Norman at the 1986 PGA Championship. Hard to believe? Not for Tway, who spent over three years searching for his game. Not for a man who seemingly spent as much time answering questions about his sudden fall as he did trying to find a way back.

Tway accomplished both at Hilton Head Island, South Carolina, when he flew a six-iron shot 30 inches from the pin at the 177-yard 17th hole to beat Nolan Henke in what had started out as a three-way playoff. Henke had pulled his shot into the deep grass and pitched long. David Frost, who birdied the final hole in regulation to make the playoff at nine-under-par 275, flew the green at that same 18th hole on the first playoff hole to make the earliest exit.

"This means more than any of the other tournaments," Tway said. "Those other tournaments I won, they all seemed easy. This wasn't easy. This was very, very special. When you've been down so long, you think you'll never get up. You wonder, 'Why bother?' I guess the key is to never give up."

Tway started the day as one of the 39 players within five shots of the lead, which was held by Frost, David Edwards, Mark McCumber and Gene Sauers. Actually, he was one of the 11 players within three shots and he wound up as one of nine players who had or shared the lead in the final round. Tway holed a 30-yard, over-a-bunker pitch shot at the 17th to get into the club-house — nearly nine holes ahead of McCumber — with the early lead. He sat and watched as one by one they fell out — even McCumber, whose five-footer for par on the 72nd hole took a left turn at the cup. Tway left with a new confidence and an exemption as a tournament winner. "This is not a miracle cure," he said. "But it's sure going to help."

Kmart Greater Greensboro Open—$1,500,000
Winner: Jim Gallagher, Jr.

An extremely damp Jim Gallagher, Jr., was shivering on the driving range at Forest Oaks Country Club in Greensboro, North Carolina, when a PGA Tour official delivered the news. There wouldn't be a playoff. He could stop hitting balls. He could dry off. He could collect the winner's check from the Kmart Greater Greensboro Open. "It was kind of a weird feeling," he said. "Since I couldn't see what was happening. I didn't know how to act."

In true Greensboro fashion, Gallagher had won from the clubhouse. He birdied four of the last six holes to close with a six-under-par 66 and a 14-under-par 274 total. He posted it, then the field shot at it. And missed.

Jeff Sluman, who started the day with a two-stroke lead over Peter Jacobsen and a seven-shot lead over Gallagher, couldn't hold on. He three-putted three times during the final round and left the biggest putt of his day — an eight-footer for par at the 17th — short. "I think my nerves got a little bit jumpy " he said. He wasn't alone. Jacobsen watched as his 20-foot birdie attempt at the 17th to tie Gallagher took a dive to the right just as it approached the cup. "It just went over the cellophane bridge," Jacobsen said. "That was a real killer."

Both came to the 18th with chances to win, but no miracles in their bags. With the wind-chill factor hovering below 40, Jacobsen lined up a bunker shot and Sluman lined up a chip. Gallagher, meanwhile, was on the range some 500 yards away wondering. And hoping. In the end, Gallagher became the fifth player in the last six years to win the tournament from behind. The comeback tied eight others — including Greensboro champions Steve Elkington (1990) and Mark Brooks (1991) — for the largest final-round comeback since 1980. All of which left Sluman, who now has two seconds and two other top fives here in 11 tries, to ponder next year.

"Maybe that should be my strategy next time," Sluman said.

Shell Houston Open—$1,400,000
Winner: Payne Stewart

Everyone thought Scott Hoch might collapse in the Shell Houston Open and he did. And in even uglier fashion than in 1989 when he missed a two-foot playoff putt to lose the Masters to Nick Faldo.

Try losing a seven-shot lead with 13 holes to play or a five-shot advantage with seven to play. Try making a clutch 35-footer to get into the playoff with your neighbor and close friend Payne Stewart. Then try giving the title to him with a horrid game plan and an off-balance bunker shot on the first playoff hole. "You can print it now," Hoch said sprinting through the TPC at The Woodlands parking lot. "That's why Hoch rhymes with choke."

Stewart shook his head. "I hate that word. It's a nasty, hard word. But who am I to argue?" Who indeed. Stewart won for the first time since the 1991 U.S. Open after surviving an afternoon of surprises. He won with a new-found patience, new set of clubs, a splendid six iron to 16 feet at the 72nd hole and a gut-churning three-footer for par in the playoff. He won with lucky bounces and touches of irony on a course where he had watched three previous chances — 1985, 1987 and 1993 — nose-dive into ponds, lakes and bunkers.

Hoch started the day up by five shots over John Cook and rookie Charlie Rymer and seven strokes ahead of Stewart, who closed with 68. He had played so flawlessly in the first three rounds, in fact, that it was easy to concede the title before he teed off. But when he found himself up by five, Hoch started to play conservatively. He bogeyed the 12th and 14th and, suddenly, Rymer and Stewart were just two behind. Hoch dumped his approach at the 17th into the water. Stewart, who had chipped in at the 11th and 13th, then got a lucky bounce off the hill at the par-three 16th for another birdie and ran one home on the 72nd hole, emerged up by one. Hoch tied Stewart at 12-under-par 276 with the birdie at No. 18, then Stewart won on the first playoff hole.

BellSouth Classic—$1,300,000
Winner. Mark Calcavecchia

Mark Calcavecchia wasn't about to be left out. As the year was moving toward the midway point he had watched Peter Jacobsen, then Bob Tway, then Payne Stewart resurrect their careers with victories. So, when Calcavecchia, who hadn't won in three years, got another chance, he took advantage of it.

Calcavecchia started the final round of the BellSouth Classic in Atlanta two shots behind Jim Gallagher, Jr., and local club pro Stephen Keppler, but separated himself from any pretenders with a back-nine 31 en route to a closing 66 and a four-day total of 17-under-par 271. Calcavecchia's run started with an eagle at the par-five 11th, stalled with a bogey at No. 12, then took off. The man who hadn't won since the 1992 Phoenix Open birdied four of the final six holes to catch, then pass Gallagher and cruise to the win.

"Mark kept making birdies and it was hard to keep up," said Gallagher, who fell short of winning his second straight tournament (he won in Greensboro, then skipped Houston). "It was kind of like chasing (race car driver) Dale Earnhardt down the straightaway."

The story for the first two rounds was defending champion John Daly. He nearly aced a par-four hole and led by one over Gallagher and Michael Bradley at the halfway point. But he faded Sunday and gave the spotlight to Keppler, a 34-year-old former British Walker Cup player who hung on and closed with a four-foot birdie at the 18th to finish alone in second place.

GTE Byron Nelson Classic—$1,300,000
Winner: Ernie Els

Maybe a runaway would have been too easy. Maybe the heat and humidity were simply too oppressive in the final round. Or maybe Ernie Els is just a bit reluctant when it comes to spotlights. Whatever the reason, Els needed a kick in the pants down the stretch to take back the GTE Byron Nelson Classic in Irving, Texas, a tournament he tried to give away on the front nine and, thus, capture his second victory in the United States — this one by three strokes over Robin Freeman, Mike Heinen and D.A. Weibring.

If it sounds a bit strange, it was. After taking three weeks off to visit his hometown of Johannesburg, South Africa, Els promptly opened with 69. Then he added 61 and 65, which broke Fred Couples' 54-hole mark of 14-under-par 196 and set a standard for the best back-to-back rounds in tournament history. He was tied with Freeman after two rounds and up by three over Freeman going into the final round. But the 1994 U.S. Open champion couldn't break away.

Els scrambled across the front nine and even lost the lead to Mike Heinen at one point early. "He was playing very tentative," Freeman said. "He was leaving the ball short on his approach shots. He wasn't hitting his driver very well." So, Els, who was two-over for the day after 12 holes, went to his irons and found the touch. A 25-foot birdie at the par-three 13th started it off as he shot four under par on the final six holes. Heinen closed with 66 and Weibring with 65 to tie Freeman at 266.

Buick Classic—$1,200,000
Winner: Vijay Singh

The rough was U.S. Open deep, the fairways tight and narrow. And the winner? Well, after stringing together 17 pars and a bogey in the final round, Vijay Singh capped his second victory in three years in the Buick Classic at Westchester Country Club in New York by beating cherubic Doug Martin in a five-hole playoff.

It was the second-longest PGA Tour playoff in the 1990s, but it seemed more like a second final round. After Nick Faldo lost a two-shot lead on the back nine with bogeys at Nos. 12, 15 and 17, and Martin birdied Nos. 15, 17 and 18 to post his six-under-par 278 total, it was Singh's tournament to win, lose or, as it turned out, send into a playoff. A birdie at the 18th would have given him the win, but he pushed his drive right and under a tree and scrambled — with a delicate chip — for a par to force the playoff.

Singh missed defending his 1993 title because of a neck injury, so he felt as though this was a second chance. Both players missed birdie putts on the first two holes, then two-putted for pars on the third extra hole. On the fourth hole, Martin's shot to the 17th came up short and in the bunker, but he blasted out and saved par from 14 feet. Singh two-putted.

The tournament ended at No. 18 — their third visit there on the day — when Martin, a 28-year-old former Walker Cupper, pushed his three-wood approach into the thick rough short of the green. Martin missed his 20-foot par putt and Singh buried his putt to join Peter Jacobsen as the second two-time winner of 1995 on the PGA Tour. Ironically, Singh's other win came in a playoff at the Phoenix Open when he beat Billy Mayfair.

The rough and winds allowed only six sub-70 closing rounds. Bobby Wadkins finished third at 279, while Faldo, Ernie Els, Fred Funk and Dillard Pruitt tied at 280. The best summation of the penal rough and tough conditions? "Without expletives?" Faldo said. "Let's just say thick and juicy."

Colonial National Invitational—$1,400,000
Winner: Tom Lehman

Tom Lehman won the tradition-laden Colonial National Invitational in Fort Worth, Texas, the way you always dream of. He charged from behind, sank a huge putt on the 72nd hole and grabbed the title away from Craig Parry. Then he thanked the Man Upstairs for simply being there.

When Lehman stole this tournament from Parry, who had pretty much led since Friday, he did it with a 30-footer and a celebration around the edge of the green that showed just how much this victory meant. Just a month earlier, Lehman had undergone surgery to remove cancerous polyps in his colon. The problem had surfaced at the Masters and continued at the MCI Classic when he watched a four-shot lead at the midway point slip away. He had the surgery the following week. "It scared my wife a lot more than it scared me," Lehman said, whose closing two-under-par 68 gave him a total of nine-under 271.

After finishing 14th at Westchester, Lehman, who won the 1994 Memorial, came into Colonial not certain what to expect. Parry came in nursing a case of conjunctivitis that was so bad he could hardly see, but by tournament time, he was feeling great. The man known as Popeye because of his huge forearms took a two-stroke lead at the midway point and, after surviving a three-club wind on Saturday, he headed into the final round with a one-shot advantage over Woody Austin and two-shot advantage over Lehman.

Austin led briefly at the turn, but fell back with bogeys at Nos. 11 and 12, then bogeyed No. 18 and fell out of a tie with D.A. Weibring for third place. Lehman had fallen one shot behind Parry when the latter birdied the 14th, but Lehman birdied Nos. 17 and 18 to go up by one. Parry missed makeable birdies at Nos. 15, 16, 17 and 18, any one of which would have forced a playoff. Brad Faxon closed with 64 to tie Justin Leonard (68) and Mark McCumber (68) at 276.

Memorial Tournament—$1,700,000
Winner: Greg Norman

Greg Norman took another tournament, the Memorial in Dublin, Ohio, and ran away with it. Norman headed into the rain-delayed (the third round had to be finished Sunday morning) final round with a one-shot lead over Robert Gamez. He backed up a third-round 67 with a closing 66. He birdied three of the last five holes and one-putted six of the last seven greens. He saved par at Nos. 15 and 16 and birdied Nos. 17 and 18 to shoot 19-under-par 269 and win by four shots over David Duval, Steve Elkington and Mark Calcavecchia.

"To finish it off the way I finished was really important," Norman said. "I said to myself walking to the 17th tee, 'Let's birdie the last two.'"

And Norman did. A nine-footer at No. 17 and a 10-footer at No. 8. Not quite his 24-under-par gala at the 1994 Players Championship, but not bad. Especially for a guy who had just spent a month at home nursing back spasms. "You're lucky to see me this week," Norman joked. "Monday night when I packed my suitcase, I said, 'I've got to get back to work.' But it was a fantastic rest. It's what I needed."

As always, the Memorial was a weatherman's nightmare. The tournament was barely an hour old when play was stopped for rain. A 12-hour day on Friday got the tournament caught up, then a four-hour delay for lightning and rain pushed the close of the third round to Sunday. As it was, Gamez was the only one hurt. He closed with a 71 to finish tied for fifth at 275 with Ben Crenshaw (69), David Frost (70), Jay Haas (65) and Tom Watson (69).

Kemper Open—$1,400,000
Winner: Lee Janzen

When Lee Janzen gets the chance, he doesn't just close the door. He slams it. Granted, Janzen needed a playoff to win the Kemper Open in Potomac, Maryland, but he also needed a nifty birdie at the 18th hole just to force the playoff. He was, after all, facing a good finisher himself in Corey Pavin. Yet when the two went down No. 18 for the fifth time of the week, it was Janzen who stood tall. He slipped in a 12-footer for his fifth birdie of the week there — only one other player even managed to net par there for the week — which he didn't even need considering Pavin had bogeyed from the back bunker.

But what the heck. After Janzen's eight-under-par 272 and playoff birdie sent him to the winner's circle, a quick check showed he has won six times and finished second just once. "When Lee gets in position to win, he wins," Pavin said. "There are few players who do that well and he's one of them."

So is Pavin, who made a pair of 10-foot pars on the final two holes of regulation — the one at No. 18 following a drive into the fairway bunker, a poor five-iron approach and a splendid pitch — to get into the playoff.

Davis Love III sizzled into the lead at the midway point with a record-tying, second-round 63 that included two shots in the water. Love led by one stroke over Payne Stewart going into the final round, by two over Pavin and his third-round 63, and by three over Janzen. But it wasn't to be.

Love who played the par-threes in seven over par, and the rest of the course 16 under, came unraveled in the final round. A weird lie at No. 13 — his drive came to rest in the branch of a pine tree and he had to take a drop — and a double-cross, pull-to-the-left and into the deep round long approach into No. 17 led to bogeys. Then, his approach at No. 18 hit the cart path and bounced over the scoreboard to lead to a double bogey.

Greg Norman was one shot back going into No. 17, but pushed his six-iron shot into the water, and Robin Freeman let a chance to join the playoff slip away with bogeys at the final two holes. Freeman finished third at 273, while Justin Leonard closed with a 67 to tie Love, Norman, Mark O'Meara and Vijay Singh at 275.

U.S. Open Championship—$2,000,000
Winner: Corey Pavin

See Chapter 4.

Canon Greater Hartford Open—$1,200,000
Winner: Greg Norman

Greg Norman picked the Canon Greater Hartford Open as the site of his second victory in a matter of four weeks, but this one was no runaway like the Memorial Tournament had been. Norman tried his best to give this one away, then pulled a shocker out of his bag to win it — a 40-foot eagle chip-in at the par-four 15th hole. It wasn't exactly sweet revenge for his runner-up finish at the U.S. Open, but Norman would take it.

"Isn't that wonderful," said Norman, who watched Corey Pavin win the U.S. Open with a killer four-wood shot from the fairway on the final hole at Shinnecock Hills. "The agony and the ecstasy." And the money. With his second victory of the season, Norman set a record for single-month earnings on the PGA Tour with $781,780. The total surpassed Fred Couples' $635,750 set in March of 1992.

Norman rebounded from the U.S. Open disappointment to share the second-round lead at Hartford with Kirk Triplett. After a third-round 65, Norman waltzed into the final round with a three-shot lead over Fuzzy Zoeller. All he needed in the final round was a closing 71 — plus that eagle and a little composure — for his 267 total that beat Triplett, Dave Stockton, Jr., and Grant Waite by two strokes.

Most of the names won't be found among the leading money winners, but a run of record scores were still out there. Triplett and Bob Estes tied the course record of 64 on Friday, Zoeller broke it with 63 Friday, and Billy Andrade lowered it again Saturday with 62. But even with overnight rains, there were no charges to be found Sunday. Norman had to double-bogey the 10th, while Zoeller birdied the 11th to forge a tie. Then, when Norman missed a three-foot birdie at the 13th and Zoeller curved in a 25-footer, Zoeller led by one. The tournament swung at the 296-yard, par-four 15th, where Zoeller chunked a wedge for an eventual bogey and Norman, whose drive kicked to the right of the green, holed his pitch for eagle.

FedEx St. Jude Classic—$1,250,000
Winner: Jim Gallagher, Jr.

Believe it or not the thought of losing never crossed Jim Gallagher, Jr.'s mind in the final round of the FedEx St. Jude Classic. Never mind that he built a four-shot lead after seven holes then, in two quick holes, blew it. Never mind that Jay Delsing, who had just made his third cut of the year, made three stretch-run birdies to tie him. And never mind that he hit one ugly seven-iron approach into No. 18. "I never for one moment," Gallagher said later, "thought I wasn't going to win."

He may have been the only one. Gallagher did indeed choose the birdie-infested TPC at Southwind in Memphis, Tennessee, to win his second tournament of the year, but it wasn't easy. Instead of cruising, he scrambled to the victory with a bunker shot that flew 10 feet past the pin. He made the putt coming back. "I saw the putt as soon as I walked over there," he said. "I made a very similar putt (to win at Greensboro in April)."

Gallagher, who led by two strokes at the midway point of the tournament and by one going into the final round, closed with 72 to finish at 15-under-par 267 — one shot better than Delsing, who closed with 67, and Ken Green, who shot 68.

As easy as the course was playing (1,662 birdies and only 987 bogeys), it would have seemed Gallagher might have blown the field away. He was, after all, looking for a spot on the Ryder Cup team. And, when he got to 21 under par after seven holes, it looked as though he would do it. But he double-bogeyed the 12th hole when his approach out of the rough failed to jump and landed in the water. Then, he bogeyed the 13th. Delsing, meanwhile, tossed out three straight birdies at Nos. 14, 15 and 16 to tie Gallagher. Delsing bogeyed the 17th to fall a shot back, leaving Gallagher to scramble for the par and the win.

Motorola Western Open—$2,000,000
Winner: Billy Mayfair

When Billy Mayfair hit his splendid downwind, seven-iron shot into Cog Hill's 18th green, he thought that shot was the one he needed to get into a playoff at the Motorola Western Open in Lemont, Illinois. Instead, it was the shot he needed to win. Mayfair's approach was, perhaps, a fitting end to the tournament no one could seem to win. More than half a dozen players had their chances and lost them, setting the stage for Mayfair to sink a five-foot birdie at the 72nd hole to finish at nine-under-par 279. That done, he waited out futile last-ditch attempts by Bob Estes, then Steve Lowery to force a playoff.

Talk about take-it-no-you-take-it finishes. Jeff Maggert fired a closing 64 to finish at eight under and left the course. Justin Leonard closed with 67 for his eight-under-par total, then waited in the clubhouse. John Huston got to eight under, too, but four-putted the 16th. Brett Ogle, who shared the third-round lead with Lowery, lost his chances at the 15th when his tee shot went into deep rough and he triple-bogeyed the hole to go from eight under to five under. Lowery bogeyed three holes on the back, and Estes, who had the outright lead at nine under standing on the 16th tee, lost his chances when he glanced at the scoreboard.

Thinking he saw nine under by Maggert's name, Estes played to win instead of protect a one-shot lead. The left-to-right player tried to draw his shot into the 16th and wound up long, left and seven under after a double bogey. Estes tried to forge a tie at No. 18 with a 40-foot putt, but came up short. So did Lowery, who tried to hole-out and force a playoff.

Mayfair, who lost to Vijay Singh in a playoff in Phoenix earlier in the year, waited behind the green until he was told he won. Leonard, Maggert, Jay Haas and Scott Simpson tied for second at 280, while Estes, Lowery, Huston and Bob Tway finished at 281.

Anheuser-Busch Golf Classic—$1,100,000
Winner: Ted Tryba

Ted Tryba missed the first green in the final round with a wedge in his hand. Then he two-putted for bogey. Then he got serious. The rest of the humid, sweat-filled day was, well, a breeze for the 28-year-old Tryba as took a four-stroke lead into the final seven holes, then held off a late charge by Scott Simpson to win the Anheuser-Busch Golf Classic for his first PGA Tour victory. Starting the day one shot behind leader Jim Carter, Tryba fired a closing 68 for his 12-under-par 272 total and a one-stroke victory over Simpson.

While the Williamsburg, Virginia, crowds were cheering for home-course favorite Curtis Strange, the six-foot-four Tryba got busy. He threw a wedge into the par-five second hole for birdie, then slid in birdies at the sixth, seventh and eighth holes to take the lead for good. His longest birdie of the day? A 10-footer at the sixth.

Tryba, who became only the second first-time winner of the season, bogeyed the ninth hole, but he didn't have much to worry about since Strange, whose third-round 65 shot him into contention, Simpson and Lennie Clements were all struggling. The big putt was a six-foot birdie at the 11th, which gave him that four-shot cushion. "I felt nervous, but I've been there before," Tryba said. "I was hitting really good shots all day. I didn't think I was going to make a bad swing. I was probably going to make a bad decision. As long as I got my thinking right, I thought I could probably bring it in."

The only player to win three straight years on the Ben Hogan Tour (1990-92) did just that. Simpson birdied three of the final six holes, but Tryba hung in with a birdie at No. 15 and solid pars on Nos. 17 and 18. Carter, Clements and Scott Hoch finished tied for third at 274.

Deposit Guaranty Golf Classic—$700,000
Winner: Ed Dougherty

Ed Dougherty finally got his due. After years of hitting practice balls and chasing his dream on the PGA Tour, the soon-to-be senior golfer finally won — and in grand style at the Deposit Guaranty Golf Classic in Madison, Mississippi. A mere three months before his 48th birthday, Dougherty came from three strokes back in the final round at Annandale Golf Club to shoot 66 and walk away with the $126,000 winner's check. He trailed third-round leader Dicky Thompson by three shots after 54 holes and beat him by four. He beat runner-up Gil Morgan by two shots, and Peter Jordan by three.

Even if the big boys were playing in the British Open, there was still enough competition here to make Dougherty feel great about the win, which will give him an exemption until he reaches his 50th birthday and a spot in the 1996 Masters. "It's the answer," Dougherty said, "to a lot of prayers." And it wasn't easy.

Dicky Pride led by two strokes with seven holes to play, but collapsed and finished in a tie for eighth place. Dougherty birdied the 17th hole with an 18-foot downhiller, but even leading by two strokes going into the final hole wasn't comfortable for Dougherty, not with Morgan behind him. So Dougherty pulled out his five wood and went for the green at the 532-yard 18th. He two-putted from 60 feet right of the hole for the win.

Ideon Classic at Pleasant Valley—$1,000,000
Winner: Fred Funk

Fred Funk blew a four-shot lead in five holes. He missed five fairways on the front nine after having missed just six in the previous three rounds. And his closing two-over-par 73 set a PGA Tour record for the 1995 season — thankfully, Funk had to admit, for the highest closing score by a winner.

Funk didn't really go out and win the Ideon Classic at Pleasant Valley Country Club in Sutton, Massachusetts. He just survived the final round better than everyone else. The closing 73, by the grace of a tap-in birdie on the final hole, sent him home with a 16-under-par total of 268 and his second PGA Tour victory. His first win came at the 1992 Shell Houston Open and, ironically, to win this number two, he had to beat 1993 Houston champion Jim McGovern.

The difference was one shot. McGovern, who lost the tournament with bogeys at the 16th and 17th, closed with 70 to finish at 269. Don Pooley closed with 68 to finish third at 270.

The two battled it out from the second round on, as Funk led McGovern by three shots after 36 holes and four after 54. After a hot start by McGovern on Sunday, it stayed close — or tied — most of the day. Funk led by two shots after the eighth hole, but bogeys at Nos. 9 and 11 forced him back into a tie with McGovern. Funk's bogey at No. 13 gave McGovern the lead, but he gave it right back with trouble at Nos. 16 and 17. Leading by one going into No. 18, Funk hit the 583-yard par-five green in two strokes with a marvelous three-wood approach and two-putted from 20 feet. McGovern drove into the trees on the right and, after hitting his second shot off a rock, had to settle for putting his approach to eight feet for second place.

"No question, all that was was survival," Funk said. "I didn't have an A game or a B game. I think I was in the D division."

Buick Open—$1,200,000
Winner: Woody Austin

The big news at Warwick Hills Golf and Country Club in Grand Blanc, Michigan, wasn't that Woody Austin won a two-hole, all-rookie playoff in the Buick Open to win his first ever PGA Tour event. It was that Fred Couples finished sixth and quite likely played his way onto the Ryder Cup team.

After years of struggling just to get onto the PGA Tour, the 31-year-old Austin finally went out and won an event and was overshadowed by one of the men he beat. The former part-time bank teller from Tampa, Florida, closed out his victory with a two-putt par on the second playoff hole, while Mike Brisky pulled an eight-iron shot into a bunker and bogeyed.

Both had chances to win the event in regulation, but both misread the break on similar short birdies at the 18th to finish tied with 18-under-par 270 totals. Ernie Els bogeyed the 18th to miss a playoff, while Couples, Payne Stewart and Tom Byrum all frittered away earlier chances to, at worst, join the playoff. Byrum and Els tied third-round leader Jeff Sluman for third at 271, while Couples finished another shot back.

Despite an aching back, defending champion Couples, playing in just his second event since missing the cut at the U.S. Open, played 72 holes with just one bogey and served notice — with just another week left before the team would be chosen — to Ryder Cup captain Lanny Wadkins he would be a good choice. Still, he missed birdies at Nos. 15 and 18 and bogeyed No. 17 to miss the playoff by two shots. Stewart bogeyed Nos. 14 and 15, and Byrum, playing on a sponsor's exemption, birdied the 11th through 13th holes, but couldn't add a final birdie down the stretch.

After Austin closed with 67, Brisky nearly holed out at No. 17, then he, too, missed a birdie at No. 18. Both parred the 18th again on the first playoff hole, then Brisky buried his eight-iron shot in the bunker on the second playoff hole.

PGA Championship—$1,750,000
Winner: Steve Elkington

See Chapter 6.

Sprint International—$1,500,000
Winner: Lee Janzen

Lee Janzen didn't do it because he was mad. He didn't do it to get even. And he certainly didn't do it to rub Lanny Wadkins' nose in it.

Janzen went out and won the Sprint International in Castle Rock, Colorado, and became the first player to win three American tournaments in a year since Steve Jones in 1989 because he had something to prove to himself. Of course, he ignited a controversy, too, since the victory came just six days after Wadkins passed him over as a captain's choice for the 1995 Ryder Cup team. "If I had done this last week (at the PGA Championship where he tied for 23rd), there wouldn't be a controversy, would there?" he said. "If I was such a lock to make the Ryder Cup team, I should have made it on points. So I've got no one to blame but myself for not making the team."

Janzen was passed over in favor of multi-Cup veterans Curtis Strange and Fred Couples, both of whom skipped this event, but showed more than ever in the last round why he is known as one of the best "closers" on the PGA Tour. After playing an average first three rounds in this modified Stableford scoring system, Janzen played very well down the stretch Sunday to finish with 34 points — one better than Ernie Els' total of 33. Mark Wiebe and third-round leader Jay Haas finished third at 28.

Janzen, whose 25 points in the first three rounds came mainly from three eagles, looked shaky when he bogeyed the eighth, ninth and 10th holes. Then Janzen got up and down out of a bunker for birdie at the par-five 14th, he wedged to six feet for another birdie at No. 15, then sent a three-iron shot careening 15 feet from the pin at No. 17 and two-putted for another birdie. Els bogeyed the 18th, while Janzen, who birdied the final hole to win the 1995 Players Championship and birdied No. 18 twice in a row (second time a playoff) to win the Kemper Open, ran a 40-foot birdie attempt seven feet past the hole and made the putt coming back for the win.

"At the end of my career, nobody will remember how many Ryder Cups I played on, just how many tournaments I won," Janzen said. "I would like to have played, definitely. I was going to ask someone on the team if they needed a caddie that week. I wouldn't mind."

NEC World Series of Golf—$2,000,000
Winner: Greg Norman

There was more than a hint of scandal. There was a train-wreck of a collapse. There were records set. And finally, there was justice. For once, Greg Norman wasn't the victim. Instead, it was Norman who got the final word — not to mention his third victory of the season and a pair of records — with a 66-foot chip shot on the first playoff hole at the NEC World Series of Golf in Akron, Ohio.

After years of losing on final holes, Norman stepped up and stunned Nick Price and a struggling Billy Mayfair to take home the $360,000 first prize and become the PGA Tour's all-time money winner. The victory vaulted Norman ($9,493,579) past Tom Kite ($9,328,776) on the list and, with several months to go in the year, set a single-season earnings mark ($1,555,709). The old mark of $1,499,927 was set by Price in 1994, while Norman's previous best was $1,330,307, also in 1994.

Norman almost withdrew from the tournament on principle after the first round when he became embroiled in a controversy with first-day playing companion Mark McCumber. On the seventh hole, Norman said he saw McCumber tap down a spike mark in McCumber's line before putting — a rules violation. McCumber said he was removing an insect, but Norman refused to believe him and, later, refused to sign McCumber's scorecard. Tournament official Mike Shea signed it instead. Norman cleaned out his locker and wanted to withdraw, but was talked into playing by his wife Laura and caddie Tony Navarro.

Mayfair took command of the tournament with a three-under-par 32 on the front nine in the final round, but he couldn't hold on. Bogeys at the 15th, 16th and 17th holes left him reeling. Then he lipped out an eight-foot birdie on the final hole that would have given him the title. Price had a chance to win at No. 18, too, but drove into the rough and had to punch out. He missed an 18-foot par putt at No. 18 to get into the playoff.

Norman had the worst drive of the playoff trio, but made up for it with that chip-in. Price then came up short on a 22-foot birdie attempt and Mayfair's chip was short. "The game of golf evens itself out," Norman said. "Sometimes you hit a tree and it lands in the water. Sometimes it lands in the fairway. Those shots have happened against me, as I've heard about so many times. Now the golfing gods have evened things out."

Greater Milwaukee Open—$1,000,000
Winner: Scott Hoch

This time there was no ugly word to rhyme with Hoch. There was no ugly final putt. There was no reason to hang his head. This time, Scott Hoch was on a roll. He took a one-shot lead into the final round of the Greater Milwaukee Open, closed with a six-under-par 65 and won the sixth PGA Tour tournament of his career — and his third event worldwide in six weeks. His 15-under-par 269 total was three better than Marco Dawson's 272, a career-best finish for him, and five shots better than the 274s posted by Jim Gallagher, Jr., Joe Acosta and Jeff Sluman.

Hoch had invoked the "choke" word on himself four months before, when he blew a five-shot lead and lost to Payne Stewart in a playoff at the Shell Houston Open, but he swore this win wasn't redemption for that loss. It was just a continuation of the run that saw him win the Heineken Dutch Open and the unofficial West Coast Classic in recent weeks. In fact, Hoch wasn't even going to play at Milwaukee until he realized he was dangerously close to missing the cut-off (30th place on the money list) for the Tour Championship and that he could bring the family since his children's school was under construction and wouldn't open for another week.

Hoch shot himself into the tournament with a third-round 65, but after three holes Sunday found himself in an nine-way tie for the lead with Bob Estes, Sluman, Gallagher, Duffy Waldorf, Acosta, Dawson, Robert Gamez and Lee Rinker. When he missed a 20-foot eagle on the fourth hole by a mere 12 inches, he tapped in for birdie and a lead he would never surrender. Dawson closed the gap to one shot on the back but Hoch pulled away with birdies from 10 and 15 feet at the 17th and 18th holes, respectively. "This was not a three-stroke victory at all, though it added up to that," Hoch said. "It was not as easy as that."

Bell Canadian Open—$1,300,000
Winner: Mark O'Meara

The week of the Bell Canadian Open started with 31 of the top 50 money winners taking off but, luckily for tournament officials, ended in a flourish as Mark O'Meara needed a playoff to beat Bob Lohr and capture his second title of the year at Glen Abbey Golf Club in Oakville, Ontario.

O'Meara started the day five strokes behind Lohr, who hadn't won in seven years, and caught him just after the turn. Until then, it looked as though Lohr just might be the winner. As it was, Lohr, who took the lead after the second round when he posted rounds of 68-67 for a nine-under-par 135 total, stayed on top for 47 holes.

A 35, one under par, on the front nine by Lohr was no match for O'Meara, who flew through with just 10 putts. A birdie at the 11th gave O'Meara the lead and he widened it to three strokes. But Lohr didn't give up. He birdied three of the last four holes to force the playoff at 14-under-par 274, then shot himself out of the title.

With O'Meara, who closed with 67, safely on the green at the first playoff hole, Lohr put his 240-yard second shot into the water to hand the tournament to O'Meara. Former Canadian Open champion Nick Price closed with 68 to finish a distant third at 277, and Hal Sutton was fourth at 278.

B.C. Open—$1,000,000
Winner: Hal Sutton

It was a Johnny Miller rerun, only this time the winner was Hal Sutton and the closing 61 that won it for him came courtesy of lift, clean and place.

Sutton charged from five shots off the pace in the final round of the B.C. Open in Endicott, New York, reeled off 11 birdies, flirted with 59 and won his first tournament in nine years. "That's the best round I've ever played in my life in competition," said Sutton, who parred the first hole, then birdied 10 of the next 12 holes. "Good drives, good irons and I followed them up with good putts. I reminded myself of the old Hal Sutton out there."

Sutton, once dubbed the Bear Apparent, hadn't been heard from since winning the 1986 Memorial Tournament. In his place was a shadow of Sutton, a guy who struggled for nine seasons, hit bottom with his game and then spent two years coming back. The B.C. Open win capped his return from nowhere.

Sutton entered the final round five strokes behind leader Skip Kendall, which meant he was playing seven groups — and more than an hour — ahead of the leaders. But when he started reeling off birdies, all he could think of was not getting caught — and 59.

Miller shot his closing 61 at the 1975 Tucson Open during a time when he was one of the hottest players in the game. Sutton's came during a time when people were questioning if he could win again. His winning total of 15-under-par 269 was one stroke better than Jim McGovern's 270, and McGovern closed with 63. Craig Stadler and Kirk Triplett tied for third at 271.

Ryder Cup
Winner: Europe

See Chapter 8.

Quad City Classic—$1,000,000
Winner: D.A. Weibring

D.A. Weibring needed two days to shoot a bone-chilling opening 64. Then he needed one final rotation of his golf ball to win his third Quad City Classic title.

Anyone surprised that he got it? Weibring doesn't just play Oakwood Country Club in Coal Valley, Illinois. He plays as if he owns it. He won there in 1979 and 1991 and then became the first three-time winner when he outlasted rookie Jonathan Kaye to take home this year's rain-shortened title. As if that wasn't enough, the victory was Weibring's fourth in his home state, the other coming in the 1987 Western Open in Oak Brook, Illinois.

After needing two days to play the first round, which was halted by rain and very cool temperatures, Weibring added a second-round 65 and took a four-stroke lead into the third and final round.

Kaye shot 30 on the front nine and pulled even with Weibring after 12 holes. The lead see-sawed back and forth from there before coming down to the 18th hole. Kaye hooked his drive, then pulled a six-iron shot into the greenside fringe. His chip went across the green and his comeback putt rolled five feet past. Weibring, meanwhile, birdied the hole from 18 feet away for a 13-under-par 197 total and the title. Kaye closed with 65 for his 198 total, while Jay Delsing was third at 200.

Buick Challenge—$1,000,000
Winner: Fred Funk

It was as perfect a six-iron shot as Fred Funk had ever hit. He needed 156 yards and got 154.9 yards. As for those final 48 inches? The putt was straight in and that's the way Funk played it to birdie the final hole at the Buick Challenge in Pine Mountain, Georgia, and win his second event of the year. "It never left the flag," Funk said of the six-iron approach. "It was like a laser."

Funk, who won the Ideon Classic in August, entered the final round tied for the lead with Steve Stricker at 11-under-par 205 and one shot ahead of a pack. By the time he got to the 16th tee, he was behind and looking to charge.

Funk birdied two of the last three holes — the real heroics coming from that six iron at the 18th — and closed with 67 for his 16-under 272 total. That birdie not only made him the ninth double winner of the season on the PGA Tour, but also ended the playoff hopes of Loren Roberts and John Morse, who were sitting not so comfortably in the clubhouse at 15-under 273. Both started the day in the pack that was one stroke off the lead and closed with 67s.

Roberts, who was coming off a disappointing Ryder Cup performance, missed his final chance at the 18th when his approach shot wound up 30 feet from the flagstick. Morse, a winner in Hawaii early in the year, let his chances get away with an eight-foot birdie attempt at the 17th that was short. Still, he claimed his first top-10 finish in eight months.

Walt Disney World/Oldsmobile Classic—$1,200,000
Winner: Brad Bryant

Fairytales do come true. Just ask Brad Bryant. One soggy Sunday afternoon in October, he was transformed from Dr. Dirt to Dr. Paydirt. All it took was a closing 68 and some steady nerves on the last two holes and — like magic — Bryant walked away from the Walt Disney World/Oldsmobile Classic in Lake Buena Vista, Florida, with his first victory ever.

That it took 18 years and 486 tries for Bryant to win, and that is was in a rain-shortened event didn't matter. What did matter was that Bryant hung on to win by one stroke over Ted Tryba and Hal Sutton. Bryant, who got his Dr. Dirt nickname from his rumpled appearance, shot an 18-under-par 198 total, while Tryba, who closed with 65, and Sutton, who closed with 66, finished at 199.

"It has been so long in coming," said Bryant, who had previously been known as the richest player ($2.7 million) never to have won a PGA Tour event. "I just know I gave hope to every golfer in the world."

Las Vegas Invitational—$1,500,000
Winner: Jim Furyk

Jim Furyk's swing looks like anything but that of a winner. It starts low and inside. It flies back, then loops in and finally finds the ball.

Yet in a city where long shots are the only way to really win, Furyk hit the $270,000 first-place jackpot. After bouncing around the top 10 at times this season, Furyk went out and shot a 28-under-par 331 total at the Las Vegas Invitational and won his first PGA Tour event. The former Nike Tour player made his charge to the top in the third round when his 65 left him tied for the lead at 18-under-par 197 with David Edwards. His fourth-round 67 left him tied with Billy Mayfair after 72 holes.

The question was whether his swing would hold up under the pressure of the final round. He led going into the final round in the 1994 event, but faded to fifth place. Would history repeat itself?

The format pairs professionals with amateurs the first four days and has them playing on three different courses, but the amateurs go outside the ropes for the final round at the TPC at Summerlin. The change did nothing to halt Furyk's momentum. He led or shared the lead for the final 16 holes and he played the last two holes — both of which set up for a hook rather than his natural fade — conservatively to par in for the victory.

"I knew if I played a solid back nine, someone would have to go nuts to catch me," Furyk said. "The whole back nine I hit the ball exactly where I wanted on every hole. I didn't miss a shot." As for his swing? It may take a long time for people to get used to, but it works for him. "I play by feel," Furyk said. "I think it's a real natural athletic swing. It's so unorthodox. I don't get caught up in mechanics or positions or angles. All that would just confuse me."

La Cantera Texas Open—$1,100,000
Winner: Duffy Waldorf

You want suspense? The La Cantera Texas Open had it. Just not in the usual place. The tournament itself wasn't even close. Duffy Waldorf, best known for colorful shirts and hats and wild golf ball markings, won the final regular-season PGA Tour event in a runaway. He took a one-stroke lead into the final round and won by six strokes. His closing 65 was even more impressive since it came on the tournament's new home — the La Cantera course in San Antonio — where Waldorf, with the wind at his back, managed to drive the green at the 410-yard 11th hole Sunday with a three wood.

Waldorf romped his way to a 20-under-par 268 total and the lowest wining score among four-round PGA Tour events this year and the biggest margin of victory since Nick Price won the 1994 PGA Championship. The only man standing in the way of a bigger margin was Texan Justin Leonard, whose closing 68 left him at 274. The next closest? John Morse and John Mahaffey finished at 280, 12 strokes back.

"I basically played the round of my life," said Waldorf, who led or shared the lead from the second round on. "I can't think of a better time to do it than when you're leading after three rounds. I just didn't make any mistakes."

Waldorf started the day tied with Jay Don Blake, who threw his chances away with a closing 77. He led by five shots going into the 17th hole and drained a 20-foot birdie putt there for good measure.

As for the suspense? It was all further down the standings where players fell in and out of the top 125 money winners who would qualify for the 1996 PGA Tour. After missing the cut in seven of the last 11 events, Mahaffey tied for third place to finish in the top 125, while Mark Wiebe, Mike Standly and Keith Fergus also hung on. Tom Byrum, who came into the event in the 125th spot, missed the cut and fell out. Others who missed were Paul Stankowski, who was disqualified; Peter Jordan, who missed the cut, and Russ Cochran, who fell one shot short of keeping his card.

Tour Championship—$3,000,000
Winner: Billy Mayfair

After the third round, Brad Bryant pretty much summed up the feelings of all 30 players in the elite Tour Championship field when he said, "I started like a doofus, finished like a dummy and putted terrible in between."

Yes, things were tough at Southern Hills Country Club in Tulsa, Oklahoma. Fast greens. Gusting winds. Soft sand. Conditions where golfers don't thrive. They merely survive.

Billy Mayfair did just that. The third-round leader was the only player to find his way into red (under par) numbers in the final round and even bogeys at the 15th and 16th holes left him with a winning score of even-par 280. It was not an impressive number, but one that gave him the $540,000 winner's check and a three-shot victory over U.S. Open champion Corey Pavin and PGA champion Steve Elkington. Pavin didn't make one birdie on his way to a closing 73 and 283 total, while Elkington, who picked up the Vardon Trophy for the lowest scoring average, had just two birdies all week in his 283.

As a group, the field shot 322 over par and Mayfair was low at even par. And, of the 120 rounds played, only 14 were under par. The course was almost unplayable at times on Thursday and Friday, but calmed down on Saturday as Mayfair, a runner-up in this event in 1990, shot 69 to take a three-stroke lead going into the final day.

The 1995 Western Open champion made three key saves down the stretch Saturday, then birdied the final hole to take the lead. The saves came at the 12th, where he saved par with a great chip; at the 13th, where he hit a wedge into a bunker, then made a 25-foot par putt, and at the 14th, where he made a 15-footer.

It was the third victory of Mayfair's career and, coupled with strong finishes in three of the other biggest money events of the season, pushed him to second on the money list behind Greg Norman. Norman won the season money title with a record $1,654,959, but lost the Vardon Trophy. Although Norman had the lowest stroke average, he withdrew from the MCI Classic during a round, which disqualified him from the Vardon race. Elkington won that title with a 68.9 scoring average. Mayfair was second on the money list with $1,543,192.

Special Events

Westinghouse-Family House Invitational—$850,000
Winner: Ernie Els

Ernie Els took advantage of the local rules, then hit two clutch shots to beat Steve Stricker in a playoff at the Westinghouse-Family House Invitational at the Pittsburgh Field Club. Els missed the green at the 15th hole and was on bare ground beside a bush, which restricted his swing. A local rule, however, deemed the area ground under repair and he got a free drop. He followed with a 15-foot par putt to tie Stricker at No. 18, then a three iron out of high grass to 10 feet to set up the winning birdie on the playoff hole. Els shot rounds of 61 and 70 to claim the $170,000 first prize, while Stricker shot 65 and 66 and collected $85,000. Scott Simpson closed with 67 to finish third at 132.

Ernst Challenge—$695,000
Winner: John Cook

John Cook fired an eight-under-par 63 in the final round to edge Jeff Gove in a shoot-out at the Ernst Challenge. Cook's 63 gave him a 36-hole total of 134 at the Overlake Golf and Country Club in Medina, Washington, and the $150,000 winner's check. Gove, a Nike Tour player, closed with a 10-under 61 to finish second at 135.

Jerry Ford Invitational—$300,000
Winner: Doug Tewell

Doug Tewell closed with a five-under-par 67 to earn a two-stroke victory in the Jerry Ford Invitational at the Country Club of the Rockies in Vail, Colorado. Tewell's two-day total of 132 earned him $20,000. Bob Lohr fired rounds of 66-68 to finish second and collect $12,500. Former President Gerald Ford, the tournament host, did not compete due to a shoulder injury.

Fred Meyer Challenge—$750,000
Winners: Greg Norman and Brad Faxon

Greg Norman set it up and Brad Faxon closed it out as the two teamed up to beat Paul Azinger and Payne Stewart in a playoff at the Fred Meyer Challenge in West Lynn, Oregon. Norman slipped in a 12-foot birdie putt on the final hole to force the playoff, then Faxon holed a 15-foot birdie on the first playoff hole to give the team the $100,000 winner's check. Azinger, who made 11 birdies in the two-day event at Oregon Golf Club, had a chance to win the event on the final regulation hole, but his 10-foot birdie attempt slid off to the left. Faxon and Norman shot 65 and 64. Stewart and Azinger, who shot 64-65, shared $80,000.

"This was the first clear opportunity (to win) that I've had since my illness," said Azinger, who missed most of the 1994 season while being treated for lymphoma. "I responded well."

Defending champions John Cook and Mark O'Meara tied Jay Haas and Curtis Strange for third place at 131.

West Coast Classic—$550,000
Winner: Scott Hoch

It took an extra day and five playoff holes, but Scott Hoch outlasted Scott Verplank to win the West Coast Classic at Swan-e-set Bay in Pitt Meadows, British Columbia. The final round was delayed because of thunderstorms, but Hoch birdied the final hole and Verplank bogeyed it to finish tied at seven-under-par 203. They played two extra holes before play was suspended because of darkness, then resumed play the following day. Hoch parred the fifth hole to take home the $100,000 winner's check. Brandel Chamblee finished third at 204.

Gene Sarazen World Open—$1,900,000
Winner: Frank Nobilo

For the better part of 45 holes, Frank Nobilo was an afterthought at The Legends at Chateau Elan. While he was playing the first two rounds in four-under-par 140, John Daly was grabbing the headlines at the Gene Sarazen World Open and Miguel Jimenez was holding the 36-hole lead. But Nobilo came from three strokes off the pace in the final seven holes to take the $350,000 winner's check.

Nobilo, the 35-year-old New Zealander, birdied four of the seven holes and survived a missed three-footer at the final hole to finish the 54-hole tournament with 68 and an eight-under-par 216 total. He edged Jimenez and Zimbabwe's Mark McNulty by one stroke. Although temperatures were in the low 40s and the wind-chill was in the 30s, Nobilo was red hot. Starting at No. 12, he birdied four of the next five holes to take the lead from Jimenez, who closed with 73. McNulty fired a final-round 67 for his 209. Daly fell out of contention at the 15th hole with a double bogey and closed with 73 to finish tied for eighth place.

Lincoln-Mercury Kapalua International—$1,000,000
Winner: Jim Furyk

Jim Furyk's swing has been likened to "an octopus falling out of a tree," but it really doesn't matter what it looks like as long as it works. It certainly did at Kapalua's Plantation course as Furyk turned in a 13-under-par 271 total to beat Jim McGovern, Russ Cochran and Barry Lane by two strokes at the Lincoln-Mercury Kapalua International in Maui, Hawaii.

Furyk, who won earlier in Las Vegas, nearly lost the $180,000 winner's check at the 16th hole when he sliced a shot into a hazard, but he saved bogey with a great three-wood shot into a heavy breeze. He closed with a tap-in for birdie at the 18th hole.

Furyk led or shared the lead all four days, turning in rounds of 65, 65, 71 and 70. Cochran finished with 67 to tie Lane (69) and McGovern (70), while Ben Crenshaw, who designed the course along with partner Bill Coore, and Tom Lehman shot 274.

MasterCard PGA Grand Slam of Golf—$1,000,000
Winner: Ben Crenshaw

It was the most dramatic shot of Ben Crenshaw's season. It was also the luckiest, the most fortunate and perhaps even accidental. After playing out of bunkers most of the day, Crenshaw holed a 50-yard pitch that dove into the cup on one bounce for an eagle, a two-day total of 140 and the victory at the MasterCard PGA Grand Slam of Golf at the Poipu Bay Resort in Kauai, Hawaii. "That's one of the luckiest shots I've ever hit," said Crenshaw, who earned his way into the tournament with his Masters victory in April. "I was trying to hit a running shot and I gave it a little too much gas with my right hand. It was going to be 20, 25 feet by the hole, by all rights. It went in on the first bounce. I'm just luckier than everybody else."

At least he was a bit luckier than U.S. Open champion Corey Pavin and PGA champion Steve Elkington, who came into the hole tied with Crenshaw. Both birdied and finished tied for second place at 141. And he was a lot luckier than British Open winner John Daly, who shot 148. Crenshaw collected $400,000, while Pavin and Elkington earned $225,000 each and Daly took $150,000.

Mexican Open—$124,395
Winner: John Cook

John Cook birdied two of the final four holes to win the Mexican Open in Mexico City by one stroke over Scott Verplank. Cook's closing three-under-par 69 set a tournament record on the Club de Golf course at 15-under-par 273. Cook, who won the Ernst Challenge earlier, started the day with a one-stroke lead over Verplank, a two-shot advantage over Bob Tway. Tway shot 33 on the front nine to take the lead, but Cook and Verplank rallied for a three-way tie after 14 holes. Cook, who earned $30,000 for the win, birdied the 15th hole to take the lead, then after lipping out a chip-in for eagle at No. 17, tapped in for the birdie.

Pebble Beach Invitational—$250,000
Winner: Ronnie Black

After six holes, Ronnie Black was trailing club pro Bob Ford by three strokes and LPGA player Kris Tschetter by one. But when second- and third-round leader Ford self-destructed, Black stayed cool, closed with a one-under-par 71 to finish with a 277 total and win the Pebble Beach Invitational by two shots over Tschetter, Ford, Kenny Perry and Kirk Triplett.

Black pocketed $50,000 for his first victory since the 1984 Anheuser-Busch Classic. Ford, a two-time National Club Pro champion, bogeyed four holes in a row on the final day and five out of six to close with 75. Tschetter shot 71, Triplett shot 70 and Perry closed with 66.

Franklin Templeton Shark Shootout—$1,100,000
Winners: Mark Calcavecchia and Steve Elkington

How low could they go at the Franklin Templeton Shark Shootout? Plenty low. Try 268 under par as a field for the 10 teams. Or 15-under as a team — for one day. Or 32 under par for three days, which happens to be what PGA champion Steve Elkington and Mark Calcavecchia shot on their way to the title at Sherwood Country Club in Thousand Oaks, California.

Elkington and Calcavecchia, who led all three days, made 13 birdies on the final-day scramble — eight on the last nine — and shot a combined 32-under 184 total to edge Chip Beck and Lee Janzen by one stroke. Elkington, who won the tournament in 1993 with Raymond Floyd, and Calcavecchia took their one-stroke lead at the 17th hole when Elkington sank a five-foot birdie putt. Calcavecchia drove into the water at No. 18 before Elkington saved par with a nine iron to eight feet.

"We just wanted to get it over with, so I thought, 'Why not stiff it and get a little attitude going?'" Elkington said.

Beck and Janzen closed with 57 for their 185 total, while defending champions Fred Couples and Brad Faxon tied Tom Lehman and David Duval for third at 187. The tournament featured one day each of alternate shot, better-ball and scramble play.

Paradise Island Invitational—$310,000
Winner: Jim McGovern

Starting the day two strokes behind leader Guy Boros, Jim McGovern shot a closing 68 to win the Paradise Island Invitational in Nassau, Bahamas. McGovern, whose only PGA Tour victory came at the 1993 Shell Houston Open, shot an eight-under-par 206 total to collect the $30,000 winner's check, while Boros closed with 73 for a 209 total. Curt Byrum, who shared the first-round lead with Boros and John Inman, finished third at 211.

Office Depot Father/Son Challenge—$650,000
Winners: Raymond Floyd and Raymond Floyd, Jr.

It wasn't even close. That's the way Raymond Floyd — both Senior and Junior — wanted it as they teamed to win the Office Depot Father/Son Challenge by a whopping six strokes over Hale and Steve Irwin. The Floyds took the lead in the opening round with 62 at the Windsor Club in Vero Beach, Florida, and closed with an impressive 57 that included 13 birdies and an eagle two on the final hole. The Floyds shot 25-under-par 119 for the 36 holes to win the $150,000 first prize. Dave and Ron Stockton and Tony and Warren Jacklin tied for third place at 127.

Diners Club Matches—$2,100,000
Winners: Tom Lehman and Duffy Waldorf
        Bob Murphy and Jim Colbert
        Kelly Robbins and Tammie Green

After trailing by two holes early in the day, Tom Lehman and Duffy Waldorf rallied to beat Kenny Perry and John Huston 1 up in the finals of the Diners Club Matches in La Quinta, California. Waldorf gave them the victory when he sank a four-foot birdie putt on the final hole. Lehman set the stage with birdies on the 12th and 13th holes to even the match, then saved par with a six-footer at the 17th. "We really needed a lift," Waldorf said. "They had a chance to put us away early, but Tom made a big birdie at the 12th and came back with another at the 13th."

Bob Murphy missed a four-foot birdie putt at the 16th, then holed a 15-

foot birdie at No. 17 to give him and partner Jim Colbert a 1-up victory over Hale Irwin and Dave Stockton in the seniors division. Kelly Robbins and Tammie Green won their second consecutive title in the women's division, defeating Laura Davies and Mardi Lunn 1 up.

Lexus Challenge—$1,000,000
Winners: Raymond Floyd and Michael Chiklis

For the second time in a month, Raymond Floyd picked up a team title, this time pairing with actor Michael Chiklis to win the Lexus Challenge in La Quinta, California, by three strokes over Jim Colbert and actor William Devane. Floyd and Chiklis, who stars in ABC's television series *The Commish*, came from one stroke behind to close with an eight-under-par 64 for a two-day total of 127. Colbert and Devane closed with 65 for a 130 total, and first-round co-leaders George Archer and former basketball star Julius Erving were third at 131.

Floyd was the host of the event, which was played on the Citrus course.

Andersen Consulting World Championship—$3,650,000
Winner: Barry Lane

Playing for a $1,000,000 first prize on New Year's Eve, Barry Lane defeated David Frost 2 up in the 36-hole final of the Andersen Consulting World Championship at the Grayhawk Golf Club's Talon Course in Scottsdale, Arizona. Frost birdied three of the first four holes, but Lane countered with three consecutive birdies from the seventh and led 1 up after the first round. They were tied with four holes to play, then Lane went ahead with a nine-foot birdie putt on the 15th hole and increased his margin with a six-footer on the 18th. Frost's runner-up prize was $500,000.

In the semi-finals the previous day, Lane won by the same 2 up score over Masahiro Kuramoto, and Frost beat Mark McCumber 2 and 1. McCumber won the third-place match 4 and 3, collecting $350,000, and Kuramoto received $300,000.

There were 32 qualifiers, the top seven available players on the Sony Ranking and one invitee from each of four regions: United States, Europe, Japan and the Rest of the World. Eight of the top 10 players on the Sony Ranking declined to enter, and only Bernhard Langer and Corey Pavin were in the field from the top 10 when the matches began. Kuramoto won in Japan in February. The other regional winners were decided over the spring and summer: McCumber (United States), Lane (Europe) and Frost (Rest of the World).

All matches except the final were played over 18 holes.

Nike Tour

Jerry Kelly set a money-winnings record and Allen Doyle earned the distinction as the PGA Tour's oldest rookie ever as the 10 money leaders from the 1995 Nike Tour advanced to the big show for 1996. Kelly, from Madison, Wisconsin, was one of six players to win two Nike Tour events and earned $188,878. A record 15 players surpassed $100,000 for the year. Doyle, from LaGrange, Georgia, was second on the money list with $176,652, was the only three-event winner and, at age 47, earned his promotion.

Kelly, age 28, led in three of the four statistical categories — birdies, eagles, par-breakers — and was third in scoring average. His total winnings broke the record of $167,148 set in 1994 by Chris Perry. Doyle and one-event winner David Toms of Bossier City, Louisiana ($174,892) also exceeded the previous high, as purses on the Nike Tour continued to grow from the inaugural 1990 season when only one player had six-figure winnings.

In addition to Kelly, Doyle and Toms, those qualifying for the PGA Tour were Franklin Langham of Duluth, Georgia (no wins, $158,990), Stuart Appleby of Sydney, Australia (two wins, $144,419), Tom Scherrer of Orlando, Florida (one win, $143,404), Chris Smith of Rochester, Indiana (two wins, $143,200), Sean Murphy of Lovington, New Mexico (one win, $118,985), Hugh Royer III of Aiken, South Carolina (two wins, $118,804) and Brad Fabel of Nashville, Tennessee (one win, $115,513).

The final positions were determined in the 30th and last tournament of the year, the Nike Tour Championship in Roswell, Georgia. Among those who lost out were Matt Peterson of Athens, Georgia, and Stan Utley of Columbia, Missouri, who came into the event in ninth and 10th place respectively. Both finished tied for 12th place in the Nike Tour Championship and fell out of the top 10 for the year. They were overtaken by Murphy, who rose from 11th to eighth place, and Fabel. Utley was the only player to win two events and not qualify for the PGA Tour.

Although Utley got both of his victories in the first half of the year, as a general rule those who played well early were also those who sustained their performances and secured top-10 positions. Seven of the 10 qualifiers had victories in the first 14 tournaments.

The 1995 Nike Tour began in late February with two events in California, then went to Mexico where Appleby took seven playoff holes to become the first of the eventual qualifiers to post a victory. The 24-year-old Australian also became the eighth player in Nike Tour history to win in his first start.

The next 11 venues were in southern states — Louisiana, Alabama, Mississippi, Florida, Georgia, South Carolina, Tennessee and Virginia — as Doyle, Fabel, Kelly, Scherrer, Toms and Royer were among the winners. Highlights included Utley's final-round 62 to erase an eight-stroke deficit and win the Louisiana Open. Kelly ended a stretch of 12 top-10 finishes without a victory when he won the Alabama Classic. Six strokes down with seven holes to play, Peterson made an eagle and five birdies, shot 65 and won the Central Georgia Open. Scherrer was in playoffs in three consecutive events, winning one then losing the next two.

Now into June, there were two tournaments in Ohio, including Utley's second victory, then one in North Carolina followed by stops in Philadelphia, Buffalo and St. Louis. Kelly took his second victory in Buffalo and replaced Scherrer as the leading money winner, the position he would hold for eight of the remaining 11 weeks.

The Nike Tour headed back west in late July, first to Kansas then South Dakota, Missouri, Texas, Arkansas, Utah, Washington, Idaho and California. Smith, Royer and Appleby all won for the second time in that stretch. Entering the Nike Tour Championship, there were four players — Toms, Langham, Scherrer and Smith — with chances to overtake Kelly and become the year's leading money winner. Kelly tied for 24th place in the final event, and the best the others could do was Toms' tie for ninth place.

Canadian Tour

The 1995 Canadian Tour was fertile territory for "thirty-something" journeymen Trevor Dodds, Scott Dunlap, Ray Freeman and Jim Rutledge. They won six of the 11 tournaments on the June-to-August circuit and took four of the top five positions on the money list.

Dodds, age 35, was the leader with C$78,468 and two victories. Dunlap, age 32, won once and was second on the money list with C$65,249, then came Freeman, age 36, who won twice and earned C$54,293. Ian Hutchings, age 27, was fourth on the money list with C$51,835, ahead of Rutledge, age 36, who won once and had earnings of C$44,631.

A native of Namibia who now lives in St. Louis, Missouri, Dodds had his best year since winning twice in South Africa, including the South African Open, in 1990. Dodds is also a veteran of the American and European circuits.

Americans won six of the tournaments and there were only two Canadian winners, in the first and last events. Norm Jarvis of Surrey, British Columbia, led off in his native province, winning the Payless Open in Victoria by two strokes over Bruce Bulina of Winnipeg.

The next two tournaments were also in British Columbia. Nick Goetze of Tampa, Florida, won on the fifth playoff hole over Hutchings, a South African, in the B.C. TEL Pacific Open in Richmond. Jeff Bloom of Seattle, Washington, birdied the first playoff hole to defeat Rutledge, who is from Victoria, in the Morningstar Classic in Parksville. Rutledge shot 65 in the last round, coming from seven strokes behind to tie Bloom.

Moving on to Ponoka, Alberta, for the Henry Singer Alberta Open, Hutchings carried a four-stroke lead into the final round and won by three over Dodds.

The next week Dodds was second again, to Freeman, who is from Lexington, North Carolina, in the Klondike Days Klassic in Edmonton.

Dodds finally won in his next outing, the Xerox Manitoba Open in Winnipeg. He led by four strokes after 54 holes and was ahead by seven after his eagle on the second hole of the final round. Four consecutive bogeys on the second nine reduced his winning margin to three strokes.

Ontario was the site of the next four tournaments. Guy Hill of Lakeland, Florida, got his first professional victory by seven strokes in the Infiniti Tournament Players Championship in Toronto. Dunlap, who is from Sarasota, Florida, had an even wider victory margin in the Canadian Masters in Alberton, winning by 10 strokes with a 16-under-par 268 total that included 62 in the third round. Freeman birdied the 72nd hole to win the Export "A" Inc. Ontario Open in London, and Dodds birdied three of the first seven holes of the final round in winning the Trafalgar CPGA Championship in Manotick.

In the concluding Montclair PEI Classic at Morelli, Prince Edward Island, Rutledge came from six strokes behind in the last round to win by one stroke. His closing 64 included birdies on four of the final six holes.

South American Tour

The South American Tour again consisted of nine tournaments from October through early December plus the independent Argentina Open, which was by far the richest event on the continent. Argentina and Paraguay provided most of the winners, although there were two from the United States and one each from Chile and South Africa.

Mark Calcavecchia won the $250,000 Argentina Open with its $50,000 first prize in a playoff against another American, Andrew Magee. The prize money was more than double that of any other South American tournament, and Calcavecchia was the fifth consecutive American winner. He also won the title in 1993.

The South American Tour began with two events in Colombia with Pedro Martinez of Paraguay winning the Farallones Open and Ron Wuensche of the United States, the San Andres Open. Fabian Montavia of Argentina won the Filanbanco Ecuador Open on the next stop, then Raul Fretes of Paraguay took the Los Inkas-Peru Open. Angel Cabrera of Argentina won two consecutive tournaments, the Paraguay Open and the Litoral Open in Argentina. The circuit ended in Chile with victories by home favorite Guillermo Encina in the Prince of Wales Open and Ian Hutchings of South Africa in the Los Leones Open.

13. European Tours

Did 1995 mark the rise of other Germans alongside Bernhard Langer on the PGA European Tour? We shall see. But for now, we have Alexander Cejka to thank for the question.

We'll be hearing a lot more of Cejka, so let's get the pronunciation right. It's "Jayka" according to the Tour's media guide. And a brief biography is in order. Cejka was born on December 2, 1970, in Marienbad, in what was then Czechoslovakia. He was nine years old when his father took him and fled the country. They landed in Germany, and Alexander eventually became a naturalized citizen — and a golfer.

Cejka turned professional in 1989, and played on the Challenge Tour until qualifying for the PGA European Tour in 1993. His best finish was a tie for fourth place in the Hohe Brucke Austrian Open in 1994. Then, in 1995, Cejka had not only his breakthrough win in the Turespana Masters Open de Andalucia in March, but also won the Hohe Brucke Austrian Open in August, and then the season-ending Volvo Masters at Valderrama, one of the toughest courses on the circuit, the last week of October.

Some might think Cejka was a flash-in-the-pan, but it might be well for skeptics to note that in the Hohe Brucke Austrian Open, he shot 61, finished 21 under par, and won by four strokes. At the Volvo Masters, he shot a first-nine 29 in the second round. Cejka was one focal point of a Tour that was more like a free-for-all. For example:

• Fred Couples kicked off the season as an American show, winning the first two events about half-a-world apart, the Dubai Desert Classic and the Johnnie Walker Classic in the Philippines.

• Colin Montgomerie was No. 1 on the money list for the third successive year, matching Seve Ballesteros with that achievement. The title came in a leapfrog battle with Sam Torrance down the stretch. Montgomerie clinched the title in the last tournament, the Volvo Masters, finishing second with 284, one stroke ahead of Torrance. In 20 events, Montgomerie won twice (Volvo German Open and Trophee Lancome) and had 14 other top-10 finishes. The four times he placed lower than 10th were 11th, 13th, 15th and 20th. He totalled £835,051 to Torrance's second-place £755,706.

• There were 23 Johnnie Walker Course Record Award winners, including Russell Claydon, with 61 in the Mercedes German Masters.

• There were nine first-time winners, including three Americans — Couples, Scott Hoch (Heineken Dutch Open) and John Daly (British Open).

Apart from Europe's upset victory in the Ryder Cup, Cejka was the surprise of 1995. And he made it the Year of the Germans, because Langer also won three times. It was the 17th consecutive year in which Langer had won at least once. Torrance also won three times.

It will be a while before Cejka can hope to match Langer in another category. Langer ran his string to a record 66 tournaments in which he made the cut. He broke Neil Coles' record of 56 back at the Volvo PGA Championship in May.

Cejka and Langer weren't the only ones putting Germany on the leaderboard. Sven Struver, a sixth-year man, missed five cuts in 25 outings and had four top-10 finishes. Heinz-Peter Thul had two eighth-place finishes in 12 starts.

While Langer and Cejka were winning six events between them, the Swedes spread it around, five of them winning one each. They were Jarmo Sandelin, Robert Karlsson, Jesper Parnevik, Mathias Gronberg and Anders Forsbrand. Sandelin won Rookie of the Year honors, and Parnevik (in the Scandinavian Masters) became the first Swede to win on Swedish soil.

As wild and wooly as the PGA European Tour was, it just didn't seem the same without Nick Faldo. He had joined the American PGA Tour for 1995, and played in just three European events. It was only the fourth time in his 20 seasons that he didn't win. With £93,188 in winnings, he finished 61st on the money list, his lowest placing since joining the circuit in 1976. He won in the United States (Doral-Ryder Open) however, and he was one of the heroes in the Ryder Cup.

It also didn't seem the same without the Spaniards. Seve Ballesteros was still slumping (one victory, three missed cuts in 11 starts), and Jose Maria Olazabal was still limping with an ailing right foot. Surgery had corrected the original problem, but now he had a new one. He even turned down the captain's pick from Bernard Gallacher for the Ryder Cup team. They did win one event as teammates, the Tournoi Perrier de Paris.

PGA European Tour

Dubai Desert Classic—£450,000
Winner: Fred Couples

Fred Couples more or less spoiled Greg Norman's plans in the European Tour's 1995 coming-out party.

The Dubai Desert Classic, with its big purse and strong field, was what Norman had had in mind for the exclusive World Tour which he unsuccessfully tried to launch late in 1993, but it wasn't the kind of finish he had in mind. He led the first round with 64, his fifth consecutive round under 70 at the par-72 Emirates Golf Club, then couldn't keep up as the rest of the starry field left him. Couples, who missed the cut here in 1994, pulled away with a closing 66 for a three-stroke victory over Colin Montgomerie.

Couples gave a hint of what was coming when he started at No. 10 and went birdie, birdie, par, eagle, par, birdie and birdie. "It was a fantastic start," said Couples, and that was an understatement. With rounds of 65, 69, 68 and 66, Couples trailed Norman by one stroke in the first round, tied with him three behind Montgomerie in the second round, and tied with Montgomerie for a one-stroke lead in the third round. He had a 20-under-par 268 total for the three-stroke victory over Montgomerie.

Couples all but locked up the victory with birdies at the two toughest holes, both long par-fours. At No. 9, he fired a six-iron approach from 160 yards to about four feet. And at No. 12, it was a three iron from 190 yards to four feet.

"He deserved to win," said Montgomerie, whose game had taken a sudden turn after he birdied the first three holes of the third round. He noted, puzzled, that he was 16 under par for the first 39 holes, then one under par for the last 33 holes. Couples certainly couldn't keep up that rampaging start, but he did stay fairly hot. Maybe it was the embarrassing memory of missing the cut in 1994. "You don't come out here to be a television commentator on the weekend," Couples observed.

Johnnie Walker Classic—£600,000
Winner: Fred Couples

Like a child on vacation, Fred Couples wanted a souvenir wherever he went. His first stop was the season-opening Dubai Desert Classic and he picked up the championship. Next came the Johnnie Walker Classic at Manila. He took that one, too. "Are you trying to wreck European morale?" someone asked. Couples broke into that slow, beaming smile. "I'll come back and win the British Open," he cracked.

The tournament was played at the new Legacy course, an Arnold Palmer layout featuring Bermuda grass rough and hard greens, along with strong winds the first day, and heat and humidity all week. Couples solved things with 72, 67, 67 and 71 for a 277 total, 11 under par, to win by two strokes over Nick Price.

The Legacy course, a par-72 layout of 7,016 yards, took a heavy toll on the world's best, and criticism came easy. "It's like the U.S. PGA," said Seve Ballesteros, who shot 296 with a lowest score of 73. "I don't need this for my first event." From the 78 who made the cut, there were only 23 rounds in the 60s. Only three men had two rounds in the 60s, all in the middle rounds — Couples, 67-67; Michael Campbell, 68-66, and Colin Montgomerie, 68-68. Robert Karlsson had the tournament low, a course-record 65 in the second round.

Price made eight birdies in the second round, but got only a 67 out of the effort, plus a one-stroke halfway lead. When he dropped a 15-footer for a birdie at the 72nd hole to take second place, it came as a relief. "I needed 65 putts on the last two days," he said, "which isn't good."

Campbell continued his hot play and tied for fourth place. He shot 66 in the third round while missing five putts from inside 10 feet. "I wouldn't have a clue to what I'm doing right," he said.

Couples' secret lay in sharp driving and the ability to make shots stop on the hard greens. In the last round, he made an early birdie and bogey, ground out 10 pars, then birdied the 16th hole for a three-stroke lead. "It's hard to believe I made only one bogey," Couples said. "It seemed as if I got it up-and-down all day. It was spectacular for me around the greens."

Madeira Island Open—£250,000
Winner: Santiago Luna

Seve Ballesteros long had said that Santiago Luna had the game to win. It just took Luna a while to turn him into a prophet. And when he did, he left no doubt. Luna was a wire-to-wire winner in the Madeira Island Open, shooting rounds of 67, 67, 68 and 70 for a 16-under-par 272 total for a four-stroke victory at Campo de Golfe.

"It has taken me 10 years to prove him right," said Luna, age 32, whose previous bests were three fourth-place finishes. His play this time took all the guesswork out of the proceedings. He led by four strokes going into the final round. He went out in 35, with birdies at the second, fifth and seventh holes. He came home bogey-free, and for good measure birdied the par-three 17th with a nine iron to seven feet. The man was in his element. "I was never tense during the final round," Luna said.

Others couldn't say the same. France's Christian Cevaer, a former British Youth champion, was a strong runner-up. He closed with 69 that included a birdie from two feet at the 17th. He also was the center of probably the strangest slow-play case ever. He was fined £500 for 18 breaches of pace-of-play regulations in the second round. His group was timed at 26 minutes out of position, and finished 19 minutes off. Said Cevaer, "It's something I have to work on."

Mats Hallberg was the victim of a rare penalty when he played from near a bush in the first round. He hit the ball, the ball hit the bush, then bounced back out and hit the shaft of his club. The ruling was "ball in motion being deflected." He made an eight, and what might have been a tie for 27th dropped eight spots, to 35th. Liam White was tied for second place going into the final round, but he shot 78 and plummeted to a tie for 18th.

Turespana Open de Canarias—£244,326
Winner: Jarmo Sandelin

Jarmo Sandelin, 27-year-old Swedish rookie known best for booming tee shots with his overlong driver, did his greatest damage with a delicate chip shot of only 60 feet. The result was his first victory after seven years of struggling. He came from behind in the final round of the Turespana Open de Canarias for a one-stroke win over Seve Ballesteros and Paul Eales.

"To win finishing ahead of Seve is a dream for me, because he is my hero," Sandelin said. It was a nightmare for Ballesteros. He led all the way and was just four holes from victory when he drove under a bush at the 15th and bogeyed, and Sandelin chipped in from 60 feet for a birdie to take the lead. Sandelin played the par-72 Maspalomas course on the Canary Islands in rounds of 74, 72, 66 and 70 for a 282 total, six under par. The 66 was a course record. Ballesteros shot 73–283, and Eales tied him with a final-round 71.

"He got more confident as the round went on," Ballesteros said. "He didn't make a mistake on the back nine."

Sandelin did on the first nine, though, after he double-bogeyed No. 2 and bogeyed No. 4. "I started off very nervous and hit the ball too soft," he said. "After those two sixes, I decided to hit everything as hard as I could, and it helped me control the ball better." He birdied three holes in a row from No. 6. Ballesteros bogeyed the 13th, then birdied the 14th from five feet. Sandelin matched him from seven feet. Then came the decisive 15th hole. Eales birdied the 13th and 18th to tie Ballesteros.

Sandelin worked a long, hard seven years' time for this. He failed in the qualifying tournament three times, and finally got on the PGA European Tour through the developmental Challenge Tour. "Now I know I did the right thing by turning professional," he said.

Turespana Open de Mediterrania—£300,000
Winner: Robert Karlsson

It was a question of pressure — specifically, could lanky Robert Karlsson, who missed five straight cuts at the end of the 1994 season, stand up to it? The answer at the Turespana Open de Mediterrania late in February: If it hadn't been for that rocky patch of over-eagerness on the final nine, he would have won by at least five strokes. Instead, he won by three.

Karlsson started with a course-record 64 in the first round and played Escorpion Club at Valencia in 276, 12 under par. His other scores were 69, 71 and 72. Karlsson, age 25, a seven-year veteran, became the eighth Swede to win on the PGA European Tour, and the fourth first-time winner of 1995. It was the breakthrough by fellow Swede Jarmo Sandelin in the Turespana Open de Canarias that inspired him.

"We young Swedes all thought, if he can handle it, so can we," said Karlsson, who more than handled it. Sam Torrance, who started the final round two strokes behind, seemed ready to apply the pressure. Torrance went out in 38, with bogeys at both par-fives, and three-putted the 14th. He closed with a flourish, though. At the 492-yard 18th, he hit a drive and a nine-iron second shot to two feet, and got the eagle three to make it a four-way tie for second place.

Karlsson took a five-stroke lead with birdies at the 10th and 11th, but then he got charged up — "A bit too aggressive," he said — and bogeyed three straight holes. He settled down, got his fourth birdie of the day at the 16th, and then his first win, crowning a Swedish holiday. There were six Swedes among the top eight finishers. Sandelin and Anders Forsbrand were in the four-way tie for second place, and Pierre Fulke, Per-Ulrik Johansson and Fredrik Lindgren tied for sixth.

Turespana Open de Andalucia—£296,025
Winner: Alexander Cejka

If anybody deserved a break, it was Alexander Cejka. First, it took him six cracks at the qualifying tournament to join the PGA European Tour. Then in 1994, he was sidelined for five weeks by sunstroke, he was disqualified from the Mercedes German Masters when a traffic jam caused him to miss his tee time after an opening 67, and a bout of food poisoning knocked him out of the Chemapol Trophy Czech Open. So when Cejka was talking about a dream come true, that's exactly what it was when he won the Turespana Open de Andalucia.

Cejka (pronounced "Chaker"), age 24, a native Czech but a naturalized German citizen, came from behind in the final two rounds to become the second German — after Bernhard Langer — to win a PGA European Tour event. "Maybe they will claim this as the first win by someone born in the

Czech Republic as well," he said. He was also the fourth first-time winner, and it was only early March. He played the par-71 Islantilla course in rounds of 71, 68, 70 and 69 for a 278 total, six under par, for a three-stroke victory over Costantino Rocca. Rocca, after shooting 65 in the second round, saw his chances pretty well die with a third-round 78.

Cejka trailed by three strokes in the first and second rounds, but was tied with Anders Forsbrand after the third round. Cejka jumped in front with a two-stroke swing off a birdie at No. 1, and birdied the second. He was four ahead on the first nine until Forsbrand birdied the eighth and ninth. The 13th, a chilling par-four of 463 yards with the green almost surrounded by trees, is where Cejka edged in front to stay. He played it shrewdly — four iron, eight iron 60 yards short, and a pitch to six feet. Then he holed the putt for his par four, which was more like a birdie. The 13th, which yielded only two birdies all week, played at an average of 4.99.

Moroccan Open—£350,000
Winner: Mark James

The Moroccan Open, in the second week of March, was something of a breakthrough — first win by a Briton after eight weeks of the 1995 PGA European Tour. It was something of a breakthrough for the winner, too.

"My putting has been bad for 18 years," Mark James said at the presentation ceremony, "but today it was brilliant." James, age 41, ended a career-long struggle with his short game — for the moment, anyway — by taking up the broomstick putter so favored by Sam Torrance. He even got some help from Torrance, and one-putted 10 times when he charged from behind with a final-round 65 that tied the fresh course record at the par-72 Royal Golf Links in Agadir, Morocco. And one of the men he overran? Torrance, of course. And then David Gilford, who set the record with 65 earlier in the afternoon.

James, picking up his 18th career victory, carded three 70s, then the 65 for a 13-under-par 275 total to edge Gilford by one stroke.

At first, it looked like a repeat victory for Alexander Cejka, the breakthrough winner the week before. Ignoring a sore knee, Cejka took the first-round lead with 66 that tied the soon-to-be-broken course record. He hit 17 greens and made six birdies. He was displaced by Torrance (70) and Robert Karlsson (69) in the second round. Going into the final round, Torrance led by one stroke over Karlsson, Cejka and James. Then it turned into a scramble.

"Every time I got a birdie, I was still only one ahead," James said. "I couldn't get away." Torrance's lead evaporated after No. 8. James made four birdies on the first nine and got to 10 under par. Karlsson led briefly with a birdie at the ninth, and saw his last chance die when he missed a four-foot birdie try at the 17th. Cejka made two birdies and an eagle on the second nine. But James and his new long putter marched on. "I've been just average for three days," he said. "I supposed today I must have been the best of a bad bunch."

Portuguese Open—£300,000
Winner: Adam Hunter

Maybe "Hunter" is Scottish for "perseverance." The PGA European Tour got its sixth first-time winner when Scotland's Adam Hunter — after 10 years and seven visits to the qualifying tournament — won the Portuguese Open in a playoff over Ireland's Darren Clarke.

"I've been making up the numbers for so long now that this is doubly sweet," said Hunter, age 31, who in six previous outings missed three cuts, and finished 55th, 68th, and then warmed up with a seventh in the Moroccan Open the week before. His career-best finish before this was fifth in 1994.

Hunter shot 73, 65, 71, 68 for a 277 total, 11 under par at Penha Longa, near Lisbon. He trailed, successively, by five strokes, then four, then was two behind co-leaders Clarke, Paul McGinley and Costantino Rocca going into the last round. Rocca started badly, and McGinley was two strokes ahead with six holes to play, but ran out of gas.

Hunter tied for the lead with a birdie at No. 11. He took sole possession of first place at the 13th with his fifth birdie of the day, but bogeys at the 14th and 16th knocked him back, thus setting up his crowning moment. At the 18th hole, he hit a driver off the fairway, 275 yards to within eight feet. The eagle putt never touched the hole — "I completely misread it," he said — but he birdied. Clarke had to birdie the 18th to win, but the best he could do was par, and they were tied. They returned to No. 18 for the playoff. Hunter tried the driver off the fairway again, but caught a greenside bunker. Clarke's approach ended up in the rough off the green. His chip was 30 feet short, and he missed the birdie putt. Hunter came out of the bunker to four feet, but he didn't miss.

Turespana Open de Baleares—£242,879
Winner: Greg Turner

Sometimes the gods of golf smile on you when you're looking the other way, as Greg Turner discovered at the Turespana Open de Baleares. Turner had played just four times in four months, and so came to Santa Ponsa II, on Majorca, hoping to work out the kinks. Much to his surprise, he ended up winning, holding off a hard-charging Costantino Rocca by two strokes.

"I'd have been happy with a top-20 finish," Turner confessed. That's better than where he was headed when he opened the tournament with a triple-bogey seven. His first-round 74, two over par, left him seven strokes behind co-leaders Mark Mouland and Pedro Linhart.

Turner exploded onto the leaderboard with a course-record 65 in the second round, took a three-stroke lead with 67 in the third, and soon the gods were smiling in the fourth. He birdied the par-three second hole and made a two-putt birdie at the eighth for an outward 34. Coming back, he birdied the 10th from seven feet, but seemed doomed when he drove deep into the trees at the 11th.

"But I knew it was my day," he said, "when I found a good lie and had a clear sight of the green." He fired a six iron to six feet and got the birdie. Turner, who finished with 68 and a 274 total, 14 under par, was 10 under for his last 35 holes, without dropping a stroke.

Rocca was out in 33, and got within two strokes with birdies at the 12th, from seven feet, and 13th, from 14 feet. His chase ran out of steam at the last four holes, where he got within about 20 feet of the hole each time but couldn't get the putts to drop. He finished with 67 and a 276 total, and was runner-up for the second time in his last four outings.

Miguel Angel Jimenez, who shot 280, birdied two of the last three holes for a solo third place. Fourth place, at 281, was shared by a couple of strong finishers. Jean Van de Velde birdied four holes coming in for 68, and Barry Lane birdied the 16th from 17 feet and the par-five 17th with two putts from 10 feet for 71.

Turespana Open de Catalonia—£300,000
Winner: Philip Walton

Even the mid-April weather was scripted for this one. The "tramontana," the fierce Pyrenees wind in northeastern Spain, blasted the Peralada course near Girona all week, but then it relented that final day to set up the decisive moment.

Ireland's Philip Walton had charged into the lead on the second nine with a burst of three birdies — a 12-foot putt at the par-three 12th, two putts at the 13th and a four-footer for another two at the 14th. Then came the pressure from Andrew Coltart, the promising young Scot. It peaked at the last hole.

"After he eagled the 17th, I knew I had to rip my drive down the last and make another birdie," Walton said. "I had only a nine-iron second, and I managed to knock it to a foot." Coltart, who started the day one stroke behind Walton and two behind leader Howard Clark, ignored a double bogey at the 11th to birdie the 15th and eagle the 17th with two three-wood shots to two feet. Then he bogeyed the 18th to Walton's birdie and finished second by three strokes.

Walton, who never led until the second-nine birdie binge, shot rounds of 68, 74, 71 and 68 for a 281 total, seven under par, for his second PGA European Tour victory. Only two others broke par on the wind-battered, par-72 course — Coltart at 284 and Clark, 285.

"I was disappointed to get a flyer from the rough at the last," Coltart said, "but I would have taken second place at the start of the week. It was a week I was starting to think would never finish." He wasn't alone in his thinking. Five players withdrew or did not return cards. Among them were Steen Tinning, who left the first day after the wind blew three drives out of bounds at the 10th, and Anders Forsbrand, who left after nine holes in the second round. Said Sam Torrance, "It might have had something to do with the fact that he was 14 over par."

Air France Cannes Open—£225,000
Winner: Andre Bossert

If anyone could say a win is a win is a win, it was Andre Bossert. Critics may note that the Air France Cannes Open was only a 36-hole tournament, cut short by heavy April showers. But Bossert did his part better than 144 others did, and that made it a victory. In winning, Bossert logged not only his own first victory in six years on the PGA European Tour, but the first win ever by a golfer from Switzerland. He was also the sixth first-time winner of the year. Bossert's 65-67–132 total, 10 under par at the par-71 Royal Mougins course, gave him a two-stroke victory over Norway's Oyvind Rojahn and France's Jean Van de Velde.

"It's my first win, and that's what I've been waiting for," Bossert said. It was hardly an empty victory. The field had its share of headliners: Colin Montgomerie tied for 13th, Costantino Rocca and Ian Woosnam tied for 21st, and Sam Torrance tied for 35th.

Bossert's opening 65 left him one stroke off the lead shared by Van de Velde and Mathias Gronberg. Then in the winds of Friday, Van de Velde shot 70 and Gronberg lifted to 72, clearing the way for Bossert. He closed hard, with birdies at the 15th and 17th holes for 67 and his first bogey-free round.

Bossert, age 31, puzzled spectators with his South African accent. Simple, he explained. He was born of Swiss parents in Johannesburg, and they still live there. But he's still Swiss and the rest of his family lives in Switzerland.

Tournoi Perrier de Paris—£350,000
Winners: Seve Ballesteros and Jose Maria Olazabal

The Spanish Armada was off and flying early, and it was only April. Anytime Seve Ballesteros and Jose Maria Olazabal are partners, it's magic, and it was again in the Tournoi Perrier de Paris. They raced through the team event with 63 in the opening fourballs, then 67 (foursomes), 64 (greensomes) and 62 (fourballs) for a 256 total, 24 under par, and a three-stroke victory over Australians Mike Clayton and Peter O'Malley at the par-70 Golf de Saint-Cloud course.

Ballesteros and Olazabal had lost only twice as a team in 15 Ryder Cup matches, and it was like old times in the cool and rainy Paris spring. "Everything went right," Ballesteros said. "When I was off, Jose was there, and when he was off, I was there." Said Olazabal: "We think the same way. You always have to be in play. That's the first key. You can't be too aggressive, but as soon as you can, we attack the flag." Everybody knows that, but doing it is another matter, and nobody does it better than they do.

Examples: At No. 4 the last day, Olazabal hit a wedge shot to three feet, but Ballesteros saved him the trouble of putting by holing his 20-foot putt. At No. 10, Ballesteros hooked his drive into the trees, but Olazabal fired a six iron from 169 yards to two feet. And at the 16th, Ballesteros lobbed his wedge to one foot, and Olazabal put his two feet and this time saved his friend the trouble.

Colin Montgomerie and Ian Woosnam, who finished third, did not enjoy the same kind of harmony. On Friday, Montgomerie overhit the green at the par-three 13th and left Woosnam in a bush. "I said sorry," Montgomerie said, deadpan, "and I was still saying sorry all the way up the next hole. He wouldn't talk to me."

The Spaniards started the final round with three birdies from No. 2, and Clayton and O'Malley poured on the pressure with eight birdies in nine holes from No. 4. The Spaniards birdied two of three around the turn, then Ballesteros birdied the 13th from seven feet, and Olazabal parred the 15th from 10 feet, and it was all but over.

In case anyone thought the Spaniards had their hearts completely in Paris, Ballesteros had a reminder. "You can send a fax immediately across the Atlantic," he said. "Tell them we want the Cup back, and we're ready."

Conte de Florence Italian Open—£370,449
Winner: Sam Torrance

The story is an old one: Sam Torrance's latest ailment is so severe, he can't possibly play. Then he goes out and wins. That's exactly what he did in the Conte de Florence Italian Open. Waking with a sore upper thigh tendon Thursday morning, he called and cancelled the bet he had placed on himself. But at the practice range, he found he could swing and didn't withdraw. "It hurt the first day," Torrance said. "I'm glad I made the effort."

The effort was rounds of 69, 70, 63 and 67 for a 269 total, 19 under par at Le Rovedine, near Milan, and a two-stroke victory over Jose Rivero, the man he also beat for the 1987 Italian Open title.

England's Neal Briggs set the early pace, shaking off a bogey at No. 3 to make six birdies plus an eagle at the 18th for 65 at the par-72 course. Ronan Rafferty (68) moved ahead in the second round, and then Torrance took over with a course-record 63 — nine birdies and nine pars — in the third round and was on his way to his first victory since 1993. It wasn't automatic, however.

Costantino Rocca trailed Torrance by one stroke going into the final round, and caught him with a birdie at No. 1. Then, with Rocca making bogey at No. 3, Torrance got three quick birdies — a chip-in at No. 3, a wedge to six inches at No. 4 and a nine iron to 12 feet at No. 6 for a three-stroke lead going out.

Things changed a bit coming in. Torrance bogeyed the 11th from rough and trees, letting Rivero get within one stroke. Rivero birdied the 11th, 15th, 16th and 18th for 66. But Torrance answered with birdies on three of the last four for his 67 and the win.

Benson & Hedges International Open—£650,000
Winner: Peter O'Malley

And sometimes the race goes to the stubborn. Australian Peter O'Malley, who won the 1992 Bell's Scottish Open with a seven-under-par sprint over the last five holes, this time took the lead in the second round, lost it in the fourth, and rallied to finish first in the Benson & Hedges International Open at St. Mellion.

"This victory is special because I've had to live with the pressure all the way," said O'Malley, after the second win in his seven years on the PGA European Tour. O'Malley grabbed the lead in the second round with a course-record-tying 65 for a five-stroke edge. That shrank to two strokes in the third round over Carl Mason, who set the course record with 63, and Costantino

Rocca, who shot 64.

It seemed the pressure was getting to O'Malley in the fourth round. His lead fell to one stroke when he bogeyed from a bunker at No. 1. Mason tied him with a birdie at No. 3, and then pulled ahead at the par-three fourth when O'Malley missed the green and bogeyed. Mason's putter cost him two bogeys heading to the turn, and Mark James edged in front with a birdie at No. 8. James faded with two quick bogeys, then flirted with victory with birdies at the 14th and 16th holes. A bogey at the tough 18th left him at 281, and a tie for second place with Rocca, who bogeyed the last two holes. Mason birdied the 15th and 17th, then also stumbled at the 18th for 73 and a tie for fourth.

O'Malley birdied the par-five 12th, fired a seven iron to three feet at the 13th, and soon was facing the dangerous par-four 18th, where he had hit a shot in the water in the third round. He figured he needed a four, and so hit a booming drive to set up a safe approach over the water. He then hit an eight iron to the fringe of the green, but bogeyed anyway with a poor chip and two putts from eight feet. The five was still good enough for a one-stroke victory on rounds of 68, 65, 74 and 73 for an eight-under-par 280 total.

Peugeot Open de Espana—£550,000
Winner: Seve Ballesteros

"I felt very uncomfortable — I had no tempo and I was hitting it all over the place," Seve Ballesteros was saying. "I knew I wasn't going to play very well today, but I still didn't expect to start with three bogeys." One might cringe at the thought of Seve playing at full steam. Because these weren't the words of a man who had just shot 100. Ballesteros had just run off with the Peugeot Open de Espana by two strokes.

Ballesteros never led. He started the tournament four strokes behind after Peter Mitchell converted three eagle-threes into 66. Ballesteros started the final round one stroke behind leader Gordon Brand, Jr. and immediately crashed to three straight bogeys. Who could ask for a deeper hole? Thus inspired, Ballesteros scrambled back for the win at the sunny and hot Club de Campo in Madrid. He shot 70, 67, 66 and 71 for a 14-under-par 274 total. Brand, closing with a three-over-par 75, slipped to fourth place, far enough for Jose Rivero (68) and Ignacio Garrido (69), age 23, son of former Ryder Cup player Antonio Garrido, to tie for second and delight Ballesteros with the Spanish showing.

Ballesteros started his comeback with a birdie at No. 4 and was out in 38 and tied at 11 under par by Rivero, who had four birdies going out, and Garrido, who had three. Rivero birdied the par-five 12th and was the early leader at 276. Garrido tied him with two birdies and a bogey coming home, while Brand bogeyed the 10th and 11th.

Ballesteros jumped through the crack. He reached the 12th in two and birdied, then locked it up with two dazzling birdies — a sand wedge to five feet at the 15th, and a pitching wedge to four at the 18th.

Volvo PGA Championship—£900,000
Winner: Bernhard Langer

Colin Montgomerie was pleased, but not without reservation. He finally holed a putt, there in a last round. "Amazing," he said. "But Langer," he added, "isn't the man you want to be chasing."

That pretty well said it all at the Volvo PGA Championship at Wentworth. A tough front-runner, Bernhard Langer was on his way to his third PGA title, in the process matching one record and setting another. The victory marked the 17th consecutive year in which he had won at least once, tying Seve Ballesteros' record of making the cut for the 57th successive time, breaking Neil Coles' record of 56. He did it all on rounds of 67, 73, 68 and 71 for a 279 total, nine under par, for a one-stroke victory.

Langer is nothing if not persistent, and he proved it again down the final stretch. He entered the last round sharing a one-stroke lead with Mark Mouland at eight under par. He dropped back with a bogey at No. 3, then came back with birdie at No. 5 on a 20-foot putt. A birdie at the 11th put him nine under par, and with Mouland slipping, Per-Ulrik Johansson made a move. He reached the par-five 12th hole with a five wood and two-putted for a birdie to go to eight under.

Michael Campbell, the young New Zealander, started the day at three under, and whipped home in a sensational finish, an eagle and three birdies for 67 and the clubhouse lead at eight under par. Langer bogeyed the 13th and slipped back to eight under, but returned to the lead at the par-three 14th with a seven iron to four feet. He parred home for the win.

Langer's secret? "There have been days when I have not felt comfortable with my swing," he said, "and my short game has always pulled me through." That and patience and persistence.

Murphy's English Open—£650,000
Winner: Philip Walton

Let's see — the man is on the verge of pneumonia, has a sore throat, a sore eye, he's loaded with antibiotics, and then he wins? Sam Torrance, of course.

No, it was Philip Walton, making Murphy's English Open his second victory of the season, and his third on the PGA European Tour, and in a playoff. The victim was Colin Montgomerie, who still had a perfect playoff record — 0-4. "I love playoffs," Montgomerie said. "No, I'll rephrase that. I hate playoffs."

Walton, on the other hand, loves playoffs. He also has a perfect record — 2-0. He beat Bernhard Langer in the 1990 French Open for his first victory. Walton and Montgomerie turned this tournament into their personal match play event, flip-flopping from the outset at Forest of Arden. Walton tied for the first-round lead with 65, and Montgomerie was four strokes behind. Montgomerie leaped three strokes ahead of Walton in the second round with 63 to go to 12 under par. "I'll be disappointed not to win from here," Montgomerie said, prophetically.

They shared the lead at 12 under par going into the final round. Montgomerie was out in 34, with four birdies. Walton, out in 35, birdied the 10th with a nine iron to two feet. Then he bogeyed the 14th from a bunker, and Montgomerie matched him by missing the green at the 15th. At the par-five 17th, Montgomerie chipped to six inches, and Walton, after watering his second, averted defeat by pitching to about that distance. They parred the 18th and ended up tied at 14-under-par 274, Walton on 65-70-69-70, Montgomerie on 69-63-72-70.

They parred the first playoff hole, and at the second, the 17th, both were short of the green in two. Walton chipped to three feet, but Montgomerie left his chip 20 feet short. Montgomerie missed his putt, but Walton didn't.

"With a sore eye and nearly having pneumonia, I win the Murphy's English Open," Walton said. "When I'm healthy next week, I start missing cuts again."

Deutsche Bank Open—£650,000
Winner: Bernhard Langer

When Bernhard Langer said he couldn't tell people how he managed to win the Deutsche Bank Open — just two weeks after his first win of the season — he meant it literally.

"It was a tough week because I had the flu and found it hard to swallow and talk," Langer said, after an easy, six-shot runaway at Gut Kaden in Hamburg. "In fact, it's hard to explain how I won."

One explanation is the beware-the-sick-golfer story. Philip Walton creaked and groaned to a victory the week before, and Sam Torrance some weeks earlier, so it was time for Langer, who is not far behind Torrance in afflictions. There was nothing wrong with his game, though, despite the chill, wind and rain that early-June week. He grabbed the lead in the first round by one stroke over Costantino Rocca and a revived Jamie Spence, and roared away from there, never so much as approaching Gut Kaden's par of 72. Expanding his lead from one to four strokes, to five, then six, Langer played the 7,029-yard course in rounds of 67, 66, 68 and 69, for an 18-under-par total of 280. Spence dogged him — if that's the word — all the way and finished second at 276.

There wasn't much left for the observers except to note the goings-on elsewhere. The U.S. Open was coming up the next week. Who was ready? Big-hitting John Daly didn't seem to be. He had trouble with the winds, made three bogeys and a double bogey in the first five holes of the second round, and with 72-77 was two strokes above the cut, which came in at a robust three-over 147. Of the two other possible contenders in the field, Ian Woosnam was encouraged by a new driver that was hitting straighter, if shorter, and Colin Montgomerie was unhappy with his putting. Langer didn't leave a great deal more to talk about.

DHL Jersey Open—£300,000
Winner: Andrew Oldcorn

Andrew Oldcorn can pinpoint the moment he sank his teeth into the DHL Jersey Open. It was at La Moye's par-four 10th hole in the third round. He was comfortably in the hunt at six under par when his sand wedge approach from 80 yards hit about 10 feet past the pin, bit hard, and spun back into the hole for an eagle two. Then at the 502-yard 11th, in chilling rain and hail, he fired a four-iron approach to 12 feet and holed the putt for another eagle.

First, that had him on his way. Second, it had him scratching his head. "It was spooky stuff," said Oldcorn, who had been consulting a psychoanalyst for his game. "There should be an inquiry. You can't shoot 30 on the back nine. Not in this weather, anyway." That gave him 66 against La Moye's par of 72, and a three-stroke lead that he kept without much trouble for his second career victory. The first was in the 1993 Andalucia Open.

Oldcorn stayed firmly in control in the fourth round with a birdie from six feet at No. 5 and another from 15 at No. 8 for 34 out. He came home in 35 with birdies at both par-fives and a bogey for his clinching 69. He shot 70-68-66-69–273, 15 under par, for a three-stroke win over Scotland's Dean Robertson, a former Walker Cup player. Robertson came home in 33 with three birdies, including a gem of a two iron to two feet at the par-three 14th for his best finish in two years on the PGA European Tour.

Peugeot Open de France—£550,000
Winner: Paul Broadhurst

The face was familiar and so was the game — Paul Broadhurst, 1989 Rookie of the Year, winner of the 1993 Benson & Hedges International Open, and something of a missing person since. Broadhurst announced his return at the Peugeot Open de France with a hot 67 in the first round and a blistering course-record 63 in the final round for an eight-stroke victory at The National Golf Club, near Versailles.

"You can't explain it," he said. "That's golf. You don't know what happens." Here's what he made happen: 67, 75, 69 and 63 for a 274 total, 14 under par and eight strokes ahead of runner-up Neal Briggs, an eight-time visitor to the qualifying tournament, in his best finish.

Broadhurst's opening 67 was better than it looked. He had eight birdies in his first 14 holes, then the late-June winds came up hard and cost him two bogeys over the last four holes. The next day, the wind nearly blew him away, to 75, and Greg Turner took the lead (70–140). Costantino Rocca was in the lead going into the final round (66–207) and had the only real chance once Broadhurst caught fire. But Rocca dropped four shots over the first two holes, and Broadhurst, down by four strokes at the start, made four birdies over his first six holes, including a 25-footer at No. 2 and a 10-footer at No. 4 that gave him the lead. He was out in 32. Then he got down to business.

At the 13th, he hit a wedge to one foot; the 14th, chip-and-putt; the 15th, seven iron to six feet; the par-three 16th, a five iron to four feet, and the par-five 18th, driver, three iron, chip to 10 feet. That's five birdies over his last six holes, followed by a huge sigh of relief. "After last season, when I only won £36,000, my aim was to keep my card," he said. "I couldn't let myself think any further than that. Now..."

BMW International Open—£550,000
Winner: Frank Nobilo

Sooner or later, it seems, everybody tries putting cross-handed, and it paid off for Frank Nobilo, but only after a visit to the eye doctor. The two are not necessarily connected, but Nobilo definitely needed the doctor more than a new putting method after his vision began to blur in May. It turned out that his condition had been misdiagnosed, and the medication was hurting instead of helping. Once he got that straightened out, he could focus on golf. The bearded New Zealander, on rounds of 67, 69, 69 and 67, came from behind to make the BMW International Open at St. Eurach, Munich, his fourth European victory, his first since 1993.

Nobilo's 16-under-par 272 total won by two strokes over Bernhard Langer, trying for his third victory of the season, and Sweden's Jarmo Sandelin, who might have had his career and season second victory except for taking a great fall. He trailed by three strokes in the second round, then shot 63 in the third round and soared to a five-stroke lead going into the final round. And then he crashed to 74.

"Defending a five-shot lead is precarious," Nobilo offered. "Somebody is always liable to do something at this level unless you produce a good score." And he was the "somebody."

Nobilo, who started the final round five shots behind Sandelin, made his move immediately. He eagled No. 1 with an iron second to six feet. He bogeyed No. 2, but at No. 5 started a harvest of five birdies in eight holes that took him into the lead. When Sandelin made six at the 16th off an errant drive, Nobilo's lead was up to three. He bogeyed the last hole, but he could afford to. "Not only is it difficult to claw five shots back in one round," a relieved Nobilo said, "but the halfway cuts are getting lower, and the standard of play is getting higher."

Murphy's Irish Open—£667,000
Winner: Sam Torrance

Murphy's Irish Open, at the Mount Juliet course in Kilkenny, had to be admired first for its diversity of attractions. There was winless Sven Struver, age 27, the German with the Scandinavian name, breathless at leading through the first two rounds for the first time (he tied for fourth). Bernhard Langer, the defending champion, stretching his record of cuts made to 60 (his try for a third 1995 victory ended up in the water at the 13th). And gloomy Seve Ballesteros, missing his third straight cut and saying his confidence, on a scale of 10, was maybe a one.

Then there was rejuvenated Howard Clark, wondering why a birdie putt wins other playoffs but not this one, and Sam Torrance explaining that eagles beat birdies. And this was a Torrance taking his second victory of the year without any known aches or pains.

A one-over-par 73 knocked Struver off the top in the third round. Colin Montgomerie, ever in the hunt, shot 69 for a one-stroke lead over David Gilford, Greg Norman and Torrance going into the final round. What happened next on that balmy Sunday early in July was a scorekeeper's carnival.

At one point, 10 players were within two strokes of the lead. That included Langer, who sank at the 13th. He tied for 20th place. Stuart Cage, who turned 22 during the week, parred in from the 11th for 69 and the clubhouse lead at 11 under par. Clark, who last won in 1988, popped into the lead with an outward 33. He lost three strokes at the 13th and 14th, rebounded for birdies at the next three. Montgomerie plunged from sight — a lost ball and a triple bogey at No. 4, a bogey at the 15th, another at the 17th.

Clark and Torrance both bogeyed the 18th, keeping Cage alive. In the playoff, Cage left at the first extra hole on a badly hooked approach. Clark and Torrance parred and went to the second playoff hole, the par-five 17th. There, Torrance hit a career shot, a 240-yard three wood that pulled up nine feet from the cup. "As good a shot as I've ever hit under pressure," Torrance said. Clark missed the fairway, then the green, then chipped poorly to 15 feet. Clark made his birdie — and then Torrance made his winning eagle.

Scottish Open—£650,000
Winner: Wayne Riley

They can't say Wayne Riley did it the easy way. Riley, a 33-year-old Australian, felt the hot breath of Nick Faldo and Colin Montgomerie, and survived to make the Scottish Open the first victory of his 12 years on the PGA European Tour.

"To go head-to-head with Monty on Friday and Nick on Saturday and come out on top — you can't ask for anything more than that," Riley said after touring classic old Carnoustie in rounds of 66, 69, 69 and 72 for a 276 total, 12 under par, for a two-stroke win over Faldo.

Riley, who was two behind Montgomerie's opening lead of 64, could add Ian Woosnam to that murderers' row of stars standing between him and his first victory. Woosnam was in the hunt in the first round, then bowed out with a 74-78 middle. Riley (69) tied Montgomerie at nine-under-par 135 through 36 holes, then surged into a five-stroke lead over Faldo with another 69 going into the final round. Montgomerie was another stroke back. Then the real pressure began.

Riley birdied No. 3 from eight feet, and Faldo bogeyed the fourth and fifth. Riley, of course, wasn't silly enough to think it was over. And it wasn't. Faldo birdied three in a row from No. 6, on putts of seven, 25 and eight feet. Riley tripped at No. 7 and dropped a shot. He was out in 36 and headed home four strokes ahead of Faldo. Montgomerie, out in 35, bogeyed No. 10. Faldo birdied the par-three 13th from four feet to cut Riley's margin to three, and then Riley added to the suspense with a bogey at No. 16. But he finished strong with a birdie from 25 feet at the 17th, then parred the 18th. Faldo birdied it, and Montgomerie had finished with three birdies over the last five holes. Faldo finished two behind, and Montgomerie two behind him.

British Open Championship—£1,340,700
Winner: John Daly

See Chapter 5.

Heineken Dutch Open—£650,000
Winner: Scott Hoch

While everyone was watching newly crowned British Open champion John Daly, another American was making off with the Heineken Dutch Open title. This was Scott Hoch, coming from behind to pluck the victory from Sam Torrance and Swedish rookie Michael Jonzon. Hoch, professing indifference to the Ryder Cup but pleased at making a Ryder Cup showing, played the par-71 Hilversum course in rounds of 65, 70, 69 and 65 for a 269 total, 15 under par, for a two-stroke victory.

"It's great to beat all your Ryder Cup guys," Hoch said. "I'm 13th on our list and though I would like to play, it won't concern me too much if I don't make it." In fact, he did beat most of the European point leaders — Torrance, Colin Montgomerie, Philip Walton, Costantino Rocca, Mark James, Ian Woosnam and Bernhard Langer.

Hoch's victory was hardly clear sailing from the start. Walton and he tied for the first-round lead with six-under-par 65s, and then Torrance, seeking his third victory of the season, stepped up the pace. Torrance jumped into the halfway lead with 64 in the second round for a two-stroke lead, and three over Hoch, who still trailed by three in the third round when Frank Nobilo, with 65, joined Torrance in the lead at 12-under-par 201.

"I knew I needed a low round, and I got one," Hoch was to say. In the fourth round, Hoch carded seven birdies and one bogey for 65. It carried him past Jonzon, who led briefly with three successive birdies for 66. Torrance, after chipping in for a birdie at the 17th, needed an eagle at the par-five 18th to tie Hoch. A bunkered approach shot ended that possibility.

Volvo Scandinavian Masters—£650,000
Winner: Jesper Parnevik

Jesper Parnevik became the first Swede to win on Swedish soil in the 22 years of the Volvo Scandinavian Masters, but a bitter memory may have had as much to do with it as a surge of national pride.

Parnevik took the lead in the second round, and he felt the pressure in the final round when Colin Montgomerie pulled within two strokes with a birdie at No. 2. Just over a year earlier, Nick Price took the 1994 British Open from him with a dramatic finish. This time, Parnevik headed Montgomerie, dropping an 18-foot putt for a birdie at No. 7. Four more birdies over the last seven holes gave him an easy five-stroke victory and left Montgomerie with his third runner-up finish and his ninth top-10 placing.

"It has to be the best win of my career," said Parnevik, after his 67-67-69-67—270 performance, in the early-August heat at Barseback in Malmo. He had one other win on the PGA European Tour and three victories on the Challenge Tour.

Only once did Parnevik open the door, and it was with his lone flaw in 72 holes. It happened at No. 3 in the third round, where a bunker and a three-putt cost him a double-bogey six. That put Michael Campbell, who threatened at the British Open, into the lead by two strokes. Not for long. Campbell stumbled to three bogeys, then Parnevik chalked up four birdies in seven holes from No. 6 en route to 69 and a three-stroke lead after the third round. Campbell birdied four of the last six holes for 70 and a tie for second with Montgomerie, but a final-round 76 dropped him to 10th.

Hohe Brucke Austrian Open—£250,000
Winner: Alexander Cejka

Alexander Cejka made it a breakthrough year when he took not only his second victory of the season but the second of his seven-year career. And he didn't leave much to the imagination doing it. Cejka set records and season-lows all over the place in running away with the Hohe Brucke Austrian Open at Waldviertel Golf Club in Litschau, Austria. The raw numbers were impressive enough: 61-68-68-70–267, 21 under par and a four-stroke victory.

Cejka, who won the Turespana Open de Andalucia in March, became the PGA European Tour's fifth double-winner of the year, and rang up these accomplishments: His opening 61 was the course record by three strokes and the lowest first round of the year on the Tour. His 129 total for two rounds was two shots lower than Colin Montgomerie's 131 in the season-opener at Dubai. His three-round total of 197 was three lower than Jarmo Sandelin's 200 in the BMW International Open. Finally, his 267 total was a stroke lower than Fred Couples' winning 268 at Dubai. And it all started at the first tee in the first round.

Cejka left the field gasping with birdies at the first six holes. He added five more along the way for the 61. "It was one of those days when the putter was hot and I didn't make any stupid mistakes," he said. And he was never in trouble. He led by four strokes after the first and second rounds, by five after the third, and then by four for the victory.

Chemapol Trophy Czech Open—£750,000
Winner: Peter Teravainen

It was a mystery of the East solving a puzzle in the West.

Most agreed that Peter Teravainen, a 39-year-old American who had played on the PGA European Tour since 1982, ought to have won long ago but victory always was denied for some reason or another. The latest problem was a painful injury to his shins. "I could hardly play golf because of the pain," he said. His wife came to the rescue, bringing some Chinese medical bandages from their Singapore home. "There has been a marked improvement," he said. So marked, in fact, that he scored the first victory of his career in the Chemapol Trophy Czech Open at Marianske Lazne Golf Club in Marienbad.

Teravainen, who tied for the lead in the second round, was one stroke behind Howard Clark and Ronan Rafferty going into the fourth round. Rafferty soon was the man to beat, but he was out in 39, losing his lead of two strokes over Teravainen and three over Clark. Clark birdied the 10th, 11th, 14th and 15th holes, and was one stroke ahead of Teravainen with three holes to play. Clark finished with two bogeys and a birdie, and Teravainen locked up the victory with a two-putt birdie at the par-five 17th and a two-putt par at the 18th. He shot rounds of 67, 66, 68 and 67 for a 268 total, 16 under par.

"It had been my worst year in Europe in 14 years," Teravainen said. "I lost my confidence because I was unable to use my legs in the swing. Now it's got to be my best year." The money should see to it. He had won only some £9,000 coming in. His best previous year was 1991, £112,536. His first prize here was £125,000. "This," he cracked, "brings me up to broke."

Volvo German Open—£650,000
Winner: Colin Montgomerie

Sam Torrance couldn't hold on in the Volvo German Open, and defending champion Colin Montgomerie whizzed by for his first victory of the year. Montgomerie also leapfrogged from fourth place and knocked Torrance off the top of the money list, strengthening his bid for a third straight No. 1 finish.

Not that Montgomerie won by default. He did his part with two closing birdies for a card of 69-64-68-67–268, 16 under par and a one-stroke win at the GolfClub Schloss Nippenburg in Stuttgart. But it had been Torrance's tournament to lose, and he did.

"It just wasn't my day," Torrance said. That pretty well sums up a round in which he three-putted only once, that at No. 1, caught a flyer and bogeyed No. 2, then hit a shot into the water at No. 9 and double-bogeyed, and tied for second with Sweden's Nicklas Fasth.

In the final round, Stuart Cage, a young Englishman, got five birdies on the first nine and birdied the 13th to reach 16 under par. Then he faded to a tie for fourth place. Fasth made four birdies going out, birdied the 10th and 13th to reach 15 under, then bogeyed the 16th. Torrance bounced back from his bogey at No. 2 with an eagle at No. 4 off a five-iron shot to six feet. He double-bogeyed the ninth hole, then made three birdies in four holes from the 12th to go to 16 under par for a one-stroke lead. He bogeyed the 16th after driving into deep grass, parred the 17th, and at the par-five 18th, he had to scramble for a par after driving into the rough.

Montgomerie clinched the victory with two closing birdies — a 30-foot putt at the 17th and a chip and a tap-in at the 18th. Reactions? Said Torrance, "I'm livid, devastated." Montgomerie wasn't exactly sympathetic. "No one deserves a victory more than I do," he said. "I didn't come here to be second."

Canon European Masters—£700,000
Winner: Mathias Gronberg

Don't look at the scoreboard? Jesper Parnevik refused to look in the 1994 British Open, and it cost him the title. But it worked for Mathias Gronberg in the Canon European Masters at Crans-sur-Sierre, Switzerland. "Concentrate on your own game and don't look at the scoreboard," said Gronberg, 25, in his third year on the PGA European Tour. And so in this first week of September, the Tour had its fourth Swedish winner of the season and the ninth first-time winner (counting American veterans Fred Couples, John Daly and Scott Hoch). He rose into contention in the third round and won by two strokes over Barry Lane and Costantino Rocca, shooting rounds of 70, 65, 66 and 69 for a 270 total, 18 under par.

Gronberg, a surprise even to himself, had caught some of those magical moments, such as his six-under-par 66 in the third round that put him on top. "I've never led a tournament at this stage," Gronberg said. "I might have shot 63, but I three-putted from 15 feet at No. 4, then missed from two feet at the 13th."

Gronberg, who had missed 12 cuts in his previous 24 starts, didn't crack in final round despite some heavy pressure. Lane, who started the day seven strokes behind, was out in 31 with six birdies, added another at the par-three 11th on a 30-foot putt, eagled the par-five 15th with a 12-footer, and birdied the 17th from 15 feet. He three-putted the 18th for a bogey and 64. Rocca was out in 32 with three birdies and an eagle two at No. 7, then birdied the 15th and 16th for 66.

Gronberg, meanwhile, birdied the par-three third hole from six feet, bogeyed No. 4, and got three more birdies for an outward 33. He missed the 12th green and bogeyed, giving Lane a brief share of the lead, then regained his lead at the 15th, chipping close for a birdie, and he parred in for the win.

The tournament was notable for two other reasons. Both Greg Norman and Seve Ballesteros missed the 36-hole cut.

Trophee Lancome—£600,000
Winner: Colin Montgomerie

The Colin and Sam Show resumed at the Trophee Lancome early in September, and it was Colin Montgomerie again, this time by one stroke over Sam Torrance at St. Nom la Breteche, near Paris, France. Last time, at the Volvo German Open three weeks earlier, Montgomerie said nobody deserved a victory more than he did. While he still felt that way, he credited a "miraculous shot" at the final hole for saving him this time.

"Sam had a six-foot putt for a birdie two, which he went on to make," Montgomerie said, "and I faced a 30-yard, downhill chip off hard ground over a bunker. I could have had 100 balls and never got it closer." With an exquisite touch, Montgomerie got to three feet, holed the par putt, and beat Torrance for his second victory of the season, tightening his grip on a third consecutive No. 1 finish on the money list.

Montgomerie totaled an 11-under-par 269 on rounds of 64, 69, 65 and 71. He led Torrance by one stroke in the first round, and Torrance (65-67-69-69–270) reversed that in the second round. Montgomerie had much the better of it going into the final round, with a three-stroke lead. Next back was Wayne Riley, seven strokes behind. The only other thing that interrupted the show was Jean Louis Guepy's course-record 62 in the second round. Guepy had opened with 77, and he tied for 26th place.

It was strictly a two-man race, and not all that much of one until the tense finish. Montgomerie, who never lost the lead, bogeyed the first and fourth holes, then made three birdies in four holes from No. 5. Torrance was still two behind coming to the par-three 18th. There, he fired a five iron to six feet, and Montgomerie hooked a six-iron shot long, into a tight, tramped-down lie with a bunker in front and water beyond the down-sloping green. "It was not my idea of fun," Montgomerie said. Not until he chipped it to three feet and holed the winner.

Torrance and Montgomerie played together all four days. "You end up running out of things to say to each other," Montgomerie said.

Collingtree British Masters—£650,000
Winner: Sam Torrance

It was clear from New Zealand rookie Michael Campbell's performance in the British Open that he would be chalking up that first victory pretty soon, and the Collingtree British Masters was just about it. But as Sam Torrance demonstrated, it was going to take a bit more seasoning.

Torrance led through the second and third rounds, but soon felt the heat in the fourth round as the 26-year-old Campbell surged ahead with three successive birdies down the stretch. Then came Campbell's fatal errors. He three-putted the 16th hole and fell back into a tie with Torrance, and they were still tied going to the par-five 18th. Torrance drove into the short rough to the left, but Campbell fired his tee shot into the water. He took a penalty drop, and forced the issue with a huge three-wood shot 257 yards over more water, to the green. "Michael hit a fantastic shot and forced me to go for it," Torrance said. "I hit a ripper."

Both were on the green, 30 feet from the hole, and both putted three feet past. Campbell holed his for a par, and then Torrance holed his for a birdie, a three-under-par 69, and his third win of the season. Torrance played Collingtree Park in rounds of 67, 66, 68 and 69 for a 270 total, 18 under par. Campbell shot 70-67-66-68—271.

Torrance jumped over Colin Montgomerie and back to the top of the money list. "What do you make of that — a 42-year-old at the top," Torrance said. "I haven't been so happy since my children were born." Montgomerie tied for seventh place.

If anybody was surprised by Torrance's performance, it wasn't his father and teacher, Bob Torrance, who told him that he would play his best golf in his 40s. And why? "I don't know," Sam said. "The old bugger wouldn't tell me. But he's right."

Smurfit European Open—£650,000
Winner: Bernhard Langer

Pity Barry Lane. His first victory in 18 months was almost in hand. He was standing on the final tee of the Smurfit European Open leading by two strokes. Then came a roar from the 18th green ahead, and what it meant was that suddenly he needed a birdie to win, or a par to tie. Bernhard Langer, two groups ahead, had eagled the 518-yard, par-five finishing hole.

For those who missed Langer's dance around the green, he had a simple explanation. "If you can't get excited about a 70-foot putt on the last green,"

Langer said, "what can you get excited about?" Langer had reached the green with a five iron, and holed the 70-footer for an eagle, finished with 68, and had the lead at eight-under-par 280 at the K Club, near Kildare, Ireland. Lane missed the green, chipped 18 feet past, and two-putted for a par and a tie. Langer shot 74-70-68-68, and Lane 67-71-71-71.

In the playoff, they halved the first extra hole — the 18th — in birdies. At the second, No. 10, Langer dropped an 18-footer for a birdie and his third victory of the season. It was a strong performance from one just recovering from the nerve-wracking heroics of the Ryder Cup the week before.

Langer trailed by three strokes going into the final round. Lane bogeyed No. 1, then birdied the fifth and sixth holes from 25 feet each. He bogeyed No. 12, then got his two-stroke margin at the 15th, dropping a 15-footer for a birdie. Langer, out in one-under 35, birdied No. 13 with a good chip and one putt, then went after the eagle at the 18th, and got it. Langer said, "It was probably the most dramatic finish I've ever had."

Mercedes German Masters—£650,000
Winner: Anders Forsbrand

Anders Forsbrand turned the Mercedes German Masters into another Swedish holiday and in the process saved it from becoming either a Bernhard Langer member-guest or a German monopoly. Forsbrand became the fifth Swede to win this season, thus snatching a fourth victory from Langer and — with Alexander Cejka's two — a sixth from Germany.

"It's always tough to beat Bernhard, especially in Germany, because you can never count him out," Forsbrand said.

Forsbrand first had to shake off Russell Claydon's 61 in the second round, then hold off Langer in the last round for his first victory since January, 1994. And in the process, the par-72 Motzener See Club at Berlin took a beating in the pleasant early October weather. For example: Steven Richardson shot four rounds in the 60s and tied for 15th place. The cut came at two-under-par 142, and Carl Mason shot level-par 288 and finished 66th, dead last.

Forsbrand did the big damage, with his scores of 64, 64, 67 and 69 for a 264 total, 24 under par. His three-round 195 total was also a season low, and his 21-under-par figure for 54 holes was a PGA European Tour record.

Forsbrand shared the lead in the first round, trailed the hot Claydon in the second round, and jumped to a five-stroke lead over Langer going into the final round. He was out in par 37 and lost ground to Per-Ulrik Johansson, who eagled the second and eighth holes, and Claydon, who birdied six of the first 10 holes and caught him at the 10th. While they had their problems, Langer, three strokes behind Forsbrand at the turn, put on a charge. He chipped in at the 11th hole then birdied four of the last six holes, but came up two strokes short. Forsbrand birdied the 12th and 15th, and holed a four-footer for a two at the 17th.

Forsbrand credited his victory to a putter made for him by a Swedish furniture maker. "It may look weird, but it's the first putter I've been able to aim straight with," he said. So it would seem. He had an eagle and 28 birdies for the week.

Toyota World Match Play Championship—£650,000
Winner: Ernie Els

See Chapter 9.

Alfred Dunhill Cup—£1,000,000
Winner: Scotland

See Chapter 10.

Volvo Masters—£750,000
Winner: Alexander Cejka

The Volvo Masters, ringing down the curtain on the 1995 PGA European Tour, might have been something of a preview of the 1997 Ryder Cup in more ways than one. First, the course, Valderrama Golf Club at Sotogrande, Spain, a beautiful and tough course, will be the venue. Only one man managed to break par — he won, of course — and that man could give the European team two German stars in 1997. He was three-time winner Alexander Cejka.

Cejka was a surprise when he scored his breakthrough victory in the Turespana Open de Andalucia in March. He was more of a surprise when he won the Hohe Brucke Austrian Open in August. And now he took his third on possibly the toughest course and against the toughest field on the circuit, joining countryman Bernhard Langer and Sam Torrance as the only three-time European winners of 1995.

"I cannot believe it," Cejka said. "I've been working very hard on my game, even indoors at night until two or three in the morning." The midnight oil paid off in a come-from-behind victory on rounds of 74, 66, 72 and 70 for a 282 total, two under par. Colin Montgomerie, whose late challenge failed, finished second at even-par 284 to beat out Sam Torrance, who tied for third place, for No. 1 on the European money list. It was Montgomerie's third straight No. 1 finish.

Cejka climbed from five strokes off the lead in the first round to within two strokes, then one behind three-round leader Anders Forsbrand. The battle came down the final nine holes, after Forsbrand faded to 39 on the first nine of the last day.

Per-Ulrik Johansson birdied three holes from the 11th and got to two under par, then bogeyed the 15th and double-bogeyed the 16th when he left a shot in a bunker. Ian Woosnam was out in 34, then destructed with two bogeys and a double bogey coming in. David Gilford came close but bogeyed the 18th from a bunker. It was Cejka's victory to take, and he took it. He birdied the 11th, then the 13th, 14th and 15th holes, the last off a three-iron shot to five feet. He bogeyed the 16th, and then with others struggling, he fired a six-iron shot to 10 feet at the 18th and holed the putt for his fifth birdie in eight holes, and his third win of the season. "I cannot find words," Cejka said. "What a year. It's been wonderful."

Johnnie Walker World Championship—£2,500,000
Winner: Fred Couples

See Chapter 11.

Challenge Tour

Thirty-eight tournaments from March to October came down to a difference of £99.93 for the final qualifiers on the European Challenge Tour in 1995. The top 10 money winners gained entry to the 1996 PGA European Tour and that margin separated No. 10 Stephen Field of England (£24,208.62) from No. 11 Patrik Sjoland of Sweden (£24,108.69).

The Challenge Tour, which has nurtured the careers of such players as Costantino Rocca, Michael Campbell and Jarmo Sandelin, found a star in 1995 in 24-year-old Thomas Bjorn of Denmark. Bjorn won four tournaments and led the Challenge Tour with earnings of £46,471.49.

In addition to Bjorn and Field, the other qualifiers for the PGA European Tour were, in order of their finish on the money list, Tim Planchin of France, Diego Borrego of Spain, Eric Giraud of France, Simon Hurley of England, Per Nyman of Sweden, Emanuele Bolognesi of Italy, Francisco Valera of Spain and Ricky Willison of England.

That is 10 players from six countries, with three from England and two each from France and Spain. Giraud, Nyman and Bolognesi each won two tournaments, as did Rolf Muntz of the Netherlands, who did not qualify after finishing 18th on the money list.

In addition to his four victories, Bjorn provided two of the most dramatic finishes of the year, both in August, as he recorded his last two triumphs.

In the Esbjerg Danish Closed, Bjorn entered the last round six strokes behind Ben Tinning. He shot 64 to tie Tinning, who missed a two-foot putt on the final regulation hole. On the first extra hole, Bjorn hit his tee shot into a bunker, played out, and then holed a nine-iron shot from 128 yards for a birdie and the victory.

In the Coca-Cola Open at East Sussex National, Bjorn came from three strokes behind with two holes to play and won. He birdied the 17th and 18th holes while the leader, Fredrik Jacobson of Sweden, bogeyed both. "Two weeks ago I holed a nine-iron shot to win a playoff in Denmark, so I guess I have all the luck right now," Bjorn said. "I feel very confident about going onto the main Tour next year."

The Challenge Tour began in early March with the Kenya Open, a hold-over from the former Safari Tour, then went to the Canary Islands in late April. Tournaments were held weekly, and sometimes two or three in the same week, from mid-May through mid-October.

14. Asia/Japan Tours

The year of 1995 in Japanese golf was all very orderly and predictable. Who would have had the audacity to even suggest that mighty Masashi (Jumbo) Ozaki would give up his mastery of the Japan PGA Tour? Of course, he didn't, although Satoshi Higashi, a hitherto-lightly-regarded veteran, gave him a run for the money until the final weeks, when Jumbo was at his best.

In contrast, tournament golf in the rest of Asia became confusing and even a bit rancorous. A new tour came into being and challenged the long-time circuit of the Asia-Pacific Golf Confederation, based on long commercial ties and the involvement of and emphasis on the development of Asian players. Neither circuit chose to align itself with the Australasian Tour, which had shown an interest in doing so and made an inroad by getting the Epson Singapore Open, a long-time fixture on the old Asia Tour, and co-sponsoring the Alfred Dunhill Asian Masters. Throw in the seemingly incongruous invasion of the PGA European Tour with its early-season events in Dubai and the Philippines and you have a problem sorting it all out.

The new circuit, which began play in late June in Thailand as the Asia PGA Tour and, acquiring a sponsor, became the Omega Tour in October, broke some new ground with tournaments in Pakistan and Vietnam, but played most of its 15-tournament schedule in the same countries in which national championships make up most of the Asia Tour structure. The old circuit also expanded and staged the first international tournament ever in China, which later hosted the venerable World Cup of Golf and the continuing domination of the powerful team of Fred Couples and Davis Love III from the United States.

With the Omega Tour continuing into January of 1996 with three tournaments, Lin Keng-Chi of Taiwan, the only multiple winner with three titles, led the money list by a sizeable margin over Thailand's Boonchu Ruangkit and India's Gaurav Ghei. American Brandt Jobe was equally impressive with three victories on the Asia Tour, which in its expansion mode had two seasons — the usual weekly February-to-April run and the start of a 1995-1996 campaign in October, when Corey Pavin demolished the field in the inaugural Volvo Asian Masters in Taiwan. Jobe, with his victories in Malaysia, Bali and Korea, finished atop the Asia Tour money list and joined five of his predecessor No. 1s on the Japan PGA Tour. In a most unusual development, all six — Frankie Minoza, Rick Gibson, Todd Hamilton, Brian Watts, Carlos Franco and Jobe — won tournaments during the long season in Japan.

The big story once again in Japan was Jumbo Ozaki, his five victories and his sixth money title with earnings of ¥192,319,800. The talented competitor, now 48, has won 27 of his 74 titles on the Japan PGA Tour since 1990. The 34-year-old Higashi, a 12-year JPGA Tour veteran who had won only three times before 1995, took four victories, including the strong Taiheiyo Masters, in his losing money duel with Ozaki. He won ¥136,854,183. Only two others — Minoza and Watts — were multiple winners, each with two victories. That, more than anything else, was the reason why the money race rested between Ozaki and Higashi.

The Japan season wasn't totally routine. The big-name international stars, who invariably make their marks in the richer events, were shut out in 1995 for the first time within memory. So were the players from Taiwan, who normally pick up a win or two during the season. None even challenged all year.

Finally, before moving into the individual accounts of the Japanese tournaments and the Asian maze, a player to watch: Hisayuki Sasaki, the 30-year-old Japan PGA champion and playoff loser to Love in the World Cup individual race, who qualified for and will play on the U.S. PGA Tour, where no Japanese player before him has ever played a full schedule and been successful.

Asia Tour

Thai International Bodharamik Thailand Open—US$300,000
Winner: Todd Hamilton

Todd Hamilton added another chapter to his success story in Asian golf when he won the Thailand Open, the first event on the revamped 1995 Asia Tour. Hamilton, 29, a regular and winner on the Japan PGA Tour since qualifying for that circuit as the Asia Tour money leader in 1992, rallied from a three-stroke deficit in the final round to force a playoff with fellow Texan Steve Veriato and took the title on the second extra hole.

The first day at Pinehurst Golf and Country Club in Bangkok belonged to American Scott Frisch, who shot an eight-under-par 64, then shot 71 and yielded the top spot to Korea's Young-Il Kim (68-66) Friday. Veriato (70-66-67) and Rick Dalpos (69-69-65), another U.S. pro, moved in front Saturday as Hamilton shot 70 for his trailing 206. Then Hamilton exploded Sunday, starting the day with an eagle, then five straight birdies. He eventually shot 65 to Veriato's 68 to forge the tie. Veriato countered Hamilton's blazing front nine with a 31 on the incoming nine that also included an eagle. Hamilton won the title with a par at the second (18th) playoff hole when Veriato missed a short par putt. Dalpos shot 72 and finished four strokes behind in a tie for fourth place.

Sabah Masters—US$250,000
Winner: Brandt Jobe

Oklahoma-born Brandt Jobe began his surge to Asia Tour supremacy in the Sabah Masters, the circuit's first of two stops in Malaysia. The 29-year-old American, runner-up to Carlos Franco on the money list in 1994, edged into the lead the third day at Sabah Golf and Country Club at Kota Kinabalu and eased to a three-stroke victory with a final-round 71 for an eight-under-par 280 total.

Jobe's only serious challengers at the end were two Malaysians — Periasamy Gunasagaran and Marimuthu Ramayah — but another American, Ron Wuensche, had the best start with 67 Thursday. Ramayah, Malaysia's most successful pro, shot 69 Friday and moved into the lead, three strokes ahead of Jobe. Brandt took charge with a five-under-par 67 Saturday. He was a shot ahead of Ramayah, but it was Gunasagaran who produced the stronger challenge Sunday with a 69. However, Jobe had been five ahead of Periasamy and his 71 carried him to the comfortable victory, the second in Asia for the former UCLA All-American. He won the Thailand Open in 1994.

Dole Philippine Open—US$300,000
Winner: Carlos Espinosa

Carlos Espinosa had been contemplating a career change, but fortunately decided against making a rash move. He gave his playing career another chance with a return to the Asia Tour and it paid off with victory in the venerable Philippine Open in late February. Espinosa, 33, a former World Cup and Alfred Dunhill Cup player for Mexico who now lives in McAllen, Texas, came from five strokes off the lead in the final round and scored a two-stroke victory in Asia's oldest tournament.

The result was a bitter pill for Kevin Wentworth, who had led from the start, then stuttered to 77 and a third-place-tie finish. He led by three shots after his opening 66 and his midway 70–136, then by two over Lee Porter and Robert Pactolerin with 208 after 54 holes. Espinosa had drawn little attention with his 69-74-70 but, in a manner reminiscent of his 1988 victory in Taiwan, he put together a 69 that vaulted him into the lead and the triumph. Olle Nordberg of Sweden, who co-led the 1995 qualifier for the circuit, also finished fast Sunday with 67–284 to snatch second place from 285-shooters Felix Casas, Young-Keun Han, Porter and Wentworth.

Classic Indian Open—US$250,000
Winner: Jim Rutledge

Nearly a decade of campaigning on the Asia Tour finally paid off for Jim Rutledge with victory in the Classic Indian Open. The 36-year-old Canadian, who had a history of faltering finishes over the seasons since he joined the circuit in the late 1980s, turned it around at Delhi Golf Club, breezing to a four-stroke victory with a final-round 68 for an eight-under-par 280 total. Rutledge became the fourth Canadian winner in Tour history, one of his predecessors, Remi Bouchard, having won in India in 1989.

Rutledge, who also has played on the PGA European Tour, seemed to be primed to win after finishing eighth, then third on the Asia money list, registering seven top-10 showings during that period, most recently second place in the Korean Open, where he lost in a playoff.

Back-to-back 69s at Delhi gave Rutledge a two-shot advantage over American Rob Moss, the first-round leader, but the Canadian yielded the top spot to India's Basad Ali (72-70-69–211) when he shot 74 Saturday. This time he rebounded strongly with the 68, the product of five birdies and a bogey. Bob May, with 67, and India-born Swedish pro Daniel Chopra, with 68, tied for second place at 284. May had started with a 77.

Benson & Hedges Malaysian Open—US$250,000
Winner: Clay Devers

Clay Devers, a long-hitting Asia Tour rookie from Kansas City, became the third American champion of the 1995 season, holding off the challenge of the experienced Darren Clarke of Northern Ireland to score a one-stroke victory in the Benson & Hedges Malaysian Open at Templer Park Golf Club in Kuala Lumpur. The 27-year-old Devers, who followed countrymen Todd Hamilton (Thailand) and Brandt Jobe (Sabah Masters) to the winners' circle, closed with 69 for 276, 12 under par, edging Clarke, fellow American Kevin Wentworth and Daniel Chopra, placing second for the second week in a row.

Devers trailed by four strokes as Clarke and Jim Rutledge, coming off his victory four days earlier in India, opened with 67s on the 7,120-yard Templer Park course. He was still three behind Clarke, 140 to 137, after 36 holes, but caught up Saturday when he gathered seven birdies and a 67 to Darren's 70. Devers' fourth birdie in Sunday's final round, a chip-in at the 13th hole on the heels of his only bogey at the 12th, gave him a one-stroke lead over the Irishman and it held up as he parred in for the 69. Clarke had a bogey and a birdie in the stretch and shot 70 to finish in the runner-up tie with Wentworth and Chopra, who both had 67s.

Sampoerna Indonesia Open—US$250,000
Winner: Jose Cantero

Another country was heard from when the Asia Tour reached Indonesia in mid-March. Jose Cantero became the first Argentinian victor on the circuit at that stop, coming from a stroke off the lead in the final round to post a one-stroke victory with his 11-under-par 277 at Pantai Indah Kapuk in Jakarta. The 35-year-old Cantero honed his game on Europe's Challenge Tour, on which he won three times to go with a 1994 victory in Chile.

Among the victims of the Argentinian was America's Hale Irwin, the three-time U.S. Open champion, who shared the 36-hole lead with Australia's Don Fardon at 138. Cantero was at 69-71–140. A third-round 74 ruined Irwin's chances as Fardon shot 70 and led Cantero and American Gary Webb, the 1993 winner, by a stroke, defending champion Frank Nobilo, the globe-trotting New Zealand star, by two, going into Sunday's finale. Cantero took charge with birdies at the 11th, 12th and 14th, moving ahead of Nobilo, who had recovered nicely from a triple bogey and 74 in the first round. Cantero made a final birdie at the 17th, holing an 18-foot putt for a two-shot lead, a cushion he needed when he bogeyed the last hole for his winning 68. Fardon shot 70 for 278 and second place, a stroke ahead of Nobilo.

Sempati Bali Open—US$250,000
Winner: Brandt Jobe

When Brandt Jobe won the inaugural Sempati Bali Open, one of the new events on the 1995 Asia Tour, he accomplished two things of particular note: The victory jumped him into what proved to be permanent possession of first place on the money list and, as his second of 1995, made him the first player in five years — since Frankie Minoza in 1990 — to win more than one Asia Tour event in a single season.

For the second time in five months, though, the exotic site of the tournament — Bali Golf and Country Club — hosted controversy as well as accomplishment. The previous November, when the Alfred Dunhill Masters was played at Bali, Nick Faldo was disqualified for an inadvertent rules infraction while leading the tournament. In the Bali Open, South Korea's Jong-Duck Kim, the 1994 Korean Open champion who had shot a second-round 64, was assessed an odd two-stroke penalty and dropped from third to ninth place for repeated improper replacements of his marked ball on the greens the last day.

A third-round 66 propelled Jobe into contention, moving him within two strokes of Taiwan's Lin Keng-Chi, the leader at 202 after his Saturday 63. Jobe shared the runner-up slot with Eric Meeks, with whom he had jointly led the first day with 66. He shot 69 Sunday for his 15-under-par 273 and won by two strokes over Lin, who closed with 73 for 275. Meeks tied for third with Roger Wessels and Glenn Joyner at 277.

Rolex Masters—US$250,000
Winner: Ron Wuensche

American domination of the Asia Tour continued in Singapore as Ron Wuensche, who had finished back in the pack in the previous seven events, caught fire in the Rolex Masters and rolled to a three-stroke victory with a 15-under-par 269 total at Singapore Island Country Club. The tournament, an independent event for many years, joined the expanded circuit at the longtime venue of the Singapore Open.

The 26-year-old University of Wisconsin graduate was never out of the 60s all week on Singapore Island's 6,674-yard, par-71 Bukit course, but trailed Canada's Rick Todd and his 65 by a stroke the first day. Strong chipping and putting enabled Wuensche to shoot 68 Friday and share first place at 134 with fellow American John Kernohan. A third-round 69 for 203 elevated him a stroke into the lead, Bob May and Nick Goetze, also Americans, posting 204s. Wuensche gave nobody a chance Sunday, zipping along to a 66 for the 269. May, who also had four rounds under 70, shot 68 to take second place at 272, three ahead of Brandt Jobe, the two-time 1995 winner, who solidified his hold on first place on the money list.

Chin Fong Republic of China Open—US$300,000
Winner: Daniel Chopra

Daniel Chopra came to the 1995 Asia Tour with a billing by others that might have seemed prematurely optimistic when tagged to a 21-year-old. The ranks of doubters dwindled as Chopra, an India-born Swedish citizen, made consistent showings through the early events and tied for second in consecutive weeks in the Indian and Malaysian Opens. Then, the promise was fully realized when he won the rain-shortened Chin Fong Republic of

China Open in early April by a stroke.

Chopra, who had started the tournament with 73, six strokes behind leader Nico Van Rensburg of South Africa, vaulted into the lead Saturday after rain washed out the second round. He reeled off seven birdies for a 65, one shot off the course record at Tong Hwa Golf and Country Club in the Taipei suburb of Linkou. His lead at 138 was tenuous with Van Rensburg and Taiwan's Hsieh Chin-Sheng and Lu Chien-Soon at 139 and five others at 140. But the young man was solid Sunday, setting off a lone bogey with three birdies for a 70 and the winning eight-under-par 208. Hsieh, the World and Alfred Dunhill Cup veteran trying to give the home country fans a fourth straight ROC Open winner, also shot 70, his third sub-par round, and took second place. The victory boosted Chopra to second place on the money list.

Maekyung Bando Fashion Korean Open—US$400,000
Winner: Brandt Jobe

Brandt Jobe clearly established why he was the leading player on the 1995 Asia Tour with his highly impressive victory in the Maekyung Bando Fashion Korean Open, his third of the season. The 29-year-old American came from nowhere and not only took the title but by a breezing four strokes at Nam Seoul Country Club at the South Korean capital. He was just the second U.S. pro to win the Korean Open and the other man was Todd Hamilton the year he, like Jobe, led the money list.

Jobe's chances seemed remote at best after he opened with rounds of 73 and 72. Kevin Wentworth had him by 10 strokes at that point (and eventually lost by seven). Then Jobe lit up the scoreboard Saturday. An eagle, seven birdies and a bogey had him a par away from a course-record 64, but he double-bogeyed the 18th for 66, still good enough to join a four-way tie for the lead with Wentworth, who shot 76; Canadian Rick Todd and Korea's Yong-Jin Shin at 211. Of the four, only Jobe handled the final-round pressure well. While the other three faded, Jobe put together a 69 for an eight-under-par 280 total. Sang-Ho Choi, the 1991 champion, closed with 70–284 to take second place.

Volvo China Open—US$400,000
Winner: Raul Fretes

Things had not gone well for Raul Fretes during much of the Asia Tour season. Twice he was on the verge of flying back to his Asuncion home in Paraguay and twice he stayed, first because of a third-place finish in Taipei and second because of the long-distance phone persuasion of his wife, Grace, that he remain for the final event of the season. Fretes had just missed the cut in the Dunlop Open when she talked him into staying. So, the 29-year-old Paraguayan went to Beijing and won the inaugural Volvo China Open by a handy three strokes.

Fretes surely had misgivings after his opening 74 at Beijing International Golf Club left him eight strokes off the lead of Taiwan's Lin Keng-Chi.

However, he brought himself back into the picture Friday with the first of three solid rounds, a 67 that included a chip-in eagle. At 141, Fretes trailed Lin by four. Then, Saturday's 68 catapulted him into first place, a shot in front of Lai Ying-Juh, as Lin skied to a 77. The final round turned into a duel between Fretes and rookie pro Lai, age 24. Fretes retained a one-stroke lead with a tough par at the 14th, then pulled away with birdies at the next two holes, posting another 68 for an 11-under-par 277 as Lai shot 70 for 280. China's Zhang Lian-Wei placed third at 282.

Brandt Jobe clinched the Asia Tour money title in absentia, having returned to his Denver home for a brief rest before beginning play on the Japan PGA Tour, the major perk for the No. 1 money winner.

Volvo Asian Masters—US$400,000
Winner: Corey Pavin

The Asia Tour launched its new (1995-96) season in Taiwan in mid-October and couldn't have gotten off on a much higher note. Corey Pavin, the U.S. Open champion, made the new event at Taipei's Sunrise Golf and Country Club a runaway victory and prelude to his later triumph in South Africa's Nedbank Million Dollar Challenge that took him to the top of the World Money List.

Pavin never was out of the lead at Sunrise and, after matching par-72 rounds the windy first day with Australia's Craig Jones, was never in danger of not winning. The rout began Friday when the 35-year-old American exploded with a six-under-par 66 and rolled to a six-stroke lead over Isao Aoki. Pavin then shot 67 to Aoki's 68 Saturday to widen the gap to seven strokes. It was a walk in the park Sunday as a 50-foot birdie putt at the third hole headed Pavin toward a final 69 for a 14-under-par 274 total and a nine-stroke edge over the 53-year-old Aoki, who double-bogeyed the last hole for 71–283. So decisive was Pavin's victory that Canada's Rick Todd, finishing third, trailed by 17 strokes.

World Cup of Golf—US$1,500,000
Winners: United States/Davis Love III

It doesn't seem to make any difference where they take the World Cup of Golf, not even to a country like China, where the game is in its infancy. Davis Love III and Fred Couples, the most successful partners in the international event since Arnold Palmer and Jack Nicklaus, just keep rolling up big victories. The Love and Couples team, which has never even trailed in the competition, racked up its fourth consecutive victory for the United States, building to a 14-stroke margin over Australia at Mission Hills Golf Club in the resort area of southern China. Love shot 267, Couples 276 for the 33-under-par 543 total, as they matched the record four titles won by the Nicklaus/Palmer team (not consecutive) in the 1960s. The only reservation to the accomplishment was the absence of top international stars from several of the teams.

The runaway at Mission Hills went like this: First round — Love (65) and

Couples (68) for 133 and a three-stroke lead over Sweden's Jesper Parnevik (67) and Jarmo Sandelin (69); second round — Love (67) and Couples (69) for 269 and a four-stroke lead over Parnevik (66) and Sandelin (71); third round — Love (68) and Couples (70) for 407 and a 10-stroke lead over Japan's Hisayuki Sasaki (198) and Hiroshi Goda (219); fourth round — Love (67) and Couples (69) for the 14-stroke victory over Australia's Brett Ogle and Robert Allenby.

The individual competition for the International Trophy was a different story. Japan's Sasaki, who later qualified for the 1996 U.S. PGA Tour, set a World Cup record with his opening 62, followed with rounds of 69, 67 and 69 to tie Love's 21-under-par 267 and carried the American five playoff holes before yielding that title.

Hong Kong Open—US$300,000
Winner: Gary Webb

The winners' circle of the long-standing Hong Kong Open has been occupied in recent years by players from other parts of the world, including international stars Tom Watson, Bernhard Langer and David Frost in 1994. Things didn't change when the 37-year-old tournament was moved to the autumn as the second stop on the Asia Tour's 1995-96 calendar.

This time the winner was an American — Gary Webb, a 34-year-old University of Texas graduate who won the 1993 Indonesian Open. Webb, who had just returned to the Orient after failing to qualify for the U.S. PGA Tour, staged a blazing finish on the composite course at Royal Hong Kong to post a two-stroke victory with his 13-under-par 271 total. With two holes to play, Webb, who had just birdied the 16th, was tied for the lead with Mexico's Rafael Alarcon, who was in front the first two days with 65-67–132 before taking 74 and yielding to Taiwan's Yeh Chang-Ting and his 203. Webb birdied the last two holes as well for 66 and the two-shot win over Alarcon. Yeh shot 71 to finish third at 274.

Tugu Pratama Indonesia PGA Championship—US$250,000
Winner: John Senden

A new tournament on the Asia Tour brought a new winner. John Senden, a 24-year-old Australian, fended off the final-round challenges of a handful of other contenders, including international veteran Frank Nobilo of New Zealand, to capture a two-stroke victory in the Tugu Pratama Indonesia PGA Championship at Jakarta's Damai Indah course. The young Queenslander birdied the 72nd hole to clinch the victory, the first of his three-year career, with 72 for a nine-under-par 279, two better than the total of Filipino Felix Casas. Nobilo closed with 69 for 282 and a third-place tie with Mohammed Ali Kadir and Glenn Joyner.

Joyner was the first-round leader with 68, but Senden moved ahead Friday with 69-67–136 and took a two-shot lead over Casas and Kadir into the final round when he followed with 71 Saturday for 207.

China Tour

When professional tournament golf came to the People's Republic of China for the first time in April of 1995, the scenario, as it unfolded, hardly could have been scripted any more appropriately. Particularly the way the first-ever Volvo China Tour started and finished.

To the delight of the organizers of the four-event Tour, one of their own — Zhang Lian-Wei — had an exciting, one-stroke victory in the inaugural Volvo Open at his home Shenzhen Golf Club. Although an Australian, an Ecuadorean and a Scot took the other three titles, Zhang was the most consistent performer throughout and led the money list handily, though with a modest US$17,325.

The purses for the four-event, 12-day swing through the sub-tropical resort area of Southern China north of Hong Kong totaled just $180,000, less than half of the prize money for the main event that followed in Beijing — the inaugural $400,000 Volvo China Open that concluded the 1995 Asia Tour season. Zhang followed his win with ties for third, fifth and 10th in the other three tournaments to secure the top spot.

Although he was never out of the lead at Shenzhen Golf Club, the 29-year-old Zhang, a three-time China Amateur champion, could never breathe easy until the final putt was struck — and missed — by Jeff Senior at the 36th hole. Zhang shot 69-73–142 and won by one stroke after Senior missed a 30-foot birdie putt on the final hole.

Tony Maloney, 34, a veteran campaigner from Australia, became the first foreigner to win in China later that first week in the Honichi Open at Honichi Golf Leisure Club. Rafael Ponce's victory in the Hugo Boss Open five days later was rather ironic. The 31-year-old pro from Ecuador was there only because he had been playing so poorly on the Asia Tour that he was not eligible for the Dunlop Open. Simon Yates, 25, of Scotland won the Coca-Cola Open, the China Tour's last stop. That victory qualified him for the Volvo China Open as Ponce's win had for him three days earlier.

Japan Tour

Token Corporation Cup—¥100,000,000
Winner: Todd Hamilton

Todd Hamilton seems to like to do first things first. The 29-year-old American, who has enjoyed great success in Asia in recent years, had won in

Thailand in the initial event on the 1995 Asia Tour. A month later, he was on hand for the opening event of the Japan PGA Tour — the Token Corporation Cup — and did the same thing, picking up his seventh title in Asia, his fifth in Japan, with a one-stroke victory over Australia's Peter Senior.

Hamilton, 29, who won twice in Japan in 1994, established a four-stroke margin in the third round at Kedoin Golf Club after sharing the 36-hole lead at 141 with Seiji Ebihara and Hideyuki Sato. He shot Saturday's best round of 68 to go seven under par at 209 with Tsuneyuki (Tommy) Nakajima, Yoshinori Kaneko, Yoshikazu Sakamoto and Shigeki Maruyama at 213. The challenge Sunday came from Senior, who came from five strokes back with 68, falling one short of Hamilton's 72–281. Masashi (Jumbo) Ozaki, Japan's No. 1 player, came on too late with 67, finishing at 285.

Daido Drinko Shizuoka Open—¥100,000,000
Winner: Brian Watts

Brian Watts followed the lead of countryman Todd Hamilton and put another win in Japan on his record. Like Hamilton, the 28-year-old Watts found his fortune in Asia and, for now at least, campaigns full-time in Japan. Watts' two-stroke victory in the Daido Drinko Shizuoka Open was his sixth in little more than two years on the Japan Tour following his Cinderella 1994 season when he won five times, was the No. 2 money winner on the circuit and 11th on the World Money List.

Watts shared the first-round lead with 69 at Shizuoka Golf Club with Hisayuki Sasaki and Chen Tze-Ming, but Australia's Richard Backwell took over the next two days. He led alone at 74-66–140 Friday and at 210 Saturday with Frankie Minoza, the fine Filipino. Watts, two back entering the final round, produced one of the day's two low-round 68s to forge the two-stroke victory at eight-under-par 280. Both Backwell and Minoza collapsed, and Shigeki Maruyama seized second with 71 for 282.

Novell KSB Open—¥70,000,000
Winner: Rick Gibson

The parade of Asia Tour season champions from North America continued to stride a victory march on the Japan PGA Tour as Canadian Rick Gibson, the 1991 Asia Tour money leader, took the Novell KSB Open title. Gibson, 33, a member of the Canadian team that surprised with its triumph in the 1994 Alfred Dunhill Cup at St. Andrews, hung on for a one-stroke victory in the Novell KSB Open, shooting a final-round 68 for a 17-under-par 271 total.

The Manila-based Gibson trailed by one shot after the first round at Kinojo Country Club at Okayama as Tsuneyuki (Tommy) Nakajima opened with 64. Gibson moved a shot in front of Nakajima Friday with 67 for 132 and maintained that lead Saturday with 71–203, then one in front of Toshimitsu Izawa and Richard Backwell. His 68 Sunday was just enough to hold off Izawa and Tsukasa Watanabe, who tied for second at 272.

Descente Classic—¥80,000,000
Winner: Satoshi Higashi

Satoshi Higashi brought the foreign monopoly on the Japan PGA Tour to an end in the Descente Classic, stepping strongly in front in the third round, then hanging on for a one-stroke victory at Century Miki Golf Club at Hyogo. His closing 73 gave him a six-under-par total of 282.

Little-known Shinichi Yokota enjoyed two days of glory before departing for the nether regions of the final standings. Yokota led for two days with his pair of 69s, his 138 after Friday's round positioning him two in front of Higashi, Peter McWhinney of Australia and Katsuyoshi Tomori. Higashi, who hadn't won since the 1991 Japan Match Play, jumped into a three-stroke lead over Tomori and Yoshimi Niizeki Saturday with 69–209 as Yokota ballooned to 80-75 the last two days. Higashi struggled to 73 Sunday, and a bogey at the last hole cut his final victory margin to one over Tomori. It was his fourth career win.

Tsuruya Open—¥100,000,000
Winner: Satoshi Higashi

Satoshi Higashi rested on his victory laurels for a week, then won again in the Tsuruya Open, the next event after an open week on the Japan PGA Tour schedule. Again Higashi survived a tight finish, this time edging five other players by the same one-stroke margin. He posted a nine-under-par 279 total at Sports Shinko Country Club, also in Hyogo Prefecture.

Katsunori Kuwahara, one of the five eventual runners-up Sunday, shot 64 Thursday and shared a three-stroke, first-round lead with Joji Furuki. Hisayuki Sasaki carried the lead the next two days — with 69-68–137 to lead Kuwahara by one Friday and with 208 to lead Kuwahara and Higashi (69-74-66) Saturday. When Sasaki slipped to 73 Sunday, Higashi inched in front. Finishing with a bogey as he had done in the Descente, Satoshi posted a 70 and the 279, just enough to beat the 280 shooters — Kuwahara, Yoshinori Mizumaki, Koki Idoki, Kiyoshi Maita and Roger Mackay — and put a fifth title on his record.

Dunlop Open—¥100,000,000
Winner: Peter Senior

The frustrations of the Japanese players returned at the Dunlop Open, the most prestigious tournament of the early season on the Japan PGA Tour, as Australian Peter Senior rang up an easy victory in the late-April event. Only Satoshi Higashi with his back-to-back wins interfered with foreign domination over the first six weeks of the season.

It was an impressive victory by Senior, who had won the Australian Masters earlier in the year and two earlier titles in Japan. He was part of a four-player group with 69s Thursday, dropped one stroke off the pace Friday when Canadian Rick Todd shot 66 for 138, then raced six strokes in front with 67–206 Saturday. The mighty Masashi (Jumbo) Ozaki was the man at 212, but he never mounted a threat Sunday as the Australian shot a respectable 73 — one birdie, two bogeys — in heavy winds to score a five-stroke victory with his nine-under-par 279 on Ibaragi Golf Club's East course. American Brian Watts came up with a 70 to take second place at 284.

Normally the final stop on the Asia Tour as well as one on the Japan circuit, the Dunlop Open was next-to-last to the new Volvo China Open. Brandt Jobe, who was to wind up as the money leader, and Daniel Chopra, the only man with a chance to catch him, both missed the 36-hole cut.

Chunichi Crowns—¥120,000,000
Winner: Masashi Ozaki

It was just a matter of time. It was a virtual certainty that Masashi (Jumbo) Ozaki would pick up the 70th victory of his marvelous career on the Japan PGA Tour during the 1995 season, but how quickly? The 48-year-old superstar took care of that matter in the year's seventh event and in decisive fashion. A week after he missed that chance with a poor finish in the Dunlop Open, Ozaki shattered the Chunichi Crowns field and the Tour record for par-70 courses with a 20-under-par 260 total on the Wago course of Nagoya Country Club. He won his third Chunichi Crowns by five strokes and was off and running on another huge season.

Even with a 66-64 start, Ozaki had to be content with second place in the halfway standings behind Katsuyoshi Tomori's 129. Then, he took command with his third-round 63 that moved him four strokes in front, with Nobuo Serizawa at 197 and Tomori at 199. He strolled to victory Sunday with 67, finishing five strokes ahead of Serizawa (68) and eight in front of Tomori (69). American Larry Mize, with 66 and 269 was fourth, while Peter Senior, the Dunlop winner, closed with 63 and 271.

Fuji Sankei Classic—¥120,000,000
Winner: Tsuneyuki Nakajima

Tsuneyuki (Tommy) Nakajima, who first won the Fuji Sankei Classic 13 years earlier, used a second victory in the event on the Fuji course of Ito's Kawana Hotel Golf Club to end a winning drought of nearly a year on the Japan PGA Tour. It was the 45th career victory for Nakajima, the circuit's leading money winner four times in the 1980s.

The 40-year-old Nakajima started and finished with 66s as he scored a two-stroke victory over Masahiro Kuramoto, another of Japan's winningest players, registering a 12-under-par 272 total. For three days, though, the tournament was in the hands of Hisayuki Sasaki. Sasaki opened with 65, followed with 68 and had a three-stroke lead over Nakajima, Kuramoto, Paraguay's Carlos Franco and Yoshinori Mizumaki. Things tightened up Saturday when Hisayuki shot 71 for 204. He then led Toru Suzuki, Kuramoto and Franco by one stroke, Nakajima and Masayuki Kawamura by two. Nakajima emerged from that pack Sunday, even though he bogeyed the first hole, as Sasaki faltered to 73 and fifth place. Six subsequent birdies produced the 66.

Franco, the Asia Tour leader in 1994, finished third at 275 and American Todd Hamilton, the Token winner, was fourth at 276.

Japan PGA Championship—¥100,000,000
Winner: Hisayuki Sasaki

Hisayuki Sasaki made a most rewarding turnaround in the Japan PGA Championship. The week before in the Fuji Sankei Classic, Sasaki came apart in the final round after leading for three days. In the PGA Championship, he struck gold the final day, shooting the best round of his career — a dazzling 63 — to annex the prestigious title, just his second win on the Japan PGA Tour. He won by four stokes with his 16-under-par 272 total.

The 30-year-old Sasaki played catch-up all week, as Toru Suzuki held sway for three rounds. He was 45th and trailed by six strokes after starting with 71 at Natsudomari Golf Links at Hiranai in northern Japan. When Suzuki repeated his 65 Friday, Sasaki was 11 strokes behind after a 70, though he advanced to 16th place. Sasaki gave himself a chance with a 68 Saturday that left him five behind when Suzuki took 74. Suzuki continued to fade Sunday and Sasaki struck his biggest blow of the day when he chipped in for an eagle at the par-five 10th, touching off a back-nine 29. Kazuhiro Takami kept pace with Sasaki until he holed a pitching-wedge approach at the par-four 15th for another eagle and Takami took a double bogey. Takami settled for second with his 71. Suzuki shot 73 and finished third at 277. Tour stars Jumbo Ozaki, complaining of a cold, and Tommy Nakajima skipped the championship.

Pepsi Ube Tournament—¥80,000,000
Winner: Mitsutaka Kusakabe

Some players should never complain about the weather. Mitsutaka Kusakabe, for instance. At the Pepsi Ube Tournament, a mid-May stop on the Japan PGA Tour, Kusakabe joined a fairly small group of players who have won tournaments without leaving the clubhouse for a final round when weather, usually heavy rains, forced cancellation of the last day's play.

In Kusababe's case, sour grapes would not have been appropriate. He had taken a three-stroke lead Saturday at Ube Country Club at Ajisu with 66, one of the best rounds of the tournament, and his 206 became the winning score when torrential downpours brought a wipeout of play Sunday. Kusakabe had lingered a few strokes off the pace the first two days with his 70-70 start. Koki Idoki, Kosaku Hirano and American Brandt Jobe led the first day with 66s. Idoki shot 71 Friday to retain a share of the lead with Katsunari Takahashi and Australian Roger Mackay at 137 with Jobe one back. The three Friday leaders all had 72s Saturday and tied for second with Harumitsu Hamano, who shot 69.

Mitsubishi Galant Tournament—¥100,000,000
Winner: Brandt Jobe

Weather continued to harass the Japan PGA Tour when the players moved on to the Aso Prince Hotel course at Akamizu for the Mitsubishi Galant Tournament. This time, though, the rains came early, wiping out the Thursday round, and officials decided to go for a 36-hole finish Sunday. That proved very much to the liking of American Brandt Jobe, playing in his third Japanese tournament after grabbing the Asia Tour money list title that qualified him to play on the Japan circuit.

The 29-year-old pro from Denver, who had made a strong showing the previous week in the Pepsi Ube, ran wild in the Mitsubishi Galant. He not only won the tournament, his fourth of 1995, but set a Japan Tour record in the process. With rounds of 65, 67, 65 and 69, Brandt posted a 266 total on the par-73 Aso Prince Hotel course. The 26-under-par score was two better than the old mark, set by Masahiro Kuramoto in the 1987 Maruman Open. Interestingly, Kuramoto unleashed a 10-under-par 63 in the opening round at Aso Prince to lead by two and finished second to Jobe Sunday, shooting 68-68 in the double round for 272.

JCB Classic Sendai—¥100,000,000
Winner: Ryoken Kawagishi

Big things had been expected of Ryoken (Ricky) Kawagishi when he joined the Japan PGA Tour in 1990 after an outstanding collegiate career in America. He lived up to those expectations with three victories in his first year and another in early 1991. Then, nothing. He didn't win another tournament on the Japan circuit for more than four years — until he scored a three-stroke victory in the JCB Classic Sendai the first week of June at Omote Zaoh Kokusai Golf Club at Sendai.

The 28-year-old Kawagishi did not give much of an indication that the drought was about to end when he began the JCB Classic with 71 and trailed leader Nichito Hashimoto by eight. However, a 68 Friday moved him within four of Hiroyuki Fujita (67-68), and he took over first place with a sparkling 64 Saturday for 203, then two in front of Hashimoto. Kawagishi then nailed down that long-sought fifth title with a final-round 68 for a 13-under-par 271 total. Toru Suzuki placed second with 67–274.

Sapporo Tokyu Open—¥100,000,000
Winner: Carlos Franco

South America's brightest star of the moment in Asia continued the successful pattern of Asia Tour champions on the Japan PGA Tour. Carlos Franco, the 30-year-old from Paraguay who led the Asia Tour money list in 1994 and later in the year won the Gene Sarazen Jun Classic in Japan, scored his second Japanese victory in the Sapporo Tokyu Open. He was the fifth former money leader to win on the JPGA circuit in 1995.

Franco never was behind on Sapporo Kokusai Country Club's Shimamatsu course on the northern island of Hokkaido, the first wire-to-wire leader of the season. The tournament started with a logjam as six players — Eduardo Herrera, Tsukasa Watanabe, Frankie Minoza, Hidezumi Shirakata, Takashi Kanemoto and Franco — shared the lead with 68s. Of the six, only Franco remained on top when he followed with 69 for 137 and tied Yoshinori Mizumaki, the defending champion (69-68). Franco then nosed two strokes in front with 69–206 Saturday as Mizumaki shot 71. The South American gave his closest pursuers a chance Sunday when he managed only a par 72 for 278. Shinji Ikeuchi, with 69, and Kazuhiro Takami, with 70, fell one stroke short and tied for second place.

Pocari Sweat Yomiuri Open—¥100,000,000
Winner: Eduardo Herrera

A South American joined the victory bandwagon on the Japan PGA Tour for the second consecutive week when Eduardo Herrera, a 30-year-old Colombian who had played in Japan for several years without a victory, captured the Pocari Sweat Yomiuri Open after Carlos Franco of Paraguay won the Sapporo Tokyu. He was the seventh non-Japanese winner in the first 14 events on JPGA circuit.

Ryoken (Ricky) Kawagishi, the winner of the JCB Sendai two weeks earlier, got the tournament off to a fast start with an eight-under-par 63 and clung to a piece of the lead with a 70 Friday. Mitsutaka Kusakabe also had 133. It was anybody's game after Saturday's play ended. Four players — Satoshi Higashi, Shigeki Maruyama, Lin Chie-Hsiang and Kusakabe — shared the lead at 204 and seven others, including Kawagishi and Herrera, were at 205. Herrera had five birdies and a bogey in the rain Sunday for 67, and his 12-under-par 272 total gave him a one-stroke victory over Hiroyuki Fujita, another 205 shooter who finished with 68 for 273.

Mizuno Open—¥100,000,000
Winner: Brian Watts

It was not a good week for the home players on the Japan PGA Tour. Not only did a foreign player — American Brian Watts — take the Mizuno Open title, but six of the next eight finishers were visitors to the country, something that usually only happens in the autumn when overseas standouts come for the big-money events. The triumph was the second of the season and seventh in less than three years in Japan for Watts, the defending champion and 1994 runner-up on the Japan money list.

It took Watts three rounds to work his way up the standings into the lead. He began the tournament with 71, five strokes off the pace of Satoshi Higashi and Tetsu Nishikawa, then rose quickly into a three-way tie for third place, two behind Eiji Mizoguchi and Canada's Rick Gibson, who shot a 10-under-par 62 Friday. Watts advanced into a two-stroke lead over Gibson Saturday with a 66 for 202 and his one-under 71 Sunday gave him a three-stroke victory over Gibson, the Novell KSB winner in March. Jobe, Roger Mackay and Peter Senior shared third place at 277 with Toshimitsu Izawa and Kiyoshi

Murota. Todd Hamilton and Anthony Gilligan were next at 278.

PGA Philanthropy Tournament—¥100,000,000
Winner: Kazuhiro Takami

A remarkable string of non-happenings came to an end in the PGA Philan-thropy Tournament in early July. For the first time all season on the Japan PGA Tour, a playoff was required to determine a champion. Kazuhiro Takami prevailed in overtime, breaking a run of three victories by foreign members of the circuit.

None of the three playoff contestants led over the first three rounds at Twinfields Golf Club at Komatsu. Takami and Brian Watts, going for two in a row, were two strokes off the lead of Tsuyoshi Yoneyama and Richard Backwell at 206, and the third overtime worker — Katsunari Takahashi — was five back after 54 holes. Takami and Watts shot 69s and Takahashi 66 to forge the tie at 277 and bring on the playoff. It ended quickly when Takahashi and Watts missed birdie putts from 16 and five feet respectively on the first extra hole before Takami holed his five-footer for the win, the second of his career.

Yonex Open Hiroshima—¥80,000,000
Winner: Masashi Ozaki

When heavy rains washed out the opening round of the Mitsubishi Galant two months earlier in the season, officials opted for a 36-hole Sunday finish to preserve the 72-hole event. When bad weather obliterated the Thursday round of the Yonex Open at Hiroshima Country Club, though, they took a different tack, declaring it a 54-hole event then and there. As a result, Masashi (Jumbo) Ozaki didn't have to go another round to keep his 54-hole lead and win his second tournament of the 1995 Japan PGA Tour season.

Ozaki passed 63 players from start to his 71st title after beginning the tournament six strokes off the pace of leader Nobuhiro Yoshino when the delayed event got underway Friday. Low scores abounded as the next six players had 68s. Ozaki came up with one himself Saturday. It was one of the day's better rounds, but his 141 left him four strokes behind Chen Tze-Ming, Shoichi Kuwabara and Yoshino. The final round turned into a battle between Satoshi Higashi and Ozaki, Jumbo prevailing with 66 for a 207 total, nine under par and one ahead of Higashi, who finished with a 68 and 208.

Nikkei Cup—¥100,000,000
Winner: Tetsu Nishikawa

Tetsu Nishikawa ended a two-year winless spell with an impressive perfor-mance in the Nikkei Cup in mid-July on the Dejima course of Fuji Golf Club in Dejimamura. Nishikawa led the final three rounds and was never out of the 60s as he scored his third victory on the Japan PGA Tour and his first since the 1993 Descente Classic early that season. He won by two strokes with his 19-under-par 269 total.

Nishikawa began the tournament with 65, yet trailed Toshimitsu Izawa by one stroke. He then moved two strokes in front Friday with his 67–132. Shigeki Maruyama, Saburo Fujiki, Yoshinori Kaneko and Isamu Sugita were at 134. When Nishikawa produced 69 Saturday, he kept a one-stroke lead over Hideki Kase, who shot 66 for 202. He stayed in front thanks to a 50-foot birdie putt on the final green, his fourth birdie of the day against a single bogey. None of the pursuers of the first three days remained in contention Sunday as Nishikawa shot 68 for his 269. Tomohiro Maruyama, with a dazzling 64, raced into second place at 271 and Kazuhiro Takami, with a 65 finish, was third at 272.

NST Niigata Open—¥60,000,000
Winner: Tomohiro Maruyama

Tomohiro Maruyama carried a hot hand into the NST Niigata Open. He had fallen just short of victory the Sunday before despite a final-round 64. He was closer to the top after 54 holes in the Niigata event at Sun Rise Golf Club at Seiro and his closing 66 zipped him to a three-stroke triumph, the first win for the 37-year-old golfer since the Daikyo Open at the end of the 1993 season and just the second of his long career on the Japan PGA Tour.

What was delight for Maruyama was disappointment for Hidemichi Tanaka, who led the tournament for three days only to finish second. Tanaka opened with 66 for a one-stroke lead over Futoshi Irino. He shot 71 Friday for 137 and retained the one-stroke lead, then over Yasunori Ida, two over Maruyama, Shinichi Yokota and Kiyoshi Maita. His Saturday 69 gave him a two-stroke advantage over Maruyama and Yokota going into the final round, in which Maruyama executed a five-stroke swing and recorded a 14-under-par 274 total. Tanaka shot 71 for 277. American Greg Meyer had 67 and tied with Yokota for third at 279.

Sanko Grand Summer Championship—¥100,000,000
Winner: Frankie Minoza

With Frankie Minoza's victory in the new Sanko Grand Summer Championship, the list of former Asia Tour money leaders with victories on the 1995 Japan PGA Tour stretched back without interruption to the 1990 season. That's when the 35-year-old standout from the Philippines capped his best season with a playoff victory in the Dunlop Open, his first in Japan, and clinched the money title. Since then, Minoza won the Maruman Open in 1993, then the Sanko Grand Summer title the first week of August at Gunma Sanko 72 Country Club.

Minoza hung close to the lead for three days at Gunma. He shot 68 Thursday. The one-two placers — Hideki Kase (64) and Tatsuo Takasaki (66) — promptly dissolved and lightly regarded Kazuhiko Hosokawa entered the picture. With matching 67s, he joined Ryoken (Ricky) Kawagishi on top Friday with 134, then moved in front alone by a stroke Saturday with 68–202. Minoza (68-

68-67) was at 203 with Kawagishi and Tomohiro Maruyama, winner of the previous week's NST Niigata Open. Minoza made Sunday's finale no contest when he stirred up an eight-under-par 64 and rolled to a four-stroke victory with his 267. Shinji Ikeuchi popped into second place with a 66–271.

Acom International—¥100,000,000
Winner: Katsunori Kuwahara

Katsunori Kuwahara staged a 12-point spurt in the final round of the off-beat Acom International to capture his first victory on the Japan PGA Tour. The final-round heroics gave Kuwahara a 46 total and a five-point triumph over Tsukasa Watanabe, who had shared the third-round lead at 36 with Takaaki Fukuzawa at the Seve Ballesteros Golf Club at Sakuragawa.

Veteran left-hander Yutaka Hagawa got off to a big start in Thursday's first round with 21 points in Stableford-style event, patterned after The International on the U.S. PGA Tour with point values ranging from five for eagles to minus one for bogeys. Watanabe and Hisashi Nakase compiled 15 points each. Hagawa faded Friday as Watanabe added 11 points and moved one in front of Takaaki Fukuzawa. Kuwahara was then seven points off the pace, but moved to 34 and within two of the co-leaders going into the final round.

Hisamitsu KBC Augusta Tournament—¥100,000,000
Winner: Kazuhiko Hosokawa

Kazuhiko Hosokawa apparently learned something from adversity — his failure to carry a lead to victory two weeks earlier in the Sanko Grand Summer Championship. He got himself into the same position as second- and third-round leader in the Hisamitsu KBC Augusta tournament at Ashiya Golf Club, Fukuoka. This time, Hosokawa was equal to the challenge. He shot a final-round 69 to edge fast-closing Todd Hamilton and a hot Tomohiro Maruyama, both 1995 winners on the Japan PGA Tour. He finished at 271, 17 under par, one shot ahead of Hamilton and Maruyama.

Hosokawa started the tournament with 69, too, and was five strokes in the hole to leader Carlos Franco, the Sapporo Tokyu winner. Hosokawa then vaulted all the way into first place with 66 Friday, his 135 leading Toru Suzuki, Frankie Minoza and Hideki Kase by one stroke. He held that margin with his 67–202, Minoza matching the 67 for 203 and Maruyama standing third with Kase at 204. Hamilton, the Token champion back in March, finished with 66-67 to climb into the runner-up tie with Maruyama, who had a final-round 68.

Japan Match Play Championship—¥80,000,000
Winner: Katsuyoshi Tomori

Katsuyoshi Tomori, one of the older players in the 32-man field, overcame the rigors of the Japan Match Play Championship and claimed the title at the Nidom Classic course in Hokkaido with a 2-and-1 victory over Shigeki

Maruyama in the 36-hole final. The 40-year-old traversed six rounds in four days in winning the sixth title in his long career on the Japan PGA Tour and first in more than a year, since the 1994 Mitsubishi Galant.

En route to the title match, Tomori took out two of the tournament's biggest names — Tsuneyuki (Tommy) Nakajima and Masahiro Kuramoto — by 2-and-1 scores in succession after beating Koki Idoki, 5 and 3, in the first round. He rolled over Toru Suzuki, 6 and 5, while Maruyama was nipping Hideki Kase, 1 up, in the semi-finals. Maruyama's path to the semis had not been easy. He eliminated David Ishii, 1 up, and went 19 holes before ousting Masayuki Kawamura around a 5-and-3 victory over Katsunari Takahashi.

Suntory Open—¥90,000,000
Winner: Masahiro Kuramoto

Victories have been fewer and farther between for Masahiro Kuramoto in recent years, so his win in the Suntory Open, the 28th of his outstanding career on the Japan PGA Tour, was particularly welcome and meaningful, since the field was at full strength and also included U.S. Open champion Corey Pavin. Kuramoto won by three strokes with his 15-under-par 273 at Narashino Country Club in Chiba.

The key to Kuramoto's victory was his second-round 64, which jumped him from a shot off the opening-day lead of KBC Augusta winner Kazuhiko Hosokawa into a five-stroke lead at 131 over Takaaki Fukuzawa. Though he took a 71 Saturday, he still led by three over Nobuo Serizawa, four over Fukuzawa, Tateo Ozaki and Satoshi Higashi. Very little changed Sunday. Kuramoto shot 71 again and posted the three-stroke victory over Higashi, Fukuzawa (70s) and Serizawa (71). Pavin finished another stroke back with Mitsutaka Kusakabe and Hajime Meshiai.

ANA Open—¥100,000,000
Winner: Masashi Ozaki

You could have bet on it. Masashi (Jumbo) Ozaki had to be the odds-on favorite to win the ANA (All Nippon Airways) Open just off his track record — six victories in the event, dating back to 1972 and including 1992 and 1994, when he was 20 under par and won by nine strokes. The 48-year-old Ozaki lived up to expectations, although the going wasn't quite so easy this time on the Watts course of Sapporo Golf Club. Still, he won by three strokes over international star Ernie Els, the South African winner of the 1994 U.S. Open, with 279, nine under par, to add victory No. 72 to his tremendous record.

Never more than two strokes behind, Ozaki led through the last two rounds in becoming the first three-time winner on the 1995 Japan PGA Tour. Tsuyoshi Yoneyama led for two days before his lights went out (78-77). He opened with 68 and followed with 72 for 140 and a two-stroke lead over Hisayuki Sasaki, Tsuneyuki Nakajima, Masahiro Kuramoto, Kiyoshi Maita and Ozaki. Jumbo slipped a stroke in front with 69–211 Saturday. Hideki Kase and Els also had 69s and positioned themselves second and third. Ozaki fashioned a solid, four-birdie 68 to tie up the victory as Els shot 69 and Kase 72 to finish third. The ¥18 million check moved Ozaki within striking distance of Satoshi Higashi, the year's leading money winner with ¥68.8 million.

Gene Sarazen Jun Classic—¥110,000,000
Winner: Satoshi Higashi

The year's top two players on the Japan PGA Tour went head to head in the stretch run of the Gene Sarazen Jun Classic. Satoshi Higashi, No. 1 on the money list and a two-time winner, against Masashi (Jumbo) Ozaki, a close No. 2 with three 1995 titles, including the previous week's ANA Open. Higashi, whose record palls when compared to Ozaki's, nonetheless won the duel on the Jun Classic Golf Club course, shooting a final-round 68 to Ozaki's 70 to edge him by one stroke with his 18-under-par 270 total The third 1995 victory gave the 34-year-old Higashi six career titles and boosted his money lead to more than ¥10 million.

Hideki Kase, playing strongly for weeks but unable to crack through with a win, made another bid in the Jun Classic with a leading 65 start. He remained in front with 70–135 Friday but was joined at the top by the veteran Nobumitsu Yuhara. Higashi and Ozaki, at 137, were among 10 players within two strokes. Ozaki charged to the front with 64 Saturday, but Higashi stayed within a stroke with 65 for 202, where Kase and Yuhara lighted after 67s, and Higashi won the title with 68 Sunday, getting the upper hand early with birdies at the first and third holes.

Japan Open Championship—¥90,000,000
Winner: Toshimitsu Izawa

It was an astonishing week at Kasumigaseki Country Club, site of the Japan Open Championship. The national championship has, as one would expect, a distinguished roll of winners, particularly in recent years. Since 1985, only Seiki Okuda (1993) broke the strangleholds of Jumbo Ozaki, Tommy Nakajima and Isao Aoki on the Open, and he had four victories already on his record when that happened. So along comes 27-year-old Toshimitsu Izawa, who had traveled the Japan PGA Tour for seven years without winning, and he outplays the powerful field, shoots a seven-under-par 277 total and walks away with the championship.

Izawa, who had two high finishes early in the season, started the week off with a bang, birdied four of his first five holes and took a one-stroke lead with 67. It was reasonable to expect that that would be all for Izawa. Instead, he shot 70 Friday and widened his margin to two strokes over Nobumitsu Yuhara. Ozaki, the five-time Open champion, kept his hopes alive at 142, but Izawa's position kept getting better. His second 70 Saturday stretched his lead to three strokes over Nobuo Serizawa and Hidemichi Tanaka, who shot 65. He needed all of that buffer Sunday when he again shot 70, just enough to nip Kazuhiko Hosokawa, who closed with 67, by a single stroke.

Tokai Classic—¥110,000,000
Winner: Masayuki Kawamura

For all intents and purposes, another first-time winner emerged on the Japan PGA Tour on the heels of Toshimitsu Izawa's victory in the Japan Open. Masayuki Kawamura had a previous victory on his record, but it was in the 1992 Chishikoku Open, one of the tournaments in the usual mid-summer week of regional events during a Tour break. However, nothing detracted from Kawamura's 1995 triumph in the Tokai Classic, which has had an impressive international array of past winners. Kawamura parlayed one sensational round into a one-stroke victory with a three-under-par 285 total at Miyoshi Country Club.

Kawamura was floating back in the pack for two days after rounds of 74-73 as first Hirofumi Miyase then Kiyoshi Maita held one-stroke leads. Then, Kawamura rocketed to the fore with an eight-under-par 64, seizing a three-stroke margin over Katsunari Kuwahara and Maita. That proved to be just enough of an edge Sunday, as he slipped back to 74 and edged a frustrated Hideki Kase by the single stroke.

Golf Digest Tournament—¥100,000,000
Winner: Stewart Ginn

The foreign contingent had been relatively quiet and the Japanese players had been winning the tournaments on the Japan PGA Tour for a couple of months. Stewart Ginn, the 44-year-old Australian who has campaigned in Asia for many years and on the Japan PGA Tour from time to time, changed things at the Golf Digest Tournament with the season's strongest 36-hole finish. Ginn, a three-time winner over a 15-year span on the Asia Tour but never a winner in Japan, shot back-to-back 64s at Tohmei Country Club, coming from nowhere to post a two-stroke victory with his 17-under-par 267 total.

Brian Watts, who won at Shizuoka early in the season but was far off the pace that led to his huge 1994 run in Asia and Japan, got off to a strong start in the Golf Digest event. He led five players by a stroke with his opening 66 and was still one shot ahead after his 68–134 Friday. Chen Tze-Ming was at 135, and six others were at 136. Ginn, who trailed by five at that point, surged into a tie for first place with Canada's Rick Gibson, the Novell KSB winner, with the first 64. They were at 203. Gibson played well Sunday with a five-under 66, but was no match for Ginn and his second straight 64.

Bridgestone Open—¥120,000,000
Winner: Shigeki Maruyama

Shigeki Maruyama, who has been trying to live up to his brilliant amateur career in his first four years on the Japan PGA Tour, took a big step in that direction in the Bridgestone Open. The 25-year-old player, whose only previous win had been in the 1993 Pepsi Ube event, outdueled American Mark

Calcavecchia down the stretch and registered a three-stroke victory at Sodegaura Golf Club. He was 14 under par at 274.

Maruyama, who piled up 37 titles as an amateur, was in or just off the lead throughout the Bridgestone Open. He launched his victory bid with 66 and shared first place with Tateo Ozaki, Yasunobu Kuramoto and Calcavecchia, the 1989 British Open champion who had won his seventh title on the U.S. PGA Tour earlier in the season at Memphis. Kuramoto nosed one stroke in front of Maruyama, Brian Watts, Hidemichi Tanaka and Hajime Meshiai with 69–135 Friday, but Maruyama spurted three strokes in front with 67 Saturday and Calcavecchia took over the runner-up position with 68–206. In the tense finish Sunday, Maruyama slipped two over par for the day through 12 holes and into a tie with the American. However, he pulled away to the three-stroke final margin over Calcavecchia, Jumbo Ozaki and Shinichi Yokota with birdies at the 13th, 16th and 18th holes.

Philip Morris Championship—¥200,000,000
Winner: Hidemichi Tanaka

Hidemichi Tanaka picked a superb time to acquire his first title on the Japan PGA Tour, in the richest tournament of the 1995 season to that late October date. Tanaka, just 25 but a professional for five years, outfought veterans Nobumitsu Yuhara and Naomichi (Joe) Ozaki to win the Philip Morris Championship by a stroke at the ABC Golf Club at Tojo with his nine-under-par 279 total.

A rare lapse by Masashi (Jumbo) Ozaki, the money leader, gave Tanaka and others the chance at the ¥36 million first prize. Jumbo Ozaki shared first place the first two days, on Thursday with Tanaka and Harumitsu Hamano at 67 and on Friday with Yuhara at 138. Tanaka dropped two behind with 73–140, then bounced back Saturday with 69–209 and led jointly with Joe Ozaki, who had recently returned to Japan after a season on the U.S. PGA Tour. The Sunday finish was exciting. Ozaki, with two birdies, led at the turn, but Tanaka's third birdie of the day at the 15th put him a stroke in front. Yuhara eagled the par-five 18th to overtake Tanaka, but Tanaka birdied there moments later to snatch the victory with his 69–278. Yuhara and Joe Ozaki tied for second at 279. Jumbo Ozaki was next at 280.

Daiwa International—¥170,000,000
Winner: Shigenori Mori

An unusual pattern in the late-season segment of the Japan PGA Tour continued at the Daiwa International. At a time when the big guns of the circuit and visiting international stars normally dominate, Japanese lesser lights were taking the victories. Shigenori Mori, a 37-year-old in his 11th season, became the fifth first-time Tour winner in six weeks when he survived a feeble finishing round and an incendiary charge by Hisayuki Sasaki and won the Daiwa by one shot with his eight-under-par 280 total.

Mori moved up the standings the first two days. He was tied for seventh with 71 behind Seiki Okuda's 66 Thursday and fourth at 138 behind Tsukasa

Watanabe's 135 Friday. A 69 Saturday elevated him into a first-place tie at 207 with Masanobu Kimura and he barely hung on Sunday. Sasaki and David Ishii closed in when Mori went three over par on the front nine. Ishii had four straight birdies on that side, but eventually shot just 69. Sasaki, the Japan PGA champion who started the round nine strokes back, had an eagle and eight birdies on the first 16 holes, but took a fatal double bogey at the 18th and his 65 tied him with Ishii at 281. Mori birdied the 10th and 12th holes, then parred in for 73 and the one-stroke victory at Daiwa Vintage Golf Club at Sudama.

Sumitomo Visa Taiheiyo Masters—¥150,000,000
Winner: Satoshi Higashi

The influx of international stars continued as usual as the Japan PGA Tour reached Gotemba for the Sumitomo Visa Taiheiyo Masters, the springboard event 23 years ago for the lucrative late-season series of tournaments. The focus, however, remained on the domestic battle for No. 1 on the Tour between Satoshi Higashi and the holder, Masashi (Jumbo) Ozaki. Higashi kept the upper hand by scoring his fourth victory of the season in convincing fashion and fattening his 1995 earnings to ¥130 million. Ozaki lost ground with his third-place finish.

Higashi held the lead from the second round on after opening the tournament with 70, two strokes behind front-runner Toru Suzuki. His second-round 66 projected him three strokes ahead of ever-present Hideki Kase. Meanwhile, Ozaki recovered from a first-round 73 with 69 for 142. Ozaki shaved two strokes off Higashi's lead with a 69 Saturday, as Colin Montgomerie, the leader of the PGA European Tour money list, entered the picture with 66–209 to take over second place, two behind Higashi. Higashi dealt well with the challenge, shooting 67 Sunday for a 14-under-par 274 total. He won by four over Shigeki Maruyama, the Bridgestone victor three weeks earlier, and by five over Ozaki, the defending champion.

Dunlop Phoenix Tournament—¥200,000,000
Winner: Masashi Ozaki

Great players usually respond positively to important challenges and Masashi (Jumbo) Ozaki is clearly a great player. Satoshi Higashi flung down the gauntlet when he won the Taiheiyo Masters and opened a sizeable lead over Ozaki on the Japan PGA Tour money list, on which Jumbo had been No. 1 five of the last seven years. Ozaki immediately took care of that circumstance in the rich Dunlop Phoenix Tournament the following week with one of the most sensational finishes of his storied career. He eagled the 72nd hole to take a one-stroke victory over Americans Robert Gamez, the 1994 Casio World winner, and Brandt Jobe, the Asia Tour qualifier with four 1995 victories, and Australia's Peter Senior, the Dunlop Open winner who led at Phoenix Country Club after the second and third rounds. His final score was 11-under-par 273.

Ozaki came from three strokes off the pace in Sunday's final round to successfully defend the Dunlop Phoenix title, the third in a string of three victories in a row he had in 1994. He had begun the tournament with 65, one shot behind England's Barry Lane, the leader. Then Senior took over for two days. He shot 64 Friday and 69 Saturday for a 202 total and a one-stroke lead over 51-year-old Graham Marsh, a fellow Aussie with a wonderful record over the years in Japan. Ozaki, after 71-69, was at 205 with American Larry Nelson. Fast forward to the par-five 18th Sunday. Jobe and Gamez were in with 274s. Ozaki needed a birdie to tie. Jumbo drilled a four-iron second shot onto the green and rolled in a 30-foot eagle putt, which became the winner when Senior, just off the back edge in two strokes, took three to hole out and tied Jobe and Gamez.

Casio World Open—¥150,000,000
Winner: Seiki Okuda

Jumbo Ozaki ran out of miracles and Seiki Okuda came up with a finish golfers usually only dream of. As a result, Okuda won his first tournament since he took the Japan Open Championship in 1993 and the sixth of his career. Okuda's once-in-a-lifetime finish in the Casio World Open was an eight-under-par 64 and he needed every stroke to beat Ozaki, the Japan PGA Tour's leading player. It gave him a 14-under-par 274 total.

Ozaki seemed on the verge of back-to-back victories at Ibusuki Golf Club in the Casio World. After journeyman Kiyoshi Maita, an 11-year non-winner on the circuit, faded following two days on top with opening rounds of 65 and 68, Jumbo, with 68, climbed into a tie for the lead at 207 with Hajime Meshiai. David Ishii, with 66, advanced into a three-way tie for third at 209 with Maita and Italy's Costantino Rocca, the British Open runner-up. Sunday belonged to Okuda, who came from three strokes behind with an eight-birdie 64, just enough to nip Ozaki, who finished well with a four-birdie 68. The victory gave Japanese pros a rare sweep of the major end-of-season events which have a significant number of overseas pros in their fields.

Japan Series of Golf—¥100,000,000
Winner: Masashi Ozaki

Masashi (Jumbo) Ozaki put the icing on the cake in the Japan Series, his final scheduled appearance of the Japan PGA Tour season. He followed up his victory in the Dunlop Phoenix and runner-up finish in the Casio World Open the two previous weeks with his fifth triumph of the year. It put his sixth money-winning title (certainly he had others in the 1970s before JPGA records were available for verification) far out of reach of Satoshi Higashi, the distant runner-up. The victory was his sixth in the Series but his first since 1980.

Higashi, a four-time winner on the 1995 circuit, had a shot at the Series title, going into the final round tied with Ozaki at 204, one stroke off the lead of Tsuneyuki (Tommy) Nakajima in the limited-field tournament, comprised of the year's tournament victors and non-winners high on the money list. However, he shot 73 Sunday and sagged into a four-way tie for fourth at 277, five shots behind Ozaki's winning 16-under-par 272 total at the Tokyo Yomiuri Country Club. Ozaki finished with a 68, gaining a two-stroke victory over Nakajima, who shot 71, and Shigenori Mori, who closed with 67 for his 274. Shigeki Maruyama, who had led the first day with a hole-in-one and 65, then slipped a stroke behind Ozaki's 66-67–133 Friday, joined the fourth-place deadlock with Higashi, Eduardo Herrera and Masahiro Kuramoto.

Daikyo Open—¥120,000,000
Winner: Frankie Minoza

The Japan PGA Tour acquired one final multiple winner, when Frankie Minoza, the Philippines' No. 1 player, took the season-ending Daikyo Open. The one-stroke victory, coupled with his triumph in the Sanko Grand Summer Championship, made Minoza just the fourth man to record more than a single victory on the 1995 circuit. Minoza, 35, the 1990 Asia Tour champion, now has three titles in Japan to go with his four victories on the Asia Tour.

Minoza lingered just off the lead for two days at Daikyo Country Club on Okinawa as Brian Watts, an American standout in Japan for two years, held first place with 67-68–135. He shared first place Thursday with Toru Nakamura and Nobuo Serizawa. The Filipino took over Saturday with 67 for 204 after his 68-69–137 start, inching one stroke ahead of Watts and two in front of Serizawa. He wrapped it up easily Sunday when Watts and Serizawa faded, Watts with 75, Serizawa with 72. Minoza shot 69 for a 273 total, 11-under-par and two strokes in front of Nakamura, who finished with 66 for 275, and Masahiro Kuramoto, who closed with 67 for 276.

Asia PGA/Omega Tour

The International—US$200,000
Winner: Nam-Sin Park

The Asia PGA Tour came off the drawing board and into reality in late June with the playing of The International at Thailand's Sriracha International Golf Club. With the new professional circuit more oriented toward and supported by the players and PGAs of the Far East than the venerable Asia Tour of the Asia-Pacific Golf Confederation, it was deemed appropriate that Nam-Sin Park, one of Korea's leading players who had been in limbo until earlier in the year because of a brush with the Korea PGA over an international faux pas, would win the inaugural event.

It was a tight squeeze for the 36-year-old Seoul pro, who sank a two-foot par putt at the 72nd hole for 66, a 17-under-par 271 total and a one-stroke victory over South Africa's Hendrik Buhrmann. Par took a beating all week at Sriracha, starting on Thursday when Buhrmann and India's Amandeep Johl led with 66s. Johl, age 29, followed with 68 to go a stroke in front of American Mike Cunning and Filipino Robert Pactolerin, two ahead of Buhrmann and four on top of Park (70-68). He remained in front with 69–203 Saturday, Buhrmann shooting 68 for 204 and Park surging with a back-nine 31 for 67–205. The 13-year Korean veteran continued his torrid play Sunday, seizing the lead with birdies on the first five holes and shaking all of the close contenders except Buhrmann, who missed a tying birdie putt on the 18th green at the end.

Canlubang Classic—US$150,000
Winner: Carlos Espinosa

Carlos Espinosa surely will always have a soft spot in his heart for the Philippines. The U.S.-based Mexican pro became the first man to win on both the Asia PGA Tour and the old Asia Tour when he followed his earlier 1995 victory in the Philippine Open with a one-stroke triumph in the Canlubang Classic, the new circuit's only stop in the Philippines. Espinosa, a frequent international representative of Mexico, shot four sub-par rounds for a 10-under-par 274 total, edging Nico Van Rensburg, the second straight South African runner-up finisher of the young season.

Only half the field completed the first round before heavy rains halted play with little-known Yeh Yeou-Tsai, a first-year pro at age 30 who got into the tournament as a standby, in with 66 and a two-stroke lead over Van Rensburg, three over Espinosa. They finally caught up with the schedule Saturday and by that time Espinosa had added rounds of 69 and 67 for 205 and a two-shot lead over Van Rensburg and American John Kernohan.

The 28-year-old South African, outdriving Espinosa Sunday by as much as 40 yards at times, caught him with a two-putt birdie at the par-five ninth and jumped two strokes ahead when he holed a bunker shot from 119 yards for an eagle at the 12th. Espinosa came back with birdies at the 14th and 16th, regained the lead when Van Rensburg bunkered his tee shot at the par-three 17th and put up a 70 with a closing par for the victory when a poor drive prevented Van Rensburg from reaching the par-five 18th in two.

Tournament Players Championship—US$150,000
Winner: Lin Keng-Chi

It took five years and the extra opportunities of the new Asia PGA Tour for Taiwan's Lin Keng-Chi to cash in his first professional victory. It came in the Tournament Players Championship at the Tanjong Puteri Golf Resort at Johor Baru when the circuit went to Malaysia even though that country's PGA had refused to sanction it. Nazamuddin Yusof, the club pro at Tanjong Puteri, was the only Malaysian professional who defied a threatened MPGA ban and played. Even with that on his mind, Yusof shot a course-record 66 in the third round.

But the final day belonged to the 29-year-old Lin, whose most recent of six career runner-up finishes came three months earlier at Bali on the Asia Tour. Wielding a hot putter, the Taiwanese pro came from a shot off the pace with a closing 68. His 10-under-par 278 total gave him a three-stroke victory over countryman Lu Wen-Ter and South Africa's Craig Kamps. The third round co-leaders — rookie pros David Bransdon, 21, of Australia and Cheng Jun, 26, of China — fell back Sunday, Bransdon to ninth place with 75 and Cheng, one of two pros from the People's Republic pioneering international play, to 17th with 77. He had shared the first-round lead at 68 with India's Jyoti Randhawa and Gaurav Ghei and was two off the 139 pace of Lin Chih-Chen and Vivek Bhandari at the midpoint. Lin had rounds of 72-70-68 going into his strong final round, in which he sank five birdie putts of nine feet or longer.

Formosa Open—US$250,000
Winner: Lin Chie-Hsiang

Although appearing on the schedule of the Asia PGA Tour as the Formosa Open, the tournament at Formosa First Golf Club at Taipei also was the Republic of China's PGA Championship, the crown jewel event on the domestic Taiwan PGA Tour. Not everything blended together that August week from administrative standpoints, but the behind-the-scenes squabbles did not detract from the tournament and its exciting finish as Lin Chie-Hsiang, the defending PGA champion and two-time winner of the China (ROC) Open on the Asia Tour, scored a thrilling, come-from-behind victory.

Eight strokes behind and far down in the standings after his opening rounds of 71-74, Lin began his move with a five-under-par 67 Saturday. Yet, he still trailed by six strokes, as Thailand's Boonchu Ruangkit added 68 to his earlier 70-68, moving from a shot behind Korea's Jong-Duck Kim, the midway leader, into a two-stroke advantage over Chul-Sang Cho. The home favorite maintained his hot pace Sunday, firing 68 that included a run of five consecutive birdies at mid-round. That was enough to catch Ruangkit, runner-up in the 1994 China Open. Lin was just on in two on the par-five 16th, the first playoff hole, and Ruangkit pitched his third four feet from the cup only to watch in disbelief as the Taiwanese pro rolled in his 40-foot eagle putt for the victory.

Yokohama Singapore PGA Championship—US$225,000
Winner: Lin Keng-Chi

Lin Keng-Chi seems to have found the key to victory on the Asia PGA Tour. Less than a month and the second tournament after he picked up the first win of his five-year career, the Taiwanese pro struck again. He did it quite differently in the Yokohama Singapore PGA Championship, though, holding at least a share of the lead throughout at Jurong Country Club, then surviving a late bid by Myanmar's Zaw Moe for a one-stroke victory, the third in a row by a Taiwan golfer on the circuit.

Lin's march to the title went this way:

He shot 68 Thursday and tied for the lead with Takehito Daijo of Japan and Aaron Meeks of the U.S. Mike Cunning and Robert Pactolerin were at 69. Lin followed with 67 Friday and took a three-stroke lead. Moe shaved one shot off Lin's lead Saturday with 68 to the leader's 69 and was the only serious challenger Sunday. Trailing by two strokes, Moe reached the green at the par-five 18th with a 235-yard, four-wood second shot that stopped 10 feet from the hole. But, he missed the eagle putt and Lin sewed up the win with two putts from just off the front edge for 71 and 275, 13 under par. Australian David Bransdon, who had taken a run at victory in the Tournament Players Championship two tournaments back, closed with 66 to tie Cunning for third at 279.

Passport Open—US$300,000
Winner: Vijay Singh

Vijay Singh, who has put Fiji on the golfing map with his outstanding play since the late 1980s throughout the world and especially in Europe and the United States, put his talents on display with a one-stop visit to the Asia PGA Tour when it staged the Passport Open at Korea's Chun Chon Country Club. Undaunted by a seven-stroke deficit halfway through the tournament, Singh produced back-to-back 65s and held off another Singh — Jeev Milkha, a 23-year-old pro from India — for a one-shot victory.

The outcome was a bitter disappointment for Jong-Duck Kim and his home country supporters. Kim, the 1994 Korean Open champion, had assumed the lead the second day, his 68-67–135 setting him two strokes in front of Jeev Singh, Masakazu Noritake of Japan and Thaworn Wiratchant of Thailand, seven ahead of Vijay Singh. Another 67 widened his lead to five, but then over Vijay. Jeev was two further back. The two Singhs simply overwhelmed him with birdies Sunday. Kim held on until Vijay made his sixth birdie at the 12th hole to go in front for good. Vijay made his last birdie at the 14th and parred in, just enough to hold off Jeev Singh, who ran off eight birdies for 64–273, falling one shot short. Kim shot 73 and finished third at 275. South Africa's standout David Frost also dropped in at Chun Chon and tied for fourth with Carlos Espinosa, the two-time 1995 winner in Asia, and Koreans Sang-Ho Choi and Yong-Jin Shin.

Langkawi Open—US$150,000
Winner: Boonchu Ruangkit

Boonchu Ruangkit is upholding his reputation as Thailand's leading playing professional with his performances on the Asia PGA Tour. The 39-year-old Ruangkit, a veteran campaigner on the old Asia Tour and winner of the Thailand Open in 1992, scored a resounding victory in the Langkawi Open when the Asia PGA circuit resumed action in Malaysia after a month's hiatus. He blistered the Datai Bay Golf Club course on the resort island of Langkawi with a 15-under-par total of 275, seven strokes better than his nearest pursuer, compatriot Jannian Chitprasong. The victory, following strong showings in three earlier events, including his runner-up playoff finish in the Formosa Open, elevated Boonchu into first place on the circuit's money list.

Ruangkit was in the lead at Datai Bay after all except the second round, when American Clay Devers, winner of the long-running Malaysian Open on the Asia Tour earlier in the year, had him by a shot with his 68-69–137. Ruangkit had begun the tournament in front, firing a back-nine 31 for 67 and a one-stroke lead over Devers and Aaron Meeks. He moved back into first place with another 67 Saturday for 205 and carried a three-stroke lead over Devers (71) and four over South African Craig Kamps into the final round. A solid 68 — four birdies, no bogeys — established the final margin over Chitprasong, who finished with 69 to edge par-shooting Kamps by a stroke.

Gadgil Western Dubai Creek Open—US$500,000
Winner: Robert Willis

The Asia PGA Tour acquired a commercial sponsor and a new name and Robert Willis became the first Australian victor on the freshly-dubbed Omega Tour. The 32-year-old Willis, whose only previous victory had come in the 1991 Fiji Open, picked a great time for the win. The $500,000 Dubai Creek Open was the first of two big-money events this year and of others in years to come that Gadgil Western Group, an Indian oil and industrial conglomerate, announced it will sponsor on the circuit, which now has the Swiss watch company as its title sponsor.

Willis, who led after two rounds and trailed by a single stroke after 54 holes, almost let the victory get away. He had shot 71-66–137 to lead at the halfway point, then slipped one stroke behind Thailand's 48-year-old Arjin Sophon when he shot 73 Saturday. Willis led most of the way Sunday only to take his lone bogey at the last hole off a poor chip for 73 and fall into a tie with Thailand's Jannian Chitprasong, runner-up to countryman Boonchu Ruangkit the previous week at Langkawi. Chitprasong closed with 69 for his five-under-par 283, one shot ahead of Ruangkit, the money list leader, and India's Jeev Milkha Singh. The playoff ended quickly on the par-five 10th hole after Chitprasong went for the green in two and put his ball in the water. Willis laid up and won with his conservative par.

Merlion Masters—US$200,000
Winner: Nico Van Rensburg

Nico Van Rensburg keeps outstanding company when he is home in South Africa and, after winning the Merlion Masters, the October stop of the Omega Tour in Singapore, figures that "I'm not so far behind" the man he frequently practices with — Ernie Els. Van Rensburg, 29, who blew a lead and finished second earlier in the season in the Canlubang Classic, almost did it again at the Laguna National Golf and Country Club. With a final-round 73 that included an eagle, four birdies, four bogeys and a triple bogey, Van Rensburg eked out a one-stroke victory over Australian Don Fardon and Thailand's Pisit Infasang with his nine-under-par 279.

Infasang led the first day with 65, Van Rensburg and Rodrigo Cuello of the Philippines took over Friday with 137s, and Fardon moved a stroke ahead of Van Rensburg and Cuello Saturday with 67–205. Van Rensburg seemed to have the title in the bag Sunday when he went three strokes ahead with a birdie at the 16th hole. But, he put his tee shot in the water at the par-three 17th and took a triple bogey, then parred the 18th, opening the door to Fardon. However, the Aussie bogeyed the 17th and missed a 30-foot birdie putt for the tie on the final green. He shot 75 for 280. Infasang shot 69 to bolt to the second-place tie. Cuello stumbled to 76 and dropped to fifth place at 282, a stroke behind Scot Kenny Walker.

Samsung Masters—US$500,000
Winner: Lin Keng-Chi

The remarkable season of Taiwan's Lin Keng-Chi reached its highest point when the Omega Tour staged its rich Samsung Masters in Korea in late October. Already the young circuit's only two-time winner, the 29-year-old Lin, who had never won before 1995, captured his third title in convincing fashion at Pusan's Dongrae Country Club, easing to a two-stroke victory over fast-closing Korean veteran Jong-Duck Kim with his nine-under-par 279. The $80,750 check boosted him far in front on the Omega Tour money list.

Lin, who had proved his mettle in faster company the preceding week in the Volvo Asian Masters in Taiwan, the first event on the Asia Tour's autumn start of its 1995-96 season, with a fourth-place finish, established his front-running position at Dongrae with a 68-67 start after American John Kernohan opened the tournament in front with 66. Even though he slipped to 74 Saturday, he lost just a stroke of his five-shot lead. Four back after 54 holes were Nam-Sin Park, Mike Cunning of the U.S. and Lu Chien-Soon, the reputable Taiwan veteran. Aware of Kim's charge Sunday, Lin remained focused and played flawlessly on the finishing holes, securing the victory with birdies on the par-five 15th and 18th holes.

Royal Perak Classic—US$150,000
Winner: Gerry Norquist

Gerry Norquist achieved a couple of firsts when the Omega Tour made its third visit to Malaysia in late October for the Royal Perak Classic. When the 27-year-old Norquist from Oregon defeated countryman Greg Hanrahan in a playoff at Ipoh's Royal Perak, he became the first American to win on the new circuit and to own titles on both operating tours in Asia. Norquist won the Malaysian Open in 1993.

The two Americans jockeyed for position during the first two rounds, then rocketed to the top Saturday when they both shot eight-under-par 64s. Hanrahan, who had earlier rounds of 69-71, took the lead at 205, one stroke in front of Norquist, who had started 71-70. Hanrahan stayed in front most of the way Sunday, leading by two after both men birdied the 16th. But Norquist holed a 12-foot birdie putt at No. 17 and birdied the 18th from the sand for 67 to force the playoff as Hanrahan posted 68. Norquist then birdied the 18th again at the start of the playoff to win the title. Singapore's Madasamy Murugiah placed third, six shots out of first place.

Kenmore Pakistan Masters—US$225,000
Winner: Young-Suk Kwon

Young-Suk Kwon, relying on the experience he had gained earlier in the year when he won the non-Tour Korean Open, put together a solid 69 finish to surge from behind and land the Kenmore Pakistan Masters, the second international tournament ever in the country. (The first was a Pakistan Open on the Asia Tour in 1989.) The three-under-par final round gave Kwon a 276 total and a four-stroke victory over Thailand's Thaworn Wiratchant and New Zealand's Tony Christie. The 25-year-old Korean led by as many as seven strokes during the final round.

The lead changed hands every day at the Karachi course in the Omega Tour's 12th event. Gaurav Ghei of India started with 68, then Kwon went in front with 69-68–137. Wiratchant slipped a stroke ahead of the Korean Saturday when he added 68 to his earlier pair of 69s for 206. However, Wiratchant could manage only a 74 Sunday and dropped into the runner-up tie with Christie, who finished with 68.

Gadgil Western Masters—US$500,000
Winner: Gaurav Ghei

The rich Gadgil Western Masters, the second $500,000 tournament on the Omega Tour sponsored by the India conglomerate, got its money's worth of excitement in its final moments at Delhi Golf Club, which had hosted the Indian Open of the Asia Tour back in March. Gaurav Ghei, needing to get down in two strokes from just off the green at the 72nd hole to bring about a playoff, ran in the 30-yard chip shot for an eagle and victory over a stunned Vijay Kumar, who was waiting to handle a three-foot putt, expecting nothing worse than an overtime duel with Ghei. Instead, the 27-year-old Ghei, with 69 and 274, had the title and the $80,750 first-place check. Kumar's subsequent putt gave him a 70 for 275.

The two men had carried the lead into the final round, Ghei with 69-69-67 and Kumar with 71-67-67 for 205s. Jyoti Randhawa and Carlos Espinosa, a 1995 winner on both the Asia and Omega Tours, also had title chances Sunday. Randhawa shot 68 and had the clubhouse lead at 276 before Ghei and Kumar reached the final holes. Espinosa killed his chances with a bad drive and bogey at the 18th, dropping into a tie for fourth at 277 with Jeev Milkha Singh and Wook-Soon Kang.

Gadgil Western Vietnam Open—US$150,000
Winner: Clay Devers

Clay Devers of the United States joined Carlos Espinosa, an American-based Mexican, with the unique distinction as a winner on both professional tours in Asia in 1995 when he won the first-ever international golf tournament in Vietnam. Devers scored a one-stroke victory over Thailand's Boonchu Ruangkit in the Omega Tour's Gadgil Western Vietnam Open at Golf Vietnam, Thu Duc in Ho Chi Minh City in early December, some nine months after winning the Benson & Hedges Malaysian Open on the Asia Tour. Espinosa had victories on both circuits in the Philippines earlier in the year.

Devers got away fast with a pair of 66s the first two days, sharing the first-round lead with Jeff Senior of Australia, then taking a three-stroke advantage on runner-up Ruangkit at the halfway point. Devers shot 70 Saturday and lost one stroke of his lead to Ruangkit (69–204) with circuit leader Lin Keng-Chi lurking at 205. None of the three fared well Sunday, but Devers' 73 for a 275 total, 13 under par, enabled him to finish with the one-stroke victory.

Philippine Classic—US$200,000
Winner: Jeev Milkha Singh

Youth was finally served in mid-December in the Philippine Classic, the final 1995 event on the Omega Tour, when 24-year-old Jeev Milkha Singh commanded the Philippine Classic at Sta Elena Golf Club in Laguna from start to finish and posted a one-stroke victory. Singh had come close to his first victory in three earlier Omega tournaments, especially in the Passport Open in Korea, where he fired a final-round 64 but fell a stroke short of the other, more-famous Singh, Vijay.

At Laguna, Jeev started fast with a 65 and was never caught. The seven-under-par round gave him a three-stroke lead over countryman Arjun Atwal. Singh lost a stroke of his margin to Atwal Friday when he had a 73 to Atwal's 72. They both had 72s Saturday, putting Singh at 210, Atwal at 212. Singh's challenge Sunday came from Thailand's Preccha Senaprom, who mustered a 71 but fell a stroke short of Singh's 73–283. Singh's birdie at the 17th made the difference. Atwal took a 76 and dropped into a third-place tie with Korea's Nam-Sin Park at 288.

15. Australasian Tour

The Australasian Tour of 1995 provided a variety of success stories, unlike some previous years when the list basically started and ended with Greg Norman. The Great White Shark was still at the forefront, but he was joined there by Steve Elkington, Craig Parry and Michael Campbell, to name but three others.

Norman led the U.S. PGA Tour money list with $1,654,959 and his five worldwide victories included his fourth Heineken Australian Open, which also was his first home victory in five years. Elkington led off the year by winning the Mercedes Championship, came up just short in the British Open, then won his first major title at the PGA Championship. He also won the late-season Franklin Templeton Shark Shootout with partner Mark Calcavecchia.

Parry was No. 1 on the Australasian Tour with A$334,803, winning the Canon Challenge and Norman's Holden Classic between hauling in $293,413 to finish 65th in the United States without a victory there. Campbell split his time between Australasia and the PGA European Tour, placing second to Parry with A$207,403 and fourth in Europe with £400,977.

Entering the year, Campbell had won only the 1993 Canon Challenge but he came to be recognized as Australasia's next emerging star. The 26-year-old New Zealander won the Alfred Dunhill Masters, but he first attracted worldwide notice in the British Open, where he led after 54 holes before tieing for third place. He placed second or third six times during the year.

Parry's comments after defeating Campbell by one stroke in November were typical. "He's going to be one of the world's top players in a couple of years. No question," Parry said. "He's got all the shots and he never gives up. He is a great ball-striker and he thinks well. If he has a weakness, it is his putting and judgement of speed."

The Australasians were again well-represented on the Sony Ranking. Norman held his usual No. 1 position and Elkington was boosted from No. 43 to No. 10 by his PGA Championship victory. Campbell rose during the year from No. 209 to No. 28, followed by Frank Nobilo at No. 37, Parry at No. 43 and Peter Senior at No. 47. Others in the top 100 of the Sony Ranking were Robert Allenby (No. 64), Brett Ogle (No. 83), Wayne Riley (No. 88), Robert O'Malley (No. 89) and Greg Turner (No. 92).

Not everyone went from strength to strength. Allenby and Ogle each fell 16 positions on the Sony Ranking but those were relatively insignificant changes compared to those of Roger Mackay (No. 94 to 138), Wayne Grady (No. 115 to 170) and Rodger Davis (No. 81 to 181). And there was Ian Baker-Finch. The 1991 British Open champion played 24 events in 1995 and earned exactly nothing. He last made a 36-hole cut in October of 1994 in Australia. His last in the United States was in August of that year.

Lucas Parsons led off 1995 on the Australasian Tour by winning the AMP New Zealand Open. Tim Elliott, who had not won in 10 years on the circuit, provided the year's biggest surprises by winning two of the next three events, the Optus Players Championship and Ford South Australian Open. In between, Allenby won the Heineken Classic. Senior, who would later win the Dunlop Open in Japan, took the Australian Masters title, and Parry concluded the January-February segment by winning the Canon Challenge.

In late October, Terry Price was the winner of the Bank of Queensland Open, which preceded Campbell's victory in the official Australasian Tour opener. Then Steve Conran won the Epson Singapore Open and Stephen Leaney won the Victorian Open. Norman and Parry were winners of the next two events. O'Malley, winner of the Benson & Hedges International Open in Europe, took the title in the AMP Air New Zealand Open and Shane Robinson wrapped up the year with a victory in the Schweppes Coolum Classic.

Other Australasian champions worldwide during the year included Turner (Turespana Open de Baleares), Nobilo (BMW International Open) and Riley (Scottish Open) on the PGA European Tour. In Japan, Stewart Ginn took the Golf Digest Open title. A golfer who bears watching, Stuart Appleby had two victories on America's Nike Tour and qualified for the primary circuit in 1996.

The year also marked the first Alfred Dunhill Challenge, a Ryder Cup-type event between Australasia and Southern Africa, won by the home team in Johannesburg.

AMP New Zealand Open—A$237,930
Winner: Lucas Parsons

Lucas Parsons plays golf in New Zealand as if he were at home, and it is, in fact, the home of his mother's family. Parsons, a 25-year-old Australian, won three amateur tournaments there and added the AMP New Zealand Open this year in an improbable finish. "Golf can be weird, it really can," Parsons said after coming from five strokes behind Mike Harwood in the final round to win by one stroke over Michael Clayton.

Harwood, who finished with 77 for a sixth-place tie, four strokes behind Parsons, bogeyed the first four holes in the final round. Parsons made an eagle three on the second hole and a birdie on the fourth, and saw his name atop the leaderboard as he went to the sixth tee. He never relinquished the advantage, had more birdies at the 11th and 14th holes, and shot 68 for a 282 total, six under par on the Heretaunga course in Wellington. It was his third professional victory.

Clayton, who had a final-round 70, missed a five-foot putt on the 18th hole that would have forced a playoff with Parsons. New Zealander Michael Campbell finished with 69 and tied for third place at 284 with David Smail and Tim Elliott.

Optus Players Championship—A$350,000
Winner: Tim Elliott

Perhaps the difference was Tim Elliott's recent gift of a lucky penny, when Elliott won for the first time after 10 years on the Australasian Tour, with a come-from-behind victory despite his three-over-par 75 in the last round of the Optus Players Championship at Kingston Heath Golf Club in Melbourne. The A$63,000 first prize came at a good time for Elliott, whose wife had recently given birth to twins.

Elliott's lucky 1938 penny was given to him by the same person who, five years earlier, had given one to his friend Craig Parry. Elliott had earlier rounds of 67, 70 and 71, and went into the final day two strokes behind Michael Clayton. The reason Elliott won with his 75 and 283 total, five under par, was that Clayton shot 80, which left him in a tie for third place at 286. Clayton had a double-bogey five on the fifth hole and a quadruple-bogey eight on the sixth, including a two-stroke penalty when his bunker shot ricocheted and hit him.

Second place at 284 went to Peter Fowler, who shot 68 after starting the day 10 strokes behind Clayton. Stuart Appleby also finished well, having 67 to share third place with Clayton, Doug Dunakey, Greg Chalmers and Peter O'Malley.

Heineken Classic—A$400,000
Winner: Robert Allenby

A week after missing the 36-hole cut with 80 in the second round, Robert Allenby secured the seventh victory of his brief career with a tense, one-stroke triumph over hometown favorite Wayne Smith in the Heineken Classic at The Vines Resort in Perth. Instead of Allenby, those missing the cut this week included American import John Daly, Craig Parry, Wayne Grady, Lucas Parsons and Tim Elliott.

Allenby was over par in the first round with 73, but his 66 brought him back within two strokes of leader David Smail after 36 holes. His 67 in the third round, against Smail's 76, sent Allenby into the last day with a five-stroke cushion over David Ecob and Brett Ogle. Smith was among those six strokes off the lead.

Smith, who had recently returned from lessons with David Leadbetter in Florida, had five birdies over the space of seven holes in the final round, shooting 31 for his first nine holes before finishing with 67 and a 279 total. Allenby heightened the suspense by scoring a double bogey on the 11th hole and a bogey on the 12th, but avoided any further disasters to finish with 72 and a 278 total, 10 under par.

Ford South Australian Open—A$200,000
Winner: Tim Elliott

Tim Elliott went 10 years without a victory, won his first professional golf tournament, missed the 36-hole cut the next time out, then won again in the Ford South Australian Open at Royal Adelaide Golf Club. "I haven't changed anything. That's the amazing thing," said Elliott, whose earnings for 1995 already surpassed those for the past decade. "It just happened. There's no secret. Maybe it's just my turn to play well, and you don't know how long it will last. These might be the only two tournaments I win, but then again I might win 20. I'll just enjoy it while it's happening."

Elliott won by three strokes over Jack O'Keefe and Anthony Painter with a 275 total, 17 under par, in conditions which provided every opportunity for low scoring. His rounds were 68, 71, 66 and 70 over what is usually one of Australia's most difficult courses. He had only three bogeys in 72 holes.

Australian Masters—A$750,000
Winner: Peter Senior

Peter Senior won the Australian Masters for a second time, having to over-come a drunken spectator and Tom Watson on the final hole. In the midst of Senior's backswing on the tee, the spectator had said, "I hope you don't choke like last year." Senior pulled his second shot badly, beside a hospi-tality marquee, took a free drop then pitched over a bunker to the green, leaving himself a 16-foot putt. Watson had an 18-foot putt on the same line for a birdie to tie Senior, but missed before Senior holed his putt for the victory.

"I would not have holed it had I not watched Watson's putt," Senior said. "Tom hit it on exactly the same line as I would have but, once I saw his ball break slightly to the right at the end, I made an adjustment and my putt went right in the center."

Senior had rounds of 69, 70, 72 and 69 for a 280 total, 12 under par at the Huntingdale Golf Club in Melbourne, while Watson, Lucas Parsons and Wayne Grady tied for second place at 281, with Michael Clayton two strokes further behind. Parsons, who opened the year with a victory in New Zealand, led entering the last round by two strokes over Senior, Watson and Clayton. Parsons and Clayton finished with 72s and Watson shot 67. John Daly was in second place after his 71-69 start, then shot 79 and 74 and finished 13 strokes behind.

In the final round, Senior moved into a tie for the lead with Watson and Grady by holing a 20-foot birdie putt on the 13th hole, and took the lead alone with another birdie on the 14th hole. He scrambled home from there. He appeared to have created an opening for Watson at the 17th, when his second shot to the long par-four hole went over the green, but he salvaged the par.

As for the disruptive spectator on the 18th hole, Senior said, "I don't want the good guys in the gallery to be grouped with the bad one." Although Senior won the Australian Masters in 1991, the spectator's remark was in reference to the 1993 event, when he three-putted the 18th hole after being distracted twice by a photographer. Generally, the Australians' respect for this gritty veteran could be noted by the line of winners outside the betting shop after the tournament.

Canon Challenge—A$350,000
Winner: Craig Parry

Craig Parry equalled the course record with seven-under-par 65 in the last round and won by three strokes in the Canon Challenge, the final tourna-ment of the January/February segment of the Australasian Tour, then raced off to Sydney airport en route to play the U.S. PGA Tour.

Both Parry and Richard Green, a left-handed newcomer from Melbourne, shot 65s on the last day at Terrey Hills Country Club, a new course on

Sydney's north shore. Green secured a share of sixth place at 282, while Parry had a 275, 13 under par, to defeat runner-up Wayne Smith. Glenn Joyner led Parry by one stroke after 54 holes, then Joyner shot 80 and fell to a tie for 33rd place. Parry began his round with an eagle and had five birdies in a near-flawless performance. Paul Moloney and Grant Kenny shot 280 and Peter Senior was alone in fifth place at 281.

Bank of Queensland Open—A$50,000
Winner: Terry Price

A long and costly trip paid dividends for Terry Price in October as the Australasian Tour resumed eight months after the Canon Challenge. Price won the Bank of Queensland Open for the second time in three years. The victory came after Price, frustrated by his putting, went to the United States for a putting school conducted by Dave Pelz.

Price won by three strokes over Rodney Pampling, Anthony Edwards and Stuart Bouvier, having a 12-under-par 276 total at Windaroo Country Club in Beenleigh. His final-round 69 featured very solid putting. His main challenger at the end was Bouvier, a fellow Queenslander. Bouvier drove out of bounds on the 14th hole and Price, playing behind him, took control with birdies on the 11th and 12th holes.

Alfred Dunhill Masters—$530,785
Winner: Michael Campbell

Despite being considered an emerging star, Michael Campbell had not won in 1995 as he returned to Australasia in October to begin a late-year run at the Alfred Dunhill Masters in Jakarta, Indonesia. Brushes with victory had included the British Open and a handful of other events on the 1995 PGA European Tour, but the 26-year-old Campbell's lone triumph remained the 1993 Canon Challenge.

Campbell came through with that victory with a 267 performance, 21 under par at the Arnold Palmer-designed Emeralda Golf and Country Club. He shot 65s in the second and fourth rounds and had 30s on the second nine for the last two days. That resulted in a five-stroke margin over Craig Parry and Mark Mouland. "I wanted to win this tournament so badly," Campbell said. "I had been so close so many times that I really needed to come through this week."

Early on Parry was the man to beat. He shot 66 and tied for the first-round lead with Mathias Gronberg and Paul Gow, while Campbell shot 69. Parry remained three strokes ahead of Campbell after the second round, as both shot 65s. In the third round Campbell took the lead with 68, despite a two-stroke penalty for grounding his club in a bunker, as Parry shot 72.

Low scoring was the rule in the final round, although Campbell proved unbeatable with an eagle and seven birdies. Stuart Appleby shot 65 but that got him only to fourth place, eight strokes behind. Mouland finished with 66 for his share of second place, and Wayne Grady and Vijay Singh also posted 66s to take fifth and sixth place, respectively.

Epson Singapore Open—A$519,210
Winner: Steve Conran

Winner Steve Conran shared the praise in the Epson Singapore Open with the tournament officials and staff at Singapore Island Country Club, who managed to keep the Bukit course in playing condition despite heavy rains. Because of the weather, Conran played 36 holes on the second day, six on the third and 30 on the fourth while compiling a 270 total, 14 under par, and winning by three strokes over Andrew Bonhomme, whose scores included 64 in the third round.

The conditions did cause a problem for Conran in the final round. Rules were in effect to permit the players to lift, clean and place their golf balls on the fairways, but Conran's caddie made the mistake of lifting a ball from light rough behind the 12th green. Conran was penalized one stroke, but he still proceeded to his second consecutive 66 and the victory.

Victorian Open—A$200,000
Winner: Stephen Leaney

Stephen Leaney played amateur golf with the likes of Robert Allenby and Michael Campbell, but while they progressed as professionals Leaney had to overcome a serious physical problem. Thus Leaney's victory in the Victorian Open, by one stroke over Allenby and Mike Clayton, was applauded by all sides. Leaney shot 283, five under par at Victoria Golf Club, and his final-round 71 included a two-putt birdie on the final hole to avoid a playoff. Earlier, Allenby had eagled the 18th while finishing with 67.

Leaney, winner of the 1992 Western Australia Amateur, was diagnosed two years ago with a blood clot in his shoulder. Doctors had to remove a rib to ease the pressure on the clot. "I think it took me six months to get back physically, but a whole lot longer mentally," the 26-year-old Leaney said. "This is the first full year I've been fully fit."

Heineken Australian Open—A$850,000
Winner: Greg Norman

Greg Norman won the Heineken Australian Open, his fourth national title and his first victory in his homeland in five years. His triumph was reminiscent of the 1988 MCI Heritage Classic, as Norman again dedicated a victory to a young cancer patient. On the evening before the final round, Norman visited 12-year-old Michael Gentile at the Royal Children's Hospital in Melbourne. After the tournament, Norman told the television audience, "I promised him I would win it. I won it for you, Michael."

Norman's fifth worldwide victory of the year was no cinch as the tightly bunched leaders struggled on the extra-fast greens at Kingston Heath Golf Club before Norman completed his 278 total, 10 under par, to win by two strokes over Peter McWhinney.

After starting the tournament with three bogeys in the first five holes, Norman fought back to post an even-par 72 to be four strokes off the lead.

He shot 69s in the second and third rounds and was tied with McWhinney entering the last day. Four players were tied for the lead with seven holes to play — Norman, McWhinney, Craig Parry and Stuart Appleby — and Frenchman Jean Louis Guepy was just behind them. Norman won with four birdies down the stretch, the last a cup-rattling putt from 35 feet.

In addition to Norman, the star attractions were Steve Elkington, returning home for the first time since winning the PGA Championship, and British Open winner John Daly. Elkington finished 13 strokes behind and Daly, 16 back, on one of those weeks when he apparently was not concentrating on golf. Daly reported that he won A$250,000 in a casino the night before he shot 80 in the third round.

Greg Norman's Holden Classic—A$700,000
Winner: Craig Parry

Everyone agrees that Michael Campbell will be an Australasian star of the future, but Campbell again came away short-handed in the present, as Craig Parry handed Campbell his third one-stroke defeat of the year in Greg Norman's Holden Classic. Parry, winless himself since the Canon Challenge in February, won with a par to Campbell's bogey on the final hole at The Lakes Golf Club in Sydney.

"Everyone tells me I'm a good player, so I need to win instead of being the bridesmaid all the time," said Campbell, whose lone 1995 victory came three weeks earlier in the Alfred Dunhill Masters, where Parry tied for second place.

Parry and Campbell battled head-to-head for four rounds, the last being described by Parry as "like a boxing match." Parry began with an eight-under-par 65 then shot 67. Campbell was just behind him with scores of 66 and 68, along with Frenchman Jean Louis Guepy, continuing his fine showing with rounds of 70 and an astonishing 63. On a very windy third day, Parry and Campbell shot 71s and Guepy, 74.

The host fared even worse in the third round. Greg Norman, who would finish tied for 13th place, shot 79 that included 11 on the 14th hole with three golf balls hit into the water. John Daly was also not a factor in the tournament, finishing one stroke behind Norman.

In the final round, Parry had a four-stroke lead with six holes to play, but Campbell fought back and finally tied him with a birdie on the 17th. On the par-three 18th, Campbell hit his tee shot over the green and Parry was in the fringe short of the green. Campbell's chip shot down a slope went 12 feet past the hole. Parry putted up within four feet, then Campbell missed his try for par before Parry holed the winning putt. "You don't get too many chances to win," Parry said, "and I told myself I had better knock this one in."

Parry finished with 73 for a 276 total, 16 under par, and Campbell had 72 for his 277 total. Brad Faxon took third place at 280, three strokes ahead of Guepy, who shot 76 in the last round, Stuart Appleby and Terry Price.

AMP Air New Zealand Open—A$550,600
Winner: Peter O'Malley

While successful in Europe, Peter O'Malley had never won on the Australasian Tour until he took the AMP Air New Zealand Open title by three strokes over American Scott Hoch. Superb driving carried the Australian on the windy final day when only eight players were able to break par 70 at the Grange Golf Club in Auckland. O'Malley finished with 72 for an eight-under-par 272 total, and Hoch shot 68 to be runner-up at 273.

O'Malley's earlier scores were 65, 67 and 68. He entered the last round with a three-stroke lead and held on. Frank Nobilo and Terry Price shot 71 and 72 respectively and tied for third place at 276. Home favorite Michael Campbell shot 69 in the first round but had to withdraw the next day because of a sore wrist.

Schweppes Coolum Classic—A$200,000
Winner: Shane Robinson

Shane Robinson gave himself a Christmas present, just as he did in 1994, by winning a late-year tournament. Last year, it was the Air New Zealand-Shell Open, his first title after five years as a professional. Fifty-three weeks later Robinson won again in the Schweppes Coolum Classic with a final-round 69 and 10-under-par 278 total to defeat Steve Conran by three strokes.

Robinson had earlier scores of 69, 69 and 71, entering the last round one stroke ahead of Conran. The last round became a duel between those two, as Jeff Senior placed third, five strokes behind, and Grant Todd and Peter Lonard tied for fourth, seven shots back. Conran started well on the final day, with four birdies on the first nine, but cooled off to finish with 71, and Robinson wrapped up the title with a 35-foot birdie putt on the 17th hole.

16. African Tours

Golf in Africa in 1995 was just about whatever anyone wanted to make of it. It had enough clear distinctions that it meant different things to different people, all of them valid. But it probably meant the most to U.S. Open champion Corey Pavin and Nick Price — Pavin because picking up a cool million in one tournament is hard to beat, and the drought-ridden Price because two quick victories at the end of 1995 might be a sign of good things to come.

Of course, you could also say this wasn't South African golf, it was America East. Four of the eight South African events were won by Americans. You could also say it was Ernie Els' year, what with his two big victories in the Bell's Cup and the Lexington PGA Championship. Then there was the Southern Africa victory over Australasia in the inaugural Alfred Dunhill Challenge, a Ryder Cup-like competition.

Of all the wrinkles in African golf, the reemergence of Price might have been the most interesting. He had been tops in the world for so long, and then, as often happens to a golfer, he mysteriously cooled. Then in November, he was on his way home to Zimbabwe when he stopped off in Morocco and won the Hassan II Trophy. It had been 14 months since he had won anything.

"It's a great feeling to win again," Price said. And just in time. Price had given himself the Hassan II Trophy, Zimbabwe Open and Nedbank Million Dollar Challenge "to try and rescue something from this year." He did more than rescue something. He came back the next week and won the Zimbabwe Open for the first time in his career. "I played well in front of people I grew up with," he said, "and it's hard to put into words how much this means to me. After 22 years, this win means as much as any other I've had."

Price's victory couldn't dim the emergence of a couple of new names in the Zimbabwe Open. Brenden Pappas, from the Hans Merensky Golf Club, challenged Price all the way, shot four rounds in the 60s, and finished second by one stroke. Behind Pappas was Mawonga Nomwa, 25, from Soweto Country Club, in only his second year of professional golf. He also shot four rounds in the 60s and was third, four strokes behind Price. "I did not know before this week whether I could handle the pressure, and I am now happy that I can," said Nomwa, who has dreams of playing the American PGA Tour.

Price was poised to make it three wins in a row in the Nedbank Million Dollar Challenge, but it was snatched away from him by a scrawny fighter named Corey Pavin. The short-hitting Pavin tamed the long, tough Gary Player Country Club course with another clinic in shotmaking. "I said at the beginning of the week this course would bring out the best in all aspects of play," Pavin said. It was his fourth victory of the year worldwide, and the $1 million first prize put him over $2.7 million for 1995.

Els had closed out 1994 by winning the Johnnie Walker World Championship in Jamaica in December, then opened 1995 by winning the Bell's Cup in January. In mid-February he won the Lexington PGA Championship. That gave him a victory a month for five straight months.

So Els had his fun, but then the Americans turned South African golf into a raiding party.

Ron Whittaker, 23, a nephew of Lanny Wadkins and a professional for only seven months, started it in the FNB Players Championship, the second event of the year. He won by six strokes against a field that included Mark McNulty, Wayne Westner and Tony Johnstone. "I feel like I'm dreaming," said Whittaker, a former Wake Forest University golfer. Next was Brad Ott in the Hollard Insurance Royal Swazi Sun Classic, coming from three strokes behind with eight holes to play, and carding five birdies over seven holes.

Scott Dunlap was next, beating McNulty in a playoff for the Telkom South African Masters for his first victory in six years on the South African Tour. This came after a curious first round. He was out in 32, back in 42. Then came the pièce de résistance — Pavin and his million-dollar finish.

Speaking for the natives, Ashley Roestoff, a club pro, scored his first victory in the ICL International, and Retief Goosen blocked Els' bid for a third South African victory at the Philips South African Open, winning by five strokes.

As vintages go, then, a lot of golfers found that 1995 was a very good year.

Bell's Cup—R600,000
Winner: Ernie Els

Ernie Els certainly didn't waste any time in the New Year, picking up where he left off. Els closed out 1994 by winning the Johnnie Walker World Championship in Jamaica. He won the Bell's Cup about three weeks later, in the first week of January. "It was great winning at home again," Els said, after taking his first victory in South Africa in two years. Els played the Fancourt Country Club course in 275, 13 under par, for a five-stroke victory over South African Hendrik Buhrmann and American Pat Horgan.

It didn't turn out exactly as Els had wanted. "I really wanted to burn up the course and pull away from the field," Els said, after his 70 in the final round. "But I battled a bit over the first nine. I missed birdie chances at one and two, and just could not find the right rhythm." Els had made his move in the third round with his 69, including an eagle at No. 8, on a five iron to eight feet, and he took a one-stroke lead into the final round. He was soon leading by four strokes when his nearest challengers began to stumble. Retief Goosen suffered three consecutive bogeys from No. 3, and Scott Dunlap, an American, double-bogeyed No. 4.

Els himself faced a big problem, but he survived brilliantly. At the par-four 11th, he hit his tee shot into the water. Unruffled, he took his penalty drop, hit his next onto the green, and holed the putt to save his par. That was his closest brush with big trouble. His card also showed four birdies and two bogeys.

FNB Players Championship—R675,000
Winner: Ron Whittaker

It was a case of like uncle, like nephew in the FNB Players Championship at Durban Country Club. Ron Whittaker, 23 and a professional golfer for only seven months, showed that he can be as determined and pressure-proof as his uncle, Lanny Wadkins. Whittaker, in only his eighth tournament as a pro, stood up to the best the FNB Tour could throw at him — Tony Johnstone, Wayne Westner and Mark McNulty, to name three — and breezed to his first victory by six strokes. They were "going to have to come and get me, because there was no way I was about to let up," Whittaker said. He had the figures to prove it: 68, 64, 68 and 70, for an 18-under-par 270 total. That also got him an invitation to the NEC World Series of Golf.

Johnstone cut Whittaker's five-stroke lead to two through No. 5 in the final round. Then Whittaker, out in 37, rushed home in 33. After a bogey at the 11th, he birdied four of the next five holes — the 12th, 14th, 15th, and finally the 16th with a breaking 20-foot putt. His 70 gave him a six-stroke victory over Johnstone (71) and John McHenry (66).

Whittaker broke out of a five-way tie for the first-round lead at 68 with an eight-birdie 64 in the second round, and led the rest of the way. In the third round, two birdies over the last four holes in the rain boosted his lead to five strokes going into the final round. "I feel like I'm dreaming," Whittaker said. "I certainly never felt I would come out here and win in South Africa."

ICL International—R550,000
Winner: Ashley Roestoff

The ICL International was full of surprises. Mark McNulty missed the 36-hole cut by one stroke. New Zealander Frank Nobilo missed it by a mile, as did De Wet Basson. And, for a final surprise, the tournament was won by Ashley Roestoff, 31-year-old South African club pro, for his first professional victory.

Roestoff enjoyed a charmed week at Zwartkop Country Club as his challengers fell away one by one. Nico van Rensburg led the first round with 65, and followed it with 72. Roestoff, Sammy Daniels and Michael Green tied at 66, then Daniels shot 73, Green 77. Ian Hutchings trailed Roestoff by one stroke after 36 holes, then shot 75. Tony Johnstone tied Roestoff in the second round, then self-destructed in the fourth. His putter sputtering, he ground out 11 consecutive pars, then bogeyed the 12th, 13th and 14th holes, suffered a quadruple-bogey seven at the 15th, and shot 78.

Still, Roestoff had to do his part, and that amounted to rounds of 66, 70, 69 and 70 for a 275 total, 13 under par, for a four-stroke victory over Michael Christie and Kevin Stone. For all of the help he received, Roestoff — who started birdie-birdie-bogey-eagle — didn't get a grip on the ICL title until the back nine of the final round. "When I holed that birdie putt on the 14th, I knew I had it in the bag," Roestoff said. It dropped him to 14 under par, while Stone, his new challenger, bogeyed. The swing gave him a four-stroke lead.

Hollard Insurance Royal Swazi Sun Classic—R450,000
Winner: Brad Ott

The FNB Tour had its tightest finish and tightest battle of the young season when American Brad Ott charged from three strokes behind with eight holes to play to win the Hollard Insurance Royal Swazi Sun Classic by a two-stroke margin that was closer than it looked. Curiously, the tournament came down not to the shot that was made, but that wasn't.

The stage was Royal Swazi's par-five 17th hole, where the golfers were faced with a tough decision all week — go for the green in two, or lay up short of the water? That was Ott's predicament in the last round. "I asked my caddie what our cut-off distance was for going for the green in two," Ott said. The answer was 200 yards, and Ott was 203. "So I just took my pitching wedge and laid up short of the water," Ott said. Chris Davison opted to go for it from the left rough with a fairway wood. He was short — and in the water. Richard Kaplan, his other challenger, lipped out his putt. Ott put his third shot within 10 feet, holed the birdie putt for a two-stroke lead, and went on to a seven-under-par 65. He won by two strokes with a 266 total, 22 under par. Davison and Kaplan shared second at 268.

Ott started the final round one stroke behind Davison and tied with Kaplan. He fell a stroke further behind when he went out in 33 to their 32s. And then his situation started to look dark — he bogeyed No. 10 and was three behind. Then came his charge: He birdied five of seven holes from the 11th, and crowned his closing 65 with that masterful birdie at the 17th.

Telkom South African Masters—R675,000
Winner: Scott Dunlap

When American Scott Dunlap finally did it, he left no doubt. When you've beaten Mark McNulty, especially on his home ground, you've underlined it. Dunlap, 31, had been winless in six years while playing in South Africa, and he picked a great way to break the dry spell, beating McNulty on the first playoff hole.

"It feels great," Dunlap said. "On the first day, I went out in 32 and came back in 42 and I didn't know what to think about this course." But after that opening 74, he solved the par-72 Lost City course at Bophuthatswana with rounds of 67, 71 and 67 for a nine-under-par 279 total. His closing 67 was the only bogey-free round the last day, and it caught McNulty, who closed with 72 after three 69s.

Dunlap, who won the Manitoba Open in Canada the previous summer, chalked up this victory by firing his tee shot within three feet of the hole at the 197-yard, par-three 16th. McNulty put his shot to 20 feet, and when he missed, Dunlap holed his putt for the win.

Dunlap was out in 34 in the final round, and came home with birdies at the 14th, 16th and 17th holes. McNulty, who led by one shot coming into the final round, needed an eagle at the par-five 18th to win outright. He fired his approach shot to 20 feet, but his eagle try just missed, and he holed for the birdie to force the playoff.

Philips South African Open—R675,000
Winner: Retief Goosen

Retief Goosen may have scored three victories in one when he took the Philips South African Open. He won his national championship, he beat Ernie Els, and he conquered some personal doubts. Goosen, 26, South Africa's Rookie of the Year for 1991, might have been the homeland's top talent if Els hadn't arrived at the same time. And now he had to go head-to-head with Els at Randpark this second week of February. Goosen later said it was nerve-wracking, having Els hot on his heels. But it didn't show in his scores, rounds of 70, 65, 70 and 70 for a 275 total, 13 under par and a five-stroke victory over Els. It was Goosen's sixth victory overall, and his first since 1993.

Goosen kept Els tagging along. In the second round, Els tied the course record with 65 but couldn't gain an inch. Goosen had already set the record minutes before, and led him by two. Els wasn't his only worry, but he got the help he needed. Tony Johnstone, who led the first round with 66, came back with 74. Veteran John Bland was within four strokes going into the final round, and blew to 76.

In the final round, Els bogeyed the par-three second hole, and birdied No. 9. Goosen bogeyed No. 4, but birdied the next two holes. Going down the stretch, he was 11 under and leading by four, and refused to crack, making great saves at the 15th and 17th. Poor Els — even a birdie at the par-five 18th didn't help. In fact, it cost him a stroke, because Goosen eagled the hole with a one iron off the tee, a 200-yard five iron to four feet, and a cool putt.

Lexington PGA Championship—£300,000
Winner: Ernie Els

Ernie Els was becoming accustomed to his one victory a month. It had been over a month since his last. So Els charged in the final round, and took the Lexington PGA Championship at Wanderers Golf Club. This victory, in mid-February, kept up his pace of one a month for five consecutive months.

There was also a bit of history here. The championship was making its debut as a stop on the PGA European Tour, adding Johannesburg to such European outposts as Dubai and Manila. Els, Mark James and Vijay Singh were the most prominent PGA European Tour pros to make the trip.

Els grabbed the lead in the final round and finished with a flourish, a long, breaking putt at the 17th hole. "I felt the tournament was mine when I sank the birdie putt," Els said. It carried him to a closing 64 after rounds of 65, 71 and 71, for a nine-under-par 271 total, and a two-stroke victory over Roger Wessels.

Challengers rose and fell. Wayne Westner shot 62 for the first-round lead, then added 75. Nic Henning led the second with 66–135, then shot 73. Trevor Dodds was next, his 68–206 giving him a one-stroke lead going into the final round. A par 70 dropped him to seventh place. Els took the lead at No. 7 in the final round with the third of three consecutive birdies. McNulty tied him with three birdies from No. 10, but three-putted the 16th for a bogey. "I hadn't seen that Mark had bogeyed 16, and I felt he could still birdie the last two holes," Els said. He wasn't taking any chances. At the 17th, he faced a 25-foot putt with a two-foot break. Els rapped it home.

Alfred Dunhill Challenge
Winner: Southern Africa

In the latest reincarnation of the Ryder Cup, captain Gary Player's Southern Africans beat Terry Gale's Australasians, 14-11, in the Alfred Dunhill Challenge at Houghton Golf Club in Johannesburg. It featured one of the most questionable pair of concessions in match play history.

It came in the singles Sunday, when Greg Norman and Nick Price conceded each other putts of 15 and nine feet for a half at the par-four 16th hole. Price said they wanted to avoid the kind of animosity that grew in the Ryder Cup. "If that's what the players saw fit to do, then so be it," Player said. Gale wasn't as agreeable. "It surprises me that putts of that length were conceded," he said.

The Southern Africans got off winging in the opening fourballs. David Frost, partnering Retief Goosen, ran off 10 birdies in a 3-and-1 victory over Norman and Michael Campbell. "I putted unbelievably well," Frost said. Frost and Goosen scored another point in the afternoon foursomes, running off five straight birdies from the 13th in a 3-and-1 win over Norman and Robert Allenby. They wouldn't be cooled off until the second morning foursomes, losing to Lucas Parsons and Vijay Singh, who sank a 12-footer at the 17th. Norman and Allenby overcame a three-hole deficit through the 10th hole and beat Wayne Westner and Fulton Allem, 1 up.

The Southern Africans needed just three points out of nine singles the last day, and Frost, continuing his rampage, got the first with a 6-and-5 romp over Wayne Grady. After the grand concessions, Norman was in the rough twice at the 18th and missed from 14 feet while Price chipped close and won, 1 up. Mark McNulty beat Frank Nobilo, 3 and 1, for the only perfect record, 5-0, leaving the Southern Africans needing just one-half point. Hendrik Buhrmann got it three matches later with a half against Clayton.

Hassan II Trophy—$407,000
Winner: Nick Price

Nick Price was planning to go home to Zimbabwe for a long break, but an invitation to the Hassan II Trophy in Morocco persuaded him to change his plans. It was a good move. He won, ending a 14-month drought dating to the 1994 Bell Canadian Open.

"I had given myself only this week, the Zimbabwe Open in Harare and the Million Dollar Challenge in Sun City to try and rescue something from this year," said Price, who had seemed invincible not so long ago.

Price toured the par-73 Red Course at Dar Es Salam in rounds of 69, 71, 74 and 72 for a 286 total, six under par. He won by two strokes over England's Roger Chapman. Price's secret was his putting. His touch seemed to have returned. He made 14 birdies in the tournament. Three birdies through the turn in the final round gave him some working room against the oncoming Chapman, who birdied the 12th hole to climb within two strokes.

Price's game had shown signs of coming back. In August, he was runner-up in a playoff to Greg Norman in the NEC World Series of Golf. Then, in October, in the Alfred Dunhill Cup at St. Andrews, he won all five of his matches, leading Zimbabwe to a runner-up finish.

Price added the Hassan II Trophy's $93,000 first prize to his war chest, and then headed home to Zimbabwe to see whether this victory had been a sign of good things to come.

Zimbabwe Open—R400,000

Winner: Nick Price

Nick Price played the first nine of the final round in seven under par. He led by four strokes through the turn. He made only one bogey in the entire tournament. So it may be hard to believe that Price would have to sweat out the victory. But that's how it went as Price returned for his home classic, the Zimbabwe Open. He had to hold off Brendan Pappas for a one-stroke victory. No matter, Price's year suddenly had brightened in November. After going winless in 1995, he now had — with the Hassan II Trophy two weeks earlier — two victories in two starts. This, by the way, was Price's first Zimbabwe Open victory in 22 years of trying.

Price, coming from five shots behind in the first round, carded a 70-65-66-65–266 total, 22 under par, but it took a rousing finish to bring in the trophy.

Price, Mark McNulty and Pappas, age 25, playing out of the Hans Merensky Golf Club, were tied for the lead at 15 under par going into the final round. Price parred No. 1, then exploded into what looked like an easy win. He played the next six holes in seven under par. The burst included eagles at both par-fives — an approach shot to four feet at No. 3, and a chip-in at No. 6. He was out in 29, and had started to look ahead. "After seven, I was actually thinking 27 for the front and perhaps 59 for the round," Price admitted. "But I guess I ran out of putts on the back nine."

Pappas eagled the par-five 13th with a shot from the trees to six feet, and birdied the 16th and 17th to close to within one stroke of Price. Both missed the green at the 18th. Pappas left his chip shot eight feet shot, and Price chipped a tad past. The gritty Pappas made his demanding putt for par, and Price tapped in for the win.

Nedbank Million Dollar Challenge—US$2,510,000

Winner: Corey Pavin

They've almost run out of courses that Corey Pavin can't handle. Last on the list for 1995 was the Gary Player Country Club course at Sun City, South Africa, in the Nedbank Million Dollar Challenge. Pavin, not realizing it was much too long for him, played it in 12-under-par 276 and beat Nick Price by five strokes.

Pavin couldn't resist. "Dare I say it?" he said. "I feel like a million bucks, minus the tax." It was his fourth victory of the year, and boosted his world-wide winnings over $2.7 million. Pavin, hardly a big-hitter, proved again that shotmaking can make up for a lack of muscle. "I like to hit low approach shots," he said, "but when the pins are tucked away into the corners of the greens, and the greens are hard like they were this week, you need to hit high floaters." Start with accurate driving, follow with floaters, and finish with good putting, and it all added up to rounds of 69, 72, 69 and 66. He also got a big boost.

Price lead Pavin by three strokes going into the third round, and lost it down the stretch, on a bogey at the par-four 15th and a double bogey at the 17th. They were tied entering the final round. They parted company at No. 6, where Pavin birdied and Price bogeyed. Pavin pulled three ahead with another birdie at No. 7, and at No. 8, Pavin picked up another stroke when Price bogeyed. It was all but over, then, when Pavin birdied the par-five 14th to Price's bogey. Pavin became the first American in 13 years to win the tournament, and the third after Johnny Miller in 1981 and Raymond Floyd in 1982.

17. Senior Tours

Jim Colbert had his heart set on being No. 1 on the U.S. Senior PGA Tour in 1995. "I had never been No. 1 in anything," Colbert said, "and I wanted it very badly." The 54-year-old Midwesterner turned Las Vegas businessman had been flirting with the top through most of his five seasons on the Senior PGA Tour after forsaking his job as a golf commentator when he reached age 50.

Colbert achieved his goal in most exciting fashion when he won the season-ending Energizer Senior Tour Championship with a wire-to-wire performance. Although he had led the money list through much of the season and won four times, Colbert was fourth behind Dave Stockton, Raymond Floyd and Bob Murphy going into that final event and needed the victory to pass the others. The $262,000 check elevated his total to a record $1,444,386.

Though Colbert prevailed at the end, the other three contenders for the money title had little cause for remorse about their own seasons and quite a few others had their moments during the year.

Floyd, in fact, led the Senior World Money List with $1,811,049 and surely would have captured the No. 1 spot on the Senior PGA Tour easily if he had played a little more often. Floyd played in 21 official events compared to Colbert's 34, yet finished just $25,000 behind him in the final accounting. Floyd won the PGA Seniors' Championship and two other events, along with the Senior Grand Slam and the extracurricular Senior Skins, Office Depot Father/Son Challenge (with Raymond Jr.) and his own Lexus Challenge (with actor Michael Chiklis). Including those last three events, Floyd's total earnings were $2,561,049. Equally impressive, Floyd finished second seven times.

Stockton, playing the same sort of busy schedule as Colbert, came up $29,000 short of a third straight money title, leading the standings for the last eight weeks before the Tour Championship. Unlike previous seasons, Stockton won his two tournaments early, the second in May. Murphy, who matched Colbert in victories with four and teamed with him to win the senior division of the Diners Club Matches in December, had his best season by far in finishing fourth on the money list with $1,241,524.

Although Lee Trevino's seventh-place finish was his lowest ever, he played through pain much of the year following late-1994 neck surgery and an ailing shoulder. Trevino was not without accomplishments of note in 1995. With his wins in the Northville and Transamerica tournaments, he built his Senior PGA Tour total to a leading 26 official individual titles to go with his third Legends of Golf victory with partner Mike Hill and other unofficial events.

Hale Irwin played in 12 tournaments on the Senior PGA Tour after turning 50 in June and was as impressive as expected. He won twice and never finished worse than 12th. Jack Nicklaus also played sparingly and well, winning The Tradition and finishing second to Tom Weiskopf in the U.S. Senior Open and second to J.C. Snead in the Ford Senior Players Championship.

Brian Barnes scored the highlight victory on the European Seniors Tour

— in the Seniors British Open at Royal Portrush, Northern Ireland — and led that circuit's money list. Brian Huggett was the only double winner on the 11-event Tour.

Between Isao Aoki's two victories at the start and finish of the Japan Senior Tour, eight players scored wins, the best known being Seiichi Kanai, a multiple winner the last two years; Teruo Sugihara, the winner of more than 50 tournaments in Japan during his long and outstanding career, and Taiwan's Hsieh Min-Nan.

U.S. Senior PGA Tour

Senior Tournament of Champions—$750,000
Winner: Jim Colbert

Jim Colbert surprised himself as the Senior Tournament of Champions launched the 1995 season at the Hyatt Dorado Beach's East course in Puerto Rico. Colbert had not been playing well when the 1994 season ended, and tied for last place in the final event. He reversed his form so drastically that he went from the bottom to the top.

First, Colbert had to contend with the likes of Lee Trevino, with whom he shared the second-round lead at 138, and Raymond Floyd, the first-round leader at 68 who was just one stroke behind going into the final round. Colbert's finishing 71 — 17 pars and one birdie — took care of that as Trevino, playing his first tournament since October back surgery, and Floyd finished uncharacteristically with 76 and 75, respectively.

Colbert's problem was dealing with Jim Albus, who was five under par after 12 holes of the final round and led by three strokes. But Albus double-bogeyed the 12th hole and bogeyed the 16th (which Colbert birdied), shooting 69 to tie Colbert and create a playoff.

The two parred the first two extra holes before Colbert made an astonishing shot from a fairway bunker between two palms and put the ball three feet from the hole. Albus missed his birdie try from 10 feet and Colbert holed the three-footer for his 10th senior win.

Royal Caribbean Classic—$850,000
Winner: J.C. Snead

J.C. Snead shot 75 and Raymond Floyd 76 in the second round of the Royal Caribbean Classic, the first full-field tournament of the Senior PGA Tour season. So they were out of it, right? Wrong. Although those scores, inflated by high winds at the Links at Key Biscayne in Miami, Florida, left them four strokes off the lead at 144, the two sailed past the six men ahead of them with seven-under-par 65s Sunday and forced another playoff.

Snead prevailed on the first extra hole with a routine par after Floyd, fresh from his $420,000 domination of the Senior Skins Game in Hawaii, flubbed an approach shot and bogeyed. It was just Snead's second win in his more than four years on the senior circuit.

Bob Murphy opened the tournament with 66 to lead Floyd, Kermit Zarley, Tom Wargo and Jack Kiefer by two strokes; Snead, Walter Morgan, Harry Toscano and Buddy Allin by three, but he was one of the worst victims of Saturday's cool winds, shooting 78. Bob Charles, who, with Jimmy Powell, had the day's low round of 71, moved in front at 141 with Wargo, who shot 73. Morgan and Zarley were at 142, and Powell and Lee Trevino, the defending champion, had 143s.

Six players had the lead at one time or another Sunday, but in the end it came down to Snead and Floyd. Floyd missed two late birdie chances and settled for 65, which Snead matched when he finished right behind him.

IntelliNet Challenge—$600,000
Winner: Bob Murphy

Bob Murphy conceded that "Irishmen are lucky, that's all there is to it" when rain erased the final round of the IntelliNet Challenge and victory was his because he had occupied first place when play ended Saturday night in Naples, Florida. Murphy wasn't apologizing about it. "I did win the tournament," he pointed out. "I played better than the other guys for two days."

In winning his fifth title on the Senior PGA Tour — and second weather-shortened 36-hole event — Murphy put together rounds of 67 and 70 for his 137 total at The Vineyards course. It relegated Raymond Floyd to the runner-up position for the second week in a row. He shot 69-69–138. The abbreviated ending also eliminated Mike Hill's shot at three consecutive wins in Naples, a feat accomplished by only three other players — Chi Chi Rodriguez, Bob Charles and George Archer. Hill tied for third place at 140 with Rocky Thompson.

Murphy may have won the tournament with a daring gamble in Friday's first round. He hooked his tee shot into a lake on the par-five sixth hole, the ball coming to rest on a rocky patch. Murphy waded in to his knees, hooked the shot around a tree back into play and salvaged a par. His 67 tied for the lead with Harry Toscano, two strokes in front of six others.

GTE Suncoast Classic—$750,000
Winner: Dave Stockton

Dave Stockton, a notorious slow starter on the Senior PGA Tour who always winds up the season at or near the top of the money standings, won the GTE Suncoast Classic in February. The leading money winner the last two years, who hadn't won any earlier than the end of April the previous three seasons, Stockton was determined to "get off to a fast start and play better early" in 1995.

The "fast start" applied to the final round at the TPC at Cheval in Tampa, Florida. Stockton, who entered the last day sharing the lead at 136 with Dave Eichelberger and Gary Player, got in front at the fifth hole when he holed an 83-yard wedge shot for an eagle and two-stroke lead. He never surrendered that margin. Stockton shot 32 on the front nine and nine pars on the back nine for 68 and a nine-under-par 204, two strokes better than Bob Charles, Jim Colbert and J.C. Snead.

Jack Nicklaus, making a rare appearance in a regular Senior PGA Tour event, shot 207 and tied for fifth place with Simon Hobday and Bruce Lehnhard. It was another disappointing week for Raymond Floyd. He opened with 66 and shared the first-round lead with Tony Jacklin, but followed with 72 and 70, and finished four strokes behind Stockton.

Chrysler Cup—$600,000
Winner: United States

The International team could not afford to be without the best eligible players for the Chrysler Cup, and it showed as the United States scored a decisive 11-5 victory after losing in 1994 for only the second time in the 10-year history of the Ryder Cup-style event. Although the American squad was not exactly star-studded, the International squad obviously missed Gary Player and Isao Aoki when the tournament, after nine years in Sarasota, Florida, was relocated to the Tres Vidas Golf Club in Acapulco, Mexico.

The Internationals held their own in the foursomes (alternate shot) competition the first day, losing 2½ to 1½ as Bob Charles, the captain, and Graham Marsh nipped U.S. captain Jim Colbert and Tom Wargo, and Simon Hobday and Harold Henning halved with Jim Dent and Bob Murphy. The longer hitters on the American squad then took charge Saturday as the U.S. swept the four-ball (better-ball) play and built a 6½-2½ advantage. The issue was decided quickly in the Sunday singles as Colbert beat Charles, 69-72, and Dent defeated Henning, 71-76, in the first two matches to clinch the victory.

FHP Health Care Classic—$750,000
Winner: Bruce Devlin

Bruce Devlin, a formidable player in his younger days but a struggler since switching from television commentary back to active competition in 1987, was delighted and even tearful when he emerged as the winner of the FHP Health Care Classic.

Heavy rains required an unusual finish at Ojai Valley Inn and Country Club after Devlin and Dave Eichelberger had taken the lead with matching 64-66—130s on the par-70 resort course in the California mountains east of Santa Barbara. It continued to rain so hard overnight Saturday that there were mudslides in the area and the course was swamped. The final round was cancelled and all except Devlin and Eichelberger were dismissed.

They wanted to determine a winner with a playoff, but while waiting until afternoon when it could be telecast on ESPN, the constant downpour made the fairways virtually unplayable. It was decided to use two par-three holes with elevated greens. They parred the first, then Devlin sank a 19-foot putt from the front fringe for the victory, the first for the 57-year-old Australian since he won the 1972 USI Classic on the PGA Tour.

Senior Grand Slam—$500,000
Winner: Raymond Floyd

Raymond Floyd couldn't quite get it done in the early tournaments, but he had no trouble with the special events. He dominated the Senior Skins at the end of January. Then in early March, he was an equally decisive victor in the Senior Grand Slam at Los Cabos in Mexico, easily putting away the winners of the other three major championships on the Senior PGA Tour with his 72-67–139. The reigning champion of The Tradition defeated Dave Stockton (Senior Players) by six strokes, Simon Hobday (U.S. Senior Open) by eight and Lee Trevino (PGA Seniors' Championship) by 16 in adding another $250,000 to his bank account.

Stockton birdied five of the first eight holes but eventually dropped back with a double bogey at the 14th hole to tie Hobday at 70 for the first-day lead in the 36-hole event. Trevino shot himself out of contention with 80. Floyd took charge in the final round with his five-under-par 67. No one else broke par, Stockton and Trevino shooting 75, Hobday 77.

SBC Presents the Dominion Seniors—$650,000
Winner: Jim Albus

The last thing Jim Albus wanted was a playoff in the Dominion Seniors in San Antonio. The last two times he had a good chance to score his fifth victory on the Senior PGA Tour, he lost in playoffs.

He couldn't quite duplicate his wire-to-wire victory in the 1994 Dominion, but he repeated the victory in more decisive fashion, closing with 69 for a 205 total and a three-stroke triumph over Raymond Floyd and Jay Sigel.

Albus had his good-luck charm — his collegian son Mark, a member of the Vanderbilt golf team — at his side as his caddie as he launched his defense at The Dominion Country Club. Mark caddied for his father during his last three wins. After a mediocre start of 71, four strokes off the lead of Lee Elder and Bob Dickson, Albus vaulted into first place with 65, the week's best round, for a 136 total and a one-stroke advantage over Dickson and Dick Rhyan.

Although Albus was never caught Sunday, Lee Trevino, a two-time winner of the Dominion, was within one stroke after he birdied the 10th hole on a windy afternoon. When Trevino bogeyed the 12th and 14th holes after Albus birdied the 11th, Albus had all the room he needed. Trevino shot 70–209 and finished fourth.

Toshiba Classic—$800,000
Winner: George Archer

George Archer played through periodic aches and pains through much of his career, yet always kept winning. With his right hip and his game deteriorating through the early stages of 1995, Archer decided that he had suffered enough, and that it was time to retire. He proceeded to make himself reverse that decision by winning his first tournament in 17 months, the inaugural

Toshiba Classic at an old Tour site, Mesa Verde Country Club in Costa Mesa, California.

Archer came from three strokes off the pace with a final-round 64 for his 11-under-par 199 total and a one-stroke victory over Dave Stockton, who also closed with 64, and Tom Wargo. Wargo had carried the lead into the final round with his 65-67–132 start, leading Larry Laoretti by one stroke, and Bob E. Smith, Tom Weiskopf and Archer by three.

Archer, who made his six birdies on the last 12 holes, won with his last birdie at the 17th hole from 25 feet after Stockton had caught him with a 35-footer at the 16th. Marion Heck shot 63 — the same score with which Dave Eichelberger led the first day — and finished fourth at 202. Said Archer, after scoring his 16th win as a senior, "I guess now I'll have to play as long as I physically can."

The Tradition—$1,000,000
Winner: Jack Nicklaus

Jack Nicklaus always seems to have been able to kick his game up another notch when a major championship came along on the schedule. This was true on the regular Tour and is even more so in the four events generally recognized as the major events of the Senior PGA Tour. In his first six years, playing a very limited schedule, Nicklaus won eight times and all except one of the victories was in a major championship.

The eighth — and his only 1995 victory — was in The Tradition at Desert Mountain near Scottsdale, Arizona, where he won the limited-field invitational for a third time. It didn't come easy as Isao Aoki, fresh from his victory in the American Express Grand Slam in Japan, carried him three extra holes after they tied for first place with 276 totals in regulation.

Jim Ferree took the first-round lead with 67. Nicklaus was among five players at 69. Aoki shot 66 for a 137 total to lead Jay Sigel by one stroke and Gary Player by two. Nicklaus and Aoki were tied after the third round with 209 totals, one ahead of Ferree, Sigel and Jim Colbert. Nicklaus, Aoki and Ferree all produced 67s in the last round, Nicklaus and Aoki to force the playoff and Ferree to fall one stroke short and finish third. After Nicklaus and Aoki parred the first two extra holes and went to the 18th for the third time that day, the Japanese star overshot the green with his third shot after Nicklaus had reached the back fringe in two. Nicklaus chipped close and won when Aoki pitched his fourth off the front edge.

PGA Seniors' Championship—$1,000,000
Winner: Raymond Floyd

Clearly, it was just a matter of time before Raymond Floyd would win on the 1995 Senior PGA Tour. Since the first of January, he had won the special-event Senior Skins and Senior Slam and had finished second in three of his six Tour starts. He was overdue and it was particularly appropriate that Floyd's first official win of the year came in the PGA Seniors' Championship, the scene of his shockingly embarrassing giveaway the previous year.

This time, in the tournament in which he went from a four-stroke lead midway through the final round to a third-place finish after going six over par on two par-three water holes, Floyd rolled to a five-stroke victory over defending champion Lee Trevino, John Paul Cain and Larry Gilbert. He posted an 11-under-par 277 total on the Champion course at PGA National Golf Club in Palm Beach Gardens, Florida, in the mid-April championship. It was his 10th Senior Tour victory in less than three years.

An opening pair of 70s put Floyd in third place, two strokes behind Jim Colbert and one back of Isao Aoki. Then Floyd moved in front with 67 for a 207 total, two ahead of Colbert, three in front of Jack Nicklaus, and four ahead of Trevino and Jim Albus. His closing 70 was so solid that no one came close to mounting a challenge.

Liberty Mutual Legends of Golf—$1,115,000
Winners: Lee Trevino and Mike Hill

It didn't make any difference to Lee Trevino and Mike Hill that Liberty Mutual moved its Legends of Golf tournament from its long-time home in Austin, Texas, to Palm Springs, California, and Pete Dye's notorious Stadium course at PGA West. They kept on winning, taking the title for the third time in the last four that were played as team competition. Their score of 21-under-par 195 was seven strokes higher than the winning total of Dale Douglass and Charles Coody at Austin's Barton Creek in 1994, the first time the event was cut back to 54 holes.

Hill, who reduced his schedule in 1994 and hadn't won in more than a year, was the stalwart performer for the winning team through the first two rounds and on the early holes the final day with 14 birdies to just three by Trevino. Then Trevino made four on the last six holes to secure a two-stroke victory over Gibby Gilbert and J.C. Snead.

Six teams were tied for the lead at different times in the last round before Trevino and Hill went in front for good with Trevino's birdies at the 13th and 14th holes. He padded the margin with a two-putt birdie at the 16th and clinched it with a 35-foot birdie putt at the final green.

Las Vegas Senior Classic—$1,000,000
Winner: Jim Colbert

Ever since moving from Kansas City to Las Vegas in 1981, Jim Colbert had been trying to win a title in the Nevada gambling mecca — to no avail. When he finally broke through in the Las Vegas Senior Classic, Colbert ranked the victory at the top of his impressive list of 10 Senior Tour titles beside his major title — the 1993 Senior Players Championship. "When I won the major, it was very important," Colbert said, "but this was just as big for me."

The triumph at the TPC at Summerlin was by two strokes over Jim Dent, Rocky Thompson and Raymond Floyd, the defending champion coming off his victory in the PGA Seniors' two weeks earlier. Colbert was 11 under par at 205, as he became the first multiple winner of the year.

Colbert opened in front at Summerlin with 65, leading Floyd, Bob Murphy and Jerry McGee by one shot. Thompson edged a stroke in front of Colbert and Floyd Saturday when he shot 65 for a 135 total. Although they eventually tied for second place, Thompson and Dent fell back early Sunday, leaving the title fight to Floyd and Colbert. Floyd trailed by one stroke after 15 holes, but made what he later conceded was a tactical mistake when he chose not to lay up from a bad lie in an old divot and put the shot in the water in front of the 16th green. That gave Colbert enough leeway that he could bogey the 17th and still win by two with his closing 69.

PaineWebber Invitational—$800,000
Winner: Bob Murphy

Bob Murphy became the Senior PGA Tour's second two-time winner in the PaineWebber Invitational, primarily because he proved a better stretch-runner at the TPC at Piper Glen in Charlotte, North Carolina. Murphy, who had won the IntelliNet Challenge in Naples, played Piper Glen's back nine in a solid 34 strokes and watched his challengers drop back on the leaderboards. His 69 for a 13-under-par 203 total gave him a two-stroke victory over Raymond Floyd and Larry Ziegler, four over Jim Colbert and Australian Graham Marsh.

Ziegler got a lot out of the back nine in the opening round. He birdied the last three holes for 66 and a one-stroke lead over Marsh and Roger Kennedy. Murphy shot 68 and Floyd was among four at 69. Murphy made his move when he matched Ziegler's 66 and set a new 36-hole record at Piper Glen with his 134, one shot ahead of Ziegler and Marsh. He began the final round with a bogey, which he described as "a wake-up call," got the stroke back at the second and posted three more birdies, including key ones at the 13th and 14th holes that cushioned his finish.

Floyd made the strongest run at Murphy. Four strokes back starting the day, he was even with Murphy after both birdied the 13th hole, but Floyd put two balls in the water and made a 10-foot putt for a double bogey at the 14th. He shot 67, but settled for the second-place tie with Ziegler, who birdied the par-five 18th for 70.

Cadillac NFL Classic—$950,000
Winner: George Archer

George Archer, who had been on the verge of retirement before he won the Toshiba Classic in March, solidified his decision to continue playing as long as he was physically able by scoring the reinforcing "extra point" of another victory on the Senior PGA Tour in the Cadillac NFL Classic in which NFL players share the stage with the golfers at Upper Montclair Country Club in Clifton, New Jersey, in mid-May.

The 56-year-old Archer, who treats his ailing right hip with daily dosages of an anti-inflammatory medicine, parlayed the low back-nine score of the year — 30 in the second round — into a one-stroke victory with his 11-under-par 205 total. The six-birdie 30 gave Archer a 66–135 total and a one-stroke lead after he trailed Bob Murphy, the first-day leader, by four strokes. Murphy drifted three shots off the lead when he followed with 73, but came back with 68 to tie Raymond Floyd for second place at 206.

Floyd made a strong run at Archer and had a one-stroke lead until Archer birdied the 14th hole to pull even. Archer then parred in for 70 and the victory, his 17th on the Senior PGA Tour, when Floyd, the leading money winner, bogeyed the par-three 17th. It was his sixth runner-up finish, and fourth in his last six starts.

Bell Atlantic Classic—$900,000
Winner: Jim Colbert

Jim Colbert made two decisions that led to his third victory of the 1995 Senior PGA Tour season. First he concluded that because he plays better on tough courses, he made a mistake in skipping Philadelphia in 1994 and, second, weary from playing 14 tournaments in 18 weeks, he got an extra day of rest at home in Las Vegas before coming to the Bell Atlantic Classic.

Refreshed, Colbert staged a final-round rally to overhaul J.C. Snead, the leader the first two days, and score a one-stroke victory with his three-under-par 207 total. Snead, who won the Royal Caribbean Classic in February, finished at 208. Jack Nicklaus, making a rare appearance in a regular event on the Senior PGA Tour, ran out of birdies on the final holes and his 68 placed him third at 209, the only other player to record a sub-par total.

Snead led Colbert and three others — Deane Beman, Isao Aoki and Dave Stockton — by two with his opening 66 and was still a stroke ahead of Colbert and Stockton despite a second-round 72 that he salvaged from a four-over-par start. Colbert needed a hole-in-one and a chip-in birdie to shoot his 71. The final round looked like Snead's day again. He built a five-stroke lead early, but Colbert began a surge with his first of five birdies in an eight-hole stretch. At the same time, Snead was faltering with three bogeys over the last 11 holes.

Quicksilver Classic—$1,100,000
Winner: Dave Stockton

The Senior PGA Tour was on the verge of crowning a successful defending champion at the Quicksilver Classic on the outskirts of Pittsburgh, then Dave Eichelberger's driver developed pull tendencies. That was all Dave Stockton needed and the circuit had a multiple 1995 winner for the fifth straight week.

Starting the final round four strokes off the lead, Stockton stormed in front with birdies on three of the last four holes, posted 67 for an eight-under-par 208 total and won by one stroke over Isao Aoki. Eichelberger, with 71, dropped into a three-way tie for third place at 210 with Tom Wargo and George Archer, who led at the start of the day in his bid for his third 1995 victory.

Archer, who was two shots in front of Eichelberger after his 69-68–137 start, went 15 holes without a birdie. Eichelberger had a two-stroke lead through 12 holes. After pulled driver shots, off the tee at the 13th and from the fairway at the par-five 15th, Eichelberger suddenly found himself two behind Stockton, who had just finished his three-birdie run at the par-five 17th to go eight under par. Eichelberger matched that birdie at the 17th, but underclubbed on his approach at the final hole, then three-putted from the front fringe.

Bruno's Memorial Classic—$1,050,000
Winner: Graham Marsh

It had seemed unfair that Graham Marsh had to go through the qualifying tournament to get on the Senior PGA Tour in 1994. He was a noted international star who had circled the globe winning 56 tournaments, mostly in Japan, Europe and his native Australia. Still, he didn't fit the exempt categories.

Qualification proved easy but winning wasn't — until Marsh made a runaway of the Bruno's Memorial Classic at Birmingham, Alabama. The 51-year-old Aussie broke it open in the second round with a dazzling 63, the season's low round to that point, and went on to a five-stroke victory with a 15-under-par 201 at Greystone Country Club.

Dave Stockton shot 66 and took a one-stroke lead over Bruce Summerhays, Bob Rawlins and Buddy Allin. Then Marsh went ahead with the 63, moving five strokes ahead of Summerhays and Tom Weiskopf with his 131 total. Marsh, who has built his reputation as a sound technical player of average length and putting skills, fashioned a steady final-round 70 that gave no one a real shot at him.

Weiskopf, playing with Marsh and outdriving him, got within three strokes when the Aussie made his second bogey of the tournament at the seventh hole. But Weiskopf, playing in his first event since breaking two ribs in a shower fall two months earlier, bogeyed the next two holes and Marsh cruised in. J.C. Snead closed with a 68 to snatch second place by one stroke from Weiskopf, Summerhays, Al Geiberger and Larry Laoretti.

BellSouth Classic at Opryland—$1,100,000
Winner: Jim Dent

So many times weather delays have had adverse effects on leaders of tournaments. To the contrary in the case of Jim Dent in the BellSouth Classic at Opryland. The interruption early in the final round came at just the right time. Leading the tournament at the start of the day, Dent had just bogeyed the third hole when the rains came. It not only gave him a 55-minute chance to forget about the lost shot but also time for a nap. Dent played flawlessly after play resumed, shot 68 for a 13-under-par 203 total at Springhouse Golf Club and secured a two-stroke victory over Bob Murphy.

Dent was in contention all week in the tournament that revolves around Nashville's famous country music industry. He opened with 66, one stroke behind leader Harold Henning, then moved one stroke ahead of Murphy with a 69–135 total, when Henning sank to 74–139.

Dave Hill, six back at 141, mounted the biggest challenge to the long-hitting Dent. Hill had eight birdies and a bogey on the first 13 holes, the birdie at the 13th putting him in a tie for the lead. But Dent made his fifth birdie at the next hole to regain first place. Murphy made a run of his own on the back nine with four consecutive birdies, starting at the 13th, and his 69 enabled him to finish second alone, a stroke in front of Dave Stockton and two ahead of Hill and Hale Irwin, making his first Senior Tour start a week after his 50th birthday.

Dallas Reunion Pro-Am—$550,000
Winner: Tom Wargo

A number of career club professionals have made their mark on the Senior PGA Tour in recent years, most notably Jim Albus with his five victories and $3 million in earnings. Not far behind and giving him a run for the money is Tom Wargo, whose wide-ranging earlier lifetime covered a lot of ground before he struck gold on the Senior PGA Tour.

Wargo punctuated his status with the most decisive victory of the year in the Dallas Reunion Pro-Am as he led from start to finish and won by seven strokes. He set tournament records for 36 and 54 holes with his 13-under-par 197 total at Oak Cliff Country Club. It was his third triumph in his three seasons, the first being the 1993 PGA Seniors Championship. He also won the 1994 Seniors British Open.

All Wargo had to avoid was a total collapse in the final round. He had established a six-stroke lead with his record-setting pair of 64s the first two days. Dave Eichelberger was at 134 and Dave Stockton at 135. Eichelberger, playing with Wargo Sunday, gave him cause for alarm early when he birdied the first three holes. When Wargo made his second bogey at the sixth, his lead was down to two strokes. That was as close as Eichelberger got.

Eichelberger bogeyed the eighth, Wargo birdied the ninth and had his big lead back after the 10th, where he birdied again and Eichelberger took a double bogey. Wargo took another bogey at the 12th, then parred to the 18th, where he finished with a flourish by holing a 40-foot birdie chip for 69. Eichelberger scored 70 and shared second place at 204 with Stockton.

Nationwide Championship—$1,200,000
Winner: Bob Murphy

Bob Murphy was determined to make amends for 1994 in Atlanta, where he came up a stroke short of Dave Stockton and his amazing final-hole par to win the Nationwide Championship. He put himself in position to do it in the 1995 event by shooting a second-round 64 for a 36-hole 135 to trail co-leaders Larry Laoretti and Bruce Summerhays by one stroke.

It wasn't those two he focused on, but rather Hale Irwin, the new senior who was tied with him. "My concentration today was to beat Hale Irwin," he said afterward. And he was right. Although Summerhays, who began the tournament at the Golf Club of Georgia with a nine-under-par 63, tied Irwin for second place at the end, Irwin had a great chance for no worse than a tie and playoff as he played the par-five finishing hole.

Murphy, who had birdied the 12th, 14th and 15th holes, held a one-stroke lead and was on the 17th green as Irwin went for the 18th green with a three wood, missed the shot off a tough lie and put the ball in the water. Seconds later, Murphy missed his par second putt at No. 17, but with Irwin's subsequent bogey at the 18th, the pressure was off and Murphy finished with a birdie for 68 and a 203 total, winning by two over Irwin and Summerhays.

U.S. Senior Open Championship—$1,000,000
Winner: Tom Weiskopf

It may not rank with his 1973 British Open title or the U.S. Opens and Masters that slipped away, but Tom Weiskopf had good reason to be proud of his victory in the U.S. Senior Open Championship that he called the best golf of his life. "Under the conditions, no, I've never played better," said Weiskopf after winning with a precision that produced a four-stroke victory over his long-time nemesis, Jack Nicklaus, at the Congressional Country Club in Bethesda, Maryland. His 13-under-par 275 total, the product of four rounds in the 60s, was the second lowest against par in U.S. Senior Open history.

The 53-year-old Weiskopf was in the thick of things all week. He was one of six 69 shooters, one stroke behind leaders J.C. Snead and Larry Ringer the first day, then went to the top for the duration with another 69, joined by Tommy Aaron in first place. Yet another 69 gave Weiskopf a one-stroke lead over Isao Aoki, although that wasn't established until early Sunday morning, when 10 players, including him, finished a round that rains prevented them from completing Saturday.

Much was made of the fact that Weiskopf had some retribution for the many setbacks he had suffered at the hands of Nicklaus in the past. In reality, although Nicklaus was the runner-up and shot 67, he had started the last round five strokes back and never really threatened Weiskopf even with the hole-in-one he made at the seventh hole. Aoki was the challenger. The Japanese great was tied for the lead after seven holes, but Weiskopf turned it on with a birdie at the eighth and led the rest of the way, closing with a 68 for the 275. Aoki shot 72 and dropped into a third-place tie with Bob Murphy at 280.

Kroger Classic—$900,000
Winner: Mike Hill

Good things had happened in the past for Mike Hill at King Island's Grizzly course outside of Cincinnati, Ohio. Like his third and last victory on the PGA Tour back in 1977. It seemed appropriate that Hill would end a 17-month winless spell on the Senior PGA Tour with a victory on that same course in the Kroger Classic. It took the lowest score of the year — a 17-under-par, tournament-record 196 total — for the 57-year-old Hill, one of the Senior Tour's surprising successes, to take a one-stroke victory over Japan's Isao Aoki.

Hill led from the start, recording the year's second wire-to-wire victory as the Grizzly course yielded to a barrage of low scoring all week. He began with 64, two strokes better than Aoki, Ben Smith, Gay Brewer and J.C. Snead. Hill remained two in front of Aoki with a 66–130 total, getting that margin when Aoki put a ball in the water guarding the 18th green and finished bogey-bogey.

The turning point in the last round came when Hill matched the ninth-hole eagle of Graham Marsh, the other player still in contention, and birdied the 10th. Aoki, who missed a 15-foot eagle putt at the ninth, had one last chance at the 18th. This time he hit the green in two, but was 40 feet from the cup. Hill elected to lay up, carved a careful par for 66 and won by one stroke when Aoki missed the eagle putt. He and Marsh, who finished two strokes back in third place, had 65s.

Ford Senior Players Championship—$1,500,000
Winner: J.C. Snead

It took three years, but J.C. Snead finally got even with the TPC of Michigan. At the scene of what he calls "the biggest disappointment I've ever had," Snead captured the Ford Senior Players Championship that he let slip away with a double bogey on the final hole in 1992. This time he dealt with the pressure of a challenge from Jack Nicklaus, eventually defeating him on the first hole of a playoff at the end of a brutally steamy week in Dearborn, Michigan. It was Snead's third win as a senior and his second of the year.

The TPC course stood up to the seniors in the first round as the four-under-par 68s of Jerry McGee, Bob Charles and Bob Zimmerman led the way. Former champion Jim Colbert, already a three-time winner in 1995, exploded with a course- and tournament-record 63 and roared to a 133 total and a four-stroke lead over Lee Trevino and Snead. Thunderstorms disrupted play Saturday afternoon, forcing the leaders to finish their rounds Sunday morning. When that had been accomplished, Colbert, bearing symptoms of heat sickness, had shot himself out of contention with 75 and Snead had edged to a one-stroke lead at 203 over Dave Stockton, two over Nicklaus, Raymond Floyd and Kermit Zarley.

All except Nicklaus killed their hopes of catching Snead early in the final round. With a birdie at the sixth hole on top of an eagle at the par-five third, Snead led Nicklaus by four strokes and he maintained that margin until a bogey at the 14th following Nicklaus' birdie cut it in half. At the par-five 17th, which has a huge carry to the green over a lake, Nicklaus did it with a three iron, holed the eight-foot eagle putt and caught him. Snead parred there, both parred the 18th for 16-under-par 272s and they returned to that tee for a playoff, which Snead won with a five-iron approach to four feet and the subsequent birdie putt.

First of America Classic—$700,000
Winner: Jimmy Powell

Jimmy Powell wrote a historic double into the Senior PGA Tour record book at the First of America Classic. At 60, Powell was eligible for the special, 36-hole Super Seniors portions of many events for the first time in 1995 and already had four wins to his credit when he ran away with a fifth at Egypt Valley Country Club at Grand Rapids, Michigan.

This time, though, Powell's winning Super Seniors score of 134 also gave him the overall tournament lead and he shot a solid 67 in the final round for a five-stroke victory. It was the first time a Super Senior ever won the main event the next day. Powell was just the third player in his 60s to win on the Senior PGA Tour and the first since 63-year-old Mike Fetchick did it at Hilton Head in 1985.

Powell trailed leaders George Archer and Chuck Montalbano by two after shooting 68 in the first round at Egypt Valley, then took over first place and wrapped up a six-stroke victory in the Super Seniors with 66 for the 134 total. That gave him a two-stroke lead over Babe Hiskey.

Hiskey birdied three of the first four holes, yet only gained a stroke on Powell, who opened the margin to four strokes by the turn, went six ahead with a birdie to Hiskey's double bogey at the 10th and coasted home to his 15-under-par 201 total, five ahead of Hiskey and six in front of Larry Laoretti, who both shot 70s.

Ameritech Open—$850,000
Winner: Hale Irwin

It took five tries, but when Hale Irwin broke through with his much-anticipated first victory on the Senior PGA Tour, he did so with an exclamation point. Irwin rocketed into a five-stroke lead in the second round and he wound up winning by seven, matching the year's previous biggest margin posted by Tom Wargo in Dallas. His 21-under-par 195 total was an Ameritech tournament record and just one stroke off Raymond Floyd's 54-hole record at Palm Desert, California, in 1993.

The second round was a particularly exciting day at Stonebridge Country Club. Deadlocked at 66 after the first round with co-leaders Bob Dickson and Jim Colbert, Irwin blazed to his five-stroke lead over Colbert and Kermit Zarley with a nine-under 63, but that wasn't even the low round of the day. Joe Jimenez, the remarkable 69-year-old, shot 62, a course record.

Irwin, the three-time U.S. Open champion and winner of 20 titles during his PGA Tour career, started the last round on the wrong foot with a bogey, but he was flawless after that. When he made a 50-footer for his fifth birdie at No. 13, he moved five ahead of runner-up Zarley, who three-putted. He went on to shoot 66 for the 195 and the seven-stroke victory over Zarley, who shot 68. Dave Stockton shot 66 to finish a distant third at 204.

VFW Championship—$900,000
Winner: Bob Murphy

Although in the middle of one of the finest years of his career, Bob Murphy did not figure to add to his victories in the VFW Championship in Kansas City. He was just back from the Seniors British Open and the jet-lag problem had to be intensified by the disappointment of his loss to Brian Barnes at Royal Portrush. But Murphy brushed off a slow start with a 63-63 finish that tied the Senior PGA Tour record and nosed out Jim Colbert, the hometown favorite, by one stroke for the title at Loch Lloyd Country Club. It made Murphy the first four-time winner of the year and pulled him within $40,000 of Colbert, the leading money winner.

While Murphy was shooting 69, Buddy Allin was firing 63 and taking the first-round lead by two strokes over Jay Sigel. Sigel edged ahead with a 66–131 total as Murphy shot his first 63 and tied for second place with Allin (69) and Jack Kiefer. It all came down to the last three holes of the final round. Colbert had a five-birdie string and shot 29 on the first nine to project himself into contention and, when he dropped a seven-foot birdie putt at the 15th, he joined Murphy at 14 under par. Murphy regained the lead when he birdied the 17th and his second 63 and 195 total was just enough when Colbert barely missed a birdie putt from 20 feet at the 18th for 61 and a tie. Colbert's 62 tied the course record and Murphy's 195 equalled the low total of the season, posted the previous week in Chicago by Hale Irwin.

Burnet Classic—$1,100,000
Winner: Raymond Floyd

On the eve of the Burnet Classic, Raymond Floyd boldly predicted: "If I putt well, I will win." Floyd putted well enough at Bunker Hills Golf Course in Coon Rapids, Minnesota — and won — by one stroke over Graham Marsh, bearing up the validity of his forecast, which he said had been a challenge to himself, and his decision to play in the Senior PGA Tour event rather than in the PGA Championship. He had no regrets, "but I would have if I had not won here."

Stormy weather plagued the tournament from start almost to finish, leading to two-tee starts and "winter rules" lifts and placings. They didn't get the first round underway until noon Friday, had two hour-long delays during the afternoon, but still completed play with Graham Marsh and Gibby Gilbert shooting 64s to lead by three strokes. Thunderstorms wreaked worse havoc Saturday and only 27 finished before play was called for the day. When they finished Sunday morning, Floyd had joined Marsh on top at 133, Raymond shooting 68 and 65.

Marsh, seeking his second victory of the season, led much of the way in better weather Sunday. However, Floyd's putter responded when he needed it most. He rolled in a 15-footer at the 17th to tie Graham at 14-under and an eight-footer at the 18th for 68 and a 201 total and the victory after Marsh had missed his birdie try from 15 feet. Gilbert and Jim Albus tied for third, four strokes behind Marsh.

Northville Long Island Classic—$800,000
Winner: Lee Trevino

It had been a painful season in more ways than one for Lee Trevino. Not only had he been playing with an aching shoulder and neck, but also his psyche was hurting in the absence of victories. The physical pain, which he had played through in 25 tournaments, finally got to him and he decided to take three weeks off after defending his title in the Northville Long Island Classic, which also happened to be his most recent victory.

When Trevino headed home from New York that Sunday night, he had another title to his credit and had become the winningest player in the history of the Senior PGA Tour. The win at the Meadow Brook Club was his 25th individual title — he and Mike Hill have won the Legends of Golf three times, including 1995 — moving him ahead of Miller Barber in that category.

John Paul Cain, the Texas amateur who turned pro to play the Senior PGA Tour and won twice during his seven years on the circuit, was headed for his third victory for two days at Meadow Brook with a 65-69–134 start, one stroke ahead of Dave Eichelberger and two in front of Trevino, Buddy Allin, Larry Gilbert and Ben Smith. Trevino, keeping his low, hooking drives in the fairways, took charge Sunday, ran off seven birdies, three-putted the 18th and still won by four strokes with his 66–202 total, 14 under par. Allin, having a good rookie season, shot 70–206 for second place, one stroke ahead of Jack Kiefer, Jay Sigel, Smith and Gilbert. Cain finished with 74–208.

Bank of Boston Classic—$800,000
Winner: Isao Aoki

Victory finally came for Japanese star Isao Aoki when the Senior PGA Tour reached New England for its only visit and the Bank of Boston Classic. Aoki, Japan's first and, thus far, only truly successful international player, had been in contention time and again among his 17 starts earlier in the year on the Senior PGA Tour, notably at the U.S. Senior Open and the Tradition, and had won the American Express Grand Slam, the Japanese tournament with an international field in March. This time at Nashawtuc Country Club outside of Boston, Aoki led from wire to wire, although out of the lead briefly in the final round, and won by one stroke with his final-round 69 and 12-under-par 204 total, gaining his fourth senior title.

The outcome came down to the final holes after Aoki shared the first-round lead with Jim Colbert, Buddy Allin, George Archer and Rocky Thompson, a former winner at Nashawtuc, at 69, then moved in front alone on Saturday with 66 for a 135 total, two ahead of Hale Irwin, Mike McCullough and another ex-champion, Bob Charles. Aoki fell behind in the last round as he ran off 14 straight pars. Then his famous short game came into play. He sank birdie putts from 24 and 30 feet to tie for the lead, parred the 17th, and birdied the par-five finishing hole with one of his trademark bunker shots — he holed a wedge shot to win the 1983 Hawaiian Open on the PGA Tour — to within inches of the cup from 60 feet. Charles and Irwin had the best chances to force a playoff, but Charles could only par the 18th after tangling himself twice in the rough and Irwin was too little too late with birdies on the last two holes. They tied for second at 205.

Franklin Quest Championship—$600,000
Winner: Tony Jacklin

Tony Jacklin survived a closing bogey to pick up his second victory on the Senior PGA Tour in the Franklin Quest Championship at Park City, Utah. Seven players came to the final hole with a chance to win or at least tie for first place. Certainly, when the former British star and Ryder Cup captain three-putted the last green for a 67–206 total, he didn't expect that score to hold up as the winning number. But it did and Jacklin, 51, who joined the U.S. circuit in 1994, had his second victory.

Jacklin had started the final round three strokes off the leading pace of Don Bies and Simon Hobday. At the turn at Park Meadows Golf Club, 12 players were within two strokes of the lead. Jacklin, playing ahead of most of the contenders, reached the 18th hole leading at 11 under par before the three-putt. "I've never three-putted the last hole and won anything," he commented wryly. "I thought I would be in a playoff or maybe be one back."

Actually, Dave Stockton had already missed his chance after charging from five strokes off the pace only to bogey the last hole for 66 and the first of six 207 totals. So had Tom Weiskopf, the defending champion, who also had made a big move but missed a birdie putt at the 18th for 206. The same fate befell Bruce Summerhays, the hometown favorite; John Paul Cain and Rives McBee, the 1990 winner. Hobday birdied the 18th but fell one short and Bies, gambling for a tying birdie, took a bogey instead and finished in a three-way tie at 208 with Jack Kiefer and Bruce Devlin.

GTE Northwest Classic—$600,000
Winner: Walter Morgan

How unlikely was it that Walter Morgan would be the winner of the 1995 GTE Northwest Classic? Consider that he began to play golf almost by accident 11 years into a military hitch because there was a golf course adjacent to the baseball field in Hawaii where he was a member of the Army nine. The Vietnam War veteran, a combat infantryman, won a couple of military golf titles, but settled into club work after his discharge in 1980 before qualifying for the Senior PGA Tour the first time in 1991 and each subsequent year, never finishing high enough on the money list to keep his playing privileges. That's all changed now that Morgan is a winner and among the top 31 on the final money list.

Morgan won by three strokes with his 13-under-par total at Inglewood Country Club. He trailed three Super Seniors — Don January, Joe Jimenez and Jimmy Powell — by one stroke the first day when he opened with 68. Morgan then took over first place with another 68 for a 136 total, one shot ahead of Bob E. Smith, then gave himself some breathing room on the last day when he birdied the first three holes. Bogeys at the sixth and 11th holes around another birdie at the par-five seventh kept things a little tight. He

Ben Crenshaw wore the green jacket as winner of his second Masters title.

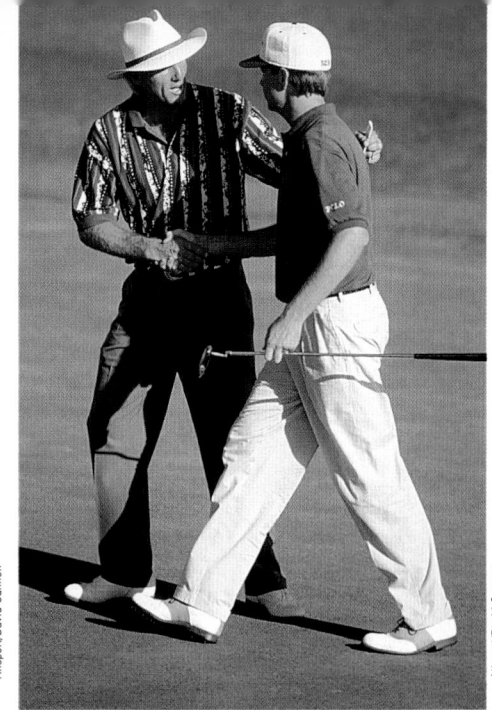

Jay Haas led with a second-round 64 and tied for third place.

Greg Norman (left) and Davis Love III were contenders to the finish.

Brian Henninger shared the 54-hole lead, but fell to a 10th-place tie.

U.S. Amateur champion Tiger Woods made his major championship debut.

Crenshaw, with caddie Carl Jackson, was overcome with emotion after his final putt.

U.S. Open

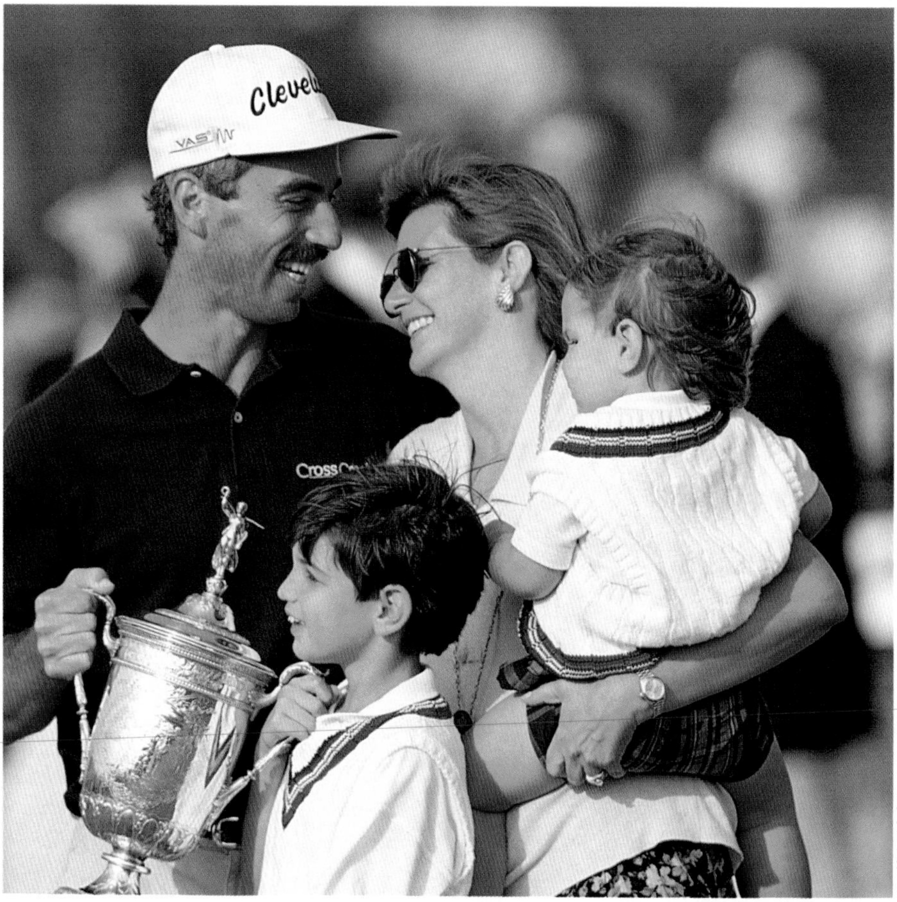

Michael C. Cohen

Corey Pavin celebrated his U.S. Open victory with his family after a stirring finish at Shinnecock Hills.

Michael C. Cohen

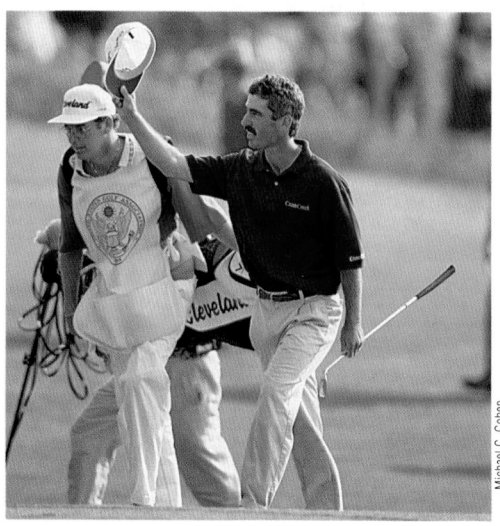

Greg Norman led for two rounds and placed second, two strokes behind.

Tied after 54 holes, Tom Lehman finished third, three strokes back.

Jumbo Ozaki shot 80 in the third round after contending for 36 holes.

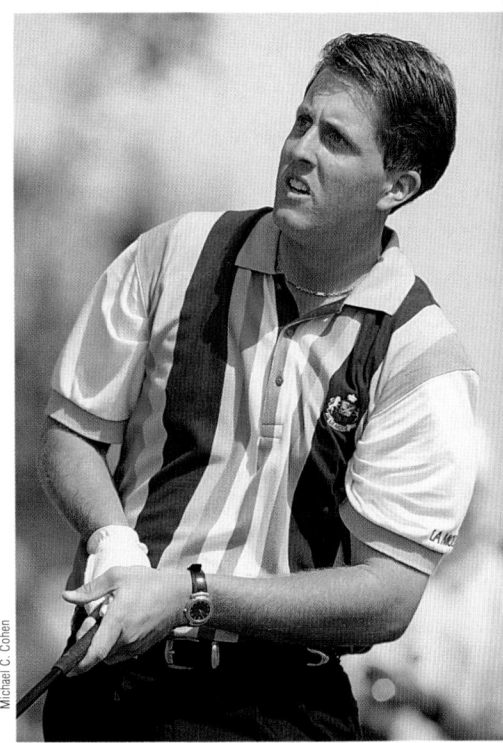

Phil Mickelson was four strokes off the pace after opening with 68.

John Daly became only the second American winner of the British Open in 12 years.

Costantino Rocca gained a playoff with a 60-foot putt, but was easily beaten.

Arnold Palmer made his farewell appearance after 35 years.

Michael Campbell had a near-perfect bunker shot at No. 17 to hold the third-round lead. He finished with 76 and was one stroke behind.

PGA Championship

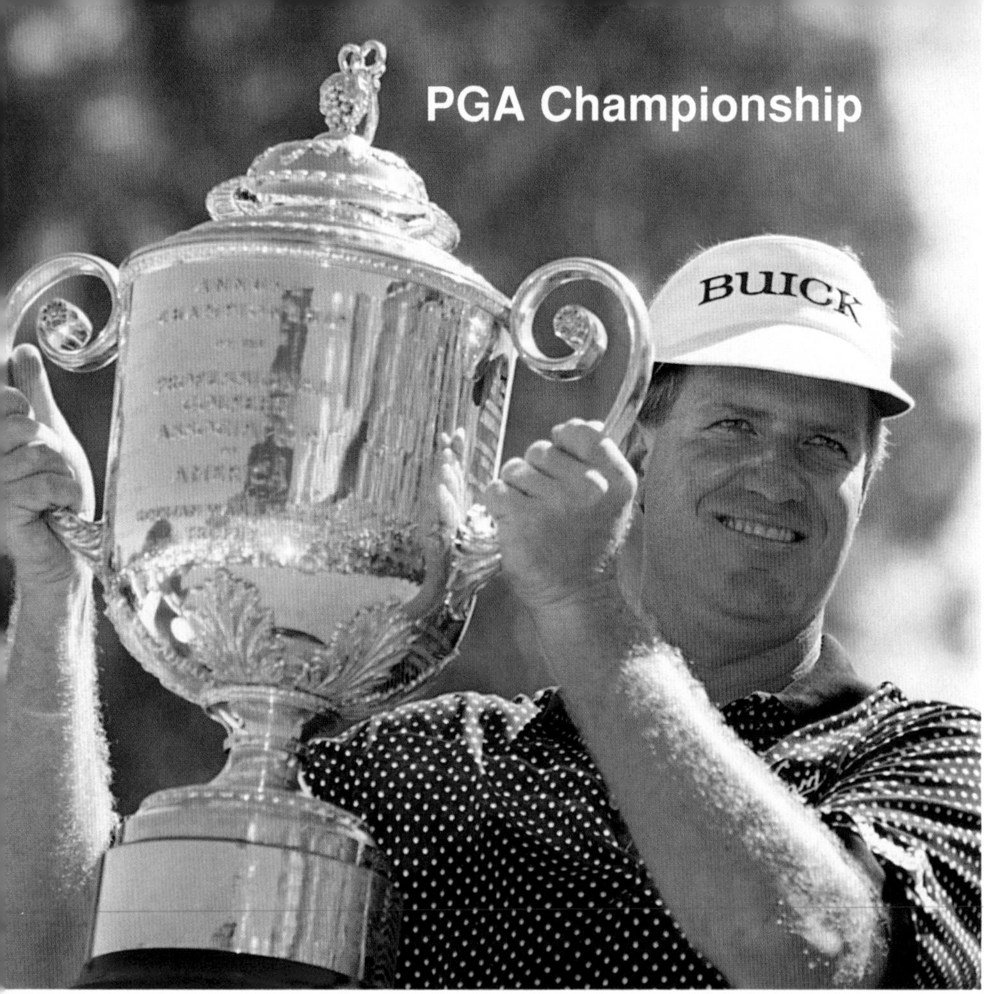

Allsport/J.D. Cuban

Allsport/J.D. Cuban

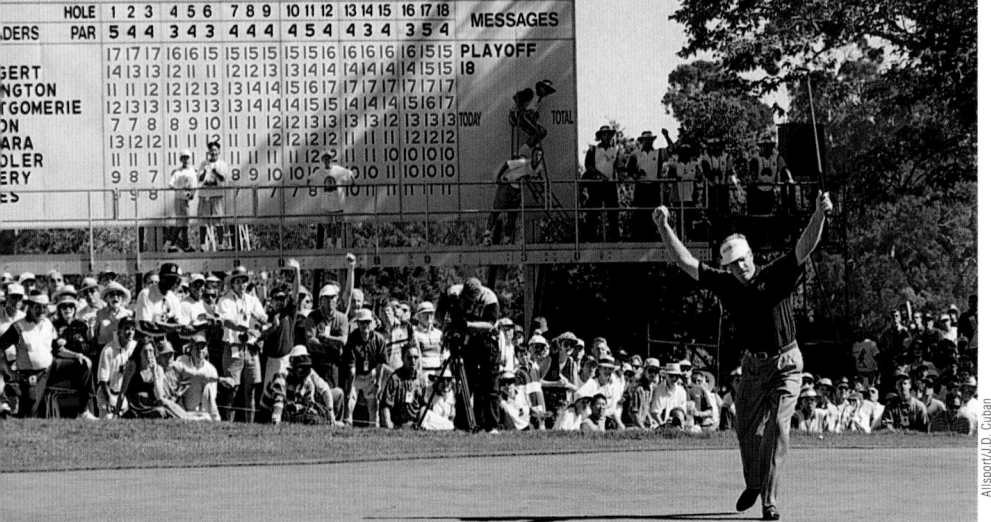

It took a 20-foot playoff birdie for Steve Elkington to win the PGA Championship.

Colin Montgomerie was close again.

Mark O'Meara shared the 36-hole record.

Ernie Els posted the record 54-hole score.

Brad Faxon's 63 took fifth place.

Ryder Cup

Down 7-9 entering the singles, Europe made an inspired comeback to win.

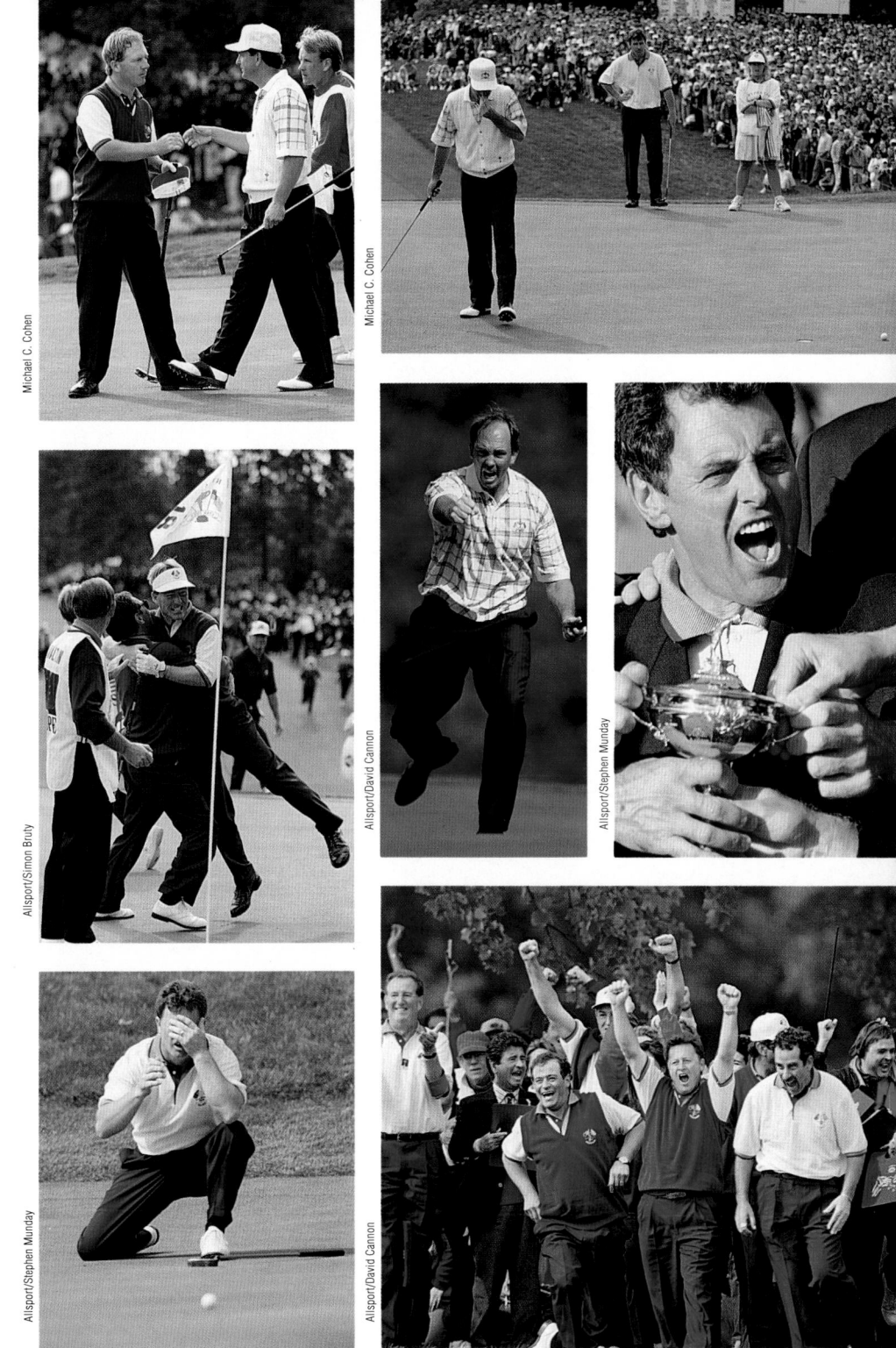

The raw emotions of the Ryder Cup were never more evident than on the last day.

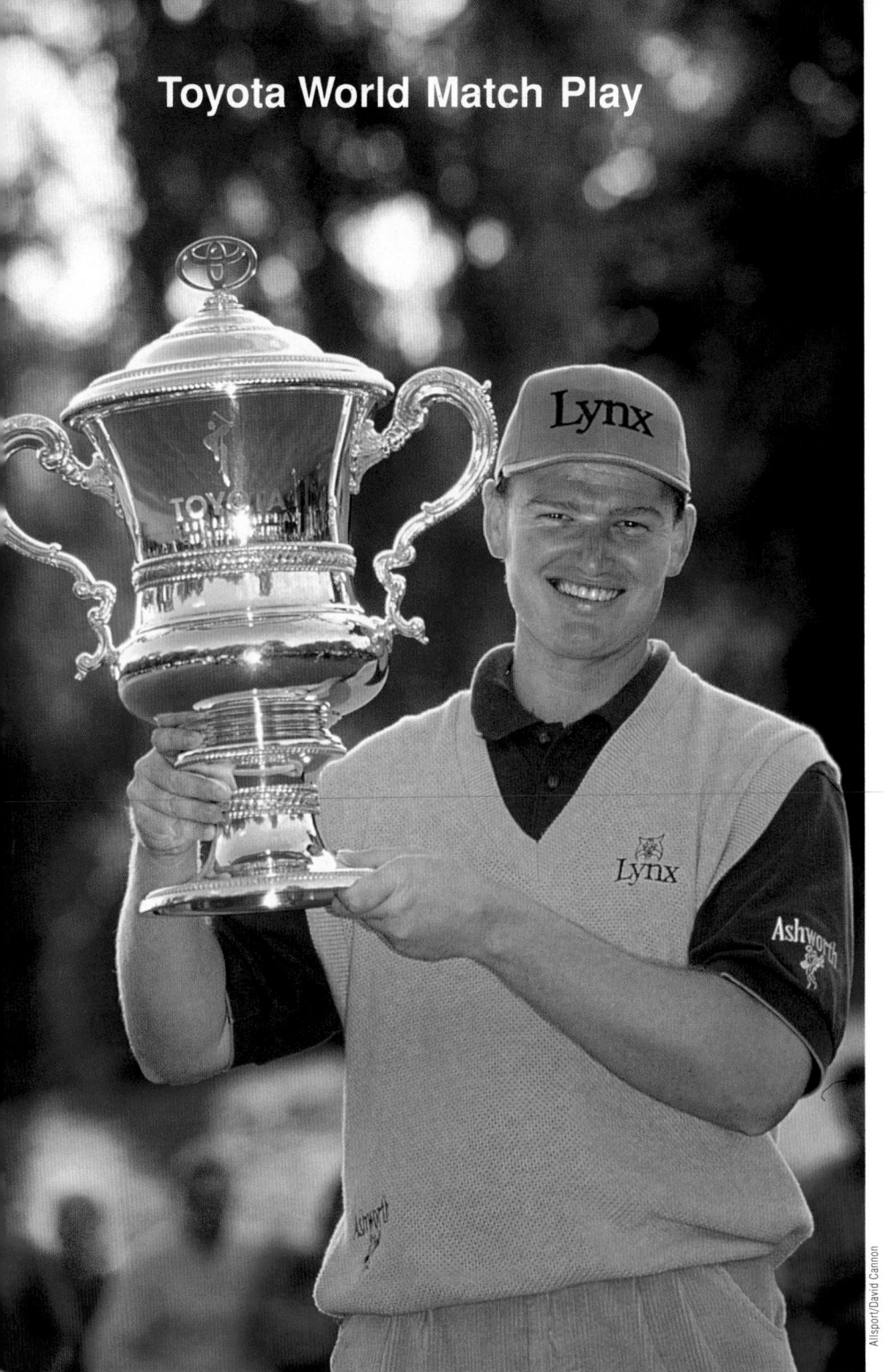

Toyota World Match Play

Ernie Els defended his Toyota World Match Play title, playing 24 under par.

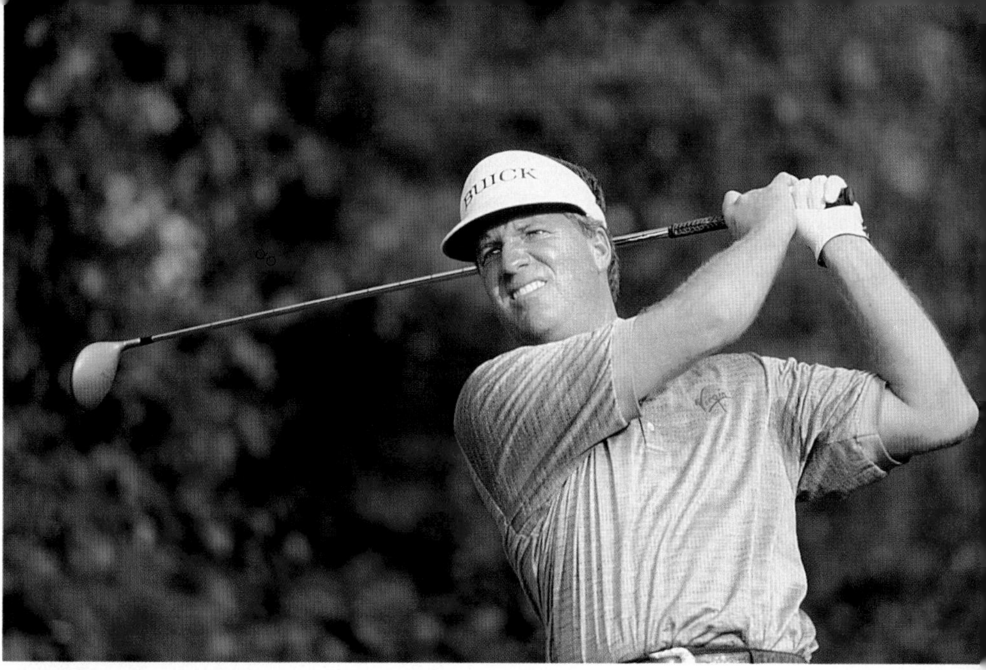

Allsport/David Cannon

Steve Elkington reached the final before losing to Els, 3 & 1.

Allsport/Tim Matthews

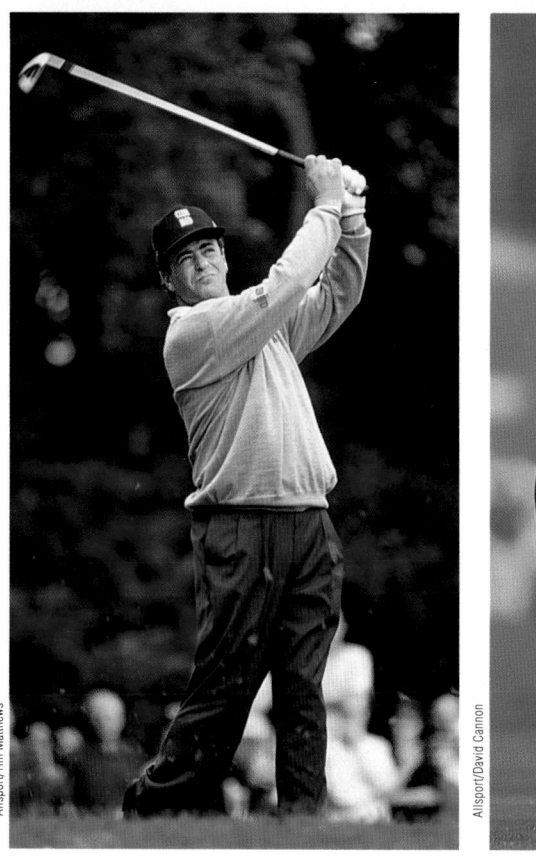

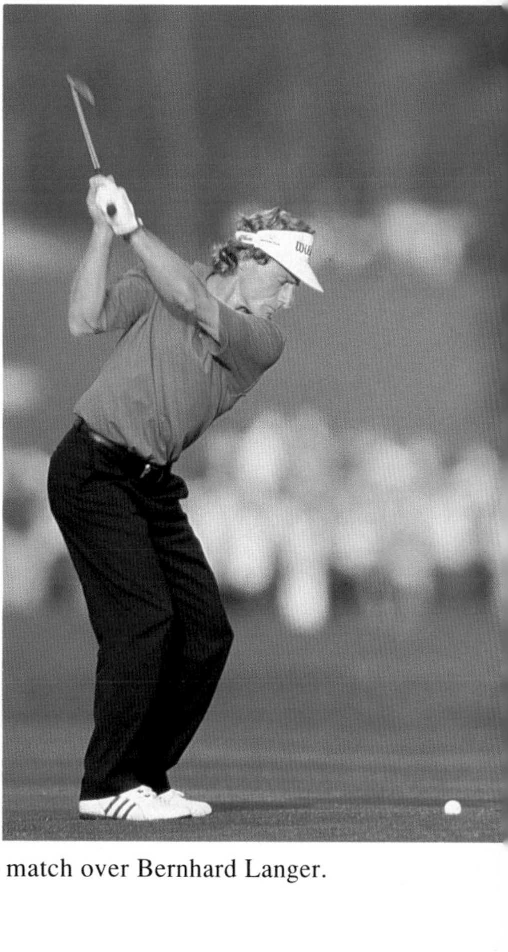

Allsport/David Cannon

Costantino Rocca (left) won the third-place match over Bernhard Langer.

In five years, Fred Couples won two World Championships and over $1.5 million.

Loren Roberts had four steady rounds — 70, 70, 70, 69 — to gain the playoff.

Vijay Singh shared second place.

John Daly finished 40 over par.

Alfred Dunhill Cup

Allsport/David Cannon

Allsport/Stephen Munday

Andrew Coltart (left and playing above), Sam Torrance and Colin Montgomerie produced Scotland's first Alfred Dunhill Cup title.

finished strong with birdies on three of the last four holes for 67 and the three-stroke margin over Dave Stockton, whose runner-up money of $52,800 elevated him to the top of the money list.

Notable sidelight: Sunday was Arnold Palmer's 66th birthday and he shot his age for the first time that day at Inglewood.

Brickyard Crossing Championship—$750,000
Winner: Simon Hobday

Simon Hobday converted a discovery on the practice tee into a self-described miracle and brought to a sudden end an aura of frustration that had dogged him all season on the PGA Senior Tour. The colorful South African, who had been "playing terrible the whole year" after an excellent 1994 campaign during which he won twice, including the U.S. Senior Open, corrected a flaw in his downswing shoulder turn and "suddenly, I'm hitting it dead perfect." With that, Hobday came from one stroke off the lead of Bob Murphy and Bob Charles with a final-round 68 in the Brickyard Crossing Championship and scored his fifth Senior PGA Tour victory with a 12-under-par 204 at Brickyard Crossing Golf Club in Indianapolis, Indiana.

Hobday had taken charge in the windy final round with three back-nine birdies, but hit a bad approach into a bunker at the 18th hole, a poor sand shot and, notoriously weak putter that he is, faced a three-foot putt for bogey to avoid a six-way tie and playoff that looked like "two-and-a-half miles." He made it.

What of the five who wound up in the second-place deadlock at 205? Murphy missed an 18-inch putt at the ninth. Lee Trevino and Kermit Zarley failed to birdie the vulnerable, par-five 15th. Isao Aoki double-bogeyed the 13th, and Hale Irwin missed a 15-footer for the tie by inches at the 18th green. Raymond Floyd, the first-round leader with 65, finished at 206 with Bruce Summerhays.

Bank One Classic—$600,000
Winner: Gary Player

It's a wonder Gary Player doesn't make his American home in Kentucky. Just being a devoted thoroughbred horseman alone would be enough, but consider what Kentucky has meant to his golf career. Thirty-seven years ago, when Player was 22, he won his first tournament in America — the Kentucky Derby Open in Louisville. In 1993 he won the Bank One Classic in Lexington and two years later, after going through that period without a Senior PGA Tour victory, he won the Bank One tournament again, the 159th title on his remarkable record.

The latest victory was an exciting one. After two days the field was bunched, the lead of 143 shared by Jim Dent, George Archer, Raymond Floyd, Mike Hill and defending champion Isao Aoki with three others just one stroke behind. Player trailed by four strokes in a tie for 16th place at 147, but he had a feeling. He told friends: "I just might sneak in there tomorrow."

It really wasn't very sneaky. He circled the field full blast with an eight-birdie, no-bogey 64 and finished at 211, five under par and two strokes in front of Jack Kiefer, who started the day at 145, tied for ninth. Aoki, Archer and Harold Henning finished at 214.

Vantage Championship—$1,500,000
Winner: Hale Irwin

Just as when he won his first tournament on the Senior PGA Tour in July, Hale Irwin left the other contenders grasping for straws when the chips were down in the rich Vantage Championship at Tanglewood Park in Clemmons, North Carolina. He won by seven strokes in the Ameritech, and by four in taking his second title the first of October against one of the year's strongest fields. Irwin broke from a 36-hole, first-place tie with Dave Stockton and shot a powerful 65 for the four-shot victory with his 17-under-par 199 total, just one stroke off the tournament record. It was his ninth straight finish on the Senior Tour at 10th or better and that included three runner-up finishes in addition to the two victories.

Irwin opened the tournament in front with 66 and shot 68 in the second round for the deadlock at 134 with Stockton. Mike Hill was next at 136 and among those within range was 66-year-old Arnold Palmer at 139. Palmer faded after an early spurt, but it wouldn't have mattered. Irwin birdied five holes in a row on the first nine to open a three-stroke lead. Stockton had mid-round problems, Hill matched an eagle with a double bogey, and Irwin was breezing. Stockton shot 69 for his runner-up 203 and the $132,000 check strengthened his hold on first place on the money list. Raymond Floyd shot 67 for 206 and finished third.

The Transamerica—$650,000
Winner: Lee Trevino

Lee Trevino knew what he had to do when he made the turn in the final round of The Transamerica and he did it. Sizing up the situation on the scoreboard, Trevino told his long-time caddie, Herman Mitchell, "I have to shoot 32 on the back," and when he did, he had his second Transamerica title, his second win of the season and the 26th victory of his career on the Senior PGA Tour. The 32 gave him 66 and a 15-under-par 201 total. Actually, he didn't need quite that good a score, since he won by three strokes, but Bruce Summerhays, finishing second for the third time this year, made a bogey at the par-five 18th which he had eagled easily the day before.

A new face appeared at Silverado and he made his presence felt. John Bland, a successful player in his native South Africa and Europe for many years, had won the London Masters on the European Seniors Tour the previous Sunday, two days after his 50th birthday and come directly to Napa, California, having already been granted a sponsor's exemption. Undaunted by the excitement of victory and the jet lag, Bland shot a seven-under 65 and led the first round. Trevino, Bob Murphy and Ben Smith trailed by one, Summerhays by two. All except Murphy merged into a first-place tie at 135 when Trevino uncharacteristically turned an eight-foot eagle chance into a careless three-putt par at the 18th.

Though Trevino was out in 34 Sunday, he trailed Summerhays by two strokes; hence, his target of 32. Trevino caught Summerhays with a birdie at the 14th, made a "turning point" chip and saved par at the 15th, then birdied the last three holes, putting himself out of reach of Summerhays, as it turned out.

Raley's Gold Rush—$700,000
Winner: Don Bies

Back in 1992 in a pre-tournament interview at the PaineWebber Invitational, Lee Trevino made a somewhat-surprising, off-the-cuff prediction that Don Bies would win the tournament. Which he did. Three-and-a-half years and no ensuing victories later, Bies finally won again and the triumph in the Raley's Gold Rush came at the expense of, who else, Lee Trevino. A short birdie putt Trevino missed on the final green gave Bies his eighth victory on the Senior PGA Tour. He made his birdie putt there for 68 and an 11-under-par 205 total on Rancho Murieta Country Club's North course near Sacramento, California.

The dramatics at the 18th hole climaxed an exciting, head-to-head battle between the two after they and Chi Chi Rodriguez began the final round in the last threesome tied for the lead at 137. The first-day front-runners — Walter Zembriski at 67, Dick Goetz, Graham Marsh and J.C. Snead at 68 — had all slipped back. In fact, no one challenged Bies or Trevino after the early holes Sunday, not even Rodriguez, winless since 1993 and struggling with his game, who faded to 18th place with 76.

Bies and Trevino, coming off his Transamerica victory the previous Sunday, exchanged the lead seven times during the round. Bies took the lead for the first time when he holed a 70-yard wedge shot for an eagle at the par-five eighth, but they were never separated by more than a stroke the rest of the way. Bies parred the last seven holes, Trevino catching up one final time with a birdie at the 17th. Both reached the green of the par-five 18th in two, but Trevino rolled his first putt five feet past the cup and missed coming back.

Ralph's Classic—$800,000
Winner: John Bland

John Bland had only one free pass when he came to America in early October to ply his trade on the Senior PGA Tour — a sponsor's exemption for The Transamerica. Despite his fifth-place finish, the South African had to play his way into any tournaments after that through Monday qualifying. At Los Angeles, Bland was one of 110 seniors seeking one of the four available spots in the Ralph's Classic. He succeeded —and it was the last time he will have to go through that grind for at least a year because he won the Ralph's Classic, which, among other things, makes him an exempt player for the next 12 months.

Bland, little known in America but a 21-tournament winner in South Africa and Europe, was getting little attention through the first two rounds of the Ralph's at Wilshire Country Club, the new tournament venue after five years at Rancho Park. Jim Colbert, trying to overtake Dave Stockton in the money race, opened in front with 65 then shared second place with Stockton at 135, three strokes behind Larry Gilbert. Bland was then at 136 after a 69-67 start. Gilbert didn't hold up in the last round, eventually shooting 73 and tying for sixth, and Bland seized the lead with a run of four consecutive birdies and a 30 on the front nine. He preserved his 12-under-par status with a six-foot par putt at the 17th hole, parred the 18th for 201, and watched as Colbert missed an eight-foot birdie putt that would have created a tie and brought Bland back for a playoff.

Hyatt Regency Maui Kaanapali Classic—$600,000
Winner: Bob Charles

Another victory drought ended when Bob Charles won the Hyatt Regency Maui Kaanapali Classic in circumstances in many ways parallel to the triumph of his good friend, Gary Player, in the Bank One Classic in September. Both are high on the victory list of the Senior PGA Tour, but had gone some two years or so without winning as their 60th birthdays approached. Charles had the tougher time of it, rallying from three strokes off the pace in the final round and going three extra holes before winning a playoff against Dave Stockton, the leading money winner. The win of the New Zealander, his first since the Quicksilver Classic in September of 1993, was his 22nd, moving him into a tie with Don January and Chi Chi Rodriguez, third best on the all-time Senior PGA Tour victory list.

Charles lingered just off the pace the first two days at Royal Kaanapali's North course as Stockton and the seemingly ever-present Bruce Summerhays led with six-under 65s. Mike McCullough, a Monday qualifier trying to duplicate the victory feat of John Bland the previous Sunday in Los Angeles, went to the front with a 66-67–133 total, but right behind were Stockton at 134, Lee Trevino at 135 and Charles at 136. McCullough was no match for them in the end. Trevino went in front with birdies at the 14th and 15th holes only to give back three shots and his chances by going bogey, double bogey on the next two holes and finishing at eight-under 205. Meanwhile, Stockton was rallying from a four-stroke deficit with four back-nine birdies for 70 and 204, and Charles, after a bogey at the 17th, matched the 204 with his 68. The playoff, just the sixth of the season and first since July, went three holes before Charles, ever the clutch putter, dropped a 12-footer for the win.

Emerald Coast Classic—$1,000,000
Winner: Raymond Floyd

It certainly wasn't the way the community wanted to bring tournament golf back to Pensacola, Florida, an annual stop on the PGA Tour for more than 30 years until escalating purse levels squeezed it out in the late 1980s, but Raymond Floyd had no objections. Weather marred and nearly wiped out the Emerald Coast Classic, the new entry on the Senior PGA Tour's schedule.

Torrential rains, measuring more than 22 inches in 48 hours, inundated The Moors, washing out the first round, shortening the event to 36 holes, the second Florida event of the season (Naples was the other) to suffer that fate. When play finally started Saturday, Floyd began his move toward his third title of the season and 12th on the circuit, at the same time establishing a serious challenge for his first money title ever.

Floyd shot 69, he and three others trailing leaders Isao Aoki and Bruce Devlin by one stroke. Then, on a cool, calm Sunday, he birdied two of his last three holes for 66 to overtake Tom Wargo, already in at 135 after tacking a seven-under 64 to his opening 71. Buddy Allin shot 63 and Bob Murphy 64, but fell one stroke short of the first-place tie. Floyd prevailed on the second hole of the playoff when he sank a six-foot birdie putt for the win. Stockton (139) and Jim Colbert (142) lost ground to Floyd and Murphy in the money race.

Energizer Senior Tour Championship—$1,500,000
Winner: Jim Colbert

It worked out just the way Senior PGA Tour officials had hoped it would. When the top 30 players of the year — No. 22 Jack Nicklaus passed — gathered for the Energizer Senior Tour Championship, the final event of the season in early November, the stakes were at a premium. Besides going for the prestigious title and its $262,000 first prize, four players — Dave Stockton, Raymond Floyd, Bob Murphy and Jim Colbert — all had shots at the No. 1 position on the final money list and the Arnold Palmer Award.

In a complete turnaround from 1994, when he tied for last place, Colbert took the lead at Myrtle Beach, South Carolina's renowned Dunes Golf and Beach Club the first day, fattened it to six after three rounds, survived a skid of his own and a familiar Floyd charge Sunday, and not only won the championship but jumped from fourth to first place and took the money title with record earnings of $1,444,386. It was his fourth win of the season and 12th of his five-year senior career.

Uncomfortable temperatures in the mid-50s greeted the field Thursday and Colbert, with 68, was the only player under 71. Colbert maintained that margin with 69 Friday, leading Isao Aoki by three, Tom Wargo and Hale Irwin by five. His lead looked insurmountable Saturday night after Wargo, his closest challenger through the third round, triple-bogeyed the 18th hole. That left Colbert at 208, six strokes ahead of Stockton, Floyd and Rocky Thompson. Hale Irwin would have been there with them but for an unusual rules infraction involving ball marking that cost him four strokes.

Floyd, the ultimate challenger, fell 10 strokes behind Colbert after five holes and was seven back at the turn. Then, things went into reverse for Colbert. He bogeyed the 11th, 13th and 15th holes while Floyd, playing ahead of him, birdied the 13th, 16th and, from 10 inches, the par-three 17th to narrow the margin to a single stroke. Colbert clinched the victory with a birdie of his own with a 20-footer at the 17th as Floyd was missing a 15-foot birdie putt at the last hole. Colbert bogeyed the 18th for a 74–282 total and a one-stroke victory over Floyd. Wargo and Thompson finished at 285 and Stockton at 286.

European Seniors Tour

Windsor Senior Masters—£54,000
Winner: Brian Huggett

The European seniors traveled to Kenya to launch their 1995 season and Brian Huggett in particular was glad he made the trip. The stocky little Welshman, now age 58, scored his sixth victory on the PGA European Seniors Tour in the Windsor Senior Masters at Nairobi's Windsor Golf and Country Club, displaying the sort of stout play in the heat of a rousing finish that brought him 19 victories in his prime years. Huggett birdied the final hole to snatch a one-stroke victory over Antonio Garrido with his seven-under-par 209 total.

Garrido and David Creamer shared the early headlines. Creamer, better known in Europe as a table tennis ace, jumped in front Friday with 66, then yielded first place to the Spaniard, who shot his second 68 Saturday and led Creamer, Huggett (70-67) and Tommy Horton (71-66) by a stroke entering Sunday's round. Creamer forged a three-shot margin after nine holes in blustery conditions, then cracked, the battle shifting to Garrido, Horton, Huggett and Italy's Alberto Croce. Ultimately, it came down to Huggett and Garrido and the final hole, where Huggett put a wind-fighting eight-iron shot three feet from the pin for his birdie and 72. Minutes later, Garrido, in the final group, missed his bid for a tying birdie from 20 feet, finishing with 74 and 210.

The tournament was played at the end of March and was the only event until the schedule resumed in Germany in July.

International German PGA Seniors Championship—£80,000
Winner: Renato Campagnoli

As a younger man, Renato Campagnoli's success in golf had been limited to victories in his home country, Italy. As a senior player, he is changing all that. After two near-misses as the leading qualifier during his initial season on the PGA European Seniors Tour in 1994, Campagnoli captured his first international title with a wire-to-wire victory in the International German PGA Seniors Championship in Frankfurt in mid-July.

After sharing the lead with four others the first day at Idstein Golf Club, Campagnoli took sole possession of first place Saturday and shot a steady, one-under-par 71 Sunday for a 208 total and a two-stroke victory over countryman Alberto Croce and Brian Huggett. Hugh Inggs, Chick Evans, Sooky Maharaj and Paul Leonard matched Campagnoli's opening 68, but not his Saturday 69, which put him two in front of Malcolm Gregson and Mike Ingham. The challenges to Campagnoli Sunday, though, came from Croce and Huggett, who had won the season opener in Kenya in April. Both shot 67s, Huggett firing 31 on the front nine to move within two shots of the lead.

But Huggett couldn't maintain that pace on the back nine and the title went to the 51-year-old Italian.

Senior British Open—£350,000
Winner: Brian Barnes

Nobody was more pleased than Brian Barnes when the Royal and Ancient Golf Club announced that it was moving the Senior British Open to Royal Portrush in Northern Ireland in 1995. That would be his first Senior Open and something special because his father-in-law, Max Faulkner, now age 79, had won the British Open at Portrush in 1951. Barnes, a standout in his younger days in European golf with 11 victories and strong performances in Ryder Cup play, dreamed of duplicating Faulkner's feat and the dream came true after a gruelling playoff finish and an astonishing putt.

Barnes, who tuned up for the Senior Open with four starts on the U.S. Senior PGA Tour after turning 50 in early June, got off flying at Portrush. He shot 67 in each of the first two days and led America's Bob Murphy by three and John Morgan by five. Then, his putting went awry. He shot 77 and wound up at 211 with John Jacobs, one stroke behind Murphy, who shot 73.

Eight players had a shot at the title well into the final round, but it came down to Barnes, who made a six-foot par putt at the 18th for 70 and 281, and Murphy, who bogeyed from the rough for 71 and his 281. Both men parred the first two playoff holes and went again to the par-five 17th. Murphy drove poorly, but Barnes reached the edge of the green with his two-iron second shot and, after Murphy put his third 20 feet from the cup, ran in the 50-foot eagle putt for the victory. Max Faulkner was the first person to congratulate him.

Lawrence Batley Seniors—£70,000
Winner: Alberto Croce

Italian golf fans, who have rarely had much to crow about where their home country golfers have been concerned internationally, found plenty to cheer about in the early events on the PGA European Seniors Tour in 1995. Three weeks after compatriot Renato Campagnoli scored his first-ever international win in the German Seniors, Alberto Croce repeated the accomplishment in the Lawrence Batley Seniors at Fixby Golf Club in Huddersfield, England.

Remarkably, for the second week in a row, the issue was decided by an eagle putt on the final hole. A week after Brian Barnes won the Senior British Open with an eagle putt on the third playoff hole, the 55-year-old Croce dropped a 25-foot eagle putt at the last green to win by one stroke with 68 and a four-under-par 209 total.

It came down to the final hole after American Deray Simon led the first day with 68 and Croce and Tommy Horton took over with 141s Saturday. With John Morgan already in with two-under 211, the final group of Croce, Horton and Malcolm Gregson all reached the green on the par-five 18th in two. Gregson missed from 30 feet before Croce holed his and Horton failed with his try for the tie from closer range. Gregson dropped into a deadlock for third with Morgan when he three-putted.

Forte PGA Seniors Championship—£90,000
Winner: John Morgan

It had been much the same as in his initial senior season. John Morgan was again playing contending golf in the early events of 1995 on the PGA European Seniors Tour ... not winning but on the verge. At just about the same point in the season, Morgan scored his fourth victory, repeating in the Forte PGA Seniors Championship at Sunningdale. The Forte win in 1994 was the third of his rookie year on his way to the money-winnings title.

This time the 51-year-old Morgan had to work overtime to win after he and Spaniard Antonio Garrido tied in regulation with six-under-par 204s. The loss was particularly disappointing for Garrido, also 51, who won the Shell Scottish Seniors in 1994. He had opened with a five-under 65 and retained a one-stroke lead over American John Jacobs with his 70–135. Morgan, starting the final round two back, failed to avoid the extra work when he missed a two-footer and three-putted the 18th green Sunday. However, Morgan won the playoff on the same hole with a bogey five when Garrido found sand twice and took six.

Brian Huggett came back from an opening 75 with 66-65 for 206 and tied for third with Jacobs, Neil Coles, Liam Higgins and Francisco Abreu.

Northern Electric Seniors—£60,000
Winner: Brian Waites

Brian Waites, the former Ryder Cupper, added another chapter to his courageous comeback story when he won the Northern Electric Seniors, his second victory since an auto accident in 1991 that was so serious that, as he puts it, "I could've wound up in a box." The 55-year-old club pro from Nottingham won the D-Day Seniors Open in 1994, as well as the venerable Forte Seniors in 1990 and 1991 before the accident.

Waites posted the only sub-par total — 215 — on the demanding Slaley Hall Golf Club course to win the Northern Electric by two strokes over five others — Bob Verwey, Peter Butler, Noel Ratcliffe, Francisco Abreu and Neil Coles. The Englishman attributed his solid play to a modified putting stroke and good mental concentration. Four shots behind Ratcliffe after the 50-year-old Australian newcomer opened the tournament with a four-under 68, Waites climbed into a first-place tie with 70–142 as Ratcliffe slipped to 74 Saturday. Although he took a 73 Sunday, Waites held off a posse of challengers with a game finish, holing par putts from four, five and seven feet over the last four holes and saving par from a bunker at the 17th.

Collingtree Seniors—£52,000

Winner: Neil Coles

You could see it coming. With runner-up finishes two weeks in a row, you figured Neil Coles was about to win again. And win he did — in the Collingtree Seniors by four strokes, the biggest margin to that point of the season on the PGA European Seniors Tour. It was the eighth Seniors victory, second at Collingtree, and the 40th triumph in the 38-year career of Britain's most enduring player and statesman of the game.

"I was delighted to strike a blow for the older seniors," remarked Coles after his August win at Collingtree Park Golf Club a month before his 61st birthday. It was his first win in two years, his play affected by an operation in 1994.

Brian Huggett had the hot hand early at Collingtree, shooting a first-round 67 to lead Peter Butler by one and Malcolm Gregson by two. Strong winds took a heavy toll Saturday — 71 was the best score. As Huggett shot 78, Coles added 72 to his first-round 71 and tied for the lead with Francisco Abreu, having his third consecutive strong tournament. Coles put the field away on the front nine Sunday with five birdies, 13 putts and a 31 and brought it home with 68 despite a double bogey at the 13th, finishing five under par at 211. Brian Barnes, the Senior Open champion who had been shelved since that win because of leg surgery to remove a blood clot, charged into second place at 215 with a course-record 66, highlighted by a 75-foot eagle putt.

Shell Scottish Seniors Open—£100,000

Winner: Brian Huggett

Brian Huggett obviously has a long memory and a patient desire to even old scores. When Huggett won what came down to a head-to-head battle with Neil Coles for the Shell Scottish Seniors Open title, he noted, "I really wanted this one. It's always great to beat Neil and this one avenges his playoff victory over me in the Scottish Open back in 1972." More to a current point, Huggett's two-stroke triumph over Coles at Royal Aberdeen Golf Club was his seventh as a senior and 33rd of his distinguished career. He became the first (and eventually the only) multiple winner of the 1995 PGA European Seniors Tour following his season-opening victory in the Windsor Masters in Kenya in April.

Low scores abounded the first day as Antonio Garrido, the defending champion, registered a seven-under-par 63 to lead Huggett by one shot, John Fourie and Maurice Bembridge by two and Coles and Tommy Horton by three. The top of the standings thinned out the second day as Garrido with 70–133, Huggett with 70–134 and Coles with 69–135 pulled away from the rest. Garrido fell away with three dropped shots to par on the front nine, leaving the two old Ryder Cup partners to slug it out. They remained tied until Coles, shooting for two in a row, overshot the 17th green and bogeyed. Huggett then birdied the 18th with a 25-footer for 66 and a tournament-record 200. Coles shot 67 for his 202. Garrido wound up third at 206.

De Vere Hotels Seniors Classic—£60,000
Winner: Tommy Horton

It seemed like a Ryder Cup reunion when play concluded in the De Vere Hotels Seniors Classic with Tommy Horton, a two-time member of the British team back in the 1970s, finishing in the winner's slot at Belton Woods Golf Club at Grantham, England, and four other Ryder Cuppers occupying the next spots in the standings. The win was Horton's seventh since joining the PGA European Seniors Tour in 1992 with at least one of those victories in each of the four seasons. It was the 20th of his career.

Belton Woods, a new course, was not amenable to low scoring. Neil Coles, Alberto Croce and Bembridge led the first day with 70s, then Horton went ahead to stay Saturday with one of just two rounds in the 60s all week. His 71-69–140 total put him one stroke ahead of Bembridge and Waites, and he was never caught Sunday, even though shooting 73–213. Garrido came within one stroke with his 71–214, one of only two sub-par rounds that day. Mike Ingham tied the course record with 68 but he had started the round in last place. Bembridge, Waites and Gregson tied for third at 215.

London Masters—£80,000
Winner: John Bland

Talk about fast starts. John Bland, a longtime and successful fixture on the South African and European Tours, won the London Masters on the PGA European Seniors Tour just two days after his 50th birthday in what obviously was his first appearance as a senior. Bland, who had accumulated 23 titles in his younger days, won decisively at the London Golf Club near Sevenoaks in England, finishing four strokes in front of four runners-up with his six-under-par 210 total.

Tony Grubb, age 59, a former British PGA champion winless for 26 years, launched a bid Friday with a course-record 68, two shots ahead of Bland and Hugh Inggs, another South African who has played frequently in Europe over the years. Then, Bland edged ahead by one stroke Saturday with 69–139 and was never seriously threatened Sunday as he shot his third straight sub-par round — 71 — for the 210. Both Grubb and Inggs had 74s Sunday, dropping into the four-way deadlock for second place with John Morgan, who shot 73, and Bob Verwey, yet another South African, who made a big jump with 69. The high finish kept alive Morgan's hopes to repeat as year-end Order of Merit leader.

Bland left immediately for America and, as noted elsewhere in this chapter, challenged in his first start on the U.S. Senior PGA Tour and won two weeks later in the Los Angeles event. He intends to play full schedules on both senior circuits in 1996.

Senior Zurich Pro-Am: Lexus Trophy—£60,000

Winner: Liam Higgins

It took familiar and favorite ground for Irishman Liam Higgins to get over the hump and back into the winner's circle on the PGA European Seniors Tour. The long-hitting Higgins, age 52, the pro at Waterville, was back at the site of one of his two 1994 victories — the season-ending Senior Zurich Pro-Am: Lexus Trophy in the Swiss Alps — and took full advantage of his last chance for a 1995 title. In contrast to 1994 when he squeezed out a one-shot victory, Liam ran away with it the second time around, his five-stroke margin the widest of the season.

Breitenloo Golf Club was damp and playing long, an advantage for Higgins, who reached all of the par-fives in two every day. He shared the first-round lead with Renato Campagnoli at 69 Friday, but fell three strokes off the pace Saturday with his 70–139 as Randall Vines, a newcomer from Australia, raced into the lead with a 66 for 136. However, Vines could not keep up that pace, shot 75 Sunday and wound up in second place with 211 as Higgins closed with 67, scoring three birdies and an eagle on the par-fives and trimming Vines' bid early with five birdies and a front-nine 31.

Brian Barnes clinched the Order of Merit title even though on the shelf with severe leg problems virtually the entire season after his lucrative victory in the Senior British Open. John Morgan had a shot at the top, but, needing a win at Zurich to do it, finished in a seven-man tie for third place at 212.

Japan Senior Tour

American Express Grand Slam—¥60,000,000

Winner: Isao Aoki

For one reason or another, Isao Aoki did not play in the richest of the Senior Japan PGA Tour tournaments — the early-season Grand Slam — the first three years that he was eligible. When he finally teed it up in the event in March of 1995, Japan's most famous and successful international star embellished his 60-victory record on his country's regular tour with a two-stroke victory in the weather-bedeviled tournament.

Before the skies turned nasty, Lee Trevino shot a seven-birdie 66 at Glen Oaks Country Club, the tournament venue for the first time, and took a one-stroke lead over Ed Sneed. Aoki was two back, tied with Dave Stockton and Marion Heck. Rain and cold temperatures toughened playing conditions Saturday and Aoki's two-under 70 for 138 gave him a two-shot advantage over Gibby Gilbert (70-70). Trevino shot 75, joining Graham Marsh (70-71) at 141. The weather deteriorated so badly Sunday — snow and temperatures at the freezing mark — that officials shortened the final round to nine holes. Aoki's 35 gave him an unusual victory total of 173. Marsh (34) and Gilbert (35) tied for second at 175, two ahead of Trevino.

TPC Starts Senior—¥50,000,000
Winner: Fujio Kobayashi

A challenger several times in 1994, Fujio Kobayashi picked up his first title on the Senior Japan PGA Tour in the TPC Starts tournament, scoring a three-stroke victory in the 72-hole event at Garden Golf Club in Ibaragi Prefecture. Kobayashi stood off Hsieh Min-Nan, the long-time Taiwanese star, after the two men led the field entering the final round with 54-hole scores of 208, shooting 71 for his nine-under-par 279 while Hsieh was slipping to 74, 282 and the runner-up slot.

Hsieh, winner of four senior events in the previous two seasons in Japan, jumped in front Thursday with 66, leading Kobayashi by a stroke. Hiroshi Ishii entered the fray Friday with 65, the week's best round. That tied him at the top with Hsieh at 138 after Hsieh and Kobayashi posted 72s. Ishii was only one back after 54 holes, but took 77 Sunday.

Daiichi Seimei Cup—¥50,000,000
Winner: Seiichi Kanai

Seiichi Kanai, Japan's most successful senior, continued his winning ways in 1995 with a May victory in the Daiichi Seimei Cup. Kanai, the winner of seven titles on the lightly scheduled Senior Japan PGA Tour the previous two seasons, captured the Daiichi Seimei Cup at Tomisato Golf Club in Chiba Prefecture by one stroke over Ryosuke Ota and Kuo Chie-Hsiung.

Mitsutaka Kono shot 67 in the opening round, taking a one-stroke lead over Kanai and Hiroshi Ishii, who had blown a chance to win in the previous seniors event with a poor finish. It happened to Ishii again at Tomisato when he skied to 80 Saturday as Kanai duplicated his 68 and took a two-stroke lead over Kuo, who also shot 68 that day. Kanai barely held on Sunday. He just matched par for a 208 total. Kuo shot 71 and Ota jumped into the runner-up deadlock with a closing 67.

Japan PGA Senior Championship—¥50,000,000
Winner: Teruo Sugihara

Teruo Sugihara enforced his reputation as Japan's most enduring champion at the Japan PGA Senior Championship, still winning at age 58. Sugihara, who remains active on the regular Japan PGA Tour where he won his most recent of 57 victories in 1992, scored his second senior victory by one stroke over Seiichi Kanai, the over-50 circuit's most dominant player, in the important event at Shimoakima Country Club at Gunma.

The ever-present Hiroshi Ishii made yet another unsuccessful run at victory in the PGA Seniors, opening in front with 66. Sugihara gave little notice with 71 and was still four back at 140 after 36 holes. Kanai, gunning for his second 1995 win, led with 67-69–136. Sugihara chipped away only one of those strokes with another 69 Saturday, but his third straight 69 Sunday fashioned the victory as Kanai slipped to 73. Ishii finished in a tie for third with Haruo Yasuda, three behind Kanai at 282.

HTB Senior Classic—¥30,000,000
Winner: Hsieh Min-Nan

Masaru Amano made a strong bid to repeat as champion of the HTB Senior Classic at the end of June, eventually yielding to Taiwan's Hsieh Min-Nan, the long-time Asian star, by a single stroke amid a final-round cavalry charge by a host of serious contenders.

Hsieh and Amano entered the Sunday round tied for the lead at 139 after matching rounds of 72-67. There were 12 players within four strokes behind them, among them Namio Takasu, who was the first-round front-runner with a surprisingly high, two-under-par 70 at Mitsui Kanko Iris Golf Club in Hokkaido. Hsieh closed with 69 to Amano's 70 to grab the title with his 208 total. Ichiro Teramoto finished one stroke behind Amano, and Norihiko Matsumoto was next at 211.

Asahi Kokusai Vintage Classic—¥30,000,000
Winner: Haruo Yasuda

Haruo Yasuda, one of the leading players in the early years of the Japan PGA Tour, has developed an affinity for the Asahi Kokusai Vintage Classic. Yasuda has won the tournament two years in a row, each time by a margin of a single stroke. In 1995, he followed a pair of four-under-par 66s with a closing 70 for 202 and the one-stroke victory over Norihiko Matsumoto.

Yasuda trailed by a stroke the first day at Asahi Kokusai Country Club as Matsumoto opened with 65. Shoji Kikuchi matched his 66. The second 66 pushed Yasuda one stroke ahead of Fujio Kobayashi, the TPC Starts winner earlier in the season, and two in front of Matsumoto and Hsieh Min-Nan, the HTB Classic winner in July. Hsieh, with 70–204, finished third and Kobayashi, with 72-205, took fourth place.

Komatsu Nagoya TV Open—¥40,000,000
Winner: Kuo Chie-Hsiung

The "horses for courses" maxim held true again on the Senior Japan PGA Tour when Kuo Chie-Hsiung captured the Komatsu Nagoya TV Open in mid-September. The Taiwanese player had scored his first victory two years earlier in the tournament at Hananoki Golf Club in Aichi Prefecture.

In contrast to a come-from-behind victory in 1993, Kuo carried a one-stroke lead into the final round and won despite a 73, as his closest early pursuers fell from contention. His six-under-par 210 total gave him a two-stroke victory over Shigeru Uchida and Haruo Yasuda, the previous week's winner. Toshikazu Izumi had his day in the sun Friday when he led with 64 as Kuo opened with 67. Kuo's 70 Saturday moved him into the one-stroke lead over Mitsuhiro Kitta as Izumi collapsed with 79. Kitta suffered the same fate Sunday, and nobody else came up with a hot hand to overtake the faltering Kuo. American Art Proctor had 69, the only round under 70.

Noboru Gotah Memorial Tokyu Senior Cup—¥30,000,000
Winner: Koji Nakajima

Koji Nakajima followed the usual pattern of an unlikely tournament winner in the Noboru Gotah Memorial Tokyu Senior Cup. Three strokes off the pace, Nakajima started the final round at Tokyu Seven Hundred Club well ahead of the second-day leaders, put 68 on the scoreboard and watched from the clubhouse as his 208 stood up as the winning score.

The lightly regarded Nakajima trailed first-round leaders Shozo Miyamoto and Fujio Kobayashi (67s) by three strokes Friday and was still three back after two rounds Saturday with his 70-70–140. Yoshihiro Takada led with 137 and nine others were ahead of Nakajima in the standings. Five players — Kikuo Arai, Seiji Ogawa, Fukuji Kikuchi, Izuru Taka and Takada — all fell one stroke short of catching Nakajima and forcing the season's first playoff.

Ho-Oh Cup—¥35,000,000
Winner: Ryokichi Jibiki

When a player takes a first-round lead of six strokes and keeps his wits and game about him, he should have no trouble winning a 54-hole tournament. Which is exactly what Ryokichi Jibiki did in the Ho-Oh Cup. Jibiki recorded a 15-under-par 201 total at Ho-Oh Golf Club and won by four strokes over Kuo Chie-Hsiung.

Jibiki's opening 62 was certainly out of the ordinary, but one is hard-pressed to come up with another example of a player taking such a huge lead the first day of any tournament. Kuo began his futile pursuit with 68, a score matched by Hsieh Min-Nan. Jibiki lost only one stroke of his margin Saturday when he shot 70, as his Taiwanese pursuers, Kuo and Hsieh, mustered 69 and 70, respectively. Jibiki breezed to the four-stroke victory with 69 Sunday. Kuo shot 68 as did Hsieh and Kikuo Arai, who tied for third at 206.

Japan Senior Open—¥50,000,000
Winner: Isao Aoki

When Isao Aoki is around the Senior Japan PGA Tour, the rest of the field usually is playing for second place. This certainly was the case in 1995 when Aoki, his country's greatest international player ever, ended the senior season in Japan as he had started it — with a victory. In between, he won a tournament and more than $1 million on the U.S. Senior PGA Tour. Back in Japan in November for the Senior Open, Aoki, who had given up the lead to Masaru Amano after running in front the first two days, came from one back and won the championship for the second year in a row. It was a one-stroke victory with his 13-under-par 275 total at Kitaura Golf Club.

Aoki began the the championship with 65 and a one-stroke lead over Kanae Nobechi and maintained the same edge Friday. He shot 67 and Amano moved into second place with 67-66–133. Amano, who flew to America immediately afterward and led the qualifying tournament for the 1996 U.S. Senior PGA Tour, slipped one stroke in front at Kitaura Saturday with 72 to Aoki's 74. However, Aoki came back strongly with 69 Sunday to finish one stroke in front of Mitoshi Tomita, as Amano took 73 and dropped into a third-place tie with South Africa's Gary Player at 278.

18. Women's Tours

Not since the arrival of Nancy Lopez and Beth Daniel more than 15 years earlier had women's golf been so invigorated by a newcomer as it was in 1995 by Annika Sorenstam. The youngster from Stockholm, Sweden, who did not reach her 25th birthday until October, became the first ever to lead the money lists on the LPGA Tour in the United States, Women's European Tour and Women's Australasian Tour in the same year.

It was an achievement which had eluded Laura Davies, a recent leading money winner on two circuits, but never more than one in the same year. The 32-year-old English golfer, who in 1994 had won eight tournaments worldwide and become the first woman to earn more than $1 million in one year, suddenly had a rival for international prominence.

Not to be ignored were the stars of the Japan LPGA Tour, Ikuyo Shiotani, Mayumi Hirase and Akiko Fukushima, but their exploits were confined to the domestic circuit while Sorenstam and Davies crisscrossed the globe.

Davies won seven tournaments worldwide in 1995 to Sorenstam's six victories. Sorenstam was the leading money winner in the United States with $663,533 to Davies' runner-up total of $530,349. She led in Europe with £130,324 as Davies again was second with £100,697. Each also had victories on other circuits, Sorenstam in Australia and Davies in Japan. Sorenstam won both the LPGA's Vardon Trophy (71.00 scoring average) and Rolex Player of the Year Award.

On the Women's World Money List, Sorenstam led with a record $1,043,121 and Davies was second with $932,246. Shiotani, with five Japanese victories, was third with $822,334, just ahead of Hirase, who earned $808,176 and won three tournaments. Fukushima was fifth with $743,131.

Sorenstam's emergence was not unexpected. She attended the University of Arizona and won the 1991 national collegiate title in her first year. She was Rookie of the Year on the 1994 U.S. LPGA Tour and tied for second in the Weetabix Women's British Open before achieving her first professional victory late in the year at the Holden Australian Open.

She began 1995 by winning twice in Europe on the newly titled American Express Tour, at the OVB Damen Open in Austria, beating Davies by three strokes, and at the Hennessy Cup in Germany. Her first American victory was a major title, the U.S. Women's Open, when she came from five strokes behind in the final round. She won the GHP Heartland Classic in St. Louis by 10 strokes.

Sorenstam and Davies went head-to-head in the Samsung World Championship of Women's Golf in South Korea. Sorenstam overcame a three-stroke deficit in the final round then holed a 45-foot chip shot for a birdie to win in a playoff. Her final victory of the year was the Alpine Australian Masters, by an eight-stroke margin.

The seven victories by Davies were two on the U.S. LPGA Tour at the Standard Register PING and Chick-Fil-A Charity Classic, four in Europe at the Evian Masters (by five strokes over Sorenstam), Guardian Irish Holidays Open (by 16 strokes), Woodpecker Welsh Open and Wilkinson Sword English Open, and the Itoen Ladies in Japan. She finished the year with 40 career victories worldwide including a record 22 wins in Europe.

Other highlights of women's golf in 1995 included Betsy King's induction into the U.S. LPGA Hall of Fame with her 30th career victory in the ShopRite Classic. Major championships were won by Nanci Bowen in the Nabisco Dinah Shore, Kelly Robbins in the McDonald's LPGA Championship and Jenny Lidback in the du Maurier Classic. Karrie Webb, a 20-year-old Australian, won the Weetabix Women's British Open.

Michelle McGann and Alison Nicholas had three worldwide victories each, including two in the United States. Dottie Mochrie and Patty Sheehan each won two U.S. LPGA titles, Marie Laure de Lorenzi won three times in Europe and Rachel Hetherington won twice. Two-time winners in Japan were Fukushima, Kaori Higo, Marnie McGuire, Aki Takamura, Huang Bie-Shyun and Hiromi Kobayashi.

Finally, there was a changing of the guard on the U.S. LPGA Tour with 41-year-old Jim Ritts of Channel One Communications, replacing Charles Mechem, who retired after five years as commissioner.

U.S. LPGA Tour

Chrysler-Plymouth Tournament of Champions—$700,000
Winner: Dawn Coe-Jones

When a cold, windswept rain hit the Grand Cypress Resort in the third round of the Chrysler-Plymouth Tournament of Champions, Dawn Coe-Jones was not disappointed.

Coe-Jones opened with 74, under sunny skies and light winds, six strokes behind leader Barb Mucha. She added 70 on Friday to pull within two of Beth Daniel. When the rains came on Saturday, Coe-Jones saw it as her chance to shine. While most of her competitors were slipping, Coe-Jones shot 68 to take a three-stroke lead. She continued on Sunday with 69 for a seven-under-par 281 total and a six-stroke victory over Daniel in the season's opener in Orlando, Florida, which brought together tournament winners from the previous year plus some invitees.

"I've never been discouraged about playing in the rain," Coe-Jones said. "I grew up in it and I'm used to it. I've had good rounds in bad weather and bad rounds in good weather. You just never know."

Putting was the key for Coe-Jones. She had only 24 putts on Saturday in the rain and 27 more in Sunday's dampness on the way to winning $115,000. Coe-Jones was never threatened during the final round. She maintained a three-stroke lead through the first five holes, then put the tournament away with a birdie on No. 6 while her closest pursuers, Daniel and Liselotte Neumann, bogeyed, giving her a commanding five-shot lead.

HealthSouth Inaugural—$450,000
Winner: Pat Bradley

After Pat Bradley won back-to-back tournaments late in 1991 to qualify for the LPGA Hall of Fame, it seemed the chase had worn her down, and she sat back and enjoyed the view for the next three years. Everyone knew the competitive Bradley would be back. It was only a matter of time. Bradley's time came in the year's second event, the HealthSouth Inaugural in Orlando, Florida, at Disney World's Eagle Pines Golf Course, where a final-round 68 put her back in the winner's circle.

"It's good to be back," said Bradley, who shot rounds of 71, 72 and 68 for a 211 total and beat Beth Daniel by one stroke. "From tee to green, I never hit the ball better in my 22-year career. This is very satisfying."

The victory didn't come easily. Bradley started the final round two strokes behind Daniel, who took the lead with a second-round 70. Bradley birdied two of the last three holes, then waited for Daniel, who was one shot and three groups behind Bradley, to finish. Daniel gave Bradley a chance with a struggling 37 on the first nine and by missing several key putts on the second nine. She missed a birdie opportunity from seven feet at No. 13, birdied No. 14 and 15, then parred in, missing from five feet at No. 16 and nine feet at No. 17. "I had my chances," Daniel said. "It was frustrating coming in. I saw Pat had finished five under and I needed to make a couple of birdies coming in. I just couldn't do it."

Cup Noodles Hawaiian Open—$550,000
Winner: Barb Thomas

For almost 12 years, Barb Thomas wondered how it would feel to win a tournament. In her wildest dreams, however, she never thought it would come as easily as it did, by a glorious five strokes in the Cup Noodles Hawaiian Open. But Hawaii seems to be the place for those seeking their first victories. In 1994, Marta Figueras-Dotti won here for the first time in 11 years. Dawn Coe-Jones and Cindy Rarick also won for the first time in Hawaii.

Thomas made easy work of it, with rounds of 68, 66 and 70 for a 204 total over the 6,250-yard Ko Olina Golf Club course in Oahu. She took a three-stroke lead into the final round, stretched her lead to five at the turn and went to the 18th hole leading by six. "It's amazing, really, considering I've been out here this long," Thomas said. "I've worked for this since I was eight. That's 26 years. You wonder if it's ever going to pay off. At times today, when I was standing over putts, I thought 'This is a dream come true.' You don't get many moments like that."

She played the first 36 holes with no bogeys, but was less than a picture of perfection on Sunday. Paired with Chris Johnson and Marianne Morris, Thomas left open the door by missing 10 greens in regulation. Despite being in constant trouble, she had honors on 14 holes. Hiromi Kobayashi and Kris Tschetter tied for second place, Kobayashi with a final-round 66 and Tschetter with 69.

PING Welch's Championship—$450,000
Winner: Dottie Mochrie

Dottie Mochrie isn't easily riled, but when it was suggested at the PING Welch's Championship that her game seemed to have slipped the last couple years, the 1992 Player of the Year bristled. "How can you say that? My worst finish in the last four years on the money list was fourth," Mochrie said to the press. "If that's a lousy year, I'll take it."

Then, as if to prove her point, Mochrie won by five strokes at Randolph Park North Golf Course in Tucson, Arizona, despite playing with several blisters on her feet. Her bogey-free, four-under-par 68 in the final round produced a 10-under 278 total, and no player got within three strokes of her down the stretch.

It had nothing to do with the fact the women hadn't played in three weeks, since mid-February in Hawaii. It had everything to do with Mochrie out-driving everyone and holing all the four- and five-foot putts that she needed. Mochrie was most impressive on Sunday, hitting 17 of 18 greens in regulation, despite playing for the first time competitively with a new set of irons. The only suspense was the battle for second place, produced by Cindy Rarick and Annika Sorenstam. Each shot 70 to tie with 283 totals. "When Dottie gets that putter working like she did this week, she's hard to beat," Rarick said. "Considering how hard the greens were, she was very, very impressive."

Mochrie shot an opening-round 70, three strokes behind Kim Williams and Karen Noble, then took the lead with a second-round 68. The weather became her friend Saturday, with a 45 mile-an-hour wind, followed by rain, slowing down any would-be threats.

Standard Register PING —$700,000
Winner: Laura Davies

The first five times Laura Davies played in the Standard Register PING at Moon Valley in Phoenix, Arizona, it was hardly love at first sight. Between 1988 and 1993, her best finish was 17th place, and three times she missed the 36-hole cut. Her problem was keeping her golf ball in bounds, and out of the many back yards that line the course. In 1994, Davies kept it between the houses and out of the swimming pools, and won by four strokes over Beth Daniel and Elaine Crosby. Armed with that confidence, Davies returned in 1995 and did it again, although not as impressively, shooting rounds of 69, 68, 70 and 73 for a 280 and a one-stroke victory over Daniel.

It took a bit of luck to get Davies through the final round. She finished with two bogeys, then closed her eyes, afraid to look as Daniel lined up a 25-foot birdie putt for a tie. "I was scared to death that Beth was going to birdie the last two holes, but she didn't and I managed to limp in," Davies said. "I didn't play well, but this just shows that if you hang in there, not make many silly shots, you can win when you're not playing well."

"Neither one of us played well on the back nine. Laura left the door open for me a couple of times and I couldn't walk in," Daniel said.

While Davies and Daniel were the LPGA headliners through the week,

Arizona State senior Wendy Ward caused quite a stir, bidding to become the first amateur since JoAnne Carner in 1969 to win an LPGA Tour event. Ward held a share of the lead after the first round, posted four subpar rounds, and tied for third place with three others.

Nabisco Dinah Shore—$850,000
Winner: Nanci Bowen

Not many people make their first victory a major championship, and Nanci Bowen didn't figure to either, when she began the final round of the Nabisco Dinah Shore four strokes out of the lead held by Tammie Green and with the likes of Nancy Lopez, Laura Davies and Brandie Burton in between.

But on Sunday afternoon, there was Bowen jumping in the lake in Rancho Mirage, California, after shooting three-under-par 285 for a one-stroke victory over Susie Redman and two over Lopez, Davies, Burton and Sherri Turner.

"I was assuming the whole day that I was back in the pack," said Bowen, who has a habit of not looking at leaderboards. It wasn't until she blocked her drive at No. 18, hit a tree with her second shot and laid up short of the water with her third that she stole a peek at the leaderboard, and saw she was leading. After holing a three-footer for bogey, all she could do was wait.

Lopez, who almost always finishes well when in contention, didn't this time. Leading by three strokes with six holes to play, she three-putted Nos. 14 and 15 for bogeys; missed the green at No. 16 for another bogey, and hit her third shot into the water at No. 18 and settled for third place. Davies' chance was a longshot at best, needing to make a 100-footer at No. 18 just to tie, and she didn't. Green led by one stroke going to No. 17, but made bogey there from the bunker, then bunkered her second shot at No. 18 and buried her third shot into the bunker's lip. She finished tied for seventh.

"Obviously, this is the highlight of my career," said Bowen, whose previous best finish was a tie for third place in the JAL Big Apple Classic. "Overall, I was just hanging in there." Bowen shared the first-round lead at 69 with Muffin Spencer-Devlin and Penny Hammel. She slipped to 75 in the second round and fell three strokes behind, forgotten as the big names moved in.

Lopez's collapse was as startling as Bowen's rise, considering her 47 career victories and Hall-of-Fame status. But Lopez hadn't won in almost two years. "I never felt nervous. I felt confident," Lopez said. "I don't know if my mind was making me swing differently or what. But I hadn't been in that situation in a long time and that probably had something to do with it."

Pinewild Women's Championship—$650,000
Winner: Rosie Jones

There was Rosie Jones on the 18th tee of the Pinewild Women's Championship, two strokes behind Dottie Mochrie. She made a bogey on the par-five hole, whereas a par would have avoided a playoff with Mochrie. All's well that ends well, as they say. Jones won, making a 12-foot birdie on the same 18th hole while Mochrie missed from six feet.

"I used to watch the leaderboard," Jones said, "but I choked too much. I'm better off not knowing what's going on until the end. In hindsight, though, maybe I was a little aggressive playing the 18th the first time."

With rounds of 72, 70 and 69 for a 211 total over the 6,426-yard Pinewild course in Pinehurst, North Carolina, Jones won for the sixth time in her career, but for the first time since 1991. Jones was a late contender. Caroline Pierce led the first round with 69; Nicole Jeray led the second round, adding 67 to her opening 71, with Liselotte Neumann only one shot behind. Jones trailed by four strokes.

The final round was hotly contested. Brandie Burton had six birdies, but four bogeys and missed the playoff by one shot; Michelle McGann birdied four of the last six holes, but needed one more birdie; Nanci Bowen birdied three holes early, but none late and fell one stroke shy. Jones and Mochrie got to the playoff in different ways. Jones had eight birdies and four bogeys in the 19 holes, while Mochrie had three birdies and a lone costly bogey, that one coming at No. 15.

Chick-fil-A Charity Championship—$500,000
Winner: Laura Davies

Dominating from start to finish, Laura Davies put three 67s on the board at Eagles Landing Country Club in Stockbridge, Georgia, and beat Kelly Robbins by four strokes in the Chick-fil-A Charity Championship. Davies, who three weeks earlier won the Standard Register PING, earned $75,000 and remained atop the LPGA money list with $282,040.

This was hardly a normal week. There were seven hours of rain delays in the first two days and the 36-hole cut couldn't be made until about noon on Sunday.

Oddly, Davies had low expectations. The Eagles Landing course played only 6,187 yards, a bit shorter than Davies prefers. But the rain turned it into a longer and softer course, putting the brakes on Davies' errant drives. Davies, who began the last day one stroke ahead of Mochrie, eagled the short par-five, 440-yard third hole; birdied the fourth from the rough, and was on her way.

"I must admit, when we found the ball at the fourth and I got up and down, I started to get the feeling that maybe this is a good day for me," Davies said. She escaped from trouble several times and gave no hope to those in pursuit. "There were a couple of times today I thought I may have made her think about the lead," Robbins said. "But I don't know if Laura thinks about much at all. She just hits it. Hard."

Sprint Championship—$1,200,000
Winner: Val Skinner

The best of Val Skinner's golf career seemed over, until noted sports psychologist Bob Rotella asked her on Thanksgiving Day, 1992, "Is golf a priority for you?" Skinner knew it was, and she began to prove it again.

Skinner, a steady player through the 1980s, dropped to 100th on the money list in 1992, but after her talk with Rotella, she won in 1993, and won again in 1994, advancing to 12th on the LPGA money list.

And in April, 1995, Skinner won the Sprint Championship, the LPGA's richest event. Her $180,000 check was the biggest of her 13-year career. Rounds of 71, 65, 70 and 67 produced a 15-under-par 273 total and a two-stroke victory over Kris Tschetter on the demanding LPGA International course in Daytona Beach, Florida.

Tschetter, Dottie Mochrie and Colleen Walker shared the first-round lead with 66s; Tschetter led the second round alone with 67, and went to the final round with a one-stroke lead over Skinner. It was Skinner's day. She birdied Nos. 2 and 3 to take the lead. Over the next seven holes, she shared the top spot with Tschetter and Michelle McGann. With four holes remaining, she led by three strokes and the win seemed to be hers. Instead, it became a struggle. Skinner bogeyed the 15th hole, while McGann birdied. Skinner got a stroke back with a birdie at No. 16 and breathed easier when McGann bogeyed the 452-yard 18th.

"I'm standing on the 18th tee, three shots ahead of Kris and I drive it in the water," Skinner said. "Then, after taking a drop, I hit the next one almost into the gallery, while Kris is on the green with a 30-footer for eagle. Things definitely were not looking good." Skinner hit her fourth shot out of deep rough to within four feet. Tschetter missed the eagle, Skinner made her par and exhaled. "It wasn't a sterling finish, but that's okay," she said. "This is probably the best I've ever played in the lead my entire career. A lot of bad things could have happened on that hole, and I didn't let them."

Sara Lee Classic—$525,000
Winner: Michelle McGann

After six winless seasons, Michelle McGann finally won the week after her toughest loss. McGann became a winner on the LPGA Tour by blowing past Laura Davies with a final-round 68 to win the Sara Lee Classic in Old Hickory, Tennessee.

McGann has long had the style, making a fashion statement with her colorful outfits, bright lipstick and Sonni hats. This time, she added the substance. Her 14-under-par 202 total at Hermitage Golf Club broke Davies' year-old record of 203. "I'm happy for Michelle," Davies said. "She should have won many times before, and did this time in fine style. It must be horrible to be a player expecting to win, but never doing it. She'll win many more now."

McGann had three consecutive birdies early in her round, but this was no walk in the park. She had to hold steady as Dottie Mochrie shot 65 to come up one stroke short; Kelly Robbins three-putted the par-five 16th to fall one shy; and Davies, tied with McGann after 15 holes, topped her second shot into the water on the 16th and also made bogey. McGann could relate to those closing-hole disasters.

"Starting with three birdies on Sunday was big for me," said McGann, who had rounds of 69, 65 and 68. "It's a relief to finally win, but a can't-win label never bothered me. I think I'm a winner in more ways than any golf tournament. I always figured if I kept putting myself in contention, one of these times I would win."

McDonald's LPGA Championship
Winner: Kelly Robbins

There was a power surge at DuPont Country Club in Wilmington, Delaware, in the final round of the McDonald's LPGA Championship. In one corner, you had the grip-it-and-rip-it style of Laura Davies, and in the other the well-balanced precision and tremendous hand action of Kelly Robbins. The decision went to Robbins, who put her precision to great use on DuPont's three par-fives, which she played in five under par. Despite her strength, Davies struggled on those same holes with only two birdies and a bogey on the shortest of the three, the 465-yard 16th.

Robbins shot steady rounds of 66, 68, 72 and 68 for a 274 total in winning her first major championship, finishing two strokes ahead of Davies, who led by as many as three strokes during the final round. No other golfer was close. Patty Sheehan, Marianne Morris and Julie Larsen tied for third place at 280, six behind Robbins. Dottie Mochrie, who had top-five finishes in her last four events, came to the final round trailing by three strokes, but bogeyed three of the first five holes, shot 73 and tied for sixth place.

Robbins led the first two rounds, Davies led the third and appeared to have things well in hand with a three-stroke lead after 11 holes on a cold, wet Sunday. Robbins cut the deficit to one stroke with birdies at Nos. 12 and 14, but Davies appeared still in control as they went to No. 16, where she ripped her tee shot and had only 203 yards to the green. Robbins pushed hers slightly, but it hit the cart path and hopped forward, leaving her only 181 yards from the flag.

Davies hit a three-iron shot short of the hole. She then missed the green, chipped to four feet and missed the putt for a bogey. The calm Robbins punched a four-iron shot under the trees and into a greenside bunker, blasted out to four feet and made the putt for an unexpected two-shot swing and one-stroke lead.

"I'm sure that's the last thing Laura expected," Robbins said. "I'm sure she was thinking birdie, or par at the most. And I was the last person to think she might hit that second shot fat. One poor shot did her in."

Davies, however, said it was two bad shots — the three iron and a pull-hook seven iron at No. 18 on Saturday that resulted in double-bogey six, shaving her lead from three shots to one. "Two bad ones, that's all it was," Davies said. "But Kelly made birdies on the back nine and I didn't. I wasn't good enough. I was beaten by a very deserving player."

Star Bank LPGA Classic—$500,000
Winner: Chris Johnson

Sometimes it isn't easy to admit that you need to start from scratch again. But Chris Johnson bit the bullet and in 1992 started from scratch, after 13 years, six victories and $1.2 million in earnings. "I never lost faith, I knew it was the right thing to do," said Johnson, after coming from six strokes behind to win the Star Bank LPGA Classic at the Country Club of the North in Dayton, Ohio.

Johnson's final-round 67 came largely on four birdies over the final seven holes to steal the victory from Juli Inkster, who needed to par the last three holes but bogeyed two of them. It was the third week in a row that the leader on the 16th tee failed to win an LPGA tournament. "I don't wish bogeys on anybody," said Johnson, whose winning score came after rounds of 68 and 75. "I did it last year in Seattle. It doesn't feel good at all. But I've worked awfully hard the last few years to get back to this point."

Winless since 1991, Johnson said her confidence level was low coming into the tournament. She hadn't played well since January and finished 38th in the McDonald's LPGA Championship. Even after posting an opening 68, Johnson wasn't confident. "I've changed my whole game," she said. "The distance is different, the ball-striking different, and flight of the ball different."

Following a second-round 75, Johnson had little hope of winning. Inkster was doing everything right, opening with two 68s for a three-stroke lead as she tried to end a three-year slump of her own. Needing to par the final three holes, Inkster missed the green at No. 16 and made a bogey. She made par on the 17th and bogeyed the 18th after pulling her drive into the rough, missing the green and leaving an 18-foot putt short.

Corning Classic—$550,000
Winner: Alison Nicholas

It seemed reasonable that Alison Nicholas' first victory would come at Corning Country Club in Corning, New York. Of all the courses Nicholas had played in North America, this one reminded her most of the courses she played as an amateur at home in England. Few were surprised when Nicholas put together rounds of 70, 67, 66 and 72 for a 275 total to win by three strokes over Danielle Ammaccapane and Barb Mucha. After all, it was here in 1993 that she bogeyed the final hole and the first playoff hole to lose to Kelly Robbins. It also didn't hurt that the weather turned very British on Sunday — wind and rain — which kept anyone from making a strong run at her down the stretch.

The 35-year-old Nicholas moved into the lead Saturday with 66 and led Pat Bradley by two strokes. After opening with two pars Sunday, Nicholas left the Hall of Famer in a wake of birdies at Nos. 2, 3 and 4. Mucha, who was eight shots behind Nicholas after seven holes, joined the fight with birdies at Nos. 11, 14 and 16 to trail by one stroke, but she self-destructed with a double bogey at No. 18, three-putting from 15 feet.

"I looked and Alison was 16 under after five holes and I'm thinking, there's nobody close to her," Mucha said. "So I told my caddie we're going to play for second place. I kept playing, made a few putts, got to 12 under and saw Alison coming back." Nicholas felt the heat. She had to make a five-foot putt to save par at the short 16th before finishing with routine pars. "Before the round and at No. 18, I thought about losing here in 1993, but most players never win when they're in contention the first time," Nicholas said. "You have to be there a few times, then you learn to win. I had eight seconds before I won in Europe."

Oldsmobile Classic—$600,000
Winner: Dale Eggeling

In a year of comebacks, Dale Eggeling's may have been the best yet as the 41-year-old veteran returned to the winner's circle in the Oldsmobile Classic in East Lansing, Michigan, 15 years after her first LPGA victory. Eggeling's victory at Walnut Hills Country Club broke Shelley Hamlin's record for the longest period between victories.

And what took so long? It seems Eggeling had been more interested in her show horses than her golf game. "I finally listened to my husband," Eggeling said, referring to Mike, a former player and now head of promotions for Tommy Armour Golf. "He told me I still had some good years left if I changed my focus."

Eggeling opened with a course-record 63 and followed with scores of 69, 71 and 71 for a 274 total and a two-stroke victory over Meg Mallon, Elaine Crosby and Sweden's Annika Sorenstam. Eggeling led wire-to-wire. Crosby took the lead briefly through the rainy third round, but fell back with 73. Mallon, with an eagle on the par-five 14th hole, shot 67 and tied for Sunday's low round, but she put herself in a hole with an opening 71 before rallying with two 69s. Her downfall was the par-fives, which she played in only three under par with one birdie and one eagle.

Edina Realty Classic—$500,000
Winner: Julie Larsen

After eight years of playing golf in Asia, Europe, the American mini-tours and six trips to the LPGA qualifying tournament, Juli Larsen found success and happiness on Edinburgh USA's 18th hole in Brooklyn Park, Minnesota. There she sank a four-footer for par to win the Edina Realty Classic by one stroke over another long-aspiring player Leigh Ann Mills. The putt gave the 32-year-old Larsen a one-under-par 71 to go with her rounds of 66 and 68, and her first victory.

Larsen started the final round leading by three strokes, but her lead was down to one stroke until she birdied the 17th hole. After Mills birdied the 18th, Larsen had to call upon the grit that comes with adversity. Needing two putts from 25 feet for the victory, she knocked her first putt six feet past the hole, but then sank the return putt. "Adrenalin took over I guess," Larsen said. "I was just trying to get it close. But it was no problem. I saw the line really well. And, I figured even if I missed, I would still be in a playoff. And if I lost, I would still have plenty of chances to win."

Larsen, who set a tournament record for the first 36 holes, was steady if not spectacular over the first 17 holes of the final round. She led by four strokes after three holes, then made several par-saving putts until a bogey at No. 13. Larsen had two hard days of labor to get to the sunny final round. Rain, wind and chilly temperatures plagued the first two rounds, prompting

Pat Bradley to comment, "Walking down the first fairway on Saturday was a joke. I think all the players got webbed feet from having to play."

Rochester International—$550,000
Winner: Patty Sheehan

Maybe it's time they renamed the Rochester International in Pittsford, New York, for Patty Sheehan. She won the tournament for the fourth time in seven years, and placed second, fourth and seventh in the other three years. Coming off a two-week layoff, Sheehan shot rounds of 73, 66, 69 and 70 for a 278 total and won by four strokes over Sherri Steinhauer. "I try to think of why I play so well here. Maybe it's because the greens are so similar to the ones I grew up on in Vermont," Sheehan said. "I guess it's just feeling like I'm at home."

While Sheehan came to Locust Hill Country Club with good memories, confidence wasn't part of the mix. And when she opened with 73, optimism was at an all-time low at this event. Sheehan fixed that with a second-round 66 and moved within three strokes of JoAnne Carner, then took the lead by one over Steinhauer with 69 on Saturday, while Carner crashed with 78. "I'm not sure what's going to happen Sunday," Sheehan said. "My game isn't where I want it to be. If someone else is hitting the ball well, thinking well and doing all the other things, they're certainly going to beat me."

That didn't happen, so it didn't matter if Sheehan was merely human on Sunday. Steinhauer was only one stroke back after nine holes, but Sheehan took control on the 10th hole with help from her playing companion. Steinhauer bogeyed, Sheehan birdied to lead by three strokes, and was never in trouble. "Sometimes you win playing just awesome, sometimes you don't," Sheehan said. "I just happened to win not playing so awesome. Every once in a while you get lucky, especially if you're patient."

ShopRite Classic—$650,000
Winner: Betsy King

Want one definition of relief? It's Betsy King not having to play in another tournament and having to address one more time her feelings on being one victory short of the LPGA Hall of Fame. The 39-year-old King took care of that, finally winning No. 30, the ShopRite Classic in Somers Point, New Jersey. The victory came one year, seven months and 18 days after No. 29 in the 1993 season-ending Toray Queens Cup in Japan.

King finally exhaled after making a 15-footer for birdie on Great Bay's 17th hole to take the lead, and secured the victory minutes later with another birdie at No. 18. Thus, did King finally become the 14th player to earn her way into one of golf's most exclusive clubs. "I'm obviously very excited, but more relieved," King said before adding, "I'm just happy I won't have to deal with it anymore."

King led by one stroke after the rain-delayed first round with 66. Following a second-round 71, she began the final 18 holes on a rather inauspicious — not to mention embarrassing — note. She hit her first drive only 30 yards, but she managed to save par, holing a 40-footer. The pressure was off. "After I hit that shot, I just said that if it wasn't going to be my day, again, that I could handle it," she said. "Making that putt was a great confidence builder."

From there, it was still a struggle. Rosie Jones took the lead with a birdie at No. 15, but then missed a one-footer for par at No. 17. That turned out to be the break King needed. She hit a seven iron to 15 feet on No. 17 and knocked it in. At No. 18, which she had bogeyed twice, she hit a perfect drive and seven iron to 10 feet and made the putt. "I'm just glad Betsy made her putt on 18. It was her day," Jones said. "When you birdie 17 and 18, you deserve all the credit. She's had a great career, played long and hard."

"I think it's been pretty tough," King said of her Hall of Fame quest. "We have standards that everyone can shoot for. That's the reason they made criteria, to be objective, instead of it being a popularity vote. ... It's been a while since I played well. It seems like I've been going backward. I'm glad I got this one, because it's only going to get tougher."

Youngstown-Warren Classic—$550,000
Winner: Michelle McGann

Say this for Michelle McGann. She's a fast learner. It took her seven years to learn how to win for the first time — Sara Lee Classic — but only a couple of months to put the second victory in her portfolio. It came much to the chagrin of Katie Peterson-Parker, who could not secure victory in the Youngstown-Warren Classic in Warren, Ohio, with a two-stroke lead on the final hole, a par-five hole at that. McGann birdied, Peterson-Parker bogeyed, and McGann won on the third playoff hole, again with a birdie on the 18th. McGann shot rounds of 65, 70 and 70 for a 205 total.

"It's just confidence," McGann said. "I'm playing well. I've never been in a playoff before, so it was fun to win the first one. Also, I've been in situations before like Katie was in today. It's a learning thing."

Peterson-Parker was a bundle of nerves when she and McGann went to the final hole of regulation. Needing a par to win, Peterson-Parker hit a 40-yard pitch shot across the green, chipped back and two-putted for bogey. "I was nervous and my heart was racing real fast," she said. "I completely blacked out."

That was totally unlike Peterson-Parker's first two rounds of 65 and 69, which enabled her to take a one-stroke lead over McGann, a lead she didn't lose until the final hole in regulation. The entire last round was like a play-off. Just Katie and Michelle. "Winning the first one is always the toughest, I don't care what anybody else says," McGann said. "Once you learn to win, it's easier the second time around."

Jamie Farr Toledo Classic—$500,000
Winner: Kathryn Marshall

Add Kathryn Marshall to the list of successful international golfers on the LPGA Tour. The England-born, Scotland-raised Marshall shot a final-round 67 to win the Jamie Farr Toledo (Ohio) Classic by one stroke over Sherri

Steinhauer for her first LPGA Tour victory after almost three years. Marshall, who lives in Dundee, Scotland, became the ninth first-time winner of 1995 on rounds of 67, 71 and 67 for a 205 total.

"Absolutely fantastic," said Marshall, who received a boost by calling home after a second-round 71 left her one shot out of the lead held by Pam Wright. Marshall's final-round effort was helped by a comfortable pairing with Wright, her friend and neighbor from Aboyne, Scotland.

There also was a tip of the hat to Bernhard Langer. After a stretch of poor putting this year, Marshall adopted Langer's style of gripping the left wrist and putter with the right hand. In the final round, she made four birdies, all from the range of six feet or more. That brought her to victory in a round that had 12 players within two strokes on the second nine and eight players still clustered over the final six holes.

The turning point for Marshall came at the par-four 13th hole where, tied with Steinhauer, she drove into deep rough and near a tree. She had an opening but barely escaped, then hit a sand wedge 75 yards to within four feet of the hole and made the putt for par. Steinhauer wasn't as fortunate on the 18th, where from the woods she played a nine iron to 20 feet and left the putt one foot short.

U.S. Women's Open—$1,000,000
Winner: Annika Sorenstam

The U.S. Women's Open is known for identifying the courageous. This Open, the 50th anniversary event, played over the East course at The Broadmoor in Colorado Springs, Colorado, lived up to that reputation.

Proving that experience is not everything was Sweden's Annika Sorenstam. Just two years out of the University of Arizona, Sorenstam, age 24, erased a five-shot deficit to third-round leader and former champion Meg Mallon and scored a victory for youth. Score one for true grit. How else to explain her march to the title with rounds of 67-71-72-68–278, two under par.

Sorenstam wasn't just five strokes behind, but five behind Mallon, one of the game's best clutch players. Sorenstam should have been all nerves. She wasn't. "Other players have won for the first time in the U.S. Open. So why not me?" said Sorenstam, who became the 13th to break through at the U.S. Women's Open. She was also the fifth non-American to win. "It's a great feeling, a dream come true."

It was a nightmare for Mallon, who led the field by two strokes, then triple-bogeyed the shortest hole on the course and spent the rest of the day trying to pick up the pieces of a dream that quickly was becoming a nightmare. "I know the nature of the Opens and I know you don't win on Saturday," Mallon said. "Annika won and played great. That is what you have to do on Sunday."

In the first round, 32 players shot par 70 or better, led by Jill Briles-Hinton's 66, which led by one stroke over Japanese Tour member Jean Bartholomew, Tania Abitbol, Pat Bradley and Sorenstam. Most groups took five hours to finish and 18 players had to finish the next morning. In the second round, 27 players failed to complete play because of a severe thunderstorm.

When all heads were counted, first-year player Leta Lindley was in a group of eight players at two under par, among them Sorenstam, Bradley and Tammie Green. Mallon was one stroke behind, but she charged to the top in the third round with a bogey-free 66 to lead by two strokes over Julie Larsen.

Mallon opened the way early in the final round, dropping four strokes on two holes, the par-four third, where she bogeyed from a poor fairway lie, and the 139-yard, par-three fourth, where she dumped an eight-iron shot into the water. A drop and three putts later, she was in a five-way tie for the lead with Sorenstam, Bradley, Larsen and Betsy King.

Sorenstam moved ahead with four straight birdies beginning at No. 9. By the time she reached the 15th hole, she had a three-stroke lead. Sorenstam stole a peek at the leaderboard and promptly made bogey there, and lost another stroke of her lead with a three-putt bogey on the par-three 16th hole. "I was nervous and losing my confidence," Sorenstam said. "I've never been that nervous."

Sorenstam almost bogeyed the 17th hole, but made a five-foot putt for par. She finished like a champion, two-putting from 30 feet, then stood near the scorer's tent waiting for Mallon, who needed a birdie on the final hole to tie. You could see Sorenstam holding her breath as Mallon's 20-footer started out on line and looked good for all but the last 10 inches when it drifted below the hole.

JAL Big Apple Classic—$700,000
Winner: Tracy Kerdyk

When it came to self-doubt, Tracy Kerdyk carried enough of it to supply the entire LPGA Tour. Then a funny thing happened. She won the JAL Big Apple Classic in New Rochelle, New York, by four strokes and vanquished the burden she had been carrying for her entire career. Kerdyk demolished one of the best fields of the year with rounds of 74, 66, 66 and 67 for a 273 total, four strokes better than runners-up Elaine Crosby, Caroline Pierce, Michelle McGann and Carin Hjalmarsson.

"I can't believe it," said Kerdyk, a former two-time All-American at the University of Miami, of her tournament-record total. "This is the kind of golf I always felt I could play, but I kept getting in my own way."

Kerdyk won 11 collegiate tournaments, the 1987 Canadian Amateur and U.S. Women's Public Links, was runner-up in the U.S. Women's Amateur, played on the 1988 U.S. Curtis Cup team and was NCAA Player of the Year. She came to the LPGA Tour expecting to win and didn't, finally hitting bottom in March at the Nabisco Dinah Shore with her fourth consecutive missed cut. That's when she made three decisions that turned around her career. Kerdyk vowed to be more positive, then she called her longtime teacher Charlie DeLucca and promised to do everything he asked, and finally, she ended a serious personal relationship where marriage and children had been discussed.

After her opening 74, Kerdyk made a putting grip change and shot 66. She was still six strokes behind leader McGann, but not for long. She shot another 66 while McGann unraveled with a third-round 74, and on the last day lapped the field with 67, making only one bogey.

Friendly's Classic—$500,000
Winner: Becky Iverson

It isn't that Becky Iverson is superstitious, but when a combination of things seem to bring results, she's not about to mess with fate. Only a year and a half out of qualifying for the LPGA Tour, Iverson won the inaugural Friendly's Classic in Agawam, Massachusetts, using the same golf ball for 54 holes and eating at the same restaurant for four days.

Iverson put together rounds of 71, 63, 72 and 70 for a 276 total to win for the first time, beating Helen Alfredsson and Kelly Robbins by one stroke.

The good life began for Iverson with a second-round 63, which gave her a one-stroke lead over Kris Tschetter. The night before, she ate fijitas from Chi-Chi's, and she played the round of 63 with an old two-piece Titleist DT golf ball.

Iverson began the third round with a different ball, but after playing the first six holes in three over par, she took the old ball. From there, she made three birdies and nine pars and was tied for the lead with Robbins. "I started to panic after going three over and made my caddie dig in the bag and come up with the old ball," Iverson said. "That ball likes the bottom of the cup better."

A birdie-par start to the final round gave Iverson a two-stroke lead. Robbins caught her at 12 under par with an eagle at No. 7, then fell behind by two strokes at the turn on a bogey and Iverson's birdie. Tschetter started only one stroke back, but couldn't make a closing rush, eventually tying for fourth place, and Robbins opened the door for Iverson's victory when she four-putted the 12th green.

Armed with a three-shot lead going to No. 18, Iverson made a bogey. After hitting a 130-yard eight-iron shot over the green, she hit a pitch shot four feet below the hole and missed for only her second bogey in a round of 70.

McCall's Classic at Stratton Mountain—$500,000
Winner: Dottie Mochrie

To most of the LPGA field that plays each year at Stratton Mountain, Vermont, the McCall's Classic is no major event. But it's different for Dottie Mochrie. As far as Mochrie's concerned, it's as major as they get. Her home is just an hour away in Saratoga Springs, New York, and winning at Stratton Mountain is special.

"This is like winning a major to me," Mochrie said after winning her second title of the year and the 10th of her career in the weather-shortened event, which lost the first round to fog. Mochrie won on rounds of 69, 67 and 68 for a 204 total, making Kelly Robbins a runner-up for the second consecutive week.

Fog took care of the first round, rain interrupted play twice on Friday and the first round wasn't completed until Saturday morning. And by Sunday, both the first and 10th tees were needed when rain caused a two-hour delay. In the confusion, Michelle McGann, who was only four strokes back after 36 holes, missed her tee time and was disqualified. Allison Finney and Catrin Nilsmark shot 67s to lead the first round, then gave way to Mochrie and Pat Bradley. But Bradley never got on track Sunday, shooting 73 and tying for fourth place.

Mochrie played as if possessed. Her father, Don, led the rooting for the home team all week, and his daughter's bogey-free play helped hold off Robbins, who started three strokes behind but caught her briefly with 32 on the first nine. Robbins' chances of winning ended at No. 12, where she hit her approach shot over the green and made bogey. "That was really a dumb shot," said Robbins, who found consolation in that her runner-up finish enabled her to pass Laura Davies and take over the top spot on the money list with $469,260.

PING Welch's Championship—$500,000
Winner: Beth Daniel

Beth Daniel came to the PING Welch's Championship in Canton, Massachusetts, needing four more LPGA Tour victories or one major to qualify for the LPGA Hall of Fame, and left needing only three wins or a major title. Daniel won for the first time in 1995 on rounds of 65, 68, 69 and 69 for a 271 total for a three-stroke margin over Meg Mallon and Colleen Walker, who entered the final round tied with Daniel.

Daniel was the only player in the field to shoot four sub-70 rounds and her 17-under-par total was three strokes better than the tournament record set in 1994 by Helen Alfredsson. But, mostly, it ended a drought. "It finally hit me on the 18th green that I had won a golf tournament and not finished second," said Daniel, who had finished second four times.

Daniel held or shared the lead all four days, but she didn't run away from the field on the last day. There were distractions, first by a photographer, then by Mallon, who made a hole-in-one at No. 7 and an eagle at No. 9 to thunderous roars each time. "Good for her," Daniel said. "You can't get comfortable with a two- or three-shot lead on this golf course. Too many things can happen."

Walker was a definite distraction. Despite starting bogey-bogey to give Daniel a two-stroke lead, she hung on and momentarily shared the lead at No. 14 until Daniel also made a birdie. The margin remained one stroke until No. 18, but Daniel made a birdie and Walker bogeyed for the final margin.

du Maurier Ltd. Classic—$1,000,000
Winner: Jenny Lidback

For someone who has played in relative obscurity for her entire career, Jenny Lidback couldn't have found a better stage from which to say, "Look at me now!" She won the LPGA's final major championship, the du Maurier Ltd. Classic in Pointe-Claire, Quebec, Canada. It was the first victory for the 32-year-old Lidback and marked the fifth time in seven years that the du Maurier event had been won by a previously winless player.

"It's almost like I'm in shock," said Lidback, who was born in Peru and has lived in Brazil, Connecticut, Louisiana, Texas and now in Arizona. "I'm very wobbly." There was nothing wobbly about the way Lidback played. She survived a nerve-racking final 18 holes — a day-long challenge from Sweden's Liselotte Neumann and greens that were in terrible condition — to become the 11th first-time winner on the LPGA Tour in 1995, the most in 46 seasons.

Lidback's victory was no fluke. She was solid on rounds of 71, 69, 68 and 72 for a 280 total. She trailed Patty Sheehan by five strokes after the first round. She was three behind Neumann after two rounds, and led by one stroke entering the final round. "In golf, it's very easy to lose your patience," Lidback said. "I made an effort to remind myself to stay patient. After seeing the golf course, I told my caddie we would have to be extra patient."

Sheehan led by five strokes after the first round, but soared to 77 in the second round and gave way to Neumann after 36 holes. She went backward in the third round with 72, leaving Lidback with a one-stroke lead on a round of 68 that included hitting all 18 greens in regulation. Only once had Lidback led going to the final round, in the 1993 LPGA Championship, where she collapsed with 78. There would be no repeat. An opening-hole bogey was like a slap in the face. She birdied the second, chipped in at the fourth, and after a bogey at No. 13, played solidly coming in, although she almost whiffed her lay-up shot at No. 18. She recovered with a solid approach and two-putted for the victory.

State Farm Rail Classic—$550,000
Winner: Mary Beth Zimmerman

While most eyes were following veteran stars Betsy King and Beth Daniel and future star Emilee Klein, Mary Beth Zimmerman, who fits into neither category, won the State Farm Rail Classic in Springfield, Illinois. Zimmerman, a 12-year veteran, came from seven strokes behind in the final round to tie 21-year-old Klein, then won on the second playoff hole.

"It's overwhelming, almost unbelievable," said Zimmerman, who won her fourth career victory, but her first since 1987. "It's great to win here in front of friends and family."

Zimmerman's name was nowhere to be found on the leaderboard after two rounds of 72 and 69, but she reeled in Klein with a final-round 65 that featured seven birdies and no bogeys.

Klein began the final round tied for the lead with King and two strokes ahead of Daniel. She managed to cling to the lead until Zimmerman, playing four groups ahead, caught her with a birdie at No. 17. Zimmerman then fell one stroke back after Klein birdied the 15th. Klein three-putted the 18th, forcing the playoff. Both players parred the first playoff hole, then moved to the par-three 16th, where Zimmerman rolled in a 35-foot uphill putt for birdie and Klein missed from 20 feet.

King, a three-time winner of this event, finished in a tie for third place with Colleen Walker and Leta Lindley. Daniel tied for sixth place.

PING AT&T Wireless Services Championship—$500,000
Winner: Alison Nicholas

After standing so long in the shadow of her countrywoman Laura Davies, Alison Nicholas stepped into the spotlight on her own, winning the PING AT&T Wireless Services Championship in Portland, Oregon. It was Nicholas' second LPGA victory of the year, a feat then matched only by Davies, Dottie Mochrie and Michelle McGann.

Although Nicholas coasted home by three strokes over Kelly Robbins with rounds of 66, 73 and 68 for a 207 total, the margin of victory was deceptive. For most of the afternoon, the leaderboard was in a state of flux as a host of contenders blazed to the top, only to drop out. "Everybody was up there," Nicholas said. "They were putting names up there, then taking them off. I just sort of tried to hang in there, to play each hole as it comes and see what happens."

Betsy King shot up there, taking the lead midway through the second nine, but she bogeyed the 16th and 17th holes. Next came Moira Dunn to lead by two strokes, but she was undone by a three-putt double bogey at No. 16. Then came Rosie Jones to tie Nicholas, only to bogey the 16th, 17th and 18th holes.

It was time to ask, "Does anybody want to win?" Nicholas answered with an 18-foot birdie putt at No. 12. And when Robbins three-putted for bogey, Nicholas, watching the leaderboard all the way, seized the moment, making birdie at No. 15 to open a three-stroke lead. "I'm thrilled to bits to win again over here," Nicholas said, referring to her Corning Classic victory earlier in the year. "It's always been a goal of mine to compete over here — the great tournaments and against the best players."

Safeco Classic—$500,000
Winner: Patty Sheehan

Say this for Patty Sheehan. She knows how to turn a season of mostly question marks into an exclamation point. Having announced that the Safeco Classic in Kent, Washington, would be her final event of the year, Sheehan made it special with a two-stroke victory over rookie Emilee Klein.

Since she played 25 events in 1990, Sheehan's schedule has diminished steadily to a career-low 17 events in 1995. And after 12 straight seasons of being eighth or better on the money list, she was destined for a second straight finish in the teens. "Winning here may not get me into the top 10 on the money list, but it does put me in a better mood going into my off-season," said Sheehan of her second victory, worth $75,000. "I let down for a while. It was no fun being 30th and 40th. I'm still very competitive, and I'll keep playing until I lose that."

Even while Sheehan was going out in style — rounds of 68, 65, 70 and 71 for a 274 total — Klein came on strong with a final-round 67 and finished second for the second time in three weeks. "You're going to be seeing more good things to come from Emilee for a long, long time," Sheehan said. "She's one of the best young players to come out here in a long time."

Klein, 21, is the youngest player on the LPGA Tour and 17 years Sheehan's junior. With her second-place earnings of $46,546, the 1994 NCAA champion from Arizona State jumped to 39th on the money list and planted herself firmly in the Rookie of the Year race. She had played in 23 events, the last nine straight and planned to make it 11 in a row. Sheehan, on the other hand, was taking the opposite approach, going home to watch her nieces and nephews play lacrosse.

GHP Heartland Classic—$525,000
Winner: Annika Sorenstam

That Annika Sorenstam was an emerging star was never more apparent than when she won the U.S. Women's Open with clutch fourth-round play, and it was only punctuated at the GHP Heartland Classic in St. Louis, Missouri.

Almost everyone took their lumps on the tight and testy 6,375-yard Forest Hills course, but Sorenstam shot rounds of 69, 67, 70 and 72 for a 278 total, 10 under par. It was 10 strokes better than the second-place finisher, Jan Stephenson. And it took four days, 65 holes and 252 swings before Sorenstam made her first bogey. "I was just kind of walking along and sort of lost my focus for a moment," she said of the lone bogey. "I was just thinking about things."

It mattered not. Sorenstam had lost the rest of the field many, many holes earlier. The unfocused bogey on the par-four 12th hole came after 13 birdies. It also mattered not that she bogeyed two more holes coming in. Sorenstam's final-round 72 enabled her to match the tournament record total.

Sorenstam's total was the same as Liselotte Neumann had in winning the inaugural GHP Heartland Classic in 1994, but Neumann's winning margin was only three strokes. Sorenstam's margin was the largest on the LPGA Tour this year. "I really enjoyed this, I was having a good time. It's such a good golf course," Sorenstam said. "At the Open, I really didn't get a chance to do that. It all happened so fast there. There was so much more pressure."

Fieldcrest Cannon Classic—$500,000
Winner: Gail Graham

For most of 1995, Gail Graham was an accident waiting to happen and more times than not, it did happen. There was the accident on in-line skates that left her in a leg brace for six weeks. Later in the year, she broke her big toe after striking it on a coffee table.

Pegged with the nickname, "The Accidental Tourist," Graham went to the Fieldcrest Cannon Classic in Cornelius, North Carolina, and beat Tammie Green by two strokes, reaffirming that accidents will happen on the golf course, too. Maybe accident is too harsh a word, but it fits considering Graham hadn't finished in the top 10 since January and only once had posted consecutive sub-70 rounds.

In the final round, Graham hit all 14 fairways, never came close to making a bogey, birdied three of the last 10 holes and beat Green, who hit 17 greens but couldn't make many putts. Such a performance earned Graham $75,000, which was more than she had made in the previous 22 starts. And it came against a field which included 33 of the LPGA Tour's top 40 money winners.

"A new event on a new golf course brings everyone in the field into play," said Graham, whose previous best finish was third in the 1993 Sun-Times Classic. "It was just my time. Thank goodness."

Graham had to work for it. She went into the last round one stroke in front of Green and Hiromi Kobayashi. Standing on the 72nd tee, she still led by one over Green. All day, she had driven past Green by 20 to 30 yards, and she did it again, leaving her 165 yards to the green. Green tried to match Graham's drive, but pulled it into a fairway bunker, and that was that.

Samsung World Championship of Women's Golf—$475,000
Winner: Annika Sorenstam

Any lingering doubts as to the LPGA Tour's Player of the Year were dispelled in dramatic fashion when Annika Sorenstam chipped in from 45 feet in a playoff to beat Laura Davies in the Samsung World Championship of Women's Golf, which was held at Cheji Island, South Korea.

Three weeks after steamrolling her competition by 10 strokes in the GHP Heartland Classic, Sorenstam took the long way around this time, coming from three strokes behind to beat Davies for her third victory this year on the LPGA Tour. It reinforced her standing atop both the American and European money lists. The victory also made anti-climactic the season-ending Toray Queens Cup in Japan. Regardless of what happened, Sorenstam would become the first player to win money titles in the same year on both sides of the Atlantic. Davies won the European money title in 1985 and 1986, and led the LPGA money list in 1994.

Sorenstam's victory on rounds of 72, 69, 71 and 70 for a 282 total came from persistence. The final round was delayed over an hour because of rain and fog, then was played in 35 mile-an-hour winds. Her score of 70 was just one of two sub-par rounds posted in the field of 16 players. Nine others shot 74 or worse.

Davies teed off on the last day leading by three strokes over Sorenstam, Dottie Mochrie and Rosie Jones. Sorenstam turned in 34, caught Davies at the 11th hole and looked like a winner in regulation play, but Davies saved par from 50 feet to gain a playoff. "It was almost like a chess match. After catching Laura, I tried to be patient. I knew I would have to beat her to win," Sorenstam said. In the playoff, they returned to the 18th, a 475-yard, par-five hole. Sorenstam missed the green with an eight-iron approach shot, then chipped in. Davies could have extended the match another hole, but missed her 12-footer for birdie.

JCPenney Classic—$1,300,000
Winners: Beth Daniel and Davis Love III

As teams and tournaments go, the pairing of Beth Daniel and Davis Love III seem to go together like beer and nuts. Daniel and Love were at it again in the JCPenney Classic, turning the better-ball event into their personal property.

Love and Daniel blistered Innisbrook course in Tarpon Springs, Florida, over the final 36 holes, shooting a pair of 63s for a 27-under-par 257 total. It was their second victory in the event, by two strokes over Robert Gamez and Helen Alfredsson, and in five tries together they have never finished worse than a tie for third. "I can't get tired of this," said Love, who turned down an invitation to the Nedbank Million Dollar Challenge. "I wouldn't come here unless it would be fun and I had a chance to win."

Love and Daniel worked their way to victory under ideal scoring conditions all week. They were tied for 11th place with 66 after the first round; shot 65 the next day to move to eighth; had 63 on Saturday to tie Jay Delsing and Val Skinner for first place, and once they got the lead Sunday, no one challenged. Love sealed the victory with a birdie on the 70th hole.

"Davis makes this golf course (7,054 yards) very short for me," said Daniel, one of the longest hitters on the LPGA Tour. "I don't worry about us making bogeys. We make plenty of birdies and eagles because both of us hit a lot of greens, and that makes us comfortable."

Women's European Tour

Ladies' Open Costa Azul—£55,000
Winner: Marie Laure de Lorenzi

Marie Laure de Lorenzi demonstrated that she was regaining her late-1980s form by winning the Ladies' Open Costa Azul over the Montado and Troia courses in Lisbon, Portugal, the first event on the newly titled American Express Tour. The 36-year-old Frenchwoman had won in Spain in the autumn of 1994 and continued playing well into 1995 with this, her 16th career victory.

De Lorenzi, who had seven victories in 1988, had rounds of 72, 67 and 66 for a 205 total, 11 under par, to win by two strokes over Evelyn Orley of Switzerland and by three over Corinne Dibnah of Australia. Valerie Michaud of France shot two 69s and led de Lorenzi and Dibnah by one stroke entering the last round. Michaud stumbled to 75 and a tie for fifth place.

Ford Classic—£110,000
Winner: Lora Fairclough

Experience in the Solheim Cup was a key factor in Lora Fairclough's victory in the Ford Classic at Chart Hills Golf Club in Kent, England. "Playing in the Solheim Cup last year was the ultimate in pressure," Fairclough said, "and the experience served me well today." She had no bogeys in her final-round 68 while posting a 277 total, 11 under par, and defeating Florence Descampe of Belgium by one stroke.

Descampe shot a course-record 67 in the second round for a two-stroke lead at 136, and she added 72 in the third round, maintaining first place by one stroke over Fairclough, whose early scores were 70, 68 and 71. Fairclough birdied three of the first five holes in the last round, was out in 33 for a three-stroke advantage and held on from there.

Evian Masters—£275,000
Winner: Laura Davies

It did not take Laura Davies long to re-establish her dominance in Europe. In her second European tournament of the year, Davies posted rounds of 68, 67, 69 and 67 for a 271 total, 17 under par, and won by five strokes over Annika Sorenstam in the Evian Masters at Royal Golf Club Evian in France. "I've won twice in America already this year which is brilliant, but I really wanted to win in Europe as well," Davies said. "This is what I set out to do — win on both sides of the Atlantic."

Davies had a three-stroke lead after 54 holes and wrapped up the title with a flawless 67. "I just played solidly all week," she said, "but today was probably the best I've played all year." Said Alison Nicholas, who placed fourth, "She's incredible, isn't she? There's just no stopping Laura when she gets going like she did this week."

OVB Damen Open—£100,000
Winner: Annika Sorenstam

Annika Sorenstam's first victory on the American Express Tour — after six runner-up finishes since starting in Europe in 1993 — came by a three-stroke margin over Laura Davies in the OVB Damen Open in Salzburg, Austria. The 24-year-old Swedish golfer, who got her first professional triumph in the 1994 Holden Australian Open, shot rounds of 66, 69, 67 and 68 for a 270 total, 12 under par.

"I am so relieved but I am still nervous," Sorenstam said. "I have been waiting for this win for a while and I just feel lucky to pull it through." Sorenstam trailed by one stroke after the first round, shared the 36-hole lead and led by two strokes over Sally Prosser entering the last day. Davies charged to 66 to take second place at 273, Corinne Dibnah was third at 274 and Prosser was fourth at 275, finishing with 71.

European Masters—£150,000
Winner: Lora Fairclough

After five tournaments in 1995, it became apparent that Lora Fairclough was a player to be reckoned with in Europe. She won the European Masters for her second victory of the year, following ties for 22nd and 21st place in her previous two events. "I didn't play as well as I did when I won the Ford Classic," she said. "After that I went into the Evian Masters and put too much pressure on myself, but that is behind me now, and it is nice to win again."

Fairclough's scores were 71, 67 and 68 for a 206 total, and she won by two strokes over Federica Dassu of Italy and by three over Alison Nicholas of England, who recently had won the Corning Classic in America. Dassu and Nicholas shared the first-round lead with 66s, and Nicholas led after 36 holes at 135 by three strokes over Fairclough and Dassu. Fairclough took the lead with a first-nine 33 on the last day as the other two fell back.

Hennessy Cup—£300,000
Winner: Annika Sorenstam

The Hennessy Cup remained in Swedish hands as Annika Sorenstam won over compatriot Liselotte Neumann, who was attempting to win for the third successive year at Golf und Landklub Koln in Bladbach, Germany. The competition went to the 72nd hole, a par-five, where Neumann missed a four-foot birdie attempt then Sorenstam holed a three-footer to secure her second American Express Tour victory.

Sorenstam's winning 271 total consisted of scores of 68, 70, 65 and 68. Neumann, who had a last-round 66, tied at 272 with Trish Johnson of England, who birdied three of the final four holes to shoot 68. Wendy Doolan of Australia led the first two rounds before dropping to an 11th-place tie. Sorenstam equalled the course record with her 65 in the third round to lead by one over Johnson. Laura Davies' 293 total for 42nd place included scores of 79 and 76.

Guardian Irish Holidays Open—£100,000
Winner: Laura Davies

In the last European tournament, four weeks earlier in Germany, Laura Davies had one of those very rare occasions when she clearly was not No. 1 in the world, or even close to it. Davies made up for that with a vengeance in the Guardian Irish Holidays Open as she won by a staggering 16 strokes with a 267 total, 25 under par at St. Margaret's Golf and Country Club in Dublin. Her scores were 67, 66, 66 and 68. Second place went to Asa Gottmo of Sweden at 283.

The 16-stroke margin broke the American Express Tour record by five strokes, the 25-under-par figure (on a par-73 course) was a record by three strokes, and the 267 total matched Davies' own record from the 1988 Biarritz Open. "It was brilliant. Excellent. I am really pleased, but I obviously can't expect to play like that every week," Davies said. "If my putting and chipping were this good all the time I wouldn't have much to worry about, would I?"

Payne & Gunter Scottish Open—£75,000
Winner: Alison Nicholas

Alison Nicholas, a winner earlier in the year in America, claimed her first European title in three years, and the 11th of her career, with a tense one-stroke victory over Patricia Meunier of France in the Payne & Gunter Scottish Open on the Dalmahoy course in Edinburgh. The 22-year-old from France battled England's Nicholas all week, leading the first round and entering the last day one stroke behind.

With nine holes to play, however, Nicholas was four strokes behind Meunier, who had six birdies in the opening seven holes. "At that moment I thought I was playing for second place," Nicholas said. Meunier's game came unravelled on the second nine and both finished with 69s, three under par, and Nicholas was in front with her 272 total.

Woodpecker Welsh Open—£60,000
Winner: Laura Davies

Not even a painful wasp sting in the final round could keep Laura Davies from winning the Woodpecker Welsh Open for her third victory of the year in Europe — and her fifth worldwide — while also equalling Dale Reid's American Express Tour record of 21 career victories. Davies now had 38 career wins worldwide.

Although Davies led after 36 and 54 holes, she was closely pursued through the tournament by the likes of Trish Johnson, Marie Laure de Lorenzi and Wendy Doolan, an Australian who placed second. Davies had a 278 total to win by three strokes on rounds of 68, 69, 71 and 70. She was stung on the right hand by the wasp on the 12th tee, but birdied that hole and guaranteed her victory with another birdie at No. 16.

Weetabix Women's British Open—£360,000
Winner: Karrie Webb

From the village of Ayr in northern Queensland, Australia, Karrie Webb's mother, Evelyn, could not believe it. "Look, it's two o'clock in the morning; you're not having me on?" she asked the caller from England, who was reporting from the fourth round of the Weetabix Women's British Open. "Six shots? You're kidding."

No, Webb indeed was leading by six strokes, and the 20-year-old won by that margin on the Dukes Course at Woburn Golf and Country Club in Milton Keynes. The runner-up was another impressive young golfer, Annika Sorenstam of Sweden, fresh off her own major triumph in the U.S. Women's Open, who shared second place with a young American, Jill McGill.

Webb, who was second to Laura Davies in the Alpine Australian Ladies Masters last December in only her second professional tournament, won on rounds of 69, 70, 69 and 70 for a 278 total, 14 under par. Two strokes behind after the first round, Webb was one stroke ahead after both 36 and 54 holes, entering the final round in front of Val Skinner, who finished with 76 and tied for fourth place.

"I had dreamed of walking up the 18th to win a tournament, but for it to be the British Open is unbelievable," Webb said. "A lot of people at home will be shocked, but happily shocked."

Ford-Stimorol Danish Open—£60,000
Winner: Caroline Hall

With a course-record 64 in the final round, England's young Caroline Hall breezed to an eight-stroke victory over Australia's Corinne Dibnah in the Ford-Stimorol Danish Open at Vejle Golf Club in Vejle, Denmark. A star of the 1992 Curtis Cup, Hall achieved her first professional victory with a 201 total, 15 under par.

Hall, age 21, was tied with Dibnah after an opening-round 67, then shot 70 for a one-stroke lead. Not even strong winds could deter Hall in the last round. She hit two drivers and a wedge shot into the par-five first green, then birdied from eight feet, and sank a 20-foot birdie putt on the second hole. "I was nervous at the start and knew that Corinne was the player I would have to beat," Hall said. "But she took three putts on the first green, and those two early birdies helped me to relax."

Wilkinson Sword English Open—£95,000
Winner: Laura Davies

Little-known Wendy Dicks led for three rounds, but on the pressure-packed final day Laura Davies came through for her fourth victory of the year in Europe, and her sixth worldwide, in the Wilkinson Sword English Open at the Oxfordshire Golf Club in Thames, England. Davies had rounds of 72, 67, 70 and 70 for her 279 total, nine under par, and won by one stroke over fast-closing Karina Orum and by two over Dicks.

Dicks, who until 1994 sold Christmas toys at Harrods to subsidize her income, had early rounds of 67, 68 and 72 to lead by one stroke over Lora Fairclough and by two over Davies. While Dicks shot a closing 74, dropping four strokes in eight holes from the ninth, Davies birdied the 11th and 12th holes to take control.

Trygg Hansa Open—£115,000
Winner: Liselotte Neumann

Spectators at the Trygg Hansa Open had much about which to cheer, as Swedish stars Liselotte Neumann and Annika Sorenstam battled to the 18th hole, where Neumann birdied to secure a one-stroke victory with her 281 total, 11 under par at Haninge Golf Club in Stockholm. Neumann, who led Sorenstam by two strokes after 54 holes, won with rounds of 70, 71, 68 and 72, while Sorenstam shot 71, 70, 70 and 71.

The victory was Neumann's first of 1995. "It was a relief to win again," Neumann said. "It was a real match play situation, and Annika played much better than I did. She has won so much this year, so it was probably my turn to win."

Staatsloteru Dutch Open—£70,000
Winner: Marie Laure de Lorenzi

It was a victory as impressive as any in her career as Marie Laure de Lorenzi crushed her opposition in winning by nine strokes in the Staatsloteru Dutch Open at Rijk van Nijmegen in Groesbeek, Netherlands. De Lorenzi shot a course-record 66, seven under par, in the second round and was not far off that score in the other two, having 67 and 68. Lora Fairclough of England was runner-up to the French ace.

Comparing this to her seven-victory year in 1988, de Lorenzi said, "I am a much better golfer than I was then. I have more experience and a better method. But there are so many more good players around now, and it is more difficult to win."

Maredo German Open—£75,000
Winner: Rachel Hetherington

Australia's Rachel Hetherington shot a blistering 64, nine under par, in the third round and won with relative ease, although by just two strokes, in the Maredo German Open at the Hotel Treudelberg course in Hamburg. Hetherington, age 23, a second-year pro, finished with 72 for a 275 total, 17 under par, edging England's Caroline Hall, who closed with 68 for her 277 total.

Evelyn Orley of Switzerland led the first round with 67, while Hetherington was deep in the pack with 71, but Hetherington's 68 in the second round brought her within one stroke of the lead and her third-round 64 gave her a five-stroke cushion over Wendy Doolan, who fell with 74 on the last day.

Italian Open di Sicilia—£100,000
Winner: Denise Booker

A third young golfer from Australia, Denise Booker, won on the American Express Tour at the Italian Open di Sicilia. Booker's victory at Il Picciolo Golf Club in Sicily was much more unlikely than those of Karrie Webb and Rachel Hetherington. Before this week, Booker had played in 13 tournaments in 1995, missed the cut in eight and earned only £2,265.

Booker held or shared second place for three rounds, then shot three-under-par 70 in the last round for a 284 total, eight under par, and won by one stroke over Spain's Amaia Arruti, who three-putted the 18th hole to allow Booker to win with a par there. "I feel very numb," Booker said. "It has not sunk in yet that I have won, and I don't know when it will."

Nestle Open de France Feminin—£60,000
Winner: Marie Laure de Lorenzi

Marie Laure de Lorenzi achieved another massive victory when she won the Nestle Open de France Feminin by 10 strokes. De Lorenzi shot rounds of 71, 68 and 71 for a 210 total, nine under par at the St. Endreol course in La Motte, France. Her closest pursuers with 220 totals were the British trio of Kathryn Marshall, Alison Nicholas and Sally Prosser.

It was de Lorenzi's 18th American Express Tour career victory, her third of the year, and her third French Open title. The French golfer, who is based in Barcelona, Spain, was one stroke behind after the first round, then surged to a four-stroke lead and proved to be unstoppable despite starting the final round with two bogeys.

La Manga Spanish Open—£50,000
Winner: Rachel Hetherington

The American Express Tour of 1995 ended with a third Australian victory in four tournaments as Rachel Hetherington added to her victory in Germany by winning the La Manga Spanish Open. Hetherington had a 202 total, 14 under par, to win by two strokes over England's Lisa Hackney and France's Stephanie Dallongeville.

Unlike her earlier victory, when she entered the final round with a five-stroke lead, Hetherington fought far into the third round before she could feel confident of winning. Hetherington, Dallongeville and Spain's Amaia Arruti were tied after 36 holes at 134. With nine holes to play, Hetherington was two strokes ahead, then made three birdies in four holes starting at No. 10 while finishing with 68.

Princess Lalla Meriem Cup—FF250,000
Winner: Amaia Arruti

Spain's Amaia Arruti won the unofficial Princess Lalla Meriem Cup in Rabat, Morocco, on the second extra hole against Sweden's Sofia Gronberg after they finished with two-over-par 221 totals for three rounds over the Blue Course at Royal Golf Dar-es-Salam. Gronberg made up a two-stroke deficit with a final-round 72, but lost with a bogey in the playoff.

Women's Australasian Tours

Malaysian JAL Mercedes-Benz Open—US$90,000
Winner: Corinne Dibnah

Corinne Dibnah said her strategy was to play conservatively, but you could not tell that from the results, as Dibnah expanded a four-stroke margin to an eight-stroke victory in the Malaysian JAL Mercedes-Benz Open on the Palm Course of Saujana Golf and Country Club in Kuala Lumpur. The Australian's scores were 73, 73 and 74 for a 220 total, four over par, while American Tina Paternostro was second with a 228 total. There were no sub-par rounds and only one player, Susan Farron of New Zealand, had an even-par 72 round. Her other scores were 79 and 82.

Singapore JAL Open—US$80,000
Winner: Estefania Knuth

Despite an opening-round 75, Spain's Estefania Knuth posted a victory in the Singapore JAL Open as she stormed back with rounds of 67 and 66 for a 208 total, eight under par, to win by two strokes over Huang Yu-Chen. The inexperienced Knuth surprised the field with her excellent iron play, holding off Huang, Lisa Hackney, Dale Reid and Corinne Dibnah. Hackney entered the last round with a one-stroke lead over Reid and Huang, then shot 73 to place fifth with 213. Huang and Dibnah finished with 69s, and Dibnah took third place at 211. Reid was fourth with 71 and a 212 total.

Indonesia JAL Open—US$100,000
Winner: Lisa Hackney

After hitting into the water on the 18th hole and being forced into a playoff, Britain's 27-year-old Lisa Hackney scored her first professional victory when she birdied the second playoff hole to defeat Mardi Lunn in the Indonesia JAL Open at Pantai Indah Kapuk Country Club in Jakarta. Hackney and Lunn tied with even-par 216 totals, after Hackney shot 74 in the final round and Lunn had 70. Hackney's earlier scores were 70 and 72, and she began the last round tied for the lead with Huang Yu-Chen, who shot 75 and placed third with a 217 total.

Thailand Open—US$110,000
Winner: Liz Earley

Liz Earley of Canada missed the cut in the first three tournaments, but her determination paid off in the Thailand Open when she won by one stroke over Amy Fruhwirth of the United States. Earley shot 69 in the first round and led Fruhwirth by one stroke. Her second-round 75 left her one stroke behind Fruhwirth and Japan's Megumi Matsuo. In the last round, Earley hit 15 greens in regulation strokes and shot 70, two under par, for her 214 total. Fruhwirth had 72 for a 215 total, then came Fusako Nagata of Japan at 216 and Matsuo at 216.

Republic of China Open—US$118,500
Winner: Cheng Mei-Chi

Local knowledge may have been a big factor in Cheng Mei-Chi's victory in the Republic of China Open, when she held on to win by one stroke over Lisa Hackney at Linkou International Golf and Country Club in Taipei. After playing in steamy conditions in Thailand, the golfers found rain and icy winds in this February event. Cheng's scores were 75, 71 and 74 for her 220 total, four over par. Hackney shot 71, 75 and 75 to have a 221 total and finish as the leading money winner. Patti Liscio of the United States was third, four strokes further behind, including her final-round 70, the best score of the tournament.

Holden Australian Open—A$250,000
Winner: Liselotte Neumann

Despite leading after each of the first three rounds, Liselotte Neumann of Sweden needed to birdie the last three holes and a playoff to win the Holden Australian Open. Tied with Neumann at 283, nine under par on the Yarra Yarra course in Melbourne, were another Swede, defending champion Annika Sorenstam, and American Jane Geddes. They went three extra holes, all on the par-five 18th, with Neumann winning on a two-putt birdie.

Neumann began the tournament with a course-record 67 and led Geddes by one stroke. She shot 74 in high winds on the second day but kept the lead because Geddes had the same score. A third-round 71 sent Neumann into the last day with a one-stroke margin over Geddes and two in front of Sorenstam and young Australian star Karrie Webb. Neumann finished with 71 while Sorenstam shot 69 and Geddes, 70. Webb had a final-round 70 and missed a birdie putt on the 18th hole that would have put her in the playoff.

Alpine Australian Masters—A$300,000
Winner: Annika Sorenstam

Young Swedish star Annika Sorenstam rolled to her sixth worldwide victory of 1995 in the Alpine Australian Masters, winning by eight strokes over Jane Geddes and by nine over Laura Davies and Liselotte Neumann. Sorenstam shot rounds of 66, 68, 67 and 69 for a 270 total, 22 under par at the Royal Pines Resort in Queensland.

Sorenstam either led or shared the lead after each round. She was tied the first day with Neumann, then was three strokes ahead with her 134 total for

36 holes. Her victory was virtually assured with her third-round 67 which provided a six-stroke margin over Neumann.

Among those who Sorenstam impressed was former Australian star Peter Thomson. "She could make a fine study for those on the men's tour who have problems getting the best out of themselves," Thomson said. "She has a keen golfing brain that applies itself to careful planning of each round. She calls herself a 'grinder' but if it is true, then so was Ben Hogan.

"For one thing, she never, ever tries to hit further than she can. Each shot is under firm control and her judgement of distance is amazing. As for her putting, she is in the Kel Nagle class."

Japan LPGA Tour

Daikin Orchid—¥60,000,000
Winner: Marnie McGuire

Marnie McGuire won the season-opening event on the Japan LPGA Tour by doing something no else managed at any time in the Daikin Orchid tournament that early March weekend. She broke 70 ... but good. The New Zealand golfer produced a five-under-par 67 in Sunday's final round to post a three-stroke victory with her six-under-par 210 total.

McGuire, who scored her first Japan victory in the 1994 Nasu Ogawa, opened with 73, trailing leader Woo-Soon Ko by three strokes. Kaori Higo moved in front Saturday with 71-70–141 as McGuire shot 70 and took over the runner-up position. No one else was close. Higo had a 72 Sunday and, though a three-stroke loser, took second place by five shots at Ryukyu Golf Club in Okinawa.

Chiyoda Ladies—¥50,000,000
Winner: Yuka Irie

It wasn't a very pretty finish, but Yuka Irie held on to capture the first victory of her Japan LPGA Tour career in the Chiyoda Ladies. Irie, who had carried a four-stroke lead into the final round at wind-swept Miyazaki Zaronbai Golf Club at Miyazaki, struggled home with 78, but her four-over-par 220 total held up for a one-shot victory over Young-Me Lee.

Akiko Fukushima, who eventually tied for third place two strokes behind the winner, grabbed the first-round lead with 70 as Irie shot her first of two 71s. The 142 jumped Irie four strokes in front of Lee, who matched 73s. Fukushima skied to 78 Saturday. In the blustery weather Sunday, when just two players broke par, the victor had a double bogey and six bogeys to go with two birdies. Lee fell one stroke short with her closing 75.

Saishunkan Ladies—¥60,000,000
Winner: Nayoko Yoshikawa

It took a playoff birdie to do it, but Nayoko Yoshikawa ended a victory drought of more than two years in the Saishunkan Ladies tournament at Takayuhbaru Country Club at Kumamoto. Yoshikawa, long a standout on the Japan LPGA Tour with 28 victories on her outstanding record, dropped a 10-foot putt on the first extra hole for No. 29 after she and Korea's able Ok-Hee Ku tied in 54-hole regulation with par 216s.

The two were well off the pace Friday as Kaori Higo and Aiko Hashimoto shot 69s and were still one back Saturday evening as Yoshikawa posted 74-70–144 and Ku 73-71–144. Aki Takamura and Mayumi Murai were at 143. Par 72s by Yoshikawa and Ku forced the playoff, with Yuko Saito, Yuko Moriguchi and Marnie McGuire, the Daikin Orchid winner two weeks earlier, missing the deadlock by one stroke.

Kenshoen Ladies—¥50,000,000
Winner: Keiko Arai

The Japan LPGA Tour had its second first-time winner of the season when tournament activity resumed after a two-week break. As was the case in the preceding event at Kumamoto, a playoff was required. Keiko Arai scored her initial victory when she parred the first extra hole as her opponent, Huang Bie-Shyun of Taiwan, incurred a bogey.

Arai and Huang had finished the 54 holes Sunday with four-under-par 212s, Arai coming from three strokes off the lead with 70, Huang from one back with 72. Kaori Higo, a contender virtually every week in the early season, and Kaori Harada were the 36-hole leaders with 139s. Huang had begun play Friday with a front-running 68, one stroke ahead of Arai, Higo, Harada and Yuko Moriguchi.

Mitsukoshi Cup—¥60,000,000
Winner: Ikuyo Shiotani

Ikuyo Shiotani seemed to have been laying in wait. Visible but not a serious contender in the first four tournaments with finishes ranging from 11th to 20th, the 32-year-old Shiotani rushed from four strokes off the pace in the final round of the Japan LPGA season's first 72-hole event to grab her initial victory of 1995 and 10th of her career.

Shiotani hardly looked to be a contender, let alone a winner, with her opening rounds of 76-77–153, although the 72s of Young-Me Lee and Yukiko Ishiguro led the first day at the Segovia Golf Course at Chiyoda. She was nine behind Chikayo Yamazaki at the midpoint. Then came a big-time move. Shiotani shot 70 Saturday to climb within four and 69 Sunday to win with her four-over-par 292. Marnie McGuire, the Daikin Orchid winner, who had shared the third-round lead with Yamazaki at 219, shot 74 and came up one stroke short but one ahead of three others — Ayako Okamoto, Michiko Hattori and Akiko Fukushima.

Nasu Ogawa—¥50,000,000
Winner: Ikuyo Shiotani

Ikuyo Shiotani followed a similar path when she scored her second victory in a row on the Japan LPGA Tour in the Nasu Ogawa tournament at Tochigi. The second time, though, the slow start and fast finish only pulled her into a first-place tie with three others at one-over-par 217 in tough weather, and she had to go five extra holes to etch an 11th title onto her record.

Shiotani rallied from an opening 75 with 72-70 on the weekend, the latter round bringing her from three shots off the leading pace of Aki Takamura and Yuko Moriguchi into a four-way deadlock at 217 at the end of regulation play. She was joined in the playoff by Mayumi Hirase (71), Japan's top player in 1994; Hisako Takada (72) and Moriguchi (73), Moriguchi surviving until Shiotani sank a 13-foot birdie putt at the fifth playoff hole.

Satake Japan Classic—¥50,000,000
Winner: Akiko Fukushima

Akiko Fukushima, the highly regarded 21-year-old star on the Japan LPGA Tour, stood up to two of the game's most successful international players and made off with the Satake Japan Classic title at the end of April at Hiroshima Country Club. Fukushima, who had been a frequent contender earlier in the season, outfought Sweden's Liselotte Neumann in the stretch to score a three-shot victory with her eight-under-par 208 total, her career second on the circuit. The other world-class visitor, Laura Davies, tied for fifth place.

Fukushima, whose father Hisaaki, a former baseball player, caddied for her, set up her victory bid with a second-round 67, equally the week's low round. With 139, Fukushima led omnipresent Kaori Higo by two, Neumann by three. That was her ultimate margin over Neumann, although Fukushima's birdie to Neumann's bogey at the last hole broke open a harrowing stretch battle after Neumann had eagled the par-five 16th.

Gunze World Cup—¥60,000,000
Winner: Kaori Higo

Kaori Higo, who had been knocking on the door through most of the early season, broke through with a victory in the Gunze World Cup at Tokyo's noted Yomiuri Country Club. Higo, who had four top-10 finishes in the first seven events of the 1995 Japan LPGA Tour, came from two strokes off the pace in the final round to score her third career victory, but got an assist when Ikuyo Shiotani, already a two-time 1995 winner, bogeyed the last hole. That gave Shiotani a 73 and 282, one stroke behind Higo, who had 70 for her seven-under-par 281.

The 26-year-old Higo sprinted to a four-stroke lead with an opening-round 65, but tumbled into third place behind Shiotani and Liselotte Neumann when she followed with a 75. Shiotani and Neumann were at 138, and

Shiotani moved one stroke ahead of Neumann with a 71 to her 72 Saturday. Higo shot 71 for 211, then regained the lead Sunday with four front-nine birdies. Two bogeys later, she and Shiotani were tied for the lead before Shiotani took her fatal bogey at the 18th.

Yakult Ladies—¥60,000,000
Winner: Akiko Fukushima

Akiko Fukushima picked up her second victory in 14 days, perhaps aided by a Sunday rainstorm that forced a cutback of the Yakult Ladies' final round to nine holes. The young Japanese star had a 37 Sunday and her 174 total, six under par, gave her a one-stroke victory over Huang Bie-Shyun, who closed the gap with a 34. It was Huang's second runner-up finish of the Japan LPGA season.

Toshimi Kimura led the first day at Fukuoka Kokusai Country Club with 69 as the eventual winner opened with 70 and Huang with 73. Fukushima took over first place Saturday with 67–137, one stroke in front of Yuko Saito, who shot the week's low round of 66. Saito dropped to third place Sunday when she shot 39 for her nine holes, finishing with 177.

Chukyo TV Bridgestone—¥60,000,000
Winner: Ikuyo Shiotani

Yukie Ueki had the wrong lady on her heels and it cost her a victory in the Chukyo TV Bridgestone tournament in mid-May at Kasugai Country Club at Nagoya. Ueki led for two days and one of her nearest pursuers at the end of each round was Ikuyo Shiotani, the hottest player on the Japan LPGA Tour. The pressure told Sunday, as Shiotani shifted into the lead and registered her third victory of the year, the 12th of her fine career.

The scoring went this way: First round — Ueki shot 66, Shiotani 69. Second round — Ueki shot 70 for 136, Shiotani another 69 for 138. Final round — Shiotani shot 74 for 212, four under par; Ueki 77 for 213. Suzuko Maeda and Nayoko Yoshikawa tied for third at 214.

Toto Motors Ladies—¥50,000,000
Winner: Mayumi Hirase

Mayumi Hirase accelerated her relatively slow start on the 1995 Japan LPGA Tour at the Toto Motors Ladies tournament at Toto Hannoh Country Club, Saitama. Hirase, the circuit's leading performer in 1994 with four victories and top position on the money list for the second year in a row, put together a steady 209, and the seven-under-par score accounted for a three-stroke victory, her first of the 1995 season. She had made only one serious title run earlier in the season, losing in a playoff a month before in the Nasu Ogawa.

Hirase, who had 13 victories on her fine record coming into the season, took over first place at Toto Hannoh with a pair of 69s after trailing Chikayo

Yamazaki (67) the first day. She then led Marnie McGuire, the New Zealander who won the year's opening Daikin Orchid, by two strokes. A final-round 71 widened the ending gap to three as McGuire shot 72 and tied for second with Young-Me Lee.

Mitsubishi Electric Ladies—¥50,000,000
Winner: Aiko Hashimoto

Aiko Hashimoto began living up to expectations in the Mitsubishi Electric Ladies tournament. Hashimoto, who had gone seven years without notching a professional victory after taking the 1986 Japan Women's Amateur, finally broke through with her triumph in the Mitsubishi at Kita Rokko Country Club in Hyogo. She was the only player to break par with her one-under 215 total. It was a particularly gratifying win for Hashimoto because she had shared first place in the tournament after two rounds the year before and wound up losing by three strokes.

Four players, including the previous Sunday's winner, Mayumi Hirase, tied for the lead at 70 in the first round. The others were Young-Me Lee, Fumiko Muraguchi and Tamayo Ueda. Koreans Ok-Hee Ku and Lee wound up on top Saturday, Ku shooting 73-70-143 and Lee reversing those totals. Hashimoto stayed close with her 72-72–144, tied for third with Hirase (70-74). Her one-under 71 edged Hashimoto to the front and victory Sunday as Muraguchi and Ku shared second place at 216.

Dunlop Twin Lakes Ladies—¥50,000,000
Winner: Mayumi Hirase

Mayumi Hirase continued playing a hot hand in the Dunlop Twin Lakes Ladies at Fujioka, winning her second title in 14 days with a contending sixth-place finish falling between the two victories. Hirase survived a stretch battle against Korea's Young-Me Lee, another player on a warm streak, to record a two-stroke victory at even-par 288 in the mid-June tournament, two Sundays after capturing the Toto Motors title. The win was the 15th of her career.

The leading money winner in Japan LPGA golf in 1993 and 1994 trailed Ai-Yu Tu of Korea by four strokes when she opened with 72, but jumped into a second-place tie at 141 with Junko Yasui when she followed with 69. Yasui had the same combination. The battle remained tight after 54 holes with Hirase, Lee and Mariko Ohtani at 216, Akiko Fukushima, Aki Nakano and Yasui at 217, but it came down to a duel between Hirase and Lee well into Sunday's final round. The winner moved in front to stay after a birdie/bogey switch with Lee at the 14th hole. Woo-Soon Ko closed with 69 to tie Lee for second place.

Japan Women's Open Championship—¥60,000,000
Winner: Ikuyo Shiotani

Displaying what in 1995 became her standard procedure, Ikuyo Shiotani won the prestigious Japan Women's Open Championship with a come-from-behind 72 for 285 and a one-stroke victory. It was a fitting climax to the first four months of her season, during which she scored four victories to run her career total to 13. Each of her previous three wins had been the product of last-round rallies.

The 33-year-old Shiotani, as steady as the rain that pelted the Ube Country Club course that Sunday afternoon, had started the day two strokes off the leading pace of Marnie McGuire, who stumbled to a 77 and finished third at 288, two behind Korean Man-Soo Kim, who blew her title hopes with bogeys at the 16th and 17th holes. McGuire, in turn, had replaced Akiko Fukushima in first place Saturday. Fukushima had led the first two days with rounds of 65 and 70 on the Mannenike course of Ube Country Club at Yamaguchi.

Tohato Ladies—¥50,000,000
Winner: Akane Ohshiro

Ikuyo Shiotani and Man-Soo Kim, fresh from their one-two finishes in the Open at Ube, were front-runners again when the following week's Tohato Ladies was played at Ichihara's Oak Village Golf Club. However, Akane Ohshiro matched them in regulation and snatched the title, the fourth of her career, on the second hole of a playoff.

Kim bounced back from her disappointing loss to Shiotani with an opening 67, then yielded the lead Saturday to Mayumi Hirase, who shot 68-77–145. Kim skied to 79 for 146, tying with Shiotani, who had 71-75. When Hirase ballooned to 79 Sunday, the other three jumped in, Ohshiro with 74, Kim and Shiotani with 75s for the playoff-forcing, five-over-par 221s. Kim bogeyed the first extra hole, and Ohshiro took the victory with a 10-foot birdie putt at the second.

Toyo Suisan Ladies—¥50,000,000
Winner: Aki Nakano

Aki Nakano came up with her strongest and most consistent performance in three years in registering a three-stroke victory in the Toyo Suisan Ladies tournament at Hokkaido's Kosaido Sapporo Country Club in early July. Nakano had not won since the Meiji Nyugyo Cup in 1992.

Nakano opened with 68, one stroke behind leader Chieko Nishida, then took command of first place the rest of the way. With 70 Saturday for 138, she established a one-stroke margin over Junko Yasui and Kumiko Hiyoshi. She balanced off two birdies with two bogeys for 72 Sunday to gain the three-stroke triumph over Mayumi Hirase, Rie Mitsuhashi, Yasui and the previous week's victor, Akane Ohshiro.

Resort Trust Cleanup Ladies—¥50,000,000
Winner: Wu Ming-Yeh

The Taiwan contingent on the Japan LPGA Tour claimed its first victory at the Resort Trust Cleanup Ladies tournament as Wu Ming-Yeh, a 10-year veteran from the island nation, scored the eighth win of her career. Though going two over par with her final-round 74, Wu came from two strokes off the pace to win by one at Maple Point Golf Club at Yamanashi with her five-under-par 211.

Yuka Irie rattled the field Friday with a 64, taking a four-stroke lead. Junko Yasui, with 68-67, overtook her Saturday when Irie followed with 71. Wu was next with 68-69–137. Wu's 74–211 Sunday was one better than the 212s of Shin Sora and Yuko Moriguchi.

Katokichi Queens Golf—¥50,000,000
Winner: Fuki Kido

Fuki Kido, who hadn't won on the Japan LPGA Tour since posting a pair of early victories in 1993, took advantage of the weather and a hot round to re-enter the winner's circle in the Katokichi Queens Golf tournament at Kagawa. Four strokes back after the first 18 holes, Kido came back Sunday after a thunderstorm wiped out the second round, produced a 68, the day's best round, and with her three-under-par 141, squeezed out a one-stroke victory.

Australia's Jennifer Sevil was the Friday leader with 69 and she wound up in a three-way tie for second Sunday at 142 with Yoko Inoue (72-70) and Junko Yasui (70-72).

SC Ladies—¥50,000,000
Winner: Huang Bie-Shyun

For the second time in three weeks, a title on the Japan LPGA Tour had a Taiwan destination. Huang Bie-Shyun, one of her country's top-ranking players, captured her second victory in Japan, coming from behind in the final round of the SC Ladies tournament to post a two-stroke win at Kousaido Saitama Golf Club. Huang's earlier victory in Japan came in the 1993 Mitsubishi Electric. She had finished second in the Yakult Ladies earlier in the season.

Three players — Michie Ohba, Tatsuko Morimoto and Miyuki Shimabukuro — shared the first-round lead with 68s, then disappeared from view. Chikako Matsuzawa took over Saturday with a second 69. She led Norimi Terasawa (70-69) by one, Huang (70-70) by two. Huang shot 69 Sunday for her winning, seven-under-par 209. Terasawa's 72–211 took second and Matsuzawa, with 74, tied for third with Toshimi Kimura and Nayoko Yoshikawa.

Mizuno Ladies—¥60,000,000
Winner: Aki Takamura

Aki Takamura had made only a few waves in earlier tournaments on the 1995 Japan LPGA Tour, her best showing back in April when she folded after sharing the second-round lead in the Nasu Ogawa. So, it was quite a surprise not just that she won the Mizuno Ladies tournament at Asahi Kokusai Tojo Country Club but that she was the first player all year to lead from wire to wire. It was the first victory for the 23-year-old professional.

It went this way: Takamura shot a six-under-par 66 in the first round for a three-stroke lead over Yuko Moriguchi. She followed with 70 Saturday and that widened her margin to five over Moriguchi, Mayumi Hirase and Aki Nakano. Another 70 Sunday established a seven-stroke victory advantage over those same three competitors, who all shot 72s. It was by far the biggest margin of victory of the 1995 season.

NEC Karuizawa 72—¥60,000,000
Winner: Mayumi Hirase

Mayumi Hirase closed in on Tour leader Ikuyo Shiotani when she collected her third victory of the Japan LPGA season in the NEC Karuizawa 72 tournament in mid-August at Karuizawa's Iriyama course. It was the 16th win of her career. Shiotani, with four in 1995, has 13 victories on her record.

Aiko Hashimoto, the Mitsubishi Electric winner in June, and little-known Megumi Matsuo led the field the first day with 68s, as Hirase began play with a par 71. Both leaders fell back Saturday and Akiko Fukushima and Nayoko Yoshikawa moved ahead with 139s. Hirase had one of the day's best rounds, 68, to advance within one stroke of the lead, along with Michiko Hattori. As it turned out, par and 212 produced the win, as Hattori, one of Japan's leading players, remained winless in 1995 when she shot 73 to finish second by one stroke. Kaori Higo and Hashimoto tied for third at 214.

Lotte Ladies—¥50,000,000
Winner: Kaori Higo

Perhaps it had something to do with the unpredictability of youth. Akiko Fukushima, who seemed to have been in constant contention all season, looked like a sure thing to post her third 1995 triumph in the Lotte Ladies at Minayoshida Country Club at Chiba. She was four shots ahead with 18 holes to play. Instead, the title went to Kaori Higo, who was tied for 46th place after the opening round.

Higo capped her splendid rally — shooting 66-71 after beginning with 74 — by defeating little-known Yukiyo Haga on the second hole of a playoff after the two tied at 211 over the 54-hole distance. It was Higo's second win of the season and fourth of the 26-year-old's career. Fukushima had established her four-stroke lead over Higo, Fuki Kido and Chikako Matsuzawa with a 69-67 start before the wheels came off Sunday. She took a 78 and dropped into a tie for eighth place at 214.

Goyo Kensetsu Cup—¥60,000,000
Winner: Marnie McGuire

Most of the components repeated from the previous week when Marnie McGuire, the New Zealand regular on the Japan LPGA Tour, won the Goyo Kensetsu Cup at Tomisato Golf Club at Chiba. The victory was McGuire's second of the season, she shot 211, and a playoff decided the winner. The same factors applied to Kaori Higo's win the previous Sunday. However, McGuire had to go three extra holes before knocking out the veteran Aiko Takasu and there were no collapses as with Akiko Fukushima.

McGuire, with 69, trailed leader Aki Takamura by one stroke after the opening round, then went in front Saturday when she shot 68 for 137. At that point, Chikayo Yamazaki (69-69) was second, Takasu (71-68) third and nobody else close. When McGuire faltered with 74 Sunday, Takasu overtook her with 72 for her 211. The 41-year-old Takasu, in her 21st professional season, failed in her bid for her 15th title and first since 1993.

Fuji Sankei Classic—¥45,000,000
Winner: Junko Yasui

They had to deal with the long and short of it when the Fuji Sankei Classic tournament took the Japan LPGA to the playoff route for the third week in a row. The "short" was the tournament proper, which became a 36-hole event when heavy fog forced cancellation of the final round. With Saturday's standings becoming the final ones, Junko Yasui and Aki Nagano finished in a first-place deadlock with 142s on the par-73 Five Hundred Club course at Shizuoka. They found a way to stage the playoff and that's where the "long" came in. It went six holes before Yasui sank a six-foot par putt to gain her first win of the season and 10th of her career.

Interestingly, the two playoff protagonists, neither a winner over the past three seasons, had matching rounds the first two days. Their 69s led the first day before they posted 73s Saturday. Akio Takasu, the playoff loser the previous Sunday, missed another playoff by one stroke with her 70-73–143.

Japan LPGA Championship—¥65,000,000
Winner: Aki Takamura

Two of the youngest players on the Japan LPGA Tour pushed conventional wisdom aside when one of the circuit's majors — the LPGA Championship — came up on the September schedule. Veteran stars, with their experience and confidence, normally dominate the prestige events. Not so at the 1995 LPGA at The Classic Golf Club at Miyata, Fukuoka. Aki Takamura, age 23, who had won her first title just a month earlier, outfought the circuit's 21-year-old standout, Akiko Fukushima, in a stretch run to a four-stroke victory.

Perhaps opening-round nerves did bother Takamura as she shot 74 and trailed co-leaders Fukushima and Jae-Sook Won by three, but she was solid the rest of the way. She shot 70 Friday to move into a tie for third with

Fukushima and two others, four back of veteran Akio Takasu, who then dropped from contention. Takamura's 69 Saturday jumped her one stroke into the lead at 213, and the finishing kick of her closing 69 secured the victory. She birdied three of the last seven holes, unaware that the omnipresent Fukushima, starting the final round three shots behind, had caught up with three early birdies of her own. Takamura's winning total was six-under-par 282. Fukushima finished second at 286.

Kosaido Asahi Cup—¥45,000,000
Winner: Huang Bie-Shyun

Bad weather again plagued the Japan LPGA Tour, forcing an abbreviation of the Kosaido Asahi Cup to 27 holes at Ichihara's Chiba Kosaido Country Club as Typhoon Oscar bore down on Japan's east coast. Taiwan's Huang Bie-Shyun was the beneficiary this time, picking up her second win of the season with the odd score of 103, which was five under par. Akemi Yamaoka was second with 104.

Yamaoka had the first-round lead with 69 and Huang was three behind her as tournament officials debated their options when steady rain arrived Saturday ahead of the typhoon. Despite the bad weather, they decided to try to get in nine holes, since 27 holes met the minimum requirements for an official tournament. The Taiwanese star then fired a sparkling 31 in the horrid conditions to land the victory.

Miyagi TV Cup—¥50,000,000
Winner: Natsuko Noro

Natsuko Noro couldn't believe it was happening to her. The obscure Japanese golfer confessed that she harbored negative thoughts until she reached the clubhouse at Hananomori Golf Club with her 212 score and knew that she had the first victory of her career on the Japan LPGA Tour. Noro, one of only a few first-time winners on the 1995 circuit, came from one stroke off the pace with a final-round 71 to take the title away from Hisako Takeda, who led after 36 holes with 70-70—140.

Noro had begun the tournament with 69, one shot off the leading pace of Yuko Motoyama. The 29-year-old winner caught up to Takeda at the 11th hole Sunday when she dropped a 23-foot birdie putt and opened the two-stroke victory margin on the last seven holes.

Tokai Classic—¥60,000,000
Winner: Fumiko Muraguchi

She had to contend with three of the year's most successful players and Japan's premier international player, but Fumiko Muraguchi, who hadn't won in four years, was equal to the task in the final round of the Tokai Classic at Ryosen Golf Club and packed away the victory in stylish fashion.

Muraguchi crafted a bogey-free 67 for a six-under-par 210 total and a one-stroke triumph, her first since she won twice in her rookie 1991 season.

Muraguchi had gone into the last round with 71-72–143 and had cause for despair, since the leader at 139 was Ayako Okamoto, the brilliant veteran with sterling world credentials, with the likes of Ikuyo Shiotani, Akiko Fukushima and Kaori Higo close by. As it turned out, Okamoto flopped to a stunning 75, and Fukushima provided the greatest challenge, shooting 70 for 211 and another of quite a few near-misses she had accumulated along with two victories during the season. Shiotani and Higo, the first-round co-leader with Jae-Sook Won, tied for third at 213.

Takara World Invitational—¥80,000,000
Winner: Michelle McGann

The Takara World Invitational, carrying the largest purse of the regular Japan LPGA season, attracted a strong international field to Chiba's Caledonian Golf Club and one of the most prominent visitors — America's Michelle McGann — carried away the title. McGann, one of the leading players on the U.S. LPGA Tour, took charge of the tournament with a third-round 69 and breezed to a four-stroke victory with her 72 and five-under-par 283 total.

Two other noted members of the international cast asserted their talents early. Sweden's Annika Sorenstam opened with 68, one stroke in front of Mayumi Hirase and Mitsuyo Hirata, then yielded first place to fellow Swede Liselotte Neumann, who was making her second visit of the year to Japan. Neumann shot 68 for 140 and a one-stroke advantage over Keiko Arai. McGann was two back after a pair of 71s and took it from there. Hirase, fighting for the JLPGA money title, got a big boost when she finished with 71 and took second place.

Fujitsu Ladies—¥60,000,000
Winner: Hiromi Kobayashi

Hiromi Kobayashi surely was happy to be home. She had enjoyed considerable success on the U.S. LPGA Tour in the past but had a mediocre season in 1995, and Kobayashi returned to Japan to play in the Fujitsu Ladies tournament two weeks before the LPGA's season-ending, two-tournament foray to the country. Good decision. She won it — posting a 12-under-par 204, as Akiko Fukushima again let a victory get away from her, finishing as runner-up for the second time in three weeks.

Fukushima began the tournament with a six-under-par 66, taking a one-stroke lead over Taiwan's Wu Ming-Yeh and three over five others, including Kobayashi. After 36 holes, it was Fukushima still on top after a 69 for 135, but Kobayashi closed to within one stroke with a 67, as did Nayoko Yoshikawa. Kobayashi's 68 Sunday forged a two-shot victory as Fukushima shot 71.

Kibun Classic—¥50,000,000
Winner: Hiromi Kobayashi

The regulars on the Japan LPGA Tour could be pardoned for wishing that Hiromi Kobayashi had stayed in America a couple of weeks longer. Bad enough the 32-year-old Kobayashi had picked off the Fujitsu title the first week home. Worse, she shut them out again the next week in the Kibun Classic at Musashi Matsuyama Country Club in Saitama, coming from four strokes off the pace with a course-record 65 in the final round.

Kobayashi started with 75 and was four strokes off the lead after Friday's round. Fuki Kido, the Katokichi Queens winner in July who was one of six 71 shooters Friday, moved one stroke in front with a 69 Saturday. At that point, Kobayashi trailed her by four strokes. Then came the seven-birdie 65, one stroke better than the previous best at Musashi Matsuyama. She won going away, her seven-under 209 three strokes better than the runner-up 212s of Kido, Kayo Yamada and Chen Li-Ying.

Nichirei International—$620,000
Winner: United States

In most years, it's been a given that the United States LPGA team will come to Japan for the Nichirei International and with little fanfare or difficulty walk away with the victory. The Japanese women had won only twice since 1979. It wasn't so easy for the U.S. women this year. In fact, it was downright scary. They had to wipe out a seven-point deficit on the last day, a comeback that brought a 19-17 victory, stunning the Japanese side.

The Japanese led 12½-5½ after the first two rounds, both best-ball matches, and needed only to win six of the 18 singles matches to score a startling upset. It didn't happen. Led by Meg Mallon and Helen Alfredsson, the LPGA team won 12½ of 14 points during one stretch of play, relying on eight sub-70 rounds (all victories) for their 11th straight Nichirei International victory.

"In the near future we'd better be really prepared if we're going to defend our title," said LPGA captain Val Skinner. "The JLPGA came to play. I hope they realize we were red hot and it easily could have gone the other way."

Mallon's 65 was by far the best on Sunday and it keyed the decisive stretch, for the Americans still trailed 16-12 when she finished birdie-birdie to begin a run of seven straight U.S. points.

Toray Japan Queens Cup—$700,000
Winner: Woo-Soon Ko

Never has a tie for 23rd place been so satisfying to Annika Sorenstam, whose performance in the Toray Japan Queens Cup was more than enough to move her into fast company. Her finish assured Sorenstam of winning the LPGA triple crown — Player of the Year, Vare Trophy and money-winning title — joining Betsy King, Dottie Mochrie, Pat Bradley and Beth Daniel as triple winners of the 1990s.

Sorenstam locked up the Vare Trophy for lowest scoring average by shooting even par over three rounds at Seta Golf Club in Ohtsu. That was nine strokes behind winner Woo-Soon Ko, who successfully defended her Toray title. On a leaderboard dominated by Japanese, Sorenstam's score mattered only because Mochrie, who trailed Sorenstam by .02 in the Vare Trophy standings entering the tournament, missed the cut. Sorenstam's final average was 71.00, just .13 ahead of Mochrie.

Having already won the money titles in Europe and the U.S., Sorenstam also confirmed her Player of the Year status over runner-up Laura Davies, who failed to break par and tied for 47th place. Sorenstam finished the season with $666,533 in LPGA Tour earnings and enough hardware to fill a trophy case.

"I thought about the Player of the Year even before I got here," Sorenstam said. "Once I got here, it was on my mind on every putt, every shot. I was watching what the others were doing and didn't play aggressively. It's hard to believe all this happened in one year."

Itoen Ladies—¥60,000,000
Winner: Laura Davies

As all outstanding players seem to be able to do, Laura Davies rose to the occasion at the Itoen Ladies tournament. Never a factor in the previous week's Toray Queens event that wrapped up the official U.S. LPGA Tour, Davies remained in Japan to defend her title in the Itoen at the Great Island Club at Chonanmachi and turned her game around in the limelight. She strung together three solid rounds and walked away with a two-stroke victory, her seventh of the year worldwide.

Davies' opening 71 was just one stroke off the lead held by Korea's Woo-Soon Ko. The British star followed with 70 and, at 141, led Ko and Tatsuko Morimoto by two. She repeated the 70 Sunday for her five-under-par 211 and the two-shot margin over Ko and Mayumi Hirase, who shot 69 and strengthened her hold on the No. 1 spot on the JLPGA money chart. Hirase had a good shot at her fourth 1995 win. She caught Davies with a birdie/bogey swing at the 11th hole, but she bogeyed the last two holes. The win was Davies' third in Japan.

Daio Seishi Elleair Ladies Open—¥60,000,000
Winner: Michiko Okada

The Japan LPGA Tour gave way to a well-respected senior citizen, an unexpected development that took the circuit's attention away from its closely contested battle for the top spot on the year's official money list. Michiko Okada, less than two months away from her 51st birthday, put together two strong rounds that brought her the title in the Daio Seishi Elleair Ladies Open. With the win, the 10th of her long career, Okada replaced herself as the oldest winner ever on the Japan LPGA Tour. She had set the record when she won the Kosaido Asahi in 1992 when she was 47.

Woo-Soon Ko, co-runner-up five days earlier in the Itoen tournament, launched another victory bid in the Elleair Open with 66, taking a two-stroke lead over Huang Bie-Shyun, Akio Takasu, Ok-Hee Ku and Mayumi Murai. Six shots back after the first round, Okada rose into a six-way tie for the lead Saturday with 67, sharing that position at 139 with Huang, Ku, Ko, Natsuko Noro and Chikako Matsuzawa. It was tight to the end. Okada holed a 16-foot birdie putt on the final green for 69–208 and a two-stroke victory over five others — Ko, Noro, Matsuzawa, Man-Soo Kim and Hiromi Kobayashi, shooting for a third straight victory.

Meiji Nyugyo Cup—¥50,000,000
Winner: Ikuyo Shiotani

Ikuyo Shiotani arose from the "dead" to capture the Meiji Nyugyo Cup title and, more importantly, to claim the No. 1 position on the 1995 money-winning standings as the season came to a close at Aoshima Golf Club at Miyazaki in southern Japan. It was a remarkable performance by the 32-year-old veteran, who had begun the tournament in fourth place on the money list and had to win to have a chance at No. 1, which she was in 1992.

To everybody except Shiotani, that chance became remote when she struggled to a 78 in the wind-swept first round at Aoshima. However, the leaders — Akiko Fukushima, Jennifer Sevil and Mitsuyo Hirata — had 74s, so a re-bounding 67 Saturday pulled Shiotani up into second place, three behind Hirata, who ironically had won the final tournament of the 1994 season. Shiotani completed her remarkable rally Sunday, forcing a playoff with her 70 to Hirata's 73 for one-under-par 215s. Then, they went three extra holes before Shiotani's par won the tournament — her fifth of the season and 14th of her career.

The ¥9 million check gave her ¥75 million for the year, ¥1.29 million more than runner-up Mayumi Hirase, the 1993 and 1994 money leader who was in front starting the week but could get nothing going in the Meiji Nyugyo Cup and tied for 16th.

APPENDIXES

The Sony Ranking
(As of December 31, 1995)

Pos.		Player	Circuit	Points Average	Total Points	No. of Events	92/94 Total	92/94 Minus	1995 Plus
1	(2)	Greg Norman	ANZ 1	21.97	1494	68	1399	-765	860
2	(1)	Nick Price	Afr 1	16.26	1203	74	1716	-949	436
3	(4)	Bernhard Langer	Eur 1	15.68	1176	75	1164	-648	660
4	(6)	Ernie Els	Afr 2	13.98	1328	95	1382	-734	680
5	(8)	Colin Montgomerie	Eur 2	13.86	1289	93	1182	-653	760
6	(10)	Corey Pavin	USA 1	13.58	1073	79	891	-506	688
7	(3)	Nick Faldo	Eur 3	13.16	921	70	1236	-767	452
8	(7)	Fred Couples	USA 2	12.02	781	65	939	-578	420
9	(9)	Masashi Ozaki	Jpn 1	10.82	790	73	797	-459	452
10	(43)	Steve Elkington	ANZ 2	10.48	765	73	399	-258	624
11	(17)	Tom Lehman	USA 3	9.62	808	84	756	-412	464
12	(5)	Jose Maria Olazabal	Eur 4	9.26	667	72	1199	-664	132
13	(20)	Loren Roberts	USA 4	8.55	650	76	597	-315	368
14	(15)	Vijay Singh	Asa 1	8.41	933	111	925	-508	516
15	(38)	Sam Torrance	Eur 5	8.28	762	92	455	-237	544
16	(32)	Lee Janzen	USA 5	8.25	759	92	545	-314	528
17	(25)	Davis Love III	USA 6	7.67	644	84	568	-372	448
18	(123)	Peter Jacobsen	USA 7	7.53	542	72	167	-89	464
19	(34)	Ben Crenshaw	USA 8	7.23	557	77	430	-241	368
20	(30)	Scott Hoch	USA 9	7.18	632	88	455	-231	408
21	(63)	Costantino Rocca	Eur 6	7.02	632	90	370	-206	468
22	(22)	Phil Mickelson	USA 10	6.89	517	75	492	-255	280
23	(19)	Mark McCumber	USA 11	6.79	421	62	507	-262	176
24	(11)	David Frost	Afr 3	6.66	633	95	968	-547	212
25	(47)	Jay Haas	USA 12	6.47	550	85	434	-256	372
26	(65)	Jim Gallagher, Jr.	USA 13	6.36	528	83	346	-210	392
27	(14)	Seve Ballesteros	Eur 7	6.36	458	72	681	-371	148
28	(209)	Michael Campbell	ANZ 3	6.28	452	72	83	-43	412
29	(54)	Payne Stewart	USA 14	6.09	499	82	376	-213	336
30	(49)	Mark Calcavecchia	USA 15	6.08	596	98	487	-271	380
31	(26)	Brad Faxon	USA 16	6.00	534	89	585	-339	288
32	(12)	Fuzzy Zoeller	USA 17	5.97	370	62	603	-309	76
33	(23)	Tom Watson	USA 18	5.95	357	60	409	-232	180
34	(27)	Jeff Maggert	USA 19	5.82	489	84	552	-303	240
35	(166)	Billy Mayfair	USA 20	5.80	539	93	166	-91	464
36	(18)	Mark McNulty	Afr 4	5.79	405	70	561	-308	152
37	(31)	Frank Nobilo	ANZ 4	5.61	471	84	471	-260	260
38	(57)	Scott Simpson	USA 21	5.54	438	79	335	-177	280
39	(437T)	David Duval	USA 22	5.49	379	69	26	-15	368
40	(39)	Jesper Parnevik	Eur 8	5.46	431	79	387	-200	244
41	(16)	Ian Woosnam	Eur 9	5.31	398	75	660	-382	120
42	(36)	Bill Glasson	USA 23	5.30	350	66	350	-188	188
43	(44)	Craig Parry	ANZ 5	5.25	509	97	473	-280	316
44	(83T)	Mark O'Meara	USA 24	5.15	443	86	268	-197	372
45	(72)	John Daly	USA 25	5.00	400	80	286	-166	280
46	(59)	Craig Stadler	USA 26	4.83	362	75	350	-200	212
47	(53)	Peter Senior	ANZ 6	4.81	462	96	437	-271	296
48	(101)	Kenny Perry	USA 27	4.79	402	84	225	-123	300

( ) : Figures in brackets indicate 1992/94 positions.

Pos.		Player	Circuit	Points Average	Total Points	No. of Events	92/94 Total	92/94 Minus	1995 Plus
49	(37)	Bob Estes	USA 28	4.77	396	83	466	-242	172
50	(42)	Miguel Angel Jimenez	Eur 10	4.70	418	89	478	-264	204
51	(55)	Mark James	Eur 11	4.63	338	73	313	-175	200
52	(35)	Barry Lane	Eur 12	4.51	437	97	553	-320	204
53	(33)	David Gilford	Eur 13	4.50	369	82	464	-259	164
54	(13)	Tom Kite	USA 29	4.46	330	74	677	-411	64
55	(28)	Larry Mize	USA 30	4.45	343	77	491	-268	120
56	(29)	Hale Irwin	USA 31	4.38	285	65	399	-206	92
57	(308T)	Bob Tway	USA 32	4.31	345	80	60	-31	316
58	(61)	Brian Watts	USA 33	4.24	335	79	318	-159	176
59	(351T)	Justin Leonard	USA 34	4.22	304	72	40	-20	284
60	(99)	Kirk Triplett	USA 35	4.19	352	84	232	-124	244
61	(21)	Paul Azinger	USA 36	4.17	288	69	522	-322	88
62	(71)	Anders Forsbrand	Eur 14	4.11	325	79	347	-226	204
63	(41)	Bruce Lietzke	USA 37	4.08	245	60	313	-196	128
64	(48)	Robert Allenby	ANZ 7	4.02	382	95	459	-257	180
65	(106)	D.A. Weibring	USA 38	3.90	261	67	176	-103	188
66	(–)	Woody Austin	USA 39	3.89	292	75	0	0	292
67	(58)	Curtis Strange	USA 40	3.79	292	77	316	-168	144
68	(68)	Per-Ulrik Johansson	Eur 15	3.78	287	76	308	-177	156
69	(78)	Duffy Waldorf	USA 41	3.76	323	86	293	-194	224
70	(110)	Fred Funk	USA 42	3.74	367	98	250	-147	264
71	(75)	Howard Clark	Eur 16	3.72	249	67	227	-118	140
72	(40)	John Huston	USA 43	3.70	322	87	475	-269	116
73	(90)	Jeff Sluman	USA 44	3.70	344	93	293	-209	260
74	(226)	Brandt Jobe	USA 45	3.70	244	66	74	-38	208
75	(133)	Steve Stricker	USA 46	3.67	257	70	138	-69	188
76	(98)	Brad Bryant	USA 47	3.65	347	95	271	-148	224
77	(45)	David Edwards	USA 48	3.65	252	69	380	-220	92
78	(46)	Tsuneyuki Nakajima	Jpn 2	3.64	313	86	430	-241	124
79	(69)	Steve Lowery	USA 49	3.63	345	95	323	-162	184
80	(258)	Satoshi Higashi	Jpn 3	3.59	316	88	81	-45	280
81	(261)	Jim Furyk	USA 50	3.53	300	85	72	-36	264
82	(119)	Hal Sutton	USA 51	3.52	310	88	199	-101	212
83	(67)	Brett Ogle	ANZ 8	3.51	263	75	299	-176	140
84	(184)	Shigeki Maruyama	Jpn 4	3.47	267	77	110	-55	212
85	(367)	Alexander Cejka	Eur 17	3.42	243	71	39	-20	224
86	(74)	Darren Clarke	Eur 18	3.40	296	87	303	-167	160
87	(66)	Gil Morgan	USA 52	3.31	222	67	277	-155	100
88	(190)	Wayne Riley	ANZ 9	3.25	289	89	143	-78	224
89	(148)	Peter O'Malley	ANZ 10	3.21	286	89	170	-116	232
90	(52)	Eduardo Romero	SAm 1	3.16	231	73	350	-203	84
91	(70)	Naomichi Ozaki	Jpn 5	3.05	302	99	375	-225	152
92	(87)	Greg Turner	ANZ 11	3.01	235	78	240	-125	120
93	(56)	Joakim Haeggman	Eur 19	3.01	241	80	349	-184	76
94	(80)	Todd Hamilton	USA 53	2.96	275	93	308	-177	144
95	(95)	Lennie Clements	USA 54	2.95	230	78	204	-102	128
96	(107)	Jose Rivero	Eur 20	2.89	202	70	194	-128	136
97	(50)	Rick Fehr	USA 55	2.77	205	74	366	-209	48
98	(24)	John Cook	USA 56	2.76	221	80	500	-339	60
99	(134)	Katsuyoshi Tomori	Jpn 6	2.76	248	90	167	-87	168
100	(88)	Robert Gamez	USA 57	2.72	234	86	245	-135	124
101	(82)	Peter Baker	Eur 21	2.72	242	89	290	-156	108
102	(122)	Frankie Minoza	Asa 2	2.71	195	72	168	-93	120
103	(131)	Jim McGovern	USA 58	2.70	275	102	222	-119	172
104	(105)	Jay Don Blake	USA 59	2.67	211	79	205	-122	128

( ) : Figures in brackets indicate 1992/94 positions.

Pos.		Player	Circuit	Points Average	Total Points	No. of Events	92/94 Total	92/94 Minus	1995 Plus
105	(51)	Mark Roe	Eur 22	2.67	208	78	393	-221	36
106	(113)	Mark Brooks	USA 60	2.64	277	105	273	-176	180
107	(150T)	Mike Heinen	USA 61	2.62	212	81	128	-64	148
108	(73)	Wayne Westner	Afr 5	2.60	208	80	307	-175	76
109	(86)	Nolan Henke	USA 62	2.60	213	82	264	-155	104
110	(116)	Masahiro Kuramoto	Jpn 7	2.57	242	94	208	-138	172
111	(260)	John Morse	USA 63	2.54	188	74	67	-43	164
112	(–)	Hidemichi Tanaka	Jpn 8	2.53	152	60	0	0	152
113	(79)	Andrew Magee	USA 64	2.51	216	86	297	-173	92
114	(206)	Philip Walton	Eur 23	2.49	207	83	116	-69	160
115	(141)	Hisayuki Sasaki	Jpn 9	2.46	187	76	129	-66	124
116	(128)	Carlos Franco	SAm 2	2.41	154	64	140	-70	84
117	(60)	Gordon Brand, Jr.	Eur 24	2.40	199	83	370	-211	40
118	(64)	Tony Johnstone	Afr 6	2.35	207	88	372	-237	72
119	(275)	Scott Verplank	USA 65	2.28	148	65	56	-28	120
120	(112)	Mike Clayton	ANZ 12	2.27	232	102	256	-140	116
121	(197T)	Andrew Oldcorn	Eur 25	2.27	145	64	90	-45	100
122	(91)	Billy Andrade	USA 66	2.26	210	93	274	-160	96
123	(100)	Retief Goosen	Afr 7	2.24	217	97	235	-126	108
124	(145T)	Nobuo Serizawa	Jpn 10	2.22	198	89	175	-93	116
125	(62)	Chip Beck	USA 67	2.22	195	88	364	-225	56
126	(138)	Paul Broadhurst	Eur 26	2.18	179	82	159	-96	116
127	(109)	Blaine McCallister	USA 68	2.18	183	84	220	-125	88
128	(93)	Sandy Lyle	Eur 27	2.17	169	78	239	-166	96
129	(162)	Bob Lohr	USA 69	2.15	183	85	150	-79	112
130	(177)	Hideki Kase	Jpn 11	2.14	171	80	127	-68	112
131	(143)	Andrew Coltart	Eur 28	2.13	175	82	142	-71	104
132	(291)	Tomohiro Maruyama	Jpn 12	2.10	166	79	72	-38	132
133	(243T)	Roger Wessels	Afr 8	2.08	137	66	67	-38	108
134	(173)	Masayuki Kawamura	Jpn 13	2.05	158	77	126	-64	96
135	(117T)	Robert Karlsson	Eur 29	2.04	159	78	177	-110	92
136	(155)	Jose Coceres	SAm 3	2.03	150	74	130	-68	88
137	(83T)	Carl Mason	Eur 30	2.02	166	82	268	-142	40
138	(94)	Roger Mackay	ANZ 13	2.02	121	60	190	-109	40
139	(127)	Joey Sindelar	USA 70	2.01	137	68	168	-111	80
140	(85)	Dan Forsman	USA 71	2.01	147	73	252	-169	64
141	(145T)	Gene Sauers	USA 72	2.01	155	77	150	-107	112
142	(92)	Ronan Rafferty	Eur 31	2.00	176	88	277	-181	80
143	(255)	Toru Suzuki	Jpn 14	1.99	145	73	67	-34	112
144	(125)	Patrick Burke	USA 73	1.98	129	65	152	-79	56
145	(223)	Kazuhiro Takami	Jpn 15	1.97	158	80	97	-55	116
146	(234)	Rick Gibson	Can 1	1.97	150	76	91	-53	112
147	(568T)	Toshimitsu Izawa	Jpn 16	1.97	118	60	12	-6	112
148	(108)	Peter Mitchell	Eur 32	1.96	190	97	258	-148	80
149	(132)	Terry Price	ANZ 14	1.94	149	77	155	-86	80
150	(104)	Tsukasa Watanabe	Jpn 17	1.92	203	106	283	-156	76
151	(152)	Sven Struver	Eur 33	1.91	153	80	137	-72	88
152	(96)	David Ishii	USA 74	1.85	157	85	253	-140	44
153	(185)	Lucas Parsons	ANZ 15	1.83	110	60	95	-53	68
154	(–)	Jarmo Sandelin	Eur 34	1.83	128	70	0	0	128
155	(161)	Paul McGinley	Eur 35	1.81	150	83	147	-77	80
156	(181T)	Eduardo Herrera	SAm 4	1.80	119	66	96	-49	72
157	(136)	Pierre Fulke	Eur 36	1.79	129	72	146	-73	56
158	(231T)	Guy Boros	USA 75	1.79	152	85	84	-48	116
159	(208)	Grant Waite	ANZ 16	1.78	166	93	115	-69	120
160	(77)	Mike Springer	USA 76	1.78	153	86	302	-157	8

( ) : Figures in brackets indicate 1992/94 positions.

Pos.		Player	Circuit	Points Average	Total Points	No. of Events	92/94 Total	92/94 Minus	1995 Plus
161	(111)	Yoshinori Mizumaki	Jpn 18	1.78	185	104	260	-139	64
162	(199)	Paul Eales	Eur 37	1.78	151	85	118	-59	92
163	(218T)	Don Pooley	USA 77	1.74	108	62	78	-46	76
164	(280)	Ignacio Garrido	Eur 38	1.74	120	69	56	-28	92
165	(–)	Kazuhiro Hosokawa	Jpn 19	1.73	104	60	0	0	104
166	(191)	Mike Hulbert	USA 78	1.72	165	96	149	-96	112
167	(102)	Rocco Mediate	USA 79	1.71	111	65	192	-117	36
168	(236)	Ted Tryba	USA 80	1.69	174	103	100	-50	124
169	(153)	Hajime Meshiai	Jpn 20	1.67	142	85	165	-87	64
170	(115)	Wayne Grady	ANZ 17	1.66	136	82	222	-134	48
171	(103)	Donnie Hammond	USA 81	1.65	127	77	197	-114	44
172	(163)	Russell Claydon	Eur 39	1.62	141	87	156	-87	72
173	(325)	Kiyoshi Maita	Jpn 21	1.62	105	65	56	-31	80
174	(139)	Katsunari Takahashi	Jpn 22	1.60	146	91	186	-100	60
175	(130)	Russ Cochran	USA 82	1.60	134	84	192	-118	60
176	(434T)	Mathias Gronberg	Eur 40	1.57	118	75	28	-14	104
177	(97)	Fulton Allem	Afr 9	1.57	130	83	250	-136	16
178	(89)	David Feherty	Eur 41	1.55	136	88	263	-155	28
179	(214)	Santiago Luna	Eur 42	1.54	125	81	111	-70	84
180	(466T)	Jean Louis Guepy	Eur 43	1.54	108	70	24	-12	96
181	(81)	Rodger Davis	ANZ 18	1.54	114	74	272	-166	8
182	(126)	Glen Day	USA 83	1.54	137	89	177	-104	64
183	(306)	Robin Freeman	USA 84	1.54	140	91	74	-42	108
184	(178)	Peter Hedblom	Eur 44	1.52	108	71	104	-52	56
185	(203)	Jay Delsing	USA 85	1.49	130	87	125	-79	84
186	(–)	Michael Jonzon	Eur 45	1.48	92	62	0	0	92
187	(–)	Steve Jones	USA 86	1.48	96	65	0	0	96
188	(267T)	Ryoken Kawagishi	Jpn 23	1.47	115	78	80	-45	80
189	(211)	Mark Wiebe	USA 87	1.46	101	69	98	-57	60
190	(227)	Dillard Pruitt	USA 88	1.46	117	80	105	-64	76
191	(373)	Marco Dawson	USA 89	1.46	127	87	54	-31	104
192	(165)	Stephen Ames	SAm 5	1.46	102	70	116	-58	44
193	(76)	Raymond Floyd	USA 90	1.45	87	60	209	-158	36
194	(160)	Mike Standly	USA 91	1.44	134	93	163	-93	64
195	(253)	Nobumitsu Yuhara	Jpn 24	1.43	107	75	86	-63	84
196	(180)	Paul Moloney	ANZ 19	1.42	111	78	109	-58	60
197	(120)	Steven Richardson	Eur 46	1.42	138	97	246	-152	44
198	(147)	Gary Orr	Eur 47	1.41	130	92	157	-79	52
199	(270)	John Adams	USA 92	1.40	123	88	91	-52	84
200	(210)	Mike Sullivan	USA 93	1.40	102	73	101	-55	56

( ) : Figures in brackets indicate 1992/94 positions.

World's Winners of 1995

U.S. PGA TOUR

Mercedes Championship	Steve Elkington
United Airlines Hawaiian Open	John Morse
Northern Telecom Open	Phil Mickelson
Phoenix Open	Vijay Singh
AT&T Pebble Beach National Pro-Am	Peter Jacobsen
Buick Invitational of California	Peter Jacobsen (2)
Bob Hope Chrysler Classic	Kenny Perry
Nissan Open	Corey Pavin
Doral-Ryder Open	Nick Faldo
Honda Classic	Mark O'Meara
The Nestle Invitational	Loren Roberts
The Players Championship	Lee Janzen
Freeport-McMoRan Classic	Davis Love III
Masters Tournament	Ben Crenshaw
MCI Classic	Bob Tway
Kmart Greater Greensboro Open	Jim Gallagher, Jr.
Shell Houston Open	Payne Stewart
BellSouth Classic	Mark Calcavecchia
GTE Byron Nelson Classic	Ernie Els (3)
Buick Classic	Vijay Singh (2)
Colonial National Invitational	Tom Lehman
Memorial Tournament	Greg Norman
Kemper Open	Lee Janzen (2)
U.S. Open Championship	Corey Pavin (2)
Canon Greater Hartford Open	Greg Norman (2)
FedEx St. Jude Classic	Jim Gallagher, Jr. (2)
Motorola Western Open	Billy Mayfair
Anheuser-Busch Golf Classic	Ted Tryba
Deposit Guaranty Golf Classic	Ed Dougherty
Ideon Classic at Pleasant Valley	Fred Funk
Buick Open	Woody Austin
PGA Championship	Steve Elkington (2)
Sprint International	Lee Janzen (3)
NEC World Series of Golf	Greg Norman (4)
Greater Milwaukee Open	Scott Hoch (3)
Bell Canadian Open	Mark O'Meara (2)
B.C. Open	Hal Sutton
Ryder Cup	Europe
Quad City Classic	D.A. Weibring
Buick Challenge	Fred Funk (2)
Walt Disney World/Oldsmobile Classic	Brad Bryant
Las Vegas Invitational	Jim Furyk
La Cantera Texas Open	Duffy Waldorf
Tour Championship	Billy Mayfair (2)

SPECIAL EVENTS

Westinghouse-Family House Invitational	Ernie Els (4)
Ernst Championship	John Cook
Jerry Ford Invitational	Doug Tewell
Fred Meyer Challenge	Greg Norman (3)/Brad Faxon
West Coast Classic	Scott Hoch (2)
Gene Sarazen World Open	Frank Nobilo (2)
Lincoln-Mercury Kapalua International	Jim Furyk (2)

MasterCard PGA Grand Slam of Golf	Ben Crenshaw (2)
Mexican Open	John Cook (2)
Pebble Beach Invitational	Ronnie Black
Franklin Templeton Shark Shootout	Mark Calcavecchia (2)/
	Steve Elkington (3)
Paradise Island Invitational	Jim McGovern
Office Depot Father/Son Challenge	Raymond Floyd (5)/
	Raymond Floyd, Jr.
Diners Club Matches	Tom Lehman (2)/Duffy
	Waldorf (2)
Lexus Challenge	Raymond Floyd (6)/
	Michael Chiklis
Andersen Consulting World Championship	Barry Lane

NIKE TOUR

San Jose Open	John Maginnes
Inland Empire Open	Jeff Brehaut
Monterrey Open	Stuart Appleby
Louisiana Open	Stan Utley
Pensacola Classic	Clarence Rose
Mississippi Gulf Coast Classic	Allen Doyle
Tallahassee Open	Bill Murchison
Shreveport Open	Brad Fabel
Alabama Classic	Jerry Kelly
South Carolina Classic	Jerry Foltz
Central Georgia Open	Matt Peterson
Knoxville Open	Thomas Scherrer
Greater Greenville Classic	David Toms
Dominion Open	Hugh Royer III
Miami Valley Open	Stan Utley (2)
Cleveland Open	Karl Zoller
Carolina Classic	Michael Christie
Philadelphia Classic	Sean Murphy
Buffalo Open	Jerry Kelly (2)
Gateway Classic	Chris Smith
Wichita Open	David Toms (2)
Dakota Dunes Open	Chris Smith (2)
Ozarks Open	Mike Schuchart
Permian Basin Open	Hugh Royer III (2)
Texarkana Open	Allen Doyle (2)
Utah Classic	Glen Hnatiuk
Tri-Cities Open	Jeff Gove
Boise Open	Frank Lickliter
Sonoma County Open	Stuart Appleby (2)
Nike Tour Championship	Allen Doyle (3)

CANADIAN TOUR

Payless Open	Norm Jarvis
B.C. TEL Pacific Open	Nick Goetze
Morningstar Classic	Jeff Bloom
Henry Singer Alberta Open	Ian Hutchings
Klondike Days Klassic	Ray Freeman
Xerox Manitoba Open	Trevor Dodds
Infiniti Championship	Guy Hill
Canadian Masters	Scott Dunlap
Export "A" Inc. Ontario Open	Ray Freeman (2)
Trafalgar CPGA Championship	Trevor Dodds (2)
Montclair PEI Classic	Jim Rutledge (2)

SOUTH AMERICAN TOUR

Farallones Open	Pedro Martinez
San Andres Open	Ron Wuensche (2)
Filanbanco Ecuador Open	Fabian Montovia
Los Inkas-Peru Open	Raul Fretes (2)
Paraguay Open	Angel Cabrera
Litoral Open	Angel Cabrera (2)
Uruguay Open	Ricardo Gonzalez
Prince of Wales Open	Guillermo Encina
Los Leones Open	Ian Hutchings (2)
Argentina Open	Mark Calcavecchia (3)

PGA EUROPEAN TOUR

Dubai Desert Classic	Fred Couples
Johnnie Walker Classic	Fred Couples (2)
Madeira Island Open	Santiago Luna
Turespana Open de Canarias	Jarmo Sandelin
Turespana Open de Mediterrania	Robert Karlsson
Turespana Open de Andalucia	Alexander Cejka
Moroccan Open	Mark James
Portuguese Open	Adam Hunter
Turespana Open de Baleares	Greg Turner
Turespana Open de Catalonia	Philip Walton
Air France Cannes Open	Andre Bossert
Tournoi Perrier de Paris	Seve Ballesteros/ Jose Maria Olazabal
Conte de Florence Italian Open	Sam Torrance
Benson & Hedges International Open	Peter O'Malley
Peugeot Open de Espana	Seve Ballesteros (2)
Volvo PGA Championship	Bernhard Langer
Murphy's English Open	Philip Walton (2)
Deutsche Bank Open	Bernhard Langer (2)
DHL Jersey Open	Andrew Oldcorn
Peugeot Open de France	Paul Broadhurst
BMW International Open	Frank Nobilo
Murphy's Irish Open	Sam Torrance (2)
Scottish Open	Wayne Riley
British Open Championship	John Daly
Heineken Dutch Open	Scott Hoch
Volvo Scandinavian Masters	Jesper Parnevik
Hohe Brucke Austrian Open	Alexander Cejka (2)
Chemapol Trophy Czech Open	Peter Teravainen
Volvo German Open	Colin Montgomerie
Canon European Masters	Mathias Gronberg
Trophee Lancome	Colin Montgomerie (2)
Collingtree British Masters	Sam Torrance (3)
Smurfit European Open	Bernhard Langer (3)
Mercedes German Masters	Anders Forsbrand
Toyota World Match Play	Ernie Els (5)
Alfred Dunhill Cup	Scotland
Volvo Masters	Alexander Cejka (3)
Johnnie Walker World Championship	Fred Couples (3)

CHALLENGE TOUR

Kenya Open	James Lee
Canarias Challenge Tour	Pedro Linhart
KB Golf Challenge	Eric Giraud
Compaq Open	Dennis Edlund
Siab Open	Anssi Kankkonen
Challenge Chargeurs	Rolf Muntz
Club Med Open	Emanuele Bolognesi

Himmerland Open	Thomas Bjorn
Cepsa APG	Fernando Roca
Italian Native Open	Emanuele Bolognesi (2)
Championnat de France Pro	Eric Giraud (2)
Nedcar National Open	Rolf Muntz (2)
Team Erhverv Danish Open	Rob Edwards
Memorial Olivier Barras	Simon Hurley
Neuchatel Open SBS Trophy	Nicolas Vanhootegem
Open Divonne	Patrik Sjoland
Volvo Finnish Open	Fredrik Plahn
Open des Volcans	Thomas Gogele
Interlaken Open	Thomas Bjorn (2)
Karsten Ping Norwegian Open	Stephen Field
UPS German PGA Championship	John O'Flynn
Audi Quattro Trophy	Joost Steenkamer
Rolex Pro-Am	Carl Suneson
Esbjerg Danish Closed	Thomas Bjorn (3)
Finnish PGA Championship	Mikael Piltz
Steelcover Dutch Challenge Open	Warren Bennett
Toyota Danish PGA	Francois Lamare
Coca-Cola Open	Thomas Bjorn (4)
Tessali Open	Andrew Collison
Perrier European Pro-Am	Diego Borrego
Open de Dijon Bourgogne	Tim Planchin
Kentab Open	Per Nyman (2)
Eulen Open Galea	Ben Tinning
Lomas Bosque Challenge	Per Nyman
Swiss PGA Championship	Steve Rey
Tunisian Open Challenge	Ricky Willison
UAP Grand Finale	Francisco Valera

ASIA TOUR

Thai International Bodharamik Thailand Open	Todd Hamilton
Sabah Masters	Brandt Jobe
Dole Philippine Open	Carlos Espinosa
Classic Indian Open	Jim Rutledge
Benson & Hedges Malaysian Open	Clay Devers
Sampoerna Indonesia Open	Jose Cantero
Sempati Bali Open	Brandt Jobe (2)
Rolex Masters	Ron Wuensche
Chin Fong Republic of China Open	Daniel Chopra
Maekyung Bando Fashion Korean Open	Brandt Jobe (3)
Volvo China Open	Raul Fretes
Volvo Asian Masters	Corey Pavin (3)
World Cup of Golf	United States/Davis Love III (2)
Hong Kong Open	Gary Webb
Tugu Pratama Indonesia PGA Championship	John Senden

CHINA TOUR

Volvo Open	Zhang Lian-Wei
Honichi Open	Tony Maloney
Hugo Boss Open	Rafael Ponce
Coca-Cola Open	Simon Yates

JAPAN TOUR

Token Corporation Cup	Todd Hamilton (2)
Daido Drinko Shizuoka Open	Brian Watts
Novell KSB Open	Rick Gibson
Descente Classic	Satoshi Higashi
Tsuruya Open	Satoshi Higashi (2)
Dunlop Open	Peter Senior (2)

Chunichi Crowns	Masashi Ozaki
Fuji Sankei Classic	Tsuneyuki Nakajima
Japan PGA Championship	Hisayuki Sasaki
Pepsi Ube Tournament	Mitsutaka Kusakabe
Mitsubishi Galant Tournament	Brandt Jobe (4)
JCB Classic Sendai	Ryoken Kawagishi
Sapporo Tokyu Open	Carlos Franco
Pocari Sweat Yomiuri Open	Eduardo Herrera
Mizuno Open	Brian Watts (2)
PGA Philanthropy Tournament	Kazuhiro Takami
Yonex Open Hiroshima	Masashi Ozaki (2)
Nikkei Cup	Tetsu Nisikawa
NST Niigata Open	Tomohiro Maruyama
Sanko Grand Summer Championship	Frankie Minoza
Acom International	Katsunori Kuwahara
Hisamitsu KBC Augusta Tournament	Kazuhiko Hosokawa
Japan Match Play Championship	Katsuyoshi Tomori
Suntory Open	Masahiro Kuramoto
ANA Open	Masashi Ozaki (3)
Gene Sarazen Jun Classic	Satoshi Higashi (3)
Japan Open Championship	Toshimitsu Izawa
Tokai Classic	Masayuki Kawamura
Golf Digest Tournament	Stewart Ginn
Bridgestone Open	Shigeki Maruyama
Philip Morris Championship	Hidemichi Tanaka
Daiwa International	Shigenori Mori
Sumitomo Visa Taiheiyo Masters	Satoshi Higashi (4)
Dunlop Phoenix Tournament	Masashi Ozaki (4)
Casio World Open	Seiki Okuda
Japan Series of Golf	Masashi Ozaki (5)
Daikyo Open	Frankie Minoza (2)

ASIA PGA/OMEGA TOUR

The International	Nam-Sin Park
Canlubang Classic	Carlos Espinosa (2)
Tournament Players Championship	Lin Keng-Chi
Formosa Open	Lin Chie-Hsiang
Yokohama Singapore PGA Championship	Lin Keng-Chi (2)
Passport Open	Vijay Singh (3)
Langkawi Open	Boonchu Ruangkit
Gadgil Western Dubai Creek Open	Robert Willis
Merlion Masters	Nico Van Rensburg
Samsung Masters	Lin Keng-Chi (3)
Royal Perak Classic	Gerry Norquist
Kenmore Pakistan Masters	Young-Suk Kwon
Gadgil Western Masters	Gaurav Ghei
Gadgil Western Vietnam Open	Clay Devers (2)
Philippine Classic	Jeev Milkha Singh

AUSTRALASIAN TOUR

AMP New Zealand Open	Lucas Parsons
Optus Players Championship	Tim Elliott
Heineken Classic	Robert Allenby
Ford South Australian Open	Tim Elliott (2)
Australian Masters	Peter Senior
Canon Challenge	Craig Parry
Bank of Queensland Open	Terry Price
Alfred Dunhill Masters	Michael Campbell
Epson Singapore Open	Steve Conran
Victorian Open	Stephen Leaney
Heineken Australian Open	Greg Norman (5)

Greg Norman's Holden Classic	Craig Parry (2)
AMP Air New Zealand Open	Peter O'Malley (2)
Schweppes Coolum Classic	Shane Robinson

AFRICAN TOURS

Bell's Cup	Ernie Els
FNB Players Championship	Ron Whittaker
ICL International	Ashley Roestoff
Hollard Insurance Royal Swazi Sun Classic	Brad Ott
Telkom South African Masters	Scott Dunlap
Philips South African Open	Retief Goosen
Lexington PGA Championship	Ernie Els (2)
Alfred Dunhill Challenge	Southern Africa
Hassan II Trophy	Nick Price
Zimbabwe Open	Nick Price (2)
Nedbank Million Dollar Challenge	Corey Pavin (4)

U.S. SENIOR PGA TOUR

Senior Tournament of Champions	Jim Colbert
Royal Caribbean Classic	J.C. Snead
IntelliNet Challenge	Bob Murphy
GTE Suncoast Classic	Dave Stockton
Chrysler Cup	United States
FHP Health Care Classic	Bruce Devlin
Senior Grand Slam	Raymond Floyd
SBC Presents the Dominion Seniors	Jim Albus
Toshiba Classic	George Archer
The Tradition	Jack Nicklaus
PGA Seniors' Championship	Raymond Floyd (2)
Liberty Mutual Legends of Golf	Mike Hill/Lee Trevino
Las Vegas Senior Classic	Jim Colbert (2)
PaineWebber Invitational	Bob Murphy (2)
Cadillac NFL Classic	George Archer (2)
Bell Atlantic Classic	Jim Colbert (3)
Quicksilver Classic	Dave Stockton (2)
Bruno's Memorial Classic	Graham Marsh
BellSouth Classic at Opryland	Jim Dent
Dallas Reunion Pro-Am	Tom Wargo
Nationwide Championship	Bob Murphy (3)
U.S. Senior Open Championship	Tom Weiskopf
Kroger Classic	Mike Hill (2)
Ford Senior Players Championship	J.C. Snead (2)
First of America Classic	Jimmy Powell
Ameritech Open	Hale Irwin
VFW Championship	Bob Murphy (4)
Burnet Classic	Raymond Floyd (3)
Northville Long Island Classic	Lee Trevino (2)
Bank of Boston Classic	Isao Aoki (2)
Franklin Quest Championship	Tony Jacklin
GTE Northwest Classic	Walter Morgan
Brickyard Crossing Championship	Simon Hobday
Bank One Classic	Gary Player
Vantage Championship	Hale Irwin (2)
The Transamerica	Lee Trevino (3)
Raley's Gold Rush	Don Bies
Ralph's Classic	John Bland (2)
Hyatt Regency Maui Kaanapali Classic	Bob Charles
Emerald Coast Classic	Raymond Floyd (4)
Energizer Senior Tour Championship	Jim Colbert (4)
Diners Club Matches	Bob Murphy (5)/Jim Colbert (5)

EUROPEAN SENIORS TOUR

Windsor Senior Masters	Brian Huggett
International German PGA Seniors Championship	Renato Campagnoli
Senior British Open	Brian Barnes
Lawrence Batley Seniors	Alberto Croce
Forte PGA Seniors Championship	John Morgan
Northern Electric Seniors	Brian Waites
Collingtree Seniors	Neil Coles
Shell Scottish Seniors Open	Brian Huggett (2)
De Vere Hotels Seniors Classic	Tommy Horton
London Masters	John Bland
Senior Zurich Pro-Am: Lexus Trophy	Liam Higgins

JAPAN SENIOR TOUR

American Express Grand Slam	Isao Aoki
TPC Starts Senior	Fujio Kobayashi
Daiichi Seimei Cup	Seiichi Kanai
Japan PGA Senior Championship	Teruo Sugihara
HTB Senior Classic	Hsieh Min-Nan
Asahi Kokusai Vintage Classic	Haruo Yasuda
Komatsu Nagoya TV Open	Kuo Chie-Hsiung
Noboru Gotah Memorial Tokyu Senior Cup	Koji Nakajima
Ho-Oh Cup	Ryokichi Jibiki
Japan Senior Open	Isao Aoki (3)

U.S. LPGA TOUR

Chrysler-Plymouth Tournament of Champions	Dawn Coe-Jones
HealthSouth Inaugural	Pat Bradley
Cup Noodles Hawaiian Open	Barb Thomas
PING Welch's Championship	Dottie Mochrie
Standard Register PING	Laura Davies
Nabisco Dinah Shore	Nanci Bowen
Pinewild Women's Championship	Rosie Jones
Chick-fil-A Charity Championship	Laura Davies (2)
Sprint Championship	Val Skinner
Sara Lee Classic	Michelle McGann
McDonald's LPGA Championship	Kelly Robbins
Star Bank LPGA Classic	Chris Johnson
Corning Classic	Alison Nicholas
Oldsmobile Classic	Dale Eggeling
Edina Realty Classic	Julie Larsen
Rochester International	Patty Sheehan
ShopRite Classic	Betsy King
Youngstown-Warren Classic	Michelle McGann (2)
Jamie Farr Toledo Classic	Kathryn Marshall
U.S. Women's Open	Annika Sorenstam (3)
JAL Big Apple Classic	Tracy Kerdyk
Friendly's Classic	Becky Iverson
McCall's Classic at Stratton Mountain	Dottie Mochrie (2)
PING Welch's Championship	Beth Daniel
du Maurier Ltd. Classic	Jenny Lidback
State Farm Rail Classic	Mary Beth Zimmerman
PING AT&T Wireless Services Championship	Alison Nicholas (3)
Safeco Classic	Patty Sheehan (2)
GHP Heartland Classic	Annika Sorenstam (4)
Fieldcrest Cannon Classic	Gail Graham
Samsung World Championship of Women's Golf	Annika Sorenstam (5)
JCPenney Classic	Davis Love III (3)/Beth Daniel (2)
Diners Club Matches	Kelly Robbins (2)/Tammie Green

WOMEN'S EUROPEAN TOUR

Ladies' Open Costa Azul	Marie Laure de Lorenzi
Ford Classic	Lora Fairclough
Evian Masters	Laura Davies (3)
OVB Damen Open	Annika Sorenstam
European Masters	Lora Fairclough (2)
Hennessy Cup	Annika Sorenstam (2)
Guardian Irish Holidays Open	Laura Davies (4)
Payne & Gunter Scottish Open	Alison Nicholas (2)
Woodpecker Welsh Open	Laura Davies (5)
Weetabix Women's British Open	Karrie Webb
Ford-Stimorol Danish Open	Caroline Hall
Wilkinson Sword English Open	Laura Davies (6)
Trygg Hansa Open	Liselotte Neumann
Staatsloteru Dutch Open	Marie Laure de Lorenzi (2)
Maredo German Open	Rachel Hetherington
Italian Open di Sicilia	Denise Booker
Nestle Open de France Feminin	Marie Laure de Lorenzi (3)
La Manga Spanish Open	Rachel Hetherington (2)
Princess Lalla Meriem Cup	Amaia Arruti

WOMEN'S AUSTRALASIAN TOURS

Malaysian JAL Mercedes-Benz Open	Corinne Dibnah
Singapore JAL Open	Estefania Knuth
Indonesian JAL Open	Lisa Hackney
Thailand Open	Liz Earley
Republic of China Open	Cheng Mei-Chi
Holden Australian Open	Liselotte Neumann (2)
Alpine Australian Masters	Annika Sorenstam (6)

JAPAN LPGA TOUR

Daikin Orchid	Marnie McGuire
Chiyoda Ladies	Yuka Irie
Saishunkan Ladies	Nayoko Yoshikawa
Kenshoen Ladies	Keiko Arai
Mitsukoshi Cup	Ikuyo Shiotani
Nasu Ogawa	Ikuyo Shiotani (2)
Satake Japan Classic	Akiko Fukushima
Gunze World Cup	Kaori Higo
Yakult Ladies	Akiko Fukushima (2)
Chukyo TV Bridgestone	Ikuyo Shiotani (3)
Toto Motors Ladies	Mayumi Hirase
Mitsubishi Electric Ladies	Aiko Hashimoto
Dunlop Twin Lakes Ladies	Mayumi Hirase (2)
Japan Women's Open Championship	Ikuyo Shiotani (4)
Tohato Ladies	Akane Ohshiro
Toyo Suisan Ladies	Aki Nakano
Resort Trust Cleanup Ladies	Wu Ming-Yeh
Katokichi Queens Golf	Fuki Kido
SC Ladies	Huang Bie-Shyun
Mizuno Ladies	Aki Takamura
NEC Karuizawa 72	Mayumi Hirase (3)
Lotte Ladies	Kaori Higo (2)
Goyo Kensetsu Cup	Marnie McGuire (2)
Fuji Sankei Classic	Junko Yasui
Japan LPGA Championship	Aki Takamura (2)
Kosaido Asahi Cup	Huang Bie-Shyun (2)
Miyagi TV Cup	Natsuko Noro
Tokai Classic	Fumiko Muraguchi
Takara World Invitational	Michelle McGann (3)

Fujitsu Ladies	Hiromi Kobayashi
Kibun Classic	Hiromi Kobayashi (2)
Nichirei International	United States
Toray Japan Queens Cup	Woo-Soon Ko
Itoen Ladies	Laura Davies (7)
Daio Seishi Elleair Ladies Open	Michiko Okada
Meiji Nyugyo Cup	Ikuyo Shiotani (5)

Multiple Winners of 1995

PLAYER	WINS	PLAYER	WINS
Laura Davies	7	Raul Fretes	2
Raymond Floyd	6	Akiko Fukushima	2
Annika Sorenstam	6	Fred Funk	2
Jim Colbert	5	Jim Furyk	2
Ernie Els	5	Jim Gallagher, Jr.	2
Bob Murphy	5	Eric Giraud	2
Greg Norman	5	Todd Hamilton	2
Masashi Ozaki	5	Rachel Hetherington	2
Ikuyo Shiotani	5	Kaori Higo	2
Thomas Bjorn	4	Mike Hill	2
Satoshi Higashi	4	Huang Bie-Shyun	2
Brandt Jobe	4	Brian Huggett	2
Corey Pavin	4	Ian Hutchings	2
Isao Aoki	3	Hale Irwin	2
Mark Calcavecchia	3	Peter Jacobsen	2
Alexander Cejka	3	Jerry Kelly	2
Fred Couples	3	Hiromi Kobayashi	2
Allen Doyle	3	Tom Lehman	2
Steve Elkington	3	Billy Mayfair	2
Mayumi Hirase	3	Marnie McGuire	2
Scott Hoch	3	Frankie Minoza	2
Lee Janzen	3	Dottie Mochrie	2
Bernhard Langer	3	Colin Montgomerie	2
Lin Keng-Chi	3	Rolf Muntz	2
Marie Laure de Lorenzi	3	Liselotte Neumann	2
Davis Love III	3	Frank Nobilo	2
Michelle McGann	3	Per Nyman	2
Alison Nicholas	3	Peter O'Malley	2
Vijay Singh	3	Mark O'Meara	2
Sam Torrance	3	Craig Parry	2
Lee Trevino	3	Nick Price	2
Stuart Appleby	2	Kelly Robbins	2
George Archer	2	Hugh Royer III	2
Seve Ballesteros	2	Jim Rutledge	2
John Bland	2	Peter Senior	2
Emanuele Bolognesi	2	Patty Sheehan	2
Angel Cabrera	2	Chris Smith	2
John Cook	2	J.C. Snead	2
Ben Crenshaw	2	Dave Stockton	2
Beth Daniel	2	Aki Takamura	2
Clay Devers	2	David Toms	2
Trevor Dodds	2	Stan Utley	2
Tim Elliott	2	Duffy Waldorf	2
Carlos Espinosa	2	Philip Walton	2
Lora Fairclough	2	Brian Watts	2
Ray Freeman	2	Ron Wuensche	2

World Money List

This list of the 350 leading money winners in the world of professional golf in 1995 was compiled from the results of men's (excluding seniors) tournaments carried in the Appendixes of this edition. This list includes tournaments with a minimum of 36 holes and four contestants and does not include such competitions as skins games, pro-ams and shootouts.

In the 30 years during which World Money Lists have been compiled, the earnings of the player in the 200th position have risen from a total of $3,326 in 1966 to $220,949 in 1995. The top-200 players in 1966 earned a total of $4,680,287. In 1995, the comparable total was $123,435,438.

Because of fluctuating values of money throughout the world, it was necessary to determine an average value of non-American currency to U.S. money to prepare this listing. The conversion rates used for 1995 were: British pound = US$1.59; Japanese yen = US$0.0109635; South African rand = US$0.27969; Australian dollar = US$0.75; Canadian dollar = US$0.74.

POS.	PLAYER, COUNTRY	TOTAL MONEY
1	Corey Pavin, U.S.	$2,746,340
2	Masashi Ozaki, Japan	2,169,824
3	Colin Montgomerie, Scotland	2,153,211
4	Greg Norman, Australia	2,001,285
5	Bernhard Langer, Germany	1,923,554
6	Steve Elkington, Australia	1,914,135
7	Ernie Els, South Africa	1,833,318
8	Sam Torrance, Scotland	1,788,798
9	Lee Janzen, U.S.	1,705,392
10	Vijay Singh, Fiji	1,674,913
11	Davis Love III, U.S.	1,646,995
12	Billy Mayfair, U.S.	1,635,599
13	Barry Lane, England	1,585,140
14	Satoshi Higashi, Japan	1,500,401
15	Fred Couples, U.S.	1,462,009
16	Mark Calcavecchia, U.S.	1,335,226
17	Tom Lehman, U.S.	1,331,915
18	Ben Crenshaw, U.S.	1,270,319
19	Masahiro Kuramoto, Japan	1,269,739
20	Nick Price, Zimbabwe	1,258,387
21	Scott Hoch, U.S.	1,192,071
22	Peter Jacobsen, U.S.	1,186,337
23	Costantino Rocca, Italy	1,154,407
24	Shigeki Maruyama, Japan	1,131,532
25	David Duval, U.S.	1,113,766
26	Nick Faldo, England	1,105,218
27	Jim Gallagher, Jr., U.S.	1,098,442
28	David Frost, South Africa	1,093,719
29	Peter Senior, Australia	1,083,870
30	Loren Roberts, U.S.	1,079,369
31	Katsuyoshi Tomori, Japan	1,057,642
32	Mark O'Meara, U.S.	1,018,957

POS.	PLAYER, COUNTRY	TOTAL MONEY
33	Phil Mickelson, U.S.	979,552
34	Jay Haas, U.S.	945,667
35	Payne Stewart, U.S.	941,789
36	Scott Simpson, U.S.	929,740
37	Michael Campbell, New Zealand	902,797
38	Hisayuki Sasaki, Japan	899,068
39	Brian Watts, U.S.	898,735
40	Bob Tway, U.S.	864,572
41	Hidemichi Tanaka, Japan	864,097
42	Kenny Perry, U.S.	859,643
43	Justin Leonard, U.S.	818,816
44	Frankie Minoza, Philippines	802,041
45	Frank Nobilo, New Zealand	800,967
46	Tomohiro Maruyama, Japan	795,241
47	Mark McCumber, U.S.	782,657
48	Jim Furyk, U.S.	779,285
49	Woody Austin, U.S.	767,756
50	Tsuneyuki Nakajima, Japan	763,253
51	Naomichi Ozaki, Japan	763,101
52	Fred Funk, U.S.	747,162
53	Brad Bryant, U.S.	731,098
54	Hideki Kase, Japan	728,766
55	Craig Parry, Australia	717,189
56	Jesper Parnevik, Sweden	716,560
57	Kirk Triplett, U.S.	709,440
58	Kazuhiro Takami, Japan	694,156
59	Brad Faxon, U.S.	684,756
60	Toru Suzuki, Japan	676,572
61	Duffy Waldorf, U.S.	669,668
62	Rick Gibson, Canada	664,401
63	John Daly, U.S.	653,030
64	Jeff Sluman, U.S.	636,075
65	Todd Hamilton, U.S.	617,796
66	Nobuo Serizawa, Japan	617,249
67	Shigenori Mori, Japan	607,139
68	Alexander Cejka, Germany	603,485
69	Robert Allenby, Australia	597,662
70	Nobumitsu Yuhara, Japan	589,767
71	Jeff Maggert, U.S.	577,514
72	Tsukasa Watanabe, Japan	577,249
73	Anders Forsbrand, Sweden	571,944
74	Katsunori Kuwabara, Japan	571,508
75	Brandt Jobe, U.S.	562,850
76	Steve Stricker, U.S.	561,185
77	Miguel Angel Jimenez, Spain	560,640
78	Craig Stadler, U.S.	558,372
79	Hal Sutton, U.S.	554,733
80	Peter O'Malley, Australia	554,693
81	Masayuki Kawamura, Japan	554,504
82	Jim McGovern, U.S.	552,387
83	Robert Gamez, U.S.	544,445
84	Carlos Franco, Paraguay	542,258
85	D.A. Weibring, U.S.	536,299
86	Kazuhiko Hosokawa, Japan	526,345

POS.	PLAYER, COUNTRY	TOTAL MONEY
87	Wayne Riley, Australia	522,291
88	Toshimitsu Izawa, Japan	517,804
89	Ryoken Kawagishi, Japan	516,621
90	Seiki Okuda, Japan	514,487
91	Steve Lowery, U.S.	506,861
92	Mark James, England	495,656
93	Seve Ballesteros, Spain	489,754
94	Philip Walton, Ireland	482,905
95	Eduardo Herrera, Argentina	482,860
96	Larry Mize, U.S.	477,620
97	Koki Idoki, Japan	476,907
98	Curtis Strange, U.S.	476,517
99	Andrew Coltart, Scotland	470,307
100	Ted Tryba, U.S.	469,833
101	Darren Clarke, Northern Ireland	467,065
102	Brett Ogle, Australia	461,659
103	Hajime Meshiai, Japan	460,740
104	Kiyoshi Maita, Japan	460,198
105	Mark Brooks, U.S.	457,052
106	Yoshinori Mizumaki, Japan	452,626
107	Tom Watson, U.S.	444,848
108	Scott Verplank, U.S.	440,854
109	John Morse, U.S.	436,190
110	Bob Estes, U.S.	433,825
111	Mark McNulty, Zimbabwe	433,686
112	Bill Glasson, U.S.	422,317
113	Mike Heinen, U.S.	411,691
114	Stewart Ginn, Australia	411,419
115	Lennie Clements, U.S.	408,345
116	John Cook, U.S.	404,935
117	Howard Clark, England	398,782
118	Paul Azinger, U.S.	395,129
119	Jose Maria Olazabal, Spain	393,038
120	John Huston, U.S.	392,559
121	David Gilford, England	392,216
122	Jose Rivero, Spain	383,038
123	Andrew Magee, U.S.	381,103
124	Yoshinori Kaneko, Japan	371,791
125	Mike Hulbert, U.S.	366,030
126	Jay Don Blake, U.S.	364,803
127	Bob Lohr, U.S.	364,584
128	Shinichi Yokota, Japan	364,379
129	Katsunari Takahashi, Japan	362,328
130	Ian Woosnam, Wales	362,177
131	Billy Andrade, U.S.	357,029
132	Per-Ulrik Johansson, Sweden	353,416
133	Guy Boros, U.S.	351,065
134	Masanobu Kimura, Japan	350,064
135	Paul Broadhurst, England	338,962
136	David Ishii, U.S.	331,976
137	Takaaki Fukuzawa, Japan	331,217
138	Toru Nakamura, Japan	330,282
139	Shinji Ikeuchi, Japan	329,453
140	Mitsutaka Kusakabe, Japan	319,856

POS.	PLAYER, COUNTRY	TOTAL MONEY
141	Gene Sauers, U.S.	317,787
142	Jarmo Sandelin, Sweden	314,282
143	Robin Freeman, U.S.	308,440
144	Ronan Rafferty, Northern Ireland	307,375
145	Bruce Lietzke, U.S.	306,894
146	Ignacio Garrido, Spain	301,048
147	Grant Waite, New Zealand	297,882
148	Eiji Mizoguchi, Japan	296,499
149	Mathias Gronberg, Sweden	294,407
150	Marco Dawson, U.S.	292,109
151	Jay Delsing, U.S.	290,062
152	Sandy Lyle, Scotland	282,626
153	Chip Beck, U.S.	281,361
154	Greg Turner, New Zealand	281,006
155	Saburo Fujiki, Japan	280,413
156	Blaine McCallister, U.S.	277,897
157	Steve Jones, U.S.	276,509
158	Hirofumi Miyase, Japan	275,004
159	Peter Teravainen, U.S.	272,025
160	Jean Louis Guepy, France	271,645
161	Tom Kite, U.S.	271,053
162	Kiyoshi Murota, Japan	270,366
163	Ken Kusumoto, Japan	260,152
164	Mike Clayton, Australia	259,569
165	Nolan Henke, U.S.	258,987
166	Brian Claar, U.S.	258,827
167	Peter Baker, England	257,360
168	John Adams, U.S.	257,066
169	Doug Martin, U.S.	256,536
170	Tatsuo Takasaki, Japan	255,940
171	Gil Morgan, U.S.	255,565
172	Fuzzy Zoeller, U.S.	253,006
173	Brandel Chamblee, U.S.	252,580
174	Sven Struver, Germany	251,768
175	Retief Goosen, South Africa	249,815
176	Eduardo Romero, Argentina	246,926
177	Roger Mackay, Australia	246,702
178	Ikuo Shirahama, Japan	246,633
179	Lin Chie-Hsiang, Taiwan	245,081
180	Michael Bradley, U.S.	244,859
181	Andrew Oldcorn, England	244,593
182	Stuart Appleby, Australia	243,146
183	Roger Chapman, England	242,929
184	David Edwards, U.S.	241,857
185	Glen Day, U.S.	239,958
186	Tetsu Nisikawa, Japan	239,350
187	Peter Mitchell, England	238,255
188	Jose Coceres, Argentina	237,869
189	Jamie Spence, England	236,612
190	Joakim Haeggman, Sweden	234,140
191	Russ Cochran, U.S.	234,113
192	Anthony Gilligan, Australia	234,083
193	Peter McWhinney, Australia	229,202
194	Jerry Kelly, U.S.	228,576

POS.	PLAYER, COUNTRY	TOTAL MONEY
195	Don Pooley, U.S.	226,784
196	Santiago Luna, Spain	226,056
197	Dillard Pruitt, U.S.	225,848
198	Derrick Cooper, England	223,145
199	Michael Jonzon, Sweden	221,264
200	Russell Claydon, England	220,949
201	Tony Johnstone, Zimbabwe	218,628
202	Stuart Cage, England	216,407
203	Paul Eales, England	211,362
204	Mike Brisky, U.S.	209,874
205	Robert Karlsson, Sweden	209,640
206	Jay Townsend, U.S.	208,316
207	Dan Forsman, U.S.	208,314
208	Jonathan Kaye, U.S.	206,964
209	Brian Henninger, U.S.	206,730
210	Emlyn Aubrey, U.S.	204,020
211	Joey Sindelar, U.S.	202,896
212	Tsutomu Higa, Japan	201,200
213	Neal Lancaster, U.S.	200,719
214	Lee Rinker, U.S.	199,216
215	Peter Hedblom, Sweden	199,166
216	Curt Byrum, U.S.	198,233
217	Tsuyoshi Yoneyama, Japan	197,520
218	Charles Rymer, U.S.	196,336
219	Akiyoshi Ohmachi, Japan	196,182
220	Mike Standly, U.S.	196,170
221	Tateo Ozaki, Japan	193,970
222	Mats Lanner, Sweden	193,960
223	Lin Keng-Chi, Taiwan	193,593
224	Mark Mouland, Wales	189,608
225	Yoshikazu Sakamoto, Japan	189,601
226	Paul McGinley, Ireland	188,506
227	Scott Gump, U.S.	187,678
228	Seiji Ebihara, Japan	186,041
229	Mark Wiebe, U.S.	183,832
230	Richard Boxall, England	182,323
231	Hideyuki Sato, Japan	182,321
232	Olle Karlsson, Sweden	181,576
233	Jim Carter, U.S.	180,664
234	Tom Byrum, U.S.	180,386
235	Franklin Langham, U.S.	180,216
236	Kelly Gibson, U.S.	180,113
237	Allen Doyle, U.S.	179,916
238	Paul Moloney, Australia	176,631
239	Pete Jordan, U.S.	176,340
240	Wayne Smith, Australia	176,038
241	Mike Sullivan, U.S.	175,786
242	Bobby Wadkins, U.S.	175,527
243	David Toms, U.S.	174,892
244	Terry Price, Australia	173,674
245	Hsieh Chin-Sheng, Taiwan	173,623
246	Ken Green, U.S.	173,545
247	Keith Fergus, U.S.	173,225
248	Dave Stockton, Jr., U.S.	173,079

POS.	PLAYER, COUNTRY	TOTAL MONEY
249	Wayne Westner, South Africa	172,983
250	John Mahaffey, U.S.	172,542
251	Ronnie Black, U.S.	172,188
252	Daisuke Serizawa, Japan	171,811
253	Dan Pohl, U.S.	171,219
254	Dean Robertson, Scotland	170,917
255	Hiroshi Makino, Japan	169,092
256	Hiroyuki Fujita, Japan	168,769
257	Joji Furuki, Japan	168,250
258	Roger Wessels, South Africa	168,136
259	Donnie Hammond, U.S.	167,672
260	Richard Backwell, Australia	167,321
261	Teruo Nakamura, Japan	166,849
262	Patrick Burke, U.S.	166,648
263	Tommy Tolles, U.S.	166,431
264	Howard Twitty, U.S.	165,645
265	Rick Fehr, U.S.	165,266
266	Brian Kamm, U.S.	165,235
267	Jean Van de Velde, France	165,223
268	David Ogrin, U.S.	164,992
269	Eamonn Darcy, Ireland	164,473
270	Yoshimi Niizeki, Japan	162,748
271	Bob Gilder, U.S.	162,694
272	Robert Willis, Australia	162,537
273	Christian Cevaer, France	162,219
274	Ed Dougherty, U.S.	162,082
275	Nicklas Fasth, Sweden	161,024
276	Sean Murphy, U.S.	159,100
277	Andrew Sherborne, England	158,472
278	Jeev Milkha Singh, India	157,063
279	Vicente Fernandez, Argentina	156,585
280	John Wilson, U.S.	155,830
281	Scott Dunlap, U.S.	155,787
282	Chris Smith, U.S.	155,700
283	Gary Orr, Scotland	155,635
284	Paul Affleck, Wales	155,565
285	Paul Goydos, U.S.	154,923
286	Phil Blackmar, U.S.	154,801
287	Joe Acosta, Jr., U.S.	153,065
288	Hiroshi Goda, Japan	152,574
289	Dave Barr, Canada	151,733
290	Adam Hunter, Scotland	150,552
291	Silvio Grappasonni, Italy	149,591
292	Tom Purtzer, U.S.	149,412
293	Ross McFarlane, England	149,394
294	Scott McCarron, U.S.	149,321
295	Mark Roe, England	148,506
296	Chen Tze-Ming, Taiwan	146,975
297	Pedro Linhart, Spain	146,199
298	Takenori Hiraishi, Japan	144,977
299	Steven Bottomley, England	144,799
300	Tom Scherrer, U.S.	144,795
301	Lucas Parsons, Australia	144,754
302	Paul Stankowski, U.S.	144,558

POS.	PLAYER, COUNTRY	TOTAL MONEY
303	Chris Perry, U.S.	144,038
304	Lee Westwood, England	143,891
305	Boonchu Ruangkit, Thailand	143,595
306	Hideto Shigenobu, Japan	143,453
307	Steven Richardson, England	142,524
308	Hiroshi Ueda, Japan	141,825
309	Toru Nakayama, Japan	141,223
310	Wayne Grady, Australia	141,188
311	Neil Briggs, England	139,413
312	Hidezumi Shirakata, Japan	139,296
313	Toshiaki Odate, Japan	138,843
314	Tommy Armour III, U.S.	138,139
315	Greg Kraft, U.S.	137,655
316	Carl Mason, England	137,167
317	Jeff Gove, U.S.	135,250
318	Steve Rintoul, Australia	132,877
319	Mark Davis, England	132,156
320	Koichi Suzuki, Japan	132,008
321	Jay Williamson, U.S.	131,313
322	Hiroya Kamide, Japan	130,667
323	Guarav Ghei, India	130,124
324	Harumitsu Hamano, Japan	127,219
325	Stephen Ames, Trinidad & Tobago	126,993
326	Joel Edwards, U.S.	126,910
327	Tray Tyner, U.S.	126,339
328	David Feherty, Northern Ireland	126,286
329	Andre Bossert, Switzerland	125,976
330	Mike Reid, U.S.	124,519
331	Yoshitaka Yamamoto, Japan	123,807
332	Rocco Mediate, U.S.	121,618
333	Mitsuo Harada, Japan	120,873
334	Kinpachi Yoshimura, Japan	119,898
335	Martin Gates, England	119,604
336	Bart Bryant, U.S.	119,201
337	Hugh Royer III, U.S.	118,804
338	Skip Kendall, U.S.	118,598
339	Gary Hallberg, U.S.	118,557
340	Des Smyth, Ireland	118,034
341	Steve Conran, Australia	117,834
342	Chen Tze-Chung, Taiwan	117,741
343	Bruce Fleisher, U.S.	116,530
344	Dudley Hart, U.S.	116,334
345	Nobuhiro Yoshino, Japan	116,277
346	Takashi Kanemoto, Japan	115,662
347	Brad Fabel, U.S.	115,513
348	Pierre Fulke, Sweden	114,814
349	Malcolm Mackenzie, England	114,555
350	Fredrik Lindgren, Sweden	113,885

Career World Money List

The following is a listing of the 50 leading money winners for their careers through the 1995 season. It includes players active on both the regular and senior tours of the world. The World Money List from this and the 29 previous editions of this annual and a table prepared for a companion book, *The Wonderful World of Professional Golf* (Atheneum, 1973), form the basis for this compilation. Additional figures were taken from official records of major golf associations, although the shortcomings in records-keeping in professional golf outside the United States in the 1950s and 1960s and exclusions from U.S. records in a few cases during those years prevent these figures from being completely accurate. Conversions of foreign currency figures to U.S. dollars are based on average values during the particular years involved.

POS.	PLAYER, COUNTRY	TOTAL MONEY
1	Greg Norman, Australia	$16,413,101
2	Bernhard Langer, Germany	14,467,643
3	Fred Couples, U.S.	13,929,225
4	Masashi Ozaki, Japan	13,700,674
5	Nick Faldo, England	13,496,005
6	Nick Price, Zimbabwe	12,052,675
7	Lee Trevino, U.S.	11,937,543
8	Tom Kite, U.S.	11,889,461
9	Raymond Floyd, U.S.	11,871,203
10	David Frost, South Africa	11,579,479
11	Seve Ballesteros, Spain	11,227,913
12	Corey Pavin, U.S.	10,337,808
13	Ian Woosnam, Wales	10,326,347
14	Isao Aoki, Japan	10,116,431
15	Payne Stewart, U.S.	10,012,220
16	Tsuneyuki Nakajima, Japan	9,605,029
17	Curtis Strange, U.S.	9,442,318
18	Ben Crenshaw, U.S.	9,041,609
19	Paul Azinger, U.S.	8,714,937
20	Jose Maria Olazabal, Spain	8,700,355
21	Jack Nicklaus, U.S.	8,650,822
22	Tom Watson, U.S.	8,598,156
23	Bob Charles, New Zealand	8,530,521
24	Mark Calcavecchia, U.S.	8,439,191
25	Davis Love III, U.S.	8,340,511
26	Hale Irwin, U.S.	8,173,937
27	Naomichi Ozaki, Japan	8,020,443
28	George Archer, U.S.	7,975,824
29	Gary Player, South Africa	7,853,955
30	Craig Stadler, U.S.	7,817,320
31	Mark O'Meara, U.S.	7,809,166
32	Lanny Wadkins, U.S.	7,797,155
33	Colin Montgomerie, Scotland	7,683,696
34	Chi Chi Rodriguez, U.S.	7,425,794

POS.	PLAYER, COUNTRY	TOTAL MONEY
35	Jim Colbert, U.S.	7,371,606
36	Scott Hoch, U.S.	7,363,122
37	Chip Beck, U.S.	7,001,529
38	Miller Barber, U.S.	6,780,931
39	Masahiro Kuramoto, Japan	6,774,894
40	Larry Mize, U.S.	6,689,310
41	Sandy Lyle, Scotland	6,685,524
42	Graham Marsh, Australia	6,612,389
43	Mike Hill, U.S.	6,565,930
44	Dave Stockton, U.S.	6,552,288
45	Steve Elkington, Australia	6,541,683
46	Mark McNulty, Zimbabwe	6,322,328
47	Bruce Lietzke, U.S.	6,310,325
48	Ernie Els, South Africa	6,269,211
49	Jay Haas, U.S.	6,196,196
50	Sam Torrance, Scotland	6,149,966

These 50 players have won $448,165,699 in their lifetimes playing professional tournament golf.

Senior World Money List

This list includes official earnings on the U.S. PGA Tour, U.S. Senior PGA Tour, European Seniors Tour and Japan Senior Tour, along with other winnings in established unofficial events when reliable figures could be obtained.

POS.	PLAYER, COUNTRY	TOTAL MONEY
1	Raymond Floyd, U.S.	$1,811,049
2	Jim Colbert, U.S.	1,645,011
3	Dave Stockton, U.S.	1,615,469
4	Bob Murphy, U.S.	1,442,149
5	Isao Aoki, Japan	1,315,076
6	Lee Trevino, U.S.	1,121,339
7	Hale Irwin, U.S.	1,098,969
8	J.C. Snead, U.S.	1,028,137
9	Graham Marsh, Australia	1,025,196
10	Tom Wargo, U.S.	903,304
11	George Archer, U.S.	844,587
12	Jim Albus, U.S.	819,936
13	Bruce Summerhays, U.S.	729,021
14	Bob Charles, New Zealand	710,548
15	Mike Hill, U.S.	675,536
16	Dave Eichelberger, U.S.	668,566
17	Rocky Thompson, U.S.	666,521
18	Jim Dent, U.S.	655,898

POS.	PLAYER, COUNTRY	TOTAL MONEY
19	Jack Nicklaus, U.S.	646,958
20	Tom Weiskopf, U.S.	645,137
21	Bud Allin, U.S.	599,142
22	Simon Hobday, South Africa	569,929
23	Jay Sigel, U.S.	567,557
24	Larry Gilbert, U.S.	540,062
25	Kermit Zarley, U.S.	525,789
26	Jack Kiefer, U.S.	473,732
27	Gibby Gilbert, U.S.	467,758
28	Tony Jacklin, England	437,839
29	Walter Morgan, U.S.	423,756
30	Jimmy Powell, U.S.	409,639
31	Larry Laoretti, U.S.	406,170
32	John Paul Cain, U.S.	404,762
33	Dale Douglass, U.S.	400,445
34	Al Geiberger, U.S.	388,496
35	Jerry McGee, U.S.	371,097
36	Gary Player, South Africa	350,764
37	Don Bies, U.S.	328,000
38	Ben Smith, U.S.	311,098
39	DeWitt Weaver, U.S.	309,210
40	Terry Dill, U.S.	289,652
41	Bob E. Smith, U.S.	287,098
42	Tommy Aaron, U.S.	282,134
43	Harold Henning, South Africa	275,447
44	Bruce Devlin, Australia	269,643
45	Bob Dickson, U.S.	261,889
46	John Bland, South Africa	260,699
47	Teruo Sugihara, Japan	248,715
48	Larry Ziegler, U.S.	246,131
49	Butch Baird, U.S.	240,198
50	Ed Sneed, U.S.	238,021
51	Chi Chi Rodriguez, U.S.	235,547
52	Dave Hill, U.S.	223,091
53	Harry Toscano, U.S.	217,547
54	Seiichi Kanai, Japan	214,273
55	Calvin Peete, U.S.	204,817
56	Hsieh Min-Nan, Taiwan	202,116
57	Walter Zembriski, U.S.	196,524
58	Charles Coody, U.S.	186,653
59	Kuo Chie-Hsiung, Taiwan	185,809
60	Tom Shaw, U.S.	185,022
61	Rives McBee, U.S.	181,216
62	Haruo Yasuda, Japan	177,904
63	Jim Ferree, U.S.	177,717
64	Deane Beman, U.S.	173,751
65	Chuck Montalbano, U.S.	167,370
66	Dick Hendrickson, U.S.	166,972
67	Brian Barnes, Scotland	165,486
68	Marion Heck, U.S.	160,849
69	Gay Brewer, U.S.	154,876
70	Dick Rhyan, U.S.	152,784
71	Fujio Kobayashi, Japan	147,843
72	Robert Zimmerman, U.S.	139,988

POS.	PLAYER, COUNTRY	TOTAL MONEY
73	Miller Barber, U.S.	137,858
74	Joe Jimenez, U.S.	136,294
75	Brian Huggett, Wales	130,419
76	Arnold Palmer, U.S.	128,893
77	Dick Goetz, U.S.	126,111
78	Masaru Amano, Japan	121,810
79	Bobby Nichols, U.S.	116,661
80	Kikuo Arai, Japan	115,881
81	Homero Blancas, U.S.	114,806
82	Bruce Crampton, Australia	109,134
83	John Morgan, England	108,812
84	Tommy Horton, England	103,970
85	Hiroshi Ishii, Japan	103,772
86	Bob Betley, U.S.	103,486
87	Mike McCullough, U.S.	101,692
88	Bobby Mitchell, U.S.	100,555
89	Gary Groh, U.S.	97,309
90	Don January, U.S.	95,717
91	Mitoshi Tomita, Japan	91,777
92	Ryosuke Ota, Japan	91,773
93	Mitsuhiro Kitsuta, Japan	90,767
94	Babe Hiskey, U.S.	89,279
95	Antonio Garrido, Spain	88,109
96	Ryokichi Jibiki, Japan	87,726
97	Orville Moody, U.S.	87,271
98	Norihiko Matsumoto, Japan	86,431
99	Shigeru Uchida, Japan	80,529
100	Seiji Ogawa, Japan	77,755

Women's World Money List

This list includes official earnings on the U.S. LPGA Tour, Women's European Tour, Women's Australasian Tours and Japan LPGA Tour, along with other winnings in established unofficial events when reliable figures could be obtained.

POS.	PLAYER, COUNTRY	TOTAL MONEY
1	Annika Sorenstam, Sweden	$1,043,121
2	Laura Davies, England	932,246
3	Ikuyo Shiotani, Japan	822,334
4	Mayumi Hirase, Japan	808,175
5	Akiko Fukushima, Japan	743,131
6	Marnie McGuire, New Zealand	739,289
7	Beth Daniel, U.S.	681,219

POS.	PLAYER, COUNTRY	TOTAL MONEY
8	Kaori Higo, Japan	673,921
9	Kelly Robbins, U.S.	662,930
10	Michelle McGann, U.S.	644,925
11	Huang Bie-Shyun, Taiwan	567,467
12	Dottie Mochrie, U.S.	560,395
13	Liselotte Neumann, Sweden	502,126
14	Aki Takamura, Japan	498,596
15	Val Skinner, U.S.	498,214
16	Betsy King, U.S.	496,149
17	Aki Nakano, Japan	490,201
18	Nayoko Yoshikawa, Japan	489,434
19	Meg Mallon, U.S.	473,581
20	Tammie Green, U.S.	464,017
21	Junko Yasui, Japan	457,502
22	Rosie Jones, U.S.	449,912
23	Hiromi Kobayashi, Japan	447,230
24	Yuko Moriguchi, Japan	409,599
25	Kris Tschetter, U.S.	399,719
26	Jane Geddes, U.S.	397,529
27	Young-Me Lee, Korea	396,966
28	Woo-Soon Ko, Korea	382,423
29	Alison Nicholas, England	379,109
30	Ok-Hee Ku, Korea	371,093
31	Pat Bradley, U.S.	368,904
32	Aiko Hashimoto, Japan	368,545
33	Helen Alfredsson, Sweden	362,551
34	Natsuko Noro, Japan	358,481
35	Michiko Hattori, Japan	351,059
36	Patty Sheehan, U.S.	350,097
37	Fuki Kido, Japan	331,023
38	Toshimi Kimura, Japan	330,316
39	Akane Ohshiro, Japan	318,612
40	Man-Soo Kim, Korea	301,295
41	Colleen Walker, U.S.	299,892
42	Jenny Lidback, U.S.	296,386
43	Dale Eggeling, U.S.	288,182
44	Julie Larsen, U.S.	285,879
45	Nanci Bowen, U.S.	285,717
46	Dawn Coe-Jones, Canada	268,665
47	Fumiko Muraguchi, Japan	266,105
48	Michiko Okada, Japan	261,318
49	Sherri Steinhauer, U.S.	256,707
50	Kaori Harada, Japan	252,720
51	Jennifer Sevil, New Zealand	246,278
52	Aiko Takasu, Japan	246,038
53	Ayako Okamoto, Japan	244,173
54	Brandie Burton, U.S.	238,889
55	Juli Inkster, U.S.	235,134
56	Barb Thomas, U.S.	235,095
57	Chris Johnson, U.S.	232,712
58	Wu Ming-Yeh, Taiwan	226,889
59	Joan Pitcock, U.S.	226,517
60	Jae-Sook Won, Korea	220,902
61	Suzuko Maeda, Japan	220,283

POS.	PLAYER, COUNTRY	TOTAL MONEY
62	Mayumi Murai, Japan	219,675
63	Yuka Irie, Japan	217,341
64	Katie Peterson-Parker, U.S.	215,831
65	Chikako Matsuzawa, Japan	214,243
66	Nancy Lopez, U.S.	210,882
67	Mitsuyo Hirata, Japan	210,069
68	Akemi Yamaoka, Japan	207,687
69	Keiko Arai, Japan	203,413
70	Marianne Morris, U.S.	200,395
71	Michele Redman, U.S.	198,756
72	Caroline Pierce, England	196,905
73	Miyuki Shimabukuro, Japan	191,645
74	Elaine Crosby, U.S.	191,284
75	Yuko Saito, Japan	190,636
76	Emilee Klein, U.S.	189,743
77	Tracy Kerdyk, U.S.	185,975
78	Danielle Ammaccapane, U.S.	181,560
79	Feng Tseng-Hsiu, Taiwan	179,019
80	Pamela Wright, Scotland	165,311
81	Barb Mucha, U.S.	161,346
82	Karrie Webb, Australia	159,353
83	Trish Johnson, England	159,217
84	Mary Beth Zimmerman, U.S.	156,741
85	Shin Sora, Korea	155,704
86	Mardi Lunn, Australia	154,479
87	Hiromi Takamura, Japan	151,298
88	Carin Hjalmarsson, Sweden	150,523
89	Cheng Mei-Chi, Taiwan	147,207
90	Fusako Nagata, Japan	144,378
91	Gail Graham, Canada	142,346
92	Kathryn Marshall, Scotland	141,503
93	Yukiyo Haga, Japan	138,092
94	Michelle Estill, U.S.	136,551
95	Cindy Rarick, U.S.	134,302
96	Susie Redman, U.S.	133,095
97	Chikayo Yamazaki, Japan	132,448
98	Lora Fairclough, England	132,272
99	Chieko Nishida, Japan	131,525
100	Hisako Takeda, Japan	131,159

American Tours

Mercedes Championship

LaCosta Country Club, Carlsbad, California
Par 36-36–72; 7,022 yards

January 5-8
purse, $1,000,000

	SCORES				TOTAL	MONEY
Steve Elkington	69	71	71	67	278	$180,000
Bruce Lietzke	71	69	71	67	278	108,000
(Elkington defeated Lietzke on second extra hole.)						
Bill Glasson	70	69	73	67	279	68,000
Craig Stadler	71	65	73	71	280	48,000
Fred Couples	73	68	68	72	281	35,250
Ben Crenshaw	71	67	75	68	281	35,250
Rick Fehr	71	74	70	66	281	35,250
Tom Lehman	75	68	72	66	281	35,250
John Huston	67	66	72	77	282	28,750
Lee Janzen	72	63	76	71	282	28,750
Scott Hoch	74	67	73	69	283	26,750
Bob Estes	69	68	74	73	284	24,750
Hale Irwin	73	69	72	70	284	24,750
Corey Pavin	74	71	69	70	284	24,750
Mark Brooks	71	71	73	70	285	22,750
Mark McCumber	70	72	72	72	286	21,250
Kenny Perry	72	70	74	70	286	21,250
Greg Norman	74	72	72	70	288	20,000
Phil Mickelson	72	73	71	73	289	19,250
John Daly	75	74	72	69	290	18,125
Dicky Pride	71	72	74	73	290	18,125
Steve Lowery	71	79	70	71	291	17,250
Neal Lancaster	72	75	70	75	292	16,750
Mike Heinen	72	75	71	75	293	16,000
Loren Roberts	71	73	75	74	293	16,000
Brian Henninger	75	74	70	78	297	15,375
Andrew Magee	75	72	75	75	297	15,375
Mike Sullivan	71	77	75	75	298	15,050
Brett Ogle	77	73	75	75	300	14,850
Mike Springer	72	72	83	75	302	14,650
Johnny Miller	71	71	77		WD	

United Airlines Hawaiian Open

Waialae Country Club, Honolulu, Hawaii
Par 36-36–72; 6,975 yards

January 12-15
purse, $1,200,000

	SCORES				TOTAL	MONEY
John Morse	71	65	65	68	269	$216,000
Tom Lehman	68	70	67	67	272	105,600
Duffy Waldorf	68	65	71	68	272	105,600
Paul Azinger	72	67	69	66	274	49,600
Bill Glasson	70	70	68	66	274	49,600
Dan Pohl	69	67	69	69	274	49,600

	SCORES				TOTAL	MONEY
Mark Brooks	68	69	68	70	275	38,700
John Huston	72	68	69	66	275	38,700
Chip Beck	71	66	66	73	276	34,800
David Ishii	71	69	68	69	277	31,200
Grant Waite	71	69	66	71	277	31,200
Robert Gamez	72	67	67	72	278	26,400
Brian Henninger	72	65	74	67	278	26,400
Dave Barr	69	70	69	71	279	21,000
Mark Calcavecchia	75	69	67	68	279	21,000
David Duval	71	73	64	71	279	21,000
Keith Fergus	67	72	70	70	279	21,000
Patrick Burke	74	70	66	70	280	16,200
Jim Furyk	67	72	72	69	280	16,200
Sean Murphy	72	70	71	67	280	16,200
Jesper Parnevik	70	75	67	68	280	16,200
Pat Bates	75	70	70	66	281	11,520
Steve Jones	68	73	69	71	281	11,520
Greg Kraft	72	71	69	69	281	11,520
Yoshinori Mizumaki	68	71	74	68	281	11,520
Charlie Rymer	71	69	72	69	281	11,520
David Edwards	73	72	68	69	282	7,820
Jim Gallagher, Jr.	75	68	71	68	282	7,820
Scott Gump	72	73	69	68	282	7,820
Jonathan Kaye	73	69	68	72	282	7,820
Jim McGovern	69	70	71	72	282	7,820
David Ogrin	70	72	70	70	282	7,820
Dave Rummells	73	71	70	68	282	7,820
Mike Sullivan	69	69	74	70	282	7,820
Craig Stadler	71	72	68	71	282	7,820
Clark Dennis	68	68	71	76	283	5,530
Doug Martin	71	68	72	72	283	5,530
Corey Pavin	69	75	69	70	283	5,530
Don Pooley	74	70	68	71	283	5,530
Steve Stricker	74	70	70	69	283	5,530
Mark Wurtz	72	66	74	71	283	5,530
Russ Cochran	73	68	71	72	284	4,200
Skip Kendall	70	71	72	71	284	4,200
Steve Lowery	72	72	70	70	284	4,200
Naomichi Ozaki	70	75	68	71	284	4,200
Curtis Strange	70	73	69	72	284	4,200
Andy Bean	75	69	71	70	285	2,960.73
Michael Bradley	73	72	67	73	285	2,960.73
Curt Byrum	70	75	69	71	285	2,960.73
Paul Goydos	75	68	73	69	285	2,960.73
Peter Jacobsen	70	72	69	74	285	2,960.73
Mark O'Meara	76	69	69	71	285	2,960.73
Vijay Singh	70	73	73	69	285	2,960.73
Richard Zokol	71	72	70	72	285	2,960.73
Kelly Gibson	69	71	74	71	285	2,960.72
Gene Sauers	70	71	74	70	285	2,960.72
Bruce Vaughan	72	68	72	73	285	2,960.72
Woody Austin	73	72	71	70	286	2,652
Brian Claar	70	74	69	73	286	2,652
Mike Heinen	73	71	74	68	286	2,652
Jeff Leonard	72	73	69	72	286	2,652
Joel Edwards	76	68	71	72	287	2,568
J.L. Lewis	69	72	76	70	287	2,568
Omar Uresti	70	71	74	72	287	2,568
Bob Burns	74	71	71	72	288	2,460
Hubert Green	72	71	74	71	288	2,460

	SCORES				TOTAL	MONEY
Dudley Hart	72	72	71	73	288	2,460
Masahiro Kuramoto	73	71	74	70	288	2,460
Dennis Paulson	70	72	71	75	288	2,460
Scott Simpson	73	70	71	74	288	2,460
Bart Bryant	70	73	74	72	289	2,352
Kawika Cotner	73	71	75	70	289	2,352
Harry Taylor	73	71	76	69	289	2,352
Fred Funk	74	71	73	72	290	2,292
Ted Tryba	74	70	69	77	290	2,292
Scott Hoch	70	74	72	76	292	2,256
Bill Britton	72	72	73	77	294	2,232
John Daly	73	71	76	78	298	2,208

Northern Telecom Open

Tucson National Golf Course
Par 36-36–72; 7,148 yards

January 19-22
purse, $1,250,000

Starr Pass Golf Club
Par 35-36–71; 6,942 yards
Tucson, Arizona

	SCORES				TOTAL	MONEY
Phil Mickelson	65	66	70	68	269	$225,000
Jim Gallagher, Jr.	68	64	69	69	270	110,000
Scott Simpson	69	65	68	68	270	110,000
Brett Ogle	68	65	68	70	271	60,000
Jim Furyk	69	69	67	67	272	50,000
Woody Austin	68	69	70	67	274	37,812.50
David Duval	67	70	67	70	274	37,812.50
Tom Kite	71	66	67	70	274	37,812.50
Naomichi Ozaki	68	67	70	69	274	37,812.50
Don Pooley	71	66	65	72	274	37,812.50
Bob Tway	70	65	69	70	274	37,812.50
Bart Bryant	70	69	67	69	275	26,250
Brandel Chamblee	70	71	68	66	275	26,250
Tom Purtzer	65	71	70	69	275	26,250
Nolan Henke	70	67	70	69	276	21,875
Hal Sutton	70	71	69	66	276	21,875
Tommy Armour III	70	66	71	70	277	15,812.50
Lennie Clements	69	71	68	69	277	15,812.50
Russ Cochran	68	69	70	70	277	15,812.50
John Cook	74	67	70	66	277	15,812.50
Peter Jordan	68	72	69	68	277	15,812.50
Gary McCord	72	68	71	66	277	15,812.50
Steve Pate	71	69	70	67	277	15,812.50
Paul Stankowski	67	66	69	75	277	15,812.50
Lee Janzen	72	70	68	68	278	9,339.29
Jeff Maggert	68	74	68	68	278	9,339.29
Steve Stricker	70	71	69	68	278	9,339.29
Bruce Vaughan	72	69	70	67	278	9,339.29
Dave Barr	71	67	70	70	278	9,339.28
Nick Faldo	70	70	70	68	278	9,339.28
Bobby Wadkins	69	69	70	70	278	9,339.28
Bob Estes	72	70	67	70	279	6,486.12
Mark Calcavecchia	69	69	74	67	279	6,486.11
Rick Fehr	68	70	70	71	279	6,486.11

	SCORES				TOTAL	MONEY
Paul Goydos	67	71	70	71	279	6,486.11
Scott Hoch	70	68	74	67	279	6,486.11
Neal Lancaster	72	67	72	68	279	6,486.11
Rocco Mediate	68	69	72	70	279	6,486.11
Ted Tryba	71	67	72	69	279	6,486.11
Tray Tyner	71	68	72	68	279	6,486.11
Jay Don Blake	67	71	71	71	280	4,750
Mike Brisky	71	68	71	70	280	4,750
Dudley Hart	72	68	69	71	280	4,750
Howard Twitty	66	69	72	73	280	4,750
Danny Briggs	70	67	74	70	281	3,575
Robin Freeman	69	67	76	69	281	3,575
Jerry Haas	71	70	71	69	281	3,575
Mike Hulbert	74	68	68	71	281	3,575
Mark O'Meara	69	71	71	70	281	3,575
Lanny Wadkins	67	73	69	72	281	3,575
John Adams	72	69	71	70	282	2,925
Andrew Magee	69	70	71	72	282	2,925
Doug Martin	70	71	72	69	282	2,925
Dan Pohl	71	71	71	69	282	2,925
Jim Thorpe	71	69	69	73	282	2,925
Ronnie Black	72	70	71	69	282	2,925
J.B. Sneve	71	71	68	72	282	2,925
Mark Brooks	68	70	74	71	283	2,762.50
Gil Morgan	72	69	69	73	283	2,762.50
Loren Roberts	72	67	72	72	283	2,762.50
John Wilson	70	68	73	72	283	2,762.50
Jeff Leonard	71	67	75	71	284	2,637.50
Yoshinori Mizumaki	69	72	68	75	284	2,637.50
Mike Standly	72	70	72	70	284	2,637.50
Mike Sullivan	71	69	70	74	284	2,637.50
Doug Tewell	73	69	74	68	284	2,637.50
Omar Uresti	71	71	74	68	284	2,637.50
Jim Carter	67	72	74	72	285	2,512.50
Brian Henninger	68	73	71	73	285	2,512.50
Bob Lohr	71	70	76	68	285	2,512.50
Dillard Pruitt	73	69	72	71	285	2,512.50
Kenny Perry	71	70	70	75	286	2,450
Brian Claar	70	70	74	73	287	2,400
Fred Funk	70	70	74	73	287	2,400
Jesper Parnevik	71	69	74	73	287	2,400
Kirk Triplett	70	70	74	74	288	2,350
Pat Bates	70	72	72	77	291	2,325
Chip Beck	68	71	76	78	293	2,300

Phoenix Open

TPC of Scottsdale, Phoenix, Arizona
Par 35-36–71; 6,992 yards

January 26-29
purse, $1,300,000

	SCORES				TOTAL	MONEY
Vijay Singh	70	67	66	66	269	$234,000
Billy Mayfair	69	67	67	66	269	140,400
(Singh defeated Mayfair on first extra hole.)						
Ben Crenshaw	68	64	70	69	271	88,400
Bruce Lietzke	72	65	69	66	272	53,733.34
Steve Jones	68	69	68	67	272	53,733.33

		SCORES			TOTAL	MONEY
Payne Stewart	71	68	67	66	272	53,733.33
John Adams	71	66	66	70	273	37,830
Mark Calcavecchia	72	67	66	68	273	37,830
Hale Irwin	66	66	72	69	273	37,830
Steve Lowery	70	68	65	70	273	37,830
Naomichi Ozaki	68	71	67	67	273	37,830
Jim Carter	70	64	73	67	274	24,700
Jim Furyk	67	68	68	71	274	24,700
Donnie Hammond	70	68	68	68	274	24,700
Tom Purtzer	69	68	69	68	274	24,700
Steve Stricker	70	68	67	69	274	24,700
Tom Watson	67	67	71	69	274	24,700
Rick Fehr	71	70	65	69	275	17,550
Blaine McCallister	68	69	71	67	275	17,550
John Morse	72	69	66	68	275	17,550
John Wilson	69	66	69	71	275	17,550
Paul Azinger	72	68	69	67	276	13,000
Dan Forsman	71	67	71	67	276	13,000
Tom Lehman	70	71	66	69	276	13,000
Doug Tewell	69	69	70	68	276	13,000
Joel Edwards	71	70	69	67	277	10,010
Steve Elkington	68	71	68	70	277	10,010
Steve Pate	71	69	71	66	277	10,010
Bob Estes	69	71	71	67	278	8,265.84
Loren Roberts	72	67	67	72	278	8,265.84
Ronnie Black	69	70	69	70	278	8,265.83
David Edwards	73	67	68	70	278	8,265.83
Gil Morgan	70	67	71	70	278	8,265.83
Grant Waite	69	71	71	67	278	8,265.83
Woody Austin	71	68	69	71	279	6,272.50
David Feherty	73	66	69	71	279	6,272.50
Bob Lohr	67	72	69	71	279	6,272.50
Andrew Magee	69	71	69	70	279	6,272.50
Phil Mickelson	70	66	70	73	279	6,272.50
Kirk Triplett	74	65	67	73	279	6,272.50
Jay Don Blake	68	70	70	72	280	4,426.50
Bill Glasson	69	70	69	72	280	4,426.50
Yoshinori Mizumaki	70	69	72	69	280	4,426.50
Kenny Perry	73	68	67	72	280	4,426.50
Dillard Pruitt	71	68	71	70	280	4,426.50
Gene Sauers	72	65	70	73	280	4,426.50
Bob Tway	73	67	69	71	280	4,426.50
Fuzzy Zoeller	70	71	67	72	280	4,426.50
Mark Carnevale	72	68	67	74	281	3,328
Bobby Wadkins	69	68	75	69	281	3,328
Skip Kendall	69	69	71	73	282	3,128.67
Jim McGovern	71	70	70	71	282	3,128.67
Pat Bates	69	70	72	71	282	3,128.66
Nick Faldo	71	69	76	67	283	2,964
Paul Goydos	72	68	73	70	283	2,964
Mike Hulbert	73	68	75	67	283	2,964
Howard Twitty	72	69	70	72	283	2,964
Duffy Waldorf	64	72	72	75	283	2,964
Brian Claar	69	72	69	74	284	2,847
Jay Delsing	72	67	70	75	284	2,847
Davis Love III	72	67	76	69	284	2,847
Dave Stockton, Jr.	72	68	74	70	284	2,847
Lee Janzen	68	71	75	71	285	2,782
Michael Bradley	68	69	73	76	286	2,743
David Ogrin	71	70	74	71	286	2,743

	SCORES				TOTAL	MONEY
Bob Burns	68	72	73	74	287	2,652
Brandel Chamblee	73	68	73	73	287	2,652
Neal Lancaster	68	70	72	77	287	2,652
Mike Standly	69	72	77	69	287	2,652
Mike Sullivan	72	69	73	73	287	2,652

AT&T Pebble Beach National Pro-Am

Pebble Beach Golf Links
Par 36-36–72; 6,799 yards

February 2-5
purse, $1,400,000

Spyglass Hill Golf Club
Par 36-36–72; 6,810 yards

Poppy Hills Golf Club
Par 36-36–72; 6,865 yards
Pebble Beach, California

	SCORES				TOTAL	MONEY
Peter Jacobsen	67	73	66	65	271	$252,000
David Duval	72	67	67	67	273	151,200
Davis Love III	65	71	71	68	275	81,200
Kenny Perry	68	68	67	72	275	81,200
Payne Stewart	71	67	69	70	277	56,000
Guy Boros	69	66	71	72	278	46,900
Brad Faxon	70	64	72	72	278	46,900
Jack Nicklaus	71	70	67	70	278	46,900
John Adams	72	66	71	70	279	36,400
Emlyn Aubrey	70	69	68	72	279	36,400
Nick Faldo	66	72	69	72	279	36,400
Mark O'Meara	73	68	70	68	279	36,400
Mark Calcavecchia	72	70	69	69	280	24,733.34
Fuzzy Zoeller	68	67	76	69	280	24,733.34
Ben Crenshaw	73	72	69	66	280	24,733.33
Andrew Magee	70	69	70	71	280	24,733.33
Steve Stricker	74	72	64	70	280	24,733.33
Tom Watson	70	65	73	72	280	24,733.33
Steve Elkington	74	70	68	69	281	18,900
Blaine McCallister	70	72	67	72	281	18,900
Mark Brooks	70	69	74	69	282	12,460
Jim Carter	70	70	69	73	282	12,460
Fred Funk	69	71	72	70	282	12,460
Jim Furyk	70	68	74	70	282	12,460
Bob Lohr	71	69	73	69	282	12,460
Steve Lowery	76	74	64	68	282	12,460
Jeff Maggert	71	68	70	73	282	12,460
Hal Sutton	69	69	70	74	282	12,460
Kirk Triplett	71	70	70	71	282	12,460
Tommy Tolles	74	66	73	69	282	12,460
Robin Freeman	72	72	69	70	283	7,140
Steve Gotsche	70	70	72	71	283	7,140
Mike Heinen	72	67	70	74	283	7,140
Ed Humenik	70	69	74	70	283	7,140
Brian Kamm	76	70	68	69	283	7,140
Tom Purtzer	72	68	73	70	283	7,140
Loren Roberts	68	72	69	74	283	7,140
Charlie Rymer	71	70	71	71	283	7,140

	SCORES				TOTAL	MONEY
Craig Stadler	72	71	70	70	283	7,140
Ray Stewart	72	70	70	71	283	7,140
Duffy Waldorf	70	71	69	73	283	7,140
Willie Wood	70	74	70	69	283	7,140
Billy Andrade	71	70	72	71	284	4,368
Rick Fehr	72	73	68	71	284	4,368
Keith Fergus	72	71	71	70	284	4,368
Bob Gilder	72	68	74	70	284	4,368
Peter Jordan	74	68	70	72	284	4,368
Justin Leonard	71	71	71	71	284	4,368
Rocco Mediate	70	69	70	75	284	4,368
John Cook	74	69	70	72	285	3,376.80
David Frost	71	72	68	74	285	3,376.80
Mike Hulbert	71	72	68	74	285	3,376.80
Gil Morgan	73	69	68	75	285	3,376.80
Jay Williamson	70	71	71	73	285	3,376.80
Chris Perry	73	69	69	75	286	3,220
Kawika Cotner	67	73	72	75	287	3,192
Paul Azinger	74	70	70	74	288	3,122
Larry Mize	72	69	72	75	288	3,122
Jeff Sluman	73	71	68	76	288	3,122
Dave Stockton	69	72	71	76	288	3,122
Howard Twitty	69	72	73	75	289	3,052
Don Reese	72	70	69	79	290	3,024
Brad Bryant	71	73	70	77	291	2,982
Steve Rintoul	72	70	69	80	291	2,982

Buick Invitational of California

Torrey Pines Golf Club, San Diego, California
South Course: Par 36-36–72; 7,000 yards
North Course: Par 36-36–72; 6,592 yards

February 9-12
purse, $1,200,000

	SCORES				TOTAL	MONEY
Peter Jacobsen	68	65	68	68	269	$216,000
Mark Calcavecchia	71	67	67	68	273	79,200
Mike Hulbert	70	65	70	68	273	79,200
Hal Sutton	67	69	68	69	273	79,200
Kirk Triplett	69	69	66	69	273	79,200
Dan Pohl	65	74	66	70	275	41,700
Dillard Pruitt	69	70	68	68	275	41,700
Brandel Chamblee	66	66	74	70	276	33,600
Nolan Henke	68	66	73	69	276	33,600
John Huston	69	71	67	69	276	33,600
David Ogrin	66	69	74	67	276	33,600
Brad Bryant	72	67	69	69	277	24,300
Brian Kamm	69	71	70	67	277	24,300
Davis Love III	69	71	72	65	277	24,300
Craig Stadler	67	69	72	69	277	24,300
Chip Beck	70	70	71	67	278	15,240
Danny Briggs	69	69	70	70	278	15,240
Bob Estes	69	69	71	69	278	15,240
J.P. Hayes	67	71	72	68	278	15,240
Ed Humenik	69	71	69	69	278	15,240
Bob Lohr	72	69	67	70	278	15,240
Phil Mickelson	65	69	75	69	278	15,240
Payne Stewart	66	73	67	72	278	15,240

	SCORES				TOTAL	MONEY
John Wilson	71	69	73	65	278	15,240
Jay Don Blake	69	72	69	68	278	15,240
Fred Funk	69	70	72	68	279	8,700
Scott Gump	70	68	70	71	279	8,700
Steve Lowery	68	69	70	72	279	8,700
Blaine McCallister	68	70	72	69	279	8,700
Dennis Paulson	67	68	72	72	279	8,700
Loren Roberts	72	69	72	66	279	8,700
John Adams	70	67	71	72	280	6,226.67
Ronnie Black	69	71	67	73	280	6,226.67
Brad Faxon	66	73	70	71	280	6,226.67
Kelly Gibson	67	73	68	72	280	6,226.67
Jerry Haas	65	73	71	71	280	6,226.67
Chris Perry	73	66	69	72	280	6,226.67
Joey Sindelar	68	67	74	71	280	6,226.66
Mike Smith	73	68	71	68	280	6,226.66
Scott Verplank	67	74	70	69	280	6,226.66
Jim Carter	69	72	69	71	281	4,200
Ben Crenshaw	73	64	69	75	281	4,200
Keith Fergus	69	68	75	69	281	4,200
Tom Kite	75	66	67	73	281	4,200
Jesper Parnevik	72	64	74	71	281	4,200
Steve Stricker	67	66	75	73	281	4,200
Howard Twitty	68	67	74	72	281	4,200
Tommy Armour III	69	67	71	75	282	3,204
Billy Mayfair	69	72	70	71	282	3,204
Billy Andrade	71	68	73	71	283	2,922
Donnie Hammond	68	72	70	73	283	2,922
Tom Hearn	69	72	73	69	283	2,922
Scott McCarron	71	68	71	73	283	2,922
Bob Burns	66	69	74	75	284	2,748
Curt Byrum	68	70	76	70	284	2,748
Chris DiMarco	65	72	79	68	284	2,748
Steve Hart	71	68	74	71	284	2,748
Lennie Clements	74	66	72	73	285	2,640
John Cook	71	70	72	72	285	2,640
Joel Edwards	65	70	76	74	285	2,640
Steve Gotsche	68	71	76	70	285	2,640
Mark O'Meara	68	70	76	71	285	2,640
Joe Acosta, Jr.	69	72	70	75	286	2,508
David Duval	69	70	76	71	286	2,508
John Mahaffey	69	71	74	72	286	2,508
Dave Stockton, Jr.	73	68	72	73	286	2,508
Bobby Wadkins	68	68	76	74	286	2,508
Curtis Strange	71	70	75	70	286	2,508
Emlyn Aubrey	69	69	76	73	287	2,352
Dan Forsman	70	70	76	71	287	2,352
Robin Freeman	71	68	75	73	287	2,352
J.L. Lewis	71	70	73	73	287	2,352
Yoshinori Mizumaki	68	70	73	76	287	2,352
Lee Rinker	67	73	73	74	287	2,352
Brad Sherfy	72	69	75	71	287	2,352
Mike Brisky	67	69	82	70	288	2,256
Craig Kanada	68	73	74	74	289	2,220
Steve Rintoul	71	70	76	72	289	2,220
Larry Nelson	67	72	76	75	290	2,172
Doug Tewell	70	71	77	72	290	2,172
Keith Clearwater	70	67	82	72	291	2,112
Paul Goydos	68	71	75	77	291	2,112
John Morse	71	68	77	75	291	2,112

	SCORES				TOTAL	MONEY
Mark Wurtz	69	71	78	74	292	2,064
Bruce Vaughan	73	68	75	77	293	2,040

Bob Hope Chrysler Classic

Bermuda Dunes Country Club, Indian Wells, California
Par 36-36–72; 6,927 yards

Indian Wells Country Club, Indian Wells, California
Par 36-36–72; 6,478 yards

La Quinta Country Club, La Quinta, California
Par 36-36–72; 6,888 yards

Indian Ridge Country Club, Palm Desert, California
Par 36-36–72; 7,037 yards

February 16-19
purse, $1,200,000

	SCORES					TOTAL	MONEY
Kenny Perry	63	71	64	67	70	335	$216,000
David Duval	67	68	65	67	69	336	129,600
Dillard Pruitt	65	70	69	68	65	337	62,400
Curtis Strange	64	73	67	63	70	337	62,400
Tommy Tolles	66	69	68	64	70	337	62,400
Robert Gamez	70	68	66	68	66	338	43,200
Tommy Armour III	66	67	69	68	69	339	34,920
Mark Brooks	67	68	69	65	70	339	34,920
Kelly Gibson	65	71	67	67	69	339	34,920
Donnie Hammond	67	69	66	69	68	339	34,920
Harry Taylor	66	64	66	71	72	339	34,920
Lee Rinker	67	69	71	68	65	340	26,400
Tray Tyner	67	68	70	65	70	340	26,400
Jim Gallagher, Jr.	64	72	70	69	66	341	22,200
Justin Leonard	68	68	67	71	67	341	22,200
Brandel Chamblee	70	68	68	67	69	342	15,760
Jim Furyk	70	65	68	68	71	342	15,760
Larry Mize	67	69	69	69	68	342	15,760
Mark O'Meara	69	68	65	67	73	342	15,760
Brad Sherfy	71	67	69	66	69	342	15,760
Scott Simpson	66	69	69	68	70	342	15,760
Paul Stankowski	71	64	66	69	72	342	15,760
Bob Tway	70	67	67	69	69	342	15,760
Kirk Triplett	70	68	67	69	68	342	15,760
Keith Fergus	65	69	69	69	71	343	9,800
Dennis Paulson	69	69	70	66	69	343	9,800
Fuzzy Zoeller	68	68	66	70	71	343	9,800
Chris DiMarco	72	73	66	66	67	344	8,160
Fred Funk	66	69	70	69	70	344	8,160
Steve Gotsche	67	72	68	69	68	344	8,160
John Huston	67	70	68	70	69	344	8,160
Steve Pate	68	68	72	71	65	344	8,160
Patrick Burke	68	67	67	74	69	345	6,205.72
Bob Burns	68	69	65	73	70	345	6,205.72
Tom Kite	71	71	64	70	69	345	6,205.72
Joe Acosta, Jr.	66	68	72	72	67	345	6,205.71
Marco Dawson	64	70	70	70	71	345	6,205.71
Neal Lancaster	68	72	69	68	68	345	6,205.71
Chris Perry	66	67	71	69	72	345	6,205.71

	SCORES				TOTAL	MONEY
Yoshinori Kaneko	70	66	69	71	70	346	4,205.34
J.L. Lewis	67	70	68	71	70	346	4,205.34
Robin Freeman	64	70	72	69	71	346	4,205.33
Skip Kendall	71	73	65	69	68	346	4,205.33
Bob Lohr	72	73	64	69	68	346	4,205.33
John Mahaffey	70	72	66	70	68	346	4,205.33
Gil Morgan	70	68	71	68	69	346	4,205.33
Tony Sills	71	71	67	70	67	346	4,205.33
Mike Reid	71	75	66	64	70	346	4,205.34
Guy Boros	67	72	68	70	70	347	2,961.60
Bob Estes	72	72	65	69	69	347	2,961.60
Bob Gilder	71	70	66	71	69	347	2,961.60
Andrew Magee	67	71	69	68	72	347	2,961.60
Steve Rintoul	73	67	69	69	69	347	2,961.60
Emlyn Aubrey	71	71	65	71	70	348	2,688
Curt Byrum	69	73	66	68	72	348	2,688
Joel Edwards	70	65	72	70	71	348	2,688
Dan Forsman	70	69	70	70	69	348	2,688
Scott Hoch	70	69	68	72	69	348	2,688
Yoshinori Mizumaki	69	69	70	71	69	348	2,688
Tim Simpson	67	68	71	67	75	348	2,688
Ted Tryba	69	69	71	68	71	348	2,688
John Wilson	69	73	66	71	69	348	2,688
Bart Bryant	70	70	70	69	70	349	2,532
Nolan Henke	69	69	70	71	70	349	2,532
Brian Henninger	71	68	69	70	71	349	2,532
Mike Springer	69	68	72	68	72	349	2,532
Woody Austin	68	71	70	68	73	350	2,448
J.P. Hayes	71	70	69	69	71	350	2,448
Mark Wurtz	67	68	70	72	73	350	2,448
Gary Hallberg	70	71	69	68	73	351	2,376
Corey Pavin	69	70	72	68	72	351	2,376
Grant Waite	68	68	70	72	73	351	2,376
Lanny Wadkins	69	74	68	68	73	352	2,328
Ikuo Shirahama	71	67	68	71	80	357	2,304

Nissan Open

Riviera Country Club, Pacific Palisades, California
Par 35-36–71; 6,946 yards

February 23-26
purse, $1,200,000

	SCORES				TOTAL	MONEY
Corey Pavin	67	66	68	67	268	$216,000
Jay Don Blake	69	67	66	69	271	105,600
Kenny Perry	70	62	68	71	271	105,600
Scott Simpson	70	66	68	68	272	52,800
Craig Stadler	67	68	67	70	272	52,800
Jodie Mudd	66	71	69	67	273	43,200
Jay Haas	69	70	68	67	274	38,700
Lanny Wadkins	67	72	66	69	274	38,700
Ronnie Black	72	68	66	70	276	30,000
Jim Furyk	67	74	65	70	276	30,000
Mike Hulbert	71	66	68	71	276	30,000
Brian Kamm	67	74	67	68	276	30,000
Mike Reid	69	69	69	69	276	30,000
Guy Boros	73	70	65	69	277	20,400
Steve Elkington	68	72	68	69	277	20,400

	SCORES				TOTAL	MONEY
Bob Estes	68	66	70	73	277	20,400
Steve Lowery	69	70	68	70	277	20,400
Jeff Sluman	72	67	69	69	277	20,400
Fred Couples	69	69	68	72	278	15,060
David Feherty	69	68	72	69	278	15,060
Blaine McCallister	72	70	69	67	278	15,060
Bob Tway	70	72	69	67	278	15,060
Lennie Clements	71	70	68	70	279	12,000
Scott Hoch	70	69	69	71	279	12,000
Emlyn Aubrey	70	69	72	69	280	8,406
Brandel Chamblee	70	72	71	67	280	8,406
Keith Clearwater	70	73	69	68	280	8,406
Jerry Haas	71	70	71	68	280	8,406
Donnie Hammond	68	73	70	69	280	8,406
Mike Heinen	70	72	71	67	280	8,406
Dennis Paulson	70	73	69	68	280	8,406
Don Pooley	72	68	71	69	280	8,406
Kirk Triplett	71	69	70	70	280	8,406
Omar Uresti	68	72	67	73	280	8,406
Peter Jacobsen	69	71	69	72	281	5,790
Davis Love III	69	74	68	70	281	5,790
Billy Mayfair	66	72	68	75	281	5,790
Dan Pohl	70	67	70	74	281	5,790
Scott Verplank	74	67	70	70	281	5,790
John Wilson	72	70	71	68	281	5,790
Mark Calcavecchia	73	69	72	68	282	4,440
John Daly·	67	69	71	75	282	4,440
David Edwards	70	72	71	69	282	4,440
Tom Kite	71	67	74	70	282	4,440
Bobby Wadkins	71	71	69	71	282	4,440
Patrick Burke	70	73	69	71	283	3,264
Dudley Hart	73	68	69	73	283	3,264
Lee Janzen	77	66	67	73	283	3,264
Skip Kendall	73	67	72	71	283	3,264
Bruce Vaughan	71	69	72	71	283	3,264
Duffy Waldorf	71	72	70	70	283	3,264
Jim Carter	68	73	70	73	284	2,784
Brad Faxon	67	75	68	74	284	2,784
Rick Fehr	72	71	71	70	284	2,784
Justin Leonard	69	70	74	71	284	2,784
Scott McCarron	70	69	73	72	284	2,784
Tony Sills	73	70	68	73	284	2,784
Robin Freeman	69	72	71	73	285	2,664
Doug Martin	73	67	71	74	285	2,664
Mark Wiebe	69	72	73	71	285	2,664
Tommy Armour III	73	69	73	71	286	2,592
Brian Claar	71	71	73	71	286	2,592
Ben Crenshaw	71	71	71	73	286	2,592
Kelly Gibson	72	66	79	70	287	2,532
Tray Tyner	72	71	73	71	287	2,532
Hale Irwin	69	72	76	71	288	2,448
Steve Pate	68	72	73	75	288	2,448
Paul Stankowski	71	72	73	72	288	2,448
Dave Stockton, Jr.	73	70	73	72	288	2,448
D.A. Weibring	68	70	77	73	288	2,448
Marco Dawson	71	72	74	72	289	2,328
Glen Day	72	69	74	74	289	2,328
J.P. Hayes	71	71	72	75	289	2,328
Tim Loustalot	69	72	72	76	289	2,328

	SCORES				TOTAL	MONEY
Kazuhiro Takami	72	71	72	74	289	2,328
Bill Porter	71	72	75	72	290	2,256
Kevin Burton	74	69	76	72	291	2,232
Jeff Leonard	71	72	74	77	294	2,196
Mike Standly	69	74	80	71	294	2,196

Doral-Ryder Open

Doral Resort & Country Club, Miami, Florida   March 2-5
Par 36-36–72; 6,939 yards   purse, $1,500,000

	SCORES				TOTAL	MONEY
Nick Faldo	67	71	66	69	273	$270,000
Peter Jacobsen	68	69	64	73	274	132,000
Greg Norman	68	68	65	73	274	132,000
Steve Elkington	67	72	67	69	275	62,000
Justin Leonard	68	68	71	68	275	62,000
Davis Love III	65	69	70	71	275	62,000
Woody Austin	66	71	68	71	276	48,375
Hale Irwin	70	70	67	69	276	48,375
Steve Stricker	70	68	71	68	277	43,500
Steve Lowery	65	72	73	68	278	39,000
Mark O'Meara	69	72	66	71	278	39,000
Fulton Allem	66	71	68	74	279	29,400
Michael Bradley	70	73	67	69	279	29,400
Mark McCumber	70	71	69	69	279	29,400
Vijay Singh	70	70	67	72	279	29,400
Jeff Sluman	69	67	70	73	279	29,400
Lennie Clements	70	70	67	73	280	17,700
David Duval	67	72	68	73	280	17,700
Ernie Els	74	67	70	69	280	17,700
Raymond Floyd	72	71	68	69	280	17,700
Bill Glasson	68	68	70	74	280	17,700
Jay Haas	69	69	70	72	280	17,700
Dudley Hart	71	67	68	74	280	17,700
Colin Montgomerie	72	68	68	72	280	17,700
Naomichi Ozaki	68	68	72	72	280	17,700
Scott Verplank	65	76	70	69	280	17,700
Jim Carter	72	65	70	74	281	10,425
Russ Cochran	71	64	71	75	281	10,425
Mike Hulbert	71	70	70	70	281	10,425
John Huston	73	69	65	74	281	10,425
Jesper Parnevik	71	66	74	70	281	10,425
Harry Taylor	71	67	69	74	281	10,425
Mark Calcavecchia	69	74	70	69	282	7,757.15
Brian Claar	68	75	69	70	282	7,757.15
Fred Funk	70	72	70	70	282	7,757.14
Jim Gallagher, Jr.	71	68	71	72	282	7,757.14
Hal Sutton	68	71	66	77	282	7,757.14
Tray Tyner	69	68	73	72	282	7,757.14
D.A. Weibring	71	70	67	74	282	7,757.14
Bernhard Langer	69	71	71	72	283	6,150
Dillard Pruitt	70	69	71	73	283	6,150
Bruce Vaughan	70	69	71	73	283	6,150
Curt Byrum	71	69	72	72	284	4,383
Chris DiMarco	71	71	70	72	284	4,383
David Edwards	73	69	68	74	284	4,383

	SCORES				TOTAL	MONEY
Scott Gump	71	69	68	76	284	4,383
Skip Kendall	69	73	69	73	284	4,383
Billy Mayfair	70	71	71	72	284	4,383
Jim McGovern	72	71	66	75	284	4,383
Loren Roberts	70	71	70	73	284	4,383
Curtis Strange	72	71	67	74	284	4,383
Grant Waite	71	71	65	77	284	4,383
Bruce Fleisher	73	69	71	72	285	3,456
Mike Heinen	68	75	73	69	285	3,456
Andrew Magee	70	68	74	73	285	3,456
Paul Stankowski	70	73	71	71	285	3,456
Bobby Wadkins	70	72	67	76	285	3,456
Paul Azinger	70	72	72	72	286	3,240
Jay Don Blake	72	67	70	77	286	3,240
John Daly	71	69	72	74	286	3,240
Jim Furyk	70	71	71	74	286	3,240
Neal Lancaster	71	72	69	74	286	3,240
Chris Perry	71	71	72	72	286	3,240
Gene Sauers	70	70	74	72	286	3,240
Lanny Wadkins	72	71	67	76	286	3,240
Mark Wiebe	70	73	71	72	286	3,240
Clark Dennis	71	72	71	73	287	3,045
John Morse	70	70	72	75	287	3,045
Mike Standly	73	67	71	76	287	3,045
Bob Tway	74	67	70	76	287	3,045
Tom Kite	66	73	71	78	288	2,970
Robert Gamez	70	69	73	77	289	2,910
Brian Henninger	71	72	70	76	289	2,910
Dave Stockton, Jr.	71	70	71	77	289	2,910
Billy Andrade	69	70	75	76	290	2,850
Payne Stewart	68	74	76	74	292	2,820
Richard Sadler	72	69	76	77	294	2,790

Honda Classic

Weston Hills Country Club, Ft. Lauderdale, Florida
Par 35-36–71; 7,069 yards

March 9-12
purse, $1,200,000

	SCORES				TOTAL	MONEY
Mark O'Meara	68	65	71	71	275	$216,000
Nick Faldo	67	71	69	69	276	129,600
Ian Woosnam	68	72	69	68	277	81,600
Andrew Magee	69	67	76	67	279	57,600
Blaine McCallister	70	66	73	71	280	48,000
Bill Britton	71	69	72	69	281	43,200
Mike Standly	71	66	75	70	282	40,200
Seve Ballesteros	70	68	76	69	283	32,400
Michael Bradley	73	69	73	68	283	32,400
Brian Claar	69	70	72	72	283	32,400
Keith Fergus	69	72	71	71	283	32,400
Scott Verplank	74	67	73	69	283	32,400
Bernhard Langer	70	71	73	70	284	18,174.55
Mark McCumber	71	67	76	70	284	18,174.55
Jim McGovern	65	74	75	70	284	18,174.55
Nick Price	71	70	69	74	284	18,174.55
Lee Rinker	68	72	76	68	284	18,174.55
Steve Stricker	69	72	71	72	284	18,174.55

		SCORES			TOTAL	MONEY
Woody Austin	73	69	70	72	284	18,174.54
Patrick Burke	73	71	67	73	284	18,174.54
Scott Gump	73	69	70	72	284	18,174.54
Mike Hulbert	70	74	69	71	284	18,174.54
Bob Tway	71	72	70	71	284	18,174.54
Glen Day	70	69	72	74	285	10,560
Eduardo Romero	70	72	73	70	285	10,560
Gene Sauers	69	72	74	70	285	10,560
Ronnie Black	73	71	70	72	286	8,700
Lee Janzen	69	73	70	74	286	8,700
Joey Sindelar	75	69	71	71	286	8,700
Paul Stankowski	70	71	73	72	286	8,700
Robin Freeman	70	70	74	73	287	6,520
Brian Henninger	72	71	71	73	287	6,520
Tom Lehman	74	67	72	74	287	6,520
Justin Leonard	71	70	76	70	287	6,520
Bob Lohr	69	71	75	72	287	6,520
Doug Martin	71	68	75	73	287	6,520
Vijay Singh	69	72	77	69	287	6,520
Curtis Strange	72	72	71	72	287	6,520
Bobby Wadkins	73	70	70	74	287	6,520
Donnie Hammond	71	69	74	74	288	4,440
Dudley Hart	71	69	76	72	288	4,440
Peter Jordan	72	71	72	73	288	4,440
Joey Rassett	73	67	74	74	288	4,440
Steve Rintoul	69	74	70	75	288	4,440
Mike Smith	72	67	77	72	288	4,440
Dicky Thompson	74	70	71	73	288	4,440
Tommy Armour III	70	71	74	74	289	3,124
Mark Calcavecchia	66	77	74	72	289	3,124
Bob Gilder	71	73	74	71	289	3,124
Craig Parry	72	71	74	72	289	3,124
Jerry Pate	71	72	72	74	289	3,124
Tray Tyner	70	74	72	73	289	3,124
Billy Andrade	70	74	73	73	290	2,752
Mike Brisky	71	72	71	76	290	2,752
Curt Byrum	72	71	72	75	290	2,752
Colin Montgomerie	69	75	71	75	290	2,752
Steve Pate	73	70	76	71	290	2,752
Howard Twitty	73	71	72	74	290	2,752
Dave Barr	67	74	76	74	291	2,592
Bob Burns	71	73	76	71	291	2,592
Brandel Chamblee	70	74	74	73	291	2,592
Marco Dawson	69	71	79	72	291	2,592
Jim Gallagher, Jr.	72	68	74	77	291	2,592
Jerry Haas	69	75	72	75	291	2,592
Mike Sullivan	68	74	74	75	291	2,592
Chip Beck	73	69	75	75	292	2,436
Chris DiMarco	71	70	78	73	292	2,436
Bruce Fleisher	73	71	73	75	292	2,436
Brian Kamm	73	71	78	70	292	2,436
Mark Wiebe	68	76	71	77	292	2,436
Chris Perry	73	69	76	74	292	2,436
Mark Carnevale	71	72	75	75	293	2,328
David Feherty	71	73	76	73	293	2,328
Grant Waite	74	67	77	75	293	2,328
Joel Edwards	72	72	71	79	294	2,232
Dan Forsman	70	71	79	74	294	2,232
Bruce Lietzke	71	72	77	74	294	2,232
Yoshinori Mizumaki	71	68	82	73	294	2,232

	SCORES				TOTAL	MONEY
Dicky Pride	72	69	78	75	294	2,232
John Daly	71	70	77	77	295	2,148
Neal Lancaster	72	71	73	79	295	2,148
Keith Clearwater	69	74	79	76	298	2,112
Bobby Tracy	71	73	77	80	301	2,088

The Nestle Invitational

Bay Hill Club, Orlando, Florida
Par 36-36–72; 7,114 yards

March 16-19
purse, $1,200,000

	SCORES				TOTAL	MONEY
Loren Roberts	68	65	68	71	272	$216,000
Brad Faxon	69	70	64	71	274	129,600
Peter Jacobsen	70	68	68	69	275	81,600
Steve Stricker	67	72	69	69	277	57,600
Nick Faldo	71	73	66	68	278	39,300
Jay Haas	72	69	69	68	278	39,300
Bob Lohr	69	70	67	72	278	39,300
Mark McCumber	69	70	69	70	278	39,300
Jesper Parnevik	67	72	67	72	278	39,300
Duffy Waldorf	71	72	70	65	278	39,300
Mark McNulty	68	72	67	72	279	27,600
Greg Norman	71	69	70	69	279	27,600
Scott Simpson	70	71	70	68	279	27,600
Patrick Burke	71	73	70	66	280	22,200
Nick Price	71	70	68	71	280	22,200
Fred Funk	70	71	68	72	281	18,600
Davis Love III	69	66	73	73	281	18,600
Jeff Maggert	73	69	69	70	281	18,600
Curtis Strange	71	70	70	70	281	18,600
Billy Andrade	67	69	74	72	282	13,000
Emlyn Aubrey	74	67	68	73	282	13,000
Mark Brooks	65	73	73	71	282	13,000
Dan Forsman	70	72	67	73	282	13,000
Bill Glasson	69	75	70	68	282	13,000
Vijay Singh	73	70	66	73	282	13,000
Kelly Gibson	74	70	65	74	283	8,880
Paul Goydos	73	67	72	71	283	8,880
Mike Heinen	69	71	70	73	283	8,880
Jeff Sluman	71	70	70	72	283	8,880
Fuzzy Zoeller	68	71	72	72	283	8,880
Paul Azinger	71	70	71	72	284	6,960
Mike Hulbert	75	69	72	68	284	6,960
Bernhard Langer	71	69	75	69	284	6,960
Masahiro Ozaki	71	73	72	68	284	6,960
Dan Pohl	72	67	69	76	284	6,960
Payne Stewart	69	70	73	72	284	6,960
Chip Beck	72	70	72	71	285	5,400
Fred Couples	68	71	70	76	285	5,400
Jim Gallagher, Jr.	70	75	70	70	285	5,400
Tom Lehman	70	75	73	67	285	5,400
Corey Pavin	71	70	71	73	285	5,400
Brandel Chamblee	71	73	69	73	286	3,966.86
Ben Crenshaw	71	70	70	75	286	3,966.86
Ernie Els	74	67	77	68	286	3,966.86
Colin Montgomerie	73	70	70	73	286	3,966.86

	SCORES				TOTAL	MONEY
Mark O'Meara	70	73	71	72	286	3,966.86
Jose Maria Olazabal	75	69	66	76	286	3,966.85
Mike Sullivan	73	72	70	71	286	3,966.85
Jim Carter	68	70	76	73	287	2,994
Steve Jones	74	69	74	70	287	2,994
Larry Nelson	70	73	71	73	287	2,994
Ian Woosnam	71	74	70	72	287	2,994
Mark Calcavecchia	73	68	73	74	288	2,739.43
John Cook	72	71	71	74	288	2,739.43
David Duval	71	72	70	75	288	2,739.43
Bob Estes	71	72	69	76	288	2,739.43
Chris Perry	71	72	73	72	288	2,739.43
Kenny Perry	74	70	68	76	288	2,739.43
Larry Mize	71	73	68	76	288	2,739.42
Andy Bean	72	73	73	72	290	2,604
Rick Fehr	67	77	74	72	290	2,604
Donnie Hammond	75	67	72	76	290	2,604
Greg Kraft	74	69	74	73	290	2,604
D.A. Weibring	74	71	72	74	291	2,544
Lee Janzen	73	70	72	77	292	2,508
Tom Kite	72	72	72	76	292	2,508
John Morse	71	74	73	75	293	2,460
David Peoples	74	70	76	73	293	2,460
Neal Lancaster	74	70	72	78	294	2,424
Brian Kamm	71	71	76	77	295	2,388
Bill Kratzert	72	72	73	78	295	2,388
John Daly	68	74	73	81	296	2,340
John Mahaffey	72	73	73	78	296	2,340
Don Pooley	70	75	78	75	298	2,304
Eddie Pearce	76	69	76	79	300	2,280

The Players Championship

TPC at Sawgrass, Ponte Vedra Beach, Florida
Par 36-36–72; 7,896 yards

March 23-26
purse, $3,000,000

	SCORES				TOTAL	MONEY
Lee Janzen	69	74	69	71	283	$540,000
Bernhard Langer	69	71	71	73	284	324,000
Corey Pavin	66	73	72	74	285	156,000
Gene Sauers	67	72	78	68	285	156,000
Payne Stewart	69	73	71	72	285	156,000
Brad Bryant	72	71	72	71	286	104,250
Davis Love III	73	67	74	72	286	104,250
Billy Andrade	74	69	73	71	287	87,000
Larry Mize	69	77	72	69	287	87,000
Naomichi Ozaki	74	70	72	71	287	87,000
Brian Claar	74	70	71	73	288	69,000
Scott Simpson	71	72	73	72	288	69,000
Steve Stricker	69	71	74	74	288	69,000
Tom Lehman	71	72	72	74	289	52,500
Phil Mickelson	78	66	75	70	289	52,500
Colin Montgomerie	79	70	71	69	289	52,500
Craig Stadler	73	73	75	68	289	52,500
Curt Byrum	73	71	76	70	290	39,120
Mark Calcavecchia	74	75	71	70	290	39,120
Lennie Clements	71	71	76	72	290	39,120

	SCORES				TOTAL	MONEY
Jeff Maggert	71	72	72	75	290	39,120
Billy Mayfair	71	77	70	72	290	39,120
Jim Gallagher, Jr.	74	72	73	72	291	25,950
Mark McCumber	71	73	72	75	291	25,950
Mark McNulty	76	72	71	72	291	25,950
Jose Maria Olazabal	78	70	74	69	291	25,950
Curtis Strange	76	71	72	72	291	25,950
Ian Woosnam	74	69	73	75	291	25,950
Michael Bradley	75	70	74	73	292	19,500
Fred Couples	73	72	73	74	292	19,500
Peter Jacobsen	74	69	71	78	292	19,500
Masahiro Ozaki	72	72	75	73	292	19,500
Tom Watson	72	71	75	74	292	19,500
Bob Estes	76	73	75	69	293	16,200
Loren Roberts	73	72	72	76	293	16,200
Justin Leonard	73	74	72	74	293	16,200
Seve Ballesteros	75	68	73	78	294	13,200
David Frost	72	74	75	73	294	13,200
Mike Heinen	74	75	67	78	294	13,200
Andrew Magee	70	75	72	77	294	13,200
Greg Norman	70	74	73	77	294	13,200
Nick Price	73	71	75	75	294	13,200
Bob Gilder	73	76	75	71	295	9,620
Tom Kite	71	74	76	74	295	9,620
Wayne Levi	73	74	74	74	295	9,620
Bruce Lietzke	78	70	75	72	295	9,620
Vijay Singh	74	72	73	76	295	9,620
D.A. Weibring	71	70	73	81	295	9,620
Brad Faxon	73	74	76	73	296	7,330
Robert Gamez	74	69	78	75	296	7,330
Paul Goydos	75	74	75	72	296	7,330
Jesper Parnevik	74	74	72	76	296	7,330
Dicky Pride	74	73	74	75	296	7,330
Jeff Sluman	74	74	78	70	296	7,330
Bob Lohr	74	75	73	75	297	6,750
John Mahaffey	76	73	72	76	297	6,750
Rocco Mediate	71	74	80	72	297	6,750
Kenny Perry	76	73	73	75	297	6,750
Fuzzy Zoeller	72	73	77	75	297	6,750
Hale Irwin	73	68	78	78	297	6,750
Chip Beck	72	75	76	75	298	6,390
Clark Dennis	78	71	77	72	298	6,390
Fred Funk	73	73	74	78	298	6,390
Ken Green	77	71	74	76	298	6,390
Nolan Henke	74	75	72	77	298	6,390
Bobby Wadkins	75	74	77	72	298	6,390
Kirk Triplett	71	75	78	75	299	6,180
Ernie Els	72	72	78	78	300	6,032.25
Gil Morgan	74	74	75	77	300	6,032.25
Dan Pohl	72	74	76	78	300	6,032.25
Bob Tway	78	71	74	77	300	6,032.25
Donnie Hammond	73	76	81	72	302	5,880
Robert Allenby	77	72	78	79	306	5,820

Freeport-McMoRan Classic

English Turn Golf & Country Club, New Orleans, Louisiana
Par 36-36–72; 7,116 yards

March 30-April 2
purse, $1,200,000

	SCORES			TOTAL	MONEY
Davis Love III	68	69	66	71	274	$216,000
Mike Heinen	66	71	71	66	274	129,600
(Love defeated Heinen on second extra hole.)					
David Duval	67	68	71	69	275	81,600
Craig Parry	71	69	66	70	276	57,600
Jeff Maggert	72	66	70	69	277	43,800
David Peoples	70	69	66	72	277	43,800
Mike Standly	70	65	69	73	277	43,800
Brad Bryant	65	74	69	70	278	36,000
Scott Simpson	68	70	71	69	278	36,000
Danny Briggs	69	71	73	66	279	27,600
Brian Claar	68	70	71	70	279	27,600
Lennie Clements	69	68	70	72	279	27,600
Kirk Triplett	66	73	71	69	279	27,600
Mark Wiebe	70	68	68	73	279	27,600
Woody Austin	68	71	70	71	280	16,880
Michael Bradley	68	71	67	74	280	16,880
Fred Couples	73	68	68	71	280	16,880
Steve Jones	69	69	66	76	280	16,880
Greg Kraft	70	71	67	72	280	16,880
Billy Mayfair	67	71	70	72	280	16,880
Naomichi Ozaki	73	70	67	70	280	16,880
Jesper Parnevik	71	67	70	72	280	16,880
Tony Sills	71	71	70	68	280	16,880
John Adams	69	69	71	72	281	10,560
Steve Lowery	73	68	72	68	281	10,560
Scott Verplank	70	67	70	74	281	10,560
Dave Barr	67	68	74	73	282	8,520
Peter Jordan	72	67	75	68	282	8,520
Mike Reid	68	69	73	72	282	8,520
Omar Uresti	70	66	74	72	282	8,520
Grant Waite	68	72	72	70	282	8,520
Tim Loustalot	71	71	70	71	283	6,497.15
John Mahaffey	70	70	73	70	283	6,497.15
Keith Clearwater	74	69	70	70	283	6,497.14
Sandy Lyle	69	72	71	71	283	6,497.14
Andrew Magee	69	73	72	69	283	6,497.14
Doug Martin	69	71	72	71	283	6,497.14
Don Pooley	67	75	71	70	283	6,497.14
Ronnie Black	66	75	72	71	284	4,920
Fred Funk	70	72	68	74	284	4,920
Steve Gotsche	73	69	71	71	284	4,920
Justin Leonard	69	73	71	71	284	4,920
Ian Woosnam	70	69	71	74	284	4,920
J.L. Lewis	64	72	72	77	285	4,080
Mark Wurtz	68	70	74	73	285	4,080
Emlyn Aubrey	69	74	73	70	286	3,496
Jim Carter	72	70	73	71	286	3,496
Mike Smith	70	72	72	72	286	3,496
Patrick Burke	69	71	80	67	287	2,932
Russ Cochran	68	74	72	73	287	2,932
Glen Day	69	74	69	75	287	2,932
Jerry Pate	71	72	73	71	287	2,932
Steve Rintoul	73	70	71	73	287	2,932

	SCORES				TOTAL	MONEY
John Wilson	72	68	72	75	287	2,932
Michael Allen	72	67	74	75	288	2,712
Marco Dawson	73	69	74	72	288	2,712
Wayne Grady	70	69	75	74	288	2,712
Scott Gump	70	71	74	73	288	2,712
Jerry Haas	73	69	74	72	288	2,712
Chris DiMarco	70	71	73	75	289	2,616
David Frost	74	69	74	72	289	2,616
Skip Kendall	69	71	75	74	289	2,616
Bobby Doolittle	71	70	73	76	290	2,508
Jim Furyk	70	72	72	76	290	2,508
Dudley Hart	71	72	71	76	290	2,508
Bob Lohr	69	74	76	71	290	2,508
Doug Tewell	68	72	77	73	290	2,508
Bruce Vaughan	70	72	74	74	290	2,508
Kelly Gibson	70	68	75	78	291	2,412
Jay Williamson	68	75	75	73	291	2,412
Duffy Waldorf	70	68	77	77	292	2,376
Brett Ogle	71	71	73	78	293	2,340
Don Reese	69	70	75	79	293	2,340
Robert Gamez	71	71	71	81	294	2,304
Kawika Cotner	71	69	78	77	295	2,268
Pete Mathews	69	74	79	73	295	2,268
David Feherty	70	73	77	80	300	2,232

Masters Tournament

Augusta National Golf Club, Augusta, Georgia   April 6-9
Par 36-36–72; 6,905 yards   purse, $2,000,000

	SCORES				TOTAL	MONEY
Ben Crenshaw	70	67	69	68	274	$396,000
Davis Love III	69	69	71	66	275	237,600
Jay Haas	71	64	72	70	277	127,600
Greg Norman	73	68	68	68	277	127,600
Steve Elkington	73	67	67	72	279	83,600
David Frost	66	71	71	71	279	83,600
Scott Hoch	69	67	71	73	280	70,950
Phil Mickelson	66	71	70	73	280	70,950
Curtis Strange	72	71	65	73	281	63,800
Fred Couples	71	69	67	75	282	57,200
Brian Henninger	70	68	68	76	282	57,200
Lee Janzen	69	69	74	71	283	48,400
Kenny Perry	73	70	71	69	283	48,400
Hale Irwin	69	72	71	72	284	39,600
Jose Maria Olazabal	66	74	72	72	284	39,600
Tom Watson	73	70	69	72	284	39,600
Paul Azinger	70	72	73	70	285	28,786
Brad Faxon	76	69	69	71	285	28,786
Raymond Floyd	71	70	70	74	285	28,786
John Huston	70	66	72	77	285	28,786
Colin Montgomerie	71	69	76	69	285	28,786
Corey Pavin	67	71	72	75	285	28,786
Ian Woosnam	69	72	71	73	285	28,786
David Edwards	69	73	73	71	286	18,260
Nick Faldo	70	70	71	75	286	18,260
David Gilford	67	73	75	71	286	18,260

		SCORES			TOTAL	MONEY
Loren Roberts	72	69	72	73	286	18,260
Duffy Waldorf	74	69	67	76	286	18,260
Bob Estes	73	70	76	68	287	15,300
Masahiro Ozaki	70	74	70	73	287	15,300
Peter Jacobsen	72	73	69	74	288	13,325
Bernhard Langer	71	69	73	75	288	13,325
Bruce Lietzke	72	71	71	74	288	13,325
Mark O'Meara	68	72	71	77	288	13,325
Chip Beck	68	76	69	77	290	10,840
Dan Forsman	71	74	74	71	290	10,840
Wayne Grady	69	73	74	74	290	10,840
Mark McCumber	73	69	69	79	290	10,840
Jack Nicklaus	67	78	70	75	290	10,840
Tom Lehman	71	72	74	75	292	9,500
Mark Calcavecchia	70	72	78	73	293	8,567
Jeff Sluman	73	72	71	77	293	8,567
Payne Stewart	71	72	72	78	293	8,567
*Tiger Woods	72	72	77	72	293	
Seve Ballesteros	75	68	78	75	296	7,500
John Daly	75	69	71	81	296	7,500
Rick Fehr	76	69	69	83	297	6,800

Out of Final 36 Holes

				TOTAL	
Clark Dennis	73	73		146	
Miguel Angel Jimenez	71	75		146	
Sandy Lyle	75	71		146	
Tsuneyuki Nakajima	72	74		146	
Craig Stadler	70	76		146	
Hal Sutton	77	69		146	
Fuzzy Zoeller	72	74		146	
Brad Bryant	77	70		147	
Charles Coody	74	73		147	
John Cook	73	74		147	
Ernie Els	72	75		147	
Mike Heinen	73	74		147	
Tom Kite	74	73		147	
Larry Mize	76	71		147	
Mike Sullivan	72	75		147	
Steve Lowery	75	73		148	
Jeff Maggert	78	70		148	
Mark McNulty	75	73		148	
John Morse	74	74		148	
Vijay Singh	77	71		148	
Gay Brewer	79	70		149	
Gary Player	76	73		149	
Nick Price	76	73		149	
Lanny Wadkins	74	75		149	
Jim McGovern	77	73		150	
Bill Glasson	71	80		151	
Neal Lancaster	74	77		151	
Arnold Palmer	79	73		152	
Dicky Pride	79	73		152	
Mark Brooks	76	77		153	
Frank Nobilo	81	73		154	
*Tim Jackson	79	76		155	
*Trip Kuehne	79	76		155	
*Lee James	77	80		157	
Mike Springer	77	80		157	
Ian Baker-Finch	79	81		160	

	SCORES		TOTAL
*Guy Yamamoto	84	77	161
Billy Casper	79	89	168
Doug Ford	88		WD

(Professionals who did not complete 72 holes received $1,500.)

MCI Classic

Harbour Town Golf Links, Hilton Head Island, South Carolina   April 13-16
Par 36-35–71; 6,916 yards   purse, $1,300,000

	SCORES				TOTAL	MONEY
Bob Tway	67	69	72	67	275	$234,000
David Frost	71	68	66	70	275	114,400
Nolan Henke	66	72	70	67	275	114,400
(Tway defeated Frost on first extra hole and Henke on second extra hole.)						
Woody Austin	71	72	69	64	276	53,733.34
Nick Faldo	74	64	70	68	276	53,733.33
Mark McCumber	70	71	64	71	276	53,733.33
Ernie Els	73	70	64	70	277	36,508.34
Nick Price	69	72	71	65	277	36,508.34
David Edwards	70	69	66	72	277	36,508.33
Steve Lowery	68	73	66	70	277	36,508.33
Gil Morgan	73	71	62	71	277	36,508.33
Tom Watson	70	68	68	71	277	36,508.33
Kelly Gibson	74	69	68	67	278	22,285.72
Blaine McCallister	73	69	71	65	278	22,285.72
Lanny Wadkins	73	67	71	67	278	22,285.72
John Daly	68	68	71	71	278	22,285.71
Phil Mickelson	68	69	71	70	278	22,285.71
Loren Roberts	72	65	70	71	278	22,285.71
Gene Sauers	66	70	69	73	278	22,285.71
Scott Hoch	70	67	69	73	279	15,145
Peter Jacobsen	69	70	68	72	279	15,145
Wayne Levi	71	71	66	71	279	15,145
Mike Sullivan	70	71	69	69	279	15,145
Paul Goydos	71	69	68	72	280	9,836.67
Hale Irwin	71	73	69	67	280	9,836.67
Brian Kamm	67	71	72	70	280	9,836.67
Steve Stricker	71	69	70	70	280	9,836.67
Scott Verplank	72	68	70	70	280	9,836.67
D.A. Weibring	69	70	69	72	280	9,836.67
Tom Lehman	67	65	75	73	280	9,836.66
Kenny Perry	72	69	67	72	280	9,836.66
Payne Stewart	70	66	70	74	280	9,836.66
Neal Lancaster	69	69	74	69	281	7,182.50
Jim McGovern	73	69	66	73	281	7,182.50
Dillard Pruitt	69	72	72	68	281	7,182.50
Mike Standly	73	70	70	68	281	7,182.50
Jay Delsing	69	68	72	73	282	5,590
Chris DiMarco	70	73	68	71	282	5,590
Steve Jones	68	72	67	75	282	5,590
Tom Kite	74	68	68	72	282	5,590
Steve Rintoul	73	70	70	69	282	5,590
Tommy Tolles	69	68	73	72	282	5,590
Duffy Waldorf	70	70	72	70	282	5,590
Clark Dennis	69	75	70	69	283	3,686.23

	SCORES				TOTAL	MONEY
Dan Forsman	70	72	71	70	283	3,686.23
Robin Freeman	70	72	71	70	283	3,686.22
Fred Funk	72	72	69	70	283	3,686.22
Greg Kraft	68	71	71	73	283	3,686.22
Justin Leonard	71	68	70	74	283	3,686.22
Brett Ogle	68	74	67	74	283	3,686.22
Jesper Parnevik	70	66	72	75	283	3,686.22
Kirk Triplett	69	73	70	71	283	3,686.22
Corey Pavin	68	72	73	71	284	3,024.67
Bobby Wadkins	74	69	69	72	284	3,024.67
Keith Fergus	70	73	69	72	284	3,024.66
Chip Beck	73	71	71	70	285	2,912
Brad Faxon	74	70	66	75	285	2,912
Jim Furyk	72	71	69	73	285	2,912
Billy Mayfair	73	71	71	70	285	2,912
John Morse	73	71	66	75	285	2,912
Michael Bradley	75	69	74	68	286	2,756
Wayne Grady	75	69	71	71	286	2,756
Mark O'Meara	73	71	70	72	286	2,756
Craig Parry	70	71	73	72	286	2,756
Steve Pate	74	69	73	70	286	2,756
Dicky Pride	72	68	68	78	286	2,756
Jim Thorpe	70	72	72	72	286	2,756
Paul Azinger	73	70	70	74	287	2,613
Robert Gamez	71	73	71	72	287	2,613
Davis Love III	70	73	73	71	287	2,613
Paul Stankowski	70	74	72	71	287	2,613
Gary Hallberg	73	71	68	76	288	2,522
John Huston	70	67	72	79	288	2,522
Larry Nelson	73	71	78	66	288	2,522
Fulton Allem	69	75	76	70	290	2,457
Ken Green	70	73	76	71	290	2,457
Mark Carnevale	75	69	72	75	291	2,418
Billy Andrade	74	67	73	78	292	2,392

Kmart Greater Greensboro Open

Forest Oaks Country Club, Greensboro, North Carolina   April 20-23
Par 36-36–72; 6,958 yards   purse, $1,500,000

	SCORES				TOTAL	MONEY
Jim Gallagher, Jr.	69	70	69	66	274	$270,000
Peter Jacobsen	69	65	69	72	275	132,000
Jeff Sluman	70	65	66	74	275	132,000
John Adams	70	66	70	70	276	72,000
Mark Calcavecchia	68	73	67	69	277	60,000
Jesper Parnevik	70	68	68	72	278	54,000
Guy Boros	73	67	70	69	279	43,650
Brad Faxon	65	71	71	72	279	43,650
Vijay Singh	65	72	69	73	279	43,650
Steve Stricker	68	73	66	72	279	43,650
Ted Tryba	69	70	69	71	279	43,650
Hal Sutton	67	68	74	71	280	33,000
Fuzzy Zoeller	70	71	70	69	280	33,000
David Duval	72	68	70	71	281	25,500
Gary Hallberg	69	71	69	72	281	25,500
Justin Leonard	70	71	72	68	281	25,500

	SCORES				TOTAL	MONEY
Loren Roberts	71	70	71	69	281	25,500
Kirk Triplett	68	65	71	77	281	25,500
Chris DiMarco	68	73	71	70	282	17,550
Robert Gamez	69	72	70	71	282	17,550
Steve Gotsche	71	70	69	72	282	17,550
Ed Humenik	73	70	68	71	282	17,550
Brian Kamm	71	71	68	72	282	17,550
Davis Love III	66	71	75	70	282	17,550
Dave Barr	71	68	72	72	283	11,962.50
Jay Don Blake	71	71	70	71	283	11,962.50
Brad Bryant	69	66	72	76	283	11,962.50
Howard Twitty	68	70	77	68	283	11,962.50
Michael Bradley	69	74	72	69	284	9,332.15
Chris Perry	73	69	70	72	284	9,332.15
Billy Andrade	72	68	72	72	284	9,332.14
Trevor Dodds	68	73	73	70	284	9,332.14
David Edwards	67	74	71	72	284	9,332.14
Scott Simpson	67	72	70	75	284	9,332.14
Mike Sullivan	69	72	70	73	284	9,332.14
Bob Burns	68	74	72	71	285	7,065
Lennie Clements	68	72	73	72	285	7,065
Bob Lohr	71	71	74	69	285	7,065
Kenny Perry	68	72	74	71	285	7,065
Scott Verplank	72	71	69	73	285	7,065
Bob Boyd	69	72	72	73	286	5,400
Billy Ray Brown	72	70	70	74	286	5,400
Curt Byrum	68	73	72	73	286	5,400
Glen Day	72	70	74	70	286	5,400
Lee Janzen	70	67	76	73	286	5,400
Ted Schulz	72	70	70	74	286	5,400
Keith Fergus	73	70	72	72	287	4,035
Jeff Maggert	72	66	75	74	287	4,035
Gene Sauers	70	71	74	72	287	4,035
Mike Taylor	70	73	73	71	287	4,035
Phil Blackmar	68	73	73	74	288	3,577.50
Jim Furyk	69	73	70	76	288	3,577.50
J.P. Hayes	70	70	75	73	288	3,577.50
Steve Lowery	65	71	74	78	288	3,577.50
David Peoples	68	72	77	72	289	3,450
Ronnie Black	68	70	78	74	290	3,360
Kelly Gibson	71	72	72	75	290	3,360
Nolan Henke	72	71	75	72	290	3,360
Blaine McCallister	71	72	73	74	290	3,360
Tommy Tolles	68	72	73	77	290	3,360
Ed Fiori	70	71	76	74	291	3,225
Mike Heinen	67	75	71	78	291	3,225
Neal Lancaster	70	72	73	76	291	3,225
Paul Stankowski	70	70	79	72	291	3,225
Bob Gilder	74	69	75	74	292	3,075
Skip Kendall	73	69	73	77	292	3,075
Doug Martin	72	69	75	76	292	3,075
Katsumasa Miyamoto	70	72	74	76	292	3,075
Jerry Pate	74	68	73	77	292	3,075
Mike Standly	71	70	75	76	292	3,075
Joel Edwards	71	72	76	74	293	2,970
Omar Uresti	75	68	72	79	294	2,940
David Feherty	69	73	76	77	295	2,910

Shell Houston Open

TPC at The Woodlands, The Woodlands, Texas
Par 36-36–72; 7,042 yards

April 27-30
purse, $1,400,000

		SCORES			TOTAL	MONEY
Payne Stewart	73	65	70	68	276	$252,000
Scott Hoch	68	64	69	75	276	151,200
(Stewart defeated Hoch on first extra hole.)						
Charlie Rymer	69	69	68	71	277	95,200
Paul Stankowski	71	68	71	68	278	61,600
Tray Tyner	70	69	68	71	278	61,600
Brian Claar	73	68	67	71	279	48,650
Brett Ogle	68	69	71	71	279	48,650
Steve Rintoul	66	70	71	73	280	40,600
Vijay Singh	70	70	70	70	280	40,600
John Wilson	71	69	68	72	280	40,600
John Cook	67	70	69	75	281	35,000
Curt Byrum	72	69	70	71	282	25,800
Clark Dennis	74	68	69	71	282	25,800
Fred Funk	71	70	72	69	282	25,800
Kirk Triplett	73	66	72	71	282	25,800
Omar Uresti	73	68	68	73	282	25,800
Willie Wood	68	66	75	73	282	25,800
Ed Fiori	71	70	71	70	282	25,800
Phil Blackmar	70	72	69	72	283	15,225
Brad Bryant	69	72	72	70	283	15,225
Jeff Maggert	76	66	74	67	283	15,225
Gil Morgan	73	70	67	73	283	15,225
Dicky Pride	71	68	71	73	283	15,225
Scott Simpson	68	71	75	69	283	15,225
Mike Sullivan	72	70	70	71	283	15,225
Greg Twiggs	71	69	73	70	283	15,225
Lennie Clements	71	72	66	75	284	9,940
David Duval	71	70	72	71	284	9,940
John Mahaffey	68	71	70	75	284	9,940
Joey Sindelar	73	67	72	72	284	9,940
Harry Taylor	69	72	69	74	284	9,940
Mark Brooks	70	70	71	74	285	7,264.45
J.P. Hayes	72	69	71	73	285	7,264.45
Andrew Magee	69	72	69	75	285	7,264.45
Curtis Strange	72	70	75	68	285	7,264.45
Scott Gump	72	67	74	72	285	7,264.44
Justin Leonard	69	67	73	76	285	7,264.44
Blaine McCallister	69	71	68	77	285	7,264.44
Doug Tewell	75	68	69	73	285	7,264.44
Jim Thorpe	69	71	71	74	285	7,264.44
Dan Forsman	70	70	69	77	286	5,180
Craig Stadler	70	69	73	74	286	5,180
Ray Stewart	70	73	69	74	286	5,180
Hal Sutton	69	73	68	76	286	5,180
Howard Twitty	70	69	73	74	286	5,180
Billy Ray Brown	67	74	74	72	287	3,640
Brandel Chamblee	72	69	67	79	287	3,640
David Feherty	68	74	72	73	287	3,640
Jim Furyk	67	76	73	71	287	3,640
Brian Kamm	71	66	71	79	287	3,640
Skip Kendall	71	71	71	74	287	3,640
Doug Martin	71	72	75	69	287	3,640
Craig Parry	70	70	69	78	287	3,640

	SCORES				TOTAL	MONEY
Joey Rassett	72	70	73	72	287	3,640
Dudley Hart	68	72	71	77	288	3,178
Steve Jones	69	71	70	78	288	3,178
Tom Kite	72	69	74	73	288	3,178
Lee Rinker	72	71	69	76	288	3,178
Tommy Armour III	70	71	77	71	289	2,996
Mark Calcavecchia	69	71	72	77	289	2,996
Ben Crenshaw	70	73	73	73	289	2,996
Steve Gotsche	71	72	72	74	289	2,996
Peter Jacobsen	67	75	78	69	289	2,996
Lee Janzen	72	68	73	76	289	2,996
Mike Smith	69	73	73	74	289	2,996
Mike Standly	72	71	73	73	289	2,996
Grant Waite	68	73	70	78	289	2,996
John Adams	71	68	74	77	290	2,842
Don Pooley	70	72	73	75	290	2,842
Clark Burroughs	71	71	74	75	291	2,758
Joel Edwards	69	72	75	75	291	2,758
Bob Lohr	70	73	77	71	291	2,758
Bill Porter	73	70	74	74	291	2,758
Kawika Cotner	71	72	74	75	292	2,632
Chris Perry	69	71	77	75	292	2,632
Dave Rummells	73	70	77	72	292	2,632
Bruce Vaughan	73	70	75	74	292	2,632
Bobby Wadkins	72	69	72	79	292	2,632
Guy Boros	73	70	76	74	293	2,520
Bart Bryant	69	71	75	78	293	2,520
Tom Hearn	69	74	78	72	293	2,520
Robin Freeman	72	69	81	73	295	2,464
Keith Clearwater	70	73	75	78	296	2,422
Bruce Fleisher	71	72	76	77	296	2,422
Jeff Leonard	72	71	77	84	304	2,380

BellSouth Classic

Atlanta Country Club, Marietta, Georgia
Par 36-36–72; 7,018 yards

May 4-7
purse, $1,300,000

	SCORES				TOTAL	MONEY
Mark Calcavecchia	67	69	69	66	271	$234,000
Jim Gallagher, Jr.	65	70	68	70	273	140,400
Stephen Keppler	67	69	67	71	274	88,400
Curtis Strange	70	71	69	65	275	53,733.34
Guy Boros	71	67	67	70	275	53,733.33
Scott Verplank	72	67	67	69	275	53,733.33
Billy Andrade	72	68	69	67	276	37,830
Brandel Chamblee	68	70	69	69	276	37,830
Lennie Clements	70	66	72	68	276	37,830
Scott Hoch	69	71	71	65	276	37,830
Tommy Tolles	70	69	68	69	276	37,830
John Daly	67	67	71	72	277	28,600
Steve Stricker	71	69	67	70	277	28,600
Brett Ogle	71	71	70	66	278	24,700
Emlyn Aubrey	71	70	70	68	279	22,100
David Duval	69	71	73	66	279	22,100
Jerry Pate	69	71	71	68	279	22,100
Phil Blackmar	66	74	72	68	280	17,550

	SCORES				TOTAL	MONEY
Bill Porter	65	73	68	74	280	17,550
Gene Sauers	71	69	71	69	280	17,550
Joey Sindelar	69	70	72	69	280	17,550
Harry Taylor	68	75	69	69	281	11,718.58
Ronnie Black	72	69	68	72	281	11,718.57
Marco Dawson	71	72	70	68	281	11,718.57
Bob Estes	67	72	68	74	281	11,718.57
J.P. Hayes	70	71	71	69	281	11,718.57
Greg Kraft	71	72	70	68	281	11,718.57
Davis Love III	67	69	70	75	281	11,718.57
Ed Fiori	72	69	71	70	282	8,645
Dan Forsman	71	71	70	70	282	8,645
Billy Mayfair	72	70	70	70	282	8,645
Larry Mize	73	69	72	68	282	8,645
Tom Kite	66	77	68	72	283	6,442.23
Mark Wurtz	72	70	70	71	283	6,442.23
Tommy Armour III	67	73	70	73	283	6,442.22
Mike Hulbert	69	72	68	74	283	6,442.22
Neal Lancaster	68	70	70	75	283	6,442.22
J.L. Lewis	69	73	71	70	283	6,442.22
David Peoples	70	71	75	67	283	6,442.22
Ray Stewart	68	74	73	68	283	6,442.22
Hal Sutton	71	70	73	69	283	6,442.22
Clark Dennis	71	69	72	72	284	4,810
Keith Fergus	70	73	67	74	284	4,810
David Frost	70	71	70	73	284	4,810
Dave Barr	70	70	75	70	285	3,471
Jay Don Blake	69	71	74	71	285	3,471
Kawika Cotner	71	69	71	74	285	3,471
Wayne Grady	68	71	72	74	285	3,471
Scott Gump	71	71	69	74	285	3,471
Hale Irwin	70	72	70	73	285	3,471
Blaine McCallister	70	72	75	68	285	3,471
Jim McGovern	70	72	69	74	285	3,471
Craig Parry	70	72	74	69	285	3,471
Don Pooley	74	69	69	73	285	3,471
Michael Bradley	70	65	73	78	286	2,964
Rick Fehr	74	68	68	76	286	2,964
John Wilson	69	68	74	75	286	2,964
Scott Ford	74	69	71	73	287	2,899
Wayne Levi	73	70	72	72	287	2,899
Dudley Hart	73	70	72	73	288	2,834
Tim Loustalot	70	73	74	71	288	2,834
Lee Rinker	70	72	72	74	288	2,834
John Adams	71	71	70	77	289	2,756
Bob Lohr	69	71	72	77	289	2,756
Don Reese	72	71	69	77	289	2,756
Mark Brooks	67	71	75	77	290	2,691
Fred Funk	71	71	77	71	290	2,691
Michael Allen	74	69	75	73	291	2,613
Nolan Henke	70	73	73	75	291	2,613
Kirk Triplett	69	72	70	80	291	2,613
Ted Tryba	68	74	81	68	291	2,613
*Stewart Cink	71	72	78	70	291	
Keith Clearwater	72	71	73	76	292	2,535
David Ogrin	72	70	79	71	292	2,535
Tony Sills	71	72	77	74	294	2,496

GTE Byron Nelson Classic

TPC at Las Colinas
Par 35-35–70; 6,899 yards

May 11-14
purse, $1,300,000

Cottonwood Valley
Par 35-36–71; 6,862 yards
Irving, Texas

		SCORES			TOTAL	MONEY
Ernie Els	69	61	65	68	263	$234,000
Mike Heinen	67	66	67	66	266	97,066.67
D.A. Weibring	65	69	67	65	266	97,066.67
Robin Freeman	65	65	68	68	266	97,066.66
Jay Don Blake	64	69	69	66	268	45,662.50
Gil Morgan	68	66	68	66	268	45,662.50
Kenny Perry	65	66	70	67	268	45,662.50
Scott Verplank	67	69	67	65	268	45,662.50
Loren Roberts	68	67	69	65	269	36,400
Bob Tway	68	66	69	66	269	36,400
Mark Brooks	68	66	69	67	270	27,560
Glen Day	63	69	67	71	270	27,560
Keith Fergus	67	66	71	66	270	27,560
Steve Lowery	72	67	69	62	270	27,560
Craig Stadler	66	67	68	69	270	27,560
Mark Calcavecchia	64	70	69	68	271	19,500
Brandel Chamblee	67	68	66	70	271	19,500
Mark O'Meara	68	66	71	66	271	19,500
Naomichi Ozaki	65	71	68	67	271	19,500
Corey Pavin	70	65	70	66	271	19,500
Bart Bryant	69	69	70	64	272	13,520
Nick Faldo	66	71	69	66	272	13,520
Scott Hoch	70	64	71	67	272	13,520
Howard Twitty	67	68	71	66	272	13,520
Mark Wurtz	66	69	69	68	272	13,520
Emlyn Aubrey	68	66	70	69	273	9,425
Tom Byrum	69	68	69	67	273	9,425
Jim Carter	68	71	69	65	273	9,425
Justin Leonard	70	66	68	69	273	9,425
John Mahaffey	71	68	66	68	273	9,425
Jeff Sluman	67	67	70	69	273	9,425
John Cook	71	66	70	67	274	6,745.56
Jeff Maggert	71	66	66	71	274	6,745.56
Brett Ogle	70	65	69	70	274	6,745.56
Charlie Rymer	66	71	67	70	274	6,745.56
Fuzzy Zoeller	68	67	64	75	274	6,745.56
Brad Bryant	70	69	69	66	274	6,745.55
Steve Elkington	71	68	68	67	274	6,745.55
Jesper Parnevik	68	66	70	70	274	6,745.55
Payne Stewart	68	66	71	69	274	6,745.55
John Daly	68	65	73	69	275	4,550
Robert Hoyt	66	69	74	66	275	4,550
Steve Jones	68	64	73	70	275	4,550
J.L. Lewis	67	68	69	71	275	4,550
David Ogrin	72	67	67	69	275	4,550
Dillard Pruitt	69	70	68	68	275	4,550
Ray Stewart	65	69	72	69	275	4,550
Curt Byrum	67	72	66	71	276	3,231.43
Ben Crenshaw	70	67	71	68	276	3,231.43
Bob Gilder	70	67	73	66	276	3,231.43
Steve Gotsche	66	69	72	69	276	3,231.43

	SCORES				TOTAL	MONEY
Billy Mayfair	68	70	70	68	276	3,231.43
Omar Uresti	71	66	71	68	276	3,231.43
Tom Purtzer	68	65	71	72	276	3,231.42
Bob Estes	67	68	72	70	277	2,912
Donnie Hammond	70	69	70	68	277	2,912
Ed Humenik	69	67	73	68	277	2,912
Doug Martin	65	66	72	74	277	2,912
Dennis Paulson	68	67	73	69	277	2,912
Scott Simpson	69	69	69	70	277	2,912
Mike Smith	70	67	72	68	277	2,912
Brian Claar	67	70	73	68	278	2,795
Harry Taylor	70	69	68	71	278	2,795
Brian Henninger	67	72	69	71	279	2,730
Roger Salazar	69	70	68	72	279	2,730
Mike Standly	66	71	68	74	279	2,730
Ronnie Black	69	70	72	69	280	2,626
Chris DiMarco	65	69	76	70	280	2,626
Tim Loustalot	69	67	71	73	280	2,626
Jerry Pate	72	66	70	72	280	2,626
Dave Stockton, Jr.	71	67	69	73	280	2,626
Tony Sills	67	66	72	76	281	2,535
Tom Watson	68	71	67	75	281	2,535
Woody Austin	67	69	72	74	282	2,457
Kawika Cotner	69	69	73	71	282	2,457
Mark Wiebe	70	67	73	72	282	2,457
Jay Williamson	66	68	72	76	282	2,457
Mark Carnevale	67	72	73	71	283	2,366
Paul Goydos	69	67	73	74	283	2,366
J.P. Hayes	68	71	76	68	283	2,366
Larry Nelson	70	69	70	75	284	2,301
Steve Pate	70	68	73	73	284	2,301
Lee Rinker	68	71	75	71	285	2,262
John Sikes	68	69	74	77	288	2,236

Buick Classic

Westchester Country Club, Harrison, New York
Par 36-35–71; 6,779 yards

May 18-21
purse, $1,200,000

	SCORES				TOTAL	MONEY
Vijay Singh	70	69	67	72	278	$216,000
Doug Martin	67	70	72	69	278	129,600
(Singh defeated Martin on fifth extra hole.)						
Bobby Wadkins	72	66	69	72	279	81,600
Ernie Els	68	69	75	68	280	47,250
Nick Faldo	70	70	68	72	280	47,250
Fred Funk	71	68	71	70	280	47,250
Dillard Pruitt	72	69	70	69	280	47,250
David Duval	69	75	67	70	281	33,600
Bruce Fleisher	68	71	69	73	281	33,600
Bob Gilder	73	70	68	70	281	33,600
Blaine McCallister	69	71	69	72	281	33,600
Chris Perry	69	67	74	72	282	26,400
Craig Stadler	70	72	71	69	282	26,400
Tom Lehman	70	72	73	68	283	21,000
Steve Lowery	73	70	66	74	283	21,000
Jim McGovern	74	70	65	74	283	21,000

		SCORES			TOTAL	MONEY
Bob Tway	73	70	68	72	283	21,000
Chip Beck	69	70	72	73	284	14,100
Mike Brisky	70	72	67	75	284	14,100
Steve Elkington	71	69	70	74	284	14,100
Jerry Haas	70	72	70	72	284	14,100
J.P. Hayes	73	71	69	71	284	14,100
Mike Hulbert	68	68	73	75	284	14,100
Lee Janzen	73	71	69	71	284	14,100
David Ogrin	73	68	68	75	284	14,100
Bart Bryant	70	71	73	71	285	9,240
Mark Carnevale	74	71	69	71	285	9,240
Ben Crenshaw	74	70	71	70	285	9,240
Brad Bryant	71	71	71	73	286	7,465.72
Jim Carter	69	72	74	71	286	7,465.72
Marco Dawson	69	72	73	72	286	7,465.72
Steve Brodie	72	69	70	75	286	7,465.71
Billy Ray Brown	75	69	68	74	286	7,465.71
Brad Faxon	72	68	70	76	286	7,465.71
Grant Waite	68	73	72	73	286	7,465.71
Tom Hearn	73	68	77	69	287	5,775
Ed Humenik	71	74	69	73	287	5,775
Wayne Levi	73	69	70	75	287	5,775
Larry Rinker	69	74	73	71	287	5,775
Michael Allen	74	70	69	75	288	4,320
Paul Azinger	69	74	72	73	288	4,320
Jim Furyk	69	72	73	74	288	4,320
Jim Gallagher, Jr.	72	69	72	75	288	4,320
Naomichi Ozaki	72	71	68	77	288	4,320
Don Pooley	70	74	71	73	288	4,320
John Wilson	70	74	71	73	288	4,320
Richard Zokol	71	72	73	72	288	4,320
David Feherty	74	71	70	74	289	3,204
Charlie Rymer	71	69	74	75	289	3,204
David Frost	71	73	75	71	290	2,894.40
Bill Porter	71	72	68	79	290	2,894.40
Ray Stewart	73	72	73	72	290	2,894.40
Harry Taylor	73	69	73	75	290	2,894.40
Greg Twiggs	73	71	75	71	290	2,894.40
Tom Byrum	74	70	71	76	291	2,712
Rocco Mediate	73	71	77	70	291	2,712
Greg Powers	72	73	72	74	291	2,712
Duffy Waldorf	73	70	75	73	291	2,712
Willie Wood	72	69	77	73	291	2,712
Bob Burns	72	71	71	78	292	2,592
J.L. Lewis	73	71	71	77	292	2,592
Mike Reid	70	73	75	74	292	2,592
Steve Stricker	72	70	73	77	292	2,592
Omar Uresti	70	75	75	72	292	2,592
Fulton Allem	69	70	81	73	293	2,448
Bill Britton	74	69	75	75	293	2,448
Clark Burroughs	69	76	73	75	293	2,448
Curt Byrum	70	73	73	77	293	2,448
Bobby Clampett	70	74	72	77	293	2,448
Buddy Gardner	75	70	77	71	293	2,448
Mike Smith	72	73	74	74	293	2,448
Mike McCullough	68	71	73	82	294	2,352
Bruce Vaughan	74	71	74	77	296	2,316
Mark Wurtz	72	72	77	75	296	2,316
Phil Blackmar	71	74	73	79	297	2,256
Brian Kamm	70	75	74	78	297	2,256

	SCORES				TOTAL	MONEY
Jay Williamson	72	73	75	77	297	2,256
Dennis Paulson	70	74	78	79	301	2,208

Colonial National Invitational

Colonial Country Club, Fort Worth, Texas
Par 35-35–70; 7,010 yards

May 25-28
purse, $1,400,000

	SCORES				TOTAL	MONEY
Tom Lehman	67	68	68	68	271	$252,000
Craig Parry	66	65	70	71	272	151,200
D.A. Weibring	66	72	69	67	274	95,200
Woody Austin	67	69	66	73	275	67,200
Brad Faxon	67	70	75	64	276	51,100
Justin Leonard	68	72	68	68	276	51,100
Mark McCumber	67	73	68	68	276	51,100
Mark Calcavecchia	70	67	68	72	277	39,200
Jeff Maggert	66	68	74	69	277	39,200
Billy Mayfair	68	71	67	71	277	39,200
Rocco Mediate	69	68	70	70	277	39,200
David Duval	67	71	76	64	278	29,400
Nick Price	73	69	70	66	278	29,400
Scott Verplank	69	68	70	71	278	29,400
Billy Andrade	65	71	72	71	279	20,335
Jay Don Blake	70	72	73	64	279	20,335
Steve Elkington	68	68	77	66	279	20,335
David Frost	69	72	70	68	279	20,335
Mike Hulbert	66	70	68	75	279	20,335
Larry Mize	72	70	69	68	279	20,335
Brett Ogle	67	72	72	68	279	20,335
Lanny Wadkins	69	73	67	70	279	20,335
Dave Barr	68	72	71	69	280	12,110
Lennie Clements	64	69	74	73	280	12,110
Peter Jacobsen	69	71	69	71	280	12,110
Jeff Sluman	69	67	76	68	280	12,110
Brad Bryant	67	74	72	67	280	12,110
Tom Kite	70	68	71	71	280	12,110
Bruce Lietzke	67	70	74	70	281	9,310
Gil Morgan	73	68	70	70	281	9,310
Mike Standly	70	72	71	68	281	9,310
Bob Tway	70	69	70	72	281	9,310
Glen Day	70	72	69	71	282	7,087.50
Fred Funk	69	71	71	71	282	7,087.50
Neal Lancaster	71	71	70	70	282	7,087.50
Steve Lowery	73	69	71	69	282	7,087.50
Phil Mickelson	69	71	73	69	282	7,087.50
Kenny Perry	73	68	74	67	282	7,087.50
Scott Simpson	74	68	70	70	282	7,087.50
Kirk Triplett	69	72	71	70	282	7,087.50
David Edwards	67	71	75	70	283	5,180
Robin Freeman	72	69	68	74	283	5,180
Mike Sullivan	70	71	72	70	283	5,180
Tom Watson	68	69	70	76	283	5,180
Fuzzy Zoeller	66	72	74	71	283	5,180
Keith Fergus	69	70	76	69	284	3,808
John Mahaffey	69	72	71	72	284	3,808
Jim McGovern	67	75	77	65	284	3,808

	SCORES				TOTAL	MONEY
Steve Pate	72	69	70	73	284	3,808
Dan Pohl	68	72	75	69	284	3,808
Loren Roberts	70	70	71	73	284	3,808
Guy Boros	73	69	75	68	285	3,248
Clark Dennis	64	74	76	71	285	3,248
Robert Gamez	68	69	75	73	285	3,248
Scott Hoch	69	70	74	72	285	3,248
Payne Stewart	66	72	74	73	285	3,248
Tray Tyner	68	70	74	73	285	3,248
Davis Love III	70	68	74	74	286	3,108
Charlie Rymer	72	70	75	69	286	3,108
Curtis Strange	66	72	71	77	286	3,108
Paul Goydos	69	68	73	77	287	3,038
Bob Lohr	68	74	73	72	287	3,038
Gary Hallberg	70	71	74	73	288	2,968
Naomichi Ozaki	68	74	73	73	288	2,968
Jerry Pate	67	73	76	72	288	2,968
Chip Beck	68	71	77	74	290	2,884
Joey Sindelar	67	72	76	75	290	2,884
Paul Stankowski	70	71	74	75	290	2,884
Michael Bradley	68	70	75	80	293	2,828
Mike Reid	68	73	80	73	294	2,800

Memorial Tournament

Muirfield Village Golf Club, Dublin, Ohio
Par 36-36–72; 7,104 yards

June 1-4
purse, $1,700,000

	SCORES				TOTAL	MONEY
Greg Norman	66	70	67	66	269	$306,000
David Duval	70	71	64	68	273	126,933.34
Mark Calcavecchia	69	71	66	67	273	126,933.33
Steve Elkington	69	68	69	67	273	126,933.33
Ben Crenshaw	67	68	71	69	275	57,630
David Frost	68	72	65	70	275	57,630
Robert Gamez	68	67	69	71	275	57,630
Jay Haas	72	72	66	65	275	57,630
Tom Watson	67	71	68	69	275	57,630
Nick Price	71	71	69	65	276	45,900
Kenny Perry	68	74	68	67	277	40,800
Vijay Singh	69	67	71	70	277	40,800
Ernie Els	72	68	70	68	278	30,033.34
Fred Funk	72	69	67	70	278	30,033.34
Nick Faldo	68	72	70	68	278	30,033.33
Bill Glasson	72	66	71	69	278	30,033.33
Peter Jacobsen	68	68	70	72	278	30,033.33
Bruce Lietzke	69	67	70	72	278	30,033.33
Jeff Sluman	72	70	70	67	279	22,950
Lee Janzen	69	73	69	68	279	22,950
Robert Allenby	71	71	69	69	280	15,958.75
Brad Bryant	69	71	69	71	280	15,958.75
Lennie Clements	71	69	66	74	280	15,958.75
David Edwards	72	71	68	69	280	15,958.75
Mark McCumber	68	73	68	71	280	15,958.75
Brett Ogle	70	71	66	73	280	15,958.75
Craig Parry	69	71	69	71	280	15,958.75
Scott Simpson	68	70	74	68	280	15,958.75
Jay Don Blake	68	71	69	73	281	11,050

	SCORES			TOTAL	MONEY
Hale Irwin	70	70 72	69	281	11,050
Tom Lehman	71	69 71	70	281	11,050
Bob Tway	72	66 70	73	281	11,050
Scott Verplank	74	69 71	67	281	11,050
Chip Beck	69	70 74	69	282	8,967.50
Donnie Hammond	72	72 70	68	282	8,967.50
Doug Martin	71	73 70	68	282	8,967.50
Gil Morgan	70	70 73	69	282	8,967.50
Woody Austin	67	76 68	72	283	6,630
Mark Brooks	69	75 69	70	283	6,630
Clark Dennis	70	71 74	68	283	6,630
Jim Gallagher, Jr.	67	75 73	68	283	6,630
Scott Hoch	67	72 72	72	283	6,630
Mike Hulbert	68	68 75	72	283	6,630
Tom Kite	72	72 67	72	283	6,630
Jim McGovern	65	73 73	72	283	6,630
Mark O'Meara	66	71 72	74	283	6,630
Brad Faxon	72	72 71	69	284	4,494.80
Lee Rinker	70	70 72	72	284	4,494.80
Craig Stadler	68	74 68	74	284	4,494.80
Duffy Waldorf	71	71 73	69	284	4,494.80
D.A. Weibring	70	73 68	73	284	4,494.80
Fuzzy Zoeller	70	67 75	73	285	4,080
Steve Jones	72	70 71	73	286	3,898.67
Davis Love III	73	70 70	73	286	3,898.67
John Mahaffey	72	72 72	70	286	3,898.67
Larry Mize	72	72 73	69	286	3,898.67
Jim Furyk	71	71 68	76	286	3,898.66
Wayne Grady	69	71 72	74	286	3,898.66
Hubert Green	71	74 71	71	287	3,740
Phil Mickelson	70	73 71	73	287	3,740
Payne Stewart	70	75 71	71	287	3,740
Don Pooley	72	72 72	72	288	3,621
Dillard Pruitt	70	74 72	72	288	3,621
Curtis Strange	73	72 73	70	288	3,621
Lanny Wadkins	69	72 73	74	288	3,621
Brian Claar	71	71 73	75	290	3,451
Keith Fergus	72	70 74	74	290	3,451
Jesper Parnevik	73	70 73	74	290	3,451
Gene Sauers	70	73 74	73	290	3,451
Steve Stricker	73	72 72	73	290	3,451
Hal Sutton	69	73 73	75	290	3,451
Mike Sullivan	67	76 77	72	292	3,332
Bob Estes	71	72 74	72	294	3,298
Allen Doyle	73	72 76	74	295	3,264
Nolan Henke	75	70 73	78	296	3,230
David Graham	73	72 78	79	302	3,196

Kemper Open

TPC at Avenel, Potomac, Maryland
Par 36-35–71; 7,005 yards

June 8-11
purse, $1,400,000

	SCORES			TOTAL	MONEY
Lee Janzen	68	69 68	67	272	$252,000
Corey Pavin	73	68 63	68	272	151,200
(Janzen defeated Pavin on first extra hole.)					
Robin Freeman	70	69 66	68	273	95,200

	SCORES				TOTAL	MONEY
Justin Leonard	71	67	70	67	275	52,780
Davis Love III	68	63	71	73	275	52,780
Greg Norman	72	66	69	68	275	52,780
Mark O'Meara	66	70	69	70	275	52,780
Vijay Singh	65	71	71	68	275	52,780
John Mahaffey	72	69	65	70	276	35,000
Larry Mize	67	70	70	69	276	35,000
Kenny Perry	72	68	69	67	276	35,000
Nick Price	70	68	70	68	276	35,000
Payne Stewart	69	69	65	73	276	35,000
Marco Dawson	67	69	73	68	277	25,900
Scott Simpson	72	69	68	68	277	25,900
John Adams	69	69	71	69	278	21,000
Billy Andrade	71	71	65	71	278	21,000
Bill Glasson	72	70	66	70	278	21,000
Steve Jones	69	68	69	72	278	21,000
Neal Lancaster	70	70	65	73	278	21,000
Fulton Allem	73	69	65	72	279	12,460
Phil Blackmar	67	68	72	72	279	12,460
Paul Goydos	76	66	68	69	279	12,460
Wayne Grady	66	69	75	69	279	12,460
Tom Hearn	70	71	73	65	279	12,460
Scott Hoch	68	65	72	74	279	12,460
Tom Kite	67	68	73	71	279	12,460
Jesper Parnevik	67	70	69	73	279	12,460
Hal Sutton	71	66	72	70	279	12,460
Bobby Wadkins	71	71	69	68	279	12,460
Bart Bryant	70	69	71	70	280	7,940
Brad Faxon	71	71	71	67	280	7,940
Scott Gump	69	73	68	70	280	7,940
Jay Haas	71	70	67	72	280	7,940
Mike Hulbert	72	70	70	68	280	7,940
Jeff Maggert	64	72	73	69	280	7,940
Don Pooley	68	72	70	70	280	7,940
Ken Green	71	68	71	71	281	6,160
Skip Kendall	72	70	69	70	281	6,160
Jeff Sluman	72	67	69	73	281	6,160
Paul Stankowski	69	70	71	71	281	6,160
Tom Byrum	71	70	73	68	282	4,396
Mark Carnevale	73	68	71	70	282	4,396
Joel Edwards	72	70	73	67	282	4,396
Dan Forsman	69	72	70	71	282	4,396
Robert Gamez	65	70	77	70	282	4,396
Steve Lowery	64	74	70	72	282	4,396
Billy Mayfair	72	67	74	69	282	4,396
Scott McCarron	69	71	71	71	282	4,396
Doug Tewell	68	72	74	68	282	4,396
Chris DiMarco	70	71	70	72	283	3,315.20
Steve Gotsche	73	69	69	72	283	3,315.20
Dudley Hart	72	68	72	71	283	3,315.20
Andrew Magee	67	70	71	75	283	3,315.20
Lee Rinker	69	69	76	69	283	3,315.20
Bill Britton	71	71	72	70	284	3,136
Jerry Haas	71	66	68	79	284	3,136
J.T. Lewis	72	68	71	73	284	3,136
Doug Martin	68	72	73	71	284	3,136
Steve Pate	69	73	72	70	284	3,136
Bruce Fleisher	69	73	76	67	285	3,024
Kelly Gibson	67	75	71	72	285	3,024
Rocco Mediate	69	71	73	72	285	3,024

	SCORES				TOTAL	MONEY
Miguel Angel Jimenez	68	74	72	72	286	2,954
Blaine McCallister	73	69	73	71	286	2,954
Jay Don Blake	70	70	73	74	287	2,884
Donnie Hammond	69	72	72	74	287	2,884
Jerry Pate	73	69	76	69	287	2,884
Ray Stewart	71	71	76	71	289	2,828
Craig Parry	73	69	75	73	290	2,800
Morris Hatalsky	72	68	78	77	295	2,772

U.S. Open Championship

Shinnecock Hills Golf Club, Southampton, New York
Par 35-35–70; 6,944 yards

June 15-18
purse, $2,000,000

	SCORES				TOTAL	MONEY
Corey Pavin	72	69	71	68	280	$350,000
Greg Norman	68	67	74	73	282	207,000
Tom Lehman	70	72	67	74	283	131,974
Bill Glasson	69	70	76	69	284	66,633.67
Neal Lancaster	70	72	77	65	284	66,633.67
Jeff Maggert	69	72	77	66	284	66,633.67
Phil Mickelson	68	70	72	74	284	66,633.67
Jay Haas	70	73	72	69	284	66,633.66
Davis Love III	72	68	73	71	284	66,633.66
Bob Tway	69	69	72	75	285	44,184.34
Frank Nobilo	72	72	70	71	285	44,184.33
Vijay Singh	70	71	72	72	285	44,184.33
Brad Bryant	71	75	70	70	286	30,934
Lee Janzen	70	72	72	72	286	30,934
Mark McCumber	70	71	77	68	286	30,934
Nick Price	66	73	73	74	286	30,934
Mark Roe	71	69	74	72	286	30,934
Jeff Sluman	72	69	74	71	286	30,934
Steve Stricker	71	70	71	74	286	30,934
Duffy Waldorf	72	70	75	69	286	30,934
Billy Andrade	72	69	74	72	287	20,085.43
Peter Jordan	74	71	71	71	287	20,085.43
Brett Ogle	71	75	72	69	287	20,085.43
Payne Stewart	74	71	73	69	287	20,085.43
Scott Verplank	72	69	71	75	287	20,085.43
Fuzzy Zoeller	69	74	76	68	287	20,085.43
Ian Woosnam	72	71	69	75	287	20,085.42
Miguel Angel Jimenez	72	72	75	69	288	13,912.13
Colin Montgomerie	71	74	75	68	288	13,912.13
Scott Simpson	67	75	74	72	288	13,912.13
David Duval	70	73	73	72	288	13,912.12
Jose Maria Olazabal	73	70	72	73	288	13,912.12
Masashi Ozaki	69	68	80	71	288	13,912.12
Mike Hulbert	74	72	72	70	288	13,912.13
Gary Hallberg	70	76	69	73	288	13,912.12
Guy Boros	73	71	74	71	289	9,812.38
Steve Elkington	72	73	73	71	289	9,812.38
Raymond Floyd	74	72	76	67	289	9,812.38
Curtis Strange	70	72	76	71	289	9,812.38
Curt Byrum	70	70	76	73	289	9,812.37
Bernhard Langer	74	67	74	74	289	9,812.37
Bill Porter	73	70	79	67	289	9,812.37

	SCORES				TOTAL	MONEY
Hal Sutton	71	74	76	68	289	9,812.37
Barry Lane	74	72	71	73	290	8,147
John Daly	71	75	74	71	291	7,146
Nick Faldo	72	68	79	72	291	7,146
Bradley Hughes	72	71	75	73	291	7,146
Jim McGovern	73	69	81	68	291	7,146
Christian Pena	74	71	76	70	291	7,146
Omar Uresti	71	74	75	71	291	7,146
Bob Burns	73	72	75	72	292	5,842.60
Matt Gogel	73	70	73	76	292	5,842.60
Peter Jacobsen	72	72	74	74	292	5,842.60
Eduardo Romero	73	71	75	73	292	5,842.60
Ted Tryba	71	75	73	73	292	5,842.60
Brad Faxon	71	73	77	72	293	4,833.84
Steve Lowery	69	72	75	77	293	4,833.84
Greg Bruckner	70	72	73	78	293	4,833.83
Scott Hoch	74	72	70	77	293	4,833.83
Chris Perry	70	74	75	74	293	4,833.83
Tom Watson	70	73	77	73	293	4,833.83
John Cook	70	75	76	73	294	3,969
David Edwards	72	74	72	76	294	3,969
Jim Gallagher	71	75	77	71	294	3,969
Paul Goydos	73	73	70	78	294	3,969
Brandt Jobe	71	72	76	75	294	3,969
Tommy Armour III	77	69	74	75	295	3,349
Mike Brisky	71	72	77	75	295	3,349
Tom Kite	70	72	82	71	295	3,349
John Connelly	75	71	74	76	296	3,039
Ben Crenshaw	72	71	79	75	297	2,806.50
John Maginnes	75	71	74	77	297	2,806.50
Joe Gullion	70	74	81	76	301	2,574

Out of Final 36 Holes

			TOTAL
Fulton Allem	77	70	147
Seve Ballesteros	74	73	147
Bob Estes	80	67	147
John Huston	74	73	147
Hale Irwin	75	72	147
Doug Martin	72	75	147
Blaine McCallister	73	74	147
Larry Mize	73	74	147
Patrick Moore	77	70	147
Dana Quigley	71	76	147
Mike Standly	75	72	147
Bruce Vaughan	74	73	147
Ernie Els	74	73	147
Paul Azinger	73	75	148
Robert Gamez	76	72	148
Tim Hobby	72	76	148
Per-Ulrik Johansson	74	74	148
Darrell Kestner	73	75	148
Mark McNulty	72	76	148
Eric Meeks	73	75	148
Olle Nordberg	71	77	148
Mike San Filippo	76	72	148
Chip Beck	75	74	149
Billy Ray Brown	73	76	149
Fred Couples	77	72	149
*Jerry Courville	72	77	149

	SCORES		TOTAL
Wayne Grady	76	73	149
Mike Heinen	75	74	149
Jeff Julian	74	75	149
John Mahaffey	74	75	149
David Morland	75	74	149
*Chris Tidland	70	79	149
Kim Young	75	74	149
Mark Calcavecchia	74	76	150
Rick Fehr	75	75	150
David Gilford	74	76	150
Tim Herron	78	72	150
Gary Koch	74	76	150
Andrew Magee	74	76	150
Brian Mogg	73	77	150
Andy North	75	75	150
Tommy Roddy	74	76	150
Don Walsworth	76	74	150
Ian Baker-Finch	76	75	151
David Frost	73	78	151
Fred Funk	76	75	151
Simon Hobday	77	74	151
Kenny Perry	76	75	151
Michael Schuchart	74	77	151
Chris Zambri	70	81	151
Bill Britton	71	81	152
Glen Day	76	76	152
Craig Marseilles	75	77	152
Jack Nicklaus	71	81	152
Todd White	73	79	152
Bobby Elliott	78	75	153
Fran Marrello	75	78	153
Bill Murchison	76	77	153
Steve Pate	78	75	153
Rafael Alarcon	74	80	154
Jon Chaffee	76	78	154
Rick Cramer	79	75	154
Geoffrey Sisk	75	79	154
D.J. Holland	75	80	155
Michael Muehr	75	80	155
John Snyder	82	73	155
John Calabria	81	75	156
Clark Dennis	78	78	156
Jim Estes	77	79	156
Mike Springer	75	81	156
Collin Stoops	79	77	156
Adam Armagost	80	77	157
Kelly Mitchum	76	81	157
Javier Sanchez	82	75	157
Larry Tedesco	78	79	157
Chris Kaufman	79	79	158
Scot Tyson	86	73	159
John Hulbert	78	81	159
Dustin Phillips	74	87	161
John Reeves	81	80	161
Brad Bell	83	81	164
Loren Roberts	73		WD
*Tiger Woods	74		WD

(Professionals who did not complete 72 holes received $1,000.)

Canon Greater Hartford Open

TPC at River Highlands, Cromwell, Connecticut
Par 35-35–70; 6,820 yards

June 22-25
purse, $1,200,000

	SCORES				TOTAL	MONEY
Greg Norman	67	64	65	71	267	$216,000
Dave Stockton, Jr.	65	68	68	68	269	89,600
Kirk Triplett	64	67	69	69	269	89,600
Grant Waite	66	67	67	69	269	89,600
Brian Henninger	66	67	72	65	270	43,800
Don Pooley	67	72	66	65	270	43,800
Fuzzy Zoeller	70	63	66	71	270	43,800
Billy Andrade	74	65	62	70	271	34,800
Michael Bradley	67	66	69	69	271	34,800
Bob Estes	64	72	68	67	271	34,800
Dave Barr	68	71	68	65	272	26,400
Guy Boros	68	70	64	70	272	26,400
David Edwards	69	67	67	69	272	26,400
Corey Pavin	70	67	66	69	272	26,400
Paul Azinger	67	70	66	70	273	20,400
Dudley Hart	72	67	68	66	273	20,400
Vijay Singh	68	66	68	71	273	20,400
Emlyn Aubrey	66	72	68	68	274	15,120
Pat Bates	70	66	67	71	274	15,120
Stewart Cink	71	67	67	69	274	15,120
Jerry Haas	68	65	71	70	274	15,120
Dan Pohl	69	69	70	66	274	15,120
Tony Sills	67	70	67	70	274	15,120
Steve Jones	68	68	68	71	275	10,230
Peter Jordan	71	68	66	70	275	10,230
Craig Parry	70	69	68	68	275	10,230
David Peoples	73	68	67	67	275	10,230
Chip Beck	67	68	71	70	276	8,160
Ronnie Black	67	66	70	73	276	8,160
Gary Hallberg	71	69	65	71	276	8,160
Andrew Magee	69	66	72	69	276	8,160
Mark O'Meara	68	70	67	71	276	8,160
Brian Claar	70	71	65	71	277	6,480
Bruce Fleisher	71	67	66	73	277	6,480
Steve Gotsche	70	68	69	70	277	6,480
Don Reese	71	68	71	67	277	6,480
Lee Rinker	68	65	73	71	277	6,480
Tommy Armour III	71	68	69	70	278	4,920
Ken Green	73	66	68	71	278	4,920
Scott Gump	70	71	68	69	278	4,920
Nolan Henke	73	68	67	70	278	4,920
Ryan Howison	73	67	67	71	278	4,920
Doug Martin	70	71	69	68	278	4,920
David Ogrin	68	72	71	67	278	4,920
Mike Brisky	72	69	65	73	279	3,432
John Cook	66	72	71	70	279	3,432
Ed Fiori	70	68	67	74	279	3,432
Donnie Hammond	68	73	71	67	279	3,432
Blaine McCallister	72	67	71	69	279	3,432
Joey Sindelar	70	71	70	68	279	3,432
Billy Ray Brown	71	70	67	72	280	2,824
Mike Heinen	70	69	73	68	280	2,824
Billy Mayfair	73	68	72	67	280	2,824
Steve Rintoul	68	68	71	73	280	2,824

	SCORES				TOTAL	MONEY
Bobby Wadkins	70	71	71	68	280	2,824
Mark Wurtz	71	66	71	72	280	2,824
Lennie Clements	76	65	69	71	281	2,700
Steve Stricker	69	71	70	71	281	2,700
Fulton Allem	69	69	74	70	282	2,592
Mark Carnevale	68	73	68	73	282	2,592
Skip Kendall	70	71	68	73	282	2,592
Greg Kraft	67	72	70	73	282	2,592
Bill Porter	74	67	69	72	282	2,592
Mike Smith	70	71	73	68	282	2,592
Mike Standly	71	69	72	70	282	2,592
Brad Faxon	74	67	71	71	283	2,448
Scott McCarron	70	67	72	74	283	2,448
Carl Paulson	72	68	69	74	283	2,448
Dicky Pride	71	69	72	71	283	2,448
Willie Wood	71	70	68	74	283	2,448
Scott Ford	69	70	75	70	284	2,364
Jay Williamson	71	70	74	69	284	2,364
Dick Mast	72	68	72	73	285	2,328
Dave Rummells	67	72	72	75	286	2,292
Ted Tryba	72	69	72	73	286	2,292
Harry Taylor	70	71	71	75	287	2,256
Roger Maltbie	73	68	78	70	289	2,232
Tom Sullivan	69	71	74	77	291	2,208

FedEx St. Jude Classic

TPC at Southwind, Memphis, Tennessee
Par 36-35–71; 7,006 yards

June 29-July 2
purse, $1,250,000

	SCORES				TOTAL	MONEY
Jim Gallagher, Jr.	65	62	68	72	267	$225,000
Jay Delsing	69	63	69	67	268	110,000
Ken Green	68	67	65	68	268	110,000
Gene Sauers	68	65	63	73	269	60,000
Brandel Chamblee	69	70	65	66	270	40,937.50
John Cook	65	70	67	68	270	40,937.50
Steve Jones	68	69	65	68	270	40,937.50
Rocco Mediate	65	71	67	67	270	40,937.50
Larry Mize	69	66	67	68	270	40,937.50
Bob Tway	65	64	70	71	270	40,937.50
Mark Brooks	69	65	68	69	271	28,750
Jay Haas	68	70	67	66	271	28,750
John Huston	67	65	68	71	271	28,750
Bob Estes	69	67	67	69	272	20,625
Brett Ogle	67	70	70	65	272	20,625
Kirk Triplett	68	68	67	69	272	20,625
Ted Tryba	68	68	67	69	272	20,625
Howard Twitty	67	70	68	67	272	20,625
D.A. Weibring	65	70	69	68	272	20,625
Curtis Strange	67	70	69	67	273	16,250
Glen Day	62	74	70	68	274	13,000
Craig Parry	67	72	67	68	274	13,000
Charlie Rymer	66	71	67	70	274	13,000
Omar Uresti	66	67	70	71	274	13,000
Duffy Waldorf	72	65	67	70	274	13,000
Jim Carter	73	64	69	69	275	8,331.50

	SCORES				TOTAL	MONEY
Lennie Clements	70	67	69	69	275	8,331.50
Ernie Els	67	67	71	70	275	8,331.50
Paul Goydos	67	68	69	71	275	8,331.50
Peter Jacobsen	66	69	70	70	275	8,331.50
Craig Stadler	66	69	68	72	275	8,331.50
Mike Standly	62	67	75	71	275	8,331.50
Mike Sullivan	70	68	68	69	275	8,331.50
Grant Waite	69	66	67	73	275	8,331.50
Mark Wurtz	68	69	70	68	275	8,331.50
Guy Boros	71	68	69	68	276	6,145
Gil Morgan	68	71	66	71	276	6,145
Jerry Pate	71	65	71	69	276	6,145
Tommy Armour III	67	71	67	72	277	5,000
Bob Lohr	68	68	70	71	277	5,000
Tom Purtzer	67	68	72	70	277	5,000
Scott Simpson	65	74	68	70	277	5,000
Bruce Vaughan	68	71	68	70	277	5,000
Scott Verplank	66	69	68	74	277	5,000
Bill Glasson	68	69	72	69	278	3,660
Brian Henninger	74	64	74	66	278	3,660
Lee Janzen	69	70	70	69	278	3,660
Dennis Paulson	64	71	72	71	278	3,660
Jay Williamson	65	68	69	76	278	3,660
Chip Beck	70	67	69	73	279	3,075
Bob Gilder	67	71	71	70	279	3,075
Mike Hulbert	68	67	69	75	279	3,075
Mike Brisky	71	67	73	69	280	2,880
Kawika Cotner	68	70	73	69	280	2,880
Ed Fiori	67	69	74	70	280	2,880
Justin Leonard	67	69	72	72	280	2,880
Tony Sills	71	68	72	69	280	2,880
John Mahaffey	69	69	74	69	281	2,775
Dillard Pruitt	68	70	74	69	281	2,775
Dave Stockton, Jr.	68	68	68	77	281	2,775
Emlyn Aubrey	70	69	72	71	282	2,700
Donnie Hammond	71	67	70	74	282	2,700
Larry Nelson	73	64	71	74	282	2,700
Carl Paulson	67	70	75	71	283	2,637.50
Lee Rinker	69	70	71	73	283	2,637.50
Greg Kraft	69	69	75	71	284	2,575
Harry Taylor	70	68	72	74	284	2,575
Dicky Thompson	70	68	72	74	284	2,575
Fulton Allem	70	69	71	75	285	2,525
Ray Stewart	71	68	77	72	288	2,500
Brian Kamm	66	73	74	76	289	2,475

Motorola Western Open

Cog Hill Golf & Country Club, Lemont, Illinois
Par 36-36–72; 7,073 yards

July 6-9
purse, $2,000,000

	SCORES				TOTAL	MONEY
Billy Mayfair	73	70	69	67	279	$360,000
Jay Haas	69	68	73	70	280	132,000
Justin Leonard	70	71	72	67	280	132,000
Jeff Maggert	74	73	69	64	280	132,000
Scott Simpson	71	72	69	68	280	132,000

	SCORES			TOTAL	MONEY
Bob Estes	72	73	66	70	281	64,750
John Huston	73	68	72	68	281	64,750
Steve Lowery	69	70	70	72	281	64,750
Bob Tway	76	69	68	68	281	64,750
Woody Austin	74	70	69	69	282	50,000
Scott Gump	74	70	72	66	282	50,000
Scott Hoch	73	69	70	70	282	50,000
Bill Glasson	77	70	66	70	283	34,285.72
Dan Pohl	73	71	69	70	283	34,285.72
Nick Price	75	71	68	69	283	34,285.72
Larry Mize	72	72	68	71	283	34,285.71
Brett Ogle	69	71	69	74	283	34,285.71
Grant Waite	72	72	67	72	283	34,285.71
Tom Watson	68	71	73	71	283	34,285.71
Jay Don Blake	74	72	69	69	284	22,480
Mark Brooks	73	71	70	70	284	22,480
Greg Kraft	71	71	75	67	284	22,480
Sean Murphy	77	66	72	69	284	22,480
Don Pooley	76	67	70	71	284	22,480
Chip Beck	74	70	72	69	285	15,950
Guy Boros	71	73	69	72	285	15,950
Mark Calcavecchia	71	73	73	68	285	15,950
Robin Freeman	74	70	71	70	285	15,950
Patrick Burke	75	72	68	71	286	11,418.19
Jay Delsing	77	70	69	70	286	11,418.19
Paul Azinger	74	67	73	72	286	11,418.18
Michael Bradley	73	73	73	67	286	11,418.18
Jim Carter	73	68	77	68	286	11,418.18
Fred Couples	70	73	71	72	286	11,418.18
Steve Elkington	76	70	69	71	286	11,418.18
David Frost	75	70	72	69	286	11,418.18
Donnie Hammond	72	72	73	69	286	11,418.18
Nolan Henke	73	72	70	71	286	11,418.18
Tom Purtzer	74	71	70	71	286	11,418.18
Ronnie Black	71	72	71	73	287	8,200
Paul Stankowski	74	73	70	70	287	8,200
Duffy Waldorf	73	69	75	70	287	8,200
Mark Carnevale	72	74	72	70	288	6,240
John Cook	76	70	69	73	288	6,240
Ed Fiori	69	75	71	73	288	6,240
Ken Green	72	71	71	74	288	6,240
Doug Martin	75	72	70	71	288	6,240
Phil Mickelson	72	73	70	73	288	6,240
Steve Stricker	78	67	74	69	288	6,240
Billy Ray Brown	72	70	73	74	289	4,980
Joel Edwards	69	74	75	71	289	4,980
Brian Claar	72	72	73	73	290	4,664
Glen Day	74	71	70	75	290	4,664
Ed Humenik	76	71	71	72	290	4,664
Chris Perry	73	72	71	74	290	4,664
D.A. Weibring	72	72	74	72	290	4,664
Pat Bates	74	70	75	72	291	4,500
Brad Bryant	73	73	73	72	291	4,500
*Tiger Woods	74	71	77	69	291	
Peter Jacobsen	75	71	72	74	292	4,380
Davis Love III	73	74	76	69	292	4,380
Corey Pavin	74	73	69	76	292	4,380
Ted Tryba	72	72	76	72	292	4,380
Bob Gilder	71	76	77	69	293	4,260
Bobby Wadkins	73	72	77	71	293	4,260

	SCORES				TOTAL	MONEY
Vijay Singh	73	73	75	73	294	4,200
Alan Pate	80	66	71	78	295	4,160
Russ Cochran	73	74	71	78	296	4,080
David Duval	74	73	74	75	296	4,080
Blaine McCallister	75	72	70	79	296	4,080
Dudley Hart	73	74	75	75	297	4,000

Anheuser-Busch Golf Classic

Kingsmill Golf Club, Williamsburg, Virginia
Par 36-35–71; 6,797 yards

July 13-16
purse, $1,100,000

	SCORES				TOTAL	MONEY
Ted Tryba	69	67	68	68	272	$198,000
Scott Simpson	69	69	68	67	273	118,800
Jim Carter	66	69	68	71	274	57,200
Lennie Clements	68	69	69	68	274	57,200
Scott Hoch	67	69	71	67	274	57,200
Marco Dawson	68	71	73	63	275	36,225
Curtis Strange	72	70	65	68	275	38,225
Fred Funk	68	68	70	71	277	31,900
David Ogrin	71	71	66	69	277	31,900
Jeff Sluman	72	69	67	69	277	31,900
Michael Bradley	67	71	71	69	278	21,842.86
Mark McCumber	74	68	69	67	278	21,842.86
Joey Rassett	71	70	69	68	278	21,842.86
Payne Stewart	70	68	71	69	278	21,842.86
Kelly Gibson	71	70	66	71	278	21,842.85
Kirk Triplett	66	71	70	71	278	21,842.85
Glen Day	70	72	69	67	278	21,842.86
Joe Acosta, Jr.	70	71	67	71	279	12,466.67
Jim McGovern	69	67	71	72	279	12,466.67
Tom Purtzer	72	69	68	70	279	12,466.67
Joey Sindelar	68	69	71	71	279	12,466.67
Howard Twitty	70	70	71	68	279	12,466.67
Willie Wood	69	69	70	71	279	12,466.67
Jim Gallagher, Jr.	69	65	70	75	279	12,466.66
Paul Goydos	71	70	65	73	279	12,466.66
Blaine McAllister	68	67	69	75	279	12,466.66
John Adams	73	68	68	71	280	7,480
Woody Austin	70	69	74	67	280	7,480
Bill Britton	71	71	68	70	280	7,480
Jonathan Kaye	68	72	72	68	280	7,480
Tony Sills	71	67	70	72	280	7,480
Scott Verplank	72	69	66	73	280	7,480
John Wilson	68	70	72	70	280	7,480
Robin Freeman	65	72	72	72	281	5,555
Scott Gump	69	68	71	73	281	5,555
Jay Haas	72	69	69	71	281	5,555
Jerry Pate	68	71	73	69	281	5,555
Don Reese	72	65	71	73	281	5,555
Scott McCarron	66	73	71	71	281	5,555
Tom Byrum	69	69	71	73	282	4,290
Mark Carnevale	72	68	68	74	282	4,290
Mike Donald	68	69	72	73	282	4,290
Rick Fehr	70	72	67	73	282	4,290
Richard Zokol	65	75	72	70	282	4,290

		SCORES			TOTAL	MONEY
Stewart Cink	68	70	71	74	283	3,146
Bob Gilder	73	67	70	73	283	3,146
J.P. Hayes	71	68	75	69	283	3,146
David Peoples	70	72	70	71	283	3,146
Dicky Pride	69	69	70	75	283	3,146
Duffy Waldorf	66	71	73	73	283	3,146
Mike Brisky	70	71	73	70	284	2,604.80
Ed Dougherty	70	71	74	69	284	2,604.80
Ken Green	68	70	72	74	284	2,604.80
John Mahaffey	73	68	74	69	284	2,604.80
Tommy Tolles	74	66	74	70	284	2,604.80
Phil Blackmar	68	71	74	72	285	2,453
Rex Caldwell	69	69	78	69	285	2,453
Russ Cochran	71	69	76	69	285	2,453
Dudley Hart	65	72	78	70	285	2,453
Jeff Leonard	70	69	75	71	285	2,453
Dave Stockton, Jr.	68	71	76	70	285	2,453
Steve Pate	70	66	73	77	286	2,376
Ronnie Black	70	71	70	76	287	2,310
Bobby Clampett	70	71	75	71	287	2,310
Mike Reid	70	69	76	72	287	2,310
Harry Taylor	68	71	74	74	287	2,310
Mark Wiebe	70	71	74	72	287	2,310
Chris Van der Velde	67	72	77	72	288	2,244
Pat Bates	76	66	75	73	290	2,211
Roger Maltbie	70	71	74	75	290	2,211
Carl Paulson	70	69	74	79	292	2,167
Dicky Thompson	71	70	75	76	292	2,167

Deposit Guaranty Golf Classic

Annadale Golf Club, Madison, Mississippi
Par 36-36–72; 7,157 yards

July 20-23
purse, $700,000

		SCORES			TOTAL	MONEY
Ed Dougherty	68	68	70	66	272	$126,000
Gil Morgan	69	69	67	69	274	75,600
Peter Jordan	71	67	69	68	275	47,600
Tom Byrum	69	69	68	70	276	27,562.50
Steve Rintoul	73	68	67	68	276	27,562.50
Dicky Thompson	67	68	68	73	276	27,562.50
Kirk Triplett	66	70	69	71	276	27,562.50
Bob Gilder	69	66	69	73	277	20,300
Dicky Pride	66	68	70	73	277	20,300
Rocky Walcher	70	68	73	66	277	20,300
John Adams	70	67	72	69	278	13,900
Marco Dawson	68	72	70	68	278	13,900
Fred Fink	67	71	70	70	278	13,900
Ed Humenik	69	73	71	65	278	13,900
Jonathan Kaye	70	72	63	73	278	13,900
Bill Porter	68	69	70	71	278	13,900
Doug Tewell	68	70	70	70	278	13,900
Glen Day	72	70	68	69	279	10,150
Willie Wood	67	71	68	73	279	10,150
Kelly Gibson	67	72	70	71	280	7,061.25
Jerry Haas	69	69	73	69	280	7,061.25
Morris Hatalsky	70	69	72	69	280	7,061.25

		SCORES			TOTAL	MONEY
Mark Hayes	68	71	70	71	280	7,061.25
Don Reese	70	71	69	70	280	7,061.25
Clarence Rose	71	70	66	73	280	7,061.25
Dave Rummells	69	73	70	68	280	7,061.25
Tommy Tolles	69	67	71	73	280	7,061.25
Mike Brisky	70	70	73	68	281	4,555
Joel Edwards	70	67	74	70	281	4,555
Dudley Hart	69	71	70	71	281	4,555
Skip Kendall	70	69	71	71	281	4,555
David Peoples	65	74	73	69	281	4,555
Dillard Pruitt	70	68	70	73	281	4,555
Paul Stankowski	68	66	72	75	281	4,555
Bobby Clampett	71	68	72	71	282	3,161.67
Carl Paulson	70	69	67	76	282	3,161.67
John Schroeder	71	70	70	71	282	3,161.67
Harry Taylor	70	72	72	68	282	3,161.67
Greg Twiggs	72	68	71	71	282	3,161.67
John Wilson	71	69	73	69	282	3,161.67
Buddy Gardner	69	69	72	72	282	3,161.66
Jimmy Green	68	70	71	73	282	3,161.66
Mike Standly	68	69	71	74	282	3,161.66
Bill Britton	68	69	72	74	283	2,175.60
Steve Lamontagne	67	72	73	71	283	2,175.60
John Mahaffey	73	69	70	71	283	2,175.60
Scott McCarron	68	69	73	73	283	2,175.60
David Ogrin	70	70	69	74	283	2,175.60
Keith Fergus	69	70	72	73	284	1,746.50
Dick Mast	68	69	74	73	284	1,746.50
Joey Rassett	73	69	68	74	284	1,746.50
Joey Sindelar	69	73	72	70	284	1,746.50
Pat Bates	72	69	70	74	285	1,620.50
Curt Byrum	70	71	71	73	285	1,620.50
Rex Caldwell	70	70	73	72	285	1,620.50
Brian Kamm	68	73	68	76	285	1,620.50
J.P. Hayes	71	70	70	75	286	1,540
Tom Hearn	71	71	76	68	286	1,540
Barry Jaeckel	72	70	72	72	286	1,540
Mac O'Grady	72	67	78	69	286	1,540
Mike Tschetter	71	66	72	77	286	1,540
Jay Williamson	68	67	78	73	286	1,540
Mark Wurtz	72	68	71	75	286	1,540
Tommy Armour III	70	66	73	78	287	1,470
Phil Blackmar	71	71	68	77	287	1,470
Mike Donald	70	72	72	73	287	1,470
Sean Murphy	74	68	69	77	288	1,435
Bobby Wadkins	71	69	72	76	288	1,435
Bruce Vaughan	70	72	78	69	289	1,414
Michael Allen	71	70	74	76	291	1,393
Omar Uresti	68	73	76	74	291	1,393
Tray Tyner	71	67	79	75	292	1,372
Joe Acosta, Jr.	69	72	75	77	293	1,358
Kawika Cotner	69	71	77	77	294	1,337
Ernie Gonzalez	71	70	74	79	294	1,337

Ideon Classic at Pleasant Valley

Pleasant Valley Country Club, Sutton, Massachusetts
Par 36-35–71; 7,110 yards

July 27-30
purse, $1,000,000

	SCORES				TOTAL	MONEY
Fred Funk	66	63	66	73	268	$180,000
Jim McGovern	66	66	67	70	269	108,000
Don Pooley	70	64	68	68	270	68,000
Lennie Clements	67	68	69	67	271	39,375
Roger Maltbie	68	67	69	67	271	39,375
Joey Sindelar	69	66	70	66	271	39,375
Jay Williamson	67	67	68	69	271	39,375
Dan Forsman	69	65	67	71	272	29,000
Greg Kraft	70	67	66	69	272	29,000
Howard Twitty	67	67	68	70	272	29,000
Woody Austin	68	66	68	71	273	22,000
Marco Dawson	69	68	68	68	273	22,000
Steve Lowery	68	66	68	71	273	22,000
Kenny Perry	70	70	66	67	273	22,000
Billy Ray Brown	69	65	69	71	274	17,000
Dudley Hart	68	69	70	67	274	17,000
D.A. Weibring	71	67	68	68	274	17,000
Billy Andrade	68	66	72	69	275	13,500
Tommy Armour III	70	66	69	70	275	13,500
Bob Estes	73	67	68	67	275	13,500
Greg Twiggs	69	68	72	66	275	13,500
Guy Boros	69	66	70	71	276	9,600
Michael Bradley	69	71	71	65	276	9,600
Brian Claar	68	66	70	72	276	9,600
Scott Gump	68	68	71	69	276	9,600
Peter Jacobsen	70	67	69	70	276	9,600
Ronnie Black	65	70	69	73	277	6,950
Curt Byrum	68	69	70	70	277	6,950
Mark Calcavecchia	68	67	70	72	277	6,950
Jim Furyk	69	68	71	69	277	6,950
Gene Sauers	66	68	69	74	277	6,950
Ted Tryba	71	65	74	67	277	6,950
Joe Acosta, Jr.	71	68	70	69	278	4,955.56
Rick Fehr	67	71	70	70	278	4,955.56
Jim Hallet	71	65	73	69	278	4,955.56
Billy Mayfair	70	68	71	69	278	4,955.56
Don Reese	70	68	71	69	278	4,955.56
Tom Byrum	67	70	70	71	278	4,955.55
Jim Carter	66	69	74	69	278	4,955.55
Jay Delsing	68	68	71	71	278	4,955.55
Sam Randolph	73	67	70	68	278	4,955.55
Paul Azinger	71	68	73	67	279	3,400
Russ Cochran	70	67	71	71	279	3,400
Paul Goydos	72	68	68	71	279	3,400
Carl Paulson	69	69	70	71	279	3,400
Tom Purtzer	71	68	70	70	279	3,400
Harry Taylor	70	65	73	71	279	3,400
John Adams	67	72	72	69	280	2,462.50
George Burns	66	69	73	72	280	2,462.50
David Feherty	70	68	68	74	280	2,462.50
P.H. Horgan III	66	73	70	71	280	2,462.50
Ryan Howison	68	71	71	70	280	2,462.50
Jonathan Kaye	69	70	73	68	280	2,462.50
Skip Kendall	68	69	71	72	280	2,462.50

	SCORES				TOTAL	MONEY
Joey Rassett	66	70	75	69	280	2,462.50
Richard Backwell	69	68	71	73	281	2,250
Dave Barr	70	69	70	72	281	2,250
Peter Jordan	68	68	73	72	281	2,250
Jeff Sluman	73	67	70	71	281	2,250
Steve Gotsche	71	68	73	70	282	2,140
Jeff Leonard	69	70	68	75	282	2,140
Scott McCarron	66	69	76	71	282	2,140
Rocco Mediate	70	69	73	70	282	2,140
David Peoples	70	67	72	73	282	2,140
Mark Wiebe	73	65	75	69	282	2,140
Mark Wurtz	66	70	74	72	282	2,140
Clark Dennis	73	65	72	73	283	2,030
J.L. Lewis	71	69	71	72	283	2,030
Dicky Thompson	68	71	70	74	283	2,030
Tray Tyner	68	71	74	70	283	2,030
Joel Edwards	70	70	74	70	284	1,960
Eduardo Romero	72	63	76	73	284	1,960
John Wilson	72	66	73	73	284	1,960
Kenny Knox	69	70	74	73	286	1,910
Jeff Maggert	69	71	69	77	286	1,910
Bob Burns	70	70	75	72	287	1,880
Rodney Butcher	68	72	76	75	291	1,860
Andy Bean	68	72	77	76	293	1,840
Ken Green	66	73	68	84	WD	
Bill Glasson	72	68	71		WD	

Buick Open

Warwick Hills Golf & Country Club, Grand Blanc, Michigan   August 3-6
Par 36-36–72; 7,105 yards   purse, $1,200,000

	SCORES				TOTAL	MONEY
Woody Austin	63	68	72	67	270	$216,000
Mike Brisky	67	68	67	68	270	129,600
(Austin defeated Brisky at second extra hole.)						
Tom Byrum	69	67	65	70	271	62,400
Ernie Els	69	68	66	68	271	62,400
Jeff Sluman	66	67	67	71	271	62,400
Fred Couples	68	67	67	70	272	43,200
Joel Edwards	69	65	68	71	273	40,200
Payne Stewart	65	65	73	71	274	37,200
Jonathan Kaye	69	67	69	70	275	33,600
Tom Lehman	71	66	70	68	275	33,600
Brad Bryant	68	67	68	73	276	24,600
Fred Funk	70	68	70	68	276	24,600
Jim Furyk	72	62	71	71	276	24,600
Gil Morgan	69	70	67	70	276	24,600
Kenny Perry	67	69	72	68	276	24,600
Scott Verplank	67	70	67	72	276	24,600
Tommy Armour III	67	71	70	69	277	15,702.86
Russ Cochran	66	70	70	71	277	15,702.86
Justin Leonard	66	71	72	68	277	15,702.86
Larry Mize	69	70	68	70	277	15,702.86
Tom Purtzer	70	69	69	69	277	15,702.86
J.L. Lewis	65	69	71	72	277	15,702.85
Nick Price	69	66	69	73	277	15,702.85

	SCORES				TOTAL	MONEY
Joe Acosta, Jr.	71	67	68	72	278	9,080
Bart Bryant	69	68	70	71	278	9,080
Clark Dennis	71	68	67	72	278	9,080
Chris DiMarco	70	69	73	66	278	9,080
Dan Forsman	69	70	67	72	278	9,080
Wayne Grady	67	73	67	71	278	9,080
Greg Kraft	71	68	68	71	278	9,080
Bruce Vaughan	65	69	75	69	278	9,080
Dillard Pruitt	70	68	72	68	278	9,080
Bob Burns	68	72	71	68	279	6,205.72
Jim McGovern	68	71	67	73	279	6,205.72
Tony Sills	69	67	73	70	279	6,205.72
Jim Carter	67	71	68	73	279	6,205.71
Jay Haas	70	67	68	74	279	6,205.71
Scott Hoch	69	70	67	73	279	6,205.71
Mark Wurtz	71	65	70	73	279	6,205.71
Dave Barr	70	69	70	71	280	4,560
Paul Goydos	65	69	73	73	280	4,560
Skip Kendall	69	68	69	74	280	4,560
Tom Kite	72	67	74	67	280	4,560
Tommy Tolles	72	63	71	74	280	4,560
Grant Waite	69	68	74	69	280	4,560
Harry Taylor	68	72	73	68	281	3,209.15
Howard Twitty	72	68	69	72	281	3,209.15
Brad Faxon	72	65	72	72	281	3,209.14
Robin Freeman	73	66	70	72	281	3,209.14
Nolan Henke	68	70	70	73	281	3,209.14
Peter Jordan	71	69	67	74	281	3,209.14
Doug Martin	68	72	67	74	281	3,209.14
Tim Loustalot	69	69	75	69	282	2,792
Bill Porter	69	69	72	72	282	2,792
J.P. Hayes	66	72	73	71	282	2,792
Marco Dawson	71	69	73	70	283	2,736
Nick Faldo	72	68	75	69	284	2,664
Scott Gump	70	69	72	73	284	2,664
Steve Rintoul	68	72	71	73	284	2,664
Ted Tryba	68	69	73	74	284	2,664
D.A. Weibring	70	70	72	72	284	2,664
Michael Allen	71	69	76	69	285	2,556
Chip Beck	70	68	72	75	285	2,556
David Peoples	67	71	73	74	285	2,556
Mike Sullivan	70	70	76	69	285	2,556
Dick Mast	71	69	72	74	286	2,484
John Wilson	69	71	70	76	286	2,484
Yoshinori Mizumaki	67	72	74	74	287	2,436
David Ogrin	68	72	78	69	287	2,436
Jeff Maggert	69	71	74	74	288	2,388
Jerry Pate	69	70	74	75	288	2,388
Phil Blackmar	71	69	75	75	290	2,352

PGA Championship

Riviera Country Club, Pacific Palisades, California
Par 35-36–71; 6,956 yards

August 10-13
purse, $1,750,000

	SCORES				TOTAL	MONEY
Steve Elkington	68	67	68	64	267	$360,000
Colin Montgomerie	68	67	67	65	267	216,000
(Elkington defeated Montgomerie at first extra hole.)						
Ernie Els	66	65	66	72	269	116,000
Jeff Maggert	66	69	65	69	269	116,000
Brad Faxon	70	67	71	63	271	80,000
Bob Estes	69	68	68	68	273	68,500
Mark O'Meara	64	67	69	73	273	68,500
Jay Haas	69	71	64	70	274	50,000
Justin Leonard	68	66	70	70	274	50,000
Steve Lowery	69	68	68	69	274	50,000
Jeff Sluman	69	67	68	70	274	50,000
Craig Stadler	71	66	66	71	274	50,000
Jim Furyk	68	70	69	68	275	33,750
Miguel Angel Jimenez	69	69	67	70	275	33,750
Payne Stewart	69	70	69	67	275	33,750
Kirk Triplett	71	69	68	67	275	33,750
Michael Campbell	71	65	71	69	276	26,000
Costantino Rocca	70	69	68	69	276	26,000
Curtis Strange	72	68	68	68	276	26,000
Greg Norman	66	69	70	72	277	21,000
Jesper Parnevik	69	69	70	69	277	21,000
Duffy Waldorf	69	69	67	72	277	21,000
Woody Austin	70	70	70	68	278	15,500
Nolan Henke	68	73	67	70	278	15,500
Peter Jacobsen	69	67	71	71	278	15,500
Lee Janzen	66	70	72	70	278	15,500
Bruce Lietzke	73	68	67	70	278	15,500
Billy Mayfair	68	68	72	70	278	15,500
Steve Stricker	75	64	69	70	278	15,500
Sam Torrance	69	69	69	71	278	15,500
Paul Azinger	70	70	72	67	279	8,906.25
Mark Brooks	67	74	69	69	279	8,906.25
Fred Couples	70	69	74	66	279	8,906.25
Nick Faldo	69	73	70	67	279	8,906.25
Gil Morgan	66	73	74	66	279	8,906.25
Jose Maria Olazabal	72	66	70	71	279	8,906.25
Naomichi Ozaki	71	70	65	73	279	8,906.25
D.A. Weibring	74	68	69	68	279	8,906.25
Lennie Clements	67	71	72	70	280	6,750
Fred Funk	70	72	68	70	280	6,750
Sandy Lyle	67	73	69	71	280	6,750
Nick Price	71	71	70	68	280	6,750
Philip Walton	71	70	71	68	280	6,750
Chip Beck	66	74	73	68	281	5,600
Ben Crenshaw	68	73	73	67	281	5,600
Jim Gallagher, Jr.	64	72	73	72	281	5,600
Gene Sauers	69	71	68	73	281	5,600
Peter Senior	68	71	74	68	281	5,600
John Adams	65	76	71	70	282	4,620
Brian Claar	68	67	73	74	282	4,620
Robin Freeman	71	69	70	72	282	4,620
Masashi Ozaki	73	68	69	72	282	4,620
Kenny Perry	75	67	70	70	282	4,620

	SCORES				TOTAL	MONEY
Michael Bradley	63	73	73	74	283	4,050
Hale Irwin	71	68	71	73	283	4,050
Tom Kite	70	69	70	74	283	4,050
Scott Simpson	71	67	71	74	283	4,050
Ed Dougherty	68	72	74	70	284	3,630
Per-Ulrik Johansson	72	69	71	72	284	3,630
Steve Pate	71	71	71	71	284	3,630
Loren Roberts	74	68	71	71	284	3,630
Tom Watson	71	71	72	70	284	3,630
Barry Lane	74	68	75	68	285	3,400
Mike Sullivan	72	69	71	73	285	3,400
Lanny Wadkins	73	69	71	72	285	3,400
Dillard Pruitt	73	69	72	72	286	3,300
David Frost	69	73	72	73	287	3,262.50
Jack Nicklaus	69	71	71	76	287	3,262.50
Fuzzy Zoeller	72	69	75	72	288	3,225
Brian Kamm	71	66	74	78	289	3,200
Curt Byrum	71	71	78	71	291	3,162.50
Wayne DeFrancesco	69	73	74	75	291	3,162.50

Out of Final 36 Holes

Billy Andrade	71	72	143
Brad Bryant	72	71	143
John Cook	70	73	143
Glen Day	70	73	143
David Duval	72	71	143
Brian Henninger	72	71	143
Darrell Kestner	72	71	143
Davis Love III	71	72	143
Ron McDougal	71	72	143
Brett Ogle	72	71	143
Don Pooley	71	72	143
Mike Springer	70	73	143
Bob Tway	71	72	143
Ian Woosnam	71	72	143
Robert Allenby	72	72	144
Frank Dobbs	67	77	144
Scott Hoch	71	73	144
Mike Hulbert	72	72	144
Masahiro Kuramoto	73	71	144
Jim McGovern	73	71	144
Larry Mize	76	68	144
John Morse	74	70	144
Frank Nobilo	68	76	144
Pete Oakley	71	73	144
Steve Rintoul	77	67	144
Hal Sutton	70	74	144
Scott Verplank	73	71	144
Grant Waite	71	73	144
Mark Calcavecchia	70	75	145
Wayne Grady	75	70	145
Hubert Green	75	70	145
Mike Heinen	75	70	145
Doug Martin	72	73	145
Mark Mielke	78	67	145
Larry Nelson	70	75	145
John Reeves	77	68	145
Brian Watts	72	73	145
Bruce Zabriski	69	76	145

	SCORES		TOTAL
Bill Glasson	74	72	146
David Graham	76	70	146
Stephen Keppler	75	71	146
Blaine McCallister	75	71	146
Guy Boros	74	73	147
Steve Brady	69	78	147
Brandel Chamblee	69	78	147
Tom Dolby	73	74	147
Greg Kraft	73	74	147
Tom Lehman	72	75	147
Bob Makoski	74	73	147
John Mahaffey	75	72	147
Mark McCumber	73	74	147
Craig Parry	76	71	147
Corey Pavin	71	76	147
Paul Stankowski	75	72	147
Phil Mickelson	77	71	148
Tsuneyuki Nakajima	76	72	148
Vijay Singh	73	75	148
Jim Sobb	72	76	148
Gary Trivisonno	71	77	148
John Daly	76	73	149
Dana Quigley	74	75	149
Ted Tryba	70	79	149
Larry Emery	76	74	150
Seve Ballesteros	76	75	151
Bobby Wadkins	75	76	151
Rick Acton	75	77	152
Ian Baker-Finch	80	72	152
Jay Don Blake	74	78	152
Drue Johnson	74	78	152
Robert Gamez	77	76	153
Michael Burke, Jr.	78	76	154
Kent Dinsdale	77	78	155
Benny Passons	80	75	155
Phil Bland	77	79	156
Denny Hepler	78	79	157
Mike Lawrence	83	77	160
Bob Lendzion	76	WD	76
John Huston	78	DQ	78

(Professionals who did not complete 72 holes received $1,200.)

Sprint International

Castle Pines Golf Club, Castle Rock, Colorado
Par 36-36—72; 7,559 yards

August 17-20
purse, $1,500,000

FINAL ROUND

	POINTS				TOTAL	MONEY
Lee Janzen	10	9	6	9	34	$270,000
Ernie Els	17	0	7	9	33	162,000
Mark Wiebe	8	15	-1	6	28	87,000
Jay Haas	3	12	13	0	28	87,000
David Duval	10	9	6	2	27	60,000
Jose Maria Olazabal	7	5	6	8	26	52,125

	POINTS			TOTAL	MONEY
Tom Watson	7	8	9	2	26	52,125
Greg Norman	14	3	-2	9	24	43,500
Dan Forsman	3	10	7	4	24	43,500
Davis Love III	11	6	6	1	24	43,500
Kirk Triplett	5	2	10	5	22	34,500
David Feherty	2	11	7	2	22	34,500
Tom Kite	11	-1	10	2	22	34,500
D.A. Weibring	3	10	6	1	20	27,000
Craig Stadler	11	-4	11	2	20	27,000
Tom Lehman	8	7	7	-2	20	27,000
Mark Carnevale	7	4	5	3	19	22,500
Glen Day	5	2	9	3	19	22,500
Mike Hulbert	1	10	10	-2	19	22,500
Wayne Westner	5	6	5	0	16	18,750
Dicky Pride	3	9	6	-2	16	18,750
Joey Sindelar	8	-1	9	-2	14	16,800
Kelly Gibson	5	2	9	-4	12	15,600
Naomichi Ozaki	6	6	5	-6	11	14,400

IN THE MONEY

				TOTAL	MONEY
Brett Ogle	9	7	-2	14	13,200
Mark Calcavecchia	-5	10	8	13	10,650
Michael Campbell	-1	7	7	13	10,650
Russ Cochran	4	3	6	13	10,650
Duffy Waldorf	-1	8	6	13	10,650
Brad Bryant	4	5	4	13	10,650
Howard Twitty	6	4	3	13	10,650
Steve Stricker	7	4	2	13	10,650
Jesper Parnevik	-3	7	8	12	7,925
Keith Clearwater	5	3	4	12	7,925
Paul Goydos	3	6	3	12	7,925
Bob Lohr	3	8	1	12	7,925
Doug Martin	4	7	1	12	7,925
Lee Rinker	9	4	-1	12	7,925
Larry Mize	3	8	0	11	6,450
Scott Verplank	2	9	0	11	6,450
Chip Beck	2	10	-1	11	6,450
Patrick Burke	3	2	5	10	4,608
Anthony Rodriguez	0	5	5	10	4,608
Tom Purtzer	-3	8	5	10	4,608
Michael Bradley	2	4	4	10	4,608
Chris DiMarco	5	1	4	10	4,608
Bob Tway	10	-3	3	10	4,608
Bruce Lietzke	5	2	3	10	4,608
Peter Senior	8	0	2	10	4,608
Jim Furyk	3	5	2	10	4,608
Dudley Hart	8	7	-5	10	4,608
Craig Parry	2	4	3	9	3,600
John Cook	5	1	2	8	3,510
Emlyn Aubrey	7	6	-5	8	3,510
Retief Goosen	0	4	3	7	3,360
Fred Funk	3	1	3	7	3,360
Chris Perry	-5	9	3	7	3,360
Neal Lancaster	1	5	1	7	3,360
Roger Maltbie	5	1	1	7	3,360
Jim Carter	7	-1	1	7	3,360
Andrew Magee	9	0	-2	7	3,360
Charlie Rymer	6	0	0	6	3,180
Dave Barr	-1	7	0	6	3,180

	POINTS			TOTAL	MONEY
Steve Rintoul	3	5	-2	6	3,180
Justin Leonard	8	1	-3	6	3,180
Jerry Haas	0	9	-3	6	3,180
Keith Fergus	-2	6	-1	3	3,075
Mike Brisky	6	-1	-2	3	3,075
Dillard Pruitt	3	1	-2	2	3,030
Mike Standly	3	2	-4	1	3,000
Skip Kendall	0	6	-6	0	2,970
Marco Gortana	4	0	-8	-4	2,940

NEC World Series of Golf

Firestone Country Club, Akron, Ohio
Par 35-35–70; 7,149 yards

August 24-27
purse, $2,000,000

	SCORES				TOTAL	MONEY
Greg Norman	73	68	70	67	278	$360,000
Billy Mayfair	70	68	70	70	278	176,000
Nick Price	72	69	69	68	278	176,000
(Norman defeated Mayfair and Price at first extra hole.)						
Phil Mickelson	69	74	70	66	279	88,000
Vijay Singh	71	69	65	74	279	88,000
Fred Couples	68	76	68	68	280	69,500
Jim Gallagher, Jr.	66	71	70	73	280	69,500
Mike Sullivan	71	67	74	69	281	62,000
Jose Maria Olazabal	68	70	69	75	282	56,000
Loren Roberts	72	74	70	66	282	56,000
Bob Tway	73	72	68	70	283	50,000
Nick Faldo	71	71	70	72	284	39,200
Davis Love III	70	73	74	67	284	39,200
Mark McCumber	68	76	68	72	284	39,200
Ted Tryba	68	72	73	71	284	39,200
Tom Lehman	68	75	69	72	284	39,200
Peter Jacobsen	74	68	72	71	285	32,000
Fred Funk	75	72	66	73	286	29,000
Lee Janzen	71	71	72	72	286	29,000
Robert Allenby	72	73	67	75	287	22,480
Mark O'Meara	72	74	70	71	287	22,480
Corey Pavin	71	73	66	77	287	22,480
Mike Springer	70	75	73	69	287	22,480
Brian Watts	72	73	73	69	287	22,480
Mark Calcavecchia	69	72	74	73	288	17,100
Bruce Lietzke	71	77	73	67	288	17,100
Payne Stewart	67	74	75	72	288	17,100
Bob Estes	71	75	70	73	289	16,000
Ernie Els	73	67	73	76	289	16,000
John Daly	78	73	71	68	290	15,700
Kenny Perry	70	76	74	71	292	15,600
Rick Fehr	75	74	75	69	293	15,500
Ed Dougherty	74	71	75	74	294	15,350
Anthony Gilligan	74	75	73	72	294	15,350
Andrew Coltart	79	78	67	71	295	15,150
Robert Gamez	70	74	76	75	295	15,150
Woody Austin	68	79	76	73	296	14,900
Retief Goosen	73	79	68	76	296	14,900
Hisayuki Sasaki	77	73	69	77	296	14,900
Eiji Mizoguchi	77	77	72	71	297	14,650

	SCORES				TOTAL	MONEY
Ron Whittaker	70	78	71	78	297	14,650
Ben Crenshaw	79	72	75	72	298	14,450
Peter Senior	72	75	75	76	298	14,450
John Morse	76	77	79	71	303	14,300

Greater Milwaukee Open

Brown Deer Park Golf Club, Milwaukee, Wisconsin August 31-September 3
Par 35-36–71; 6,716 yards purse, $1,000,000

	SCORES				TOTAL	MONEY
Scott Hoch	68	71	65	65	269	$180,000
Marco Dawson	70	65	70	67	272	108,000
Joe Acosta, Jr.	68	69	69	68	274	52,000
Jim Gallagher, Jr.	68	71	68	67	274	52,000
Jeff Sluman	72	71	65	66	274	52,000
Steve Lowery	70	69	71	65	275	32,375
Lee Rinker	70	68	67	70	275	32,375
Joey Sindelar	74	68	68	65	275	32,375
Duffy Waldorf	69	73	65	68	275	32,375
Bob Estes	71	70	71	64	276	22,166.67
Jay Haas	74	68	67	67	276	22,166.67
Andrew Magee	69	72	69	66	276	22,166.67
Mark O'Meara	69	71	68	68	276	22,166.67
Robert Gamez	67	69	70	70	276	22,166.66
D.A. Weibring	70	69	71	66	276	22,166.66
Ted Schulz	69	72	68	68	277	17,000
Lennie Clements	70	72	69	67	278	11,800
Ed Fiori	70	70	69	69	278	11,800
Nolan Henke	75	66	69	68	278	11,800
Mike Hulbert	69	73	67	69	278	11,800
Peter Jordan	68	69	71	70	278	11,800
Justin Leonard	71	70	72	65	278	11,800
Steve Pate	70	68	69	71	278	11,800
Curtis Strange	71	66	75	66	278	11,800
Richard Zokol	65	70	73	70	278	11,800
Howard Twitty	71	67	71	69	278	11,800
Russ Cochran	74	68	71	66	279	6,800
Greg Kraft	70	72	65	72	279	6,800
Tom Purtzer	73	69	65	72	279	6,800
Loren Roberts	72	69	71	67	279	6,800
Ray Stewart	68	71	68	72	279	6,800
Hal Sutton	68	71	70	70	279	6,800
Dicky Thompson	74	67	67	71	279	6,800
Tom Byrum	70	72	69	69	280	4,733.34
John Huston	72	69	73	66	280	4,733.34
J.L. Lewis	72	69	66	73	280	4,733.34
Dave Barr	73	70	71	66	280	4,733.33
Lee Janzen	70	72	67	71	280	4,733.33
Jerry Kelly	72	68	71	69	280	4,733.33
Bob Lohr	69	71	67	73	280	4,733.33
Billy Mayfair	66	72	68	74	280	4,733.33
Jerry Pate	70	70	71	69	280	4,733.33
Phil Blackmar	73	70	73	65	281	3,400
Patrick Burke	73	68	73	67	281	3,400
Don Pooley	68	71	71	71	281	3,400
Dave Rummells	68	73	74	66	281	3,400

		SCORES			TOTAL	MONEY
Brian Kamm	69	72	70	71	282	2,568.58
Bart Bryant	72	70	70	70	282	2,568.57
Bruce Fleisher	74	68	70	70	282	2,568.57
Scott Gump	71	71	70	70	282	2,568.57
Wayne Levi	71	72	68	71	282	2,568.57
Doug Martin	69	73	70	70	282	2,568.57
Tom Watson	71	72	72	67	282	2,568.57
Woody Austin	70	72	72	69	283	2,290
Paul Goydos	71	72	72	68	283	2,290
John Morse	71	70	75	67	283	2,290
Don Reese	71	70	70	72	283	2,290
Tommy Armour III	69	71	74	70	284	2,200
Bill Britton	69	74	72	69	284	2,200
Kawika Cotner	69	73	72	70	284	2,200
Robin Freeman	73	70	70	71	284	2,200
Jim Furyk	71	72	72	69	284	2,200
Jay Don Blake	72	70	72	71	285	2,110
Gary Hallberg	67	74	74	70	285	2,110
Ed Humenik	71	67	76	71	285	2,110
Craig Parry	69	72	74	70	285	2,110
John Daly	67	75	76	68	286	2,050
Neal Lancaster	72	71	76	67	286	2,050
Kelly Gibson	73	69	70	75	287	2,010
Dave Stockton, Jr.	69	70	72	76	287	2,010
Skip Kendall	72	71	77	71	291	1,980

Bell Canadian Open

Glen Abbey Golf Club, Oakville, Ontario, Canada
Par 35-37–72; 7,112 yards

September 7-10
purse, $1,300,000

		SCORES			TOTAL	MONEY
Mark O'Meara	72	67	68	67	274	$234,000
Bob Lohr	68	67	69	70	274	140,400
(O'Meara defeated Lohr at first extra hole.)						
Nick Price	72	69	68	68	277	88,400
Hal Sutton	69	72	68	69	278	62,400
Bill Glasson	68	74	68	70	280	49,400
Andrew Magee	68	68	73	71	280	49,400
Tony Sills	72	68	73	69	282	43,550
Scott Dunlap	71	67	73	72	283	40,300
Brian Kamm	74	71	70	69	284	36,400
Bob Tway	69	72	68	75	284	36,400
Dan Forsman	69	72	69	75	285	31,200
John Wilson	76	67	68	74	285	31,200
J.P. Hayes	68	71	74	73	286	27,300
Phil Blackmar	70	73	74	70	287	20,150
Jay Don Blake	74	73	67	73	287	20,150
Mark Brooks	68	73	69	77	287	20,150
Brad Bryant	71	71	72	73	287	20,150
Kawika Cotner	70	71	74	72	287	20,150
David Frost	72	71	72	72	287	20,150
Joey Sindelar	75	67	72	73	287	20,150
Bobby Wadkins	69	76	71	71	287	20,150
Gary Hallberg	68	74	70	76	288	14,040
Mark McCumber	72	75	68	73	288	14,040
Jay Delsing	72	73	71	73	289	10,790

	SCORES				TOTAL	MONEY
Trevor Dodds	72	73	72	72	289	10,790
Bruce Fleisher	72	69	72	76	289	10,790
Jim Gallagher, Jr.	69	68	75	77	289	10,790
Grant Waite	67	72	77	73	289	10,790
Brandel Chamblee	72	71	71	76	290	8,450
Justin Leonard	70	72	75	73	290	8,450
Scott McCarron	72	75	70	73	290	8,450
John Morse	70	70	71	79	290	8,450
Tommy Tolles	74	67	76	73	290	8,450
Fred Couples	71	71	72	77	291	6,857.50
Dudley Hart	71	76	68	76	291	6,857.50
Billy Mayfair	72	73	70	76	291	6,857.50
Dave Stockton, Jr.	72	75	71	73	291	6,857.50
Pat Bates	73	73	69	77	292	5,330
Scott Gump	70	71	71	80	292	5,330
Blaine McCallister	70	70	72	80	292	5,330
David Ogrin	69	75	69	79	292	5,330
Craig Parry	74	70	73	75	292	5,330
Mike Springer	74	73	73	72	292	5,330
Scott Verplank	72	72	77	71	292	5,330
Joe Acosta, Jr.	74	70	71	78	293	3,471
Curt Byrum	73	73	75	72	293	3,471
Mark Calcavecchia	74	71	71	77	293	3,471
Brian Claar	71	74	72	76	293	3,471
Glen Day	72	75	72	74	293	3,471
Steve Lowery	69	77	74	73	293	3,471
Jim McGovern	74	72	71	76	293	3,471
Jerry Pate	74	69	73	77	293	3,471
Dennis Paulson	69	70	76	78	293	3,471
Bruce Vaughan	73	69	74	77	293	3,471
Bart Bryant	74	72	75	73	294	2,938
Jim Carter	71	74	73	76	294	2,938
Russ Cochran	66	80	69	79	294	2,938
Charlie Rymer	70	77	72	75	294	2,938
D.A. Weibring	75	72	70	77	294	2,938
Mike Brisky	75	71	73	76	295	2,860
Joel Edwards	71	73	77	75	296	2,782
Greg Kraft	72	72	77	75	296	2,782
Neal Lancaster	75	72	74	75	296	2,782
Mike Reid	78	69	74	75	296	2,782
Mike Smith	76	69	74	77	296	2,782
Dicky Pride	70	75	71	81	297	2,704
Woody Austin	72	73	72	81	298	2,652
Lee Rinker	70	75	75	78	298	2,652
Mark Wiebe	74	73	73	78	298	2,652
Keith Fergus	70	72	75	82	299	2,587
Steve Jones	70	75	73	81	299	2,587
Steve Rintoul	74	71	79	76	300	2,535
Mike Sullivan	70	76	78	76	300	2,535
John Huston	71	74	73	83	301	2,483
Sandy Lyle	74	72	77	78	301	2,483
David Feherty	71	75	75	81	302	2,444
Ed Dougherty	72	73	81	77	303	2,392
Retief Goosen	73	74	79	77	303	2,392
Paul Stankowski	73	74	76	80	303	2,392
Jay Williamson	78	69	75	82	304	2,340
Ray Freeman	73	74	78	83	308	2,314

B.C. Open

En-Joie Golf Club, Endicott, New York
Par 37-34–71; 6,966 yards

September 14-17
purse, $1,000,000

	SCORES				TOTAL	MONEY
Hal Sutton	71	69	68	61	269	$180,000
Jim McGovern	71	67	69	63	270	108,000
Craig Stadler	67	69	68	67	271	58,000
Kirk Triplett	69	67	69	66	271	58,000
Stewart Cink	71	70	66	65	272	38,000
Jay Haas	68	69	71	64	272	38,000
Skip Kendall	66	69	68	70	273	29,100
Jeff Leonard	69	66	71	67	273	29,100
Joey Sindelar	68	68	70	67	273	29,100
Jeff Sluman	67	69	68	69	273	29,100
Jay Williamson	67	68	69	69	273	29,100
Guy Boros	68	67	70	69	274	21,000
Tom Byrum	71	68	71	64	274	21,000
David Edwards	70	66	68	70	274	21,000
Gary Hallberg	73	63	68	71	275	17,500
Neal Lancaster	70	70	67	68	275	17,500
Ed Fiori	67	70	71	68	276	15,000
Jim Furyk	70	69	73	64	276	15,000
Steve Pate	67	69	72	68	276	15,000
Fred Couples	68	69	72	68	277	10,087.50
Brad Faxon	67	68	71	71	277	10,087.50
Bruce Fleisher	71	69	67	70	277	10,087.50
Peter Jacobsen	71	65	71	70	277	10,087.50
Peter Jordan	69	69	74	65	277	10,087.50
Jonathan Kaye	70	69	71	67	277	10,087.50
Wayne Levi	68	70	69	70	277	10,087.50
Billy Ray Brown	69	70	71	67	277	10,087.50
Michael Allen	69	69	74	66	278	5,730.77
Kawika Cotner	71	70	69	68	278	5,730.77
Marco Dawson	68	71	73	66	278	5,730.77
Joel Edwards	72	69	69	68	278	5,730.77
Rick Fehr	71	70	70	67	278	5,730.77
Fred Funk	69	72	69	68	278	5,730.77
Steve Lowery	66	74	69	69	278	5,730.77
Andrew Magee	67	70	69	72	278	5,730.77
Anthony Rodriguez	71	70	69	68	278	5,730.77
Ray Stewart	72	69	67	70	278	5,730.77
Mike Sullivan	73	66	71	68	278	5,730.77
Tommy Tolles	70	70	68	70	278	5,730.77
Bill Britton	68	68	74	68	278	5,730.76
Phil Blackmar	67	72	69	71	279	3,700
Scott Dunlap	69	71	74	65	279	3,700
Ken Green	67	72	71	69	279	3,700
Mike Hulbert	69	69	73	68	279	3,700
David Peoples	70	69	72	68	279	3,700
Kelly Gibson	68	72	69	71	280	2,674.29
Mike Springer	70	70	74	66	280	2,674.29
Dicky Thompson	68	72	70	70	280	2,674.29
John Wilson	69	70	68	73	280	2,674.29
Tommy Armour III	69	69	69	73	280	2,674.28
Steve Rintoul	67	70	74	69	280	2,674.28
Dave Stockton, Jr.	70	68	72	70	280	2,674.28
Pat Bates	72	69	68	72	281	2,293.34
Don Reese	73	68	71	69	281	2,293.34

	SCORES				TOTAL	MONEY
Patrick Burke	69	68	76	68	281	2,293.33
Curt Byrum	74	67	69	71	281	2,293.33
Nolan Henke	70	71	71	69	281	2,293.33
Howard Twitty	71	68	74	68	281	2,293.33
Jay Delsing	69	69	75	69	282	2,160
Bill Kratzert	71	70	71	70	282	2,160
Carl Paulson	68	72	73	69	282	2,160
Ted Schulz	75	65	74	68	282	2,160
Ted Tryba	67	71	76	68	282	2,160
Greg Twiggs	72	69	73	68	282	2,160
Bobby Wadkins	68	72	74	68	282	2,160
Ed Dougherty	71	70	73	69	283	2,070
Omar Uresti	69	72	72	70	283	2,070
Dennis Paulson	71	69	75	69	284	2,020
Bill Porter	69	69	74	72	284	2,020
Willie Wood	70	71	76	67	284	2,020
Ed Humenik	69	69	76	71	285	1,980
John Schroeder	68	73	73	73	287	1,960
Billy Andrade	71	69	73	76	289	1,940

Ryder Cup

Oak Hill Country Club, Rochester, New York   September 22-24
Par 443 543 444–35; 434 543 444–35–70; 6,902 yards

FIRST DAY
Morning Foursomes

Corey Pavin and Tom Lehman (USA) defeated Nick Faldo and Colin Montgomerie
(Europe), 1 up

Faldo/Montgomerie	4 6 3	5 5 2	4 4 4	4 3 4	4 4 3	4 5 5
Pavin/Lehman	3 4 2	5 4 3	6 5 4	4 3 4	5 3 4	4 5 4

Sam Torrance and Costantino Rocca (Europe) defeated Jay Haas and Fred Couples
(USA), 3 and 2

Torrance/Rocca	4 4 3	5 4 3	4 4 4	4 3 4	6 5 3	4
Haas/Couples	4 4 4	4 4 4	5 5 5	5 3 3	5 3 4	4

Davis Love III and Jeff Maggert (USA) defeated Howard Clark and Mark James
(Europe), 4 and 3

Clark/James	4 4 3	4 5 4	5 4 4	5 3 4	5 4 3
Love/Maggert	3 4 2	5 3 3	3 4 4	4 3 4	6 4 3

Bernhard Langer and Per-Ulrik Johansson (Europe) defeated Ben Crenshaw and Curtis
Strange (USA), 1 up

Langer/Johansson	4 4 4	4 4 3	4 4 3	4 3 4	7 5 3	5 6 4
Crenshaw/Strange	5 4 3	5 3 3	4 4 4	5 4 4	5 4 3	5 5 5

POINTS: Europe 2, United States 2

Afternoon Fourball

David Gilford and Seve Ballesteros (Europe) defeated Brad Faxon and Peter Jacobsen (USA), 4 and 3

Gilford	5 4 3	5 4 2	4 4 4	4 3 4	4 4 2
Ballesteros	4 5 3	4 5 3	5 5 4	3 3 4	6 4 3
Faxon	4 4 3	5 4 3	5 4 4	4 3 4	5 4 3
Jacobsen	5 3 3	4 5 3	4 4	4 3 5	5 4 3

Jeff Maggert and Loren Roberts (USA) defeated Sam Torrance and Costantino Rocca (Europe), 6 and 5

Torrance	4 5 3	5 4 3	5 5 4	4 3 5	5
Rocca	5 3	5 3 3	4 5 4	4 3 5	6
Maggert	4 4 3	5 4 3	4 4 4	4 3 4	5
Roberts	4 4 3	4 4 3	3 4 3	4 2 4	5

Fred Couples and Davis Love III (USA) defeated Nick Faldo and Colin Montgomerie (Europe), 3 and 2

Faldo	4 4 3	5 5 4	4 4 4	4 3 4	5 4 4	4
Montgomerie	4 4 3	5 5 4	4 4 4	4 3 3	6 3 4	4
Couples	4 3 3	5 4	4 4 4	4 3 4	6 4 3	4
Love	4 4 4	4 4 3	4 4 4	4 3 4	5 4 4	4

Corey Pavin and Phil Mickelson (USA) defeated Bernhard Langer and Per-Ulrik Johansson (Europe), 6 and 4

Langer	5 5	3	4 4 4	5 2 4	5 4
Johansson	4 5 4	5 3 4	5 5 4	5 3 4	5 4
Pavin	3 4 3	5 4 3	4 5 4	4 3 4	5 3
Mickelson	5 4 3	4 4 3	4 4 3	4 3 3	5 4

POINTS: Europe 3, United States 5

SECOND DAY
Morning Foursomes

Nick Faldo and Colin Montgomerie (Europe) defeated Curtis Strange and Jay Haas (USA), 4 and 2

Faldo/Montgomerie	4 4 3	4 5 4	4 4 3	5 3 5	4 4 3	W
Strange/Haas	5 4 3	5 4 4	5 4 5	5 3 4	5 4 3	C

Sam Torrance and Costantino Rocca (Europe) defeated Davis Love III and Jeff Maggert (USA), 6 and 5

Torrance/Rocca	4 3 3	6 4 1	4 4 4	4 3 3	5
Love/Maggert	6 4 4	5 5 2	4 4 5	4 4 3	5

Loren Roberts and Peter Jacobsen (USA) defeated Ian Woosnam and Philip Walton (Europe), 1 up

Woosnam/Walton	4 4 3	4 6 2	5 5 4	4 2 5	5 6 2	5 4 4
Roberts/Jacobsen	5 4 3	5 5 3	4 4 4	4 3 4	4 4 3	5 4 4

Bernhard Langer and David Gilford (Europe) defeated Corey Pavin and Tom Lehman (USA), 4 and 3

Langer/Gilford	4 3 2	5 5 3	4 4 5	5 3 3	5 4 3
Pavin/Lehman	4 3 4	5 5 3	5 5 4	5 3 4	5 4 4

POINTS: Europe 6, United States 6

Afternoon Fourball

Brad Faxon and Fred Couples (USA) defeated Sam Torrance and Colin Montgomerie (Europe), 4 and 2

Torrance	4 4 2	5 4 4	4 4 4	4 3 4	4 4 3	4
Montgomerie	4 4 4	5 4 4	4 4 4	3 3 4	4 4 3	4
Faxon	4 4 2	5 4 4	4 6 5	3 2 4	5 4 3	3
Couples	4 4 3	5 4 3	5 4 4	4 3 3	4	4

Ian Woosnam and Costantino Rocca (Europe) defeated Davis Love III and Ben Crenshaw (USA), 3 and 2

Woosnam	4 5 2	5 4 3	4 4 4	4 3 4	5 4 3	4
Rocca	4 3 3	5 4 3	4 4 4	5 2 3	6 4 3	4
Love	5 4 3	5 4 3	4 4 4	3 3 4	6 4 3	4
Crenshaw	4 4 4	5 4 3	4 4 4	4 3 4	5 4 3	4

Jay Haas and Phil Mickelson (USA) defeated Seve Ballesteros and David Gilford (Europe), 3 and 2

Ballesteros	4 4 3	5 4 3	5 4 4	4 3 4	5 4 3	4
Gilford	4 5 3	5 5 3	4 4 4	4 3 4	5 4 3	4
Haas	4 3 3	4 4 3	4 4 4	4 4 4	5 4 3	4
Mickelson	4 4 3	5 4 3	5 4 4	4 2 4	5 4 3	4

Corey Pavin and Loren Roberts (USA) defeated Nick Faldo and Bernhard Langer (Europe), 1 up

Faldo	4 4 3	4 4 3	5 4 4	4 3 4	4 4 3	4 4 4
Langer	4 4 3	4 4 3	5 5 3	4 3 4	5 4 4	4 4 4
Pavin	3 4 4	4 3 3	4 4 4	5 3 3	5 4 3	4 4 3
Roberts	4 4 4	4 5 3	4 4 4	5 3 4	5 4 3	4 4 4

POINTS: Europe 7, United States 9

THIRD DAY
Singles

Tom Lehman (USA) defeated Seve Ballesteros (Europe), 4 and 3

Ballesteros	5 3 3	5 4 3	4 5 4	4 4 4	6 4 3
Lehman	4 4 3	5 4 3	4 3 4	4 3 4	5 3 3

Howard Clark (Europe) defeated Peter Jacobsen (USA), 1 up

Clark	4 4 3	5 4 3	4 4 4	4 1 4	6 4 3	4 4 4
Jacobsen	4 4 3	4 5 2	5 4 4	3 2 4	5 5 3	5 4 4

Mark James (Europe) defeated Jeff Maggert (USA), 4 and 3

James	4 3 3	4 4 2	5 4 5	4 3 3	5 4 3
Maggert	4 4 3	5 6 2	3 4 5	5 2 4	5 4 4

Ian Woosnam (Europe) halved with Fred Couples (USA)

Woosnam	5 4 3	5 4 3	5 3 3	4 4 4	5 4 3	4 4 4
Couples	4 4 4	6 5 3	4 3 4	4 3 4	5 4 3	4 3 4

Davis Love III (USA) defeated Costantino Rocca (Europe), 3 and 2

Rocca	4 4 3	5 4 3	4 5 4	5 3 4	5 4 3	3
Love	4 5 3	4 4 3	3 3 4	3 2 4	6 4 3	3

David Gilford (Europe) defeated Brad Faxon (USA), 1 up

Gilford	4 4 3	4 5 2	5 4 4	4 3 4	5 4 3	4 4 5
Faxon	4 4 3	5 4 2	4 4 5	4 3 4	5 5 3	4 4 5

Colin Montgomerie (Europe) defeated Ben Crenshaw (USA), 3 and 1

Montgomerie	4 5 3	5 4 3	4 4 5	4 3 6	5 3 3	3 3
Crenshaw	4 4 4	5 5 3	4 5 4	4 3 4	5 4 3	4 4

Nick Faldo (Europe) defeated Curtis Strange (USA), 1 up

Faldo	4 4 3	5 4 3	4 3 4	4 3 4	5 4 3	5 4 4
Strange	4 4 3	5 5 2	4 3 4	4 2 4	5 4 3	5 5 5

Sam Torrance (Europe) defeated Loren Roberts (USA), 2 and 1

Torrance	4 4 3	5 5 3	4 4 4	4 2 5	5 5 3	3 4
Roberts	4 4 4	5 4 4	4 4 5	4 2 4	5 5 3	4 4

Corey Pavin (USA) defeated Bernhard Langer (Europe), 3 and 2

Langer	5 4 3	5 3 3	4 4 3	4 3 5	5 4 3	4
Pavin	5 4 2	4 4 3	4 3 4	4 3 4	4 4 3	4

Philip Walton (Europe) defeated Jay Haas (USA), 1 up

Walton	5 4 4	5 4 3	5 3 4	4 3 4	5 4 2	4 5 5
Haas	6 5 3	5 3 3	5 4 5	4 3 4	5 4 3	3 4 5

Phil Mickelson (USA) defeated Per-Ulrik Johansson (Europe), 2 and 1

Johansson	5 3 2	4 4 2	5 4 5	4 3 4	5 4 4	4 5
Mickelson	4 3 3	5 5 3	4 4 5	3 2 3	5 5 3	4 4

TOTAL POINTS: Europe 14½, United States 13½

LEGEND: C—conceded hole to opponent; W—won hole by concession without holing out.

Quad City Classic

Oakwood Country Club, Coal Valley, Illinois
Par 35-35–70; 6,796 yards
(Shortened to 54 holes — rain.)

September 21-24
purse, $1,000,000

	SCORES			TOTAL	MONEY
D.A. Weibring	64	65	68	197	$180,000
Jonathan Kaye	67	66	65	198	108,000
Jay Delsing	69	64	67	200	68,000
Jim McGovern	64	71	66	201	48,000
Michael Allen	66	70	66	202	36,500
Scott Hoch	71	65	66	202	36,500
Dennis Paulson	71	66	65	202	36,500
Curt Byrum	66	68	69	203	30,000
Bob Gilder	68	69	66	203	30,000
Bruce Fleisher	72	66	66	204	26,000
Scott Verplank	65	73	66	204	26,000
Russ Cochran	64	72	69	205	17,875
Clark Dennis	73	65	67	205	17,875
Joel Edwards	66	70	69	205	17,875
Robin Freeman	68	68	69	205	17,875
J.P. Hayes	67	69	69	205	17,875
Dick Mast	70	69	66	205	17,875
Chris Perry	66	72	67	205	17,875
Mike Small	70	67	68	205	17,875
David Edwards	69	68	69	206	11,650
Steve Jones	71	66	69	206	11,650
Greg Kraft	67	75	64	206	11,650
Carl Paulson	70	67	69	206	11,650

	SCORES			TOTAL	MONEY
Chris DiMarco	71	68	68	207	8,800
Paul Goydos	73	65	69	207	8,800
Tommy Tolles	69	71	67	207	8,800
Kenny Knox	70	67	71	208	7,100
Jeff Leonard	71	66	71	208	7,100
Andrew Magee	71	65	72	208	7,100
Bill Porter	68	69	71	208	7,100
Bob Tway	70	71	67	208	7,100
Keith Fergus	68	70	71	209	5,533.34
Dillard Pruitt	72	69	68	209	5,533.34
Patrick Burke	73	69	67	209	5,533.33
Peter Jordan	73	69	67	209	5,533.33
Greg Twiggs	68	70	71	209	5,533.33
Mark Wiebe	71	69	69	209	5,533.33
Joe Acosta, Jr.	72	70	68	210	4,200
Tom Hearn	73	67	70	210	4,200
Ed Humenik	69	71	70	210	4,200
Mark McCumber	69	74	67	210	4,200
David Peoples	70	69	71	210	4,200
Larry Rinker	69	70	71	210	4,200
Phil Blackmar	71	71	69	211	2,890
Ernie Gonzalez	71	70	70	211	2,890
Donnie Hammond	70	70	71	211	2,890
Mark Pfeil	72	71	68	211	2,890
Lee Rinker	73	66	72	211	2,890
Dave Rummells	71	71	69	211	2,890
Gene Sauers	71	69	71	211	2,890
Ted Schulz	67	72	72	211	2,890
Emlyn Aubrey	72	71	69	212	2,308.58
Doug Dunakey	72	69	71	212	2,308.57
Gary Hallberg	71	71	70	212	2,308.57
J.L. Lewis	68	71	73	212	2,308.57
Dicky Pride	68	73	71	212	2,308.57
Hal Sutton	70	71	71	212	2,308.57
Harry Taylor	73	70	69	212	2,308.57
John Cook	69	72	72	213	2,150
Jerry Haas	71	71	71	213	2,150
Tom Kite	70	70	73	213	2,150
Don Reese	69	71	73	213	2,150
Joey Sindelar	71	71	71	213	2,150
Tray Tyner	70	72	71	213	2,150
Omar Uresti	68	73	72	213	2,150
Bruce Vaughan	72	71	70	213	2,150
Steve Brodie	70	71	73	214	1,960
Barry Cheesman	73	70	71	214	1,960
Lennie Clements	74	69	71	214	1,960
Ed Dougherty	72	71	71	214	1,960
David Frost	71	70	73	214	1,960
Kelly Gibson	70	73	71	214	1,960
Steve Gotsche	73	70	71	214	1,960
John Huston	70	73	71	214	1,960
Ken Schall	70	72	72	214	1,960
Ray Stewart	71	67	76	214	1,960
Willie Wood	73	69	72	214	1,960
Kawika Cotner	74	65	76	215	1,780
Bob Lohr	70	73	72	215	1,780
Scott McCarron	70	73	72	215	1,780
Steve Rintoul	68	75	72	215	1,780
Dave Rueter	70	70	75	215	1,780
Dave Stockton, Jr.	73	70	72	215	1,780

	SCORES			TOTAL	MONEY
Mike Heinen	69	74	72	215	1,780
Robert Gamez	69	74	73	216	1,690
Vance Heafner	72	71	73	216	1,690
Ryan Howison	71	72	74	217	1,660
Stephen Keppler	75	68	76	219	1,640

Buick Challenge

Callaway Gardens Resort, Mountain Course,
Pine Mountain, Georgia
Par 36-36–72; 7,057 yards

September 28-October 1
purse, $1,000,000

	SCORES				TOTAL	MONEY
Fred Funk	69	67	69	67	272	$180,000
John Morse	71	68	67	67	273	88,000
Loren Roberts	70	69	67	67	273	88,000
Kirk Triplett	71	66	69	68	274	41,333.34
Guy Boros	68	69	72	65	274	41,333.33
Jeff Sluman	67	69	70	68	274	41,333.33
David Ogrin	70	68	70	67	275	33,500
Scott Hoch	70	70	69	67	276	28,000
John Huston	67	71	70	68	276	28,000
Larry Nelson	71	65	70	70	276	28,000
Steve Stricker	66	67	72	71	276	28,000
Brad Bryant	70	69	70	68	277	19,000
Bob Burns	71	71	68	67	277	19,000
Glen Day	68	67	74	68	277	19,000
Scott Gump	69	73	67	68	277	19,000
Mike Heinen	68	73	73	63	277	19,000
Bob Lohr	74	68	65	70	277	19,000
Steve Jones	70	69	69	70	278	14,500
Justin Leonard	69	67	71	71	278	14,500
John Adams	68	68	72	71	279	11,650
Jim Gallagher, Jr.	71	70	69	69	279	11,650
Greg Norman	71	68	72	68	279	11,650
Mike Smith	69	73	66	71	279	11,650
Emlyn Aubrey	70	73	70	67	280	8,100
Woody Austin	68	69	70	73	280	8,100
Dave Barr	70	70	70	70	280	8,100
Steve Lowery	66	70	72	72	280	8,100
Scott McCarron	70	72	71	67	280	8,100
Duffy Waldorf	68	71	71	70	280	8,100
Russ Cochran	72	67	73	69	281	6,350
Ben Crenshaw	70	70	69	72	281	6,350
Jay Delsing	68	69	73	71	281	6,350
Tony Sills	70	69	70	72	281	6,350
Dan Forsman	68	73	69	72	282	5,050
David Frost	72	68	71	71	282	5,050
Brian Kamm	70	69	72	71	282	5,050
Neal Lancaster	71	72	66	73	282	5,050
J.L. Lewis	68	71	73	70	282	5,050
Gene Sauers	70	68	74	70	282	5,050
Michael Bradley	69	70	73	71	283	3,600
Lennie Clements	70	71	71	71	283	3,600
Larry Mize	66	72	71	74	283	3,600
Carl Paulson	70	70	72	71	283	3,600
Lee Rinker	70	71	75	67	283	3,600

	SCORES				TOTAL	MONEY
Hal Sutton	73	68	70	72	283	3,600
Ted Tryba	69	67	73	74	283	3,600
Grant Waite	71	71	71	70	283	3,600
Billy Ray Brown	69	71	70	74	284	2,580
Curt Byrum	68	72	71	73	284	2,580
Mike Hulbert	71	72	71	70	284	2,580
Craig Parry	72	71	70	71	284	2,580
Fulton Allem	71	72	72	70	285	2,345
Keith Clearwater	69	71	72	73	285	2,345
Scott Ford	71	72	75	67	285	2,345
Dicky Thompson	72	71	73	69	285	2,345
Jim Furyk	68	73	70	75	286	2,270
Howard Twitty	68	70	74	74	286	2,270
Mike Brisky	70	71	70	76	287	2,160
Bill Britton	71	72	72	72	287	2,160
Bart Bryant	71	70	75	71	287	2,160
Patrick Burke	71	72	73	71	287	2,160
Stewart Cink	70	73	70	74	287	2,160
Robin Freeman	70	71	77	69	287	2,160
Kelly Gibson	70	73	78	66	287	2,160
Billy Mayfair	68	74	74	71	287	2,160
Tray Tyner	69	74	74	70	287	2,160
John Daly	71	70	74	73	288	2,040
John Godwin	70	73	75	70	288	2,040
Dave Stockton, Jr.	71	68	79	70	288	2,040
Bruce Fleisher	69	74	79	67	289	1,970
Chris Perry	70	73	72	74	289	1,970
Bill Porter	65	76	74	74	289	1,970
Omar Uresti	71	70	73	75	289	1,970
Joe Acosta, Jr.	72	71	75	72	290	1,900
Bill Glasson	68	73	78	71	290	1,900
Greg Kraft	72	70	76	72	290	1,900
Blaine McCallister	69	73	76	73	291	1,860
Ted Schulz	71	72	78	71	292	1,840
Steve Rintoul	71	70	75	77	293	1,820
Dudley Hart	70	72	76	76	294	1,800

Walt Disney World/Oldsmobile Classic

Walt Disney World Resort, Orlando, Florida
Palm Course: Par 36-36–72; 6,957 yards
Magnolia Course: Par 36-36–72; 7,190 yards
Lake Buena Vista Course: Par 36-36–72; 6,819 yards
(Shortened to 54 holes — rain.)

October 5-8
purse, $1,200,000

	SCORES			TOTAL	MONEY
Brad Bryant	67	63	68	198	$216,000
Hal Sutton	67	66	66	199	105,600
Ted Tryba	69	65	65	199	105,600
Joe Acosta, Jr.	68	67	66	201	49,600
Mike Reid	68	66	67	201	49,600
Bob Tway	65	70	66	201	49,600
Patrick Burke	66	65	71	202	31,275
Russ Cochran	66	67	69	202	31,275
Mike Heinen	65	68	69	202	31,275
Mike Hulbert	68	66	68	202	31,275
Lee Rinker	68	67	67	202	31,275

	SCORES			TOTAL	MONEY
Charlie Rymer	68	68	66	202	31,275
Jay Williamson	69	65	68	202	31,275
Carl Paulson	62	68	72	202	31,275
Chip Beck	70	66	67	203	18,600
John Cook	66	68	69	203	18,600
Bob Gilder	68	64	71	203	18,600
Scott Gump	69	64	70	203	18,600
Doug Martin	69	68	66	203	18,600
Grant Waite	67	67	69	203	18,600
Ronnie Black	67	68	69	204	11,605.72
Lee Janzen	69	67	68	204	11,605.72
Brian Kamm	68	66	70	204	11,605.72
Curt Byrum	71	68	65	204	11,605.71
Scott Hoch	72	64	68	204	11,605.71
Bob Lohr	67	67	70	204	11,605.71
Steve Lowery	65	70	69	204	11,605.71
Paul Azinger	68	70	67	205	7,480
Keith Fergus	64	69	72	205	7,480
Ken Green	68	68	69	205	7,480
Tom Hearn	71	69	65	205	7,480
John Mahaffey	71	67	67	205	7,480
Larry Mize	70	66	69	205	7,480
Craig Parry	64	69	72	205	7,480
Payne Stewart	70	64	71	205	7,480
Tray Tyner	67	69	69	205	7,480
John Adams	68	68	70	206	4,564
Emlyn Aubrey	68	68	70	206	4,564
Jay Don Blake	69	67	70	206	4,564
Mark Brooks	67	70	69	206	4,564
Glen Day	67	71	68	206	4,564
Ed Fiori	66	71	69	206	4,564
Dan Forsman	66	69	71	206	4,564
Fred Funk	66	67	73	206	4,564
Skip Kendall	70	69	67	206	4,564
Tom Kite	67	71	68	206	4,564
Scott Verplank	71	66	69	206	4,564
Duffy Waldorf	70	66	70	206	4,564
Michael Bradley	68	72	67	207	2,785.72
Chris DiMarco	67	67	73	207	2,785.72
Kelly Gibson	66	71	70	207	2,785.72
Paul Goydos	69	67	71	207	2,785.72
Jeff Leonard	70	68	69	207	2,785.72
Steve Rintoul	67	69	71	207	2,785.72
Phil Blackmar	66	70	71	207	2,785.71
Bruce Fleisher	69	68	70	207	2,785.71
Jim Furyk	66	69	72	207	2,785.71
Jim Gallagher, Jr.	69	66	72	207	2,785.71
Roger Maltbie	69	72	66	207	2,785.71
Corey Pavin	69	69	69	207	2,785.71
Mike Standly	71	65	71	207	2,785.71
Dicky Thompson	72	68	67	207	2,785.71
Rick Fehr	67	72	69	208	2,484
Donnie Hammond	71	67	70	208	2,484
John Morse	68	72	68	208	2,484
David Ogrin	71	68	69	208	2,484
Naomichi Ozaki	71	68	69	208	2,484
Chris Perry	66	70	72	208	2,484
Tommy Tolles	69	70	69	208	2,484
Mark Wurtz	70	66	72	208	2,484

Las Vegas Invitational

TPC at Summerlin
Par 36-36–72; 7,243 yards

October 12-15
purse, $1,500,000

Las Vegas Country Club
Par 36-36–72; 7,164 yards

Las Vegas Hilton Country Club
Par 36–35–71; 6,815 yards
Las Vegas, Nevada

	SCORES					TOTAL	MONEY
Jim Furyk	67	65	65	67	67	331	$270,000
Billy Mayfair	66	65	67	66	68	332	162,000
Scott McCarron	71	65	69	64	65	334	102,000
Phil Blackmar	69	66	71	64	65	335	62,000
Brad Bryant	65	68	67	69	66	335	62,000
Mark O'Meara	67	67	66	65	70	335	62,000
Glen Day	70	67	65	68	66	336	46,750
David Edwards	67	66	64	69	70	336	46,750
Davis Love III	67	67	68	67	67	336	46,750
Rick Fehr	64	68	71	67	67	337	36,000
Bill Glasson	68	68	71	65	65	337	36,000
Naomichi Ozaki	63	69	71	66	68	337	36,000
Kirk Triplett	66	67	69	68	67	337	36,000
John Cook	67	64	69	67	71	338	28,500
Patrick Burke	66	67	69	68	69	339	23,250
Lennie Clements	70	68	68	66	67	339	23,250
Kelly Gibson	66	65	74	65	69	339	23,250
Paul Goydos	72	65	68	66	68	339	23,250
Dennis Paulson	68	67	65	71	68	339	23,250
Dave Stockton, Jr.	68	65	70	67	69	339	23,250
Jay Don Blake	72	66	68	69	65	340	17,400
Andrew Magee	70	67	67	67	69	340	17,400
Justin Leonard	70	69	67	69	66	341	15,000
Bruce Vaughan	70	69	68	67	67	341	15,000
Bart Bryant	69	68	69	67	69	342	11,700
Marco Dawson	68	64	73	66	71	342	11,700
Roger Maltbie	70	65	70	69	68	342	11,700
Jim McGovern	68	65	70	70	69	342	11,700
Bob Tway	65	65	69	71	72	342	11,700
Mark Brooks	66	66	71	71	69	343	8,533.34
Phil Mickelson	71	65	70	69	68	343	8,533.34
Mike Smith	69	69	67	69	69	343	8,533.34
Curt Byrum	66	65	70	72	70	343	8,533.33
Jonathan Kaye	67	66	67	69	74	343	8,533.33
Doug Martin	65	72	69	67	70	343	8,533.33
Blaine McCallister	67	67	67	68	74	343	8,533.33
Craig Parry	64	70	71	68	70	343	8,533.33
Chris Perry	71	68	67	68	69	343	8,533.33
John Adams	70	70	68	68	68	344	6,150
Mark Calcavecchia	66	69	69	72	68	344	6,150
Russ Cochran	68	69	67	69	71	344	6,150
Mike Hulbert	68	69	71	68	68	344	6,150
Skip Kendall	67	67	69	68	73	344	6,150
Steve Jones	65	70	69	66	75	345	5,100
Tommy Tolles	68	70	68	69	70	345	5,100
Tom Byrum	66	67	67	73	73	346	3,952.50
Clark Dennis	69	68	70	67	72	346	3,952.50

	SCORES					TOTAL	MONEY
Steve Gotsche	69	67	70	68	72	346	3,952.50
Bruce Lietzke	68	70	69	68	71	346	3,952.50
Omar Uresti	72	68	67	70	69	346	3,952.50
Scott Verplank	66	68	69	74	69	346	3,952.50
Duffy Waldorf	67	68	68	72	71	346	3,952.50
Paul Stankowski	69	66	70	69	72	346	3,952.50
Chip Beck	69	67	72	68	71	347	3,420
Ronnie Black	68	68	67	77	67	347	3,420
Jeff Sluman	67	68	71	70	71	347	3,420
Grant Waite	69	70	69	70	69	347	3,420
Lee Rinker	67	69	71	70	70	347	3,420
Jim Carter	69	69	67	70	73	348	3,285
Ken Green	67	69	71	73	68	348	3,285
Steve Lowery	66	67	72	72	71	348	3,285
John Wilson	64	73	69	73	69	348	3,285
Bruce Fleisher	70	67	71	67	74	349	3,210
Brad Faxon	67	69	72	74	68	350	3,090
Jerry Haas	66	69	73	70	72	350	3,090
Donnie Hammond	68	68	70	75	69	350	3,090
Mike Heinen	68	67	72	73	70	350	3,090
Brian Henninger	69	69	69	73	70	350	3,090
Steve Pate	72	68	68	69	73	350	3,090
Charlie Rymer	66	72	69	71	72	350	3,090
Woody Austin	66	73	69	73	70	351	2,940
Ray Stewart	69	68	71	74	69	351	2,940
Ted Tryba	70	72	63	71	75	351	2,940
Emlyn Aubrey	67	68	71	73	73	352	2,850
Paul Azinger	67	67	67	77	74	352	2,850
Kawika Cotner	72	67	68	74	71	352	2,850
Craig Stadler	69	69	68	73	75	354	2,790
Brian Kamm	67	71	68	78	76	360	2,745
Bill Porter	69	68	71	75	77	360	2,745
Tony Sills	73	64	71	76	84	368	2,700

La Cantera Texas Open

La Cantera Country Club, San Antonio, Texas
Par 36-36–72; 6,885 yards

October 19-22
purse, $1,100,000

	SCORES				TOTAL	MONEY
Duffy Waldorf	66	66	71	65	268	$198,000
Justin Leonard	67	70	69	68	274	118,800
John Mahaffey	67	71	71	71	280	57,200
John Morse	70	69	71	70	280	57,200
Loren Roberts	64	72	73	71	280	57,200
Jay Don Blake	67	67	70	77	281	38,225
Mike Standly	68	71	74	68	281	38,225
Jay Haas	68	68	74	72	282	34,100
Lee Rinker	70	66	72	75	283	30,800
Mark Wiebe	74	69	70	70	283	30,800
Bart Bryant	67	72	73	72	284	26,400
Steve Jones	70	73	73	68	284	26,400
Blaine McCallister	68	73	73	71	285	22,000
Jim McGovern	72	70	71	72	285	22,000
Tommy Armour III	69	71	75	71	286	16,500
Paul Azinger	68	74	76	68	286	16,500
Mike Brisky	74	65	77	70	286	16,500

	SCORES				TOTAL	MONEY
Donnie Hammond	65	76	74	71	286	16,500
Kenny Perry	69	72	74	71	286	16,500
Payne Stewart	69	71	78	68	286	16,500
Omar Uresti	72	70	71	73	286	16,500
Brandel Chamblee	69	74	74	70	287	10,211.67
Bob Estes	68	73	74	72	287	10,211.67
Paul Goydos	69	72	75	71	287	10,211.67
Bruce Vaughan	72	72	75	68	287	10,211.67
Ken Green	71	69	74	73	287	10,211.66
Dudley Hart	69	72	72	74	287	10,211.66
Frank Conner	68	72	75	73	288	7,480
Keith Fergus	68	72	74	74	288	7,480
Kelly Gibson	67	71	73	77	288	7,480
Chris Perry	65	76	75	72	288	7,480
Mike Springer	69	74	75	70	288	7,480
David Edwards	73	71	71	74	289	5,940
Joel Edwards	73	71	70	75	289	5,940
Steve Gotsche	68	72	72	77	289	5,940
Mike Hulbert	72	72	71	74	289	5,940
Bob Lohr	70	73	73	73	289	5,940
Rex Caldwell	68	76	73	73	290	4,620
Russ Cochran	70	74	72	74	290	4,620
Jerry Haas	70	75	71	74	290	4,620
Jeff Maggert	68	77	71	74	290	4,620
Scott McCarron	71	74	73	72	290	4,620
Larry Mize	72	71	70	77	290	4,620
Kawika Cotner	72	72	75	72	291	3,325.67
Mike Heinen	70	73	73	75	291	3,325.67
David Ogrin	71	70	76	74	291	3,325.67
Steve Rintoul	76	68	76	71	291	3,325.67
Dan Forsman	67	77	71	76	291	3,325.66
Scott Gump	69	75	69	78	291	3,325.66
David Duval	70	75	74	73	292	2,678.50
Ed Humenik	68	71	74	79	292	2,678.50
Steve Pate	73	71	75	73	292	2,678.50
Kirk Triplett	69	74	76	73	292	2,678.50
Phil Blackmar	73	70	75	75	293	2,508
Mark Carnevale	70	73	75	75	293	2,508
Jim Carter	68	73	71	81	293	2,508
Tom Kite	72	66	79	76	293	2,508
Anthony Rodriguez	67	73	76	77	293	2,508
Billy Andrade	72	73	75	74	294	2,387
Lennie Clements	70	72	76	76	294	2,387
Greg Kraft	72	71	77	74	294	2,387
Dicky Pride	71	74	76	73	294	2,387
Dillard Pruitt	69	72	79	74	294	2,387
Hal Sutton	67	76	79	72	294	2,387
Curt Byrum	73	69	79	74	295	2,266
David Feherty	71	73	75	76	295	2,266
Ed Fiori	71	71	76	77	295	2,266
Tom Hearn	71	72	74	78	295	2,266
Ken McDonald	74	69	77	75	295	2,266
Dick Mast	72	73	73	78	296	2,189
John Wilson	74	69	80	73	296	2,189
Billy Ray Brown	71	72	77	77	297	2,134
Robin Freeman	71	73	76	77	297	2,134
D.A. Weibring	75	70	74	78	297	2,134
John Cook	71	74	82	72	299	2,079
Jay Delsing	71	74	75	79	299	2,079
Steve Brodie	72	71	77	81	301	2,035

	SCORES				TOTAL	MONEY
Ryan Howison	73	70	80	78	301	2,035
Carl Paulson	71	74	81	79	305	2,002
Bruce Lietzke	72	73	82	79	306	1,980

Tour Championship

Southern Hills Country Club, Tulsa, Oklahoma   October 26-29
Par 35-35–70; 6,834 yards   purse, $3,000,000

	SCORES				TOTAL	MONEY
Billy Mayfair	68	70	69	73	280	$540,000
Steve Elkington	71	72	67	73	283	265,500
Corey Pavin	72	70	68	73	283	265,500
Woody Austin	71	68	73	72	284	132,000
Scott Simpson	71	70	74	69	284	132,000
Vijay Singh	69	71	72	73	285	108,000
Brad Bryant	69	68	73	76	286	99,000
Justin Leonard	70	70	72	74	286	99,000
David Duval	74	69	71	73	287	87,600
Greg Norman	72	70	74	71	287	87,600
Loren Roberts	73	68	74	73	288	81,000
Tom Lehman	71	70	73	76	290	76,800
Nick Faldo	76	72	73	70	291	71,400
Mark O'Meara	71	74	71	75	291	71,400
Bob Tway	70	75	72	75	292	66,000
Ernie Els	71	74	75	73	293	60,900
Peter Jacobsen	73	70	73	77	293	60,900
Davis Love III	74	73	74	72	293	60,900
Payne Stewart	69	75	74	75	293	60,900
Jay Haas	75	74	73	72	294	55,800
Lee Janzen	75	70	71	78	294	55,800
Kenny Perry	76	72	70	76	294	55,800
Kirk Triplett	77	71	69	77	294	55,800
Phil Mickelson	79	73	68	75	295	52,800
Ben Crenshaw	74	73	73	76	296	51,000
Jim Gallagher, Jr.	74	73	75	74	296	51,000
Mark Calcavecchia	72	75	73	77	297	49,200
Fred Funk	74	75	72	76	297	49,200
Scott Hoch	75	72	71	79	297	49,200
Nick Price	77	73	74	75	299	48,000

Special Events

Westinghouse-Family House Invitational

Pittsburgh Field Club, Pittsburgh, Pennsylvania
Par 36-35–71; 6,611 yards

June 26-27
purse, $850,000

	SCORES		TOTAL	MONEY
Ernie Els	61	70	131	$170,000
Steve Stricker	65	66	131	85,000
(Els defeated Stricker at first extra hole.)				
Scott Simpson	65	67	132	50,000
Scott Hoch	68	66	134	40,000
Mike Hulbert	66	69	135	28,750
Jeff Maggert	65	70	135	28,750
Gary McCord	71	64	135	28,750
Bob Tway	66	69	135	28,750
Lee Janzen	69	67	136	17,500
Phil Mickelson	68	68	136	17,500
David Duval	67	69	136	17,500
Fred Couples	61	75	136	17,500
Larry Mize	71	66	137	16,000
David Edwards	68	69	137	16,000
Justin Leonard	70	68	138	16,000
Davis Love III	69	69	138	16,000
Vijay Singh	64	74	138	16,000
Rocco Mediate	70	69	139	16,000
John Huston	74	66	140	16,000
Craig Stadler	72	68	140	16,000
Jay Haas	67	73	140	16,000
D.A. Weibring	66	74	140	16,000
Curtis Strange	69	72	141	16,000

Ernst Championship

Overlake Golf and Country Club, Medina, Washington
Par 36-35–71; 6,616 yards

August 14-15
purse, $695,000

	SCORES		TOTAL	MONEY
John Cook	71	63	134	$150,000
Jeff Gove	74	61	135	75,000
Scott Simpson	70	66	136	50,000
Brad Faxon	71	66	137	35,000
Fred Couples	70	68	138	21,333
Davis Love III	67	71	138	21,333
Craig Stadler	71	67	138	21,333
Ernie Els	69	70	139	16,200
Mark O'Meara	71	68	139	16,200
Mark McCumber	71	68	139	16,200
Steve Elkington	72	67	139	16,200
Jay Haas	74	65	139	16,200
Mike Hulbert	69	72	141	15,000

	SCORES		TOTAL	MONEY
Billy Andrade	72	69	141	15,000
Andrew Magee	72	69	141	15,000
Rick Fehr	73	68	141	15,000
Phil Mickelson	76	65	141	15,000
David Feherty	73	68	141	15,000
Jeff Sluman	71	71	142	15,000
Tom Kite	73	69	142	15,000
Peter Jacobsen	76	67	143	15,000
Curtis Strange	69	75	144	15,000
Chip Beck	74	70	144	15,000
Tom Lehman	75	69	144	15,000
Blaine McCallister	71	75	146	15,000
Doug Doxsie	72	74	146	15,000
Mike Reid	76	73	149	15,000
Payne Stewart	76	73	149	15,000

Jerry Ford Invitational

Country Club of the Rockies
Par 36-36–72; 7,090 yards

August 14-15
purse, $300,000

Vail Golf Club
Par 36-35–71; 6,980 yards
Vail, Colorado

	SCORES		TOTAL	MONEY
Doug Tewell	65	67	132	$20,000
Bob Lohr	66	68	134	12,500
Howard Twitty	69	66	135	6,250
John Schroeder	66	69	135	6,250
Donnie Hammond	69	67	136	5,000
Jerry Pate	70	66	136	5,000
Jay Don Blake	71	66	137	5,000
Morris Hatalsky	68	69	137	5,000
Chris Perry	68	69	137	5,000
Jim Thorpe	68	69	137	5,000
John Mahaffey	68	70	138	5,000
Gary Hallberg	70	68	138	5,000
Mark Wiebe	68	71	139	5,000
Lennie Clements	70	69	139	5,000
Buddy Gardner	71	68	139	5,000
Ted Schultz	73	67	140	5,000
Steve Jones	68	72	140	5,000
Bill Kratzert	69	71	140	5,000
Greg Twiggs	66	74	140	5,000
Charles Coody	72	69	141	5,000
Mike Standly	72	69	141	5,000
Dan Pohl	68	74	142	5,000
Fred Funk	72	70	142	5,000
Jay Delsing	74	68	142	5,000
Andy North	69	73	142	5,000
Kirk Triplett	69	74	143	5,000
Robin Freeman	71	72	143	5,000
Dave Stockton, Jr.	72	71	143	5,000
John Huston	74	69	143	5,000
Lon Hinkle	71	72	143	5,000
Richard Zokol	74	69	143	5,000

	SCORES		TOTAL	MONEY
George Burns	72	72	144	5,000
Dale Douglass	72	72	144	5,000
Mark Pfeil	72	72	144	5,000
Dave Stockton, Sr.	72	72	144	5,000
Brian Claar	73	71	144	5,000
Deane Beman	76	69	145	5,000
Tom Sieckmann	72	73	145	5,000
Keith Clearwater	73	73	146	5,000
Gary McCord	75	71	146	5,000
Jim Nelford	77	69	146	5,000
Tom Clary	72	75	147	5,000
Tom Purtzer	73	74	147	5,000
Dave Eichelberger	73	74	147	5,000
Leonard Thompson	73	74	147	5,000
Andy Bean	73	76	149	5,000
Barry Jaeckel	74	75	149	5,000
Ed Fiori	76	73	149	5,000
Hubert Green	72	78	150	5,000
Mark Lye	73	77	150	5,000
Bruce Devlin	76	75	151	5,000
Steve Satterstrom	72	81	153	5,000
Lee Elder	80	76	156	5,000
Dow Finsterwald	79		DQ	5,000

Fred Meyer Challenge

Oregon Golf Club, West Linn, Oregon   August 21-22
Par 35-36–71; 6,889 yards   purse, $750,000

	SCORES		TOTAL	MONEY (Team)
Greg Norman/Brad Faxon	65	64	129	$100,000
Payne Stewart/Paul Azinger	64	65	129	80,000
(Norman/Faxon defeated Stewart/Azinger on first extra hole.)				
John Cook/Mark O'Meara	66	65	131	65,000
Jay Haas/Curtis Strange	67	64	131	65,000
Steve Elkington/Craig Stadler	68	64	132	55,000
Ben Crenshaw/Phil Mickelson	67	66	133	50,000
Jack Nicklaus/Gary Nicklaus	68	65	133	50,000
Lee Janzen/Brian Henninger	68	65	133	50,000
Tom Lehman/Bob Gilder	65	69	134	46,667
Fred Couples/Davis Love III	68	66	134	46,667
Ernie Els/Fulton Allem	69	65	134	46,667
Peter Jacobsen/Arnold Palmer	69	68	137	45,000

West Coast Classic

Swan-e-set Bay's Country Club, Pitt Meadows, British Columbia   August 21-23
Par 36-36–72; 7,105 yards   purse, $550,000

	SCORES			TOTAL	MONEY
Scott Hoch	70	67	66	203	$100,000
Scott Verplank	68	64	71	203	55,000
(Hoch defeated Verplank on fifth extra hole.)					
Brandel Chamblee	65	67	72	204	30,000

	SCORES			TOTAL	MONEY
Dave Barr	67	66	72	205	20,000
Russ Cochran	66	71	69	206	17,500
Pete Jordan	69	68	69	206	17,500
Brett Ogle	65	69	73	207	16,000
Skip Kendall	69	67	72	208	12,625
Bob Lohr	73	64	71	208	12,625
Clarence Rose	66	71	71	208	12,625
Joel Edwards	69	67	72	208	12,625
Rex Caldwell	68	69	72	209	10,000
Greg Twiggs	71	70	69	210	8,500
Paul Goydos	74	71	65	210	8,500
Gary Hallberg	70	67	73	210	8,500
Barry Jaeckel	69	71	71	211	6,560
Ed Humenik	71	69	71	211	6,560
Larry Rinker	69	70	72	211	6,560
Ed Fiori	68	71	72	211	6,560
David Peoples	68	70	73	211	6,560
Ray Stewart	70	67	75	212	5,100
Carl Paulson	68	68	76	212	5,100
Brian Mogg	69	73	70	212	5,100
Jonathan Kaye	71	72	69	212	5,100
Richard Zokol	73	70	69	212	5,100
Gerry Foltz	75	70	68	213	4,700
Ted Schultz	69	72	73	214	4,550
Mark Lye	71	70	73	214	4,550
Steve Lamontagne	69	75	70	214	4,550
Mike Standly	69	72	73	214	4,550
Mac O'Grady	69	70	75	214	4,550
John Jacobs	77	70	68	215	4,050
Tommy Masters	74	72	69	215	4,050
David Ogrin	76	72	67	215	4,050
David DeLong	68	74	73	215	4,050
Jeff Woodland	71	71	73	215	4,050
Jay Don Blake	69	71	75	215	4,050
Dave Rummells	69	73	74	216	3,650
Jim Hallet	70	70	76	216	3,650
Patrick Burke	70	69	78	217	3,300
Bill Kratzert	69	73	75	217	3,300
Mark Pfeil	71	71	75	217	3,300
Michael Campbell	70	73	74	217	3,300
Darryl Harrington	73	71	73	217	3,300
Len Mattiace	72	74	72	218	3,000
Roger Maltbie	76	72	71	219	3,000
Buddy Gardner	71	74	74	219	3,000
John Daly	67	80	72	219	3,000
Perry Moss	73	72	74	219	3,000
Johnny Gonzales	73	73	74	220	3,000
Bobby Wilson	76	71	74	221	3,000
Mark Wurtz	70	77	74	221	3,000
Dan Halldorson	73	73	75	221	3,000
E.J. Pfister	72	75	75	222	3,000
Mike Donald	73	73	76	222	3,000
Bobby Friend	73	73	81	227	3,000
Mike Dunaay	79	80	74	233	3,000
Gary Schaal	85	82	79	236	3,000

Gene Sarazen World Open

The Legends at Chateau Elan, Braselton, Georgia
Par 36-36–72; 6,900 yards
(Shortened to 54 holes — inclement weather.)

November 2-5
purse, $1,900,000

	SCORES			TOTAL	MONEY
Frank Nobilo	70	70	68	208	$350,000
Mark McNulty	72	70	67	209	162,500
Miguel Angel Jimenez	67	69	73	209	162,500
Mark Calcavecchia	71	70	69	210	67,000
Anders Forsbrand	69	72	69	210	67,000
Eduardo Romero	69	71	70	210	67,000
Emlyn Aubrey	70	70	70	210	67,000
John Daly	70	68	73	211	52,000
Craig Stadler	68	70	73	211	52,000
Retief Goosen	70	72	70	212	41,600
Lucas Parsons	70	72	70	212	41,600
Ernie Els	71	70	71	212	41,600
Brad Faxon	73	71	69	213	32,300
Fuzzy Zoeller	67	71	75	213	32,300
Paul Curry	73	71	70	214	25,650
Lee Janzen	73	70	71	214	25,650
Per-Ulrik Johansson	72	71	71	214	25,650
Sam Torrance	71	69	74	214	25,650
Neil Kerry	73	71	71	215	20,900
Todd Hamilton	71	72	73	216	18,050
Paul Moloney	74	70	72	216	18,050
Andrew Oldcorn	71	75	70	216	18,050
Christian Post	70	74	73	217	12,910
Eric Carlberg	73	71	73	217	12,910
Chris Perry	72	72	73	217	12,910
Brandt Jobe	69	74	74	217	12,910
Mark Davis	72	73	72	217	12,910
Chris Williams	67	75	75	217	12,910
Mike Cunning	75	71	71	217	12,910
Mark O'Meara	73	68	76	217	12,910
James Lee	72	75	70	217	12,910
Mark James	76	68	74	218	9,310
Joakim Haeggman	73	72	73	218	9,310
Raymond Burns	70	75	73	218	9,310
Raul Fretes	72	73	73	218	9,310
Robert Allenby	76	70	72	218	9,310
Steve Alker	74	73	71	218	9,310
Paul Broadhurst	72	72	75	219	7,552
Carl Mason	72	74	73	219	7,552
David Frost	73	74	72	219	7,552
Anssi Kankonnen	77	70	72	219	7,552
Philip Walton	70	72	78	220	6,935
Jeff Wagner	76	71	73	220	6,935
Ronan Rafferty	72	73	76	221	6,650
Fred Funk	73	71	79	223	6,080
Daniel Chopra	68	74	81	223	6,080
Jesus Amaya	75	71	77	223	6,080
Jose Cantero	76	71	76	223	6,080
Ryan Howison	73	74	76	223	6,080
Kyi-Hla Han	71	76	77	224	5,500
Stuart Hendley	73	71	81	225	5,500
Jeff Leonard	74	73	78	225	5,500

	SCORES			TOTAL	MONEY
Gary Marks	75	72	78	225	5,500
Abdul Hameed	74	72	83	229	5,500

Lincoln-Mercury Kapalua International

Kapalua Resort, Plantation Course, Maui, Hawaii
Par 36-37–73; 7,263 yards

November 2-5
purse, $1,000,000

	SCORES				TOTAL	MONEY
Jim Furyk	65	65	71	70	271	$180,000
Russ Cochran	67	66	73	67	273	70,950
Barry Lane	66	69	69	69	273	70,950
Jim McGovern	66	69	68	70	273	70,950
Ben Crenshaw	67	67	71	69	274	34,000
Tom Lehman	67	69	69	69	274	34,000
Steve Jones	73	65	72	65	275	26,500
Marco Dawson	67	67	73	68	275	26,500
Fred Couples	68	72	69	67	276	21,333.34
Kirk Triplett	68	66	74	68	276	21,333.33
Hale Irwin	68	67	68	73	276	21,333.33
Dave Stockton, Jr.	69	68	74	66	277	18,500
Neal Lancaster	72	68	68	69	277	18,500
Jay Delsing	72	67	72	67	278	14,485.72
John Schroeder	67	72	72	67	278	14,485.71
Guy Boros	68	70	74	66	278	14,485.71
Bob Lohr	66	73	71	68	278	14,485.71
Sandy Lyle	68	68	73	69	278	14,485.71
Peter Jacobsen	68	66	71	73	278	14,485.71
Steve Pate	71	67	65	75	278	14,485.71
Billy Andrade	69	70	69	71	279	11,850
Davis Love III	69	64	73	73	279	11,850
Lennie Clements	69	72	69	70	280	10,612.50
Nolan Henke	69	68	73	70	280	10,612.50
Mike Heinen	67	67	74	72	280	10,612.50
Gary McCord	66	72	70	72	280	10,612.50
Jay Don Blake	69	67	75	70	281	9,550
Duffy Waldorf	70	69	73	69	281	9,550
Brian Claar	69	71	66	75	281	9,550
Scott Simpson	72	68	70	72	282	9,050
Blaine McCallister	69	73	70	70	282	9,050
Jerry Pate	67	72	74	70	283	8,700
John Adams	66	71	72	74	283	8,700
Howard Twitty	67	72	69	75	283	8,700
Mike Standly	65	70	72	76	283	8,700
Robin Freeman	71	71	70	72	284	8,450
Mike Hulbert	72	65	75	73	285	8,300
Tom Purtzer	73	65	72	75	285	8,300
Mike Sullivan	73	62	78	72	285	8,300
Doug Martin	73	69	71	73	286	8,175
Chip Beck	72	70	72	72	286	8,175
Woody Austin	75	65	73	74	287	8,025
Roger Maltbie	67	68	79	73	287	8,025
Andy Bean	75	66	74	72	287	8,025
Steve Lowery	70	70	78	69	287	8,025
Darren Clarke	65	70	78	75	288	7,850
Ted Tryba	70	70	75	73	288	7,850
John Cook	74	67	76	71	288	7,850

	SCORES			TOTAL	MONEY
Brandel Chamblee	67	75 74	73	289	7,750
John Mahaffey	70	71 75	74	290	7,700
John Morse	74	70 77	70	291	7,650
Michael Bradley	74	68 75	75	292	7,635
Ed Dougherty	74	71 75	72	292	7,635
David Feherty	71	75 72	75	293	7,620
Grant Waite	68	78 75	77	298	7,610
Robert Gamez	DQ				7,600

MasterCard PGA Grand Slam of Golf

Poipu Bay Resort, Kauai, Hawaii
Par 36-36–72; 6,957 yards

November 7-8
purse, $1,000,000

	SCORES		TOTAL	MONEY
Ben Crenshaw	72	68	140	$400,000
Steve Elkington	71	70	141	225,000
Corey Pavin	71	70	141	225,000
John Daly	75	73	148	150,000

Mexican Open

Club de Golf Chapultepec, Mexico City, Mexico
Par 36-36–72; 7,153 yards

November 9-12
purse, $124,395

	SCORES				TOTAL	MONEY
John Cook	68	69	67	69	273	$27,643
Scott Verplank	69	67	69	69	274	17,968
Bob Tway	69	70	67	69	275	12,440
Jay Don Blake	72	70	66	69	277	8,224
Chris Perry	71	68	70	68	277	8,224
Tom Byrum	71	67	70	70	278	4,354
Tommy Amour III	71	70	70	67	278	4,354
Lee Rinker	72	69	71	68	280	3,455
Lennie Clements	67	70	72	73	282	3,144
Mike Mitchell	70	73	71	68	282	3,144
Jeff Klein	72	71	70	71	284	2,626
Walter Hartleben	70	71	70	73	284	2,626
Jorge Perez Leon	72	69	74	69	284	2,626
Juan Brito	73	72	70	71	286	2,004
Eddie Grace	72	69	74	71	286	2,004
Bob Lohr	70	74	73	69	286	2,004
Andy Spooner	72	71	67	78	288	1,520
Carlos Espinosa	73	73	74	68	288	1,520
Octavio Gonzalez	75	72	74	67	288	1,520
*Viviano Villarreal	69	71	76	73	289	
Oscar Serna	69	75	75	71	290	1,313
Sixto Torres	74	69	71	77	291	1,244
Cesar Perez	69	73	73	77	292	1,202
Rodolfo Cazaubon	74	71	73	74	292	1,202
Carlos Peleaz	73	72	74	73	292	1,202
Vicente Osnaya	73	71	78	71	293	1,168
Pablo Del Olmo	74	77	72	70	293	1,168
*Juan Salazar	77	72	72	73	294	
Efren Serna	75	71	77	71	294	1,147

	SCORES				TOTAL	MONEY
Enrique Ramirez	74	70	73	76	295	1,120
Rudy Asbun	72	76	73	74	295	1,120
Billy Sitton	79	75	73	69	295	1,120

Pebble Beach Invitational

Pebble Beach Golf Links, Pebble Beach, California
Par 36-36–72; 6,799 yards

November 16-17
purse, $250,000

	SCORES				TOTAL	MONEY
Ronnie Black	73	68	65	71	277	$50,000
Kenny Perry	66	70	77	66	279	13,500
Kirk Triplett	72	69	68	70	279	13,500
Kris Tschetter	68	73	67	71	279	13,500
Bob Ford	67	66	71	75	279	13,500
Bruce Fleisher	68	73	68	71	280	5,750
Gary Hallberg	68	71	70	71	280	5,750
Andy North	74	69	66	72	281	5,000
Val Skinner	76	65	72	69	282	4,166
Roger Maltbie	71	67	72	72	282	4,166
Keith Fergus	68	71	70	73	282	4,166
Dave Eichelberger	74	72	70	68	284	3,700
Dan Forsman	71	71	72	71	285	3,500
Mick Soli	70	70	73	74	287	3,200
Duffy Waldorf	71	66	75	75	287	3,200
Todd Fischer	72	74	69	73	288	2,900
Jeff McMillian	69	71	75	74	289	2,500
Rick Fehr	76	71	69	73	289	2,500
Brent Geiberger	73	73	67	76	289	2,500
Bruce Summerhays	72	78	71	69	290	2,080
Ted Goin	73	71	72	74	290	2,080
Brett Upper	70	76	69	75	290	2,080
Charlie Gibson	73	70	73	75	291	2,040
Marion Dantzler	74	75	72	71	292	1,990
Brian Mogg	72	75	73	72	292	1,990
Chuck Milne	73	73	72	74	292	1,990
Al Geiberger	75	76	67	74	292	1,990
Barry Jaeckel	66	71	77	79	293	1,940
Jim Dent	73	77	73	71	294	1,870
Elaine Crosby	73	75	72	74	294	1,870
Larry Ziegler	72	73	73	76	294	1,870
Juli Inkster	73	70	76	75	294	1,870
Cindy Rarick	73	72	72	77	294	1,870
Steve Jones	73	68	73	80	294	1,870
Glen Stubblefield	75	74	74	72	295	1,790
Tommy Masters	73	73	74	75	295	1,790
Lon Hinkle	74	73	73	76	296	1,730
Rob Boldt	73	71	76	76	296	1,730
Shawn McEntee	68	78	73	77	296	1,730
Colin Campbell	68	72	76	80	296	1,730
Butch Baird	76	78	72	71	297	1,650
Clayton Cole	74	73	74	76	297	1,650
Mike Weir	75	70	74	78	297	1,650
Heinz P. Thul	75	70	77	75	297	1,650
Terry Dill	73	76	72	77	298	1,600
Mark Lye	73	75	78	73	299	1,570
Mike Parrish	71	75	74	79	299	1,570

	SCORES				TOTAL	MONEY
Bruce Soulsby	76	72	73	79	300	1,540
Laird Small	71	74	81	76	302	1,520
Tracy Kerdyk	74	74	74	81	303	1,500
Johnny Gonzales	79	70	76	79	304	1,500
Ron Cerrudo	76	74	76	80	306	1,500
Al Krueger	68	76	82	81	307	1,500

Franklin Templeton Shark Shootout

Sherwood Country Club, Thousand Oaks, California
Par 36-36–72; 7,025 yards

November 17-19
purse, $1,100,000

	SCORES			TOTAL	MONEY (Team)
Mark Calcavecchia/Steve Elkington	64	61	59	184	$300,000
Lee Janzen/Chip Beck	65	63	57	185	170,000
Tom Lehman/David Duval	66	61	60	187	102,000
Fred Couples/Brad Faxon	68	62	57	187	102,000
Greg Norman/Raymond Floyd	65	65	58	188	83,000
Hale Irwin/Bruce Lietzke	67	63	59	189	75,000
Tom Kite/Jay Haas	64	66	59	189	75,000
Peter Jacobsen/Arnold Palmer	66	67	59	192	68,000
Curtis Strange/Mark O'Meara	69	67	58	194	64,000
Fuzzy Zoeller/John Daly	69	68	60	197	60,000

Paradise Island Invitational

Paradise Island Golf Club, Paradise Island, Bahamas
Par 36-36–72; 6,770 yards

November 17-19
purse, $310,000

	SCORES			TOTAL	MONEY
Jim McGovern	71	67	68	206	$60,000
Guy Boros	70	66	73	209	30,000
Curt Byrum	70	69	72	211	20,000
Paul Azinger	72	71	69	212	15,000
Tom Purtzer	73	68	72	213	11,000
Dillard Pruitt	74	68	71	213	11,000
Donnie Hammond	74	72	68	214	10,000
Howard Twitty	73	72	69	214	10,000
John Inman	70	70	74	214	10,000
Ted Tryba	72	71	72	215	10,000
Dicky Pride	71	71	74	216	10,000
Mark Wiebe	74	73	70	217	10,000
Billy Andrade	72	74	71	217	10,000
Andrew Magee	78	71	69	218	10,000
Bobby Wadkins	77	72	71	220	9,000
Hubert Green	76	73	71	220	9,000
Robin Freeman	75	71	76	222	8,000
Lanny Wadkins	76	75	72	223	8,000
Vernon Lockhardt	76	73	76	225	8,000
Nolan Henke	77	72	77	226	8,000

Office Depot Father/Son Challenge

The Windsor Club, Vero Beach, Florida
Par 36-36–72; 6,709 yards

December 2-3
purse, $650,000

	SCORES		TOTAL	MONEY (Won by professional)
Raymond Floyd/Raymond Floyd, Jr.	62	57	119	$150,000
Hale Irwin/Steve Irwin	66	59	125	100,000
Dave Stockton/Ron Stockton	64	63	127	72,500
Tony Jacklin/Warren Jacklin	64	63	127	72,500
Larry Nelson/Drew Nelson	68	60	128	55,000
Lee Trevino/Tony Lee Trevino	68	63	131	50,000
Billy Casper/Bobby Casper	67	65	132	42,500
Tom Weiskopf/Eric Weiskopf	67	65	132	42,500
Johnny Miller/John Miller	70	63	133	32,500
David Graham/Andrew Graham	69	64	133	32,500

Diners Club Matches

PGA West, Jack Nicklaus Course, La Quinta, California
Par 36-36–72; 6,546 yards

December 7-10
purse, $890,000

FIRST ROUND

Kirk Triplett and Steve Striker defeated Jeff Maggert and Jim McGovern, 2 up
Tom Lehman and Duffy Waldorf defeated Jay Haas and Curtis Strange, 1 up
Bob Tway and Scott Verplank defeated Billy Mayfair and Mark Calcavecchia, 1 up
David Duval and Woody Austin defeated Jeff Leonard and Jeff Sluman, 2 and 1
Tom Kite and Billy Andrade defeated Fred Funk and Blaine McCallister, 1 up, 19 holes
Kenny Perry and John Huston defeated Peter Jacobsen and Brian Henninger, 3 and 2
Phil Mickelson and Paul Azinger defeated Lee Janzen and Payne Stewart, 2 up
Jim Gallagher, Jr. and Steve Lowery defeated Scott Simpson and Larry Mize, 2 and 1

(Losers in first round received $15,000 each.)

SECOND ROUND

Lehman and Waldorf defeated Triplett and Stricker, 1 up
Tway and Verplank defeated Duval and Austin, 2 up
Perry and Huston defeated Kite and Andrade, 2 and 1
Gallagher, Jr. and Lowery defeated Mickelson and Azinger, 2 and 1

(Losers in second round received $20,000 each.)

THIRD ROUND

Lehman and Waldorf defeated Tway and Verplank, 23 holes
Perry and Huston defeated Gallagher, Jr. and Lowery, 5 and 4

(Losers in third round received $35,000 each.)

FOURTH ROUND

Lehman and Waldorf defeated Perry and Huston, 1 up

(Lehman and Waldorf received $125,000 each; Perry and Huston received $50,000 each.)

Lexus Challenge

La Quinta Golf Club, Citrus Course, La Quinta, California
Par 36-36–72; 6,888 yards

December 15-16
purse, $1,000,000

	SCORES		TOTAL	MONEY (Won by professional)
Raymond Floyd/Michael Chiklis	63	64	127	$180,000
Jim Colbert/William Devane	65	65	130	120,000
Hale Irwin/Julius Erving	62	69	131	105,000
Tom Weiskopf/Chris O'Donnell	63	69	132	90,000
George Archer/Glenn Frey	62	70	132	90,000
Lee Trevino/Jimmy Connors	66	67	133	75,000
Gary Player/Bryant Gumbel	66	68	134	60,833.34
Dave Stockton, Sr./Robert Wagner	68	66	134	60,833.33
Arnold Palmer/Grant Show	68	66	134	60,833.33
Jack Nicklaus/Alan Thicke	66	69	135	55,000
Bob Murphy/Clint Eastwood	67	70	137	52,500
Chi Chi Rodriguez/Bobby Rahal	66	74	140	50,000

Andersen Consulting World Championship

Grayhawk Golf Club, Talon Course, Scottsdale, Arizona
Par 36-36–72; 7,005 yards

December 30-31
purse, $3,650,000

SEMI-FINALS

Barry Lane defeated Masahiro Kuramoto, 2 up
David Frost defeated Mark McCumber, 2 and 1

THIRD-PLACE PLAYOFF

McCumber defeated Kuramoto, 4 and 3

(McCumber received $350,000; Kuramoto received $300,000.)

FINAL

Lane defeated Frost, 2 up

(Lane received $1,000,000; Frost received $500,000.)

Japan Qualifying

Golden Palm Club, Kagoshima, Japan
Par 36-36–72; 6,947 yards

February 25-26

QUARTER-FINALS

Hideki Kase defeated Tsuneyuki Nakajima, 6 and 4
Masahiro Kuramoto defeated Yoshinori Mizumaki, 19 holes
Eiji Mizoguchi defeated Tsukasa Watanabe, 5 and 4
Naomichi Ozaki defeated Katsuyoshi Tomori, 3 and 2

(Each losing quarter-finalist received $20,000.)

SEMI-FINALS

Kuramoto defeated Kase, 4 and 2
Ozaki defeated Mizoguchi, 4 and 3

(Each losing semi-finalist received $70,000.)

FINAL

Kuramoto defeated Ozaki, 1 up

(Ozaki received $150,000.)

European Qualifying

La Moraleja II Golf Course, Madrid, Spain   May 23
Par 36-36–72; 7,051 yards

QUARTER-FINALS

Jesper Parnevik defeated David Gilford, 2 and 1
Seve Ballesteros defeated Miguel Angel Jimenez, 3 and 2
Bernhard Langer defeated Sandy Lyle, 3 and 2
Barry Lane defeated Sam Torrance, 2 and 1

(Each losing quarter-finalist received $20,000.)

Oxfordshire Golf Club, Thames, England   July 24-25
Par 36-36–72; 7,187 yards

SEMI-FINALS

Ballesteros defeated Parnevik, 3 and 1
Lane defeated Langer, 3 and 1

(Each losing semi-finalist received $70,000.)

FINAL

Lane defeated Ballesteros, 4 and 3

(Ballesteros received $150,000.)

United States Qualifying

Reynolds Plantation, Great Waters Course, Lake Oconee, Georgia   April 10-11
Par 36-36–72; 7,048 yards

QUARTER-FINALS

Corey Pavin defeated Phil Mickelson, 3 and 1
Mark McCumber defeated Tom Lehman, 1 up
Paul Azinger defeated Fuzzy Zoeller, 1 up
Loren Roberts defeated Tom Kite, 3 and 2

(Each losing quarter-finalist received $20,000.)

Blackwolf Run, River Course, Kohler, Wisconsin   July 31-August 1
Par 36-36–72; 6,991 yards

SEMI-FINALS

McCumber defeated Pavin, 1 up
Roberts defeated Azinger, 2 and 1

(Each losing semi-finalist received $70,000.)

FINAL

McCumber defeated Roberts, 2 up

(Roberts received $150,000.)

Rest of the World Qualifying

Reynolds Plantation, Great Waters Course, Lake Oconee, Georgia   April 10-11
Par 36-36–72; 7,048 yards

QUARTER-FINALS

David Frost defeated Eduardo Romero, 2 and 1
Steve Elkington defeated Frank Nobilo, 4 and 5
Robert Allenby defeated Vijay Singh, 1 up
Craig Parry defeated Mark McNulty, 1 up

(Each losing quarter-finalist received $20,000.)

Oxfordshire Golf Club, Thames, England   July 24-25
Par 36-36–72; 7,187 yards

SEMI-FINALS

Frost defeated Elkington, 4 and 3
Allenby defeated Parry, 2 and 1

(Each losing semi-finalist received $70,000.)

FINAL

Frost defeated Allenby, 3 and 2

(Allenby received $150,000.)

Nike Tour

San Jose Open

Almaden Country Club, San Jose, California   February 23-26
Par 36-36–72; 6,960 yards   purse, $200,000

	SCORES				TOTAL	MONEY
John Maginnes	69	72	68	68	277	$36,000
Larry Silveira	75	68	71	66	280	22,700
Brent Geiberger	71	72	71	68	282	16,500
Shane Bertsch	73	72	66	72	283	8,285.72
John Dowdall	74	71	68	70	283	8,285.72
Franklin Langham	73	72	69	69	283	8,285.72
Jeff Brehaut	72	70	72	69	283	8,285.71
Joey Gullion	73	68	73	69	283	8,285.71
Tim Herron	72	72	70	69	283	8,285.71
Thomas Scherrer	72	71	70	70	283	8,285.71
Joe Cioe	69	74	74	67	284	3,475
Sam Randolph	73	71	72	68	284	3,475
Tim Simpson	74	68	72	70	284	3,475
Chris Smith	72	67	72	73	284	3,475
Tom Byrum	73	71	71	70	285	2,580
Jaime Gomez	73	70	73	69	285	2,580
Jerry Kelly	70	71	73	71	285	2,580
Frank Lickliter	73	71	70	71	285	2,580
Roger Maltbie	69	76	72	68	285	2,580
Don Walsworth	72	71	72	70	285	2,580
R.W. Eaks	70	75	71	70	286	2,200
Olin Browne	69	71	72	75	287	1,900
Chris Hunsucker	71	74	73	69	287	1,900
Tom Pernice, Jr.	72	73	72	70	287	1,900
Matt Peterson	72	73	73	69	287	1,900
Stan Utley	67	77	74	69	287	1,900
Morris Hatalsky	72	71	72	73	288	1,455
Gerry Norquist	75	70	72	71	288	1,455
Greg Twiggs	74	68	76	70	288	1,455
Jeff Wilson	71	73	73	71	288	1,455

Inland Empire Open

Moreno Valley Ranch Golf Club, Moreno Valley, California   March 2-4
Par 36-36–72; 6,680 yards   purse, $200,000
(Fourth round cancelled — heavy rain.)

	SCORES			TOTAL	MONEY
Jeff Brehaut	70	66	68	204	$36,000
Danny Briggs	71	66	68	205	19,600
David Toms	70	69	66	205	19,600
Jeff Barlow	68	69	69	206	9,400
Greg Bruckner	71	66	69	206	9,400
Jeff Gove	71	65	70	206	9,400

	SCORES			TOTAL	MONEY
Taylor Smith	66	69	71	206	9,400
Jeff Woodland	67	68	71	206	9,400
Mitch Adcock	73	67	67	207	3,971.43
Edward Fryatt	66	74	67	207	3,971.43
Jon Hough	71	66	70	207	3,971.43
Jonathan Kaye	71	68	68	207	3,971.43
Hugh Royer III	69	68	70	207	3,971.43
Tim Simpson	67	70	70	207	3,971.43
Morris Hatalsky	70	65	72	207	3,971.42
Scott Ford	69	70	69	208	2,570
Esteban Toledo	71	66	71	208	2,570
Willie Wood	71	68	69	208	2,570
Robert Wrenn	69	70	69	208	2,570
Clark Burroughs	72	69	68	209	2,100
Jeff Cook	70	70	69	209	2,100
David Peoples	71	69	69	209	2,100
Matt Peterson	69	72	68	209	2,100
Mike Smith	71	70	68	209	2,100
Olin Browne	70	72	68	210	1,346.67
Bill Buttner	72	68	70	210	1,346.67
R.W. Eaks	71	69	70	210	1,346.67
Jerry Foltz	68	69	73	210	1,346.67
Brent Geiberger	69	70	71	210	1,346.67
Peter Persons	71	68	71	210	1,346.67
Larry Rinker	71	70	69	210	1,346.67
Gary Rusnak	71	68	71	210	1,346.67
Chris Hunsucker	69	66	75	210	1,346.66
Sonny Skinner	70	72	68	210	1,346.66
Stan Utley	67	69	74	210	1,346.66
Don Walsworth	70	72	68	210	1,346.66

Monterrey Open

Club Campestre, Monterrey, Mexico
Par 36-36–72; 6,920 yards

March 16-19
purse, $225,000

	SCORES				TOTAL	MONEY
Stuart Appleby	68	70	67	68	273	$40,500
Rafael Alarcon	64	69	69	71	273	25,537.50
(Appleby defeated Alarcon on seventh extra hole.)						
Brad Greer	68	73	66	67	274	18,562.50
Jerry Kelly	70	69	64	72	275	14,062.50
Ben Bates	68	70	68	70	276	10,968.75
Greg Twiggs	69	71	66	70	276	10,968.75
Stan Utley	72	67	69	69	277	8,437.50
Jay Williamson	69	67	72	69	277	8,437.50
Robert Friend	66	72	71	69	278	5,203.13
Peter Persons	71	68	69	70	278	5,203.13
Frank Lickliter	69	68	70	71	278	5,203.12
Esteban Toledo	69	65	72	72	278	5,203.12
Brent Geiberger	68	72	70	69	279	3,303
Greg Hamilton	67	73	68	71	279	3,303
Peter Jordan	67	70	69	73	279	3,303
Ron Philo, Jr.	72	70	66	71	279	3,303
Phil Tataurangi	72	67	71	69	279	3,303
Jeff Brehaut	71	71	68	70	280	2,700
Joe Cioe	69	65	71	75	280	2,700

	SCORES				TOTAL	MONEY
R.W. Eaks	69	71	68	72	280	2,700
Olin Browne	68	67	71	75	281	2,081.25
Mike Donald	73	65	75	68	281	2,081.25
John Flannery	68	72	75	66	281	2,081.25
Jeff Hart	69	70	70	72	281	2,081.25
Matthew Lane	71	69	69	72	281	2,081.25
Hugh Royer III	73	70	66	72	281	2,081.25
Bob Wolcott	68	71	69	73	281	2,081.25
Willie Wood	71	67	74	69	281	2,081.25
Jaime Gomez	69	71	71	71	282	1,451.25
Jeff Gove	71	69	70	72	282	1,451.25
Ronnie McCann	74	69	68	71	282	1,451.25
Rene Rangel	66	77	68	71	282	1,451.25

Louisiana Open

Le Triomphe Country Club, Broussard, Louisiana
Par 36-36–72; 7,004 yards

March 23-26
purse, $200,000

	SCORES				TOTAL	MONEY
Stan Utley	70	70	66	62	268	$36,000
Keith Fergus	64	68	66	72	270	22,700
J.L. Lewis	69	64	70	68	271	16,500
Jerry Kelly	64	71	71	68	274	12,500
Skip Kendall	69	71	68	67	275	9,166.67
Joey Rassett	66	70	74	65	275	9,166.67
Jerry Foltz	68	71	67	69	275	9,166.66
Bill Buttner	70	68	68	70	276	6,500
Jeff Hart	71	69	67	69	276	6,500
Shane Bertsch	68	68	69	72	277	4,500
David Peoples	72	66	67	72	277	4,500
Tom Byrum	70	66	71	71	278	3,400
Joe Cioe	71	67	68	72	278	3,400
Kawika Cotner	68	69	71	71	279	2,920
Lee Rinker	68	70	70	71	279	2,920
Ray Stewart	67	71	69	72	279	2,920
Charlie Rymer	70	67	69	74	280	2,560
Bruce Vaughan	68	69	72	71	280	2,560
Danny Briggs	70	70	71	70	281	2,250
Morris Hatalsky	67	68	74	72	281	2,250
Tom Hearn	68	70	71	72	281	2,250
Thomas Scherrer	68	71	71	71	281	2,250
Stuart Appleby	69	71	71	71	282	1,750
Jeff Cook	70	70	69	73	282	1,750
Bill Porter	63	69	74	76	282	1,750
Roger Rowland	70	68	71	73	282	1,750
Omar Uresti	68	69	74	71	282	1,750
Robert Wrenn	70	69	70	73	282	1,750
Chad Magee	71	67	73	72	283	1,290
Bill Murchison	67	69	74	73	283	1,290
Chris Patton	69	71	75	68	283	1,290
Matt Peterson	72	66	72	73	283	1,290

Pensacola Classic

The Moors, Milton, Florida
Par 36-35–71; 6,912 yards
(Second round cancelled — heavy rain.)

March 30-April 2
purse, $200,000

	SCORES			TOTAL	MONEY
Clarence Rose	64	71	66	201	$36,000
Hicks Malonson	67	71	66	204	17,233.34
Bill Buttner	68	69	67	204	17,233.33
Joe Cioe	65	70	69	204	17,233.33
Brad Fabel	68	71	66	205	8,100
Brad Greer	65	71	69	205	8,100
Thomas Scherrer	67	70	68	205	8,100
Tim Simpson	66	73	66	205	8,100
Kevin Sutherland	68	68	69	205	8,100
Frank Conner	66	70	70	206	3,780
Joe Durant	71	68	67	206	3,780
John Elliott	66	71	69	206	3,780
Sam Randolph	66	69	71	206	3,780
Brian Wright	70	70	66	206	3,780
Stuart Appleby	68	68	71	207	2,580
Ty Armstrong	67	70	70	207	2,580
Frank Dobbs	71	70	66	207	2,580
Tom Pernice, Jr.	67	71	69	207	2,580
Gary Rusnak	69	67	71	207	2,580
Phil Tataurangi	69	69	69	207	2,580
Paul Claxton	67	74	67	208	1,900
Allen Doyle	69	71	68	208	1,900
Edward Fryatt	67	71	70	208	1,900
Damon Green	64	72	72	208	1,900
Tim Herron	71	69	68	208	1,900
Matt Peterson	70	71	67	208	1,900
Tom Stankowski	69	72	67	208	1,900
Rex Caldwell	66	73	70	209	1,097.34
Bobby Collins	71	69	69	209	1,097.34
R.W. Eaks	69	71	69	209	1,097.34
John Maginnes	66	74	69	209	1,097.34
Steve Runge	71	68	70	209	1,097.34
George Burns	67	73	69	209	1,097.33
Jimmy Green	68	72	69	209	1,097.33
Jeff Hart	68	70	71	209	1,097.33
Jerry Kelly	69	71	69	209	1,097.33
Bill Malley	67	70	72	209	1,097.33
Peter Persons	69	72	68	209	1,097.33
Stan Utley	67	69	73	209	1,097.33
Vance Veazey	71	70	68	209	1,097.33
Jason Widener	73	68	68	209	1,097.33
Robert Wrenn	67	70	72	209	1,097.33

Mississippi Gulf Coast Classic

Windance Golf & Country Club, Gulfport, Mississippi
Par 35-37–72; 6,670 yards

April 6-9
purse, $200,000

	SCORES				TOTAL	MONEY
Allen Doyle	66	70	67	70	273	$36,000
Franklin Langham	70	68	70	65	273	22,700
(Doyle defeated Langham on second extra hole.)						
Eric Johnson	73	66	66	70	275	13,166.67
Willie Wood	65	74	72	64	275	13,166.67
Tim Herron	69	66	72	68	275	13,166.66
Brad Fabel	68	69	69	70	276	9,000
Jerry Kelly	71	69	69	68	277	6,000
Chris Perry	66	70	68	73	277	6,000
Larry Rinker	69	71	69	68	277	6,000
Gary Rusnak	70	68	72	67	277	6,000
Kevin Sutherland	68	71	72	66	277	6,000
Peter Jordan	70	68	71	69	278	3,400
John Maginnes	70	71	68	69	278	3,400
Barrett Brinker	68	71	71	70	280	2,776
Ryan Howison	66	73	70	71	280	2,776
Jonathan Kaye	72	70	69	69	280	2,776
Lee Rinker	69	70	71	70	280	2,776
Bob Wolcott	71	71	69	69	280	2,776
Danny Briggs	70	72	71	68	281	1,950
Tom Carr	69	69	73	70	281	1,950
Joe Cioe	68	71	70	72	281	1,950
Paul Claxton	65	72	74	70	281	1,950
Mike Donald	71	71	67	72	281	1,950
John Dowdall	68	73	73	67	281	1,950
Steve Haskins	72	69	72	68	281	1,950
Roger Rowland	67	68	72	74	281	1,950
Esteban Toledo	69	70	73	69	281	1,950
Greg Whisman	70	72	70	69	281	1,950
Dave Rummells	66	76	71	69	282	1,217.15
Mike Schuchart	69	73	71	69	282	1,217.15
Olin Browne	68	68	71	75	282	1,217.14
Brent Geiberger	69	69	71	73	282	1,217.14
Frank Lickliter	65	75	71	71	282	1,217.14
Tim Simpson	69	68	73	72	282	1,217.14
Mike Smith	69	67	74	72	282	1,217.14

Tallahassee Open

Golden Eagle Country Club, Tallahassee, Florida
Par 36-36–72; 6,965 yards

April 13-16
purse, $200,000

	SCORES				TOTAL	MONEY
Bill Murchison	72	70	67	67	276	$36,000
Olin Browne	73	71	69	68	281	17,233.34
Peter Persons	73	70	69	69	281	17,233.33
Tom Byrum	73	71	68	69	281	17,233.33
Allen Doyle	70	73	68	71	282	9,750
Franklin Langham	74	71	65	72	282	9,750
Brad Fabel	75	72	67	69	283	6,500
Morris Hatalsky	75	67	70	71	283	6,500
Charlie Rymer	76	70	69	68	283	6,500

	SCORES				TOTAL	MONEY
Rex Caldwell	72	71	71	69	283	6,500
Bobby Gage	76	68	70	70	284	3,750
Carl Paulson	71	71	75	67	284	3,750
John Elliott	69	74	72	70	285	3,200
Mike Schuchart	75	70	72	68	285	3,200
Tom Hearn	73	70	71	72	286	2,368
Frank Lickliter	69	74	75	68	286	2,368
John Maginnes	70	73	76	67	286	2,368
Chris Patton	69	77	73	67	286	2,368
Sam Randolph	69	75	72	70	286	2,368
Joey Rassett	71	72	72	71	286	2,368
Gary Rusnak	70	73	71	72	286	2,368
Willie Wood	71	68	73	74	286	2,368
Stuart Appleby	71	74	70	71	286	2,368
Darrett Brinker	72	70	72	72	286	2,368
Tim Herron	75	71	72	69	287	1,650
Jon Hough	67	76	73	71	287	1,650
Bill Kratzert	72	70	75	70	287	1,650
Matt Peterson	71	73	71	72	287	1,650
Bobby Clampett	71	75	72	70	288	1,290
Jerry Kelly	73	74	70	71	288	1,290
Ted Schulz	75	72	73	68	288	1,290
Taylor Smith	69	73	75	71	288	1,290

Shreveport Open

Southern Trace Country Club, Shreveport, Louisiana
Par 36-36–72; 6,916 yards
(Rounds 3 and 4 cancelled — heavy rains.)

April 20-23
purse, $200,000

	SCORES		TOTAL	MONEY
Brad Fabel	64	67	131	$36,000
Chris Smith	69	66	135	22,700
Frank Lickliter	65	71	136	16,500
Jaime Gomez	69	68	137	10,000
Glen Hnatiuk	68	69	137	10,000
Matthew Lane	65	72	137	10,000
Vic Wilk	68	69	137	10,000
Joe Durant	70	68	138	4,800
Robert Friend	69	69	138	4,800
Edward Fryatt	69	69	138	4,800
Jerry Kelly	67	71	138	4,800
Dean Larsson	72	66	138	4,800
Peter Persons	66	72	138	4,800
Ty Armstrong	71	68	139	2,713.34
David Toms	71	68	139	2,713.34
John Elliott	66	73	139	2,713.33
Tim Herron	70	69	139	2,713.33
David Jackson	71	68	139	2,713.33
Sean Murphy	67	72	139	2,713.33
R.W. Eaks	69	71	140	1,950
Bruce Fleisher	69	71	140	1,950
Jeff Gove	71	69	140	1,950
Joey Gullion	68	72	140	1,950
Greg Hamilton	69	71	140	1,950
Scott McCarron	74	66	140	1,950
Dave Rummells	68	72	140	1,950

	SCORES				TOTAL	MONEY
Willie Wood	70	70			140	1,950
Shane Bertsch	69	72			141	1,206
Joe Cioe	71	70			141	1,206
Scott Ford	69	72			141	1,206
John Maginnes	68	73			141	1,206
Dave Miley	70	71			141	1,206
Sam Randolph	70	71			141	1,206
Mike Schuchart	69	72			141	1,206
Sonny Skinner	69	72			141	1,206
Kevin Sutherland	72	69			141	1,206
Robert Wrenn	70	71			141	1,206

Alabama Classic

Cherokee Ridge Country Club, Huntsville, Alabama
Par 36-36–72; 6,965 yards

April 27-30
purse, $200,000

	SCORES				TOTAL	MONEY
Jerry Kelly	65	70	70	68	273	$36,000
Buddy Gardner	68	69	66	70	273	22,700
(Kelly defeated Gardner on first extra hole.)						
Brent Geiberger	67	69	67	71	274	14,500
Chris Smith	68	70	71	65	274	14,500
Danny Briggs	70	63	72	70	275	9,750
Bobby Gage	68	69	70	68	275	9,750
Greg Bruckner	69	68	70	69	276	7,500
Sonny Skinner	69	68	69	70	276	7,500
Sean Murphy	72	68	68	69	277	6,000
Mitch Adcock	67	67	74	70	278	3,780
Paul Claxton	73	70	66	69	278	3,780
Tim Herron	70	71	67	70	278	3,780
Franklin Langham	66	66	73	73	278	3,780
Kevin Sutherland	71	71	69	67	278	3,780
Glen Hnatiuk	71	71	68	69	279	2,580
David Kirkpatrick	69	69	70	71	279	2,580
Kelly Mitchum	70	71	69	69	279	2,580
Larry Rinker	72	69	69	69	279	2,580
Clarence Rose	69	72	68	70	279	2,580
Thomas Scherrer	67	67	75	70	279	2,580
Stuart Appleby	70	71	67	72	280	2,050
Jimmy Johnston	70	68	74	68	280	2,050
Chris Patton	72	71	68	69	280	2,050
Tom Pernice, Jr.	66	74	73	67	280	2,050
Steve Haskins	73	69	69	70	281	1,750
Rick Pearson	73	71	72	65	281	1,750
Allen Doyle	71	72	72	67	282	1,455
Hicks Malonson	70	69	73	70	282	1,455
Tommy Masters	69	72	69	72	282	1,455
Phil Tataurangi	73	71	69	69	282	1,455

South Carolina Classic

Country Club of South Carolina, Florence, South Carolina
Par 35-37–72; 7,150 yards

May 4-7
purse, $200,000

	SCORES				TOTAL	MONEY
Jerry Foltz	71	70	71	67	279	$36,000
Morris Hatalsky	71	72	71	66	280	17,233.34
Tim Simpson	70	69	73	68	280	17,233.33
Robert Wrenn	69	72	71	68	280	17,233.33
Rick Smallridge	71	73	71	66	281	9,166.67
Greg Twiggs	70	69	75	67	281	9,166.67
Chris Tucker	70	72	70	69	281	9,166.66
Shane Bertsch	72	71	70	69	282	5,100
John Elliott	72	69	70	71	282	5,100
Tim Herron	73	70	71	68	282	5,100
Chris Patton	73	71	70	68	282	5,100
Sam Randolph	70	70	68	74	282	5,100
Stuart Appleby	72	72	70	69	283	2,936
Brad Fabel	69	74	71	69	283	2,936
Brent Geiberger	72	71	67	73	283	2,936
Tom Pernice, Jr.	69	70	70	74	283	2,936
Thomas Scherrer	71	70	73	69	283	2,936
Bryan Sullivan	71	73	71	69	284	2,500
Matt Peterson	72	70	73	70	285	2,400
Jeff Brehaut	72	69	75	70	286	1,850
Olin Browne	70	71	70	75	286	1,850
Tom Byrum	70	73	73	70	286	1,850
Rex Caldwell	67	74	70	75	286	1,850
Damon Green	74	70	72	70	286	1,850
Craig Kanada	74	69	73	70	286	1,850
Jerry Kelly	71	73	74	68	286	1,850
Franklin Langham	72	71	72	71	286	1,850
Clarence Rose	70	73	71	72	286	1,850
Steve Runge	75	69	69	73	286	1,850
Larry Rinker	72	71	74	70	287	1,253.34
Gary Rusnak	73	71	73	70	287	1,253.33
Chris Smith	71	72	72	72	287	1,253.33

Central Georgia Open

River North Country Club, Macon, Georgia
Par 36-36–72; 6,714 yards

May 11-14
purse, $200,000

	SCORES				TOTAL	MONEY
Matt Peterson	72	66	65	65	268	$36,000
Jeff Barlow	65	67	65	73	270	22,700
Franklin Langham	68	68	67	70	273	14,500
Frank Lickliter	68	70	69	66	273	14,500
Olin Browne	71	71	69	65	276	6,625
Clark Burroughs	68	70	66	72	276	6,625
Rex Caldwell	67	69	67	73	276	6,625
Allen Doyle	69	69	65	73	276	6,625
Eric Johnson	73	65	68	70	276	6,625
Jerry Kelly	68	67	67	74	276	6,625
Peter Persons	64	73	67	72	276	6,625
Bill Smith	72	67	68	69	276	6,625

	SCORES				TOTAL	MONEY
Michael Allen	69	73	69	66	277	3,100
Ted Schulz	69	68	68	72	277	3,100
Esteban Toledo	70	70	68	69	277	3,100
Ben Bates	69	73	70	66	278	2,570
Jody Bellflower	71	71	71	65	278	2,570
Dick Mast	66	72	67	73	278	2,570
Mike Sposa	65	72	70	71	278	2,570
Stuart Appleby	74	67	67	71	279	2,150
Joe Cioe	75	66	67	71	279	2,150
Tom Pernice, Jr.	73	69	69	68	279	2,150
Rick Smallridge	71	72	67	69	279	2,150
Jaxon Brigman	68	70	73	69	280	1,650
Jon Hough	71	70	69	70	280	1,650
David Jackson	67	71	72	70	280	1,650
Jimmy Johnston	66	71	71	72	280	1,650
Bill Murchison	68	71	71	70	280	1,650
Kevin Sutherland	70	73	68	69	280	1,650
Derek Gilchrist	75	65	71	70	281	1,186.67
Jaime Gomez	68	71	70	72	281	1,186.67
Craig Kanada	72	70	68	71	281	1,186.67
David Kirkpatrick	66	76	68	71	281	1,186.67
Larry Rinker	74	67	68	72	281	1,186.66
Tim Simpson	70	66	70	75	281	1,186.66

Knoxville Open

Three Ridges Golf Club, Knoxville, Tennessee
Par 36-36–72; 6,825 yards

May 18-21
purse, $200,000

	SCORES				TOTAL	MONEY
Thomas Scherrer	71	69	68	67	275	$36,000
Mike Sposa	70	73	65	67	275	22,700
(Scherrer defeated Sposa on first extra hole.)						
Tim Conley	67	74	67	68	276	14,500
Matt Peterson	68	72	69	67	276	14,500
Jimmy Johnston	66	73	71	67	277	9,166.67
David Toms	68	74	69	66	277	9,166.67
Michael Christie	69	71	66	71	277	9,166.66
Craig Kanada	71	72	67	68	278	6,500
Rick Pearson	68	72	72	66	278	6,500
Jake Reeves	69	73	69	68	279	4,166.67
Rick Smallridge	70	74	68	67	279	4,166.67
Vance Veazey	70	71	69	69	279	4,166.66
Rafael Alarcon	73	71	73	63	280	2,735
Olin Browne	70	71	70	69	280	2,735
Paul Claxton	71	70	68	71	280	2,735
Jeff Cook	71	73	67	69	280	2,735
Jeff Gallagher	67	74	70	69	280	2,735
Sam Randolph	69	72	70	69	280	2,735
Dave Rummells	71	72	71	66	280	2,735
Larry Silveira	67	74	69	70	280	2,735
Joey Gullion	74	67	69	71	281	2,100
Len Mattiace	70	72	70	69	281	2,100
Mike Schuchart	71	72	70	68	281	2,100
Jeff Barlow	70	70	72	70	282	1,557.50
Russell Beiersdorf	70	74	68	70	282	1,557.50
Ken Duke	74	68	68	72	282	1,557.50

		SCORES			TOTAL	MONEY
Greg Hamilton	73	69	70	70	282	1,557.50
Jeff Hart	69	69	73	71	282	1,557.50
Bill Murchison	71	71	70	70	282	1,557.50
Peter Persons	71	72	69	70	282	1,557.50
Gary Rusnak	70	70	70	72	282	1,557.50

Greater Greenville Classic

Verdae Greens Golf Club, Greenville, South Carolina   May 25-28
Par 36-36–72; 6,773 yards   purse, $200,000

		SCORES			TOTAL	MONEY
David Toms	67	66	68	66	267	$36,000
Thomas Scherrer	72	64	67	64	267	22,700
(Toms defeated Scherrer on first extra hole.)						
Franklin Langham	70	66	71	64	271	16,500
Jeff Gallagher	68	67	66	71	272	10,000
Brent Geiberger	65	69	70	68	272	10,000
Jerry Kelly	69	65	69	69	272	10,000
David Thore	67	68	71	66	272	10,000
Ben Bates	69	67	68	69	273	6,500
Edward Fryatt	68	65	71	69	273	6,500
Kevin Giancola	67	70	69	68	274	4,166.67
Bill Murchison	70	69	66	69	274	4,166.67
Jeff Hart	64	68	71	71	274	4,166.66
Bobby Gage	70	71	67	67	275	3,100
Buddy Gardner	65	72	67	71	275	3,100
Chris Smith	65	70	68	72	275	3,100
Greg Whisman	64	72	70	70	276	2,760
Paul Claxton	70	69	71	67	277	2,302.86
Allen Doyle	69	70	70	68	277	2,302.86
Joe Durant	68	71	73	65	277	2,302.86
Steve Jurgensen	69	72	69	67	277	2,302.86
Tom Pernice, Jr.	69	69	71	68	277	2,302.86
Joe Cioe	73	64	70	70	277	2,302.85
Jon Hough	70	68	69	70	277	2,302.85
Chris Patton	69	69	70	70	278	1,900
Rafael Alarcon	66	70	73	70	279	1,470
Russell Beiersdorf	67	70	71	71	279	1,470
Frank Conner	70	69	69	71	279	1,470
Brian Fogt	68	73	71	67	279	1,470
Jerry Foltz	68	72	70	69	279	1,470
Sam Randolph	69	69	72	69	279	1,470
Vance Veazey	70	67	71	71	279	1,470
Vic Wilk	68	72	70	69	279	1,470

Dominion Open

The Dominion Club, Richmond, Virginia   June 1-4
Par 36-36–72; 7,089 yards   purse, $200,000

		SCORES			TOTAL	MONEY
Hugh Royer III	67	65	69	69	270	$36,000
Thomas Scherrer	70	66	69	65	270	22,700
(Royer defeated Scherrer on first extra hole.)						

	SCORES				TOTAL	MONEY
Sam Randolph	68	67	70	67	272	14,500
Gary Rusnak	66	70	67	69	272	14,500
Bobby Gage	66	68	67	73	274	10,500
Jeff Gallagher	68	69	71	67	275	8,500
Joey Gullion	68	68	67	72	275	8,500
R.W. Eaks	69	66	72	69	276	6,500
John Elliott	69	67	72	68	276	6,500
Jerry Kelly	70	68	69	70	277	4,166.67
Dave Miley	71	68	69	69	277	4,166.67
Sean Murphy	72	65	70	70	277	4,166.66
Jeff Cook	68	71	69	70	278	3,200
Skip Kendall	69	66	70	73	278	3,200
Mitch Adcock	69	69	70	71	279	2,695
Ben Bates	72	67	71	69	279	2,695
Frank Conner	69	70	68	72	279	2,695
Robert Wrenn	72	69	69	69	279	2,695
Clark Burroughs	67	72	70	71	280	2,000
John Connelly	68	70	73	69	280	2,000
Tim Herron	73	68	73	66	280	2,000
Glen Hnatiuk	70	66	73	71	280	2,000
Tim Loustalot	72	69	71	68	280	2,000
Bill Malley	70	70	71	69	280	2,000
Carl Paulson	70	69	71	70	280	2,000
Stan Utley	68	70	75	67	280	2,000
Vic Wilk	69	69	70	72	280	2,000
Brad Fabel	68	71	72	70	281	1,303.34
Larry Silveira	68	71	69	73	281	1,303.34
Jeff Barlow	69	68	75	69	281	1,303.33
Paul Claxton	67	68	74	72	281	1,303.33
Damon Green	72	69	70	70	281	1,303.33
Greg Powers	70	71	69	71	281	1,303.33

Miami Valley Open

Heatherwood Golf Club, Springboro, Ohio
Par 36-35–71; 6,730 yards

June 8-11
purse, $200,000

	SCORES				TOTAL	MONEY
Stan Utley	71	62	66	65	264	$36,000
Jon Hough	67	67	67	67	268	19,600
Steve Jurgensen	64	68	68	68	268	19,600
Ryan Howison	70	66	69	64	269	11,500
Hugh Royer III	65	69	70	65	269	11,500
Stuart Appleby	68	68	69	66	271	8,500
Karl Zoller	66	67	70	68	271	8,500
Larry Silveira	68	68	70	66	272	6,500
Kevin Sutherland	69	69	68	66	272	6,500
Greg Bruckner	72	67	68	66	273	3,950
Allen Doyle	67	69	71	66	273	3,950
Brad Fabel	68	70	68	67	273	3,950
John Maginnes	67	69	69	68	273	3,950
Danny Briggs	66	69	74	65	274	2,542.23
Joe Cioe	72	67	68	67	274	2,542.23
Mitch Adcock	70	67	67	70	274	2,542.22
Jeff Gallagher	66	69	70	69	274	2,542.22
Tim Herron	66	67	70	71	274	2,542.22
Dean Larsson	72	66	67	69	274	2,542.22

	SCORES				TOTAL	MONEY
Sean Murphy	68	67	70	69	274	2,542.22
Dave Rummells	67	70	69	68	274	2,542.22
Esteban Toledo	70	70	67	67	274	2,542.22
Tim Conley	69	66	69	71	275	1,850
Len Mattiace	69	71	68	67	275	1,850
Gary Rusnak	70	66	72	67	275	1,850
Dennis Trixler	70	67	69	69	275	1,850
Joey Gullion	67	70	70	69	276	1,455
Jimmy Johnston	67	71	71	67	276	1,455
Dave Miley	67	73	70	66	276	1,455
Kelly Mitchum	69	68	67	72	276	1,455

Cleveland Open

Quail Hollow Resort, Concord, Ohio
Par 36-36–72; 6,712 yards

June 15-18
purse, $200,000

	SCORES				TOTAL	MONEY
Karl Zoller	72	66	69	67	274	$36,000
Larry Silveira	66	69	67	72	274	22,700
(Zoller defeated Silveira on first extra hole.)						
Tom Stankowski	69	68	67	71	275	16,500
Gary Rusnak	74	70	63	69	276	12,500
Brad Fabel	72	68	70	67	277	8,625
Len Mattiace	71	68	68	70	277	8,625
Sean Murphy	68	69	70	70	277	8,625
Dennis Trixler	72	68	68	69	277	8,625
Danny Briggs	71	71	67	69	278	4,625
Allen Doyle	73	70	68	67	278	4,625
Frank Lickliter	72	67	65	74	278	4,625
Kevin Sutherland	71	72	67	68	278	4,625
Jeff Gallagher	74	67	70	68	279	3,200
Jimmy Johnston	67	69	73	70	279	3,200
David Ogrin	70	73	69	68	280	2,830
Lee Porter	68	64	73	75	280	2,830
Joe Durant	68	71	73	69	281	2,455
Tim Loustalot	70	72	70	69	281	2,455
Matt Peterson	70	74	68	69	281	2,455
Taylor Smith	69	75	68	69	281	2,455
Olin Browne	71	71	69	71	282	2,050
Tom Byrum	71	67	73	71	282	2,050
Frank Conner	70	69	73	70	282	2,050
David Toms	70	69	71	72	282	2,050
Todd Barranger	72	70	70	71	283	1,650
Rob Boldt	70	70	75	68	283	1,650
Peter Persons	72	69	71	71	283	1,650
Clarence Rose	68	70	74	71	283	1,650
Jeff Barlow	71	73	69	71	284	1,195
Ben Bates	72	70	70	72	284	1,195
Shane Bertsch	72	70	72	70	284	1,195
Kevin Giancola	71	71	68	74	284	1,195
David Jackson	72	71	71	70	284	1,195
Roger Rowland	70	73	70	71	284	1,195
Robert Thompson	72	72	70	70	284	1,195
Greg Twiggs	70	74	68	72	284	1,195

Carolina Classic

Prestonwood Country Club, Cary, North Carolina
Par 36-36–72; 6,879 yards

June 22-25
purse, $200,000

	SCORES				TOTAL	MONEY
Michael Christie	68	66	66	66	266	$36,000
Sean Murphy	67	67	67	67	268	22,700
Greg Bruckner	70	65	68	68	271	14,500
David Toms	69	68	66	68	271	14,500
Jeff Barlow	71	67	66	68	272	9,750
Larry Silveira	69	68	65	70	272	9,750
Craig Kanada	70	68	67	68	273	7,500
Thomas Scherrer	67	69	68	69	273	7,500
Jeff Brehaut	71	67	70	66	274	4,360
Chad Ginn	66	71	69	68	274	4,360
Kelly Korleski	67	73	67	67	274	4,360
Lee Porter	69	66	69	70	274	4,360
Mike Sposa	68	72	70	64	274	4,360
Joe Cioe	69	70	67	69	275	3,000
Phil Tataurangi	71	69	67	68	275	3,000
Jeff Cook	74	67	68	67	276	2,626.67
John Elliott	70	70	70	66	276	2,626.67
Bill Buttner	66	68	72	70	276	2,626.66
J.C. Anderson	72	69	68	68	277	2,150
Tom Byrum	71	69	68	69	277	2,150
Vance Heafner	70	71	67	69	277	2,150
P.H. Horgan III	65	75	66	71	277	2,150
Kevin Sutherland	65	69	72	71	277	2,150
Karl Zoller	69	67	70	71	277	2,150
Joey Gullion	71	69	71	67	278	1,508.58
Dave Benson	71	69	69	69	278	1,508.57
Mark Bucek	71	70	68	69	278	1,508.57
Michael Clark	66	71	70	71	278	1,508.57
Frank Lickliter	71	69	70	68	278	1,508.57
Clarence Rose	70	70	69	69	278	1,508.57
Robert Thompson	71	70	66	71	278	1,508.57

Philadelphia Classic

Philmont Country Club, Huntingdon Valley, Pennsylvania
Par 35-35–70; 6,412 yards

June 29-July 2
purse, $200,000

	SCORES				TOTAL	MONEY
Sean Murphy	65	68	67	67	267	$36,000
Allen Doyle	69	66	69	64	268	22,700
Matt Peterson	69	66	67	67	269	14,500
Gary Rusnak	65	69	69	66	269	14,500
Tom Pernice, Jr.	63	70	69	68	270	10,500
Jerry Kelly	70	68	66	68	272	8,500
Brett Quigley	66	68	68	70	272	8,500
Lee Porter	70	70	69	64	273	7,000
Ben Bates	68	70	67	69	274	5,000
Bill Buttner	69	66	71	68	274	5,000
Karl Zoller	69	70	71	64	274	5,000
Mitch Adcock	68	70	69	68	275	3,300
Greg Bruckner	70	69	66	70	275	3,300
Mike Sposa	71	68	67	69	275	3,300

	SCORES				TOTAL	MONEY
Paul Claxton	70	67	72	67	276	2,760
Jim Hallet	69	66	71	70	276	2,760
Dave Miley	70	69	66	71	276	2,760
Russell Beiersdorf	68	72	66	71	277	2,250
Shane Bertsch	70	67	69	71	277	2,250
Joe Cioe	65	69	75	68	277	2,250
Matthew Lane	67	72	69	69	277	2,250
Greg Lesher	65	72	67	73	277	2,250
Clarence Rose	68	68	69	72	277	2,250
Olin Browne	71	70	67	70	278	1,650
Joe Durant	67	70	70	71	278	1,650
Chad Ginn	71	67	72	68	278	1,650
Joey Gullion	69	70	69	70	278	1,650
Glen Hnatiuk	72	67	69	70	278	1,650
Hugh Royer III	71	68	73	66	278	1,650
Brent Geiberger	73	68	68	70	279	1,165.72
Greg Hamilton	70	70	68	71	279	1,165.72
P.H. Horgan III	68	68	73	70	279	1,165.72
Jeff Brehaut	67	66	74	72	279	1,165.71
Michael Clark	69	70	69	71	279	1,165.71
Jimmy Johnston	70	70	71	68	279	1,165.71
Chad Magee	67	74	71	67	279	1,165.71

Buffalo Open

Brierwood Country Club, Hamburg, New York
Par 36-36–72; 7,031 yards

July 13-16
purse, $200,000

	SCORES				TOTAL	MONEY
Jerry Kelly	70	72	67	65	274	$36,000
Tim Simpson	72	72	65	66	275	22,700
P.H. Horgan III	71	72	68	65	276	16,500
Joe Durant	71	69	66	71	277	12,500
Rafael Alarcon	74	70	68	67	279	8,625
Michael Christie	71	73	68	67	279	8,625
Len Mattiace	73	71	65	70	279	8,625
Taylor Smith	69	71	68	71	279	8,625
Billy Downes	70	69	71	70	280	4,625
Tim Herron	73	68	68	71	280	4,625
Thomas Scherrer	71	69	70	70	280	4,625
Karl Zoller	75	69	64	72	280	4,625
Robert Friend	72	70	70	69	281	2,863.34
Joey Gullion	71	71	70	69	281	2,863.34
Doug Barron	70	74	66	71	281	2,863.33
Jeff Gallagher	72	68	70	71	281	2,863.33
Greg Lesher	72	72	68	69	281	2,863.33
Bill Murchison	71	73	68	69	281	2,863.33
Edward Fryatt	70	70	74	68	282	2,400
Jerry DiPhilippo	70	72	70	71	283	1,850
R.W. Eaks	72	69	71	71	283	1,850
John Elliott	76	67	66	74	283	1,850
Brent Geiberger	69	72	70	72	283	1,850
Jimmy Johnston	73	70	69	71	283	1,850
Tom Pernice, Jr.	69	73	72	69	283	1,850
E.J. Pfister	70	73	73	67	283	1,850
Larry Silveira	70	71	72	70	283	1,850
Chris Smith	70	71	74	68	283	1,850

	SCORES				TOTAL	MONEY
Esteban Toledo	70	70	70	73	283	1,850
Sean Murphy	72	72	74	66	284	1,253.34
Brad Fabel	69	74	70	71	284	1,253.33
Eric Johnson	74	69	69	72	284	1,253.33

Gateway Classic

Lake Forest Golf & Country Club, Lake Saint Louis, Missouri   July 20-23
Par 36-36–72; 6,730 yards   purse, $200,000
(First round cancelled — rain.)

	SCORES			TOTAL	MONEY
Chris Smith	68	65	70	203	$36,000
Glen Hnatiuk	68	66	69	203	22,700
(Smith defeated Hnatiuk at first extra hole.)					
Olin Browne	72	66	67	205	14,500
David Toms	70	66	69	205	14,500
Joe Durant	68	70	68	206	9,166.67
Hugh Royer III	68	71	67	206	9,166.67
John Elliott	70	66	70	206	9,166.66
Thomas Scherrer	69	67	71	207	6,500
Mike Sposa	66	72	69	207	6,500
Greg Bruckner	70	73	66	209	3,633.34
Christian Pena	69	72	68	209	3,633.34
Joe Cioe	70	71	68	209	3,633.33
Jerry Kelly	67	72	70	209	3,633.33
Tim Simpson	71	67	71	209	3,633.33
Kevin Sutherland	69	72	68	209	3,633.33
Ben Bates	71	70	69	210	2,308.89
Allen Doyle	68	71	71	210	2,308.89
Jimmy Johnston	71	70	69	210	2,308.89
Franklin Langham	72	69	69	210	2,308.89
Bill Murchison	72	70	68	210	2,308.89
Roger Rowland	68	74	68	210	2,308.89
Sonny Skinner	74	65	71	210	2,308.89
Karl Zoller	72	70	68	210	2,308.89
John Maginnes	71	67	72	210	2,308.88
Danny Briggs	72	68	71	211	1,600
Craig Kanada	73	69	69	211	1,600
Chad Magee	71	72	68	211	1,600
Larry Silveira	69	73	69	211	1,600
Stan Utley	71	69	71	211	1,600
Jaxon Brigman	71	70	71	212	1,208
Tim Herron	69	70	73	212	1,208
Dave Miley	70	70	72	212	1,208
Kelly Mitchum	71	70	71	212	1,208
Gary Webb	70	69	73	212	1,208

Wichita Open

Reflection Ridge Golf Club, Wichita, Kansas
Par 36-36–72; 6,730 yards

July 27-30
purse, $200,000

	SCORES				TOTAL	MONEY
David Toms	67	67	68	67	269	$36,000
E.J. Pfister	68	68	63	70	269	22,700
(Toms defeated Pfister at second extra hole.)						
Mike Sposa	64	69	69	68	270	13,166.67
Greg Whisman	68	71	64	67	270	13,166.67
Gary Rusnak	68	66	66	70	270	13,166.66
Brad Fabel	66	70	68	68	272	9,000
Jeff Barlow	69	67	69	68	273	7,500
Tom Scherrer	67	72	67	67	273	7,500
Olin Browne	71	66	66	71	274	4,150
Jimmy Johnston	71	68	65	70	274	4,150
Peter Persons	71	68	67	68	274	4,150
Lee Porter	68	68	71	67	274	4,150
Larry Silveira	70	71	64	69	274	4,150
Chris Smith	72	68	66	68	274	4,150
Greg Bruckner	70	70	65	70	275	2,580
Jeff Hart	72	68	68	67	275	2,580
Glen Hnatiuk	70	69	69	67	275	2,580
Matt Peterson	71	68	67	69	275	2,580
Sonny Skinner	69	68	70	68	275	2,580
Karl Zoller	72	68	66	69	275	2,580
Doug Barron	68	70	68	70	276	1,950
Ben Bates	74	67	69	66	276	1,950
Tim Conley	70	70	70	66	276	1,950
Frank Lickliter	69	67	69	71	276	1,950
Len Mattiace	68	70	68	70	276	1,950
Mike Tschetter	68	69	68	71	276	1,950
Edward Fryatt	68	69	73	67	277	1,345.72
Steve Haskins	70	70	69	68	277	1,345.72
Phil Tataurangi	69	68	70	70	277	1,345.72
Danny Briggs	69	70	66	72	277	1,345.71
Joe Durant	68	68	70	71	277	1,345.71
Matthew Lane	70	69	68	70	277	1,345.71
Clarence Rose	72	68	67	70	277	1,345.71

Dakota Dunes Open

Dakota Dunes Country Club, Dakota Dunes, South Dakota
Par 36-36–71; 6,731 yards

August 3-6
purse, $200,000

	SCORES				TOTAL	MONEY
Chris Smith	70	69	66	67	272	$36,000
Greg Hamilton	66	70	68	69	273	19,600
Clarence Rose	70	69	68	66	273	19,600
Jon Hough	66	69	70	69	274	11,500
David Toms	70	70	66	68	274	11,500
Matt Peterson	68	67	73	67	275	9,000
Brent Geiberger	66	75	68	67	276	7,500
Greg Whisman	69	66	71	70	276	7,500
Chris Patton	68	70	70	69	277	4,625
Mike Schuchart	69	71	68	69	277	4,625
Larry Silveira	70	73	64	70	277	4,625

		SCORES			TOTAL	MONEY
Robert Thompson	70	70	66	71	277	4,625
Doug Barron	70	71	69	68	278	3,300
Stuart Appleby	71	69	70	69	279	2,713.34
Roger Rowland	69	71	71	68	279	2,713.34
Tim Herron	71	68	70	70	279	2,713.33
Hicks Malonson	68	76	68	67	279	2,713.33
Sonny Skinner	69	65	74	71	279	2,713.33
Kevin Sutherland	72	72	67	68	279	2,713.33
Cameron Beckman	72	70	69	69	280	2,000
Danny Briggs	68	71	68	73	280	2,000
Barry Fabyan	68	75	65	72	280	2,000
John Flannery	71	73	68	68	280	2,000
Eric Johnson	67	72	72	69	280	2,000
Don Walsworth	70	70	70	70	280	2,000
Vic Wilk	72	68	70	70	280	2,000
Jeff Barlow	68	70	68	75	281	1,412
Tony Mollica	73	70	70	68	281	1,412
Lee Porter	73	69	69	70	281	1,412
Tom Scherrer	72	71	68	70	281	1,412
Esteban Toledo	67	71	75	68	281	1,412

Ozarks Open

Highland Springs Country Club, Springfield, Missouri
Par 36-36–72; 7,058 yards

August 10-13
purse, $200,000

		SCORES			TOTAL	MONEY
Mike Schuchart	69	70	65	67	271	$36,000
Stuart Appleby	66	71	68	66	271	19,600
P.H. Horgan III	63	68	70	70	271	19,600
(Schuchart defeated Appleby at first extra hole and Horgan at second extra hole.)						
John Connelly	61	69	72	70	272	11,500
Phil Tataurangi	64	71	70	67	272	11,500
Jerry Haas	66	66	69	72	273	9,000
David Toms	71	69	66	68	274	8,000
Joe Durant	69	67	70	69	275	5,500
Tim Loustalot	72	64	69	70	275	5,500
Dennis Trixler	69	70	70	66	275	5,500
Robert Wrenn	64	68	72	71	275	5,500
Clark Burroughs	68	68	73	67	276	3,300
Tim Herron	69	70	67	70	276	3,300
Esteban Toledo	70	69	69	68	276	3,300
Mitch Adcock	68	70	68	71	277	2,695
Tim Conley	66	74	66	71	277	2,695
Mike Sposa	70	70	67	70	277	2,695
Jay Williamson	69	69	70	69	277	2,695
Glen Hnatiuk	66	70	68	74	278	2,350
Frank Lickliter	68	64	73	73	278	2,350
Olin Browne	65	69	74	71	279	1,950
Michael Christie	67	70	70	72	279	1,950
Craig Kanada	69	70	67	73	279	1,950
John Maginnes	69	71	67	72	279	1,950
Jack O'Keefe	67	69	72	71	279	1,950
Ron Whittaker	68	71	67	73	279	1,950
Billy Downes	68	70	71	71	280	1,317.50
John Elliott	65	72	75	68	280	1,317.50
Steve Gotsche	65	70	68	77	280	1,317.50

	SCORES				TOTAL	MONEY
Jon Hough	70	70	73	67	280	1,317.50
Dave Miley	70	69	68	73	280	1,317.50
Rick Smallridge	71	69	66	74	280	1,317.50
Kevin Sutherland	72	65	70	73	280	1,317.50
Vic Wilk	69	71	66	74	280	1,317.50

Permian Basin Open

The Club at Mission Dorado, Odessa, Texas
Par 36-36–72; 7,135 yards

August 17-20
purse, $200,000

	SCORES				TOTAL	MONEY
Hugh Royer III	69	68	68	70	275	$36,000
Paul Claxton	71	69	70	66	276	12,314.29
Kawika Cotner	69	73	67	67	276	12,314.29
Chris Smith	69	72	64	71	276	12,314.29
Phil Tataurangi	70	70	69	67	276	12,314.29
Frank Conner	67	72	72	65	276	12,314.28
Franklin Langham	70	70	69	67	276	12,314.28
Dave Miley	70	70	72	64	276	12,314.28
Joe Acosta, Jr.	70	73	68	66	277	4,360
Michael Christie	69	69	71	68	277	4,360
Brent Geiberger	70	69	69	69	277	4,360
Eric Johnson	71	70	66	70	277	4,360
Jerry Kelly	71	68	69	69	277	4,360
Glen Hnatiuk	75	69	69	65	278	2,713.34
Sean Murphy	70	73	68	67	278	2,713.34
Russell Beiersdorf	70	68	68	72	278	2,713.33
Jaxon Brigman	71	69	66	72	278	2,713.33
Jeff Hart	70	74	67	67	278	2,713.33
Roger Salazar	66	72	67	73	278	2,713.33
Brad Fabel	72	72	66	69	279	1,950
Jeff Gove	70	69	71	69	279	1,950
David Jackson	70	72	69	68	279	1,950
Chad Magee	68	73	68	70	279	1,950
Tom Pernice, Jr.	74	71	71	63	279	1,950
Mike Schuchart	70	70	71	68	279	1,950
Kevin Sutherland	72	73	67	67	279	1,950
Vic Wilk	70	74	69	66	279	1,950
Doug Barron	72	70	69	69	280	1,332
Danny Briggs	69	73	69	69	280	1,332
Tim Conley	70	71	67	72	280	1,332
Roger Rowland	70	72	71	67	280	1,332
Robert Wrenn	72	69	69	70	280	1,332

Texarkana Open

Texarkana Country Club, Texarkana, Arkansas
Par 36-36–72; 6,588 yards

August 24-27
purse, $200,000

	SCORES				TOTAL	MONEY
Allen Doyle	66	70	67	66	269	$36,000
Gary Rusnak	69	70	66	65	270	22,700
Paul Claxton	72	67	65	70	274	14,500
Peter Persons	67	65	72	70	274	14,500

	SCORES				TOTAL	MONEY
Sean Murphy	69	67	71	68	275	10,500
J.C. Anderson	68	68	72	68	276	8,000
Ben Bates	67	67	69	73	276	8,000
Bobby Collins	72	65	67	72	276	8,000
Stuart Appleby	72	68	68	69	277	4,625
Greg Bruckner	69	71	71	66	277	4,625
Bill Murchison	69	71	69	68	277	4,625
Robert Wrenn	73	69	63	72	277	4,625
Stewart Cink	68	69	68	74	279	2,936
Jimmy Johnston	70	69	70	70	279	2,936
Franklin Langham	72	67	75	65	279	2,936
John Maginnes	69	71	71	68	279	2,936
Monte Scheinblum	73	69	70	67	279	2,936
Olin Browne	72	69	73	66	280	2,250
Bill Buttner	69	72	69	70	280	2,250
Joe Cioe	72	68	72	68	280	2,250
Chris Hunsucker	68	68	71	73	280	2,250
Tom Pernice, Jr.	68	71	72	69	280	2,250
Robert Thompson	70	72	69	69	280	2,250
Mitch Adcock	72	70	68	71	281	1,800
Edward Fryatt	73	68	71	69	281	1,800
David Toms	70	67	73	71	281	1,800
Kevin Giancola	75	65	69	73	282	1,376.67
Dean Larsson	68	73	69	72	282	1,376.67
Tim Simpson	71	70	69	72	282	1,376.67
Sonny Skinner	73	69	67	73	282	1,376.67
Brad Fabel	70	70	67	75	282	1,376.66
Morris Hatalsky	70	69	71	72	282	1,376.66

Utah Classic

Riverside Country Club, Provo, Utah
Par 36-36–72; 7,001 yards

September 8-10
purse, $200,000

	SCORES			TOTAL	MONEY
Glen Hnatiuk	65	68	70	203	$36,000
Franklin Langham	69	68	66	203	19,600
Harry Rudolph	69	67	67	203	19,600
(Hnatiuk defeated Langham and Rudolph at first extra hole.)					
Bill Murchison	68	66	71	205	12,500
John Schroeder	68	70	68	206	10,500
Milan Swilor	68	67	72	207	9,000
Spencer Ahrend	70	67	71	208	7,000
Olin Browne	72	66	70	208	7,000
Damon Green	71	68	69	208	7,000
Jeff Barlow	69	70	70	209	3,633.34
Jeff Thomsen	69	72	68	209	3,633.34
Joey Gullion	69	69	71	209	3,633.33
Tim Herron	68	68	73	209	3,633.33
Jerry Kelly	70	68	71	209	3,633.33
Bob Wolcott	69	69	71	209	3,633.33
Joe Durant	74	65	71	210	2,308.89
Buddy Gardner	64	76	70	210	2,308.89
David Jackson	68	72	70	210	2,308.89
Mike Schuchart	66	73	71	210	2,308.89
Larry Silveira	73	68	69	210	2,308.89
Sonny Skinner	69	71	70	210	2,308.89

	SCORES			TOTAL	MONEY
Rick Smallridge	71	71	68	210	2,308.89
Taylor Smith	74	68	68	210	2,308.89
Clarence Rose	67	70	73	210	2,308.88
Stuart Appleby	73	69	69	211	1,374.55
Doug Barron	73	69	69	211	1,374.55
Brian Fogt	71	71	69	211	1,374.55
Cliff Kresge	71	70	70	211	1,374.55
Matt Peterson	69	72	70	211	1,374.55
Willie Wood	69	73	69	211	1,374.55
Rafael Alarcon	71	68	72	211	1,374.54
Paul Claxton	71	68	72	211	1,374.54
John Connelly	66	74	71	211	1,374.54
Steve Schneiter	68	71	72	211	1,374.54
Mike Sposa	68	69	74	211	1,374.54

Tri-Cities Open

Meadow Springs Country Club, Richland, Washington
Par 36-36–72; 6,926 yards

September 15-17
purse, $200,000

	SCORES			TOTAL	MONEY
Jeff Gove	65	68	69	202	$36,000
Franklin Langham	70	67	65	202	22,700
(Gove defeated Langham at second extra hole.)					
Tim Simpson	63	69	71	203	14,500
Robert Wrenn	68	65	70	203	14,500
Pat Fitzsimons	67	68	69	204	9,166.67
Jerry Kelly	69	66	69	204	9,166.67
Eric Johnson	68	67	69	204	9,166.66
Rafael Alarcon	67	68	70	205	5,100
John Connelly	71	65	69	205	5,100
Brent Geiberger	67	66	72	205	5,100
Craig Kanada	65	70	70	205	5,100
Larry Silveira	69	69	67	205	5,100
Ben Bates	65	66	75	206	3,100
Steve Runge	69	68	69	206	3,100
Taylor Smith	70	69	67	206	3,100
Olin Browne	72	68	67	207	2,463.34
Tom Scherrer	71	67	69	207	2,463.34
Paul Claxton	69	67	71	207	2,463.33
Clarence Rose	67	67	73	207	2,463.33
David Toms	69	68	70	207	2,463.33
Don Walsworth	70	68	69	207	2,463.33
Kevin Burton	71	66	71	208	1,900
Joe Durant	68	69	71	208	1,900
Brian Fogt	66	73	69	208	1,900
Bobby Gage	73	67	68	208	1,900
Tony Mollica	74	67	67	208	1,900
Brad Fabel	68	72	69	209	1,412
Barry Fabyan	67	71	71	209	1,412
Chad Magee	67	70	72	209	1,412
Sean Murphy	71	68	70	209	1,412
Karl Zoller	73	65	71	209	1,412

Boise Open

Hillcrest Country Club, Boise, Idaho
Par 36-35–71; 6,773 yards

September 22-24
purse, $250,000

	SCORES			TOTAL	MONEY
Frank Lickliter	66	66	68	200	$45,000
Kevin Burton	69	68	64	201	24,500
Craig Kanada	64	67	70	201	24,500
Don Walsworth	68	67	68	203	15,625
Danny Briggs	72	67	66	205	11,458.34
Glen Hnatiuk	67	67	71	205	11,458.33
Stan Utley	64	68	73	205	11,458.33
Stuart Appleby	66	71	69	206	5,437.50
Jerry Foltz	71	67	68	206	5,437.50
Franklin Langham	67	67	72	206	5,437.50
John Maginnes	68	69	69	206	5,437.50
Bill Malley	68	67	71	206	5,437.50
Tom Pernice, Jr.	70	70	66	206	5,437.50
Chris Smith	74	67	65	206	5,437.50
David Toms	68	66	72	206	5,437.50
Tim Herron	71	70	66	207	3,079.17
Tom Scherrer	68	72	67	207	3,079.17
Kevin Sutherland	69	70	68	207	3,079.17
Esteban Toledo	70	71	66	207	3,079.17
Sean Murphy	69	68	70	207	3,079.16
Chris Patton	66	72	69	207	3,079.16
Bill Murchison	67	71	70	208	2,625
John Elliott	67	71	71	209	2,250
Robert Friend	70	69	70	209	2,250
Jeff Gallagher	67	72	70	209	2,250
Jerry Kelly	68	71	70	209	2,250
Chad Magee	68	67	74	209	2,250
Gary Rusnak	70	67	73	210	1,629.17
Mike Schuchart	70	71	69	210	1,629.17
Sonny Skinner	70	69	71	210	1,629.17
Greg Whisman	70	67	73	210	1,629.17
Steve Jurgensen	71	65	74	210	1,629.16
Kelly Korleski	66	69	75	210	1,629.16

Sonoma County Open

Windsor Golf Club, Windsor, California
Par 36-36–72; 6,650 yards

September 28-October 1
purse, $200,000

	SCORES				TOTAL	MONEY
Stuart Appleby	69	69	65	66	269	$36,000
Jerry Kelly	66	72	68	67	273	17,233.34
Bobby Collins	72	65	68	68	273	17,233.33
Joe Durant	65	72	69	67	273	17,233.33
Matt Peterson	66	73	69	66	274	10,500
Jeff Gallagher	72	67	71	65	275	8,500
Kevin Sutherland	68	72	66	69	275	8,500
Frank Conner	69	73	66	68	276	6,000
Franklin Langham	71	72	70	63	276	6,000
Robert Wrenn	69	70	67	70	276	6,000
R.W. Eaks	71	69	66	71	277	3,600
Hugh Royer III	67	71	70	69	277	3,600

	SCORES				TOTAL	MONEY
Mike Sposa	69	71	68	69	277	3,600
Greg Bruckner	70	67	71	70	278	2,845
John Elliott	72	69	70	67	278	2,845
Brad Greer	73	67	68	70	278	2,845
Clarence Rose	70	70	71	67	278	2,845
Notah Begay	68	72	73	66	279	2,400
Chad Magee	72	68	69	70	279	2,400
David Toms	70	71	71	67	279	2,400
Allen Doyle	71	71	72	66	280	1,950
Robert Friend	69	70	71	70	280	1,950
Tim Herron	68	71	68	73	280	1,950
Tom Scherrer	70	73	70	67	280	1,950
Esteban Toledo	70	72	68	70	280	1,950
Vic Wilk	70	74	68	68	280	1,950
Chris Hunsucker	74	68	68	71	281	1,600
Chad Ginn	68	71	72	71	282	1,500
Doug Barron	73	70	69	71	283	1,264
Jaime Gomez	70	69	74	70	283	1,264
Larry Silveira	72	72	67	72	283	1,264
Sonny Skinner	73	71	70	69	283	1,264
Vance Veazey	73	70	71	69	283	1,264

Nike Tour Championship

Settindown Creek Golf Club, Roswell, Georgia
Par 36-36–72; 7,024 yards

October 19-22
purse, $250,000

	SCORES				TOTAL	MONEY
Allen Doyle	72	68	72	71	283	$45,000
John Maginnes	68	73	73	69	283	28,375
(Doyle defeated Maginnes at first extra hole.)						
Brad Fabel	69	74	73	69	285	21,250
Sean Murphy	69	73	72	72	286	16,250
Olin Browne	72	74	73	68	287	12,500
Joe Durant	78	66	71	72	287	12,500
Stuart Appleby	72	72	71	74	289	9,375
Hugh Royer III	70	72	71	76	289	9,375
Franklin Langham	72	70	76	72	290	6,875
David Toms	75	68	72	75	290	6,875
Tim Herron	75	72	74	70	291	5,000
Ben Bates	72	70	74	76	292	3,850
Jeff Gallagher	70	76	75	71	292	3,850
Jeff Gove	73	73	74	72	292	3,850
Matt Peterson	76	76	70	70	292	3,850
Mike Sposa	71	70	76	75	292	3,850
Stan Utley	69	75	76	72	292	3,850
Craig Kanada	71	70	78	74	293	3,000
Clarence Rose	69	73	79	72	293	3,000
Tim Simpson	71	71	78	73	293	3,000
Joe Cioe	71	76	69	78	294	2,625
Glen Hnatiuk	72	70	76	76	294	2,625
Jon Hough	77	73	74	70	294	2,625
Danny Briggs	73	70	74	78	295	2,130
Bill Buttner	75	74	75	71	295	2,130
Jerry Kelly	73	76	75	71	295	2,130
Gary Rusnak	72	71	77	75	295	2,130
Robert Wrenn	76	74	70	75	295	2,130

	SCORES				TOTAL	MONEY
Greg Bruckner	70	80	73	73	296	1,662.50
Michael Christie	73	73	79	71	296	1,662.50
Bill Murchison	68	78	78	72	296	1,662.50
Karl Zoller	69	74	83	70	296	1,662.50

Canadian Tour

Payless Open

Uplands Golf Club, Victoria, British Columbia
Par 35-35–70; 6,315 yards

June 1-4
purse, C$100,000

	SCORES				TOTAL	MONEY
Norm Jarvis	66	65	66	70	267	C$18,000
Bruce Bulina	67	68	68	66	269	10,000
Ian Hutchings	70	66	65	69	270	5,400
Stephen Leaney	69	66	67	68	270	5,400
Ian Leggatt	68	66	67	70	271	4,200
Mike Weir	69	63	70	70	272	3,700
Daniel Pelczarski	67	69	66	71	273	3,200
Chris Locker	69	68	68	69	274	2,575
Scott Dunlap	70	65	70	69	274	2,575
Jean-Louis Lamarre	67	69	70	69	275	2,033.33
Blair Piercy	68	67	69	71	275	2,033.33
Marcus Meloan	69	65	72	69	275	2,033.33
Ben Weir	72	69	66	69	276	1,650
Darren Griff	71	69	68	68	276	1,650
Carlos Espinosa	69	66	71	70	276	1,650
Blair Philip	66	66	75	69	276	1,650
Dennis Harrington	72	69	66	70	277	1,300
John Randle	73	67	66	71	277	1,300
Jeff Bloom	65	74	71	67	277	1,300
Derek James	68	71	67	71	277	1,300
Jim Rutledge	68	70	73	66	277	1,300
Matt Jackson	72	64	70	71	277	1,300
Todd Spain	68	67	70	72	277	1,300
Mike Grob	70	70	72	66	278	1,058.33
Kent Fukushima	72	68	72	66	278	1,058.33
Rich Massey	69	70	70	69	278	1,058.33
Dean Wilson	68	71	68	72	279	950
Jason Spitler	66	71	73	69	279	950
Stuart Hendley	68	69	69	73	279	950
Arden Knoll	65	71	74	69	279	950
Remi Bouchard	69	67	71	72	279	950

B.C. TEL Pacific Open

Mayfair Lakes Golf & Country Club, Richmond, British Columbia   June 8-11
Par 35-36–72; 6,641 yards   purse, C$125,000

	SCORES				TOTAL	MONEY
Nick Goetze	70	69	65	66	270	C$22,500
Ian Hutchings	70	71	64	65	270	12,500
(Goetze defeated Hutchings on fifth extra hole.)						
Ian Leggatt	69	71	64	68	272	7,500
Scott Dunlap	67	68	67	72	274	6,000
Pat Fitzsimons	68	73	66	69	276	4,062.50
Remi Bouchard	67	73	67	69	276	4,062.50
Mike Weir	70	70	67	69	276	4,062.50
Brian Mogg	70	70	70	66	276	4,062.50
Stuart Hendley	66	73	68	69	276	4,062.50
Todd Spain	69	72	71	66	278	2,750
Jason Samuelian	71	71	67	70	279	2,375
Ray Freeman	67	69	70	73	279	2,375
Jean-Louis Lamarre	67	69	72	71	279	2,375
Kip Byrne	71	71	68	70	280	2,062.50
Frank Edmonds	71	71	70	68	280	2,062.50
David Rueter	73	70	65	73	281	1,750
Ted Norby	71	72	69	69	281	1,750
Davidson Matyczuk	68	73	71	69	281	1,750
Richard Zokol	69	71	70	71	281	1,750
Eric Woods	68	72	74	67	281	1,750
Rick Todd	73	68	72	69	282	1,500
Stephen Leaney	68	72	72	70	282	1,500
Manny Zerman	67	70	73	72	282	1,500
Joe Tamburino	72	70	69	72	283	1,206.25
Brian Wright	72	70	67	74	283	1,206.25
Daniel Pelczarski	68	74	68	73	283	1,206.25
Derek James	68	74	70	71	283	1,206.25
Trevor Dodds	70	71	72	70	283	1,206.25
Blaise Giroso	70	71	70	72	283	1,206.25
Cam Emerson	70	70	71	72	283	1,206.25
Oswald Drawdy	69	71	68	75	283	1,206.25
Rob Anderson	67	72	74	70	283	1,205.25
David Armstrong	69	70	70	74	283	1,206.25

Morningstar Classic

Morningstar International Golf Club, Parksville, British Columbia   June 15-18
Par 36-36–72; 6,920 yards   purse, C$100,000

	SCORES				TOTAL	MONEY
Jeff Bloom	65	69	67	72	273	C$18,000
Jim Rutledge	70	70	68	65	273	10,000
(Bloom defeated Rutledge on first extra hole.)						
Scott Dunlap	67	64	73	70	274	6,000
Nick Goetze	66	69	72	71	278	4,800
Tim Balmer	72	70	66	71	279	3,950
Mike Weir	68	68	75	68	279	3,950
Trevor Dodds	69	73	71	67	280	3,200
Eric Woods	71	72	70	68	281	2,575
David Rueter	68	66	74	73	281	2,575
Rick Todd	70	72	73	67	282	1,975

	SCORES				TOTAL	MONEY
Ian Hutchings	70	72	69	71	282	1,975
Blair Piercy	70	69	69	74	282	1,975
Drew Hartt	67	69	72	74	282	1,975
Ray Freeman	72	70	71	70	283	1,650
Frank Edmonds	66	71	68	78	283	1,650
Todd Spain	72	72	71	69	284	1,400
Jason Samuelian	73	71	67	73	284	1,400
Brad Wilson	69	74	71	70	284	1,400
Daniel Pelczarski	71	71	75	67	284	1,400
Guy Hill	71	69	71	73	284	1,400
Ian Leggatt	69	71	76	69	285	1,200
Greg Petersen	68	72	71	74	285	1,200
Ben Weir	71	69	77	68	285	1,200
Robert Meyer	74	70	72	70	286	1,043.75
Philip Jonas	68	75	72	71	286	1,043.75
Rich Massey	71	71	72	72	286	1,043.75
Jim Wahl	72	68	71	75	286	1,043.75
Terry Berry	72	71	72	72	287	937.50
Mike Grob	71	72	69	75	287	937.50
Dean Wilson	70	73	73	71	287	937.50
J.J. West	69	69	75	74	287	937.50

Henry Singer Alberta Open

Wolf Creek Golf Resort, Ponoka, Alberta
Par 36-36–72; 7,004 yards

June 22-25
purse, C$100,000

	SCORES				TOTAL	MONEY
Ian Hutchings	67	63	66	72	268	C$18,000
Trevor Dodds	67	70	66	68	271	10,000
Greg Petersen	66	68	71	67	272	6,000
Davidson Matyczuk	67	65	68	73	273	4,800
Matt Jackson	72	64	68	70	274	3,950
Stuart Hendley	67	67	74	66	274	3,950
Mike Weir	71	66	70	68	275	2,950
Ray Freeman	71	64	72	68	275	2,950
Scott Dunlap	67	68	68	73	276	2,325
Jeff Bloom	64	69	70	73	276	2,325
Jim Rutledge	66	76	69	66	277	1,750
Brad Klapprott	71	69	70	67	277	1,750
Eric Woods	69	71	68	69	277	1,750
Adam Kase	71	67	69	70	277	1,750
Duane Bock	68	70	69	70	277	1,750
Craig Marseilles	70	67	68	72	277	1,750
Daniel Pelczarski	70	69	70	69	278	1,400
Robert Meyer	68	69	68	73	278	1,400
Marshall Butler	71	66	73	68	278	1,400
Derek James	68	70	72	69	279	1,275
Jim Wahl	67	71	72	69	279	1,275
Todd Spain	66	73	74	67	280	1,087.50
Mike Flynn	68	71	68	73	280	1,087.50
David DeLong	72	67	71	70	280	1,087.50
Arden Knoll	73	65	75	67	280	1,087.50
Danny Ellis	67	68	74	71	280	1,087.50
Oswald Drawdy	65	70	78	67	280	1,087.50
Jason Andrew	70	73	72	66	281	862.50
Stephen Leaney	74	69	71	67	281	862.50

	SCORES			TOTAL	MONEY
Rick Todd	73	69	70	69	281	862.50
Nick Goetze	69	70	75	67	281	862.50
Frank Edmonds	70	69	69	73	281	862.50
Dennis Harrington	72	67	72	70	281	862.50
J.J. West	70	69	70	72	281	862.50
Kip Byrne	68	70	72	71	281	862.50
Rich Massey	71	67	71	72	281	862.50
Trey Maples	67	70	73	71	281	862.50

Klondike Days Klassic

The Ranch Golf & Country Club, Edmonton, Alberta
Par 35-35–70; 6,912 yards

June 29-July 2
purse, C$100,000

	SCORES			TOTAL	MONEY
Ray Freeman	71	63	63	68	265	C$18,000
Trevor Dodds	69	65	66	67	267	10,000
Ian Doig	70	69	67	63	269	5,400
Ian Leggatt	72	67	67	63	269	5,400
Duane Bock	68	67	68	67	270	4,200
Dean Wilson	65	69	67	70	271	3,700
Arden Knoll	68	68	70	67	273	2,783.33
David Morland	70	66	66	71	273	2,783.33
Davidson Matyczuk	67	68	71	67	273	2,783.33
Scott Dunlap	73	67	68	66	274	1,814.29
Craig Marseilles	68	72	67	67	274	1,814.29
Martin Quinney	71	68	67	68	274	1,814.29
Eric Woods	71	68	65	70	274	1,814.29
Mike Weir	69	68	70	67	274	1,814.29
Greg Petersen	70	66	68	70	274	1,814.29
Bruce Bulina	68	68	71	67	274	1,814.29
Todd Spain	70	70	69	66	275	1,275
Dan Halldorson	71	69	67	68	275	1,275
Blair Piercy	69	71	69	66	275	1,275
Frank Edmonds	70	69	69	67	275	1,275
Dean Spriddle	72	67	70	66	275	1,275
J.J. West	68	69	71	67	275	1,275
Stuart Hendley	65	71	72	67	275	1,275
Danny Ellis	65	69	71	70	275	1,275
Stephane Talbot	68	69	71	68	276	1,012.50
David DeLong	66	71	70	69	276	1,012.50
Daniel Pelczarski	69	67	68	72	276	1,012.50
Jack Ray, Jr.	70	64	73	69	276	1,012.50
Robert Meyer	68	73	66	70	277	887.50
Brad Klapprott	71	69	67	70	277	887.50
Britt Pavelonis	72	67	71	67	277	887.50
Brian Wright	70	69	69	69	277	887.50
Philip Jonas	70	67	69	71	277	887.50
Rick Todd	64	66	70	77	277	887.50

Xerox Manitoba Open

Pine Ridge Golf Club, Winnipeg, Manitoba
Par 35-37–72; 6,670 yards

July 6-9
purse, C$100,000

	SCORES				TOTAL	MONEY
Trevor Dodds	69	71	67	72	279	C$18,000
*Rob McMillan	75	71	68	68	282	
Manny Zerman	71	71	69	72	283	8,000
Ian Leggatt	68	73	70	72	283	8,000
Stuart Hendley	69	69	77	69	284	4,800
Phillip Hatchett	71	73	68	73	285	3,700
Jim Rutledge	71	72	75	67	285	3,700
Richard Zokol	74	67	73	71	285	3,700
Paul Devenport	76	71	70	69	286	2,337.50
Philip Jonas	73	71	68	74	286	2,337.50
Jack Kay	68	73	72	73	286	2,337.50
Craig Howard	69	70	75	72	286	2,337.50
Scott Dunlap	72	71	72	72	287	1,900
Brian Mogg	72	76	71	69	288	1,610
Adam Kase	74	71	71	72	288	1,610
Craig Marseilles	74	71	68	75	288	1,610
Ian Hutchings	75	70	70	73	288	1,610
Jeff Bloom	71	72	77	68	288	1,610
Bruce Bulina	72	75	67	75	289	1,350
Derek James	71	75	75	68	289	1,350
Brent Dorman	72	70	72	75	289	1,350
Norm Jarvis	75	71	69	75	290	1,110.71
Kip Byrne	73	73	73	71	290	1,110.71
Jeff Stavroff	73	73	71	73	290	1,110.71
John Randle	73	71	77	69	290	1,110.71
Dan Halldorson	70	73	77	70	290	1,110.71
Brian Wright	68	73	73	76	290	1,110.71
Greg Petersen	74	67	75	74	290	1,110.71
Joong Mo	76	74	69	72	291	925
Ted Norby	76	73	70	72	291	925
Davidson Matyczuk	73	74	73	71	291	925
Robert Meyer	68	75	70	78	291	925
Stephen Leaney	69	72	72	78	291	925

Infiniti Championship

Royal Woodbine Golf Club, Toronto, Ontario
Par 36-35–71; 6,446 yards

July 20-23
purse, C$125,000

	SCORES				TOTAL	MONEY
Guy Hill	65	64	66	71	266	C$22,500
Duane Bock	66	69	67	71	273	10,000
Mike Weir	67	66	72	68	273	10,000
Jean-Paul Hebert	69	70	71	65	275	6,000
Arden Knoll	72	69	66	69	276	4,625
Ian Hutchings	72	68	68	68	276	4,625
Trey Maples	72	67	67	70	276	4,625
Ian Leggatt	68	69	69	71	277	3,375
Robert Meyer	73	70	67	68	278	2,906.25
Mike Grob	69	73	70	66	278	2,906.25
Bruce Heuchan	73	69	67	70	279	2,312.50
Blair Piercy	69	72	69	69	279	2,312.50

	SCORES				TOTAL	MONEY
Paul Devenport	69	69	69	72	279	2,312.50
Remi Bouchard	69	67	71	72	279	2,312.50
Daniel Pelczarski	73	68	69	70	280	1,937.50
John McMullen	70	69	71	70	280	1,937.50
David Rueter	72	72	66	71	281	1,562.50
Martin Price	70	73	70	68	281	1,562.50
Darryl James	69	74	68	70	281	1,562.50
Matt Jackson	72	71	68	70	281	1,562.50
Bruce Bulina	72	70	72	67	281	1,562.50
Todd Fanning	76	66	65	74	281	1,562.50
Kip Byrne	72	70	68	71	281	1,562.50
Nick Goetze	68	70	70	73	281	1,562.50
Jason Spitler	70	66	75	70	281	1,562.50
Jeff Mills	74	69	68	71	282	1,234.38
Jerry Springer	70	72	66	74	282	1,234.38
J.J. West	71	70	71	70	282	1,234.38
Keith Whitecotton	69	70	74	69	282	1,234.38
Adam Weinstein	69	75	68	71	283	1,078.12
Wes Martin	74	70	71	68	283	1,078.12
Craig Marseilles	74	69	66	74	283	1,078.12
David Armstrong	70	72	69	72	283	1,078.12
Dean Wilson	68	73	70	72	283	1,078.12
Craig Howard	71	68	75	69	283	1,078.12

Canadian Masters

Heron Point Golf Links, Ancaster, Ontario
Par 36-35–71; 6,841 yards

August 3-6
purse, C$200,000

	SCORES				TOTAL	MONEY
Scott Dunlap	66	72	62	68	268	C$36,000
Greg Petersen	70	73	69	66	278	12,500
Phillip Hatchett	69	71	70	68	278	12,500
Danny Ellis	72	66	67	73	278	12,500
Roger Wessels	68	69	69	72	278	12,500
Trevor Dodds	69	71	69	70	279	6,025
Craig Marseilles	72	67	69	71	279	6,025
Remi Bouchard	67	70	68	74	279	6,025
Guy Hill	69	67	71	72	279	6,025
Rick Todd	76	67	68	69	280	4,066.67
Nick Goetze	70	72	69	69	280	4,066.67
Bruce Heuchan	69	71	68	72	280	4,066.67
Mike Grob	72	71	67	71	281	3,220
Philip Jonas	74	68	69	70	281	3,220
Ben Weir	71	69	71	70	281	3,220
Trey Maples	69	69	70	73	281	3,220
Dan Halldorson	71	67	68	75	281	3,220
Blaise Giroso	70	71	69	72	282	2,650
Daniel Pelczarski	72	68	69	73	282	2,650
Todd Fanning	70	70	72	70	282	2,650
Ashley Chinner	69	69	70	74	282	2,650
Stephen Leaney	73	70	70	70	283	2,210
Matt Jackson	74	68	75	66	283	2,210
Bruce Bulina	73	69	69	72	283	2,210
Davidson Matyczuk	71	69	67	76	283	2,210
Ian Hutchings	70	68	67	78	283	2,210
Ian Leggatt	73	70	67	74	284	1,950

	SCORES				TOTAL	MONEY
Craig Howard	70	72	71	71	284	1,950
Dennis Harrington	71	69	75	69	284	1,950
Kent Jones	72	72	68	73	285	1,675
Stuart Hendley	71	73	68	73	285	1,675
Darryl James	72	72	71	70	285	1,675
John Randle	74	70	72	69	285	1,675
Ted Norby	75	68	71	71	285	1,675
Mike Weir	70	69	70	76	285	1,675
Stephane Talbot	70	69	72	74	285	1,675
Norm Jarvis	67	68	74	76	285	1,675

Export "A" Inc. Ontario Open

Forest City National Golf Club, London, Ontario
Par 36-36–72; 6,820 yards

August 10-13
purse, C$125,000

	SCORES				TOTAL	MONEY
Ray Freeman	70	66	70	67	273	C$22,500
Mike Weir	71	65	67	71	274	12,500
Trevor Dodds	67	70	71	67	275	6,750
Kent Jones	66	70	73	66	275	6,750
Blair Piercy	71	68	70	67	276	5,250
Todd Spain	69	71	71	68	279	3,765.62
Paul Devenport	69	70	71	69	279	3,765.62
Mike Flynn	67	69	75	68	279	3,765.62
Davidson Matyczuk	67	69	74	69	279	3,765.62
Jerry Springer	67	67	73	73	280	2,750
Ian Hutchings	68	74	71	68	281	2,312.50
Adam Weinstein	69	70	70	72	281	2,312.50
Tim Balmer	72	67	71	71	281	2,312.50
Jean-Paul Hebert	69	68	73	71	281	2,312.50
Ian Leggatt	70	71	68	73	282	1,895.83
Dennis Harrington	71	68	72	71	282	1,895.83
Arden Knoll	69	68	72	73	282	1,895.83
Cam Emerson	73	70	72	68	283	1,593.75
Scott Dunlap	69	73	75	66	283	1,593.75
Ben Weir	67	74	69	73	283	1,593.75
Brad Klapprott	68	73	70	72	283	1,593.75
David Rueter	69	71	69	74	283	1,593.75
Philip Jonas	66	70	77	70	283	1,593.75
Bruce Bulina	70	72	71	71	284	1,287.50
Remi Bouchard	67	72	72	73	284	1,287.50
Robert Meyer	70	69	73	72	284	1,287.50
Blaise Giroso	68	69	73	74	284	1,287.50
Duane Bock	68	69	78	69	284	1,287.50
Rick Todd	71	72	68	74	285	1,109.38
Chris Locker	69	74	71	71	285	1,109.38
Daniel Pelczarski	70	72	74	69	285	1,109.38
Kip Byrne	71	70	70	74	285	1,109.38
Drew Hartt	68	72	74	71	285	1,109.38
Jim Wahl	68	71	73	73	285	1,109.38

Trafalgar CPGA Championship

Rideau View Golf & Country Club, Manotick, Ontario

Par 36-36–72; 6,893 yards

August 17-20

purse, C$125,000

	SCORES				TOTAL	MONEY
Trevor Dodds	68	67	71	70	276	C$22,500
J.J. West	70	70	68	69	277	12,500
Jerry Springer	68	69	68	73	278	7,500
Davidson Matyczuk	71	68	66	74	279	5,291.67
Scott Dunlap	69	70	69	71	279	5,291.67
Robert Meyer	64	73	69	73	279	5,291.67
Ian Leggatt	72	70	66	73	281	4,000
Jim Rutledge	68	73	72	69	282	3,375
Arden Knoll	66	76	69	72	283	2,671.88
Mike Grob	68	72	70	73	283	2,671.88
Cam Emerson	66	74	71	72	283	2,671.88
Paul Devenport	69	70	71	73	283	2,671.88
Daniel Pelczarski	71	74	73	66	284	1,968.75
Pete McCutcheon	76	68	72	68	284	1,968.75
Stephane Talbot	70	73	72	69	284	1,968.75
Manny Zerman	69	72	75	68	284	1,968.75
Dennis Harrington	68	71	76	69	284	1,968.75
Brad Klapprott	69	69	72	74	284	1,968.75
Remi Bouchard	69	75	71	70	285	1,625
Nick Goetze	69	73	74	69	285	1,625
David Rueter	74	66	72	73	285	1,625
Greg Petersen	71	70	73	72	286	1,468.75
Yvan Beauchemin	72	68	72	74	286	1,468.75
Adam Kase	72	71	71	73	287	1,322.92
Jean-Paul Hebert	68	72	72	75	287	1,322.92
Frank Edmonds	73	68	73	73	287	1,322.92
Kent Fukushima	67	79	68	74	288	1,140.62
Tim Balmer	75	70	75	68	288	1,140.62
Marcus Meloan	72	73	69	74	288	1,140.62
Jim Wahl	71	72	74	71	288	1,140.62
Jay Cooper	73	70	74	71	288	1,140.62
Guy Hill	70	70	80	68	288	1,140.62
Chris Locker	69	71	79	69	288	1,140.62
Duane Bock	67	71	75	75	288	1,140.62

Montclair PEI Classic

Links at Crowbush Cove, Morell, P.E.I.

Par 36-36–72; 6,903 yards

August 24-27

purse, C$125,000

	SCORES				TOTAL	MONEY
Jim Rutledge	72	76	68	64	280	C$22,500
Manny Zerman	76	75	65	67	283	10,000
Guy Hill	75	73	66	69	283	10,000
Ron Philo	73	74	69	68	284	5,625
Ray Freeman	73	73	66	72	284	5,625
Nick Goetze	75	73	68	69	285	4,312.50
Danny Ellis	72	70	73	70	285	4,312.50
Matt Jackson	69	76	71	71	287	3,375
Mike Weir	70	79	68	71	288	2,906.25
David Morland	74	73	69	72	288	2,906.25
Jack Kay	74	77	71	67	289	2,500

	SCORES				TOTAL	MONEY
Kip Byrne	71	75	74	70	290	2,375
Remi Bouchard	74	74	72	71	291	2,250
Wes Martin	74	80	69	69	292	2,000
Fran Quinn	75	75	68	74	292	2,000
Robert Meyer	73	76	74	69	292	2,000
Scott Dunlap	73	80	71	69	293	1,750
Ian Hutchings	75	74	67	77	293	1,750
Martin Quinney	72	76	69	76	293	1,750
Tim Balmer	78	76	67	73	294	1,562.50
Tom Jackson	74	75	77	68	294	1,562.50
Bruce Heuchan	72	74	70	78	294	1,562.50
Paul Devenport	71	77	72	75	295	1,406.25
Frank Edmonds	72	75	77	71	295	1,406.25
Todd Doohan	76	79	71	70	296	1,250
Mike Grob	74	81	72	69	296	1,250
Blaise Giroso	74	79	71	72	296	1,250
Daniel Pelczarski	77	75	70	74	296	1,250
Jay Jamieson	75	74	76	71	296	1,250
Duane Bock	70	84	73	70	297	1,140.62
Jean-Paul Hebert	77	76	69	75	297	1,140.62

South American Tour

Farallones Open

Club Campestre Farallones, Cali, Colombia
Par 37-36–73; 7,402 yards

October 5-8
purse, $80,000

	SCORES				TOTAL	MONEY
Pedro Martinez	66	69	69	68	272	$14,400
Jorge Berendt	69	68	68	69	274	9,120
Angel Cabrera	71	73	64	67	275	6,400
Miguel Fernandez	68	68	70	70	276	4,640
Jose Cantero	68	73	66	69	276	4,640
Ron Wuensche	71	67	68	71	277	3,040
Jesus Amaya	71	73	67	66	277	3,040
Luis Felipe Graf	71	68	71	69	279	2,240
Fabian Montovia	68	70	72	71	281	2,000
Miguel Guzman	70	67	73	71	281	2,000
*Bernardo Gonzalez	68	72	70	72	282	
Gustavo Rojas	70	64	76	72	282	1,536
Gustavo Mendoza	72	72	67	71	282	1,536
Mauro Gonzalez	72	73	68	69	282	1,536
Ted Gleason	68	75	70	69	282	1,536
Diego Serna	72	72	71	67	282	1,536
Marten Olander	69	70	74	70	283	1,280
Eduardo Caballero	76	67	67	74	284	1,080
Karl Brink	76	70	68	70	284	1,080
Guillermo Encina	72	72	70	70	284	1,080

	SCORES				TOTAL	MONEY
Rigoberto Velasquez	73	65	77	69	284	1,080
Jorge Benedetti	73	70	71	71	285	821
Angel Romero	74	70	72	69	285	821
Mauricio Molina	72	73	71	69	285	821
Roberto Coceres	74	69	68	75	286	704
Albert Evers	74	68	72	72	286	704
Jay Hunter	73	73	71	69	286	704
Dan Olsen	75	69	70	73	287	613
Jeff Schmid	70	73	75	69	287	613
Ruberley Felizardo	74	72	72	69	287	613

San Andres Open

San Andres Golf Club, Bogota, Colombia
Par 36-36–72; 7,023 yards

October 12-15
purse, $80,000

	SCORES				TOTAL	MONEY
Ron Wuensche	71	64	68	70	273	$14,400
Gustavo Mendoza	70	69	69	67	275	9,120
Jeff Schmid	69	73	66	68	276	5,227
Pedro Martinez	67	72	69	68	276	5,227
Angel Franco	70	71	64	71	276	5,227
Roy Mackenzie	70	70	67	70	277	3,360
Mauricio Molina	66	70	68	74	278	2,720
Angel Romero	72	69	69	69	279	2,160
Karl Brink	70	69	69	71	279	2,160
Trevor Dodds	72	69	71	68	280	1,600
Marten Olander	72	70	69	69	280	1,600
Rigoberto Velasquez	71	68	71	70	280	1,600
Rafael Gomez	71	72	66	71	280	1,600
Jose Cantero	72	67	70	71	280	1,600
Angel Cabrera	70	66	73	71	280	1,600
Jay Hunter	67	73	66	76	282	1,280
Acacio Jorge Pedro	73	68	73	69	283	1,160
Cesar Monasterio	69	75	69	70	283	1,160
Guillermo Encina	71	72	72	69	284	843
Eduardo Caballero	71	72	71	70	284	843
Miguel Fernandez	71	71	72	70	284	843
Erik Andersson	73	70	70	71	284	843
Jorge Benedetti	71	72	70	71	284	843
Joey Rassett	72	67	71	74	284	843
Rickard Strangert	71	67	71	75	284	843
Fredrick Mansson	67	73	75	70	285	628
Roberto Coceres	70	72	72	71	285	628
Tom Mackay	70	72	72	71	285	628
Antonio Ortiz	72	69	71	73	285	628
Ted Gleason	73	71	72	70	286	544
Sean Gioffre	70	73	71	72	286	544
Arnaud Langenaeken	72	71	70	73	286	544
Gustavo Rojas	75	67	70	74	286	544
Emil Madsen	71	69	72	74	286	544

Filanbanco Ecuador Open

Guayaquil Country Club, Guayaquil, Ecuador
Par 36-36–72; 6,760 yards

October 19-22
purse, $100,000

	SCORES				TOTAL	MONEY
Fabian Montovia	69	73	66	65	273	$18,000
Scott Dunlap	70	67	70	68	275	11,400
Jeff Schmid	70	74	68	66	278	7,200
Ruben Alvarez	71	72	68	67	278	7,200
Rigoberto Velasquez	69	67	75	69	280	5,200
Frank Edmonds	71	70	73	68	282	4,200
Gustavo Rojas	73	74	70	66	283	3,100
Phillip Hatchett	71	74	69	69	283	3,100
Trevor Dodds	72	70	73	69	284	2,400
Jose Cantero	68	72	71	73	284	2,400
Roy Mackenzie	69	70	72	73	284	2,400
Miguel Fernandez	73	74	69	69	285	1,950
Jesus Amaya	73	72	69	71	285	1,950
Jay Hunter	70	73	72	71	286	1,700
Angel Romero	74	70	71	71	286	1,700
Angel Cabrera	72	70	72	72	286	1,700
Andrew Pitts	70	77	74	66	287	1,400
Ricardo Gonzalez	74	74	69	70	287	1,400
Luis Felipe Graf	71	75	71	70	287	1,400
Angel Franco	75	74	72	67	288	1,107
Raul Fretes	74	74	69	71	288	1,107
Brad Klapprott	76	69	71	72	288	1,107
Pedro Martinez	77	71	72	69	289	920
Jorge Berendt	76	67	72	74	289	920
Richard Massey	72	72	71	74	289	920
Ted Gleason	77	72	72	69	290	800
Antonio Ortiz	80	69	68	73	290	800
Roberto Coceres	74	73	67	76	290	800
Esteban Isasipecci	77	71	71	72	291	730
Mauricio Molina	71	71	73	76	291	730

Los Inkas-Peru Open

Los Inkas Country Club, Lima, Peru
Par 36-36–72; 6,828 yards

October 26-29
purse, $120,000

	SCORES				TOTAL	MONEY
Raul Fretes	65	70	68	66	269	$21,600
Angel Franco	72	63	70	68	273	11,150
Angel Cabrera	67	69	68	69	273	11,150
Ricardo Gonzalez	68	70	69	68	275	7,400
Ruben Alvarez	68	67	70	72	277	6,000
Gustavo Rojas	71	72	69	66	278	4,800
Trevor Dodds	69	70	72	68	279	3,036
Jorge Berendt	71	66	73	69	279	3,036
Roy Mackenzie	70	68	71	70	279	3,036
Richard Massey	70	67	71	71	279	3,036
Rigoberto Velasquez	68	77	69	68	282	2,340
Luis Felipe Graf	69	74	71	68	282	2,340
Rodolfo Gonzalez	74	68	71	70	283	2,100
Brad Klapprott	72	68	72	71	283	2,100
Frank Edmonds	77	69	70	68	284	1,693

	SCORES				TOTAL	MONEY
Andres Morales	67	74	74	69	284	1,693
Pedro Martinez	70	74	70	70	284	1,693
Eduardo Caballero	75	68	69	72	284	1,693
David Ogrin	70	71	71	72	284	1,693
Acacio Jorge Pedro	71	68	72	73	284	1,693
Jeff Schmid	77	69	70	69	285	1,380
Ron Wuensche	75	70	71	69	285	1,380
Sebastian Fernandez	71	73	71	71	286	1,199
Carlos Dluhosch	70	71	73	72	286	1,199
Rafael Gonzalez	72	74	66	74	286	1,199
Remi Bouchard	74	71	73	69	287	925
Marten Olander	76	71	70	70	287	925
Aquino Fernandez	70	72	74	71	287	925
Phillip Hatchet	71	72	68	76	287	925
Fernando Pasqualucci	69	72	70	76	287	925
Mark Stevenson	73	69	74	71	287	925

Paraguay Open

Paraguay Yacht & Golf Club, Asuncion, Paraguay
Par 36-35–71; 6,489 yards

November 2-5
purse, $100,000

	SCORES				TOTAL	MONEY
Angel Cabrera	70	65	70	70	275	$18,000
Stefane Talbot	70	71	69	69	279	11,400
Acacio Jorge Pedro	69	75	64	72	280	8,000
Jorge Benedetti	73	68	71	69	281	6,400
Ruben Alvarez	71	72	69	71	283	5,200
Jorge Berendt	73	72	69	71	285	3,800
Angel Franco	67	76	70	72	285	3,800
Gustavo Rojas	78	69	70	70	287	2,800
Richard Massey	71	77	70	70	288	2,400
Rafael Gonzalez	70	77	71	70	288	2,400
Rafael Gomez	74	72	71	71	288	2,400
Fabian Montovia	75	74	72	68	289	1,950
Esteban Isasipecci	69	74	72	74	289	1,950
Ramon Franco	76	70	69	75	290	1,800
Jeff Schmid	76	75	68	72	291	1,600
Ian Leggatt	72	76	71	72	291	1,600
Roy Mackenzie	67	75	73	76	291	1,600
Phillip Hatchett	71	75	75	72	293	1,400
Sebastian Fernandez	75	76	72	71	294	1,250
Eladio Franco	73	73	73	75	294	1,250
Miguel Suarez	80	71	75	69	295	953
Ted Gleason	75	74	75	71	295	953
Sebastian Franco	75	74	75	71	295	953
Miguel Fernandez	78	71	73	73	295	953
Miguel Guzman	73	70	77	75	295	953
Brad Klapprott	70	71	75	79	295	953
Remi Bouchard	77	72	76	71	296	767
Ken Staton	72	74	78	72	296	767
Tom Mackay	70	77	73	76	296	767
Armando Saavedra	75	74	74	74	297	720

Litoral Open

Rosario Golf Club, Rosario, Argentina
Par 35-36–71; 6,355 yards

November 9-12
purse, $90,000

	SCORES				TOTAL	MONEY
Angel Cabrera	68	70	66	70	274	$16,200
Gustavo Piovano	66	66	73	72	277	8,730
Miguel Fernandez	65	72	67	73	277	8,730
Jeff Schmid	66	69	73	70	278	5,760
Jorge Berendt	67	69	75	68	279	4,230
Mauricio Molina	69	65	71	74	279	4,230
Stefane Talbot	69	72	69	70	280	2,520
Roberto Coceres	69	69	71	71	280	2,520
Sebastian Fernandez	68	71	68	73	280	2,520
Marten Olander	67	69	70	74	280	2,520
Karl Brink	75	68	69	69	281	1,890
Rodolfo Gonzalez	68	69	69	75	281	1,890
Fabian Montovia	67	70	74	71	282	1,575
Jose Luis Castro	65	69	77	71	282	1,575
Anai Fuentes	68	68	74	72	282	1,575
Jay Hunter	70	70	69	73	282	1,575
Miguel Guzman	69	73	71	70	283	1,305
Horacio Carbonetti	71	68	73	71	283	1,305
Rickard Strangert	66	72	74	72	284	1,125
Fredrik Carlsson	71	70	68	75	284	1,125
Gustavo Acosta	69	73	71	72	285	924
Steve Sear	69	69	75	72	285	924
Rafael Gomez	67	68	75	75	285	924
Eleuterio Solis	70	72	74	70	286	774
Phillip Hatchett	69	73	74	70	286	774
Ronnie Damm	73	71	71	71	286	774
Tom Mackay	69	74	72	71	286	774
Gustavo Rojas	69	71	73	74	287	675
Sebastian Franco	71	71	70	75	287	675
Luis Carbonetti	70	74	75	69	288	630
Raul Albarasin	74	70	73	71	288	630
Omar Solis	74	66	73	75	288	630

Uruguay Open

Uruguay Golf Club, Montevideo, Uruguay
Par 36-37–73; 6,458 yards

November 16-19
purse, $70,000

	SCORES				TOTAL	MONEY
Ricardo Gonzalez	67	68	68	72	275	$12,600
Angel Franco	67	73	70	67	277	6,790
Scott Dunlap	66	70	72	69	277	6,790
Jorge Benedetti	72	72	66	68	278	4,060
Jorge Berendt	69	70	68	71	278	4,060
Sebastian Fernandez	71	65	68	75	279	2,940
Erik Andersson	72	70	68	70	280	2,380
Pedro Martinez	69	74	70	68	281	1,820
Vicente Fernandez	70	69	71	71	281	1,820
Jose Cantero	70	73	66	72	281	1,820
Gary Rusnak	74	69	69	71	283	1,470
Acacio Jorge Pedro	72	72	66	73	283	1,470
Miguel Fernandez	72	72	70	70	284	1,225

	SCORES			TOTAL	MONEY
Roberto Coceres	69	77 67	71	284	1,225
Pablo Benzadon	71	72 70	71	284	1,225
Marten Olander	70	71 70	73	284	1,225
Ruben Alvarez	72	71 74	68	285	945
Ian Hutchings	74	73 69	69	285	945
John Maginnes	75	67 73	70	285	945
Antonio Ortiz	72	69 73	71	285	945
Ian Leggatt	71	74 70	71	286	770
Richard Massey	74	73 70	70	287	693
Jeff Schmid	72	71 74	70	287	693
Karl Brink	76	71 70	71	288	616
Andy Wada	68	70 77	73	288	616
Ariel Canete	72	72 70	74	288	616
Carlos Perez	74	73 68	74	289	560
Horacio Carbonetti	72	74 73	71	290	504
Gustavo Rojas	73	72 72	73	290	504
Omar Solis	71	70 76	73	290	504
Ruberlei Felizardo	72	74 70	74	290	504
Antonio Barcellos	70	72 69	79	290	504

Prince of Wales Open

Prince of Wales Golf Club, Santiago, Chile
Par 36-36–72; 6,697 yards

November 23-26
purse, $120,000

	SCORES			TOTAL	MONEY
Guillermo Encina	69	70 70	65	274	$21,600
Gustavo Rojas	67	74 65	70	276	13,200
Jorge Berendt	66	71 72	68	277	9,120
Jose Coceres	70	69 67	74	280	7,440
Ricardo Gonzalez	70	72 71	68	281	4,880
Miguel Fernandez	68	72 72	69	281	4,880
Angel Franco	70	67 71	73	281	4,880
Roy Mackenzie	69	71 71	72	283	2,940
Eduardo Caballero	73	69 68	73	283	2,940
Jorge Benedetti	73	73 68	70	284	2,472
Eduardo Romero	75	68 69	72	284	2,472
Miguel Guzman	75	72 70	69	286	2,160
Ian Hutchings	74	72 69	71	286	2,160
Remi Bouchard	68	72 72	74	286	2,160
*Hugo Leon	73	72 73	70	288	
Tom Mackay	69	73 76	70	288	1,776
Alvaro Ortiz	73	72 72	71	288	1,776
Richard Massey	70	71 75	72	288	1,776
Roberto Coceres	69	69 76	74	288	1,776
Ramon Franco	70	74 73	72	289	1,452
Nilson Cabrera	73	76 67	73	289	1,452
Pedro Martinez	70	76 69	74	289	1,452
Omar Solis	71	72 72	74	289	1,452
Albert Evers	72	76 73	69	290	1,128
Rigoberto Velasquez	73	69 76	72	290	1,128
Fabian Montovia	70	79 68	73	290	1,128
Mauricio Molina	72	69 76	73	290	1,128
Brad Klapprott	72	72 71	75	290	1,128
Carlos Dluhosch	76	72 73	70	291	840
Ian Leggatt	73	75 72	71	291	840
Rafael Barcellos	69	74 76	72	291	840

	SCORES				TOTAL	MONEY
Esteban Isasi	75	71	72	73	291	840
Karl Brink	72	73	71	75	291	840
Luis Martins	74	73	68	76	291	840

Los Leones Open

Los Leones Golf Club, Santiago, Chile
Par 36-36–72; 6,653 yards

November 30-December 3
purse, $100,000

	SCORES				TOTAL	MONEY
Ian Hutchings	65	74	70	71	280	$18,000
Phillip Hatchett	70	67	74	72	283	11,400
Jorge Berendt	74	72	71	67	284	5,950
Guillermo Encina	71	71	73	69	284	5,950
Raul Fretes	71	71	71	71	284	5,950
Angel Romero	70	72	71	71	284	5,950
Frank Edmonds	68	75	69	73	285	3,100
Pedro Martinez	68	74	70	73	285	3,100
Roy Mackenzie	74	67	75	71	287	2,300
Brad Klapprott	71	75	69	72	287	2,300
Ramon Franco	74	71	70	72	287	2,300
Anai Fuentes	69	74	72	72	287	2,300
Ian Leggatt	73	72	69	74	288	1,900
Miguel Suarez	68	76	74	71	289	1,750
Acacio Jorge Pedro	73	73	69	74	289	1,750
Marten Olander	73	75	68	74	290	1,600
Karl Brink	74	72	74	71	291	1,211
Rafael Gonzalez	70	77	72	72	291	1,211
Ricardo Gonzalez	73	75	70	73	291	1,211
Steve Sear	71	72	75	73	291	1,211
Jorge Benedetti	69	76	72	74	291	1,211
Richard Massey	69	75	71	76	291	1,211
Chris Davison	70	71	72	78	291	1,211
Angel Fernandez	74	71	75	72	292	920
*Neville Clarke	76	72	76	69	293	
Esteban Isasi	71	71	74	72	293	880
Miguel Fernandez	70	78	72	74	294	820
Angel Franco	71	73	75	75	294	820
Juan Pablo Velasco	76	70	77	72	295	710
Erik Andersson	75	73	74	73	295	710
Jay Hunter	74	73	75	73	295	710
Andy Wada	75	71	76	73	295	710
Jose Aderbal	71	75	75	74	295	710
Rigoberto Velasquez	74	73	72	76	295	710

Argentina Open

Le Cancha Colorada Del Jockey Club,
Buenos Aires, Argentina
Par 34-36–70; 6,581 yards

November 30-December 3
purse, $250,000

	SCORES				TOTAL	MONEY
Mark Calcavecchia	71	70	69	69	279	$50,000
Andrew Magee	69	72	69	69	279	28,750

(Calcavecchia defeated Magee at third extra hole.)

	SCORES				TOTAL	MONEY
Angel Cabrera	74	69	69	68	280	21,250
Jose Coceres	73	71	67	70	281	15,000
Gustavo Rojas	73	71	71	67	282	11,250
Mark O'Meara	68	73	70	71	282	11,250
Eduardo Romero	72	73	69	70	284	7,500
Kelly Gibson	69	72	75	69	285	6,688
Jorge Soto	70	73	71	71	285	6,688
Armando Saavedra	74	70	74	69	287	5,226
Franklin Langham	75	73	74	65	287	5,226
Miguel Guzman	69	75	71	72	287	5,226
Roberto Coceres	74	70	73	70	287	5,226
Sebastian Fernandez	80	68	69	70	287	5,226
Juan Carlos Nunez	70	72	76	70	288	4,167
Craig Stadler	67	73	73	75	288	4,167
Raul Albarrasin	69	74	70	75	288	4,167
Cesar Monasterio	71	71	72	75	289	3,700
Ruben Alvarez	71	75	74	70	290	3,376
Ken Staton	68	72	78	72	290	3,376
Ricardo Marzorati	75	74	73	69	291	2,876
*Martin Lonardi	72	71	75	73	291	
Vicente Fernandez	72	73	74	72	291	2,876
Daniel Lobos	79	71	72	70	292	2,060
Mauricio Molina	74	71	72	75	292	2,060
Jay Townsend	75	72	73	72	292	2,060
Adan Sowa	76	72	70	74	292	2,060
Tom Mackay	69	73	78	72	292	2,060
Omar Peralta	75	70	77	71	293	1,367
Rafael Gomez	74	68	78	73	293	1,367
Luis Carbonetti	72	72	76	73	293	1,367

European Tours

Dubai Desert Classic

Emirates Golf Club, Dubai, United Arab Emirates
Par 35-37–72; 7,100 yards

January 19-22
purse, £450,000

	SCORES				TOTAL	MONEY
Fred Couples	65	69	68	66	268	£75,000
Colin Montgomerie	68	63	71	69	271	50,000
Michael Campbell	69	71	65	67	272	23,243.33
Nick Price	66	69	69	68	272	23,243.33
Wayne Riley	67	71	67	67	272	23,243.33
Greg Norman	64	70	69	70	273	15,750
Ernie Els	68	68	67	71	274	13,500
Wayne Westner	71	70	70	64	275	10,100
Retief Goosen	69	68	68	70	275	10,100
Raymond Burns	67	69	70	69	275	10,100
Samson Gimson	69	72	70	66	277	7,535
Pierre Fulke	70	66	68	73	277	7,535
Howard Clark	68	67	72	70	277	7,535
Costantino Rocca	70	69	71	67	277	7,535
Eoghan O'Connell	67	70	72	69	278	6,600
Bernhard Langer	70	68	73	68	279	5,744.17
Paul Curry	69	70	72	68	279	5,744.17
Stephen Ames	70	72	70	67	279	5,744.17
Steven Richardson	69	69	71	70	279	5,744.17
Stuart Cage	68	68	70	73	279	5,744.17
Alexander Cejka	69	71	69	70	279	5,744.17
Paul McGinley	72	68	72	68	280	5,130
Sven Struver	70	70	67	74	281	4,590
Andrew Sherborne	73	67	71	70	281	4,590
Joakim Haeggman	73	70	65	73	281	4,590
Steen Tinning	67	70	74	70	281	4,590
Paul Eales	71	70	69	71	281	4,590
Jarmo Sandelin	72	69	68	72	281	4,590
David Gilford	70	70	71	70	281	4,590
Michel Besanceney	69	73	68	72	282	3,858.75
Philip Walton	69	69	74	70	282	3,858.75
Mark Mouland	72	68	72	70	282	3,858.75
Jay Townsend	71	69	70	72	282	3,858.75
Ross McFarlane	71	71	69	72	283	3,420
Darren Clarke	71	68	73	71	283	3,420
Pedro Linhart	71	67	72	73	283	3,420
Mark James	71	67	74	71	283	3,420
Miguel Angel Martin	73	70	71	69	283	3,420
Gavin Levenson	72	68	72	72	284	2,835
Carl Mason	71	71	71	71	284	2,835
Klas Eriksson	69	72	71	72	284	2,835
Andrew Murray	70	71	71	72	284	2,835
Craig Cassells	68	74	74	68	284	2,835
Mark Davis	71	70	71	72	284	2,835
Peter Baker	67	73	74	70	284	2,835
Ignacio Garrido	70	73	71	70	284	2,835
Tsukasa Watanabe	73	69	69	74	285	2,295
Mark Roe	73	70	73	69	285	2,295

	SCORES				TOTAL	MONEY
Gordon J. Brand	67	73	71	74	285	2,295
Stephen McAllister	71	70	74	70	285	2,295
Barry Lane	70	73	73	70	286	2,025
Jeremy Robinson	70	73	71	72	286	2,025
Scott Watson	71	71	70	75	287	1,800
David Carter	70	72	75	70	287	1,800
Steven Bottomley	71	67	74	75	287	1,800
Mats Lanner	70	69	71	78	288	1,530
Richard Boxall	69	73	71	75	288	1,530
Jeff Hawkes	70	73	74	71	288	1,530
Malcolm Mackenzie	69	73	70	77	289	1,327.50
Andrew Oldcorn	70	70	73	76	289	1,327.50
Fredrik Lindgren	75	68	74	72	289	1,327.50
Ricky Willison	69	71	76	73	289	1,327.50
Anders Gillner	71	72	74	74	291	1,192.50
Peter Hedblom	69	73	74	75	291	1,192.50
Mats Hallberg	70	73	77	72	292	786
David Williams	73	70	74	75	292	786
Christian Cevaer	71	72	74	75	292	786
Paul Moloney	71	70	70	81	292	786
Jean Van de Velde	71	70	75	77	293	669

Johnnie Walker Classic

The Orchard Golf and Country Club, Manila, Philippines   January 26-29
Par 36-36–72; 7,016 yards   purse, £600,000

	SCORES				TOTAL	MONEY
Fred Couples	72	67	67	71	277	£100,000
Nick Price	71	67	71	70	279	66,660
Robert Allenby	71	70	68	71	280	37,560
Andrew Coltart	70	72	69	70	281	25,466.67
Greg Norman	72	70	70	69	281	25,466.67
Michael Campbell	74	68	66	73	281	25,466.67
Colin Montgomerie	73	68	68	74	283	18,000
Peter Senior	71	72	71	70	284	15,000
David Frost	74	71	71	69	285	12,720
Darren Clarke	72	69	72	72	285	12,720
Philip Walton	73	73	70	70	286	11,020
Robert Karlsson	74	65	72	76	287	9,485
Per-Ulrik Johansson	71	73	73	70	287	9,485
Mats Hallberg	69	73	74	71	287	9,485
Sven Struver	73	71	72	71	287	9,485
Brandt Jobe	76	70	69	73	288	8,100
Andrew Sherborne	74	73	71	70	288	8,100
Mats Lanner	74	73	70	71	288	8,100
Mike Clayton	75	73	70	71	289	7,125
Pedro Linhart	75	70	74	70	289	7,125
Ignacio Garrido	74	72	71	72	289	7,125
Mike McLean	75	74	68	72	289	7,125
Costantino Rocca	73	69	74	74	290	6,300
Bernhard Langer	74	70	71	75	290	6,300
Sam Torrance	71	71	72	76	290	6,300
Silvio Grappasonni	70	73	73	74	290	6,300
Jean Louis Guepy	78	71	69	72	290	6,300
Mark Davis	72	70	74	75	291	5,400
Ian Palmer	73	72	79	67	291	5,400

	SCORES				TOTAL	MONEY
Peter Fowler	75	69	74	73	291	5,400
Peter O'Malley	74	70	73	74	291	5,400
Roger Chapman	71	73	73	74	291	5,400
Russell Claydon	75	73	70	74	292	4,740
Alexander Cejka	76	71	67	78	292	4,740
Stephen Ames	76	71	73	72	292	4,740
Stephen McAllister	74	69	74	75	292	4,740
Peter Hedblom	76	73	72	72	293	4,260
Brian Watts	75	72	73	73	293	4,260
Isao Aoki	72	70	78	73	293	4,260
Joakim Haeggman	70	76	76	71	293	4,260
Paul Broadhurst	73	74	75	72	294	3,900
Scott Watson	72	77	75	70	294	3,900
Paul Eales	70	73	76	76	295	3,480
Ross Drummond	74	74	76	71	295	3,480
Ernie Els	78	71	75	71	295	3,480
Chen Tze-Chung	76	72	73	74	295	3,480
Cassius Casas	73	74	71	77	295	3,480
*Hong Chiao-Yu	74	75	71	75	295	
Seve Ballesteros	73	73	74	76	296	3,000
Don Walsworth	76	72	79	69	296	3,000
Jeev Milkha Singh	75	74	74	73	296	3,000
Lee Westwood	75	69	72	81	297	2,460
Craig Cassells	74	74	75	74	297	2,460
Marimuthu Ramayah	70	74	75	78	297	2,460
Danilo Cruz	77	72	72	76	297	2,460
Zhang Lian-Wei	77	72	73	75	297	2,460
Steve Flesch	74	73	73	77	297	2,460
Miguel Angel Martin	73	76	71	78	298	1,808.57
Wayne Riley	75	74	75	74	298	1,808.57
Boonchu Ruangkit	73	72	78	75	298	1,808.57
Kyi-Hla Han	78	71	72	77	298	1,808.57
Anders Sorensen	73	74	78	73	298	1,808.57
Gordon J. Brand	72	74	77	75	298	1,808.57
Carl Mason	76	73	74	75	298	1,808.57
Jung-Duck Kim	75	72	76	76	299	1,214.50
Hsieh Yu-Shu	76	71	75	77	299	1,214.50
Periasamy Gunasagaran	74	74	77	74	299	1,214.50
Paul Way	76	73	73	77	299	1,214.50
Lee Porter	74	74	76	76	300	892
Stuart Cage	74	75	76	75	300	892
Mathias Gronberg	74	75	78	73	300	892
Samson Gimson	73	74	76	77	300	892
Rodger Davis	78	70	76	76	300	892
Mike Harwood	74	71	76	81	302	885
Philip Talbot	73	76	76	77	302	885
Neal Briggs	77	72	76	78	303	882
Daniel Westermark	76	72	79	77	304	880
David Ray	77	70	77	82	306	878

Madeira Island Open

Madeira Golf Club, Madeira, Spain
Par 36-36–72; 6,606 yards

February 2-5
purse, £250,000

	SCORES				TOTAL	MONEY
Santiago Luna	67	67	68	70	272	£41,660
Christian Cevaer	70	69	68	69	276	27,770

	SCORES			TOTAL	MONEY
Paul Curry	73	67	68	71	279	15,650
Olle Karlsson	72	66	75	68	281	9,120
Dean Robertson	73	70	68	70	281	9,120
Jose Coceres	72	67	71	71	281	9,120
Iain Pyman	75	68	66	72	281	9,120
Steen Tinning	74	65	67	75	281	9,120
John Hawksworth	72	72	71	67	282	5,066.67
Ruben Alvarez	71	70	72	69	282	5,066.67
Mathias Gronberg	71	72	69	70	282	5,066.67
David J. Russell	75	71	71	66	283	3,782.50
Paul Mayo	74	68	72	69	283	3,782.50
David Williams	70	74	70	69	283	3,782.50
Dennis Edlund	73	67	73	70	283	3,782.50
Paul Lawrie	68	72	71	72	283	3,782.50
Paul Affleck	72	71	67	73	283	3,782.50
Robert Karlsson	75	69	70	70	284	3,020
Andrew Sherborne	68	71	73	72	284	3,020
Neal Briggs	71	71	68	74	284	3,020
Kenny Cross	72	67	70	75	284	3,020
Liam White	69	67	70	78	284	3,020
Juan Pinero	70	74	73	68	285	2,662.50
David R. Jones	75	69	70	71	285	2,662.50
Mark Litton	76	70	64	75	285	2,662.50
Rolf Muntz	72	66	71	76	285	2,662.50
Scott Watson	74	70	71	71	286	2,221.88
Peter Mitchell	70	76	71	69	286	2,221.88
Jay Townsend	72	73	69	72	286	2,221.88
Carlos Larrain	71	72	69	74	286	2,221.88
Eamonn Darcy	69	71	71	75	286	2,221.88
Bill Malley	68	72	71	75	286	2,221.88
John McHenry	75	66	70	75	286	2,221.88
Lee Westwood	68	72	69	77	286	2,221.88
Andrew Coltart	69	74	72	72	287	1,800
Michael Archer	70	72	73	72	287	1,800
Paul Broadhurst	69	72	74	72	287	1,800
Brian Marchbank	69	71	75	72	287	1,800
Joakim Gronhagen	72	72	72	71	287	1,800
Mats Hallberg	74	71	72	70	287	1,800
Jesus Maria Arruti	68	77	69	73	287	1,800
Brian Barnes	71	71	73	73	288	1,500
Mark James	69	75	73	71	288	1,500
Andrew Clapp	74	71	73	70	288	1,500
Eoghan O'Connell	72	72	70	74	288	1,500
Jamie Spence	72	67	74	75	288	1,500
John Mellor	71	72	72	74	289	1,250
Gordon Brand, Jr.	73	72	71	73	289	1,250
Jose Manuel Carriles	74	72	72	71	289	1,250
Emanuele Canonica	71	74	69	75	289	1,250
Wayne Riley	73	70	68	78	289	1,250
Jeremy Robinson	71	72	74	73	290	1,050
Keith Waters	73	70	74	73	290	1,050
Ian Spencer	72	71	75	72	290	1,050
Jon Robson	77	69	72	73	291	900
Des Smyth	72	71	71	77	291	900
Jarmo Sandelin	69	70	72	80	291	900
Frederic Regard	69	72	73	78	292	762.50
Adam Mednick	72	73	71	76	292	762.50
Peter Baker	72	71	73	76	292	762.50
Phil Golding	70	73	78	71	292	762.50
Gary Emerson	70	74	71	78	293	675

	SCORES				TOTAL	MONEY
Thomas Gogele	73	71	74	75	293	675
Heinz P. Thul	72	74	75	72	293	675
Martyn Roberts	73	71	74	76	294	625
Jonathan Wilshire	71	72	75	77	295	399
Stephen Ames	73	73	75	74	295	399
Michael Jonzon	73	70	76	77	296	395
Gordon J. Brand	72	68	82	74	296	399
*Jose Correia	73	72	74	82	301	
Daren Lee	74	72	75	82	303	392

Turespana Open de Canarias

Maspalomas Golf Club, Gran Canaria, Spain
Par 36-36–72; 6,904 yards

February 9-12
purse, £244,325

	SCORES				TOTAL	MONEY
Jarmo Sandelin	74	72	66	70	282	£40,719.29
Paul Eales	68	72	72	71	283	21,219.68
Seve Ballesteros	68	69	73	73	283	21,219.68
Anders Forsbrand	72	69	72	71	284	12,216.28
Sven Struver	70	72	73	70	285	8,746.85
Darren Clarke	72	69	71	73	285	8,746.85
Gary Emerson	69	72	71	73	285	8,746.85
Paolo Quirici	76	70	73	68	287	6,108.14
John McHenry	74	72	74	68	288	4,448.35
Paul Curry	71	74	70	73	288	4,448.35
Gordon Brand, Jr.	71	72	74	71	288	4,448.35
Pedro Linhart	76	68	73	71	288	4,448.35
Gary Orr	68	75	71	74	288	4,448.35
Derrick Cooper	74	69	75	70	288	4,448.35
Phillip Price	73	69	73	74	289	3,591.59
Paul R. Simpson	70	75	69	76	290	3,026.58
Steen Tinning	72	72	74	72	290	3,026.58
Paul Lawrie	72	77	68	73	290	3,026.58
Jamie Spence	69	75	74	72	290	3,026.58
Raymond Burns	73	72	74	71	290	3,026.58
Des Smyth	75	69	72	74	290	3,026.58
Steven Bottomley	72	73	73	72	290	3,026.58
Brian Marchbank	76	68	74	72	290	3,026.58
Robert Karlsson	69	75	74	73	291	2,345.53
Anders Gillner	74	72	74	71	291	2,345.53
Jose Maria Canizares	75	71	72	73	291	2,345.53
Manuel Pinero	76	71	70	74	291	2,345.53
Mike McLean	74	73	71	73	291	2,345.53
Stuart Cage	72	73	77	69	291	2,345.53
Christy O'Connor, Jr.	74	69	75	73	291	2,345.53
Eamonn Darcy	72	73	74	72	291	2,345.53
Paul Way	74	73	74	70	291	2,345.53
Steven Richardson	73	74	74	71	292	1,881.31
Philip Walton	68	76	75	73	292	1,881.31
Joakim Gronhagen	74	73	71	74	292	1,881.31
Peter Baker	71	74	77	70	292	1,881.31
Richard Boxall	73	70	73	76	292	1,881.31
Jon Robson	72	72	71	77	292	1,881.31
Francisco Valera	76	71	74	72	293	1,563.68
Jose Coceres	74	71	76	72	293	1,563.68
Ruben Alvarez	76	70	76	71	293	1,563.68

	SCORES				TOTAL	MONEY
Mark Nichols	76	72	74	71	293	1,563.68
Per Haugsrud	74	73	73	73	293	1,563.68
David Gilford	78	71	70	74	293	1,563.68
John Bickerton	74	71	75	73	293	1,563.68
Anders Sorensen	72	72	77	73	294	1,172.76
Michael Archer	72	74	72	76	294	1,172.76
Mark Mouland	75	71	72	76	294	1,172.76
Alexander Cejka	74	73	74	73	294	1,172.76
Peter Mitchell	74	72	72	76	294	1,172.76
Santiago Luna	72	71	74	77	294	1,172.76
Miguel Angel Martin	72	73	77	72	294	1,172.76
John Mellor	74	75	73	72	294	1,172.76
Dean Robertson	72	75	71	76	294	1,172.76
Michel Besanceney	72	75	73	75	295	835.59
David Ray	71	75	76	73	295	835.59
Iain Pyman	74	72	74	75	295	835.59
Jesus Maria Arruti	76	68	71	80	295	835.59
Fabrice Tarnaud	76	72	77	70	295	835.59
Juan Quiros	73	72	79	72	296	708.54
Rolf Muntz	75	72	72	77	296	708.54
Carl Suneson	76	72	71	77	296	708.54
Andrew Sherborne	73	74	71	79	297	576.43
Stephen McAllister	75	72	73	77	297	576.43
Mark Litton	73	76	73	75	297	576.43
Fredrik Jacobson	76	72	73	76	297	576.43
*Oscar Sanchez	71	73	74	80	298	
Juan Pinero	76	71	76	76	299	398
Jose Rozadilla	78	68	73	81	300	396
Keith Waters	77	72	78	74	301	394

Turespana Open de Mediterrania

Club de Golf Escorpion, Valencia, Spain
Par 36-36–72; 6,909 yards

February 23-26
purse, £300,000

	SCORES				TOTAL	MONEY
Robert Karlsson	64	69	71	72	276	£50,000
Miguel Angel Jimenez	73	69	69	68	279	19,952.50
Anders Forsbrand	69	71	67	72	279	19,952.50
Jarmo Sandelin	68	71	71	69	279	19,952.50
Sam Torrance	68	67	71	73	279	19,952.50
Pierre Fulke	74	68	68	70	280	9,000
Per-Ulrik Johansson	69	71	69	71	280	9,000
Fredrik Lindgren	66	68	77	69	280	9,000
Lee Westwood	68	72	69	72	281	5,640
Paul Affleck	71	69	69	72	281	5,640
Diego Borrego	70	69	70	72	281	5,640
Wayne Riley	69	70	72	70	281	5,640
Ross McFarlane	65	70	75	71	281	5,640
Ian Palmer	71	70	70	71	282	4,230
David Gilford	69	74	72	67	282	4,230
Andrew Sherborne	66	72	72	72	282	4,230
Mark James	69	67	73	73	282	4,230
Costantino Rocca	69	66	74	73	282	4,230
Malcolm Mackenzie	69	72	74	68	283	3,288
Derrick Cooper	72	69	73	69	283	3,288
Howard Clark	70	71	71	71	283	3,288

	SCORES				TOTAL	MONEY
Alberto Binaghi	71	70	68	74	283	3,288
Liam White	71	69	70	73	283	3,288
Jose Maria Canizares	67	73	71	72	283	3,288
Manuel Pinero	71	68	72	72	283	3,288
Peter Baker	68	70	71	74	283	3,288
Brian Barnes	71	65	74	73	283	3,288
Vicente Fernandez	68	67	71	77	283	3,288
Stuart Cage	72	68	70	74	284	2,745
Paul Curry	69	70	72	73	284	2,745
Olle Karlsson	73	67	75	70	285	2,565
Paul Way	69	69	70	77	285	2,565
Peter Mitchell	72	69	73	72	286	2,370
Des Smyth	69	73	73	71	286	2,370
Roger Chapman	71	72	71	72	286	2,370
Gary Emerson	70	68	74	74	286	2,370
Mike Miller	70	72	72	73	287	2,040
Alexander Cejka	71	71	72	73	287	2,040
Silvio Grappasonni	70	72	71	74	287	2,040
Roger Wessels	72	71	73	71	287	2,040
Darren Clarke	70	73	76	68	287	2,040
Mike McLean	71	70	71	75	287	2,040
John Bickerton	69	71	73	74	287	2,040
Mark Roe	68	73	67	80	288	1,500
Steven Richardson	73	69	74	72	288	1,500
Richard Boxall	69	73	75	71	288	1,500
David Williams	69	73	73	73	288	1,500
Jose Rivero	73	69	73	73	288	1,500
Steven Bottomley	74	68	73	73	288	1,500
Joakim Haeggman	70	73	71	74	288	1,500
Sandy Lyle	73	70	75	70	288	1,500
Barry Lane	72	71	73	72	288	1,500
Mark Litton	70	70	72	76	288	1,500
Phil Golding	69	71	72	76	288	1,500
Jon Robson	71	71	69	78	289	1,005
Iain Pyman	72	71	72	74	289	1,005
Adam Hunter	74	69	71	75	289	1,005
Eamonn Darcy	70	73	70	76	289	1,005
Paul Broadhurst	69	72	73	75	289	1,005
Jose Coceres	73	66	75	75	289	1,005
Manuel Calero	72	70	73	75	290	840
Scott Watson	70	71	76	73	290	840
Russell Claydon	69	71	74	76	290	840
Miguel Angel Martin	71	72	76	72	291	765
Gordon Brand, Jr.	69	72	75	75	291	765
Peter Teravainen	72	70	76	74	292	445
Nicklas Fasth	72	70	76	74	292	445
Emanuele Canonica	73	70	78	71	292	445
Paul Mayo	75	68	71	78	292	445
Gary Orr	74	69	76	73	292	445
Bernard Gallacher	71	72	75	74	292	445
*Sergio Garcia	73	70	73	76	292	
Mats Hallberg	71	72	73	77	293	438
Mats Lanner	74	69	75	76	294	436
Eoghan O'Connell	71	72	74	81	298	434
John Mellor	71	71	81	76	299	432
Yago Beamonte	71	72	79	80	302	430

Turespana Open de Andalucia

Islantilla Golf Club, Islantilla, Spain
Par 36-35–71; 6,677 yards

March 2-5
purse, £296,025

	SCORES				TOTAL	MONEY
Alexander Cejka	71	68	70	69	278	£49,344.95
Costantino Rocca	71	65	78	67	281	32,893.34
Paul McGinley	71	74	69	69	283	16,668.72
Wayne Riley	70	73	68	72	283	16,668.72
Olle Karlsson	72	76	69	67	284	11,448.03
Anders Forsbrand	73	72	64	75	284	11,448.03
Paolo Quirici	71	71	69	74	285	8,882.09
Des Smyth	68	71	76	71	286	6,093.11
Fabrice Tarnaud	70	72	73	71	286	6,093.11
Mark Mouland	70	75	70	71	286	6,093.11
Barry Lane	74	70	70	72	286	6,093.11
Jon Robson	71	69	72	74	286	6,093.11
Jose Rivero	75	72	71	69	287	4,187.27
Andrew Sherborne	72	75	70	70	287	4,187.27
Pedro Linhart	72	73	71	71	287	4,187.27
David Williams	74	72	69	72	287	4,187.27
Peter Mitchell	73	73	69	72	287	4,187.27
Phillip Price	69	71	74	73	287	4,187.27
Marc Farry	72	71	69	75	287	4,187.27
John Bickerton	71	72	74	71	288	3,286.37
Jose Maria Olazabal	72	76	70	70	288	3,286.37
Juan Pinero	72	72	74	70	288	3,286.37
Russell Claydon	72	72	74	70	288	3,286.37
Ian Palmer	70	74	75	69	288	3,286.37
Mike McLean	75	73	68	72	288	3,286.37
John Mellor	72	74	70	72	288	3,286.37
Mathias Gronberg	73	74	71	71	289	2,631.32
Tomas Jesus Munoz	72	72	74	71	289	2,631.32
Peter Hedblom	71	72	75	71	289	2,631.32
Ross McFarlane	73	71	73	72	289	2,631.32
Jose Maria Canizares	72	76	69	72	289	2,631.32
Peter Baker	76	71	70	72	289	2,631.32
Santiago Luna	68	73	74	74	289	2,631.32
Jonathan Lomas	74	71	69	75	289	2,631.32
Ignacio Garrido	77	69	73	71	290	2,125.36
Paul R. Simpson	73	70	76	71	290	2,125.36
Sam Torrance	70	74	73	73	290	2,125.36
John McHenry	73	74	69	74	290	2,125.36
Domingo Hospital	70	74	71	75	290	2,125.36
Eoghan O'Connell	71	75	69	75	290	2,125.36
David Carter	73	66	75	76	290	2,125.36
Stephen McAllister	73	71	74	73	291	1,776.42
Alberto Binaghi	74	72	73	72	291	1,776.42
Paul Way	76	72	72	71	291	1,776.42
Daren Lee	74	70	76	71	291	1,776.42
Andre Bossert	72	76	73	70	291	1,776.42
Stephen Dodd	76	72	70	74	292	1,421.13
Roger Chapman	74	71	74	73	292	1,421.13
Miguel Angel Jimenez	72	75	74	71	292	1,421.13
Jesus Maria Arruti	74	71	71	76	292	1,421.13
Mats Hallberg	72	75	69	76	292	1,421.13
Carl Mason	75	72	68	77	292	1,421.13
Paul Mayo	72	71	71	78	292	1,421.13
Mark Litton	81	67	72	73	293	1,184.28

	SCORES				TOTAL	MONEY
Philip Talbot	76	71	74	73	294	1,065.85
Vicente Fernandez	72	75	74	73	294	1,065.85
Diego Borrego	72	72	73	77	294	1,065.85
Liam White	72	72	73	78	295	947.42
Derrick Cooper	73	74	72	77	296	903.02
Silvio Grappasonni	74	72	74	76	296	903.02
Mark Davis	72	73	74	78	297	799.39
Francisco Valera	70	75	75	77	297	799.39
Steen Tinning	74	73	74	76	297	799.39
Sandy Lyle	73	71	77	76	297	799.39
Joakim Gronhagen	75	73	74	75	297	799.39
Manuel Moreno	74	74	76	74	298	444
Lee Westwood	73	74	73	81	301	442

Moroccan Open

Royal Golf Links, Agadir, Morocco
Par 36-36–72; 6,657 yards

March 9-12
purse, £350,000

	SCORES				TOTAL	MONEY
Mark James	70	70	70	65	275	£58,330
David Gilford	71	71	69	65	276	38,880
Robert Karlsson	68	69	73	67	277	21,910
Alexander Cejka	66	72	72	68	278	17,500
Phillip Price	71	72	69	68	280	13,540
Sam Torrance	67	70	72	71	280	13,540
Adam Hunter	75	68	69	71	283	9,625
Russell Claydon	69	75	69	70	283	9,625
Andrew Coltart	70	72	72	70	284	7,820
Anders Gillner	68	73	73	71	285	6,272.50
Roger Chapman	74	70	69	72	285	6,272.50
Jeff Hawkes	73	70	72	70	285	6,272.50
Howard Clark	70	77	70	68	285	6,272.50
David Carter	69	73	71	73	286	4,833.33
Eamonn Darcy	68	74	70	74	286	4,833.33
Malcolm Mackenzie	68	72	73	73	286	4,833.33
Paul Affleck	73	70	72	71	286	4,833.33
Antoine LeBouc	72	75	66	73	286	4,833.33
Per-Ulrik Johansson	73	70	73	70	286	4,833.33
Neal Briggs	73	74	69	71	287	4,042.50
Olle Karlsson	74	70	69	74	287	4,042.50
Mike McLean	73	70	73	71	287	4,042.50
Anders Forsbrand	75	71	70	71	287	4,042.50
Paul McGinley	70	74	75	69	288	3,570
Paolo Quirici	72	72	71	73	288	3,570
Michael Jonzon	70	74	76	68	288	3,570
Costantino Rocca	72	70	71	75	288	3,570
Per Haugsrud	75	72	72	69	288	3,570
Mats Lanner	71	76	73	69	289	3,010
Andre Bossert	69	74	74	72	289	3,010
Peter Mitchell	71	72	75	71	289	3,010
Pedro Linhart	71	75	69	74	289	3,010
Jose Coceres	74	70	68	77	289	3,010
Steven Bottomley	77	69	72	71	289	3,010
Rolf Muntz	71	73	77	69	290	2,485
Liam White	73	74	71	72	290	2,485
Raymond Burns	71	74	73	72	290	2,485

	SCORES				TOTAL	MONEY
Paul R. Simpson	72	74	74	70	290	2,485
Steven Richardson	70	71	75	74	290	2,485
Peter Baker	77	70	71	72	290	2,485
Gordon Brand, Jr.	70	77	74	69	290	2,485
Vicente Fernandez	69	75	74	72	290	2,485
Paul Eales	69	78	72	72	291	2,100
Gavin Levenson	69	71	77	74	291	2,100
Ross Drummond	77	69	70	75	291	2,100
Dennis Edlund	74	72	74	72	292	1,855
Gary Orr	70	74	75	73	292	1,855
Brian Marchbank	72	73	78	69	292	1,855
Jeremy Robinson	70	73	74	75	292	1,855
Barry Lane	71	75	74	73	293	1,505
Tony Johnstone	72	72	76	73	293	1,505
Michel Besanceney	68	75	74	76	293	1,505
Martyn Roberts	75	72	72	74	293	1,505
Ian Spencer	72	70	80	71	293	1,505
Jay Townsend	71	76	74	72	293	1,505
Anders Sorensen	75	69	76	74	294	1,190
David Way	71	72	75	76	294	1,190
Nicolas Vanhootegem	72	73	78	71	294	1,190
David Williams	71	73	77	74	295	1,067.50
Ross McFarlane	74	72	76	73	295	1,067.50
George Ryall	72	73	80	72	297	997.50
David R. Jones	69	75	78	75	297	997.50
Jean Louis Guepy	71	73	75	79	298	945
Joakim Gronhagen	74	71	79	75	299	892.50
Stephen Ames	73	73	73	80	299	892.50
Jonathan Lomas	72	74	80	76	302	525
Emanuele Canonica	73	74	75	83	305	523

Portuguese Open

Penha Longa Golf Club, Sintra, Lisbon, Portugal   March 16-19
Par 36-36–72; 6,864 yards   purse, £300,000

	SCORES				TOTAL	MONEY
Adam Hunter	73	65	71	68	277	£50,000
Darren Clarke	72	69	66	70	277	33,330
(Hunter defeated Clarke on first extra hole.)						
Jose Coceres	69	72	68	69	278	18,780
Jon Robson	70	71	68	71	280	12,733.33
Tony Johnstone	71	68	71	70	280	12,733.33
Paul McGinley	74	65	68	73	280	12,733.33
Fredrik Lindgren	71	73	69	68	281	7,730
Paul Curry	68	70	73	70	281	7,730
Miguel Angel Jimenez	68	66	75	72	281	7,730
Russell Claydon	70	74	69	69	282	4,962.86
Carl Mason	72	71	71	68	282	4,962.86
Paul Lawrie	75	67	68	72	282	4,962.86
Ross McFarlane	70	71	70	71	282	4,962.86
Jamie Spence	74	67	69	72	282	4,962.86
Mark Davis	71	67	72	72	282	4,962.86
Costantino Rocca	68	69	70	75	282	4,962.86
Peter Mitchell	75	69	67	72	283	3,880
Ian Palmer	77	66	66	74	283	3,880
Paul Broadhurst	69	71	71	72	283	3,880

	SCORES				TOTAL	MONEY
Mike Clayton	76	70	66	72	284	3,465
Jean Van de Velde	72	69	68	75	284	3,465
Peter Hedblom	72	69	74	69	284	3,465
David Ray	72	68	74	70	284	3,465
Christian Cevaer	71	74	70	70	285	3,105
Jeff Hawkes	75	70	70	70	285	3,105
Andrew Sherborne	70	71	73	71	285	3,105
David Gilford	69	70	75	71	285	3,105
Gordon Brand, Jr.	76	68	71	71	286	2,700
Andre Bossert	75	69	71	71	286	2,700
Barry Lane	74	71	73	68	286	2,700
David J. Russell	76	69	71	70	286	2,700
David Carter	72	69	74	71	286	2,700
Mike Harwood	78	68	70	71	287	2,370
Ignacio Garrido	76	67	72	72	287	2,370
Paul Way	70	72	75	70	287	2,370
Richard Boxall	72	69	72	74	287	2,370
Mark James	72	73	72	71	288	2,100
Malcolm Mackenzie	71	72	74	71	288	2,100
Eamonn Darcy	74	68	71	75	288	2,100
Andrew Murray	68	73	71	76	288	2,100
John Bickerton	72	68	74	74	288	2,100
Antonio Sobrinho	76	69	70	74	289	1,770
Robert Karlsson	76	69	73	71	289	1,770
Mathias Gronberg	74	72	70	73	289	1,770
Craig Cassells	73	73	70	73	289	1,770
Paolo Quirici	75	67	67	80	289	1,770
Neal Briggs	71	69	73	76	289	1,770
Santiago Luna	73	72	73	72	290	1,500
Daniel Westermark	73	72	72	73	290	1,500
Andrew Oldcorn	74	72	71	73	290	1,500
Jose Maria Canizares	74	71	71	75	291	1,290
Liam White	74	72	75	70	291	1,290
Pedro Linhart	72	74	69	76	291	1,290
Howard Clark	71	70	73	77	291	1,290
Alberto Binaghi	77	68	72	75	292	1,110
Ronan Rafferty	72	72	76	72	292	1,110
Jay Townsend	77	67	76	73	293	990
Mark Roe	74	72	73	74	293	990
Gavin Levenson	69	76	75	75	295	930
Wayne Riley	71	73	77	75	296	870
Darrell Kestner	73	73	76	74	296	870
Michel Besanceney	73	71	80	72	296	870
Wayne Westner	75	70	75	79	299	795
Keith Ashdown	73	73	76	77	299	795
Daniel Silva	76	70	75	79	300	600
Scott Watson	73	71	80	76	300	600

Turespana Open de Baleares

Santa Ponsa II, Majorca, Spain   March 23-26
Par 36-36–72; 6,620 yards   purse, £242,879

	SCORES				TOTAL	MONEY
Greg Turner	74	65	67	68	274	£40,478.18
Costantino Rocca	71	67	71	67	276	26,983.83
Miguel Angel Jimenez	72	73	66	69	280	15,204.21

	SCORES				TOTAL	MONEY
Jean Van de Velde	70	72	71	68	281	11,221
Barry Lane	71	70	69	71	281	11,221
Ross McFarlane	70	69	71	72	282	8,500.76
Sven Struver	75	69	68	71	283	7,286.36
Jarmo Sandelin	70	70	75	69	284	5,448.58
Fredrik Lindgren	69	72	70	73	284	5,448.58
Paul Eales	73	69	68	74	284	5,448.58
Michael Jonzon	77	70	70	68	285	3,965.73
Andrew Coltart	74	69	70	72	285	3,965.73
Darren Clarke	76	71	66	72	285	3,965.73
Peter Mitchell	76	68	68	73	285	3,965.73
Mark Mouland	67	69	74	75	285	3,965.73
Gary Emerson	68	72	76	70	286	3,152.57
Keith Waters	75	72	68	71	286	3,152.57
Mike Clayton	74	69	71	72	286	3,152.57
Iain Pyman	71	70	71	74	286	3,152.57
Phil Golding	70	73	68	75	286	3,152.57
Anders Sorensen	76	70	70	71	287	2,768.82
Mark James	73	69	73	72	287	2,768.82
Pierre Fulke	77	68	69	73	287	2,768.82
Stephen McAllister	71	73	72	72	288	2,550.23
Adam Hunter	73	73	69	73	288	2,550.23
Francisco Valera	73	70	70	75	288	2,550.23
Jonathan Lomas	72	75	71	71	289	2,189.38
Roger Chapman	73	73	73	70	289	2,189.38
Jose Rozadilla	68	74	77	70	289	2,189.38
Daniel Westermark	72	68	77	72	289	2,189.38
Fabrice Tarnaud	75	71	71	72	289	2,189.38
Anders Gillner	74	73	69	73	289	2,189.38
Pedro Linhart	67	74	74	74	289	2,189.38
Jose Manuel Carriles	73	71	72	74	290	1,894.45
Lee Westwood	75	71	70	74	290	1,894.45
Marco Gortana	72	75	66	77	290	1,894.45
Scott Watson	70	76	72	73	291	1,724.44
Ignacio Garrido	75	70	73	73	291	1,724.44
Des Smyth	70	71	80	70	291	1,724.44
Peter Hedblom	75	70	71	75	291	1,724.44
Paul Affleck	71	72	75	74	292	1,578.71
John Hawksworth	77	69	71	75	292	1,578.71
Mark Davis	74	72	72	75	293	1,432.99
Mike McLean	78	70	75	70	293	1,432.99
Eoghan O'Connell	77	71	75	70	293	1,432.99
Andre Bossert	70	73	74	76	293	1,432.99
Christian Cevaer	77	71	70	76	294	1,214.39
Andrew Oldcorn	76	71	73	74	294	1,214.39
Stephen Ames	68	80	72	74	294	1,214.39
Paul Moloney	79	69	79	67	294	1,214.39
Steven Richardson	70	77	70	77	294	1,214.39
David R. Jones	74	72	73	76	295	1,020.09
Paul Mayo	74	72	74	75	295	1,020.09
Jean Louis Guepy	75	71	75	74	295	1,020.09
Carl Suneson	78	69	72	77	296	813.64
Miguel Angel Martin	74	73	74	75	296	813.64
Martyn Roberts	73	75	74	74	296	813.64
Juan Quiros	74	74	75	73	296	813.64
Paul McGinley	71	74	78	73	296	813.64
Jose Rivero	71	74	81	70	296	813.64
Alexander Cejka	76	71	71	79	297	582.41
Mark Litton	71	73	74	79	297	582.41
Thomas Levet	74	72	74	77	297	582.41

	SCORES				TOTAL	MONEY
Mathias Gronberg	74	74	73	76	297	582.41
Jose Maria Canizares	74	74	75	74	297	582.41
Fredrik Jacobson	75	72	77	73	297	582.41
Ross Drummond	76	72	76	73	297	582.41
Brian Nelson	77	70	76	75	298	395
Daren Lee	76	72	77	73	298	395
Robert Lee	75	71	77	76	299	392
Carlos Larrain	70	72	75	83	300	390
Mark Nichols	74	70	75	82	301	387
David Carter	73	74	75	79	301	387

Turespana Open de Catalonia

Golf Club Peralada, Girona, Spain
Par 36-36–72; 6,839 yards

April 13-16
purse, £300,000

	SCORES				TOTAL	MONEY
Philip Walton	68	74	71	68	281	£50,000
Andrew Coltart	72	74	68	70	284	33,330
Howard Clark	70	70	72	73	285	18,780
Mark Davis	71	72	74	71	288	15,000
Paul Affleck	73	73	73	70	289	11,600
Retief Goosen	67	75	75	72	289	11,600
Sam Torrance	73	72	73	72	290	9,000
Michael Campbell	70	75	76	70	291	6,730
Pierre Fulke	74	76	70	71	291	6,730
Dean Robertson	73	74	71	73	291	6,730
David Williams	73	76	71	72	292	5,340
Stuart Cage	69	74	72	77	292	5,340
Ross McFarlane	74	76	71	72	293	4,242.86
Russell Claydon	70	73	77	73	293	4,242.86
Fabrice Tarnaud	69	74	77	73	293	4,242.86
Silvio Grappasonni	76	72	72	73	293	4,242.86
Roger Wessels	72	78	70	73	293	4,242.86
Wayne Riley	74	69	75	75	293	4,242.86
Ronan Rafferty	78	71	69	75	293	4,242.86
Frank Nobilo	73	71	79	71	294	3,420
Vicente Fernandez	78	72	72	72	294	3,420
Paul Eales	69	73	79	73	294	3,420
Mats Lanner	74	73	74	73	294	3,420
Joakim Haeggman	73	77	66	78	294	3,420
Richard Boxall	72	78	73	72	295	2,716.36
Barry Lane	73	76	74	72	295	2,716.36
Peter Hedblom	73	69	81	72	295	2,716.36
Andrew Sherborne	73	77	74	71	295	2,716.36
Anders Gillner	74	76	74	71	295	2,716.36
Gordon Brand, Jr.	68	78	78	71	295	2,716.36
Steven Richardson	75	75	75	70	295	2,716.36
Stephen Dodd	72	71	78	74	295	2,716.36
Jose Maria Canizares	73	77	71	74	295	2,716.36
Santiago Luna	72	72	76	75	295	2,716.36
Phillip Price	67	71	76	81	295	2,716.36
Paul Curry	75	75	74	72	296	2,070
David Carter	71	74	79	72	296	2,070
Robert Karlsson	73	75	77	71	296	2,070
Peter Mitchell	69	74	79	74	296	2,070
Gary Orr	74	71	77	74	296	2,070

	SCORES				TOTAL	MONEY
Christian Cevaer	73	73	76	74	296	2,070
David R. Jones	73	72	76	75	296	2,070
George Ryall	71	73	75	77	296	2,070
Adam Hunter	70	76	79	72	297	1,710
Peter O'Malley	75	75	77	70	297	1,710
Jose Rivero	74	75	78	70	297	1,710
Martyn Roberts	72	74	74	77	297	1,710
Paul Mayo	72	76	76	74	298	1,530
Ruben Alvarez	72	78	77	71	298	1,530
Jose Manuel Carriles	77	73	76	73	299	1,350
Lee Westwood	72	75	79	73	299	1,350
Miguel Angel Martin	74	70	82	73	299	1,350
Mathias Gronberg	75	71	76	77	299	1,350
Stephen Ames	72	77	75	76	300	1,055
Paul Moloney	71	73	80	76	300	1,055
Jon Robson	76	72	77	75	300	1,055
Ignacio Gervas	73	77	77	73	300	1,055
David Gilford	69	75	83	73	300	1,055
Paul R. Simpson	69	79	80	72	300	1,055
Paul Way	76	73	74	79	302	840
Gary Emerson	72	77	77	76	302	840
Carl Suneson	74	75	78	75	302	840
Carlos Larrain	76	74	82	70	302	840
Michael Jonzon	75	74	72	81	302	840
Neal Briggs	70	80	74	79	303	549.33
Jarmo Sandelin	70	79	79	75	303	549.33
Ignacio Garrido	76	74	80	73	303	549.33
Öyvind Rojahn	75	75	77	78	305	446
Anders Sorensen	72	77	79	80	308	444
Peter Baker	74	72	84	80	310	442

Air France Cannes Open

Royal Mougins Golf Club, Cannes, France   April 20-23
Par 35-36–71; 6,566 yards   purse, £300,000
(Rounds 3 and 4 cancelled — heavy rains.)

	SCORES		TOTAL	MONEY
Andre Bossert	65	67	132	£37,500
Oyvind Rojahn	67	67	134	19,541.25
Jean Van de Velde	64	70	134	19,541.25
David Gilford	70	65	135	10,387.50
Andrew Coltart	66	69	135	10,387.50
Domingo Hospital	66	70	136	6,316.88
Jon Robson	67	69	136	6,316.88
Mathias Gronberg	64	72	136	6,316.88
Ove Sellberg	66	70	136	6,316.88
Dean Robertson	68	69	137	4,170
Adam Hunter	68	69	137	4,170
Richard Boxall	67	70	137	4,170
Ross Drummond	70	68	138	3,247.50
Ignacio Garrido	69	69	138	3,247.50
Alberto Binaghi	67	71	138	3,247.50
Peter Hedblom	69	69	138	3,247.50
Roger Chapman	68	70	138	3,247.50
Colin Montgomerie	68	70	138	3,247.50
Iain Pyman	72	67	139	2,745

	SCORES	TOTAL	MONEY
Nicklas Fasth	67 72	139	2,745
Paul Moloney	68 72	140	2,396.25
John Bickerton	71 69	140	2,396.25
Mike Miller	70 70	140	2,396.25
Costantino Rocca	74 66	140	2,396.25
Ian Palmer	68 72	140	2,396.25
Ian Woosnam	67 73	140	2,396.25
David Curry	70 70	140	2,396.25
Emanuele Canonica	69 71	140	2,396.25
Tony Johnstone	73 68	141	1,935
Peter O'Malley	69 72	141	1,935
Frank Nobilo	69 72	141	1,935
John Bland	66 75	141	1,935
Sven Struver	71 70	141	1,935
Jeff Remesy	71 70	141	1,935
Paul McGinley	71 71	142	1,620
Peter Mitchell	70 72	142	1,620
Joakim Haeggman	68 74	142	1,620
Sam Torrance	70 72	142	1,620
Robert Karlsson	71 71	142	1,620
Eric Giraud	68 74	142	1,620
Michael Campbell	69 73	142	1,620
Howard Clark	71 72	143	1,170
Greg Turner	70 73	143	1,170
Jeff Hawkes	74 69	143	1,170
Eamonn Darcy	67 76	143	1,170
Russell Claydon	72 71	143	1,170
Jonathan Lomas	67 76	143	1,170
Miguel Angel Martin	70 73	143	1,170
Retief Goosen	71 72	143	1,170
Fabrice Tarnaud	72 71	143	1,170
Stephen McAllister	68 75	143	1,170
Silvio Grappasonni	73 70	143	1,170
Anders Gillner	72 71	143	1,170
Gary Orr	71 72	143	1,170
Manuel Pinero	69 75	144	633.35
Christian Cevaer	71 73	144	633.35
Jarmo Sandelin	69 75	144	633.35
Steen Tinning	70 74	144	633.35
Fredrik Jacobson	74 70	144	633.35
Vicente Fernandez	72 72	144	633.35
Mark Mouland	73 71	144	633.35
Fredrik Andersson	75 69	144	633.35
Paul Way	71 73	144	633.35
Ronan Rafferty	70 74	144	633.35
Pierre Fulke	69 75	144	633.35
Gavin Levenson	73 71	144	633.35
David Ray	72 72	144	633.35

Tournoi Perrier de Paris

Golf de Saint-Cloud, Paris, France
Par 35-35–70; 6,539 yards

April 27-30
purse, £350,000

	SCORES	TOTAL	MONEY (Each)
Seve Ballesteros/Jose Maria Olazabal	63 67 64 62	256	£35,000
Mike Clayton/Peter O'Malley	66 70 63 60	259	25,000

	SCORES				TOTAL	MONEY (Each)
Colin Montgomerie/Ian Woosnam	64	65	67	64	260	17,500
Gavin Levenson/Ian Palmer	66	66	70	60	262	10,750
Darren Clarke/Paul McGinley	63	69	68	62	262	10,750
Russell Claydon/Paul Eales	63	74	66	61	264	5,312.50
Paul Broadhurst/Ross McFarlane	63	71	67	63	264	5,312.50
Malcolm Mackenzie/David Ray	63	69	68	64	264	5,312.50
Stuart Cage/Iain Pyman	63	69	65	67	264	5,312.50
Frederic Cupillard/Fabrice Tarnaud	61	72	70	62	265	3,875
Ignacio Garrido/Miguel Angel Martin	67	68	68	62	265	3,875
Ruben Alvarez/Jose Coceres	66	66	69	64	265	3,875
Raymond Burns/Carl Mason	63	68	69	65	265	3,875
Fredrik Andersson/Jean Charles Cambon	67	70	67	62	266	3,050
John Bland/Jeff Hawkes	65	70	68	63	266	3,050
Jose Manuel Carriles/Juan Pinero	67	66	66	67	266	3,050
Barry Lane/Mark Roe	65	72	69	62	268	2,600
Stephen Dodd/Mark Litton	66	68	70	64	268	2,600
Phil Golding/Ricky Willison	66	68	69	65	268	2,600
Richard Boxall/Derrick Cooper	62	68	70	68	268	2,600
John Bickerton/Daren Lee	59	72	69	68	268	2,600
Emanuele Canonica/Costantino Rocca	66	70	69	64	269	2,200
Michel Besanceney/Vicente Fernandez	64	73	67	65	269	2,200
Peter Baker/David J. Russell	64	68	71	66	269	2,200
Roger Chapman/Paul Way	64	72	71	63	270	1,850
Rolf Muntz/Martyn Roberts	66	71	68	65	270	1,850
Carlos Larrain/Daniel Westermark	65	69	70	66	270	1,850
Paul Moloney/Terry Price	65	70	69	66	270	1,850
Alexander Cejka/Heinz P. Thul	62	74	72	64	272	1,550
Jon Robson/Scott Watson	62	72	70	68	272	1,550
Mark Davis/David Williams	68	67	69	69	273	525
John Mellor/Jonathan Wilshire	67	70	72	68	277	522
Dean Robertson/Craig Ronald	63	70	72	72	277	522

Conte de Florence Italian Open

Le Rovedine Golf Club, Milan, Italy
Par 36-36–72; 6,845 yards

May 4-7
purse, £370,449

	SCORES				TOTAL	MONEY
Sam Torrance	69	70	63	67	269	£61,716.73
Jose Rivero	66	70	69	66	271	41,119.79
Ronan Rafferty	67	68	68	73	276	16,299.74
Emanuele Canonica	68	69	73	66	276	16,299.74
Paul Broadhurst	69	67	71	69	276	16,299.74
Costantino Rocca	68	68	67	73	276	16,299.74
Mark Litton	68	68	72	68	276	16,299.74
Tony Johnstone	70	69	69	69	277	7,946.12
Neal Briggs	65	73	70	69	277	7,946.12
Peter Baker	71	68	71	67	277	7,946.12
Silvio Grappasonni	71	68	69	69	277	7,946.12
Peter Hedblom	73	66	69	70	278	6,001.27
Ross Drummond	72	70	66	70	278	6,001.27
Oyvind Rojahn	72	67	68	71	278	6,001.27
Anders Forsbrand	71	67	71	70	279	5,112.19
Greg Turner	72	69	72	66	279	5,112.19
Andrew Sherborne	71	68	68	72	279	5,112.19
Gary Orr	69	71	70	69	279	5,112.19
Stephen Dodd	68	70	72	70	280	4,457.73

		SCORES			TOTAL	MONEY
Mark James	70	73	68	69	280	4,457.73
Vicente Fernandez	69	72	67	72	280	4,457.73
Carl Mason	70	73	70	68	281	3,945.28
Phil Golding	71	70	71	69	281	3,945.28
Fredrik Andersson	71	68	74	68	281	3,945.28
Andrew Coltart	68	71	71	71	281	3,945.28
Stephen Ames	74	70	70	67	281	3,945.28
Keith Waters	72	68	73	68	281	3,945.28
Stephen McAllister	68	70	68	76	282	3,445.17
Jarmo Sandelin	68	69	72	73	282	3,445.17
Michel Besanceney	70	72	71	69	282	3,445.17
Gavin Levenson	70	73	68	72	283	3,083.99
Terry Price	70	73	74	66	283	3,083.99
Richard Boxall	70	74	67	72	283	3,083.99
Jose Manuel Carriles	69	74	68	72	283	3,083.99
Ricky Willison	68	71	71	74	284	2,667.23
Steen Tinning	69	71	72	72	284	2,667.23
Christian Cevaer	69	73	69	73	284	2,667.23
Carlos Larrain	71	73	69	71	284	2,667.23
Jon Robson	69	72	72	71	284	2,667.23
Fredrik Lindgren	73	71	69	71	284	2,667.23
John McHenry	70	72	70	72	284	2,667.23
Rolf Muntz	71	73	71	70	285	2,148.60
Paolo Quirici	70	74	72	69	285	2,148.60
Michael Jonzon	72	72	67	74	285	2,148.60
Wayne Riley	70	74	70	71	285	2,148.60
Derrick Cooper	72	68	72	73	285	2,148.60
Andrew Oldcorn	68	72	72	73	285	2,148.60
Ian Spencer	70	70	78	67	285	2,148.60
David R. Jones	75	69	70	72	286	1,778.15
Michael Archer	71	69	76	70	286	1,778.15
Fabrice Tarnaud	72	71	72	71	286	1,778.15
Martyn Roberts	69	74	73	71	287	1,444.75
Jim Payne	72	71	74	70	287	1,444.75
Michele Reale	66	71	77	73	287	1,444.75
Paul R. Simpson	77	67	74	69	287	1,444.75
Marco Durante	67	73	73	74	287	1,444.75
Joakim Gronhagen	72	68	71	76	287	1,444.75
Heinz P. Thul	71	72	73	72	288	1,074.30
Stuart Cage	68	72	70	78	288	1,074.30
Fredrik Jacobson	73	71	72	72	288	1,074.30
Andre Bossert	75	65	73	75	288	1,074.30
Manuel Pinero	70	70	74	74	288	1,074.30
Jonathan Lomas	72	72	73	71	288	1,074.30
Marc Farry	70	71	72	75	288	1,074.30
Daren Lee	71	72	71	75	289	604.59
Malcolm Mackenzie	67	73	75	74	289	604.59
Marcello Santi	71	70	74	74	289	604.59
Juan Quiros	73	71	70	75	289	604.59
Gary Emerson	69	74	76	70	289	604.59
Mike Harwood	71	69	76	73	289	604.59
Gabriel Hjertstedt	70	73	74	72	289	604.59
Steven Bottomley	72	72	72	74	290	542
Massimo Florioli	75	68	73	74	290	542
Giuseppe Cali	71	70	75	74	290	542
Jeremy Robinson	73	71	73	74	291	538
Antoine LeBouc	72	70	75	75	292	536
Tierri Corte	71	71	78	73	293	534
Rodger Davis	74	70	72	78	294	532
Retief Goosen	70	74	77	75	296	530

Benson & Hedges International Open

St. Mellion Golf & Country Club, Plymouth, England
Par 36-36–72; 7,054 yards

May 11-14
purse, £650,000

	SCORES			TOTAL	MONEY
Peter O'Malley	68	65	74	73	280	£108,330
Mark James	71	68	71	71	281	56,450
Costantino Rocca	72	73	64	72	281	56,450
Andrew Oldcorn	70	74	73	65	282	27,593.33
Colin Montgomerie	67	71	75	69	282	27,593.33
Carl Mason	71	75	63	73	282	27,593.33
Wayne Westner	74	73	71	66	284	16,753.33
Sandy Lyle	71	77	71	65	284	16,753.33
Steen Tinning	68	78	70	68	284	16,753.33
Jose Maria Olazabal	70	74	71	70	285	12,480
Eamonn Darcy	69	73	74	69	285	12,480
Raymond Burns	76	67	73	70	286	10,526.67
Paul Broadhurst	68	77	70	71	286	10,526.67
Gary Evans	70	73	71	72	286	10,526.67
Michael Campbell	78	70	67	72	287	8,967.50
Roger Wessels	73	73	71	70	287	8,967.50
Peter Senior	69	74	71	73	287	8,967.50
Jose Coceres	73	73	71	70	287	8,967.50
Barry Lane	74	71	73	70	288	7,518.33
Derrick Cooper	76	73	69	70	288	7,518.33
Bernhard Langer	74	70	70	74	288	7,518.33
Frank Nobilo	73	71	73	71	288	7,518.33
Sven Struver	73	73	71	71	288	7,518.33
Richard Boxall	68	73	73	74	288	7,518.33
Sam Torrance	71	73	75	70	289	6,727.50
Marc Farry	75	72	71	71	289	6,727.50
Paul Affleck	71	77	69	73	290	6,240
Miguel Angel Jimenez	75	73	70	72	290	6,240
Andrew Sherborne	74	75	72	69	290	6,240
Seve Ballesteros	72	76	70	73	291	5,573.75
Christian Cevaer	71	75	73	72	291	5,573.75
Scott Watson	74	71	77	69	291	5,573.75
Lucas Parsons	73	74	76	68	291	5,573.75
Darren Clarke	71	74	72	75	292	4,875
Gavin Levenson	72	73	73	74	292	4,875
Martin Gates	69	78	71	74	292	4,875
Greg Turner	72	71	72	77	292	4,875
Domingo Hospital	71	75	73	73	292	4,875
Jamie Spence	75	73	70	74	292	4,875
Russell Claydon	74	73	73	73	293	4,160
Mark Mouland	76	72	72	73	293	4,160
Gary Emerson	74	70	78	71	293	4,160
Steven Richardson	76	72	71	74	297	4,160
Andrew Murray	73	76	73	71	293	4,160
Stephen McAllister	74	74	73	73	294	3,640
Philip Walton	72	77	73	72	294	3,640
Gordon Brand, Jr.	71	77	73	73	294	3,640
Steven Bottomley	77	70	75	73	295	3,250
Ignacio Garrido	73	76	71	75	295	3,250
Mike Harwood	73	75	75	72	295	3,250
David Williams	74	74	73	75	296	2,990
Eoghan O'Connell	75	73	74	75	297	2,665
Jeremy Robinson	75	73	76	73	297	2,665
Andrew Coltart	75	73	74	75	297	2,665

	SCORES				TOTAL	MONEY
Alberto Binaghi	73	74	80	70	297	2,665
David Curry	72	76	78	72	298	1,971.67
Adam Hunter	72	76	75	75	298	1,971.67
Alexander Cejka	74	72	80	72	298	1,971.67
Mark Roe	73	74	71	80	298	1,971.67
Emanuele Canonica	71	75	75	77	298	1,971.67
David R. Jones	74	75	80	69	298	1,971.67
Paul Way	75	74	75	74	298	1,971.67
Mats Hallberg	74	69	78	77	298	1,971.67
Bernard Gallacher	74	72	77	75	298	1,971.67
Jarmo Sandelin	74	75	74	76	299	1,625
Antonio Garrido	76	73	75	77	301	975
Pierre Fulke	74	74	77	79	304	973

Peugeot Open de Espana

Club de Campo, Madrid, Spain
Par 36-36–72; 6,928 yards

May 18-21
purse, £550,000

	SCORES				TOTAL	MONEY
Seve Ballesteros	70	67	66	71	274	£91,660
Jose Rivero	68	69	71	68	276	47,765
Ignacio Garrido	67	66	74	69	276	47,765
Peter Baker	69	72	68	68	277	25,400
Gordon Brand, Jr.	71	66	65	75	277	25,400
Eduardo Romero	70	69	69	70	278	17,875
Peter Mitchell	66	67	73	72	278	17,875
Russell Claydon	72	69	70	68	279	11,785
Derrick Cooper	70	72	70	67	279	11,785
Bernhard Langer	71	70	69	69	279	11,785
Jay Townsend	69	67	71	72	279	11,785
Anders Sorensen	70	73	68	69	280	8,906.67
Jon Robson	69	70	74	67	280	8,906.67
Mark Roe	69	69	68	74	280	8,906.67
Pedro Linhart	74	69	70	68	281	6,954.44
Frank Nobilo	73	70	69	69	281	6,954.44
Mark Mouland	70	73	70	68	281	6,954.44
Jose Maria Olazabal	73	71	68	69	281	6,954.44
Jesper Parnevik	73	68	69	71	281	6,954.44
Colin Montgomerie	70	71	70	70	281	6,954.44
Wayne Riley	69	71	71	70	281	6,954.44
Howard Clark	69	69	73	70	281	6,954.44
Costantino Rocca	68	69	73	71	281	6,954.44
Barry Lane	69	73	71	69	282	5,775
Mike McLean	71	72	70	69	282	5,775
Ross McFarlane	72	68	71	71	282	5,775
Michael Jonzon	71	71	68	73	283	5,032.50
Greg Turner	72	72	69	70	283	5,032.50
Peter O'Malley	73	68	70	72	283	5,032.50
Sam Torrance	70	69	71	73	283	5,032.50
Mike Harwood	69	70	77	67	283	5,032.50
David Gilford	69	69	72	73	283	5,032.50
Andrew Sherborne	72	71	68	73	284	4,070
Ross Drummond	73	70	71	70	284	4,070
Jean Van de Velde	71	73	73	67	284	4,070
Phillip Price	68	73	70	73	284	4,070
John Bland	71	69	74	70	284	4,070

	SCORES				TOTAL	MONEY
Gavin Levenson	69	71	72	72	284	4,070
Domingo Hospital	71	68	70	75	284	4,070
Eamonn Darcy	69	69	76	70	284	4,070
David Carter	70	68	75	71	284	4,070
Jarmo Sandelin	69	72	72	72	285	3,410
Jose Coceres	70	72	69	74	285	3,410
Paul Broadhurst	75	69	71	70	285	3,410
Olle Karlsson	72	70	76	68	286	2,860
Juan Pinero	72	71	72	71	286	2,860
Mats Lanner	71	73	66	76	286	2,860
Malcolm Mackenzie	69	65	68	74	286	2,860
Steven Richardson	71	70	73	72	286	2,860
Rodger Davis	70	71	74	71	286	2,860
Stuart Cage	73	68	72	73	286	2,860
Paolo Quirici	72	71	71	73	287	2,255
Roger Chapman	74	70	71	72	287	2,255
Alberto Binaghi	71	70	74	72	287	2,255
Manuel Pinero	73	68	70	76	287	2,255
Paul Eales	72	71	73	72	288	1,828.75
Mark Litton	72	71	74	71	288	1,828.75
Sven Struver	71	73	72	72	288	1,828.75
Liam White	72	72	74	70	288	1,828.75
Raymond Burns	72	72	75	70	289	1,622.50
Per-Ulrik Johansson	73	68	75	73	289	1,622.50
Mike Clayton	72	70	72	76	290	1,485
Phil Golding	74	70	75	71	290	1,485
Silvio Grappasonni	70	68	78	74	290	1,485
Fabrice Tarnaud	71	71	78	71	291	961
Ignacio Gervas	70	72	77	72	291	961
Retief Goosen	69	75	77	70	291	961
Rolf Muntz	71	73	78	69	291	961
John Bickerton	71	70	73	78	292	819
Richard Boxall	73	70	78	72	293	817
Stephen McAllister	69	67	80	80	296	815

Volvo PGA Championship

Wentworth Club, West Course, Surrey, England
Par 35-37–72; 6,957 yards

May 26-29
purse, £900,000

	SCORES				TOTAL	MONEY
Bernhard Langer	67	73	68	71	279	£150,000
Michael Campbell	69	73	71	67	280	78,165
Per-Ulrik Johansson	71	69	69	71	280	78,165
Jesper Parnevik	68	73	70	71	282	32,828
Andrew Sherborne	68	69	72	73	282	32,828
Peter Senior	66	73	73	70	282	32,828
Peter O'Malley	74	71	70	67	282	32,828
Thomas Levet	72	68	71	71	282	32,828
Mark Mouland	72	71	65	75	283	18,203.33
Colin Montgomerie	70	72	69	72	283	18,203.33
Silvio Grappasonni	72	69	71	71	283	18,203.33
Jose Maria Canizares	69	70	71	74	284	13,928
Nick Faldo	67	72	71	74	284	13,928
Richard Boxall	72	71	70	71	284	13,928
Miguel Angel Jimenez	73	69	71	71	284	13,928
Gary Orr	70	67	75	72	284	13,928

	SCORES				TOTAL	MONEY
Jonathan Lomas	74	68	74	69	285	10,777.50
Stephen Ames	74	69	72	70	285	10,777.50
Paul Eales	73	68	73	71	285	10,777.50
Mark James	73	72	67	73	285	10,777.50
Sven Struver	69	69	74	73	285	10,777.50
Phillip Price	72	73	71	69	285	10,777.50
Michel Besanceney	70	71	71	73	285	10,777.50
Sandy Lyle	74	71	71	69	285	10,777.50
Santiago Luna	72	73	70	71	286	8,640
Jose Maria Olazabal	69	72	72	73	286	8,640
Barry Lane	74	70	73	69	286	8,640
Joakim Haeggman	73	72	72	69	286	8,640
Peter Baker	70	72	74	70	286	8,640
Andrew Oldcorn	70	73	73	70	286	8,640
Lee Westwood	73	68	73	72	286	8,640
Gordon Brand, Jr.	73	69	71	74	287	7,200
Mike McLean	73	70	70	74	287	7,200
Mike Harwood	75	70	75	67	287	7,200
Mark Roe	71	71	74	71	287	7,200
Philip Walton	70	68	74	75	287	7,200
Frank Nobilo	68	68	77	75	288	6,120
Costantino Rocca	72	70	77	69	288	6,120
Eamonn Darcy	71	72	72	73	288	6,120
Seve Ballesteros	72	73	69	74	288	6,120
Retief Goosen	72	67	74	75	288	6,120
Mike Clayton	74	69	73	72	288	6,120
Wayne Riley	69	72	73	74	288	6,120
Vicente Fernandez	72	72	72	73	289	5,040
Jose Rivero	74	66	75	74	289	5,040
Rodger Davis	70	73	71	75	289	5,040
Mats Lanner	73	72	70	74	289	5,040
Paul McGinley	76	68	72	73	289	5,040
Robert Karlsson	72	72	70	76	290	3,960
Vijay Singh	72	70	73	75	290	3,960
Greg Turner	74	70	75	71	290	3,960
Paul Curry	70	72	75	73	290	3,960
Darren Clarke	71	70	82	67	290	3,960
Martin Gates	73	70	76	71	290	3,960
Jay Townsend	72	71	73	74	290	3,960
Ignacio Garrido	72	70	74	75	291	2,992.50
Mark Davis	70	75	74	72	291	2,992.50
Peter Mitchell	69	73	73	76	291	2,992.50
Kevin Stables	74	71	71	75	291	2,992.50
Derrick Cooper	72	72	75	73	292	2,700
Russell Claydon	74	71	76	72	293	2,610
Jean Van de Velde	70	72	73	79	294	2,475
Scott Watson	75	69	71	79	294	2,475
Alexander Cejka	72	72	77	74	295	2,295
Wayne Westner	73	72	75	75	295	2,295
Peter Fowler	73	72	77	75	297	1,350
Zhang Lian-Wei	70	72	78	80	300	1,348

Murphy's English Open

Forest of Arden Country Club Resort, Warwickshire, England
Par 35-37–72; 7,102 yards

June 1-4
purse, £650,000

	SCORES				TOTAL	MONEY
Philip Walton	65	70	69	70	274	£108,330
Colin Montgomerie	69	63	72	70	274	72,210
(Walton defeated Montgomerie on second extra hole.)						
Roger Chapman	68	70	70	69	277	40,690
Peter Senior	66	70	69	74	279	27,593.33
Darren Clarke	72	67	69	71	279	27,593.33
Wayne Westner	68	72	71	68	279	27,593.33
Terry Price	68	71	73	68	280	17,875
Barry Lane	68	69	71	72	280	17,875
Howard Clark	68	73	71	69	281	14,510
Dean Robertson	70	72	74	66	282	12,046.67
Derrick Cooper	70	66	73	73	282	12,046.67
Jay Townsend	72	69	69	72	282	12,046.67
Jose Rivero	70	66	71	76	283	9,983.33
Malcolm Mackenzie	74	68	68	73	283	9,983.33
Sandy Lyle	70	68	73	72	283	9,983.33
Martin Gates	72	70	70	72	284	8,051.25
Ignacio Garrido	74	68	72	70	284	8,051.25
Gary Evans	71	69	73	71	284	8,051.25
Greg Turner	74	68	71	71	284	8,051.25
Mike Clayton	70	71	72	71	284	8,051.25
Paul McGinley	72	68	72	72	284	8,051.25
Peter Baker	69	68	74	73	284	8,051.25
Eamonn Darcy	70	69	74	71	284	8,051.25
Michael Campbell	67	71	74	73	285	6,149
Sam Torrance	70	72	75	68	285	6,149
Costantino Rocca	69	71	71	74	285	6,149
Anders Forsbrand	68	75	69	73	285	6,149
Paul Affleck	71	70	68	76	285	6,149
Jean Louis Guepy	68	75	67	75	285	6,149
John McHenry	71	71	71	72	285	6,149
Joakim Haeggman	71	72	69	73	285	6,149
Mark Roe	70	72	71	72	285	6,149
Mathias Gronberg	68	71	77	69	285	6,149
Mark Mouland	71	66	73	76	286	4,810
Peter Mitchell	72	68	70	76	286	4,810
Gary Emerson	72	70	74	70	286	4,810
Juan Quiros	70	71	75	70	286	4,810
Gary Orr	72	71	70	73	286	4,810
Oyvind Rojahn	72	67	74	73	286	4,810
Mats Hallberg	71	69	72	74	286	4,810
Ross Drummond	70	71	75	71	287	3,900
Nicklas Fasth	71	71	72	73	287	3,900
Raymond Burns	74	69	70	74	287	3,900
Wayne Riley	68	74	75	70	287	3,900
Jose Maria Canizares	69	74	73	71	287	3,900
Paul Broadhurst	70	71	74	72	287	3,900
Craig Cassells	75	67	72	73	287	3,900
Stephen Ames	70	73	73	72	288	3,315
Alexander Cejka	65	72	75	76	288	3,315
Andrew Coltart	69	68	79	73	289	3,055
Anders Gillner	72	71	71	75	289	3,055
Mark Davis	67	72	77	74	290	2,795
Rodger Davis	70	73	71	76	290	2,795

	SCORES				TOTAL	MONEY
Peter Teravainen	74	67	78	72	291	2,285.83
Mike Harwood	68	73	75	75	291	2,285.83
Peter Hedblom	70	72	74	75	291	2,285.83
Jon Robson	73	70	74	74	291	2,285.83
Paul Curry	73	70	73	75	291	2,285.83
Russell Claydon	71	68	80	72	291	2,285.83
David Williams	74	69	73	76	292	1,885
Fabrice Tarnaud	71	71	76	74	292	1,885
Ronan Rafferty	73	68	72	79	292	1,885
Phillip Price	68	71	74	80	293	1,690
Jamie Spence	67	72	80	74	293	1,690
Jarmo Sandelin	72	71	73	77	293	1,690
Jean Van de Velde	70	71	79	74	294	975
David Feherty	70	72	73	80	295	973

Deutsche Bank Open

Gut Kaden, Hamburg, Germany
Par 36-36–72; 7,029 yards

June 8-11
purse, £650,000

	SCORES				TOTAL	MONEY
Bernhard Langer	67	66	68	69	270	£108,330
Jamie Spence	68	69	69	70	276	72,210
Mats Lanner	69	74	68	66	277	40,690
Anders Forsbrand	75	72	65	67	279	32,500
Sam Torrance	71	67	71	71	280	25,140
Costantino Rocca	68	70	71	71	280	25,140
Roger Wessels	73	70	71	67	281	16,753.33
Michael Campbell	71	68	74	68	281	16,753.33
Stephen McAllister	73	68	69	71	281	16,753.33
Jarmo Sandelin	71	69	73	69	282	12,480
Gary Orr	70	74	71	67	282	12,480
Mark Litton	71	68	73	71	283	10,058
Jean Louis Guepy	75	70	69	69	283	10,058
Peter Baker	69	74	71	69	283	10,058
Santiago Luna	71	74	69	69	283	10,058
Stephen Ames	70	69	71	73	283	10,058
Darren Clarke	73	68	75	68	284	8,406.67
Domingo Hospital	73	73	67	71	284	8,406.67
Paul McGinley	71	75	67	71	284	8,406.67
Paul R. Simpson	72	70	71	72	285	7,215
Michel Besanceney	71	74	67	73	285	7,215
Colin Montgomerie	72	69	72	72	285	7,215
Malcolm Mackenzie	73	68	74	70	285	7,215
Sandy Lyle	74	71	67	73	285	7,215
Michael Archer	74	70	69	72	285	7,215
Pierre Fulke	74	73	69	69	285	7,215
Paul Affleck	75	69	72	70	286	5,859.29
Lee Westwood	74	73	70	69	286	5,859.29
Russell Claydon	71	72	72	71	286	5,859.29
Stephen Dodd	73	70	73	70	286	5,859.29
John Bickerton	72	73	71	70	286	5,859.29
Ignacio Garrido	69	71	72	74	286	5,859.29
Emanuele Canonica	69	77	69	71	286	5,859.29
Jim Payne	73	74	68	72	287	4,680
Peter Teravainen	73	70	71	73	287	4,680
Antoine LeBouc	71	73	75	68	287	4,680

	SCORES				TOTAL	MONEY
Peter O'Malley	72	72	70	73	287	4,680
Olle Karlsson	74	71	72	70	287	4,680
Ian Woosnam	74	72	74	67	287	4,680
Jean Van de Velde	73	70	73	71	287	4,680
Wayne Riley	73	70	73	71	287	4,680
Paul Moloney	71	71	73	72	287	4,680
Ross Drummond	71	71	71	75	288	3,835
David Carter	77	69	73	69	288	3,835
Fredrik Lindgren	71	71	78	68	288	3,835
Liam White	71	75	71	71	288	3,835
Gavin Levenson	77	69	75	68	289	3,055
Mark James	71	74	72	72	289	3,055
Peter Mitchell	71	72	74	72	289	3,055
Mark Mouland	74	67	77	71	289	3,055
Andrew Sherborne	71	73	69	76	289	3,055
Jose Manuel Carriles	73	73	75	68	289	3,055
Alberto Binaghi	72	75	69	73	289	3,055
Craig Cassells	72	73	74	70	289	3,055
Roger Chapman	73	71	74	72	290	2,340
Sven Struver	70	69	77	74	290	2,340
Andrew Coltart	76	71	70	73	290	2,340
Fredrik Andersson	76	71	71	73	291	1,950
Mike McLean	70	71	76	74	291	1,950
Paul Lawrie	76	71	72	72	291	1,950
Scott Watson	75	71	71	74	291	1,950
Ian Spencer	73	69	77	72	291	1,950
Jonathan Lomas	73	74	74	71	292	1,511.25
Paul Way	74	73	70	75	292	1,511.25
Nicklas Fasth	75	72	76	69	292	1,511.25
David J. Russell	71	73	76	72	292	1,511.25
Paul Mayo	75	71	75	72	293	973
Carl Mason	74	73	72	75	294	971
Ove Sellberg	71	72	77	75	295	968
Gary Emerson	73	74	75	73	295	968
George Ryall	74	73	77	72	296	965
Neal Briggs	72	73	79	75	299	963

DHL Jersey Open

La Moye Golf Club, Jersey
Par 36-36–72; 6,813 yards

June 15-18
purse, £300,000

	SCORES				TOTAL	MONEY
Andrew Oldcorn	70	68	66	69	273	£50,000
Dean Robertson	66	70	72	68	276	33,330
Paul Moloney	68	71	70	68	277	16,890
Olle Karlsson	69	69	70	69	277	16,890
Brian Davis	68	70	75	65	278	10,733.33
Mark James	71	69	70	68	278	10,733.33
Roger Wessels	69	68	74	67	278	10,733.33
Malcolm Mackenzie	64	72	72	71	279	6,427.50
David Williams	68	70	72	69	279	6,427.50
Martin Gates	70	72	71	66	279	6,427.50
Wayne Stephens	70	68	69	72	279	6,427.50
Philip Walton	73	69	71	67	280	4,995
David Carter	68	77	69	66	280	4,995
Glenn Ralph	70	71	71	69	281	4,145

		SCORES			TOTAL	MONEY
Richard Boxall	69	68	75	69	281	4,145
Paul Affleck	69	70	72	70	281	4,145
Derrick Cooper	70	71	71	69	281	4,145
Lee Westwood	67	70	78	66	281	4,145
Peter Mitchell	73	69	70	69	281	4,145
Carl Mason	70	72	71	69	282	3,465
Paul Curry	64	74	70	74	282	3,465
Peter Baker	71	70	72	69	282	3,465
Des Smyth	72	69	73	68	282	3,465
Ronan Rafferty	66	69	78	70	283	3,105
John Bickerton	71	70	69	73	283	3,105
Eamonn Darcy	68	72	74	69	283	3,105
Paul Broadhurst	70	73	69	71	283	3,105
Howard Clark	68	71	72	73	284	2,835
Greg Turner	70	74	72	68	284	2,835
John Mellor	72	71	72	70	285	2,610
John McHenry	69	70	73	73	285	2,610
Stuart Cage	71	70	74	70	285	2,610
Gavin Levenson	68	70	74	74	286	2,340
Jim Payne	69	71	76	70	286	2,340
Gary Emerson	74	71	69	72	286	2,340
Heinz P. Thul	72	69	74	71	286	2,340
Fabrice Tarnaud	72	68	73	73	286	2,340
Joakim Gronhagen	69	76	69	73	287	1,980
Ian Palmer	70	70	77	70	287	1,980
Robert Lee	75	70	71	71	287	1,980
Ross Drummond	70	70	78	69	287	1,980
Paul McGinley	75	66	73	73	287	1,980
David J. Russell	74	70	74	69	287	1,980
George Ryall	75	70	73	69	287	1,980
Liam White	73	71	74	70	288	1,680
Philip Talbot	73	72	75	68	288	1,680
Jeremy Robinson	71	70	75	72	288	1,680
David Ray	64	77	74	74	289	1,500
Steven Richardson	70	72	72	75	289	1,500
Keith Waters	73	72	74	70	289	1,500
Mike Miller	73	71	73	73	290	1,290
Christy O'Connor, Jr.	71	72	76	71	290	1,290
John Hawksworth	71	69	77	73	290	1,290
Craig Cassells	70	72	75	73	290	1,290
Jonathan Wilshire	72	73	74	72	291	1,080
Mark Litton	72	66	82	71	291	1,080
Gabriel Hjertstedt	70	70	78	73	291	1,080
Ricky Willison	71	73	80	68	292	930
Martyn Roberts	74	68	72	78	292	930
Ian Spencer	74	70	74	74	292	930
Bill Longmuir	72	71	77	75	295	855
Andrew Sherborne	71	73	78	73	295	855
Mark Nichols	68	75	75	78	296	795
Carlos Larrain	73	71	78	74	296	795
Ross McFarlane	69	73	82	77	301	750

Peugeot Open de France

National Golf Club, Paris, France

Par 36-36–72; 6,928 yards

June 22-25

purse, £550,000

	SCORES				TOTAL	MONEY
Paul Broadhurst	67	75	69	63	274	£91,660
Neal Briggs	73	69	68	72	282	61,100
Pierre Fulke	69	76	71	68	284	34,430
Greg Turner	70	70	71	74	285	23,350
Sandy Lyle	75	69	70	71	285	23,350
Costantino Rocca	69	72	66	78	285	23,350
Anders Sorensen	68	76	73	69	286	14,176.67
Peter O'Malley	72	73	69	72	286	14,176.67
Jose Rivero	72	71	74	69	286	14,176.67
Jamie Spence	71	71	76	69	287	11,000
Paul Affleck	72	71	72	74	289	9,471.67
Jose Maria Olazabal	69	79	71	70	289	9,471.67
Peter Baker	74	75	73	67	289	9,471.67
Adam Hunter	69	73	76	72	290	7,755
Frank Nobilo	72	73	73	72	290	7,755
Paul Moloney	77	70	74	69	290	7,755
Olle Karlsson	74	71	72	73	290	7,755
Eamonn Darcy	74	74	69	73	290	7,755
Phil Golding	71	73	77	70	291	6,618.33
Ronan Rafferty	72	74	70	75	291	6,618.33
Wayne Riley	72	73	73	74	291	6,618.33
Liam White	69	76	73	74	292	5,692.50
David Williams	73	73	74	73	292	5,692.50
Jonathan Lomas	71	73	74	74	292	5,692.50
Jean Van de Velde	76	71	74	71	292	5,692.50
Barry Lane	75	75	72	70	292	5,692.50
Eoghan O'Connell	73	76	72	71	292	5,692.50
Ross McFarlane	72	72	73	75	292	5,692.50
Sven Struver	74	73	73	72	292	5,692.50
John Hawksworth	70	80	73	70	293	4,716.25
Marc Farry	70	77	72	74	293	4,716.25
Jose Coceres	74	76	72	71	293	4,716.25
Mark Davis	75	73	72	73	293	4,716.25
Michael Jonzon	72	76	74	72	294	4,180
Terry Price	72	78	75	69	294	4,180
Des Smyth	71	77	74	72	294	4,180
David Carter	72	75	78	69	294	4,180
Paul Lawrie	77	72	74	71	294	4,180
Silvio Grappasonni	73	77	75	70	295	3,520
Stephen Dodd	70	78	73	74	295	3,520
Michael Archer	70	78	73	74	295	3,520
Gordon Brand, Jr.	74	76	75	70	295	3,520
Steven Richardson	75	75	71	74	295	3,520
Paul Eales	73	73	71	78	295	3,520
Mark Mouland	75	73	76	71	295	3,520
Jean Louis Guepy	77	71	73	75	296	3,025
Peter Mitchell	77	71	74	74	296	3,025
Christian Cevaer	78	71	77	71	297	2,695
Paul Mayo	71	77	78	71	297	2,695
Ignacio Garrido	75	74	76	72	297	2,695
Fredrik Andersson	73	75	76	73	297	2,695
David J. Russell	73	71	78	76	298	2,310
Roger Chapman	74	72	77	75	298	2,310
Tim Planchin	72	73	81	72	298	2,310

	SCORES				TOTAL	MONEY
Stuart Cage	74	75	72	78	299	1,881
Retief Goosen	78	72	75	74	299	1,881
Lee Westwood	76	73	77	73	299	1,881
Peter Teravainen	73	76	74	76	299	1,881
Tony Johnstone	76	73	74	76	299	1,881
Martin Gates	71	78	77	74	300	1,540
Juan Quiros	73	77	78	72	300	1,540
Mike Clayton	79	71	80	70	300	1,540
Santiago Luna	76	73	78	73	300	1,540
Raymond Burns	76	72	82	70	300	1,540
Joakim Haeggman	72	78	79	72	301	932.60
Roger Wessels	75	73	76	77	301	932.60
Antoine LeBouc	73	75	79	74	301	932.60
Paul Curry	77	71	79	74	301	932.60
Stephen McAllister	76	73	75	77	301	932.60
Malcolm Mackenzie	75	75	78	74	302	816
Frederic Regard	78	72	76	76	302	816
Per Haugsrud	73	71	78	81	303	813
Russell Claydon	75	75	80	74	304	811
David Curry	72	75	78	80	305	809
Paul R. Simpson	74	76	83	80	313	807

BMW International Open

St. Eurach Land Und Golfclub, Munich, Germany
Par 37-35–72; 7,090 yards

June 29-July 2
purse, £550,000

	SCORES				TOTAL	MONEY
Frank Nobilo	67	69	69	67	272	£91,660
Bernhard Langer	73	67	67	67	274	47,765
Jarmo Sandelin	68	69	63	74	274	47,765
Mike Clayton	73	67	67	68	275	25,400
Jean Louis Guepy	70	72	65	68	275	25,400
Fredrik Lindgren	72	67	68	69	276	19,250
Philip Talbot	70	68	72	67	277	11,706.43
David Gilford	70	69	69	69	277	11,706.43
Silvio Grappasonni	72	70	66	69	277	11,706.43
Raymond Burns	65	72	69	71	277	11,706.43
Peter Baker	72	67	67	71	277	11,706.43
Martin Gates	72	67	67	71	277	11,706.43
Marc Farry	67	67	71	72	277	11,706.43
Derrick Cooper	73	69	70	66	278	8,250
Mark McNulty	69	72	69	68	278	8,250
Peter Mitchell	70	69	71	69	279	7,425
Peter Hedblom	74	67	68	70	279	7,425
Eoghan O'Connell	72	65	70	72	279	7,425
Mark James	68	70	74	68	280	6,446
Emanuele Canonica	73	69	72	66	280	6,446
Jamie Spence	70	72	69	69	280	6,446
Thomas Gogele	70	73	68	69	280	6,446
David Carter	70	68	70	72	280	6,446
Klas Eriksson	71	71	69	70	281	5,692.50
Jay Townsend	75	67	69	70	281	5,692.50
Mats Hallberg	65	74	71	71	281	5,692.50
Mark Roe	70	68	71	72	281	5,692.50
Russell Claydon	72	73	68	69	282	4,876.67
Joakim Gronhagen	71	70	71	70	282	4,876.67

	SCORES			TOTAL	MONEY
Mathias Gronberg	72	70	70	70	282	4,876.67
John Bickerton	70	71	70	71	282	4,876.67
Christian Cevaer	71	72	68	71	282	4,876.67
Gary Evans	71	73	64	74	282	4,876.67
Jonathan Lomas	72	71	70	70	283	4,235
Jose Rivero	71	69	73	70	283	4,235
Peter Fowler	71	69	71	72	283	4,235
Mark Mouland	71	69	71	72	283	4,235
Terry Price	67	71	76	70	284	3,850
Costantino Rocca	71	71	69	73	284	3,850
Fredrik Jacobson	71	72	67	74	284	3,850
John Mellor	72	72	70	71	285	3,575
Retief Goosen	71	72	72	70	285	3,575
Paul Mayo	71	72	72	71	286	3,355
Jeff Cranford	72	70	73	71	286	3,355
Stephen Dodd	73	72	68	74	287	2,860
Steven Bottomley	74	68	72	73	287	2,860
David Feherty	71	72	72	72	287	2,860
Andrew Sherborne	69	73	73	72	287	2,860
Jean Van de Velde	72	71	73	71	287	2,860
Craig Cassells	70	73	74	70	287	2,860
Roger Wessels	70	73	67	77	287	2,860
Dean Robertson	73	70	70	75	288	2,200
Mark Nichols	71	72	71	74	288	2,200
Paul Moloney	74	69	71	74	288	2,200
Juan Quiros	70	70	74	74	288	2,200
Darren Clarke	71	73	73	71	288	2,200
Scott Watson	74	71	68	76	289	1,716
Gabriel Hjertstedt	72	71	70	76	289	1,716
Peter O'Malley	73	72	69	75	289	1,716
Phillip Price	71	74	74	70	289	1,716
John Bland	75	70	76	68	289	1,716
David Curry	71	71	73	75	290	1,540
Ronan Rafferty	71	73	70	77	291	1,430
Richard Boxall	72	73	70	76	291	1,430
Sven Struver	74	68	74	75	291	1,430
*Florian Bruhns	73	71	74	74	292	
Gary Orr	75	69	74	75	293	825

Murphy's Irish Open

Mount Juliet Country Club, Thomastown, Kilkenny, Ireland   July 6-9
Par 36-36–72; 7,143 yards   purse, £667,000

	SCORES			TOTAL	MONEY
Sam Torrance	68	68	70	71	277	£111,107.69
Stuart Cage	70	69	69	69	277	57,897.44
Howard Clark	71	68	68	70	277	57,897.44
(Torrance defeated Cage at first extra hole and Clark at second extra hole.)
Robert Allenby	67	72	70	69	278	21,397.80
Derrick Cooper	74	69	66	69	278	21,397.80
David Gilford	70	69	67	72	278	21,397.80
Sven Struver	65	70	73	70	278	21,397.80
Peter Baker	72	69	67	70	278	21,397.80
Craig Stadler	69	73	70	66	278	21,397.80
Colin Montgomerie	68	68	69	73	278	21,397.80
Greg Norman	70	71	65	73	279	12,266.67

	SCORES				TOTAL	MONEY
Roger Wessels	70	68	71	71	280	10,546.16
Ian Woosnam	73	67	71	69	280	10,546.16
Wayne Riley	68	71	68	73	280	10,546.16
Michael Campbell	68	69	70	73	280	10,546.16
Miguel Angel Jimenez	68	73	67	73	281	8,815.39
Wayne Westner	70	67	73	71	281	8,815.39
Domingo Hospital	68	71	70	72	281	8,815.39
Jean Van de Velde	71	73	66	71	281	8,815.39
Gary Orr	70	68	73	71	282	7,700
John Mellor	74	69	71	68	282	7,700
Bernhard Langer	72	72	69	69	282	7,700
Sandy Lyle	68	71	72	71	282	7,700
Martin Gates	68	74	69	72	283	6,900
Andrew Coltart	71	71	68	73	283	6,900
Ross McFarlane	73	71	67	72	283	6,900
Des Smyth	71	71	72	69	283	6,900
Rodger Davis	74	70	69	71	284	6,000
Frank Nobilo	71	70	70	73	284	6,000
Ronan Rafferty	71	71	70	72	284	6,000
Paul McGinley	73	66	71	74	284	6,000
Eamonn Darcy	71	68	73	72	284	6,000
Olle Karlsson	70	74	66	75	285	4,933.33
Barry Lane	73	71	73	68	285	4,933.33
David Carter	72	72	74	67	285	4,933.33
Terry Price	69	69	72	75	285	4,933.33
Dean Robertson	74	68	68	75	285	4,933.33
Jonathan Lomas	72	68	72	73	285	4,933.33
Jarmo Sandelin	72	72	68	73	285	4,933.33
Philip Walton	69	69	71	76	285	4,933.33
Michael Jonzon	72	71	72	70	285	4,933.33
Anders Forsbrand	70	68	72	76	286	4,066.67
Steven Richardson	71	71	70	74	286	4,066.67
Phil Golding	70	69	73	74	286	4,066.67
Retief Goosen	74	70	67	75	286	4,066.67
Christian Cevaer	68	74	71	74	287	3,533.33
Liam White	72	67	73	75	287	3,533.33
Michel Besanceney	72	72	70	73	287	3,533.33
Miguel Angel Martin	72	69	70	76	287	3,533.33
Silvio Grappasonni	71	73	71	73	288	2,800
Adam Hunter	73	69	73	73	288	2,800
Darren Clarke	73	71	76	68	288	2,800
Martyn Roberts	71	71	72	74	288	2,800
Andrew Sherborne	73	68	73	74	288	2,800
Richard Boxall	72	70	75	71	288	2,800
John McHenry	73	71	71	73	288	2,800
Per-Ulrik Johansson	72	72	73	72	289	2,116.67
Marc Farry	71	70	74	74	289	2,116.67
Paul Way	68	74	73	74	289	2,116.67
Lucas Parsons	70	71	73	75	289	2,116.67
Mike Clayton	69	75	72	74	290	1,833.33
Paolo Quirici	69	75	69	77	290	1,833.33
Rolf Muntz	72	72	73	73	290	1,833.33
Ove Sellberg	72	71	71	76	290	1,833.33
Andrew Oldcorn	70	73	74	74	291	1,333.34
Mats Lanner	72	72	72	75	291	1,333.34
John Bickerton	72	71	74	75	292	994
Stephen Hamill	73	70	75	74	292	994
John Hawksworth	71	68	76	77	292	994
Paul R. Simpson	68	74	77	73	292	994
Joakim Gronhagen	69	74	70	79	292	994

	SCORES				TOTAL	MONEY
Roger Chapman	67	73	79	74	293	986
Michael Archer	74	69	73	77	293	986
David J. Russell	70	74	73	76	293	986
Jay Townsend	75	68	82	70	295	982
Peter Hedblom	76	67	74	81	298	980
Mats Hallberg	72	72	83	72	299	978

Scottish Open

Carnoustie Golf Club, Carnoustie, Scotland
Par 36-36–72; 7,187 yards

July 12-15
purse, £650,000

	SCORES				TOTAL	MONEY
Wayne Riley	66	69	69	72	276	£108,330
Nick Faldo	70	68	71	69	278	72,210
Colin Montgomerie	64	71	75	70	280	40,690
Craig Parry	67	73	72	71	283	32,500
*Gordon Sherry	73	70	71	69	283	
Ronan Rafferty	74	68	70	72	284	21,507.50
Peter O'Malley	71	73	72	68	284	21,507.50
Martin Gates	74	69	74	67	284	21,507.50
David Duval	72	69	75	68	284	21,507.50
Katsuyoshi Tomori	70	66	77	72	285	14,510
Olle Karlsson	69	71	73	73	286	10,750
Anders Forsbrand	72	71	73	70	286	10,750
Sam Torrance	69	72	75	70	286	10,750
Domingo Hospital	67	77	69	73	286	10,750
Mark Davis	72	68	71	75	286	10,750
Jose Rivero	69	73	74	70	286	10,750
Mark McNulty	75	71	71	69	286	10,750
Michael Campbell	66	77	72	72	287	8,580
Greg Turner	71	71	73	72	287	8,580
Peter Mitchell	72	72	74	70	288	7,518.33
Robert Karlsson	73	72	75	68	288	7,518.33
Steve Stricker	74	70	76	68	288	7,518.33
Sandy Lyle	74	70	72	72	288	7,518.33
Roger Chapman	69	75	72	72	288	7,518.33
Lee Westwood	73	71	75	69	288	7,518.33
Des Smyth	72	72	75	70	289	6,337.50
Mark James	74	71	74	70	289	6,337.50
Costantino Rocca	73	71	73	72	289	6,337.50
Andrew Coltart	74	72	69	74	289	6,337.50
Jean Louis Guepy	69	73	76	71	289	6,337.50
Jay Delsing	73	70	74	72	289	6,337.50
David Gilford	72	71	74	73	290	5,411.25
Ian Woosnam	66	74	78	72	290	5,411.25
Vicente Fernandez	71	74	77	68	290	5,411.25
Jose Coceres	71	73	71	75	290	5,411.25
Brian Marchbank	70	75	74	72	291	4,615
Robert Allenby	73	72	73	73	291	4,615
David Feherty	71	68	74	78	291	4,615
Santiago Luna	71	75	73	72	291	4,615
Jay Townsend	73	71	74	73	291	4,615
Jamie Spence	69	72	76	74	291	4,615
Barry Lane	68	74	76	73	291	4,615
Mike Harwood	71	71	77	72	291	4,615
Iain Pyman	72	73	75	72	292	3,835

	SCORES				TOTAL	MONEY
Retief Goosen	75	71	73	73	292	3,835
Ignacio Garrido	74	71	73	74	292	3,835
Philip Walton	70	75	74	73	292	3,835
Terry Price	69	73	79	72	293	3,445
Scott Watson	69	71	79	74	293	3,445
*Tiger Woods	69	71	75	78	293	
Paul Lawrie	70	69	77	78	294	2,795
Russell Claydon	73	73	74	74	294	2,795
Manuel Pinero	74	71	78	71	294	2,795
David Frost	72	73	75	74	294	2,795
Vijay Singh	67	75	73	79	294	2,795
Mark Roe	70	75	79	70	294	2,795
Peter Hedblom	72	73	76	73	294	2,795
Eamonn Darcy	74	70	74	76	294	2,795
Raymond Burns	70	74	80	71	295	2,101.67
Andre Bossert	72	73	78	72	295	2,101.67
Stephen Ames	72	72	76	75	295	2,101.67
Tony Johnstone	71	75	72	78	296	1,852.50
Stephen McAllister	73	73	75	75	296	1,852.50
Steven Richardson	73	72	74	77	296	1,852.50
Jim Payne	71	74	76	75	296	1,852.50
Steen Tinning	71	73	77	76	297	1,315.75
Gary Orr	71	75	75	76	297	1,315.75
Andrew Oldcorn	72	73	73	79	297	1,315.75
Jean Van de Velde	72	73	77	75	297	1,315.75
Klas Eriksson	69	72	79	78	298	971
Colin Gillies	72	74	73	80	299	968
Ross Drummond	73	71	75	80	299	968
Peter Fowler	74	72	74	80	300	963
Gordon Brand, Jr.	70	74	80	76	300	963
John Morse	71	74	78	77	300	963
Craig Ronald	73	73	76	79	301	959
Donnie Hammond	72	74	82	74	302	957
Gary Evans	69	77	77	81	304	955

British Open Championship

Old Course, St. Andrews, Scotland
Par 36-36–72; 6,933 yards

July 20-23
purse, £1,340,700

	SCORES				TOTAL	MONEY
John Daly	67	71	73	71	282	£125,000
Costantino Rocca	69	70	70	73	282	100,000
(Daly defeated Rocca in four-hole playoff.)						
Michael Campbell	71	71	65	76	283	65,667
Steven Bottomley	70	72	72	69	283	65,667
Mark Brooks	70	69	73	71	283	65,667
Vijay Singh	68	72	73	71	284	40,500
Steve Elkington	72	69	69	74	284	40,500
Corey Pavin	69	70	72	74	285	33,333
Mark James	72	75	68	70	285	33,333
Bob Estes	72	70	71	72	285	33,333
Brett Ogle	73	69	71	73	286	26,000
Sam Torrance	71	70	71	74	286	26,000
Payne Stewart	72	68	75	71	286	26,000
Ernie Els	71	68	72	75	286	26,000
Greg Norman	71	74	72	70	287	18,200

	SCORES				TOTAL	MONEY
Brad Faxon	71	67	75	74	287	18,200
Ben Crenshaw	67	72	76	72	287	18,200
Robert Allenby	71	74	71	71	287	18,200
Per-Ulrik Johansson	69	78	68	72	287	18,200
David Duval	71	75	70	72	288	13,500
Barry Lane	72	73	68	75	288	13,500
Peter Mitchell	73	74	71	70	288	13,500
Andrew Coltart	70	74	71	73	288	13,500
Bernhard Langer	72	71	73	73	289	10,316.67
Mark Calcavecchia	71	72	72	74	289	10,316.67
Jesper Parnevik	75	71	70	73	289	10,316.67
Lee Janzen	73	73	71	72	289	10,316.67
Katsuyoshi Tomori	70	68	73	78	289	10,316.67
Bill Glasson	68	74	72	75	289	10,316.67
*Steve Webster	70	72	74	73	289	
David Frost	72	72	74	72	290	8,122
David Feherty	68	75	71	76	290	8,122
Tom Watson	67	76	70	77	290	8,122
Darren Clarke	69	77	70	74	290	8,122
Ross Drummond	74	68	77	71	290	8,122
Jose Maria Olazabal	72	72	74	72	290	8,122
Hisayuki Sasaki	74	71	72	73	290	8,122
John Huston	71	74	72	73	290	8,122
Peter Jacobsen	71	76	70	73	290	8,122
Nick Price	70	74	70	77	291	7,050
Mark McNulty	67	76	74	74	291	7,050
Nick Faldo	74	67	75	75	291	7,050
Seve Ballesteros	75	69	76	71	291	7,050
Brian Watts	72	71	73	75	291	7,050
John Cook	69	70	75	77	291	7,050
Phil Mickelson	70	71	77	73	291	7,050
Warren Bennett	72	74	73	72	291	7,050
*Gordon Sherry	70	71	74	76	291	
Mark O'Meara	72	72	75	73	292	6,350
Ian Woosnam	71	74	76	71	292	6,350
Brian Claar	71	75	71	75	292	6,350
Tsuneyuki Nakajima	73	72	72	75	292	6,350
Ken Green	71	72	73	76	292	6,350
Anders Forsbrand	70	74	75	73	292	6,350
Russell Claydon	70	74	71	78	293	5,900
Jim Gallagher, Jr.	69	76	75	73	293	5,900
Peter O'Malley	71	73	74	75	293	5,900
Raymond Floyd	72	74	72	76	294	5,475
Tom Kite	72	76	71	75	294	5,475
Peter Senior	71	75	78	70	294	5,475
Paul Broadhurst	73	72	76	73	294	5,475
Paul Lawrie	73	71	74	76	294	5,475
David Gilford	69	72	75	78	294	5,475
Justin Leonard	73	67	77	77	294	5,475
Martin Gates	73	73	72	76	294	5,475
Eduardo Herrera	74	72	73	75	294	5,475
Derrick Cooper	71	76	74	73	294	5,475
Jonathan Lomas	74	73	75	73	295	4,975
Olle Karlsson	71	76	73	75	295	4,975
Gary Hallberg	72	74	72	77	295	4,975
Gary Player	71	73	77	74	295	4,975
Peter Baker	70	74	81	70	295	4,975
Scott Hoch	74	72	73	76	295	4,975
Jose Rivero	70	72	75	78	295	4,975
Jeff Maggert	75	70	78	72	295	4,975

	SCORES				TOTAL	MONEY
Frank Nobilo	70	71	80	74	295	4,975
Mats Hallberg	68	76	75	76	295	4,975
*Tiger Woods	74	71	72	78	295	
Patrick Burke	75	72	78	71	296	4,500
Jay Haas	76	72	70	78	296	4,500
Ryoken Kawagishi	72	76	80	68	296	4,500
Steve Lowery	69	74	76	77	296	4,500
Bob Lohr	76	68	79	73	296	4,500
Sandy Lyle	71	71	79	75	296	4,500
Jack Nicklaus	78	70	77	71	296	4,500
Jarmo Sandelin	75	71	77	73	296	4,500
Dean Robertson	71	73	74	78	296	4,500
Miguel Angel Jimenez	75	73	76	73	297	4,125
Mark Davis	74	71	76	76	297	4,125
Eduardo Romero	74	74	72	77	297	4,125
Jay Delsing	72	75	73	77	297	4,125
Gene Sauers	69	73	75	80	297	4,125
Wayne Riley	70	72	75	80	297	4,125
John Hawksworth	73	74	75	76	298	4,000
Bill Longmuir	72	76	72	78	298	4,000
Lee Westwood	71	72	82	74	299	4,000
Jose Coceres	71	76	78	74	299	4,000
Simon Burnell	72	76	75	77	300	4,000
Davis Love III	70	78	74	78	300	4,000
*Gary Clark	71	76	80	74	301	
Mark Nichols	75	68	78	81	302	4,000
Don Pooley	76	71	80	75	302	4,000
Pedro Linhart	72	75	77	79	303	4,000

Out of Final 36 Holes

Paul Azinger	74	75		149
Mike Springer	75	74		149
Masashi Ozaki	70	79		149
Bob Charles	73	76		149
Scott Simpson	72	77		149
Howard Clark	76	73		149
John Morse	75	74		149
Curtis Strange	73	76		149
Peter Fowler	74	75		149
Nigel Graves	72	77		149
John Watson	76	73		149
Bob Tway	71	78		149
Loren Roberts	76	74		150
Wayne Grady	75	75		150
Tony Johnstone	75	75		150
Brandt Jobe	74	76		150
Colin Montgomerie	75	75		150
Craig Stadler	74	76		150
Mark McCumber	73	77		150
Miguel Angel Martin	73	77		150
Michel Besanceney	73	77		150
Jamie Spence	77	73		150
Mark Roe	75	75		150
Stephen Leaney	76	74		150
Michael Clayton	74	77		151
Andrew Crerar	77	74		151
Tom Wargo	72	79		151
Robert Karlsson	77	74		151
Paul Carman	72	79		151

	SCORES	TOTAL
John Bickerton	71 80	151
Larry Mize	74 77	151
*Stephen Gallacher	72 79	151
Carl Mason	75 77	152
Billy Andrade	76 76	152
Lee Trevino	75 77	152
Brad Bryant	78 74	152
Tom Weiskopf	76 76	152
Kazuhiro Takami	76 77	153
Craig Parry	76 77	153
Russell Weir	71 82	153
Neil Roderick	74 79	153
Richard Boxall	72 81	153
Fredrik Andersson	77 76	153
Ian Baker-Finch	77 76	153
Toru Suzuki	80 73	153
Ronan Rafferty	75 78	153
Adam Tillman	75 78	153
John Wither	75 78	153
Mathias Gronberg	81 72	153
Martyn Thompson	76 79	155
Brandel Chamblee	80 78	158
Arnold Palmer	83 75	158
Paul Mayo	77 82	159
Gary Stafford	78 84	162
Andrew Oldcorn	73	WD
Philip Walton	75	WD

(Professionals who did not complete 72 holes received £650.)

Heineken Dutch Open

Hilversum Golf Club, Utrecht, Netherlands — July 27-30
Par 36-35–71; 6,636 yards — purse, £650,000

	SCORES	TOTAL	MONEY
Scott Hoch	65 70 69 65	269	£108,330
Sam Torrance	68 64 69 70	271	56,450
Michael Jonzon	70 65 70 66	271	56,450
Derrick Cooper	68 69 66 69	272	32,500
Terry Price	66 70 67 71	274	25,140
Frank Nobilo	68 68 65 73	274	25,140
Richard Boxall	68 72 64 71	275	15,815
Colin Montgomerie	67 70 67 71	275	15,815
Peter Mitchell	68 69 69 69	275	15,815
Darren Clarke	68 69 73 65	275	15,815
Paul Eales	69 65 71 71	276	11,570
Philip Walton	65 69 73 69	276	11,570
Costantino Rocca	70 71 68 68	277	9,983.33
Ross McFarlane	67 69 73 68	277	9,983.33
Phil Golding	71 68 69 69	277	9,983.33
Thomas Levet	66 73 70 69	278	7,936.67
Mark James	70 65 71 72	278	7,936.67
Rodger Davis	70 71 67 70	278	7,936.67
John Huston	70 69 75 64	278	7,936.67
Russell Claydon	69 71 70 68	278	7,936.67
Christy O'Connor, Jr.	72 68 69 69	278	7,936.67

	SCORES				TOTAL	MONEY
Silvio Grappasonni	73	66	69	70	278	7,936.67
Ian Woosnam	70	66	71	71	278	7,936.67
Mark Mouland	73	65	67	73	278	7,936.67
Oyvind Rojahn	67	71	72	69	279	6,435
John Hawksworth	73	67	70	69	279	6,435
Greg Turner	75	65	68	71	279	6,435
Peter O'Malley	69	70	70	70	279	6,435
David Williams	72	68	64	75	279	6,435
Domingo Hospital	69	68	73	70	280	5,499
Howard Clark	69	72	75	64	280	5,499
Miguel Angel Jimenez	71	70	69	70	280	5,499
Vicente Fernandez	73	67	70	70	280	5,499
Nicklas Fasth	68	70	72	70	280	5,499
Christian Cevaer	71	69	69	72	281	4,290
Jim Payne	71	69	70	71	281	4,290
Paul Broadhurst	69	72	68	72	281	4,290
Andrew Sherborne	69	70	72	70	281	4,290
Paul Affleck	70	70	66	75	281	4,290
Rolf Muntz	71	66	76	68	281	4,290
Mike McLean	70	68	72	71	281	4,290
Peter Hedblom	69	70	70	72	281	4,290
Stuart Cage	70	70	66	75	281	4,290
Jose Coceres	72	64	70	75	281	4,290
Gary Emerson	74	67	69	71	281	4,290
Bernhard Langer	72	69	71	69	281	4,290
Lee Westwood	70	71	69	71	281	4,290
Jonas Saxton	67	73	71	71	282	3,315
Roger Chapman	70	68	74	70	282	3,315
Jonathan Lomas	70	70	69	74	283	2,925
John Daly	72	66	73	72	283	2,925
Pierre Fulke	71	68	72	72	283	2,925
Dean Robertson	71	70	73	69	283	2,925
Manuel Pinero	70	67	75	72	284	2,285.83
Paul Way	70	69	74	71	284	2,285.83
Mats Lanner	69	71	71	73	284	2,285.83
Ignacio Garrido	71	70	71	72	284	2,285.83
Tony Johnstone	71	70	74	69	284	2,285.83
Vijay Singh	66	70	76	72	284	2,285.83
Alexander Cejka	66	70	73	76	285	1,885
Steven Bottomley	72	69	71	73	285	1,885
Paul Moloney	68	73	76	68	285	1,885
Emanuele Canonica	69	70	75	72	286	1,690
Joakim Gronhagen	72	67	74	73	286	1,690
Jean Louis Guepy	68	71	76	71	286	1,690
Hendrick Buhrmann	68	70	75	74	287	975
Daniel Westermark	69	71	71	78	289	973

Volvo Scandinavian Masters

Barseback, Stockholm, Sweden
Par 35-37–72; 7,301 yards

August 3-6
purse, £650,000

	SCORES				TOTAL	MONEY
Jesper Parnevik	67	67	69	67	270	£108,330
Colin Montgomerie	70	69	67	69	275	72,210
Vijay Singh	72	70	70	65	277	40,690
Robert Allenby	67	72	70	69	278	30,015

	SCORES				TOTAL	MONEY
Eamonn Darcy	72	70	69	67	278	30,015
Miguel Angel Jimenez	67	73	70	69	279	22,750
Ross McFarlane	66	76	67	71	280	17,875
Paul Broadhurst	66	74	72	68	280	17,875
John Daly	71	74	67	69	281	14,510
Ian Woosnam	67	71	70	74	282	11,650
Michael Jonzon	70	72	68	72	282	11,650
Michael Campbell	69	67	70	76	282	11,650
Paul Way	71	71	67	73	282	11,650
Andre Bossert	70	72	71	70	283	9,162
Emanuele Canonica	71	71	69	72	283	9,162
Paul McGinley	72	69	72	70	283	9,162
Barry Lane	68	68	74	73	283	9,162
Jamie Spence	70	67	74	72	283	9,162
Lee Westwood	70	71	71	72	284	8,060
Paolo Quirici	71	71	70	73	285	7,410
Gary Orr	69	74	69	73	285	7,410
Mats Lanner	71	73	68	73	285	7,410
Richard Boxall	72	72	69	72	285	7,410
Frank Nobilo	66	73	74	72	285	7,410
Des Smyth	71	72	74	69	286	5,967
Thomas Levet	69	69	76	72	286	5,967
Gary Emerson	70	74	69	73	286	5,967
Peter O'Malley	72	72	72	70	286	5,967
Mathias Gronberg	72	71	71	72	286	5,967
Anders Forsbrand	68	70	75	73	286	5,967
Roger Chapman	75	69	66	78	286	5,967
Ronan Rafferty	71	73	75	67	286	5,967
Carl Mason	69	73	71	73	286	5,967
Joakim Gronhagen	73	72	71	70	286	5,967
Ignacio Garrido	72	71	73	71	287	4,745
Juan Quiros	73	70	69	75	287	4,745
David Carter	70	68	76	73	287	4,745
Mike McLean	66	72	75	74	287	4,745
Philip Talbot	75	70	69	73	287	4,745
Paul Affleck	70	69	75	73	287	4,745
Stephen Ames	74	71	71	72	288	4,030
Klas Eriksson	74	70	75	69	288	4,030
Retief Goosen	68	75	73	72	288	4,030
Silvio Grappasonni	71	71	73	73	288	4,030
Adam Hunter	71	68	72	77	288	4,030
Sven Struver	74	70	73	72	289	3,445
Paul Eales	70	72	73	74	289	3,445
Nicklas Fasth	69	75	73	72	289	3,445
Rolf Muntz	69	74	74	72	289	3,445
Jean Van de Velde	73	71	76	70	290	2,795
Santiago Luna	73	71	72	74	290	2,795
Michel Besanceney	73	72	71	74	290	2,795
Jarmo Sandelin	69	76	75	70	290	2,795
Ian Palmer	71	73	73	73	290	2,795
Pedro Linhart	74	71	71	74	290	2,795
John Mellor	73	71	74	73	291	2,080
Fredrik Andersson	71	71	72	77	291	2,080
Steen Tinning	72	72	76	71	291	2,080
Phillip Price	71	73	75	72	291	2,080
Fredrik Lindgren	69	76	72	74	291	2,080
Stuart Cage	67	72	78	74	291	2,080
Martyn Roberts	72	73	76	71	292	1,401.29
Fredrik Jacobson	71	74	75	72	292	1,401.29
Keith Waters	72	71	75	74	292	1,401.29

	SCORES				TOTAL	MONEY
Mike Harwood	69	72	79	73	292	1,401.29
Adam Mednick	73	71	73	75	292	1,401.29
Greg Turner	73	72	72	75	292	1,401.29
Mark Litton	70	73	75	74	292	1,401.29
Jeremy Robinson	72	73	77	72	294	967
Steven Bottomley	68	75	73	78	294	967
Olle Nordberg	70	73	79	72	294	967
Fabrice Tarnaud	71	72	75	77	295	963
Raymond Burns	77	68	75	76	296	961
*Johan Selberg	75	70	75	76	296	
Gabriel Hjertstedt	72	70	77	78	297	959
Rodger Davis	69	72	78	79	298	957
Mark Roe	71	72	75		DQ	955

Hohe Brucke Austrian Open

Golf Club Waldviertel, Litschau, Austria
Par 36-36–72; 6,937 yards

August 10-13
purse, £250,000

	SCORES				TOTAL	MONEY
Alexander Cejka	61	68	68	70	267	£41,660
Rolf Muntz	68	65	70	68	271	18,640
Ronan Rafferty	69	66	67	69	271	18,640
Ignacio Garrido	68	67	68	68	271	18,640
Pedro Linhart	68	67	71	68	274	8,950
Paul McGinley	67	67	69	71	274	8,950
Michel Besanceney	67	68	71	68	274	8,950
Heinz P. Thul	67	69	71	68	275	5,362.50
Phil Golding	68	73	67	67	275	5,362.50
Nic Henning	69	71	69	66	275	5,362.50
Andrew Clapp	70	69	70	66	275	5,362.50
Philip Talbot	72	66	69	69	276	4,043.33
Warren Bennett	68	70	67	71	276	4,043.33
Gavin Levenson	68	68	73	67	276	4,043.33
Stephen Dodd	72	67	64	74	277	3,521.67
Mathias Gronberg	69	72	70	66	277	3,521.67
John Bickerton	69	67	72	69	277	3,521.67
Ricky Willison	69	68	71	70	278	3,020
Craig Ronald	66	70	70	72	278	3,020
Mark Mouland	75	66	69	68	278	3,020
Stephen McAllister	72	68	71	67	278	3,020
Stephen Pullan	70	71	68	69	278	3,020
Steven Richardson	65	71	71	72	279	2,625
Jean Van de Velde	69	71	72	67	279	2,625
Magnus Persson	72	69	69	69	279	2,625
Brendan McGovern	65	69	70	75	279	2,625
Massimo Scarpa	67	70	71	71	279	2,625
Per Haugsrud	72	70	71	67	280	2,325
Joakim Gronhagen	69	70	68	73	280	2,325
David Carter	67	71	73	69	280	2,325
Jonathan Hodgson	73	68	72	68	281	2,137.50
Pierre Corte	71	66	73	71	281	2,137.50
*Markus Brier	70	72	69	70	281	
Miguel Angel Martin	69	72	69	72	282	1,875
Chris Davison	67	74	70	71	282	1,875
Marc Farry	68	68	71	75	282	1,875
Brian Marchbank	69	70	72	71	282	1,875

A playoff chip-in at the NEC World Series of Golf gave Greg Norman his third U.S. PGA Tour title of the year. Norman led the American money list with $1,654,959.

Allsport/J.D. Cuban

Billy Mayfair was second on the U.S. money list after winning the Tour Championship.

Allsport/J.D. Cuban

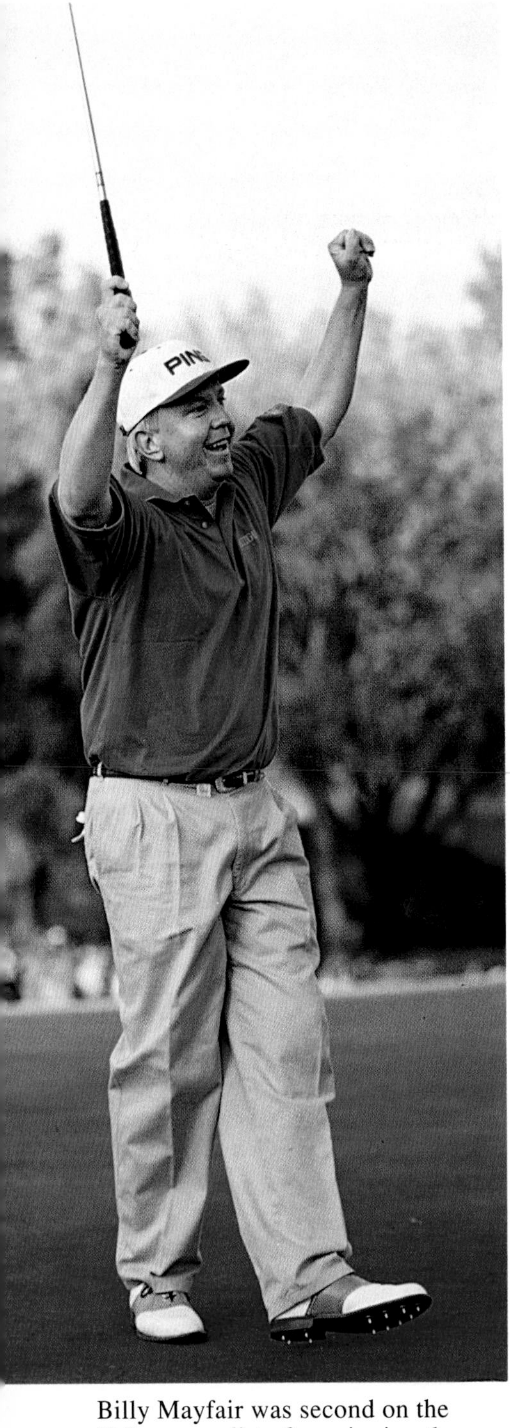

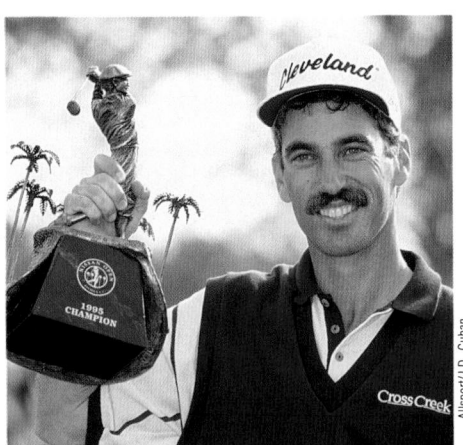

Corey Pavin defended in Los Angeles.

Allsport/J.D. Cuban

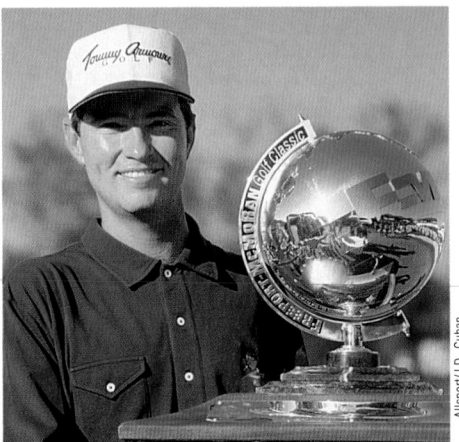

Davis Love III got in the Masters.

Allsport/J.D. Cuban

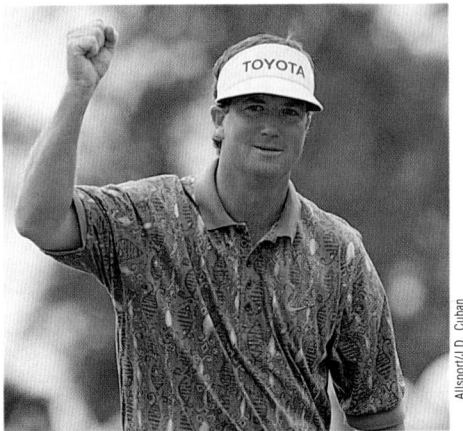

Peter Jacobsen won two in a row.

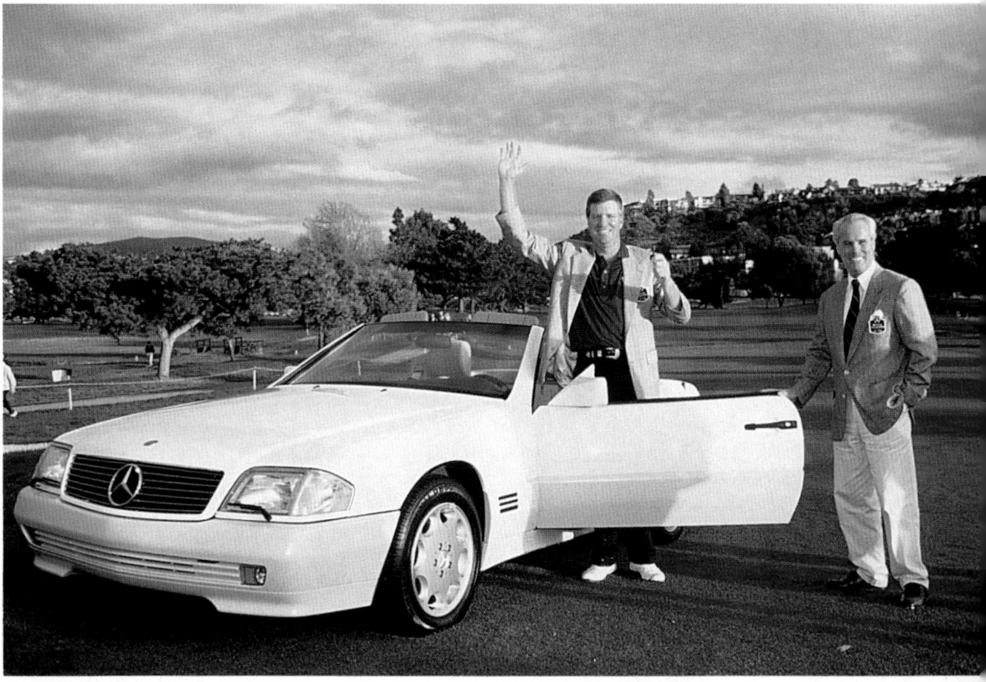

Allsport/Gary Newkirk

Steve Elkington led off with a victory in the Mercedes Championship.

Allsport/J.D. Cuban

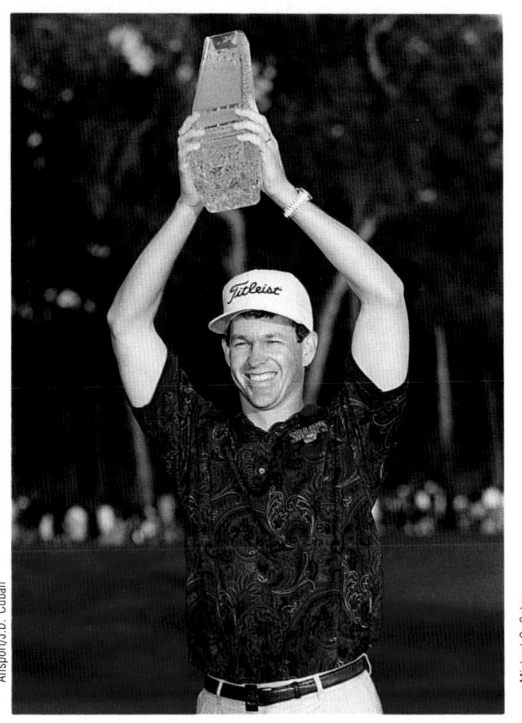

Lee Janzen was The Players champion.

Michael C. Cohen

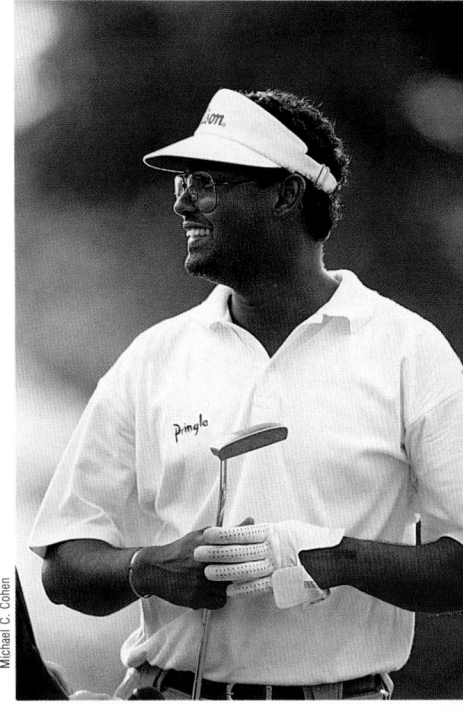

Vijay Singh had two 1995 titles.

Jim Gallagher, Jr., won twice.

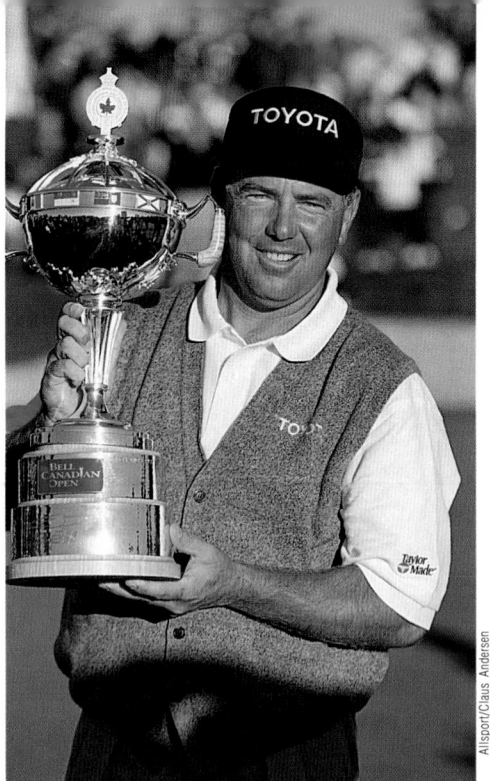

Mark O'Meara had two victories.

Rookie David Duval was impressive.

Payne Stewart ended his drought.

Mark Calcavecchia took the BellSouth Classic.   Loren Roberts repeated at Bay Hill.

Tom Lehman (left) and Nick Faldo both won, but Nick Price was shut out in the United States before two victories in Africa.

European Tour

Colin Montgomerie won twice and was No. 1 in Europe for the third successive year.

Fred Couples took two titles.

Sam Torrance celebrated his third victory in the British Masters.

Allsport/Andrew Redington

Mark James won in Morocco.

Allsport/Mike Cooper

The European Open was Bernhard Langer's third title.

Allsport/Clive Mason

Barry Lane was eighth on the money list.

Allsport/Graham Chadwick

Alexander Cejka posted three victories including the Volvo Masters.

Peter O'Malley won the Benson &
Hedges International Open.

Jesper Parnevik had a home victory in the
Scandinavian Masters.

Anders Forsbrand took the
Mercedes German Masters.

Wayne Riley won the Scottish Open.

Allsport/David Cannon

Jarmo Sandelin had his first victory.

Allsport/Graham Chadwick

Philip Walton won twice.

Allsport/Stephen Munday

Jose Maria Olazabal and Seve Ballesteros won in the Tournoi Perrier de Paris.

Allsport/Stephen Munday

Howard Clark earned a Ryder Cup place with a solid year.

Australasian/Japan Tours

Robert Allenby completed a Heineken double — Open and Classic.

Peter Senior won the Australian Masters.

Craig Parry had two Australasian titles.

Brian Watts won twice in Japan.

Michael Campbell claimed the Alfred Dunhill Masters.

Fred Couples and Davis Love III won in China.

Satoshi Higashi (left) won four and Jumbo Ozaki won five on the Japan Tour.

Senior Tours

Four victories made Jim Colbert No. 1 on the Senior PGA Tour money list with $1,444,386.

With a limited schedule, Raymond Floyd was second again on the money list.

Dave Stockton didn't win after May but was third on the money list.

Tom Weiskopf with the Open cup.

Lee Trevino had two victories.

Bob Murphy won four times.

Senior British champion Brian Barnes.

Hale Irwin was an immediate success.

Women's Tours

Allsport/J.D. Cuban

Annika Sorenstam won six events and led the American and European Tours.

Michael C. Cohen

Michael C. Cohen

Michael C. Cohen

Betsy King (left) qualified for the Hall of Fame, while Dottie Mochrie and Beth Daniel had top-10 years on the American LPGA Tour.

Laura Davies had seven titles worldwide.

Nanci Bowen won the Dinah Shore.

Jenny Lidback won a major in Canada.

Kelly Robbins took the LPGA title.

Young Australian star Karrie Webb won the Weetabix Women's British Open.

Mayumi Hirase had three wins.

Ikuyo Shiotani won five titles.

	SCORES				TOTAL	MONEY
Raymond Burns	73	70	69	70	282	1,875
Roger Chapman	70	67	68	77	282	1,875
Fabrice Tarnaud	71	71	68	72	282	1,875
Antoine LeBouc	69	69	73	71	282	1,875
Ian Palmer	68	71	74	70	283	1,600
Marc Pendaries	71	71	72	69	283	1,600
Mike Miller	71	70	73	69	283	1,600
Vanslow Phillips	71	70	72	71	284	1,400
Paul Page	71	71	72	70	284	1,400
Matthias Debove	70	73	69	72	284	1,400
Keith Waters	70	73	72	69	284	1,400
Daniel Chopra	76	65	77	66	284	1,400
Kalle Vainola	71	72	73	69	285	1,175
Robert Edwards	68	75	77	65	285	1,175
Klas Eriksson	73	70	73	69	285	1,175
Mats Hallberg	71	69	74	71	285	1,175
Paul R. Simpson	70	73	71	72	286	1,025
Fredrik Jacobson	74	69	71	72	286	1,025
Robert Lee	69	71	71	76	287	925
Tim Planchin	70	72	73	72	287	925
Mark Litton	68	73	72	75	288	808.33
Claude Grenier	68	73	74	73	288	808.33
Daniel Westermark	70	73	71	74	288	808.33
Matthew Hazelden	71	72	72	74	289	737.50
Adam Hunter	73	69	74	73	289	737.50
Carl Magnus Stromberg	74	68	70	78	290	675
Mikael Krantz	72	68	75	75	290	675
Mark Stevenson	70	73	70	77	290	675
Patrick Platz	73	70	77	71	291	625
Peter Teravainen	67	74	77	74	292	400
*Nikolaus Zitny	71	71	73	77	292	
Marco Durante	71	71	76	75	293	398
Thomas Nielsen	67	75	77	75	294	396
Gianluca Pietrobono	72	70	80	73	295	394
Craig Cassells	71	72	83	77	303	392

Chemapol Trophy Czech Open

Marianske Lazne Golf Club, Czech Republic
Par 34-37–71; 6,753 yards

August 17-20
purse, £750,000

	SCORES				TOTAL	MONEY
Peter Teravainen	67	66	68	67	268	£125,000
Howard Clark	66	68	66	69	269	83,320
Peter Hedblom	68	66	68	69	271	42,220
Ronan Rafferty	65	68	67	71	271	42,220
Darren Clarke	67	72	65	69	273	24,817.50
Santiago Luna	69	67	68	69	273	24,817.50
Jean Louis Guepy	68	68	69	68	273	24,817.50
Nicklas Fasth	66	69	66	72	273	24,817.50
Lee Westwood	69	71	69	66	275	14,610
Klas Eriksson	71	67	69	68	275	14,610
Gary Orr	68	69	69	69	275	14,610
Greg Turner	69	70	69	67	275	14,610
Sven Struver	71	68	68	69	276	11,282.50
Barry Lane	67	67	70	72	276	11,282.50
Jose Rivero	70	68	66	72	276	11,282.50

	SCORES				TOTAL	MONEY
Sam Torrance	66	71	69	70	276	11,282.50
Paul Moloney	71	68	69	69	277	9,900
Roger Chapman	69	66	71	71	277	9,900
Domingo Hospital	69	66	71	72	278	8,675
Costantino Rocca	69	71	70	68	278	8,675
Gary Emerson	70	70	69	69	278	8,675
Alexander Cejka	68	68	73	69	278	8,675
Des Smyth	70	69	69	70	278	8,675
Marc Farry	73	67	70	68	278	8,675
Mark Davis	69	67	73	70	279	6,885
Richard Boxall	70	70	67	72	279	6,885
Christian Cevaer	71	70	69	69	279	6,885
Derrick Cooper	72	69	70	68	279	6,885
David Gilford	68	71	71	69	279	6,885
Rodger Davis	70	69	68	72	279	6,885
Mark James	67	73	74	65	279	6,885
Andre Bossert	70	70	71	68	279	6,885
Paul Eales	72	68	69	70	279	6,885
Joakim Haeggman	69	71	67	72	279	6,885
Jim Payne	69	72	70	69	280	5,175
Dean Robertson	66	73	74	67	280	5,175
Paul Way	69	71	71	69	280	5,175
Sandy Lyle	68	72	73	67	280	5,175
Mark Litton	73	64	72	71	280	5,175
Fredrik Lindgren	68	70	72	70	280	5,175
Olle Karlsson	71	70	69	70	280	5,175
Malcolm Mackenzie	71	70	70	69	280	5,175
Raymond Burns	67	74	65	74	280	5,175
Philip Walton	71	67	72	70	280	5,175
Phil Golding	69	72	67	73	281	4,275
Peter Mitchell	66	72	74	69	281	4,275
Silvio Grappasonni	74	67	71	70	282	4,050
Joakim Gronhagen	67	70	76	70	283	3,525
Nic Henning	69	70	73	71	283	3,525
Ross Drummond	69	71	69	74	283	3,525
Peter Fowler	74	67	69	73	283	3,525
Jon Robson	75	66	67	75	283	3,525
Oyvind Rojahn	69	71	70	73	283	3,525
John Bland	70	70	72	72	284	2,775
David Williams	71	69	73	71	284	2,775
Stephen Dodd	67	71	75	71	284	2,775
Jarmo Sandelin	70	71	72	71	284	2,775
Robert Karlsson	69	69	74	73	285	2,287.50
Vicente Fernandez	71	69	75	70	285	2,287.50
Daniel Westermark	73	68	71	73	285	2,287.50
John Bickerton	71	70	70	74	285	2,287.50
Jose Maria Canizares	70	69	73	74	286	2,062.50
Neal Briggs	71	70	71	74	286	2,062.50
Paul Lawrie	70	69	74	74	287	1,650
Ross McFarlane	68	70	78	71	287	1,650
Gordon J. Brand	72	69	77	69	287	1,650
Steven Bottomley	72	69	75	75	291	1,123

Volvo German Open

GolfClub Schloss Nippenburg, Stuttgart, Germany
Par 36-35–71; 6,705 yards

August 24-27
purse, £650,000

	SCORES				TOTAL	MONEY
Colin Montgomerie	69	64	68	67	268	£108,330
Sam Torrance	68	65	66	70	269	56,450
Nicklas Fasth	68	67	68	66	269	56,450
Stuart Cage	70	64	68	68	270	27,593.33
Pedro Linhart	68	66	68	68	270	27,593.33
Paul Moloney	67	65	68	70	270	27,593.33
Mark James	67	67	70	67	271	17,875
Jay Townsend	72	66	67	66	271	17,875
Jose Coceres	67	67	70	68	272	13,755
Joakim Haeggman	70	69	66	67	272	13,755
Paul Eales	66	67	70	70	273	11,570
Des Smyth	69	66	69	69	273	11,570
Gary Orr	69	63	71	71	274	9,577
Gordon Brand, Jr.	67	66	69	72	274	9,577
Andrew Oldcorn	67	71	67	69	274	9,577
Eduardo Romero	69	69	69	67	274	9,577
Paul McGinley	68	68	67	71	274	9,577
Darren Clarke	66	73	68	68	275	8,385
Ronan Rafferty	67	70	69	70	276	7,821.67
David Gilford	68	67	71	70	276	7,821.67
Oyvind Rojahn	67	71	68	70	276	7,821.67
Mike McLean	66	71	70	70	277	6,435
Andrew Murray	71	69	71	66	277	6,435
Thomas Levet	67	71	69	70	277	6,435
Jesper Parnevik	66	70	72	69	277	6,435
Barry Lane	69	69	70	69	277	6,435
Heinz P. Thul	68	68	71	70	277	6,435
Sven Struver	67	71	66	73	277	6,435
Miguel Angel Martin	70	70	71	66	277	6,435
Eamonn Darcy	69	70	68	70	277	6,435
Roger Wessels	69	68	67	73	277	6,435
Paul Affleck	64	68	73	72	277	6,435
Mats Lanner	70	68	73	67	278	5,135
Ian Woosnam	69	69	66	74	278	5,135
Paul Lawrie	65	71	73	69	278	5,135
Mark Litton	69	69	70	70	278	5,135
Ian Palmer	68	70	73	68	279	4,485
Paul Way	69	65	73	72	279	4,485
Bernhard Langer	70	69	70	70	279	4,485
Peter O'Malley	68	72	72	67	279	4,485
David J. Russell	67	67	73	72	279	4,485
Jonathan Lomas	70	67	72	70	279	4,485
Daniel Westermark	70	70	72	68	280	3,770
Marc Farry	70	68	74	68	280	3,770
Malcolm Mackenzie	67	72	73	68	280	3,770
Paolo Quirici	67	72	73	68	280	3,770
John Hawksworth	71	68	70	71	280	3,770
Steven Richardson	69	69	68	75	281	2,925
Fredrik Lindgren	67	73	68	73	281	2,925
Santiago Luna	69	71	70	71	281	2,925
Mike Miller	70	66	75	70	281	2,925
Adam Hunter	72	68	68	73	281	2,925
David Carter	67	67	74	73	281	2,925
Olle Karlsson	68	68	74	71	281	2,925

	SCORES				TOTAL	MONEY
Fabrice Tarnaud	70	66	70	75	281	2,925
Peter Mitchell	72	67	74	69	282	2,080
Jose Rivero	66	73	70	73	282	2,080
Nic Henning	69	71	70	72	282	2,080
Christian Cevaer	67	70	74	71	282	2,080
Anders Sorensen	67	71	73	71	282	2,080
Michael Archer	69	71	72	70	282	2,080
Juan Quiros	71	67	72	73	283	1,573
John Bickerton	70	70	76	67	283	1,573
Jon Robson	72	68	69	74	283	1,573
Alberto Binaghi	69	69	73	72	283	1,573
Andre Bossert	70	66	72	75	283	1,573
Paul Broadhurst	71	68	70	75	284	972
Jose Maria Canizares	71	68	75	70	284	972
Philip Walton	68	69	71	77	285	968
Scott Watson	69	67	73	76	285	968
Stephen Ames	69	69	71	77	286	965
Peter Teravainen	69	71	71	76	287	963
Gary Emerson	70	69	76	73	288	961
Mark Davis	69	70	72	78	289	959
Erol Simsek	67	73	77	73	290	957
John Mellor	71	69	75	78	293	955
Stephen McAllister	72	68	76	80	296	953

Canon European Masters

Crans-sur-Sierre Golf Club, Crans-sur-Sierre, Switzerland August 31-September 3
Par 36-36–72; 6,745 yards purse, £700,000

	SCORES				TOTAL	MONEY
Mathias Gronberg	70	65	66	69	270	£116,660
Barry Lane	67	71	70	64	272	60,795
Costantino Rocca	70	69	67	66	272	60,795
Eduardo Romero	67	66	69	71	273	32,320
Joakim Haeggman	71	66	66	70	273	32,320
Darren Clarke	67	68	70	69	274	21,000
Sandy Lyle	71	66	70	67	274	21,000
Steven Richardson	67	64	71	72	274	21,000
Sam Torrance	73	70	64	68	275	14,805
Mats Lanner	71	67	68	69	275	14,805
Michael Campbell	71	66	69	70	276	11,725
Vicente Fernandez	68	69	71	68	276	11,725
Colin Montgomerie	68	70	68	70	276	11,725
Michael Jonzon	72	65	67	72	276	11,725
Olle Karlsson	70	71	69	67	277	10,080
Jamie Spence	71	70	70	66	277	10,080
Oyvind Rojahn	73	70	67	68	278	8,382.50
David J. Russell	74	67	70	67	278	8,382.50
Domingo Hospital	67	69	70	72	278	8,382.50
Alexander Cejka	73	69	70	66	278	8,382.50
Sven Struver	69	70	68	71	278	8,382.50
Ignacio Garrido	68	66	70	74	278	8,382.50
Paul Lawrie	70	71	68	69	278	8,382.50
Peter Mitchell	67	69	66	76	278	8,382.50
Stuart Cage	68	75	70	66	279	6,825
Jay Townsend	69	72	69	69	279	6,825
Jose Rivero	67	74	69	69	279	6,825

	SCORES				TOTAL	MONEY
Dean Robertson	68	70	71	70	279	6,825
Jean Louis Guepy	69	71	70	69	279	6,825
Peter O'Malley	71	70	69	69	279	6,825
Paolo Quirici	74	68	72	66	280	5,827.50
Corey Pavin	73	68	71	68	280	5,827.50
Mike Harwood	71	68	70	71	280	5,827.50
Roger Chapman	73	67	72	68	280	5,827.50
Paul Affleck	73	68	69	71	281	4,830
Andrew Oldcorn	71	71	69	70	281	4,830
Fabrice Tarnaud	73	69	66	73	281	4,830
Jean Van de Velde	69	66	74	72	281	4,830
Jose Maria Canizares	73	69	71	68	281	4,830
Tony Johnstone	72	69	71	69	281	4,830
Jeremy Robinson	74	69	69	69	281	4,830
Joakim Gronhagen	72	71	69	69	281	4,830
Christian Cevaer	69	74	68	70	281	4,830
Jon Robson	71	69	70	71	281	4,830
Jose Coceres	71	72	68	71	282	3,920
Robert Karlsson	74	68	74	66	282	3,920
Per-Ulrik Johansson	71	70	70	71	282	3,920
Peter Fowler	70	71	68	74	283	3,570
Scott Watson	72	70	70	71	283	3,570
Philip Talbot	69	67	74	74	284	2,940
Russell Claydon	73	69	70	72	284	2,940
Peter Hedblom	74	69	72	69	284	2,940
Miguel Angel Martin	68	68	73	75	284	2,940
Eamonn Darcy	71	69	72	72	284	2,940
Anders Forsbrand	72	68	71	73	284	2,940
Klas Eriksson	70	70	71	73	284	2,940
Richard Boxall	72	71	71	71	285	2,222.50
Iain Pyman	70	69	75	71	285	2,222.50
Andrew Sherborne	70	70	72	73	285	2,222.50
Mike Miller	72	67	73	73	285	2,222.50
Mark Mouland	67	73	73	73	286	1,574.25
Gary Orr	72	70	67	77	286	1,574.25
Alberto Binaghi	68	75	73	70	286	1,574.25
Wayne Riley	71	67	73	75	286	1,574.25
Christy O'Connor, Jr.	73	68	71	74	286	1,574.25
Paul Moloney	71	70	76	69	286	1,574.25
Paul Broadhurst	72	70	72	72	236	1,574.25
Jim Payne	72	69	72	73	286	1,574.25
Phil Golding	74	68	73	72	287	1,042
Ross Drummond	70	73	74	70	287	1,042
Malcolm Mackenzie	71	68	73	75	287	1,042
Steen Tinning	71	70	71	77	289	1,038
Chris Moody	70	73	73	74	290	1,036
Derrick Cooper	71	72	74	74	291	1,034
John Bickerton	72	71	73	76	292	1,031
Manuel Pinero	73	67	77	75	292	1,031
Thomas Levet	73	70	71	80	294	1,028
*John Lee	73	70	78	74	295	

Trophee Lancome

St. Nom la Breteche, Paris, France
Par 35-35–70; 6,758 yards

September 7-10
purse, £600,000

		SCORES			TOTAL	MONEY
Colin Montgomerie	64	69	65	71	269	£100,000
Sam Torrance	65	67	69	69	270	66,660
David Gilford	70	71	67	63	271	37,560
Tom Lehman	67	70	69	67	273	30,000
Bernhard Langer	70	69	69	66	274	25,400
Michael Jonzon	72	67	70	66	275	19,500
Wayne Riley	68	69	68	70	275	19,500
Paul Broadhurst	69	69	70	68	276	15,000
Costantino Rocca	70	70	68	69	277	13,440
Steven Richardson	70	68	68	72	278	10,740
David J. Russell	69	67	74	68	278	10,740
Mike Clayton	73	72	70	63	278	10,740
Jose Coceres	71	72	69	66	278	10,740
Michael Campbell	66	68	74	71	279	7,866.67
Oyvind Rojahn	66	72	72	69	279	7,866.67
Paul McGinley	71	70	67	71	279	7,866.67
Doug Martin	71	73	68	67	279	7,866.67
Mathias Gronberg	72	68	72	67	279	7,866.67
Peter Hedblom	72	70	70	67	279	7,866.67
Greg Turner	73	72	69	65	279	7,866.67
Darren Clarke	70	70	70	69	279	7,866.67
Seve Ballesteros	67	73	70	69	279	7,866.67
Peter O'Malley	73	71	68	68	280	6,480
Vicente Fernandez	67	70	70	73	280	6,480
David Carter	69	71	70	70	280	6,480
Christian Cevaer	73	72	69	67	281	5,497.50
Vijay Singh	70	71	69	71	281	5,497.50
Jose Maria Olazabal	71	67	70	73	281	5,497.50
Jose Rivero	73	71	70	67	281	5,497.50
Jean Louis Guepy	77	62	70	72	281	5,497.50
Mark James	73	73	67	68	281	5,497.50
Roger Wessels	72	71	71	67	281	5,497.50
Carl Mason	70	70	71	70	281	5,497.50
Richard Boxall	72	72	72	66	282	4,500
Gordon Brand, Jr.	71	67	72	72	282	4,500
Malcolm Mackenzie	73	70	69	70	282	4,500
Alexander Cejka	69	70	73	70	282	4,500
Ian Woosnam	69	72	72	69	282	4,500
Silvio Grappasonni	74	70	70	68	282	4,500
Robert Karlsson	71	73	70	69	283	4,080
Gary Orr	70	73	72	69	284	3,780
Mats Lanner	71	75	71	67	284	3,780
Olle Karlsson	76	70	70	68	284	3,780
Eduardo Romero	71	75	71	67	284	3,780
Paul Affleck	68	72	76	69	285	3,240
Jay Townsend	69	74	70	72	285	3,240
Marc Farry	74	68	70	73	285	3,240
Thomas Levet	73	70	71	71	285	3,240
Andrew Coltart	73	72	69	71	285	3,240
Des Smyth	73	73	70	70	286	2,880
Peter Baker	70	73	75	69	287	2,460
Miguel Angel Jimenez	71	73	71	72	287	2,460
Rodger Davis	71	71	71	74	287	2,460
Pedro Linhart	71	73	71	72	287	2,460

	SCORES				TOTAL	MONEY
Nicklas Fasth	73	70	72	72	287	2,460
Paul Moloney	74	71	73	69	287	2,460
Ignacio Garrido	71	70	74	73	288	1,980
Jean Van de Velde	70	71	73	74	288	1,980
Iain Pyman	69	66	80	74	289	1,740
Derrick Cooper	70	74	75	70	289	1,740
Paul Eales	71	73	73	72	289	1,740
Mark Mouland	73	69	75	72	289	1,740
Jamie Spence	72	74	74	69	289	1,740
Mike McLean	70	70	75	75	290	1,214.50
Peter Mitchell	74	72	71	73	290	1,214.50
Barry Lane	72	74	76	68	290	1,214.50
Mark Litton	73	71	75	71	290	1,214.50
Jarmo Sandelin	71	75	75	70	291	895
Stewart Cink	74	71	73	73	291	895
*Raphael Eyraud	75	69	74	73	291	
Andre Bossert	72	72	78	74	296	892
Lee Westwood	74	70	74	79	297	890

Collingtree British Masters

Collingtree Park ETC, Northampton, England
Par 36-36–72; 6,768 yards

September 14-17
purse, £650,000

	SCORES				TOTAL	MONEY
Sam Torrance	67	66	68	69	270	£108,330
Michael Campbell	70	67	66	68	271	72,210
Miguel Angel Jimenez	73	65	68	67	273	40,690
Vicente Fernandez	70	68	67	69	274	32,500
Iain Pyman	69	67	71	69	276	25,140
Andrew Oldcorn	67	70	68	71	276	25,140
Stephen Ames	68	67	71	71	277	15,815
Peter Baker	70	69	67	71	277	15,815
Colin Montgomerie	69	69	67	72	277	15,815
Peter Hedblom	70	69	66	72	277	15,815
Pedro Linhart	69	69	74	66	278	10,146.43
Jose Coceres	70	69	72	67	278	10,146.43
Santiago Luna	67	67	75	69	278	10,146.43
Greg Turner	69	71	69	69	278	10,146.43
Des Smyth	68	67	72	71	278	10,146.43
Mark James	67	67	72	72	278	10,146.43
Peter Mitchell	68	69	67	74	278	10,146.43
Miguel Angel Martin	67	74	71	67	279	7,962.50
Roger Chapman	68	72	70	69	279	7,962.50
Darren Clarke	73	62	74	70	279	7,962.50
Jose Rivero	70	67	71	71	279	7,962.50
Paul Moloney	71	69	72	68	280	7,020
Retief Goosen	70	69	73	68	280	7,020
Sven Struver	72	71	69	68	280	7,020
Jonathan Lomas	68	67	75	70	280	7,020
Steven Richardson	69	71	67	73	280	7,020
Joakim Haeggman	70	73	71	67	281	6,045
Jean Louis Guepy	66	76	70	69	281	6,045
Jamie Spence	70	72	70	69	281	6,045
Brian Marchbank	70	72	70	69	281	6,045
Ian Palmer	74	69	66	72	281	6,045
Mats Hallberg	66	73	74	69	282	5,330

	SCORES				TOTAL	MONEY
Andrew Coltart	69	74	69	70	282	5,330
Carl Mason	69	70	71	72	282	5,330
John Bickerton	72	69	72	70	283	4,745
Ross McFarlane	72	70	72	69	283	4,745
Christy O'Connor, Jr.	69	71	74	69	283	4,745
Mike Clayton	70	71	71	71	283	4,745
Robert Karlsson	69	69	72	73	283	4,745
Sandy Lyle	66	71	71	75	283	4,745
Jim Payne	69	68	75	72	284	3,770
Mike McLean	69	73	71	71	284	3,770
Marc Farry	72	69	72	71	284	3,770
Mats Lanner	70	73	71	70	284	3,770
Frank Nobilo	70	71	74	69	284	3,770
Ronan Rafferty	72	70	74	68	284	3,770
Ross Drummond	73	70	68	73	284	3,770
Nic Henning	68	70	72	74	284	3,770
Olle Karlsson	71	68	70	75	284	3,770
Christian Cevaer	69	73	71	72	285	3,055
Derrick Cooper	72	70	69	74	285	3,055
Seve Ballesteros	69	69	74	74	286	2,795
Tony Johnstone	70	71	76	69	286	2,795
Gary Orr	69	73	72	73	287	2,237.86
Paul McGinley	72	70	72	73	287	2,237.86
Phillip Price	73	70	72	72	287	2,237.86
Wayne Riley	71	70	75	71	287	2,237.86
David Carter	71	69	76	71	287	2,237.86
Adam Hunter	70	73	74	70	287	2,237.86
Peter Teravainen	73	70	76	68	287	2,237.86
Anders Sorensen	71	70	71	76	288	1,787.50
Peter Fowler	68	71	73	76	288	1,787.50
Barry Lane	71	72	71	74	288	1,787.50
Howard Clark	70	70	74	74	288	1,787.50
Rodger Davis	70	73	72	74	289	1,625
Dean Robertson	76	67	75	73	291	974
Gordon Brand, Jr.	72	70	79	70	291	974
Peter O'Malley	68	70	77	77	292	969
Rolf Muntz	75	68	73	76	292	969
Keith Waters	69	74	76	73	292	969
Mathias Gronberg	69	70	83	72	294	965
Domingo Hospital	69	67	67		DQ	963

Smurfit European Open

The K Club, Kildare, Ireland
Par 36-36–72; 7,159 yards

September 28-October 1
purse, £650,000

	SCORES				TOTAL	MONEY
Bernhard Langer	74	70	68	68	280	£108,330
Barry Lane	67	71	71	71	280	72,210
(Langer defeated Lane at second extra hole.)						
Jay Townsend	68	76	67	72	283	36,595
Colin Montgomerie	71	69	73	70	283	36,595
Costantino Rocca	69	75	70	70	284	27,530
Steen Tinning	69	75	70	71	285	21,125
Fabrice Tarnaud	68	73	69	75	285	21,125
Joakim Haeggman	71	70	71	74	286	16,250
Paul Lawrie	69	72	73	73	287	12,222

	SCORES				TOTAL	MONEY
Anders Forsbrand	70	71	72	74	287	12,222
Carl Mason	67	73	71	76	287	12,222
Dean Robertson	73	72	71	71	287	12,222
Tom Lehman	70	72	73	72	287	12,222
Peter Teravainen	73	75	70	70	288	9,162
Stephen Ames	69	71	77	71	288	9,162
Mark Davis	73	71	72	72	288	9,162
Mark James	72	70	74	72	288	9,162
Santiago Luna	71	72	73	72	288	9,162
Per-Ulrik Johansson	72	71	70	76	289	7,821.67
Miguel Angel Martin	73	73	70	73	289	7,821.67
Ian Woosnam	72	72	72	73	289	7,821.67
Sandy Lyle	70	70	74	76	290	7,410
Paul Broadhurst	70	72	75	74	291	7,215
Fredrik Lindgren	73	70	75	74	292	6,532.50
Russell Claydon	73	70	74	75	292	6,532.50
Sam Torrance	73	73	73	73	292	6,532.50
Lee Westwood	71	77	73	71	292	6,532.50
Mats Lanner	75	73	67	77	292	6,532.50
John Bickerton	79	69	73	71	292	6,532.50
Sven Struver	71	71	77	74	293	5,573.75
Jimmy Heggarty	76	69	70	78	293	5,573.75
Iain Pyman	73	70	74	76	293	5,573.75
Miguel Angel Jimenez	76	72	71	74	293	5,573.75
Christian Cevaer	73	75	70	76	294	4,745
Klas Eriksson	70	72	79	73	294	4,745
Andrew Coltart	76	69	79	70	294	4,745
Anders Gillner	76	70	70	78	294	4,745
Wayne Riley	70	75	74	75	294	4,745
Oyvind Rojahn	73	68	75	78	294	4,745
Jose Maria Canizares	74	73	67	80	294	4,745
Steven Bottomley	75	72	74	73	294	4,745
Michael Campbell	68	77	75	75	295	3,900
Roger Chapman	77	66	74	78	295	3,900
Jean Louis Guepy	74	72	72	77	295	3,900
Mats Hallberg	72	75	69	79	295	3,900
Olle Karlsson	74	72	73	76	295	3,900
Howard Clark	72	76	71	77	296	3,380
Michael Jonzon	73	73	77	73	296	3,380
Pedro Linhart	74	71	74	77	296	3,380
Mike Clayton	75	73	72	77	297	2,860
Christy O'Connor, Jr.	74	74	74	75	297	2,860
Ronan Rafferty	75	71	73	78	297	2,860
Phillip Price	71	73	77	76	297	2,860
David Carter	72	72	75	78	297	2,860
Steven Richardson	73	72	76	77	298	2,223
Mathias Gronberg	74	74	73	77	298	2,223
Derrick Cooper	74	72	72	80	298	2,223
David Gilford	72	72	72	82	298	2,223
Paul Way	72	74	72	80	298	2,223
Raymond Burns	72	69	74	84	299	1,917.50
Jonathan Lomas	74	73	76	76	299	1,917.50
Gordon J. Brand	71	72	77	80	300	1,787.50
Andrew Murray	72	73	76	79	300	1,787.50
Stuart Cage	72	74	76	79	301	1,690
Paul Curry	75	71	73	83	302	1,625
Domingo Hospital	75	71	72	85	303	973
Peter Hedblom	72	76	73	82	303	973
David J. Russell	76	72	76	79	303	973

Mercedes German Masters

Motzener See Golf & Country Club, Berlin, Germany
Par 37-35–72; 6,848 yards

October 5-8
purse, £650,000

		SCORES			TOTAL	MONEY
Anders Forsbrand	64	64	67	69	264	£108,330
Bernhard Langer	67	66	67	66	266	72,210
Russell Claydon	66	61	74	67	268	40,690
Per-Ulrik Johansson	64	66	71	68	269	30,015
Jesper Parnevik	68	64	70	67	269	30,015
Paul Eales	65	69	70	67	271	21,125
Joakim Haeggman	67	67	68	69	271	21,125
Heinz P. Thul	70	70	66	66	272	13,380
Jose Coceres	68	73	65	66	272	13,380
Richard Boxall	71	66	67	68	272	13,380
Sven Struver	69	71	65	67	272	13,380
Ignacio Garrido	70	66	67	69	272	13,380
Tom Lehman	67	67	70	69	273	10,200
Jarmo Sandelin	67	67	70	69	273	10,200
Silvio Grappasonni	68	71	67	68	274	8,217.78
Greg Turner	67	68	69	70	274	8,217.78
Peter Teravainen	69	69	69	67	274	8,217.78
Jim Payne	68	66	69	71	274	8,217.78
Sandy Lyle	67	72	66	69	274	8,217.78
Robert Allenby	71	67	71	65	274	8,217.78
Steven Richardson	69	68	68	69	274	8,217.78
Jay Townsend	68	74	66	66	274	8,217.78
Robert Karlsson	69	70	69	66	274	8,217.78
Malcolm Mackenzie	67	72	69	67	275	6,532.50
Peter Mitchell	68	64	71	72	275	6,532.50
Miguel Angel Jimenez	66	67	74	68	275	6,532.50
Vijay Singh	73	63	71	68	275	6,532.50
Retief Goosen	64	69	70	72	275	6,532.50
Peter Hedblom	67	66	75	67	275	6,532.50
Stephen Ames	69	70	67	70	276	5,655
Jose Rivero	69	70	70	67	276	5,655
Fredrik Lindgren	68	63	72	73	276	5,655
Ronan Rafferty	71	70	71	65	277	4,810
Klas Eriksson	64	73	70	70	277	4,810
Erol Simsek	74	64	67	72	277	4,810
Miguel Angel Martin	68	72	69	68	277	4,810
Andrew Coltart	69	71	68	69	277	4,810
Andrew Sherborne	69	65	71	72	277	4,810
Ross McFarlane	73	64	71	69	277	4,810
Sam Torrance	71	70	68	68	277	4,810
Santiago Luna	67	67	72	71	277	4,810
Andre Bossert	69	67	72	70	278	4,095
Andrew Murray	71	70	70	67	278	4,095
Ralf Berhorst	71	67	68	73	279	3,900
Peter O'Malley	70	70	69	71	280	3,575
Peter Baker	71	69	70	70	280	3,575
Mats Lanner	69	70	69	72	280	3,575
Brian Marchbank	69	68	69	74	280	3,575
Paul Way	71	70	72	68	281	3,055
Paul Curry	70	69	70	72	281	3,055
Paul Broadhurst	71	70	71	69	281	3,055
Fabrice Tarnaud	75	64	72	70	281	3,055
Vicente Fernandez	71	68	69	74	282	2,535
Jamie Spence	70	71	69	72	282	2,535

	SCORES				TOTAL	MONEY
Ross Drummond	71	69	70	72	282	2,535
Gary Orr	75	67	70	70	282	2,535
Michel Besanceney	73	69	72	69	283	2,028
Jean Van de Velde	70	72	72	69	283	2,028
Michael Campbell	74	67	70	72	283	2,028
Steen Tinning	67	70	71	75	283	2,028
Wayne Westner	71	70	70	72	283	2,028
Eoghan O'Connell	70	68	69	77	284	1,787.50
Gavin Levenson	67	73	69	75	284	1,787.50
David J. Russell	67	69	78	72	286	1,657.50
Mark Davis	69	71	72	74	286	1,657.50
Carl Mason	72	67	76	73	288	975

Toyota World Match Play

Wentworth Club, Surrey, England
Par 434 534 444–35; 345 434 455–37–72; 6,957 yards

October 12-15
purse, £650,000

FIRST ROUND

Lee Janzen defeated Katsuyoshi Tomori, 7 and 6

Janzen	5 3 4	5 3 4	4 4 4	36	2 4 4	4 3 4	4 4 5	34	70
Tomori	4 3 5	4 3 4	5 4 4	36	3 4 4	4 3 4	5 5 5	37	73

Janzen leads, 3 up

Janzen	4 2 4	4 4 3	4 4 4	33	3 4 3				
Tomori	3 3 5	5 2 4	3 4 5	34	4 4 4				

Bernhard Langer defeated Sam Torrance, 5 and 4

Torrance	4 3 5	4 2 4	5 4 4	35	4 4 4	4 4 4	5 4 4	37	72
Langer	4 2 4	4 2 4	4 3 4	31	3 4 5	4 3 4	4 5 5	37	68

Langer leads, 4 up

Torrance	5 3 6	4 4 4	3 4 4	37	3 4 4	4 3			
Langer	4 3 4	4 3 4	3 4 4	33	5 4 4	5 3			

Colin Montgomerie defeated David Duval, 2 up

Montgomerie	4 3 5	4 3 4	3 3 4	33	3 3 4	4 3 4	4 4 4	33	66
Duval	4 4 4	4 4 3	4 4 4	35	3 4 5	4 3 4	4 5 4	36	71

Montgomerie leads, 5 up

Montgomerie	4 3 5	5 2 3	4 4 4	34	3 C4	4 3 5	5 4 4		
Duval	4 3 4	4 3 4	4 3 5	34	2 3 3	5 3 4	4 4 C		

Costantino Rocca defeated Vijay Singh, 4 and 3

Rocca	4 3 4	3 2 4	4 3 4	31	3 3 4	4 3 4	4 5 4	34	65
Singh	4 3 4	4 4 3	4 4 4	34	3 4 4	4 4 4	4 4 4	35	69

Rocca leads, 3 up

Rocca	4 2 4	4 4 4	C4 3	X	2 4 5	4 3 4			
Singh	4 2 4	4 4 4	W4 4	X	3 4 4	5 3 4			

SECOND ROUND

Ernie Els defeated Lee Janzen, 4 and 3

Els	4 2 3	4 3 4	4 4 4	32	3 3 4	4 2 4	4 4 4	32	64
Janzen	4 3 4	4 3 4	4 5 4	35	3 4 4	4 4 4	3 5 4	35	70

Els leads, 5 up

Els	4 2 4	C3 4	4 4 3	X	3 4 4	3 3 4			
Janzen	4 3 4	W3 4	3 4 4	X	2 5 3	4 2 4			

Bernhard Langer defeated Nick Price, 1 up

Langer	4 3 4	5 3 4	5 4 4	36	2 3 5	5 3 4	4 4 4	34	70
Price	4 2 5	4 4 3	4 4 4	34	C 5 3	4 3 4	4 5 5	X	X

Match all-square

Langer	4 2 4	5 3 4	3 4 3	32	3 4 5	4 2 4	4 5 5	36	68
Price	5 2 4	4 3 4	4 4 4	34	3 4 4	4 3 4	4 4 5	35	69

Steve Elkington defeated Colin Montgomerie, 3 and 1

Elkington	4 3 4	5 3 3	4 4 4	34	3 4 3	4 3 4	4 4 4	33	67
Montgomerie	4 3 4	4 3 4	4 4 4	34	3 3 4	4 3 4	4 5 5	35	69

Elkington leads, 2 up

Elkington	4 3 4	C 3 4	4 3 4	X	2 4 4	3 3 4	4 4	
Montgomerie	4 2 4	4 3 5	4 4 4	34	2 3 4	4 3 5	3 C	

Costantino Rocca defeated Ben Crenshaw, 3 and 2

Rocca	4 3 4	4 4 3	4 4 5	35	2 4 4	3 3 4	3 5 4	32	67
Crenshaw	4 4 5	4 3 4	5 4 4	37	3 4 4	4 3 5	4 6 4	37	74

Rocca leads, 7 up

Rocca	4 2 5	4 4 4	4 4 4	35	4 4 3	5 4 4	4
Crenshaw	4 3 4	4 3 4	4 3 3	32	3 4 4	5 3 4	4

SEMI-FINALS

Ernie Els defeated Bernhard Langer, 1 up

Els	4 3 4	4 3 4	3 4 4	33	3 4 4	4 3 4	4 5 4	35	68
Langer	4 3 4	3 3 5	4 4 3	33	4 3 4	3 3 5	4 5 5	36	69

Els leads, 1 up

Els	4 3 4	5 3 4	4 5 4	36	3 3 4	4 3 4	3 4 5	33	69
Langer	4 3 4	5 3 4	4 4 5	36	3 3 4	3 3 3	4 5 5	33	69

Steve Elkington defeated Costantino Rocca, 3 and 1

Elkington	4 3 4	4 4 4	4 4 4	35	2 4 4	4 3 4	4 4 4	33	68
Rocca	4 3 4	4 4 4	4 3 4	34	3 4 3	5 3 4	4 5 4	35	69

Elkington leads, 1 up

Elkington	4 3 4	4 3 3	4 4 4	33	3 5 3	4 3 4	3 4	
Rocca	4 3 4	4 3 4	3 4 4	33	4 4 4	4 2 4	4 5	

FINAL

Ernie Els defeated Steve Elkington, 3 and 1

Els	4 3 4	4 3 4	4 3 4	33	3 3 4	4 4 3	C 6 4	X	X
Elkington	4 2 4	4 3 4	5 4 4	34	3 4 5	4 3 5	W 5 5	X	X

Els leads, 2 up

Els	4 2 4	5 4 4	4 4 4	35	3 4 4	4 3 4	4 4	
Elkington	4 3 5	4 3 4	3 5 4	35	3 4 4	4 3 4	4 C	

THIRD-PLACE PLAYOFF

Costantino Rocca defeated Bernhard Langer, 2 and 1

Langer	3 3 5	4 3 4	4 4 4	34	3 5 4	5 3 3	4 5	
Rocca	4 3 4	4 4 3	4 4 4	34	3 3 5	4 3 4	3 4	

PRIZE MONEY: Els £170,000; Elkington £90,000; Rocca £60,000; Langer £50,000; Janzen, Price, Montgomerie, Crenshaw £40,000 each; Tomori, Torrance, Duval, Singh £30,000 each.

LEGEND: C—conceded hole to opponent; W—won hole by concession without holing out; X—no total score.

Alfred Dunhill Cup

Old Course, St. Andrews, Scotland
Par 36-36–72; 6,933 yards

October 19-22
purse, £1,000,000

FIRST ROUND

NEW ZEALAND DEFEATED JAPAN, 2-1
Michael Campbell (NZ) defeated Hideki Kase, 68-73; Frank Nobilo (NZ) defeated
Tsukasa Watanabe, 71-75; Nobuo Serizawa (J) defeated Greg Turner, 72-73.

ZIMBABWE DEFEATED WALES, 3-0
Tony Johnstone (Z) defeated Mark Mouland, 73-75; Nick Price (Z) defeated Paul
Affleck, 67-70; Mark McNulty (Z) defeated Ian Woosnam, 69-74.

AUSTRALIA DEFEATED ARGENTINA, 2-1
Jose Coceres (Arg) defeated Greg Norman, 72-75; Steve Elkington (Aus) defeated
Eduardo Romero, 72-74; Craig Parry (Aus) defeated Vicente Fernandez, 70-71.

SPAIN DEFEATED ENGLAND, 2-1
Barry Lane (E) defeated Jose Rivero, 74-75; Miguel Angel Jimenez (Sp) defeated
Mark James, 73-77; Ignacio Garrido (Sp) defeated Howard Clark, 75-76.

SCOTLAND DEFEATED REPUBLIC OF CHINA, 3-0
Andrew Coltart (Sc) defeated Chen Liang-Hsi, 66-73; Sam Torrance (Sc) defeated Lu
Wen-Ter (75-81); Colin Montgomerie (Sc) defeated Chung Chun-Hsing, 71-80.

SOUTH AFRICA DEFEATED GERMANY, 2-1
Retief Goosen (SA) defeated Heinz P. Thul, 70-72; Sven Struver (G) defeated David
Frost, 73-74; Ernie Els (SA) defeated Alexander Cejka, 70-72.

IRELAND DEFEATED UNITED STATES, 3-0
Darren Clarke (I) defeated Lee Janzen, 71-73; Ronan Rafferty (I) defeated Ben
Crenshaw, 70-71; Philip Walton (I) defeated Peter Jacobsen, 72-73.

SWEDEN DEFEATED CANADA, 3-0
Jesper Parnevik (Sw) defeated Dave Barr, 70-77; Jarmo Sandelin (Sw) defeated Ray
Stewart, 72-73; Per-Ulrik Johansson (Sw) defeated Rick Gibson, 69-71.

SECOND ROUND

SOUTH AFRICA DEFEATED REPUBLIC OF CHINA, 3-0
Retief Goosen (SA) defeated Chung Chun-Hsing, 73-77; David Frost (SA) defeated Lu
Wen-Ter, 68-75; Ernie Els (SA) defeated Chen Liang-Hsi, 70-72.

SCOTLAND DEFEATED GERMANY, 3-0
Andrew Coltart (Sc) defeated Alexander Cejka, 68-70; Sam Torrance (Sc) defeated
Heinz P. Thul, 71-74; Colin Montgomerie (Sc) defeated Sven Struver, 72-73.

IRELAND DEFEATED CANADA, 2-1
Darren Clarke (I) defeated Rick Gibson, 69-73; Philip Walton (I) defeated Ray Stewart,
71-73; Dave Barr (Can) defeated Ronan Rafferty, 71-72.

UNITED STATES DEFEATED SWEDEN, 2-1
Peter Jacobsen (US) defeated Jesper Parnevik, 67-71; Ben Crenshaw (US) defeated
Jarmo Sandelin, 67-69; Per-Ulrik Johansson (Sw) defeated Lee Janzen, 72-72, first
extra hole.

ARGENTINA DEFEATED ENGLAND, 2-1
Vicente Fernandez (Arg) defeated Barry Lane, 68-76; Jose Coceres (Arg) defeated
Mark James, 73-74; Howard Clark (E) defeated Eduardo Romero, 68-72.

AUSTRALIA DEFEATED SPAIN, 2-1
Greg Norman (Aus) defeated Miguel Angel Jimenez, 67-68; Jose Rivero (Sp) defeated Steve Elkington, 70-72; Craig Parry (Aus) defeated Ignacio Garrido, 67-70.

WALES DEFEATED NEW ZEALAND, 3-0
Ian Woosnam (W) defeated Michael Campbell, 68-71; Mark Mouland (W) defeated Greg Turner, 71-74; Paul Affleck (W) defeated Frank Nobilo, 69-70.

ZIMBABWE DEFEATED JAPAN, 2-1
Tsukasa Watanabe (J) defeated Tony Johnstone, 71-73; Mark McNulty (Z) defeated Hideki Kase, 66-73; Nick Price (Z) defeated Nobuo Serizawa, 68-71.

THIRD ROUND

SPAIN DEFEATED ARGENTINA, 2-1
Vicente Fernandez (Arg) defeated Miguel Angel Jimenez, 68-74; Jose Rivero (Sp) defeated Eduardo Romero, 70-72; Ignacio Garrido (Sp) defeated Jose Coceres, 71-73.

ENGLAND DEFEATED AUSTRALIA, 3-0
Barry Lane (E) defeated Steve Elkington, 72-73; Mark James (E) defeated Greg Norman, 68-69; Howard Clark (E) defeated Craig Parry, 69-70.

WALES DEFEATED JAPAN, 2-1
Ian Woosnam (W) defeated Hideki Kase, 72-73; Tsukasa Watanabe (J) defeated Mark Mouland, 70-71; Paul Affleck (W) defeated Nobuo Serizawa, 69-71.

ZIMBABWE DEFEATED NEW ZEALAND, 3-0
Tony Johnstone (Z) defeated Greg Turner, 73-74; Nick Price (Z) defeated Frank Nobilo, 68-71; Mark McNulty (Z) defeated Michael Campbell, 70-72.

CANADA DEFEATED UNITED STATES, 2-1
Ray Stewart (Can) defeated Peter Jacobsen, 71-71, first extra hole; Rick Gibson (Can) defeated Lee Janzen, 72-73; Ben Crenshaw (US) defeated Dave Barr, 68-72.

IRELAND DEFEATED SWEDEN, 2-1
Jarmo Sandelin (Sw) defeated Darren Clarke, 67-70; Philip Walton (I) defeated Jesper Parnevik, 72-72, first extra hole; Ronan Rafferty (I) defeated Per-Ulrik Johansson, 68-71.

SCOTLAND DEFEATED SOUTH AFRICA, 2-1
Ernie Els (SA) defeated Andrew Coltart, 70-75; Sam Torrance (Sc) defeated Retief Goosen, 68-70; Colin Montgomerie (Sc) defeated David Frost, 69-71.

GERMANY DEFEATED REPUBLIC OF CHINA, 2-1
Sven Struver (G) defeated Chung Chun-Hsing, 68-75; Heinz P. Thul (G) defeated Lu Wen-Ter, 77-78; Chen Liang-Hsi (Ch) defeated Alexander Cejka, 68-70.

SEMI-FINALS

SCOTLAND DEFEATED IRELAND, 2-1
Andrew Coltart (Sc) defeated Philip Walton, 75-76; Colin Montgomerie (Sc) defeated Darren Clarke, 70-72; Ronan Rafferty (I) defeated Sam Torrance, 73-74.

ZIMBABWE DEFEATED SPAIN, 2-1
Miguel Angel Jimenez (Sp) defeated Tony Johnstone, 70-71; Nick Price (Z) defeated Jose Rivero, 69-70; Mark McNulty (Z) defeated Ignacio Garrido, 73-DQ.

FINAL

SCOTLAND DEFEATED ZIMBABWE, 2-1
Andrew Coltart (Sc) defeated Tony Johnstone, 67-71; Sam Torrance (Sc) defeated Mark McNulty, 68-70; Nick Price (Z) defeated Colin Montgomerie, 68-74.

	MATCHES WON	INDIVIDUAL GAMES WON (After Round 3)	PRIZE MONEY TEAM	PRIZE MONEY PLAYER
GROUP 1				
Ireland	3	7	£95,000	£31,666
Sweden	1	5	45,000	15,000
Canada	1	3	25,500	8,500
United States	1	3	19,500	6,500
GROUP 2				
Scotland	3	8	300,000	100,000
South Africa	2	6	45,000	15,000
Germany	1	3	25,500	8,500
Republic of China	0	1	19,500	6,500
GROUP 3				
Zimbabwe	3	8	150,000	50,000
Wales	2	5	45,000	15,000
New Zealand	1	2	25,500	8,500
Japan	0	3	19,500	6,500
GROUP 4				
Spain	2	5	95,000	31,666
Australia	2	4	45,000	15,000
England	1	5	25,500	8,500
Argentina	1	4	19,500	6,500

Volvo Masters

Valderrama Country Club, Sotogrande, Spain
Par 35-36–71; 6,819 yards

October 26-29
purse, £750,000

	SCORES			TOTAL	MONEY
Alexander Cejka	74	66	72	70	282	£125,000
Colin Montgomerie	71	72	69	72	284	83,400
David Gilford	74	68	71	72	285	42,225
Sam Torrance	73	71	73	68	285	42,225
Jose Rivero	75	68	70	73	286	23,680
Per-Ulrik Johansson	75	71	66	74	286	23,680
Bernhard Langer	74	68	71	73	286	23,680
Ian Woosnam	70	71	71	74	286	23,680
Anders Forsbrand	68	70	73	75	286	23,680
Howard Clark	73	70	73	71	287	14,900
Paul Eales	71	71	74	71	287	14,900
Peter Baker	77	70	70	71	288	12,375
Frank Nobilo	76	70	69	73	288	12,375
Costantino Rocca	74	70	71	73	288	12,375
Jesper Parnevik	74	70	70	74	288	12,375
Tony Johnstone	77	71	71	70	289	10,550
Mark James	74	73	68	74	289	10,550
Miguel Angel Jimenez	71	73	71	74	289	10,550
Andrew Coltart	75	72	71	72	290	9,525
Santiago Luna	73	74	71	72	290	9,525
Sandy Lyle	72	71	72	75	290	9,525
Jean Louis Guepy	72	72	71	75	290	9,525
Jose Coceres	69	72	78	72	291	8,900
Greg Turner	78	72	70	73	293	8,275
Peter O'Malley	75	70	75	73	293	8,275
Mats Lanner	74	74	72	73	293	8,275

	SCORES				TOTAL	MONEY
Jamie Spence	73	76	72	72	293	8,275
Michael Campbell	78	73	72	71	294	7,210
Andrew Oldcorn	76	73	73	72	294	7,210
Peter Mitchell	75	73	72	74	294	7,210
Sven Struver	73	70	70	81	294	7,210
Barry Lane	70	74	73	77	294	7,210
Wayne Riley	78	72	73	72	295	6,500
Darren Clarke	77	76	71	71	295	6,500
Ignacio Garrido	74	73	70	78	295	6,500
Derrick Cooper	79	72	71	74	296	6,500
Joakim Haeggman	77	72	77	71	297	6,050
Peter Hedblom	73	70	75	80	298	5,900
Russell Claydon	78	75	72	74	299	5,600
Paul Broadhurst	77	76	72	74	299	5,600
Michael Jonzon	75	69	77	78	299	5,600
Mathias Gronberg	75	76	73	77	301	5,225
Roger Chapman	72	74	71	84	301	5,225
Jay Townsend	80	72	75	75	302	4,925
Stuart Cage	77	80	73	72	302	4,925
Jarmo Sandelin	76	77	73	77	303	4,550
Philip Walton	76	77	72	78	303	4,550
Olle Karlsson	76	76	71	80	303	4,550
Robert Karlsson	75	77	76	76	304	4,250
Peter Teravainen	78	74	76	78	306	4,100
Paul Way	82	73	76	77	308	3,950
Mike Harwood	82	73	73	81	309	3,800
Robert Allenby	77	74	77 WD			3,575
Ronan Rafferty	DQ					3,575

Johnnie Walker World Championship

Tryall Golf & Beach Resort, Montego Bay, Jamaica
Par 35-36–73; 6,760 yards

December 14-17
purse, $2,500,000

	SCORES				TOTAL	MONEY
Fred Couples	70	67	71	71	279	$550,000
Loren Roberts	70	70	70	69	279	250,000
Vijay Singh	69	68	72	70	279	250,000
(Couples defeated Roberts and Singh on second extra hole.)						
Bernhard Langer	71	73	73	68	285	115,000
Mark Calcavecchia	72	70	70	73	285	115,000
Wayne Riley	66	71	76	75	288	85,000
Alexander Cejka	73	75	65	75	288	85,000
Phil Mickelson	72	72	72	72	288	85,000
Nick Faldo	74	75	72	68	289	74,000
Ernie Els	79	73	66	71	289	74,000
Paul Azinger	75	74	68	73	290	66,500
Peter Senior	77	70	71	72	290	66,500
Lee Janzen	75	73	74	69	291	64,000
Billy Mayfair	75	73	68	76	292	63,000
David Duval	72	77	70	74	293	62,000
Sam Torrance	77	75	67	77	296	60,500
Colin Montgomerie	75	72	72	77	296	60,500
Toshimitsu Izawa	80	71	72	78	301	59,000
John Daly	80	80	84	80	324	58,000
Anders Forsbrand	83	78 WD				57,000

Challenge Tour

Kenya Open

Muthaiga Golf Club, Nairobi, Kenya
Par 35-36–71; 6,676 yards

March 2-5
purse, £65,000

	SCORES				TOTAL	MONEY
James Lee	66	66	65	68	265	£10,500
Thomas Bjorn	64	68	67	71	270	5,495
Chris Williams	65	73	65	67	270	5,495
Jean Francois Remesy	71	66	65	69	271	3,170
Stuart Little	67	66	70	69	272	2,890
William Guy	70	66	68	69	273	2,367.50
Vanslow Phillips	67	68	68	70	273	2,367.50
Adilson Da Silva	69	68	70	67	274	2,090
Rob Edwards	69	72	69	65	275	1,707.50
Brendan McGovern	68	69	67	71	275	1,707.50
Jonathan Sewell	68	69	72	66	275	1,707.50
Russell Weir	70	69	69	67	275	1,707.50
Thomas Gogele	72	68	71	65	276	1,235
John Mashego	68	70	68	70	276	1,235
John Vingoe	67	69	72	68	276	1,235
Wayne Bradley	73	67	70	67	277	899.67
David Jones	71	67	69	70	277	899.67
Bill McColl	70	68	73	66	277	899.67
Stephen Field	68	71	72	67	278	720
Paul Friedlander	67	70	72	69	278	720
James Kingston	69	67	72	70	278	720
Frederik Larsson	74	66	70	68	278	720
Tim Planchin	70	68	72	68	278	720
Philip Harrison	71	66	71	71	279	638
Craig Maltman	70	68	73	68	279	638
Mikael Krantz	70	70	70	70	280	588
Robert Coles	68	71	70	72	281	564
Phil Horgan	71	70	68	72	281	564
Anssi Kankkonen	71	69	71	71	282	524
Magnus Persson	74	67	72	69	282	524
Ashley Roestoff	71	70	71	70	282	524

Canarias Challenge Tour

Las Palmas Golf Club, Gran Canaria, Canary Islands
Par 35-36–71; 6,221 yards

April 27-30
purse, £48,471

	SCORES				TOTAL	MONEY
Pedro Linhart	67	67	69	72	275	£8,660.85
Ignacio Feliu	66	71	69	70	276	5,770.43
Emanuele Bolognesi	70	71	65	71	277	2,520.02
Carl Suneson	67	70	67	73	277	2,520.02
Richard Walker	67	69	73	68	277	2,520.02
Tomas Jesus Munoz	65	74	68	70	277	2,520.02

	SCORES				TOTAL	MONEY
Michele Reale	69	73	69	67	278	1,788.31
Alfonso Pinero	71	67	69	71	278	1,788.31
Ian Garbutt	66	68	71	74	279	1,459.07
Miles Tunnicliff	69	74	65	71	279	1,459.07
Antonio Garrido	69	71	68	71	279	1,459.07
Eric Carlberg	70	70	70	70	280	1,119.43
Andrew Clapp	70	67	70	73	280	1,119.43
Simon Hurley	64	71	72	73	280	1,119.43
Magnus Persson	66	70	72	73	281	857.77
Thomas Bjorn	71	67	70	73	281	857.77
Per Nyman	72	68	71	71	282	684.48
Christian Post	69	70	71	72	282	684.48
Andrew Sandywell	69	73	68	72	282	684.48
Mikael Krantz	75	68	67	73	283	540
Eric Giraud	69	74	70	70	283	540
Diego Borrego	69	66	73	75	283	540
Manuel Moreno	68	75	67	73	283	540
Frederik Lundgren	69	70	71	73	283	540
Kalle Vainola	71	70	72	70	283	540
Jamie Taylor	69	73	71	70	283	540
Warren Bennett	69	69	73	72	283	540
Hans Karlsson	70	70	72	72	284	440.58
Vanslow Phillips	68	71	72	73	284	440.58
Massimo Florioli	70	70	69	75	284	440.58
Manuel Montes	70	69	73	72	284	440.58

KB Golf Challenge

Praha Karlstejn, Czech Republic   May 11-14
Par 36-36–72; 6,966 yards   purse, £61,728

	SCORES				TOTAL	MONEY
Eric Giraud	66	68	73	72	279	£10,043.38
Ian Garbutt	70	68	73	71	282	6,691.57
Ben Tinning	66	70	77	70	283	3,773.80
Richard Walker	69	71	74	70	284	2,785.14
Stuart Little	72	67	74	71	284	2,785.14
Marcello Santi	69	71	72	73	285	2,164.21
Tim Planchin	69	70	74	72	285	2,164.21
Olivier Edmond	70	67	75	73	285	2,164.21
Ricky Willison	70	72	74	70	286	1,495.06
Massimo Scarpa	69	70	74	73	286	1,495.06
Andrew Collison	69	71	74	72	286	1,495.06
Emmanuel Dussart	70	69	76	71	286	1,495.06
Thomas Bjorn	72	66	76	72	286	1,495.06
Stephen Field	69	69	77	71	286	1,495.06
Andrew Clapp	69	72	73	73	287	874.13
Benoit Teilleria	75	66	73	73	287	874.13
Quentin Dabson	71	72	72	72	287	874.13
Frederik Larsson	69	70	77	71	287	874.13
Kalle Vainola	71	72	73	71	287	874.13
Michele Reale	71	72	74	71	288	658.31
Massimo Florioli	70	71	76	71	288	658.31
Laurent Lassalle	66	70	77	75	288	658.31
Raymond Russell	73	69	74	72	288	658.31
Martyn Roberts	71	70	80	67	288	658.31
Warren Bennett	70	69	78	72	289	572.70

	SCORES				TOTAL	MONEY
Martin Sludds	71	69	78	71	289	572.70
Joakim Nilsson	74	69	77	69	289	572.70
Patrik Sjoland	72	71	73	74	290	510.91
Tierri Corte	71	70	74	75	290	510.91
Alan Hogg	73	69	75	73	290	510.91
Pehr Magnebrant	70	73	73	74	290	510.91

Compaq Open

Osterakers Golf Club, Stockholm, Sweden
Par 36-36–72; 6,334 yards

May 25-28
purse, £30,000

	SCORES				TOTAL	MONEY
Dennis Edlund	72	71	73	71	287	£4,873.05
Thomas Nielsen	70	70	74	76	290	2,538.90
Thomas Bjorn	69	74	78	69	290	2,538.90
Henrik Edin	75	73	76	68	292	1,462.50
Marcello Santi	73	74	71	75	293	1,240.20
Daniel Ageflod	74	73	76	71	294	1,092.49
Joakim Rask	73	74	73	74	294	1,092.49
Lars Tingvall	77	74	72	72	295	965.25
Simon Brown	77	70	72	77	296	788.29
Stuart Little	78	71	73	74	296	788.29
Stephen Field	78	70	76	72	296	788.29
Marcus Westerberg	75	72	77	72	296	788.29
Nicklas Fasth	73	78	71	75	297	599.63
Kalle Vainola	73	73	74	77	297	599.63
Gary Marks	72	73	77	76	298	482.63
Simon Burnell	78	72	73	75	298	482.63
Fredrik Jakobsson	74	75	72	78	299	366.21
Frederik Larsson	75	71	72	81	299	366.21
Niclas Johnsson	78	73	74	74	299	366.21
Vanslow Phillips	76	74	75	74	299	366.21
Frederik Andersson	75	75	75	74	299	366.21
Frederik Lundgren	75	76	71	78	300	318.83
Joost Steenkamer	75	75	77	74	301	282.75
Fredrik Plahn	77	73	74	77	301	282.75
Rikard Strangert	73	76	75	77	301	282.75
Tony Nilsson	75	74	76	76	301	282.75
Jesper Thuen	75	72	76	78	301	282.75
Matthew McGuire	78	72	76	75	301	282.75
Anders Haglund	79	72	76	75	302	247.17
Joakim Nilsson	73	74	77	78	302	247.17

Siab Open

Soderasens Golf Club, Stockholm, Sweden
Par 35-36–71; 5,532 yards

June 1-4
purse, £30,000

	SCORES				TOTAL	MONEY
Anssi Kankkonen	74	69	68	72	283	£4,873.05
Kalle Vainola	75	74	71	65	285	3,246.75
Dennis Edlund	71	74	70	71	286	1,646.78
Joakim Gronhagen	70	69	74	73	286	1,646.78
Per Nyman	73	75	69	70	287	1,141.73

	SCORES				TOTAL	MONEY
Joakim Rask	74	72	69	72	287	1,141.73
Per Haugsrud	68	71	74	74	287	1,141.73
Niclas Bjornsson	71	77	72	68	288	891.15
Johan Rystrom	75	73	69	71	288	891.15
Vilhelm Forsbrand	72	73	71	72	288	891.15
Inigo Moral	75	75	70	69	289	631.22
Mikael Lundberg	73	77	69	70	289	631.22
Fredrik Plahn	70	78	73	68	289	631.22
Johan Omander	73	74	72	70	289	631.22
Pehr Magnebrant	69	78	72	70	289	631.22
Per Jacobson	75	69	74	72	290	431.44
Raimo Sjoberg	69	74	73	74	290	431.44
Marcus Westerberg	71	79	71	70	291	355.39
Frederik Andersson	73	71	71	76	291	355.39
Johan Andersson	69	74	75	73	291	355.39
Thomas Nilsson	70	71	74	76	291	355.39
Peter Malmgren	74	75	74	69	292	297.18
David Tapping	74	74	74	70	292	297.18
Morten Backhausen	77	70	73	72	292	297.18
Frederik Lundgren	74	72	72	74	292	297.18
Frederik Larsson	71	74	74	73	292	297.18
Marcus Rosenlund	74	75	72	72	293	252.14
Joakim Nilsson	76	72	72	73	293	252.14
Ove Sellberg	73	74	74	72	293	252.14
Yngve Nilsson	73	72	74	74	293	252.14
Jesper Thuen	73	71	80	69	293	252.14

Challenge Chargeurs

Golf de Bondues, Lille, France
Par 35-36–71; 5,633 yards

June 2-5
purse, £61,728

	SCORES				TOTAL	MONEY
Rolf Muntz	65	69	69	65	268	£8,744.56
Eric Giraud	66	69	69	70	274	4,555.99
Heinz P. Thul	67	66	71	70	274	4,555.99
Warren Bennett	71	70	71	64	276	2,297.24
Thomas Bjorn	69	72	65	70	276	2,297.24
Martyn Roberts	68	66	68	74	276	2,297.24
Andrew Clapp	67	72	69	69	277	1,879.08
Francisco Valera	71	71	71	65	278	1,663.88
Ricky Willison	72	67	67	72	278	1,663.88
Marc Pendaries	70	72	70	68	280	1,411.94
Marco Durante	69	72	68	71	280	1,411.94
Antoine LeBouc	68	71	71	72	282	1,183.61
Quentin Dabson	72	64	74	72	282	1,183.61
Miles Tunnicliff	74	64	75	70	283	835.61
Massimo Florioli	72	68	73	70	283	835.61
Richard Walker	69	70	73	71	283	835.61
Benoit Teilleria	70	71	69	73	283	835.61
Matthias Debove	68	74	67	74	283	835.61
Ignacio Feliu	71	72	75	66	284	575.87
Massimo Scarpa	71	72	72	69	284	575.87
James Lee	72	70	70	72	284	575.87
David R. Jones	69	72	71	72	284	575.87
William Guy	68	68	76	72	284	575.87
Thomas Gogele	72	67	73	72	284	575.87

	SCORES				TOTAL	MONEY
Martin Sludds	72	70	64	78	284	575.87
Gary Marks	69	69	76	71	285	482.89
Matthew McGuire	69	71	72	73	285	482.89
Dominique Nouailhac	71	69	71	74	285	482.89
Marcelle Manieteka	69	72	73	72	286	437.40
John Vingoe	68	74	72	72	286	437.40
Daren Lee	75	68	70	73	286	437.40

Club Med Open

Margara Golf Club, Margara, Italy
Par 36-36–72; 5,667 yards

June 8-11
purse, £59,043

	SCORES				TOTAL	MONEY
Emanuele Bolognesi	70	64	69	68	271	£9,590.58
Olivier Edmond	66	68	68	72	274	6,389.88
Warren Bennett	68	70	70	68	276	3,240.99
Jean Francois Remesy	67	71	69	69	276	3,240.99
Patrik Sjoland	68	67	70	72	277	2,440.82
Ian Garbutt	68	70	73	67	278	2,150.11
Antonio Sobrinho	72	68	68	70	278	2,150.11
Nicolas Joakimides	70	71	67	71	279	1,753.86
Jamie Taylor	65	71	71	72	279	1,753.86
Dennis Edlund	68	69	70	72	279	1,753.86
Rob Edwards	73	69	69	69	280	1,485.22
David R. Jones	69	75	72	65	281	1,181.55
Renato Campagnoli	72	72	70	67	281	1,181.55
Robert Coles	70	69	71	71	281	1,181.55
Raymond Russell	67	73	70	71	281	1,181.55
Quentin Dabson	72	72	70	68	282	715.98
Christophe Bovet	66	70	77	69	282	715.98
Jean-Pierre Cixous	73	70	70	69	282	715.98
Massimo Scarpa	73	70	69	70	282	715.98
Carl Watts	68	72	71	71	282	715.98
William Guy	72	68	71	71	282	715.98
Daniel Chopra	71	68	71	72	282	715.98
Eric Giraud	70	69	69	74	282	715.98
Marcello Santi	72	70	72	69	283	529.61
Silvano Locatelli	70	74	70	69	283	529.61
Robert Huxtable	69	70	74	70	283	529.61
Paul Page	70	73	69	71	283	529.61
Roger Winchester	69	67	75	72	283	529.61
John Vingoe	68	70	73	72	283	529.61
Baldovino Dassu	70	71	70	72	283	529.61

Himmerland Open

Himmerlands Golf Club, Himmerland, Denmark
Par 36-36–72; 4,889 yards

June 9-11
purse, £30,000

	SCORES			TOTAL	MONEY
Thomas Bjorn	70	70	76	216	£4,873.05
Anssi Kankkonen	75	70	71	216	2,538.90
Nicolas Vanhootegem	75	71	70	216	2,538.90

(Bjorn defeated Kankkonen and Vanhootegem on first extra hole.)

	SCORES			TOTAL	MONEY
Marten Olander	76	70	71	217	1,170.59
Max Anglert	75	71	71	217	1,170.59
Per Nyman	74	74	69	217	1,170.59
Bruno Petit	74	72	71	217	1,170.59
Andreas Jernberg	70	69	78	217	1,170.59
Alan Hogg	75	71	73	219	820.95
Jens Nilsson	72	70	77	219	820.95
Ben Tinning	69	73	77	219	820.95
Soren Kjeldsen	76	75	69	220	659.59
Michael Welch	72	71	77	220	659.59
Fredrik Plahn	76	75	70	221	511.88
Mikael Krantz	73	76	72	221	511.88
Rikard Strangert	72	73	76	221	511.88
Ulrik Gustafsson	75	71	76	222	366.21
Johan Andersson	75	70	77	222	366.21
Daniel Fornstam	74	73	75	222	366.21
Robert Jonsson	72	77	73	222	366.21
Lars Logstrup	71	78	73	222	366.21
Richard Hussey	75	71	77	223	312.98
Jesper Thuen	74	76	73	223	312.98
*Soren Hansen	78	68	77	223	
Niclas Bjornsson	78	71	75	224	277.88
Jorgen Eriksson	77	73	74	224	277.88
Patrik Johansson	74	78	72	224	277.88
Simon Brown	74	77	73	224	277.88
Daniel Ageflod	73	74	77	224	277.88
Eric Carlberg	75	75	75	225	243.75
Kalle Vainola	75	73	77	225	243.75
Joakim Rask	72	78	75	225	243.75

Cepsa APG

Sotogrande Golf Club, Sotogrande, Spain
Par 36-36–72; 5,691 yards

June 13-16
purse, £58,165

	SCORES				TOTAL	MONEY
Fernando Roca	72	69	72	68	281	£8,121.75
Manuel Pinero	71	72	68	71	282	5,411.25
Santiago Luna	74	74	66	69	283	3,051.75
Alvaro Prat	71	71	75	67	284	2,252.25
Ignacio Garrido	72	70	70	72	284	2,252.25
Jose Rozadilla	74	70	68	73	285	1,896.38
Juan Pinero	74	70	72	71	287	1,745.25
Manuel Blanco	72	78	69	69	288	1,545.38
Diego Borrego	77	68	68	75	288	1,545.37
Antonio Garrido	74	75	69	71	289	1,365
Pedro Linhart	72	72	74	72	290	1,204.13
Angel Sierra	74	74	68	74	290	1,204.12
Francisco Valera	74	75	73	69	291	950.63
Manuel Moreno	74	74	73	70	291	950.63
Bernardo Solanes	71	74	73	73	291	950.63
Felix Ortiz	75	73	72	72	292	692.25
Jesus Maria Arruti	73	72	75	72	292	692.25
Tomas Jesus Munoz	72	74	73	73	292	692.25
Mariano Aparicio	74	77	72	70	293	589.88
Inigo Moral	76	73	70	74	293	589.87
Jose Canizares	78	74	71	71	294	531.38

	SCORES				TOTAL	MONEY
Manuel Ramos	73	75	74	72	294	531.38
Juan Quiros	77	75	69	73	294	531.38
Alfonso Pinero	73	76	74	72	295	470.44
Manuel Linan	75	71	74	75	295	470.44
Francisco Navarro	77	71	70	77	295	470.44
Manuel Velasco	72	72	74	77	295	470.44
Manuel Montes	74	72	76	74	296	413.16
Antonio Cortes	76	71	74	75	296	413.16
Jose Romero	73	70	77	76	296	413.16
Miguel Angel Martin	73	75	69	79	296	413.16

Italian Native Open

Garlenda Golf Club, Garlenda, Italy
Par 35-36–71; 5,454 yards

June 14-17
purse, £51,170

	SCORES				TOTAL	MONEY
Emanuele Bolognesi	66	77	70	68	281	£8,121.75
Massimo Florioli	70	70	70	71	281	5,411.25
(Bolognesi defeated Florioli at second extra hole.)						
Silvano Locatelli	70	70	71	71	282	2,744.63
Emanuele Canonica	68	70	72	72	282	2,744.63
Baldovino Dassu	72	70	72	70	284	1,902.88
Michele Reale	73	70	71	70	284	1,902.88
Alberto Croce	74	70	68	72	284	1,902.88
Giorgio Merletti	72	68	71	76	287	1,485.25
Renato Campagnoli	70	74	71	72	287	1,485.25
Alessandro Tadini	71	69	73	74	287	1,485.25
Giuseppe Cali	72	71	72	73	288	1,204.13
Gianluca Crespi	74	71	73	70	288	1,204.13
Pietro Molteni	72	72	71	74	289	1,048.13
Alessandro Rogato	73	75	73	69	290	950.63
Marcello Santi	77	72	73	70	292	763.75
Massimo Scarpa	75	72	72	73	292	763.75
Mario Tadini	71	67	79	75	292	763.75
Tierri Corte	72	71	77	73	293	606.13
Paolo Pustetto	73	73	74	73	293	606.13
Niccolo Bisazza	72	70	73	78	293	606.13
Giovanno Ciprandi	75	72	75	72	294	550.88
Federico Bisazza	76	74	72	73	295	495.30
Delio Lovato	75	73	71	76	295	495.30
Gianluca Pietrobono	68	74	75	78	295	495.30
Francesco Guermani	70	74	78	73	295	495.30
Alessandro Carrara	76	73	71	75	295	495.30
Stefano Betti	74	77	71	74	296	448.50
Roberto Bernardini	73	73	75	76	297	413.16
Stefano Pietrobono	74	72	74	77	297	413.16
Alain Vergari	70	78	75	74	297	413.16
Felice Crotti	75	75	74	73	297	413.16

Championnat de France Pro

AA St. Omer Golf Club, St. Omer, France
Par 36-36–72; 5,773 yards

June 15-18
purse, £50,239

	SCORES				TOTAL	MONEY
Eric Giraud	75	71	72	70	288	£8,121.75
Roger Sabarros	74	68	72	74	288	4,231.50
Frederic Regard	74	72	73	69	288	4,231.50
(Giraud defeated Sabarros and Regard at third extra hole.)						
Tim Planchin	74	69	76	70	289	2,437.50
Benoit Telleria	69	72	77	72	290	1,981.69
Nicolas Joakimides	72	74	74	70	290	1,981.69
Fabrice Honnorat	74	71	72	74	291	1,612
Quentin Dabson	74	70	73	74	291	1,612
Jean Francois Remesy	73	68	74	76	291	1,612
Romain Victor	70	76	75	71	292	1,365
Stephane De Marboeuf	73	71	74	75	293	1,101.75
Franck Aumonier	77	74	69	73	293	1,101.75
Emmanuel Dussart	73	73	76	71	293	1,101.75
Frederic Grosset-Grange	74	73	74	72	293	1,101.75
Jean-Pierre Cixous	76	74	71	73	294	763.75
Michel Tapia	72	75	76	71	294	763.75
Philippe Uranga	74	70	80	70	294	763.75
Matthias Debove	76	74	70	75	295	638.63
Claudio Muskus	71	73	74	78	296	576.88
Bruno Petit	73	70	81	72	296	576.88
Jean Pierre Sallat	70	77	76	73	296	576.88
Pascal Edmond	71	75	76	75	297	503.35
Stephane Lahary	74	71	77	75	297	503.35
Paul Brown	68	82	75	72	297	503.35
Marc Pendaries	75	73	77	72	297	503.35
Christophe De Aizpurua	77	75	74	72	298	455.82
Cyrille Duplessis	75	71	78	74	298	455.82
Jean-Yann Dusson	75	73	81	70	299	407.55
Stephane Chauffour	73	79	77	70	299	407.55
Olivier Edmond	72	76	80	71	299	407.55
Francois Lamare	74	76	77	72	299	407.55
Stephan Catherine	76	75	75	73	299	407.55

Nedcar National Open

Rosendealsche Golf Club, Arnhem, Holland
Par 36-36–72; 6,916 yards

June 21-24
purse, £22,451

	SCORES				TOTAL	MONEY
Rolf Muntz	71	74	68	72	285	£3,680.53
Joost Steenkamer	70	71	72	72	285	2,392.34
(Muntz defeated Steenkamer at second extra hole.)						
Alan Saddington	74	71	72	71	288	1,472.21
Chris Van der Velde	73	76	68	76	293	1,177.77
Willem Swart	72	76	78	69	295	966.14
Ruben Wechgelaar	76	75	72	72	295	966.14
Phil Helsby	69	78	81	68	296	742.24
John Woof	74	77	74	71	296	742.24
Tim Giles	74	76	77	69	296	742.24
Jonas Saxton	75	80	75	68	298	607.29
Brian Gee	76	77	71	75	299	533.68

	SCORES				TOTAL	MONEY
Allan McLean	76	71	80	72	299	533.68
Ruud Bos	75	74	77	74	300	460.07
Constant Smits Van Waesbe	69	72	84	75	300	460.07
*Robert Jan Derksen	80	76	71	73	300	
Roddy Watkins	76	79	75	73	303	404.86
*Niels Boysen	73	74	82	74	303	
*Rob Van Den Berg	76	81	76	71	304	
David Burnside	75	80	77	73	305	349.65
Wilfred Lemmens	77	73	77	78	305	349.65
G. McIlwain	79	76	78	72	305	349.65
*Alain Ruiz Fonhof	77	77	75	76	305	
*J. Germes	76	73	78	78	305	
F. Schulte	79	78	78	71	306	312.85
Cees Borst	81	75	77	74	307	290.76
H. Bensdorp	75	81	75	76	307	290.76
*M. Lafeber	78	78	80	71	307	
Alain Christiaens	77	78	77	76	308	279.72
Stephane Lovey	79	75	76	79	309	261.32
Iain Scott	77	76	77	79	309	261.32
D. Blok	75	74	81	79	309	261.32
Jan Dorrestein	78	79	76	76	309	261.32
A. Allen	80	77	73	80	310	242.91
*R. Buschow	74	78	82	76	310	
Joost Huurman	78	75	76	82	311	235.55
I. Forrester	79	80	76	77	312	224.51
John Balvert	75	80	80	77	312	224.51

Team Erhverv Danish Open

Simons Golf Club, Copenhagen, Denmark
Par 36-36–72; 6,780 yards

June 22-25
purse, £55,706

	SCORES				TOTAL	MONEY
Rob Edwards	74	72	64	71	281	£8,933.92
Magnus Persson	73	75	70	68	286	3,270.05
Anders R. Hansen	71	74	71	70	286	3,270.05
Gary Marks	72	73	69	72	286	3,270.05
Nicolas Joakimides	71	72	73	70	286	3,270.05
Inigo Moral	70	70	75	71	286	3,270.05
Stephen Field	75	75	66	71	287	1,773.20
Vilhelm Forsbrand	74	73	72	68	287	1,773.20
*Knud Jensen	73	74	67	73	287	
Joakim Rask	72	75	66	74	287	1,773.20
Stephen Hamill	78	72	69	69	288	1,383.53
Matthew McGuire	74	74	72	68	288	1,383.53
Thomas Bjorn	70	71	72	75	288	1,383.53
Per Nyman	76	71	73	69	289	943.80
Warren Bennett	72	75	70	72	289	943.80
Laurent Lassalle	73	72	72	72	289	943.80
Soren Kjeldsen	71	74	71	73	289	943.80
Carl Magnus Stromberg	71	69	76	73	289	943.80
Marcello Santi	75	75	70	70	290	651.55
Per Jacobson	72	78	69	71	290	651.55
Nigel Graves	74	74	72	70	290	651.55
James Lee	76	70	69	75	290	651.55
Jean Charles Cambon	74	74	70	73	291	563.06
David Fisher	73	74	76	68	291	563.06

	SCORES				TOTAL	MONEY
Patrik Sjoland	73	74	69	75	291	563.06
Arild Townhill	76	74	70	72	292	501.40
Anders Haglund	75	72	75	70	292	501.40
Henrik Nystrom	73	74	70	75	292	501.40
Jean Pierre Sallat	75	71	71	75	292	501.40
Rudi Sailer	75	74	71	73	293	418.95
Jesper Bjorklund	75	74	71	73	293	418.95
Paul Page	73	76	69	75	293	418.95
Hans Karlsson	75	73	73	72	293	418.95
Pehr Magnebrant	74	73	76	70	293	418.95
Romain Victor	73	74	75	71	293	418.95
Nicolas Vanhootegem	72	75	74	72	293	418.95
Max Anglert	72	74	74	73	293	418.95

Memorial Olivier Barras

Crans-sur-Sierre Golf Club, Crans-sur-Sierre, Switzerland
Par 36-36–72; 6,748 yards

June 23-25
purse, £34,261

	SCORES			TOTAL	MONEY
Simon Hurley	72	71	71	214	£8,784.77
Stefan Gort	74	73	68	215	5,856.52
Lothar Jahn	74	72	70	216	3,416.30
Renato Campagnoli	72	72	72	216	3,416.30
Juan Ciola	72	77	68	217	780.87
Kevin Carissimi	76	72	69	217	780.87
Emanuele Bolognesi	73	74	70	217	780.87
Silvano Locatelli	75	72	70	217	780.87
Massimo Florioli	77	70	70	217	780.87
Nicolas Kalouguine	75	71	71	217	780.87
Dimitri Bieri	72	71	74	217	780.87
Nicholas Leconte	72	76	70	218	414.84
Alberto Croce	74	73	71	218	414.84
Christophe Pottier	77	73	69	219	341.63
Steve Rey	78	70	71	219	341.63
Giorgio Merletti	76	71	72	219	341.63
Manuel Garcia	75	70	74	219	341.63
Ricky Willison	71	74	74	219	341.63
Michele Reale	71	71	77	219	341.63
David R. Jones	75	75	70	220	292.83
John Vingoe	77	73	70	220	292.83
Yves Auberson	75	73	72	220	292.83
Gianluca Pietrobono	74	74	72	220	292.83
Jesus Maria Arruti	68	73	79	220	292.83
Carlos Duran	74	72	75	221	292.83
Christophe Bovet	77	70	75	222	244.02
Patrick Kressig	71	73	78	222	244.02
Roger Winchester	75	76	72	223	244.02
Emilio Rodriguez	76	74	74	224	244.02
Jiri Janda	76	72	76	224	244.02

Neuchatel Open SBS Trophy

Neuchatel Golf and Country Club, Neuchatel, Switzerland
Par 35-35–72; 6,368 yards

June 30-July 2
purse, £33,171

	SCORES			TOTAL	MONEY
Nicolas Vanhootegem	66	66	68	200	£5,856.52
Michele Reale	64	67	71	202	3,904.34
Matthew McGuire	67	67	69	203	2,440.21
Andrew Collison	71	70	64	205	1,830.16
Frederik Larsson	73	66	66	205	1,830.16
Simon Hurley	69	69	68	206	1,342.12
Daren Lee	67	69	70	206	1,342.12
Ian Garbutt	70	68	69	207	1,073.69
Miles Tunnicliff	68	69	70	207	1,073.69
Marcello Santi	71	70	67	208	927.28
James Lee	71	70	68	209	727.18
Raymond Russell	71	67	71	209	727.18
Joost Steenkamer	69	70	70	209	727.18
Simon Burnell	65	72	72	209	727.18
John Woof	69	68	72	209	727.18
Richard Walker	73	70	67	210	440.86
Ben Tinning	70	72	68	210	440.86
Christophe Pottier	73	67	70	210	440.86
Stephen Field	68	73	69	210	440.86
David Higgins	70	69	71	210	440.86
Stuart Little	69	69	72	210	440.86
Stephen Pullan	72	72	67	211	356.27
Robert Coles	71	70	70	211	356.27
Olivier Edmond	74	68	70	212	328.61
Francisco Valera	74	68	70	212	328.61
Gavin Healey	69	69	74	212	328.61
Pehr Magnebrant	73	69	71	213	294.45
Marco Scopetta	74	68	71	213	294.45
Dimitri Bieri	71	71	71	213	294.45
Uli Zilg	70	73	71	214	270.86
Vanslow Phillips	73	69	72	214	270.86

Open Divonne

Divonne Golf Club, Divonne, France
Par 36-36–72; 6,600 yards

July 6-9
purse, £47,847

	SCORES				TOTAL	MONEY
Patrik Sjoland	68	66	66	69	269	£7,772.94
Nicolas Kalouguine	71	65	69	69	274	4,049.77
Christophe Pottier	65	73	64	72	274	4,049.77
Daren Lee	66	71	70	68	275	2,155.52
Stephen Field	71	65	71	68	275	2,155.52
Andrew Collison	67	71	71	67	276	1,610.81
Nicolas Vanhootegem	66	72	70	68	276	1,610.81
Anders R. Hansen	66	69	67	74	276	1,610.81
James Lee	67	64	71	74	276	1,610.81
Heinz P. Thul	70	68	73	66	277	1,153.58
Per Nyman	68	71	70	68	277	1,153.58
Stephane De Marboeuf	68	70	71	68	277	1,153.58
Jonathan Sewell	69	73	67	68	277	1,153.58
Miles Tunnicliff	67	73	70	68	278	775.66

	SCORES				TOTAL	MONEY
Tim Planchin	67	70	70	71	278	775.66
Simon Hurley	70	67	69	72	278	775.66
Carlos Larrain	70	70	65	73	278	775.66
Pehr Magnebrant	75	66	70	68	279	555.21
Jean Francois Remesy	66	73	72	68	279	555.21
Thomas Gogele	70	72	68	69	279	555.21
Carl Suneson	68	71	69	71	279	555.21
Marc Pendaries	67	69	72	71	279	555.21
Jean Marie Kula	69	72	72	67	280	480.56
Thomas Bjorn	75	67	65	73	280	480.56
Vanslow Phillips	69	72	71	69	281	436.24
Frederic Cupillard	72	71	69	69	281	436.24
Michele Reale	70	69	72	70	281	436.24
Roger Sabarros	73	68	69	71	281	436.24
Olivier Edmond	70	69	73	70	282	401.24
Ignacio Feliu	71	72	70	70	283	340.59
Eric Galardi	71	71	71	70	283	340.59
Eric Giraud	67	72	72	72	283	340.59
Christophe Muniesa	75	67	69	72	283	340.59
Andrew Sandywell	68	74	69	72	283	340.59
Ricky Willison	67	71	72	73	283	340.59
Carl Watts	70	70	70	73	283	340.59
Frederik Larsson	71	69	70	73	283	340.59
Raymond Russell	71	67	71	74	283	340.59
Frederic Grosset-Grange	65	74	70	74	283	340.59
Ian Garbutt	67	71	71	74	283	340.59

Volvo Finnish Open

Espo Golf Club, Espo, Finland
Par 36-36–72; 6,720 yards

July 7-9
purse, £30,000

	SCORES			TOTAL	MONEY
Fredrik Plahn	71	73	68	212	£4,873.05
Dennis Edlund	71	75	68	214	2,180.10
Magnus Persson	71	72	71	214	2,180.10
Robert Jonsson	68	73	73	214	2,180.10
Niklas Diethelm	69	71	75	215	1,240.20
Tony Edlund	76	73	67	216	1,137.83
Mikael Piltz	75	72	70	217	930.15
Mikael Lundberg	73	73	71	217	930.15
Kalle Vainola	72	70	75	217	930.15
Henrik Bergquist	71	76	70	217	930.15
Eric Carlberg	75	74	69	218	631.22
Matthew Hazelden	75	73	70	218	631.22
Johan Omander	74	69	75	218	631.22
Hans Karlsson	73	71	74	218	631.22
Henrik Nystrom	71	77	70	218	631.22
Joakim Nilsson	76	74	69	219	415.35
Vincente Danielsen	74	73	72	219	415.35
Juha Selin	73	72	74	219	415.35
Simon Burnell	77	71	72	220	346.13
Emanuele Bolognesi	72	75	73	220	346.13
Thomas Nilsson	71	76	73	220	346.13
Soren Kjeldsen	76	71	74	221	297.18
Jesper Kjaerbye	74	74	73	221	297.18
Morten Backhausen	72	78	71	221	297.18

	SCORES			TOTAL	MONEY
Ola Eliasson	72	74	75	221	297.18
Niclas Bjornsson	71	74	76	221	297.18
Marcus Norgren	76	71	75	222	264.72
Fredrick Mansson	74	75	73	222	264.72
Anssi Kankkonen	76	75	72	223	240.59
Raimo Sjoberg	74	77	72	223	240.59
Simon Brown	73	74	76	223	240.59
Erik Andersson	70	75	78	223	240.59

Open des Volcans

Golf des Volcans, Volcans, France
Par 36-36–72; 6,874 yards

July 12-15
purse, £53,029

	SCORES				TOTAL	MONEY
Thomas Gogele	72	67	67	68	274	£8,744.56
Per Nyman	69	68	66	72	275	4,555.99
Rolf Muntz	67	71	65	72	275	4,555.99
Dennis Edlund	69	68	66	73	276	2,624.42
Juan Pinero	70	68	69	70	277	2,133.65
Miles Tunnicliff	66	76	68	67	277	2,133.65
Frederik Larsson	70	69	70	69	278	1,879.08
Nicholas Leconte	71	68	69	71	279	1,663.88
Patrik Sjoland	71	71	68	69	279	1,663.88
Jesus Maria Arruti	68	69	70	73	280	1,411.94
Jean Francois Remesy	70	69	70	71	280	1,411.94
Marcello Santi	71	69	71	70	281	1,238.72
Daren Lee	73	68	67	74	282	851.06
Kalle Vainola	68	73	68	73	282	851.06
Jonathan Sewell	74	69	67	72	282	851.06
Emanuele Bolognesi	67	69	74	72	282	851.06
Dominique Nouailhac	68	69	73	72	282	851.06
Warren Bennett	70	68	73	71	282	851.06
Anssi Kankkonen	71	72	73	66	282	851.06
Carl Suneson	71	69	66	77	283	606.24
Vanslow Phillips	73	68	71	71	283	606.24
Ian Garbutt	70	69	71	74	284	551.13
Francois Lamare	71	69	71	73	284	551.13
Nicolas Joakimides	67	74	71	72	284	551.13
Steve Rey	68	68	71	78	285	490.77
Juan Ciola	68	73	70	74	285	490.77
Jonathan Hodgson	73	69	71	72	285	490.77
John Lawson	71	71	71	72	285	490.77
Roger Sabarros	70	68	69	79	286	437.40
Ramuncho Artola	72	67	74	73	286	437.40
Diego Borrego	72	70	73	71	286	437.40

Interlaken Open

Interlaken Golf Club, Interlaken, Switzerland
Par 36-36–72; 5,540 yards

July 21-23
purse, £48,780

	SCORES			TOTAL	MONEY
Thomas Bjorn	64	71	65	200	£7,927.53
Andre Bossert	68	68	67	203	5,281.84

	SCORES			TOTAL	MONEY
Heinz P. Thul	70	70	65	205	2,678.99
John McHenry	66	69	70	205	2,678.99
Simon Hurley	69	69	68	206	1,934.30
Frederik Larsson	67	71	68	206	1,934.30
Juan Ciola	70	69	68	207	1,703.51
Nicholas Leconte	72	69	67	208	1,449.73
Marcello Santi	72	68	68	208	1,449.73
Massimo Scarpa	70	70	68	208	1,449.73
Marten Olander	76	67	66	209	1,075.40
Carl Watts	71	71	67	209	1,075.40
Joakim Rask	70	70	69	209	1,075.40
Joe Higgins	67	74	68	209	1,075.40
Dominique Nouailhac	70	73	67	210	618.59
David Fisher	69	73	68	210	618.59
Fernando Roca	71	72	67	210	618.59
Andrew Clapp	70	71	69	210	618.59
Stephen Hamill	71	69	70	210	618.59
James Lee	72	68	70	210	618.59
Antonio Sobrinho	70	67	73	210	618.59
Kalle Vainola	69	74	67	210	618.59
Rob Edwards	66	72	72	210	618.59
Christophe Bovet	72	72	67	211	452.05
Stephen Field	70	71	70	211	452.05
Paolo Quirici	68	72	71	211	452.05
Ricky Willison	70	70	71	211	452.05
Stefan Gort	69	70	72	211	452.05
Stephen Pullan	74	70	68	212	371.75
Jesus Maria Arruti	71	72	69	212	371.75
Andrew Collison	72	71	69	212	371.75
Robert Coles	72	70	70	212	371.75
Anssi Kankkonen	66	76	70	212	371.75
Carlos Larrain	72	69	71	212	371.75
Michele Reale	71	69	72	212	371.75
Vanslow Phillips	70	70	72	212	371.75

Karsten Ping Norwegian Open

Bogstad Golf Club, Oslo, Norway
Par 36-36–72; 6,623 yards

July 27-30
purse, £60,000

	SCORES				TOTAL	MONEY
Stephen Field	73	66	69	67	275	£9,746.10
Andrew Collison	70	69	69	70	278	6,493.50
Miles Tunnicliff	70	70	71	68	279	3,662.10
John McHenry	70	69	69	72	280	2,443.84
Stephen Pullan	71	68	73	68	280	2,443.84
Diego Borrego	72	68	69	71	280	2,443.84
Patrik Sjoland	71	72	72	65	280	2,443.84
Lucas Parsons	72	70	71	68	281	1,930.50
James Lee	73	69	70	70	282	1,778.40
*Knut Ekjord	73	67	69	73	282	
Anssi Kankkonen	71	73	72	67	283	1,446.41
David Fisher	74	72	69	68	283	1,446.41
Nicolas Vanhootegem	71	71	73	68	283	1,446.41
Per Nyman	73	71	71	68	283	1,446.41
Michael Welch	75	70	72	67	284	1,082.25
Massimo Florioli	74	72	68	70	284	1,082.25

	SCORES				TOTAL	MONEY
Thomas Bjorn	73	70	69	73	285	727.59
Roger Winchester	73	70	69	73	285	727.59
Warren Bennett	72	73	69	71	285	727.59
Nicholas Leconte	72	71	70	72	285	727.59
Tim Planchin	74	70	70	71	285	727.59
Daren Lee	76	67	73	69	285	727.59
Carl Watts	71	68	72	74	285	727.59
Paul Gareth Simpson	70	76	71	68	285	727.59
Kalle Vainola	74	70	72	70	286	555.75
Max Anglert	76	69	70	71	286	555.75
Ben Tinning	72	70	72	72	286	555.75
Keith Waters	73	72	69	72	286	555.75
Antoine LeBouc	74	70	74	68	286	555.75
Daniel Chopra	74	72	70	71	287	481.16
Andrew Clapp	72	73	72	70	287	481.16
Wayne Henry	71	70	72	74	287	481.16
Nicolas Joakimides	72	71	74	70	287	481.16

UPS German PGA Championship

Wendlohe Golf Club, Hamburg-Wendlohe, Germany
Par 36-36–72; 6,616 yards

July 29-31
purse, £26,749

	SCORES			TOTAL	MONEY
John O'Flynn	71	69	70	210	£4,344.97
Erol Simsek	69	67	75	211	2,894.91
Patrick Platz	68	70	74	212	1,632.62
Simon Brown	74	70	69	213	1,089.50
Thomas Gogele	71	73	69	213	1,089.50
Howard Francis	74	67	72	213	1,089.50
Oliver Eckstein	68	74	73	213	1,089.50
Guido Tillmanns	74	66	74	214	860.65
Steve Chadwick	75	71	69	215	674.44
Richard Fries	75	70	70	215	674.44
Phil Gresswell	72	73	70	215	674.44
Martin Coup	71	71	73	215	674.44
Rainer Numd	69	70	76	215	674.44
Steve Marr	74	73	70	217	433.58
Stuart McGregor	71	71	75	217	433.58
Martin Pyatt	70	72	75	217	433.58
Uwe Venohr	70	72	75	217	433.58
Michael Elliott	74	72	72	218	324.27
Ulrich Eckhardt	75	69	74	218	324.27
Michael Terwort	69	72	77	218	324.27
Marc Amort	75	71	73	219	284.27
Ralf Berhorst	75	69	75	219	284.27
Carl E. Robinson	71	73	75	219	284.27
Uli Zilg	72	77	71	220	251.68
Lee Michael Spencer	74	71	75	220	251.68
Alan Hogg	72	71	77	220	251.68
John Brennand	72	70	78	220	251.68
Dirk Randolff	74	76	71	221	218.03
Alan Murdoch	74	75	72	221	218.03
Lothar Jahn	78	70	73	221	218.03
Sandy Walker	74	73	74	221	218.03
Uwe Haasmann	73	73	75	221	218.03

Audi Quattro Trophy

Eschenried Golf Club, Munich, Germany
Par 36-36–72; 6,657 yards

August 3-6
purse, £72,000

	SCORES				TOTAL	MONEY
Joost Steenkamer	70	63	69	66	268	£11,695.32
Diego Borrego	69	67	69	64	269	7,792.20
Marcello Santi	66	66	69	69	270	3,952.26
Juan Pinero	67	67	68	68	270	3,952.26
Olivier Edmond	65	68	71	67	271	2,976.48
Simon Brown	72	67	64	69	272	2,520.18
Raymond Russell	68	68	68	68	272	2,520.18
Jean Francois Remesy	70	69	66	67	272	2,520.18
Tim Planchin	70	64	68	71	273	2,134.08
Christophe Pottier	67	67	71	69	274	1,735.70
Magnus Persson	70	70	66	68	274	1,735.70
Anssi Kankkonen	68	71	69	66	274	1,735.70
Stephen Hamill	69	66	68	71	274	1,735.70
Simon Hurley	69	70	69	67	275	1,117.58
Miles Tunnicliff	66	67	75	67	275	1,117.58
Nicolas Joakimides	67	64	74	70	275	1,117.58
Oliver Eckstein	70	65	72	68	275	1,117.58
Warren Bennett	68	72	66	69	275	1,117.58
Peter Smith	68	71	67	70	276	783.90
Mikael Krantz	66	73	72	65	276	783.90
Daren Lee	69	70	64	73	276	783.90
David Fisher	72	68	71	65	276	783.90
Jonathan Hodgson	72	68	70	66	276	783.90
Jesus Maria Arruti	68	72	67	69	276	783.90
Simon Yates	72	69	68	68	277	645.84
Dominique Nouailhac	68	68	72	69	277	645.84
Joakim Rask	69	67	67	74	277	645.84
Massimo Florioli	72	69	67	69	277	645.84
Roger Winchester	68	70	71	68	277	645.84
Stephen Field	70	71	70	67	278	568.62
Andrew Clapp	67	71	73	67	278	568.62
Frederik Larsson	71	68	68	71	278	568.62
*Philipp Neels	69	72	66	71	278	

Rolex Pro-Am

Geneva Golf Club, Geneva, Switzerland
Par 36-36–72; 6,878 yards

August 3-6
purse, £48,780

	SCORES				TOTAL	MONEY
Carl Suneson	66	70	69	67	272	£6,246.95
Simon Burnell	69	71	65	68	273	3,904.34
Francisco Valera	66	65	72	72	275	3,025.87
Patrik Sjoland	71	70	70	68	279	2,318.20
George Ryall	68	69	70	72	279	2,318.20
Roger Sabarros	72	70	70	70	282	2,245
Gary Marks	67	72	73	70	282	2,245
Henrik Simonsen	66	75	70	71	282	2,245
Per Nyman	70	68	74	71	283	1,220.11
Martin Sludds	68	68	73	74	283	1,220.11
Jonathan Sewell	71	71	72	70	284	976.09
Alvaro Prat	73	72	70	69	284	976.09

	SCORES				TOTAL	MONEY
Christian Post	73	70	71	70	284	976.09
Rob Edwards	71	70	70	74	285	805.27
Jamie Taylor	73	71	67	74	285	805.27
Andrew Sandywell	72	69	70	75	286	732.06
John Vingoe	67	71	76	73	287	683.26
Emanuele Bolognesi	73	66	75	74	288	634.46

Esbjerg Danish Closed

Esbjerg Golf Club, Esbjerg, Denmark
Par 35-36–71; 6,941 yards

August 10-13
purse, £10,000

	SCORES			TOTAL	MONEY
Thomas Bjorn	73	75	64	212	£1,655.30
Ben Tinning	70	72	70	212	1,286.34
(Bjorn defeated Tinning on first extra hole.)					
Christian Post	70	72	73	215	997.17
Soren Kjeldsen	70	75	73	218	797.73
Soren Rolner	73	72	74	219	698.02
Anders R. Hansen	76	73	72	221	623.23
Rene Michelsen	71	74	76	221	623.23
Danny Jorgensen	76	75	71	222	548.44
Morten Backhausen	75	74	74	223	473.65
Jesper Thuen	72	77	74	223	473.65
Per Ove Moller	75	75	76	226	398.87
Lars Logstrup	70	78	79	227	378.92
Michael Jacobsen	76	72	80	228	358.98
Arne Tinning	71	80	78	229	339.04
Ronny Kert	75	75	83	233	319.09

Finnish PGA Championship

Tuusula Golf Club, Tuusula, Finland
Par 36-36–72; 6,829 yards

August 10-13
purse, £3,368

	SCORES			TOTAL	MONEY
Mikael Piltz	75	71	69	215	£808.30
Sami Wachter	70	75	71	216	623.06
Mikko Rantanen	73	73	75	221	454.67
Juha Selin	75	76	72	223	353.63
Erkki Valimaa	79	76	71	226	286.27
Timo Sipponen	75	77	75	227	235.75
Mark Galvin	77	78	73	228	185.24
Lassi-Pekka Tilander	76	79	73	228	185.24
Riku Soravuo	79	76	74	229	134.72
Jouni Vilmunen	77	81	73	231	50.52
Markku Louhio	76	79	76	231	50.52

Steelcover Dutch Challenge Open

Broekpolder Golf Club, Rotterdam, Holland
Par 36-36–72; 7,020 yards

August 17-20
purse, £60,000

	SCORES				TOTAL	MONEY
Warren Bennett	68	71	70	67	276	£9,746.10
Francisco Valera	71	70	69	66	276	6,493.50
(Bennett defeated Valera on second extra hole.)						
Massimo Florioli	69	73	69	67	278	3,662.10
Carlos Larrain	71	73	68	68	280	2,702.70
Thomas Gogele	68	72	70	70	280	2,702.70
Ricky Willison	68	73	70	70	281	1,943.37
Frederik Larsson	74	67	68	72	281	1,943.37
Andrew Collison	73	73	66	69	281	1,943.37
Stephen Leaney	72	66	72	71	281	1,943.37
Nicolas Joakimides	67	72	68	74	281	1,943.37
Ian Garbutt	71	71	74	66	282	1,148.27
Martin Sludds	67	68	73	74	282	1,148.27
Dennis Edlund	71	72	71	68	282	1,148.27
Benoit Telleria	74	70	69	69	282	1,148.27
Mikael Krantz	71	69	71	71	282	1,148.27
Tomas Jesus Munoz	71	70	71	70	282	1,148.27
Simon Burnell	71	74	68	69	282	1,148.27
Nigel Graves	74	68	73	68	283	696.15
Jean Francois Remesy	73	70	69	71	283	696.15
Marcello Santi	74	70	71	68	283	696.15
Roger Winchester	75	70	67	71	283	696.15
Tim Planchin	72	70	71	70	283	696.15
Lucas Parsons	72	70	74	68	284	592.80
Carl Suneson	72	74	68	70	284	592.80
Pascal Edmond	72	72	69	71	284	592.80
Jonathan Hodgson	70	72	69	74	285	546.98
Vanslow Phillips	73	73	68	71	285	546.98
Nicholas Leconte	71	70	72	73	286	482.63
Keith Waters	75	69	73	69	286	482.63
Eric Giraud	76	70	66	74	286	482.63
Ian Spencer	68	72	74	72	286	482.63
Ignacio Feliu	71	71	73	71	286	482.63
Fernando Roca	73	70	70	73	286	482.63

Toyota Danish PGA

Sollerod Golf Club, Sollerod, Denmark
Par 36-36–72; 6,570 yards

August 18-20
purse, £29,551

	SCORES			TOTAL	MONEY
Francois Lamare	71	67	71	209	£4,873.05
Magnus Persson	68	72	71	211	3,246.75
*Jesper Happel	69	68	74	211	
Stephen Pullan	71	70	71	212	1,831.05
Thomas Bjorn	68	70	75	213	1,280.18
Patrik Gottfridson	68	69	76	213	1,280.18
Jesper Thuen	67	74	72	213	1,280.18
Markus Rosenlund	75	70	70	215	827.78
Per Jacobson	74	74	67	215	827.78
Raimo Sjoberg	74	71	70	215	827.78
Rene Michelsen	73	70	72	215	827.78

	SCORES			TOTAL	MONEY
Anders R. Hansen	72	71	72	215	827.78
Rikard Strangert	68	77	70	215	827.78
Adam Frontal-Gay	67	77	71	215	827.78
Henrik Nystrom	77	69	70	216	448.50
Henrik Simonsen	75	72	69	216	448.50
Mark Stevenson	73	73	70	216	448.50
Marten Olander	73	72	71	216	448.50
Leif Nyholm	72	74	70	216	448.50
Anders Sandgren	69	74	73	216	448.50
Andreas Jernberg	74	70	73	217	331.50
Karl-Henrik Brink	72	73	72	217	331.50
Frederic Grosset-Grange	72	73	72	217	331.50
Vilhelm Forsbrand	76	70	72	218	296.40
Per Nyberg	69	74	75	218	296.40
Tony Edlund	69	72	77	218	296.40
Emil Madsen	77	69	73	219	246.03
Petter Skantze	74	74	71	219	246.03
Peter Bolle	74	71	74	219	246.03
Hans Karlsson	74	69	76	219	246.03
Jorgen Aker	73	73	73	219	246.03
Thomas Persson	73	73	73	219	246.03
Juan Sanchez	72	74	73	219	246.03
Vincente Danielsen	70	76	73	219	246.03
Peter Hendriksson	69	73	77	219	246.03

Coca-Cola Open

East Sussex National, Uckfield, England
Par 36-36–72; 7,081 yards

August 23-26
purse, £65,834

	SCORES				TOTAL	MONEY
Thomas Bjorn	70	70	69	71	280	£10,558.28
Fredrik Jacobsson	66	70	72	73	281	7,034.63
Diego Borrego	67	71	73	72	283	3,967.28
Magnus Persson	71	71	70	72	284	3,168.75
Stuart Little	70	71	75	69	285	2,473.74
Paul Gareth Simpson	71	73	69	72	285	2,473.74
Dennis Edlund	69	69	73	74	285	2,473.74
Massimo Florioli	73	70	75	68	286	1,856.89
Antoine LeBouc	70	74	72	70	286	1,856.89
Ian Garbutt	75	67	73	71	286	1,856.89
Vanslow Phillips	72	73	72	69	286	1,856.89
Andrew Sandywell	71	71	71	74	287	1,364.67
Patrik Sjoland	73	72	68	74	287	1,364.67
Miles Tunnicliff	71	72	72	72	287	1,364.67
John McHenry	75	70	70	73	288	952.21
Ralf Berhorst	76	70	71	71	288	952.21
Eric Giraud	72	72	73	71	288	952.21
Martyn Roberts	71	71	75	71	288	952.21
Carl Suneson	73	71	73	72	289	766.84
George Ryall	74	73	74	68	289	766.84
Jean Francois Remesy	72	74	76	68	290	666.71
Stephen Field	68	73	78	71	290	666.71
Andrew Clapp	75	72	71	72	290	666.71
Carlos Larrain	70	73	73	74	290	666.71
Dominique Nouailhac	72	72	74	72	290	666.71
Joe Higgins	75	72	75	69	291	564.04
Jamie Taylor	74	72	76	69	291	564.04

	SCORES				TOTAL	MONEY
Simon Hurley	72	70	74	75	291	564.04
Glenn Ralph	76	71	74	70	291	564.04
Carl Watts	71	76	72	72	291	564.04

Tessali Open

Riva dei Tessali, Taranto, Italy   August 30-September 2
Par 35-36–71; 6,518 yards   purse, £38,773

	SCORES				TOTAL	MONEY
Andrew Collison	70	71	68	70	279	£6,393.72
Jonathan Sewell	70	71	68	72	281	4,259.92
Nicolas Vanhootegem	67	71	72	72	282	2,160.66
Massimo Florioli	72	68	70	72	282	2,160.66
Raymond Russell	72	67	74	70	283	1,627.21
Martyn Roberts	76	72	69	67	284	1,492.89
Vanslow Phillips	73	73	71	68	285	1,269.02
Tim Planchin	69	71	71	74	285	1,269.02
Antoine LeBouc	70	70	70	75	285	1,269.02
Emanuele Bolognesi	71	72	67	76	286	1,032.36
Michele Reale	73	72	69	72	286	1,032.36
Stephen Pullan	69	73	72	73	287	826.40
Roberto Zappa	69	77	72	69	287	826.40
Roger Winchester	70	74	70	73	287	826.40
Anders R. Hansen	73	75	69	71	288	601.25
Morten Backhausen	72	75	71	70	288	601.25
Giuseppe Cali	72	72	74	70	288	601.25
Emmanuel Dussart	71	71	75	72	289	456.69
James Lee	73	73	69	74	289	456.69
Marcello Santi	73	74	73	69	289	456.69
Tierri Corte	74	72	68	75	289	456.69
John Woof	76	70	70	73	289	456.69
Massimo Scarpa	73	77	72	70	292	395.29
Paolo Pustetto	73	78	71	70	292	395.29
Matthew McGuire	77	74	72	70	293	353.07
Stephane Chauffour	74	76	72	71	293	353.07
Baldovino Dassu	73	71	75	74	293	353.07
Martin Sludds	72	72	70	79	293	353.07
Stefano Betti	79	72	70	72	293	353.07
Gianluca Pietrobono	79	73	69	73	294	310.86
Richard Hussey	78	71	68	77	294	310.86
Peter Alabaster	74	74	71	75	294	310.86

Perrier European Pro-Am

Three Courses, Waterloo La Marache, Belgium   September 7-10
Par 36-36–72; 6,135 yards   purse, £55,000

	SCORES				TOTAL	MONEY
Diego Borrego	71	74	71	63	279	£8,933.92
Jonathan Lomas	73	69	67	71	280	5,952.38
Miguel Angel Martin	70	68	72	71	281	3,019.09
Carlos Larrain	72	75	71	63	281	3,019.09
Per Nyman	71	71	70	71	283	2,093.16
Ove Sellberg	70	72	70	71	283	2,093.16

	SCORES				TOTAL	MONEY
Daniel Chopra	69	73	73	68	283	2,093.16
Stephen Field	70	73	72	69	284	1,571.22
Ian Garbutt	69	78	70	67	284	1,571.22
Andrew Murray	67	77	69	71	284	1,571.22
Vanslow Phillips	68	75	72	69	284	1,571.22
Ricky Willison	68	77	73	67	285	1,100.66
Thomas Gogele	74	74	70	67	285	1,100.66
Joost Steenkamer	68	77	72	68	285	1,100.66
Carl Suneson	71	74	68	72	285	1,100.66
Raymond Russell	73	73	70	70	286	790.97
Marcello Santi	70	73	76	67	286	790.97
Olivier Edmond	66	76	75	70	287	651.55
John Bland	70	74	71	72	287	651.55
Patrik Sjoland	72	73	73	69	287	651.55
Ian Spencer	69	77	73	68	287	651.55
Warren Bennett	75	72	75	66	288	536.25
Nicolas Vanhootegem	70	75	77	66	288	536.25
Francisco Valera	71	76	70	71	288	536.25
Dennis Edlund	72	76	70	70	288	536.25
Anssi Kankkonen	71	77	70	70	288	536.25
Jose Carriles	73	77	71	67	288	536.25
Antoine LeBouc	73	72	71	73	289	461.18
Rob Edwards	74	76	69	70	289	461.18
John Vingoe	72	76	72	69	289	461.18

Open de Dijon Bourgogne

Golf de Dijon, Dijon, France
Par 36-36–72; 6,753 yards

September 14-17
purse, £34,814

	SCORES				TOTAL	MONEY
Tim Planchin	69	69	69	70	277	£5,685.23
Matthew McGuire	70	67	70	70	277	3,787.88
(Planchin defeated McGuire on third extra hole.)						
Andrew Clapp	68	69	69	73	279	1,763.13
Massimo Florioli	70	73	67	69	279	1,763.13
Carl Watts	67	70	74	68	279	1,763.13
Ian Garbutt	69	73	68	70	280	1,327.46
Rob Edwards	69	74	71	68	282	1,221.68
Jean Francois Remesy	74	70	69	70	283	1,126.13
Miles Tunnicliff	70	69	70	75	284	882.47
Philip Talbot	72	70	68	74	284	882.47
Paul Gareth Simpson	68	75	69	72	284	882.47
Jean-Louis Schneider	68	69	73	74	284	882.47
Simon Hurley	70	69	73	72	284	882.47
Michael Welch	67	68	75	75	285	543.27
Jonathan Sewell	73	69	70	73	285	543.27
Stephen Field	67	74	71	73	285	543.27
Vanslow Phillips	73	72	71	69	285	543.27
Nicolas Vanhootegem	73	70	70	72	285	543.27
Antoine LeBouc	70	69	75	72	286	412.92
Franck Aumonier	72	73	70	71	286	412.92
Carlos Larrain	73	70	70	74	287	331.35
Jean-Pierre Cixous	73	72	74	68	287	331.35
Jean Baptiste Levet	72	71	69	75	287	331.35
Mikael Krantz	73	72	70	72	287	331.35
Oliver Eckstein	73	73	69	72	287	331.35

	SCORES			TOTAL	MONEY
Thomas Gogele	71	70 77	69	287	331.35
Frederic Regard	74	65 77	71	287	331.35
Stuart Little	70	72 74	71	287	331.35
Jonathan Wilshire	72	71 73	71	287	331.35
Nicolas Joakimides	71	70 71	75	287	331.35

Kentab Open

Frosakers Golf Club, Stockholm, Sweden
Par 36-36–72; 6,365 yards

September 15-17
purse, £29,250

	SCORES			TOTAL	MONEY
Per Nyman	68	72	73	213	£4,873.05
Anders Gillner	72	72	70	214	3,246.75
Fredrik Jacobsson	72	73	70	215	1,646.78
Magnus Sunesson	71	73	71	215	1,646.78
Ian Spencer	74	72	70	216	1,141.73
Scott Henderson	71	74	71	216	1,141.73
Jens Nilsson	68	79	69	216	1,141.73
Yngve Nilsson	71	70	76	217	965.25
Johan Selberg	76	74	68	218	889.20
Thomas Nielsen	75	70	74	219	786.83
Jesper Thuen	71	78	70	219	786.83
Markus Westerberg	77	73	70	220	600.36
Anders Haglund	77	71	72	220	600.36
Johan Annerfelt	76	74	70	220	600.36
Claes Hovstadius	75	71	74	220	600.36
Hans Karlsson	74	77	70	221	363.80
Johan Axgren	74	75	72	221	363.80
Matthew Hazelden	74	74	73	221	363.80
Johan Rystrom	73	76	72	221	363.80
Patrik Gottfridsson	71	78	72	221	363.80
Raimo Sjoberg	71	77	73	221	363.80
Joakim Rask	71	75	75	221	363.80
Fredrik Plahn	70	76	75	221	363.80
*Viktor Gustavsson	74	73	74	221	
Marcus Norgren	75	76	71	222	282.27
Tony Edlund	74	77	71	222	282.27
Stephen Chadwick	74	76	72	222	282.27
Frederik Andersson	74	74	74	222	282.27
Mikael Lundberg	76	74	73	223	241.32
Patrik Sjoland	75	74	74	223	241.32
Magnus Persson	75	74	74	223	241.32
Anders Sandgren	74	75	74	223	241.32
Juha Selin	74	75	74	223	241.32
Pehr Magnebrant	73	78	72	223	241.32

Eulen Open Galea

RSG de Neguri, Bilbao, Spain
Par 36-36–72; 6,868 yards

September 20-23
purse, £70,591

	SCORES			TOTAL	MONEY
Ben Tinning	74	70 67	70	281	£11,370.45
Kalle Vainola	71	71 68	72	282	5,924.10

	SCORES				TOTAL	MONEY
Diego Borrego	73	71	70	68	282	5,924.10
Manuel Moreno	73	72	71	67	283	2,987.08
Juan Quiros	73	69	71	70	283	2,987.08
Ricky Willison	72	70	71	70	283	2,987.08
Matthew McGuire	72	73	71	68	284	2,170.35
Joakim Gronhagen	71	68	72	73	284	2,170.35
Max Anglert	73	70	70	71	284	2,170.35
Michele Reale	72	71	74	67	284	2,170.35
Tim Planchin	74	70	70	71	285	1,472.84
Inigo Moral	72	73	70	70	285	1,472.84
Tomas Jesus Munoz	74	71	71	69	285	1,472.84
Jamie Taylor	77	67	71	70	285	1,472.84
Simon Hurley	74	70	71	70	285	1,472.84
Patrik Sjoland	75	70	67	74	286	1,006.69
Joost Steenkamer	70	71	72	73	286	1,006.69
Thomas Bjorn	74	70	73	70	287	812.18
Morten Backhausen	73	70	72	72	287	812.18
Eduardo Fernandez	71	69	74	73	287	812.18
Jean Charles Cambon	71	71	73	72	287	812.18
Stephen Field	71	75	72	69	287	812.18
Antoine LeBouc	71	73	69	75	288	611.77
Ian Spencer	67	74	72	75	288	611.77
Thomas Nielsen	73	73	73	69	288	611.77
Ralf Berhorst	69	74	72	73	288	611.77
Andrew Sandywell	72	74	72	70	288	611.77
Marc Pendaries	74	71	71	72	288	611.77
Frederik Andersson	71	72	72	73	288	611.77
Juan Pinero	71	73	73	71	288	611.77
Jose Buendia	71	71	76	70	288	611.77
Massimo Florioli	74	68	74	72	288	611.77
Stephane De Marboeuf	72	70	75	71	288	611.77

Lomas Bosque Challenge

Lomas Bosque Golf Club, Madrid, Spain
Par 36-36–72; 6,723 yards

September 26-29
purse, £29,841

	SCORES				TOTAL	MONEY
Per Nyman	71	69	67	65	272	£4,873.05
Manuel Moreno	73	69	66	68	276	2,180.10
Raimo Sjoberg	71	67	69	69	276	2,180.10
Simon Hurley	72	66	65	73	276	2,180.10
Tim Planchin	74	67	69	67	277	1,240.20
Juan Pinero	70	70	71	67	278	1,137.83
Ricky Willison	71	71	71	66	279	1,006.20
Manuel Alvarez	68	71	71	69	279	1,006.20
Alfonso Pinero	70	69	73	68	280	889.20
Andrew Sandywell	71	73	69	68	281	819
Warren Bennett	70	71	71	70	282	661.05
Thomas Bjorn	70	67	74	71	282	661.05
Jesus Maria Arruti	67	70	73	72	282	661.05
Frederik Larsson	68	73	68	73	282	661.05
Martyn Roberts	71	73	71	68	283	458.25
Kalle Vainola	68	73	71	71	283	458.25
Massimo Florioli	70	73	68	72	283	458.25
Andrew Clapp	73	69	72	70	284	383.18
Nicholas Leconte	73	71	72	69	285	339.30

	SCORES				TOTAL	MONEY
Miles Tunnicliff	72	71	73	69	285	339.30
Rolf Muntz	73	68	72	72	285	339.30
Fredrik Jacobsson	71	69	70	75	285	339.30
Jorgen Aker	70	74	75	67	286	301.28
Dennis Edlund	71	75	68	72	286	301.28
Manuel Linan	70	76	74	67	287	264.72
Francisco Valera	75	71	73	68	287	264.72
Mikael Krantz	76	69	74	68	287	264.72
Fernando Roca	73	72	71	71	287	264.72
Magnus Persson	72	73	70	72	287	264.72
Stephen Field	75	70	69	73	287	264.72

Swiss PGA Championship

Blumisberg Golf Club, Blumisberg, Switzerland
Par 36-36–72; 6,614 yards

October 2-4
purse, £14,178

	SCORES			TOTAL	MONEY
Steve Rey	74	69	72	215	£2,928.26
Dimitri Bieri	75	74	67	216	2,196.19
Carlos Duran	75	73	70	218	1,342.12
Tim Huyton	71	71	76	218	1,342.12
Gary Owens	74	71	74	219	951.68
Yves Auberson	71	72	76	219	951.68
Christophe Bovet	74	75	71	220	683.26
Alisdair Malcolm	76	73	71	220	683.26
Stephane Lovey	78	72	72	222	512.45
Gavin Healey	76	73	73	222	512.45
Lloyd Freeman	75	76	72	223	463.64
Marco Scopetta	76	73	75	224	414.84
Stefan Gort	74	73	77	224	414.84
Tony Price	73	76	75	224	414.84

Tunisian Open Challenge

Tabarka Golf Club, Tabarka, Tunisia
Par 36-36–72; 7,306 yards

October 4-7
purse, £70,000

	SCORES				TOTAL	MONEY
Ricky Willison	71	70	72	70	283	£11,370.45
Simon Hurley	69	72	73	71	285	5,924.10
Tim Planchin	69	72	74	70	285	5,924.10
Nicholas Leconte	71	74	70	72	287	3,412.50
Anders Hansen	76	75	67	70	288	2,893.80
Kalle Vainola	70	78	75	66	289	2,549.14
Robert Lee	70	72	77	70	289	2,549.14
Jon Robson	75	76	74	65	290	2,163.53
Ian Garbutt	72	75	71	72	290	2,163.53
Raymond Russell	79	69	70	73	291	1,911
Joakim Rask	69	78	73	72	292	1,685.78
Vanslow Phillips	74	74	73	71	292	1,685.78
Francisco Valera	73	77	73	70	293	1,399.13
Andrew Sandywell	74	75	75	69	293	1,399.13
Thomas Bjorn	74	70	72	78	294	1,126.13
Jonathan Sewell	76	73	71	74	294	1,126.13

	SCORES				TOTAL	MONEY
Morten Backhausen	74	74	76	71	295	875.31
Andrew Collison	76	75	73	71	295	875.31
Stephen Field	75	73	71	76	295	875.31
Miles Tunnicliff	74	71	72	78	295	875.31
John Woof	78	68	73	77	296	757.58
Patrik Sjoland	72	77	73	74	296	757.58
Marcello Santi	70	75	76	76	297	680.80
Martin Sludds	77	74	71	75	297	680.80
Mikael Krantz	77	73	71	76	297	680.80
Daren Lee	72	74	76	75	297	680.80
Uli Zilg	76	74	74	74	298	607.43
Dennis Edlund	76	76	70	76	298	607.43
Nicolas Vanhootegem	76	76	70	76	298	607.43
Simon Brown	76	76	75	72	299	539.18
Eric Giraud	77	75	77	70	299	539.18
Romain Victor	75	70	82	72	299	539.18
Olivier Edmond	75	77	78	69	299	539.18
Frederik Larsson	80	70	77	72	299	539.18

UAP Grand Finale

Quinta do Peru, Lisbon, Portugal
Par 36-36–72; 6,033 yards

October 12-15
purse, £60,000

	SCORES				TOTAL	MONEY
Francisco Valera	71	67	68	69	275	£10,000
Tim Planchin	71	68	67	70	276	6,660
Joakim Rask	70	68	70	69	277	3,756
Andrew Sandywell	70	69	70	69	278	2,626
Stuart Little	68	71	73	66	278	2,626
Juan Pinero	72	72	67	67	278	2,626
Patrik Sjoland	68	72	71	68	279	2,148
Miles Tunnicliff	68	74	67	71	280	1,902
Thomas Bjorn	70	72	70	68	280	1,902
Ricky Willison	73	64	72	72	281	1,546.67
Michele Reale	70	75	68	68	281	1,546.67
Nicholas Leconte	76	67	67	71	281	1,546.67
Dennis Edlund	75	70	66	71	282	1,230
Matthew McGuire	72	74	68	68	282	1,230
Fernando Roca	79	66	70	68	283	940
Emanuele Bolognesi	69	70	69	75	283	940
Frederik Larsson	71	68	70	74	283	940
Andrew Collison	73	73	66	72	284	746
Raymond Russell	72	66	72	74	284	746
Ben Tinning	71	72	70	71	284	746
Marcello Santi	72	70	69	74	285	678
Thomas Gogele	70	74	72	70	286	630
Stephen Field	72	71	71	72	286	630
Daren Lee	73	70	71	72	286	630
Simon Hurley	71	69	75	72	287	561
Per Nyman	77	71	69	70	287	561
Nicolas Vanhootegem	71	69	75	72	287	561
Magnus Persson	70	70	74	73	287	561
Rob Edwards	71	69	73	75	288	516
Rolf Muntz	73	73	73	70	289	498

Asia/Japan Tours

Thai International Bodharamik Thailand Open

Pinehurst Golf & Country Club, Bangkok, Thailand
Par 36-36–72; 6,851 yards

February 2-5
purse, $300,000

	SCORES				TOTAL	MONEY
Todd Hamilton	68	68	70	65	271	$50,000
Steve Veriato	70	66	67	68	271	33,330
(Hamilton defeated Veriato on second extra hole.)						
Lee Porter	70	69	66	69	274	18,780
Bjorn Nordberg	69	69	70	67	275	12,740
Mike Cunning	68	70	70	67	275	12,740
Rick Dalpos	69	69	65	72	275	12,740
Kazunari Matsunaga	69	68	70	69	276	9,000
Frank Edmonds	70	70	69	68	277	5,815.71
Kevin Baker	68	69	72	68	277	5,815.71
Sang-Ho Choi	68	69	72	68	277	5,815.71
Brandt Jobe	69	71	68	69	277	5,815.71
David Berganio	69	70	69	69	277	5,815.71
Bob May	67	69	72	69	277	5,815.71
Brian Watts	69	70	67	71	277	5,815.71
Veerawut Supavarangoon	70	71	69	68	278	4,132.50
Don Walsworth	68	73	68	69	278	4,132.50
Raul Fretes	68	71	70	69	278	4,132.50
Tom Pernice	70	70	68	70	278	4,132.50
Shoichi Kuwabara	68	73	71	67	279	3,516
Daniel Chopra	75	68	66	70	279	3,516
Boonchu Ruengkit	67	72	70	70	279	3,516
Scott Frisch	64	71	72	72	279	3,516
Rafael Ponce	70	69	67	73	279	3,516
Jerry Smith	70	70	71	69	280	3,135
Rick Todd	67	72	72	69	280	3,135
Brad Montgomery	70	69	70	71	280	3,135
Young-Il Kim	68	66	72	74	280	3,135
Periasamy Gunasagaran	70	73	69	69	281	2,782.50
Mark Strickland	71	66	74	70	281	2,782.50
Carlos Espinosa	71	70	68	72	281	2,782.50
Gerry Norquist	68	73	68	72	281	2,782.50

Sabah Masters

Sabah Golf & Country Club, Kota Kinabalu, Malaysia
Par 36-36–72; 6,969 yards

February 9-12
purse, $250,000

	SCORES				TOTAL	MONEY
Brandt Jobe	69	73	67	71	280	$41,650
Periasamy Gunasagaran	72	71	71	69	283	27,775
Marimuthu Ramayah	70	69	71	74	284	15,650
Lee Porter	74	72	73	67	286	9,837.50
Don Walsworth	74	71	70	71	286	9,837.50
Brian Tennyson	73	71	71	71	286	9,837.50

	SCORES			TOTAL	MONEY
Gerry Norquist	73	72	68	73	286	9,837.50
Gary Nicklaus	74	75	70	68	287	5,925
Daniel Chopra	76	70	70	71	287	5,925
Jim Rutledge	70	73	73	72	288	4,666.67
Pedro Martinez	75	69	71	73	288	4,666.67
Mike Tschetter	69	74	70	75	288	4,666.67
Greg Lesher	72	76	73	69	290	3,493.75
Danny Zarate	71	76	73	70	290	3,493.75
Jose Cantero	73	76	70	71	290	3,493.75
Eric Meeks	73	75	71	71	290	3,493.75
Jong-Duck Kim	73	72	74	71	290	3,493.75
Scott Frisch	79	68	71	72	290	3,493.75
Rick Dalpos	72	72	73	73	290	3,493.75
Lu Wen-Ter	74	70	69	77	290	3,493.75
Mardan Mamat	78	72	71	70	291	2,750
Robert Boldt	75	73	72	71	291	2,750
Nobuhito Sato	72	75	73	71	291	2,750
Craig Kamps	73	75	69	74	291	2,750
Jeev Milkha Singh	73	72	70	76	291	2,750
Antonio Barcellos	70	74	70	77	291	2,750
Don Fardon	71	72	76	73	292	2,387.50
Steve Flesch	72	74	72	74	292	2,387.50
Gustavo Rojas	75	72	70	75	292	2,387.50
Clay Devers	73	71	72	76	292	2,387.50

Dole Philippine Open

APO Golf & Country Club, Davao City, Philippines
Par 36-36–72; 6,709 yards

February 23-26
purse, $300,000

	SCORES			TOTAL	MONEY
Carlos Espinosa	69	74	70	69	282	$49,980
Olle Nordberg	74	70	73	67	284	33,330
Young-Keun Han	72	72	73	68	285	14,250
Felix Casas	74	71	68	72	285	14,250
Lee Porter	69	70	71	75	285	14,250
Kevin Wentworth	66	70	72	77	285	14,250
Manny Zerman	72	73	72	70	287	6,670
Eric Meeks	73	74	69	71	287	6,670
Pedro Martinez	69	76	68	74	287	6,670
Frankie Minoza	70	71	72	74	287	6,670
Jerry Smith	74	69	69	75	287	6,670
Robert Pactolerin	69	71	70	77	287	6,670
Bob May	70	74	75	69	288	4,980
Bob Mattiace	71	73	75	70	289	4,342.50
Frank Edmonds	74	73	68	74	289	4,342.50
Ray Cragun	72	74	69	74	289	4,342.50
Lee Lien-Fu	70	71	70	78	289	4,342.50
Todd Barranger	70	74	73	73	290	3,795
Steve Flesch	70	70	74	76	290	3,795
Brian Wilson	79	67	73	72	291	3,342.86
Jim Rutledge	71	73	74	73	291	3,342.86
Mike Tschetter	71	78	68	74	291	3,342.86
Chang Tse-Peng	72	72	73	74	291	3,342.86
Danny Zarate	72	71	74	74	291	3,342.86
Rob Moss	72	69	76	74	291	3,342.86
Scott Taylor	73	72	70	76	291	3,342.86

	SCORES				TOTAL	MONEY
*Antonio Lascuna	71	74	72	74	291	
John Jacobs	78	71	75	68	292	2,955
David Podlich	75	70	72	75	292	2,955
Matt Gogel	78	69	70	76	293	2,820

Classic Indian Open

Delhi Golf Club, Delhi, India
Par 36-36–72; 6,835 yards

March 2-5
purse, $250,000

	SCORES				TOTAL	MONEY
Jim Rutledge	69	69	74	68	280	$41,650
Bob May	77	71	69	67	284	21,712.50
Daniel Chopra	72	69	75	68	284	21,712.50
Rick Todd	72	72	72	69	285	10,616.67
Gaurav Ghei	71	72	73	69	285	10,616.67
Basad Ali	72	70	69	74	285	10,616.67
Eric Meeks	73	71	73	70	287	6,875
Gary Webb	73	70	70	74	287	6,875
Jerry Wood	75	71	74	68	288	5,300
Olle Nordberg	72	74	72	70	288	5,300
Mike Cunning	72	74	70	72	288	5,300
Ray Cragun	73	76	72	68	289	4,268.75
Jyoti Randhawa	70	75	73	71	289	4,268.75
Kevin Wentworth	74	70	70	75	289	4,268.75
Rob Moss	68	72	74	75	289	4,268.75
Chang Tse-Peng	75	74	74	67	290	3,257.14
Anthony Painter	77	73	72	68	290	3,257.14
Greg Lesher	77	70	75	68	290	3,257.14
Jose Cantero	71	74	75	70	290	3,257.14
Ali Sher	75	72	72	71	290	3,257.14
Steve Veriato	71	75	72	72	290	3,257.14
Raul Fretes	76	72	68	74	290	3,257.14
Rick Dalpos	75	73	74	69	291	2,783.33
Mark Strickland	70	76	76	69	291	2,783.33
Brian Wilson	72	72	75	72	291	2,783.33
Glenn Joyner	71	79	73	69	292	2,575
Uttam Singh Mundy	74	74	73	71	292	2,575
Jeev Milkha Singh	69	74	76	73	292	2,575
George Zorkic	75	73	75	70	293	2,318.75
Vivek Bhandari	75	72	75	71	293	2,318.75
Don Fardon	72	75	74	72	293	2,318.75
Scott Frisch	69	74	76	74	293	2,318.75
*Amit Luthra	71	75	74	73	293	

Benson & Hedges Malaysian Open

Templer Park Country Club, Kuala Lumpur, Malaysia
Par 36-36–72; 7,120 yards

March 9-12
purse, $250,000

	SCORES				TOTAL	MONEY
Clay Devers	71	69	67	69	276	$41,650
Kevin Wentworth	71	70	69	67	277	18,641.67
Daniel Chopra	70	71	69	67	277	18,641.67
Darren Clarke	67	70	70	70	277	18,641.67

	SCORES				TOTAL	MONEY
Frank Nobilo	69	74	69	67	279	9,675
Rick Todd	74	73	64	68	279	9,675
Jim Rutledge	67	75	72	66	280	6,450
David Podlich	69	72	69	70	280	6,450
Carlos Espinosa	72	66	72	70	280	6,450
Lee Porter	68	71	73	69	281	4,825
Michael Campbell	69	72	69	71	281	4,825
Brandt Jobe	71	70	72	69	282	4,350
Roger Wessels	73	73	68	69	283	3,933.33
Mark Roe	73	70	69	71	283	3,933.33
Danny Ellis	71	71	70	71	283	3,933.33
Lee Westwood	72	73	72	67	284	3,287.50
Bob May	72	70	73	69	284	3,287.50
Mike Cunning	70	74	70	70	284	3,287.50
Jong-Duck Kim	71	72	71	70	284	3,287.50
Steve Flesch	70	71	75	69	285	2,925
Nico Van Rensburg	73	71	70	71	285	2,925
Jerry Smith	68	74	71	72	285	2,925
Todd Barranger	71	74	72	69	286	2,716.67
Greg Lesher	71	73	71	71	286	2,716.67
Manny Zerman	71	74	69	72	286	2,716.67
Jose Cantero	70	77	75	65	287	2,425
Andre Cruse	76	69	73	69	287	2,425
Robert Allenby	72	72	74	69	287	2,425
Joakim Haeggman	71	75	70	71	287	2,425
Jerry Wood	73	73	69	72	287	2,425

Sampoerna Indonesia Open

Pantai Indah Kapuk Course, Jakarta, Indonesia   March 15-18
Par 36-36–72; 7,186 yards   purse, $250,000

	SCORES				TOTAL	MONEY
Jose Cantero	69	71	69	68	277	$41,650
Don Fardon	68	70	70	70	278	27,775
Frank Nobilo	74	68	68	69	279	15,650
Roger Wessels	68	72	70	70	280	12,500
Johan Tumba	76	71	67	67	281	7,740
Bob May	73	72	69	67	281	7,740
Gustavo Rojas	69	72	71	69	281	7,740
Gary Simpson	69	71	72	69	281	7,740
Gary Webb	69	74	66	72	281	7,740
Andre Cruse	74	70	72	66	282	4,666.67
Hale Irwin	70	68	74	70	282	4,666.67
Todd Hamilton	70	71	70	71	282	4,666.67
Blair Philip	76	71	67	69	283	4,037.50
Craig McClellan	70	70	73	70	283	4,037.50
Jim Rutledge	71	72	71	70	284	3,443.75
Eric Meeks	72	69	72	71	284	3,443.75
Dustin Phillips	70	71	71	72	284	3,443.75
Mardan Mamat	71	69	69	75	284	3,443.75
Brian Wilson	74	72	73	66	285	2,930
Glenn Joyner	68	73	78	66	285	2,930
Robert Boldt	71	73	72	69	285	2,930
Greg Lesher	72	70	73	70	285	2,930
Andrew Bonhomme	73	69	71	72	285	2,930
Gary Nicklaus	73	70	74	69	286	2,650

	SCORES				TOTAL	MONEY
David Podlich	69	73	72	72	286	2,650
Kevin Wentworth	72	69	72	73	286	2,650
Lee Porter	72	72	78	65	287	2,316.67
John Senden	77	70	70	70	287	2,316.67
Mike Cunning	73	72	71	71	287	2,316.67
Nico Van Rensburg	70	72	73	72	287	2,316.67
Danny Ellis	70	70	74	73	287	2,316.67
Raul Fretes	71	73	69	74	287	2,316.67

Sempati Bali Open

Bali Golf & Country Club, Denpasar, Indonesia March 22-25
Par 36-36–72; 6,849 yards purse, $250,000

	SCORES				TOTAL	MONEY
Brandt Jobe	66	72	66	69	273	$41,650
Lin Keng-Chi	71	68	63	73	275	27,775
Roger Wessels	72	67	69	69	277	12,916.67
Glenn Joyner	67	67	72	71	277	12,916.67
Eric Meeks	66	67	71	73	277	12,916.67
Bob May	69	67	71	71	278	7,500
Kevin Wentworth	69	65	73	71	278	7,500
Jong-Duck Kim	71	64	71	72	278	7,500
Felix Casas	67	75	70	67	279	5,300
Michael Welch	70	68	69	72	279	5,300
John Kernohan	69	70	72	69	280	3,856.25
Anthony Painter	67	72	72	69	280	3,856.25
Steve Veriato	70	68	73	69	280	3,856.25
Dominique Boulet	69	68	72	71	280	3,856.25
Jim Rutledge	69	68	72	71	280	3,856.25
Norikazu Kawakami	71	70	67	72	280	3,856.25
Brian Tennyson	69	71	68	72	280	3,856.25
Daniel Chopra	67	71	70	72	280	3,856.25
Rick Todd	72	69	70	70	281	2,825
Gustavo Rojas	70	70	71	70	281	2,825
Jose Cantero	67	72	72	70	281	2,825
John Senden	70	68	73	70	281	2,825
Nico Van Rensburg	71	69	70	71	281	2,825
Stephen Leaney	68	70	72	71	281	2,825
Carlos Espinosa	72	68	69	72	281	2,825
Lu Wen-Ter	70	71	67	73	281	2,825
Raul Fretes	71	70	70	71	282	2,387.50
Robert Boldt	68	71	71	72	282	2,387.50
Jerry Smith	67	71	72	72	282	2,387.50
Todd Barranger	72	69	68	73	282	2,387.50

Rolex Masters

Singapore Island Club, Bukit Course, Singapore March 30-April 2
Par 35-36–71; 6,674 yards purse, $250,000

	SCORES				TOTAL	MONEY
Ron Wuensche	66	68	69	66	269	$41,650
Bob May	69	67	68	68	272	27,775
Brandt Jobe	71	68	69	67	275	15,650

	SCORES				TOTAL	MONEY
Jim Rutledge	72	68	71	65	276	10,616.67
John Kernohan	68	66	71	71	276	10,616.67
Nick Goetze	69	69	66	72	276	10,616.67
Jerry Smith	69	71	69	68	277	6,875
Roger Wessels	71	65	68	73	277	6,875
Greg Lesher	70	70	72	66	278	4,900
Blair Philip	70	72	66	70	278	4,900
Antonio Barcellos	67	73	68	70	278	4,900
Pedro Martinez	68	70	70	70	278	4,900
Steve Flesch	72	71	70	66	279	3,825
Danny Cabajar	69	72	69	69	279	3,825
Johan Tumba	67	69	71	72	279	3,825
Per Haugsrud	70	66	70	73	279	3,825
Lu Wen-Ter	71	71	68	70	280	3,275
Jerry Wood	70	68	69	73	280	3,275
Steve Scahill	70	70	73	68	281	2,930
Chou Hung-Nan	68	71	74	68	281	2,930
Matt Gogel	70	73	69	69	281	2,930
Felix Casas	67	71	74	69	281	2,930
Eric Meeks	72	70	69	70	281	2,930
Manny Zerman	73	68	71	70	282	2,575
Mardan Mamat	69	68	74	71	282	2,575
Carlos Espinosa	70	70	70	72	282	2,575
Mohammed Ali Kadir	70	69	71	72	282	2,575
Young Nam	69	68	71	74	282	2,575
David Podlich	69	73	71	70	283	2,312.50
Gary Simpson	69	71	72	71	283	2,312.50

Chin Fong Republic of China Open

Tong Hwa Golf & Country Club, Taipei, Taiwan
Par 36-36–72; 7,165 yards
(Third round cancelled — heavy rains.)

April 6-9
purse, $300,000

	SCORES			TOTAL	MONEY
Daniel Chopra	73	65	70	208	$50,000
Hsieh Chin-Sheng	69	70	70	209	32,200
Raul Fretes	72	68	71	211	15,000
Chang Tse-Peng	68	72	71	211	15,000
Nico Van Rensburg	67	72	72	211	15,000
*Kao Bo-Song	71	73	68	212	
Yu Chin-Han	71	73	69	213	7,700
Manny Zerman	71	72	70	213	7,700
Jim Rutledge	72	70	71	213	7,700
Bob May	71	69	73	213	7,700
Mike Tschetter	70	70	73	213	7,700
Lin Chie-Hsiang	73	72	69	214	4,948
Kevin Wentworth	74	70	70	214	4,948
Robert Boldt	73	71	70	214	4,948
Greg Lesher	72	70	72	214	4,948
George Zorkic	75	69	71	215	4,190
Chen Tze-Chung	70	74	71	215	4,190
Ron Wuensche	74	71	71	216	3,465
Bob Mattiace	73	70	73	216	3,465
Jerry Wood	71	72	73	216	3,465
Shen Chung-Shyang	73	69	74	216	3,465
Max Stevens	70	72	74	216	3,465

	SCORES	TOTAL	MONEY
Glenn Joyner	69 73 74	216	3,465
Nick Goetze	70 71 75	216	3,465
Anthony Painter	73 67 76	216	3,465
Andre Cruse	77 70 70	217	2,769
Chen Tze-Ming	76 71 70	217	2,769
Matt Gogel	75 71 71	217	2,769
Olle Nordberg	74 72 71	217	2,769
Philip Jonas	76 68 73	217	2,769
Ken Mattiace	73 71 73	217	2,769
Brandt Jobe	71 72 74	217	2,769
Michael Welch	71 70 76	217	2,769

Maekyung Bando Fashion Korean Open

Nam Seoul Country Club, Seoul, Korea   April 13-16
Par 36-36–72; 6,923 yards   purse, $400,000

	SCORES			TOTAL	MONEY
Brandt Jobe	73	72 66 69		280	$66,640
Sang-Ho Choi	72	72 70 70		284	44,440
Hyung-Soo Lim	71	68 73 73		285	25,040
You-Hyun Kwak	69	74 71 72		286	14,592
Jong-Duck Kim	73	69 71 73		286	14,592
Brian Tennyson	70	71 72 73		286	14,592
Eric Meeks	73	66 73 74		286	14,592
Rick Todd	73	71 67 75		286	14,592
Rob Moss	73	73 70 71		287	8,480
Kevin Wentworth	68	67 76 76		287	8,480
Clay Devers	76	72 72 68		288	7,200
Suk-No Kim	75	71 69 73		288	7,200
Mike Cunning	73	73 72 71		289	6,120
Tony Christie	71	72 74 72		289	6,120
Ken Mattiace	70	72 73 74		289	6,120
Bob May	70	72 72 75		289	6,120
Zaw Moe	72	75 73 70		290	4,984
Hong-Sik Kim	73	75 70 72		290	4,984
Scott Dunlap	74	70 72 74		290	4,984
Kwang-Soo Choi	74	69 72 75		290	4,984
Yong-Jin Shin	71	68 72 79		290	4,984
Philip Jonas	76	72 72 71		291	4,286.67
Do-Man Jung	74	73 73 71		291	4,286.67
Wan-Tae Kim	73	74 73 71		291	4,286.67
Nam-Sin Park	72	71 76 72		291	4,286.67
Jeev Milkha Singh	77	71 70 73		291	4,286.67
Oh-Chul Kwon	69	71 75 76		291	4,286.67
Gerry Norquist	71	71 76 74		292	3,760
Don Fardon	71	73 72 76		292	3,760
Olle Nordberg	71	72 73 76		292	3,760

Volvo China Open

Beijing International Golf Club, Beijing
Par 36-36–72; 7,120 yards

April 27-30
purse, $400,000

	SCORES				TOTAL	MONEY
Raul Fretes	74	67	68	68	277	$72,000
Lai Ying-Juh	70	69	71	70	280	42,000
Zhang Lian-Wei	70	72	71	69	282	28,800
Lin Keng-Chi	66	71	77	71	285	14,966.67
Ray Cragun	72	72	70	71	285	14,966.67
Rob Moss	73	73	72	67	285	14,966.67
M. Ramayah	73	70	75	67	285	14,966.67
Daniel Chopra	73	72	72	68	285	14,966.67
Matt Gogel	72	71	70	72	285	14,966.67
Manny Zerman	70	73	73	70	286	9,800
Tony Maloney	72	71	69	74	286	9,800
Mike Cunning	72	73	70	71	286	9,800
Steve Conran	68	73	77	69	287	7,050
Glenn Joyner	73	73	70	71	287	7,050
Wang Ter-Chang	71	72	75	69	287	7,050
Jeff Wagner	77	71	72	67	287	7,050
Jong-Duck Kim	72	76	72	68	288	4,936
Phil Jonas	69	71	77	71	288	4,936
Jeev Milkha Singh	75	72	75	66	288	4,936
Jim Rutledge	74	72	74	68	288	4,936
Lu Chien-Soon	73	69	73	73	288	4,936
Kevin Wentworth	77	73	67	72	289	4,360
Young-Keun Han	77	72	71	69	289	4,360
Greg Lesher	75	74	72	69	290	3,826.67
Lu Wen-Ter	77	72	72	69	290	3,826.67
Zaw Moe	71	71	77	71	290	3,826.67
Eric Meeks	73	73	75	70	291	3,280
Gerry Norquist	77	72	73	69	291	3,280
John Kernohan	75	72	73	71	291	3,280
Gustavo Rojas	71	72	74	74	291	3,280

Volvo Asian Masters

Sunrise Golf & Country Club, Taoyuan, Taiwan
Par 36-36–72; 6,922 yards

October 12-15
purse, $400,000

	SCORES				TOTAL	MONEY
Corey Pavin	72	66	67	69	274	$66,640
Isao Aoki	75	69	68	71	283	44,400
Rick Todd	76	71	72	72	291	25,040
Lin Keng-Chi	76	71	74	72	293	18,480
Yuan Ching-Chi	73	77	70	73	293	18,480
Chen Liang-Hsi	81	72	70	71	294	13,000
Craig Jones	72	77	73	72	294	13,000
David Smail	77	78	70	70	295	9,480
Sang-Ho Choi	77	76	70	72	295	9,480
Hsieh Yu-Shu	73	73	75	75	296	8,000
Terry Gale	78	76	74	69	297	7,440
Wang Ter-Chang	80	75	74	69	298	6,460
Chang Tse-Peng	81	72	75	70	298	6,460
Kuo Chie-Hsiung	73	76	72	77	298	6,460
Chen Tsang-Ter	74	74	72	78	298	6,460

	SCORES				TOTAL	MONEY
Chung Chun-Hsing	74	78	74	73	299	5,460
Li Wen-Sheng	74	76	72	77	299	5,460
Evan Droop	79	75	71	75	300	4,832
Yeh Wei-Tse	77	74	74	75	300	4,832
Glen Joyner	77	72	75	76	300	4,832
Anthony Painter	77	74	72	77	300	4,832
Bob Mattiace	76	74	71	79	300	4,832
Hsu Tien-Lai	76	75	77	73	301	4,400
Yeh Chang-Ting	77	75	72	77	301	4,400
Hsu Kun-Te	81	76	73	72	302	4,120
Boonchu Ruengkit	79	71	74	78	302	4,120
Lee Lien-Fu	76	76	71	79	302	4,120
Lu Wen-Ter	75	79	79	70	303	3,537.14
Michael Etherington	80	77	74	72	303	3,537.14
Darren Cole	77	78	76	72	303	3,537.14
Yeh Chang-Ming	80	76	74	73	303	3,537.14
Craig McClellan	80	74	75	74	303	3,537.14
Lucas Parsons	78	77	72	76	303	3,537.14
Andre Cruse	76	75	76	76	303	3,537.14

World Cup of Golf

Mission Hills Golf Club, Shenzhen, China
Par 36-36—72; 7,102 yards

November 9-12
purse, $1,500,000

	INDIVIDUAL SCORES				TOTAL
UNITED STATES (543)—$200,000					
Davis Love III	65	67	68	67	267
Fred Couples	68	69	70	69	276
AUSTRALIA (557)—$100,000					
Brett Ogle	70	71	69	68	278
Robert Allenby	68	73	68	70	279
SCOTLAND (558)—$56,250					
Sam Torrance	68	70	64	69	271
Andrew Coltart	70	74	72	71	287
JAPAN (558)—$56,250					
Hisayuki Sasaki	62	69	67	69	267
Hiroshi Goda	77	72	70	72	291
NEW ZEALAND (559)—$40,000					
Frank Nobilo	73	70	70	71	284
Michael Campbell	69	71	67	68	275
FRANCE (561)—$26,250					
Jean Van de Velde	69	72	68	69	278
Jean-Louis Guepy	72	69	72	70	283
IRELAND (561)—$26,250					
Philip Walton	73	71	71	71	286
Darren Clarke	68	69	69	69	275
SOUTH AFRICA (563)—$16,000					
Hendrick Buhrmann	74	73	70	71	288
Retief Goosen	71	66	66	72	275

	INDIVIDUAL SCORES				TOTAL
SWEDEN (564)—$14,000					
Jarmo Sandelin	69	71	73	74	287
Jesper Parnevik	67	66	73	71	277
ZIMBABWE (565)—$11,000					
Tony Johnstone	67	78	68	71	284
Mark McNulty	71	72	69	69	281
MEXICO (565)—$11,000					
Esteban Toledo	70	67	68	73	278
Rafael Alarcon	72	70	73	72	287
SWITZERLAND (566)—$8,000					
Andre Bossert	71	73	72	67	283
Paolo Quirici	73	72	72	66	283
ITALY (566)—$8,000					
Silvio Grappasonni	72	75	72	73	292
Costantino Rocca	70	68	64	72	274
GERMANY (567)—$6,500					
Sven Struver	73	73	69	70	285
Alexander Cejka	71	70	72	69	282
SPAIN (569)—$5,500					
Santiago Luna	66	71	69	70	276
Ignacio Garrido	74	75	75	69	293
WALES (570)—$5,000					
Phillip Price	73	70	72	72	287
Mark Mouland	68	74	71	70	283
CANADA (571)—$4,500					
Jim Rutledge	72	76	71	73	292
Rick Gibson	67	73	71	68	279
HOLLAND (572)—$4,400					
Rolf Muntz	73	75	68	70	286
Joost Steenkamer	70	70	73	73	286
FINLAND (578)—$4,300					
Anssi Kankkonen	72	71	73	68	284
Kalle Vainola	76	70	75	73	294
PHILIPPINES (580)—$4,100					
Frankie Minoza	71	74	71	71	287
Robert Pactolerin	72	74	74	73	293
PARAGUAY (580)—$4,100					
Gregorio Nelson Cabrera	70	74	75	75	294
Marco Ruiz	74	71	71	70	286
ENGLAND (580)—$4,100					
Paul Broadhurst	73	74	76	75	298
Mark Roe	68	69	72	73	282
ARGENTINA (582)—$3,900					
Cesar Monasterio	75	77	74	76	302
Eduardo Romero	67	76	70	67	280

	INDIVIDUAL SCORES				TOTAL
REPUBLIC OF KOREA (583)—$3,750					
Sang-Ho Choi	71	72	72	72	287
Kwang-Soo Choi	78	73	73	72	296
DENMARK (583)—$3,750					
Steen Tinning	75	71	72	74	292
Anders Sorensen	73	74	69	75	291
THAILAND (585)—$3,600					
Thamnoon Sriroj	70	67	74	73	284
Udorn Duangdecha	80	76	73	72	301
CHINA (588)—$3,500					
Cheng Jun	76	74	74	72	296
Zhang Lian-Wei	75	74	68	75	292
VENEZUELA (589)—$3,400					
Henrique Lavie	78	72	73	70	293
Emilio Miartuz	76	74	72	74	296
MALAYSIA (590)—$3,300					
Mohammed Ali Kadir	70	76	78	73	297
Marimuthu Ramayah	70	76	74	73	293
COLOMBIA (596)—$3,200					
Jesus Amaya	76	73	74	80	303
Angel Romero	73	72	75	73	293
SRI LANKA (603)—$3,100					
Nandesena Perera	77	71	75	74	297
Koswinna Chandradasa	78	74	77	77	306
PERU (634)—$3,000					
Luis Felipe Graf	74	77	84	81	316
Niceforo Quispe	84	81	77	76	318

INTERNATIONAL TROPHY

WINNER (after playoff): Love - 267 - $100,000. RUNNER-UP: Sasaki - 267 - $50,000. ORDER OF FINISH: Torrance - 271 - $25,000; Rocca - 274 - $15,000; Clarke, Goosen, Campbell - 275 - $3,333 each.

Hong Kong Open

Royal Hong Kong Golf Club, Composite Course, Hong Kong
Par 35-36–71; 6,671 yards

November 16-19
purse, $300,000

	SCORES				TOTAL	MONEY
Gary Webb	68	69	68	66	271	$49,980
Rafael Alarcon	65	67	74	67	273	33,330
Yeh Chang-Ting	67	68	68	71	274	18,780
Mike Cunning	73	68	69	66	276	13,860
Joost Steenkamer	68	72	68	68	276	13,860
Dominique Boulet	71	72	66	69	278	9,750
Eduardo Romero	70	71	67	70	278	9,750
Mark Mouland	69	72	71	67	279	7,500
Payne Stewart	69	75	71	66	281	5,700
Lee Porter	66	75	71	69	281	5,700

	SCORES				TOTAL	MONEY
Anthony Painter	69	68	75	69	281	5,700
Gary Nicklaus	67	72	72	70	281	5,700
Ray Cragun	69	70	70	72	281	5,700
Jim Rutledge	71	71	72	68	282	3,879
Chang Tse-Peng	72	71	69	70	282	3,879
Raul Fretes	70	73	69	70	282	3,879
Lin Keng-Chi	68	74	70	70	282	3,879
Steve Haskins	73	67	72	70	282	3,879
George Zorkic	70	70	71	71	282	3,879
Rick Todd	67	73	71	71	282	3,879
Sang-Ho Choi	69	71	70	72	282	3,879
Zhang Lian-Wei	67	73	69	73	282	3,879
Arjun Atwal	70	69	70	73	282	3,879
Mike Tschetter	74	73	71	65	283	3,000
Rodrigo Cuello	74	72	65	72	283	3,000
Jean Van de Velde	68	72	71	72	283	3,000
Norikazu Kawakami	68	72	70	73	283	3,000
Chen Liang-Hsi	70	70	69	74	283	3,000
Felix Casas	72	64	73	74	283	3,000
Andre Cruse	68	67	71	76	283	3,000

Tugu Pratama Indonesia PGA Championship

Bumi Serpong, Damai Course, Jakarta, Indonesia
Par 36-36–72; 7,109 yards

November 22-25
purse, $250,000

	SCORES				TOTAL	MONEY
John Senden	69	67	71	72	279	$41,650
Felix Casas	72	70	67	72	281	27,775
Frank Nobilo	73	69	71	69	282	12,917
Glen Joyner	68	71	72	71	282	12,917
Mohammed Ali Kadir	69	70	70	73	282	12,917
Tony Carolan	75	71	68	69	283	8,750
Kasyadi	72	72	71	69	284	7,500
Martin Roberts	70	71	73	72	286	6,250
Rodrigo Cuello	69	73	72	73	287	5,600
Brian Wilson	72	71	76	70	289	4,825
Fran Quinn	71	73	74	71	289	4,825
Ken Mattiace	76	72	73	69	290	4,142
Bob Mattiace	76	72	72	70	290	4,142
Danny Mijovic	75	73	70	72	290	4,142
*Sukamdi	68	72	75	75	290	
Raul Fretes	71	75	68	77	291	3,725
Kevin Baker	75	71	76	70	292	3,230
Ray Cragun	74	74	73	71	292	3,230
Stuart Bouvier	73	75	73	71	292	3,230
Philip Hodge	75	72	74	71	292	3,230
Philip Jonas	71	74	75	72	292	3,230
Olle Nordberg	72	73	76	72	293	2,888
Gary Webb	75	69	70	79	293	2,888
Tod Power	74	77	73	70	294	2,717
Morten Backhausen	75	73	72	74	294	2,717
Stuart Deane	76	72	70	76	294	2,717
Ron Wuensche	75	74	74	72	295	2,538
Andre Cruse	75	73	74	73	295	2,538
Neil Kerry	77	73	74	72	296	2,350
Jun Jung	74	74	76	72	296	2,350
Maan Nasim	74	72	75	75	296	2,350

China Tour

Volvo Open

Shenzhen Golf Club, Shenzhen
Par 36-36–72; 7,250 yards

April 10-11
purse, $50,000

	SCORES		TOTAL	MONEY
Zhang Lian-Wei	69	73	142	$9,000
Jeff Senior	70	73	143	4,625
Tod Power	73	70	143	4,625
Tony Maloney	70	75	145	2,125
David Smail	74	71	145	2,125
Cheng Jun	70	75	145	2,125
Chen Liang-Hsi	73	72	145	2,125
Grant Dodd	70	76	146	1,600
Lai Ying-Juh	74	73	147	1,375
Valen Tan	77	70	147	1,375
Hsu Tien-Lai	73	75	148	1,056.25
Lin Tieh-Shun	72	76	148	1,056.25
Mohammed Ali Kadir	75	73	148	1,056.25
Tsai Chie-Huang	74	74	148	1,056.25
Lu Wen-Ter	76	73	149	755
Tsai Ching-Ming	75	74	149	755
Yeh Chang-Ming	76	73	149	755
Glenn Joyner	75	74	149	755
Bill Fung	77	72	149	755
Kao Yu-Huang	75	75	150	625
Yeh Wei-Tse	76	74	150	625
Lai Chum-Hui	74	76	150	625
Cesar Ababa	76	74	150	625
Steve Collins	75	75	150	625
Chang Chin-Kuo	76	75	151	500
Joon Lee	78	73	151	500
Mok Yuk-Lun	75	76	151	500
Ajay Gupta	79	72	151	500
Amandeep Johl	75	76	152	500
Wu Xiang-Bin	75	77	152	387.50
Chen Jung-Hsin	76	76	152	387.50
Michael Welsh	79	73	152	387.50
Eddie Bagtas	77	75	152	387.50

Honichi Open

Honichi Golf Leisure Club, Shenzhen
Par 36-36–72; 7,009 yards

April 13-14
purse, $30,000

	SCORES		TOTAL	MONEY
Tony Maloney	74	67	141	$5,400
Michael Welch	73	69	142	3,450
Lu Wen-Ter	70	73	143	1,875
Mohammed Ali Kadir	73	70	143	1,875

	SCORES		TOTAL	MONEY
Amandeep Johl	70	74	144	1,150
Zhang Lian-Wei	73	71	144	1,150
Yang Wen-Lai	72	72	144	1,150
Kao Yu-Huang	70	75	145	765
Hsu Tien-Lai	73	72	145	765
Lai Chum-Hui	71	74	145	765
Jeff Wagner	74	71	145	765
Chen Tsang-Ter	71	74	145	765
Richard Kan	74	71	145	765
Grant Dodd	73	73	146	525
David Thompson	76	70	146	525
Tod Power	75	72	147	457.50
Jeff Senior	73	74	147	457.50
Yeh Wei-Tse	72	76	148	412.50
Brian Dunbar	77	71	148	412.50
Tang Man-Kee	76	72	148	412.50
Yeh Chang-Ming	73	75	148	412.50
Eddie Bagtas	73	76	149	337.50
Danilo Z. Cabajar	75	74	149	337.50
Tang Shu-Chuen	74	75	149	337.50
Jyoti Randhawa	77	72	149	337.50
Chou Chin-Yi	74	75	149	337.50
Jimmy Qi	78	71	149	337.50
Cesar Ababa	76	74	150	277.50
Mario Siodina	76	74	150	277.50
Bill Fung	76	75	151	210
Lin Tieh-Shun	77	74	151	210
Tsai Ching-Ming	75	76	151	210
Chen Ming-Wen	74	77	151	210
Tang Shu-Wing	75	76	151	210
Joon Lee	77	74	151	210
Chen Liang-Hsi	76	75	151	210

Hugo Boss Open

Shenzhen Xili Golf Club, Shenzhen
Par 36-36—72; 6,576 yards

April 18-19
purse, $50,000

	SCORES		TOTAL	MONEY
Rafael Ponce	69	66	135	$9,000
Lu Wen-Ter	68	67	135	5,750
(Ponce defeated Lu at second extra hole.)				
Zhang Lian-Wei	70	66	136	3,125
Jeff Wagner	68	68	136	3,125
Michael Welch	69	68	137	2,000
Jeff Senior	67	70	137	2,000
Steve Collins	68	70	138	1,600
Matt Gogel	70	68	138	1,600
Andre Stolz	66	72	138	1,600
Jyoti Randhawa	71	68	139	1,250
Yeh Chang-Ming	68	71	139	1,250
Cesar Ababa	71	69	140	895.83
Steve Conran	68	72	140	895.83
Amandeep Johl	73	67	140	895.83
Yeh Yeou-Tsai	70	70	140	895.83
David Thompson	72	68	140	895.83
Tony Maloney	70	70	140	895.83

	SCORES		TOTAL	MONEY
Grant Dodd	73	68	141	675
Aaron Meeks	69	72	141	675
Leonard Sorensen	71	70	141	675
Gary Harvey	69	72	141	675
Mohammed Ali Kadir	72	69	141	675
Danilo Z. Cabajar	75	67	142	500
Lai Ying-Juh	71	71	142	500
Tseng Chin-Fa	69	73	142	500
Chen Liang-Hsi	72	70	142	500
Ajay Gupta	74	68	142	500
Mario Siodina	72	70	142	500
Cheng Jun	70	72	142	500
Yeh Wei-Tse	73	69	142	500
Anthony Painter	70	72	142	500

Coca-Cola Open

Mission Hills Golf Club, Shenzhen
Par 36-36–72; 6,709 yards

April 21-22
purse, $300,000

	SCORES		TOTAL	MONEY
Simon Yates	69	71	140	$9,000
David Smail	67	74	141	5,750
Mohammed Ali Kadir	72	71	143	3,125
Michael Welch	71	72	143	3,125
Craig Kamps	73	71	144	1,916.67
Steve Conran	71	73	144	1,916.67
Steve Collins	72	72	144	1,916.67
Danilo Z. Cabajar	71	74	145	1,525
Jyoti Randhawa	72	73	145	1,525
Jeff Wagner	71	75	146	1,150
Aaron Meeks	71	75	146	1,150
Zhang Lian-Wei	73	73	146	1,150
Andre Stolz	72	74	146	1,150
Anthony Painter	72	75	147	875
Zaw Moe	71	76	147	875
Kao Yu-Huang	74	73	147	875
Cesar Ababa	68	80	148	775
Derek Fung	69	80	149	725
David Thompson	73	76	149	725
Grant Dodd	72	77	149	725
Lai Ying-Juh	80	70	150	625
Hsu Chie-San	72	78	150	625
Cheng Jun	74	76	150	625
Tod Power	74	76	150	625
Jeff Senior	79	71	150	625
Gary Harvey	78	73	151	525
Mario Siodina	78	73	151	525
Richard Kan	79	72	151	525
Matt Gogel	71	81	152	475
Tang Man-Kee	72	81	153	387.50
Chen Tsang-Ter	75	78	153	387.50
Huang Huan-Jen	77	76	153	387.50
Rafael Ponce	76	77	153	387.50
Yeh Wei-Tse	72	81	153	387.50
Kyi-Hla Han	77	76	153	387.50

Japan Tour

Token Corporation Cup

Kedoin Golf Club, Kagoshima
Par 36-36–72; 7,097 yards

March 9-12
purse, ¥100,000,000

	SCORES				TOTAL	MONEY
Todd Hamilton	70	71	68	72	281	¥18,000,000
Peter Senior	72	72	70	68	282	10,000,000
Shigeki Maruyama	69	74	70	70	283	6,800,000
Tsuneyuki Nakajima	69	74	70	71	284	4,800,000
Masashi Ozaki	71	75	72	67	285	3,800,000
Yoshikazu Yokoshima	73	70	72	70	285	3,800,000
Tsuyoshi Yoneyama	73	74	71	68	286	2,900,000
Yoshinori Kaneko	71	72	70	73	286	2,900,000
Hiroshi Goda	70	72	71	73	286	2,900,000
Masahiro Kuramoto	73	72	74	68	287	1,955,000
Kazuo Kanayama	74	71	71	71	287	1,955,000
Isamu Sugita	73	74	69	71	287	1,955,000
Hajime Meshiai	70	74	71	72	287	1,955,000
Kiyoshi Maita	74	72	73	69	288	1,440,000
Ken Kusumoto	72	74	73	69	288	1,440,000
Shoichi Miyazato	69	75	70	74	288	1,440,000
Pete Izumikawa	74	72	69	74	289	1,120,000
Kazuhiro Takami	71	72	72	74	289	1,120,000
Yoshikazu Sakamoto	73	70	70	76	289	1,120,000
Shinji Ikeuchi	70	76	71	73	290	980,000
Mitsutaka Kuwakabe	68	74	75	73	290	980,000
Shoichi Kuwabara	74	72	76	69	291	853,000
Norihiro Yoshino	73	74	73	71	291	853,000
Roger Mackay	72	71	77	71	291	853,000
Craig Warren	68	77	74	72	291	853,000
Rick Gibson	76	71	72	72	291	853,000
Seiji Ebihara	74	67	74	76	291	853,000
Ikuo Shirahama	75	71	78	68	292	687,000
Nobuo Serizawa	75	72	75	70	292	687,000
Tomohiro Maruyama	74	74	73	71	292	687,000
Satoshi Higashi	77	71	73	71	292	687,000
Katsuyoshi Tomori	73	73	73	73	292	687,000
Chen Tze-Chung	76	66	77	73	292	687,000
Richard Backwell	74	71	74	73	292	687,000
Harumitsu Hamano	70	76	72	74	292	687,000
Akiyoshi Ohmachi	74	72	72	74	292	687,000
Hiromasa Kimura	72	71	73	76	292	687,000
Hideyuki Sato	70	71	75	76	292	687,000

Daido Drinko Shizuoka Open

Shizuoka Golf Club, Shizuoka
Par 36-36–72; 6,902 yards

March 16-19
purse, ¥100,000,000

		SCORES			TOTAL	MONEY
Brian Watts	69	72	71	68	280	¥18,000,000
Shigeki Maruyama	70	75	66	71	282	10,000,000
Toru Suzuki	73	69	70	72	284	5,800,000
Toru Nakayama	72	72	67	73	284	5,800,000
Akio Nakamura	72	72	71	70	285	4,000,000
Eduardo Herrera	70	77	69	70	286	3,233,000
Tsutomu Higa	70	76	69	71	286	3,233,000
Frankie Minoza	71	72	67	76	286	3,233,000
Saburo Fujiki	73	71	72	71	287	2,185,000
Carlos Franco	71	73	71	72	287	2,185,000
Ikuo Shirahama	74	72	68	73	287	2,185,000
Nobuo Serizawa	71	70	73	73	287	2,185,000
Seiichi Koizumi	70	75	75	68	288	1,386,000
Masayuki Kawamura	73	72	71	72	288	1,386,000
Ken Kusumoto	75	71	68	74	288	1,386,000
Anthony Gilligan	73	72	69	74	288	1,386,000
Yoshikazu Sakamoto	75	67	71	75	288	1,386,000
Hisayuki Sasaki	69	73	70	76	288	1,386,000
Noboru Sugai	73	72	74	70	289	1,000,000
Satoshi Higashi	70	74	72	73	289	1,000,000
Richard Backwell	74	66	70	79	289	1,000,000
Kiyoshi Maita	70	76	72	72	290	853,000
Katsuyoshi Tomori	73	73	72	72	290	853,000
Koichi Suzuki	70	72	75	73	290	853,000
Toru Nakamura	75	73	69	73	290	853,000
Lin Chie-Hsiang	73	72	71	74	290	853,000
Keiichiro Fukahori	75	70	71	74	290	853,000
Peter Senior	72	74	74	71	291	721,000
Gohei Sato	73	73	73	72	291	721,000
Hiroshi Makino	73	72	72	74	291	721,000
Tsukasa Watanabe	72	74	71	74	291	721,000
Tatsuo Takasaki	71	76	70	74	291	721,000
Tsuyoshi Yoneyama	72	73	69	77	291	721,000
Taisei Inagaki	72	71	71	77	291	721,000

Novell KSB Open

Kinojo Country Club, Okayama
Par 36-36–72; 6,883 yards

March 23-26
purse, ¥70,000,000

		SCORES			TOTAL	MONEY
Rick Gibson	65	67	71	68	271	¥12,600,000
Tsukasa Watanabe	65	72	69	66	272	5,880,000
Toshimitsu Izawa	68	69	67	68	272	5,880,000
Toru Suzuki	68	67	71	67	273	3,080,000
Yoshinori Kaneko	70	68	67	68	273	3,080,000
Kazuhiro Takami	67	72	68	67	274	2,520,000
Seiki Okuda	72	68	69	66	275	2,030,000
Masanobu Kimura	65	74	68	68	275	2,030,000
Richard Backwell	66	69	69	71	275	2,030,000
Lin Chie-Hsiang	68	68	69	71	276	1,610,000
Tsutomu Higa	70	69	70	68	277	1,288,000

	SCORES				TOTAL	MONEY
Masayuki Kawamura	70	67	70	70	277	1,288,000
Hisayuki Sasaki	71	67	69	70	277	1,288,000
Hiroshi Goda	68	69	75	66	278	929,000
Peter McWhinney	70	69	72	67	278	929,000
Craig McClellan	73	68	70	67	278	929,000
Katsuyoshi Tomori	69	67	72	70	278	929,000
Tatsuo Takasaki	67	67	72	72	278	929,000
Hsieh Chin-Sheng	70	69	72	68	279	660,000
Carlos Franco	72	69	69	69	279	660,000
Akio Nakamura	70	69	70	70	279	660,000
Frankie Minoza	73	68	68	70	279	660,000
Ken Kusumoto	70	68	69	72	279	660,000
Tsuneyuki Nakajima	64	69	72	74	279	660,000
Eduardo Herrera	70	73	72	65	280	546,000
Yoshikazu Sakamoto	71	70	71	68	280	546,000
Teruo Sugihara	68	74	70	68	280	546,000
Eiji Mizoguchi	70	68	73	69	280	546,000
Motomasa Aoki	68	70	73	69	280	546,000
Brian Watts	73	67	69	71	280	546,000
Takenori Hiraishi	72	68	69	71	280	546,000

Descente Classic

Century Miki Golf Club, Hyogo
Par 36-36–72; 6,952 yards

March 30-April 2
purse, ¥80,000,000

	SCORES				TOTAL	MONEY
Satoshi Higashi	72	68	69	73	282	¥14,400,000
Katsuyoshi Tomori	73	67	72	71	283	8,000,000
Yoshimi Niizeki	73	68	71	72	284	5,440,000
Ryoken Kawagishi	74	70	72	70	286	3,306,000
Eduardo Herrera	72	70	73	71	286	3,306,000
Takaaki Fukuzawa	72	69	74	71	286	3,306,000
Kinpachi Yoshimura	73	70	73	71	287	2,440,000
Peter McWhinney	72	68	73	74	287	2,440,000
Chen Tze-Ming	73	72	75	68	288	1,474,000
Kikuo Arai	77	71	71	69	288	1,474,000
Katsumi Kuwabara	75	69	72	72	288	1,474,000
Masayuki Kawamura	75	67	73	73	288	1,474,000
Yoshinori Mizumaki	78	69	68	73	288	1,474,000
Eiji Mizoguchi	71	71	72	74	288	1,474,000
Hideki Kase	70	71	72	75	288	1,474,000
Katsunari Takahashi	73	69	71	75	288	1,474,000
Masahiro Kuramoto	72	73	73	71	289	928,000
Akiyoshi Ohmachi	73	72	71	73	289	928,000
Hisashi Nakase	78	67	74	71	290	721,000
Samson Gimson	77	68	73	72	290	721,000
Frankie Minoza	72	72	74	72	290	721,000
Tatsuo Takasaki	71	73	74	72	290	721,000
Todd Hamilton	79	67	71	73	290	721,000
Toshimitsu Izawa	71	74	72	73	290	721,000
Tsutomu Higa	73	71	73	73	290	721,000
Kazuhiro Takami	71	73	73	73	290	721,000
Hiroshi Makino	73	70	71	76	290	721,000
Richard Backwell	72	72	76	71	291	600,000
Brian Watts	73	72	74	72	291	600,000
Stewart Ginn	72	72	75	72	291	600,000
Seiji Ebihara	75	69	72	75	291	600,000

Tsuruya Open

Sports Shinko Country Club, Hyogo
Par 36-36–72; 6,842 yards

April 13-16
purse, ¥100,000,000

	SCORES				TOTAL	MONEY
Satoshi Higashi	69	74	66	70	279	¥18,000,000
Yoshinori Mizumaki	70	70	72	68	280	5,840,000
Roger Mackay	73	69	70	68	280	5,840,000
Koki Idoki	67	76	69	68	280	5,840,000
Kiyoshi Maita	71	69	70	70	280	5,840,000
Katsunori Kuwahara	64	74	71	71	280	5,840,000
Rick Gibson	70	72	69	70	281	3,050,000
Hisayuki Sasaki	69	68	71	73	281	3,050,000
Peter Senior	69	72	70	71	282	2,600,000
Hirofumi Miyase	74	71	69	69	283	2,300,000
Tsuneyuki Nakajima	75	70	71	68	284	1,704,000
Katsuyoshi Tomori	68	71	75	70	284	1,704,000
Akiyoshi Ohmachi	72	73	69	70	284	1,704,000
Nobuo Serizawa	73	69	70	72	284	1,704,000
Shinichi Yokota	70	71	69	74	284	1,704,000
Hideyuki Sato	70	70	72	73	285	1,320,000
Eiji Mizoguchi	72	74	69	71	286	1,160,000
Toshimitsu Izawa	68	74	72	72	286	1,160,000
Ken Kusumoto	69	74	75	69	287	960,000
Yoshitaka Yamamoto	71	75	72	69	287	960,000
Yoshinori Kaneko	76	71	70	70	287	960,000
Ryoken Kawagishi	69	75	73	70	287	960,000
Tsukasa Watanabe	67	73	73	74	287	960,000
Hiroshi Ueda	70	75	75	68	288	790,000
Chen Tze-Chung	72	75	71	70	288	790,000
Shoutei You	71	75	72	70	288	790,000
Shigeki Maruyama	77	69	70	72	288	790,000
Seiki Okuda	71	73	72	72	288	790,000
Wayne Smith	70	75	71	72	288	790,000
Koichi Suzuki	68	73	74	73	288	790,000
Joji Furuki	64	79	72	73	288	790,000

Dunlop Open

Ibaragi Golf Club, Ibaragi
Par 36-36–72; 7,122 yards

April 20-23
purse, ¥100,000,000

	SCORES				TOTAL	MONEY
Peter Senior	69	70	67	73	279	¥16,200,000
Brian Watts	71	74	69	70	284	9,000,000
Katsuyoshi Tomori	74	73	70	68	285	6,120,000
Masashi Ozaki	73	68	71	74	286	4,320,000
Shigeki Maruyama	72	72	70	74	288	3,600,000
Masahiro Kuramoto	69	78	70	72	289	2,910,000
Kisho Rin	75	72	70	72	289	2,910,000
Steve Flesch	73	69	71	76	289	2,910,000
Gerry Norquist	72	72	73	73	290	1,966,000
Brian Wilson	72	69	76	73	290	1,966,000
Akiyoshi Ohmachi	72	69	75	74	290	1,966,000
Carlos Franco	70	73	72	75	290	1,966,000
Hsieh Chin-Sheng	71	72	74	74	291	1,512,000
Nobuo Serizawa	70	73	76	73	292	1,242,000

	SCORES				TOTAL	MONEY
Yoshinori Mizumaki	72	72	74	74	292	1,242,000
Jong-Duck Kim	72	71	75	74	292	1,242,000
Anthony Gilligan	72	73	69	78	292	1,242,000
Eiji Mizoguchi	74	74	73	72	293	888,000
Chang Tse-Peng	73	72	75	73	293	888,000
Hideto Shigenobu	72	71	74	76	293	888,000
Isao Aoki	73	75	69	76	293	888,000
Manny Zerman	69	73	75	76	293	888,000
Ron Wuensche	74	69	74	76	293	888,000
Hisayuki Sasaki	72	74	76	72	294	711,000
Kazuhiro Takami	70	73	77	74	294	711,000
Koki Idoki	71	72	76	75	294	711,000
Masahiro Kawamura	74	72	73	75	294	711,000
Teruo Sugihara	72	75	72	75	294	711,000
Harumitsu Hamano	75	72	72	75	294	711,000
Don Fardon	74	70	74	76	294	711,000
Rick Todd	72	66	77	79	294	711,000

Chunichi Crowns

Nagoya Golf Club, Wago Course, Aichi
Par 35-35–70; 6,473 yards

April 27-30
purse, ¥120,000,000

	SCORES				TOTAL	MONEY
Masashi Ozaki	66	64	63	67	260	¥21,600,000
Nobuo Serizawa	64	67	66	68	265	12,000,000
Katsuyoshi Tomori	64	65	70	69	268	8,160,000
Larry Mize	65	72	66	66	269	5,760,000
Peter Senior	71	68	69	63	271	4,320,000
Masahiro Kuramoto	65	70	70	66	271	4,320,000
Yoshinori Mizumaki	68	66	67	70	271	4,320,000
Richard Backwell	68	68	70	66	272	3,330,000
Shigeki Maruyama	64	69	70	69	272	3,330,000
Robert Gamez	67	69	69	68	273	2,760,000
Masanobu Kimura	66	72	67	69	274	2,208,000
Toru Nakamura	66	70	69	69	274	2,208,000
Hsieh Chin-Sheng	67	70	67	70	274	2,208,000
Hisayuki Sasaki	68	71	70	66	275	1,872,000
Anthony Gilligan	72	72	70	62	276	1,385,000
Saburo Fujiki	69	73	70	64	276	1,385,000
Toru Nakayama	69	72	70	65	276	1,385,000
Tsukasa Watanabe	69	68	71	68	276	1,385,000
Satoshi Higashi	66	71	70	69	276	1,385,000
Kiyoshi Maita	71	73	63	69	276	1,385,000
Tsuneyuki Watanabe	66	69	72	69	276	1,385,000
Toru Suzuki	71	71	70	66	278	1,050,000
Mitsuo Harada	70	72	69	67	278	1,050,000
Kiyoshi Murota	70	69	71	68	278	1,050,000
Hajime Meshiai	66	76	67	69	278	1,050,000
Frankie Minoza	72	69	72	66	279	948,000
Tomohiro Maruyama	69	72	71	67	279	948,000
Hiroya Kamide	68	72	72	67	279	948,000
Todd Hamilton	71	69	70	69	279	948,000
Glen Day	72	68	71	69	280	832,000
Katsunari Takahashi	71	72	67	70	280	832,000
Seiji Ebihara	69	74	67	70	280	832,000
Naomichi Ozaki	70	71	69	70	280	832,000

		SCORES			TOTAL	MONEY
Seiichi Kanai	70	71	68	71	280	832,000
Hidemichi Tanaka	72	68	65	75	280	832,000

Fuji Sankei Classic

Kawana Golf Club, Fuji Course, Shizuoka   May 4-7
Par 35-36–71; 6,694 yards   purse, ¥120,000,000

		SCORES			TOTAL	MONEY
Tsuneyuki Nakajima	66	70	70	66	272	¥21,600,000
Masahiro Kuramoto	67	69	69	69	274	12,000,000
Carlos Franco	67	69	69	70	275	8,160,000
Todd Hamilton	68	69	71	68	276	5,760,000
Hisayuki Sasaki	65	68	71	73	277	4,800,000
Toru Suzuki	68	69	68	73	278	4,320,000
Daisuke Serizawa	69	73	70	67	279	3,330,000
Yoshinori Mizumaki	66	70	75	68	279	3,330,000
Toshimitsu Izawa	69	73	69	68	279	3,330,000
Masayuki Kawamura	70	69	67	73	279	3,330,000
Hsieh Chin-Sheng	71	69	73	67	280	2,044,000
Kiyoshi Maita	65	73	72	70	280	2,044,000
Seiji Ebihara	70	69	71	70	280	2,044,000
Masashi Ozaki	71	70	68	71	280	2,044,000
Shinichi Yokota	71	67	71	71	280	2,044,000
Ken Kusumoto	68	69	75	69	281	1,584,000
Saburo Fujiki	74	69	68	71	282	1,344,000
Tsukasa Watanabe	70	69	71	72	282	1,344,000
Joji Furuki	70	70	68	74	282	1,344,000
Tadashi Ezure	72	70	72	69	283	1,128,000
Hiroya Kamide	72	70	71	70	283	1,128,000
Nobuo Serizawa	70	71	70	72	283	1,128,000
Hideyuki Sato	71	72	67	73	283	1,128,000
Hajime Meshiai	71	70	72	71	284	1,008,000
Kiyoshi Murota	73	67	71	73	284	1,008,000
Tetsu Oide	70	70	70	74	284	1,008,000
Peter McWhinney	72	71	75	67	285	912,000
Tomohiro Maruyama	69	72	75	69	285	912,000
Masanobu Kimura	70	71	73	71	285	912,000
Katsunari Takahashi	71	72	70	72	285	912,000
Brent Franklin	68	69	72	76	285	912,000

Japan PGA Championship

Natsudomari Golf Links, Aomori   May 11-14
Par 36-36–72; 7,058 yards   purse, ¥100,000,000

		SCORES			TOTAL	MONEY
Hisayuki Sasaki	71	70	68	63	272	¥18,000,000
Kazuhiro Takami	67	70	68	71	276	10,000,000
Toru Suzuki	65	65	74	73	277	6,800,000
Tateo Ozaki	70	70	70	68	278	4,133,000
Frankie Minoza	68	70	71	69	278	4,133,000
Yoshinori Mizumaki	71	67	68	72	278	4,133,000
Toshimitsu Izawa	70	67	72	70	279	3,200,000
Teruo Sugihara	69	69	71	71	280	2,900,000

	SCORES				TOTAL	MONEY
Katsunori Kuwahara	70	71	71	70	282	2,450,000
Nobumitsu Yuhara	71	71	69	71	282	2,450,000
Lin Chie-Hsiang	72	70	74	67	283	1,770,000
Masahiro Kuramoto	70	70	72	71	283	1,770,000
Tomohiro Maruyama	71	71	70	71	283	1,770,000
Hirofumi Miyase	70	69	72	72	283	1,770,000
Chen Tze-Chung	73	70	73	68	284	1,154,000
Hiroshi Makino	70	70	76	68	284	1,154,000
Hidezumi Shirakata	70	71	74	69	284	1,154,000
Yoshinori Kaneko	69	74	71	70	284	1,154,000
Masanobu Kimura	68	73	73	70	284	1,154,000
Toru Nakamura	70	72	72	70	284	1,154,000
Hideyuki Sato	72	72	67	73	284	1,154,000
Todd Hamilton	70	74	68	73	285	900,000
Masahiko Akazawa	69	72	71	73	285	900,000
Koki Idoki	69	71	76	70	286	810,000
Nobuo Serizawa	71	73	71	71	286	810,000
Tsutomu Higa	68	71	76	71	286	810,000
Noboru Sugai	72	70	71	73	286	810,000
Kazunari Matsunaga	71	71	71	73	286	810,000
Yoshimitsu Fukuzawa	69	69	74	74	286	810,000
Shinji Ikeuchi	74	70	72	71	287	685,000
Shigeki Maruyama	68	75	72	72	287	685,000
Saburo Fujiki	70	69	75	73	287	685,000
Takaaki Fukuzawa	70	72	72	73	287	685,000
Wayne Smith	68	74	72	73	287	685,000
Joji Furuki	70	70	73	74	287	685,000
Eduardo Herrera	72	71	69	75	287	685,000

Pepsi Ube Tournament

Ube Country Club, Mannenike-Higashi Course, Yamaguchi
Par 36-36–72; 6,952 yards

May 19-21
purse, ¥80,000,000

	SCORES			TOTAL	MONEY
Mitsutaka Kusakabe	70	70	66	206	¥10,800,000
Harumitsu Hamano	71	69	69	209	3,840,000
Koki Idoki	66	71	72	209	3,840,000
Roger Mackay	68	69	72	209	3,840,000
Katsunari Takahashi	67	70	72	209	3,840,000
Toru Suzuki	71	69	70	210	1,940,000
Jack O'Keefe	68	71	71	210	1,940,000
Brandt Jobe	66	72	72	210	1,940,000
Akiyoshi Ohmachi	71	72	68	211	1,560,000
Kazuhiko Hosokawa	73	70	69	212	1,228,000
Hirofumi Miyase	71	70	71	212	1,228,000
Hidemichi Tanaka	70	71	71	212	1,228,000
Teruo Nakamura	70	73	70	213	802,000
Anthony Gilligan	72	71	70	213	802,000
Nobuo Serizawa	70	72	71	213	802,000
Teruo Sugihara	68	74	71	213	802,000
Nobuhiro Yoshino	68	74	71	213	802,000
Satoshi Furuyama	69	73	71	213	802,000
Tomohiro Maruyama	73	68	72	213	802,000
Todd Hamilton	70	74	70	214	554,000
Hideto Shigenobu	72	71	71	214	554,000
Shinji Kuraoka	70	73	71	214	554,000

	SCORES			TOTAL	MONEY
Shinji Ikeuchi	68	74	72	214	554,000
Katsunori Kuwahara	68	73	73	214	554,000
Toshiaki Sudo	73	72	70	215	492,000
Kazunari Matsunaga	70	74	71	215	492,000
Mitsuo Harada	69	72	74	215	492,000
Masanobu Kimura	72	73	71	216	433,000
Kosaku Hirano	66	79	71	216	433,000
Shinichi Yokota	73	70	73	216	433,000
Hiroyuki Fujita	69	74	73	216	433,000
Yoshimi Niizeki	70	72	74	216	433,000
Jonathan Lomas	69	73	74	216	433,000
Seiji Ebihara	69	72	75	216	433,000

Mitsubishi Galant Tournament

Aso Prince Hotel Golf Club, Kumamoto   May 25-28
Par 36-37–73; 6,913 yards   purse, ¥100,000,000

	SCORES				TOTAL	MONEY
Brandt Jobe	65	67	65	69	266	¥18,000,000
Masahiro Kuramoto	63	73	68	68	272	10,000,000
Tatsuo Takasaki	69	66	71	67	273	6,800,000
Kiyoshi Maita	67	65	71	71	274	4,400,000
Wayne Smith	71	65	67	71	274	4,400,000
Eduardo Herrera	67	69	72	67	275	3,400,000
Tsuneyuki Nakajima	70	71	63	71	275	3,400,000
Rick Gibson	70	67	70	69	276	2,900,000
Hisayuki Sasaki	72	68	71	66	277	2,450,000
Nobuo Serizawa	71	69	68	69	277	2,450,000
Kazuhiro Takami	71	68	70	69	278	1,840,000
Tomohiro Maruyama	69	66	73	70	278	1,840,000
Masayuki Kawamura	66	69	69	74	278	1,840,000
Anthony Gilligan	71	70	71	67	279	1,240,000
Todd Hamilton	71	67	72	69	279	1,240,000
Ryoken Kawagishi	66	71	73	69	279	1,240,000
Nobumitsu Yuhara	69	72	67	71	279	1,240,000
Noboru Sugai	68	73	67	71	279	1,240,000
Saburo Fujiki	72	68	66	73	279	1,240,000
Hideki Kase	70	69	67	73	279	1,240,000
Satoshi Higashi	71	67	71	71	280	920,000
Katsunari Takahashi	70	68	70	72	280	920,000
Joji Furuki	71	66	69	74	280	920,000
Toru Nakamura	71	71	67	72	281	850,000
Toru Suzuki	68	69	71	73	281	850,000
Hajime Meshiai	73	68	72	69	282	750,000
Toshimitsu Izawa	70	71	71	70	282	750,000
Seiki Okuda	71	70	71	70	282	750,000
Lin Chie-Hsiang	69	69	73	71	282	750,000
Tsutomu Higa	69	70	72	71	282	750,000
Koki Idoki	69	69	72	72	282	750,000
Isamu Sugita	71	68	70	73	282	750,000
Koichi Suzuki	67	69	70	76	282	750,000

JCB Classic Sendai

Omate Zaoh Kokusai Golf Club, Miyagi
Par 36-35–71; 6,645 yards

June 1-4
purse, ¥100,000,000

	SCORES				TOTAL	MONEY
Ryoken Kawagishi	71	68	64	68	271	¥18,000,000
Toru Suzuki	69	72	66	67	274	10,000,000
Takaaki Fukuzawa	70	71	70	64	275	5,200,000
Hisayuki Sasaki	74	69	67	65	275	5,200,000
Nichito Hashimoto	63	73	69	70	275	5,200,000
Hirofumi Miyase	71	72	69	64	276	3,400,000
Masashi Ozaki	73	67	69	67	276	3,400,000
Koki Idoki	70	73	71	63	277	2,750,000
Tatsuo Takasaki	66	74	68	69	277	2,750,000
Rick Gibson	71	73	70	64	278	1,955,000
Hiroshi Makino	70	67	71	70	278	1,955,000
Mitsutaka Kusakabe	67	69	71	71	278	1,955,000
Eduardo Herrera	69	69	69	71	278	1,955,000
Hideyuki Sato	70	72	69	68	279	1,500,000
Satoshi Higashi	66	70	73	70	279	1,500,000
Hiroya Kamide	70	72	69	69	280	1,106,000
Toshimitsu Izawa	69	68	73	70	280	1,106,000
Saburo Fujiki	71	68	70	71	280	1,106,000
Masanobu Kimura	71	68	70	71	280	1,106,000
Kazuhiro Takami	67	72	69	72	280	1,106,000
Kyi-Hla Han	69	69	69	73	280	1,106,000
Lin Chie-Hsiang	69	72	74	66	281	875,000
Craig Warren	71	71	71	68	281	875,000
Shigenori Mori	74	70	66	71	281	875,000
Mitsuo Harada	71	68	68	74	281	875,000
Yurio Akitomi	70	73	73	66	282	760,000
Hajime Meshiai	73	69	71	69	282	760,000
Koichi Suzuki	70	74	69	69	282	760,000
Katsunari Takahashi	69	73	69	71	282	760,000
Koichi Nogami	69	72	70	71	282	760,000
Nobuo Serizawa	71	70	69	72	282	760,000
Hiroyuki Fujita	67	68	73	74	282	760,000

Sapporo Tokyu Open

Sapporo Kokusai Country Club, Shimamatsu Course, Hokkaido
Par 36-36–72; 6,949 yards

June 8-11
purse, ¥100,000,000

	SCORES				TOTAL	MONEY
Carlos Franco	68	69	69	72	278	¥18,000,000
Shinji Ikeuchi	73	67	70	69	279	8,400,000
Kazuhiro Takami	71	68	70	70	279	8,400,000
Katsuyoshi Tomori	72	69	73	67	281	4,400,000
Yoshinori Mizumaki	69	68	71	73	281	4,400,000
Tsukasa Watanabe	68	76	69	69	282	2,766,000
Tomohiro Maruyama	69	74	70	69	282	2,766,000
Kiyoshi Maita	71	73	68	70	282	2,766,000
David Ishii	70	71	71	70	282	2,766,000
Toshiaki Odate	71	67	73	71	282	2,766,000
Masahiro Kuramoto	70	72	68	72	282	2,766,000
Hajime Meshiai	71	76	68	68	283	1,840,000
Chen Tze-Ming	73	74	69	68	284	1,560,000

	SCORES				TOTAL	MONEY
Hideto Shigenobu	69	75	72	68	284	1,560,000
Toru Suzuki	70	73	72	69	284	1,560,000
Satoshi Higashi	70	72	74	69	285	1,213,000
Tsuneyuki Nakajima	75	68	72	70	285	1,213,000
Seiichi Kanai	70	70	70	75	285	1,213,000
Tsuyoshi Yoneyama	74	73	69	70	286	960,000
Hideyuki Sato	75	70	70	71	286	960,000
Anthony Gilligan	72	71	71	72	286	960,000
Katsunori Kuwahara	70	72	71	73	286	960,000
Takashi Kanemoto	68	75	70	73	286	960,000
Yeh Chang-Ting	73	72	74	68	287	830,000
Hsieh Chin-Sheng	70	71	72	74	287	830,000
Koichi Suzuki	71	68	73	75	287	830,000
Frankie Minoza	68	74	69	76	287	830,000
Taichi Teshima	72	75	72	69	288	750,000
Richard Backwell	73	70	72	73	288	750,000
Hiroshi Goda	74	71	70	73	288	750,000
Toru Nakamura	73	73	68	74	288	750,000

Pocari Sweat Yomiuri Open

Yomiuri Country Club, Hyogo
Par 36-35–71; 6,973 yards

June 15-18
purse, ¥100,000,000

	SCORES				TOTAL	MONEY
Eduardo Herrera	70	67	68	67	272	¥18,000,000
Hiroyuki Fujita	67	73	65	68	273	10,000,000
Shigeki Maruyama	65	71	68	70	274	6,800,000
Saburo Fujiki	71	69	68	67	275	3,700,000
Roger Mackay	72	68	67	68	275	3,700,000
Yoshikazu Sakamoto	69	69	69	68	275	3,700,000
Koki Idoki	71	69	66	69	275	3,700,000
Rick Gibson	67	68	70	70	275	3,700,000
Kiyoshi Murota	71	71	69	65	276	2,185,000
Carlos Franco	68	69	69	70	276	2,185,000
Ryoken Kawagishi	63	70	72	71	276	2,185,000
Mitsutaka Kusakabe	67	66	71	72	276	2,185,000
Tsutomu Higa	68	67	73	69	277	1,560,000
Hisayuki Sasaki	69	68	69	71	277	1,560,000
Satoshi Higashi	68	68	68	73	277	1,560,000
Takaaki Fukuzawa	71	71	70	66	278	1,106,000
Masayuki Kawamura	74	67	68	69	278	1,106,000
Kinpachi Yoshimura	69	73	67	69	278	1,106,000
Hideki Kase	73	65	68	72	278	1,106,000
Frankie Minoza	69	68	68	73	278	1,106,000
Yoshimi Niizeki	68	70	67	73	278	1,106,000
Hideyuki Sato	70	71	72	66	279	842,000
Hsieh Chin-Sheng	71	68	73	67	279	842,000
Toru Nakamura	70	69	71	69	279	842,000
Wayne Smith	70	70	70	69	279	842,000
Craig Warren	72	70	68	79	279	842,000
Yoshitaka Yamamoto	71	71	68	69	279	842,000
Nobuhito Sato	67	67	71	74	279	842,000
Tomohiro Maruyama	71	70	73	66	280	686,000
Tatsuo Takasaki	70	70	72	68	280	686,000
Katsunari Takahashi	69	71	72	68	280	686,000
Shigenori Mori	73	68	71	68	280	686,000

	SCORES				TOTAL	MONEY
Hirofumi Miyase	69	67	74	70	280	686,000
Satoshi Oide	67	72	71	70	280	686,000
Hajime Meshiai	68	69	72	71	280	686,000
Yoshinori Kaneko	70	70	68	72	280	686,000
Yasunori Ida	69	71	67	73	280	686,000

Mizuno Open

Tokinodai Country Club, Bigjodai Course, Ishikawa
Par 36-36–72; 6,814 yards

June 22-25
purse, ¥100,000,000

	SCORES				TOTAL	MONEY
Brian Watts	71	65	66	71	273	¥18,000,000
Rick Gibson	72	62	70	72	276	10,000,000
Roger Mackay	67	73	71	66	277	4,480,000
Toshimitsu Izawa	74	65	70	68	277	4,480,000
Peter Senior	69	69	69	70	277	4,480,000
Kiyoshi Murota	70	71	65	71	277	4,480,000
Brandt Jobe	68	68	69	72	277	4,480,000
Anthony Gilligan	68	71	70	69	278	2,750,000
Todd Hamilton	69	70	68	71	278	2,750,000
Tsuneyuki Nakajima	69	69	71	70	279	2,150,000
Eiji Mizoguchi	67	67	72	73	279	2,150,000
Frankie Minoza	72	69	69	70	280	1,840,000
Teruo Nakamura	71	69	71	70	281	1,620,000
Kiyoshi Maita	72	71	67	71	281	1,620,000
Toru Suzuki	70	70	74	68	282	1,097,000
Carlos Franco	73	70	70	69	282	1,097,000
Takashi Kanemoto	72	70	71	69	282	1,097,000
Katsuyoshi Tomori	71	72	68	71	282	1,097,000
Koki Idoki	68	71	71	72	282	1,097,000
Lin Chie-Hsiang	72	70	68	72	282	1,097,000
Daisuke Serizawa	73	68	69	72	282	1,097,000
Koichi Suzuki	74	68	68	72	282	1,097,000
Kyi-Hla Han	72	69	69	72	282	1,097,000
Hiroshi Makino	71	71	72	69	283	820,000
Nobuhito Sato	73	71	70	69	283	820,000
Satoshi Higashi	66	71	76	70	283	820,000
Shinji Ikeuchi	73	70	70	70	283	820,000
Masami Ito	70	70	71	72	283	820,000
Yutaka Hagawa	75	64	74	71	284	740,000
Masahiro Kuramoto	70	70	69	75	284	740,000
Takaaki Fukuzawa	70	68	70	76	284	740,000

PGA Philanthropy Tournament

Twinfields Golf Club, Ishikawa
Par 36-36–72; 7,072 yards

June 29-July 2
purse, ¥100,000,000

	SCORES				TOTAL	MONEY
Kazuhiro Takami	69	71	68	69	277	¥12,600,000
Katsunari Takahashi	71	72	68	66	277	5,880,000
Brian Watts	72	67	69	69	277	5,880,000
(Takami defeated Takahashi and Watts at first extra hole.)						
Brandt Jobe	71	71	69	67	278	2,730,000

		SCORES			TOTAL	MONEY
Peter Senior	72	70	68	68	278	2,730,000
Nobuhito Sato	76	67	67	68	278	2,730,000
Kazuhiko Hosokawa	70	69	71	68	278	2,730,000
Frankie Minoza	70	74	68	67	279	1,925,000
Nobuo Serizawa	68	71	70	70	279	1,925,000
Hiroya Kamide	68	71	71	70	280	1,432,000
Richard Backwell	68	69	69	74	280	1,432,000
Tsuyoshi Yoneyama	66	73	67	74	280	1,432,000
Tsutomu Higa	73	70	68	70	281	1,176,000
Lin Chie-Hsiang	68	75	68	71	282	1,050,000
Hiroshi Ueda	69	70	69	74	282	1,050,000
Hideki Kase	74	70	73	66	283	795,000
Toru Nakamura	69	70	72	72	283	795,000
Tsuneyuki Nakajima	70	69	71	73	283	795,000
Roger Mackay	69	72	69	73	283	795,000
Yoshinori Kaneko	71	70	67	75	283	795,000
Seiki Okuda	73	70	73	68	284	585,000
Saburo Fujiki	71	70	73	70	284	585,000
Masayuki Kawamura	71	70	73	70	284	585,000
Kyi-Hla Han	71	72	71	70	284	585,000
Eiichi Itai	70	72	71	71	284	585,000
Shinji Ikeuchi	70	71	71	72	284	585,000
Masahiro Kuramoto	69	67	75	73	284	585,000
Rick Gibson	69	70	72	73	284	585,000
Shigeki Maruyama	70	71	70	73	284	585,000
Anthony Gilligan	72	67	70	75	284	585,000

Yonex Open Hiroshima

Hiroshima Country Club, Hachihonmatsu Course, Hiroshima
Par 36-36–72; 6,782 yards
(Tournament shortened to 54 holes — heavy rain.)

July 6-9
purse, ¥80,000,000

		SCORES		TOTAL	MONEY
Masashi Ozaki	73	68	66	207	¥10,800,000
Satoshi Higashi	71	69	68	208	6,000,000
Takashi Kanemoto	75	68	67	210	4,080,000
Kiyoshi Maita	71	71	69	211	2,480,000
Hiroya Kamide	71	68	72	211	2,480,000
Nobuhiro Yoshino	67	70	74	211	2,480,000
Masayuki Kawamura	72	72	68	212	1,560,000
Toru Nakamura	73	71	68	212	1,560,000
Shinichi Yokota	68	75	69	212	1,560,000
Hiroshi Makino	69	71	72	212	1,560,000
Toyokazu Hioki	69	70	73	212	1,560,000
Hideyuki Sato	73	71	69	213	978,000
Lin Chie-Hsiang	70	72	71	213	978,000
Hajime Meshiai	69	73	71	213	978,000
Wayne Levi	70	72	71	213	978,000
Tateo Ozaki	74	70	70	214	578,000
Yoshitaka Yamamoto	69	75	70	214	578,000
Kyi-Hla Han	68	75	71	214	578,000
Hiroshi Ueda	69	74	71	214	578,000
Koki Idoki	69	73	72	214	578,000
Masanobu Kimura	71	71	72	214	578,000
Seiji Ebihara	71	71	72	214	578,000
Hideto Shigenobu	75	67	72	214	578,000

	SCORES			TOTAL	MONEY
Takenori Hiraishi	72	69	73	214	578,000
Stewart Ginn	73	68	73	214	578,000
Masahiro Kuramoto	69	71	74	214	578,000
Kiyoshi Murota	69	69	76	214	578,000
Shoichi Kuwabara	68	69	77	214	578,000
Craig Warren	72	70	73	215	444,000
Saburo Fujiki	69	72	74	215	444,000
Chen Tze-Ming	68	69	78	215	444,000

Nikkei Cup

Fuji Golf Club, Dejima Course, Ibargi
Par 36-36–72; 6,980 yards

July 13-16
purse, ¥100,000,000

	SCORES				TOTAL	MONEY
Tetsu Nisikawa	65	67	69	68	269	¥18,000,000
Tomohiro Maruyama	68	68	71	64	271	10,000,000
Kazuhiro Takami	72	69	66	65	272	6,800,000
Frankie Minoza	69	67	71	66	273	4,400,000
Nobumitsu Yuhara	70	65	71	67	273	4,400,000
Satoshi Higashi	67	70	71	66	274	3,233,000
Hidemichi Tanaka	68	68	68	70	274	3,233,000
Hideki Kase	68	68	66	72	274	3,233,000
Yoshikazu Sakamoto	70	69	70	67	276	1,996,000
Toshiyuki Hiyama	70	70	69	67	276	1,996,000
Shigeki Maruyama	68	66	74	68	276	1,996,000
Kinpachi Yoshimura	71	67	70	68	276	1,996,000
Masahiro Kuramoto	70	68	68	70	276	1,996,000
Koki Idoki	67	68	70	71	276	1,996,000
Seiichi Koizumi	68	73	71	65	277	1,154,000
Keisuke Goi	69	70	70	68	277	1,154,000
Saburo Fujiki	67	67	74	69	277	1,154,000
Shinji Ikeuchi	72	69	67	69	277	1,154,000
Kiyoshi Murota	68	69	71	69	277	1,154,000
Toshiaki Odate	69	70	69	69	277	1,154,000
Isamu Sugita	65	69	73	70	277	1,154,000
Eiichi Itai	70	69	69	70	278	900,000
Toshimitsu Izawa	64	71	69	74	278	900,000
Takaaki Fukuzawa	69	71	70	69	279	790,000
Yoshinori Kaneko	67	67	76	69	279	790,000
Yoshimitsu Fukuzawa	71	70	69	69	279	790,000
Tatsuo Takasaki	69	69	71	70	279	790,000
Satoshi Oide	69	72	67	71	279	790,000
Toshiaki Sudo	70	68	70	71	279	790,000
Yoshimi Niizeki	69	66	71	73	279	790,000
Shinichi Yokota	67	70	69	73	279	790,000

NST Niigata Open

Sun Rise Golf Club, Niigata
Par 36-36–72; 7,145 yards

July 27-30
purse, ¥60,000,000

	SCORES				TOTAL	MONEY
Tomohiro Maruyama	69	70	69	66	274	¥10,800,000
Hidemichi Tanaka	66	71	69	71	277	6,000,000

	SCORES				TOTAL	MONEY
Gregory Meyer	70	74	68	67	279	3,480,000
Shinichi Yokota	72	67	69	71	279	3,480,000
Hajime Meshiai	69	71	74	67	281	2,280,000
Kazuo Kanayama	72	69	69	71	281	2,280,000
Isamu Sugita	73	71	72	66	282	1,830,000
Shoichi Kuwabara	72	71	70	69	282	1,830,000
Shinji Ikeuchi	72	71	71	69	283	1,150,000
Katsunori Kuwahara	73	70	71	69	283	1,150,000
Hisayuki Sasaki	70	73	70	70	283	1,150,000
Masayuki Kawamura	71	71	71	70	283	1,150,000
Hikaru Emoto	71	74	68	70	283	1,150,000
Tsutomu Higa	70	72	70	71	283	1,150,000
Seiichi Koizumi	73	68	71	71	283	1,150,000
Teruo Nakamura	71	74	71	68	284	633,000
Yurio Akitomi	68	76	71	69	284	633,000
Ken Kusumoto	73	71	70	70	284	633,000
Taichi Teshima	71	72	71	70	284	633,000
Mitsutaka Kusakabe	74	68	71	71	284	633,000
Yasunori Ida	70	68	75	71	284	633,000
Kiyoshi Masaka	71	68	72	73	284	633,000
Hiroshi Ueda	69	71	69	75	284	633,000
Yoshimi Niizeki	70	74	72	69	285	480,000
Daisuke Serizawa	72	69	75	69	285	480,000
Joji Furuki	73	71	72	69	285	480,000
Nobuo Serizawa	72	72	71	70	285	480,000
Keiichiro Fukahori	71	71	72	71	285	480,000
Yoshiyuki Omori	74	71	69	71	285	480,000
Yoshikazu Sakamoto	69	75	68	73	285	480,000

Sanko Grand Summer Championship

Gunma Sanko 72 County Club, Gunma
Par 36-36–72; 7,041 yards

August 3-6
purse, ¥100,000,000

	SCORES				TOTAL	MONEY
Frankie Minoza	68	68	67	64	267	¥18,000,000
Shinji Ikeuchi	71	69	65	66	271	10,000,000
Joji Furuki	69	69	67	68	273	5,200,000
Tomohiro Maruyama	70	68	65	70	273	5,200,000
Kazuhiko Hosokawa	67	67	68	71	273	5,200,000
Koki Idoki	71	68	69	66	274	3,600,000
Kiyoshi Maita	67	72	67	69	275	2,900,000
Hidemichi Tanaka	69	68	68	70	275	2,900,000
Ryoken Kawagishi	67	67	69	72	275	2,900,000
Seiichi Koizumi	70	66	72	68	276	1,955,000
Yoshimitsu Fukuzawa	69	69	70	68	276	1,955,000
Tsutomu Higa	71	70	66	69	276	1,955,000
Teruo Nakamura	69	70	68	69	276	1,955,000
Hisayuki Sasaki	71	69	71	66	277	1,440,000
Tsukasa Watanabe	70	69	69	69	277	1,440,000
Mitsuo Harada	69	71	67	70	277	1,440,000
Toshiaki Odate	69	73	68	68	278	997,000
Hideto Shigenobu	70	66	73	69	278	997,000
Satoshi Higashi	70	71	67	70	278	997,000
Nobuhiro Yoshino	69	70	69	70	278	997,000
Stewart Ginn	71	69	68	70	278	997,000
Taisuke Kitajima	69	67	71	71	278	997,000

	SCORES				TOTAL	MONEY
Toru Suzuki	69	68	69	72	278	997,000
Hidezumi Shirako	70	67	67	74	278	997,000
Shigenori Mori	69	70	70	70	279	820,000
Masami Ito	72	69	68	70	279	820,000
Eiji Mizoguchi	68	70	69	72	279	820,000
Hiroshi Ueda	68	71	72	69	280	780,000
Hisao Inoue	71	67	73	70	281	730,000
Shinichi Yokota	71	69	69	72	281	730,000
Jun Murota	69	70	70	72	281	730,000
Tatsuo Takasaki	66	71	70	74	281	730,000

Acom International

Seve Ballesteros Golf Club, Ibaragi
Par 36-36–72; 6,828 yards

August 18-20
purse, ¥100,000,000

	POINTS				TOTAL	MONEY
Katsunori Kuwahara	6	13	15	12	46	¥18,000,000
Tsukasa Watanabe	15	11	10	5	41	10,000,000
Tomohiro Maruyama	4	11	11	14	40	6,800,000
Takaaki Fukuzawa	14	11	11	3	39	4,800,000
Mark Brooks	7	14	6	9	36	3,800,000
Mark Roe	10	7	10	9	36	3,800,000
Hidemichi Tanaka	8	4	9	14	35	3,050,000
Kazuhiko Hosokawa	7	5	10	13	35	3,050,000
Satoshi Higashi	9	5	9	11	34	2,300,000
Yurio Akitomi	5	8	10	11	34	2,300,000
Koki Idoki	5	5	13	11	34	2,300,000
Tsutomu Higa	4	13	6	10	33	1,840,000
Kazuhiro Takami	8	11	5	8	32	1,500,000
Yutaka Hagawa	21	-2	9	4	32	1,500,000
Daisuke Serizawa	10	11	-2	13	32	1,500,000
Shoichi Kuwabara	5	7	11	9	32	1,500,000
Keisuke Goi	9	10	3	9	31	1,120,000
Kyi-Hla Han	10	8	9	4	31	1,120,000
Takashi Kanemoto	1	18	6	6	31	1,120,000
Masami Ito	11	6	-1	14	30	960,000
Masanobu Kimura	3	11	7	9	30	960,000
Brent Franklin	8	7	4	11	30	960,000
Junji Kawase	2	8	11	8	29	870,000
Todd Hamilton	7	11	5	6	29	870,000
Carlos Franco	1	11	9	6	27	840,000
Toshiaki Sudo	5	9	10	2	26	820,000
Taisei Inagaki	11	5	1	8	25	790,000
Toshiaki Odate	1	12	8	4	25	790,000
Motomasa Aoki	9	7	4	4	24	720,000
Kiyoshi Murota	2	8	2	12	24	720,000
Yoshikazu Sakamoto	4	6	6	8	24	720,000
Hisashi Nakase	15	0	7	2	24	720,000
Wayne Riley	1	11	5	7	24	720,000

Hisamitsu KBC Augusta Tournament

Ashiya Golf Club, Fukuoka
Par 36-36–72; 7,154 yards

August 24-27
purse, ¥100,000,000

	SCORES				TOTAL	MONEY
Kazuhiko Hosokawa	69	66	67	69	271	¥18,000,000
Todd Hamilton	69	70	66	67	272	8,400,000
Tomohiro Maruyama	69	68	67	68	272	8,400,000
Nobumitsu Yuhara	70	71	67	65	273	4,800,000
Satoshi Higashi	70	69	68	67	274	3,800,000
Frankie Minoza	67	69	67	71	274	3,800,000
Hidemichi Tanaka	67	71	69	68	275	3,200,000
Toru Suzuki	68	68	69	71	276	2,900,000
Katsunari Takahashi	71	69	70	67	277	2,185,000
Carlos Franco	64	73	70	70	277	2,185,000
Ikuo Shirahama	66	71	69	71	277	2,185,000
Hideki Kase	65	71	68	73	277	2,185,000
Chen Tze-Ming	68	72	68	70	278	1,680,000
Nobuo Serizawa	71	69	71	68	279	1,440,000
Katsuyoshi Tomori	71	70	68	70	279	1,440,000
Masanobu Kimura	69	71	69	70	279	1,440,000
Masashi Ozaki	75	68	69	68	280	1,120,000
Shinichi Yokota	71	69	71	69	280	1,120,000
Tsutomu Higa	70	67	72	71	280	1,120,000
Hajime Meshiai	73	70	73	65	281	910,000
Tsuyoshi Yoneyama	70	70	71	70	281	910,000
Toshimitsu Izawa	70	73	67	71	281	910,000
Eduardo Herrera	72	68	69	72	281	910,000
Yasunobu Kuramoto	70	70	69	72	281	910,000
Tatsuo Takasaki	71	69	68	73	281	910,000
Koki Idoki	65	75	73	69	282	790,000
Akiyoshi Ohmachi	69	73	71	69	282	790,000
Seiki Okuda	72	69	72	69	282	790,000
Toru Nakayama	70	72	68	72	282	790,000
Kiyoshi Maita	69	74	70	70	283	702,000
Kinpachi Yoshimura	72	69	72	70	283	702,000
Seiichi Koizumi	70	71	71	71	283	702,000
Yoshinori Kaneko	69	71	70	73	283	702,000
Keisuke Goi	73	67	69	74	283	702,000

Japan Match Play Championship

Nidom Classic Course, Hokkaido
Par 36-36–72; 6,941 yards

August 31-September 3
purse, ¥80,000,000

FIRST ROUND

Brian Watts defeated Yoshinori Kaneko, 2 and 1
Toru Suzuki defeated Eduardo Herrera, 2 up
Katsunari Takahashi defeated Eiji Mizoguchi, 1 up, 19 holes
Tomohiro Maruyama defeated Hsieh Chin-Sheng, 5 and 4
Masahiro Kuramoto defeated Hiroshi Ueda, 3 and 2
Rick Gibson defeated Ryoken Kawagishi, 3 and 2
Tsuneyuki Nakajima defeated Shinji Ikeuchi, 5 and 4
Katsuyoshi Tomori defeated Koki Idoki, 5 and 3
Ikuo Shirahama defeated Hisayuki Sasaki, 3 and 2
Shigeki Maruyama defeated David Ishii, 1 up

Masayuki Kawamura defeated Carlos Franco, 1 up
Kiyoshi Murota defeated Kazuhiro Takami, 2 and 1
Todd Hamilton defeated Kazuhiko Hosokawa, 3 and 2
Nobuo Serizawa defeated Yoshinori Mizumaki, 1 up, 23 holes
Satoshi Higashi defeated Katsunori Kuwahara, 2 and 1
Hideki Kase defeated Tsukasa Watanabe, 1 up, 20 holes

(Each losing player received ¥450,000.)

SECOND ROUND

Suzuki defeated Watts, 1 up
Maruyama defeated Takahashi, 5 and 3
Kuramoto defeated Gibson, 3 and 1
Tomori defeated Nakajima, 2 and 1
Maruyama defeated Shirahama, 3 and 2
Kawamura defeated Murota, 1 up
Hamilton defeated Serizawa, 4 and 3
Kase defeated Higashi, 5 and 4

(Each losing player received ¥850,000.)

QUARTER-FINALS

Suzuki defeated Maruyama, 1 up
Tomori defeated Kuramoto, 2 and 1
Maruyama defeated Kawamura, 1 up, 19 holes
Kase defeated Hamilton, 4 and 3

(Each losing player received ¥1,600,000.)

SEMI-FINALS

Tomori defeated Suzuki, 6 and 5
Maruyama defeated Kase, 1 up

THIRD-FOURTH PLACE PLAYOFF

Kase defeated Suzuki, 1 up

(Kase received ¥6,000,000; Suzuki received ¥4,500,000.)

FINAL

Tomori defeated Maruyama, 2 and 1

(Tomori received ¥25,000,000; Maruyama received ¥12,500,000.)

Suntory Open

Narashino Country Club, Chiba
Par 36-36–72; 7,052 yards

September 7-10
purse, ¥90,000,000

	SCORES				TOTAL	MONEY
Masahiro Kuramoto	67	64	71	71	273	¥16,200,000
Satoshi Higashi	68	70	68	70	276	6,480,000
Takaaki Fukuzawa	68	68	70	70	276	6,480,000
Nobuo Serizawa	68	69	68	71	276	6,480,000
Mitsutaka Kusakabe	71	72	67	67	277	3,240,000

		SCORES			TOTAL	MONEY
Corey Pavin	71	69	70	67	277	3,240,000
Hajime Meshiai	74	68	66	69	277	3,240,000
Katsunori Kuwahara	70	72	69	67	278	2,340,000
Yuichi Takano	71	68	72	67	278	2,340,000
Masashi Ozaki	74	68	65	71	278	2,340,000
Carlos Franco	70	72	69	69	280	1,656,000
Yeh Chang-Ting	70	68	70	72	280	1,656,000
Wayne Grady	68	71	68	73	280	1,656,000
Ryoken Kawagishi	67	76	71	67	281	1,116,000
Nobumitsu Yuhara	75	68	69	69	281	1,116,000
Akiyoshi Ohmachi	71	69	71	70	281	1,116,000
Tsuneyuki Nakajima	72	71	67	71	281	1,116,000
Brian Watts	67	72	70	72	281	1,116,000
Kazuhiko Hosokawa	66	72	71	72	281	1,116,000
Eiji Mizoguchi	69	73	67	72	281	1,116,000
Hideki Kase	73	69	69	71	282	846,000
Seiji Ebihara	69	69	73	71	282	846,000
Hisayuki Sasaki	69	71	74	69	283	756,000
Hiroshi Makino	71	73	70	69	283	756,000
Yutaka Hagawa	76	67	70	70	283	756,000
Brandt Jobe	69	69	74	71	283	756,000
Tateo Ozaki	70	70	66	77	283	756,000
Atsushi Takamatsu	70	72	74	68	284	675,000
Kiyoshi Murota	73	70	72	69	284	675,000
Katsunari Takahashi	71	70	70	73	284	675,000
Kinpachi Yoshimura	68	73	70	73	284	675,000

ANA Open

Sapporo Golf Club, Watts Course, Sapporo
Par 36-36–72; 7,063 yards

September 14-17
purse, ¥100,000,000

		SCORES			TOTAL	MONEY
Masashi Ozaki	70	72	69	68	279	¥18,000,000
Ernie Els	72	72	69	69	282	10,000,000
Hideki Kase	70	73	69	72	284	6,800,000
Masayuki Kawamura	74	70	71	72	287	4,800,000
Hisayuki Sasaki	73	69	77	69	288	3,800,000
Masahiro Kuramoto	70	72	73	73	288	3,800,000
Katsuyoshi Tomori	73	71	74	71	289	3,200,000
Tsuneyuki Nakajima	73	69	76	72	290	2,450,000
Eiji Mizoguchi	75	70	72	73	290	2,450,000
Pete Izumikawa	74	71	72	73	290	2,450,000
Yoshinori Kaneko	74	70	72	74	290	2,450,000
Kiyoshi Maita	72	70	78	71	291	1,506,000
Hideyuki Sato	72	74	74	71	291	1,506,000
Satoshi Higashi	76	70	73	72	291	1,506,000
Yoshikazu Sakamoto	77	70	72	72	291	1,506,000
Larry Nelson	77	72	69	73	291	1,506,000
Wayne Grady	72	71	74	74	291	1,506,000
Lin Chie-Hsiang	72	77	73	70	292	968,000
Shigeki Maruyama	76	72	73	71	292	968,000
Takaaki Fukuzawa	77	72	71	72	292	968,000
Rick Gibson	74	72	73	73	292	968,000
Anthony Gilligan	74	72	73	73	292	968,000
Hsieh Chin-Sheng	72	75	69	76	292	968,000
Tateo Ozaki	76	69	71	76	292	968,000

	SCORES				TOTAL	MONEY
Yoshimi Niizeki	73	74	76	70	293	790,000
Kiyoshi Murota	72	74	76	71	293	790,000
Peter Senior	75	69	76	73	293	790,000
Katsunari Takahashi	73	70	76	74	293	790,000
Akihito Yokoyama	76	73	70	74	293	790,000
Yoshinori Mizumaki	72	74	71	76	293	790,000

Gene Sarazen Jun Classic

Jun Classic County Club, Tochigi
Par 36-36–72; 7,094 yards

September 21-24
purse, ¥110,000,000

	SCORES				TOTAL	MONEY
Satoshi Higashi	68	69	65	68	270	¥19,800,000
Masashi Ozaki	69	68	64	70	271	11,000,000
Hajime Meshiai	72	71	61	68	272	6,380,000
Hideki Kase	65	70	67	70	272	6,380,000
Nobumitsu Yuhara	69	66	67	72	274	4,400,000
Daisuke Serizawa	68	69	69	69	275	3,740,000
Masayuki Kawamura	70	73	62	70	275	3,740,000
Tateo Ozaki	71	70	67	68	276	2,695,000
Rick Gibson	68	69	70	69	276	2,695,000
Gohei Sato	69	70	68	69	276	2,695,000
Peter McWhinney	71	70	65	70	276	2,695,000
Tomohiro Maruyama	71	72	67	67	277	1,793,000
Carlos Franco	71	69	68	69	277	1,793,000
Hidemichi Tanaka	71	68	67	71	277	1,793,000
Taisei Inagaki	70	66	70	71	277	1,793,000
Todd Hamilton	69	67	72	70	278	1,287,000
Yoshikazu Sakamoto	72	70	64	72	278	1,287,000
Pete Izumikawa	68	69	67	74	278	1,287,000
David Ishii	68	69	66	75	278	1,287,000
Seiji Ebihara	70	68	74	67	279	1,100,000
Anthony Gilligan	72	67	70	71	280	1,034,000
Frankie Minoza	72	69	66	73	280	1,034,000
Yoshimi Niizeki	68	74	69	70	281	946,000
Motomasa Aoki	69	70	72	70	281	946,000
Toru Suzuki	72	70	68	71	281	946,000
Brandt Jobe	71	72	70	69	282	869,000
Tsuneyuki Nakajima	70	71	70	71	282	869,000
Nobuo Serizawa	72	65	72	63	282	869,000
Shigeki Maruyama	71	69	68	74	282	869,000
Masanobu Kimura	75	69	71	68	283	792,000
Kiyoshi Murota	70	72	71	70	283	792,000
Tsuyoshi Yoneyama	69	70	71	73	283	792,000

Japan Open Championship

Kasumigaseki Country Club, Saitama
Par 35-36–71; 6,995 yards

September 28-October 1
purse, ¥90,000,000

	SCORES				TOTAL	MONEY
Toshimitsu Izawa	67	70	70	70	277	¥16,200,000
Kazuhiko Hosokawa	72	69	70	67	278	9,000,000
Hidemichi Tanaka	72	73	65	71	281	6,390,000

	SCORES				TOTAL	MONEY
Masashi Ozaki	71	71	71	70	283	4,455,000
Masahiko Akazawa	75	73	69	67	284	3,369,000
Frankie Minoza	68	73	71	72	284	3,369,000
Nobuo Serizawa	70	73	67	74	284	3,369,000
Brandt Jobe	69	75	72	69	285	2,511,000
Todd Hamilton	70	72	71	72	285	2,511,000
Satoshi Higashi	72	71	72	71	286	1,782,000
Peter Senior	70	74	70	72	286	1,782,000
Shigeki Maruyama	69	74	70	73	286	1,782,000
Nobumitsu Yuhara	68	71	74	73	286	1,782,000
*Yasuharu Imano	74	71	70	72	287	
Yoshitaka Yamamoto	70	74	70	73	287	1,422,000
Ryoken Kawagishi	73	73	72	70	288	1,314,000
Katsunori Kuwahara	77	67	75	70	289	930,000
Hirofumi Miyase	74	76	69	70	289	930,000
Katsuyoshi Tomori	75	72	71	71	289	930,000
Toru Suzuki	71	79	68	71	289	930,000
Hiroshi Ueda	72	73	73	71	289	930,000
Kiyoshi Murota	75	70	72	72	289	930,000
Hidezumi Shirakata	72	74	71	72	289	930,000
Ken Kusumoto	73	72	70	74	289	930,000
Chen Tze-Chung	74	71	70	74	289	930,000
Naomichi Ozaki	75	70	69	75	289	930,000
Seiki Okuda	74	71	76	69	290	746,000
Seiji Ebihara	75	70	73	72	290	746,000
Motomasa Aoki	70	78	72	71	291	710,000
Brian Watts	75	73	71	72	291	710,000

Tokai Classic

Miyoshi Country Club, Aichi
Par 36-36–72; 7,089 yards

October 5-8
purse, ¥110,000,000

	SCORES				TOTAL	MONEY
Masayuki Kawamura	74	73	64	74	285	¥19,800,000
Hideki Kase	70	75	71	70	286	11,000,000
Ryoken Kawagishi	70	74	74	69	287	7,480,000
Tomohiro Maruyama	69	77	72	70	288	4,546,000
Hirofumi Miyase	68	75	73	72	288	4,546,000
Tsuneyuki Nakajima	72	74	69	73	288	4,546,000
Eiichi Itai	70	77	71	71	289	3,190,000
Katsunori Kuwahara	73	71	70	75	289	3,190,000
Kiyoshi Maita	72	70	72	75	289	3,190,000
Brian Watts	72	77	71	71	291	2,251,000
Tateo Ozaki	71	79	70	71	291	2,251,000
Katsunari Takahashi	71	74	71	75	291	2,251,000
Akiyoshi Ohmachi	74	74	74	70	292	1,782,000
Kazuhiro Takami	75	72	70	75	292	1,782,000
Shigenori Mori	73	76	74	70	293	1,269,000
Satoshi Higashi	74	73	75	71	293	1,269,000
Chen Tze-Ming	75	74	73	71	293	1,269,000
Nobumitsu Yuhara	70	75	75	73	293	1,269,000
Seiki Okuda	76	74	70	73	293	1,269,000
Yutaka Hagawa	74	76	70	73	293	1,269,000
Hiroshi Ueda	76	69	72	76	293	1,269,000
Nobuo Serizawa	71	75	75	73	294	962,000
Toru Nakayama	74	74	73	73	294	962,000

	SCORES			TOTAL	MONEY
Nobuhiro Yasuno	71	78	71	74	294	962,000
Wayne Smith	71	75	73	75	294	962,000
Kazuhiko Hosokawa	72	78	75	70	295	825,000
Masahiro Kuramoto	69	74	81	71	295	825,000
Mitsutaka Kusakabe	72	76	75	72	295	825,000
Ken Kusumoto	70	78	75	72	295	825,000
Yoshitaka Yamamoto	74	72	75	74	295	825,000
Lin Chie-Hsiang	75	72	73	75	295	825,000
Peter McWhinney	71	74	75	75	295	825,000
Hitoshi Kato	70	76	74	75	295	825,000

Golf Digest Tournament

Tohmei Country Club, Shizuoka
Par 35-36–71; 6,801 yards

October 12-15
purse, ¥100,000,000

	SCORES			TOTAL	MONEY
Stewart Ginn	70	69	64	64	267	¥18,000,000
Rick Gibson	68	68	67	66	269	10,000,000
Tsukasa Watanabe	70	66	68	67	271	6,800,000
Tomohiro Maruyama	68	68	70	67	273	4,400,000
Tsuneyuki Nakajima	67	70	69	67	273	4,400,000
Brian Watts	66	68	71	69	274	3,400,000
Nobumitsu Yuhara	67	69	68	70	274	3,400,000
Satoshi Higashi	68	68	68	71	275	2,900,000
Nobuo Serizawa	69	70	69	69	277	2,185,000
Yoshinori Kaneko	73	68	67	69	277	2,185,000
Toru Nakamura	72	72	64	69	277	2,185,000
Teruo Sugihara	71	66	70	70	277	2,185,000
Masahiro Kuramoto	67	71	74	66	278	1,337,000
Kazuhiko Hosokawa	72	68	71	67	278	1,337,000
Shigenori Mori	70	70	71	67	278	1,337,000
Toshiaki Odate	72	67	71	68	278	1,337,000
Hidemichi Tanaka	71	66	71	70	278	1,337,000
Hajime Meshiai	71	68	69	70	278	1,337,000
Hiroshi Makino	68	70	69	71	278	1,337,000
Yoshitaka Yamada	76	63	71	69	279	924,000
Chen Tze-Ming	69	66	74	70	279	924,000
Tatsuo Takasaki	68	68	72	71	279	924,000
Joji Furuki	70	68	70	71	279	924,000
Seiji Ebihara	70	68	69	72	279	924,000
Saburo Fujiki	72	70	70	68	280	760,000
Masanobu Kimura	74	68	70	68	280	760,000
Lin Chie-Hsiang	73	66	71	70	280	760,000
Yoshinori Mizumaki	74	67	68	71	280	760,000
Shinichi Yokota	68	74	67	71	280	760,000
Peter McWhinney	71	71	67	71	280	760,000
Hisayuki Sasaki	71	68	69	72	280	760,000
Nobuhiro Yoshino	69	68	71	72	280	760,000
Takaaki Fukuzawa	69	69	69	73	280	760,000

Bridgestone Open

Sodegaura Country Club, Chiba
Par 36-36–72; 7,120 yards

October 19-22
purse, ¥120,000,000

	SCORES				TOTAL	MONEY
Shigeki Maruyama	66	70	67	71	274	¥21,600,000
Masashi Ozaki	67	74	68	68	277	8,640,000
Shinichi Yokota	67	71	71	68	277	8,640,000
Mark Calcavecchia	66	72	68	71	277	8,640,000
Kaname Yoko	68	71	69	70	278	4,800,000
Hajime Meshiai	68	68	72	71	279	4,080,000
Carlos Franco	68	75	66	70	279	4,080,000
Naomichi Ozaki	72	72	70	66	280	2,940,000
Ken Kusumoto	69	70	69	72	280	2,940,000
Hidemichi Tanaka	68	68	74	70	280	2,940,000
Brian Watts	68	68	72	72	280	2,940,000
Hsieh Min-Nan	73	69	67	72	281	1,881,600
Katsunari Takahashi	70	71	69	71	281	1,881,600
Takaaki Fukuzawa	71	72	69	69	281	1,881,600
Anthony Gilligan	70	70	70	71	281	1,881,600
Glen Day	68	69	72	72	281	1,881,600
Yoshinori Mizumaki	67	74	70	71	282	1,344,000
Koki Idoki	67	73	69	73	282	1,344,000
Eiji Mizoguchi	73	71	70	68	282	1,344,000
Motomasa Aoki	69	68	71	75	283	1,128,000
Hiroshi Makino	71	71	70	71	283	1,128,000
David Ishii	68	70	75	70	283	1,128,000
Jim Furyk	72	70	71	70	283	1,128,000
Seiji Ebihara	72	71	71	70	284	924,480
Tateo Ozaki	66	72	76	70	284	924,480
Yoshinori Kaneko	68	74	71	71	284	924,480
Masanobu Kimura	68	73	72	71	284	924,480
Ryoken Kawagishi	67	74	70	73	284	924,480
Mitsutaka Kusakabe	71	72	68	73	284	924,480
Yasunobu Kuramoto	66	69	72	77	284	924,480
Stewart Ginn	77	66	71	70	284	924,480
Hidezumi Shirakata	73	71	71	69	284	924,480
Andrew Magee	71	72	71	70	284	924,480

Philip Morris Championship

ABC Golf Club, Hyogo
Par 36-36–72; 7,176 yards

October 26-29
purse, ¥200,000,000

	SCORES				TOTAL	MONEY
Hidemichi Tanaka	67	73	69	69	278	¥36,000,000
Nobumitsu Yuhara	69	69	72	69	279	16,800,000
Naomichi Ozaki	69	70	70	70	279	16,800,000
Masashi Ozaki	67	69	75	69	280	9,600,000
Brian Watts	71	70	71	69	281	7,600,000
Ikuo Shirahama	69	70	71	71	281	7,600,000
Takenori Hiraishi	74	70	69	70	283	6,400,000
Andrew Magee	69	74	72	69	284	5,500,000
Katsunari Takahashi	72	71	71	70	284	5,500,000
Jim Furyk	70	69	74	72	285	4,300,000
Shinichi Yokota	70	75	67	73	285	4,300,000
Hirofumi Miyase	71	72	76	67	286	3,260,000

	SCORES			TOTAL	MONEY
Tsuyoshi Yoneyama	68	75 73	70	286	3,260,000
Tomohiro Maruyama	71	71 73	71	286	3,260,000
Stewart Ginn	69	72 73	72	286	3,260,000
Saburo Fujiki	76	72 75	64	287	2,340,000
Lin Chie-Hsiang	75	72 74	66	287	2,340,000
Masahiro Kuramoto	72	70 76	69	287	2,340,000
Shigenori Mori	72	74 71	70	287	2,340,000
David Ishii	69	71 77	71	288	1,920,000
Tsukasa Watanabe	71	73 72	72	288	1,920,000
Yutaka Hagawa	71	72 70	75	288	1,920,000
Yoshitaka Yamamoto	72	74 76	67	289	1,700,000
Hajime Meshiai	74	72 74	69	289	1,700,000
Yasunobu Kuramoto	70	74 74	71	289	1,700,000
Katsunori Kuwabara	72	71 73	73	289	1,700,000
Frankie Minoza	73	73 77	67	290	1,445,000
Duffy Waldorf	69	78 75	68	290	1,445,000
Hideki Kase	74	72 75	69	290	1,445,000
Hideto Shigenobu	74	74 73	69	290	1,445,000
Yoshinori Kaneko	70	76 74	70	290	1,445,000
Satoshi Higashi	75	72 72	71	290	1,445,000
Harumitsu Hamano	67	75 76	72	290	1,445,000
Mitsuo Harada	70	73 74	73	290	1,445,000
Tatsuo Takasaki	72	70 72	76	290	1,445,000

Daiwa International

Daiwa Vintage Golf Club, Tochigi
Par 36-36–72; 6,938 yards

November 2-5
purse, ¥170,000,000

	SCORES			TOTAL	MONEY
Shigenori Mori	71	67 69	73	280	¥30,600,000
Hisayuki Sasaki	72	73 71	65	281	14,280,000
David Ishii	70	72 70	69	281	14,280,000
Satoshi Higashi	72	73 70	67	282	7,026,666
Masanobu Kimura	71	65 71	75	282	7,026,666
Koki Idoki	71	71 70	70	282	7,026,666
Ken Kusumoto	76	69 70	68	283	4,930,000
Shigeki Maruyama	67	69 73	74	283	4,930,000
Justin Leonard	73	69 71	70	283	4,930,000
Hideki Kase	72	68 74	70	284	3,189,200
Koichi Suzuki	76	70 68	70	284	3,189,200
Tsukasa Watanabe	72	63 77	72	284	3,189,200
Peter Senior	74	69 72	69	284	3,189,200
Jerry Kelly	74	71 69	70	284	3,189,200
Phil Mickelson	73	70 68	74	285	2,448,000
Yoshinori Kaneko	71	73 70	72	286	1,931,200
Nobuo Serizawa	75	72 66	73	286	1,931,200
Toru Nakamura	70	75 71	70	286	1,931,200
Richard Boxall	72	76 74	64	286	1,931,200
Jesper Parnevik	76	72 72	66	286	1,931,200
Joji Furuki	73	72 72	70	287	1,538,500
Kiyoshi Murota	73	69 74	71	287	1,538,500
Seiki Okuda	66	75 74	72	287	1,538,500
Eiji Mizoguchi	73	69 72	73	287	1,538,500
Hiroyuki Fujita	72	73 70	73	288	1,428,000
Shinji Ikeuchi	76	71 75	67	289	1,343,000
Hiroshi Makino	77	72 70	70	289	1,343,000

	SCORES				TOTAL	MONEY
Hajime Meshiai	73	71	73	72	289	1,343,000
Shinichi Yokota	70	76	74	69	289	1,343,000
Hideyuki Sato	72	76	72	70	290	1,151,750
Kazuhiro Takami	69	73	75	73	290	1,151,750
Saburo Fujiki	76	70	74	70	290	1,151,750
Yoshinori Mizumaki	74	70	74	72	290	1,151,750
Masahiro Kuramoto	74	73	73	70	290	1,151,750
Eduardo Herrera	75	71	71	73	290	1,151,750
Toshiaki Odate	77	71	72	70	290	1,151,750
Peter McWhinney	74	70	71	75	290	1,151,750

Sumitomo Visa Taiheiyo Masters

Taiheiyo Club, Gotenba Course, Shizuoka
Par 36-36–72; 7,072 yards

November 9-12
purse, ¥150,000,000

	SCORES				TOTAL	MONEY
Satoshi Higashi	70	66	71	67	274	¥27,000,000
Shigeki Maruyama	70	72	68	68	278	15,000,000
Masashi Ozaki	73	69	69	68	279	10,200,000
Colin Montgomerie	74	69	66	61	280	7,200,000
Hideki Kase	70	69	74	68	281	6,000,000
Stewart Ginn	72	71	67	72	282	5,400,000
Tsukasa Watanabe	73	68	70	72	283	4,575,000
Mike Heinen	72	75	69	67	283	4,575,000
Nobuo Serizawa	76	70	67	71	284	3,450,000
Kazuhiro Takami	73	72	72	67	284	3,450,000
Bernhard Langer	74	74	68	68	284	3,450,000
Hidemichi Tanaka	72	75	73	65	285	2,760,000
Seiki Okuda	72	73	69	72	286	2,430,000
Shinichi Yokota	76	69	69	72	286	2,430,000
Larry Mize	75	75	69	68	287	2,070,000
Greg Norman	74	71	71	71	287	2,070,000
Yoshinori Kaneko	72	75	71	70	288	1,635,000
Kiyoshi Murota	73	71	73	71	288	1,635,000
Hirofumi Miyase	74	75	68	71	288	1,635,000
Peter Senior	73	71	71	73	288	1,635,000
Saburo Fujiki	72	74	73	70	289	1,320,000
Kiyoshi Maita	72	74	70	73	289	1,320,000
Masahiro Kuramoto	74	70	74	71	289	1,320,000
Ryoken Kawagishi	73	76	69	71	289	1,320,000
Hsieh Chin-Sheng	80	69	71	69	289	1,320,000
Phil Mickelson	74	74	68	73	289	1,320,000
Seiji Ebihara	73	74	72	71	290	1,110,857
Toru Suzuki	68	73	73	76	290	1,110,857
Mitsutaka Kusakabe	75	73	70	72	290	1,110,857
Lin Chie-Hsiang	70	77	70	73	290	1,110,857
Kazuhiko Hosokawa	74	73	71	72	290	1,110,857
Todd Hamilton	74	74	70	72	290	1,110,857
Barry Lane	73	74	69	74	290	1,110,857

Dunlop Phoenix Tournament

Phoenix Country Club, Miyazaki
Par 35-36–71; 6,798 yards

November 16-19
purse, ¥200,000,000

	SCORES				TOTAL	MONEY
Masashi Ozaki	65	71	69	68	273	¥36,000,000
Brandt Jobe	69	67	71	67	274	14,400,000
Robert Gamez	66	69	72	67	274	14,400,000
Peter Senior	69	64	69	72	274	14,400,000
Tom Watson	66	70	70	70	276	7,600,000
Graham Marsh	68	69	66	73	276	7,600,000
Larry Mize	66	71	71	69	277	6,400,000
Scott Hoch	73	66	73	66	278	4,900,000
Naomichi Ozaki	68	72	69	69	278	4,900,000
Toru Suzuki	70	68	70	70	278	4,900,000
Yoshinori Kaneko	67	70	70	71	278	4,900,000
David Frost	70	70	73	66	279	3,520,000
Vijay Singh	68	70	71	70	279	3,520,000
Hidemichi Tanaka	71	72	71	66	280	2,560,000
Jeff Sluman	72	69	72	67	280	2,560,000
Shigeki Maruyama	66	71	73	70	280	2,560,000
Hisayuki Sasaki	69	67	74	70	280	2,560,000
Masahiro Kuramoto	68	68	72	72	280	2,560,000
Larry Nelson	68	68	69	75	280	2,560,000
Todd Hamilton	71	70	72	68	281	1,880,000
Ernie Els	68	73	71	69	281	1,880,000
Miguel Angel Jimenez	70	71	68	72	281	1,880,000
Nobuo Serizawa	69	67	72	73	281	1,880,000
Seiki Okuda	72	68	72	70	282	1,680,000
Barry Lane	64	72	75	71	282	1,680,000
Craig Parry	70	69	72	71	282	1,680,000
Eduardo Herrera	71	71	75	66	283	1,580,000
Hajime Meshiai	69	73	70	71	283	1,580,000
Ryoken Kawagishi	73	68	75	68	284	1,500,000
Costantino Rocca	74	68	72	70	284	1,500,000

Casio World Open

Ibusuki Golf Club, Kaimon Course, Kagoshima
Par 36-36–72; 7,014 yards

November 23-26
purse, ¥150,000,000

	SCORES				TOTAL	MONEY
Seiki Okuda	69	72	69	64	274	¥27,000,000
Masashi Ozaki	70	69	68	68	275	15,000,000
Katsuyoshi Tomori	69	70	71	66	276	10,200,000
Hajime Meshiai	66	71	70	70	277	7,200,000
Costantino Rocca	70	70	69	70	279	6,000,000
Kiyoshi Maita	65	68	76	71	280	5,100,000
Nobumitsu Yuhara	72	69	71	68	280	5,100,000
Robert Gamez	72	74	70	65	281	4,350,000
Yoshinori Mizumaki	76	72	65	69	282	3,126,000
David Ishii	72	71	66	73	282	3,126,000
Mark Brooks	72	71	72	67	282	3,126,000
Brian Watts	65	73	70	70	282	3,126,000
Miguel Angel Jimenez	73	71	70	68	282	3,126,000
Hideki Kase	72	75	70	66	283	1,860,000
Toru Suzuki	76	70	69	68	283	1,860,000

	SCORES				TOTAL	MONEY
Todd Hamilton	70	74	70	69	283	1,860,000
Philip Walton	70	72	72	69	283	1,860,000
Lee Janzen	70	73	68	72	283	1,860,000
Vijay Singh	70	71	71	71	283	1,860,000
Carlos Franco	70	70	70	73	283	1,860,000
Masayuki Kawamura	68	75	69	72	284	1,357,500
Hirofumi Miyase	74	73	67	70	284	1,357,500
Hidemichi Tanaka	71	75	72	66	284	1,357,500
Richard Backwell	69	71	73	71	284	1,357,500
Yoshinori Kaneko	68	71	72	74	285	1,260,000
Tateo Ozaki	72	74	70	70	286	1,140,000
Tsuneyuki Nakajima	71	71	73	71	286	1,140,000
Yoshimi Niizeki	72	74	69	71	286	1,140,000
Tsuyoshi Yoneyama	68	76	71	71	286	1,140,000
Chen Tze-Chung	74	71	71	70	286	1,140,000
Rick Gibson	72	72	71	71	286	1,140,000
Joakim Haeggman	70	72	71	73	286	1,140,000

Japan Series of Golf

Tokyo Yomiuri Country Club, Tokyo
Par 36-36–72; 7,022 yards

November 30-December 3
purse, ¥100,000,000

	SCORES				TOTAL	MONEY
Masashi Ozaki	66	67	71	68	272	¥30,000,000
Shigenori Mori	68	70	69	67	274	11,250,000
Tsuneyuki Nakajima	67	68	68	71	274	11,250,000
Shigeki Maruyama	65	69	72	71	277	4,450,000
Masahiro Kuramoto	69	69	68	71	277	4,450,000
Eduardo Herrera	70	65	70	72	277	4,450,000
Satoshi Higashi	68	68	68	73	277	4,450,000
Toru Suzuki	67	70	69	72	278	3,200,000
Hidemichi Tanaka	72	72	62	73	279	2,800,000
Katsuyoshi Tomori	71	73	69	67	280	2,375,000
Todd Hamilton	69	76	67	68	280	2,375,000
Rick Gibson	69	74	69	69	281	1,900,000
Stewart Ginn	71	72	68	70	281	1,900,000
Kazuhiro Takami	73	71	67	73	284	1,600,000
Toshimitsu Izawa	73	71	71	70	285	1,350,000
Carlos Franco	71	74	67	73	285	1,350,000
Brandt Jobe	72	71	67	75	285	1,350,000
Mitsutaka Kusakabe	75	65	70	75	285	1,350,000
Kazuhiko Hosokawa	74	73	67	72	286	1,075,000
Nobumitsu Yuhara	71	70	72	73	286	1,075,000
Seiki Okuda	70	70	73	73	286	1,075,000
Brian Watts	72	68	68	78	286	1,075,000
Frankie Minoza	72	70	73	73	288	925,000
Katsunori Kuwabara	74	72	69	73	288	925,000
Tomohiro Maruyama	71	76	70	72	289	825,000
Masayuki Kawamura	73	72	69	75	289	825,000
Hideki Kase	68	73	72	77	290	750,000
Tetsu Nishikawa	75	75	75	73	298	700,000

Daikyo Open

Daikyo Country Club, Okinawa
Par 36-35–71; 6,268 yards

November 30-December 3
purse, ¥120,000,000

	SCORES				TOTAL	MONEY
Frankie Minoza	68	69	67	69	273	¥21,600,000
Toru Nakamura	67	72	70	66	275	12,000,000
Masahiro Kuramoto	71	68	70	67	276	8,160,000
Katsuyoshi Tomori	69	71	67	70	277	5,280,000
Katsuyoshi Kuwahara	69	72	67	69	277	5,280,000
Nobuo Serizawa	67	71	68	72	278	3,690,000
Kazuhiro Takami	71	68	72	67	278	3,690,000
Masanobu Kimura	71	67	71	69	278	3,690,000
Ken Kusumoto	71	70	72	65	278	3,690,000
Peter McWhinney	72	72	66	69	279	2,760,000
Shigeki Maruyama	71	71	69	69	280	2,304,000
Brian Watts	67	68	70	75	280	2,304,000
Teruo Sugihara	66	73	71	71	281	2,016,000
Hideyuki Sato	71	70	74	67	282	1,593,600
Toshiaki Sudo	70	74	71	67	282	1,593,600
Saburo Fujiki	69	70	74	69	282	1,593,600
Masami Ito	68	76	74	64	282	1,593,600
Yasunobu Kuramoto	68	73	66	75	282	1,593,600
Yoshinori Kaneko	70	73	68	72	283	1,176,000
Shigenori Mori	68	69	71	75	283	1,176,000
Hajime Meshiai	67	75	70	71	283	1,176,000
Tatsuo Takasaki	72	71	69	71	283	1,176,000
Tomohiro Maruyama	72	72	74	66	284	1,044,000
Hidezumi Shirakata	75	67	71	71	284	1,044,000
Hideto Shigenobu	72	71	70	72	285	960,000
Anthony Gilligan	69	73	75	68	285	960,000
Keisuke Goi	70	73	71	71	285	960,000
Kazuhiko Hosokawa	74	70	69	72	285	960,000
Shinichi Yokota	72	72	76	65	285	960,000
Motomasa Aoki	69	70	74	73	286	853,200
Toru Nakayama	72	72	73	69	286	853,200
Nobumitsu Yuhara	73	69	73	71	286	853,200
David Ishii	72	73	69	72	286	853,200

Asia PGA/Omega Tour

The International

Srirach International Golf Club, Pattaya, Thailand
Par 36-36–72; 6,964 yards

June 22-25
purse, $200,000

	SCORES				TOTAL	MONEY
Nam-Sin Park	70	68	67	66	271	$32,300
Hendrik Buhrmann	66	70	68	68	272	22,260

	SCORES				TOTAL	MONEY
Amandeep Singh Johl	66	68	69	71	274	12,400
Clayton Devers	69	68	68	71	276	10,000
Shigemasa Higaki	70	70	67	70	277	7,500
Robert Glenn Willis	71	69	68	69	277	7,500
Wang Ter-Chang	70	70	67	71	278	4,626
John Kernohan	69	69	69	71	278	4,626
Robert Pactolerin	69	66	72	71	278	4,626
Jeev Milkha Singh	70	72	69	67	278	4,626
Thannoon Sriroj	67	69	69	73	278	4,626
Michael Cunning	67	68	73	71	279	3,236.66
Makoto Komura	69	68	72	70	279	3,236.66
No-Sook Park	68	69	69	73	279	3,236.66
Mardan Mamat	70	69	70	71	280	2,760
Zaw Moe	73	69	70	68	280	2,760
Rafael Ponce	69	70	72	69	280	2,760
Kyung-Joo Choi	73	70	66	71	280	2,760
Lin Keng-Chi	72	68	69	72	281	2,344
Tony Maloney	70	68	69	74	281	2,344
Tony Mills	69	70	70	72	281	2,344
Gerry Norquist	69	70	71	71	281	2,344
Chen Liang-Hsi	70	71	67	73	281	2,344
Andrew Bonhomme	69	70	71	72	282	2,040
Craig Kamps	71	69	71	71	282	2,040
Young-Suk Kwon	69	72	70	71	282	2,040
Supoj Meesawad	68	71	70	73	282	2,040
Lu Wen-Ter	69	69	74	70	282	2,040
Lin Chih-Chen	69	71	69	74	283	1,697.14
Jannian Chitprasong	73	69	71	70	283	1,697.14
Wook-Soon Kang	69	69	75	70	283	1,697.14
Scott Taylor	69	74	69	71	283	1,697.14
Nico Van Rensburg	68	70	72	73	283	1,697.14
Yong-Nam Yang	74	68	72	69	283	1,697.14
Pisit Infasang	71	72	67	73	283	1,697.14

Canlubang Classic

Canlubang Golf & Country Club, Laguna, Philippines
Par 35-36–71; 6,757 yards

June 29-July 2
purse, $150,000

	SCORES				TOTAL	MONEY
Carlos Espinosa	69	69	67	69	274	$24,225
Nico Van Rensburg	68	73	66	68	275	16,695
John Kernohan	71	69	67	71	278	9,300
Sang-Ho Choi	69	67	72	71	279	7,500
Greg Chalmers	73	69	69	69	280	5,625
Scott Taylor	67	70	71	72	280	5,625
Chul-Sang Cho	70	71	72	68	281	4,125
Robert Willis	69	71	70	71	281	4,125
Craig Kamps	74	70	68	71	283	2,918.25
Wook-Soon Kang	68	72	70	73	283	2,918.25
Nam-Sin Park	70	71	70	72	283	2,918.25
Li Wen-Sheng	71	69	69	74	283	2,918.25
Sung-Ho Kim	70	74	68	72	284	2,353.50
Yeh Yeou-Tsai	66	75	68	75	284	2,353.50
Bradley Andrews	69	74	69	73	285	2,070
David Bransdon	71	70	71	73	285	2,070
Mike Cunning	71	71	75	68	285	2,070

	SCORES				TOTAL	MONEY
Don Fardon	69	71	72	73	285	2,070
Tony Christie	74	67	71	74	286	1,805
Eijiro Koyama	69	71	74	72	286	1,805
Masakazu Noritake	74	71	72	69	286	1,805
Gaurav Ghei	77	70	68	72	287	1,575
Lin Keng-Chi	72	70	73	72	287	1,575
Chung Chun-Hsing	72	72	72	71	287	1,575
Oh-Chul Kwon	71	68	80	68	287	1,575
Tony Maloney	72	71	70	74	287	1,575
Jeev Milkha Singh	74	68	75	70	287	1,575
Zhang Lian-Wei	69	75	72	71	287	1,575
Cesar Ababa	69	73	71	75	288	1,256.25
Darren Barnes	70	71	70	77	288	1,256.25
Felix Casas	75	72	73	68	288	1,256.25
Lin Chih-Chen	72	72	73	71	288	1,256.25
Greg Hanrahan	73	73	70	72	288	1,256.25
Zaw Moe	71	73	67	77	288	1,256.25
Rafael Ponce	72	70	73	73	288	1,256.25
Yasuo Sone	70	75	73	70	288	1,256.25

Tournament Players Championship

Tanjong Puteri Golf Resort, Johor Baru, Malaysia
Par 36-36–72; 7,058 yards

July 27-30
purse, $150,000

	SCORES				TOTAL	MONEY
Lin Keng-Chi	72	70	68	68	278	$24,225
Craig Kamps	69	72	70	70	281	12,997.50
Lu Wen-Ter	71	73	69	68	281	12,997.50
Lin Chih-Chen	70	69	72	71	282	7,500
Aaron Meeks	69	73	68	73	283	4,875
Gerry Norquist	75	71	68	69	283	4,875
Stephen Scahill	71	75	70	67	283	4,875
Dominique Boulet	70	74	70	69	283	4,875
David Bransdon	74	68	67	75	284	3,032.50
Tony Maloney	76	67	71	70	284	3,032.50
Scott Taylor	69	74	70	71	284	3,032.50
Vivek Bhandari	69	70	74	72	285	2,320.50
Gaurav Ghei	68	74	73	70	285	2,320.50
Zaw Moe	70	70	75	70	285	2,320.50
Shimoi Masashi	75	71	71	68	285	2,320.50
Boonchu Ruangkit	73	72	71	69	285	2,320.50
Darren Barnes	73	69	72	72	286	1,875
Mike Cunning	74	71	68	73	286	1,875
Thannoon Sriroj	71	73	72	70	286	1,875
Robert Willis	75	72	69	70	286	1,875
Cheng Jun	68	73	68	77	286	1,875
Chung Chun-Hsing	74	69	73	71	287	1,597.50
Tony Mills	71	75	67	74	287	1,597.50
Ghulam Nabi	74	69	72	72	287	1,597.50
Chang Tse-Peng	76	72	71	68	287	1,597.50
Jeff Senior	71	70	74	72	287	1,597.50
Nico Van Rensburg	71	69	75	72	287	1,597.50
Andrew Bonhomme	69	71	70	78	288	1,417.50
Yasuo Sone	70	73	74	71	288	1,417.50
Makoto Komura	74	72	71	72	289	1,350

Formosa Open

Formosa First Golf Club, Taipei, Taiwan
Par 36-36–72; 6,932 yards

August 17-20
purse, $250,000

	SCORES				TOTAL	MONEY
Lin Chie-Hsiang	71	74	67	68	280	$65,536.44
Boonchu Ruangkit	70	68	68	74	280	41,194.33
(Lin defeated Ruangkit on first extra hole.)						
Chul-Sang Cho	72	68	68	73	281	23,218.62
Jong-Duck Kim	70	67	75	70	282	17,226.72
Lu Wen-Ter	70	69	72	71	282	17,226.72
Lin Keng-Chi	71	71	71	70	283	9,542.10
Nam-Sin Park	73	67	74	69	283	9,542.10
S. Fukunaha	71	70	70	72	283	9,542.10
Jose Cantero	72	69	74	68	283	9,542.10
Chen Liang-Hsi	70	71	69	73	283	9,542.10
Masakazu Noritake	69	76	69	70	284	6,391.36
Ron Wuensche	71	68	73	72	284	6,391.36
Hsieh Chin-Sheng	71	70	73	70	284	6,391.36
Felix Casas	70	69	74	72	285	5,145.54
Chung Chun-Hsing	70	72	73	70	285	5,145.54
Nico Van Rensburg	76	70	70	69	285	5,145.54
Andre Cruse	68	73	71	73	285	5,145.54
H. Nimiki	72	74	71	68	285	5,145.54
Hendrik Buhrmann	72	72	72	70	286	4,198.07
Yu Chin-Han	69	74	71	72	286	4,198.07
Chen Tze-Chung	71	71	74	70	286	4,198.07
Hsieh Min-Nan	70	70	75	71	286	4,198.07
Chen Tze-Ming	74	73	71	68	286	4,198.07
Wang Ter-Chang	75	70	68	74	287	3,473.43
Gaurav Ghei	73	70	72	72	287	3,473.43
Mike Cunning	73	73	67	74	287	3,473.43
Hsu Tien-Lai	72	73	70	72	287	3,473.43
Aaron Meeks	74	70	74	69	287	3,473.43
Zaw Moe	73	75	70	69	287	3,473.43
Yasuo Sone	75	70	72	70	287	3,473.43
Dominique Boulet	73	70	72	72	287	3,473.43
Olle Nordberg	72	71	71	73	287	3,473.43
Bob May	71	72	70	74	287	3,473.43

Yokohama Singapore PGA Championship

Jurong Country Club, Singapore
Par 36-36–72; 6,896 yards

August 24-27
purse, $225,000

	SCORES				TOTAL	MONEY
Lin Keng-Chi	68	67	69	71	275	$36,337.50
Zaw Moe	70	68	68	70	276	25,042.50
David Bransdon	71	70	72	66	279	12,600
Mike Cunning	69	70	72	68	279	12,600
Gaurav Ghei	70	70	71	69	280	7,875
Richard Kaplan	72	70	71	67	280	7,875
Boonchu Ruangkit	71	70	67	72	280	7,875
Jyoti Randhawa	71	75	68	67	281	5,625
Greg Chalmers	72	69	73	70	284	4,225.50
John Kernohan	71	70	71	72	284	4,225.50
Masakazu Noritake	70	73	69	72	284	4,225.50

	SCORES				TOTAL	MONEY
Robert Pactolerin	69	71	73	71	284	4,225.50
Thannoon Sriroj	72	71	70	71	284	4,225.50
Takehito Daijo	68	76	72	69	285	3,375
Aaron Meeks	68	73	71	73	285	3,375
Hendrik Buhrmann	70	72	73	71	286	2,920.50
Craig Kamps	76	70	71	69	286	2,920.50
Eijiro Koyama	75	68	70	73	286	2,920.50
Gerry Norquist	70	72	73	71	286	2,920.50
Preecha Senaprom	73	72	69	72	286	2,920.50
Eddie Bagtas	73	73	72	69	287	2,430
Poh Eing-Chong	73	71	71	72	287	2,430
Rodrigo Cuello	72	73	71	71	287	2,430
Carlos Espinosa	71	72	74	70	287	2,430
Greg Hanrahan	77	69	71	70	287	2,430
Simon Owen	73	73	71	70	287	2,430
Yasuo Sone	73	73	71	70	287	2,430
Mardan Mamat	75	71	71	71	288	2,126.25
Jeev Milkha Singh	76	68	70	74	288	2,126.25
George Olaybar	74	71	70	74	289	1,903.50
Scott Taylor	74	72	70	73	289	1,903.50
Suphavaarangoon Veerawut	68	74	77	70	289	1,903.50
Thaworn Wiratchant	72	74	72	71	289	1,903.50
Poh Eng-Wah	76	71	69	73	289	1,903.50

Passport Open

Chun Chon Country Club, Chun Chon, Korea
Par 36-36–72; 6,874 yards

August 31-September 3
purse, $300,000

	SCORES				TOTAL	MONEY
Vijay Singh	70	72	65	65	272	$48,450
Jeev Milkha Singh	67	70	72	64	273	33,390
Jong-Duck Kim	68	67	67	73	275	18,060
Sang-Ho Choi	69	69	70	70	278	11,625
Carlos Espinosa	70	69	70	69	278	11,625
David Frost	69	69	73	67	278	11,625
Yong-Jin Shin	73	69	70	66	278	11,625
Don Fardon	66	72	74	67	279	6,730
Young-Keun Han	67	73	70	69	279	6,730
Young-Suk Kwon	72	72	68	67	279	6,730
Masakazu Noritake	68	69	73	70	280	5,017.50
Nam-Sin Park	71	70	68	71	280	5,017.50
Joselito Rempojo	71	68	71	70	280	5,017.50
Thaworn Wiratchant	69	68	71	72	280	5,017.50
Clay Devers	71	69	68	73	281	4,230
Nozomi Kawahara	70	71	68	72	281	4,230
Scott Taylor	70	72	68	71	281	4,230
Hendrik Buhrmann	70	71	70	71	282	3,730
John Kernohan	70	69	71	72	282	3,730
Joon Chung	67	71	71	73	282	3,730
Tae-Ha Bong	74	68	68	73	283	3,420
Preecha Senaprom	70	71	71	71	283	3,420
Dominique Boulet	68	77	72	66	283	3,420
Derek Fung	73	70	71	70	284	3,105
Alan Murdoch	73	71	68	72	284	3,105
Robert Pactolerin	71	69	73	71	284	3,105
Chip Beck	71	73	72	68	284	3,105

	SCORES				TOTAL	MONEY
Bradley Andrews	70	68	74	73	285	2,745
Chul-Sang Cho	70	74	71	70	285	2,745
Amandeep Johl	70	71	69	75	285	2,745
Sung-Ho Kim	69	71	71	74	285	2,745

Langkawi Open

Datai Bay Golf Club, Langkawi, Malaysia
Par 36-36–72; 6,666 yards

September 28-October 1
purse, $150,000

	SCORES				TOTAL	MONEY
Boonchu Ruangkit	67	71	67	68	273	$24,225
Jannian Chitprasong	69	71	71	69	280	16,695
Craig Kamps	69	72	68	72	281	9,300
Clay Devers	68	69	71	75	283	6,750
John Kernohan	72	71	72	68	283	6,750
Gaurav Ghei	72	73	68	72	285	4,500
Mardan Mamat	69	73	73	70	285	4,500
Lu Chien-Soon	75	69	70	71	285	4,500
Madasamy Murugiah	71	76	72	67	286	3,345
Rodrigo Cuello	74	69	72	72	287	2,776
Tsai Chie-Huang	73	70	74	70	287	2,776
Andrew Bonhomme	74	72	72	69	287	2,776
Lu Wen-Ter	70	73	73	72	288	2,210.40
Cheng Jun	74	69	73	72	288	2,210.40
Shimoi Masashi	69	75	72	72	288	2,210.40
Carlos Espinosa	75	71	70	72	288	2,210.40
Eddie Bagtas	71	73	75	69	288	2,210.40
Scott Taylor	71	72	72	74	289	1,812
Simon Yates	74	72	69	74	289	1,812
Udorn Duangdecha	70	74	71	74	289	1,812
Zhang Lian-Wei	74	72	70	73	289	1,812
Tsao Chien-Teng	70	75	72	72	289	1,812
Lin Keng-Chi	72	73	71	74	290	1,642.50
Zaw Moe	77	73	70	70	290	1,642.50
Poh Eing-Chong	71	71	74	75	291	1,552.50
Makoto Komura	75	73	72	71	291	1,552.50
Greg Chalmers	74	72	70	76	292	1,372.50
Danny Zarate	72	72	73	75	292	1,372.50
Derek Fung	72	68	78	74	292	1,372.50
Chung Chun-Hsing	72	73	74	73	292	1,372.50
Lin Chih-Chen	69	76	74	73	292	1,372.50
Tony Mills	75	76	70	71	292	1,372.50

Gadgil Western Dubai Creek Open

Dubai Creek Golf & Yacht Club, Dubai, United Arab Emirates
Par 35-36–71; 6,781 yards

October 5-8
purse, $500,000

	SCORES				TOTAL	MONEY
Robert Willis	71	66	73	73	283	$80,750
Jannian Chitprasong	72	69	73	69	283	55,650
(Willis defeated Chitprasong on first extra hole.)						
Jeev Milkha Singh	75	72	68	70	285	28,000
Boonchu Ruangkit	74	70	72	69	285	28,000

	SCORES			TOTAL	MONEY
Wang Ter-Chang	73	67	73	73	286	16,250
Gaurav Ghei	69	69	77	71	286	16,250
Greg Hanrahan	68	73	74	71	286	16,250
Zaw Moe	71	67	77	71	286	16,250
David Bransdon	71	76	69	71	287	9,727.50
Mike Cunning	70	70	74	73	287	9,727.50
John Kernohan	74	65	73	75	287	9,727.50
Arjin Sophon	68	71	70	78	287	9,727.50
Nico Van Rensburg	71	73	74	70	288	7,845
Zhang Lian-Wei	74	69	72	73	288	7,845
Simon Owen	71	74	73	71	289	7,350
Hendrik Buhrmann	72	73	76	69	290	6,020
Felix Casas	73	74	71	72	290	6,020
Lin Keng-Chi	75	70	77	68	290	6,020
Shigemasa Higaki	72	72	75	71	290	6,020
Mardan Mamat	77	67	73	73	290	6,020
Supoj Meesawad	73	71	72	74	290	6,020
Ghulam Nabi	75	72	70	73	290	6,020
Masakazu Noritake	72	69	78	71	290	6,020
Gerry Norquist	74	70	72	74	290	6,020
Simon Yates	73	70	77	70	290	6,020
Chung Chun-Hsing	70	70	76	75	291	4,950
Tony Mills	71	77	73	70	291	4,950
Scott Taylor	72	73	77	69	291	4,950
Bradley Andrews	71	69	75	77	292	4,500
Carlos Espinosa	69	73	77	73	292	4,500
Jyoti Randhawa	72	73	75	72	292	4,500

Merlion Masters

Laguna National Golf & Country Club, Singapore   October 12-15
Par 36-36–72; 6,991 yards   purse, $200,000

	SCORES			TOTAL	MONEY
Nico Van Rensburg	68	69	69	73	279	$32,300
Don Fardon	71	67	67	75	280	17,330
Pisit Infasang	65	75	71	69	280	17,330
Kenny Walker	69	72	72	68	281	10,000
Rodrigo Cuello	67	70	69	76	282	8,000
Thannoon Sriroj	69	72	74	70	285	7,000
David Bransdon	71	73	71	71	286	5,500
Craig Kamps	70	74	70	72	286	5,500
Felix Casas	70	73	71	74	288	4,230
Simon Owen	73	70	72	73	288	4,230
Mardan Mamat	76	72	73	68	289	3,440
Preecha Senaprom	71	74	73	71	289	3,440
Scott Taylor	73	73	71	72	289	3,440
Jannian Chitprasong	68	73	73	76	290	2,940
Nozomi Kawahara	73	70	79	68	290	2,940
Zaw Moe	70	74	74	72	290	2,940
Greg Chalmers	71	73	76	71	291	2,700
Eddie Bagtas	74	74	70	74	292	2,486.66
Madasamy Murugiah	72	74	74	72	292	2,486.66
Gerry Norquist	66	80	73	73	292	2,486.66
Robert Willis	75	72	71	75	293	2,340
Cesar Ababa	70	76	75	73	294	2,160
Brad Andrews	72	75	70	77	294	2,160

	SCORES				TOTAL	MONEY
Richard Kaplan	70	71	77	76	294	2,160
Makoto Komura	72	72	73	77	294	2,160
Masakazu Noritake	69	73	72	80	294	2,160
Derek Fung	70	76	71	78	295	1,950
Tony Maloney	72	75	71	77	295	1,950
Takehito Daijo	69	77	75	75	296	1,720
Greg Hanrahan	69	81	73	73	296	1,720
Tony Mills	75	76	73	72	296	1,720
Alan Murdoch	73	75	74	74	296	1,720
George Olaybar	69	71	76	80	296	1,720
Shimoi Masashi	75	73	74	74	296	1,720

Samsung Masters

Dongrae Country Club, Pusan, Korea
Par 36-36–72; 7,443 yards

October 19-22
purse, $500,000

	SCORES				TOTAL	MONEY
Lin Keng-Chi	68	67	74	70	279	$80,750
Jong-Duck Kim	71	71	72	67	281	55,650
Lu Chien-Soon	75	65	73	71	284	28,000
No-Sook Park	73	71	70	70	284	28,000
Nam-Sin Park	68	75	70	73	286	17,500
Richard Kaplan	71	71	75	69	286	17,500
Robert Willis	70	74	73	69	286	17,500
Jin-Kyu Choi	73	77	68	69	287	12,500
Scott Taylor	71	70	75	72	288	10,575
Gerry Norquist	70	77	70	71	288	10,575
Derek Fung	71	74	76	68	289	9,175
Mike Cunning	72	70	71	77	290	7,906
John Kernohan	66	76	73	75	290	7,906
Yong-Jun Ahn	70	77	71	72	290	7,906
Jeev Milkha Singh	71	72	76	71	290	7,906
Hendrik Buhrmann	75	70	74	72	291	6,613
Jae-Chul Yoo	75	72	72	72	291	6,613
Shimoi Masashi	72	69	79	71	291	6,613
Choon-Bok Moon	75	72	75	69	291	6,613
Heung-Soo Kwak	72	75	74	71	292	5,925
Wook-Soon Kang	74	71	79	68	292	5,925
Tseng Kuo-Chang	72	74	71	76	293	5,550
Cesar Ababa	72	70	77	74	293	5,550
Shigemasa Higaki	73	73	73	74	293	5,550
Young-Keun Han	71	74	73	76	294	4,725
Simon Owen	78	67	74	75	294	4,725
Kyung-Joo Choi	77	72	71	74	294	4,725
Boo-Won Park	74	75	71	74	294	4,725
Wang Ter-Chang	75	74	71	74	294	4,725
Simon Yates	75	71	75	73	294	4,725
Takehito Daijo	71	77	73	73	294	4,725
Yasuo Sone	73	76	76	69	294	4,725

Royal Perak Classic

Royal Perak Golf Club, Ipoh, Malaysia
Par 36-36–72; 6,299 yards

October 26-29
purse, $150,000

	SCORES				TOTAL	MONEY
Gerry Norquist	71	70	64	67	272	$24,225
Greg Hanrahan	69	71	64	68	272	16,695
(Norquist defeated Hanrahan at first extra hole.)						
Madasamy Murugiah	69	68	70	71	278	9,300
Jeff Senior	69	70	69	71	279	7,500
Derek Fung	69	69	70	72	280	4,875
Craig Kamps	74	68	66	72	280	4,875
Prayad Marksaeng	74	68	66	72	280	4,875
Zaw Moe	69	70	66	75	280	4,875
Lin Keng-Chi	72	66	69	74	281	3,172.50
Merciano Pucay	68	74	67	72	281	3,172.50
Scott Taylor	73	72	68	70	283	2,664
Boonchu Ruangkit	72	72	67	72	283	2,664
Eddie Bagtas	68	73	70	73	284	2,353.50
Lu Wen-Ter	69	74	71	70	284	2,353.50
Aaron Meeks	71	70	74	70	285	2,115
Stephen Scahill	68	69	76	72	285	2,115
David Hill	68	72	72	73	285	2,115
Yeh Chang-Ming	69	64	76	77	286	1,897.50
Kenny Walker	73	69	73	71	286	1,897.50
Preecha Senaprom	75	70	69	73	287	1,755
Tsao Chien-Teng	71	74	72	70	287	1,755
Mohammed Khalid Yusof	69	73	71	74	287	1,755
Adam Henwood	73	72	74	69	288	1,620
Mardan Mamat	76	71	67	74	288	1,620
Simon Yates	72	70	72	74	288	1,620
Bill Fung Hee Kwan	73	72	74	70	289	1,462.50
Tony Maloney	71	73	75	70	289	1,462.50
George Olaybar	78	68	71	72	289	1,462.50
Chang Tse-Peng	75	71	72	71	289	1,462.50
Cesar Ababa	71	72	75	72	290	1,269
Poh Eing-Chong	74	74	69	73	290	1,269
Chung Chun-Hsing	71	73	71	75	290	1,269
Dino Kwek Deng Kwee	67	74	76	73	290	1,269
Beom Tiger Lee	74	70	74	72	290	1,269

Kenmore Pakistan Masters

Karachi Golf Club, Karachi, Pakistan
Par 36-36–72; 7,010 yards

November 16-19
purse, $225,000

	SCORES				TOTAL	MONEY
Young-Suk Kwon	69	68	70	69	276	$36,337.50
Thaworn Wiratchant	69	69	68	74	280	19,496.25
Tony Christie	71	69	72	68	280	19,496.25
Lu Wen-Ter	70	72	70	70	282	10,125
Amritinder Singh	70	71	71	70	282	10,125
Jeff Senior	69	70	73	71	283	6,750
Gaurav Ghei	68	73	72	70	283	6,750
Richard Kaplan	69	71	72	71	283	6,750
Cesar Ababa	70	74	73	68	285	4,758.75
Ghulam Nabi	71	71	73	70	285	4,758.75

	SCORES				TOTAL	MONEY
Simon Yates	68	71	75	72	286	4,128.75
Simon Owen	70	72	72	73	287	3,641.25
Javed Inayat	72	73	72	70	287	3,641.25
Mardan Mamat	69	75	72	71	287	3,641.25
Tae-Ha Bong	72	72	70	74	288	3,042
Li Wen-Sheng	70	67	77	74	288	3,042
George Olaybar	71	73	71	73	288	3,042
Oh-Chul Kwon	71	71	74	72	288	3,042
Craig Kamps	75	70	72	71	288	3,042
Wook-Soon Kang	72	71	72	74	289	2,632.50
Rohtas Singh	77	74	69	69	289	2,632.50
Hendrik Buhrmann	75	70	74	70	289	2,632.50
Rafael Ponce	71	69	73	77	290	2,430
Lin Chih-Chen	71	73	73	73	290	2,430
Nadeem Inayat	73	69	76	72	290	2,430
Amandeep Johl	70	72	74	75	291	2,160
Supoj Meesawad	74	70	75	72	291	2,160
Tsao Chien-Teng	73	75	71	72	291	2,160
Hsu Tien-Lai	72	76	71	72	291	2,160
Young-Il Kim	73	73	75	70	291	2,160

Gadgil Western Masters

Delhi Golf Club, Delhi, India
Par 36-36–72; 6,493 yards

November 23-25
purse, $500,000

	SCORES				TOTAL	MONEY
Gaurav Ghei	69	69	67	69	274	$80,750
Vijay Kumar	71	67	67	70	275	55,650
Jyoti Randhawa	67	72	69	68	276	31,000
Carlos Espinosa	70	71	66	70	277	20,833.33
Wook-Soon Kang	71	66	70	70	277	20,833.33
Jeev Milkha Singh	67	71	70	69	277	20,833.33
Arjun Atwal	72	71	68	69	280	11,565
Mike Cunning	68	71	70	71	280	11,565
Rafael Ponce	67	69	70	74	280	11,565
Scott Taylor	73	72	68	67	280	11,565
Boonchu Ruangkit	72	70	70	68	280	11,565
Chul-Sang Cho	65	72	71	73	281	8,312.50
Rohtas Singh	73	68	71	69	281	8,312.50
Zaw Moe	72	71	71	68	282	7,500
Jim Rutledge	72	72	72	66	282	7,500
Andrew Bonhomme	72	75	69	67	283	6,490
Wang Ter-Chang	70	72	69	72	283	6,490
Ajay Gupta	69	73	73	68	283	6,490
Richard Kaplan	71	73	73	66	283	6,490
Supoj Meesawad	71	72	71	69	283	6,490
Amritinder Singh	70	71	70	73	284	5,775
Ali Sher	72	69	71	72	284	5,775
Brad Andrews	74	71	72	68	285	5,475
Chen Liang-Hsi	75	70	71	69	285	5,475
Mardan Mamat	72	71	74	69	286	5,025
Nam-Sin Park	70	74	70	72	286	5,025
Jeff Senior	74	70	72	70	286	5,025
Li Wen-Sheng	67	77	73	69	286	5,025
Prayad Marksaeng	71	74	72	70	287	4,575
Chang Tse-Peng	71	70	72	74	287	4,575

	SCORES				TOTAL	MONEY
*Harmeet Kahlon	67	79	70	71	287	
*Amit Luthra	73	72	68	74	287	

Gadgil Western Vietnam Open

Golf Vietnam, Thu Due, Ho Chi Minh City, Vietnam
Par 36-36–72; 6,777 yards

December 7-10
purse, $150,000

	SCORES				TOTAL	MONEY
Clay Devers	66	66	70	73	275	$24,225
Boonchu Ruangkit	69	66	69	72	276	16,695
Chen Liang-Hsi	72	71	69	65	277	9,300
Carlos Espinosa	72	69	68	70	279	7,500
Lin Keng-Chi	67	72	66	75	280	5,625
Dominique Boulet	68	69	72	71	280	5,625
Prayad Marksaeng	71	70	69	71	281	4,500
Jeff Senior	66	72	68	76	282	3,547.50
Thaworn Wiratchant	73	72	71	66	282	3,547.50
Mardan Mamat	70	71	69	73	283	2,876.25
Scott Taylor	69	74	72	68	283	2,876.25
Tony Maloney	71	73	71	69	284	2,493.75
No-Sook Park	70	73	70	71	284	2,493.75
Danny Mijovic	69	70	74	72	285	2,250
Craig Kamps	71	72	70	72	285	2,250
Yasuo Sone	69	72	69	76	286	1,983.75
Chul-Sang Cho	71	68	73	74	286	1,983.75
Andrew Bonhomme	74	70	72	70	286	1,983.75
Simon Yates	74	68	73	71	286	1,983.75
Lu Wen-Ter	71	71	71	74	287	1,755
Greg Hanrahan	77	70	67	73	287	1,755
Uttam Singh Mundy	76	69	71	71	287	1,755
Vivek Bhandari	72	72	72	72	288	1,575
Saneh Saengsui	72	75	73	68	288	1,575
Kenny Walker	72	72	74	70	288	1,575
Suphavaarangoon Veerawut	73	76	69	70	288	1,575
Derek Fung	76	71	70	71	288	1,575
Kwang-Soo Choi	72	74	68	75	289	1,395
Nam-Sin Park	72	70	73	74	289	1,395
Tae-Hwa Jee	72	72	73	72	289	1,395

Philippine Classic

Sta. Elena Golf Club, Laguna, Philippines
Par 36-36–72; 7,114 yards

December 14-17
purse, $200,000

	SCORES				TOTAL	MONEY
Jeev Milkha Singh	65	73	72	73	283	$32,300
Preecha Senaprom	72	70	71	71	284	22,260
Arjun Atwal	68	72	72	76	288	11,200
Nam-Sin Park	71	74	73	70	288	11,200
Carlos Espinosa	75	74	71	69	289	8,000
Andrew Bonhomme	71	75	72	72	290	6,500
Joselito Rempojo	74	75	70	71	290	6,500
Rey Alit	71	72	74	74	291	4,112.80
Robert Pactolerin	77	73	69	72	291	4,112.80

	SCORES				TOTAL	MONEY
Tony Mills	70	77	76	68	291	4,112.80
Scott Taylor	72	74	74	71	291	4,112.80
Brad Andrews	76	73	71	71	291	4,112.80
Clay Devers	76	68	72	76	292	3,072
Lu Wen-Ter	72	77	70	73	292	3,072
Chang Tse-Peng	75	71	76	70	292	3,072
Dominique Boulet	73	73	71	76	293	2,820
Rudolfo Cuello	73	75	70	76	294	2,640
Danny Zarate	75	73	71	75	294	2,640
Danny Mijovic	70	73	75	77	295	2,252.50
No-Sook Park	75	71	74	75	295	2,252.50
Eleuterio Nival	74	71	76	74	295	2,252.50
Uttam Singh Mundy	77	74	71	73	295	2,252.50
Vivek Bhandari	75	75	72	73	295	2,252.50
George Olaybar	76	70	76	73	295	2,252.50
Rafael Ponce	72	76	75	72	295	2,252.50
Nico Van Rensburg	74	77	73	71	295	2,252.50
Greg Hanrahan	76	75	70	75	296	1,830
Jung-Ki Park	76	75	70	75	296	1,830
Edwin Estrera	72	75	74	75	296	1,830
Rodrigo Cuello	69	77	75	75	296	1,830
Amritinder Singh	74	76	74	72	296	1,830
Felix Casas	74	78	74	74	296	1,830

Australasian Tour

AMP New Zealand Open

Wellington Golf Club, Heretaunga Course,   January 12-15
Wellington, New Zealand   purse, A$237,930
Par 37-35–72; 6,771 yards

		SCORES			TOTAL	MONEY
Lucas Parsons	72	72	70	68	282	A$42,827.40
Mike Clayton	71	69	73	70	283	24,268.86
Michael Campbell	70	74	71	69	284	12,332.70
David Smail	69	71	70	74	284	12,332.70
Tim Elliott	71	71	69	73	284	12,332.70
Greg Turner	71	73	71	71	286	8,089.62
Mike Harwood	66	71	72	77	286	8,089.62
Evan Droop	77	68	74	68	287	6,126.69
Stephen Collins	71	73	73	70	287	6,126.69
Matthew Lane	73	73	68	73	287	6,126.69
Neale Smith	73	69	72	73	287	6,126.69
*Mark Brown	72	72	69	74	287	
Darren Cole	73	73	73	69	288	4,362.05
David Podlich	75	70	71	72	288	4,362.05
Chris Taylor	72	68	74	74	288	4,362.05
Don Fardon	72	70	77	70	289	3,616.53
Craig Jones	69	75	74	71	289	3,616.53
Michael Barry	74	73	73	70	290	2,798.65
Matthew King	75	71	72	72	290	2,798.65
Shane Robinson	72	73	72	73	290	2,798.65
David Armstrong	74	70	71	75	290	2,798.65
Robert Stephens	71	75	72	73	291	2,426.88
David Diaz	76	69	73	73	291	2,426.88
Paul Devenport	74	71	70	76	291	2,426.88
Andre Stolz	74	73	75	70	292	2,012.88
Richard Green	75	73	72	72	292	2,012.88
David McKenzie	73	72	73	74	292	2,012.88
Rob Willis	71	73	73	75	292	2,012.88
Stephen Moriarty	76	72	68	76	292	2,012.88
*Marcus Wheelhouse	73	70	74	75	292	

Optus Players Championship

Kingston Heath Golf Club, Melbourne, Australia   January 19-22
Par 36-36–72; 6,814 yards   purse, A$350,000

		SCORES			TOTAL	MONEY
Tim Elliott	67	70	71	75	283	A$63,000
Peter Fowler	69	74	73	68	284	35,700
Stuart Appleby	69	75	75	67	286	15,645
Doug Dunakey	70	73	73	70	286	15,645
Greg Chalmers	77	67	71	71	286	15,645
Peter O'Malley	67	72	74	73	286	15,645
Mike Clayton	65	70	71	80	286	15,645

	SCORES				TOTAL	MONEY
Richard Backwell	74	70	75	68	287	9,800
David McKenzie	67	71	80	69	287	9,800
Peter Senior	70	73	76	69	288	7,140
Rob Willis	70	70	78	70	288	7,140
Ben Jackson	70	75	72	71	288	7,140
Stephen Scahill	75	69	73	71	288	7,140
Scott Laycock	71	72	71	74	288	7,140
David Ecob	73	70	72	74	289	5,063.33
David Armstrong	71	69	73	76	289	5,063.33
Michael Long	68	72	71	78	289	5,063.33
Tony Carolan	75	71	72	72	290	3,642.18
Craig Warren	78	68	72	72	290	3,642.18
Simon Owen	69	67	79	75	290	3,642.18
Mike Ferguson	71	73	72	74	290	3,642.18
Mike Harwood	69	73	74	74	290	3,642.18
Jamie Taylor	68	71	75	76	290	3,642.18
Rodger Davis	68	72	72	78	290	3,642.18
Max Stevens	71	66	76	77	290	3,642.18
Andre Stolz	68	75	80	68	291	2,765
Leith Wastle	72	72	75	72	291	2,765
David Hill	74	72	72	73	291	2,765
David Smail	70	73	76	73	292	2,432.50
David Iwasaki-Smith	72	74	71	75	292	2,432.50

Heineken Classic

The Vines Resort, Perth, Australia
Par 36-36–72; 7,778 yards

February 2-5
purse, A$400,000

	SCORES				TOTAL	MONEY
Robert Allenby	73	66	67	72	278	A$72,000
Wayne Smith	75	71	66	67	279	40,800
David Ecob	68	71	72	70	281	27,000
Michael Campbell	70	73	69	70	282	19,200
Steve Conran	72	70	72	70	284	14,400
Brad Hughes	69	74	71	70	284	14,400
Brett Ogle	71	72	68	73	284	14,400
Peter O'Malley	72	69	72	72	285	11,600
Mike Clayton	71	72	71	72	286	9,400
Rob Willis	73	72	69	72	286	9,400
Peter McWhinney	74	70	70	72	286	9,400
Craig Parry	72	73	69	72	286	9,400
Perry Moss	66	72	78	72	288	6,272
Peter Senior	76	67	73	72	288	6,272
Stephen Leaney	73	69	72	74	288	6,272
Peter Zidar	71	70	71	76	288	6,272
David Smail	67	69	76	76	288	6,272
Ian Garbutt	70	74	73	73	290	4,800
Stephen Moriarty	72	73	77	69	291	4,150
Peter Teravainen	75	71	72	73	291	4,150
Craig Warren	74	70	72	75	291	4,150
Jack O'Keefe	74	69	72	76	291	4,150
Mark Allen	72	69	73	77	291	4,150
Glenn Joyner	74	69	76	72	291	4,150
Phillip Tataurangi	73	72	74	73	292	3,184
Darren Cole	74	72	73	73	292	3,184
Jon Evans	71	74	73	74	292	3,184

	SCORES				TOTAL	MONEY
Richard Green	74	65	77	76	292	3,184
Elliot Boult	72	74	69	77	292	3,184
Terry Price	74	73	74	72	293	2,600
Lucas Parsons	73	74	72	74	293	2,600
Jean Van de Velde	74	69	70	80	293	2,600

Ford South Australian Open

Royal Adelaide Golf Club, Adelaide, Australia   February 9-12
Par 37-36–73; 6,985 yards   purse, A$200,000

	SCORES				TOTAL	MONEY
Tim Elliott	68	71	66	70	275	A$36,000
Jack O'Keefe	68	71	70	69	278	16,950
Anthony Painter	70	68	70	70	278	16,950
Peter McWhinney	72	72	68	68	280	9,600
Andre Stolz	73	69	71	68	281	7,600
Chris Gray	68	72	69	72	281	7,600
Todd Hamilton	74	72	69	67	282	5,866.66
Michael Long	67	76	71	68	282	5,866.66
Scott Laycock	73	69	71	69	282	5,866.66
Lucas Parsons	76	69	70	68	283	5,000
Evan Droop	75	72	68	69	284	3,440
David Ecob	73	69	72	70	284	3,440
David Iwasaki-Smith	71	72	71	70	284	3,440
Richard Backwell	71	75	67	71	284	3,440
Richard Green	73	69	70	72	284	3,440
Grant Moorhead	71	71	70	72	284	3,440
Phil Brew	71	75	66	72	284	3,440
Wayne Smith	68	77	70	70	285	2,186
Peter O'Malley	73	70	71	71	285	2,186
David Armstrong	69	75	69	72	285	2,186
Marcus Cain	72	71	68	74	285	2,186
Leith Wastle	73	74	65	73	285	2,186
Rick Gibson	72	74	72	68	286	1,855
*Justin Cooper	73	71	72	70	286	
Tom Scherrer	72	74	70	70	286	1,855
Simon Owen	73	72	70	71	286	1,855
Mark Allen	71	70	71	74	286	1,855
David McKenzie	72	75	72	68	287	1,424
Paul Powell	76	69	72	70	287	1,424
Jeff Wagner	75	72	68	72	287	1,424
Craig Warren	74	73	68	72	287	1,424
Perry Moss	70	75	69	73	287	1,424

Australian Masters

Huntingdale Golf Club, Melbourne, Australia   February 16-19
Par 37-36–73; 6,994 yards   purse, A$750,000

	SCORES				TOTAL	MONEY
Peter Senior	69	70	72	69	280	A$135,000
Wayne Grady	72	72	70	67	281	54,375
Tom Watson	69	72	70	70	281	54,375
Lucas Parsons	73	68	68	72	281	54,375

	SCORES				TOTAL	MONEY
Mike Clayton	75	68	68	72	283	30,000
Anthony Gilligan	75	69	71	70	285	25,500
Craig Parry	73	72	70	70	285	25,500
Robert Allenby	69	73	71	73	286	21,750
Richard Green	75	72	74	66	287	20,250
Bob Shearer	75	72	74	67	288	18,750
*Jarrod Moseley	72	74	73	70	289	
Perry Moss	72	72	74	71	289	13,950
*Craig Spence	70	75	72	72	289	
Stephen Scahill	74	71	71	73	289	13,950
Stephen Collins	75	71	71	72	289	13,950
Stephen Leaney	73	73	71	72	289	13,950
Rob Whitlock	72	73	69	75	289	13,950
Stuart Appleby	75	73	72	70	290	9,850
Rob Willis	77	71	71	71	290	9,850
Michael Long	74	75	71	70	290	9,850
Brad Hughes	74	71	76	70	291	7,633.92
Grant Kenny	74	71	73	73	291	7,633.92
Tim Elliott	72	74	72	73	291	7,633.92
Robert Stephens	73	70	74	74	291	7,633.92
Peter O'Malley	71	73	72	75	291	7,633.92
Zoran Zorkic	71	75	70	75	291	7,633.92
Ian Garbutt	68	73	73	77	291	7,633.92
Mike Ferguson	73	75	74	70	292	5,640
Stuart Bouvier	76	73	72	71	292	5,640
Paul Powell	73	73	73	73	292	5,640
Darren Cole	70	75	71	76	292	5,640
Rick Gibson	74	71	69	78	292	5,640

Canon Challenge

Terrey Hills Country Club, Sydney, Australia
Par 36-36–72; 7,019 yards

February 23-26
purse, A$350,000

	SCORES				TOTAL	MONEY
Craig Parry	69	69	72	65	275	A$63,000
Wayne Smith	72	68	72	66	278	35,700
Paul Moloney	75	67	71	67	280	20,212.50
Grant Kenny	69	68	74	69	280	20,212.50
Peter Senior	70	70	70	71	281	14,000
Richard Green	71	74	72	65	282	10,850
David Bransdon	74	68	72	68	282	10,850
David Armstrong	70	70	72	70	282	10,850
Phillip Tataurangi	70	71	71	70	282	10,850
Darren Cole	71	70	74	68	283	7,816.66
Jack O'Keefe	72	70	71	70	283	7,816.66
Peter O'Malley	71	72	68	72	283	7,816.66
Don Fardon	68	70	78	68	284	5,950
Stephen Leaney	74	68	74	68	284	5,950
Stephen Scahill	70	70	73	71	284	5,950
Ian Garbutt	71	72	70	72	285	5,040
John Senden	72	71	75	68	286	3,946.25
Taichi Teshima	72	69	75	70	286	3,946.25
Grant Moorhead	75	67	74	70	286	3,946.25
Kyi-Hla Han	72	72	71	71	286	3,946.25
Tim Elliott	68	69	75	74	286	3,946.25
Mark Allen	72	70	68	76	286	3,946.25
Mike Weir	68	74	76	69	287	3,246.25

	SCORES				TOTAL	MONEY
Zoran Zorkic	67	74	75	71	287	3,246.25
Perry Moss	73	73	65	76	287	3,246.25
Leith Wastle	70	70	73	74	287	3,246.25
Stephen Collins	73	70	75	70	288	2,438.33
Stuart Appleby	74	72	71	71	288	2,438.33
Terry Price	73	73	72	70	288	2,438.33
Bradley Forrester	74	71	72	71	288	2,438.33
Greg Chalmers	70	72	74	72	288	2,438.33
Richard Backwell	71	68	76	73	288	2,438.33

Bank of Queensland Open

Windaroo Country Club, Beenligh, Australia
Par 36-36–72; 6,850 yards

October 19-22
purse, A$50,000

	SCORES				TOTAL	MONEY
Terry Price	69	66	72	69	276	A$9,000
Rodney Pampling	71	67	70	71	279	3,883.33
Anthony Edwards	66	72	68	73	279	3,883.33
Stuart Bouvier	69	70	70	70	279	3,883.33
Leith Wastle	72	69	72	68	281	2,100
Jeff Wagner	70	69	71	71	281	2,100
David Diaz	76	66	72	67	281	2,100
Paul Gow	70	72	73	67	282	1,450
Kenny Druce	72	71	71	68	282	1,450
Richard Buczynsky	69	73	74	66	282	1,450
Leigh Hunter	71	71	71	70	283	1,250
Richard Green	73	71	68	71	283	1,250
Max Stevens	70	68	75	71	284	950
Jeff Senior	71	77	65	71	284	950
Lucas Parsons	71	71	69	73	284	950
Marcus Cain	71	67	70	76	284	950
Anthony Painter	72	76	67	70	285	750
Russell Swanson	71	74	69	72	286	700
Darren Cole	69	72	71	75	287	625
Anthony Summers	71	72	73	71	287	625
Lucien Tinkler	73	73	68	74	288	482
David Podlich	73	74	75	66	288	482
Craig Parker	75	69	75	69	288	482
Ossie Moore	71	71	74	72	288	482
Craig Hanson	73	73	72	70	288	482
Josh Willard	70	74	71	74	289	396.67
Glenn Joyner	74	72	69	74	289	396.67
John Clifford	68	75	73	73	289	396.67
Brett Officer	75	72	72	72	291	357.50
Philip Hodge	74	73	70	74	291	357.50

Alfred Dunhill Masters

Emeralda Golf & Country Club, Jakarta, Indonesia
Par 36-36–70; 7,081 yards

November 2-5
purse, A$530,785

	SCORES				TOTAL	MONEY
Michael Campbell	69	65	68	65	267	A$95,541.30
Craig Parry	66	65	72	69	272	44,984.02

		SCORES			TOTAL	MONEY
Mark Mouland	70	67	69	66	272	44,984.02
Stuart Appleby	69	69	72	65	275	25,477.68
Wayne Grady	72	70	68	66	276	21,231.40
Vijay Singh	72	72	67	66	277	19,108.26
Greg Chalmers	68	67	75	68	278	16,985.12
Rodney Pampling	74	70	67	68	279	13,057.31
Jeev Milkha Singh	72	66	71	70	279	13,057.31
Mark Allen	69	72	68	70	279	13,057.31
Gavin Coles	71	67	67	74	279	13,057.31
Mathias Gronberg	66	70	69	74	279	13,057.31
Stephen Leaney	70	71	71	68	280	9,023.34
Gerry Norquist	70	73	68	69	280	9,023.34
Anthony Painter	71	72	66	71	280	9,023.34
Aaron Byrnes	72	71	71	67	281	6,721.06
Danny Zarate	68	71	73	69	281	6,721.06
Evan Droop	68	69	73	71	281	6,721.06
David Bransdon	69	72	68	72	281	6,721.06
Thaworn Wiratchant	70	70	72	70	282	5,555.54
Chang Tse-Peng	72	70	70	70	282	5,555.54
Hsieh Yu-Shu	70	69	71	72	282	5,555.54
David Ecob	73	70	69	71	283	4,923.03
David Diaz	70	69	70	74	283	4,923.03
Darren Cole	69	70	70	74	283	4,923.03
David Podlich	67	71	68	77	283	4,923.03
Paul Gow	66	78	72	68	284	3,861.46
Scott Laycock	68	76	69	71	284	3,861.46
Ian Woosnam	67	72	68	77	284	3,861.46
Shane Tait	73	69	67	75	284	3,861.46

Epson Singapore Open

Singapore Island Club, Bukit Course, Singapore   November 9-12
Par 35-36–71; 6,749 yards   purse, A$519,210

		SCORES			TOTAL	MONEY
Steve Conran	70	68	66	66	270	A$93,457.80
Andrew Bonhomme	69	71	64	69	273	52,959.42
Lu Wen-Ter	70	69	69	66	274	35,046.67
Madasamy Murugiah	71	69	69	66	275	22,845.24
Greg Chalmers	70	71	69	65	275	22,845.24
Peter Teravainen	65	70	70	71	276	17,653.14
Robert Farley	67	71	69	69	276	17,653.14
Terry Price	72	68	68	69	277	15,057.00
Don Fardon	71	70	70	67	278	10,755.06
Stephen Leaney	66	70	68	74	278	10,755.06
David Bransdon	70	70	67	71	278	10,755.06
Jeff Senior	69	72	67	70	278	10,755.06
Dominique Boulet	68	70	71	69	278	10,755.06
Ron Wuensche	70	73	71	64	278	10,755.06
Kyi-Hla Han	72	69	69	68	278	10,755.06
Stuart Appleby	73	69	70	67	279	7,476.62
Craig Jones	71	69	73	67	280	5,854.09
Richard Green	71	71	70	68	280	5,854.09
John Senden	74	70	70	66	280	5,854.09
Simon Owen	67	70	67	76	280	5,854.09
Mike Clayton	72	68	68	72	280	5,854.09
Maan Nasim	71	69	68	72	280	5,854.09

	SCORES			TOTAL	MONEY
Shane Tait	71	72	69	69	281	4,815.67
Anthony Painter	74	69	68	70	281	4,815.67
Leith Wastle	72	71	68	70	281	4,815.67
Rodney Pampling	70	73	71	67	281	4,815.67
Lucas Parsons	71	70	72	69	282	3,777.25
Danny Zarate	72	72	68	70	282	3,777.25
Guan Soon Chua	69	69	74	70	282	3,777.25
John Clifford	69	69	70	74	282	3,777.25

Victorian Open

Victoria Golf Club, Melbourne, Australia
Par 36-36–72; 6,801 yards

November 16-19
purse, A$200,000

	SCORES				TOTAL	MONEY
Stephen Leaney	72	72	68	71	283	A$36,000
Robert Allenby	74	70	73	67	284	16,950
Mike Clayton	75	68	69	72	284	16,950
David McKenzie	73	71	69	72	285	9,600
Mike Harwood	72	71	69	74	286	7,600
Lyndsay Stephen	72	70	72	72	286	7,600
Lucas Parsons	70	73	74	70	287	6,400
*Gavin Vearing	71	70	75	71	287	
John Clifford	69	72	75	72	288	5,600
David Smail	71	75	70	72	288	5,600
*Stephen Allan	75	69	71	73	288	
Brett Ogle	71	76	74	68	289	4,250
Peter Lonard	74	70	76	69	289	4,250
Grant Dodd	71	75	73	70	289	4,250
Shane Tait	73	71	73	72	289	4,250
*Geoff Ogilvy	70	70	71	78	289	
Darren Cole	72	75	73	70	290	2,788.33
Chris Gray	73	74	72	71	290	2,788.33
Craig Jones	71	75	72	72	290	2,788.33
Gavin Stratfold	74	73	71	72	290	2,788.33
David Bransdon	74	74	70	72	290	2,788.33
*Robbie Brook	77	70	70	73	290	
Peter Fowler	71	79	67	73	290	2,788.33
Alexander Cejka	72	75	74	70	291	2,160
*Matthew Goggin	73	73	69	76	291	
Don Fardon	72	74	76	70	292	1,736
Andrew Gott	77	72	72	71	292	1,736
Scott Laycock	73	74	74	71	292	1,736
Mark Allen	74	70	76	72	292	1,736
Ben Jackson	74	74	72	72	292	1,736
*John Sutherland	72	73	74	73	292	
Marcus Cain	73	74	71	74	292	1,736
Terry Gale	77	71	70	74	292	1,736
Ian Stanley	75	70	71	76	292	1,736
Jeff Wagner	74	74	68	76	292	1,736
Glenn Joyner	71	75	69	77	292	1,736

Heineken Australian Open

Kingston Heath Golf Club, Melbourne, Australia
Par 36-36–72; 6,814 yards

November 23-26
purse, A$850,000

	SCORES				TOTAL	MONEY
Greg Norman	72	69	69	68	278	A$153,000
Peter McWhinney	68	70	72	70	280	86,700
Jean Louis Guepy	73	69	69	70	281	49,087.50
Craig Parry	70	72	71	68	281	49,087.50
Stuart Appleby	72	72	70	68	282	34,000
Mats Hallberg	72	72	71	69	284	28,900
Grant Waite	69	73	72	70	284	28,900
Peter Lonard	76	72	70	67	285	23,800
David Hill	73	70	69	73	285	23,800
Rob Willis	71	74	70	71	286	19,975
Terry Gale	71	70	73	72	286	19,975
Terry Price	70	76	74	67	287	15,583.33
Craig Mann	73	73	71	70	287	15,583.33
Robert Allenby	71	74	71	71	287	15,583.33
Brad Faxon	70	76	73	69	288	12,296.66
*Geoff Ogilvy	70	75	73	70	288	
Lucien Tinkler	68	74	75	71	288	12,296.66
Paul Fitzgibbon	70	78	68	72	288	12,296.66
Grant Dodd	72	76	70	71	289	9,290.50
John Morse	70	72	74	73	289	9,290.50
Paul Devenport	69	73	73	74	289	9,290.50
Mike Clayton	73	69	73	74	289	9,290.50
Peter Fowler	72	71	71	75	289	9,290.50
Ben Jackson	73	71	74	72	290	7,633
David Iwasaki-Smith	71	77	70	72	290	7,633
Perry Moss	69	76	72	73	290	7,633
David McKenzie	72	72	72	74	290	7,633
Rodney Pampling	70	73	71	76	290	7,633
David Podlich	72	72	76	71	291	5,780
Michael Campbell	69	78	72	72	291	5,780
Steve Elkington	71	75	72	73	291	5,780
Paul Gow	74	73	71	73	291	5,780
Mike Harwood	71	71	75	74	291	5,780

Greg Norman's Holden Classic

The Lakes Golf Club, Sydney, Australia
Par 36-37–73; 6,904 yards

November 30-December 3
purse, A$750,000

	SCORES				TOTAL	MONEY
Craig Parry	65	67	71	73	276	A$126,000
Michael Campbell	66	68	71	72	277	71,400
Brad Faxon	68	70	70	72	280	47,250
Stuart Appleby	67	73	75	68	283	28,933.33
Jean Louis Guepy	70	63	74	76	283	28,933.33
Terry Price	68	69	71	75	283	28,933.33
Stephen Scahill	73	67	73	71	284	20,533.33
Jon Evans	72	72	69	71	284	20,533.33
Grant Waite	66	70	72	76	284	20,533.33
Wayne Riley	70	71	75	69	285	17,500
Mike Clayton	72	71	73	70	286	14,700
Peter Senior	68	67	76	75	286	14,700

	SCORES				TOTAL	MONEY
Greg Norman	72	67	79	69	287	11,445
Paul Devenport	71	69	76	71	287	11,445
Andre Stolz	71	70	75	71	287	11,445
Richard Backwell	73	68	75	71	287	11,445
John Clifford	70	71	69	78	288	7,892.50
Gary Evans	69	74	74	71	288	7,892.50
Jean Van de Velde	73	67	74	74	288	7,892.50
Robert Stephens	72	68	74	74	288	7,892.50
John Daly	74	71	68	75	288	7,892.50
Frank Nobilo	64	70	74	80	288	7,892.50
Brett Ogle	72	70	77	70	289	6,492.50
Perry Moss	73	72	72	72	289	6,492.50
David Smail	72	71	72	74	289	6,492.50
Doug Dunakey	70	73	70	76	289	6,492.50
*Matthew Goggin	70	74	74	72	290	
Simon Owen	72	73	72	73	290	5,092.50
Alexander Cejka	72	73	70	75	290	5,092.50
Neale Smith	71	69	74	76	290	5,092.50
John Senden	71	70	73	76	290	5,092.50

AMP Air New Zealand Open

Grange Golf Club, Auckland, New Zealand
Par 35-35–70; 6,533 yards

December 7-10
purse, A$550,600

	SCORES				TOTAL	MONEY
Peter O'Malley	65	67	68	72	272	A$78,795
Scott Hoch	71	69	67	68	275	44,650.50
Frank Nobilo	70	69	66	71	276	25,280.06
Terry Price	69	69	66	72	276	25,280.06
Elliot Boult	69	66	73	69	277	16,634.50
Grant Waite	72	66	69	70	277	16,634.50
Don Fardon	70	70	70	69	279	12,366.43
Steve Conran	72	66	72	69	279	12,366.43
Doug Dunakey	65	72	69	73	279	12,366.43
Craig Parry	68	68	70	73	279	12,366.43
Martyn Roberts	71	68	70	71	280	9,192.75
David Smail	68	67	71	74	280	9,192.75
Scott Laycock	70	71	71	69	281	6,356.75
Peter Fowler	71	69	72	69	281	6,356.75
Peter Lonard	69	71	71	70	281	6,356.75
Stephen Moriarty	70	63	75	73	281	6,356.75
Leith Wastle	68	73	69	71	281	6,356.75
Shane Tait	68	68	71	74	281	6,356.75
Greg Turner	68	68	67	78	281	6,356.75
Ashley Andrews	75	66	72	69	282	4,530.71
Jeev Milkha Singh	70	72	70	70	282	4,530.71
Rodney Pampling	66	71	71	74	282	4,530.71
Mike Harwood	67	68	72	75	282	4,530.71
*Mark Brown	70	68	74	71	283	
John Senden	69	72	70	72	283	4,071.07
Craig Jones	68	74	69	72	283	4,071.07
Simon Owen	69	68	78	69	284	3,291.88
Bob Charles	71	70	72	71	284	3,291.88
Rob Whitlock	71	67	74	72	284	3,291.88
Peter Senior	72	70	70	72	284	3,291.88
Stuart Bouvier	72	69	70	73	284	3,291.88

Schweppes Coolum Classic

Hyatt Regency Resort, Queensland, Australia

December 14-17

Par 36-36–72; 6,918 yards

purse, A$200,000

	SCORES				TOTAL	MONEY
Shane Robinson	69	69	71	69	278	A$36,000
Steve Conran	75	67	68	71	281	20,400
Jeff Senior	68	76	69	70	283	13,500
Grant Dodd	68	74	73	70	285	8,800
Peter Lonard	71	72	71	71	285	8,800
Stuart Appleby	67	74	73	72	286	6,200
Gavin Stratfold	71	71	72	72	286	6,200
Anthony Gilligan	67	71	75	73	286	6,200
Paul Powell	72	70	68	76	286	6,200
Craig Parry	70	77	69	71	287	4,466.66
Robert Stephens	69	76	70	72	287	4,466.66
David Iwasaki-Smith	73	72	69	73	287	4,466.66
Rob Whitlock	72	75	74	68	289	3,136
Lyndsay Stephen	71	75	74	69	289	3,136
Martyn Roberts	73	69	76	71	289	3,136
Jon Evans	71	69	77	72	289	3,136
Ben Jackson	70	70	75	74	289	3,136
David Ecob	76	70	74	70	290	2,222.50
Stephen Leaney	72	67	78	73	290	2,222.50
Neale Smith	72	69	76	73	290	2,222.50
John Senden	72	73	71	74	290	2,222.50
Mike Clayton	73	71	74	73	291	1,940
Greg Chalmers	68	79	70	74	291	1,940
Lucien Tinkler	71	70	76	74	291	1,940
Steve Alker	70	70	76	75	291	1,940
Martin Peterson	72	70	76	74	292	1,630
Don Fardon	74	72	71	75	292	1,630
Stuart Bouvier	72	70	77	74	293	1,390
Russell Swanson	73	68	76	76	293	1,390
Tod Power	71	71	75	76	293	1,390
Taylor Murphy	73	70	74	76	293	1,390

African Tours

Bell's Cup

Fancourt Hotel and Country Club, George, South Africa
Par 36-36–72; 6,812 yards

January 5-8
purse, R600,000

	SCORES				TOTAL	MONEY
Ernie Els	69	67	69	70	275	R94,800
Hendrik Buhrmann	72	65	72	71	280	55,260
Pat Horgan	66	74	69	71	280	55,260
Wayne Bradley	72	68	72	69	281	20,150
Scott Dunlap	70	68	68	75	281	20,150
Retief Goosen	68	68	71	74	281	20,150
Stuart Hendley	71	73	71	66	281	20,150
Jimmy Johnson	75	68	69	69	281	20,150
Stuart Little	68	69	72	72	281	20,150
Deane Pappas	71	67	74	70	282	11,250
Andrew Pitts	72	69	75	66	282	11,250
Darren Clarke	72	71	73	67	283	9,195
Nic Henning	67	68	79	69	283	9,195
Nico van Rensburg	74	70	71	68	283	9,195
Chris Williams	71	66	74	72	283	9,195
Lan Gooch	70	73	72	69	284	7,830
Barry Lane	66	69	77	72	284	7,830
Malcolm Mackenzie	71	64	74	75	284	7,830
John Snyder	72	72	70	70	284	7,830
Andre Cruse	74	69	71	71	285	6,397.50
Trevor Dodds	72	69	72	72	285	6,397.50
Dion Fourie	74	69	74	68	285	6,397.50
Ian Hutchings	68	72	73	72	285	6,397.50
Philip Jonas	68	73	70	74	285	6,397.50
Mark McNulty	69	70	74	72	285	6,397.50
Sean Pappas	71	71	73	70	285	6,397.50
Dave Schreyer	72	67	71	75	285	6,397.50
Ray Freeman	71	69	69	77	286	5,062.50
Craig Kamps	70	69	75	72	286	5,062.50
Ashley Roestoff	69	70	74	73	286	5,062.50
Tom Sutter	74	69	72	71	286	5,062.50
Graeme Watson	70	74	71	71	286	5,062.50
Michael Welch	68	72	76	70	286	5,062.50
Roger Wessels	72	67	71	76	286	5,062.50
Wayne Westner	70	67	78	71	286	5,062.50

FNB Players Championship

Durban Country Club, Durban, South Africa
Par 36-36–72; 6,643 yards

January 12-15
purse, R675,000

	SCORES				TOTAL	MONEY
Ron Whittaker	68	64	68	70	270	R106,650
Tony Johnstone	68	68	69	71	276	62,167.50
John McHenry	69	70	71	66	276	62,167.50

		SCORES			TOTAL	MONEY
Wayne Westner	70	68	69	70	277	33,142.50
John Bland	68	71	67	72	278	22,072.50
Malcolm Mackenzie	71	63	72	72	278	22,072.50
Mark McNulty	69	74	65	70	278	22,072.50
Warren Schutte	69	68	68	73	278	22,072.50
David Gilford	70	72	72	65	279	14,580
Dave Schreyer	71	69	68	72	280	12,656.25
Steve van Vuuren	69	74	68	69	280	12,656.25
Kyle Coody	69	70	74	68	281	11,272.50
Michael Green	68	73	70	71	282	10,035
Richard Kaplan	72	67	71	72	282	10,035
Greg Reid	75	64	73	70	282	10,035
Jeff Hawkes	69	70	70	74	283	8,341.07
P.H. Horgan	74	69	73	67	283	8,341.07
Derek James	69	73	69	72	283	8,341.07
David Smith	74	71	68	70	283	8,341.07
Roger Wessels	71	69	73	70	283	8,341.07
Clinton Whitelaw	72	68	70	73	283	8,341.07
Wilhelm Winsnes	73	73	69	68	283	8,341.07
Hugh Baiocchi	74	71	71	68	284	6,986.25
Hendrik Buhrmann	77	68	66	73	284	6,986.25
Chris Davison	68	74	72	70	284	6,986.25
Trevor Dodds	73	74	67	70	284	6,986.25
Retief Goosen	76	70	70	69	285	6,277.50
James Kingston	69	69	77	70	285	6,277.50
Neil Wallace	71	74	69	71	285	6,277.50
Michael Archer	69	74	69	74	286	5,602.50
Jack Ferenz	70	70	71	75	286	5,602.50
Nic Henning	70	77	66	73	286	5,602.50
Stuart Hendley	73	72	72	69	286	5,602.50
Robbie Stewart	69	70	75	72	286	5,602.50

ICL International

Zwartkop Country Club, Pretoria, South Africa
Par 36-36–72; 6,621 yards

January 19-22
purse, R550,000

		SCORES			TOTAL	MONEY
Ashley Roestoff	66	70	69	70	275	R86,900
Michael Christie	69	71	68	71	279	50,665
Kevin Stone	68	70	69	72	279	50,665
Jimmy Johnson	70	73	70	68	281	23,063.33
Brandon Knight	71	72	67	71	281	23,063.33
Van Phillips	73	68	72	68	281	23,063.33
Scott Dunlap	74	70	67	71	282	16,225
Ian Hutchings	67	70	75	71	283	11,044
Brad Ott	70	71	73	69	283	11,044
Warren Schutte	71	72	69	71	283	11,044
Des Terblanche	69	72	73	69	283	11,044
Steve van Vuuren	72	71	71	69	283	11,044
A.P. Botes	71	68	75	70	284	8,030
Ian Leggatt	67	75	73	69	284	8,030
Sean Pappas	71	73	67	73	284	8,030
Bryan Prytz	67	72	76	69	284	8,030
Hendrik Buhrmann	69	72	73	71	285	6,462.50
Andre Cruse	71	68	73	73	285	6,462.50
Paul Friedlander	70	72	70	73	285	6,462.50

	SCORES				TOTAL	MONEY
Nic Henning	71	72	70	72	285	6,462.50
Tony Johnstone	68	68	71	78	285	6,462.50
Jannie le Grange	72	71	70	72	285	6,462.50
John McHenry	71	72	73	69	285	6,462.50
Nico van Rensburg	65	72	73	75	285	6,462.50
John Bland	71	69	69	77	286	5,280
Brad Diffenthal	71	70	73	72	286	5,280
Thomas Goegele	71	73	70	72	286	5,280
Michael Scholz	71	70	75	70	286	5,280
Roger Wessels	67	72	73	74	286	5,280
Mike Board	70	74	71	72	287	4,400
Desvonde Botes	72	72	71	72	287	4,400
Kyle Coody	68	75	70	74	287	4,400
P.H. Horgan	74	70	71	72	287	4,400
Derek James	69	71	72	75	287	4,400
Stuart Little	68	71	74	74	287	4,400
Deane Pappas	74	69	71	73	287	4,400
Chris Williams	71	71	72	73	287	4,400

Hollard Insurance Royal Swazi Sun Classic

Royal Swazi Country Club, Mbabane, Swaziland
Par 36-36–72; 6,694 yards

January 26-29
purse, R450,000

	SCORES				TOTAL	MONEY
Brad Ott	67	67	67	65	266	R71,100
Chris Davison	68	67	65	68	268	41,445
Richard Kaplan	69	63	69	67	268	41,445
Ashley Roestoff	65	68	69	68	270	22,095
Michael Christie	70	69	65	67	271	17,257.50
Ray Freeman	68	67	70	66	271	17,257.50
Sammy Daniels	69	69	70	64	272	13,275
Steve Ford	69	71	64	69	273	9,416.25
Retief Goosen	67	68	69	69	273	9,416.25
P.H. Horgan	69	68	67	69	273	9,416.25
Ron Whittaker	69	68	67	69	273	9,416.25
Hendrik Buhrmann	70	69	67	68	274	6,759
Scott Dunlap	71	67	66	70	274	6,759
Guy Hill	69	71	66	68	274	6,759
Ian Hutchings	71	67	67	69	274	6,759
Roger Wessels	71	69	62	72	274	6,759
Wayne Bradley	70	67	69	69	275	5,872.50
Greg Reid	66	72	66	71	275	5,872.50
Mike Board	72	66	69	69	276	5,422.50
Desvonde Botes	68	70	71	67	276	5,422.50
De Wet Basson	73	69	65	70	277	4,927.50
Mervyn Galant	67	74	68	68	277	4,927.50
Stuart Hendley	71	68	67	71	277	4,927.50
Brandon Knight	69	66	68	74	277	4,927.50
Kyle Coody	69	70	71	68	278	4,191.42
Trevor Dodds	69	69	68	72	278	4,191.42
Michael Green	71	67	68	72	278	4,191.42
Bryan Prytz	69	70	66	73	278	4,191.42
Kevin Stone	72	70	67	69	278	4,191.42
Brook Tully	69	69	69	71	278	4,191.42
David White	72	68	67	71	278	4,191.42

Telkom South African Masters

Lost City Golf Club, Sun City, South Africa
Par 36-36–72; 7,637 yards

February 2-5
purse, R675,000

	SCORES				TOTAL	MONEY
Scott Dunlap	74	67	71	67	279	R106,650
Mark McNulty	69	69	69	72	279	77,625
(Dunlop defeated McNulty on first extra hole.)						
John Bland	74	68	70	70	282	46,710
Kevin Johnson	73	71	72	67	283	30,510
Schalk van der Merwe	72	74	71	66	283	30,510
James Kingston	70	71	69	74	284	23,896
Cameron Beckman	71	68	69	77	285	17,032.50
Retief Goosen	77	69	70	69	285	17,032.50
Marco Gortana	70	75	66	74	285	17,032.50
Trevor Dodds	70	70	77	69	286	11,795.62
Oswald Drawdy	73	71	72	70	286	11,795.62
Ian Hutchings	72	72	69	73	286	11,795.62
Michael Muehr	71	73	71	71	286	11,795.62
Des Terblanche	75	73	73	66	287	9,753.75
Steve van Vuuren	70	72	73	72	287	9,753.75
Hendrik Buhrmann	71	71	73	73	288	8,977.50
Jeff Hawkes	75	69	73	71	288	8,977.50
Stuart Hendley	73	71	71	73	288	8,977.50
P.H. Horgan	73	70	75	71	289	7,863.75
Derek James	70	69	78	72	289	7,853.75
Sean Pappas	76	71	71	71	289	7,863.75
Roger Wessels	70	76	68	75	289	7,863.75
Hugh Baiocchi	75	72	69	74	290	6,783.75
Eric Booker	73	72	73	72	290	6,783.75
Desvonde Botes	77	70	69	74	290	6,783.75
Michael Christie	73	73	69	75	290	6,783.75
Chris Davison	74	70	74	72	290	6,783.75
David White	72	72	72	74	290	6,783.75
Mawonga Nomwa	76	71	74	70	291	6,075
Lan Gooch	73	76	73	70	292	5,670
Jimmy Johnson	72	72	73	75	292	5,670
John Mashego	73	72	76	71	292	5,670
Michael Teague	74	74	71	73	292	5,670

Philips South African Open

Randpark Golf Club, Johannesburg, South Africa
Par 36-36–72; 6,806 yards

February 9-12
purse, R675,000

	SCORES				TOTAL	MONEY
Retief Goosen	70	65	70	70	275	R106,650
Ernie Els	72	65	72	71	280	77,625
Michael Christie	71	72	67	73	283	39,926.25
Mark McNulty	68	72	71	72	283	39,926.25
Schalk van der Merwe	74	72	70	68	284	27,877.50
John Bland	71	70	68	76	285	23,895
Marco Gortana	71	67	77	71	286	17,032.50
Fran Quinn	71	72	70	73	286	17,032.50
Warren Schutte	74	75	68	69	286	17,032.50
Mike Harwood	73	70	72	72	287	12,195
Tony Johnstone	66	74	75	72	287	12,195

		SCORES			TOTAL	MONEY
Ben Weir	73	75	69	70	287	12,195
Scott Dunlap	77	69	73	69	288	10,260
Richard Kaplan	71	76	73	68	288	10,260
Andre Cruse	72	72	75	70	289	9,450
Roger Wessels	71	71	79	68	289	9,450
Jeff Hawkes	73	70	76	71	290	8,808.75
Stuart Hendley	68	76	72	74	290	8,808.75
Kyle Coody	72	72	73	74	291	7,425
Trevor Dodds	71	77	74	69	291	7,425
David Frost	74	73	66	78	291	7,425
Mervyn Galant	75	74	73	69	291	7,425
P.H. Horgan	74	73	72	72	291	7,425
Ian Hutchings	70	73	74	74	291	7,425
*Andrew McLardy	68	73	79	71	291	
Van Phillips	73	75	69	74	291	7,425
David White	74	73	72	72	291	7,425
Cameron Beckman	73	75	76	68	292	5,930.35
Nic Henning	74	72	72	74	292	5,930.35
David Higgins	74	73	70	75	292	5,930.35
Bobby Lincoln	73	73	74	72	292	5,930.35
Mawonga Nomwa	75	72	74	71	292	5,930.35
Brenden Pappas	71	75	73	73	292	5,930.35
Greg Reid	76	71	74	71	292	5,930.35

Lexington PGA Championship

Wanderers Golf Club, Johannesburg, South Africa
Par 35-35–70; 6,960 yards

February 16-19
purse, £300,000

		SCORES			TOTAL	MONEY
Ernie Els	65	71	71	64	271	£39,478.70
Roger Wessels	68	72	69	64	273	28,748.08
Vanslow Phillips	66	71	71	66	274	12,190.49
Tony Johnstone	68	70	69	67	274	12,190.49
Warren Schutte	68	71	68	67	274	12,190.49
Mark McNulty	68	72	67	67	274	12,190.49
Trevor Dodds	66	71	68	70	275	7,386.66
Mats Hallberg	73	68	69	66	276	5,789.55
Michael Jonzon	71	71	70	64	276	5,789.55
Nic Henning	69	66	74	68	277	4,385.83
Robbie Stewart	69	70	70	68	277	4,385.83
Jay Townsend	67	74	70	66	277	4,385.83
Mark James	71	71	69	66	277	4,385.83
Wayne Westner	62	75	73	68	278	3,643.42
Jimmy Johnson	68	74	68	68	278	3,643.42
Alexander Cejka	66	72	74	67	279	3,306.53
James Kingston	71	69	71	68	279	3,306.53
Michael Scholz	73	69	71	66	279	3,306.53
Mike Christie	72	72	70	65	279	3,306.53
Fran Quinn	69	71	69	71	280	2,863.58
De Wet Basson	71	70	70	69	280	2,863.58
Sammy Daniels	72	70	69	69	280	2,863.58
Marc Farry	70	74	66	70	280	2,863.58
Jeff Hawkes	71	69	71	70	281	2,515.46
Richard Kaplan	71	70	68	72	281	2,515.46
P.H. Horgan	74	68	70	69	281	2,515.46
David Carter	69	74	68	70	281	2,515.46

	SCORES				TOTAL	MONEY
Ricky Willison	72	72	67	70	281	2,515.46
Deane Pappas	69	72	70	71	282	2,229.31
Wayne Riley	70	71	71	70	282	2,229.31
Mark Wiltshire	71	70	72	69	282	2,229.31

Alfred Dunhill Challenge

Houghton Golf Club, Johannesburg, South Africa   February 24-26
Par 36-36–72; 7,036 yards

FIRST DAY
Morning Fourballs

Nick Price and Mark McNulty (SA) defeated Wayne Grady and Lucas Parsons (A), 2 and 1
Ernie Els and Tony Johnstone (SA) defeated Robert Allenby and Michael Clayton (A), 1 up
David Frost and Retief Goosen (SA) defeated Greg Norman and Michael Campbell (A), 3 and 1
Vijay Singh and Frank Nobilo (A) defeated Fulton Allem and Hendrik Buhrmann (SA), 6 and 5

Afternoon Foursomes

Els and Johnstone (SA) defeated Singh and Nobilo (A), 4 and 3
Price and McNulty (SA) defeated Clayton and Greg Turner (A), 3 and 2
Frost and Goosen (SA) defeated Norman and Allenby (A), 3 and 1
Grady and Campbell (A) halved with Allem and Wayne Westner (SA)

Southern Africa 6½, Australasia 1½

SECOND DAY
Morning Foursomes

Els and Johnstone (SA) halved with Clayton and Turner (A)
Price and McNulty (SA) defeated Campbell and Grady (A), 3 and 2
Singh and Parsons (A) defeated Frost and Goosen (SA), 1 up
Norman and Allenby (A) defeated Allem and Westner (SA), 1 up

Afternoon Fourballs

Price and Frost (SA) halved with Singh and Parsons (A)
Els and McNulty (SA) defeated Clayton and Turner (A), 2 and 1
Norman and Grady (A) defeated Goosen and Buhrmann (SA), 2 and 1
Allenby and Nobilo (A) defeated Allem and Johnstone (SA), 1 up

Southern Africa 9½, Australasia 6½

THIRD DAY
Singles

Frost (SA) defeated Grady (A), 6 and 5
Price (SA) defeated Norman (A), 1 up
McNulty (SA) defeated Nobilo (A), 3 and 1
Singh (A) defeated Els (SA), 3 and 1
Parsons (A) defeated Goosen (SA), 2 and 1
Buhrmann (SA) halved with Clayton (A)
Campbell (A) defeated Westner (SA), 1 up

Allem (SA) halved with Turner (A)
Johnstone (SA) halved with Allenby (A)

FINAL RESULTS: Southern Africa 14, Australasia 11

Hassan II Trophy

Royal Golf Dar-es-Salam, Red Course, Rabat, Morocco
Par 36-37–73; 7,350 yards

November 9-12
purse, $407,000

		SCORES			TOTAL	MONEY
Nick Price	69	71	74	72	286	$93,000
Roger Chapman	71	73	73	71	288	50,000
Christian Cevaer	73	70	78	69	290	27,000
Wayne Westner	69	75	72	74	290	27,000
Steve Rintoul	71	74	72	74	291	20,000
Lee Westwood	71	76	73	72	292	16,000
Franklin Langham	73	73	71	75	292	16,000
Jay Williamson	71	76	73	73	293	13,500
Chris Smith	72	78	73	71	294	12,500
Jose Maria Canizares	70	76	73	76	295	11,500
Donnie Hammond	71	74	74	77	296	10,000
Mathias Gronberg	73	73	75	75	296	10,000
Mike Brisky	73	73	76	74	296	10,000
Neil Briggs	72	76	74	75	297	8,500
David J. Russell	70	74	80	73	297	8,500
Peter Mitchell	75	74	73	75	297	8,500
Martin Gates	73	76	79	70	298	7,600
Billy Casper	75	74	78	73	300	7,300
Charlie Rymer	76	76	76	73	301	6,875
Ronan Rafferty	73	76	77	75	301	6,875
John Wilson	76	74	73	80	303	6,550
Mohammed Makroun	76	77	79	79	311	6,350
Abdellah Bendiab	79	81	76	79	315	6,250
Peter Townsend	76	76	80	84	316	6,150
Mustapha Sabri	79	80	80	79	318	5,525
Bobby Casper	80	77	82	79	318	5,525

Zimbabwe Open

Royal Harare Golf Club, Harare, Zimbabwe
Par 36-36–72; 7,060 yards

November 16-19
purse, R400,000

		SCORES			TOTAL	MONEY
Nick Price	70	65	66	65	266	R63,200
Brenden Pappas	67	67	67	66	267	46,000
Mawonga Nomwa	69	67	67	67	270	27,680
Mark McNulty	69	66	66	70	271	19,640
Des Terblanche	70	68	67	70	275	16,520
Chris Williams	71	66	69	70	276	14,160
Bobby Lincoln	67	67	72	71	277	10,820
Ashley Roestoff	72	68	65	72	277	10,820
Adilson da Silva	70	71	65	72	278	8,240
Robbie Stewart	69	68	70	71	278	8,240
A.P. Botes	71	67	73	68	279	6,706.66
Andrew McKenzie	68	69	70	72	279	6,706.66
Bradford Vaughan	69	68	76	66	279	6,706.66

	SCORES				TOTAL	MONEY
Greg Reid	72	71	66	71	280	5,880
Simon Hobday	72	72	68	69	281	5,506.66
Grant Muller	68	70	72	71	281	5,506.66
Steve van Vuuren	69	70	71	71	281	5,506.66
Wayne Bradley	70	69	73	70	282	4,611.42
James Kingston	72	71	69	70	282	4,611.42
Noel Maart	69	73	72	68	282	4,611.42
Ian Palmer	73	71	71	67	282	4,611.42
Dean van Staden	69	69	73	71	282	4,611.42
Schalk van der Merwe	68	70	73	71	282	4,611.42
Bobby Verwey, Jr.	70	71	72	69	282	4,611.42
Alan McLean	69	75	69	70	283	4,020
Wayne Westner	66	75	72	70	283	4,020
Gerry Coetzee	72	70	72	70	284	3,660
Derek Crawford	70	71	70	73	284	3,660
John Mashego	70	73	70	71	284	3,660
John Nelson	72	71	71	70	284	3,660

Nedbank Million Dollar Challenge

Gary Player Country Club, Sun City, South Africa
Par 36-36–72; 7,691 yards

November 30-December 3
purse, $2,510,000

	SCORES				TOTAL	MONEY
Corey Pavin	69	72	69	66	276	$1,000,000
Nick Price	71	67	72	71	281	250,000
Bernhard Langer	72	69	71	71	283	200,000
Sam Torrance	69	73	70	72	284	175,000
Tom Lehman	71	70	73	73	287	150,000
David Frost	74	76	71	68	289	125,000
Nick Faldo	72	78	69	72	291	103,333
Costantino Rocca	76	75	67	73	291	103,333
Ernie Els	72	72	69	78	291	103,333
Vijay Singh	75	72	74	72	293	100,000
Colin Montgomerie	79	76	71	71	297	100,000
Phil Mickelson	73	77	72	76	298	100,000

Senior Tours

Senior Tournament of Champions

Hyatt Dorado Beach, East Course, Dorado, Puerto Rico
Par 36-36–72; 6,740 yards

January 13-15
purse, $750,000

	SCORES			TOTAL	MONEY
Jim Colbert	72	66	71	209	$148,000
Jim Albus	70	70	69	209	87,000
(Colbert defeated Albus on third extra hole.)					
Jim Dent	69	72	69	210	65,000
Larry Gilbert	73	67	70	210	65,000
Tom Wargo	73	72	66	211	47,000
Raymond Floyd	68	71	75	214	35,500
Dave Stockton	72	71	71	214	35,500
Lee Trevino	70	68	76	214	35,500
Jack Nicklaus	75	72	68	215	27,500
Tony Jacklin	71	70	75	216	24,500
Jack Kiefer	69	73	74	216	24,500
Bob Murphy	75	71	71	217	20,166.67
Rocky Thompson	76	69	72	217	20,166.67
Mike Hill	74	71	72	217	20,166.66
Dave Eichelberger	73	76	70	219	18,000
John Paul Cain	77	70	74	221	16,500
Kermit Zarley	75	71	75	221	16,500
Jay Sigel	74	77	71	222	15,000
Tom Weiskopf	76	76	72	224	14,500
Simon Hobday	78	76	71	225	14,000

Royal Caribbean Classic

The Links at Key Biscayne, Key Biscayne, Florida
Par 35-36–71; 6,725 yards

February 3-5
purse, $850,000

	SCORES			TOTAL	MONEY
J.C. Snead	69	75	65	209	$127,500
Raymond Floyd	68	76	65	209	74,800
(Snead defeated Floyd on first extra hole.)					
Bob Charles	70	71	69	210	61,200
Walter Morgan	69	73	69	211	45,900
Kermit Zarley	68	74	69	211	45,900
Jack Kiefer	68	76	68	212	32,300
Lee Trevino	70	73	69	212	32,300
Roger Kennedy	71	74	68	213	25,500
Tom Wargo	68	73	72	213	25,500
Bob Murphy	66	78	70	214	22,100
Chi Chi Rodriguez	70	74	72	216	19,550
Bob Toski	73	75	68	216	19,550
Jim Colbert	72	74	71	217	16,150
Ted Hayes	70	74	73	217	16,150
Jimmy Powell	72	71	74	217	16,150
Al Geiberger	72	75	71	218	13,600
Tony Jacklin	70	76	72	218	13,600

	SCORES			TOTAL	MONEY
Jerry McGee	73	74	71	218	13,600
Butch Baird	74	77	68	219	10,313.34
Mike Hill	71	74	74	219	10,313.34
Bud Allin	69	76	74	219	10,313.33
Miller Barber	71	74	74	219	10,313.33
Bruce Summerhays	70	78	71	219	10,313.33
Harry Toscano	69	79	71	219	10,313.33
Marty Bohen	71	75	74	220	7,926.25
Gay Brewer	72	77	71	220	7,926.25
Rives McBee	72	77	71	220	7,926.25
Gary Player	70	79	71	220	7,926.25
Jim Albus	71	78	72	221	6,290
Don Bies	71	79	71	221	6,290
Jim Dent	72	77	72	221	6,290
Bob Dickson	74	77	70	221	6,290
Don January	76	76	69	221	6,290
Ben Smith	73	78	70	221	6,290
Tommy Aycock	72	77	73	222	4,802.50
Simon Hobday	71	80	71	222	4,802.50
Graham Marsh	72	81	69	222	4,802.50
Ed Sneed	71	78	73	222	4,802.50
DeWitt Weaver	73	77	72	222	4,802.50
Larry Ziegler	71	76	75	222	4,802.50

IntelliNet Challenge

The Vineyards, Naples, Florida
Par 36-36—72; 6,787 yards
(Third round cancelled — rain.)

February 10-12
purse, $600,000

	SCORES		TOTAL	MONEY
Bob Murphy	67	70	137	$90,000
Raymond Floyd	69	69	138	52,800
Mike Hill	71	69	140	39,600
Rocky Thompson	70	70	140	39,600
Jim Albus	69	72	141	22,080
Bob Charles	69	72	141	22,080
Larry Gilbert	74	67	141	22,080
Richie Karl	71	70	141	22,080
Jerry McGee	72	69	141	22,080
Bob Brue	70	72	142	15,600
Jack Kiefer	73	70	143	11,657.15
Graham Marsh	74	69	143	11,657.15
Bobby Nichols	72	71	143	11,657.14
Jay Sigel	69	74	143	11,657.14
Roger Stern	71	72	143	11,657.14
Harry Toscano	67	76	143	11,657.14
Lee Trevino	71	72	143	11,657.14
Tommy Aaron	75	69	144	7,730
George Archer	72	72	144	7,730
Tommy Aycock	77	67	144	7,730
Dale Douglass	74	70	144	7,730
Gibby Gilbert	73	71	144	7,730
J.C. Snead	72	72	144	7,730
Agim Bardha	72	73	145	5,246.67
Gay Brewer	72	73	145	5,246.67
Walter Morgan	71	74	145	5,246.67
Gary Player	73	72	145	5,246.67

	SCORES			TOTAL	MONEY
Bob E. Smith	72	73		145	5,246.67
Larry Ziegler	73	72		145	5,246.67
Bob Dickson	71	74		145	5,246.66
Gary Groh	71	74		145	5,246.66
Dick Hendrickson	71	74		145	5,246.66
Butch Baird	74	72		146	3,625.72
Chuck Montalbano	76	70		146	3,625.72
Tom Shaw	74	72		146	3,625.72
Marion Heck	69	77		146	3,625.71
Richard Rhyan	73	73		146	3,625.71
Bruce Summerhays	73	73		146	3,625.71
DeWitt Weaver	73	73		146	3,625.71
Don Bies	73	74		147	2,580
Robert Gaona	69	78		147	2,580
Dick Goetz	72	75		147	2,580
Simon Hobday	73	74		147	2,580
Robert Landers	73	74		147	2,580
Rives McBee	73	74		147	2,580
Ben Smith	76	71		147	2,580
Dave Stockton	75	72		147	2,580
Walter Zembriski	76	71		147	2,580

GTE Suncoast Classic

TPC of Tampa Bay, Lutz, Florida
Par 35-36–71; 6,638 yards

February 17-19
purse, $750,000

	SCORES			TOTAL	MONEY
Dave Stockton	70	66	68	204	$112,500
Bob Charles	68	69	69	206	55,000
Jim Colbert	71	68	67	206	55,000
J.C. Snead	68	69	69	206	55,000
Simon Hobday	68	71	68	207	31,000
Bruce Lehnhard	70	68	69	207	31,000
Jack Nicklaus	69	70	68	207	31,000
Dale Douglass	71	67	70	208	19,800
Raymond Floyd	66	72	70	208	19,800
Graham Marsh	70	68	70	208	19,800
Bob Murphy	70	69	69	208	19,800
Lee Trevino	69	72	67	208	19,800
Jim Albus	72	67	70	209	14,250
Tommy Aycock	68	72	69	209	14,250
Jack Kiefer	67	71	71	209	14,250
Jim Dent	72	69	69	210	10,962.50
Dave Eichelberger	70	66	74	210	10,962.50
Gibby Gilbert	67	72	71	210	10,962.50
Gary Player	69	67	74	210	10,962.50
Bob E. Smith	68	71	71	210	10,962.50
Tom Wargo	71	69	70	210	10,962.50
Bud Allin	69	71	71	211	8,081.25
Jerry McGee	68	75	68	211	8,081.25
Bruce Summerhays	70	68	73	211	8,081.25
Tom Weiskopf	73	66	72	211	8,081.25
Tommy Aaron	73	70	69	212	6,825
Don Bies	71	69	72	212	6,825
Calvin Peete	70	74	68	212	6,825
Miller Barber	70	69	74	213	5,200
Deane Beman	72	70	71	213	5,200

	SCORES			TOTAL	MONEY
Terry Dill	72	70	71	213	5,200
Chi Chi Rodriguez	71	73	69	213	5,200
Tom Shaw	77	72	70	213	5,200
Jay Sigel	68	70	75	213	5,200
Rocky Thompson	69	73	71	213	5,200
Tom Ulozas	69	73	71	213	5,200
Tony Jacklin	66	76	71	213	5,200
Jim Ferree	70	72	72	214	3,975
Al Geiberger	72	69	73	214	3,975
Gary Groh	72	73	69	214	3,975

Chrysler Cup

Tres Vidas Golf Club, Acapulco, Mexico
Par 36-36–72; 7,082 yards

February 24-26
purse, $600,000

FIRST DAY
Alternate Shot

Jim Dent and Bob Murphy (USA) halved with Simon Hobday and Harold Henning (International), 73-73
Tom Weiskopf and Jim Albus (USA) defeated Tommy Horton and Tony Jacklin (International), 69-74
George Archer and Larry Gilbert (USA) defeated Bruce Crampton and Antonio Garrido (International), 72-78
Bob Charles and Graham Marsh (International) defeated Jim Colbert and Tom Wargo (USA), 72-73

United States 2½, International 1½

SECOND DAY
Fourball

Dent and Murphy (USA) defeated Horton and Jacklin (International), 66-67
Archer and Gilbert (USA) defeated Hobday and Henning (International), 66-70
Weiskopf and Albus (USA) defeated Charles and Marsh (International), 65-69
Colbert and Wargo (USA) defeated Crampton and Garrido (International), 67-68

United States 4, International 0

THIRD DAY
Singles

Colbert (USA) defeated Charles (International), 69-72
Dent (USA) defeated Henning (International), 71-76
Garrido (International) defeated Archer (USA), 71-76
Wargo (USA) halved with Horton (International), 71-71
Gilbert (USA) defeated Crampton (International), 68-73
Murphy (USA) defeated Hobday (International), 72-78
Jacklin (International) defeated Weiskopf (USA), 71-74
Marsh (International) defeated Albus (USA), 69-74

United States 4½, International 3½

FINAL RESULTS: United States 11, International 5

(Each United States player received $50,000; each International player received $25,000.)

FHP Health Care Classic

Ojai Valley Inn & Golf Club, Ojai, California
Par 35-35–70; 6,190 yards

March 3-5
purse, $750,000

	SCORES		TOTAL	MONEY
Bruce Devlin	64	66	130	$112,500
Dave Eichelberger	64	66	130	66,000
(Devlin defeated Eichelberger at second extra hole.)				
Dale Douglass	67	65	132	54,000
Bud Allin	72	61	133	34,500
Dave Hill	68	65	133	34,500
Dave Stockton	63	70	133	34,500
Tom Wargo	70	63	133	34,500
Bob Charles	64	70	134	19,000
Jim Colbert	68	66	134	19,000
Jim Dent	66	68	134	19,000
Jay Sigel	67	67	134	19,000
Harry Toscano	67	67	134	19,000
Larry Ziegler	68	66	134	19,000
Deane Beman	69	66	135	13,125
Al Geiberger	68	67	135	13,125
Tony Jacklin	67	68	135	13,125
Jimmy Powell	67	68	135	13,125
Isao Aoki	68	68	136	10,575
Dick Goetz	67	69	136	10,575
Jack Kiefer	71	65	136	10,575
Bruce Summerhays	68	69	137	8,531.25
DeWitt Weaver	66	71	137	8,531.25
Tom Weiskopf	69	68	137	8,531.25
Kermit Zarley	72	65	137	8,531.25
Butch Baird	68	70	138	7,150
Homero Blancas	70	68	138	7,150
Ed Sneed	67	71	138	7,150
Jim Ferree	66	73	139	5,940
Gary Groh	71	68	139	5,940
Don January	71	68	139	5,940
Chuck Montalbano	72	67	139	5,940
Bob Wynn	72	67	139	5,940
George Archer	70	70	140	4,837.50
Tommy Aycock	69	71	140	4,837.50
Walter Morgan	68	72	140	4,837.50
Bob E. Smith	69	71	140	4,837.50
Jim Albus	71	70	141	3,900
Bruce Crampton	72	69	141	3,900
Bob Dickson	70	71	141	3,900
Al Kelley	73	68	141	3,900
Orville Moody	72	69	141	3,900
Arnold Palmer	70	71	141	3,900

Senior Grand Slam

Los Cabos Resort, Los Cabos, Mexico
Par 36-36-72; 7,037 yards

March 6-7
purse, $500,000

	SCORES		TOTAL	MONEY
Raymond Floyd	72	67	139	$250,000
Dave Stockton	70	75	145	125,000

	SCORES	TOTAL	MONEY
Simon Hobday	70 77	147	75,000
Lee Trevino	80 75	155	50,000

SBC Presents the Dominion Seniors

The Dominion Country Club, San Antonio, Texas
Par 36-36–72; 6,814 yards

March 10-12
purse, $650,000

	SCORES			TOTAL	MONEY
Jim Albus	71	65	69	205	$97,500
Raymond Floyd	72	68	68	208	52,000
Jay Sigel	69	73	66	208	52,000
Lee Trevino	72	67	70	209	39,000
Tommy Aaron	72	68	70	210	28,600
Dave Stockton	74	69	67	210	28,600
Dave Eichelberger	71	70	70	211	22,100
Dick Hendrickson	70	71	70	211	22,100
Isao Aoki	74	69	69	212	15,058.34
Jim Ferree	75	69	68	212	15,058.33
Gay Brewer	72	71	69	212	15,058.33
John Paul Cain	76	66	70	212	15,058.33
Jim Dent	72	67	73	212	15,058.33
Lee Elder	67	72	73	212	15,058.33
George Archer	73	72	68	213	9,815
Homero Blancas	70	70	73	213	9,815
Bob Dickson	67	70	76	213	9,815
Al Geiberger	70	73	70	213	9,815
Simon Hobday	68	72	73	213	9,815
Chi Chi Rodriguez	71	68	74	213	9,815
Tom Wargo	72	73	68	213	9,815
Gary Groh	73	71	70	214	7,003.75
Richard Rhyan	71	66	77	214	7,003.75
Tom Shaw	71	72	71	214	7,003.75
Larry Ziegler	72	71	71	214	7,003.75
Miller Barber	70	72	73	215	5,655
Gibby Gilbert	72	72	71	215	5,655
Marion Heck	72	70	73	215	5,655
Jerry McGee	70	74	71	215	5,655
Bobby Nichols	73	71	71	215	5,655
Jim Colbert	75	69	72	216	4,485
Terry Dill	71	72	73	216	4,485
Walter Morgan	72	73	71	216	4,485
Ben Smith	71	75	70	216	4,485
Rocky Thompson	72	69	75	216	4,485
Bud Allin	70	71	76	217	3,656.25
Bobby Mitchell	71	74	72	217	3,656.25
J.C. Snead	75	67	75	217	3,656.25
Ed Sneed	71	76	70	217	3,656.25
Dale Douglass	69	74	75	218	3,185
Joe Jimenez	71	75	72	218	3,185
Charles Sifford	72	72	74	218	3,185

Toshiba Classic

Mesa Verde Country Club, Costa Mesa, California
Par 35-35–70; 6,163 yards

March 17-19
purse, $800,000

	SCORES			TOTAL	MONEY
George Archer	67	68	64	199	$120,000
Dave Stockton	69	67	64	200	64,000
Tom Wargo	65	67	68	200	64,000
Marion Heck	67	72	63	202	48,000
DeWitt Weaver	72	65	66	203	38,400
J.C. Snead	67	70	68	205	30,400
Terry Dill	69	72	64	205	30,400
Bob Murphy	68	73	65	206	20,266.67
Rocky Thompson	68	70	68	206	20,266.67
Al Geiberger	71	69	66	206	20,266.67
Bob E. Smith	70	65	71	206	20,266.67
Jim Dent	70	66	70	206	20,266.66
Tom Weiskopf	68	67	71	206	20,266.67
Ed Sneed	71	69	67	207	14,400
Lee Trevino	69	69	69	207	14,400
Bob Charles	68	69	70	207	14,400
Larry Ziegler	70	69	69	208	10,662.86
Richard Rhyan	71	71	66	208	10,662.86
Jim Albus	69	70	69	208	10,662.86
Bud Allin	69	71	68	208	10,662.86
Dave Eichelberger	63	75	70	208	10,662.86
Simon Hobday	73	66	69	208	10,662.85
Jim Colbert	68	70	70	208	10,662.85
Robert Zimmerman	72	70	67	209	7,314.29
Tom Shaw	71	69	69	209	7,314.29
Dale Douglass	71	70	68	209	7,314.29
Dick Goetz	69	71	69	209	7,314.29
Dave Hill	67	71	71	209	7,314.28
Calvin Peete	73	67	69	209	7,314.28
Isao Aoki	65	74	70	209	7,314.28
Dick Hendrickson	69	70	71	210	5,170
Jack Kiefer	71	69	70	210	5,170
Larry Laoretti	65	68	77	210	5,170
Jerry McGee	69	69	72	210	5,170
Chuck Montalbano	70	71	69	210	5,170
Walter Morgan	67	75	68	210	5,170
Bruce Summerhays	71	68	71	210	5,170
Gibby Gilbert	71	71	68	210	5,170
Jimmy Powell	71	71	69	211	4,080
Tommy Aaron	68	70	73	211	4,080
Gay Brewer	69	72	70	211	4,080

The Tradition

Desert Mountain Golf Club, Scottsdale, Arizona
Par 36-36–72; 6,864 yards

March 30-April 2
purse, $1,000,000

	SCORES				TOTAL	MONEY
Jack Nicklaus	69	71	69	67	276	$150,000
Isao Aoki	71	66	72	67	276	88,000
(Nicklaus defeated Aoki at third extra hole.)						
Jim Ferree	67	74	69	67	277	72,000

	SCORES				TOTAL	MONEY
Jim Colbert	76	64	70	70	280	60,000
Jimmy Powell	75	68	69	69	281	48,000
Raymond Floyd	70	72	71	69	282	38,000
Jay Sigel	70	69	71	72	282	38,000
Dale Douglass	74	74	67	68	283	27,500
Bob Murphy	73	71	69	70	283	27,500
Bruce Summerhays	71	77	66	69	283	27,500
Tom Weiskopf	75	74	67	67	283	27,500
Bob Charles	69	76	70	69	284	19,200
Jim Dent	75	73	68	68	284	19,200
Larry Gilbert	71	70	71	72	284	19,200
Dave Stockton	73	68	74	69	284	19,200
Rocky Thompson	73	71	69	71	284	19,200
George Archer	70	72	72	71	285	15,033.34
Graham Marsh	72	69	72	72	285	15,033.33
Gary Player	69	70	72	74	285	15,033.33
Tommy Aaron	73	69	73	71	286	11,740
Gary Groh	72	73	70	71	286	11,740
J.C. Snead	75	70	71	70	286	11,740
Lee Trevino	70	68	74	74	286	11,740
Kermit Zarley	71	74	70	71	286	11,740
Tom Shaw	82	70	69	66	287	9,533.34
Jack Kiefer	74	74	69	70	287	9,533.33
Arnold Palmer	71	74	71	71	287	9,533.33
Don Bies	73	72	70	73	288	8,100
Dave Eichelberger	73	72	70	73	288	8,100
Calvin Peete	69	71	73	75	288	8,100
Larry Ziegler	72	74	71	71	288	8,100
Harold Henning	75	73	69	72	289	7,050
Bobby Nichols	74	75	71	69	289	7,050
DeWitt Weaver	72	77	70	71	290	6,600
Bobby Mitchell	74	73	72	72	291	6,300
John Paul Cain	73	75	74	70	292	5,625
Charles Coody	72	70	76	74	292	5,625
Gibby Gilbert	72	71	73	76	292	5,625
Jerry McGee	69	76	73	74	292	5,625
Al Geiberger	74	74	72	73	293	5,100

PGA Seniors' Championship

PGA National Golf Club, Palm Beach Gardens, Florida
Par 36-36–72; 6,702 yards

April 13-16
purse, $1,150,000

	SCORES				TOTAL	MONEY
Raymond Floyd	70	70	67	70	277	$180,000
John Paul Cain	72	71	70	69	282	75,000
Larry Gilbert	71	70	72	69	282	75,000
Lee Trevino	72	70	69	71	282	75,000
Graham Marsh	71	71	70	71	283	40,000
Isao Aoki	70	69	73	71	283	40,000
Bob Charles	70	75	68	70	283	40,000
Jack Nicklaus	76	66	68	74	284	30,000
Jim Colbert	69	69	71	76	285	25,000
Bob Murphy	71	73	70	72	286	17,833.34
Jim Albus	69	73	69	75	286	17,833.33
George Archer	73	71	68	74	286	17,833.33
Gibby Gilbert	74	73	68	72	287	15,500

	SCORES				TOTAL	MONEY
Bob Dickson	74	73	71	70	288	14,750
Ed Sneed	73	73	69	73	288	14,750
Terry Dill	72	72	71	74	289	13,000
Dale Douglass	77	70	71	71	289	13,000
Noel Ratcliffe	76	67	74	72	289	13,000
J.C. Snead	71	70	76	72	289	13,000
DeWitt Weaver	68	73	72	76	289	13,000
Seiichi Kanai	73	75	71	71	290	10,500
Bill Kennedy	72	70	76	72	290	10,500
Harry Toscano	68	76	73	73	290	10,500
Kermit Zarley	74	73	72	71	290	10,500
Larry Ziegler	73	72	70	75	290	10,500
Calvin Peete	68	76	70	77	291	8,250
Chi Chi Rodriguez	73	73	75	70	291	8,250
Bruce Summerhays	71	77	71	72	291	8,250
Rocky Thompson	74	69	77	71	291	8,250
Jack Kiefer	73	73	75	71	292	5,281.25
Larry Laoretti	69	76	76	71	292	5,281.25
Dick Hendrickson	70	73	74	75	292	5,281.25
Tommy Horton	78	69	70	75	292	5,281.25
Orville Moody	71	78	72	71	292	5,281.25
Jay Sigel	74	75	73	70	292	5,281.25
Tom Wargo	72	74	77	69	292	5,281.25
Walter Zembriski	70	78	76	68	292	5,281.25
Dave Eichelberger	74	75	72	72	293	3,500
Bud Allin	74	71	74	75	294	2,768.75
Gay Brewer	71	76	72	75	294	2,768.75
Malcolm Gregson	73	75	73	73	294	2,768.75
Marion Heck	72	76	70	76	294	2,768.75
Harold Henning	70	80	70	74	294	2,768.75
Roger Kennedy	73	76	72	73	294	2,768.75
Randy Petri	72	74	75	73	294	2,768.75
Robert Zimmerman	71	75	73	75	294	2,768.75

Liberty Mutual Legends of Golf

PGA West, Stadium Course, La Quinta, California
Par 36-36–72; 6,843 yards

April 21-23
purse, $1,115,000

	SCORES			TOTAL	MONEY (Each)
Mike Hill/Lee Trevino	64	66	65	195	$100,000
Gibby Gilbert/J.C. Snead	65	64	68	197	50,000
Chi Chi Rodriguez/Jim Dent	64	70	64	198	25,625
Bob Murphy/Jim Colbert	65	67	66	198	25,625
Bobby Nichols/Dave Hill	68	63	67	198	25,625
Tony Jacklin/Bob Charles	66	65	67	198	25,625
Charles Coody/Dale Douglass	63	68	68	199	18,500
Orville Moody/Jimmy Powell	68	64	68	200	16,500
Al Geiberger/Dave Stockton	65	65	70	200	16,500
Harold Henning/Dave Eichelberger	69	67	65	201	14,000
Bud Allin/Deane Beman	68	63	60	201	14,000
Homero Blancas/Tom Shaw	68	69	65	202	11,500
Bruce Crampton/Ed Sneed	70	67	66	203	10,000
Jim Albus/Larry Laoretti	69	65	69	203	10,000
George Archer/Simon Hobday	70	66	68	204	7,500
Miller Barber/Jim Ferree	69	69	66	204	7,500
Don Bies/Bruce Devlin	73	61	70	204	7,500

	SCORES			TOTAL	MONEY (Each)
Gay Brewer/Billy Casper	70	70	65	205	4,833.34
Joe Jimenez/Charles Sifford	69	70	66	205	4,833.33
Arnold Palmer/Tom Wargo	69	71	65	205	4,833.33
Frank Beard/Larry Mowry	71	69	70	210	4,500
Lee Elder/Calvin Peete	71	66	74	211	4,000
Don January/Gene Littler	69	71	71	211	4,000
Mike Fetchick/Bob Toski	73	68	71	212	4,000
Lionel Hebert/Tommy Jacobs	79	68	71	218	4,000
Roberto De Vicenzo/Peter Thomson	73	71	75	219	3,000
Paul Harney/Mike Souchak	70	74	77	221	3,000
Bob Goalby/Billy Maxwell	75	71	77	223	3,000
Dave Marr/Bob Rosburg	74	84	71	229	3,000
Dow Finsterwald/Mason Rudolph	84	77	69	230	3,000

Las Vegas Senior Classic

TPC at Summerlin, Las Vegas, Nevada
Par 36-36–72; 6,963 yards

April 28-30
purse, $1,000,000

	SCORES			TOTAL	MONEY
Jim Colbert	65	71	69	205	$150,000
Jim Dent	67	70	70	207	74,266.67
Rocky Thompson	70	65	72	207	74,266.67
Raymond Floyd	66	70	71	207	74,266.66
Tom Weiskopf	72	69	67	208	48,800
Gibby Gilbert	72	70	68	210	33,280
Mike Hill	75	66	69	210	33,280
Jack Kiefer	73	69	68	210	33,280
Graham Marsh	73	64	73	210	33,280
Dave Stockton	70	72	68	210	33,280
Bob Charles	67	73	71	211	24,000
Tom Shaw	76	67	68	211	24,000
Harold Henning	69	72	71	212	19,500
Tony Jacklin	72	68	72	212	19,500
J.C. Snead	71	69	72	212	19,500
Tom Wargo	70	72	70	212	19,500
Chi Chi Rodriguez	68	76	69	213	17,000
John Paul Cain	69	71	74	214	14,000
Bruce Crampton	77	68	69	214	14,000
Bob Dickson	72	71	71	214	14,000
Dave Eichelberger	72	71	71	214	14,000
Larry Gilbert	70	73	71	214	14,000
Gay Brewer	73	69	73	215	10,475
Jerry McGee	66	75	74	215	10,475
Jimmy Powell	76	68	71	215	10,475
Kermit Zarley	71	72	72	215	10,475
Don Bies	73	71	72	216	8,700
Charles Coody	70	70	76	216	8,700
Bruce Devlin	70	72	74	216	8,700
Bob Murphy	66	75	75	216	8,700
Dale Douglass	72	72	73	217	7,400
Bobby Nichols	73	73	71	217	7,400
Larry Ziegler	75	72	70	217	7,400
Deane Beman	74	70	74	218	6,500
Don January	76	73	69	218	6,500
Jay Sigel	68	74	76	218	6,500
Butch Baird	73	73	73	219	5,900

	SCORES			TOTAL	MONEY
George Archer	69	76	75	220	5,400
Miller Barber	76	70	74	220	5,400
Larry Laoretti	70	73	77	220	5,400
Dave Hill	71	74	75	220	5,400

PaineWebber Invitational

TPC at Piper Glen, Charlotte, North Carolina
Par 36-36–70; 6,774 yards

May 5-7
purse, $800,000

	SCORES			TOTAL	MONEY
Bob Murphy	68	66	69	203	$120,000
Raymond Floyd	69	69	67	205	64,000
Larry Ziegler	66	69	70	205	64,000
Jim Colbert	70	71	66	207	43,200
Graham Marsh	67	68	72	207	43,200
Larry Gilbert	74	68	66	208	28,800
Jerry McGee	70	69	69	208	28,800
Kermit Zarley	73	66	69	208	28,800
Walter Morgan	69	72	68	209	20,800
Tom Shaw	70	68	71	209	20,800
Dave Stockton	72	70	67	209	20,800
Butch Baird	73	66	71	210	16,800
DeWitt Weaver	70	70	70	210	16,800
Gibby Gilbert	71	74	66	211	13,600
Mike Hill	70	71	70	211	13,600
Roger Kennedy	67	75	69	211	13,600
Bruce Summerhays	69	69	73	211	13,600
Lee Trevino	72	70	69	211	13,600
Bud Allin	69	70	73	212	9,968
Bob Dickson	72	71	69	212	9,968
Jay Sigel	73	68	71	212	9,968
J.C. Snead	71	69	72	212	9,968
Rocky Thompson	70	69	73	212	9,968
Dave Eichelberger	74	68	72	214	7,480
Tony Jacklin	74	69	71	214	7,480
Larry Laoretti	71	71	72	214	7,480
Jimmy Powell	72	73	69	214	7,480
Tom Wargo	71	74	69	214	7,480
Tom Weiskopf	77	66	71	214	7,480
Gary Groh	71	72	72	215	6,160
Marion Heck	75	71	69	215	6,160
Jim Albus	77	69	70	216	5,051.43
George Archer	72	73	71	216	5,051.43
Dick Hendrickson	70	72	74	216	5,051.43
Bob Menne	73	69	74	216	5,051.43
Bob E. Smith	72	74	70	216	5,051.43
Ed Sneed	74	70	72	216	5,051.43
Dick Goetz	71	70	75	216	5,051.42
Jim Ferree	75	70	72	217	4,000
Bruce Lehnhard	76	69	72	217	4,000
Dick Lotz	73	72	72	217	4,000
Arnold Palmer	76	69	72	217	4,000

Cadillac NFL Classic

Upper Montclair Country Club, Clifton, New Jersey   May 12-14
Par 36-36–72; 6,816 yards   purse, $950,000

	SCORES			TOTAL	MONEY
George Archer	69	66	70	205	$142,500
Raymond Floyd	67	71	68	206	76,000
Bob Murphy	65	73	68	206	76,000
Lee Trevino	70	66	71	207	57,000
Isao Aoki	68	69	71	208	45,600
Dave Stockton	70	67	72	209	36,100
Larry Ziegler	69	69	71	209	36,100
Al Geiberger	69	69	72	210	28,500
Jerry McGee	70	70	70	210	28,500
Bob Charles	69	70	72	211	23,750
Dale Douglass	69	71	71	211	23,750
Don Bies	66	73	73	212	19,950
Kermit Zarley	68	72	72	212	19,950
Bob Dickson	73	70	70	213	16,625
Tony Jacklin	71	70	72	213	16,625
Rocky Thompson	68	71	74	213	16,625
Tom Wargo	67	74	72	213	16,625
Jim Dent	69	74	71	214	12,991.25
Jack Kiefer	68	76	70	214	12,991.25
Chi Chi Rodriguez	71	70	73	214	12,991.25
Bruce Summerhays	69	73	72	214	12,991.25
Dave Eichelberger	71	72	72	215	10,735
DeWitt Weaver	72	71	72	215	10,735
Deane Beman	72	71	73	216	9,500
Dick Lotz	69	74	73	216	9,500
Mike Still	74	67	75	216	9,500
Larry Laoretti	70	74	73	217	8,645
Bud Allin	70	73	75	218	8,075
J.C. Snead	70	75	73	218	8,075
Bob Betley	73	72	74	219	6,859
Charles Coody	72	74	73	219	6,859
Bruce Devlin	69	76	74	219	6,859
Gibby Gilbert	74	73	72	219	6,859
Jimmy Powell	74	72	73	219	6,859
Dick Hendrickson	74	74	72	220	5,265.72
Harold Henning	72	79	69	220	5,265.72
Larry Mowry	74	75	71	220	5,265.72
Butch Baird	71	73	76	220	5,265.71
Robert Landers	71	75	74	220	5,265.71
Walter Morgan	72	70	78	220	5,265.71
Ed Sneed	74	73	73	220	5,265.71

Bell Atlantic Classic

Chester Valley Golf Club, Malvern, Pennsylvania   May 19-21
Par 35-35–70; 6,608 yards   purse, $900,000

	SCORES			TOTAL	MONEY
Jim Colbert	68	71	68	207	$135,000
J.C. Snead	66	72	70	208	79,200
Jack Nicklaus	72	69	68	209	64,800
Calvin Peete	71	73	67	211	54,000

	SCORES			TOTAL	MONEY
Charles Coody	72	69	71	212	35,100
Ed Sneed	72	71	69	212	35,100
Dave Stockton	68	71	73	212	35,100
Bruce Summerhays	70	70	72	212	35,100
Lee Trevino	69	72	72	213	25,200
Deane Beman	68	74	72	214	22,500
Dave Eichelberger	71	71	72	214	22,500
Jim Albus	75	68	72	215	19,800
Bob Carson	74	69	73	216	17,550
Bob Dickson	70	72	74	216	17,550
Isao Aoki	68	73	76	217	12,830
Miller Barber	72	73	72	217	12,830
Billy Casper	72	75	70	217	12,830
Jim Dent	70	75	72	217	12,830
Rives McBee	74	75	68	217	12,830
Bobby Mitchell	72	74	71	217	12,830
Jay Sigel	76	72	69	217	12,830
Bob E. Smith	73	71	73	217	12,830
Tom Wargo	73	74	70	217	12,830
Joe Jimenez	70	75	73	218	8,797.50
Richie Karl	72	72	74	218	8,797.50
Larry Laoretti	72	75	71	218	8,797.50
Chi Chi Rodriguez	75	74	69	218	8,797.50
Butch Baird	73	74	72	219	7,290
Bruce Devlin	73	74	72	219	7,290
Dale Douglass	72	73	74	219	7,290
Al Kelley	73	73	73	219	7,290
Homero Blancas	75	69	76	220	5,940
Walter Morgan	78	73	69	220	5,940
Bob Murphy	73	76	71	220	5,940
Bob Thatcher	75	74	71	220	5,940
Harry Toscano	73	75	72	220	5,940
Lee Elder	75	75	71	221	4,500
Mike Hill	76	71	74	221	4,500
Graham Marsh	77	70	74	221	4,500
Jerry McGee	74	73	74	221	4,500
Larry Mowry	74	78	69	221	4,500
Gary Player	73	75	73	221	4,500
Jimmy Powell	72	75	74	221	4,500
Fred Ruiz	77	75	69	221	4,500

Quicksilver Classic

Quicksilver Golf Club, Midway, Pennsylvania
Par 36-36–72; 6,896 yards

May 26-28
purse, $1,100,000

	SCORES			TOTAL	MONEY
Dave Stockton	72	69	67	208	$165,000
Isao Aoki	68	72	69	209	96,800
George Archer	69	68	73	210	66,000
Dave Eichelberger	71	68	71	210	66,000
Tom Wargo	71	72	67	210	66,000
Tony Jacklin	73	69	69	211	44,000
J.C. Snead	69	72	71	212	39,600
Bud Allin	68	76	69	213	29,040
John Paul Cain	71	72	70	213	29,040
Graham Marsh	70	71	72	213	29,040

	SCORES			TOTAL	MONEY
Jerry McGee	69	71	73	213	29,040
DeWitt Weaver	71	75	67	213	29,040
Jim Albus	70	72	72	214	20,350
Gibby Gilbert	71	72	71	214	20,350
Jimmy Powell	71	72	71	214	20,350
Kermit Zarley	74	67	73	214	20,350
Tommy Aaron	68	73	74	215	14,272.50
Don Bies	72	73	70	215	14,272.50
Jim Colbert	74	72	69	215	14,272.50
Larry Gilbert	67	75	73	215	14,272.50
Mike Hill	72	71	72	215	14,272.50
Larry Laoretti	70	70	75	215	14,272.50
Jay Sigel	72	71	72	215	14,272.50
Bob E. Smith	73	74	68	215	14,272.50
Miller Barber	73	71	72	216	10,257.50
Jim Dent	75	69	72	216	10,257.50
Simon Hobday	72	73	71	216	10,257.50
Bruce Summerhays	73	73	70	216	10,257.50
Al Geiberger	73	72	72	217	8,910
Calvin Peete	73	75	69	217	8,910
Deane Beman	74	72	72	218	8,085
Chuck Montalbano	70	70	78	218	8,085
Dick Goetz	73	72	74	219	7,425
Walter Zembriski	73	68	78	219	7,425
Walter Morgan	72	71	77	220	6,462.50
Ron Skiles	77	69	74	220	6,462.50
Mike Still	72	73	75	220	6,462.50
Robert Zimmerman	72	73	75	220	6,462.50
Harold Henning	75	74	72	221	5,500
Dave Hill	71	75	75	221	5,500
Jack Kiefer	74	75	72	221	5,500
Gary Player	75	72	74	221	5,500

Bruno's Memorial Classic

Greyston Golf Club, Birmingham, Alabama
Par 36-36–72; 7,012 yards

June 2-4
purse, $1,050,000

	SCORES			TOTAL	MONEY
Graham Marsh	68	63	70	201	$157,500
J.C. Snead	71	67	68	206	92,400
Bud Allin	67	70	70	207	57,750
Larry Laoretti	70	67	70	207	57,750
Bruce Summerhays	67	69	71	207	57,750
Tom Weiskopf	68	68	71	207	57,750
Al Geiberger	70	68	70	208	37,800
Tom Wargo	71	67	71	209	33,600
Isao Aoki	72	69	69	210	28,350
Raymond Floyd	69	72	69	210	28,350
Butch Baird	72	69	70	211	22,312.50
Dick Hendrickson	72	69	70	211	22,312.50
Mike Hill	68	73	70	211	22,312.50
Dave Stockton	66	74	71	211	22,312.50
Jim Colbert	71	70	71	212	16,821
Bruce Devlin	70	69	73	212	16,821
Jerry McGee	72	68	72	212	16,821
DeWitt Weaver	72	72	68	212	16,821

	SCORES			TOTAL	MONEY
Walter Zembriski	72	71	69	212	16,821
John Paul Cain	71	70	72	213	13,440
Kermit Zarley	72	74	67	213	13,440
George Archer	76	68	70	214	10,560
Bob Carson	70	71	73	214	10,560
Dave Eichelberger	73	69	72	214	10,560
Gibby Gilbert	74	68	72	214	10,560
Dave Hill	77	68	69	214	10,560
Jack Kiefer	71	70	73	214	10,560
Jay Sigel	69	74	71	214	10,560
Jim Albus	70	73	72	215	8,295
Bill Hall	72	70	73	215	8,295
Tony Jacklin	69	74	72	215	8,295
Don Bies	73	72	71	216	7,087.50
Larry Mowry	71	74	71	216	7,087.50
Gary Player	75	67	74	216	7,087.50
Lee Trevino	70	67	79	216	7,087.50
Tommy Aaron	74	74	69	217	5,906.25
Miller Barber	72	73	72	217	5,906.25
Charles Coody	72	70	75	217	5,906.25
Jim Ferree	74	70	73	217	5,906.25
Gay Brewer	76	69	73	218	5,250
Simon Hobday	70	73	75	218	5,250

BellSouth Classic at Opryland

Springhouse Golf Club, Nashville, Tennessee
Par 36-36–72; 6,783 yards

June 9-11
purse, $1,100,000

	SCORES			TOTAL	MONEY
Jim Dent	66	69	68	203	$165,000
Bob Murphy	70	66	69	205	96,800
Dave Stockton	71	67	68	206	79,200
Dave Hill	67	74	66	207	59,400
Hale Irwin	70	68	69	207	59,400
Tommy Aaron	70	68	70	208	39,600
Jim Albus	69	70	69	208	39,600
Rocky Thompson	71	67	70	208	39,600
Harold Henning	65	74	70	209	30,800
Isao Aoki	70	74	66	210	24,420
Dave Eichelberger	68	70	72	210	24,420
Jay Sigel	73	68	69	210	24,420
Bruce Summerhays	73	70	67	210	24,420
Kermit Zarley	69	71	70	210	24,420
George Archer	71	70	70	211	17,622
John Paul Cain	72	72	67	211	17,622
Larry Laoretti	72	69	70	211	17,622
Mike McCullough	69	75	67	211	17,622
Calvin Peete	70	70	71	211	17,622
Mike Joyce	72	69	71	212	14,080
Walter Zembriski	71	72	69	212	14,080
Lee Trevino	72	71	70	213	12,760
Bud Allin	71	71	72	214	10,312.50
John Brodie	70	71	73	214	10,312.50
Gibby Gilbert	69	75	70	214	10,312.50
Mike Hill	67	74	73	214	10,312.50
Jack Kiefer	73	71	70	214	10,312.50

	SCORES			TOTAL	MONEY
Harry Toscano	68	72	74	214	10,312.50
Tom Wargo	72	68	74	214	10,312.50
Tom Weiskopf	73	71	70	214	10,312.50
Butch Baird	70	70	75	215	7,425
Miller Barber	74	73	68	215	7,425
Al Geiberger	74	72	69	215	7,425
Tony Jacklin	71	74	70	215	7,425
Ed Sneed	70	75	70	215	7,425
DeWitt Weaver	70	74	71	215	7,425
Terry Dill	71	70	75	216	5,500
Simon Hobday	72	70	74	216	5,500
Robert Landers	74	72	70	216	5,500
Jerry McGee	68	77	71	216	5,500
Larry Mowry	69	72	75	216	5,500
Arnold Palmer	73	72	71	216	5,500
Gary Player	74	72	70	216	5,500
Larry Ziegler	72	73	71	216	5,500

Dallas Reunion Pro-Am

Oak Cliff Country Club, Dallas, Texas
Par 35-35–70; 6,579 yards

June 16-18
purse, $600,000

	SCORES			TOTAL	MONEY
Tom Wargo	64	64	69	197	$82,500
Dave Eichelberger	66	68	70	204	44,000
Dave Stockton	67	68	69	204	44,000
Bruce Summerhays	69	70	69	208	27,133.34
Jim Albus	70	71	67	208	27,133.33
Brian Barnes	68	70	70	208	27,133.33
Jim Dent	72	73	64	209	18,700
Marion Heck	73	70	66	209	18,700
Bud Allin	69	72	69	210	14,300
Harold Henning	71	71	68	210	14,300
Ben Smith	71	74	65	210	14,300
Charles Coody	73	67	71	211	10,560
Dale Douglass	68	72	71	211	10,560
Rives McBee	69	72	70	211	10,560
J.C. Snead	73	65	73	211	10,560
Lee Trevino	66	70	75	211	10,560
Dick Goetz	69	69	74	212	8,525
Bob Wynn	69	72	71	212	8,525
Tommy Aaron	75	72	66	213	6,853
Mike Hill	73	75	65	213	6,853
Jack Kiefer	70	68	75	213	6,853
Mike McCullough	71	69	73	213	6,853
Ed Sneed	71	70	72	213	6,853
John Paul Cain	70	72	72	214	5,258
Dick Hendrickson	72	71	71	214	5,258
Graham Marsh	67	73	74	214	5,258
Mike Still	72	74	68	214	5,258
Ron Widby	73	71	70	214	5,258
Bob Betley	71	72	72	215	4,158
Terry Dill	71	70	74	215	4,158
Richie Karl	73	68	74	215	4,158
Bobby Mitchell	71	70	74	215	4,158
Chi Chi Rodriguez	72	72	71	215	4,158

	SCORES			TOTAL	MONEY
Larry Gilbert	74	73	69	216	3,547.50
John Jacobs	72	75	69	216	3,547.50
Bruce Devlin	73	73	71	217	2,979.17
Jerry McGee	70	74	73	217	2,979.17
Bob Murphy	73	73	71	217	2,979.17
Robert Zimmerman	72	72	73	217	2,979.17
Robert Gaona	75	73	69	217	2,979.16
Harry Toscano	76	71	70	217	2,979.16

Nationwide Championship

The Golf Club of Georgia, Alpharetta, Georgia

Par 36-36–72; 6,777 yards

June 23-25

purse, $1,200,000

	SCORES			TOTAL	MONEY
Bob Murphy	71	64	68	203	$180,000
Hale Irwin	70	65	70	205	96,000
Bruce Summerhays	63	71	71	205	96,000
Isao Aoki	69	70	67	206	72,000
Graham Marsh	69	67	71	207	52,800
Tom Weiskopf	75	66	66	207	52,800
Jay Sigel	71	67	70	208	43,200
Deane Beman	66	73	70	209	33,000
Dale Douglass	71	72	66	209	33,000
Larry Laoretti	66	68	75	209	33,000
Tom Wargo	69	69	71	209	33,000
Jim Colbert	71	71	68	210	25,200
Mike Hill	73	68	69	210	25,200
Al Geiberger	73	69	69	211	22,200
Orville Moody	67	74	70	211	22,200
Tommy Aaron	71	73	69	213	18,072
Jim Albus	73	67	73	213	18,072
Bobby Nichols	71	68	74	213	18,072
Jimmy Powell	70	71	72	213	18,072
DeWitt Weaver	72	71	70	213	18,072
George Archer	72	72	70	214	14,400
Dave Hill	71	75	68	214	14,400
Butch Baird	75	71	69	215	11,502.86
Homero Blancas	74	69	72	215	11,502.86
Jack Kiefer	74	69	72	215	11,502.86
Richard Rhyan	74	74	67	215	11,502.86
Tom Shaw	74	71	70	215	11,502.86
Gary Groh	70	70	75	215	11,502.86
J.C. Snead	71	71	73	215	11,502.86
Don Bies	70	73	73	216	7,788
Bob Charles	70	77	69	216	7,788
Jim Ferree	69	73	74	216	7,788
Gibby Gilbert	71	71	74	216	7,788
Dick Hendrickson	71	74	71	216	7,788
Harold Henning	70	73	73	216	7,788
Simon Hobday	74	72	70	216	7,788
Gary Player	75	71	70	216	7,788
Rocky Thompson	71	72	73	216	7,788
Harry Toscano	71	73	72	216	7,788
John Paul Cain	73	71	73	217	5,640
Charlie Epps	74	71	72	217	5,640
Ed Sneed	76	69	72	217	5,640

	SCORES			TOTAL	MONEY
Dave Stockton	75	72	70	217	5,640
Lee Trevino	72	74	71	217	5,640

U.S. Senior Open Championship

Congressional Country Club, Bethesda, Maryland
Par 36-36–72; 6,945 yards

June 29-July 2
purse, $1,000,000

	SCORES				TOTAL	MONEY
Tom Weiskopf	69	69	69	68	275	$175,000
Jack Nicklaus	71	71	70	67	279	103,500
Isao Aoki	70	70	68	72	280	51,998
Bob Murphy	69	70	71	70	280	51,998
Hale Irwin	72	68	71	71	282	32,625
J.C. Snead	68	73	70	71	282	32,625
Lee Trevino	73	68	74	68	283	28,073
Raymond Floyd	70	72	69	73	284	24,810.50
Graham Marsh	69	70	74	71	284	24,810.50
DeWitt Weaver	73	71	70	71	285	22,043
Brian Barnes	69	72	71	74	286	19,093.67
Bob Betley	76	67	71	72	286	19,093.67
Bob Charles	74	70	71	71	286	19,093.67
Larry Laoretti	69	73	71	75	288	15,595.67
Rocky Thompson	72	73	69	74	288	15,595.67
Kermit Zarley	74	69	74	71	288	15,595.67
Mike Joyce	71	74	74	70	289	13,330.50
John Morgan	74	68	76	71	289	13,330.50
Calvin Peete	73	71	72	74	290	11,850.50
Gary Player	73	71	75	71	290	11,850.50
Harold Henning	76	73	71	71	291	9,797.60
Mike McCullough	73	76	68	74	291	9,797.60
Larry Ringer	68	80	69	74	291	9,797.60
Jay Sigel	70	73	73	75	291	9,797.60
Dave Stockton	69	70	74	78	291	9,797.60
Don Bies	71	72	75	74	292	8,355
Bob Leaver	73	69	77	74	293	7,757.50
Tom Wargo	72	75	71	75	293	7,757.50
Tommy Aaron	70	68	79	77	294	6,439.17
Jim Albus	73	72	74	75	294	6,439.17
Babe Hiskey	72	77	77	68	294	6,439.17
Chi Chi Rodriguez	73	77	71	73	294	6,439.17
Bruce Summerhays	72	72	74	76	294	6,439.17
Walter Zembriski	74	71	73	76	294	6,439.17
Dick Goetz	75	71	76	73	295	5,253.33
Simon Hobday	72	72	75	76	295	5,253.33
Bob Wynn	71	73	73	78	295	5,253.33
John Paul Cain	76	73	71	76	296	4,821
*Robert Housen	76	70	73	77	296	
Dave Ojala	71	75	74	77	297	4,531
Jimmy Powell	73	74	72	78	297	4,531

Kroger Classic

The Golf Center at Kings Island, Grizzly Course, Mason, Ohio   July 7-9
Par 36-35–71; 6,628 yards   purse, $900,000

	SCORES			TOTAL	MONEY
Mike Hill	64	66	66	196	$135,000
Isao Aoki	66	66	65	197	79,200
Graham Marsh	70	63	65	198	64,800
J.C. Snead	66	68	67	201	48,600
Rocky Thompson	70	67	64	201	48,600
Ed Sneed	67	70	65	202	36,000
Jim Colbert	69	68	66	203	27,450
Al Geiberger	68	67	68	203	27,450
Gibby Gilbert	70	66	67	203	27,450
Lee Trevino	72	66	65	203	27,450
Bud Allin	70	67	67	204	18,540
Gay Brewer	66	71	67	204	18,540
Bob Charles	71	69	64	204	18,540
Joe Jimenez	68	68	68	204	18,540
Jay Sigel	68	67	69	204	18,540
Walter Morgan	70	65	70	205	13,972.50
Calvin Peete	69	71	65	205	13,972.50
Harry Toscano	67	72	66	205	13,972.50
Tom Wargo	68	71	66	205	13,972.50
Jim Dent	67	69	70	206	10,305
Don January	69	67	70	206	10,305
Chi Chi Rodriguez	69	68	69	·206	10,305
Bruce Summerhays	70	70	66	206	10,305
Walter Zembriski	68	71	67	206	10,305
Larry Ziegler	69	69	68	206	10,305
Brian Barnes	72	66	69	207	7,650
Tony Jacklin	69	70	68	207	7,650
Bobby Mitchell	67	71	69	207	7,650
Ben Smith	66	69	72	207	7,650
DeWitt Weaver	70	66	71	207	7,650
Robert Zimmerman	72	68	67	207	7,650
Miller Barber	67	70	71	208	5,805
Bob Dickson	70	66	72	208	5,805
Dick Goetz	70	68	70	208	5,805
Bob Hauer	69	69	70	208	5,805
Simon Hobday	72	70	66	208	5,805
Tom Ulozas	69	71	68	208	5,805
John Paul Cain	71	70	68	209	4,590
Billy Casper	71	68	70	209	4,590
Dale Douglass	69	72	68	209	4,590
Gene Littler	69	69	71	209	4,590
Rives McBee	74	64	71	209	4,590

Ford Senior Players Championship

TPC of Michigan, Dearborn, Michigan   July 13-16
Par 36-36–72; 6,876 yards   purse, $1,500,000

	SCORES				TOTAL	MONEY
J.C. Snead	69	68	66	69	272	$225,000
Jack Nicklaus	71	68	66	67	272	132,000

(Snead defeated Nicklaus on first extra hole.)

	SCORES				TOTAL	MONEY
Jim Colbert	70	63	75	68	276	90,000
Jerry McGee	68	73	67	68	276	90,000
Ben Smith	73	67	67	69	276	90,000
Isao Aoki	71	68	68	70	277	60,000
Don Bies	74	71	68	65	278	48,000
Bob Murphy	71	68	69	70	278	48,000
Dave Stockton	69	69	66	74	278	48,000
Raymond Floyd	69	70	66	74	279	34,500
Al Geiberger	71	69	68	71	279	34,500
Hale Irwin	74	69	72	64	279	34,500
Tom Weiskopf	70	71	69	69	279	34,500
Larry Laoretti	74	69	69	68	280	26,250
Graham Marsh	72	70	70	68	280	26,250
Walter Morgan	74	67	69	70	280	26,250
Kermit Zarley	69	69	67	75	280	26,250
Jim Dent	75	69	69	68	281	19,890
Mike Hill	71	69	66	75	281	19,890
Tony Jacklin	73	71	70	67	281	19,890
Jay Sigel	69	72	68	72	281	19,890
Rocky Thompson	70	69	72	70	281	19,890
DeWitt Weaver	71	73	70	68	282	14,378.58
Tommy Aaron	74	72	67	69	282	14,378.57
Bob Charles	68	73	73	68	282	14,378.57
Gibby Gilbert	73	70	70	69	282	14,378.57
Simon Hobday	71	72	69	70	282	14,375.57
Richard Rhyan	74	69	69	70	282	14,375.57
Robert Zimmerman	68	74	72	68	282	14,378.57
George Archer	73	67	75	68	283	10,830
Robert Gaona	74	67	65	77	283	10,830
Jimmy Powell	70	72	71	70	283	10,830
Lee Trevino	70	67	74	72	283	10,830
Tom Wargo	69	74	73	67	283	10,830

First of America Classic

Egypt Valley Golf Club, Ada, Michigan
Par 36-36–72; 6,874 yards

July 21-23
purse, $700,000

	SCORES			TOTAL	MONEY
Jimmy Powell	68	66	67	201	$105,000
Babe Hiskey	71	65	70	206	61,600
Larry Laoretti	68	69	70	207	50,400
Jim Albus	69	70	69	208	28,466.67
Jim Colbert	69	70	69	208	28,466.67
Simon Hobday	69	71	68	208	28,466.67
Richard Rhyan	72	69	67	208	28,466.67
George Archer	66	72	70	208	28,466.66
Walter Morgan	69	69	70	208	28,466.66
Bob Wynn	69	70	70	209	18,200
Dave Eichelberger	71	70	69	210	15,400
Larry Gilbert	72	71	67	210	15,400
Mike Hill	71	72	67	210	15,400
Graham Marsh	68	71	72	211	12,600
Ed Sneed	71	70	70	211	12,600
Harry Toscano	67	70	74	211	12,600
Bud Allin	71	72	69	212	9,601.67
Marion Heck	74	70	68	212	9,601.67

	SCORES			TOTAL	MONEY
Dave Stockton	70	74	68	212	9,601.67
Walter Zembriski	73	68	71	212	9,601.67
Gay Brewer	70	70	72	212	9,601.66
Bruce Summerhays	70	70	72	212	9,601.66
Wally Armstrong	67	72	74	213	7,175
Chuck Montalbano	66	72	75	213	7,175
Chi Chi Rodriguez	75	67	71	213	7,175
Ken Still	75	65	73	213	7,175
Tommy Aaron	68	72	74	214	5,950
Deane Beman	73	69	72	214	5,950
Jack Kiefer	73	72	69	214	5,950
Mike Still	74	70	70	214	5,950
John Brodie	73	70	72	215	4,725
Jim Ferree	71	71	73	215	4,725
Harold Henning	74	70	71	215	4,725
Tony Jacklin	68	74	73	215	4,725
Rives McBee	74	70	71	215	4,725
Jerry McGee	68	72	75	215	4,725
Butch Baird	77	70	69	216	3,640
Bruce Devlin	77	69	70	216	3,640
Bob Dickson	73	71	72	216	3,640
Robert Gaona	72	72	72	216	3,640
Joe Jimenez	72	74	70	216	3,640
Denny Spencer	70	75	71	216	3,640

Ameritech Open

Stonebridge Country Club, Chicago, Illinois
Par 36-36–72; 6,840 yards

July 28-30
purse, $850,000

	SCORES			TOTAL	MONEY
Hale Irwin	66	63	66	195	$127,500
Kermit Zarley	69	65	68	202	74,800
Dave Stockton	73	65	66	204	61,200
Mike Hill	67	72	66	205	51,000
Jim Colbert	66	68	72	206	37,400
Raymond Floyd	69	69	68	206	37,400
Gay Brewer	74	68	65	207	25,925
Dave Hill	69	68	70	207	25,925
Joe Jimenez	74	62	71	207	25,925
Ben Smith	69	68	70	207	25,925
John Paul Cain	69	72	67	208	18,700
Gibby Gilbert	68	68	72	208	18,700
Bob E. Smith	67	70	71	208	18,700
Bob Dickson	66	74	69	209	15,300
Al Geiberger	73	65	71	209	15,300
Chuck Montalbano	69	68	72	209	15,300
Dick Goetz	73	68	69	210	11,659.17
Gary Groh	71	70	69	210	11,659.17
Graham Marsh	71	72	67	210	11,659.17
Bruce Summerhays	72	70	68	210	11,659.17
Lee Trevino	72	68	70	210	11,659.16
Walter Zembriski	69	69	72	210	11,659.16
Bob Betley	72	70	69	211	8,712.50
Dave Eichelberger	72	68	71	211	8,712.50
Jerry McGee	71	71	69	211	8,712.50
Mike Still	74	67	70	211	8,712.50

	SCORES			TOTAL	MONEY
Tony Jacklin	74	73	65	212	6,899.17
Robert Rawlins	73	69	70	212	6,899.17
Rocky Thompson	73	72	67	212	6,899.17
Harry Toscano	74	70	68	212	6,899.17
Larry Gilbert	73	68	71	212	6,899.16
Richard Rhyan	72	68	72	212	6,899.16
Bruce Devlin	72	70	71	213	5,482.50
Terry Dill	77	71	65	213	5,482.50
Jim Ferree	71	72	70	213	5,482.50
Rives McBee	69	73	71	213	5,482.50
George Archer	72	73	69	214	4,080
Deane Beman	72	70	72	214	4,080
Dick Hendrickson	70	71	73	214	4,080
Jack Kiefer	73	68	73	214	4,080
Walter Morgan	73	67	74	214	4,080
Jimmy Powell	75	67	72	214	4,080
Chi Chi Rodriguez	70	73	71	214	4,080
Tom Shaw	75	66	73	214	4,080
Jay Sigel	73	66	75	214	4,080
Robert Zimmerman	71	71	72	214	4,080

VFW Championship

Loch Lloyd Country Club, Belton, Missouri   August 4-6
Par 35-35–70; 6,608 yards   purse, $900,000

	SCORES			TOTAL	MONEY
Bob Murphy	69	63	63	195	$135,000
Jim Colbert	68	66	62	196	79,200
Jay Sigel	65	66	67	198	64,800
Bud Allin	63	69	68	200	48,600
Simon Hobday	66	68	66	200	48,600
Isao Aoki	68	67	66	201	36,000
Larry Gilbert	70	67	65	202	26,280
Hale Irwin	67	68	67	202	26,280
Dave Stockton	69	68	65	202	26,280
Bruce Summerhays	69	64	69	202	26,280
Lee Trevino	70	68	64	202	26,280
Walter Morgan	70	69	64	203	19,800
Dave Eichelberger	68	67	69	204	17,100
Jack Kiefer	67	65	72	204	17,100
Robert Zimmerman	68	71	65	204	17,100
Bob Betley	71	66	68	205	13,554
Dale Douglass	70	70	65	205	13,554
Raymond Floyd	68	69	68	205	13,554
Graham Marsh	67	67	71	205	13,554
Tom Wargo	69	66	70	205	13,554
Rives McBee	71	67	68	206	10,237.50
Ben Smith	68	71	67	206	10,237.50
Harry Toscano	68	69	69	206	10,237.50
Kermit Zarley	72	66	68	206	10,237.50
Tony Jacklin	70	68	69	207	8,208
Larry Mowry	73	67	67	207	8,208
Tom Shaw	70	66	71	207	8,208
Rocky Thompson	71	68	68	207	8,208
Jim Albus	68	68	71	207	8,208
Don Bies	68	74	66	208	6,498

	SCORES			TOTAL	MONEY
Bob Dickson	73	67	68	208	6,498
Jerry McGee	67	69	72	208	6,498
Richard Rhyan	68	73	67	208	6,498
Bob E. Smith	70	69	69	208	6,498
John Paul Cain	73	70	66	209	5,535
Gibby Gilbert	68	71	70	209	5,535
Tommy Aaron	73	68	69	210	4,590
Dick Goetz	66	73	71	210	4,590
Marion Heck	69	72	69	210	4,590
Ron Skiles	69	77	64	210	4,590
Ed Sneed	71	70	69	210	4,590
Mike Still	71	69	70	210	4,590
Bob Wynn	71	70	69	210	4,590

Burnet Classic

Bunker Hills Golf Club, Coon Rapids, Minnesota
Par 36-36–72; 6,909 yards

August 11-13
purse, $1,100,000

	SCORES			TOTAL	MONEY
Raymond Floyd	68	65	68	201	$165,000
Graham Marsh	64	69	69	202	96,800
Jim Albus	68	69	69	206	72,600
Gibby Gilbert	64	70	72	206	72,600
Dave Stockton	68	71	68	207	45,466.67
Kermit Zarley	72	67	68	207	45,466.67
Butch Baird	67	70	70	207	45,466.66
Terry Dill	68	69	71	208	31,533.34
George Archer	68	69	71	208	31,533.33
Lee Trevino	68	66	74	208	31,533.33
Bob Dickson	70	71	68	209	26,400
Bud Allin	68	68	74	210	21,725
Isao Aoki	69	71	70	210	21,725
Bob E. Smith	69	69	72	210	21,725
Rocky Thompson	71	68	71	210	21,725
Tommy Aaron	73	67	71	211	16,566
Dave Eichelberger	69	72	70	211	16,566
Harry Toscano	67	72	72	211	16,566
Tom Wargo	70	71	70	211	16,566
Robert Zimmerman	70	69	72	211	16,566
Dave Hill	70	71	71	212	11,644.29
Simon Hobday	71	70	71	212	11,644.29
Robert Landers	71	73	68	212	11,644.29
Jay Sigel	72	71	69	212	11,644.29
Bob Charles	70	71	71	212	11,644.28
Dale Douglass	70	70	72	212	11,644.28
Dick Hendrickson	71	67	74	212	11,644.28
Deane Beman	71	71	71	213	7,993.34
Jim Colbert	71	71	71	213	7,993.34
Larry Gilbert	71	72	70	213	7,993.34
Al Geiberger	74	70	69	213	7,993.33
Gary Groh	74	69	70	213	7,993.33
Walter Morgan	74	72	67	213	7,993.33
Richard Rhyan	71	70	72	213	7,993.33
Bruce Summerhays	70	72	71	213	7,993.33
Walter Zembriski	71	72	70	213	7,993.33
Jerry McGee	70	71	73	214	6,160

	SCORES			TOTAL	MONEY
Ed Sneed	71	69	74	214	6,160
Agim Bardha	70	72	73	215	5,280
John Paul Cain	73	72	70	215	5,280
Harold Henning	72	72	71	215	5,280
Jack Kiefer	69	72	74	215	5,280
Larry Laoretti	73	69	73	215	5,280
DeWitt Weaver	70	72	73	215	5,280

Northville Long Island Classic

Meadow Brook Club, Jericho, New York
Par 36-36–72; 6,775 yards

August 18-20
purse, $800,000

	SCORES			TOTAL	MONEY
Lee Trevino	67	69	66	202	$120,000
Bud Allin	67	69	70	206	70,400
Larry Gilbert	68	68	71	207	44,000
Jack Kiefer	72	69	66	207	44,000
Jay Sigel	68	70	69	207	44,000
Ben Smith	68	68	71	207	44,000
John Paul Cain	65	69	74	208	28,800
Jim Albus	68	69	72	209	20,266.67
George Archer	71	66	72	209	20,266.67
Larry Laoretti	69	71	69	209	20,266.67
Bob Murphy	69	71	69	209	20,266.67
Dave Eichelberger	69	66	74	209	20,266.66
Tony Jacklin	66	71	72	209	20,266.66
Bruce Summerhays	69	71	70	210	15,200
Chuck Montalbano	72	67	72	211	14,400
Jimmy Powell	72	69	71	212	13,600
Terry Dill	73	70	70	213	12,026.67
Tom Joyce	75	70	68	213	12,026.67
Bob E. Smith	70	73	70	213	12,026.66
Mike Joyce	68	73	73	214	10,560
Jim Colbert	73	73	69	215	9,333.34
Snell Lancaster	73	69	73	215	9,333.33
Calvin Peete	70	74	71	215	9,333.33
Charles Coody	71	74	71	216	8,400
Isao Aoki	74	73	70	217	6,971.43
Butch Baird	76	72	69	217	6,971.43
Bob Betley	76	73	68	217	6,971.43
Dick Goetz	72	70	75	217	6,971.43
Harold Henning	72	75	70	217	6,971.43
Walter Morgan	73	72	72	217	6,971.43
Dick Rhyan	72	69	76	217	6,971.42
Simon Hobday	74	71	73	218	5,520
Mike McCullough	79	68	71	218	5,520
Bob Thatcher	70	72	76	218	5,520
Bob Charles	70	74	75	219	4,800
Ken Still	71	76	72	219	4,800
Larry Ziegler	74	70	75	219	4,800
Don Davis	70	74	76	220	4,080
Don Massengale	78	74	68	220	4,080
Steve Robbins	74	74	72	220	4,080
Ed Sneed	77	70	73	220	4,080
Tom Wargo	74	71	75	220	4,080

Bank of Boston Classic

Nashawtuc Country Club, Concord, Massachusetts   August 25-27
Par 36-36–72; 6,755 yards   purse, $800,000

	SCORES			TOTAL	MONEY
Isao Aoki	69	66	69	204	$120,000
Bob Charles	70	67	68	205	64,000
Hale Irwin	71	66	68	205	64,000
Bruce Summerhays	72	69	66	207	43,200
Walter Zembriski	71	69	67	207	43,200
George Archer	69	70	69	208	28,800
Terry Dill	75	68	65	208	28,800
Jay Sigel	74	68	66	208	28,800
Bud Allin	69	69	71	209	22,400
Dave Eichelberger	71	72	67	210	19,200
Bob Murphy	71	70	69	210	19,200
Rocky Thompson	69	70	71	210	19,200
Homero Blancas	73	72	66	211	15,200
Larry Gilbert	71	68	72	211	15,200
Mike McCullough	71	66	74	211	15,200
Tommy Aaron	75	64	73	212	12,048
Bob Brue	74	70	68	212	12,048
Chuck Montalbano	76	69	67	212	12,048
Walter Morgan	73	70	69	212	12,048
Kermit Zarley	75	67	70	212	12,048
Jim Albus	75	69	69	213	9,333.34
Miller Barber	74	67	72	213	9,333.33
Jim Ferree	72	69	72	213	9,333.33
Butch Baird	70	71	73	214	7,648
Jim Colbert	69	74	71	214	7,648
Mike Hill	70	75	69	214	7,648
Rives McBee	73	73	68	214	7,648
Denny Spencer	70	74	70	214	7,648
Bob Dickson	77	70	68	215	6,180
Simon Hobday	73	73	69	215	6,180
Calvin Peete	73	73	69	215	6,180
DeWitt Weaver	73	70	72	215	6,180
Dick Goetz	73	70	73	216	5,280
Jimmy Powell	73	71	72	216	5,280
Dick Rhyan	72	70	74	216	5,280
Bob Betley	74	75	68	217	4,416
Joe Jimenez	73	72	72	217	4,416
Bruce Lehnhard	73	72	72	217	4,416
Ben Smith	73	76	68	217	4,416
Bob E. Smith	71	72	74	217	4,416

Franklin Quest Championship

Park Meadows Country Club, Park City, Utah   September 1-3
Par 36-36–72; 7,026 yards   purse, $600,000

	SCORES			TOTAL	MONEY
Tony Jacklin	72	67	67	206	$90,000
John Paul Cain	69	70	68	207	34,400
Simon Hobday	66	70	71	207	34,400
Rives McBee	70	68	69	207	34,400
Dave Stockton	71	70	66	207	34,400

	SCORES			TOTAL	MONEY
Bruce Summerhays	70	68	69	207	34,400
Tom Weiskopf	69	72	66	207	34,400
Don Bies	69	67	72	208	17,200
Bruce Devlin	69	70	69	208	17,200
Jack Kiefer	72	67	69	208	17,200
George Archer	73	65	71	209	13,800
Don January	70	71	68	209	13,800
Tommy Aaron	69	71	70	210	10,800
Bob Charles	71	72	67	210	10,800
Gibby Gilbert	71	68	71	210	10,800
Joe Jimenez	72	69	69	210	10,800
Tom Shaw	71	72	67	210	10,800
Jim Albus	72	69	70	211	7,730
Dick Hendrickson	70	70	71	211	7,730
Larry Laoretti	65	72	74	211	7,730
Jerry McGee	74	68	69	211	7,730
Bob E. Smith	69	73	69	211	7,730
J.C. Snead	73	67	71	211	7,730
Butch Baird	71	72	69	212	6,000
Gay Brewer	67	74	71	212	6,000
Kermit Zarley	69	72	71	212	6,000
Charles Coody	72	71	70	213	4,870
Robert Landers	73	71	69	213	4,870
Gary Player	69	76	68	213	4,870
Jay Sigel	72	70	71	213	4,870
Ben Smith	63	80	70	213	4,870
Harry Toscano	72	71	70	213	4,870
Bob Betley	72	71	71	214	3,700
Dick Goetz	68	74	72	214	3,700
Harold Henning	73	70	71	214	3,700
Babe Hiskey	72	74	68	214	3,700
Ron Skiles	70	75	69	214	3,700
Larry Ziegler	71	72	71	214	3,700
Joe Huber	70	71	74	215	3,120
Walter Morgan	71	74	70	215	3,120

GTE Northwest Classic

Inglewood Country Club, Kenmore, Washington
Par 36-36—72; 6,440 yards

September 8-10
purse, $600,000

	SCORES			TOTAL	MONEY
Walter Morgan	68	68	67	203	$90,000
Dave Stockton	69	69	68	206	52,800
George Archer	70	68	69	207	36,000
Al Geiberger	69	71	67	207	36,000
Rocky Thompson	71	69	67	207	36,000
Jimmy Powell	67	72	69	208	21,600
Bob E. Smith	68	69	71	208	21,600
Bruce Summerhays	72	66	70	208	21,600
Butch Baird	70	71	69	210	16,800
John Paul Cain	71	68	72	211	12,150
Jim Colbert	70	69	72	211	12,150
Bob Dickson	69	74	68	211	12,150
Terry Dill	71	69	71	211	12,150
Dale Douglass	71	68	72	211	12,150
Don January	67	71	73	211	12,150

	SCORES			TOTAL	MONEY
Joe Jimenez	67	77	67	211	12,150
Robert Zimmerman	68	73	70	211	12,150
Bud Allin	69	76	67	212	8,205
Simon Hobday	69	74	69	212	8,205
Jack Kiefer	71	72	69	212	8,205
Chuck Montalbano	74	67	71	212	8,205
Jim Albus	71	74	68	213	6,312
Tony Jacklin	69	71	73	213	6,312
Gary Player	70	72	71	213	6,312
Tom Shaw	70	69	74	213	6,312
Ed Sneed	71	70	72	213	6,312
Miller Barber	71	74	69	214	5,220
Rives McBee	70	73	71	214	5,220
Arnold Palmer	70	78	66	214	5,220
Don Bies	72	73	70	215	4,240
Marion Heck	73	71	71	215	4,240
Snell Lancaster	69	73	73	215	4,240
Robert Landers	70	71	74	215	4,240
Larry Laoretti	72	71	72	215	4,240
J.C. Snead	71	72	72	215	4,240
Tommy Aaron	73	73	70	216	3,375
Babe Hiskey	69	71	76	216	3,375
Bobby Mitchell	71	73	72	216	3,375
Bill Tindall	76	67	73	216	3,375
John Brodie	69	71	77	217	2,940
Dick Goetz	69	74	74	217	2,940
Harry Toscano	75	70	72	217	2,940

Brickyard Crossing Championship

Brickyard Crossing Golf Club, Speedway, Indiana
Par 36-36–72; 6,721 yards

September 15-17
purse, $750,000

	SCORES			TOTAL	MONEY
Simon Hobday	71	65	68	204	$112,500
Isao Aoki	69	69	67	205	46,200
Hale Irwin	70	66	69	205	46,200
Bob Murphy	67	68	70	205	46,200
Lee Trevino	67	69	69	205	46,200
Kermit Zarley	68	70	67	205	46,200
Raymond Floyd	65	72	69	206	25,500
Bruce Summerhays	69	73	64	206	25,500
Jim Albus	70	67	70	207	20,250
Tom Wargo	71	66	70	207	20,250
Larry Laoretti	66	72	70	208	17,250
Gary Player	68	69	71	208	17,250
Bud Allin	70	67	72	209	14,625
Walter Morgan	71	69	69	209	14,625
Jim Dent	66	70	74	210	12,375
Terry Dill	69	69	72	210	12,375
Graham Marsh	69	73	68	210	12,375
Tom Weiskopf	69	71	70	210	12,375
Tommy Aaron	74	70	67	211	8,653.13
Bob Carson	68	72	71	211	8,653.13
Jim Colbert	74	70	67	211	8,653.13
Jay Sigel	69	71	71	211	8,653.13
John Paul Cain	66	72	73	211	8,653.12

	SCORES			TOTAL	MONEY
Bob Charles	67	68	76	211	8,653.12
Dave Stockton	70	67	74	211	8,653.12
DeWitt Weaver	70	70	71	211	8,653.12
Larry Gilbert	73	67	72	212	6,225
Joe Jimenez	70	67	75	212	6,225
Jack Kiefer	70	69	73	212	6,225
Bob E. Smith	69	73	70	212	6,225
J.C. Snead	71	68	73	212	6,225
Bruce Devlin	70	69	74	213	5,175
Tony Jacklin	70	73	70	213	5,175
Calvin Peete	68	71	74	213	5,175
Robert Landers	72	70	72	214	4,320
Gene Littler	72	69	73	214	4,320
Rives McBee	73	70	71	214	4,320
Chi Chi Rodriguez	74	71	69	214	4,320
Harry Toscano	72	71	71	214	4,320
Jim Ferree	75	65	75	215	3,450
Gibby Gilbert	73	72	70	215	3,450
Dick Goetz	71	74	70	215	3,450
Gary Groh	69	72	74	215	3,450
Mike Hill	72	71	72	215	3,450
Dick Rhyan	70	73	72	215	3,450

Bank One Classic

Kearney Hill Links, Lexington, Kentucky
Par 36-36–72; 6,798 yards

September 22-24
purse, $600,000

	SCORES			TOTAL	MONEY
Gary Player	72	75	64	211	$90,000
Jack Kiefer	72	73	68	213	52,800
Isao Aoki	72	71	71	214	33,000
George Archer	73	70	71	214	33,000
Harold Henning	76	70	68	214	33,000
J.C. Snead	72	72	70	214	33,000
John Paul Cain	71	74	70	215	18,300
Dave Eichelberger	72	75	68	215	18,300
Mike Hill	71	72	72	215	18,300
Tom Wargo	72	72	71	215	18,300
Jim Dent	69	74	73	216	12,360
Raymond Floyd	71	72	73	216	12,360
Chuck Montalbano	73	74	69	216	12,360
Mike Still	76	73	67	216	12,360
Bob E. Smith	74	70	72	216	12,360
Larry Gilbert	75	75	67	217	9,036
Dave Hill	74	73	70	217	9,036
Larry Laoretti	77	74	66	217	9,036
Calvin Peete	73	74	70	217	9,036
DeWitt Weaver	72	76	69	217	9,036
Butch Baird	77	70	71	218	7,200
Bruce Summerhays	72	74	72	218	7,200
Bob Betley	78	68	73	219	6,300
Walter Morgan	74	72	73	219	6,300
Dave Stockton	75	72	72	219	6,300
Bobby Mitchell	81	71	68	220	5,580
Walter Zembriski	77	72	71	220	5,580
Charles Coody	71	76	74	221	4,551.43

	SCORES			TOTAL	MONEY
Gary Cowan	78	74	69	221	4,551.43
Terry Dill	72	80	69	221	4,551.43
Gibby Gilbert	72	79	70	221	4,551.43
Don Massengale	73	76	72	221	4,551.43
Ben Smith	74	76	71	221	4,551.43
Marion Heck	73	73	75	221	4,551.42
Bud Allin	80	75	67	222	3,780
Gay Brewer	77	73	73	223	3,440
Dale Douglass	75	72	76	223	3,440
Bob Irving	77	76	70	223	3,440
Deane Beman	77	75	72	224	3,000
Simon Hobday	80	70	74	224	3,000
Bob Leaver	79	70	75	224	3,000
Rocky Thompson	77	73	74	224	3,000

Vantage Championship

Tanglewood Golf Club, Clemmons, North Carolina
Par 36-36–72; 6,680 yards

September 29-October 1
purse, $1,500,000

	SCORES			TOTAL	MONEY
Hale Irwin	66	68	65	199	$225,000
Dave Stockton	68	66	69	203	132,000
Raymond Floyd	70	69	67	206	108,000
Jim Albus	71	66	70	207	64,800
Isao Aoki	68	70	69	207	64,800
Mike Hill	67	69	71	207	64,800
Gary Player	70	67	70	207	64,800
Rocky Thomson	69	69	69	207	64,800
Dale Douglass	71	70	67	208	42,000
Jack Kiefer	71	72	66	209	31,285.72
J.C. Snead	74	68	67	209	31,285.72
Tom Wargo	69	71	69	209	31,285.72
Dave Eichelberger	71	69	69	209	31,285.71
Simon Hobday	73	65	71	209	31,285.71
Bob E. Smith	67	72	70	209	31,285.71
Lee Trevino	70	67	72	209	31,285.71
Bud Allin	73	70	67	210	22,550
Jay Sigel	71	70	69	210	22,550
Robert Zimmerman	72	70	68	210	22,550
George Archer	74	71	66	211	19,200
DeWitt Weaver	70	71	70	211	19,200
Gibby Gilbert	74	70	68	212	15,780
Dick Hendrickson	71	71	70	212	15,780
Harold Henning	74	68	70	212	15,780
Graham Marsh	71	74	67	212	15,780
Jimmy Powell	69	71	72	212	15,780
Larry Gilbert	70	73	70	213	11,914.29
Marion Heck	72	71	70	213	11,914.29
Jerry McGee	72	73	68	213	11,914.29
Ben Smith	71	72	70	213	11,914.29
Bob Charles	70	70	73	213	11,914.28
Jim Dent	72	70	71	213	11,914.28
Larry Laoretti	73	67	73	213	11,914.28
Butch Baird	69	72	73	214	8,190
Bob Betley	71	72	71	214	8,190
Al Geiberger	71	71	72	214	8,190

	SCORES			TOTAL	MONEY
Dick Goetz	69	73	72	214	8,190
Gary Groh	71	76	67	214	8,190
Tony Jacklin	71	71	72	214	8,190
Don January	71	76	67	214	8,190
Arnold Palmer	71	68	75	214	8,190
Ed Sneed	72	73	69	214	8,190
Bob Murphy	73	73	68	214	8,190

The Transamerica

Silverado Country Club & Resort, Napa, California
Par 35-37–72; 6,632 yards

October 6-8
purse, $650,000

	SCORES			TOTAL	MONEY
Lee Trevino	66	69	66	201	$97,500
Bruce Summerhays	67	68	69	204	57,200
Ben Smith	66	69	70	205	46,800
Bob Murphy	66	72	68	206	39,000
Jim Albus	69	69	69	207	26,866.67
Walter Morgan	69	67	71	207	26,866.67
John Bland	65	70	72	207	26,866.66
Tommy Aaron	71	68	70	209	17,875
Graham Marsh	71	70	68	209	17,875
Jimmy Powell	70	71	68	209	17,875
Dave Stockton	71	70	68	209	17,875
Jim Colbert	70	71	69	210	12,837.50
Mike McCullough	68	70	72	210	12,837.50
Bobby Mitchell	75	68	67	210	12,837.50
Kermit Zarley	75	66	69	210	12,837.50
Bob Charles	71	69	71	211	10,725
Harry Toscano	71	71	69	211	10,725
Don Bies	73	68	71	212	9,165
Al Geiberger	69	71	72	212	9,165
Tom Weiskopf	69	71	72	212	9,165
John Paul Cain	71	71	71	213	7,393.75
Dave Eichelberger	72	72	69	213	7,393.75
Dick Lotz	72	74	67	213	7,393.75
Tom Shaw	74	71	68	213	7,393.75
Bob Brue	73	72	69	214	5,795.84
Larry Gilbert	71	74	69	214	5,795.84
Bob Betley	73	73	68	214	5,795.83
Jack Kiefer	70	72	72	214	5,795.83
Dick Rhyan	71	71	72	214	5,795.83
J.C. Snead	73	71	70	214	5,795.83
Charles Coody	68	76	71	215	4,582.50
Bob Dickson	73	71	71	215	4,582.50
Tony Jacklin	68	73	74	215	4,582.50
Don January	68	73	74	215	4,582.50
Bud Allin	73	72	71	216	3,997.50
John Brodie	70	72	74	216	3,997.50
Marion Heck	69	76	72	217	3,445
John Jacobs	74	75	68	217	3,445
Gary Player	73	73	71	217	3,445
Jay Sigel	77	70	70	217	3,445
Bob E. Smith	74	70	73	217	3,445

Raley's Gold Rush

Rancho Murieta Country Club, Rancho Murieta, California
Par 36-36–72; 6,685 yards

October 13-15
purse, $700,000

	SCORES			TOTAL	MONEY
Don Bies	69	68	68	205	$105,000
Lee Trevino	72	65	69	206	61,600
Jim Colbert	69	71	68	208	38,500
Graham Marsh	68	71	69	208	38,500
Bob Murphy	70	71	67	208	38,500
J.C. Snead	68	71	69	208	38,500
Bob Charles	69	72	68	209	23,800
Jay Sigel	70	71	68	209	23,800
Bud Allin	71	67	72	210	18,200
Rives McBee	72	69	69	210	18,200
Tom Wargo	70	68	72	210	18,200
Jack Kiefer	72	69	70	211	14,233.34
Hale Irwin	69	71	71	211	14,233.33
Bob E. Smith	71	73	67	211	14,233.33
George Archer	75	71	66	212	11,900
Charles Coody	73	71	68	212	11,900
Bruce Summerhays	74	69	69	212	11,900
Dale Douglass	72	69	72	213	9,870
Gary Player	74	71	68	213	9,870
Chi Chi Rodriguez	69	68	76	213	9,870
Tommy Aaron	70	69	75	214	7,962.50
Dick Goetz	68	74	72	214	7,962.50
Chuck Montalbano	72	68	74	214	7,962.50
Kermit Zarley	70	71	73	214	7,962.50
Bruce Crampton	73	70	72	215	6,241.67
Bob Dickson	73	70	72	215	6,241.67
Joe Jimenez	73	67	75	215	6,241.67
Dave Stockton	72	71	72	215	6,241.67
Jim Albus	69	73	73	215	6,241.66
Harry Toscano	72	71	72	215	6,241.66
Al Geiberger	74	72	70	216	4,935
Gibby Gilbert	69	70	77	216	4,935
Larry Laoretti	70	71	75	216	4,935
Walter Zembriski	67	75	74	216	4,935
John Paul Cain	76	69	72	217	4,305
Walter Morgan	76	71	70	217	4,305
Jerry McGee	73	73	72	218	3,850
Tom Shaw	70	73	75	218	3,850
Ben Smith	73	72	73	218	3,850
Butch Baird	72	73	75	220	3,150
Billy Casper	75	71	74	220	3,150
Larry Gilbert	75	72	73	220	3,150
Robert Landers	73	72	75	220	3,150
Orville Moody	69	77	74	220	3,150
Jimmy Powell	77	70	73	220	3,150
Larry Ziegler	77	70	73	220	3,150

Ralph's Classic

Wilshire Country Club, Los Angeles, California
Par 35-36–71; 6,295 yards

October 20-22
purse, $800,000

	SCORES			TOTAL	MONEY
John Bland	69	67	65	201	$120,000
Jim Colbert	65	70	67	202	70,400
Terry Dill	67	69	67	203	52,800
Dave Stockton	68	67	68	203	52,800
Al Geiberger	69	69	66	204	38,400
Larry Gilbert	67	65	73	205	30,400
Chi Chi Rodriguez	68	68	69	205	30,400
Hale Irwin	70	72	64	206	22,933.34
Bud Allin	67	70	69	206	22,933.33
Miller Barber	70	68	68	206	22,933.33
Rives McBee	67	70	70	207	17,600
Calvin Peete	69	69	69	207	17,600
Kermit Zarley	69	67	71	207	17,600
Chuck Montalbano	70	69	69	208	14,800
Harry Toscano	71	71	66	208	14,800
Bob Charles	71	69	69	209	13,600
Bruce Devlin	68	69	73	210	11,660
Gibby Gilbert	74	68	68	210	11,660
Bob Murphy	74	68	68	210	11,660
Bob E. Smith	69	69	72	210	11,660
Tommy Aaron	76	70	65	211	8,880
Jim Albus	74	65	72	211	8,880
George Archer	72	69	70	211	8,880
Bob Dickson	71	73	67	211	8,880
Jimmy Powell	74	69	68	211	8,880
Homero Blancas	74	67	71	212	6,800
Dale Douglass	68	73	71	212	6,800
Dick Hendrickson	71	70	71	212	6,800
Graham Marsh	71	72	69	212	6,800
Gary Player	69	72	71	212	6,800
Dick Rhyan	73	67	72	212	6,800
Deane Beman	67	74	72	213	5,051.43
Gay Brewer	71	71	71	213	5,051.43
Dave Eichelberger	69	71	73	213	5,051.43
Joe Jimenez	70	73	70	213	5,051.43
Jerry McGee	69	72	72	213	5,051.43
Jay Sigel	70	72	71	213	5,051.43
Rocky Thompson	68	71	74	213	5,051.42
Billy Casper	69	73	72	214	3,760
Robert Landers	71	70	73	214	3,760
Walter Morgan	69	71	74	214	3,760
Tom Shaw	70	72	72	214	3,760
Ben Smith	71	70	73	214	3,760
Bruce Summerhays	70	71	73	214	3,760
Larry Ziegler	73	72	69	214	3,760

Hyatt Regency Maui Kaanapali Classic

Kaanapali Resort, North Course, Maui, Hawaii
Par 35-36–71; 6,590 yards

October 27-29
purse, $600,000

	SCORES			TOTAL	MONEY
Bob Charles	69	67	68	204	$90,000
Dave Stockton	65	69	70	204	52,800
(Charles defeated Stockton at third extra hole.)					
Lee Trevino	69	66	70	205	43,200
Harold Henning	67	70	69	206	29,600
Graham Marsh	68	69	69	206	29,600
Mike McCullough	66	67	73	206	29,600
Don Bies	69	70	68	207	21,600
Terry Dill	72	65	71	208	16,500
Jerry McGee	70	67	71	208	16,500
Bob Murphy	68	68	72	208	16,500
Bruce Summerhays	65	71	72	208	16,500
Joe Jimenez	69	72	68	209	13,200
George Archer	67	69	74	210	10,800
Deane Beman	68	68	74	210	10,800
Charles Coody	69	72	69	210	10,800
Rocky Thompson	68	67	75	210	10,800
DeWitt Weaver	67	70	73	210	10,800
Tommy Aaron	71	68	72	211	7,730
Jim Albus	70	71	70	211	7,730
Tony Jacklin	71	65	75	211	7,730
Chuck Montalbano	70	68	73	211	7,730
Walter Morgan	71	69	71	211	7,730
Mike Still	72	71	68	211	7,730
Bob Brue	72	67	73	212	5,610
John Jacobs	73	67	72	212	5,610
Tom Shaw	72	71	69	212	5,610
Ed Sneed	72	72	68	212	5,610
Harry Toscano	68	75	69	212	5,610
Larry Ziegler	75	67	70	212	5,610
John Paul Cain	72	67	74	213	4,425
Dave Eichelberger	68	74	71	213	4,425
Dick Hendrickson	68	70	75	213	4,425
Larry Laoretti	70	69	74	213	4,425
Bud Allin	72	69	73	214	3,780
Dale Douglass	68	75	71	214	3,780
Bob Lunn	66	76	72	214	3,780
Jim Colbert	69	70	76	215	3,180
Gibby Gilbert	71	71	73	215	3,180
Babe Hiskey	72	70	73	215	3,180
Gene Littler	70	72	73	215	3,180
Bob E. Smith	73	73	69	215	3,180

Emerald Coast Classic

The Moors Golf Club, Milton, Florida
Par 36-35–71; 6,691 yards
(Shortened to 36 holes — rain.)

November 3-5
purse, $1,000,000

	SCORES		TOTAL	MONEY
Raymond Floyd	69	66	135	$150,000
Tom Wargo	71	64	135	88,000
(Floyd defeated Wargo at second extra hole.)				
Bud Allin	73	63	136	66,000
Bob Murphy	72	64	136	66,000
Isao Aoki	68	69	137	48,000
John Bland	70	68	138	38,000
Bruce Devlin	68	70	138	38,000
Bob Dickson	70	69	139	28,666.67
Dave Stockton	70	69	139	28,666.67
Bruce Summerhays	70	69	139	28,666.66
Dave Eichelberger	72	68	140	22,000
Gary Player	72	68	140	22,000
Ed Sneed	69	71	140	22,000
Chuck Montalbano	73	68	141	18,000
Rocky Thompson	72	69	141	18,000
Tom Weiskopf	72	69	141	18,000
Jim Colbert	73	69	142	15,033.34
Chi Chi Rodriguez	70	72	142	15,033.33
Lee Trevino	72	70	142	15,033.33
Jim Dent	75	68	143	11,171.43
Al Geiberger	75	68	143	11,171.43
Simon Hobday	73	70	143	11,171.43
Larry Laoretti	72	71	143	11,171.43
Graham Marsh	73	70	143	11,171.43
Rives McBee	75	68	143	11,171.43
Butch Baird	70	73	143	11,171.42
Jim Albus	73	71	144	7,290.91
Gay Brewer	71	73	144	7,290.91
John Paul Cain	74	70	144	7,290.91
Bob Charles	76	68	144	7,290.91
Charles Coody	74	70	144	7,290.91
Terry Dill	71	73	144	7,290.91
Dale Douglass	73	71	144	7,290.91
Marion Heck	73	71	144	7,290.91
Jack Kiefer	72	72	144	7,290.91
Bob E. Smith	73	71	144	7,290.91
DeWitt Weaver	69	75	144	7,290.90
George Archer	73	72	145	5,300
Homero Blancas	75	70	145	5,300
Tony Jacklin	73	72	145	5,300

Energizer Senior Tour Championship

The Dunes Golf & Beach Club, Myrtle Beach, South Carolina
Par 36-36–72; 6,815 yards

November 10-12
purse, $1,500,000

	SCORES				TOTAL	MONEY
Jim Colbert	68	69	71	74	282	$262,000
Raymond Floyd	71	74	69	69	283	151,000
Rocky Thompson	71	75	68	71	285	115,500

	SCORES				TOTAL	MONEY
Tom Wargo	73	69	73	70	285	115,500
Dave Stockton	74	71	69	72	286	83,900
Dave Eichelberger	73	72	70	72	287	69,800
Bob Charles	76	70	69	73	288	62,800
George Archer	72	75	71	71	289	48,000
Mike Hill	75	74	71	69	289	48,000
Hale Irwin	72	70	75	72	289	48,000
Graham Marsh	74	70	71	74	289	48,000
Jim Dent	74	70	72	74	290	36,900
Tom Weiskopf	72	74	71	73	290	36,900
Jack Kiefer	73	72	74	72	291	28,933.34
Bob Murphy	73	71	76	71	291	28,933.34
Jim Albus	72	73	74	72	291	28,933.33
Isao Aoki	71	69	75	76	291	28,933.33
Larry Gilbert	71	73	75	72	291	28,933.33
Bruce Summerhays	75	71	69	76	291	28,933.33
Jay Sigel	74	76	70	73	293	22,550
Kermit Zarley	73	72	72	76	293	22,550
Simon Hobday	71	74	75	75	295	19,950
Lee Trevino	74	70	77	74	295	19,950
Bud Allin	73	76	73	75	297	18,050
Walter Morgan	77	71	73	76	297	18,050
J.C. Snead	80	69	77	72	298	16,800
Larry Laoretti	74	78	69	79	300	16,300
Tony Jacklin	71	75	81	74	301	15,800
John Paul Cain	80	76	72	75	303	15,050
Jimmy Powell	77	78	76	72	303	15,050

Diners Club Matches

PGA West, Jack Nicklaus Course, La Quinta, California   December 7-10
Par 36-36–72; 6,546 yards   purse, $890,000

FIRST ROUND

Raymond Floyd and Dave Eichelberger defeated Jack Nicklaus and Arnold Palmer, 3 and 2
Dave Stockton and Hale Irwin defeated Tom Weiskopf and Isao Aoki, 2 and 1
George Archer and Dale Douglass defeated Chi Chi Rodriguez and Jim Albus, 1 up
Jim Colbert and Bob Murphy defeated Sam Snead and Gibby Gilbert, 2 and 1

(Losers in first round received $15,000 each.)

SECOND ROUND

Stockton and Irwin defeated Floyd and Eichelberger, 5 and 3
Colbert and Murphy defeated Archer and Douglass, 24 holes

(Losers in second round received $35,000 each.)

THIRD ROUND

Colbert and Murphy defeated Stockton and Irwin, 1 up

(Colbert and Murphy received $125,000 each; Stockton and Irwin received $50,000 each.)

European Seniors Tour

Windsor Senior Masters

Windsor Golf & Country Club, Nairobi, Kenya
Par 36-36–72; 7,063 yards

March 30-April 1
purse, £54,000

	SCORES			TOTAL	MONEY
Brian Huggett	70	67	72	209	£8,887.50
Antonio Garrido	68	68	74	210	5,812.50
Tommy Horton	71	66	74	211	3,387.50
David Creamer	66	71	75	212	2,345.83
John Morgan	70	70	72	212	2,345.83
Alberto Croce	70	70	72	212	2,345.83
David Jimenez	70	70	74	214	1,893.75
Joe Carr	74	69	73	216	1,668.75
Malcolm Gregson	68	75	73	216	1,668.75
Michael Murphy	73	69	75	217	1,362.50
Hugh Inggs	72	70	75	217	1,362.50
Brian Waites	68	71	78	217	1,362.50
Terry Fine	72	72	74	218	1,181.25
Gordon Gray	71	70	78	219	1,008.75
John Fourie	72	75	72	219	1,008.75
Renato Campagnoli	72	74	73	219	1,008.75
Ramon Sota	72	71	76	219	1,008.75
Roger Fidler	72	73	74	219	1,008.75
Vincent Tshabalala	73	71	77	221	846.88
Rafe Botts	71	72	78	221	846.88
Liam Higgins	70	75	77	222	738.54
DeRay Simon	72	75	75	222	738.54
Francisco Abreu	75	74	73	222	738.54
David Butler	72	73	78	223	656.25
Denis Hutchinson	77	70	78	225	579.17
Howell Fraser	74	76	75	225	579.17
Ross Whitehead	74	71	80	225	579.17
Phil Ferranti	72	75	79	226	521.88
Hugh Boyle	76	74	76	226	521.88
Frank Hill	71	80	76	227	503.13
Bobby Browne	74	75	78	227	503.13
Terry Squires	75	75	77	227	503.13

International German PGA Seniors Championship

Idstein Golf Club, Frankfurt, Germany
Par 36-36–72; 6,742 yards

July 14-16
purse, £80,000

	SCORES			TOTAL	MONEY
Renato Campagnoli	68	69	71	208	£13,350
Alberto Croce	70	73	67	210	6,950
Brian Huggett	69	74	67	210	6,950
Malcolm Gregson	72	67	72	211	3,543.33
Hugh Inggs	68	73	70	211	3,543.33

	SCORES			TOTAL	MONEY
John A. Jacobs	71	71	69	211	3,543.33
Doug Dalziel	71	71	70	212	2,835
Chick Evans	68	73	71	212	2,835
Mike Ingham	70	69	74	213	2,375
Liam Higgins	71	71	71	213	2,375
Neil Coles	71	73	70	214	1,712
John Morgan	73	75	66	214	1,712
Peter Headland	75	66	73	214	1,712
David Creamer	71	69	74	214	1,712
Antonio Garrido	73	69	72	214	1,712
Arthur Proctor	74	74	67	215	1,150
Sooky Maharaj	68	74	73	215	1,150
Peter Butler	75	71	69	215	1,150
Tommy Horton	70	75	71	216	930
Brian Waites	73	73	70	216	930
Bobby Verwey	73	70	73	216	930
Randall Vines	69	71	76	216	930
Harry Flatman	76	69	72	217	786.67
Vincent Tshabalala	73	71	73	217	786.67
DeRay Simon	72	72	73	217	786.67
Gordon Gray	75	67	76	218	725
Fred Boobyer	74	72	73	219	650.83
Paul Leonard	68	74	77	219	650.83
Noel Ratcliffe	72	72	75	219	650.83
Francisco Abreu	77	71	71	219	650.83
Ross Whitehead	73	75	71	219	650.83
Michel Damiano	75	72	72	219	650.83

Senior British Open

Royal Portrush Golf Club, Portrush, Northern Ireland
Par 36-36–72; 6,672 yards

July 27-30
purse, £350,000

	SCORES				TOTAL	MONEY
Brian Barnes	67	67	77	70	281	£58,330
Bob Murphy	68	69	73	71	281	38,850
(Barnes defeated Murphy on second extra hole.)						
John Morgan	71	68	75	68	282	19,705
Bob Charles	70	73	73	66	282	19,705
Tommy Horton	78	68	67	70	283	13,545
John Fourie	70	71	73	69	283	13,545
John A. Jacobs	69	71	71	73	284	10,500
Larry Laoretti	69	74	72	70	285	8,750
Hugh Inggs	72	70	75	70	287	7,840
Brian Huggett	74	71	72	71	288	7,000
Malcolm Gregson	72	69	75	73	289	6,440
Tom Wargo	75	71	69	75	290	6,020
Frank Hill	74	70	73	74	291	5,497.50
Vincent Tshabalala	74	73	73	71	291	5,497.50
Neil Coles	72	75	74	71	292	5,040
Michael Murphy	68	74	78	72	292	5,040
David Huish	71	79	71	72	293	4,445
Dale Douglass	76	68	76	73	293	4,445
Paul Leonard	74	71	72	76	293	4,445
Jim Albus	77	71	73	72	293	4,445
Liam Higgins	71	73	77	73	294	4,000
Randall Vines	77	69	75	73	294	4,000

	SCORES				TOTAL	MONEY
Maurice Bembridge	73	73	77	71	294	4,000
*Kenny Stevenson	77	70	75	72	294	
Arne Dokka	71	73	76	76	296	3,650
Gary Player	77	69	75	75	296	3,650
Peter Headland	72	74	77	73	296	3,650
Frank Rennie	75	74	73	74	296	3,650
*Marvin Giles III	78	72	72	74	296	
Billy Dunk	75	74	77	71	297	3,250
Akio Toyoda	72	77	75	73	297	3,250
DeRay Simon	72	74	74	77	297	3,250
Alberto Croce	76	76	72	73	297	3,250

Lawrence Batley Seniors

Fixby Golf Club, Huddersfield, England
Par 35-36–71; 6,096 yards

August 2-4
purse, £70,000

	SCORES			TOTAL	MONEY
Alberto Croce	69	72	68	209	£11,000
Tommy Horton	74	67	69	210	7,200
Malcolm Gregson	73	69	69	211	3,750
John Morgan	71	73	67	211	3,750
Liam Higgins	71	73	68	212	2,840
Brian Huggett	70	74	69	213	2,475
Neil Coles	70	72	71	213	2,475
Antonio Garrido	72	73	70	215	2,160
Bobby Verwey	76	70	70	216	1,980
Renato Campagnoli	72	75	70	217	1,830
DeRay Simon	68	79	71	218	1,566.67
Francisco Abreu	77	68	73	218	1,566.67
Bob Thatcher	74	73	71	218	1,566.67
Maurice Bembridge	74	72	73	219	1,340
David Creamer	73	70	76	219	1,340
Bernard Hunt	71	72	77	220	1,210
Tienie Britz	75	75	70	220	1,210
John A. Jacobs	73	75	73	221	1,120
Roger Fidler	77	73	72	222	1,035
Mike Ingham	72	76	74	222	1,035
Vincent Tshabalala	76	73	74	223	835
Walter Sauer	75	74	74	223	835
Chick Evans	76	71	76	223	835
Jose Maria Roca	76	75	72	223	835
David Butler	75	74	74	223	835
Tony Grubb	73	80	70	223	835
John Fourie	78	73	73	224	665
Doug Dalziel	76	77	71	224	665
Ross Whitehead	78	74	73	225	618
David Jimenez	75	76	74	225	618
Peter Butler	76	70	79	225	618
David Snell	73	72	80	225	618

Forte PGA Seniors Championship

Sunningdale Golf Club, Sunningdale, Berkshire, England
Par 35-35–70; 6,341 yards

August 11-13
purse, £90,000

	SCORES			TOTAL	MONEY
John Morgan	67	70	67	204	£15,000
Antonio Garrido	65	70	69	204	10,000
(Morgan defeated Garrido on first extra hole.)					
John A. Jacobs	68	68	70	206	4,248
Liam Higgins	69	68	69	206	4,248
Francisco Abreu	68	69	69	206	4,248
Neil Coles	71	67	68	206	4,248
Brian Huggett	75	66	65	206	4,248
Bobby Verwey	68	70	69	207	3,100
Tommy Horton	67	71	70	208	2,650
Malcolm Gregson	67	71	70	208	2,650
Brian Waites	70	67	72	209	2,200
Alberto Croce	71	68	70	209	2,200
Maurice Bembridge	70	68	72	210	1,740
Renato Campagnoli	69	70	71	210	1,740
Peter Butler	73	70	67	210	1,740
Hugh Inggs	68	69	75	212	1,330
Noel Ratcliffe	69	70	73	212	1,330
Harry Flatman	68	72	72	212	1,330
Jack Wilkshire	70	73	69	212	1,330
Hugh Boyle	71	72	70	213	1,040
David Creamer	75	69	69	213	1,040
Frank Hill	70	71	73	214	880
Jose Maria Roca	71	72	71	214	880
Christy O'Connor	69	75	70	214	880
Randall Vines	74	67	74	215	766.67
Chick Evans	69	73	73	215	766.67
Frank Rennie	73	70	72	215	766.67
Peter Thomson	68	76	72	216	690
Rafe Botts	73	72	71	216	690
Doug Dalziel	72	73	71	216	690
John Hamilton	73	73	70	216	690

Northern Electric Seniors

Slaley Hall Golf & Country Club, Hexham, England
Par 36-36–72; 6,435 yards

August 18-20
purse, £60,000

	SCORES			TOTAL	MONEY
Brian Waites	72	70	73	215	£9,700
Bobby Verwey	73	73	71	217	3,546
Peter Butler	73	75	69	217	3,546
Noel Ratcliffe	68	74	75	217	3,546
Francisco Abreu	73	75	69	217	3,546
Neil Coles	70	75	72	217	3,546
John Morgan	72	71	75	218	1,985
Doug Dalziel	71	74	73	218	1,985
Malcolm Gregson	72	76	71	219	1,680
John Fourie	72	75	72	219	1,680
Vincent Tshabalala	73	76	71	220	1,430
Liam Higgins	69	76	75	220	1,430
David Creamer	72	77	73	222	1,290

	SCORES			TOTAL	MONEY
Renato Campagnoli	74	73	76	223	1,220
Bernard Hunt	75	71	78	224	1,127.50
David Huish	78	75	71	224	1,127.50
Chick Evans	72	78	75	225	975
Tony Grubb	74	74	77	225	975
Tony Coveney	74	74	77	225	975
Hugh Boyle	73	76	76	225	975
Phil Ferranti	77	75	74	226	850
DeRay Simon	75	77	76	228	805
Howell Fraser	78	79	72	229	760
Antonio Garrido	75	77	78	230	637.20
Ross Whitehead	75	79	76	230	637.20
Frank Hill	76	78	76	230	637.20
Alberto Croce	76	77	77	230	637.20
Maurice Bembridge	83	74	73	230	637.20
Tommy Horton	81	80	70	231	550
Walter Sauer	81	76	74	231	550

Collingtree Seniors

Collingtree Park Golf Club, Northampton, England
Par 36-36–72; 6,695 yards

August 24-26
purse, £52,000

	SCORES			TOTAL	MONEY
Neil Coles	71	72	68	211	£8,085
Brian Barnes	74	75	66	215	5,290
Noel Ratcliffe	72	75	69	216	3,085
Francisco Abreu	70	73	75	218	2,415
David Huish	74	71	75	220	1,903.33
Brian Huggett	67	78	75	220	1,903.33
Maurice Bembridge	73	71	76	220	1,903.33
John Morgan	70	77	75	222	1,585
Malcolm Gregson	69	79	75	223	1,400
Peter Butler	68	77	78	223	1,400
David Butler	78	76	70	224	1,235
Chick Evans	73	77	75	225	1,024
David Creamer	74	73	78	225	1,024
John Fourie	74	82	69	225	1,024
Tienie Britz	74	76	75	225	1,024
Alberto Croce	78	76	71	225	1,024
Renato Campagnoli	73	75	78	226	730
Vincent Tshabalala	75	75	76	226	730
Liam Higgins	75	74	77	226	730
Hugh Boyle	72	78	76	226	730
Howell Fraser	74	73	79	226	730
Roger Fidler	75	77	74	226	730
Doug Dalziel	72	74	80	226	730
Michael Murphy	78	75	73	226	730
Antonio Garrido	74	77	76	227	537.50
Tony Coveney	76	73	78	227	537.50
Hugh Inggs	73	75	81	229	490
Terry Squires	77	77	75	229	490
Phil Ferranti	76	75	79	230	455
Bobby Verwey	75	78	77	230	455
Brian Waites	74	77	79	230	455

Shell Scottish Seniors Open

Royal Aberdeen Golf Club, Aberdeen, Scotland
Par 35-35–70; 6,372 yards

September 1-3
purse, £100,000

	SCORES			TOTAL	MONEY
Brian Huggett	64	70	66	200	£16,660
Neil Coles	66	69	67	202	11,100
Antonio Garrido	63	70	73	206	6,260
Malcolm Gregson	70	69	68	207	5,000
John Fourie	65	72	71	208	4,240
Noel Ratcliffe	67	72	70	209	3,735
Maurice Bembridge	65	75	69	209	3,735
John Morgan	67	73	70	210	3,300
Tommy Horton	66	73	72	211	3,040
Brian Waites	69	72	71	212	2,800
John Hudson	67	76	70	213	2,260
Renato Campagnoli	68	71	74	213	2,260
Robert Webster	69	75	69	213	2,260
Alberto Croce	67	76	70	213	2,260
Bobby Browne	67	77	70	214	1,650
Doug Dalziel	73	73	68	214	1,650
Michael Murphy	73	74	68	215	1,400
Ross Whitehead	74	73	69	216	1,215
Liam Higgins	71	71	74	216	1,215
Tony Coveney	72	76	68	216	1,215
David Huish	69	73	74	216	1,215
David Creamer	69	75	73	217	1,070
Hugh Inggs	68	81	68	217	1,070
Paul Leonard	70	76	72	218	1,010
Vincent Tshabalala	73	72	74	219	920
Fred Boobyer	68	77	74	219	920
Frank Hill	69	76	74	219	920
Francisco Abreu	73	75	71	219	920
Peter Gill	70	77	72	219	920
David Butler	71	74	75	220	810
Kenneth Magnusson	67	81	72	220	810
Peter Butler	75	73	72	220	810

De Vere Hotels Seniors Classic

Belton Woods Golf Club, Grantham, England
Par 36-36–72; 6,792 yards

September 8-10
purse, £60,000

	SCORES			TOTAL	MONEY
Tommy Horton	71	69	73	213	£9,380
Antonio Garrido	71	72	71	214	6,140
Malcolm Gregson	71	72	72	215	2,933.33
Maurice Bembridge	70	71	74	215	2,933.33
Brian Waites	71	70	74	215	2,933.33
Alberto Croce	70	73	74	217	2,200
Tony Grubb	72	74	72	218	2,000
David Jimenez	72	74	73	219	1,830
David Creamer	73	74	73	220	1,690
Neil Coles	70	76	75	221	1,550
Joe Carr	75	70	77	222	1,258
Derek Craik	77	73	72	222	1,258
Terry Squires	73	70	79	222	1,258

	SCORES			TOTAL	MONEY
Chick Evans	78	72	72	222	1,258
Noel Ratcliffe	73	75	74	222	1,258
Liam Higgins	76	71	76	223	917.14
Hugh Boyle	78	70	75	223	917.14
Francisco Abreu	76	74	73	223	917.14
John Morgan	72	76	75	223	917.14
Rafe Botts	75	74	74	223	917.14
Bobby Verwey	78	73	72	223	917.14
Renato Campagnoli	78	72	73	223	917.14
DeRay Simon	79	76	69	224	690
Harry Flatman	77	72	75	224	690
Mike Ingham	74	82	68	224	690
Michael Murphy	76	77	72	225	587.50
John Fourie	76	76	73	225	587.50
Gordon Gray	76	73	77	226	550
Roger Fidler	72	80	75	227	533
Sooky Maharaj	71	78	78	227	533

London Masters

London Club, International Course, Kent, England
Par 36-36–72; 6,658 yards

September 29-October 1
purse, £80,000

	SCORES			TOTAL	MONEY
John Bland	70	69	71	210	£13,350
Hugh Inggs	70	70	74	214	5,332.50
Tony Grubb	68	72	74	214	5,332.50
John Morgan	71	70	73	214	5,332.50
Bobby Verwey	72	73	69	214	5,332.50
Chick Evans	73	70	73	216	3,200
Neil Coles	73	70	74	217	2,720
Noel Ratcliffe	74	69	74	217	2,720
Brian Waites	75	71	71	217	2,720
Bernard Hunt	72	72	74	218	1,888
Liam Higgins	72	72	74	218	1,888
John Fourie	73	72	73	218	1,888
Brian Huggett	71	75	72	218	1,888
Tommy Horton	74	73	71	218	1,888
Francisco Abreu	72	72	75	219	1,207.50
Malcolm Gregson	74	72	73	219	1,207.50
Antonio Garrido	75	72	72	219	1,207.50
Renato Campagnoli	77	74	68	219	1,207.50
Christy O'Connor	73	71	76	220	909
David Creamer	74	72	74	220	909
Randall Vines	74	73	73	220	909
John Hudson	75	73	72	220	909
George Will	71	78	71	220	909
Frank Hill	72	71	78	221	740
Jose Maria Roca	75	73	73	221	740
Paul Leonard	74	75	72	221	740
Sooky Maharaj	74	76	71	221	740
Howell Fraser	74	73	75	222	675
Alberto Croce	75	72	76	223	647.50
Vincent Tshabalala	77	74	72	223	647.50

Senior Zurich Pro-Am: Lexus Trophy

Breitenloo Golf Club, Zurich, Switzerland
Par 36-36–72; 6,698 yards

October 5-7
purse, £60,000

	SCORES			TOTAL	MONEY
Liam Higgins	69	70	67	206	£9,170
Randall Vines	70	66	75	211	6,000
Tommy Horton	72	72	68	212	2,315.71
Vincent Tshabalala	71	70	71	212	2,315.71
David Butler	71	70	71	212	2,315.71
Brian Waites	72	69	71	212	2,315.71
Malcolm Gregson	72	69	71	212	2,315.71
John Morgan	72	69	71	212	2,315.71
David Creamer	70	69	73	212	2,315.71
Peter Butler	71	75	67	213	1,426.67
Chick Evans	73	70	70	213	1,426.67
Neil Coles	71	70	72	213	1,426.67
Noel Ratcliffe	75	72	67	214	1,210
Helmuth Schumacher	73	73	68	214	1,210
Antonio Garrido	71	68	75	214	1,210
Roger Fidler	73	69	73	215	1,000
Renato Campagnoli	69	72	74	215	1,000
John Fourie	70	70	75	215	1,000
David Snell	75	71	71	217	880
David Huish	76	71	71	218	780
Francisco Abreu	75	69	74	218	780
Jose Maria Roca	71	72	75	218	780
Bobby Verwey	72	74	73	219	630
Terry Squires	76	70	73	219	630
Phil Ferranti	76	71	72	219	630
DeRay Simon	75	73	73	221	560
Howell Fraser	77	73	73	223	540
Michael Murphy	74	75	75	224	520
Maurice Bembridge	74	77	74	225	515
Tienie Britz	75	77	76	228	505
David Jimenez	78	74	76	228	505
Hedley Muscroft	77	77	74	228	505

Japan Senior Tour

American Express Grand Slam

Glen Oaks Country Club, Kurimoto Machi
Par 36-36–72; 6,741 yards
(Final round shortened to nine holes — snow.)

March 24-26
purse, ¥60,000,000

	SCORES			TOTAL	MONEY
Isao Aoki	68	70	35	173	¥9,000,000
Gibby Gilbert	70	70	35	175	3,750,000

	SCORES			TOTAL	MONEY
Graham Marsh	70	71	34	175	3,750,000
Lee Trevino	66	75	36	177	2,400,000
Bob Menne	70	74	35	179	2,100,000
Ed Sneed	67	75	38	180	1,540,000
Hiroshi Ishii	69	74	37	180	1,540,000
Marion Heck	68	74	38	180	1,540,000
Fujio Kobayashi	71	75	35	181	1,096,000
Bob Dickson	70	75	36	181	1,096,000
Haruo Yasuda	70	72	39	181	1,096,000
Ryosuke Ota	70	76	36	182	957,000
Jim Colbert	71	74	37	182	957,000
Ryokichi Jibiki	72	75	36	183	891,000
Gary Groh	73	75	35	183	891,000
Dave Stockton	68	77	38	183	891,000
Mitoshi Tomita	74	72	37	183	891,000
Kenichi Tsurumoto	75	73	36	184	819,000
Seiji Ogawa	71	76	37	184	819,000
DeWitt Weaver	69	77	38	184	819,000
Bob Betley	69	76	39	184	819,000
John Paul Cain	71	77	37	185	774,000
Hisashi Suzumura	71	77	38	186	738,000
Sadao Ogawa	74	74	38	186	738,000
Masaru Amano	72	76	38	186	738,000
Mitsutaka Kono	75	77	35	187	690,000
Kuo Chie-Hsiung	74	77	36	187	690,000
Gary Player	72	77	38	187	690,000
Ichiro Togawa	70	78	39	187	690,000
Dave Eichelberger	78	74	36	188	618,000
Ichiro Teramoto	73	77	38	188	618,000
Akio Toyoda	74	75	39	188	618,000
Simon Hobday	77	71	40	188	618,000
Dick Goetz	71	77	40	188	618,000
Jimmy Powell	73	74	41	188	618,000
Katsumi Hara	69	77	42	188	618,000
Tom Shaw	69	77	42	188	618,000

TPC Starts Senior

Garden Golf Club, Ibaragi
Par 36-36–72; 6,538 yards

April 6-9
purse, ¥50,000,000

	SCORES				TOTAL	MONEY
Fujio Kobayashi	67	72	69	71	279	¥7,500,000
Hsieh Min-Nan	66	72	70	74	282	3,500,000
Seiichi Kaneda	69	71	72	71	283	2,375,000
Mitsuhiro Kitta	70	71	71	71	283	2,375,000
Kuo Chie-Hsiung	69	71	73	72	285	1,750,000
Hiroshi Ishii	73	65	71	77	286	1,287,500
Teruo Suzumura	68	72	75	71	286	1,287,500
Kenichi Tsurumoto	73	76	66	72	287	1,000,000
Norihiko Matsumoto	70	74	74	70	288	900,000
Hisashi Iwamoto	71	72	69	77	289	800,000
Shichiro Enomoto	70	73	72	75	290	750,000
Seiji Ogawa	74	74	68	74	290	750,000
Seiji Katayama	73	74	70	73	290	750,000
Akio Toyoda	69	74	75	72	290	750,000
Tetsuhiro Ueda	73	74	75	69	291	670,000

	SCORES				TOTAL	MONEY
Shigeru Ueda	75	70	69	77	291	670,000
Kunio Koike	73	74	75	69	291	670,000
Katsumi Hara	69	75	72	75	291	670,000
Hsu Chie-San	72	73	71	75	291	670,000
Masaru Amano	73	75	71	73	292	602,500
Kikuo Arai	72	72	74	74	292	602,500
Isao Matsui	74	72	70	76	292	602,500
Ichiro Togawa	75	67	74	76	292	602,500
Kesao Uchida	73	72	72	76	293	551,666
Hiroshi Tahara	71	72	74	76	293	551,666
Kenji Ueda	75	71	74	73	293	551,666
Sadao Ogawa	72	77	69	76	294	520,000
Ryosuke Ota	72	74	74	74	294	520,000
Ichiro Teramoto	73	70	74	77	294	520,000
Namio Takasu	75	75	74	71	295	480,000
Chen Ching-Po	73	72	75	75	295	480,000
Kanae Nobechi	75	74	72	74	295	480,000
Katsutoshi Miura	73	76	75	71	295	480,000
Koichi Okuno	73	73	74	75	295	480,000

Daiichi Seimei Cup

Tomisato Golf Club, Chiba
Par 36-36–72; 6,428 yards

May 19-21
purse, ¥50,000,000

	SCORES			TOTAL	MONEY
Seiichi Kanai	68	68	72	208	¥7,500,000
Ryosuke Ota	71	71	67	209	3,125,000
Kuo Chie-Hsiung	70	68	71	209	3,125,000
Haruo Yasuda	70	72	69	211	2,000,000
Mitsuhiro Kitta	70	71	71	212	1,625,000
Billy Dunk	70	70	72	212	1,625,000
Yoshihiro Takada	73	70	70	213	1,250,000
Namio Takasu	72	72	70	214	1,000,000
Chen Ching-Po	73	71	70	214	1,000,000
Norihiko Matsumoto	70	72	72	214	1,000,000
Ichiro Teramoto	73	73	69	215	811,666
Mitoshi Tomita	71	72	72	215	811,666
Kenichi Tsurumoto	69	74	72	215	811,666
Sadao Ogawa	73	73	70	216	727,500
Mitsutaka Kono	67	75	74	216	727,500
Hsieh Min-Nan	70	70	76	216	727,500
Kunio Koike	73	70	73	216	727,500
Hisashi Suzumura	73	75	68	216	727,500
Teruo Suzumura	74	72	70	216	727,500
Kikuo Arai	75	74	68	217	652,500
Ryokichi Jibiki	75	68	74	217	652,500
Hiroshi Ishii	68	80	69	217	652,500
Hsu Chie-San	73	73	71	217	652,500
Masaru Amano	78	69	71	218	596,250
Seiichi Sato	70	76	72	218	596,250
Hideo Jibiki	70	75	73	218	596,250
Eleuterio Nival	71	72	75	218	596,250
Shigeru Uchida	73	73	73	219	560,000
Akio Toyoda	72	73	74	219	560,000
Katsumi Hara	73	72	74	219	560,000

Japan PGA Senior Championship

Shimoakima Country Club, Gunma
Par 36-36–72; 6,694 yards

June 1-4
purse, ¥50,000,000

	SCORES				TOTAL	MONEY
Teruo Sugihara	71	69	69	69	278	¥7,500,000
Seiichi Kanai	67	69	70	73	279	3,500,000
Haruo Yasuda	71	72	68	71	282	2,375,000
Hiroshi Ishii	66	73	71	72	282	2,375,000
Hsieh Min-Nan	67	73	71	72	283	1,750,000
Shigeru Uchida	73	71	71	71	286	1,425,000
Mitsuo Hirukawa	74	71	68	76	289	1,075,000
Kennichi Sasamoto	68	72	76	73	289	1,075,000
Seiji Ogawa	75	69	74	72	290	812,500
Takaaki Kono	77	69	70	74	290	812,500
Fujio Kobayashi	69	70	75	76	290	812,500
Kuo Chie-Hsiung	72	74	73	71	290	812,500
Ichiro Teramoto	74	69	76	72	291	735,000
Ryosuke Ota	78	72	72	71	293	700,000
Akio Kanemoto	72	74	71	76	293	700,000
Mitoshi Tomita	71	70	76	76	293	700,000
Masaru Amano	76	70	73	75	294	655,000
Kesao Uchida	72	76	69	77	294	655,000
Chen Ching-Po	73	74	76	71	294	655,000
Kikuo Arai	75	72	76	72	295	617,500
Makoto Nanbu	75	72	75	73	295	617,500
Hiroshi Tahara	77	75	71	73	296	587,500
Mitsuhiro Kitta	73	72	76	75	296	587,500
Katsuji Murakami	78	74	69	76	297	551,666
Sato Hirokazu	76	70	77	74	297	551,666
Katsumi Hara	77	73	73	74	297	551,666
Hiroshi Gunji	75	72	79	72	298	530,000
Namio Takasu	78	72	78	71	299	515,000
Kunio Koike	70	73	75	81	299	515,000
Takahiro Takeyasu	76	69	77	78	300	480,000
Chen Chen-Chung	76	70	77	77	300	480,000
Keiichi Hoshino	76	75	75	74	300	480,000
Izuru Taka	72	75	80	73	300	480,000
Ichiro Togawa	75	75	77	73	300	480,000

HTB Senior Classic

Mitsui Kanko Golf Club, Hokkaido
Par 36-36–72; 6,427 yards

June 30-July 2
purse, ¥30,000,000

	SCORES			TOTAL	MONEY
Hsieh Min-Nan	72	67	69	208	¥4,500,000
Masaru Amano	72	67	70	209	2,100,000
Ichiro Teramoto	72	69	69	210	1,650,000
Norihiko Matsumoto	71	69	71	211	1,200,000
Haruo Yasuda	72	70	71	213	975,000
Ryosuke Ota	72	71	70	213	975,000
Seiji Ogawa	75	69	70	214	670,000
Yoshihiro Takada	73	71	70	214	670,000
Kenichi Tsurumoto	74	65	75	214	670,000
Namio Takasu	70	72	73	215	540,000

	SCORES			TOTAL	MONEY
Shichiro Enomoto	73	72	71	216	495,000
Isao Matsui	73	72	71	216	495,000
Hideo Jibiki	74	73	70	217	465,000
Mitsuhiro Kitta	76	70	71	217	465,000
Shoji Kikuchi	73	70	75	218	436,500
Ryokichi Jibiki	72	74	72	218	436,500
Chen Chen-Chung	72	74	72	218	436,500
Hiroshi Hanabusa	73	72	73	218	436,500
Masao Kikuchi	71	75	73	219	409,500
Mitoshi Tomita	73	73	73	219	409,500
Shinzo Arai	74	74	72	220	382,500
Hiroshi Tahara	75	73	72	220	382,500
Katsumi Hara	75	72	73	220	382,500
Kuo Chie-Hsiung	74	73	73	220	382,500
Yasuo Kuninaka	74	70	77	221	360,000
Sadao Ogawa	75	74	73	222	330,000
Kiyokuni Kimoto	72	73	77	222	330,000
Chen Ching-Po	73	73	76	222	330,000
Shigeru Uchida	74	74	74	222	330,000
Kunio Koike	75	73	74	222	330,000
Ichiro Togawa	73	75	74	222	330,000
Tatsuyoshi Nishimiya	72	70	80	222	330,000
Hsu Chie-San	78	71	73	222	330,000
Billy Dunk	73	74	75	222	330,000

Asahi Kokusai Vintage Classic

Asahi Kokusai Country Club, Hyogo
Par 35-35–70; 6,332 yards

September 8-10
purse, ¥30,000,000

	SCORES			TOTAL	MONEY
Haruo Yasuda	66	66	70	202	¥4,500,000
Norihiko Matsumoto	65	69	69	203	2,100,000
Hsieh Min-Nan	68	66	70	204	1,650,000
Fujio Kobayashi	68	65	72	205	1,200,000
Masaru Amano	69	65	72	206	1,050,000
Seiichi Kanai	74	66	69	209	770,000
Akio Kanemoto	70	70	69	209	770,000
Mitsuhiro Kitta	70	68	71	209	770,000
Kuo Chie-Hsiung	74	67	69	210	600,000
Mitsutaka Kono	71	69	71	211	500,250
Yoshiaki Inada	68	71	72	211	500,250
Shigeru Uchida	67	74	70	211	500,250
Takuo Terashima	71	69	71	211	500,250
Sadao Ogawa	70	71	71	212	445,500
Koji Nakajima	75	72	65	212	445,500
Teruo Suzuki	74	65	73	212	445,500
Kenichi Tsurumoto	67	71	74	212	445,500
Hiroshi Ishii	74	71	68	213	409,500
Katsumi Hara	73	69	71	213	409,500
Toshiki Matsui	71	72	70	213	409,500
Hsu Chie-San	70	70	73	213	409,500
Shoji Kikuchi	66	73	75	214	362,571
Seiichi Sato	72	70	72	214	362,571
Misao Jitsukata	70	73	71	214	362,571
Takahiro Takeyasu	75	67	72	214	362,571
Hideo Jibiki	71	71	72	214	362,571

	SCORES			TOTAL	MONEY
Ryosuke Ota	72	70	72	214	362,571
Kiyotaka Mochida	71	71	72	214	362,571
Kesahiko Uchida	72	69	74	215	327,000
Izuru Taka	69	74	72	215	327,000
Ichiro Teramoto	70	71	74	215	327,000
Mitsuo Hirukawa	72	73	70	215	327,000

Komatsu Nagoya TV Open

Hananoki Golf Club, Aichi
Par 36-36–72; 6,742 yards

September 15-17
purse, ¥40,000,000

	SCORES			TOTAL	MONEY
Kuo Chie-Hsiung	67	70	73	210	¥6,000,000
Haruo Yasuda	70	71	71	212	2,500,000
Shigeru Uchida	70	72	70	212	2,500,000
Masaru Amano	69	73	72	214	1,400,000
Shoji Kikuchi	71	70	73	214	1,400,000
Hiroshi Ishii	70	71	73	214	1,400,000
Seiji Ogawa	70	72	73	215	1,000,000
Ichiro Teramoto	74	71	71	216	880,000
Seiichi Kanai	71	74	72	217	710,000
Fujio Kobayashi	74	72	71	217	710,000
Mitsuhiro Kitta	66	72	79	217	710,000
Art Proctor	71	77	69	217	710,000
Seiichi Sato	71	72	75	218	613,333
Hsieh Min-Nan	69	73	76	218	613,333
Teruo Suzumura	76	71	71	218	613,333
Toshiki Matsui	66	75	78	219	582,000
Toshikazu Izumi	64	79	76	219	582,000
Ichio Sato	73	72	75	220	546,000
Kenji Ueda	76	74	70	220	546,000
Yoshihiro Takada	72	73	75	220	546,000
Norihiko Matsumoto	71	76	73	220	546,000
*Yoshikazu Miyajima	75	73	72	220	
Kikuo Arai	73	71	77	221	498,000
Takuo Terashima	75	71	75	221	498,000
Billy Dunk	69	74	78	221	498,000
Kenichi Tsurumoto	70	74	77	221	498,000
Shichiro Enomoto	75	73	74	222	456,000
Hisao Kinoshita	68	78	76	222	456,000
Takahiro Takeyasu	75	75	72	222	456,000
Tetsuhiro Ueda	71	77	74	222	456,000
Katsumi Hara	70	73	79	222	456,000

Noboru Gotah Memorial Tokyu Senior Cup

Tokyu 700 Country Club, Chiba
Par 36-36–72; 6,687 yards

September 22-24
purse, ¥30,000,000

	SCORES			TOTAL	MONEY
Koji Nakajima	70	70	68	208	¥4,500,000
Kikuo Arai	70	69	70	209	1,380,000
Seiji Ogawa	70	68	71	209	1,380,000
Fukuji Kikuchi	70	70	69	209	1,380,000

	SCORES			TOTAL	MONEY
Izuru Taka	71	67	71	209	1,380,000
Yoshihiro Takada	69	68	72	209	1,380,000
Masao Kikuchi	71	68	71	210	610,800
Akiro Chiba	71	71	68	210	610,800
Hideo Jibiki	70	71	69	210	610,800
Norihiko Matsumoto	70	70	70	210	610,800
Billy Dunk	71	68	71	210	610,800
Fujio Kobayashi	67	72	72	211	466,500
Haruo Yasuda	71	69	71	211	466,500
Mitoshi Tomita	74	67	70	211	466,500
Katsumi Hara	76	70	65	211	466,500
Seiichi Kanai	73	69	70	212	427,500
Shoji Kikuchi	74	66	72	212	427,500
Kiyokuni Kimoto	76	68	68	212	427,500
Hsieh Min-Nan	70	68	74	212	427,500
Kesahiko Uchida	71	70	72	213	374,625
Jun Nobechi	70	71	72	213	374,625
Tetsuhiro Ueda	73	66	74	213	374,625
Ichiro Teramoto	74	69	70	213	374,625
Shozo Miyamoto	67	72	74	213	374,625
Kiyotaka Mochida	69	72	72	213	374,625
Hsu Chie-San	70	74	69	213	374,625
Eleuterio Nival	71	71	71	213	374,625
Sadao Ogawa	68	72	74	214	327,000
Mitsutaka Kono	75	70	69	214	327,000
Chen Chen-Chung	71	70	73	214	327,000
Teruo Suzuki	77	66	71	214	327,000
Toshiki Matsui	74	66	74	214	327,000
Art Proctor	75	70	69	214	327,000

Ho-Oh Cup

Ho-Oh Golf Club, Gunma
Par 36-36–72; 6,641 yards

October 27-29
purse, ¥35,000,000

	SCORES			TOTAL	MONEY
Ryokichi Jibiki	62	70	69	201	¥5,250,000
Kuo Chie-Hsiung	68	69	68	205	2,450,000
Kikuo Arai	70	68	68	206	1,662,500
Hsieh Min-Nan	68	70	68	206	1,662,500
Masaru Amano	70	68	69	207	1,225,000
Seiichi Kanae	71	68	69	208	1,050,000
Kenichi Tsurumoto	72	66	72	210	875,000
Fujio Kobayashi	74	69	69	212	770,000
Shoji Kikuchi	77	70	66	213	606,900
Mitsutaka Kono	70	73	70	213	606,900
Jun Nobechi	75	65	73	213	606,900
Haruo Yasuda	77	69	67	213	606,900
Shigeru Uchida	73	68	72	213	606,900
Mitoshi Tomita	73	70	71	214	535,500
Sadao Ogawa	76	67	72	215	477,750
Hiroshi Kaihata	69	71	75	215	477,750
Takaaki Kono	71	72	72	215	477,750
Koji Nakajima	74	71	70	215	477,750
Ryosuke Ota	72	75	68	215	477,750
Yoshihiro Takada	76	67	72	215	477,750
Chen Chien-Chin	70	73	72	215	477,750

	SCORES			TOTAL	MONEY
Ichiro Teramoto	69	71	75	215	477,750
Katsumi Hara	73	72	70	215	477,750
Norihiko Matsumoto	73	72	70	215	477,750
Teruo Suzumura	70	73	73	216	420,000
Hisao Kinoshita	72	70	75	217	406,000
Tetsuhiro Ueda	69	72	76	217	406,000
Tetsuyuki Nishimiya	75	71	71	217	406,000
Hiroshi Ishii	77	71	70	218	385,000
Ichiro Togawa	72	73	73	218	385,000
Hsu Chie-San	73	70	75	218	385,000

Japan Senior Open

Kitaura Golf Club, Nara
Par 36-36–72; 6,753 yards

November 23-26
purse, ¥50,000,000

	SCORES				TOTAL	MONEY
Isao Aoki	65	67	74	69	275	¥7,500,000
Mitoshi Tomita	70	67	70	69	276	3,500,000
Masaru Amano	67	66	72	73	278	2,375,000
Gary Player	69	69	71	69	278	2,375,000
Seiichi Kanai	71	66	73	70	280	1,750,000
Haruo Yasuda	70	72	70	69	281	1,287,500
Graham Marsh	72	66	70	73	281	1,287,500
Hiroshi Ishii	70	73	70	69	282	1,000,000
Kuo Chie-Hsiung	72	69	70	72	283	850,000
Billy Dunk	74	71	69	69	283	850,000
Seiji Ogawa	69	74	72	69	284	761,666
Kanae Nobechi	66	78	69	71	284	761,666
Kenichi Tsurumoto	73	72	70	69	284	761,666
Kiyokuni Kimoto	70	73	72	70	285	692,500
Hsieh Min-Nan	74	70	71	70	285	692,500
Ryosuke Ota	71	72	73	69	285	692,500
Katsumi Hara	71	72	73	69	285	692,500
Kesahiko Uchida	71	73	70	72	286	647,500
Hideo Jibiki	70	71	73	72	286	647,500
Kikuo Arai	68	69	76	74	287	625,000
Shoji Kikuchi	69	73	74	72	288	587,500
Namio Takasu	73	73	71	71	288	587,500
Mitsuhiro Kitsuta	72	76	72	68	288	587,500
Toshiki Matsui	73	72	69	74	288	587,500
Mitsutaka Kono	75	67	76	71	289	545,000
Norihiko Matsumoto	73	72	72	72	289	545,000
Fukuji Kikuchi	71	71	75	73	290	515,000
Hsieh Yung-Yo	73	75	74	68	290	515,000
Kunio Koike	72	69	79	70	290	515,000
Eleuterio Nival	72	73	73	72	290	515,000

Women's Tours

Chrysler-Plymouth Tournament of Champions

Grand Cypress Resort, Orlando, Florida
Par 36-36–72; 6,387 yards

January 12-15
purse, $700,000

		SCORES			TOTAL	MONEY
Dawn Coe-Jones	74	70	68	69	281	$115,000
Beth Daniel	69	73	74	71	287	72,000
Pat Bradley	79	71	70	68	288	46,750
Betsy King	71	74	71	72	288	46,750
Helen Alfredsson	74	73	70	72	289	33,100
Val Skinner	74	72	74	70	290	23,466
Laura Davies	72	74	71	73	290	23,466
Liselotte Neumann	73	71	71	75	290	23,466
Hiromi Kobayashi	74	74	74	69	291	17,325
Meg Mallon	75	71	73	72	291	17,325
Tammie Green	71	75	73	73	292	14,918
Deb Richard	74	72	77	70	293	12,976
Dottie Mochrie	72	73	75	73	293	12,976
Brandie Burton	75	71	72	75	293	12,976
Marta Figueras-Dotti	75	75	71	73	294	10,768
Barb Mucha	68	75	75	76	294	10,768
Martha Nause	73	75	69	77	294	10,768
JoAnne Carner	73	73	78	71	295	9,492
Missie McGeorge	74	74	73	74	295	9,492
Nancy Lopez	74	72	74	75	295	9,492
Lisa Walters	73	72	74	77	296	8,673
Jane Geddes	76	74	76	73	299	7,844
Lauri Merten	75	74	77	73	299	7,844
Patty Sheehan	76	72	76	75	299	7,844
Kelly Robbins	74	77	71	77	299	7,844
Lisa Kiggens	73	73	78	76	300	7,212
Sherri Steinhauer	77	76	78	72	303	6,979
Trish Johnson	76	80	74	74	304	6,630
Shelley Hamlin	73	76	80	75	304	6,630
Missie Berteotti	79	75	75	77	306	6,164
Elaine Crosby	76	76	77	77	306	6,164

HealthSouth Inaugural

Eagles Pines Golf Course, Orlando, Florida
Par 36-36–72; 6,256 yards

January 20-22
purse, $450,000

		SCORES		TOTAL	MONEY
Pat Bradley	71	72	68	211	$67,500
Beth Daniel	71	70	71	212	41,891
Val Skinner	71	72	70	213	30,569
Laura Davies	73	69	72	214	23,776
Joan Pitcock	74	71	70	215	19,247
Missie McGeorge	72	70	74	216	15,850
Meg Mallon	70	74	73	217	12,567

	SCORES			TOTAL	MONEY
Helen Alfredsson	71	72	74	217	12,567
Jackie Gallagher-Smith	78	72	68	218	7,189
Dawn Coe-Jones	75	73	70	218	7,189
Lauri Merten	73	75	70	218	7,189
Kelly Robbins	75	72	71	218	7,189
Barb Mucha	73	74	71	218	7,189
Stephanie Maynor	75	71	72	218	7,189
Dale Eggeling	74	72	72	218	7,189
Margaret Platt	74	70	74	218	7,189
Pat Hurst	74	70	74	218	7,189
Jerilyn Britz	73	70	75	218	7,189
Gail Graham	70	73	75	218	7,189
Cathy Johnston-Forbes	70	72	76	218	7,189
Deb Richard	76	73	70	219	4,785
Chris Johnson	68	79	72	219	4,785
Hiromi Kobayashi	73	73	73	219	4,785
Jane Crafter	75	75	70	220	3,687
Lisa Walters	74	76	70	220	3,687
Catriona Matthew	75	74	71	220	3,687
Nanci Bowen	74	75	71	220	3,687
Katie Peterson-Parker	73	76	71	220	3,687
Tammie Green	73	76	71	220	3,687
Dottie Mochrie	71	77	72	220	3,687
Jill Briles-Hinton	73	74	73	220	3,687
Sherri Steinhauer	72	75	73	220	3,687
Liselotte Neumann	71	76	73	220	3,687
Vicki Fergon	73	72	75	220	3,687
Cindy Rarick	72	73	75	220	3,687

Cup Noodles Hawaiian Open

Ko Olina Golf Club, Ewa Beach, Oahu, Hawaii
Par 36-36–72; 6,250 yards

February 16-18
purse, $550,000

	SCORES			TOTAL	MONEY
Barb Thomas	68	66	70	204	$82,500
Hiromi Kobayashi	72	71	66	209	39,208
Kris Tschetter	69	71	69	209	39,208
Chris Johnson	69	68	72	209	39,208
Brandie Burton	68	74	69	211	17,324
Colleen Walker	70	70	71	211	17,324
Dale Eggeling	69	71	71	211	17,324
Marianne Morris	71	68	72	211	17,324
Annika Sorenstam	69	70	72	211	17,324
Denise Baldwin	69	73	70	212	10,240
Mitsuyo Hirata	67	75	70	212	10,240
Betsy King	70	71	71	212	10,240
Michele Redman	69	70	73	212	10,240
Cathy Mockett	71	75	67	213	8,579
Missie McGeorge	72	73	69	214	7,250
Muffin Spencer-Devlin	73	69	72	214	7,250
Carin Hjalmarsson	70	71	73	214	7,250
LaRee Pearl Sugg	69	71	74	214	7,250
Dawn Coe-Jones	67	73	74	214	7,250
Jill Briles-Hinton	72	74	69	215	5,177
Sherri Steinhauer	75	70	70	215	5,177
Elaine Crosby	73	71	71	215	5,177

	SCORES			TOTAL	MONEY
Leta Lindley	72	72	71	215	5,177
Ellie Gibson	73	70	72	215	5,177
Allison Finney	73	70	72	215	5,177
Julie Larsen	72	71	72	215	5,177
Kristal Parker-Gregory	71	72	72	215	5,177
Lisa Kiggens	69	74	72	215	5,177
Missie Berteotti	70	71	74	215	5,177
Katie Peterson-Parker	69	72	74	215	5,177
Jenny Lidback	71	69	75	215	5,177

PING Welch's Championship

Randolph Park Golf Course, Tucson, Arizona
Par 35-37–72; 6,222 yards

March 9-12
purse, $450,000

	SCORES				TOTAL	MONEY
Dottie Mochrie	70	68	72	68	278	$67,500
Cindy Rarick	72	74	67	70	283	36,230
Annika Sorenstam	70	70	73	70	283	36,230
Kim Williams	67	74	75	68	284	23,776
Rosie Jones	74	72	70	69	285	17,548
Amy Alcott	70	69	73	73	285	17,548
Kris Tschetter	74	73	74	65	286	10,778
Katie Peterson-Parker	73	73	71	69	286	10,778
Barb Thomas	69	74	74	69	286	10,778
Juli Inkster	71	71	72	72	286	10,778
Caroline Pierce	75	67	70	74	286	10,778
Sherri Steinhauer	77	70	74	66	287	7,472
Pat Bradley	72	75	71	69	287	7,472
Jane Geddes	74	71	72	70	287	7,472
Sherri Turner	70	74	79	65	288	5,932
Val Skinner	73	70	76	69	288	5,932
Stephanie Maynor	71	76	70	71	288	5,932
Tracy Hanson	73	68	75	72	288	5,932
Suzanne Strudwick	73	73	69	73	288	5,932
Marianne Morris	74	69	77	69	289	4,690
Laura Davies	74	71	74	70	289	4,690
Nanci Bowen	73	72	74	70	289	4,690
Pat Hurst	71	71	76	71	289	4,690
Alicia Dibos	71	72	73	73	289	4,690
Carin Hjalmarsson	74	70	70	75	289	4,690
Betsy King	73	71	75	71	290	3,985
Beth Daniel	68	73	78	71	290	3,985
Helen Alfredsson	75	70	71	74	290	3,985
Cathy Mockett	76	71	74	70	291	3,107
Jennifer Wyatt	73	70	77	71	291	3,107
Hiromi Kobayashi	75	72	72	72	291	3,107
Marta Figueras-Dotti	72	73	74	72	291	3,107
Janet Anderson	72	71	76	72	291	3,107
Tammie Green	75	67	77	72	291	3,107
Michele Redman	76	69	73	73	291	3,107
Lisa Walters	76	68	74	73	291	3,107
Danielle Ammaccapane	69	75	74	73	291	3,107
Gail Graham	74	68	76	73	291	3,107
Michelle McGann	71	73	73	74	291	3,107

Standard Register PING

Moon Valley Country Club, Phoenix, Arizona
Par 36-37–73; 6,495 yards

March 16-19
purse, $700,000

	SCORES				TOTAL	MONEY
Laura Davies	69	68	70	73	280	$105,000
Beth Daniel	69	69	71	72	281	65,165
Katie Peterson-Parker	71	70	73	69	283	38,159
Rosie Jones	73	70	70	70	283	38,159
Joan Pitcock	70	70	73	70	283	38,159
*Wendy Ward	69	71	71	72	283	
Mitzi Edge	71	73	68	72	284	24,656
Annika Sorenstam	72	71	73	69	285	19,549
Jane Geddes	73	75	67	70	285	19,549
Marta Figueras-Dotti	70	76	70	70	286	14,265
Marianne Morris	71	72	71	72	286	14,265
Michele Redman	71	69	73	73	286	14,265
Betsy King	73	71	68	74	286	14,265
Colleen Walker	73	72	71	71	287	10,567
Julie Larsen	73	70	73	71	287	10,567
Karen Weiss	70	73	71	73	287	10,567
Michelle Estill	72	70	72	73	287	10,567
Alicia Dibos	76	71	71	70	288	8,629
Lisa Kiggens	75	69	73	71	288	8,629
Trish Johnson	72	72	73	71	288	8,629
Michelle McGann	70	73	71	74	288	8,629
Kelly Robbins	72	74	74	69	289	7,264
Liselotte Neumann	72	74	73	70	289	7,264
Florence Descampe	75	72	71	71	289	7,264
Nancy Lopez	72	70	72	75	289	7,264
Hollis Stacy	73	73	72	72	290	6,304
Jennifer Wyatt	70	71	77	72	290	6,304
Nicole Jeray	73	70	74	73	290	6,304
Gail Graham	71	73	72	74	290	6,304
Ellie Gibson	75	70	78	68	291	5,468
Jenny Lidback	74	74	74	69	291	5,468
Vicki Fergon	72	72	73	74	291	5,468
Missie McGeorge	73	72	71	75	291	5,468

Nabisco Dinah Shore

Mission Hills Country Club, Rancho Mirage, California
Par 36-36–72; 6,460 yards

March 23-26
purse, $850,000

	SCORES				TOTAL	MONEY
Nanci Bowen	69	75	71	70	285	$127,500
Susie Redman	75	70	70	71	286	79,129
Brandie Burton	76	71	71	69	287	42,237
Sherri Turner	72	74	71	70	287	42,237
Laura Davies	75	69	70	73	287	42,237
Nancy Lopez	74	71	68	74	287	42,237
Colleen Walker	74	73	69	72	288	23,738
Tammie Green	71	70	70	77	288	23,738
Dawn Coe-Jones	71	75	71	72	289	20,103
Caroline Pierce	77	71	73	69	290	17,964
Betsy King	77	75	71	68	291	14,200
Dottie Mochrie	78	73	70	70	291	14,200

	SCORES				TOTAL	MONEY
Barb Mucha	74	74	72	71	291	14,200
Sandra Palmer	72	73	74	72	291	14,200
Debbie Massey	71	75	72	73	291	14,200
Alicia Dibos	77	74	75	66	292	10,056
Sherri Steinhauer	78	74	72	68	292	10,056
Alison Nicholas	75	74	73	70	292	10,056
Pat Bradley	74	75	71	72	292	10,056
Juli Inkster	76	70	73	73	292	10,056
Terry-Jo Myers	77	68	73	74	292	10,056
Michelle Estill	72	72	74	74	292	10,056
Meg Mallon	74	72	71	75	292	10,056
Annika Sorenstam	76	74	74	69	293	8,040
Muffin Spencer-Devlin	69	79	74	71	293	8,040
Kristi Albers	76	72	72	73	293	8,040
Jane Geddes	76	75	74	69	294	7,014
Kris Tschetter	75	74	73	72	294	7,014
Lori West	74	75	71	74	294	7,014
Kelly Robbins	76	67	76	75	294	7,014
Barb Thomas	79	69	70	76	294	7,014

Pinewild Women's Championship

Pinewild Country Club, Pinehurst, North Carolina
Par 36-36–72; 6,426 yards

April 14-16
purse, $650,000

	SCORES			TOTAL	MONEY
Rosie Jones	72	70	69	211	$97,500
Dottie Mochrie	72	69	70	211	60,510
(Jones defeated Mochrie on first extra hole.)					
Michelle McGann	75	70	67	212	32,299
Nanci Bowen	71	72	69	212	32,299
Annika Sorenstam	73	69	70	212	32,299
Brandie Burton	70	71	71	212	32,299
Helen Alfredsson	71	75	67	213	17,226
Carin Hjalmarsson	72	73	68	213	17,226
Joan Pitcock	75	67	71	213	17,226
Page Dunlap	72	72	70	214	10,999
Meg Mallon	72	71	71	214	10,999
Juli Inkster	70	73	71	214	10,999
Sally Little	74	68	72	214	10,999
Caroline Pierce	69	72	73	214	10,999
Liselotte Neumann	70	69	75	214	10,999
Nicole Jeray	71	67	76	214	10,999
Val Skinner	73	72	70	215	7,871
Laura Davies	73	72	70	215	7,871
Dawn Coe-Jones	72	71	72	215	7,871
Beth Daniel	73	69	73	215	7,871
Lisa Walters	72	70	73	215	7,871
Margaret Platt	73	71	72	216	6,617
Susie Redman	71	70	75	216	6,617
Missie McGeorge	70	70	76	216	6,617
Muffin Spencer-Devlin	76	70	71	217	5,582
Suzanne Strudwick	73	72	72	217	5,582
Colleen Walker	74	70	73	217	5,582
Sherri Turner	74	70	73	217	5,582
Jane Crafter	73	71	73	217	5,582
Jill Briles-Hinton	73	71	73	217	5,582
Nancy Ramsbottom	73	70	74	217	5,582

Chick-fil-A Charity Championship

Eagle's Landing Country Club, Stockbridge, Georgia
Par 36-36–72; 6,187 yards

April 21-23
purse, $500,000

	SCORES			TOTAL	MONEY
Laura Davies	67	67	67	201	$75,000
Kelly Robbins	67	72	66	205	46,546
Kristi Albers	67	69	70	206	33,966
Sherri Turner	73	71	63	207	21,805
Vicki Fergon	69	69	69	207	21,805
Dottie Mochrie	69	66	72	207	21,805
Liselotte Neumann	72	70	67	209	12,579
Michelle McGann	70	72	67	209	12,579
Brandie Burton	72	69	68	209	12,579
Karen Weiss	69	72	68	209	12,579
Barb Mucha	70	73	67	210	9,561
Kris Tschetter	68	74	69	211	8,554
Susie Redman	71	68	72	211	8,554
Deb Richard	75	68	69	212	7,296
Lisa Kiggens	73	69	70	212	7,296
Nancy Ramsbottom	73	68	71	212	7,296
Trish Johnson	74	68	71	213	6,415
Kathryn Marshall	71	66	76	213	6,415
Pat Hurst	75	71	68	214	5,236
Colleen Walker	71	75	68	214	5,236
Jane Geddes	73	71	70	214	5,236
Tracy Hanson	73	71	70	214	5,236
Gail Graham	72	72	70	214	5,236
Lisa Walters	73	70	71	214	5,236
Helen Alfredsson	71	72	71	214	5,236
Danielle Ammaccapane	69	73	72	214	5,236
Marta Figueras-Dotti	73	73	69	215	3,786
Emilee Klein	72	74	69	215	3,786
Allison Finney	71	75	69	215	3,786
Melissa McNamara	74	71	70	215	3,786
Jill Briles-Hinton	72	72	71	215	3,786
Kim Saiki	71	73	71	215	3,786
Leigh Ann Mills	72	71	72	215	3,786
Michelle Estill	69	74	72	215	3,786
Cathy Mockett	74	68	73	215	3,786
Stephanie Maynor	73	68	74	215	3,786

Sprint Championship

LPGA International, Daytona Beach, Florida
Par 36-36–72; 6,435 yards

April 27-30
purse, $1,200,000

	SCORES				TOTAL	MONEY
Val Skinner	71	65	70	67	273	$180,000
Kris Tschetter	66	67	72	70	275	111,711
Michelle McGann	70	65	72	69	276	81,519
Meg Mallon	69	69	70	69	277	57,365
Dottie Mochrie	66	72	69	70	277	57,365
Dawn Coe-Jones	67	68	75	68	278	36,431
Colleen Walker	66	72	70	70	278	36,431
Beth Daniel	72	67	68	71	278	36,431
Trish Johnson	73	70	70	66	279	26,871

	SCORES				TOTAL	MONEY
Kelly Robbins	68	75	70	66	279	26,871
Sherri Steinhauer	73	67	71	69	280	20,109
Chris Johnson	76	66	68	70	280	20,109
Joan Pitcock	69	71	70	70	280	20,109
Annika Sorenstam	69	70	68	73	280	20,109
Alice Ritzman	69	69	69	73	280	20,109
Tracy Kerdyk	71	70	71	69	281	16,063
Jane Crafter	69	69	71	72	281	16,063
Susie Redman	71	71	71	69	282	14,252
Stephanie Maynor	69	74	69	70	282	14,252
Carin Hjalmarsson	69	70	73	70	282	14,252
Jane Geddes	69	73	69	71	282	14,252
Nicole Jeray	70	73	72	68	283	11,456
Emilee Klein	72	70	73	68	283	11,456
Danielle Ammaccapane	71	72	71	69	283	11,456
Florence Descampe	68	75	70	70	283	11,456
Kristi Albers	68	69	75	71	283	11,456
Helen Alfredsson	74	68	69	72	283	11,456
Kim Saiki	70	72	67	74	283	11,456
Kim Williams	73	70	71	70	284	9,276
Barb Thomas	70	72	72	70	284	9,276
Julie Larsen	70	72	72	70	284	9,276
Elaine Crosby	69	70	72	73	284	9,276
Michelle Estill	69	71	70	74	284	9,276

Sara Lee Classic

Hermitage Golf Course, Old Hickory, Tennessee
Par 36-36–72; 6,290 yards

May 5-7
purse, $525,000

	SCORES			TOTAL	MONEY
Michelle McGann	69	65	68	202	$78,750
Dottie Mochrie	67	71	65	203	37,425
Kelly Robbins	68	67	68	203	37,425
Laura Davies	64	69	70	203	37,425
Jane Geddes	69	70	66	205	22,455
Helen Alfredsson	70	68	68	206	17,039
Jenny Lidback	69	68	69	206	17,039
Colleen Walker	67	69	71	207	13,737
Betsy King	72	71	65	208	10,699
Barb Thomas	71	70	67	208	10,699
Marta Figueras-Dotti	70	70	68	208	10,699
Caroline Pierce	68	69	71	208	10,699
Maggie Will	67	72	70	209	8,718
Joan Pitcock	74	71	65	210	7,925
Katie Peterson-Parker	69	70	71	210	7,925
Dawn Coe-Jones	71	73	67	211	6,340
Martha Nause	70	74	67	211	6,340
Denise Philbrick	70	70	71	211	6,340
Nancy Harvey	69	70	72	211	6,340
Hollis Stacy	71	67	73	211	6,340
Kris Tschetter	67	71	73	211	6,340
Lenore Rittenhouse	68	68	75	211	6,340
Alicia Dibos	74	69	69	212	4,971
Susie Redman	72	69	71	212	4,971
Page Dunlap	72	69	71	212	4,971
Tina Barrett	68	72	72	212	4,971

	SCORES			TOTAL	MONEY
Michele Redman	68	71	73	212	4,971
Carin Hjalmarsson	74	71	68	213	4,107
Ayako Okamoto	69	76	68	213	4,107
Helen Dobson	74	68	71	213	4,107
Laurie Brower	67	75	71	213	4,107
Mardi Lunn	67	74	72	213	4,107
Julie Larsen	70	70	73	213	4,107

McDonald's LPGA Championship

Du Pont Country Club, Wilmington, Delaware
Par 35-36–71; 6,386 yards

May 11-14
purse, $1,200,000

	SCORES				TOTAL	MONEY
Kelly Robbins	66	68	72	68	274	$180,000
Laura Davies	68	68	69	70	275	111,711
Julie Larsen	71	68	70	71	280	65,416
Marianne Morris	67	71	70	72	280	65,416
Patty Sheehan	67	68	72	73	280	65,416
Barb Thomas	70	66	73	72	281	38,947
Dottie Mochrie	67	70	71	73	281	38,947
Pat Bradley	71	70	70	71	282	29,890
Tammie Green	69	72	70	71	282	29,890
Annika Sorenstam	71	71	72	69	283	25,362
Kristi Albers	71	71	72	70	284	20,681
Dale Eggeling	72	72	68	72	284	20,681
Joan Pitcock	75	66	71	72	284	20,681
Betsy King	69	71	72	72	284	20,681
Lisa Kiggens	70	70	75	70	285	16,504
Meg Mallon	70	72	71	72	285	16,504
Barb Mucha	71	69	71	74	285	16,504
Beth Daniel	71	73	72	70	286	13,080
Nancy Scranton	71	75	69	71	286	13,080
Susie Redman	73	71	71	71	286	13,080
Lori Garbacz	71	71	72	72	286	13,080
Kris Tschetter	73	69	71	73	286	13,080
Nancy Lopez	73	71	68	74	286	13,080
Colleen Walker	70	70	72	74	286	13,080
Allison Finney	71	68	70	77	286	13,080
Sherri Turner	73	74	70	70	287	10,626
Kathy Guadagnino	72	73	68	74	287	10,626
Nanci Bowen	71	71	71	74	287	10,626
Kim Williams	72	71	75	70	288	9,374
Michele Redman	75	68	72	73	288	9,374
Jane Geddes	71	71	71	75	288	9,374
Michelle Estill	72	73	67	76	288	9,374

Star Bank LPGA Classic

Country Club of the North, Dayton, Ohio
Par 36-36–72; 6,319 yards

May 19-21
purse, $500,000

	SCORES			TOTAL	MONEY
Chris Johnson	68	75	67	210	$75,000
Juli Inkster	69	68	74	211	46,546

	SCORES			TOTAL	MONEY
Michele Redman	72	70	70	212	33,966
Dawn Coe-Jones	71	75	67	213	26,418
Patty Sheehan	70	73	71	214	19,499
Pat Hurst	70	70	74	214	19,499
Jane Geddes	75	71	69	215	13,250
Rosie Jones	71	74	70	215	13,250
Tammie Green	71	71	73	215	13,250
Tracy Kerdyk	75	70	71	216	10,064
Mardi Lunn	70	73	73	216	10,064
Lori West	69	79	69	217	7,233
Martha Faulconer	75	71	71	217	7,233
Liselotte Neumann	76	68	73	217	7,233
Allison Finney	73	70	74	217	7,233
Alison Nicholas	72	71	74	217	7,233
Stephanie Farwig	71	72	74	217	7,233
Lisa Walters	68	74	75	217	7,233
Danielle Ammaccapane	68	74	75	217	7,233
Donna Andrews	77	71	70	218	5,415
Melissa McNamara	74	72	72	218	5,415
Janet Anderson	71	74	73	218	5,415
Lenore Rittenhouse	71	73	74	218	5,415
Tina Barrett	73	76	70	219	4,209
Cindy Rarick	72	76	71	219	4,209
Catriona Matthew	72	75	72	219	4,209
Marianne Morris	71	76	72	219	4,209
Patti Berendt	76	70	73	219	4,209
Amy Alcott	72	74	73	219	4,209
Emilee Klein	71	75	73	219	4,209
Karen Noble	72	73	74	219	4,209
Missie McGeorge	71	73	75	219	4,209
Tracy Hanson	67	74	78	219	4,209

Corning Classic

Corning Country Club, Corning, New York
Par 36-36–72; 6,070 yards

May 25-28
purse, $550,000

	SCORES				TOTAL	MONEY
Alison Nicholas	70	67	66	72	275	$82,500
Danielle Ammaccapane	72	67	70	69	278	44,282
Barb Mucha	71	69	68	70	278	44,282
Pat Bradley	67	68	70	74	279	29,060
Meg Mallon	74	70	66	71	281	21,448
Rosie Jones	72	66	70	73	281	21,448
Annika Sorenstam	70	69	72	71	282	15,359
Alice Ritzman	75	67	67	73	282	15,359
Lauri Merten	71	71	70	71	283	12,316
Amy Fruhwirth	73	68	71	71	283	12,316
Caroline Pierce	71	69	75	69	284	8,667
Elaine Crosby	73	72	69	70	284	8,667
Shelley Hamlin	70	72	70	72	284	8,667
Lori Tatum	73	69	69	73	284	8,667
Colleen Walker	71	68	72	73	284	8,667
Tammie Green	71	69	70	74	284	8,667
Beth Daniel	70	71	67	76	284	8,667
Nancy Ramsbottom	70	75	70	70	285	6,512
Mary Beth Zimmerman	71	72	72	70	285	6,512

	SCORES				TOTAL	MONEY
Suzanne Strudwick	69	74	72	70	285	6,512
Karen Noble	73	69	69	74	285	6,512
Sherri Steinhauer	73	70	74	69	286	5,589
Muffin Spencer-Devlin	72	70	73	71	286	5,589
Catriona Matthew	70	75	69	72	286	5,589
JoAnne Carner	70	73	73	71	287	4,879
Kim Shipman	70	71	74	72	287	4,879
Denise Baldwin	71	71	70	75	287	4,879
Connie Chillemi	72	68	72	75	287	4,879
Renee Heiken	70	71	69	77	287	4,879
Helen Alfredsson	71	73	73	71	288	4,082
Stephanie Maynor	72	70	74	72	288	4,082
Jody Anschutz	70	72	74	72	288	4,082
Martha Nause	71	71	72	74	288	4,082
Kelly Robbins	71	71	69	77	288	4,082

Oldsmobile Classic

Walnut Hills Country Club, East Lansing, Michigan
Par 36-36–72; 6,191 yards

June 1-4
purse, $600,000

	SCORES				TOTAL	MONEY
Dale Eggeling	63	69	71	71	274	$90,000
Meg Mallon	71	69	69	67	276	42,772
Annika Sorenstam	73	65	70	68	276	42,772
Elaine Crosby	67	68	73	68	276	42,772
Michelle McGann	70	69	68	70	277	23,398
Katie Peterson-Parker	68	69	70	70	277	23,398
Danielle Ammaccapane	69	68	71	70	278	15,901
Kris Tschetter	69	66	72	71	278	15,901
Joan Pitcock	66	69	70	73	278	15,901
Michele Redman	69	68	73	69	279	12,111
Helen Alfredsson	65	74	69	71	279	12,111
Amy Benz	68	71	74	67	280	9,427
Lisa Walters	71	68	69	72	280	9,427
Cindy Rarick	71	67	70	72	280	9,427
Tracy Hanson	73	67	67	73	280	9,427
Jane Geddes	66	71	70	73	280	9,427
Michelle Estill	71	68	72	70	281	7,162
Colleen Walker	67	72	72	70	281	7,162
Tina Barrett	72	65	73	71	281	7,162
Nanci Bowen	66	71	73	71	281	7,162
Pam Wright	71	69	69	72	281	7,162
Leta Lindley	71	69	69	72	281	7,162
Karen Noble	71	69	74	68	282	6,030
Betsy King	68	68	75	71	282	6,030
Amy Fruhwirth	75	67	73	68	283	5,562
Tracy Kerdyk	68	74	71	70	283	5,562
Hiromi Kobayashi	73	69	70	71	283	5,562
Vicki Fergon	70	74	71	69	284	4,928
Caroline Pierce	70	71	73	70	284	4,928
Barb Thomas	68	69	74	73	284	4,928
Jean Zedlitz	69	69	71	75	284	4,928

Edina Realty Classic

Edinburgh USA Golf Course, Brooklyn Park, Minnesota
Par 36-36–72; 6,141 yards

June 9-11
purse, $500,000

	SCORES			TOTAL	MONEY
Julie Larsen	66	68	71	205	$75,000
Leigh Ann Mills	69	69	68	206	46,546
Nancy Lopez	75	67	67	209	24,845
Liselotte Neumann	70	71	68	209	24,845
Michelle McGann	70	69	70	209	24,845
Pat Bradley	67	70	72	209	24,845
Betsy King	70	72	68	210	13,963
Cindy Rarick	66	71	73	210	13,963
Amy Fruhwirth	69	71	71	211	11,196
Sherri Steinhauer	70	69	72	211	11,196
Vicki Fergon	71	74	67	212	7,673
Val Skinner	68	77	67	212	7,673
Jane Geddes	68	75	69	212	7,673
Vicki Goetze	68	75	69	212	7,673
Meg Mallon	72	69	71	212	7,673
Kathryn Marshall	71	70	71	212	7,673
Elaine Crosby	70	71	71	212	7,673
Caroline Pierce	67	72	73	212	7,673
Sally Little	72	72	69	213	5,912
Terry-Jo Myers	69	70	74	213	5,912
Lisa Kiggens	70	76	68	214	5,535
Barb Mucha	74	71	70	215	4,670
Chris Johnson	72	73	70	215	4,670
Tina Barrett	69	76	70	215	4,670
Lenore Rittenhouse	72	72	71	215	4,670
Joan Pitcock	72	72	71	215	4,670
Janice Gibson	70	74	71	215	4,670
Karen Weiss	71	72	72	215	4,670
Jody Anschutz	70	73	72	215	4,670
Tracy Kerdyk	75	71	70	216	3,703
Leta Lindley	71	75	70	216	3,703
Penny Hammel	74	71	71	216	3,703
Tina Tombs	66	75	75	216	3,703
Gail Graham	69	70	77	216	3,703

Rochester International

Locust Hill Country Club, Rochester, New York
Par 35-37–72; 6,162 yards

June 15-18
purse, $550,000

	SCORES				TOTAL	MONEY
Patty Sheehan	73	66	69	70	278	$82,500
Sherri Steinhauer	70	67	72	73	282	51,201
Pam Wright	75	67	74	67	283	37,363
Helen Alfredsson	69	69	72	75	285	29,060
Jane Geddes	69	75	72	70	286	18,404
Caroline Pierce	74	72	69	71	286	18,404
Dale Eggeling	69	72	71	74	286	18,404
Alice Ritzman	70	73	67	76	286	18,404
Michelle Estill	74	73	68	72	287	12,316
JoAnne Carner	68	68	78	73	287	12,316
Michele Redman	68	77	72	71	288	8,931

	SCORES				TOTAL	MONEY
Danielle Ammaccapane	73	70	74	71	288	8,931
Allison Finney	72	70	75	71	288	8,931
Tracy Kerdyk	73	71	72	72	288	8,931
Barb Mucha	72	70	72	74	288	8,931
Barb Thomas	70	68	76	74	288	8,931
Hollis Stacy	73	75	70	71	289	6,808
Marianne Morris	76	71	71	71	289	6,808
Denise Baldwin	71	72	71	75	289	6,808
Nancy Lopez	72	70	72	75	289	6,808
Tracy Hanson	78	67	75	70	290	5,848
Colleen Walker	69	74	77	70	290	5,848
Dawn Coe-Jones	74	72	71	73	290	5,848
Alicia Dibos	74	73	72	72	291	4,981
Brandie Burton	72	75	72	72	291	4,981
Hiromi Kobayashi	72	73	74	72	291	4,981
Rosie Jones	73	70	75	73	291	4,981
Alice Miller	74	68	74	75	291	4,981
Nanci Bowen	68	76	68	79	291	4,981
Tina Barrett	73	73	73	73	292	4,243
Nancy Ramsbottom	72	74	73	73	292	4,243
Katie Peterson-Parker	76	69	72	75	292	4,243

ShopRite Classic

Great Bay Resort & Country Club, Somers Point, New Jersey
Par 36-35–71; 6,235 yards

June 23-25
purse, $650,000

	SCORES			TOTAL	MONEY
Betsy King	66	71	67	204	$97,500
Rosie Jones	68	71	67	206	52,333
Beth Daniel	68	70	68	206	52,333
Val Skinner	72	68	67	207	28,346
Tammie Green	69	70	68	207	28,346
Michele Redman	68	68	71	207	28,346
Muffin Spencer-Devlin	71	67	70	208	17,226
Dottie Mochrie	70	68	70	208	17,226
Brandie Burton	70	67	71	208	17,226
Helen Alfredsson	75	70	65	210	12,118
Liselotte Neumann	73	68	69	210	12,118
Alicia Dibos	71	70	69	210	12,118
Michelle Estill	67	69	74	210	12,118
Marianne Morris	75	67	69	211	9,261
Carin Hjalmarsson	71	71	69	211	9,261
Colleen Walker	72	67	72	211	9,261
Danielle Ammaccapane	71	67	73	211	9,261
Hiromi Kobayashi	71	72	69	212	8,035
Vicki Fergon	69	71	72	212	8,035
Patty Sheehan	74	72	67	213	7,062
Kris Tschetter	73	70	70	213	7,062
Debbie Massey	73	69	71	213	7,062
Allison Finney	69	72	72	213	7,062
Carolyn Hill	72	73	69	214	5,585
Connie Chillemi	72	73	69	214	5,585
Michelle McGann	73	71	70	214	5,585
Pat Bradley	74	69	71	214	5,585
Lenore Rittenhouse	72	71	71	214	5,585
Nanci Bowen	74	68	72	214	5,585

	SCORES			TOTAL	MONEY
Jane Geddes	70	72	72	214	5,585
Missie Berteotti	72	69	73	214	5,585
Mitzi Edge	70	70	74	214	5,585

Youngstown-Warren Classic

Avalon Lakes Golf Course, Warren, Ohio
Par 36-36–72; 6,308 yards

June 30-July 2
purse, $550,000

	SCORES			TOTAL	MONEY
Michelle McGann	65	70	70	205	$82,500
Katie Peterson-Parker	65	69	71	205	51,201
(McGann defeated Peterson-Parker on third extra hole.)					
Nancy Lopez	71	66	69	206	37,363
Tammie Green	72	68	67	207	29,060
Michelle Bell	70	69	69	208	23,524
Kelly Robbins	69	70	70	209	19,373
Cathy Mockett	70	69	71	210	15,359
Val Skinner	69	70	71	210	15,359
Rosie Jones	66	77	68	211	12,316
Muffin Spencer-Devlin	69	69	73	211	12,316
Betsy King	72	72	68	212	8,440
Chris Johnson	72	72	68	212	8,440
Mary Beth Zimmerman	72	70	70	212	8,440
Elaine Crosby	70	72	70	212	8,440
Cindy Rarick	69	72	71	212	8,440
Dottie Mochrie	70	70	72	212	8,440
Sherrin Smyers	69	71	72	212	8,440
Nancy Harvey	69	71	72	212	8,440
Gail Graham	75	69	69	213	6,226
Colleen Walker	71	71	71	213	6,226
Melissa McNamara	71	71	71	213	6,226
Patty Sheehan	71	70	72	213	6,226
Judy Dickinson	73	73	68	214	4,793
Missie Berteotti	72	74	68	214	4,793
Danielle Ammaccapane	71	74	69	214	4,793
Cathy Johnston-Forbes	71	73	70	214	4,793
Margaret Platt	71	73	70	214	4,793
Kathryn Marshall	70	73	71	214	4,793
Martha Nause	74	68	72	214	4,793
Missie McGeorge	73	69	72	214	4,793
Lenore Rittenhouse	72	68	74	214	4,793
Amy Benz	71	69	74	214	4,793

Jamie Farr Toledo Classic

Highland Meadows Golf Club, Sylvania, Ohio
Par 34-37–71; 6,319 yards

July 7-9
purse, $500,000

	SCORES			TOTAL	MONEY
Kathryn Marshall	67	71	67	205	$75,000
Sherri Steinhauer	69	70	67	206	46,546
Pam Wright	71	66	70	207	33,966
Pat Bradley	71	70	67	208	17,528
Kelly Robbins	69	71	68	208	17,528

	SCORES			TOTAL	MONEY
Deb Richard	72	67	69	208	17,528
Beth Daniel	71	68	69	208	17,528
Betsy King	68	71	69	208	17,528
Brandie Burton	68	71	69	208	17,528
Laura Brown	70	73	66	209	9,309
Vicki Fergon	73	69	67	209	9,309
Lenore Rittenhouse	68	72	69	209	9,309
Muffin Spencer-Devlin	67	71	71	209	9,309
Tammie Green	71	71	68	210	7,296
Michelle McGann	72	69	69	210	7,296
Colleen Walker	66	72	72	210	7,296
Meg Mallon	74	70	67	211	6,289
Liselotte Neumann	75	68	68	211	6,289
Barb Mucha	69	73	69	211	6,289
Jean Zedlitz	72	70	70	212	5,535
Melissa McNamara	71	71	70	212	5,535
Annika Sorenstam	70	70	72	212	5,535
Lori West	75	70	68	213	4,079
Kris Tschetter	72	73	68	213	4,079
Tracy Kerdyk	74	70	69	213	4,079
Danielle Ammaccapane	73	71	69	213	4,079
Marianne Morris	72	72	69	213	4,079
Renee Heiken	72	72	69	213	4,079
Juli Inkster	71	73	69	213	4,079
Julie Larsen	72	71	70	213	4,079
Jane Geddes	66	77	70	213	4,079
Janet Anderson	72	70	71	213	4,079
Amy Alcott	71	71	71	213	4,079
Stephanie Maynor	72	69	72	213	4,079
Nancy Lopez	71	70	72	213	4,079
Tracy Hanson	71	70	72	213	4,079

U.S. Women's Open

The Broadmoor, Colorado Springs, Colorado
Par 35-35–70; 6,398 yards

July 13-16
purse, $1,000,000

	SCORES				TOTAL	MONEY
Annika Sorenstam	67	71	72	68	278	$175,000
Meg Mallon	70	69	66	74	279	103,500
Betsy King	72	69	72	67	280	56,238
Pat Bradley	67	71	72	70	280	56,238
Leta Lindley	70	68	74	69	281	35,285
Rosie Jones	69	70	70	72	281	35,285
Tammie Green	68	70	75	69	282	28,009
Dawn Coe-Jones	68	70	74	70	282	28,009
Julie Larsen	68	71	68	75	282	28,009
Marianne Morris	73	73	70	67	283	22,190
Patty Sheehan	70	73	71	69	283	22,190
Val Skinner	68	72	72	71	283	22,190
Dottie Mochrie	73	70	69	72	284	18,007
Kris Tschetter	68	74	69	73	284	18,007
Kelly Robbins	74	68	68	74	284	18,007
Chris Johnson	71	70	74	70	285	14,454
Jill Briles-Hinton	66	72	74	73	285	14,454
Tania Abitbol	67	72	72	74	285	14,454
Dale Eggeling	70	68	73	74	285	14,454

	SCORES				TOTAL	MONEY
Michele Redman	70	75	71	70	286	12,449
Liselotte Neumann	70	71	75	71	287	11,154
Ayako Okamoto	70	73	71	73	287	11,154
Alice Ritzman	75	69	69	74	287	11,154
Carolyn Hill	74	73	70	71	288	9,287
Joan Pitcock	72	73	72	71	288	9,287
Laura Davies	72	73	69	74	288	9,287
Mary Beth Zimmerman	72	72	68	76	288	9,287
Amy Fruhwirth	75	72	72	70	289	6,841
Brandie Burton	72	74	73	70	289	6,841
Nancy Lopez	72	73	74	70	289	6,841
Mayumi Hirase	70	74	73	72	289	6,841
Colleen Walker	69	73	75	72	289	6,841
Pam Wright	72	73	71	73	289	6,841
Debbi Miho Koyama	74	68	73	74	289	6,841
Jean Bartholomew	67	71	77	74	289	6,841
Gail Graham	71	72	71	75	289	6,841

JAL Big Apple Classic

Wykagyl Country Club, New Rochelle, New York
Par 35-36–72; 6,176 yards

July 20-23
purse, $700,000

	SCORES				TOTAL	MONEY
Tracy Kerdyk	74	66	66	67	273	$105,000
Elaine Crosby	72	71	65	69	277	44,910
Caroline Pierce	70	68	70	69	277	44,910
Michelle McGann	66	68	74	69	277	44,910
Carin Hjalmarsson	69	71	65	72	277	44,910
Kris Tschetter	70	70	69	70	279	24,656
Pam Wright	70	71	70	69	280	19,549
Mary Beth Zimmerman	69	70	71	70	280	19,549
Stefania Croce	74	69	68	70	281	16,555
Amy Alcott	68	72	73	69	282	14,794
Muffin Spencer-Devlin	74	66	74	69	283	12,064
Hiromi Kobayashi	70	71	72	70	283	12,064
Trish Johnson	68	73	72	70	283	12,064
Amy Fruhwirth	72	68	70	73	283	12,064
Meg Mallon	75	69	71	69	284	9,228
Rosie Jones	74	69	70	71	284	9,228
Jan Stephenson	69	71	73	71	284	9,228
Joan Pitcock	70	69	73	72	284	9,228
Betsy King	70	71	69	74	284	9,228
Sharon Barrett	73	73	70	69	285	7,581
Val Skinner	73	72	68	72	285	7,581
Chris Johnson	75	69	69	72	285	7,581
Emilee Klein	70	69	72	74	285	7,581
Mitzi Edge	74	74	70	68	286	6,199
Brandie Burton	68	75	75	68	286	6,199
Vicki Fergon	70	73	73	70	286	6,199
Mayumi Hirase	73	69	74	70	286	6,199
Lori West	71	75	69	71	286	6,199
Katie Peterson-Parker	72	69	74	71	286	6,199
Allison Finney	72	68	73	73	286	6,199

Friendly's Classic

Crestview Country Club, Agawam, Massachusetts   July 27-30
Par 36-36–72; 6,381 yards   purse, $500,000

	SCORES				TOTAL	MONEY
Becky Iverson	71	63	72	70	276	$75,000
Helen Alfredsson	71	68	70	69	278	40,256
Kelly Robbins	70	71	65	72	278	40,256
Pat Hurst	74	69	69	67	279	23,902
Kris Tschetter	67	68	72	72	279	23,902
Sherri Steinhauer	71	69	71	69	280	16,228
Tracy Hanson	69	68	71	72	280	16,228
Val Skinner	69	72	70	70	281	11,825
Beth Daniel	69	69	72	71	281	11,825
Dottie Mochrie	70	69	70	72	281	11,825
Cathy Johnston-Forbes	71	73	69	69	282	8,916
Jane Geddes	69	71	72	70	282	8,916
Elaine Crosby	70	69	70	73	282	8,916
Michelle Estill	68	74	71	70	283	6,969
Rosie Jones	71	70	71	71	283	6,969
Michele Redman	71	70	71	71	283	6,969
Sally Little	69	69	74	71	283	6,969
Jane Crafter	68	69	74	72	283	6,969
Kristi Albers	71	74	70	69	284	5,938
Mardi Lunn	71	70	73	70	284	5,938
Hollis Stacy	73	73	71	68	285	5,317
Danielle Ammaccapane	75	70	69	71	285	5,317
Maggie Will	68	72	74	71	285	5,317
Joan Pitcock	73	72	72	69	286	4,680
Alicia Dibos	70	72	74	70	286	4,680
Melissa McNamara	70	71	75	70	286	4,680
Nancy Ramsbottom	74	70	70	72	286	4,680
Missie Berteotti	75	70	74	68	287	4,076
Barb Thomas	68	71	76	72	287	4,076
Julie Larsen	69	73	71	74	287	4,076
Sherrin Smyers	68	73	71	75	287	4,076

McCall's Classic at Stratton Mountain

Stratton Mountain Country Club, Stratton Mountain, Vermont   August 4-6
Par 36-36–72; 6,087 yards   purse, $500,000

	SCORES			TOTAL	MONEY
Dottie Mochrie	69	67	68	204	$75,000
Kelly Robbins	70	69	68	207	46,546
Jane Geddes	71	68	69	208	33,966
Cathy Johnston-Forbes	70	70	69	209	20,065
Kris Tschetter	71	68	70	209	20,065
Amy Fruhwirth	71	66	72	209	20,065
Pat Bradley	69	67	73	209	20,065
Missie McGeorge	70	71	69	210	11,825
Vicki Fergon	70	68	72	210	11,825
Rosie Jones	69	69	72	210	11,825
Gail Graham	69	71	71	211	8,947
Jenny Lidback	70	69	72	211	8,947
Mardi Lunn	70	69	72	211	8,947
Muffin Spencer-Devlin	68	74	70	212	7,164

	SCORES			TOTAL	MONEY
Terry-Jo Myers	69	72	71	212	7,164
Alice Miller	69	72	71	212	7,164
Colleen Walker	68	70	74	212	7,164
Penny Hammel	68	75	70	213	5,722
Marianne Morris	73	69	71	213	5,722
Mary Beth Zimmerman	72	69	72	213	5,722
Eva Dahllof	72	69	72	213	5,722
Allison Finney	67	74	72	213	5,722
Pat Hurst	69	71	73	213	5,722
Michelle Bell	69	74	71	214	4,484
Carin Hjalmarsson	72	70	72	214	4,484
Tammie Green	71	71	72	214	4,484
Katie Peterson-Parker	69	72	73	214	4,484
Patty Sheehan	71	68	75	214	4,484
Kim Williams	69	70	75	214	4,484
Catrin Nilsmark	67	71	76	214	4,484

PING Welch's Championship

Blue Hill Country Club, Canton, Massachusetts
Par 36-36—72; 6,137 yards

August 10-13
purse, $450,000

	SCORES				TOTAL	MONEY
Beth Daniel	65	68	69	69	271	$67,500
Meg Mallon	68	68	70	68	274	36,230
Colleen Walker	67	68	67	72	274	36,230
Betsy King	69	72	68	66	275	21,511
Jane Geddes	65	71	71	68	275	21,511
Maggie Will	70	69	68	69	276	15,850
Elaine Crosby	70	70	73	66	279	13,360
Missie McGeorge	72	70	70	68	280	9,691
Dottie Mochrie	72	71	68	69	280	9,691
Jill Briles-Hinton	72	69	70	69	280	9,691
Sharon Barrett	70	68	73	69	280	9,691
Julie Larsen	66	72	72	70	280	9,691
Stephanie Maynor	72	69	69	71	281	7,472
Dale Eggeling	71	74	69	68	282	5,984
Catrin Nilsmark	69	75	69	69	282	5,984
Tracy Kerdyk	70	69	73	70	282	5,984
Brandie Burton	73	72	65	72	282	5,984
Tonya Gill	72	71	67	72	282	5,984
Barb Thomas	73	69	68	72	282	5,984
Emilee Klein	69	72	69	72	282	5,984
Alicia Dibos	71	75	69	68	283	4,669
Dina Ammaccapane	71	71	73	68	283	4,669
Sally Little	71	69	73	70	283	4,669
Katie Peterson-Parker	69	71	72	71	283	4,669
Margaret Platt	72	74	69	69	284	3,917
Deb Richard	70	72	73	69	284	3,917
Pat Bradley	70	74	70	70	284	3,917
Sue Thomas	72	71	71	70	284	3,917
Tammie Green	68	72	73	71	284	3,917
Liselotte Neumann	68	72	70	74	284	3,917

du Maurier Ltd. Classic

Beaconsfield Golf Club, Ponte-Claire, Quebec, Canada
Par 36-36–72; 6,261 yards

August 24-27
purse, $1,000,000

	SCORES				TOTAL	MONEY
Jenny Lidback	71	69	68	72	280	$150,000
Liselotte Neumann	71	66	72	72	281	93,093
Juli Inkster	72	71	70	70	283	67,933
Tammie Green	75	71	68	70	284	52,837
Betsy King	76	70	67	72	285	38,998
Jane Geddes	71	73	69	72	285	38,998
Michelle Estill	73	77	69	67	286	27,928
Laurie Rinker-Graham	71	71	70	74	286	27,928
Helen Alfredsson	76	70	70	71	287	21,314
Danielle Ammaccapane	76	71	68	72	287	21,314
Hollis Stacy	73	73	69	72	287	21,314
Dottie Mochrie	74	73	72	69	288	16,136
Meg Mallon	73	72	73	70	288	16,136
Val Skinner	74	72	71	71	288	16,136
Kris Tschetter	75	70	71	72	288	16,136
Rosie Jones	79	70	73	67	289	13,369
Joan Pitcock	76	70	69	74	289	13,369
Emilee Klein	79	71	69	71	290	11,859
Cindy Schreyer	73	74	72	71	290	11,859
Hiromi Kobayashi	76	70	72	72	290	11,859
Dana Dormann	74	72	72	72	290	11,859
Cindy Rarick	73	72	75	71	291	10,180
Tracy Kerdyk	76	72	71	72	291	10,180
Patty Jordan	72	72	74	73	291	10,180
Michele Redman	75	75	75	67	292	8,442
Amy Fruhwirth	77	72	75	68	292	8,442
Kathryn Marshall	74	75	73	70	292	8,442
Elaine Crosby	73	72	76	71	292	8,442
Julie Larsen	76	72	72	72	292	8,442
Pat Hurst	73	72	74	73	292	8,442
Barb Scherbak	73	74	70	75	292	8,442
Patty Sheehan	66	77	74	75	292	8,442

State Farm Rail Classic

Rail Golf Club, Springfield, Illinois
Par 36-36–72; 6,403 yards

September 2-4
purse, $550,000

	SCORES			TOTAL	MONEY
Mary Beth Zimmerman	72	69	65	206	$82,500
Emilee Klein	67	67	72	206	51,201
(Zimmerman defeated Klein on second extra hole.)					
Colleen Walker	71	68	68	207	29,982
Leta Lindley	71	66	70	207	29,982
Betsy King	67	67	73	207	29,982
Beth Daniel	69	67	72	208	19,373
Michelle McGann	72	68	69	209	16,328
Nancy Lopez	71	69	70	210	14,391
Stephanie Maynor	71	71	69	211	12,316
Meg Mallon	68	71	72	211	12,316
Stefania Croce	74	70	68	212	9,188
Moira Dunn	70	73	69	212	9,188

	SCORES			TOTAL	MONEY
Jenny Lidback	72	70	70	212	9,188
Becky Iverson	69	72	71	212	9,188
Eva Dahllof	68	71	73	212	9,188
Hiromi Kobayashi	75	71	67	213	6,918
Danielle Ammaccapane	73	70	70	213	6,918
Robin Hood	70	73	70	213	6,918
Allison Finney	74	66	73	213	6,918
Tina Paternostro	71	68	74	213	6,918
Barb Thomas	70	75	69	214	5,069
Marianne Morris	73	71	70	214	5,069
Catriona Matthew	70	74	70	214	5,069
Laurel Kean	71	72	71	214	5,069
Cindy Schreyer	71	71	72	214	5,069
Alice Ritzman	71	71	72	214	5,069
Alicia Dibos	70	72	72	214	5,069
Kristi Albers	74	67	73	214	5,069
Kelly Robbins	72	69	73	214	5,069
Kathryn Marshall	69	72	73	214	5,069
Amy Fruhwirth	71	69	74	214	5,069

PING AT&T Wireless Services Championship

Columbia Edgewater Country Club, Portland, Oregon
Par 36-36–72; 6,319 yards

September 8-10
purse, $500,000

	SCORES			TOTAL	MONEY
Alison Nicholas	66	73	68	207	$75,000
Kelly Robbins	73	67	70	210	46,546
Vicki Goetze	73	68	70	211	33,966
Betsy King	74	71	67	212	23,902
Rosie Jones	68	73	71	212	23,902
Tracy Hanson	72	70	71	213	15,179
Laurie Brower	72	69	72	213	15,179
Patty Sheehan	70	69	74	213	15,179
Laura Davies	75	73	66	214	9,812
Joan Pitcock	70	75	69	214	9,812
Dale Eggeling	72	71	71	214	9,812
Hiromi Kobayashi	70	73	71	214	9,812
Alicia Dibos	70	70	74	214	9,812
Stephanie Maynor	72	72	71	215	6,509
Cindy Rarick	69	75	71	215	6,509
Danielle Ammaccapane	70	73	72	215	6,509
Jane Geddes	72	70	73	215	6,509
Missie McGeorge	71	71	73	215	6,509
Moira Dunn	70	72	73	215	6,509
Becky Iverson	71	70	74	215	6,509
Jenny Lidback	68	72	75	215	6,509
Cindy Schreyer	70	73	73	216	4,987
Mitzi Edge	75	67	74	216	4,987
Barb Mucha	71	68	77	216	4,987
Stefania Croce	68	71	77	216	4,987
Pam Wright	75	73	69	217	4,129
Marianne Morris	74	74	69	217	4,129
Val Skinner	73	74	70	217	4,129
Elaine Crosby	72	73	72	217	4,129
Michelle McGann	69	76	72	217	4,129
Mardi Lunn	71	73	73	217	4,129
Jean Zedlitz	75	68	74	217	4,129

Safeco Classic

Meridian Valley Country Club, Kent, Washington
Par 36-36–72; 6,234 yards

September 14-17
purse, $500,000

	SCORES				TOTAL	MONEY
Patty Sheehan	68	65	70	71	274	$75,000
Emilee Klein	73	65	71	67	276	46,546
Alison Nicholas	68	70	70	69	277	33,966
Liselotte Neumann	68	69	68	74	279	26,418
Jane Geddes	68	72	67	73	280	21,386
Annika Sorenstam	76	70	67	68	281	15,179
Moira Dunn	72	74	66	69	281	15,179
Julie Larsen	70	70	69	72	281	15,179
Rosie Jones	72	70	72	68	282	10,651
Pam Wright	73	70	70	69	282	10,651
Mitzi Edge	67	70	71	74	282	10,651
Tammie Green	71	72	70	70	283	8,051
Beth Daniel	71	71	71	70	283	8,051
Nancy Ramsbottom	70	72	71	70	283	8,051
Laura Davies	69	72	71	71	283	8,051
Dale Eggeling	73	72	72	67	284	6,289
Vicki Fergon	76	69	70	69	284	6,289
Leta Lindley	70	73	71	70	284	6,289
Caroline Pierce	70	74	68	72	284	6,289
Dottie Mochrie	72	69	70	73	284	6,289
Cindy Figg-Currier	70	73	72	70	285	4,927
Martha Richards	72	69	74	70	285	4,927
Barb Mucha	70	74	70	71	285	4,927
Meg Mallon	74	69	71	71	285	4,927
Danielle Ammaccapane	71	71	72	71	285	4,927
Michelle Estill	71	71	70	73	285	4,927
Jenny Lidback	68	70	73	74	285	4,927
Jodi Renner	72	72	75	67	286	4,126
Kim Williams	73	72	73	68	286	4,126
Carin Hjalmarsson	70	73	72	71	286	4,126

GHP Heartland Classic

Forest Hills Country Club, St. Louis, Missouri
Par 36-36–72; 6,375 yards

September 21-24
purse, $525,000

	SCORES				TOTAL	MONEY
Annika Sorenstam	69	67	70	72	278	$78,750
Jan Stephenson	71	76	69	72	288	48,873
Dale Eggeling	74	74	71	70	289	35,664
Michele Redman	73	70	74	73	290	22,895
Tracy Hanson	68	75	74	73	290	22,895
Pat Hurst	71	74	71	74	290	22,895
Mitzi Edge	73	72	71	75	291	15,586
Leta Lindley	74	77	69	72	292	11,821
Nancy Ramsbottom	72	76	72	72	292	11,821
Mardi Lunn	73	72	75	72	292	11,821
Tina Barrett	75	70	73	74	292	11,821
Cindy Rarick	77	73	73	70	293	8,717
Cathy Johnston-Forbes	72	74	75	72	293	8,717
Page Dunlap	71	71	78	73	293	8,717
Danielle Ammaccapane	74	76	76	68	294	6,780

	SCORES				TOTAL	MONEY
Kris Tschetter	74	76	75	69	294	6,780
Wendy Ward	78	72	74	70	294	6,780
Kelly Robbins	78	73	72	71	294	6,780
Amy Fruhwirth	75	71	75	73	294	6,780
Robin Walton	74	73	69	78	294	6,780
Janice Gibson	74	75	73	73	295	5,679
Renee Heiken	71	72	78	74	295	5,679
Stephanie Maynor	77	72	74	73	296	5,133
Nancy Lopez	76	72	75	73	296	5,133
Sherri Turner	72	72	74	78	296	5,133
Muffin Spencer-Devlin	78	71	78	70	297	4,051
Kristi Albers	77	75	73	72	297	4,051
Vicki Fergon	76	75	73	73	297	4,051
Nancy Harvey	72	75	77	73	297	4,051
Suzanne Strudwick	77	74	72	74	297	4,051
Kim Williams	70	77	76	74	297	4,051
Jodi Renner	75	76	71	75	297	4,051
Laurie Rinker-Graham	72	78	71	76	297	4,051
Catriona Matthew	72	74	75	76	297	4,051
Hiromi Kobayashi	71	75	74	77	297	4,051
Liselotte Neumann	70	73	76	78	297	4,051

Fieldcrest Cannon Classic

Peninsula Country Club, Charlotte, North Carolina
Par 36-36–72; 6,328 yards

September 28-October 1
purse, $500,000

	SCORES				TOTAL	MONEY
Gail Graham	67	68	69	69	273	$75,000
Tammie Green	67	71	67	70	275	46,546
Juli Inkster	67	71	70	69	277	27,256
Karen Lunn	70	67	71	69	277	27,256
Hiromi Kobayashi	65	71	69	72	277	27,256
Helen Alfredsson	66	73	72	68	279	17,612
Jane Geddes	72	68	72	68	280	12,579
Moira Dunn	72	69	70	69	280	12,579
Nancy Lopez	68	70	71	71	280	12,579
Stephanie Farwig	71	72	65	72	280	12,579
Colleen Walker	71	71	71	68	281	8,617
Tracy Hanson	69	72	71	69	281	8,617
Brandie Burton	69	69	70	73	281	8,617
Beth Daniel	66	71	71	73	281	8,617
Vicki Fergon	70	69	74	69	282	6,876
Emilee Klein	71	70	71	70	282	6,876
Sally Little	70	71	70	71	282	6,876
Pat Hurst	68	70	76	69	283	5,450
Laura Baugh	68	72	73	70	283	5,450
Meg Mallon	72	71	69	71	283	5,450
Amy Fruhwirth	67	72	73	71	283	5,450
Danielle Ammaccapane	70	72	69	72	283	5,450
Eva Dahllof	71	70	70	72	283	5,450
Rosie Jones	70	70	71	72	283	5,450
Elaine Crosby	67	71	72	73	283	5,450
Liselotte Neumann	71	73	72	68	284	4,428
Suzy Green	70	71	71	72	284	4,428
Leta Lindley	70	70	71	73	284	4,428
Kim Saiki	69	70	77	69	285	3,709

	SCORES				TOTAL	MONEY
Marianne Morris	71	72	72	70	285	3,709
Pat Bradley	69	74	72	70	285	3,709
Lori West	72	71	71	71	285	3,709
Carin Hjalmarsson	70	71	73	71	285	3,709
Lisa Walters	70	74	69	72	285	3,709
Cindy Schreyer	69	71	71	74	285	3,709

Samsung World Championship of Women's Golf

Paradise Golf Club, Cheji Island, South Korea
Par 36-36–72; 6,188 yards

October 12-15
purse, $475,000

	SCORES				TOTAL	MONEY
Annika Sorenstam	72	69	71	70	282	$117,500
Laura Davies	67	71	71	73	282	65,000
(Sorenstam defeated Davies on first extra hole.)						
Dottie Mochrie	72	68	72	72	284	40,000
Pat Bradley	68	70	76	72	286	30,000
Meg Mallon	73	72	71	71	287	22,500
Rosie Jones	67	73	72	75	287	22,500
Val Skinner	70	69	77	72	288	18,000
Betsy King	68	70	77	74	289	17,000
Tammie Green	69	72	74	75	290	16,000
Jenny Lidback	71	71	74	75	291	15,000
Beth Daniel	71	68	76	79	294	14,500
Ikuyo Shiotani	74	72	77	73	296	14,000
Kris Tschetter	73	74	73	78	298	13,500
Oh-Soon Lee	72	75	79	74	300	13,000
Michelle McGann	76	74	77	74	301	12,812
Nanci Bowen	73	71	79	78	301	12,812

JCPenney Classic

Innisbrook Hilton Resort, Tarpon Springs, Florida
Par 36-35–71; 6,394 yards

November 30-December 3
purse, $1,300,000

	SCORES				TOTAL	MONEY (Each)
Davis Love III/Beth Daniel	66	65	63	63	257	$162,500
Robert Gamez/Helen Alfredsson	63	67	65	64	259	79,000
Jesper Parnevik/Annika Sorenstam	67	66	64	63	260	52,000
Mark McCumber/Laura Davis	63	65	67	67	262	39,500
Jay Delsing/Val Skinner	62	67	65	69	263	29,750
Kenny Perry/Michelle McGann	69	63	68	64	264	22,755
Michael Bradley/Katie Peterson-Parker	63	68	64	69	264	22,755
Billy Mayfair/Brandie Burton	69	68	64	64	265	14,406.67
John Huston/Liselotte Neumann	66	68	64	67	265	14,406.67
Billy Andrade/Kris Tschetter	66	65	65	69	265	14,406.67
Bill Glasson/Kelly Robbins	70	65	66	65	266	10,275
Dan Forsman/Pam Wright	64	67	67	68	266	10,275
Doug Martin/Carin Hjalmarsson	66	64	69	68	267	8,390
Steve Jones/Barb Thomas	65	65	68	69	267	8,390
Glen Day/Melissa McNamara	68	63	67	69	267	8,390
Bob Lohr/Marianne Morris	68	64	66	69	267	8,390
Jim Gallagher/Jackie Gallagher-Smith	65	70	66	67	268	6,230

	SCORES				TOTAL	MONEY (Each)
Brad Bryant/Marta Figueras-Dotti	70	64	65	69	268	6,230
Jay Haas/Cathy Gerring	66	68	63	71	268	6,230
Gene Sauers/Hollis Stacy	64	66	65	73	268	6,230
Steve Stricker/Vicki Goetze	65	65	67	72	269	5,300
Kirk Triplett/Julie Larsen	66	67	68	69	270	5,000
Gary Koch/Tammie Green	67	66	68	69	270	5,000
Mike Brisky/Barb Mucha	68	67	66	69	270	5,000
John Adams/Alice Miller	65	66	67	62	270	5,000
Mark Brooks/Cindy Figg-Currier	67	68	67	69	271	4,395
Jeff Sluman/Dottie Mochrie	67	69	66	69	271	4,395
Curt Byrum/Jan Stephenson	68	69	66	68	271	4,395
Jim Furyk/Lisa Kiggens	68	70	65	68	271	4,395
Dillard Pruitt/Amy Fruhwirth	66	69	69	67	271	4,395
Marco Dawson/Elaine Crosby	66	70	70	65	271	4,395
Tom Purtzer/Juli Inkster	67	73	66	65	271	4,395
Jim McGovern/Dale Eggeling	68	68	67	69	272	3,850
Fred Funk/Tina Barrett	70	67	68	67	272	3,850
Larry Rinker/Laurie Rinker-Graham	66	70	68	69	273	3,627.50
Jim Albus/Margaret Platt	67	70	67	69	273	3,627.50
Nolan Henke/Terry-Jo Myers	69	67	67	71	274	3,233.75
Brian Claar/Jane Geddes	67	68	69	70	274	3,233.75
Woody Austin/Page Dunlap	67	70	68	69	274	3,233.75
Jonathan Kaye/Tracy Hanson	67	66	65	76	274	3,233.75
Robin Freeman/Amy Alcott	67	70	69	68	274	3,233.75
John Mahaffey/Cindy Rarick	68	70	68	68	274	3,233.75
Jay Overton/Tracy Kerdyk	69	69	68	68	274	3,233.75
D.A. Weibring/Chris Johnson	69	67	71	67	274	3,233.75
Lee Rinker/Colleen Walker	68	69	69	69	275	3,000
Guy Boros/Michele Redman	69	70	68	69	276	2,925
Mike Hulbert/Donna Andrews	67	72	69	68	276	2,925
Scott Gump/Karen Weiss	69	70	67	71	277	2,850
Jim Dent/Kim Williams	67	68	70	73	278	2,800
Tom Wargo/Nancy Scranton	68	70	70	72	280	2,750
Jay Don Blake/Emilee Klein	70	71	68	76	285	2,700
Larry Laoretti/Karen Noble	72	73	70	72	287	2,650

Diners Club Matches

PGA West, Jack Nicklaus Course, La Quinta, California
Par 36-36—72; 6,546 yards

December 8-10
purse, $610,000

FIRST ROUND

Kelly Robbins and Tammie Green defeated Jenny Lidback and Alicia Dibos, 3 and 2
Nanci Bowen and Annika Sorenstam defeated Beth Daniel and Meg Mallon, 1 up, 19 holes
Laura Davies and Mardi Lunn defeated Michelle McGann and Donna Andrews, 4 and 3
Dottie Mochrie and Juli Inkster defeated Betsy King and Val Skinner, 1 up

(Losers in first round received $15,000 each.)

SECOND ROUND

Robbins and Green defeated Bowen and Sorenstam, 3 and 2
Davies and Lunn defeated Mochrie and Inkster, 2 and 1

(Losers in second round received $35,000 each.)

THIRD ROUND

Robbins and Green defeated Davies and Lunn, 1 up

(Robbins and Green received $125,000 each; Davies and Lunn received $50,000 each.)

Women's European Tour

Ladies' Open Costa Azul

Montado Golf Club
Par 36-36–72; 5,986 yards

May 11-13
purse, £55,000

Troia Golf Club
Par 36-36–72; 5,996 yards
Lisbon, Portugal

	SCORES			TOTAL	MONEY
Marie Laure de Lorenzi	72	67	66	205	£8,250
Evelyn Orley	68	72	67	207	5,580
Corinne Dibnah	67	72	69	208	3,850
Karrie Webb	67	76	69	212	2,970
Lora Fairclough	73	67	73	213	2,127.50
Valerie Michaud	69	69	75	213	2,127.50
Stephanie Dallongeville	73	73	69	215	1,418.33
Patricia Meunier	74	70	71	215	1,418.33
Sarah Bennett	76	70	69	215	1,418.33
Kitrina Douglas	74	72	70	216	917.71
Debbie Dowling	75	71	70	216	917.71
Susan Hodge	73	68	75	216	917.71
Karina Orum	72	75	69	216	917.71
Alison Brighouse	72	72	72	216	917.71
Petra Rigby	71	70	75	216	917.71
Lisa Hackney	72	72	72	216	917.71
Helena Koch	75	76	66	217	759
Shani Waugh	71	76	70	217	759
Kathryn Marshall	69	76	72	217	759
Federica Dassu	75	74	69	218	698
Estefania Knuth	75	76	67	218	698
Martina Koch	78	70	70	218	698
Dale Reid	75	73	71	219	639
Mandy Sutton	73	74	72	219	639
Amaia Arruti	70	76	73	219	639
Aideen Rogers	72	75	72	219	639
Claire Duffy	73	76	71	220	559.16
Susan Moon	71	77	72	220	559.16
Mary Grace Estuesta	77	75	68	220	559.16
Caroline Hall	75	73	72	220	559.16
Rachel Hetherington	71	76	73	220	559.16
Joanne Morley	70	78	72	220	559.16

Ford Classic

Chart Hills Golf Club, Kent, England
Par 36-36–72; 5,845 yards

May 18-21
purse, £110,000

	SCORES				TOTAL	MONEY
Lora Fairclough	70	68	71	68	277	£16,500
Florence Descampe	69	67	72	70	278	11,125
Carin Hjalmarsson	71	69	75	66	281	7,700
Laura Davies	73	73	67	69	282	5,302
Dale Reid	72	73	66	71	282	5,302
Marie Laure de Lorenzi	71	74	69	69	283	2,912.80
Corinne Dibnah	74	73	69	67	283	2,912.80
Trish Johnson	71	71	69	72	283	2,912.80
Tracy Loveys	68	73	73	69	283	2,912.80
Karrie Webb	70	70	74	69	283	2,912.80
Karen Davies	72	72	70	70	284	2,024
Martina Koch	72	71	70	72	285	1,831.50
Helen Wadsworth	75	71	71	68	285	1,831.50
Sally Prosser	72	70	74	70	286	1,677.50
Karen Pearce	76	70	69	71	286	1,677.50
Estefania Knuth	69	73	71	74	287	1,499.50
Karina Orum	71	74	72	70	287	1,499.50
Patricia Meunier	76	69	69	73	287	1,499.50
Alison Brighouse	76	68	71	72	287	1,499.50
Julie Forbes	74	70	69	74	287	1,499.50
Evelyn Orley	72	70	73	72	287	1,499.50
Shani Waugh	74	68	73	73	288	1,347.50
Kathryn Marshall	74	73	68	73	288	1,347.50
Wendy Doolan	70	74	70	75	289	1,298
Diane Barnard	71	70	74	75	290	1,199
Janet Soulsby	74	71	74	71	290	1,199
Lara Tadiotto	73	73	72	72	290	1,199
Caroline Hall	72	72	70	76	290	1,199
Deborah Eckroth	71	75	74	70	290	1,199
Debbie Dowling	75	72	70	74	291	1,050.50
Amaia Arruti	73	74	70	74	291	1,050.50
Laura Navarro	72	73	71	75	291	1,050.50
Sara Robinson	76	72	75	68	291	1,050.50

Evian Masters

Royal Golf Club Evian, Evian, France
Par 36-36–72; 5,827 yards

June 8-11
purse, £275,000

	SCORES				TOTAL	MONEY
Laura Davies	68	67	69	67	271	£40,630
Annika Sorenstam	68	72	68	68	276	27,750
Catrin Nilsmark	68	69	70	70	277	19,255
Alison Nicholas	71	66	72	70	279	14,755
Corinne Dibnah	70	70	70	72	282	11,600
Trish Johnson	68	71	72	72	283	8,196.66
Carin Hjalmarsson	70	72	71	70	283	8,196.66
Helen Wadsworth	67	72	73	71	283	8,196.66
Mardi Lunn	70	72	70	72	284	5,792.50
Evelyn Orley	71	71	74	68	284	5,792.50
*Kristel Mourgue D'Algue	71	73	72	68	284	
Diane Barnard	74	70	71	70	285	5,000

	SCORES				TOTAL	MONEY
Karrie Webb	76	71	69	70	286	4,680
Marie Laure de Lorenzi	72	75	69	71	287	4,203.75
Charlotta Sorenstam	73	69	73	72	287	4,203.75
Stephanie Dallongeville	72	71	74	70	287	4,203.75
Helen Alfredsson	76	71	68	72	287	4,203.75
Sofia Gronberg	70	72	74	72	288	3,855
Lisa Hackney	68	72	73	75	288	3,855
Laurette Maritz-Atkins	74	68	77	70	289	3,705
Karine Espinasse	76	69	73	72	290	3,605
Karen Davies	75	70	72	74	291	3,417.50
Asa Gottmo	77	73	71	70	291	3,417.50
Lora Fairclough	71	72	70	78	291	3,417.50
Karen Pearce	71	72	75	74	292	3,067.50
Mette Hageman	75	72	73	72	292	3,067.50
Amaia Arruti	72	71	76	73	292	3,067.50
Caroline Hall	74	72	76	70	292	3,067.50
*Amandine Vincent	73	74	71	74	292	
Maria Bertilskold	70	76	75	71	292	3,067.50

OVB Damen Open

Golf Club Europa-Sportregion Zell am See, Salzburg, Austria
Par 36-37–73; 6,008 yards

June 15-18
purse, £100,000

	SCORES				TOTAL	MONEY
Annika Sorenstam	66	69	67	68	270	£15,000
Laura Davies	70	67	70	66	273	10,150
Corinne Dibnah	67	69	70	68	274	7,000
Sally Prosser	70	69	65	71	275	5,400
Marie Laure de Lorenzi	69	69	69	71	278	3,580
Mardi Lunn	68	74	69	67	278	3,580
Karrie Webb	72	68	68	70	278	3,580
Wendy Doolan	66	71	74	68	279	2,246.66
Helen Wadsworth	68	71	68	72	279	2,246.66
Evelyn Orley	68	67	74	70	279	2,246.66
Sofia Gronberg	74	68	70	69	281	1,723.33
Raquel Carriedo-Tomas	68	71	73	69	281	1,723.33
Lisa Hackney	74	67	73	67	281	1,723.33
Laurette Maritz-Atkins	65	74	70	73	282	1,550
Diane Barnard	69	69	72	73	283	1,500
Susan Moon	70	71	74	70	285	1,380
Florence Descampe	72	68	71	74	285	1,380
Karen Davies	70	73	71	71	285	1,380
Amaia Arruti	70	73	72	70	285	1,380
Joanne Morley	73	70	71	71	285	1,380
Rachel Hetherington	71	72	69	74	286	1,255
Lora Fairclough	70	72	72	72	286	1,255
Xonia Wunsch-Ruiz	74	68	72	73	287	1,210
Petra Rigby	75	69	71	73	288	1,165
Tina Fischer	70	72	75	71	288	1,165
Wendy Dicks	75	69	74	71	289	1,060
Karina Orum	74	71	72	72	289	1,060
Natascha Fink	75	71	74	69	289	1,060
Helen Dobson	74	71	73	71	289	1,060
Marina Arruti	74	73	73	69	289	1,060

European Masters

Cleydael Golf Club, Antwerp, Belgium
Par 36-36–72; 5,794 yards

June 23-25
purse, £150,000

	SCORES			TOTAL	MONEY
Lora Fairclough	71	67	68	206	£22,500
Federica Dassu	66	72	70	208	15,225
Alison Nicholas	66	69	74	209	10,500
Natascha Fink	74	68	69	211	8,100
Laurette Maritz-Atkins	76	70	66	212	5,370
Karina Orum	71	70	71	212	5,370
Mette Hageman	72	71	69	212	5,370
Rachel Hetherington	70	71	72	213	3,555
Karrie Webb	72	73	68	213	3,555
Karine Espinasse	69	74	71	214	2,688.75
Karen Davies	71	71	72	214	2,688.75
Amaia Arruti	73	70	71	214	2,688.75
Evelyn Orley	72	71	71	214	2,688.75
Helen Dobson	74	71	70	215	2,325
Marie Laure de Lorenzi	73	74	69	216	2,072.14
Sally Prosser	71	71	74	216	2,072.14
Wendy Doolan	72	76	68	216	2,072.14
Stephanie Dallongeville	75	71	70	216	2,072.14
Patricia Meunier	74	71	71	216	2,072.14
Alison Brighouse	72	69	75	216	2,072.14
Joanne Morley	70	72	74	216	2,072.14
Allison Shapcott	74	73	71	218	1,680
Estefania Knuth	76	72	70	218	1,680
Sarah Nicklin	75	69	74	218	1,680
Caroline Hall	71	71	76	218	1,680
Lynette Brooky	74	71	73	218	1,680
Petra Rigby	74	73	71	218	1,680
Loraine Lambert	74	72	72	218	1,680
Helen Wadsworth	73	70	75	218	1,680
Kirsty Speak	75	74	69	218	1,680

Hennessy Cup

Golf und Landklub Koln, Bladbach, Germany
Par 36-36–72; 6,177 yards

June 29-July 2
purse, £300,000

	SCORES				TOTAL	MONEY
Annika Sorenstam	68	70	65	68	271	£45,000
Trish Johnson	70	66	68	68	272	25,700
Liselotte Neumann	71	68	67	66	272	25,700
Marie Laure de Lorenzi	69	70	67	69	275	16,150
Jane Geddes	67	69	72	69	277	12,700
Alison Nicholas	69	70	70	69	278	10,500
Helen Alfredsson	73	67	69	70	279	9,000
Rachel Hetherington	70	69	70	71	280	7,500
Karina Orum	71	66	72	72	281	6,350
Karrie Webb	71	70	71	69	281	6,350
Corinne Dibnah	70	67	74	71	282	5,163.33
Wendy Doolan	65	68	72	77	282	5,163.33
Helen Wadsworth	72	66	73	71	282	5,163.33
Diane Barnard	73	72	70	68	283	4,490
Mardi Lunn	72	71	68	72	283	4,490

	SCORES				TOTAL	MONEY
Joanne Morley	70	70	70	73	283	4,490
Helen Dobson	72	73	68	70	283	4,490
Evelyn Orley	68	72	70	73	283	4,490
Gillian Stewart	72	70	70	72	284	4,160
Sofia Gronberg	69	73	68	76	286	4,050
Karine Espinasse	75	70	70	72	287	3,775
Sally Prosser	73	66	75	73	287	3,775
Mette Hageman	69	74	72	72	287	3,775
Patricia Meunier	73	72	68	74	287	3,775
Dale Reid	71	74	72	71	288	3,400
Karen Davies	68	75	70	75	288	3,400
Julie Forbes	72	70	74	72	288	3,400
Stefania Croce	73	72	73	71	289	3,150
Liz Weima	78	69	68	74	289	3,150
Maureen Madill	72	75	74	69	290	2,750
Laurette Maritz-Atkins	71	71	75	73	290	2,750
Florence Descampe	76	73	71	70	290	2,750
Shani Waugh	72	72	72	74	290	2,750
Charlotta Sorenstam	74	69	74	73	290	2,750
Jill McGill	72	72	76	70	290	2,750

Guardian Irish Holidays Open

St. Margaret's Golf & Country Club, Co. Dublin, Ireland   July 27-30
Par 37-36–73; 6,044 yards   purse, £100,000

	SCORES				TOTAL	MONEY
Laura Davies	67	66	66	68	267	£15,000
Asa Gottmo	69	74	69	71	283	10,150
Lora Fairclough	69	73	71	74	286	7,000
Jill McGill	67	74	72	75	288	5,400
Gillian Stewart	69	73	74	73	289	3,580
Shani Waugh	70	76	71	72	289	3,580
Martina Koch	70	72	73	74	289	3,580
Patricia Meunier	70	74	74	72	290	2,246.66
Helen Wadsworth	70	78	71	71	290	2,246.66
Lisa Hackney	70	71	75	74	290	2,246.66
Trish Johnson	71	78	69	73	291	1,840
Karina Orum	71	72	74	75	292	1,720
Claire Duffy	73	76	70	74	293	1,553.33
Emma-Jane Smith	67	76	76	74	293	1,553.33
Rachel Hetherington	73	73	75	72	293	1,553.33
Federica Dassu	69	78	72	75	294	1,344.28
Dale Reid	74	68	77	75	294	1,344.28
Suzanne Strudwick	71	71	73	79	294	1,344.28
Lana Freund	73	76	74	71	294	1,344.28
Natascha Fink	77	69	76	72	294	1,344.28
Laura Navarro	70	73	73	78	294	1,344.28
Amy DuBois	74	74	76	70	294	1,344.28
Debbie Dowling	71	73	74	77	295	1,120
Linda Percival	69	74	75	77	295	1,120
Wendy Dicks	73	74	75	73	295	1,120
Charlotta Sorenstam	69	79	71	76	295	1,120
Sophie Gustafson	71	74	75	75	295	1,120
Julie Forbes	70	76	76	73	295	1,120
Evelyn Orley	72	73	74	76	295	1,120
Penny Grice-Whittaker	72	77	72	75	296	895

	SCORES				TOTAL	MONEY
Mette Hageman	71	73	77	75	296	895
Liz Weima	73	72	73	78	296	895
Nicola Buxton	73	73	74	76	296	895
Raquel Carriedo-Tomas	73	73	74	76	296	895
Loraine Lambert	74	73	72	77	296	895
Karrie Webb	74	75	74	73	296	895
Deborah Eckroth	75	68	80	73	296	895

Payne & Gunter Scottish Open

Dalmahoy Hotel Country Club Resort, Edinburgh, Scotland   August 3-6
Par 36-36–72; 6,202 yards   purse, £75,000

	SCORES				TOTAL	MONEY
Alison Nicholas	66	67	70	69	272	£11,250
Patricia Meunier	65	71	68	69	273	7,610
Marie Laure de Lorenzi	66	70	70	68	274	5,250
Laura Davies	72	71	68	67	278	3,615
Corinne Dibnah	69	69	72	68	278	3,615
Trish Johnson	68	70	71	70	279	2,625
*Janice Moodie	70	73	69	69	281	
Kathryn Marshall	72	71	71	68	282	2,250
Joanne Morley	72	70	68	73	283	1,875
Laurette Maritz-Atkins	74	72	70	68	284	1,520
Sally Prosser	70	71	69	74	284	1,520
Evelyn Orley	69	72	69	74	284	1,520
Karrie Webb	69	72	72	72	285	1,290
Estefania Knuth	69	73	74	70	286	1,184.50
Helen Wadsworth	74	68	72	72	286	1,184.50
Dale Reid	76	68	71	72	287	1,095
Karina Orum	73	69	74	71	287	1,095
Malin Landehag	71	71	69	76	287	1,095
Penny Grice-Whittaker	75	70	73	70	288	979.20
Wendy Doolan	70	72	76	70	288	979.20
Aideen Rogers	70	73	74	71	288	979.20
Julie Forbes	73	69	73	73	288	979.20
Jill McGill	69	73	71	75	288	979.20
Gillian Stewart	74	72	74	69	289	860
Helene Koch	69	72	76	72	289	860
Caroline Hall	70	71	77	71	289	860
Nicola Moult	69	72	76	72	289	860
Fiona Pike	72	73	68	76	289	860
Diane Barnard	68	71	76	75	290	734
Shani Waugh	73	74	72	71	290	734
Sarah Burnell	71	75	70	74	290	734
Franca Fehlauer	72	74	70	74	290	734
Sarah Bennett	78	69	71	72	290	734
Lisa Hackney	73	73	72	72	290	734

Woodpecker Welsh Open

St. Pierre Hotel Country Club Resort, Chepstow, Wales
Par 36-36–72; 6,204 yards

August 10-13
purse, £60,000

		SCORES			TOTAL	MONEY
Laura Davies	68	69	71	70	278	£9,000
Wendy Doolan	67	72	71	71	281	6,090
Marie Laure de Lorenzi	70	70	70	72	282	3,720
Mardi Lunn	74	70	70	68	282	3,720
Trish Johnson	68	70	73	75	286	2,322
Dale Reid	76	70	70	70	286	2,322
Amaia Arruti	68	70	76	73	287	1,650
Joanne Morley	70	70	73	74	287	1,650
Alison Nicholas	73	71	72	72	288	1,344
Corinne Dibnah	68	74	70	77	289	1,112
Barbara Pestana	73	73	70	73	289	1,112
Rachel Hetherington	71	73	72	73	289	1,112
Karina Orum	72	75	71	72	290	966
Annika Sorenstam	70	74	74	73	291	902
Tina Fischer	70	74	73	74	291	902
Evelyn Orley	76	68	75	72	291	902
Asa Gottmo	76	70	74	72	292	828
Helen Wadsworth	67	77	74	74	292	828
Karrie Webb	74	71	76	71	292	828
Sally Prosser	74	72	76	71	293	762
Laura Navarro	72	72	77	72	293	762
Jill McGill	74	72	71	76	293	762
Valerie Michaud	74	71	73	76	294	726
Petra Rigby	73	75	71	76	295	708
Sofia Gronberg	74	70	75	77	296	645
Laurette Maritz-Atkins	77	73	72	74	296	645
Gillian Stewart	77	72	71	76	296	645
Karen Davies	71	73	76	76	296	645
Kathryn Marshall	75	74	73	74	296	645
Lisa Hackney	74	72	76	74	296	645

Weetabix Women's British Open

Woburn Golf & Country Club, Milton Keynes, England
Par 35-38–73; 6,258 yards

August 17-20
purse, £360,000

		SCORES			TOTAL	MONEY
Karrie Webb	69	70	69	70	278	£60,000
Annika Sorenstam	70	72	71	71	284	30,000
Jill McGill	71	73	71	69	284	30,000
Val Skinner	74	68	67	76	285	14,333.33
Caroline Pierce	70	70	72	73	285	14,333.33
Michelle Berteotti	73	71	71	70	285	14,333.33
Suzanne Strudwick	73	68	71	74	286	9,500
Marie Laure de Lorenzi	68	74	73	73	288	6,937.50
Liselotte Neumann	67	74	71	76	288	6,937.50
Wendy Doolan	73	71	70	74	288	6,937.50
Nancy Lopez	71	73	70	74	288	6,937.50
Patricia Meunier	73	71	71	74	289	4,957.50
Vicki Goetze	73	72	71	73	289	4,957.50
Catriona Matthew	74	71	73	71	289	4,957.50
Kris Tschetter	73	75	74	67	289	4,957.50

	SCORES				TOTAL	MONEY
Sally Prosser	70	74	74	72	290	4,430
Julie Forbes	69	73	77	71	290	4,430
Hiromi Kobayashi	72	70	74	74	290	4,430
Karen Pearce	74	71	72	74	291	4,032.50
Asa Gottmo	70	73	74	74	291	4,032.50
Brandie Burton	72	70	74	75	291	4,032.50
Lynette Brooky	69	74	76	72	291	4,032.50
Rachel Hetherington	74	76	76	66	292	3,710
Joanne Morley	72	72	74	74	292	3,710
Evelyn Orley	71	73	74	74	292	3,710
Alison Nicholas	73	72	76	72	293	3,215
Mardi Lunn	73	67	73	80	293	3,215
Stephanie Dallongeville	76	72	72	73	293	3,215
Tina Fischer	76	66	77	74	293	3,215
Lora Fairclough	76	68	72	77	293	3,215
Valerie Michaud	76	73	75	69	293	3,215
Lisa Hackney	74	74	70	75	293	3,215
Marnie McGuire	68	78	73	74	293	3,215

Ford-Stimorol Danish Open

Vejle Golf Club, Vejle, Denmark
Par 36-36–72; 5,621 yards

August 25-27
purse, £60,000

	SCORES			TOTAL	MONEY
Caroline Hall	67	70	64	201	£9,000
Corinne Dibnah	67	71	71	209	6,090
Mette Hageman	72	72	68	212	3,720
Raquel Carriedo-Tomas	70	72	70	212	3,720
Dale Reid	72	74	69	215	2,322
Aideen Rogers	70	71	74	215	2,322
Maureen Madill	69	75	72	216	1,548
Barbara Pestana	72	71	73	216	1,548
Laura Navarro	71	73	72	216	1,548
Xonia Wunsch-Ruiz	77	72	68	217	1,112
Karina Orum	77	71	69	217	1,112
Anna-Carin Jonasson	73	72	72	217	1,112
*Iben Tinning	73	74	70	217	
Amaia Arruti	70	77	71	218	918
Nicola Buxton	71	75	72	218	918
Marina Arruti	76	73	69	218	918
Caroline Rasmussen	71	72	75	218	918
Nicola Moult	72	74	73	219	852
Debbie Dowling	74	74	72	220	783.60
Laree Sugg	73	74	73	220	783.60
Lynette Brooky	74	74	72	220	783.60
Denise Booker	75	73	72	220	783.60
Maria Bertilskold	77	74	69	220	783.60
Lara Tadiotto	74	73	74	221	708
Sarah Burnell	74	74	73	221	708
Sandrine Mendiburu	78	73	70	221	708
Federica Dassu	76	75	71	222	618
Sarah Nicklin	78	74	70	222	618
Lana Freund	72	77	73	222	618
Loraine Lambert	77	72	73	222	618
Valerie Michaud	75	72	75	222	618
Charlotta Eliasson Wharton	72	76	74	222	618
Kirsty Speak	73	76	73	222	618

Wilkinson Sword English Open

Oxfordshire Golf Club, Thames, England
Par 36-36–72; 6,031 yards

August 31-September 3
purse, £95,000

	SCORES				TOTAL	MONEY
Laura Davies	72	67	70	70	279	£13,500
Karina Orum	71	73	68	68	280	9,135
Wendy Dicks	67	68	72	74	281	6,300
Diane Barnard	68	73	70	71	282	3,631.50
Trish Johnson	71	68	71	72	282	3,631.50
Dale Reid	69	75	68	70	282	3,631.50
Julie Forbes	74	70	66	72	282	3,631.50
Laura Navarro	74	69	75	65	283	2,250
Marie Laure de Lorenzi	71	72	73	68	284	1,908
Joanne Morley	70	70	72	72	284	1,908
Corinne Dibnah	73	71	70	71	285	1,512
Alison Nicholas	74	70	68	73	285	1,512
Carin Hjalmarsson	70	72	71	72	285	1,512
Lora Fairclough	71	70	67	77	285	1,512
Sally Prosser	74	67	72	73	286	1,332
Aideen Rogers	76	71	70	69	286	1,332
Pernilla Sterner	71	72	71	73	287	1,260
Anna Radford	73	72	70	72	287	1,260
Rica Comstock	72	71	73	72	288	1,188
Amaia Arruti	71	68	73	76	288	1,188
Federica Dassu	69	70	74	76	289	1,089
Xonia Wunsch-Ruiz	76	67	76	70	289	1,089
Lara Tadiotto	72	71	73	73	289	1,089
Stephanie Dallongeville	74	70	75	70	289	1,089
Maria Bertilskold	70	75	73	71	289	1,089
Karen Pearce	73	75	71	71	290	954
Mette Hageman	77	71	70	72	290	954
Barbara Pestana	74	72	75	69	290	954
Caroline Hall	75	73	74	68	290	954
Isabella Maconi	71	68	75	76	290	954

Trygg Hansa Open

Haninge Golf Club, Stockholm, Sweden
Par 36-37–73; 6,188 yards

September 7-10
purse, £115,000

	SCORES				TOTAL	MONEY
Liselotte Neumann	70	71	68	72	281	£17,250
Annika Sorenstam	71	70	70	71	282	11,672.50
Lora Fairclough	71	70	73	71	285	8,050
Sophie Gustafson	72	72	68	74	286	6,210
Charlotta Sorenstam	71	69	74	74	288	4,450.50
Julie Forbes	76	73	69	70	288	4,450.50
Helen Alfredsson	70	74	76	69	289	3,450
Maureen Madill	73	76	71	70	290	2,583.66
Mette Hageman	72	71	72	75	290	2,583.66
Karrie Webb	80	72	69	69	290	2,583.66
Federica Dassu	77	71	74	70	292	1,981.83
Claire Duffy	73	72	75	72	292	1,981.83
Asa Gottmo	76	75	71	70	292	1,981.83
Anna-Carin Jonasson	75	71	76	71	293	1,753.75
Lisa Hackney	70	75	76	72	293	1,753.75

	SCORES				TOTAL	MONEY
Wendy Dicks	73	73	74	74	294	1,679
*Maria Hjorth	76	76	72	70	294	
Shani Waugh	74	75	74	72	295	1,610
Barbara Pestana	73	73	76	73	295	1,610
Caroline Hall	73	78	75	70	296	1,541
Sofia Gronberg	74	75	74	74	297	1,477.75
Susann Norberg	70	74	80	73	297	1,477.75
Aideen Rogers	73	76	75	74	298	1,426
*Anna Berg	71	76	76	75	298	
Susan Moon	75	75	75	74	299	1,305.25
Carin Hjalmarsson	76	72	76	75	299	1,305.25
Raquel Carriedo-Tomas	74	77	73	75	299	1,305.25
Rachel Hetherington	74	74	77	74	299	1,305.25
Pernilla Sterner	73	73	77	76	299	1,305.25
Maria Bertilskold	80	72	75	72	299	1,305.25

Staatsloteru Dutch Open

Rijk van Nijmegen, Groesbeek, Netherlands
Par 37-36–73; 5,981 yards

September 15-17
purse, £70,000

	SCORES			TOTAL	MONEY
Marie Laure de Lorenzi	67	66	68	201	£10,500
Lora Fairclough	71	70	69	210	7,105
Federica Dassu	70	72	69	211	3,882.66
Nicola Moult	69	71	71	211	3,882.66
Shoko Yamamoto	72	70	69	211	3,882.66
Nicola Buxton	71	71	70	212	2,275
Fiona Pike	69	71	72	212	2,275
Mette Hageman	70	70	73	213	1,442
Amaia Arruti	73	68	72	213	1,442
Lynette Brooky	71	73	69	213	1,442
Sarah Bennett	69	73	71	213	1,442
Kirsty Speak	72	72	69	213	1,442
Karina Orum	73	68	73	214	1,071
Caroline Hall	72	71	71	214	1,071
Natascha Fink	77	71	66	214	1,071
Morag Wright	69	73	72	214	1,071
Lara Tadiotto	69	74	72	215	980
Marika Preti	71	70	74	215	980
Shani Waugh	69	72	75	216	912.33
Rachel Hetherington	71	70	75	216	912.33
Karrie Webb	74	72	70	216	912.33
Diane Barnard	71	73	73	217	794.50
Rica Comstock	71	74	72	217	794.50
Claire Duffy	73	74	70	217	794.50
Tracey Craik	71	72	74	217	794.50
Mary Grace Estuesta	73	71	73	217	794.50
Petra Rigby	73	72	72	217	794.50
Franca Fehlauer	72	74	71	217	794.50
Julie Forbes	72	74	71	217	794.50
Laurette Maritz-Atkins	71	75	72	218	658
Karen Pearce	70	73	75	218	658
Liz Weima	71	75	72	218	658
Laura Navarro	76	70	72	218	658
Maria Bertilskold	74	72	72	218	658

Maredo German Open

Hotel Treudelberg Golf & Country Club, Hamburg, Germany   September 21-24
Par 36-37–73; 6,042 yards   purse, £75,000

	SCORES				TOTAL	MONEY
Rachel Hetherington	71	68	64	72	275	£11,250
Caroline Hall	72	69	68	68	277	7,610
Corinne Dibnah	72	69	68	70	279	5,250
Claire Duffy	69	70	73	68	280	4,050
Marie Laure de Lorenzi	68	71	72	70	281	2,902.50
Sandrine Mendiburu	70	71	70	70	281	2,902.50
Wendy Doolan	68	70	70	74	282	2,250
Sofia Gronberg	73	69	71	70	283	1,685
Lynette Brooky	70	69	71	73	283	1,685
Julie Forbes	68	70	71	74	283	1,685
Dale Reid	69	70	75	70	284	1,335
Jill McGill	72	72	69	71	284	1,335
Estefania Knuth	71	71	71	72	285	1,207
Evelyn Orley	67	72	74	73	286	1,162
Petra Rigby	70	74	70	73	287	1,125
Anna-Carin Jonasson	73	74	69	72	288	1,080
Pernilla Sterner	69	75	73	71	288	1,080
Janet Soulsby	70	71	75	73	289	991.75
Barbara Pestana	68	72	74	75	289	991.75
Martina Koch	71	74	77	67	289	991.75
Joanne Morley	71	71	74	73	289	991.75
Charlotta Sorenstam	74	70	73	73	290	883
Amaia Arruti	71	71	70	78	290	883
Natascha Fink	71	75	71	73	290	883
Valerie Michaud	71	72	72	75	290	883
Fiona Pike	69	76	71	74	290	883
Laurette Maritz-Atkins	72	73	72	74	291	814
Shani Waugh	72	75	72	73	292	745.20
Mette Hageman	76	73	73	70	292	745.20
Lana Freund	75	73	74	70	292	745.20
Tracy Loveys	75	71	73	73	292	745.20
Raquel Carriedo-Tomas	70	72	76	74	292	745.20

Italian Open di Sicilia

Il Picciolo Golf Club, Castiglione di Sicilia, Sicily   September 28-October 1
Par 36-37–73; 5,608 yards   purse, £100,000

	SCORES				TOTAL	MONEY
Denise Booker	70	72	72	70	284	£15,000
Amaia Arruti	71	69	73	72	285	10,150
Federica Dassu	74	73	74	68	289	7,000
Lora Fairclough	68	79	73	70	290	5,400
Karen Davies	78	67	75	72	292	3,580
Stefania Croce	77	72	71	72	292	3,580
Julie Forbes	72	70	73	77	292	3,580
Mary Grace Estuesta	72	72	73	76	293	2,500
Gillian Stewart	75	70	74	75	294	1,950
Helen Hopkins	72	75	77	70	294	1,950
Caryn Louw	72	74	72	76	294	1,950
Valerie Michaud	74	75	74	71	294	1,950
Marie Laure de Lorenzi	70	75	75	75	295	1,465.71

	SCORES				TOTAL	MONEY
Corinne Dibnah	73	78	76	68	295	1,465.71
Maureen Madill	75	74	71	75	295	1,465.71
Estefania Knuth	78	72	73	72	295	1,465.71
Barbara Pestana	76	72	72	75	295	1,465.71
Caroline Hall	73	77	73	72	295	1,465.71
Helen Wadsworth	72	72	75	76	295	1,465.71
Aideen Rogers	75	76	73	73	297	1,300
Loraine Lambert	72	74	76	76	298	1,270
Janet Soulsby	72	77	74	76	299	1,225
Sally Prosser	75	76	75	73	299	1,225
Karina Orum	79	75	71	75	300	1,150
Anna-Carin Jonasson	78	77	75	70	300	1,150
Asa Gottmo	72	78	76	74	300	1,150
Laurette Maritz-Atkins	76	75	76	74	301	1,000
Susan Moon	76	72	75	78	301	1,000
Xonia Wunsch-Ruiz	77	75	77	72	301	1,000
Lynette Brooky	71	73	83	74	301	1,000
Laura Navarro	79	70	77	75	301	1,000
Maria Bertilskold	78	74	76	73	301	1,000
Lisa Hackney	79	74	75	73	301	1,000

Nestle Open de France Feminin

Golf De St. Endreol, La Motte, France
Par 36-37–73; 5,635 yards

October 13-15
purse, £60,000

	SCORES			TOTAL	MONEY
Marie Laure de Lorenzi	71	68	71	210	£9,000
Alison Nicholas	71	75	74	220	4,510
Sally Prosser	73	76	71	220	4,510
Kathryn Marshall	76	71	73	220	4,510
Karina Orum	79	70	72	221	2,148
Rachel Hetherington	74	76	71	221	2,148
Julie Forbes	75	68	78	221	2,148
Trish Johnson	75	77	70	222	1,422
Evelyn Orley	72	73	77	222	1,422
Federica Dassu	74	74	75	223	1,075.50
Susan Moon	75	69	79	223	1,075.50
Lana Freund	77	72	74	223	1,075.50
Joanne Morley	71	77	75	223	1,075.50
Regine Lautens	74	78	72	224	889.50
Axelle Semo	75	73	76	224	889.50
Emma-Jane Smith	73	75	76	224	889.50
Amaia Arruti	72	77	75	224	889.50
Claire Duffy	74	76	75	225	755.25
Corinne Soules	74	77	74	225	755.25
Gillian Stewart	73	76	76	225	755.25
Stefania Croce	74	76	75	225	755.25
Caryn Louw	74	78	73	225	755.25
Sarah Burnell	72	76	77	225	755.25
Raquel Carriedo-Tomas	75	74	76	225	755.25
Nicola Moult	75	74	76	225	755.25
Debbie Dowling	73	80	73	226	627
Charlotta Sorenstam	70	79	77	226	627
Mary Grace Estuesta	75	75	76	226	627
Martina Koch	74	78	74	226	627
Valerie Michaud	78	74	74	226	627

	SCORES			TOTAL	MONEY
Sandrine Mendiburu	77	75	74	226	627
Wendy Dicks	79	75	73	227	555
Barbara Pestana	76	75	76	227	555

La Manga Spanish Open

Hyatt La Manga Club Resort, South Course, North Murcia, Spain   October 19-21
Par 36-36–72; 6,114 yards   purse, £50,000

	SCORES			TOTAL	MONEY
Rachel Hetherington	68	66	68	202	£7,500
Stephanie Dallongeville	66	68	70	204	5,075
Lisa Hackney	70	65	70	205	3,500
Amaia Arruti	69	65	72	206	2,700
Marie Laure de Lorenzi	68	70	69	207	1,935
Sophie Gustafson	70	69	68	207	1,935
Emma-Jane Smith	72	68	68	208	1,500
Pamela Wright	69	70	70	209	1,250
Helen Wadsworth	68	71	71	210	1,060
Marina Arruti	69	72	69	210	1,060
Diane Barnard	72	71	69	212	803.33
Penny Grice-Whittaker	72	70	70	212	803.33
Wendy Dicks	68	71	73	212	803.33
Anna-Carin Jonasson	73	68	71	212	803.33
Raquel Carriedo-Tomas	75	68	69	212	803.33
Valerie Michaud	69	68	75	212	803.33
Xonia Wunsch-Ruiz	70	74	69	213	700
Lora Fairclough	72	69	72	213	700
Maureen Madill	74	71	69	214	613.12
Sofia Gronberg	68	75	71	214	613.12
Gillian Stewart	71	70	73	214	613.12
Stefania Croce	72	71	71	214	613.12
Lisa Jensen	74	71	69	214	613.12
Caroline Hall	73	73	63	214	613.12
Martina Koch	71	74	69	214	613.12
Sarah Bennett	70	74	70	214	613.12
Laurette Maritz-Atkins	72	71	72	215	500
Janet Soulsby	74	68	73	215	500
Barbara Pestana	71	72	72	215	500
Aideen Rogers	70	75	70	215	500
Loraine Lambert	71	69	75	215	500
Denise Booker	71	71	73	215	500
Rachel Bates	71	73	71	215	500

Princess Lalla Meriem Cup

Royal Golf Dar-es-Salam, Blue Course, Rabat, Morocco   November 10-12
Par 73; 6,400 yards   purse, FF250,000

	SCORES			TOTAL	MONEY
Amaia Arruti	72	75	74	221	FF50,000
Sofia Gronberg	71	78	72	221	35,000
(Arruti defeated Gronberg on second extra hole.)					
Martina Koch	77	74	72	223	18,125
Xonia Wunsch-Ruiz	75	72	76	223	18,125

	SCORES			TOTAL	MONEY
Sandrine Mendiburu	72	76	75	223	18,125
Diane Barnard	76	75	72	223	18,125
Sally Prosser	73	76	76	225	11,500
Regine Lautens	76	77	74	227	10,500
Lora Fairclough	79	76	72	227	10,500
Veronique Palli	70	82	76	228	10,000
Federica Dassu	76	74	79	229	10,000
Joanne Morley	79	76	75	230	10,000
Gillian Stewart	79	76	78	233	10,000
Susan Hodge	84	75	76	235	10,000
Valerie Michaud	79	78	79	236	10,000

Women's Australasian Tours

Malaysian JAL Mercedes-Benz Open

Saujana Golf & Country Club, Palm Course,
Kuala Lumpur, Malaysia
Par 36-36–72; 6,218 yards

January 19-21
purse, US$90,000

	SCORES			TOTAL	MONEY
Corinne Dibnah	73	73	74	220	US$12,750
Tina Paternostro	75	80	73	228	8,500
Huang Yu-Chen	78	76	75	229	5,737
Jae-Sook Won	80	72	77	229	5,737
Laura Navarro	79	76	75	230	3,230
Lisa Depaulo	74	76	80	230	3,230
Xonia Wunsch	80	77	74	231	2,380
Mitsuyo Hirata	78	75	78	231	2,380
Wendy Doolan	77	76	78	231	2,380
Rachel Hetherington	76	83	73	232	1,627
Mardi Lunn	81	75	76	232	1,627
Kayo Fukumoto	79	75	78	232	1,627
Estefania Knuth	78	75	79	232	1,627
*Hsiao Chuan Lu	80	75	78	233	
Regine Lautens	79	76	78	233	1,419
Loraine Lambert	78	77	78	233	1,419
Susan Farron	72	79	82	233	1,419
Michiko Okada	84	76	74	234	1,228
Susan Hodge	79	80	75	234	1,228
Kim Cathrein	79	80	75	234	1,228
Karen Davies	80	78	76	234	1,228
Shani Waugh	77	81	76	234	1,228
Janet Soulsby	78	76	80	234	1,228
Dale Reid	76	83	76	235	994
Sandrine Mendiburu	83	75	77	235	994
Liz Bowman	82	75	78	235	994
Mayumi Morioka	81	75	79	235	994
Masako Ishihara	77	79	79	235	994

	SCORES			TOTAL	MONEY
Yoshiko Ito	80	78	78	236	773
Lisa Hackney	77	81	78	236	773
Evelyn Orley	80	77	79	236	773
Mary Estuesta	79	77	80	236	773
Sarah Nicklin	77	79	80	236	773
Valerie Michaud	77	79	80	236	773

Singapore JAL Open

Tanah Merah Country Club, Garden Course, Singapore
Par 36-36–72; 6,111 yards

January 26-28
purse, US$80,000

	SCORES			TOTAL	MONEY
Estefania Knuth	75	67	66	208	US$11,250
Huang Yu-Chen	72	69	69	210	7,500
Corinne Dibnah	72	70	69	211	5,625
Dale Reid	70	71	71	212	4,500
Lisa Hackney	70	70	73	213	3,150
Lisa Depaulo	69	74	73	216	2,550
Kumiko Fuchi	73	71	74	218	2,325
Wendy Doolan	73	73	73	219	1,572
Loraine Lambert	72	74	73	219	1,572
Young-Me Lee	74	71	74	219	1,572
Mary Estuesta	71	76	72	219	1,572
Maria Bertilskold	72	72	75	219	1,572
Sally Prosser	73	71	75	219	1,572
Janet Soulsby	75	71	73	219	1,572
Kayo Fukumoto	69	78	73	220	1,177
Mayumi Ishii	76	72	72	220	1,177
Nobuko Kizawa	75	75	70	220	1,177
Jill McGill	75	75	70	220	1,177
Carri Wood	72	74	74	220	1,177
Valerie Michaud	75	73	73	221	933
Sachiko Oshima	75	70	76	221	933
Irene Yeoh	75	75	71	221	933
Asa Gottmo	74	73	74	221	933
Sarah Bennett	73	75	73	221	933
Debbie Dowling	74	74	73	221	933
Karen Davies	73	77	71	221	933
Mardi Lunn	74	69	78	221	933
*Hsiao Chuan Lu	74	78	70	222	
Michiko Okada	77	73	72	222	727
Kiyoe Yamazaki	73	76	73	222	727
Patti Liscio	73	78	71	222	727

Indonesian JAL Open

Pantai Indah Kapuk Country Club, Jakarta, Indonesia
Par 36-36–72; 6,154 yards

February 2-4
purse, US$100,000

	SCORES			TOTAL	MONEY
Lisa Hackney	70	72	74	216	US$13,500
Mardi Lunn	74	72	70	216	9,000
(Hackney defeated Lunn on second extra hole.)					
Huang Yu-Chen	71	71	75	217	6,750

	SCORES			TOTAL	MONEY
*Hsiao Chuan Lu	73	71	75	219	
Patti Liscio	75	73	71	219	4,590
Sarah Bennett	71	76	72	219	4,590
Susan Hodge	72	76	72	220	2,790
Valerie Michaud	69	77	74	220	2,790
Alison Munt	73	73	74	220	2,790
Wendy Doolan	69	74	78	221	2,250
Amy Fruhwirth	71	78	73	222	1,723
Estefania Knuth	72	77	73	222	1,723
Kayo Fukumoto	74	72	76	222	1,723
Corinne Dibnah	73	77	72	222	1,723
*Jui-Hui Lee	72	75	76	223	
Sally Prosser	76	72	75	223	1,525
Julie Shumaker	75	71	77	223	1,525
Julie Forbes	79	71	74	224	1,413
Kiyoe Yamazaki	78	73	73	224	1,413
Masayo Nishibata	77	74	73	224	1,413
Fusako Nagata	74	75	76	225	1,255
Tina Paternostro	72	75	78	225	1,255
Young-Me Lee	72	74	79	225	1,255
Karen Davis	73	80	72	225	1,255
Asa Gottmo	73	75	78	226	1,075
Elizabeth Makings	74	74	78	226	1,075
Mary Estuesta	75	73	78	226	1,075
Mikiko Furuya	80	73	73	226	1,075
Rachel Hetherington	72	75	80	227	874
Diane Barnard	72	75	80	227	874
Kim Cathrein	72	78	77	227	874
Sachiko Oshima	78	73	76	227	874
Sally Dee	75	78	74	227	874

Thailand Open

Thana City Golf & Country Club, Samutprakarn, Thailand
Par 36-36–72; 6,160 yards

February 9-11
purse, US$110,000

	SCORES			TOTAL	MONEY
Liz Earley	69	75	70	214	US$15,000
Amy Fruhwirth	70	73	72	215	10,000
Fusako Nagata	72	73	71	216	7,500
Megumi Matsuo	73	70	74	217	6,000
Patti Liscio	72	75	71	218	4,200
Julie Forbes	73	77	70	220	3,400
Sarah Bennett	73	75	73	221	3,100
Jill McGill	75	74	73	222	2,800
Jean Bartholomew	78	74	71	223	1,935
Young-Me Lee	73	76	74	223	1,935
Wendy Doolan	80	69	74	223	1,935
Loraine Lambert	73	76	74	223	1,935
Jennifer Steiner	75	73	75	223	1,935
Eui-Young Shim	77	71	75	223	1,935
Debbie Dowling	77	70	76	223	1,935
Corinne Dibnah	73	77	74	224	1,620
Kim Cathrein	81	71	73	225	1,520
Kiyoe Yamazaki	71	79	75	225	1,520
Lisa Hackney	78	69	78	225	1,520
Susan Farron	73	79	74	226	1,320

	SCORES			TOTAL	MONEY
Mette Hageman	75	75	76	226	1,320
Sally Prosser	74	74	78	226	1,320
Susan Hodge	71	76	79	226	1,320
Mitsuyo Hirata	76	71	79	226	1,320
Xonia Wunsch	77	75	75	227	1,120
Janet Soulsby	78	74	75	227	1,120
Valerie Michaud	74	75	78	227	1,120
Lisa Depaulo	74	76	78	228	892
Shani Waugh	76	76	76	228	892
Elizabeth Makings	75	74	79	228	892
Franca Fehlauer	74	75	79	228	892
Rachel Hetherington	75	74	79	228	892
Michie Ohba	81	73	74	228	892
Laura Navarro	76	78	74	228	892

Republic of China Open

Linkou International Golf & Country Club, Taipei, Taiwan

Par 36-36–72; 6,277 yards

February 16-18

purse, US$118,500

	SCORES			TOTAL	MONEY
Cheng Mei-Chi	75	71	74	220	US$16,500
Lisa Hackney	71	75	75	221	11,000
Patti Liscio	76	79	70	225	8,250
Diane Barnard	77	77	75	229	5,610
Huang Bie-Shyun	72	76	81	229	5,610
Julie Forbes	77	81	72	230	3,580
Maria Bertilskold	75	75	80	230	3,580
*Hsiao Chuan Lu	78	78	74	230	
Sarah Nicklin	77	80	75	232	2,310
Huang Yu-Chen	77	79	76	232	2,310
Wendy Doolan	75	80	77	232	2,310
Yoshiko Ito	72	82	78	232	2,310
Mary Estuesta	73	81	78	232	2,310
Feng Tseng-Hsiu	71	82	79	232	2,310
Shani Waugh	73	79	80	232	2,310
Karen Davies	74	81	78	233	1,840
Fukumi Tani	78	81	75	234	1,750
Laura Navarro	74	81	79	234	1,750
Susan Farron	76	82	77	235	1,450
Liz Earley	78	80	77	235	1,450
Tai Yu-Hsia	78	80	77	235	1,450
Kim Cathrein	79	79	77	235	1,450
Keiko Okano	75	84	76	235	1,450
Eui-Young Shim	77	79	79	235	1,450
Chen Li-Ying	78	78	79	235	1,450
Asa Gottmo	78	82	75	235	1,450
Su Ching Lu	74	80	81	235	1,450
Huang Hui-Fan	77	82	77	236	1,050
Susan Hodge	81	79	76	236	1,050
Ai-Yu Tu	78	82	76	236	1,050
Estefania Knuth	81	80	75	236	1,050
Young-Me Lee	84	78	74	236	1,050
Rachel Hetherington	73	81	82	236	1,050

Holden Australian Open

Yarra Yarra Golf Club, Melbourne, Australia
Par 37-36–73; 5,958 yards

November 9-12
purse, A$250,000

	SCORES				TOTAL	MONEY
Liselotte Neumann	67	74	71	71	283	A$37,500
Annika Sorenstam	70	75	69	69	283	20,000
Jane Geddes	68	74	71	70	283	20,000
(Neumann defeated Geddes on second extra hole and Sorenstam on third extra hole.)						
Karrie Webb	73	74	67	70	284	12,500
Alison Nicholas	76	72	68	73	289	10,000
Robin Walton	74	71	75	72	292	9,000
Helen Wadsworth	75	74	67	76	292	9,000
Emilee Klein	75	74	74	70	293	7,125
Caroline Hall	69	79	73	72	293	7,125
Sheree Higgens	76	73	77	69	295	5,375
Brandie Burton	74	75	69	77	295	5,375
Alison Munt	76	75	71	74	296	4,066.66
Dale Reid	73	75	72	76	296	4,066.66
Rachel Hetherington	74	71	73	78	296	4,066.66
Kristal Parker-Gregory	75	79	75	68	297	3,500
Catriona Matthew	77	77	75	69	298	3,225
Emma-Jane Smith	73	76	74	75	298	3,225
Carin Hjalmarsson	79	73	74	73	299	2,812.50
Joanne Mills	78	74	71	76	299	2,812.50
Patti Rizzo	75	72	75	77	299	2,812.50
Li Wen-Lin	79	71	72	77	299	2,812.50
Jane Crafter	76	72	75	77	300	2,550
Maureen Madill	73	81	75	72	301	2,400
Karina Orum	72	77	78	74	301	2,400
Anne-Marie Knight	75	79	75	73	302	2,150
Fiona Pike	75	77	73	77	302	2,150
Catrin Nilsmark	74	72	73	83	302	2,150
Shani Waugh	78	78	73	74	303	1,900
Loraine Lambert	70	78	78	77	303	1,900
Tina Fischer	77	78	75	74	304	1,700
Helen Hopkins	77	73	79	75	304	1,700
Michelle Scerri	74	79	76	75	304	1,700

Alpine Australian Masters

Royal Pines Resort, Queensland, Australia
Par 37-36–73; 6,153 yards

November 16-19
purse, A$300,000

	SCORES				TOTAL	MONEY
Annika Sorenstam	66	68	67	69	270	A$45,000
Jane Geddes	70	73	65	70	278	30,000
Laura Davies	72	70	69	68	279	16,500
Liselotte Neumann	66	72	69	72	279	16,500
Kristal Parker-Gregory	70	73	68	70	281	12,000
Catrin Nilsmark	69	70	73	70	282	10,800
Alison Nichols	68	70	72	72	282	10,800
Brandie Burton	69	75	70	69	283	8,000
Anne-Marie Knight	71	70	72	70	283	8,000
Karrie Webb	68	72	72	71	283	8,000
Li Wen-Lin	70	72	71	71	284	6,000
Jennifer Sevil	67	77	71	70	285	4,560

		SCORES			TOTAL	MONEY
Corinne Dibnah	69	76	69	71	285	4,560
Loraine Lambert	69	75	70	71	285	4,560
Carin Hjalmarsson	70	72	71	72	285	4,560
Robin Walton	70	73	70	72	285	4,560
Cathy Stolz	73	74	71	68	286	3,525
Nicole Jeray	74	70	73	69	286	3,525
Nicole Lowien	71	70	73	72	286	3,525
Karina Orum	68	73	72	73	286	3,525
Helen Wadsworth	73	74	71	69	287	3,000
Karina Lunn	67	75	72	73	287	3,000
Joanne Mills	72	69	72	74	287	3,000
Shani Waugh	68	73	72	74	287	3,000
Patti Rizzo	71	74	72	71	288	2,580
Sandra Beikoff	70	71	74	73	288	2,580
Dale Reid	71	75	69	73	288	2,580
Rachel Hetherington	72	72	74	71	289	2,280
Catriona Matthew	70	74	72	73	289	2,280
Emma-Jane Smith	72	73	75	70	290	1,980
Irene Yeoh	73	76	71	70	290	1,980
Alison Munt	69	77	71	73	290	1,980
Caroline Hall	68	78	70	74	290	1,980
Maureen Madill	70	72	74	74	290	1,980
*Simone Williams	68	69	78	75	290	

Japan LPGA Tour

Daikin Orchid

Ryukyu Golf Club, Okinawa
Par 36-36–72; 6,252 yards

March 3-5
purse, ¥60,000,000

		SCORES		TOTAL	MONEY
Marnie McGuire	73	70	67	210	¥10,800,000
Kaori Higo	71	70	72	213	5,280,000
Huang Bie-Shyun	71	76	71	218	4,200,000
Kaori Harada	75	72	73	220	3,600,000
Chihiro Nakajima	73	78	70	221	2,700,000
Ai-Yu Tu	71	77	73	221	2,700,000
Mitsuyo Hirata	74	75	73	222	1,546,000
Michiko Hattori	76	73	73	222	1,546,000
Fuki Kido	76	72	74	222	1,546,000
Miyuki Shimabukuro	77	71	74	222	1,546,000
Patty Sheehan	77	71	74	222	1,546,000
Mayumi Hirase	76	77	70	223	924,000
Jean Bartholomew	78	75	70	223	924,000
Yuko Moriguchi	76	75	72	223	924,000
Kumiko Hiyoshi	73	77	73	223	924,000
Akiko Fukushima	75	75	73	223	924,000
Woo-Soon Ko	70	78	75	223	924,000

	SCORES			TOTAL	MONEY
Man-Soo Kim	75	77	72	224	654,000
Jennifer Sevil	75	76	73	224	654,000
Ikuyo Shiotani	76	73	75	224	654,000
Nayoko Yoshikawa	75	78	72	225	546,000
Mayumi Murai	75	78	72	225	546,000
Ae-Sook Kim	78	74	73	225	546,000
Ayako Okamoto	76	75	74	225	546,000
Kikuko Shibata	76	75	74	225	546,000
Yuko Saito	74	76	75	225	546,000
Ray Bell	77	73	75	225	546,000
Li Wen-Lin	81	72	73	226	486,000
Yukiko Ishiguro	75	77	74	226	486,000
Young-Me Lee	76	75	75	226	486,000

Chiyoda Ladies

Miyazaki Zaronbai Golf Club, Miyazaki
Par 36-36–72; 6,211 yards

March 10-12
purse, ¥50,000,000

	SCORES			TOTAL	MONEY
Yuka Irie	71	71	78	220	¥9,000,000
Young-Me Lee	73	73	75	221	4,400,000
Akiko Fukushima	70	78	74	222	3,250,000
Aki Takamura	74	73	75	222	3,250,000
Suzuko Maeda	74	74	75	223	2,500,000
Yuko Saito	80	74	70	224	1,875,000
Nayoko Yoshikawa	75	75	74	224	1,875,000
Yukiyo Haga	80	72	73	225	1,172,000
Mayumi Hirase	78	73	74	225	1,172,000
Aiko Takasu	73	76	76	225	1,172,000
Seiko Watanabe	74	74	77	225	1,172,000
Ok-Hee Ku	80	75	71	226	840,000
Man-Soo Kim	73	74	79	226	840,000
Marnie McGuire	74	73	79	226	840,000
Ai-Yu Tu	76	75	76	227	640,000
Aki Nakano	76	75	76	227	640,000
Huang Bie-Shyun	76	73	78	227	640,000
Michiko Hattori	77	72	78	227	640,000
Yukiko Ishiguro	78	71	78	227	640,000
Cheng Mei-Chi	78	76	74	228	480,000
Ikuyo Shiotani	81	74	73	228	480,000
Miyuki Shimabukuro	75	73	80	228	480,000
Mitsuyo Hirata	79	73	77	229	455,000
Chieko Nishida	76	79	74	229	455,000
Yoshiko Ito	79	74	77	230	415,000
Michiko Okada	77	75	78	230	415,000
Mikino Kubo	77	75	78	230	415,000
Shoko Asano	79	73	78	230	415,000
Ae-Sook Kim	80	74	76	230	415,000
Aiko Hashimoto	77	73	80	230	415,000

Saishunkan Ladies

Takayuhbaru Country Club, Kumamoto
Par 36-36–72; 6,329 yards

March 17-19
purse, ¥60,000,000

	SCORES			TOTAL	MONEY
Nayoko Yoshikawa	74	70	72	216	¥10,800,000
Ok-Hee Ku	73	71	72	216	5,280,000
(Yoshikawa defeated Ku on first extra hole.)					
Yuko Saito	72	74	71	217	3,600,000
Yuko Moriguchi	74	72	71	217	3,600,000
Marnie McGuire	71	73	73	217	3,600,000
Michiko Hattori	72	73	73	218	2,100,000
Aiko Hashimoto	69	76	73	218	2,100,000
Mayumi Murai	69	74	75	218	2,100,000
Li Wen-Lin	74	73	72	219	1,184,000
Kaori Higo	69	77	73	219	1,184,000
Fumiko Muraguchi	72	73	74	219	1,184,000
Kikuko Shibata	71	74	74	219	1,184,000
Aki Takamura	70	73	76	219	1,184,000
Young-Me Lee	74	75	72	221	864,000
Mayumi Ishii	74	75	72	221	864,000
Ikuyo Shiotani	72	75	74	221	864,000
Huang Bie-Shyun	71	74	76	221	864,000
Miyuki Shimabukuro	73	73	76	222	684,000
Hiromi Takamura	73	73	76	222	684,000
Yukie Ueki	74	76	73	223	576,000
Jennifer Sevil	74	74	75	223	576,000
Wu Ming-Yeh	72	75	76	223	576,000
Michiko Okada	73	71	79	223	576,000
Misayo Fujisawa	78	72	74	224	540,000
Fusako Nagata	73	76	75	224	540,000
Yoshiko Ito	77	73	75	225	480,000
Chikako Matsuzawa	73	77	75	225	480,000
Feng Tseng-Hsiu	77	73	75	225	480,000
Natsuko Noro	75	74	76	225	480,000
Woo-Soon Ko	76	72	77	225	480,000
Junko Yasui	78	70	77	225	480,000
Megumi Matsuo	75	73	77	225	480,000
Tai Yu-Chuan	70	77	78	225	480,000

Kenshoen Ladies

Dogo Golf Club, Ehime
Par 36-36–72 yards; 6,194 yards

April 7-9
purse, ¥50,000,000

	SCORES			TOTAL	MONEY
Keiko Arai	69	73	70	212	¥9,000,000
Huang Bie-Shyun	68	72	72	212	4,400,000
(Arai defeated Huang on first extra hole.)					
Yuko Moriguchi	69	72	74	215	3,500,000
Akiko Fukushima	73	71	72	216	2,500,000
Feng Tseng-Hsiu	73	71	72	216	2,500,000
Kaori Higo	69	70	77	216	2,500,000
Marnie McGuire	73	72	72	217	1,500,000
Hiromi Takamura	72	73	72	217	1,500,000
Mayumi Hirase	72	72	73	217	1,500,000
Michiko Hattori	73	72	73	218	1,000,000

	SCORES			TOTAL	MONEY
Aki Takamura	75	74	70	219	695,000
Woo-Soon Ko	73	74	72	219	695,000
Ikuyo Shiotani	75	71	73	219	695,000
Tamayo Ueda	75	71	73	219	695,000
Ayako Okamoto	73	71	75	219	695,000
Akemi Yamaoka	73	70	76	219	695,000
Ritsu Imahori	71	72	76	219	695,000
Mitsuyo Hirata	72	70	77	219	695,000
Kaori Harada	69	70	80	219	695,000
Li Wen-Lin	76	71	73	220	435,000
Man-Soo Kim	76	71	73	220	435,000
Jennifer Sevil	71	74	75	220	435,000
Mikino Kubo	73	76	72	221	380,000
Fusako Nagata	73	75	73	221	380,000
Aki Nakano	74	73	74	221	380,000
Miyuki Shimabukuro	74	72	75	221	380,000
Yuko Motoyama	74	72	75	221	380,000
Chikayo Yamazaki	74	72	75	221	380,000
Mieko Nomura	76	70	75	221	380,000
Aiko Hashimoto	73	71	77	221	380,000

Mitsukoshi Cup

Segovia Golf Course, Chiyoda, Ibaraki
Par 36-36–72; 6,091 yards

April 13-16
purse, ¥60,000,000

	SCORES				TOTAL	MONEY
Ikuyo Shiotani	76	77	70	69	292	¥10,800,000
Marnie McGuire	77	70	72	74	293	5,280,000
Michiko Hattori	77	74	75	68	294	3,600,000
Ayako Okamoto	76	72	76	70	294	3,600,000
Akiko Fukushima	75	71	75	73	294	3,600,000
Kaori Higo	74	74	72	75	295	2,400,000
Aki Nakano	74	74	76	73	297	1,800,000
Junko Yasui	77	72	75	73	297	1,800,000
Chikayo Yamazaki	74	70	75	78	297	1,800,000
Yuko Moriguchi	75	75	77	71	298	1,155,000
Kumiko Hiyoshi	74	77	71	76	298	1,155,000
Young-Me Lee	72	78	75	74	299	1,050,000
Yukiko Ishiguro	72	80	75	73	300	930,000
Akemi Yamaoka	75	75	77	73	300	930,000
Mayumi Hirase	75	72	79	74	300	930,000
Ok-Hee Ku	76	71	81	73	301	750,000
Jennifer Sevil	79	71	77	74	301	750,000
Aiko Hashimoto	79	73	71	78	301	750,000
Feng Tseng-Hsiu	78	76	72	76	302	600,000
Akane Ohshiro	77	71	77	77	302	600,000
Rie Fujiwara	81	74	79	69	303	534,000
Hiromi Takamura	75	75	80	73	303	534,000
Man-Soo Kim	76	79	75	73	303	534,000
Hisako Takeda	76	74	78	75	303	534,000
Aiko Takasu	75	74	78	76	303	534,000
Fumiko Muraguchi	76	77	73	78	304	492,000
Minako Wada	78	72	76	78	304	492,000
Miyuki Shimabukuro	77	77	77	74	305	468,000
Megumi Matsuo	77	74	79	75	305	468,000
Cheng Mei-Chi	79	75	77	75	306	438,000

	SCORES			TOTAL	MONEY
Yukiyo Haga	78	74 78	76	306	438,000
Yoshiko Ito	77	76 77	76	306	438,000

Nasu Ogawa

Nasu Ogawa Golf Club, Tochigi
Par 36-36–72; 6,137 yards

April 21-23
purse, ¥50,000,000

	SCORES			TOTAL	MONEY
Ikuyo Shiotani	75	72	70	217	¥9,000,000
Mayumi Hirase	73	73	71	217	3,633,000
Hisako Takeda	74	71	72	217	3,633,000
Yuko Moriguchi	72	72	73	217	3,633,000
(Shiotani defeated Takeda and Hirase on second extra hole and Moriguchi on fifth extra hole.)					
Hiromi Hirakata	75	71	72	218	2,250,000
Aki Takamura	75	69	74	218	2,250,000
Yukie Ueki	71	76	72	219	1,750,000
Junko Yasui	79	71	71	221	1,175,000
Nagata Fusako	76	74	71	221	1,175,000
Chikako Matsuzawa	76	73	72	221	1,175,000
Michiko Okada	72	76	73	221	1,175,000
Michiko Hattori	71	79	72	222	825,000
Kaori Harada	76	74	72	222	825,000
Marnie McGuire	75	73	74	222	825,000
Nayoko Yoshikawa	77	70	75	222	825,000
Man-Soo Kim	78	74	71	223	625,000
Mayumi Murai	75	76	72	223	625,000
Mikino Kubo	76	75	72	223	625,000
Junko Ishii	76	75	72	223	625,000
Kikuko Shibata	76	76	72	224	470,000
Natsuko Noro	74	78	72	224	470,000
Miyuki Shimabukuro	76	75	73	224	470,000
Hiromi Takamura	78	73	73	224	470,000
Li Wen-Lin	78	73	73	224	470,000
Hiroe Tani	76	74	74	224	470,000
Ai-Yu Tu	78	71	75	224	470,000
Sheree Higgens	77	75	73	225	425,000
Mayumi Uchida	76	72	77	225	425,000
Toshimi Kimura	78	74	74	226	390,000
Huang Bie-Shyun	78	73	75	226	390,000
Aki Nakano	77	74	75	226	390,000
Junko Kitajima	76	75	75	226	390,000
Megumi Matsuo	76	73	77	226	390,000

Satake Japan Classic

Hiroshima Country Club, Hiroshima
Par 36-36–72; 6,196 yards

April 28-30
purse, ¥50,000,000

	SCORES			TOTAL	MONEY
Akiko Fukushima	72	67	69	208	¥9,000,000
Liselotte Neumann	70	72	69	211	4,400,000
Kaori Harada	73	71	70	214	3,250,000
Kaori Higo	70	71	73	214	3,250,000

	SCORES			TOTAL	MONEY
Yoko Inoue	76	72	67	215	1,937,000
Yukiyo Haga	75	70	70	215	1,937,000
Laura Davies	71	74	70	215	1,937,000
Marnie McGuire	69	75	71	215	1,937,000
Yukie Ueki	74	72	70	216	1,250,000
Mayumi Murai	73	76	68	217	854,000
Young-Me Lee	72	74	71	217	854,000
Yukiko Ishiguro	76	70	71	217	854,000
Yuka Irie	71	73	73	217	854,000
Miyuki Shimabukuro	71	73	73	217	854,000
Michiko Hattori	73	70	74	217	854,000
Nayoko Yoshikawa	72	74	72	218	650,000
Aiko Hashimoto	75	70	73	218	650,000
Suzuko Maeda	76	74	69	219	475,000
Norimi Terasawa	76	73	70	219	475,000
Yuko Saito	75	73	71	219	475,000
Aki Nakano	77	71	71	219	475,000
Li Wen-Lin	75	73	71	219	475,000
Aki Takamura	71	75	73	219	475,000
Hisako Takeda	75	71	73	219	475,000
Tomoe Fumihira	69	76	74	219	475,000
Man-Soo Kim	73	76	71	220	405,000
Kumiko Hiyoshi	75	73	72	220	405,000
Natsuko Noro	74	74	72	220	405,000
Ikuyo Shiotani	74	75	72	221	370,000
Michiko Okada	73	74	74	221	370,000
Mayumi Uchida	73	74	74	221	370,000
Megumi Matsuo	73	71	77	221	370,000

Gunze World Cup

Tokyo Yomiuri Country Club, Tokyo
Par 36-36–72; 6,387 yards

May 5-7
purse, ¥60,000,000

	SCORES				TOTAL	MONEY
Kaori Higo	65	75	71	70	281	¥10,800,000
Ikuyo Shiotani	69	69	71	73	282	5,280,000
Marnie McGuire	71	71	71	70	283	4,200,000
Huang Bie-Shyun	72	71	69	72	284	3,300,000
Liselotte Neumann	70	68	72	74	284	3,300,000
Natsuko Noro	73	72	71	70	286	2,400,000
Aki Nakano	71	72	72	72	287	1,950,000
Mayumi Murai	69	73	69	76	287	1,950,000
Miyuki Shimabukuro	73	70	75	70	288	1,350,000
Kaori Harada	70	73	75	70	288	1,350,000
Sherri Steinhauer	73	70	74	72	289	1,110,000
Hiromi Hirakata	72	74	72	71	289	1,110,000
Chikako Matsuzawa	72	72	76	71	291	1,020,000
Mitsuyo Hirata	76	72	74	70	292	840,000
Toshimi Kimura	71	76	74	71	292	840,000
Megumi Matsuo	72	76	72	72	292	840,000
Man-Soo Kim	71	77	71	73	292	840,000
Ok-Hee Ku	76	71	69	76	292	840,000
Akane Ohshiro	75	73	73	72	293	630,000
Cheng Mei-Chi	72	76	72	73	293	630,000
Aki Takamura	73	73	77	71	294	570,000
Fusako Nagata	71	76	74	73	294	570,000
Mayumi Uchida	75	70	75	74	294	570,000

	SCORES				TOTAL	MONEY
Yuko Moriguchi	72	74	73	75	294	570,000
Junko Kitajima	74	73	75	73	295	516,000
Karina Orum	70	75	78	72	295	516,000
Chie Yoshida	73	72	75	75	295	516,000
Yukiyo Haga	74	70	76	75	295	516,000
Jennifer Sevil	72	73	74	76	295	516,000
*Kaori Watanabe	71	72	78	74	295	

Yakult Ladies

Fukuoka Kokusai Country Club, Fukuoka
Par 36-36–72; 6,199 yards
(Third round shortened to nine holes.)

May 12-14
purse, ¥60,000,000

	SCORES			TOTAL	MONEY
Akiko Fukushima	70	67	37	174	¥10,800,000
Huang Bie-Shyun	73	68	34	175	5,280,000
Yuko Saito	72	66	39	177	4,200,000
Mayumi Hirase	76	69	34	179	2,580,000
Mitsuyo Hirata	71	72	36	179	2,580,000
Aiko Takasu	74	69	36	179	2,580,000
Toshimi Kimura	69	73	37	179	2,580,000
Shin Sora	72	67	40	179	2,580,000
Junko Yasui	73	72	35	180	1,264,000
Fuki Kido	73	72	35	180	1,264,000
Jae-Sook Won	71	74	35	180	1,264,000
Kaori Harada	73	73	35	181	882,000
Aki Nakano	73	73	35	181	882,000
Man-Soo Kim	74	72	35	181	882,000
Kaori Higo	75	70	36	181	882,000
Norimi Terasawa	73	71	37	181	882,000
Mitsuko Hamada	72	71	38	181	882,000
Yuka Irie	75	72	35	182	570,000
Suzuko Maeda	75	72	35	182	570,000
Kumiko Hiyoshi	71	75	36	182	570,000
Hiromi Takamura	72	73	37	182	570,000
Aki Takamura	74	70	38	182	570,000
Mieko Nomura	73	71	38	182	570,000
Woo-Soon Ko	76	72	35	183	462,000
Rie Mitsuhashi	76	72	35	183	462,000
Fusako Nagata	74	73	36	183	462,000
Miyuki Shimabukuro	74	72	37	183	462,000
Megumi Matsuo	75	71	37	183	462,000
Tomiko Ikebuchi	72	73	38	183	462,000
Mariko Ohtani	72	73	38	183	462,000
Hiromi Hirakata	71	73	39	183	462,000

Chukyo TV Bridgestone

Kasugai Country Club, Nagoya
Par 36-36–72; 6,216 yards

May 19-21
purse, ¥60,000,000

	SCORES			TOTAL	MONEY
Ikuyo Shiotani	69	69	74	212	¥9,000,000
Yukie Ueki	66	70	77	213	4,400,000

	SCORES			TOTAL	MONEY
Suzuko Maeda	73	70	71	214	3,250,000
Nayoko Yoshikawa	72	69	73	214	3,250,000
Junko Yasui	70	70	75	215	2,500,000
Chikako Matsuzawa	74	72	70	216	2,000,000
Fusako Nagata	72	74	71	217	1,500,000
Hiroko Inoue	73	73	71	217	1,500,000
Michiko Hattori	71	73	73	217	1,500,000
Mayumi Hirase	74	71	73	218	943,000
Yuko Moriguchi	72	71	75	218	943,000
Akiko Fukushima	70	72	76	218	943,000
Toshimi Kimura	73	74	72	219	815,000
Akane Ohshiro	72	75	72	219	815,000
Kumiko Hiyoshi	74	71	75	220	690,000
Yuko Motoyama	74	71	75	220	690,000
Chieko Nishida	72	71	77	220	690,000
Aiko Hashimoto	76	74	71	221	514,000
Kaori Harada	73	75	73	221	514,000
Ok-Hee Ku	75	72	74	221	514,000
Li Wen-Lin	74	71	76	221	514,000
Yuri Kawanami	76	69	76	221	514,000
Norimi Terasawa	75	74	73	222	440,000
Yuko Saito	67	81	74	222	440,000
Aki Nakano	74	74	74	222	440,000
Shin Sora	73	75	74	222	440,000
Cheng Mei-Chi	69	78	75	222	440,000
Keiko Arai	76	74	73	223	370,000
Aki Takamura	79	71	73	223	370,000
Michiko Okada	76	74	73	223	370,000
Rie Fujiwara	76	74	73	223	370,000
Huang Bie-Shyun	73	76	74	223	370,000
Yuka Irie	74	74	75	223	370,000
Akemi Yamaoka	74	74	75	223	370,000
Jae-Sook Won	74	73	76	223	370,000
Woo-Soon Ko	72	73	78	223	370,000

Toto Motors Ladies

Toto Hannoh Country Club, Saitama
Par 36-36–72; 6,185 yards

May 26-28
purse, ¥50,000,000

	SCORES			TOTAL	MONEY
Mayumi Hirase	69	69	71	209	¥9,000,000
Young-Me Lee	73	69	70	212	3,950,000
Marnie McGuire	68	72	72	212	3,950,000
Natsuko Noro	71	74	68	213	3,000,000
Junko Yasui	74	73	67	214	2,500,000
Mayumi Murai	68	75	72	215	1,750,000
Yukiko Ishiguro	73	70	72	215	1,750,000
Chikayo Yamazaki	67	75	73	215	1,750,000
Chikako Matsuzawa	68	75	73	216	1,250,000
Aki Takamura	74	73	70	217	917,000
Mieko Nomura	71	74	72	217	917,000
Rie Fujiwara	74	70	73	217	917,000
Aki Nakano	72	71	74	217	917,000
Wu Ming-Yeh	73	73	72	218	765,000
Mikino Kubo	71	71	76	218	765,000
Ok-Hee Ku	73	75	71	219	590,000

	SCORES			TOTAL	MONEY
Kumiko Hiyoshi	77	70	72	219	590,000
Megumi Matsuo	75	72	72	219	590,000
Woo-Soon Ko	70	77	72	219	590,000
Ikuyo Shiotani	73	72	74	219	590,000
Michiko Okada	75	74	71	220	460,000
Junko Ishii	73	75	72	220	460,000
Ae-Sook Kim	72	75	73	220	460,000
Michiko Hattori	74	72	74	220	460,000
Yuko Moriguchi	71	73	76	220	460,000
Akiko Fukushima	72	77	72	221	400,000
Kaori Imai	73	76	72	221	400,000
Akane Ohshiro	75	73	73	221	400,000
Ai-Yu Tu	74	73	74	221	400,000
Kaori Higo	74	72	75	221	400,000
Fuki Kido	73	73	75	221	400,000
Suzuko Maeda	71	73	77	221	400,000

Mitsubishi Electric Ladies

Kita Rokko Country Club, Hyogo
Par 36-37–73; 6,297 yards

June 2-4
purse, ¥50,000,000

	SCORES			TOTAL	MONEY
Aiko Hashimoto	72	72	71	215	¥9,000,000
Fumiko Muraguchi	70	75	71	216	3,950,000
Ok-Hee Ku	73	70	73	216	3,950,000
Junko Yasui	73	72	72	217	2,750,000
Young-Me Lee	70	73	74	217	2,750,000
Ikuyo Shiotani	71	76	71	218	1,875,000
Mayumi Hirase	70	74	74	218	1,875,000
Yuko Motoyama	72	75	72	219	1,500,000
Kaori Higo	73	75	72	220	1,055,000
Marnie McGuire	74	73	73	220	1,055,000
Natsuko Noro	71	75	74	220	1,055,000
Aki Takamura	74	76	71	221	790,000
Aki Nakano	72	75	74	221	790,000
Fuki Kido	73	73	75	221	790,000
Jeong-Soo Kim	74	72	75	221	790,000
Suzuko Maeda	73	76	73	222	565,000
Kaori Harada	73	75	74	222	565,000
Toshimi Kimura	72	76	74	222	565,000
Akiko Fukushima	73	74	75	222	565,000
Yukiyo Haga	71	76	75	222	565,000
Michiko Hattori	75	74	74	223	445,000
Woo-Soon Ko	73	75	75	223	445,000
Chieko Nishida	76	72	75	223	445,000
Ae-Sook Kim	71	79	74	224	400,000
Man-Soo Kim	74	75	75	224	400,000
Michiko Okada	76	73	75	224	400,000
Mitsuyo Hirata	76	72	76	224	400,000
Kumiko Hiyoshi	75	73	76	224	400,000
Li Wen-Lin	73	75	76	224	400,000
Hiromi Takamura	77	75	73	225	350,000
Hiroko Inoue	73	79	73	225	350,000
Akane Ohshiro	77	74	74	225	350,000
Rie Fujiwara	76	73	76	225	350,000

Dunlop Twin Lakes Ladies

Twin Lakes Country Club, Gunma
Par 36-36–72; 6,256 yards

June 15-18
purse, ¥50,000,000

	SCORES				TOTAL	MONEY
Mayumi Hirase	72	69	75	72	288	¥9,000,000
Woo-Soon Ko	75	72	74	69	290	3,950,000
Young-Me Lee	72	71	73	74	290	3,950,000
Ok-Hee Ku	76	70	75	71	292	2,750,000
Aki Nakano	73	71	73	75	292	2,750,000
Jae-Sook Won	72	72	76	73	293	1,750,000
Aiko Hashimoto	74	73	71	75	293	1,750,000
Mariko Ohtani	71	76	69	77	293	1,750,000
Marnie McGuire	74	77	74	69	294	1,125,000
Ikuyo Shiotani	77	72	72	73	294	1,125,000
Akane Ohshiro	74	74	76	71	295	880,000
Yukiyo Haga	75	74	73	73	295	880,000
Akiko Fukushima	73	74	70	78	295	880,000
Ae-Sook Kim	73	75	75	73	296	680,000
Huang Bie-Shyun	75	76	71	74	296	680,000
Akemi Yamaoka	74	71	77	74	296	680,000
Yuko Motoyama	74	76	72	74	296	680,000
Junko Yasui	72	69	76	79	296	680,000
Fuki Kido	73	75	74	75	297	505,000
Toshimi Kimura	74	73	73	77	297	505,000
Nayoko Yoshikawa	75	75	75	73	298	440,000
Junko Ishii	76	73	76	73	298	440,000
Rie Mitsuhashi	74	72	79	73	298	440,000
Suzuko Maeda	70	77	77	74	298	440,000
Mitsuyo Hirata	70	78	76	74	298	440,000
Chikako Matsuzawa	74	76	73	75	298	440,000
Kumiko Hiyoshi	76	73	74	75	298	440,000
Hiromi Hirakata	75	73	79	72	299	390,000
Michiko Hattori	75	75	76	73	299	390,000
Natsuko Noro	75	72	75	77	299	390,000

Japan Women's Open Championship

Ube Country Club, Mannenike Course, Yamaguchi
Par 36-36–72; 6,448 yards

June 22-25
purse, ¥60,000,000

	SCORES				TOTAL	MONEY
Ikuyo Shiotani	69	71	73	72	285	¥9,720,000
Man-Soo Kim	68	72	72	74	286	5,400,000
Marnie McGuire	71	68	72	77	288	3,834,000
Woo-Soon Ko	71	69	75	75	290	2,673,000
Akiko Fukushima	65	70	81	75	291	2,021,000
Wu Ming-Yeh	72	69	74	76	291	2,021,000
Michiko Hattori	69	74	71	77	291	2,021,000
Hiromi Hirakata	69	79	73	71	292	1,274,000
Akemi Yamaoka	74	74	72	72	292	1,274,000
Mitsuyo Hirata	72	73	74	73	292	1,274,000
Chieko Nishida	75	73	71	73	292	1,274,000
Ok-Hee Ku	72	72	73	75	292	1,274,000
Kaori Higo	76	71	77	69	293	885,000
Yuko Moriguchi	72	71	73	77	293	885,000
Aiko Hashimoto	73	73	76	72	294	651,000

	SCORES				TOTAL	MONEY
Akane Ohshiro	75	74	72	73	294	651,000
Jae-Sook Won	70	74	75	75	294	651,000
Mayumi Murai	71	73	73	77	294	651,000
Mayumi Hirase	69	72	75	78	294	651,000
Miyuki Shimabukuro	72	70	73	79	294	651,000
Jennifer Sevil	73	75	76	71	295	507,000
*Han-Lee Won	73	69	80	73	295	
Suzuko Maeda	72	76	72	75	295	507,000
Kikuko Shibata	72	76	71	76	295	507,000
*Mie Nakata	72	69	76	78	295	
*Yuri Fudo	72	72	78	74	296	
Junko Yasui	69	74	78	75	296	453,000
Megumi Matsuo	75	72	74	75	296	453,000
Kayoko Ikoma	73	73	75	75	296	453,000
Toshimi Kimura	75	71	74	76	296	453,000
Huang Yueh-Chyn	72	76	72	76	296	453,000

Tohato Ladies

Oak Village Golf Club, Chiba
Par 36-36–72; 6,248 yards

June 30-July 2
purse, ¥50,000,000

	SCORES			TOTAL	MONEY
Akane Ohshiro	73	74	74	221	¥9,000,000
Ikuyo Shiotani	71	75	75	221	3,950,000
Man-Soo Kim	67	79	75	221	3,950,000
(Ohshiro defeated Shiotani and Kim at second extra hole.)					
Marnie McGuire	70	84	70	224	2,500,000
Natsuko Noro	74	79	71	224	2,500,000
Mayumi Hirase	68	77	79	224	2,500,000
Toshimi Kimura	79	76	71	226	1,625,000
Mayumi Murai	68	83	75	226	1,625,000
Young-Me Lee	77	77	73	227	987,000
Wu Ming-Yeh	71	82	74	227	987,000
Fuki Kido	73	79	75	227	987,000
Jennifer Sevil	73	78	76	227	987,000
Yuko Motoyama	70	80	77	227	987,000
Aki Takamura	77	76	75	228	720,000
Kaori Higo	71	81	76	228	720,000
Michiko Okada	72	79	77	228	720,000
Fusako Nagata	75	75	78	228	720,000
Kyoe Fumihira	75	79	75	229	495,000
Miyuki Shimabukuro	75	78	76	229	495,000
Junko Yasui	75	77	77	229	495,000
Yukiko Ishiguro	78	74	77	229	495,000
Aiko Hashimoto	72	79	78	229	495,000
Keiko Arai	76	75	78	229	495,000
Ayako Okamoto	68	83	78	229	495,000
Yuko Tsurumaki	75	76	78	229	495,000
Mieko Nomura	73	83	74	230	410,000
Michiko Hattori	74	81	75	230	410,000
Yuka Irie	73	81	76	230	410,000
Miki Oda	74	80	76	230	410,000
Jae-Sook Won	73	80	77	230	410,000
*Mie Nakata	73	79	78	230	
Yukie Ueki	73	77	80	230	410,000

Toyo Suisan Ladies

Kosaido Sapporo Country Club, Hokkaido
Par 36-36–72; 6,412 yards

July 7-9
purse, ¥50,000,000

	SCORES			TOTAL	MONEY
Aki Nakano	68	70	72	210	¥9,000,000
Akane Ohshiro	72	69	72	213	3,350,000
Rie Mitsuhashi	71	70	72	213	3,350,000
Mayumi Hirase	73	67	73	213	3,350,000
Junko Yasui	70	69	74	213	3,350,000
Fuki Kido	71	72	71	214	1,875,000
Kumiko Hiyoshi	68	71	75	214	1,875,000
Huang Bie-Shyun	71	71	73	215	1,500,000
Nayoko Yoshikawa	72	73	71	216	1,051,000
Mayumi Murai	73	71	72	216	1,051,000
Man-Soo Kim	72	71	73	216	1,051,000
Aiko Takasu	74	72	71	217	730,000
Cheng Mei-Chi	71	75	71	217	730,000
Shoko Asano	71	73	73	217	730,000
Toshimi Kimura	73	70	74	217	730,000
Hisako Takeda	72	70	75	217	730,000
Keiko Arai	72	68	77	217	730,000
Natsuko Noro	73	72	73	218	479,000
Aiko Hashimoto	70	74	74	218	479,000
Jennifer Sevil	74	70	74	218	479,000
Mieko Nomura	72	71	75	218	479,000
Chieko Nishida	67	73	78	218	479,000
Wu Ming-Yeh	76	72	71	219	420,000
Woo-Soon Ko	70	72	77	219	420,000
Marnie McGuire	74	74	72	220	390,000
Huang Yueh-Chyn	77	71	72	220	390,000
Michiko Hattori	77	69	74	220	390,000
Ae-Sook Kim	73	71	76	220	390,000
Megumi Matsuo	71	77	73	221	335,000
Tai Yu-Chuan	76	72	73	221	335,000
Ray Bell	72	76	73	221	335,000
Chikako Matsuzawa	75	71	75	221	335,000
Yuka Shirato	78	67	76	221	335,000
Yoko Kobayashi	71	73	77	221	335,000
Yukie Ueki	74	69	78	221	335,000

Resort Trust Cleanup Ladies

Maple Point Golf Club, Yamanashi
Par 36-36–72; 6,346 yards

July 14-16
purse, ¥50,000,000

	SCORES			TOTAL	MONEY
Wu Ming-Yeh	68	69	74	211	¥9,000,000
Shin Sora	72	70	70	212	3,950,000
Yuko Moriguchi	72	69	71	212	3,950,000
Nayoko Yoshikawa	75	70	68	213	2,312,000
Toshimi Kimura	69	75	69	213	2,312,000
Aki Takamura	72	71	70	213	2,312,000
Yuka Irie	64	71	78	213	2,312,000
Kazumi Takada	75	70	69	214	1,172,000
Ok-Hee Ku	71	73	70	214	1,172,000
Suzuko Maeda	70	70	74	214	1,172,000

	SCORES			TOTAL	MONEY
Junko Yasui	68	67	79	214	1,172,000
Akemi Yamaoka	71	73	71	215	890,000
Kumiko Hiyoshi	72	73	71	216	790,000
Hiromi Hirakata	69	73	74	216	790,000
Fumiko Muraguchi	71	71	74	216	790,000
Kaori Harada	71	75	71	217	590,000
Kikuko Shibata	74	71	72	217	590,000
Reiko Kashiwado	74	71	72	217	590,000
Chikako Matsuzawa	73	71	73	217	590,000
Ae-Sook Kim	72	72	73	217	590,000
Midori Wakaura	72	76	70	218	460,000
Sheree Higgens	73	75	70	218	460,000
Michiko Okada	73	73	72	218	460,000
Hisako Higuchi	74	72	72	218	460,000
Fusako Nagata	72	73	73	218	460,000
Huang Hui-Fan	73	75	71	219	415,000
Kaori Higo	75	71	73	219	415,000
Man-Soo Kim	71	74	74	219	415,000
Natsuko Noro	69	74	76	219	415,000
Akiko Fukushima	73	75	72	220	365,000
Young-Me Lee	72	76	72	220	365,000
Huang Bie-Shyun	75	72	73	220	365,000
Miyuki Shimabukuro	73	73	74	220	365,000
Jennifer Sevil	72	74	74	220	365,000
Michie Ohba	71	75	74	220	365,000

Katokichi Queens Golf

Kotodaira Country Club, Kagawa
Par 36-36–72; 6,340 yards
(First round cancelled — inclement weather.)

July 21-23
purse, ¥50,000,000

	SCORES		TOTAL	MONEY
Fuki Kido	73	68	141	¥6,750,000
Yoko Inoue	72	70	142	2,725,000
Junko Yasui	70	72	142	2,725,000
Jennifer Sevil	69	73	142	2,725,000
Chie Yoshida	73	70	143	1,453,000
Aiko Takasu	72	71	143	1,453,000
Ikuyo Shiotani	71	72	143	1,453,000
Toshimi Kimura	71	72	143	1,453,000
Suzuko Maeda	74	70	144	796,000
Michiko Hattori	73	71	144	796,000
Miki Oda	71	73	144	796,000
Jae-Sook Won	74	71	145	607,000
Hiromi Takamura	71	74	145	607,000
Ray Bell	71	74	145	607,000
Kayo Yamada	70	75	145	607,000
Reiko Kashiwado	74	72	146	438,000
Keiko Arai	73	73	146	438,000
Rie Mitsuhashi	72	74	146	438,000
Michiko Okada	71	75	146	438,000
Megumi Matsuo	71	75	146	438,000
Ok-Hee Ku	76	71	147	337,000
Miyuki Shimabukuro	75	72	147	337,000
Fusako Nagata	74	73	147	337,000
Kaori Harada	71	76	147	337,000

	SCORES		TOTAL	MONEY
Hisako Higuchi	71	76	147	337,000
Tomiko Ikebuchi	71	76	147	337,000
Aki Nakano	74	74	148	292,000
Aiko Hashimoto	73	75	148	292,000
Jan Higgins	73	75	148	292,000
Misayo Fujisawa	73	75	148	292,000
Cheng Mei-Chi	72	76	148	292,000
Midori Wakaura	71	77	148	292,000

SC Ladies

Kousaido Saitama Golf Club, Saitama
Par 36-36–72; 6,291 yards

July 28-30
purse, ¥50,000,000

	SCORES			TOTAL	MONEY
Huang Bie-Shyun	70	70	69	209	¥9,000,000
Norimi Terasawa	70	69	72	211	4,400,000
Toshimi Kimura	71	71	70	212	3,000,000
Nayoko Yoshikawa	73	68	71	212	3,000,000
Chikako Matsuzawa	69	69	74	212	3,000,000
Fuki Kido	72	70	71	213	1,875,000
Rie Mitsuhashi	73	68	72	213	1,875,000
Suzuko Maeda	72	74	69	215	1,116,000
Akemi Yamaoka	78	67	70	215	1,116,000
Huang Yueh-Chyn	75	70	70	215	1,116,000
Yuko Moriguchi	70	73	72	215	1,116,000
Fumiko Muraguchi	73	70	72	215	1,116,000
Jae-Sook Won	71	72	73	216	840,000
Junko Yasui	74	74	69	217	620,000
Aki Nakano	71	77	69	217	620,000
Marnie McGuire	74	73	70	217	620,000
Kayo Yamada	75	72	70	217	620,000
Ok-Hee Ku	72	73	72	217	620,000
Huang Hui-Fan	71	74	72	217	620,000
Michie Ohba	68	73	76	217	620,000
Mitsuko Hamada	69	71	77	217	620,000
Cheng Mei-Chi	73	73	72	218	460,000
Mayumi Ishii	74	70	74	218	460,000
Chie Yoshida	71	71	76	218	460,000
Dahlke Kei Jeanne	75	73	71	219	415,000
Masumi Inaba	72	74	73	219	415,000
Ae-Sook Kim	73	72	74	219	415,000
Tatsuko Morimoto	68	77	74	219	415,000
Kaori Higo	72	72	75	219	415,000
Akane Ohshiro	72	71	76	219	415,000

Mizuno Ladies

Asahi Kokusai Tojo Country Club, Hygo
Par 36-36–72; 6,468 yards

August 4-6
purse, ¥60,000,000

	SCORES			TOTAL	MONEY
Aki Takamura	66	70	70	206	¥10,800,000
Mayumi Hirase	72	69	72	213	4,360,000
Aki Nakano	70	71	72	213	4,360,000

	SCORES			TOTAL	MONEY
Yuko Moriguchi	69	72	72	213	4,360,000
Nayoko Yoshikawa	70	72	72	214	3,000,000
Jae-Sook Won	71	78	66	215	2,400,000
Akane Ohshiro	73	74	69	216	2,100,000
Ai-Yu Tu	74	73	70	217	1,402,000
Kaori Higo	72	73	72	217	1,402,000
Kaori Harada	70	74	73	217	1,402,000
Chieko Nishida	71	72	74	217	1,402,000
Jennifer Sevil	75	74	69	218	930,000
Ayako Okamoto	72	74	72	218	930,000
Natsuko Noro	71	74	73	218	930,000
Michiko Okada	73	72	73	218	930,000
Junko Yasui	71	73	74	218	930,000
Ikuyo Shiotani	72	76	71	219	600,000
Young-Me Lee	77	71	71	219	600,000
Marnie McGuire	74	73	72	219	600,000
Akemi Yamaoka	75	72	72	219	600,000
Misayo Fujisawa	74	72	73	219	600,000
Huang Bie-Shyun	71	74	74	219	600,000
Mayumi Murai	74	71	74	219	600,000
Woo-Soon Ko	71	74	74	219	600,000
Cheng Mei-Chi	73	76	71	220	480,000
Mikino Kubo	74	75	71	220	480,000
Ayako Hashimoto	71	77	72	220	480,000
Yukiyo Haga	74	74	72	220	480,000
Feng Tseng-Hsiu	73	74	73	220	480,000
Michiko Hattori	71	75	74	220	480,000

NEC Karuizawa 72

Karuizawa 72 Higashi, Iriyama Course, Nagano
Par 36-36–72; 6,440 yards

August 11-13
purse, ¥60,000,000

	SCORES			TOTAL	MONEY
Mayumi Hirase	72	68	72	212	¥10,800,000
Michiko Hattori	71	69	73	213	5,280,000
Kaori Higo	69	72	73	214	3,900,000
Aiko Hashimoto	68	73	73	214	3,900,000
Aki Nakano	69	76	71	216	2,500,000
Akiko Fukushima	69	70	77	216	2,500,000
Nayoko Yoshikawa	71	68	77	216	2,500,000
Jennifer Sevil	75	69	73	217	1,405,000
Norimi Terasawa	70	74	73	217	1,405,000
Junko Yasui	71	70	76	217	1,405,000
Kayoko Ikoma	70	71	76	217	1,405,000
Megumi Matsuo	68	75	75	218	1,062,000
Chikako Matsuzawa	74	74	71	219	912,000
Huang Hui-Fan	71	77	71	219	912,000
Shin Sora	73	74	72	219	912,000
Huang Yueh-Chyn	76	71	72	219	912,000
Nadene Golu	73	75	72	220	672,000
Cheng Mei-Chi	73	74	73	220	672,000
Misayo Fujisawa	73	74	73	220	672,000
Ai-Yu Tu	73	73	74	220	672,000
Ikuyo Shiotani	76	73	72	221	558,000
Young-Me Lee	75	73	73	221	558,000
Yuko Nakamura	74	71	76	221	558,000

	SCORES			TOTAL	MONEY
Wu Ming-Yeh	74	75	73	222	510,000
Fukumi Tani	71	78	73	222	510,000
Dahlke Kei Jeanne	74	74	74	222	510,000
Akemi Yamaoka	74	72	76	222	510,000
Aiko Takasu	72	71	79	222	510,000
Jae-Sook Won	70	78	75	223	414,000
Fusako Nagata	73	75	75	223	414,000
Chikayo Yamazaki	77	71	75	223	414,000
Mieko Nomura	75	73	75	223	414,000
Kikuko Shibata	75	73	75	223	414,000
Midori Wakaura	74	74	75	223	414,000
Chieko Nishida	71	76	76	223	414,000
Mikino Kubo	76	71	76	223	414,000
Mayumi Asada	72	75	76	223	414,000
Fuki Kido	77	69	77	223	414,000
Natsuko Noro	73	73	77	223	414,000

Lotte Ladies

Minayoshida Country Club, Chiba
Par 36-36–72; 6,528 yards

August 18-20
purse, ¥50,000,000

	SCORES			TOTAL	MONEY
Kaori Higo	74	66	71	211	¥9,000,000
Yukiyo Haga	72	69	70	211	4,400,000
(Higo defeated Haga on second extra hole.)					
Yuko Moriguchi	71	71	70	212	3,000,000
Aiko Hashimoto	70	72	70	212	3,000,000
Fuki Kido	70	70	72	212	3,000,000
Jennifer Sevil	71	72	70	213	1,875,000
Yuko Saito	71	71	71	213	1,875,000
Ayako Okamoto	71	73	70	214	1,375,000
Akiko Fukushima	69	67	78	214	1,375,000
Aki Takamura	75	71	69	215	913,000
Tomoyo Taguchi	71	73	71	215	913,000
Sheree Higgens	70	73	72	215	913,000
Fumiko Omata	70	73	72	215	913,000
Jae-Sook Won	74	74	68	216	685,000
Tai Yu-Chuan	72	74	70	216	685,000
Suzuko Maeda	74	71	71	216	685,000
Fukumi Tani	71	73	72	216	685,000
Chikako Matsuzawa	72	68	76	216	685,000
Shin Sora	72	74	71	217	483,000
Keiko Arai	71	74	72	217	483,000
Akemi Yamaoka	74	71	72	217	483,000
Mayumi Murai	70	74	73	217	483,000
Feng Tseng-Hsiu	70	74	73	217	483,000
Ok-Hee Ku	70	78	70	218	410,000
Woo-Soon Ko	74	73	71	218	410,000
Reiko Kashiwado	72	75	71	218	410,000
Norimi Terasawa	70	76	72	218	410,000
Jean Bartholomew	75	71	72	218	410,000
Toshimi Kimura	72	73	73	218	410,000
Aki Nakano	72	72	74	218	410,000
Mitsuko Hamada	72	72	74	218	410,000

Goyo Kensetsu Cup

Tomisato Golf Club, Chiba
Par 36-36–72; 6,187 yards

August 25-27
purse, ¥60,000,000

	SCORES			TOTAL	MONEY
Marnie McGuire	69	68	74	211	¥10,800,000
Aiko Takasu	71	68	72	211	5,280,000
(McGuire defeated Takasu on third extra hole.)					
Chikayo Yamazaki	69	69	76	214	4,200,000
Huang Bie-Shyun	72	73	71	216	3,600,000
Hiromi Takamura	69	75	73	217	2,700,000
Cheng Mei-Chi	71	72	74	217	2,700,000
Junko Yasui	73	73	72	218	1,950,000
Michiko Okada	72	71	75	218	1,950,000
Natsuko Noro	74	72	73	219	1,270,000
Fumiko Muraguchi	73	71	75	219	1,270,000
Sachiko Ohshima	70	74	75	219	1,270,000
Hisako Higuchi	73	73	74	220	1,020,000
Yuko Saito	72	71	77	220	1,020,000
Feng Tseng-Hsiu	72	77	72	221	750,000
Michie Ohba	74	75	72	221	750,000
Chikako Matsuzawa	72	76	73	221	750,000
Hisako Ohgane	73	75	73	221	750,000
Chie Yoshida	73	72	76	221	750,000
Miyuki Shimabukuro	69	75	77	221	750,000
Masumi Inaba	73	71	77	221	750,000
Keiko Arai	75	74	73	222	546,000
Aiko Hashimoto	73	74	75	222	546,000
Jennifer Sevil	74	71	77	222	546,000
Kaori Higo	74	75	74	223	444,000
Aki Nakano	75	73	75	223	444,000
Man-Soo Kim	74	74	75	223	444,000
Wu Ming-Yeh	71	77	75	223	444,000
Jae-Sook Won	73	74	76	223	444,000
Yoko Inoue	70	77	76	223	444,000
Kozue Azuma	72	75	76	223	444,000
Shin Sora	74	72	77	223	444,000
Kikuo Shibata	70	76	77	223	444,000
Aki Takamura	68	77	78	223	444,000
Akane Ohshiro	73	72	78	223	444,000
Mitsuyo Hirata	72	73	78	223	444,000
Tomoko Ueda	74	71	78	223	444,000
Masako Ichiguchi	71	73	79	223	444,000

Fuji Sankei Classic

Five Hundred Club, Shizuoka
Par 36-37–73; 6, 610 yards
(Tournament shortened to 36 holes.)

September 2-3
purse, ¥45,000,000

	SCORES		TOTAL	MONEY
Junko Yasui	69	73	142	¥8,100,000
Aki Nakano	69	73	142	3,960,000
(Yasui defeated Nakano on sixth extra hole.)				
Akemi Yamaoka	74	69	143	2,700,000
Jae-Sook Won	72	71	143	2,700,000
Aiko Takasu	70	73	143	2,700,000

	SCORES			TOTAL	MONEY
Jeong-Soo Kim	72	72		144	1,575,000
Ae-Sook Kim	71	73		144	1,575,000
Fuki Kido	70	74		144	1,575,000
Tomiko Ikebuchi	76	69		145	955,000
Ayako Okamoto	72	73		145	955,000
Fumiko Muraguchi	71	74		145	955,000
Yuko Moriguchi	74	72		146	774,000
Reiko Kashiwado	74	72		146	774,000
Ai-Yu Tu	75	72		147	594,000
Mayumi Murai	74	73		147	594,000
Mayumi Yamada	74	73		147	594,000
Kaori Higo	73	74		147	594,000
Young-Me Lee	72	75		147	594,000
Ikuyo Shiotani	71	76		147	594,000
Nadene Golu	76	72		148	409,000
Woo-Soon Ko	75	73		148	409,000
Hiromi Hirakata	75	73		148	409,000
Kayo Yamada	74	74		148	409,000
Suzuko Maeda	73	75		148	409,000
Aki Takamura	72	76		148	409,000
Ok-Hee Ku	72	76		148	409,000
Kikuko Shibata	75	74		149	346,000
Yuko Saito	74	75		149	346,000
Chikako Matsuzawa	74	75		149	346,000
Chieko Nishida	74	75		149	346,000
Kaori Imai	74	75		149	346,000
Keiko Arai	72	77		149	346,000
Midori Wakaura	71	78		149	346,000

Japan LPGA Championship

The Classic Golf Club, Fukuoka
Par 36-36–72; 6,463 yards

September 7-10
purse, ¥65,000,000

	SCORES				TOTAL	MONEY
Aki Takamura	74	70	69	69	282	¥11,700,000
Akiko Fukushima	71	73	72	70	286	5,720,000
Akane Ohshiro	72	72	74	69	287	4,550,000
Marnie McGuire	72	74	73	70	289	3,250,000
Kaori Higo	73	72	72	72	289	3,250,000
Ok-Hee Ku	74	71	72	72	289	3,250,000
Nicole Lowien	72	72	71	75	290	2,275,000
Yuka Irie	79	72	69	71	291	1,950,000
Yuko Moriguchi	73	72	72	75	292	1,462,000
Aki Nakano	72	73	69	78	292	1,462,000
Mikino Kubo	76	76	70	71	293	1,137,000
Mayumi Murai	75	71	74	73	293	1,137,000
Ayako Okamoto	79	71	74	70	294	942,000
Mayumi Hirase	75	71	74	74	294	942,000
Miki Oda	75	71	74	74	294	942,000
Kaori Harada	72	73	74	75	294	942,000
Young-Me Lee	73	77	74	71	295	780,000
Ae-Sook Kim	74	72	79	71	296	630,000
Toshimi Kimura	72	76	74	74	296	630,000
Jae-Sook Won	71	77	73	75	296	630,000
Li Wen-Lin	74	71	73	78	296	630,000
Yukiyo Haga	73	75	77	72	297	552,000

	SCORES				TOTAL	MONEY
Kayo Yamada	74	72	74	77	297	552,000
Yoko Inoue	76	73	73	76	298	520,000
Man-Soo Kim	75	74	71	78	298	520,000
Aiko Takasu	73	67	78	80	298	520,000
Tomoko Ueda	77	74	75	73	299	461,000
Aiko Hashimoto	73	76	76	74	299	461,000
Tai Yu-Chuan	75	73	77	74	299	461,000
Mitsuyo Hirata	76	74	74	75	299	461,000
Yuri Kawanami	74	73	77	75	299	461,000
Yuko Motoyama	72	71	75	81	299	461,000

Kosaido Asahi Cup

Chiba Kosaido Country Club, Chiba
Par 36-36–72; 6,183 yards
(Third round cancelled — typhoon.)

September 15-17
purse, ¥45,000,000

	SCORES		TOTAL	MONEY
Huang Bie-Shyun	72	31	103	¥8,100,000
Akemi Yamaoka	69	35	104	3,960,000
Ok-Hee Ku	71	35	106	3,150,000
Aiko Hashimoto	72	35	107	2,250,000
Feng Tseng-Hsiu	70	37	107	2,250,000
Ae-Sook Kim	70	37	107	2,250,000
Natsuko Noro	71	37	108	1,575,000
Marnie McGuire	75	34	109	1,050,000
Mayumi Hirase	74	35	109	1,050,000
Nayoko Yoshikawa	72	37	109	1,050,000
Midori Wakaura	70	39	109	1,050,000
Man-Soo Kim	76	34	110	648,000
Yuko Moriguchi	75	35	110	648,000
Fusako Nagata	75	35	110	648,000
Yoko Inoue	75	35	110	648,000
Mikino Kubo	75	35	110	648,000
Rie Fujiwara	73	37	110	648,000
Miyuki Shimabukuro	72	38	110	648,000
Ikuyo Shiotani	77	34	111	410,000
Fuki Kido	75	36	111	410,000
Kayo Fukumoto	75	36	111	410,000
Young-Me Lee	73	38	111	410,000
Miki Oda	73	38	111	410,000
Mitsuko Hamada	73	38	111	410,000
Huang Hui-Fan	72	39	111	410,000
Kayo Yamada	77	35	112	342,000
Hiromi Takamura	76	36	112	342,000
Tai Yu-Chuan	76	36	112	342,000
Ritsu Imahori	76	36	112	342,000
Ayako Okamoto	75	37	112	342,000
Kayoko Motoki	75	37	112	342,000
Huang Yueh-Chyn	73	39	112	342,000

Miyagi TV Cup

Hananomori Golf Club, Miyagi
Par 36-36–72; 6,283 yards

September 22-24
purse, ¥50,000,000

	SCORES			TOTAL	MONEY
Natsuko Noro	69	72	71	212	¥9,000,000
Hisako Takeda	70	70	74	214	4,400,000
Marnie McGuire	73	71	71	215	3,250,000
Mayumi Hirase	74	70	71	215	3,250,000
Aki Takamura	74	72	71	217	2,083,000
Jennifer Sevil	71	72	74	217	2,083,000
Yuko Motoyama	68	75	74	217	2,083,000
Huang Bie-Shyun	70	73	76	219	1,500,000
Hiromi Takamura	74	76	70	220	1,012,000
Mikino Kubo	74	72	74	220	1,012,000
Nayoko Yoshikawa	71	74	75	220	1,012,000
Feng Tseng-Hsiu	74	71	75	220	1,012,000
Young-Me Lee	76	74	71	221	700,000
Miyuki Shimabukuro	75	75	71	221	700,000
Ae-Sook Kim	77	72	72	221	700,000
Tomoko Ueda	76	73	72	221	700,000
Akemi Yamaoka	73	75	73	221	700,000
Shin Sora	72	74	75	221	700,000
Michiko Hattori	76	75	71	222	455,000
Jeong-Soo Kim	73	77	72	222	455,000
Keiko Arai	71	78	73	222	455,000
Tatsuko Morimoto	74	75	73	222	455,000
Aki Nakano	71	77	74	222	455,000
Jae-Sook Won	74	74	74	222	455,000
Sadae Kumagai	73	73	76	222	455,000
Huang Yueh-Chyn	69	76	77	222	455,000
Wu Ming-Yeh	74	77	72	223	390,000
Ikuyo Shiotani	73	76	74	223	390,000
Junko Yasui	71	77	75	223	390,000
Kaori Harada	70	77	76	223	390,000

Tokai Classic

Ryosen Golf Club, Mie
Par 36-36–72; 6,351 yards

September 29-October 1
purse, ¥60,000,000

	SCORES			TOTAL	MONEY
Fumiko Muraguchi	71	72	67	210	¥10,800,000
Akiko Fukushima	72	69	70	211	5,280,000
Ikuyo Shiotani	72	71	70	213	3,900,000
Kaori Higo	69	72	72	213	3,900,000
Jae-Sook Won	69	78	67	214	2,000,000
Feng Tseng-Hsiu	72	74	68	214	2,000,000
Yuko Moriguchi	70	72	72	214	2,000,000
Mitsuyo Hirata	72	69	73	214	2,000,000
Chie Yoshida	70	71	73	214	2,000,000
Ayako Okamoto	70	69	75	214	2,000,000
Aiko Hashimoto	72	75	68	215	1,080,000
Suzuko Maeda	74	71	70	215	1,080,000
Fusako Nagata	73	71	71	215	1,080,000
Ok-Hee Ku	74	72	70	216	840,000
Yuka Irie	72	73	71	216	840,000

	SCORES			TOTAL	MONEY
Chieko Nishida	75	70	71	216	840,000
Aki Nakano	75	68	73	216	840,000
Miki Oda	71	71	74	216	840,000
Satoko Hirase	73	73	71	217	597,000
Hiromi Takamura	72	73	72	217	597,000
Patti Rizzo	72	72	73	217	597,000
Mayumi Hirase	73	70	74	217	597,000
Toshimi Kimura	72	71	74	217	597,000
Michiko Hattori	74	74	70	218	522,000
Jennifer Sevil	73	75	70	218	522,000
Norimi Terasawa	71	75	72	218	522,000
Ritsu Imahori	72	74	72	218	522,000
Kaori Harada	70	75	73	218	522,000
Mikino Kubo	70	72	76	218	522,000
Kyoko Isoda	75	73	71	219	468,000
Midori Wakaura	73	74	72	219	468,000
Keiko Arai	73	71	75	219	468,000

Takara World Invitational

Caledonian Golf Club, Chiba
Par 36-36–72; 6,214 yards

October 5-8
purse, ¥80,000,000

	SCORES				TOTAL	MONEY
Michelle McGann	71	71	69	72	283	¥14,400,000
Mayumi Hirase	69	74	73	71	287	7,040,000
Young-Me Lee	73	72	69	74	288	5,600,000
Michiko Hattori	76	70	69	74	289	4,800,000
Kaori Higo	72	71	72	75	290	4,000,000
Annika Sorenstam	68	76	75	72	291	3,000,000
Liselotte Neumann	72	68	75	76	291	3,000,000
Jennifer Sevil	73	73	73	73	292	2,200,000
Nayoko Yoshikawa	73	74	71	74	292	2,200,000
Alison Nicholas	70	74	72	77	293	1,600,000
Aki Nakano	72	72	75	75	294	1,456,000
Mayumi Murai	74	71	74	75	294	1,456,000
Midori Wakaura	72	76	72	75	295	1,336,000
Akiko Fukushima	71	76	74	75	296	1,136,000
Kaori Harada	72	72	74	78	296	1,136,000
Keiko Arai	70	71	77	78	296	1,136,000
Junko Yasui	73	69	75	79	296	1,136,000
Toshimi Kimura	76	72	75	74	297	814,000
Mitsuyo Hirata	69	75	78	75	297	814,000
Aiko Takasu	75	71	75	76	297	814,000
Miyuki Shimabukuro	70	76	74	77	297	814,000
Marnie McGuire	72	71	75	79	297	814,000
Cheng Mei-Chi	72	75	77	74	298	704,000
Tatsuko Morimoto	77	72	74	75	298	704,000
Suzuko Maeda	75	74	73	76	298	704,000
Fumiko Muraguchi	73	71	77	77	298	704,000
Carin Hjalmarsson	70	78	79	72	299	640,000
Akane Ohshiro	75	72	78	74	299	640,000
Feng Tseng-Hsiu	71	77	75	76	299	640,000
Kyoko Isoda	72	70	79	78	299	640,000

Fujitsu Ladies

Hamano Golf Club, Chiba
Par 36-36–72; 6,369 yards

October 13-15
purse, ¥60,000,000

	SCORES			TOTAL	MONEY
Hiromi Kobayashi	69	67	68	204	¥10,800,000
Akiko Fukushima	66	69	71	206	5,280,000
Aki Nakano	71	72	66	209	3,900,000
Nayoko Yoshikawa	69	67	73	209	3,900,000
Ayako Okamoto	71	71	68	210	3,000,000
Toshimi Kimura	69	70	72	211	2,400,000
Kaori Higo	74	71	68	213	1,950,000
Chie Yoshida	74	70	69	213	1,950,000
Feng Tseng-Hsiu	76	67	71	214	1,184,000
Chikayo Yamazaki	71	72	71	214	1,184,000
Aiko Takasu	72	70	72	214	1,184,000
Keiko Arai	70	72	72	214	1,184,000
Fuki Kido	69	71	74	214	1,184,000
Junko Yasui	71	73	71	215	894,000
Young-Me Lee	71	73	71	215	894,000
Woo-Soon Ko	69	73	73	215	894,000
Jennifer Sevil	74	72	70	216	684,000
Kaori Harada	74	72	70	216	684,000
Ai-Yu Tu	70	75	71	216	684,000
Mikino Kubo	72	72	72	216	684,000
Akane Ohshiro	74	72	71	217	552,000
Tai Yu-Chuan	70	76	71	217	552,000
Fusako Nagata	72	73	72	217	552,000
Miyuki Shimabukuro	71	73	73	217	552,000
Sheree Higgens	72	72	73	217	552,000
Ok-Hee Ku	72	71	74	217	552,000
Mayumi Murai	74	73	71	218	474,000
Chikako Matsuzawa	71	76	71	218	474,000
Michie Ohba	75	72	71	218	474,000
Akemi Yamaoka	72	73	73	218	474,000
Ae-Sook Kim	72	73	73	218	474,000
Wu Ming-Yeh	67	76	75	218	474,000
Mariko Ohtani	70	72	76	218	474,000

Kibun Classic

Musashi Matsuyama Country Club, Saitama
Par 36-36–72; 6,295 yards

October 20-22
purse, ¥50,000,000

	SCORES			TOTAL	MONEY
Hiromi Kobayashi	75	69	65	209	¥9,000,000
Kayo Yamada	71	71	70	212	3,633,000
Chen Li-Ying	71	70	71	212	3,633,000
Fuki Kido	71	69	72	212	3,633,000
Tai Yu-Chuan	75	72	67	214	2,250,000
Chieko Nishida	74	69	71	214	2,250,000
Kaori Harada	76	70	69	215	1,375,000
Huang Bie-Shyun	72	72	71	215	1,375,000
Man-Soo Kim	71	73	71	215	1,375,000
Cheng Mei-Chi	71	72	72	215	1,375,000
Mikino Kubo	75	73	68	216	850,000
Nicole Lowien	74	74	68	216	850,000

	SCORES			TOTAL	MONEY
Toshimi Kimura	73	72	71	216	850,000
Fusako Nagata	75	70	71	216	850,000
Masako Ichiguchi	74	68	74	216	850,000
Megumi Matsuo	73	75	69	217	625,000
Ok-Hee Ku	73	73	71	217	625,000
Wu Ming-Yeh	75	70	72	217	625,000
Miyuki Shimabukuro	74	71	72	217	625,000
Aiko Takasu	72	74	72	218	490,000
Reiko Kashiwado	75	71	72	218	490,000
Tomoko Ueda	77	69	72	218	490,000
Jae-Sook Won	76	73	70	219	445,000
Norimi Terasawa	75	74	70	219	445,000
Kikuko Shibata	75	74	70	219	445,000
Ae-Sook Kim	74	74	71	219	445,000
Yuko Motoyama	75	72	72	219	445,000
Yoko Inoue	73	68	78	219	445,000
Akemi Yamaoka	74	75	71	220	375,000
Nayoko Yoshikawa	78	70	72	220	375,000
Chikako Matsuzawa	73	75	72	220	375,000
Mitsuyo Hirata	77	71	72	220	375,000
Midori Wakaura	74	74	72	220	375,000
Fukumi Tani	78	70	72	220	375,000
Marnie McGuire	77	70	73	220	375,000
Chie Yoshida	76	70	74	220	375,000

Nichirei International

Tsukuba Country Club, Ibaragi
Par 36-36–72; 6,294 yards

October 27-29
purse, US$618,750

FIRST DAY
Better Ball

Ikuyo Shiotani and Aki Takamura (Japan) defeated Jane Geddes and Liselotte Neumann, 64-67
Barb Thomas and Jenny Lidback (U.S.) tied Fuki Kido and Natsuko Noro, 65-65
Young-Me Lee and Huang Bie-Shyun (Japan) defeated Chris Johnson and Nanci Bowen, 65-70
Nayoko Yoshikawa and Akane Ohshiro (Japan) defeated Val Skinner and Julie Larsen, 68-69
Junko Yasui and Aiko Hashimoto (Japan) defeated Joan Pitcock and Sherri Steinhauer, 65-69
Yuko Moriguchi and Akiko Fukushima (Japan) defeated Dale Eggeling and Colleen Walker, 68-70
Kris Tschetter and Rosie Jones (U.S.) defeated Michiko Hattori and Fumiko Muraguchi, 69-73
Helen Alfredsson and Alison Nicholas (U.S.) defeated Aki Nakano and Kaori Higo, 65-69
Mayumi Hirase and Marnie McGuire (Japan) defeated Beth Daniel and Meg Mallon, 65-66

POINTS: Japan 6½, United States 2½

SECOND DAY
Better Ball

Shiotani and Takamura (Japan) defeated Thomas and Lidback, 68-71
Walker and Eggeling (U.S.) tied Kido and Noro, 69-69

Geddes and Neumann (U.S.) defeated Lee and Huang, 61-69
Yoshikawa and Ohshiro (Japan) defeated Steinhauer and Pitcock, 68-69
Skinner and Johnson (U.S.) defeated Yasui and Hashimoto, 65-71
Bowen and Larsen (U.S.) tied Moriguchi and Fukushima, 68-68
Hattori and Muraguchi (Japan) defeated Daniel and Mallon, 66-68
Nakano and Higo (Japan) defeated Alfredsson and Nicholas, 69-70
Hirase and McGuire (Japan) defeated Tschetter and Jones, 64-67

POINTS: Japan 12½, United States 5½

THIRD DAY
Singles

Alfredsson (U.S.) defeated Yoshikawa, 68-71
Kido (Japan) defeated Walker, 73-76
Huang (Japan) defeated Lidback, 69-71
Pitcock (U.S.) defeated Lee, 72-73
Thomas (U.S.) defeated Noro, 69-71
Tschetter (U.S.) defeated Moriguchi, 69-75
Daniel (U.S.) defeated Yasui, 71-73
Nakano (Japan) defeated Johnson, 70-74
Bowen (U.S.) defeated Hattori, 70-73
Steinhauer (U.S.) tied Muraguchi, 71-71
Mallon (U.S.) defeated Higo, 65-69
Larsen (U.S.) defeated Ohshiro, 69-72
Eggeling (U.S.) defeated Hashimoto, 71-75
Skinner (U.S.) defeated Fukushima, 68-71
Neumann (U.S.) defeated Takamura, 68-72
Geddes (U.S.) defeated Shiotani, 68-71
Jones (U.S.) defeated Hirase, 72-74
McGuire (Japan) defeated Nicholas, 73-74

TOTAL POINTS: United States 19, Japan 17

(Each member of U.S. team received $22,000; each member of Japanese team received $12,375.)

Toray Japan Queens Cup

Seta Golf Club, Shiga
Par 36-36—72; 6,423 yards

November 3-5
purse, US$700,000

	SCORES			TOTAL	MONEY
Woo-Soon Ko	69	67	71	207	¥10,710,000
Toshimi Kimura	70	70	69	209	5,748,000
Hiromi Kobayashi	73	67	69	209	5,748,000
Akiko Fukushima	67	74	69	210	3,772,000
Liselotte Neumann	74	68	69	211	2,389,000
Jill Briles-Hinton	72	70	69	211	2,389,000
Nayoko Yoshikawa	72	69	70	211	2,389,000
Jane Geddes	72	69	70	211	2,389,000
Ok-Hee Ku	70	72	70	212	1,688,000
Beth Daniel	71	72	70	213	1,377,000
Meg Mallon	72	71	70	213	1,377,000
Pam Wright	73	70	70	213	1,377,000
Val Skinner	73	73	68	214	1,049,000
Kaori Harada	71	72	71	214	1,049,000
Allison Finney	71	72	71	214	1,049,000
Hisako Takeda	69	73	72	214	1,049,000

	SCORES			TOTAL	MONEY
Colleen Walker	74	68	72	214	1,049,000
Ikuyo Shiotani	75	71	69	215	826,000
Natsuko Noro	75	68	72	215	826,000
Helen Alfredsson	72	71	72	215	826,000
Marianne Morris	75	68	72	215	826,000
Rosie Jones	70	72	73	215	826,000
Alison Nicholas	71	74	71	216	644,000
Miyuki Shimabukuro	74	70	72	216	644,000
Annika Sorenstam	74	70	72	216	644,000
Chris Johnson	72	72	72	216	644,000
Emilee Klein	72	72	72	216	644,000
Jennifer Sevil	73	70	73	216	644,000
Kristi Albers	72	71	73	216	644,000
Ae-Sook Kim	70	72	74	216	644,000

Itoen Ladies

Great Island Course, Chiba
Par 36-36–72; 6,440 yards

November 10-12
purse, ¥60,000,000

	SCORES			TOTAL	MONEY
Laura Davies	71	70	70	211	¥10,800,000
Mayumi Hirase	72	72	69	213	4,740,000
Woo-Soon Ko	70	73	70	213	4,740,000
Akiko Fukushima	71	77	69	217	3,000,000
Suzuko Maeda	75	70	72	217	3,000,000
Tatsuko Morimoto	73	70	74	217	3,000,000
Wu Ming-Yeh	73	73	72	218	1,950,000
Toshimi Kimura	75	70	73	218	1,950,000
Kikuko Shibata	76	71	72	219	1,350,000
Young-Me Lee	72	73	74	219	1,350,000
Yuko Moriguchi	75	76	70	221	1,026,000
Ayako Okamoto	79	72	70	221	1,026,000
Yoshiko Ito	75	74	72	221	1,026,000
Marnie McGuire	76	75	71	222	846,000
Chie Yoshida	76	72	74	222	846,000
Hiromi Takamura	74	70	78	222	846,000
Man-Soo Kim	73	76	74	223	666,000
Mayumi Murai	77	72	74	223	666,000
Shin Sora	74	74	75	223	666,000
Aiko Takasu	77	76	71	224	534,000
Akane Ohshiro	78	74	72	224	534,000
Fusako Nagata	77	71	76	224	534,000
Jennifer Sevil	75	77	73	225	486,000
Yuko Saito	75	77	73	225	486,000
Ikuyo Shiotani	77	74	74	225	486,000
Hiromi Kobayashi	76	73	76	225	486,000
Junko Yasui	72	74	79	225	486,000
Kaori Higo	77	77	72	226	402,000
Aki Nakano	76	78	72	226	402,000
Aki Takamura	79	75	72	226	402,000
Midori Wakaura	78	76	72	226	402,000
Junko Yoshida	78	76	72	226	402,000
Aiko Hashimoto	77	76	73	226	402,000
Fuki Kido	76	75	75	226	402,000
Yuka Irie	76	75	75	226	402,000
Tomoko Ueda	73	78	75	226	402,000

Daio Seishi Elleair Ladies Open

Elleair Golf Club, Kagawa
Par 36-36–72; 6,244 yards

November 17-19
purse, ¥60,000,000

	SCORES			TOTAL	MONEY
Michiko Okada	72	67	69	208	¥10,800,000
Man-Soo Kim	71	70	69	210	3,696,000
Hiromi Kobayashi	71	70	69	210	3,696,000
Woo-Soon Ko	66	73	71	210	3,696,000
Natsuko Noro	69	70	71	210	3,696,000
Chikako Matsuzawa	72	67	71	210	3,696,000
Miyuki Shimabukuro	73	71	68	212	1,950,000
Ok-Hee Ku	68	71	73	212	1,950,000
Marnie McGuire	72	69	72	213	1,350,000
Huang Bie-Shyun	68	71	74	213	1,350,000
Ikuyo Shiotani	72	76	67	215	1,032,000
Young-Me Lee	72	71	72	215	1,032,000
Aiko Takasu	68	75	72	215	1,032,000
Yuko Nakamura	72	71	72	215	1,032,000
Mayumi Murai	68	79	69	216	762,000
Vicki Goetze	73	72	71	216	762,000
Akiko Fukushima	72	71	73	216	762,000
Feng Tseng-Hsiu	73	70	73	216	762,000
Tomoko Ueda	71	71	74	216	762,000
*Chika Arito	72	70	74	216	
Misayo Fujisawa	74	73	70	217	540,000
Yoko Inoue	74	71	72	217	540,000
Kikuko Shibata	69	76	72	217	540,000
Kaori Higo	70	74	73	217	540,000
Nayoko Yoshikawa	74	70	73	217	540,000
Hiromi Takamura	72	72	73	217	540,000
Mikiko Furuya	73	71	73	217	540,000
Huang Yueh-Chyn	74	70	73	217	540,000
Shihomi Suzuki	76	72	70	218	462,000
Junko Yasui	73	74	71	218	462,000
Suzuko Maeda	77	70	71	218	462,000
Mikino Kubo	73	71	74	218	462,000
Junko Yoshida	71	73	74	218	462,000

Meiji Nyugyo Cup

Aoshima Golf Club, Miyazaki
Par 36-36–72; 6,346 yards

November 24-26
purse, ¥50,000,000

	SCORES			TOTAL	MONEY
Ikuyo Shiotani	78	67	70	215	¥9,000,000
Mitsuyo Hirata	74	68	73	215	4,500,000
(Shiotani defeated Hirata on third extra hole.)					
Aki Takamura	77	72	68	217	2,750,000
Ayako Okamoto	76	73	68	217	2,750,000
Akiko Fukushima	74	74	71	219	1,700,000
Jennifer Sevil	74	74	71	219	1,700,000
Yuko Moriguchi	76	73	71	220	1,500,000
Feng Tseng-Hsiu	76	72	72	220	1,500,000
Kaori Harada	79	72	70	221	1,266,000
Marnie McGuire	76	73	72	221	1,266,000
Michiko Hattori	77	70	74	221	1,266,000

	SCORES			TOTAL	MONEY
Junko Yasui	79	72	71	222	1,100,000
Mayumi Murai	79	70	73	222	1,100,000
Akemi Yamaoka	75	74	73	222	1,100,000
Yuka Irie	76	75	72	223	1,000,000
Aiko Hashimoto	76	75	73	224	900,000
Mayumi Hirase	75	75	74	224	900,000
Jae-Sook Won	81	69	74	224	900,000
Aiko Takasu	78	74	73	225	800,000
Hiromi Kobayashi	82	73	71	226	687,000
Young-Me Lee	79	75	72	226	687,000
Woo-Soon Ko	76	77	73	226	687,000
Huang Bie-Shyun	75	75	76	226	687,000
Kaori Higo	76	73	77	226	687,000
Yuko Saito	79	68	79	226	687,000
Natsuko Noro	79	72	76	227	600,000
Ok-Hee Ku	79	77	72	228	562,000
Toshimi Kimura	83	73	72	228	562,000
Wu Ming-Yeh	81	77	71	229	512,000
Suzuko Maeda	76	76	77	229	512,000